THE PAPERS OF
THOMAS JEFFERSON

BARBARA B. OBERG
GENERAL EDITOR

THE PAPERS OF
Thomas Jefferson

Volume 35
1 August to 30 November 1801

BARBARA B. OBERG, EDITOR

JAMES P. McCLURE AND ELAINE WEBER PASCU,
SENIOR ASSOCIATE EDITORS

MARTHA J. KING, ASSOCIATE EDITOR

TOM DOWNEY AND AMY SPECKART,
ASSISTANT EDITORS

LINDA MONACO, EDITORIAL ASSISTANT

JOHN E. LITTLE, RESEARCH ASSOCIATE

PRINCETON AND OXFORD
PRINCETON UNIVERSITY PRESS
2008

SUPPORTERS

THIS EDITION was made possible by an initial grant of $200,000 from The New York Times Company to Princeton University. Contributions from many foundations and individuals have sustained the endeavor since then. Among these are the Ford Foundation, the Lyn and Norman Lear Foundation, the Lucius N. Littauer Foundation, the Charlotte Palmer Phillips Foundation, the L. J. Skaggs and Mary C. Skaggs Foundation, the John Ben Snow Memorial Trust, Time, Inc., Robert C. Baron, B. Batmanghelidj, David K. E. Bruce, and James Russell Wiggins. In recent years generous ongoing support has come from The New York Times Company Foundation, the Dyson Foundation, the Barkley Fund (through the National Trust for the Humanities), the Florence Gould Foundation, the Andrew W. Mellon Foundation, the Pew Charitable Trusts, and the Packard Humanities Institute (through Founding Fathers Papers, Inc.). Benefactions from a greatly expanded roster of dedicated individuals have underwritten this volume and those still to come: Sara and James Adler, Helen and Peter Bing, Diane and John Cooke, Judy and Carl Ferenbach III, Mary-Love and William Harman, Frederick P. and Mary Buford Hitz, Governor Thomas H. Kean, Ruth and Sidney Lapidus, Lisa and Willem Mesdag, Tim and Lisa Robertson, Ann and Andrew C. Rose, Sara Lee and Axel Schupf, the Sulzberger family through the Hillandale Foundation, Richard W. Thaler, Tad and Sue Thompson, The Wendt Family Charitable Foundation, and Susan and John O. Wynne. For their vision and extraordinary efforts to provide for the future of this edition, we owe special thanks to John S. Dyson, Governor Kean, H. L. Lenfest and the Lenfest Foundation, Rebecca Rimel and the Pew Charitable Trusts, and Jack Rosenthal. In partnership with these individuals and foundations, the National Historical Publications and Records Commission and the National Endowment for the Humanities have been crucial to the editing and publication of *The Papers of Thomas Jefferson*. For their unprecedented generous support we are also indebted to Jeremy Adelman, chair of the Princeton History Department, and to Christopher L. Eisgruber, provost of the university.

FOREWORD

FOR THE first two months covered by this volume, August and September 1801, Thomas Jefferson resided at Monticello, avoiding summer in the nation's capital. Although the house remained unfinished, it finally had a roof, and both daughters and their families could stay with him. A healthy granddaughter, Virginia Jefferson Randolph, was born there in August, and a grandson, Francis Eppes, weak but surviving, in late September. After Jefferson had to depart for Washington on 27 September, the family kept him informed about their health and activities and progress on the renovations to Monticello. Five-year-old granddaughter Ellen wrote after he left that her sisters had the "Hooping cough." In reply to her note, her grandfather sent off two books as a mark of his pleasure at her ability to read and write and observed that she might grow up to become "a learned lady and publish books herself." Jefferson also had many visitors, invited and uninvited, some on public business. Among these was Matthew L. Davis of New York, Aaron Burr's candidate for a naval office, who refused to be dissuaded by Secretary of the Treasury Albert Gallatin, and appeared at Monticello with numerous recommendations of his qualifications in hand.

Shortly after he arrived home on 2 August, Jefferson began the systematic arm-to-arm inoculation of family members and slaves against smallpox. He had been corresponding for some months with Benjamin Waterhouse, Edward Gantt, and others about Edward Jenner's experiments with live cowpox vaccine in England, and Waterhouse furnished him with a portion of vaccine to begin the process. Albemarle County physician William Wardlaw, busy with other cases, could only be at Monticello twice before 21 August, and Jefferson performed many of the inoculations with his own hand. He kept a record of individuals vaccinated and added to the list as late as 1826. Physicians elsewhere were having poorer luck sustaining the live virus through a succession of inoculations, and Waterhouse placed great importance on the success of what Jefferson called "my experiment" at Monticello. Jefferson remarked that he hoped his actions would encourage others in his neighborhood to follow his lead.

The president observed that he conducted, through correspondence, almost as much public business at home in Virginia as he did in his quarters in Washington. Although he did not have with him his "bundle of claims" containing requests for jobs and appointments, lengthy letters on important public matters passed back and forth between Jefferson and his department heads throughout

August and September. In fact, Jefferson remarked that he was "much more pressed" at Monticello by the chores of his office, because he had to write long letters instead of being able to have a few words of conversation to accomplish the same end.

The cabinet was to reassemble in the nation's capital on "the last day of September," he advised Gallatin, Secretary of War Henry Dearborn, and Attorney General Levi Lincoln. During much of the "rather sickly" time in the city in the late summer, Secretary of State James Madison was in Virginia and Dearborn in New England. Gallatin and Robert Smith, secretary of the navy, were the only department heads remaining in Washington, and Smith spent some of his time at home in Baltimore. Gallatin moved his family up to Capitol Hill, above the swamps, in order to stay healthy and he confessed that he greatly looked forward to the president's return: "I can go on with the routine of this Department; but I have not been used to be so long left to myself for every thing." He reported that some of the Federalist newspapers had begun to attack the absence of so many members of the administration.

Jefferson left Monticello on 27 September and arrived in Washington, as he had proposed, on the 30th. During his two-month absence, construction and interior decoration of the President's House had moved forward: the partition in his bedroom was going up; a "handsome carpet" was ready for the floor; the circular room was furnished with drapery, carpet, girandoles, and chandelier; the upholsterer was finishing up in the drawing room. Étienne Lemaire, the successor to Joseph Rapin as steward of the house, arrived on 4 September, and John Barnes dined with him, reporting to the president that he was favorably impressed. Back in Washington, Jefferson also learned of the "melancholy circumstance" of James Hemings's suicide.

In addition to a more comfortable residence than the President's House had provided John Adams, Jefferson acquired other accoutrements of his office. His carriage, on which much care had been lavished, was at last finished in Philadelphia; it was "spotless, & beautiful." Enoch Edwards wrote that he desired to keep the vehicle safe in the hands of the carriage maker as long as possible, but Jefferson should feel free to send for it whenever he wanted. The carriage would be covered securely in a way that would keep the "Eyes & the Fingers of the curious" from doing any damage in transit. John Barnes would receive the vehicle and arrange for payment.

Indeed, active work on many aspects of the capital city was moving forward. The walls of the chamber of the House of Representatives had been raised "up to the window heads," with only three feet more to go. For Jefferson, the completion of the House chamber, as well as the construction of a good gravel road on Rock Creek along Pennsylvania and New Jersey Avenues, was crucial for "ensuring the destinies of the city." Everything else he deemed subordinate. He thought it advisable to postpone the circular street around the Capitol because a practicable route already ascended the north side and the funds could be used instead to support the road along Rock Creek.

"Shall two nations, turning tygers, break up in one instant the peaceable relations of the whole world?" In a lengthy letter of 9 September to Robert R. Livingston, who was about to sail as America's minister to France, Jefferson laid out his thoughts on neutral rights and how best to navigate between the two great warring European powers. On 12 September, the president informed Napoleon Bonaparte that Livingston was coming to France to advance "the interest and happiness of the two nations." In late November, word reached the United States that a preliminary peace treaty between Britain and France had been signed on 1 October. Jefferson wrote that he was "overjoyed," and that this fortunate event of peace removed the last stumbling block to the success of his administration. This optimistic assessment was a reflection of his firm conviction that with Republicans in office and moderate Federalists beginning to see the light, only war with other nations could stand in the way of the vision he had sketched out in his First Inaugural Address.

Writing in August 1801 to Levi Lincoln, President Thomas Jefferson observed that he had foreseen "years ago" that the first Republican president to take office after the government had so long been the exclusive province of the Federalists would have a "dreadful operation" to perform in finding offices for members of his party, who felt they had so long been denied access to jobs and influence. The several letters of enthusiastic praise that he received from his fellow Republicans convinced him that he had taken the right course in candidly explaining his policies to the merchants of New Haven, Connecticut, the month before. Gallatin reported that a leading Republican from Hartford observed that Jefferson's answer to New Haven had done "much good" and that the September elections would show gains as a result. On the other hand, the president's address had encouraged Republicans to expect more removals than Jefferson deemed necessary. This was the dilemma that Jefferson continued to face.

In June 1801, Virginia Governor James Monroe forwarded to Jefferson a resolution of the Virginia legislature asking that the president and governor communicate on finding a location where persons "dangerous to the peace of society" could be transported.

Not until late November, and after he consulted with Madison, did Jefferson answer. Responding to the problem posed in the resolution—finding a place to deport slaves guilty of, in Jefferson's words, "Conspiracy, insurgency, treason, rebellion"—he thought the prospects in North America were scant, although he speculated that Toussaint-Louverture might consider rebellious slaves a "meritorious" addition to Saint-Domingue. "Africa," he concluded, "would offer a last & undoubted resort" if no other location could be found. At the same time he considered this question, the president gave orders for the prosecution of a ship, the schooner *Sally*, which, according to evidence collected, had been secretly fitted out for the slave trade. Jefferson determined the traffic in slaves to be "so odious that no indulgences" could be allowed.

Two important documents appearing in this volume demonstrate President Jefferson's collaborative methods of leading and epitomize the way in which he took command of the executive office. On 6 November, he dispatched a circular letter to the heads of the departments, which outlined "the mode & degrees of communication" by which the president and his officers would operate. Jefferson took as his model the procedures followed by George Washington, and he praised the late president for having participated in the decision process to just the extent he should have and for having been able to preserve "an unity of object and action" among the members of the cabinet. Before sending the circular letter, Jefferson first sent a copy to Madison inquiring whether this was a good way of communicating or whether he should take Madison up on his offer to speak with his colleagues on the president's behalf. But might the cabinet infer "a want of confidence on my part" if Madison were to speak for him? asked Jefferson. Much could be accomplished by written communication, and important issues could be handled in a conference, Jefferson concluded. Gallatin advocated "regular meetings"—a general conference weekly as well as private conversations with each secretary once or twice a week. Jefferson seemed less convinced that regular weekly meetings were necessary.

Shortly after sending the circular letter, at least by 12 November, Jefferson turned to the composition of his first annual message to Congress. He commenced a period of intense activity that lasted about fifteen days, during which he sought data on the annual funded debt payment, government income and expenses, internal revenues, and information on the judiciary system and circuit court cases; he also arranged for the collection of supplementary materials. While Jefferson prepared the first draft of his address himself, he sought, and incorporated, suggestions from Madison, Gallatin, Smith, and Lincoln, with Dearborn also supplying information. He desired, as he told Madison, "a serious revisal, not only as to matter, but diction." The most significant alteration he made in response to their opinions was the removal, very late in the drafting process, of a section on the Sedition Act, which he had first called "unconstitutional" and a "nullity." He accepted other changes in wording that appear in the finished address, which was dispatched to the House and Senate on December 8. Our Editorial Note preceding the fifteen documents that lead up to that address presents all the stages of the composition of this significant document.

The circular letter and the first annual message to Congress offer both the guidelines for procedures and a concrete example of how his administration would function. They answer the critical and fundamental question: What would be the process of government under a Jeffersonian-Republican administration? Jefferson set a system in place by which all heads of department could play a role. They would meet with the president individually and he would delegate responsibility to them. They would advise him and they would make decisions. These advisors would also communicate in writing, regularly and systematically. Jefferson's would be an administration of communication by the written word. He was collaborative, but his direct involvement and active, individual participation never faltered. He sent his annual message out for suggestions, but he drafted it himself, just as he had explained his views on neutral rights directly to Livingston, rather than asking the secretary of state to formulate a policy for him. He often did his own gathering of statistics and numbers, and he did his own calculations of the national population growth making sophisticated use of geometric progression.

Not yet through the first year of his term as president, Jefferson was already being asked to think about the leadership of the Republican party and the next presidential election. Gallatin was adamant that the Republicans had to make up their minds. Did they not intend to support Aaron Burr when Jefferson thought fit to retire, and did they not plan to back him for vice president at the next election? What would be the repercussions if they decided not to support Burr? These were astute and momentous questions, but Jefferson did not answer.

We take this opportunity to report the loss of two distinguished members from the list of our Advisory Committee. Noble Cunningham and Arthur Schlesinger, Jr., both died in 2007. The author of several books on the Jeffersonian Republicans and Jefferson's eight years as chief executive, Cunningham shaped historians' understanding not just of Jefferson but of the very nature and development of party politics in the early republic. His insightful and informative correspondence with Julian P. Boyd over many decades laid the foundation for our annotation of Jefferson's presidency. Arthur Schlesinger, Jr., historian of several modern American presidencies, always looked forward to the momentous time when the Jefferson edition would reach the presidential years and his great contributions to the institution of the American presidency were fully presented. Schlesinger was one of the strongest advocates of the importance of documentary editions to American scholarship, and he was articulate and vocal in the public forum. We will miss their knowledge and wisdom.

ACKNOWLEDGMENTS

MANY individuals have given the Editors the benefit of their aid in the preparation of this volume, and we offer them our thanks. Those who helped us use manuscript collections, answered research queries, assisted with translations, or advised in other ways are Lionel Gossman, William C. Jordan, Robert A. Kaster, Angel G. Loureiro, Michael S. Mahoney, Francisco Prado-Vilar, Michael Strauss, Joseph P. Younger, Princeton University; in the libraries at Princeton, Karin A. Trainer, University Librarian, and Elizabeth Z. Bennett, Colleen M. Burlingham, Stephen Ferguson, Andrea Immel, Daniel J. Linke, Roel Muñoz, Deborah T. Paparone, AnnaLee Pauls, Ben Primer, and Don C. Skemer; Ute Mehnert, Peter Paret, emeritus faculty, Institute for Advanced Study; Timothy Connelly of the NHPRC; James H. Hutson and the staff at the Manuscript Division of the Library of Congress, especially Lia Apodaca, Barbara J. Bair, Jennifer Brathovde, Jeffrey Flannery, Joseph Jackson, Patrick Kerwin, and Bruce Kirby; Peter Drummey and the library staff of the Massachusetts Historical Society, especially Nancy Heywood for providing digital scans; Rachel Howarth at Houghton Library, Harvard University; Robert C. Ritchie, Olga Tsapina, and others at the Huntington Library; Anna Berkes, Lucia C. Stanton, and Susan R. Stein of the Thomas Jefferson Foundation at Monticello; Christian Dupont, Regina Rush, and the staff of Special Collections at the University of Virginia Library; Sidney H. Lawrence, Emeritus Professor of Mathematics and Susan A. Riggs, Swem Library, the College of William and Mary; Richard Nicoll of the Colonial Williamsburg Foundation; Molly Kodner, Dennis Northcott, and the staff of the Missouri Historical Society; Martin Levitt, Roy Goodman, and Charles B. Greifenstein of the American Philosophical Society; Frank C. Mevers of the New Hampshire Division of Archives and Records Management; the staff of the New York Public Library; the Gilder Lehrman Institute of American History and Jean W. Ashton and Edward O'Reilly of the New-York Historical Society; Charles M. Harris of the Papers of William Thornton, and our fellow editors at the Thomas Jefferson Retirement Series at Monticello, the Adams Papers at the Massachusetts Historical Society, the Papers of George Washington and the Papers of James Madison at the University of Virginia, and the Papers of Benjamin Franklin at Yale University. For assistance with illustrations we are indebted to Alfred L. Bush of Princeton, Bonnie Coles and Barbara Moore of the Library of

ACKNOWLEDGMENTS

Congress, Ellen Miles and Linda Thrift of the National Portrait Gallery, and the Duke of Sotomayor, Don Ignacio Martínez de Irujo, of Madrid, Spain, for gracious permission to reproduce two portraits. Josh Allen of T-prime Consulting provided expert IT support in the design and development of our database and Web site. Scott Mc-Clure analyzed Jefferson's use of geometric progression to calculate population growth. Brian Solomon has contributed to the project in myriad ways, including additions to the documents database that is the foundation of the presidential volumes. We thank Alice Calaprice for careful reading and Jan Lilly for her unparalleled mastery of what a Jefferson volume must be. We thank those at Princeton University Press who never fail to give these volumes the benefit of their expertise: Peter J. Dougherty, Director, Chuck Creesy, Daphne Ireland, Dimitri Karetnikov, Neil Litt, Elizabeth Litz, Clara Platter, Linny Schenck, and Brigitta van Rheinberg.

EDITORIAL METHOD AND APPARATUS

1. RENDERING THE TEXT

Julian P. Boyd eloquently set forth a comprehensive editorial policy in Volume 1 of *The Papers of Thomas Jefferson*. Adopting what he described as a "middle course" for rendering eighteenth-century handwritten materials into print, Boyd set the standards for modern historical editing. His successors, Charles T. Cullen and John Catanzariti, reaffirmed Boyd's high standards. At the same time, they made changes in textual policy and editorial apparatus as they deemed appropriate. For Boyd's policy and subsequent modifications to it, readers are encouraged to consult Vol. 1: xxix-xxxviii; Vol. 22: vii-xi; and Vol. 24: vii-viii.

The revised, more literal textual method, which appeared for the first time in Volume 30, adheres to the following guidelines: Abbreviations will be retained as written. Where the meaning is sufficiently unclear to require editorial intervention, the expansion will be given in the explanatory annotation. Capitalization will follow the usage of the writer. Because the line between uppercase and lowercase letters can be a very fine and fluctuating one, when it is impossible to make an absolute determination of the author's intention, we will adopt modern usage. Jefferson rarely began his sentences with an uppercase letter, and we conform to his usage. Punctuation will be retained as written, and double marks of punctuation, such as a period followed by a dash, will be allowed to stand. Misspellings or so-called slips of the pen will be allowed to stand or will be recorded in a subjoined textual note.

English translations or translation summaries will be supplied for foreign-language documents. In some instances, when documents are lengthy and not especially pertinent to Jefferson's concerns or if our edition's typography cannot adequately represent the script of a language, we will provide only a summary in English. In most cases we will print in full the text in its original language and also provide a full English translation. If a contemporary translation that Jefferson made or would have used is extant, we may print it in lieu of a modern translation. Our own translations are designed to provide a basic readable English text for the modern user rather than to preserve all aspects of the original diction and language.

2. TEXTUAL DEVICES

The following devices are employed throughout the work to clarify the presentation of the text.

[. . .]	Text missing and not conjecturable.
[ ]	Number or part of a number missing or illegible.
[roman]	Conjectural reading for missing or illegible matter. A question mark follows when the reading is doubtful.
[*italic*]	Editorial comment inserted in the text.
<*italic*>	Matter deleted in the MS but restored in our text.

3. DESCRIPTIVE SYMBOLS

The following symbols are employed throughout the work to describe the various kinds of manuscript originals. When a series of versions is recorded, the first to be recorded is the version used for the printed text.

Dft	draft (usually a composition or rough draft; later drafts, when identifiable as such, are designated "2d Dft," &c.)
Dupl	duplicate
MS	manuscript (arbitrarily applied to most documents other than letters)
N	note, notes (memoranda, fragments, &c.)
PoC	polygraph copy
PrC	press copy
RC	recipient's copy
SC	stylograph copy
Tripl	triplicate

All manuscripts of the above types are assumed to be in the hand of the author of the document to which the descriptive symbol pertains. If not, that *fact is stated.* On the other hand, the following types of manuscripts are assumed *not* to be in the hand of the author, and exceptions will be noted:

FC	file copy (applied to all contemporary copies retained by the author or his agents)
Lb	letterbook (ordinarily used with FC and Tr to denote texts copied into bound volumes)

Tr   transcript (applied to all contemporary and later copies except file copies; period of transcription, unless clear by implication, will be given when known)

4. LOCATION SYMBOLS

The locations of documents printed in this edition from originals in private hands and from printed sources are recorded in self-explanatory form in the descriptive note following each document. The locations of documents printed from originals held by public and private institutions in the United States are recorded by means of the symbols used in the National Union Catalog in the Library of Congress; an explanation of how these symbols are formed is given in Vol. 1:xl. The symbols DLC and MHi by themselves stand for the collections of Jefferson Papers proper in these repositories; when texts are drawn from other collections held by these two institutions, the names of those collections will be added. Location symbols for documents held by institutions outside the United States are given in a subjoined list.

CSmH	The Huntington Library, San Marino, California
Ct	Connecticut State Library, Hartford
DLC	Library of Congress
DNDAR	Daughters of the American Revolution, Washington, D.C.
DeGH	Hagley Museum and Library, Greenville, Delaware
GHi	Georgia Historical Society, Savannah
MBCo	Countway Library of Medicine, Boston
MH	Harvard University, Cambridge, Massachusetts
MHi	Massachusetts Historical Society, Boston
MWA	American Antiquarian Society, Worcester, Massachusetts
MdHi	Maryland Historical Society, Baltimore
MeHi	Maine Historical Society, Portland
MiU-C	University of Michigan, William L. Clements Library, Ann Arbor
MoSHi	Missouri Historical Society, St. Louis
NHi	New-York Historical Society, New York City
NN	New York Public Library
NNC	Columbia University, New York City
NNFoM	Forbes Magazine, Inc., New York City
NNMus	Museum of the City of New York

NNPM	Pierpont Morgan Library, New York City
NjP	Princeton University
PHC	Haverford College Library, Pennsylvania
PHi	Historical Society of Pennsylvania, Philadelphia
PPAmP	American Philosophical Society, Philadelphia
PPCP	College of Physicians of Philadelphia, Pennsylvania
PPL	Library Company of Philadelphia, Pennsylvania
PWacD	David Library of the American Revolution, Washington Crossing, Pennsylvania
PWbH	Wyoming Historical and Geological Society, Wilkes-Barre, Pennsylvania
RNHi	Newport Historical Society, Rhode Island
Vi	Virginia State Library, Richmond
ViHan	Hanover County Historical Society, Hanover, Virginia
ViHi	Virginia Historical Society, Richmond
ViU	University of Virginia, Charlottesville
ViW	College of William and Mary, Williamsburg, Virginia

The following symbol represents a repository located outside of the United States:

AHN	Archivo Histórico Nacional, Madrid

5. NATIONAL ARCHIVES DESIGNATIONS

The National Archives, recognized by the location symbol DNA, with identifications of series (preceded by record group number) as follows:

RG 11	General Records of the United States Government
RG 21	Records of District Courts
RG 26	Records of the United States Coast Guard
	LDC Lighthouse Deeds and Contracts
	MLR Misc. Letters Received
RG 28	Records of the Post Office Department
	LPG Letters Sent by the Postmaster General
RG 36	Records of the United States Customs Service
	LFT Letters from the Treasury
RG 42	Records of the Office of Public Buildings and Public Parks of the National Capital
	DCLB District of Columbia Letterbook

	LR	Letters Received
	PC	Proceedings of the Board of Commissioners of the District of Columbia
RG 45		Naval Records Collection of the Office of Naval Records and Library
	LSO	Letters Sent to Officers
	LSP	Letters Sent to the President
	MLR	Misc. Letters Received
	MLS	Misc. Letters Sent
RG 46		Records of the United States Senate
	EPFR	Executive Proceedings, Foreign Relations
RG 59		General Records of the Department of State
	CD	Consular Dispatches
	DCI	Diplomatic and Consular Instructions
	DD	Diplomatic Dispatches
	DL	Domestic Letters
	GPR	General Pardon Records
	LAR	Letters of Application and Recommendation
	LOAG	Letters from and Opinions of Attorneys General
	MCL	Misc. Commissions and Lists
	MLR	Misc. Letters Received
	MPTPC	Misc. Permanent and Temporary Presidential Commissions
	NFC	Notes from Foreign Consuls
	NL	Notes from Legations
	PTCC	Permanent and Temporary Consular Commissions
	RD	Resignations and Declinations
RG 75		Records of the Bureau of Indian Affairs
	LSIA	Letters Sent by the Secretary of War Relating to Indian Affairs
	RCIAT	Records of the Cherokee Indian Agency in Tennessee
RG 76		Records of Boundary and Claims Commissions and Arbitrations
RG 104		Records of the Mint
	DL	Domestic Letters

RG 107   Records of the Office of the Secretary of War
   LRUS   Letters Received by the Secretary of
               War, Unregistered Series
   LSMA   Letters Sent by the Secretary of War
               Relating to Military Affairs
   MLS   Misc. Letters Sent
   RLRMS   Register of Letters Received, Main
               Series
RG 125   Records of the Office of the Judge Advocate
           General (Navy)
   GCMCI   Transcripts of Proceedings of General
               Courts-Martial and Courts of Inquiry
RG 233   Records of the United States House of
           Representatives
   PM   President's Messages
   TRC   Transcribed Reports of Committees

6. OTHER SYMBOLS AND ABBREVIATIONS

The following symbols and abbreviations are commonly employed in the annotation throughout the work.

Second Series   The topical series to be published as part of this edition, comprising those materials which are best suited to a topical rather than a chronological arrangement (see Vol. 1: xv-xvi)

TJ   Thomas Jefferson

TJ Editorial Files   Photoduplicates and other editorial materials in the office of The Papers of Thomas Jefferson, Princeton University Library

TJ Papers   Jefferson Papers (applied to a collection of manuscripts when the precise location of an undated, misdated, or otherwise problematic document must be furnished, and always preceded by the symbol for the institutional repository; thus "DLC: TJ Papers, 4:628-9" represents a document in the Library of Congress, Jefferson Papers, volume 4, pages 628 and 629. Citations to volumes and folio numbers of the Jefferson Papers at the Library of Congress refer to the collection as it was arranged at the time the first microfilm edition was made in 1944-45. Access to the microfilm edition of the collection as it was rearranged under the Library's Presidential Papers Program is provided by the Index to the Thomas Jefferson Papers [Washington, D.C., 1976])

RG   Record Group (used in designating the location of documents in the National Archives)

SJL   Jefferson's "Summary Journal of Letters" written and received for the period 11 Nov. 1783 to 25 June 1826 (in DLC: TJ Papers). This register, kept in Jefferson's hand, has been checked against the TJ Editorial Files. It is to be assumed that all outgoing letters are recorded in SJL unless there is a note to the contrary. When the date of receipt of an incoming letter is recorded in SJL, it is incorporated in the notes. Information and discrepancies revealed in SJL but not found in the letter itself are also noted. Missing letters recorded in SJL are, where possible, accounted for in the notes to documents mentioning them or in related documents. A more detailed discussion of this register and its use in this edition appears in Vol. 6: vii-x

SJPL   "Summary Journal of Public Letters," an incomplete list of letters and documents written by TJ from 16 Apr. 1784 to 31 Dec. 1793, with brief summaries, in an amanuensis's hand. This is supplemented by six pages in TJ's hand, compiled at a later date, listing private and confidential memorandums and notes as well as official reports and communications by and to him as Secretary of State, 11 Oct. 1789 to 31 Dec. 1793 (in DLC: TJ Papers, Epistolary Record, 514-59 and 209-11, respectively; see Vol. 22: ix-x). Since nearly all documents in the amanuensis's list are registered in SJL, while few in TJ's list are so recorded, it is to be assumed that all references to SJPL are to the list in TJ's hand unless there is a statement to the contrary

V   Ecu

ƒ   Florin

£   Pound sterling or livre, depending upon context (in doubtful cases, a clarifying note will be given)

s   Shilling or sou (also expressed as /)

d   Penny or denier

₶   Livre Tournois

℔   Per (occasionally used for pro, pre)

7. SHORT TITLES

The following list includes short titles of works cited frequently in this edition. Since it is impossible to anticipate all the works to be cited in abbreviated form, the list is revised from volume to volume.

Alberts, *Golden Voyage*   Robert C. Alberts, *The Golden Voyage: The Life and Times of William Bingham, 1752-1804*, Boston, 1969

Ammon, *Monroe*   Harry Ammon, *James Monroe: The Quest for National Identity*, New York, 1971

ANB   John A. Garraty and Mark C. Carnes, eds., *American National Biography*, New York and Oxford, 1999, 24 vols.

Annals   *Annals of the Congress of the United States: The Debates and Proceedings in the Congress of the United States . . . Compiled from Authentic Materials*, Washington, D.C., Gales & Seaton, 1834-56, 42 vols. All editions are undependable and pagination varies from one printing to another. The first two volumes of the set cited here have "Compiled . . . by Joseph Gales, Senior" on the title page and bear the caption "Gales & Seatons History" on verso and "of Debates in Congress" on recto pages. The remaining volumes bear the caption "History of Congress" on both recto and verso pages. Those using the first two volumes with the latter caption will need to employ the date of the debate or the indexes of debates and speakers.

APS   American Philosophical Society

ASP   *American State Papers: Documents, Legislative and Executive, of the Congress of the United States*, Washington, D.C., 1832-61, 38 vols.

Bear, *Family Letters*   Edwin M. Betts and James A. Bear, Jr., eds., *Family Letters of Thomas Jefferson*, Columbia, Mo., 1966

Bedini, *Statesman of Science*   Silvio A. Bedini, *Thomas Jefferson: Statesman of Science*, New York, 1990

Betts, *Farm Book*   Edwin M. Betts, ed., *Thomas Jefferson's Farm Book*, Princeton, 1953

Betts, *Garden Book*   Edwin M. Betts, ed., *Thomas Jefferson's Garden Book, 1766-1824*, Philadelphia, 1944

Biog. Dir. Cong.   *Biographical Directory of the United States Congress, 1774-1989*, Washington, D.C., 1989

Blanton, *Medicine in Virginia*   Wyndham B. Blanton, *Medicine in Virginia in the Eighteenth Century*, Richmond, 1931

Brigham, *American Newspapers*   Clarence S. Brigham, *History and Bibliography of American Newspapers, 1690-1820*, Worcester, Mass., 1947, 2 vols.

Bryan, *National Capital*   Wilhelmus B. Bryan, *A History of the National Capital from Its Foundation through the Period of the Adoption of the Organic Act*, New York, 1914-16, 2 vols.

Bush, *Life Portraits*　　Alfred L. Bush, *The Life Portraits of Thomas Jefferson*, rev. ed., Charlottesville, 1987

Cooke, *Coxe*　　Jacob E. Cooke, *Tench Coxe and the Early Republic*, Chapel Hill, 1978

Cunningham, *Process of Government*　　Noble E. Cunningham, Jr., *The Process of Government under Jefferson*, Princeton, 1978

CVSP　　William P. Palmer and others, eds., *Calendar of Virginia State Papers . . . Preserved in the Capitol at Richmond*, Richmond, 1875-93, 11 vols.

DAB　　Allen Johnson and Dumas Malone, eds., *Dictionary of American Biography*, New York, 1928-36, 20 vols.

Dangerfield, *Livingston*　　George Dangerfield, *Chancellor Robert R. Livingston of New York, 1746-1813*, New York, 1960

Daniels, *Randolphs of Virginia*　　Jonathan Daniels, *The Randolphs of Virginia*, Garden City, N.Y., 1972

Dexter, *Yale*　　Franklin Bowditch Dexter, *Biographical Sketches of the Graduates of Yale College with Annals of the College History*, New York, 1885-1912, 6 vols.

DHSC　　Maeva Marcus and others, eds., *The Documentary History of the Supreme Court of the United States, 1789-1800*, New York, 1985-2007, 8 vols.

Dictionnaire　　*Dictionnaire de biographie française*, Paris, 1933- , 19 vols.

DNB　　H. C. G. Matthew and Brian Harrison, eds., *Oxford Dictionary of National Biography, In Association with The British Academy, From the Earliest Times to the Year 2000*, Oxford, 2004, 60 vols.

DSB　　Charles C. Gillispie, ed., *Dictionary of Scientific Biography*, New York, 1970-80, 16 vols.

EG　　Dickinson W. Adams and Ruth W. Lester, eds., *Jefferson's Extracts from the Gospels*, Princeton, 1983, *The Papers of Thomas Jefferson*, Second Series

Evans　　Charles Evans, Clifford K. Shipton, and Roger P. Bristol, comps., *American Bibliography: A Chronological Dictionary of All Books, Pamphlets and Periodical Publications Printed in the United States of America from . . . 1639 . . . to . . . 1820*, Chicago and Worcester, Mass., 1903-59, 14 vols.

Ford　　Paul Leicester Ford, ed., *The Writings of Thomas Jefferson*, Letterpress Edition, New York, 1892-99, 10 vols.

Foster, *Hawkins*　　Thomas Foster, ed., *The Collected Works of Benjamin Hawkins, 1796-1810*, Tuscaloosa, Ala., 2003

Gallatin, *Papers*   Carl E. Prince and Helene E. Fineman, eds., *The Papers of Albert Gallatin*, microfilm edition in 46 reels, Philadelphia, 1969, and Supplement, Barbara B. Oberg, ed., reels 47-51, Wilmington, Del., 1985

Grainger, *Amiens Truce*   John D. Grainger, *The Amiens Truce: Britain and Bonaparte, 1801-1803*, Rochester, N.Y., 2004

Harris, *Thornton*,   C. M. Harris, ed., *Papers of William Thornton: Volume One, 1781-1802*, Charlottesville, 1995

HAW   Henry A. Washington, ed., *The Writings of Thomas Jefferson*, New York, 1853-54, 9 vols.

Heitman, *Dictionary*   Francis B. Heitman, comp., *Historical Register and Dictionary of the United States Army*, Washington, D.C., 1903, 2 vols.

Heitman, *Register*   Francis B. Heitman, *Historical Register of Officers of the Continental Army during the War of the Revolution, April, 1775, to December, 1793*, new ed., Washington, D.C., 1914

JEP   *Journal of the Executive Proceedings of the Senate of the United States . . . to the Termination of the Nineteenth Congress*, Washington, D.C., 1828, 3 vols.

JHR   *Journal of the House of Representatives of the United States*, Washington, D.C., 1826, 9 vols.

JS   *Journal of the Senate of the United States*, Washington, D.C., 1820-21, 5 vols.

King, *Life*   Charles R. King, ed. *The Life and Correspondence of Rufus King: Comprising His Letters, Private and Official, His Public Documents and His Speeches*, New York, 1894-1900, 6 vols.

Kline, *Burr*   Mary-Jo Kline, ed., *Political Correspondence and Public Papers of Aaron Burr*, Princeton, 1983, 2 vols.

L & B   Andrew A. Lipscomb and Albert E. Bergh, eds., *The Writings of Thomas Jefferson*, Washington, D.C., 1903-04, 20 vols.

LCB   Douglas L. Wilson, ed., *Jefferson's Literary Commonplace Book*, Princeton, 1989, *The Papers of Thomas Jefferson*, Second Series

Leonard, *General Assembly*   Cynthia Miller Leonard, comp., *The General Assembly of Virginia, July 30, 1619-January 11, 1978: A Bicentennial Register of Members*, Richmond, 1978

List of Patents   *A List of Patents granted by the United States from April 10, 1790, to December 31, 1836*, Washington, D.C., 1872

Longworth's   *Longworth's American Almanac, New-York Register, and City Directory*, New York
>   *for the Twenty-Fifth Year of American Independence*, 1800
>   *for the Twenty-Sixth Year of American Independence*, 1801

Madison, *Papers*   William T. Hutchinson, Robert A. Rutland, J. C. A. Stagg, and others, eds., *The Papers of James Madison*, Chicago and Charlottesville, 1962-   , 30 vols.
>   *Sec. of State Ser.*, 1986-   , 8 vols.
>   *Pres. Ser.*, 1984-   , 5 vols.

Malone, *Jefferson*   Dumas Malone, *Jefferson and His Time*, Boston, 1948-81, 6 vols.

Marshall, *Papers*   Herbert A. Johnson, Charles T. Cullen, Charles F. Hobson, and others, eds., *The Papers of John Marshall*, Chapel Hill, 1974-2006, 12 vols.

Mathews, *Ellicott*   Catharine Van Cortlandt Mathews, *Andrew Ellicott: His Life and Letters*, New York, 1908

MB   James A. Bear, Jr., and Lucia C. Stanton, eds., *Jefferson's Memorandum Books: Accounts, with Legal Records and Miscellany, 1767-1826*, Princeton, 1997, *The Papers of Thomas Jefferson*, Second Series

McLachlan, *Princetonians, 1748-1768*   James McLachlan, *Princetonians, 1748-1768: A Biographical Dictionary*, Princeton, 1976

Miller, *Alexandria Artisans*   T. Michael Miller, comp., *Artisans and Merchants of Alexandria, Virginia, 1780-1820*, Bowie, Md., 1991-92, 2 vols.

Miller, *Treaties*   Hunter Miller, ed., *Treaties and Other International Acts of the United States of America*, Washington, D.C., 1931-48, 8 vols.

Mirsky and Nevins, *Eli Whitney*   Jeannette Mirsky and Allan Nevins, *The World of Eli Whitney*, New York, 1952

Monroe, *Writings*   Stanislaus Murray Hamilton, ed., *The Writings of James Monroe*, New York, 1898-1903, 7 vols.

National State Papers: Adams   Martin P. Claussen, ed., *National State Papers of the United States, 1789-1817. Part II: Texts of Documents. Administration of John Adams, 1797-1801*, Wilmington, 1980, 24 vols.

NDBW   Dudley W. Knox, ed., *Naval Documents Related to the United States Wars with the Barbary Powers*, Washington, D.C., 1939-44, 6 vols. and *Register of Officer Personnel and Ships' Data, 1801-1807*, Washington, D.C., 1945

NDQW   Dudley W. Knox, ed., *Naval Documents Related to the Quasi-War between the United States and France, Naval Operations*, Washington, D.C., 1935-38, 7 vols. (cited by years)

Notes, ed. Peden   Thomas Jefferson, *Notes on the State of Virginia*, ed. William Peden, Chapel Hill, 1955

OED   J. A. Simpson and E. S. C. Weiner, eds., *The Oxford English Dictionary*, Oxford, 1989, 20 vols.

Palmer, *Stoddert's War*   Michael A. Palmer, *Stoddert's War: Naval Operations during the Quasi-War with France, 1798-1801*, Columbia, S.C., 1987

Papenfuse, *Maryland Legislature*   Edward C. Papenfuse, Alan F. Day, David W. Jordan, Gregory A. Stiverson, eds., *A Biographical Dictionary of the Maryland Legislature, 1635-1789*, Baltimore, 1979-85, 2 vols.

Parry, *Consolidated Treaty Series*   Clive Parry, ed., *The Consolidated Treaty Series*, Dobbs Ferry, N.Y., 1969-81, 231 vols.

Pasley, *Tyranny of Printers*   Jeffrey L. Pasley, *"The Tyranny of Printers": Newspaper Politics in the Early American Republic*, Charlottesville, 2001

Peale, *Papers*   Lillian B. Miller and others, eds., *The Selected Papers of Charles Willson Peale and His Family*, New Haven, 1983-2000, 5 vols. in 6

PMHB   *Pennsylvania Magazine of History and Biography*, 1877-

Preston, *Catalogue*   Daniel Preston, *A Comprehensive Catalogue of the Correspondence and Papers of James Monroe*, Westport, Conn., 2001, 2 vols.

Prince, *Federalists*   Carl E. Prince, *The Federalists and the Origins of the U.S. Civil Service*, New York, 1977

PW   Wilbur S. Howell, ed., *Jefferson's Parliamentary Writings*, Princeton, 1988, *The Papers of Thomas Jefferson*, Second Series

RCHS   *Records of the Columbia Historical Society*, 1895-1989

Rowe, *McKean*   G. S. Rowe, *Thomas McKean, The Shaping of an American Republicanism*, Boulder, Colo., 1978

RS   J. Jefferson Looney and others, eds., *The Papers of Thomas Jefferson: Retirement Series*, Princeton, 2004-   , 4 vols.

Saricks, *Du Pont*   Ambrose Saricks, *Pierre Samuel Du Pont de Nemours*, Lawrence, Kans., 1965

S.C. Biographical Directory, House of Representatives   J. S. R. Faunt, Walter B. Edgar, N. Louise Bailey, and others, eds., *Biographical Directory of the South Carolina House of Representatives*, Columbia, S.C., 1974-92, 5 vols.

S.C. Biographical Directory, Senate   N. Louise Bailey and others, eds., *Biographical Directory of the South Carolina Senate, 1776-1985,* Columbia, S.C., 1986, 3 vols.

Seale, *The President's House*   William Seale, *The President's House*, Washington, D.C., 1986, 2 vols.

Shackelford, *Jefferson's Adoptive Son*   George Green Shackelford, *Jefferson's Adoptive Son: The Life of William Short, 1759-1848*, Lexington, Ky., 1993

Shaw-Shoemaker   Ralph R. Shaw and Richard H. Shoemaker, comps., *American Bibliography: A Preliminary Checklist for 1801-1819*, New York, 1958-63, 22 vols.

Smith, *Napoleonic Wars*   Digby G. Smith, *The Greenhill Napoleonic Wars Data Book*, London, 1998

Sowerby   E. Millicent Sowerby, comp., *Catalogue of the Library of Thomas Jefferson*, Washington, D.C., 1952-59, 5 vols.

Sprague, *American Pulpit*   William B. Sprague, *Annals of the American Pulpit, or, Commemorative Notices of Distinguished American Clergymen of Various Denominations*, New York, 1857-69, 9 vols.

Stafford, *Philadelphia Directory*   Cornelius William Stafford, *The Philadelphia Directory*, Philadelphia, 1797-1801 (cited by year)

Stanton, *Free Some Day*   Lucia Stanton, *Free Some Day*, Thomas Jefferson Foundation, Inc., 2000

Stein, *Worlds*   Susan R. Stein, *The Worlds of Thomas Jefferson at Monticello*, New York, 1993

Stets, *Postmasters*   Robert J. Stets, *Postmasters & Postoffices of the United States, 1782-1811*, Lake Oswego, Ore., 1994

Stewart, *First United States Mint*   Frank H. Stewart, *History of the First United States Mint, Its People and Its Operations,* Camden, N.J. 1924

Stewart, *French Revolution*   John H. Stewart, *A Documentary Survey of the French Revolution*, New York, 1951

Sturtevant, *Handbook*   William C. Sturtevant, gen. ed., *Handbook of North American Indians*, Washington, 1978-   , 14 vols.

Syrett, *Hamilton*   Harold C. Syrett and others, eds., *The Papers of Alexander Hamilton*, New York, 1961-87, 27 vols.

Terr. Papers   Clarence E. Carter and John Porter Bloom, eds., *The Territorial Papers of the United States*, Washington, D.C., 1934-75, 28 vols.

TJR   Thomas Jefferson Randolph, ed., *Memoir, Correspondence, and Miscellanies, from the Papers of Thomas Jefferson*, Charlottesville, 1829, 4 vols.

Tulard, *Dictionnaire Napoléon*   Jean Tulard, *Dictionnaire Napoléon*, Paris, 1987

U.S. Statutes at Large   Richard Peters, ed., *The Public Statutes at Large of the United States . . . 1789 to March 3, 1845*, Boston, 1855-56, 8 vols.

VMHB   *Virginia Magazine of History and Biography*, 1893-

Wagstaff, *John Steele*   Henry M. Wagstaff, ed., *The Papers of John Steele*, Raleigh, N.C., 1924, 2 vols.

Walsh, *Early Banks in D.C.*   John Joseph Walsh, *Early Banks in the District of Columbia, 1792-1818*, Washington, 1940

Washington, *Papers*   W. W. Abbot, Dorothy Twohig, Philander D. Chase, Theodore J. Crackel, and others, eds., *The Papers of George Washington*, Charlottesville, 1983- , 48 vols.

    Col. Ser., 1983-95, 10 vols.

    Pres. Ser., 1987- , 12 vols.

    Ret. Ser., 1998-99, 4 vols.

    Rev. War Ser., 1985- , 16 vols.

White, *Genealogical Abstracts*   Virgil D. White, *Genealogical Abstracts of Revolutionary War Pension Files*, Waynesboro, Tenn., 1990-92, 4 vols.

WMQ   *William and Mary Quarterly*, 1892-

Woods, *Albemarle*   Edgar Woods, *Albemarle County in Virginia*, Charlottesville, 1901

CONTENTS

·‹⟪ 1801 ⟫›·

CONTENTS

CONTENTS

CONTENTS

CONTENTS

CONTENTS

CONTENTS

CONTENTS

CONTENTS

CONTENTS

CONTENTS

CONTENTS

CONTENTS

CONTENTS

CONTENTS

[xliii]

CONTENTS

APPENDICES

ILLUSTRATIONS

Following page 382

SUMMARY JOURNAL OF LETTERS, 17-31 AUG. 1801

Jefferson's Summary Journal of Letters documents the weekly delivery and the volume of mail forwarded from Washington to the president while he was at Monticello in August and September 1801. The page illustrated in this volume covers the latter half of August. In the right-hand column, under "Recieved," Jefferson recorded the approximately thirty letters that arrived at Monticello on each of two Thursdays, 20 and 27 Aug. Letters delivered in person came on other days. James Madison, for example, wrote to Jefferson from Montpelier on 27 Aug. by a "private opportunity." Jefferson received the letter the next day, as recorded at the bottom of the illustrated page.

As was his practice, Jefferson recorded in SJL the origin, date, and sometimes a word or phrase indicating the contents of the letters he received. He also kept track of many of the letters he wrote, by the date and recipient's name. The lines drawn to the left of each entry on the illustrated page are of unknown date and authorship (Vol. 6:vii-x).

Courtesy of the Library of Congress.

CARLOS MARTÍNEZ DE IRUJO

This image, painted by Gilbert Stuart about 1801, is of Carlos Martínez de Irujo, the Spanish minister to the United States. Irujo came to America in 1796. Through his father's family, he had ties to the Basque provinces of far northern Spain, while his mother's family came from the country's southernmost region. Irujo, who was born in 1763, studied at the university in Salamanca before entering the diplomatic service. Prior to his posting to the United States, when he was first secretary of the Spanish legation in London, he produced a distillation in Spanish of Adam Smith's *Wealth of Nations*. The American Philosophical Society elected him a member in 1802. He belonged to the Royal Order of Carlos III, and in 1802 the king of Spain made him the first marqués of Casa-Irujo.

In letters to his government, Irujo characterized John Adams as a "Machiavellist" and represented Timothy Pickering as "violent," crude, and wedded to British interests. In 1797, a disagreement between Irujo and Pickering, who was then secretary of state, erupted into a newspaper war between pseudonymous letter writers, in which Irujo, using the name "Verus," participated. He also engaged in an acrimonious dispute with William Cobbett. In 1800, responding to a request from the Adams administration for Irujo's recall, King Carlos IV's ministers found another diplomatic assignment for Irujo and appointed a new envoy to the United States. Irujo did not hurry to depart, however, saying that he should remain until his successor arrived, and Jefferson, when he became president, asked the Spanish government to keep Irujo in the United States. Irujo's letter of gratitude, dated 6 Oct. 1801, is printed in this volume. This portrait by Stuart, painted in oil on canvas, measures $30\frac{3}{4}$ by $31\frac{7}{8}$ inches (Eric Beerman, "Spanish Envoy to the United States

{ xlv }

ILLUSTRATIONS

[1796-1809]: Marques de Casa Irujo and His Philadelphia Wife Sally McKean," *The Americas*, 37 [1981], 445-56; Sandra Sealove, "The Founding Fathers as Seen by the Marqués de Casa-Irujo," *The Americas*, 20 [1963], 37-42; Carrie Rebora Barratt and Ellen G. Miles, *Gilbert Stuart* [New York, 2004], 243; Rowe, *McKean*, 295-303; James Tagg, *Benjamin Franklin Bache and the Philadelphia* Aurora [Philadelphia, 1991], 324; Carlos Martínez de Irujo, *Compendio de la Obra Inglesa Intitulada Riqueza de las Naciones* [Madrid, 1792]; APS, *Proceedings*, 22, pt. 3 [1884], 320; Vol. 30:53, 54-5n, 194n; Vol. 32:397n; Vol. 33:230, 322, 430, 453; Vol. 34:419-20).
Courtesy of the Duke of Sotomayor.

SARAH McKEAN IRUJO

Sarah (Sally) McKean met Carlos Martínez de Irujo at a dinner party in June 1796, soon after the diplomat's arrival in Philadelphia. They married in April 1798. In his request for permission to marry a foreigner, Irujo assured his government that his bride was a Catholic and that her father, Thomas McKean, was a prominent American statesman. McKean, who at the time of his daughter's wedding was chief justice of Pennsylvania, won the governorship of the state in 1799 and became an important supporter of Jefferson's election to the presidency. Of Irujo, McKean remarked to Jefferson in March 1801: "I love him as a child."

After the king made her husband a marqués, Sarah called herself the "Marchioness de Casa Yrujo" and enjoyed the prestige claimed by high-ranking European diplomats. The pair of portraits illustrated here, which is owned by the Irujos' descendants in Spain, was the first set that Gilbert Stuart painted of the couple. Although the paintings are undated, a letter from Sarah McKean Irujo to the artist in December 1801 implies that she was sitting for her portrait at that time. Her picture is in oil on wood, identical in size to her husband's portrait. Stuart, who was a guest at the dinner party where the Irujos first met, made at least one other set of portraits of the couple, completed in 1804, which remained in the possession of the McKean family. The marqués and marquesa de Irujo left the United States for Spain in 1808 (Barratt and Miles, *Gilbert Stuart*, 243-7; Beerman, "Spanish Envoy," 447-9; Vol. 33:392).
Courtesy of the Duke of Sotomayor.

PLAT OF ALLOTMENTS OF HENDERSON ESTATE

This plat, drawn by Albemarle County surveyor William Woods in 1801, shows four tracts of land belonging to the estate of Bennett Henderson, Sr., with each tract divided into ten allotments. In a drawing by lots ordered by the county court and carried out on 1 Oct. 1801, each of the ten heirs received one parcel of land in each tract. Earlier, Jefferson had begun to buy some of the Hendersons' shares in the estate. He made those purchases covertly, not in his own name but through Craven Peyton, an Albemarle County businessman who was married to one of Jefferson's nieces. As Woods noted on the plat, he made this copy at Peyton's request. Peyton sent it to Jefferson on 6 Nov., and Jefferson meticulously wrote the Hendersons' names in the allotments assigned to them in the 1 Oct. apportionment. He also added the locations of certain features of interest to him, such as the Hendersons' mill and milldam in the bend of the Rivanna River and a prospective mill seat in the narrow tract between the river and the town of Milton. To make a sheet of the right size and proportion for the plat, Woods pasted together with an overlap two pieces of paper, one of which is larger than the other. Those pieces have subsequently become detached. When they were together, the plat measured about 13 by 23 inches. Woods oriented the plat with south at the top. In that configuration, the river is on the left and the direction of its flow is from the bottom to the top of the plat. Jefferson had made his own diagram of the Henderson lands prior to their division among the heirs, and he oriented that drawing with north at the top and the Rivanna on the right (see Valuation of Henderson Property for Dower, [before 1 Oct. 1801]). When he worked with Woods's plat, he apparently rotated the paper to put north at the top. As a result, his neat and economically written notations are upside down when the plat is viewed as Woods created it. Turn the illustration upside down to see it as Jefferson used it.

With the plat oriented as Woods made it, south to the top, the town of Milton is the rectangle on the left, near the river. Woods did not indicate the town's acreage, which was unrelated to the distribution of the four tracts among the Henderson heirs. The 1789 act of the Virginia legislature that created Milton stipulated that the town should be laid out on 70 acres, and Jefferson added that figure, "70 as.," next to the town's name on the plat. The statute called for the town to be made up of half-acre lots, and more than 20 lots were sold by 1799. Again, however, showing the details of the town's layout was not within the surveyor's purpose when he drew this plat (Woods, *Albemarle*, 57, 58; William Waller Hening, ed., *The Statutes at Large; Being a Collection of All the Laws of Virginia*, 13 vols. [Richmond, 1809-23], 13:87).

Woods did not label the four tracts of the Henderson estate, but they are easily identified. Each is divided into ten allotments. Above Milton on the plat—that is, downstream from the town—is the tract that was referred to as the "Lower Field" (see Peyton to Jefferson, 1 Oct. 1801). A narrow strip between the riverbank and the town's edge was a tract called the "lands below the town." Upriver, which is to say below and somewhat to the right of Milton on the plat, is the "Upper Field" tract. Finally, stretching across the plat from Milton and the edge of the "Lower Field" is the largest of the tracts. In 1801 it was called the "Back Lands," and its irregular shape obviously prevented Woods from allotting it into ten simple rectangles. Running across the "Back Lands" is a band that Woods labeled a "Widow's dower" of 262 acres (see the Valuation of Henderson Property for Dower, printed at the end of September 1801). Another portion of land set aside for the dower right lay within the bend of the river. Labeled "Eliz. Hendersons Land" by the surveyor, that tract was not divided among the heirs in the drawing of lots. On it stood the residence occupied by Bennett Henderson's widow, Elizabeth Lewis Henderson, and the family's mill. Jefferson's nearby Shadwell and Monticello properties are indicated by the surveyor's sweeping notation, "Thos Jeffersons Lands," at the bottom of the plat and his name again in the upper right corner. Woods's labels around the edge of the map also locate other properties around the Henderson lands.

Within each tract, the allotments that went to Susan Henderson Kerr and three of her brothers, James, Isham, and Charles, have been outlined in red ink. That highlighting was very likely by Jefferson, since when he received the plat, those four people were the members of the Henderson family with whom Peyton had already made purchase arrangements. The Rivanna River is colored blue on the plat, probably in pencil. It is not known if that coloring was the surveyor's handiwork or Jefferson's.

Courtesy of the Tracy W. McGregor Library of American History, Special Collections, University of Virginia Library.

"THE EXHUMATION OF THE MASTODON" BY CHARLES WILLSON PEALE

This painting by Charles Willson Peale portrays the artist's recovery of mastodon bones in the Hudson Valley in the summer of 1801. In a letter to Jefferson of 11 Oct. 1801 printed in this volume, Peale described the excavation of the watery pit and the machinery that dominates this picture: a bucket hoist, supported by a derrick and powered by men walking inside a large wheel. Peale and his sons used fossils from the pit and from other sites in the vicinity, and made reproductions of missing bones, to assemble a composite skeleton of a mastodon. They opened it to public view in Philadelphia in December 1801. At that time the animal—an extinct mammal similar to an elephant—was called a "mammoth," or sometimes the "*incognitum.*" In 1806, the French naturalist Georges Cuvier distinguished the mastodon from the mammoth and gave the former animal its name.

In his picture, Peale located himself to the right of the pumping apparatus, with one hand gesturing toward the pit and the other hand clutching a diagram. As Peale informed Jefferson, the excavation and the exotic water-removal contraption attracted numbers of onlookers "of all sexes and ages." Although the painting illustrates a varied crowd of observers, some individuals in the picture never actually saw the excavation, including several members of Peale's family. The ornithologist Alexander Wilson, the figure standing with folded arms to the left of the derrick, also did not visit the site. Lillian B. Miller, an authority on Peale, argued that this work was an attempt to create a great historical painting of the neoclassical style rather than a simple factual record. For artists of Peale's day, paintings of dramatic, heroic events from classical or more recent times were the highest and most challenging achievement. Peale, who had studied under Benjamin West, a master of the form, used such terms as "historical" and "emblematical" to characterize this painting. Although he had it in mind by 1804, he did not paint it until 1806 and continued to add figures and retouch the image until 1808. The work, in oil on canvas, measures 50 by 62½ inches, or slightly more than four feet tall by five feet wide. The background depicts a "dreadful" thunderstorm that had threatened the excavation; Peale borrowed that feature from a picture that his son Rembrandt had begun but not completed. When Peale finally stopped working on this painting, there were 75 human figures in the scene. All are dwarfed by the machinery of the bucket hoist, and in Miller's and other scholars' assessment the picture lacks the unity required of a successful historical painting of that era. Peale considered it a test of his ability, threatening to abandon painting if he failed with this work. Ultimately, however, he was pleased with the results and purchased "a fine Mahogany *Easel*" to seal his commitment to artistic expression. He displayed the picture in his museum near the skeleton of the mastodon (Lillian B. Miller, "Charles Willson Peale as History Painter: *The Exhumation of the Mastodon*," *American Art Journal*, 13 [Winter 1981], 47-68; Peale, *Papers*, v. 2, pt. 2:752-3, 982, 983n, 984, 985, 996, 1010, 1036, 1039n, 1054, 1136; Christopher Brooks, "Charles Willson Peale: Painting and Natural History in Eighteenth-Century North America," *Oxford Art Journal*, 5 [1982], 39; Paul Semonin, *American Monster: How the Nation's First Prehistoric Creature Became a Symbol of National Identity* [New York, 2000], 354-61; Peale to TJ, 10 Jan. 1803, 19 Aug. 1804).

Courtesy of the Maryland Historical Society.

BREAST OF VENUS PEACH

The pit of the Poppa di Venere, or Breast of Venus, peach was one of four varieties that Philip Mazzei sent to Jefferson from Pisa with his letter of 28 Sep. He sent additional stones and cuttings of the fruit tree to Jefferson later in his presidency. This distinctive large and round peach was, observed William Coxe, "divided by a furrow on one side running from the stem to the point at the head of the fruit, which is so large as to characterize it." The illustrated engraving is reproduced from M. Duhamel du Monceau's *Traité des arbres fruitiers; contenant leur figure, leur description, leur culture, &c.*, published in Paris in 1768 in two volumes, this being Plate 23 in the second volume (Coxe, *A View of the Cultivation of Fruit Trees, and the Management of Orchards and Cider* . . . [Philadelphia, 1817]; Peter J. Hatch, *The Fruits and Fruit Trees at Monticello* [Charlottesville, 1998], 89-90; MB, 2:1182).

Courtesy of Princeton University Library.

COWPOX ON A HAND

This image, reproduced from a facsimile of the original engraving in Edward Jenner's first major treatise on vaccination, represents the hand of a dairy worker who contracted cowpox from an infected cow. In an experiment, Jenner drew "matter" from the woman's pustules to inoculate a youth. The youth successfully developed the disease and demonstrated resistance to smallpox (*An Inquiry into the Causes and Effects of the Variolæ Vaccinæ* [London, 1798; repr., Milan, 1923], 31-4, and Plate 1).

Jefferson, whom Benjamin Waterhouse tutored in methods of vaccination in 1801, emphasized the importance of observing subjects after attempted inoculation. The look of the pustules that appeared several days after inoculation indicated whether or not the vaccination was successful. While Jefferson was at Monticello in August and September of 1801, he conducted multiple inoculations and concluded that drawing matter on the eighth day after inoculation gave the most consistent results. Cowpox, an animal disease, was difficult to obtain in its "genuine" form, and vaccinators had to be wary of spurious or adulterated cowpox, which did not protect against smallpox and could harm the patient (Hervé Bezin, *The Eradication of Smallpox: Edward Jenner and the First and Only Eradication of a Human Infectious Disease*, trans. Andrew and Glenise Morgan [San Diego, 2000], 34-41, 120-2; List of Inoculations, printed at 7 Aug.; TJ to John Shore, 12 Sep.; TJ to John Vaughan, 5 Nov.).

Volume 35

1 August to 30 November 1801

JEFFERSON CHRONOLOGY
1743 · 1826

1743	Born at Shadwell, 13 Apr. (New Style).
1760	Entered the College of William and Mary.
1762	"quitted college."
1762-1767	Self-education and preparation for law.
1769-1774	Albemarle delegate to House of Burgesses.
1772	Married Martha Wayles Skelton, 1 Jan.
1775-1776	In Continental Congress.
1776	Drafted Declaration of Independence.
1776-1779	In Virginia House of Delegates.
1779	Submitted Bill for Establishing Religious Freedom.
1779-1781	Governor of Virginia.
1782	His wife died, 6 Sep.
1783-1784	In Continental Congress.
1784-1789	In France as Minister Plenipotentiary to negotiate commercial treaties and as Minister Plenipotentiary resident at Versailles.
1790-1793	Secretary of State of the United States.
1797-1801	Vice President of the United States.
1801-1809	President of the United States.
1814-1826	Established the University of Virginia.
1826	Died at Monticello, 4 July.

VOLUME 35
1 August to 30 November 1801

1 Aug.	U.S. schooner *Enterprize* defeats Tripolitan corsair near Malta.
7 Aug.	Smallpox vaccinations commence at Monticello.
13 Aug.	Receives first letter from "Nicholas Geffroy."
22 Aug.	Virginia Jefferson Randolph, TJ's granddaughter, born at Monticello.
29 Aug.	Samuel Meredith tenders his resignation as Treasurer of the U.S.
6 Sep.	Étienne Lemaire assumes stewardship of the President's House.
11 Sep.	Robert Smith reports Republican success in Maryland elections.
18 Sep.	Matthew L. Davis visits TJ at Monticello.
20 Sep.	Francis Eppes, TJ's grandson, born at Monticello.
27 Sep.	Leaves Monticello for Washington, arriving on 30 Sep.
1 Oct.	Preliminary peace treaty signed between France and Great Britain.
7 Oct.	Danbury Baptist Association assembles at Colebrook, Connecticut.
11 Oct.	Acknowledges receipt of new chariot from Philadelphia.
15 Oct.	Robert R. Livingston sails for Europe in the frigate *Boston*.
22 Oct.	Receives "Mammoth veal" from Philadelphia.
25 Oct.	Gideon Granger accepts appointment as postmaster general.
1 Nov.	Inquires into the suicide of James Hemings.
5 Nov.	Forwards vaccine matter to John Vaughan in Philadelphia.
6 Nov.	Issues circular to heads of departments on communications between president and cabinet officers.
ca.12 Nov.	Prepares first draft of annual message to Congress.
24 Nov.	Sends James Monroe opinion on removal of rebellious slaves from Virginia.
28 Nov.	Approves prosecution of the schooner *Sally* for preparing to engage in the slave trade.

THE PAPERS OF
THOMAS JEFFERSON

·《 ══════ 》·

From "Nicholas Geffroy"

New-Port August 1st 1801.

Encouraged, great & good Sir, by the character you sustain of being accesible to all of your fellow Citizens, I take the liberty of obtruding myself upon your precious time, to offer you my homage, & to assure you of the sentiments of veneration & respect with which I have been inspired by your wise, virtuous, & popular administration. The People of America would have gained but little by placing you in the presidential chair if the abuses of the past administrations had been continued, & you having commenced the correction of them (with the hope of your making a complete reform) have filled with contentment & delight all good men in this State.[1] Under the administration of John Adams very extensive fortifications were commenced & nearly completed in this harbour, merely I believe for the purpose of benefiting Genl Knox. How, you will ask, was Genl Knox to be advantaged by the building of forts at New-Port? The fact is, Sir, the engineer had it in charge from the President to obtain all the materials from Genl Knox—Colo Toussard went, at the public expence, to St. Georges river to make contracts which were paid for in advance, & the forts here were built of timber Bricks &c &c sent here in vessels by Knox all the way from the province of maine & at an enormous expence—the very lime was brought here in barrels from Knox's estate, & when the engineer was once asked at our Coffee-House why he did not refuse it on account of its badness, he answer'd "because my orders are to take all my materials from Knox's estate." This as you can easily imagine greatly scandalized the honest part of our community. After fort Adams was built eight acres of land were bought in that neighbourhood for the accommodation of the Garrison, *as 'was said*, at the price of two hundred dollars the acre—this was an unheard of price for land here, and the purchase was made of an old lady of Massachusetts who is Sister to Mrs. Adams.[2] All the offices here have been filled by persons who were recommended only

[3]

by their violence of character—the rule of appointing violent & hot headed men has governed from the office of Collector downwards. The system of which these things were parts have greatly disgusted a great majority of the People of this State—particularly the Quakers who make a large portion of 'em—Your beginning to correct the abuses of your Predecessor gives us infinite joy. Stopping the building of forts here is highly satisfactory.[3] The appointing Mr Howell attorney receives general approbation, tho' the appointment of Mr Barnes does not—Barnes is feeble in point of talents, & in politics is any thing every thing & nothing—with Tories a tory & with Wigs he is a wig. This State is at present decidedly in the wig interest (in the Genl Assembly we have a majority of more than one third) & there is a prospect of its being permanently so. In Connecticut New-Hampshire & Massachusetts political heresies are so rooted, & priest-craft is so fully in operation, that you cannot conciliate those States—but some attentions from you may do much here; & in Vermont may be useful tho' in a less degree. Gov Fenner, Mr Christopher Ellery (a Senator in Congress) Gen Joseph Staunton, Mr Paul Mumford & Wm Vernon senr are vastly influential characters in Rhode Island. The union of their interests in the parts of the State they respectively reside makes a majority of our People. I don't know if there be any reason for it but 'tis confidently said here that either Christopher Ellery or Paul Mumford will be the successor of the present Collector old Mr Ellery—they are both of them excellent men & the promotion of either would give equal pleasure. The answer you condescended to give to the remonstrance of the Satellites of old Hillhouse at new Haven, has afforded us much pleasure; & even some of our most high toned Tories acknowledge the correctness of the principle which requires that the subordinates should be of the same politics with the chief. Some young englishmen who scribble for the Papers at Providence will censure this as they will every measure of yours, but the great bulk of the People in this State think 'tis your duty to take care of yourself—that you should give fair play to your own administration—that wig principles ought to go freely into operation—that the measures of administration ought not to be fettered by being entrusted to those who disapprove 'em. These sentiments are universal among the wigs of New England. They are anathematized by Tories, but depend upon it Sir *you* cannot please *them*! Every thing from *you they* will censure (I mean the leaders of the party) Some time past they said you did not *dare* to turn men out of office, for that your nerves were too weak, now they begin to shake in their shoes & suppose you will turn 'em all out. Unless Sir the Tories are dismissed from Office (& all offices in New England are occupied by tories) you will be betrayed. Your meeting the wishes of the People (as expressed at the late election) and putting the government into the hands of Wigs is deemed essential here to our well doing. A purification is necessary, & we cannot be purified unless you cleanse the Augean Stable *completely*. The People of new-Haven (set on by old-Hillhouse) bluster about the appointment of Mr Bishop, because (as they *say*) he is old, & yet these very People abuse you, *in advance*, for the dismissal of old Ellery here & Genl. Lincoln in Boston (taking it for granted they will be dismissed) & both of these gentlemen are as old, and much more infirm than Bishop. I had the honor of being presented to you Sir, when you accompanied Genl Washington in his visit to this town, & I wish you may think that circumstance & my wish to give you some local information an excuse for troubling you with this letter & of assuring you of my respect & veneration. Should your Excellency visit this country it will give me unspeakable delight to tender my respect & services in person. Your time is so fully & usefully employed that I can hardly expect the honor of an answer from you, but should you deign in some moment of leisure to favor me with a line 'twill gladden the heart of an old man now sixty nine years of age, whose heart is sound with affection for you, & who seeing the affairs of this Country deposited in your Hands, says, sincerely, *now good Lord let thy Servant depart in Peace* for the first object of his wishes is complete. With unfeigned respect & esteem, great & good Sir, I am your humble Servant NICHOLAS GEFFROY—

Printed in the Newport *Rhode-Island Republican*, 18 Sep. 1802; at head of text: "Rutledge's Letters To the President of the United States." RC recorded in SJL as received 13 Aug., but not found. PrC (Charles M. Storey, Boston, 1958), being an extract consisting of several sentences (see notes below); entirely in TJ's hand; faint and frayed; at head of text: "Extract of a letter from Newport dated Aug. 1. 1801." Extract enclosed in TJ to Dearborn and TJ to Madison, 14 Aug.

The *Rhode-Island Republican* described Nicholas Geffroy as a native of France, about 40 years of age, and a jeweler and watchmaker of Newport. Although he possessed some mastery of spoken English, it was doubted that Geffroy could write, "with any degree of correctness, a single sentence of the language" (*Rhode-Island Republican*, 18 Sep. 1802).

TJ appointed David HOWELL U.S. attorney for Rhode Island in May 1801. He appointed David Leonard BARNES U.S. district judge for the state in April (Vol. 33:675).

A brigadier general of the Rhode Island militia, JOSEPH Stanton (STAUNTON), Jr., represented his state in the U.S. Senate from 1790 to 1793 and in the House of Representatives from 1801 to 1807 (Heitman, *Register*, 514; *Biog. Dir. Cong.*). Newport lawyer PAUL MUMFORD was a former chief justice of Rhode Island and a member of the state senate (*National Cyclopaedia of American Biography*, 63 vols. [New York; Clifton, N.J., 1898-1984], 9:393; Dexter, *Yale*, 2:346). William VERNON, Sr., was a prominent Newport merchant, who chaired the Eastern Navy Board during the American Revolution. In 1790 he sought TJ's assistance in securing the return of his son from France (DAB; Vol. 17:483-4; Vol. 19:247).

A signer of the Declaration of Independence, William Ellery, the PRESENT COLLECTOR at Newport, was appointed in 1790 and remained in office until his death in 1820 (ANB; JEP, 1:51).

TJ accompanied George WASHINGTON on a brief VISIT to Newport on 17-18 Aug. 1790 (Washington, *Papers, Pres. Ser.,* 6:281-2; Vol. 17:390, 402).

REMONSTRANCE OF THE SATELLITES: see the Remonstrance of the New Haven Merchants, printed at 18 June 1801, and TJ's reply to them of 12 July.

On 20 Aug., TJ received another letter from Newport, dated 7 Aug. and signed "Nics Jeffroy." The second letter informed TJ that Henry Dearborn had just visited Newport and declared that additional forts would be completed there. The news gave "much uneasiness" to residents, the author stated, who feared that the project would inflate local wages and inundate the town with "Bands of licentious Soldiers." The letter also claimed that TJ's reply to the New Haven merchants was well received in Boston, although the "Essex Junto write against it." Republicans were a solid majority in the Rhode Island legislature, but Federalists still held the federal offices in the state. The author recommended that the collector at Providence, Jeremiah Olney, be replaced by Arthur Fenner, and he again recommended Christopher Ellery, Mumford, and Vernon to TJ's attention. He also claimed to share TJ's interest in botany, and offered to send "some bushes of the *Daily Rose*" if TJ wished. The letter concluded by reporting that David Leonard Barnes spoke "unhandsomely" of TJ at a recent public dinner and

claimed that he owed his appointment to the federal bench to his friend Levi Lincoln (printed in the Newport *Rhode-Island Republican*, 18 Sep. 1802; at head of text: "Rutledge's Letters To the President of the United States"; RC recorded in SJL as received 20 Aug., but not found).

On 28 Aug., Christopher Ellery wrote TJ to inform him that the letters of 1 and 7 Aug. were not written by Nicholas Geffroy, but were in fact forgeries. He hinted that the actual author was John Rutledge, Jr. TJ apparently gave the original Geffroy letters to Ellery sometime in 1802. The letters were printed on 18 Sep. 1802 in the *Rhode-Island Republican*, whose editor invited the public to examine the original copies for themselves. The publication of the Geffroy letters touched off a brief but rancorous public contest over their authorship, which culminated in a physical assault on Ellery by Rutledge in January 1803. Although Rutledge vehemently maintained his innocence in the affair, including sending a written appeal to TJ on 20 Oct. 1802, the negative publicity resulted in his decision not to seek reelection in 1803 (Elizabeth Cometti, "John Rutledge, Jr., Federalist," *Journal of Southern History*, 13 [1947], 201-11; Robert Kent Ratzlaff, "John Rutledge, Jr., South Carolina Federalist, 1766-1819" [Ph.D. diss., University of Kansas, 1975], 212-20; Ellery to TJ, 28 Aug. 1801, 29 Apr. 1802; TJ to Ellery, 17 Sep. 1801; Rutledge to TJ, 20 Oct. 1802).

[1] PrC extract begins here.
[2] PrC extract breaks off here.
[3] Sentence included in PrC, ending extract.

From Philippe de Létombe

MONSIEUR LE PRÉSIDENT, Philadelphie, 1er aoust 1801. (v. St.)

J'ai reçu la lettre dont Vous avez bien voulu m'honorer le 15 du mois dernier, en réponse à la mienne du 11 précédent.

Monsieur Bingham devant partir incessamment, Le Maire est venu me dire, avant hier, à mon arrivée de New york, qu'il accepte l'honneur de Vous servir à *trente* dollars par mois, son voyage d'ici à Washington à vos frais. il pourra se rendre, dans quinze Jours ou trois Semaines, auprès de Rapin qui lui a promis de le mettre, en peu de tems, au fait des fonctions de maître d'hotel. Monsieur de Ternant (qui l'a amené ici) m'a dit que Vous ne pouvez avoir un Officier plus fidèle, plus actif et plus habile. Je serai très flatté, Monsieur le Président, que Vous vouliez bien m'adresser vos ordres pour les lui transmettre.

Monsieur Livingston se trouvant à Clermont, à mon arrivée à New york, je lui ai écrit. Mais je n'en ai reçu encore aucune réponse. J'aurai l'honneur de Vous informer de l'époque de mon départ et d'attendre, avec confiance, la dépêche dont Vous daignerez m'honorer à ce Sujet.

Je Vous supplie, Monsieur le Président, de vouloir bien agréér l'hommage de mon profond respect. LÉTOMBE

EDITORS' TRANSLATION

MISTER PRESIDENT, Philadelphia, 1st Aug. 1801 (old style)
I received the letter with which you kindly honored me the 15th of last month in reply to mine of the 11th of the preceding one.

Mr. Bingham being about to leave very shortly, Lemaire came to tell me, the day before yesterday, upon my arrival from New York, that he accepts the honor of serving you at *thirty* dollars per month, with his travel from here to Washington at your expense. He will be able to arrive within two or three weeks at Rapin's, who has promised to acquaint him in a short time with his functions as maître d'hôtel. Monsieur de Ternant (who brought him here) told me that you could not have an officer in your service more faithful, more active and more skillful. I shall be most flattered, Mister President, should you be willing to address to me your orders to transmit to him.

Mr. Livingston, being at Clermont upon my arrival in New York, I wrote to him, but I have not yet received any answer. I shall be honored to advise you of the time of my departure and to await confidently the dispatch with which you will deign to honor me on that subject.

I beg you, Mister President, kindly to accept the homage of my deep respect. LÉTOMBE

RC (DLC); endorsed by TJ as received 13 Aug. and so recorded in SJL.

From Peyton Short

DEAR SIR, Cincin[nati]—1st. Augst. 1801
I beg leave to return my thanks for the Letter you were so good as to forward me from my Brother, some short time ago—

I am sorry you shd. have thought it necessary to give me any explanation respecting the Seal— Even had I not conceived of you far more highly than of the best of Characters, I shd., not have thought of ascribing the Circumstance to any other than the Cause assigned by you—and divested of that Consideration, I could not have had the Vanity to suppose any thing in an epistolary intercourse in which I was a party, worthy of your Observation—

I again take the Liberty of enclosing you another Letter to my Brother, as he still assures me that I may continue to use that freedom on Acct. of the Friendship that subsists between yourself & him—

Accept, Dr Sir, Assurances of the highest Respect & Esteem of Yr. Obt. Sert.   PEYTON SHORT

RC (MiU-C); torn at seal; addressed: "Thomas Jefferson Esquire President of the U. States City of Washington"; franked; postmarked 4 Aug.; endorsed by TJ as received 21 Aug., but recorded in SJL as received 27 Aug. Enclosure: Peyton Short to William Short, 30 July 1801, acknowledged in summary of William

Short to Peyton Short, 19 Dec. 1801, in William's epistolary record in DLC: Short Papers; see also TJ to William Short, 3 Oct. 1801.

SO GOOD AS TO FORWARD ME: see note to TJ to William Short, 17 Mch. 1801.

From Benjamin Waterhouse

Cambridge August 1st. 1801.

Vaccine matter on the tooth-pick taken July 31.st. in the evening. The thread taken at the same time.—The two plates of glass, which he[1] have covered with lead is just come to hand from Dr. Jenner being taken May 19th. in London. Two other plates containing some of the virus taken at the same time has been proved to be perfectly active. It adheres to the glass like gum. water, warm steam, or a little hot water is necessary to dilute it for use.—Dr Waterhouse is anxious to hear from Washington respecting the success of his endeavours—

RC (DLC); endorsed by TJ as received 13 Aug. from Waterhouse, and so recorded in SJL.

VACCINE MATTER: for two previous

supplies of smallpox vaccine, or cowpox, that Waterhouse sent to TJ, see Waterhouse to TJ, 24 July.

[1] Word interlined in place of "I."

From George Douglas

SIR,   Petersburg, 2d. Aug. 1801

Some time ago I took the liberty of sending you a copy of our last year's *Register*—It was put under the care of a young Gentleman, who promised to have it delivered at the Presidential house as he passed thro' Washington—

Two reasons made me hesitate in writing to you along with the Book—I was apprehensive lest you should think that I wished to force myself upon your notice—and, I was fearful of intruding in the important avocations of your present high & very arduous office—

Finding at length, by the News-papers, that you had left the Federal City & gone to Monticello, I have seized the opportunity of acknowledging my grateful obligations for the honor you did me in writing your letter of the 21st. of Decr. last—

Agreeable to my plan, I had a drawing, or front elevation of the Capitol taken by a person in Richmond, & I got it engraved by one of the most eminent Artists in Philadelphia—The work was completed in the month of Decr. & I had every reason to expect the copies, or impressions, here in January—After waiting two months for them, in March they sent me the plate itself, but the copies, by some unlucky accident or other, were lost or mislaid, & have not yet been found—

I need scarcely say, that this very unpleasant affair has given me much uneasiness—And it has shewn me that I am placed in too remote & too inconsequential a situation, to execute such a plan with any sort of propriety, and or with any rational prospect of success—

I hope you will not think this letter an intrusion on your great or necessary employments, but that you will believe I thought it an incumbent duty on me for your goodness in writing on this subject.—

I most sincerely pray, that your Presidency may not only be a source of inward satisfaction & public honor to yourself, but that it may tend to illustrate the *theory* & establish the *practice* of Republicansim in the United States of America to the remotest posterity.

G: Douglas.

RC (DLC); endorsed by TJ as received 13 Aug. and so recorded in SJL.

Douglas had earlier sent TJ a COPY of his *Annual Register, and Virginian Repository*, and a BOOK, *Washingtoniana: A Collection of Papers Relative to the Death and Character of General George Washington*; see Vol. 32:220-1.

TJ left Washington for MONTICELLO on 30 July (Vol. 34:684-5).

The DRAWING of the Virginia Capitol was done by the Richmond miniaturist Lawrence Sully, older brother of Thomas Sully, and was ENGRAVED by Alexander Lawson. The engraved plate did not arrive from Philadelphia in time for Douglas to use in his 1801 almanac, but it was used for his *Virginia and North Carolina Almanack for the Year 1802*, published by Douglas and Ross in 1801 (Fiske Kimball, *The Capitol of Virginia: A Landmark of American Architecture*, rev. ed. [Richmond, 2002], 31-32, 78).

From Lyon Lehman

WORTHY SIR   Philadelphia 2d. August 1801

I take the liberty to adress a few lines to you, to inform you my unhappy situation, and my suffrings, and no doubt my worthy President can not help to feel for me. I am a Native of Amsterdam emigrated to France, till we marched to Holland again were I received several wounds when we Batavians entered into Holland, as I had a little property of my own as merchant made severel voyages to America and brought to this country on duties above $9000 I was taken then by the English 350 miles from the land and have put us in a long boat where I was in situation for 18 hours till we were saved at last by a pilot-boat this loss of mine amounted to $14000 even every Steatch of Cloth took those pirates of us, of my unhappy situation I have every bit of paper to Produce. Esqr. Edward Livingston presented a petition in Congress for a remission on duties last cession which amounted to $1684. our Vice President Aaron Bur knows me well as I am now in Such a melancholly situation to ask any small situation which would suport me in any degree as my correctories known in the United States. Not troubling you any longer with this writing therefore will conclude with every sincerly good wishes, health, long live, and Happiness, is the intimate wish of your friend & Humble Servant   LYON LEHMAN

N.B. Edward Livingston has seen all my papers likewise Mr Keltetus & knows my Situation

The President will therefore Honour his faithfull Servant by dressing an answer to Lyon Lehman Philadelphia

RC (DNA: RG 59, LAR); in an unidentified hand, signed by Lehman; at head of text: "Thomas Jefferson Esqr. President of the United States of America"; endorsed by TJ as received 13 Aug. and so recorded in SJL with notation "Off."

On 5 Feb. 1800, EDWARD LIVINGSTON presented Lehman's PETITION, requesting a remission of duties on firearms imported from Hamburg, to the House of Representatives, where it was referred to the Committee of Commerce and Manufactures. The committee reported on 10 Feb., but no further action was taken. On 7 Feb., New York Senator James Watson presented the same petition to the Senate.

As president of the Senate, TJ endorsed it "Feb. 7 recd. & commd." In the memorial Lehman explained that he had imported firearms in October 1799 with the intention of selling them to the War Department, but James McHenry refused to purchase them. The government then prevented Lehman from exporting the firearms to the West Indies. In the end he was forced to sell the rifles for less than cost. Because he was prohibited from exporting the arms, Lehman petitioned for a refund of the $1,684 he had paid in duties at New York (MS in DNA: RG 233, 7th Cong., 1st sess., undated, in an unidentified hand, at head of text: "To the Honourable the Senate, and House of Representatives, of the United States of

America, in Congress assembled: The Memorial of Lyon Lehman a Citizen of the united States"; JHR, 3:786, 792; JS, 3:27). A committee reported on the petition on 21 Feb. and brought in a bill for the relief of Lehman on 5 Mch. TJ endorsed the bill on that date, but no further action was taken in the Senate. On 19 Jan. 1802, the House of Representatives again considered Lehman's petition. This time the House and Senate acted on it favorably. TJ signed the "Act for the relief of Lyon Lehman," authorizing the refund of $1,684 in duties, on 6 Mch. 1802 (JS, 3:33, 42, 189; JHR, 4:54, 123; U.S. Statutes at Large, 6:45; Vol. 31:604).

From John Barnes

SIR   Geo: Town 3d Augst. 1801—

—free from the pressing Cares of Government I hope you may enjoy at last sir [. . .] [the sweets] of Domestic happiness—without [allay].

—The master of the sloop with whom I intrusted your packages of groceries, and 5 lbs. plaister of Paris—from hence to Alexandria intended for the Sloop Abigal & Rebecca from there to Richmond as the latter had left Alexandria the Evening before—was so obliging as to pursue and with some difficulty overhauled and delivered them safe on Board the A & R—with promise of delivering them as expressed in Bills Lading—tho unsigned, nor had Capt. L[. . .] time or opportunity to return me one as desired—. he suspects however from Contrary winds, & weather the A & R must have had a tedious passage. Still I hope she is ere this arrived at Richmond and that I may Venture, to send on the plaisterers, in the Course of a day or two, without risque.

—Mr Richards at Philada. in his late advices says "I have paid Doct Jackson $112.—as well as Mr. Mercer the Amt. of his Acct. for 6 Boxes sirup of punch [a] $10 [is] $60 (at request of Mr Rapin) on the Presidents a/c—and further he says "I still hold your check on Bank US. for $4000 of 16th June not hearing anything from Mr Dinsmore—to whom I sent your letter as ℔ address &c—in this Case you will be pleased to inform his Brother or Cousin with you—for his [. . .] [government therein?]—

Mr Rapin sent me a Key—(I presume) for his Room & [. . .]—I purpose calling to see if any thing is needfull or wanting at Washington—and abt the 10th Inst. expect to Obtain another warrant from the Treasury for $2000—if therefore, you should have, any [Occasional?] paymts. to make, I shall be fully prepared to answer them—

I am most Respectfully Sir, your Obed: & very hum Sev

JOHN BARNES

P.S. Your wt each figs: prunes, Raisins & Almonds, with 2 Books, are still in my stores without a present Chance of conveyance—unless I can meet with one from Alexandria—

Mr Conrads pair of looking glasses shall be procured and Mr Carpenters Bill paid when Called upon

―――――

Mr Richards also advises I shall in a few day rendr Invoices of your last order shipped for Richmond, on a/c of the President, Glass &c. &c.

RC (ViU: Edgehill-Randolph Papers); words illegible from bleeding of ink; addressed: "Thomas Jefferson Esqr. President U States at, Monticello—Virga."; franked and postmarked; endorsed by TJ as received 6 Aug. and so recorded in SJL.

TJ had ordered Barnes on 22 July to pay David JACKSON on William Wardlaw's account (TJ to Wardlaw, 16 July). SIRUP OF PUNCH: in a statement of TJ's account for the president's household, Barnes recorded a payment to John Richards at Philadelphia on 29 July for six boxes of syrup of punch for $60 (statement of household account from John Barnes, 30 Sep. 1801, in ViU).

The CHECK on the Bank of the U.S. for $400 was intended for Andrew DINSMORE (TJ to James Dinsmore, 10 June).

The WARRANT of $2,000 expected from the TREASURY was part of the president's annual compensation (Barnes to TJ, 5 May). On 7 Sep. Barnes received from the Treasury $4,000 for the months of July and August (MB, 2:1040; Barnes to TJ, 7 Sep. 1801).

TJ received an invoice for $24 from Conrad & McMunn, dated 24 Oct., for one pair of LOOKING GLASSES. Two days later, on the same sheet, below the invoice TJ dated and signed an order on Barnes for payment of $24 to Conrad & McMunn to discharge the bill (MS in ViU; acknowledgment of payment in full on verso, written and signed by David Dobbins for Conrad & McMunn, Georgetown, 26 Oct.; endorsed by TJ: "Conrad & McMunn"; endorsed by Barnes: "Private a/c"). TJ recorded the order on Barnes in his financial memoranda at 26 Oct. The next day, Barnes charged $24 to TJ's account (MB, 2:1056; statement of private account from John Barnes, 5 Nov. 1801, in ViU).

MR CARPENTERS BILL: Thomas Carpenter's latest bill is printed at 1 July.

On 15 Aug., Barnes entered in the statement of TJ's private account, the payment of $42.53 to John Richards per the invoices of sundries SHIPPED FOR RICHMOND from Philadelphia and another $5.40 for extra charges and postage for a total payment of $47.93 (statement of private account from John Barnes, 30 Sep. 1801, in ViU).

From Albert Gallatin

DR SIR   City of Washington August 3d 1801

I enclose a letter this day received from St. Th. Mason in relation to South Carolina politics. My impression had been, on that subject, altogether different from yours, as I thought I had understood it from Mr Pinckney that immediate changes were necessary, whilst you conceived them improper for near two years. I concluded that I had been mistaken; but this letter again revives my suspicion that the true situation of that State is not perfectly understood. Would it not be well to enquire?

When I requested a commission for a collector at Michillimakinac, I neglected to mention that it was necessary that you should designate a port of entry in that district. There being no doubt that Michillimakinac itself is the proper place, I enclose an *order* for that purpose, which when signed will be wanted here as the foundation of instructions to the Collector.

The vessel chartered by Eben. Stevens sub-agent of the Depart. of State at New York, for the purpose of carrying the stipulated naval stores to Tunis, after being loaded & ready to sail under convoy of the George Washington, has been discovered to be a *foreign built* vessel. The Collector according to general instructions refused a Mediterranean pass. The vessel was chartered only *to* Tunis & to return at her own risk & for account of her owner. The owner wrote that Captain & seamen would probably refuse to sail, that his vessel was entitled to protection &c.—. It was a blunder of Stevens; but there was no remedy & I sent a pass to the Collector with directions to give it on condition that it shall be returned after this voyage.

I enclose a correct amount of the Warrants issued from 1st July to Saturday last (1st. instt.) inclusive, & will hereafter send a weekly amount as you desired. I also enclose the amount of Warrants issued during the six first months of this year; (those for payt. of public debt & interest excepted) but it has not been corrected by myself, & I will substitute another one by next mail.

With sincere respect & attachment Your obt. Servt.

ALBERT GALLATIN

The new Danish minister came here one day too late to see you. He does not appear extremely bright & as he left Denmark in January, I suspect that he is too late in every point of view.

RC (DLC); addressed: "The President of the United States"; endorsed by TJ as received from the Treasury Department on 6 Aug. and "Michillim. S. Carola. Mediterrn. pass" and so recorded in SJL. Enclosures: (1) Stevens Thomson Mason to Gallatin, Raspberry Plain, 1 Aug. 1801, noting that considerable impatience prevailed in different parts of the United States on the subject of federal offices, with the continuance of several incumbents giving "great uneasiness," and lamenting "I believe you are all rather too good naturedly disposed"; that he had lately received a letter from Daniel D'Oyley of Charleston, treasurer and a "man of some political weight in that State," who wrote: "'I am persuaded that mr Jefferson is not correctly informed of our positions and though I know it is erronious to expect important measures should be hurried, and I would be chagrined to see a single act concluded which might cause a moment of repentance, yet I would wish to know what is the situation of the Presdt repecting the Federal officers in Charleston'" and warning that if decisions were postponed until the next meeting of Congress, he knew it would be positively too late for South Carolina and that "mr Pinckney knows it and every Republican and every Federalist of the least political attainment knows full well the certainty" of the case, though, Mason observed, he gave no reasons for the opinion; that Mason had also received letters on behalf of candidates for marshal of Kentucky, and although the subject pertained to Madison's department, since he was no longer in Washington, Mason gave Gallatin several names, including John Fowler and John Jouett (RC in DNA: RG 59, LAR, 3:378-9; endorsed by TJ: "Mason St. T. to mr Gallatin"). (2) Statement of amount of warrants drawn from 1 July to 1 Aug. 1801, with the sum of $70,326.44 for the civil list; $18,236.93 for foreign intercourse; $290,061.47 for payments on the public debt, the largest being $188,024.47 for the "Dutch debt, on account of both principal & interest falling due in 1802"; $150,000 for the military department; $160,000 for the Navy Department; and $14,062.93 for miscellaneous, including $1,500 for furniture for the president's house, $1,999.92 for repairs at the Treasury due to the fire, and $2,000 for the purchase of paper for stamps; for a total of $702,687.37 (MS in DLC: TJ Papers, 115:19763; entirely in Gallatin's hand; at head of text: "Amount of Warrants drawn on the

Treasurer of the United States from the 1st July 1801 to 1st August 1801 both days inclusive being one month & 1 day"). (3) Statement of amount of warrants drawn from 1 Jan. to 30 June 1801, including $108,809.03 for the civil list, $963,339.83 for the War Department, $1,656,907.08 for the Navy Department, and 18 other designations for a total sum of $2,952,866.07 (MS in DLC: TJ Papers, 114:19573; in a clerk's hand; at head of text in Gallatin's hand: "Amount of Warrants from 1st Jany. to 30th June 1801"; below total in Gallatin's hand: "not examined"). Other enclosure not found.

REQUESTED A COMMISSION: see Albert Gallatin's Report on Collector for Michilimackinac, printed at 16 July, and TJ to Gallatin, 17 July.

In May 1801, Ebenezer STEVENS chartered *Peace and Plenty*, owned by Stephen Kingston of Philadelphia, to carry NAVAL STORES TO TUNIS. Captain Richard Wood served as master of the ship. On 3 Aug., Jacob Wagner wrote Madison that he was "much mortified" to learn that Stevens had chartered a foreign-built vessel that, according to precedent, was not entitled to a Mediterranean passport (Madison, *Papers, Sec. of State Ser.*, 1:221, 2:12-14; NDBW, 1:513-14).

DANISH MINISTER: Peder Blicher Olsen, the Danish consul general empowered to act as resident minister; see Vol. 34:451n.

From Thomas Heyward, Jr.

Charleston, South Carolina
SIR   3d. Augst. 1801
This Letter is intended to be handed to you by Mr. John Huger a friend of mine & a respectable Inhabitant of this State. he is gone from hence to Rhode-Island on Account of his Health & proposes returning by Land to Carolina, taking the City of Washington in his Way—He has requested that I would remind you of our Acquaintance in the years 1776, 77, & 78, when we attended Congress—I do it with Chearfulness from a Conviction of his Claim on me for every Service that I can render & whatever Attentions you confer on him

will be esteemed an Obligation confered on me—With great Respect I am

your Excelys Most obedt humble Servt.   THOS. HEYWARD

RC (Facsimile in Anderson Galleries Catalogue, J. H. Manning Sale, No. 350, January 1926); according to catalogue, text is endorsed by TJ as received 22 Oct. Recorded in SJL as received 23 Oct.

Thomas Heyward, Jr. (1746-1809) represented South Carolina in the Continental Congress from 1776 to 1778 and was a signer of the Declaration of Independence. After many years of service as a state legislator and jurist, he retired from public life in 1790 to concentrate on his agricultural interests, especially tidal rice cultivation. In 1791, TJ had recommended him for the office of comptroller of the Treasury (ANB; Vol. 20:146).

Heyward's friend, JOHN HUGER, was a wealthy South Carolina planter, former state legislator, and intendant of Charleston from 1793 to 1795 (*S.C. Biographical Directory, Senate*, 2:775-7).

From Robert Leslie

SIR   Philadelphia August 3d 1801

On the 2d of June, I took the liberty of writeing you by Post, some account of the conversation that I had with Mr Boudinot, and others, at the mint, in consequence of the letter you favoured me with, among other things I informed you, that Mr Voight said, that each Dollar had to go through thirty two proceses before it was ready to receive the impression from the Die, and that it took thirty two Days, to prepair as maney, as[1] could be struck in one day,   this was so different from what I had seen done in England, that I at once concluded they ware working to vast disadvantage, but haveing no Authority to investigate the business and they not being desposed to explain any part of it, I was unable to ascertain whare the fault lay. however the subject has frequently since, employed my thoughts, and revived an opinion I formerly had entertained, which is, that Silver could be cast in Metal moulds, and notwithstanding, I had been told by several Silversmiths both here and in England, that it had often been tryed and found impossible, I was determined to make an experiment, I therefore made a Brass mould, to cast the Blanks (as they are called) for Dollars, and haveing no furnice of my own, I went to a silversmiths shop to melt the metal, and made three casts with as much care as possible, without getting the mould half full at either, one of the workmen in the shop, who had been maney years in the constant practice of Casting silver, then requested I would let him try, which I did, he made five attempts without any better success, when I agane tryd three more, but without ever getting the mould half full, after which I give it up for the time, and went home, but the disappointment only made me more determined to persue the object, and after a veriety of reflections, it ocured to me, that the cause of failure must be, that the Metal moulds, being so much better a conductor of heat than sand, that as soon as the melted Silver came in contact with the moulds, they absorbed the heat, and the Silver became Chiled, I therefore resolved to try one more experriment, and heat the moulds, which I did, and got the moulds full the first cast, and herewith send you the piece, tho it is not perfect in every respect, it has convinced me, that I have discovered the art of Casting Silver in metal moulds, and am certain that the Blanks for Dollars, may be made that way, and I think with more expedition and less expence, than any other, as the moulds may be made like those for casting shot, long enough for to contain, from five to ten Dollars, with which one man may cast as fast as the Silver can be melted,

And in addition to the dispatch, I am of opinion this mode will have the folowing adventages over any other, Viz, after the moulds are properly adjusted, the blanks will to a certainty, be all of the proper weight, the letters, or figures, may be cast on the edge, and save the operation of what is called milling, the metal will be much more soft and malleable, than after hammering, or roaling, and by that means receive a better impression from the Die,

The imperfections of the piece I here send, arises from the following Causes, the moulds ware mad of Brass, and smoked to prevent the Silvers adhering to them, but which give a rough surface, the Brass will not bair with safety, so much heat as is necessary, which I found by my moulds cracking, when I went to open them, which prevented me making another casting, Iron moulds will remedy both those evils, as the Silver will not stick to it without Smoke, and the Iron will bair any heat required, without injury,

I have sent this piece in its most imperfect state, as thare has been no tuch of a file on it, only whare the metal run in at, it has only been boiled in alum water, to whitein it, but to show that it is not too rough to answer, I have struck it in two or three places and in the roughest part, very lightly with a smooth hammer, which has very much improved the appearence, and showes that the Dies, will effectually remove all the defects,

I am Sir with the greates respect your very Humble Servent

ROBERT LESLIE

RC (DLC); addressed: "The President of the United States"; endorsed by TJ as received 13 Aug. and so recorded in SJL.

[1] MS: "a."

From Lewis Littlepage

SIR,   London—3d. of August—1801.

In continuation of the letter which I took the liberty to write to you from Altona of, I think, the 17th. of January last, I have now to inform you that my will deposited in the hands of Messrs. Coutts & Co. remains unaltered, and should any accident happen to me between this and America, I entreat you, as my *sole Executor* in America, to demand from Mr. Bonnet, Notary Public in this City, through the medium of Messrs. Coutts & Co. the register of nine thousand five hundred pounds sterling worth of American Stock, which I take out in Certificates transferred to me. The whole amount in *6, 8, pr. cts* and *Bank Shares*, bears interest from the 1st. of July last.

I shall not touch upon any thing respecting European Politics untill we meet.—In the mean time I have the honor to be with the highest respect,

Sir, your most obedient humble Servant.

LEWIS LITTLEPAGE.

RC (DLC); at foot of text: "T. Jefferson Esqr.—President of the United States"; endorsed by TJ as received 14 Nov. and so recorded in SJL.

From William C. C. Claiborne

DEAR SIR,   Near Nashville, August 4th. 1801.

Your friendly Letter of the 13th. of last Month, I had the honor to receive, on the 1st. Instant, accompanied with a Letter from the Secretary of State, enclosing me a Commission, as Governor of the Mississippi Territory.—I acknowledge with Gratitude, my Obligations to you, for this high proof of Confidence and Esteem, and, I trust, that every Act of my public Life, will evince my great desire, to merit a Continuance of Your good Opinion.—Conscious that very many, important *duties* attach to the Station, to which, I am called, I distrust my qualifications to execute *them*, with Justice; But I pledge myself to you, that whatsoever Talents I may possess, shall be employed, in promoting *those Objects*, which you have been pleased to suggest, and I indulge a hope, that my best endeavours to support the Interest of my Country, but more particularly to advance the happiness of the people, I am to Govern, will not prove entirely abortive.

The contiguity of the Territory, to the Spanish Dominions, and the great intercourse, between the Citizens of the U. States, and the Subjects of Spain, at New-Orleans, will probably be sources of some *Misunderstanding*;—But in all the Communications, which it may become my duty to make on this head, I shall observe "temper and Justice, the best guides in intricacies," and manifest all that "spirit of Conciliation, and mutual Accomodation, which may tend to strengthen, rather than weaken the Good Understanding, at present existing between the two Countries."—

It seems to be particularly the wish, of the Western Citizens, that *Spain* should, in preference to any other foreign Power, retain *her* present *possessions*, on the Mississippi, and there is certainly cause to fear, that a *Cession of them*, to France, might prove injurious to the U. States;—A Report, that an *event* of this kind, has actually taken place, is, at this time, in circulation, in this quarter; This Report is said, to come immediately from New-Orleans, where it is believed & regretted:—But I rather think, this is an *old Rumour* revived, and hope it may be incorrect.—

I have very lately understood, that the division among the people of the Mississippi Territory, as to the 1st. and 2nd. Grade of Government still exists, and that the *cause* you state, is the most plausible objection, with the disaffected to the present order of things.—I flatter myself however, that this Objection will soon be removed;—A just regard to Œconemy, shall be my first governing principle;—Will be encouraged by my example, and shall be enforced by all the Power, with which I am possessed.—My Mind is fully impressed, with the baneful effects of party spirit in Society, and the first Wish of my Heart, will be accomplished, should I be enabled to restore to the people of the Territory, that Harmony and mutual Confidence, which sweeten Life, and make a Community happy.—From principle and duty Sir, I shall co-operate with the friends of the 2nd. Grade, but to *each Party*, I shall be equally just, and equally solicitous to acquire their Confidence and Support.—

From Mr. Daniel Clarke, our Consul at *New-Orleans*, I anticipate "powerful Aid in the interfering claims of those who go"[1] and who reside *there*; Mr. Clarke is much esteemed by his Acquaintances, and I am sure, you do not overrate his "Worth and influence."—

The favorable sentiments, you are pleased to express of Mr. William Dunbar, has raised that Gentleman, very high in my estimation; I shall seek his Acquaintance; cultivate his friendship, and endeavour to avail myself, of his public services.—

I am very desirous, to be at my post;—But I fear, it will not be in my power, to take my departure from Tennessee, previous to the 20th. of next Month, or perhaps the first of October;—I have arrangements to make of my property in this State, that cannot be completed in less than Six Weeks.—

A Representative to Congress, from this State, will be chosen, the day after Tomorrow;—On this occasion, my name is with the people;—I have an Opponent, and the circumstance of my Appointment to the Government of the M.T. (which has been reported for several Weeks past) will detach from me, many Votes, it being generally believed, that I have, or will accept;—It is nevertheless, *highly probable*, that I shall be honored, with a majority of the suffrages of my fellow Citizens; In which case, I shall immediately decline serving, and then the Governor will order a second Election;—Official Information of my late Appointment, *did not reach me in time*, to withdraw my Name, as a Candidate for Congress.—

The amount of the Census of this State, is not certainly ascertained;—the Returns from all the Counties, had not a few days ago, reached the Marshall; But I am warranted in giving an Opinion, that our Numbers (including Slaves) will equal one hundred thousand;—Of this number, the proportion of Slaves, is not considerable.—It is the general opinion, that our Census has been incorrectly taken, and indeed, from the dispersed situation of our settlements, accuracy could not well be attained.

I shall frequently, do myself the honor to write you, "inofficially," and shall esteem myself, peculiarly fortunate, to be numbered among your Correspondents.

Your *Communication*, to which I reply, is viewed as Confidential, and "shall be confined to myself alone"; But *its Contents* will always be fresh in my memory, and shall shape the course of my Administration.—

Accept the Homage of a grateful Heart, and believe me to be—With very sincere Esteem, Your mo: obt. hble servt

WILLIAM C. C. CLAIBORNE.

RC (DLC); at foot of text: "The President of the U. States"; endorsed by TJ as received 17 Sep. and so recorded in SJL.

William Dickson, a member of the Tennessee legislature, became the state's at-large REPRESENTATIVE TO CONGRESS for the Seventh Congress. The GOVERNOR was John Sevier (*Biog. Dir. Cong.*; ANB).

[1] Closing quotation mark supplied.

From Nicolas Gouin Dufief

MONSIEUR, à Philadelphie, ce 4 d'Août. 1801—

Je vous envoye par Mr. *Duane, la morale de Jesus-Christ & des Apôtres*, édition de *Didot*; cet ouvrage manquoit à votre Collection des Moralistes anciens, pour qu'elle fut complete, lorsque j'eus l'honneur de vous voir à Philadelphie. S'il vous convient vous le Garderez, sinon Mr. *Duane* me fera l'amitié de me le rapporter; le prix en est de 250 Cts.

J'attends par les premiers bâtimens qui arriveront de France, une collection nombreuse des ouvrages nouveaux les plus piquans; Je vous en ferai passer le Catalogue dès qu'il Sera imprimé. Sûr d'être bien servi par mes Correspondans, je serais charmé, lorsque vous desirerez faire venir des livres d'Europe, que vous vous adressassiez à moi.

J'ai l'honneur d'être, Monsieur, avec tous les Sentimens qui vous Sont dus à tant de titres Votre très dévoué Serviteur.

N. GOÜIN DUFIEF

EDITORS' TRANSLATION

SIR, Philadelphia, today 4 August 1801

I am sending you, by way of Mr. Duane, *The Moral Philosophy of Jesus Christ and the Apostles* in the Didot edition; this work was missing, for it to be complete, from your collection of the ancient moral philosophers when I had the honor of seeing you in Philadelphia. If it suits you, keep it; if not, Mr. Duane will do me the favor of bringing it back to me; its price is 250 cents.

I am expecting, by the first ships that arrive from France, an ample collection of the most lively new works; I shall have a catalogue of them sent to you as soon as it is printed. Certain of being well served by my correspondents, I should be delighted, when you desire to have books sent from Europe, that you should address yourself to me.

I have the honor of being, Sir, with all the sentiments to which you are entitled for so many reasons, Your very devoted Servant.

N. GOÜIN DUFIEF

RC (DLC); at head of text: "Le Président des Etats-Unis"; endorsed by TJ as received 13 Aug. and so recorded in SJL.

ÉDITION DE DIDOT: the Didot firm published a two-volume compilation from the New Testament, the *Morale de Jésus-Christ et des Apôtres; ou, La Vie et les Instructions de Jésus-Christ*, in Paris in 1790.

From John W. Maddux

SIR   Washington County Kentucky august 4th 1801

you may think it strange when you Receive these lines pardon me Sir if it be offince you must constrew it to the ancity I have for you wellfare fo we the people of Washington county feel our Selves So happy under your administration that the name of Jefferson Echoes through the state we are ready to say that god has blest us with another Washington we Ever pray that God may bless all your administration, & that your presidents may always be such that it may meet the general approbation of Every Repubblickcan we feel ourselves happy to think we have once more a president that feels for the United States of America we feel it a duty to inform you that we have obtained our choice in consiquence of which we all appear to be United all satisfied for the present four years) to which we have felt that little Satisfaction for the Last four years it is hard for true Repubbliccan people to be happy under a tirannicle King

Your friend &c.   JOHN W. MADDUX

RC (ViW); addressed: "Thomas Jefferson President of the United States City of Washington Merriland"; franked; postmarked Danville, Kentucky, 17 Aug.; endorsed by TJ as received 10 Sep. and so recorded in SJL.

To Wilson Cary Nicholas

DEAR SIR   Monticello Aug. 4. 1801.

I was in [hopes] we should have had the pleasure of seeing you here during the court, but I learn you were not at court yesterday. you once intimated to me a possibility that you might be able to spare me a superlative overseer which you had. I do not remember his name. this possibility seems to be strengthened by a late resolution (which your friends lament) of changing the form of your property & perhaps of leaving us. should you have determined to break up your plantations, you will probably have no further occasion for this overseer, in which case he might become [my salvation] on losing Clarke who leaves me this year. certainly if I get my Bedford establishment into indifferent hands I shall be bankrupt. I will therefore pray you, if not wanting for yourself, that you would be so good as to procure me the offer of your overseer, & at the same time to give me previously some idea of what proportion of the crop, you think he would agree to [take?] or what sum of money if we should not agree as to the proportion of produce. this you can judge of by what you have given yourself, and [judging by] [. . .] Clarke's [way] is so [. . .]ant that, [. . .] of hands, I ought to put an end to it, & return it to what [. . .] gives. should there be no chance of getting this man, I will thank you for a line that I may not lose [. . .] any other [. . .]. in that case too a recommendation of some other would be recieved with thankfulness. accept assurances of my sincere friendship & respect.   TH: JEFFERSON

P.S. Your friends at Baltimore [. . .] Rob. Smith had entered on the duties of Secy. of the Navy before I left Washington. he moves his family there in the fall.

PrC (MHi); faint; at foot of text: "W. C. Nicholas"; endorsed by TJ in ink on verso.

LATE RESOLUTION: Nicholas advertised the sale of land, including the 7,000 acres he held on the north side of the James River in Albemarle County, making up five plantations, a large distillery, tobacco warehouses, the tavern at Warren, and the Warren mills (*National Intelligencer*, 11 Sep.).

Having heard that Bowling Clark was leaving Poplar Forest, Charles Clay wrote TJ from BEDFORD County on 30 July recommending Daniel Fuqua, who was the bearer of the letter, as Clark's replacement. Clay noted that Fuqua was known in Bedford "as one of the cleverest young Men on a plantation that we have ever had among us, and as paying particular attention to the improvement as well as the produce of the farm." He claimed that

if TJ had not engaged someone else, he "would hardly do wrong by making a tryal of him." Clay, who had last written TJ in October 1799, concluded by inquiring whether the president planned to visit Bedford during the summer (RC in DLC, endorsed by TJ as received 11 Aug. and so recorded in SJL; Vol. 31:208-9).

On 12 Aug., Nicholas wrote TJ a brief answer from Warren, noting that he had informed Burgess Griffin of TJ's offer to employ him to manage his estate in Bedford County. Nicholas continued: "he desires me to inform you he will be at your house by the 16th. instant. I have told him that you are willing to give the 12th. part of the crop, which I think is full enough for twenty five hands" (RC in DLC; endorsed by TJ as received 13 Aug. and so recorded in SJL).

TJ hired Griffin, who held the position as overseer at Poplar Forest until 1811 (MB, 2:1080).

From Samuel Smith

SIR,   Balte. 4. Augt. 1801

Mr Yznardi, the Elder is thus far on his Way to Washington to pay you his Respects, his State of Health will not permit him to go further—I shewed him your letter he will Accept with pleasure the Consulate &c its Duties untill there shall be a general Peace, again which time he expects he Can settle all American Claims for French Capt[ures] now under his Management—He no longer supports his Son's pretension—I am Sir,

with sincere friendship your Obedt Serv   S. SMITH

NB—All will go very well in Harford County

RC (DNA: RG 59, LAR); torn; endorsed by TJ as received 13 Aug. and so recorded in SJL; also endorsed by TJ: "Yznardi."

YOUR LETTER: TJ to Smith, 25 July.

From Sarah Franklin Bache

SIR   Settle August 5th. 1801

Knowing as I do the worth of the Person that will deliver you this, I cannot resist the impulse I feel in writing to you by him—

Mr Clay has been intimately known to this Family from an Infant and has invariably sustain'd the best Character. his intimacy with my Son Benjamin who had the highest opinion of his Integrity and who knew him thoroughly, taught us his Value—the knowledge of his being a Man of Genius, and always a firm Republican, must long ere this have reach'd you, he could I am sure have had a number of letters to you, but his modesty in this respect, I fear will stand in his way, as I know no person whose advancement would rejoice more true Americans, and all that know him say he has tallents to adorn any Situation—I shall not take up Your valuable time by apologies for this liberty, it will not I trust be thought too great a one from the daughter of a Man who had the highest Friendship for you—

I am with the greatest esteem & &c   SARAH BACHE

RC (DNA: RG 59, LAR); endorsed by TJ as received 27 Aug. and so recorded in SJL with notation "Clay for office"; TJ canceled "Bache Sarah" and added "Clay Joseph" to the endorsement.

Sarah Franklin Bache (1743-1808) was the only daughter of Benjamin Franklin and Deborah Read Franklin. A committed Whig, she followed Pennsylvania politics and during the American Revolution became active in the Ladies Association of Philadelphia, enthusiastically supporting its relief efforts for American troops. In 1794 her large family moved from Philadelphia to a farm on the Delaware River named "Settle" (ANB; Vol. 31:246n).

Philadelphia native Joseph CLAY was the executor of the estate of Benjamin Franklin Bache. In May, Clay had joined William Duane, Thomas Cooper, and other Philadelphia Republicans in recommending William Henderson for the post of naval officer (Richard N. Rosenfeld, *American Aurora: A Democratic Republican Returns* [New York, 1997], 231; Vol. 30:567n; Thomas Cooper and Others to TJ, 23 May 1801).

From Thomas Claxton

HONORD SIR   City of Washington 5th Aug. 1801.

I yesterday received from Philadelphia a Bill of Lading for your chairs, which I have this day forwarded to Messrs Gibson & Jefferson at Richmond—I have thought it proper to forward this information, in order that the first opportunity of getting them to Monticello may be embraced

I have the honor to be with the greatest esteem Sir Your Hble Svt

THOS CLAXTON

RC (MHi); endorsed by TJ as received 13 Aug. and so recorded in SJL.

YOUR CHAIRS: according to an invoice dated 31 July, Claxton owed Adam Snyder $204 for four dozen "Armd Chairs Blak & Gould" and their packaging for shipment (MS in MHi; in an unidentified hand, with note by TJ: "Oct. 13. 1801 Mr. Barnes will be pleased to pay the above," followed by his signature; endorsed by Barnes, who wrote the acknowledgment of payment on 19 Oct., signed by Claxton). TJ recorded the order on Barnes in his financial memoranda on 13 Oct. Barnes entered the payment to Claxton in TJ's private account at 19 Oct. (MB, 2:1055; statement of private account from John Barnes, 4 Nov. 1801, in ViU). Snyder was a Philadelphia windsor chair maker located at the corner of Second and Green Streets. At the end of TJ's life, the entrance hall at Monticello had twenty-eight black painted chairs, some portion of which, it is believed, were from this order (Stafford, *Philadelphia Directory, for 1801*, 142; Stein, *Worlds*, 262-3).

From Philippe de Létombe

MONSIEUR LE PRÉSIDENT,   Philadelphie 5 aoust 1801. (v. St.)

Je m'empresse de Vous informer que Rapin m'a remis, avant hier, la lettre dont Vous m'avez honoré le 29 ulto. Mais Vous aurez vû, par celle que J'ai eu l'honneur de Vous écrire le premier du courant, qu'il a trouvé ici cette besogne faite et que des arrangemens, définitifs et conformes à vos vües, avoient été pris deux jours auparavant avec Le Maire. Ils sortent tous deux de chez moi où ils sont convenus de leurs arrangemens ultérieurs. Le premier retournera demain à Washington; le second demeurera ici jusqu'au 1er du mois prochain, jour où il partira pour aller rejoindre Rapin et prendre de Lui des leçons sur ses nouvelles fonctions. J'espère que Vous serez aussi satisfait du second que Vous l'avez été du premier. Chacun trouve son bonheur à Vous plaire. J'avois aussi cru Schroeder moins éligible, attendu les circonstances critiques où il se trouve et c'est pour cela que J'avois prié mon ami, Mr. Flamand, d'épier, pendant mon absence, le moment où Lemaire seroit libre. Mr. Bingham est parti.

Vous daignez me reparler, Monsieur le Président, des remercîmens que Vous dittes me devoir à propos de cette Negociation? Je voudrois que vous fussiez moins modeste et que Je pusse Vous exprimer combien Je trouve de satisfaction à servir un grand homme, même dans les petites choses. Çest moi qui Vous doit mille remercîmens sur cette préférence que Vous avez bien voulu me donner sur des Rivaux qui se seroient empressés à mieux faire. Mais ne mettrez Vous pas le comble à vos bontés en me chargeant de vos commissions pour Paris? Ne voulez Vous point de livres, de nouveautés? N'avez Vous rien à y faire passer? Permettez Moi de Vous dire, comme Pline à Trajan: *tuus sum.* Je vais avoir l'honneur de Vous accuser la reception de votre dépêche incluse.

Je Vous supplie, Monsieur le Président, de vouloir bien agréér mon profond Respect.

LÉTOMBE

E D I T O R S '   T R A N S L A T I O N

MISTER PRESIDENT,   Philadelphia, 5 Aug. 1801 (old style)
I hasten to inform you that Rapin turned over to me, the day before yesterday, the letter with which you honored me on the 29th of last month. But you will have seen, by the one I had the honor of writing to you on the first of the present month, that he found here that task completed and that definitive arrangements, in accordance with your designs, had been made two days before with Lemaire. They have both just left my house where they agreed upon their final arrangements. The first one will go back tomorrow to Washington; the second one will remain here until the first of next month, the day on which he will leave to rejoin Rapin and take lessons from him concerning his new functions. I hope you will be as satisfied with the second one as you have been with the first. Each one finds his happiness in pleasing you. I also had thought Schroeder less eligible, given his present critical circumstances, and that is why I had requested my friend, Mr. Flamand, during my absence, to look out for the moment when Lemaire would be free. Mr. Bingham has left.

You were kind enough, Mister President, to speak again of the thanks you say you owe me concerning that negotiation? I could wish that you were less modest and that I could express to you how much satisfaction I find in serving a great man, even in the small things. I am the one who owes you a thousand thanks for that preference you have kindly shown me over rivals who would have hastened to do better. But will you not put a climax to your kindness by commissioning me to do errands for you in Paris? Do you not wish some books, some novelties? Have you nothing to send there? Allow me to say to you as Pliny did to Trajan: *tuus sum.* I am going to have the honor of acknowledging receipt of your enclosed dispatch.

I beg you, Mister President, kindly to accept my deep respect.

LÉTOMBE

RC (DLC); endorsed by TJ as received 13 Aug. and so recorded in SJL.

TUUS SUM: "I am yours." Early in the second century, Pliny the Younger corresponded with the Emperor Trajan from a province on the Black Sea, where Pliny was governor. Pliny, as consul, also composed a testimony of thanks to the emperor, the *Panegyricus* (Betty Radice, trans., *The Letters of the Younger Pliny* [Baltimore, 1963], 14-20).

To Andrew Moore

Dear Sir Monticello Aug. 5. 1801

A marshal for the Western district of Virginia having been wanting I had appointed a mr Caruthers, who however has declined. it has been suggested to me as possible that you might be willing to accept the office. had this been supposed at first you would unquestionably have had the first offer, as I deem it highly advantageous to the U.S. to have their offices filled not only with men of probity & understanding, but who are extensively known to be such. in the possibility of your acceptance I now take the liberty of proposing this office to you. I have with me a blank commission, which on recieving your permission I will fill up with your name & forward it. let me only ask the favor of an answer by the first post, as I am told some inconvenience is experienced from the delay already occasioned by mr Caruther's declining. accept assurances of my high esteem & consideration.

Th: Jefferson

PrC (DLC); at foot of text: "Colo. Andrew Moore."

Andrew Moore (1752-1821), born near Staunton, Virginia, of Scotch-Irish parents, read law under George Wythe at William and Mary, and was admitted to the bar in 1774. During the Revolutionary War, Moore raised a company of riflemen from Augusta County, which became a part of Daniel Morgan's select corp known as Morgan's Rangers. Promoted to captain, Moore fought with his company at Saratoga in the fall of 1777. After the war he rose to the rank of major general in the Virginia militia. In 1780, Moore began serving as a delegate from Rockbridge County in the Virginia General Assembly, allying himself with Madison. He voted for ratification of the U.S. Constitution in 1788 and served in Congress from 1789 to 1797, where he opposed Hamilton's policies. Moore briefly retired from politics to rebuild his law practice but again entered the Virginia assembly in 1799 to help secure passage of Madison's Virginia Resolutions in opposition to the Alien and Sedition Acts. Moore was elected to the Eighth Congress but served only a few months before being appointed to fill a vacancy in the U.S. Senate, where he served as a Jeffersonian Republican until 1809. Upon his retirement from the Senate, he accepted an appointment as U.S. marshal of Virginia, a position he held until shortly before his death (ANB; Leonard, *General Assembly*, 139, 217).

On 29 July, TJ informed Valentine White, of Hot Springs in Bath County, Virginia, that the office of MARSHAL for the western district of Virginia was still vacant because TJ's candidate had returned the commission. TJ noted that he would fill the position shortly from Monticello, where he planned to spend August and September. The president was responding to White's letter of 21 July (now missing), which was being sent to the secretary of the Treasury "to [give] you the information you desire" (PrC in MoSHi: Jefferson Papers; faint; at foot of text: "Mr Valentine White"; endorsed by TJ in ink on verso).

From Andrew Moore

SIR   Rockbridge Cy. Augt 5th 1801.

I receiv'd a Letter by the Mail from the Secretary of State—Informing me of your offer of the Marshalls place to me—I have prevaild. with Two young men to Undertake the riding—And will accept the Appointment—Should you think proper to forward the Commission—Or notify me—It will be necessary for me to Go to Williamsburgh to Qualify. I will apply for the Commission on my Way—Permit me to express my Wish that the Law making new Arrangments in the Judiciary—may be repeald—I am sure the Business in this District will not Justify the Expence—I have other reasons perhaps not well founded—

I am Sir With Since Esteem Yours &c   ANDREW MOORE

RC (ViW); endorsed by TJ as received 8 Aug. and so recorded in SJL.

Moore needed two MEN TO UNDERTAKE THE RIDING because he was recovering from an illness which had kept him confined for almost five months (Moore to Madison, 9 Apr., in DNA: RG 59, LAR, 1:0110-11).

To Archibald Stuart

DEAR SIR   Monticello Aug. 5. 1801.

Mr. Caruthers, to whom I addressed the commission of Marshal for the Western district of Virginia, having been late in signifying his declining the office, some inconvenience may perhaps have arisen from the long vacancy. I have now proposed it to Colo. Andrew Moore with but little hope however of his acceptance. in case of his declining the two who stand most recommeded are a capt. Croudson of Woodstock by yourself, and a mr Joseph Grigsby by two or three others. will you be so good as to give me, by return of post, your opinion between these two persons. I have brought a blank commission with me, which will enable me to supply the office as soon as I know whether Colo. Moore will accept. I shall be here till the last of September and happy to see you should any thing lead you this way. accept assurances of my sincere friendship & high consideration.

                                                TH: JEFFERSON

RC (ViHi); addressed: "The honble Archibald Stuart Staunton"; franked. PrC (DLC).

CAPT. CROUDSON: Samuel Croudson

(see Hugh Holmes to TJ, 17 Dec. 1801). For the recommendation of JOSEPH GRIGSBY, see John Coalter to TJ, 3 July.

Stuart responded to TJ on 7 Aug. He noted that either candidate would be

[27]

satisfactory. He described Grigsby as "a young man of Cleverness" who had adhered to his principles even while he held a commission in the U.S. provisional army. Croudson's advantage over Grigsby was that he was "More Generally Known in The district" and esteemed in that part, "which was our sheet anchor during the late struggle" (RC in MHi, endorsed by TJ as received 8 Aug. and so recorded in SJL; JEP, 1:298-9, 301, 305).

To John Barnes

DEAR SIR   Monticello Aug. 6. 1801.

This will be handed you by mr David Higginbotham, a merchant of Milton,[1] who with a mr Watson of the same place, having acted heretofore as chief factors for the houses of Brown Reeves & co. and McLure Brydie & co. are now about to set up themselves. they are both men of extraordinary attention to business, prudent, honest, & in great esteem, and will undoubtedly carry into their own concern all their former customers who are free to leave the antient houses. mr Higginbotham going on to N. York & being a stranger there, is apprehensive he may find difficulty in learning, in the short space of time he will stay there, who are the best houses for him to establish dealings with. I have told him you were perfectly acquainted there, & could probably give him good indications of the mercantile houses there with whom it would be eligible for him to establish dealings, and for that single object, to wit, of information, I give him this letter, asking the favor of you to guide his steps so as to prevent his falling into bad hands. I mean to transfer my own dealings at this place from his quondam employers to his new concern. this I do from having had long experience of the personal merit of himself and partner. accept assurances of my sincere esteem.

TH: JEFFERSON

PrC (CSmH); at foot of text: "Mr. John Barnes"; endorsed by TJ in ink on verso.

[1] Word interlined in place of "this place."

From Philippe de Létombe

MONSIEUR LE PRÉSIDENT,   Philadelphie, 6 aoust 1801. (v. St.)

J'ai reçû et lû, avec émotion, avec attendrissement, avec gratitude, la dépêche dont Vous avez bien voulu m'honorer le 27 ulto. Elle fera le bonheur de ma vieillesse. Elle me sera la recommandation la plus honorable auprès de mon Gouvernement. Elle m'est un brevet pour l'immortalité.

Je n'ai point encore reçu la dépêche de Monsieur le Sécrétaire d'Etat que Vous daignez m'annoncer. Peut être devrois-je la provoquer moi même par une dépêche *ad hoc*. Je ne l'ai osé jusqu'a présent. Ma situation officielle n'a point ici suivi le cours ordinaire des formes diplomatiques et ç'est à vos bontés généreuses seules, Monsieur le President, que Je devrai cette faveur de Monsieur le Sécrétaire d'Etat.

Quant à mon départ, dont Vous avez bien voulu Vous enquérir par votre lettre du 15 ulto., j'ai lieu de craindre aujourd'hui que ma lettre envoyée successivement à Clermont, à Albany, à Cohoe's Springs, ne soit point parvenue à Monsieur Livingston. Je lui ai écrit de nouveau hier: car je suis au milieu des transes (le Franklin ne partant plus en parlementaire) que je ne trouve aucune autre occasion sûre pour ma Personne et mes comptes. D'un autre côté, on prétend, à New york, que Monsieur Livingston ne voulant rien prendre sur lui, renvoit ces sortes de demandes au Gouvernement.

Je Vous demande humblement pardon, Monsieur le Président, de toutes ces explications. Mais Vous êtes comme la Providence qui traite les grandes et les petites Choses avec la même bonté et la même indulgence.

Daignez agréér, Monsieur le Président, l'hommage de mon profond respect.   LÉTOMBE

EDITORS' TRANSLATION

MISTER PRESIDENT,   Philadelphia, 6 Aug. 1801 (old style)
I have received and read with emotion, with tender feelings, with gratitude, the dispatch with which you honored me on the 27th of last month. It will make the happiness of my old age. It will be for me the most honorable recommendation to my Government. It is for me a certificate for immortality.

I have not yet received the dispatch from the secretary of state of which you kindly advise me. Perhaps I should prompt it myself by an ad hoc dispatch. I have not dared to until now. My official situation here has not followed the normal course of diplomatic forms, and I shall owe to your kind generous acts alone, Mister President, this favor from the secretary of state.

As for my departure, about which you were kind enough to inquire in your letter of the 15th of last month, I now have reason to fear that my letter sent successively to Clermont, to Albany, to Cohoes Springs, did not reach Mr. Livingston. I wrote him again yesterday, for I am now in an agony of suspense (the *Franklin* no longer leaving as a cartel ship) that I may find no other chance for my person and my affairs. In addition, they claim in New York that Mr. Livingston, not wanting to take anything upon himself, is sending these kinds of requests to the government.

I humbly ask your pardon, Mister President, for all these discussions, but you are like Providence, which treats great and small things with the same kindness and the same indulgence.

Kindly accept, Mister President, the homage of my deep respect.

LÉTOMBE

RC (DLC); endorsed by TJ as received 13 Aug. and so recorded in SJL.

To Robert Maxwell

SIR   Monticello Aug. 6. 1801.

I recieved your favor of July 17 in the moment I was setting out from Washington for this place. that of May 15 had come to hand May 20. as I find on recurring to my letter list. if I expressed a doubt of it to mr Rodney it must have been from memory only, without recurring to my letter list. I find it was referred to the Secretary of state (then mr Lincoln) to act on. but of what was done on it I have no means of information here. in truth the affairs of the post office needed too much to be done to be meddled with[1] until we had materials for doing all which is to be done. such local complaints therefore as were not too pressing have been suffered to lie until the whole subject can be taken up. I think it probable that the [subject] of your letter has been postponed with this view. if so it will be attended to in due season. desirous of having the public business in every department faithfully done, I am thankful to those who are kind enough to give me information of anything amiss & to put it in my power to have it rectified. accept my thanks for your communication & my best wishes.

TH: JEFFERSON

PrC (DLC); faint; at foot of text: "Mr. Robert Maxwell. Middletown. Del."; endorsed by TJ in ink on verso.

[1] Preceding four words interlined.

To John Barnes

DEAR SIR   Monticello Aug. 7. 1801

Yours of the 3d. came to hand yesterday morning. I shall be happy to hear of the arrival of the groceries &c. in Richmond, as we are much in want of them: so also of the glass when shipped from Philadelphia—a mr Andrews, who lives near the former post office in Washington & works on ornaments for architecture, was to make for me some Doric ornaments, which should be ready before this time. he should pack them himself in a box, and I should be very glad if they could be sent on to Richmond immediately so as to arrive & be put on while I am here. I have some plaister of Paris here which would do for the plaisterers to go on till the arrival of that from Washington. but my lime is still to be burnt which will take ten days. if they arrive sooner we can find something for them to do preparatory to their work—mr Andrew Dinsmore will be sure to call in due time on mr Richards for the 400. Dollars.—I hope by the next post to hear of the success of mr Rapin's mission to Philadelphia—when the ornaments from mr Andrews come, if you could procure & send at the same time a couple of dozen of barrel glass tumblers (I mean of this shape (◡) they would be acceptable as none of any kind are to be had here. accept assurances of my sincere esteem & attachment.

TH: JEFFERSON

PrC (CSmH); at foot of text: "Mr. John Barnes"; endorsed by TJ in ink on verso.

George ANDREWS sold composition ornaments at the corner of 9th and E Streets in Washington (MB, 2:1055).

To Albert Gallatin

DEAR SIR   Monticello Aug. 7. 1801.

Your favor of the 3d. came to hand yesterday. in it I recieved the list of warrants issued from your department as I did from the Secy. of the Navy those of his & the war department. none came from the office of state. perhaps mr Madison forgot to direct it, or mr Wagner to execute. a word from you to the latter will probably suffice. I think you expressed a wish to[1] see weekly this communication. this shall be done regularly after my return, and in the mean time if you desire it, by forwarding the originals as I have no Secretary here for copying.—I inclose you the act establishing Michillimakinac as the port of entry & delivery for that district.—you did unquestionably right in giving a Mediterranean pass to the vessel, tho foreign built, chartered for carrying our stores to Tunis. I have no doubt that all vessels *owned* by American citizens are entitled to such passes.—I imagine the Danish minister has been sent to engage us in the Northern confederacy. he never would have been soon enough to obtain our consent, & is now too late to bring even their own.—I return you mr Mason's letter. at the time he wrote it he had not seen the New haven papers. I think these will satisfy him. as to S. Carola, mr Pinckney was so particular in his observations to me that it was impossible to mistake him; & I have a note of what he said, at Washington. mr D'oyley is a most respectable republican, & his opinion of weight. but as mr Pinckney promised to write to me on the subject after his return, & I have some hopes that Genl. Sumpter will do the same, we had better wait. their election does not come on till at the end of two years, and mr Doyley does not explain what harm can be done provided the proper changes are made in time to prevent official weight from being then thrown into the federal scale. he is one of those destined for office. surely if we can wait till Congress meets, it will be better that arrangements should be made on the broad counsel we can then have, than on the very limited information we now possess.   I conversed with mr Madison on the subject of Rodney's letter. we both think that as the appointment of mr Lewis is made, we ought not to meddle in it. if he offers to resign, certainly we may accept it; but not propose it to him. he is admitted to be a good republican, & not a word alledged against his moral character, nor any reason given why he should be removed but that he is disagreeable, without saying for what. I think it would shew too great versatility in us to be the first movers for the purpose of undoing what has been done. mr Madison promised to write to you on this subject.— I have proposed the Marshalsea of the Western district of Virginia to Colo. Moore, and taken measures to fix on the next best character if he declines. I suppose the place will be filled in a fortnight from this time.—accept assurances of my affectionate attachment & high respect.

Th: Jefferson

RC (NHi: Gallatin Papers); at foot of first page: "The Secretary of the Treasury"; endorsed by Gallatin. PrC (DLC). Enclosure not found.

The WARRANTS for the Navy and War Departments, enclosed in Robert Smith's short transmittal letter to TJ of 3 Aug., have not been found (RC in DLC; in a clerk's hand, signed by Smith; at foot of text: "The President"; endorsed by TJ as received 6 Aug. from the Navy Department and "warrants" and so recorded in SJL).

NORTHERN CONFEDERACY: the armistice Great Britain imposed on Denmark in April 1801 and the convention between Russia and Britain in June had undermined the Baltic states' league of armed

neutrality (David Humphreys to TJ, 8 May 1801; Paine to TJ, 9 June 1801).

For Pinckney's OBSERVATIONS on South Carolina appointments, see Memorandum from Charles Pinckney, printed at 17 Mch. 1801.

For Caesar A. RODNEY'S LETTER to Madison concerning the appointment of Joel Lewis as marshal of Delaware, see enclosure at Gallatin to TJ, 29 July (third letter). MADISON PROMISED TO WRITE TO YOU: a letter from the secretary of state to Gallatin has not been found, but on 6 Aug. Madison informed Rodney that "any thing short of resignation" by Lewis "would involve the idea of removal, and as a removal without adequate objections personal to the officer, would exhibit the Executive under a disadvantageous appearance, the least embarrassing course would be to trust for a proper result to some voluntary arrangement that may grow out of the case"

(Madison, *Papers, Sec. of State Ser.,* 2:19-20).

[1] TJ canceled "know."

From Ephraim Kirby

SIR   Litchfield August 7th. 1801

I take the liberty to offer for your perusal and amusement the enclosed effusion of *anti-republican malice*. It is a true specimen of the present temper of the party in Connecticut.—The mass of the People begin to discern the danger which they have escaped, & to resort to the republican standard; but the work of reformation will be slow.—The priesthood are armed against us with all the powers of their order. Hypocrisy, *rank hypocrisy*, is more cherished and respected than true religion.—While this state of things continues, the people will in a degree continue to be the dupes of Clerical deception.—

Accept Sir, the assurances of my high respect and steem

EPHM KIRBY

RC (DLC); at foot of text: "His Excely. Thos. Jefferson"; endorsed by TJ as a letter of 17 Aug., received 3 Sep., and so recorded in SJL. Enclosure: probably "Brutus" to TJ, undated, printed in the Litchfield *Monitor,* 5 Aug. 1801 (see below).

EFFUSION OF ANTI-REPUBLICAN MALICE: Kirby probably referred to "Brutus," who, in his response to TJ's reply to the New Haven merchants, charged that the president admitted the time "may come" when honesty, capability, and adherence to the Constitution were the questions raised about candidates for office. "Brutus" conjectured that the questions now asked by TJ were "did Linn agree to vote against Burr? Did Livingston compound for the place of District Attorney, and desert Colonel Burr? Did M. Lyon agree

that he would remain unshaken if Willard might be Marshall of Vermont? Has this candidate laboured for my election? Did this man malign Washington? did that man curse Adams? Has this competitor ridiculed the institutions of religion? Has this anxious face been set 'like a flint' against the ministers of the gospel? Will you all, gentlemen, with one heart and voice, join in anathemas against that 'Sect' of which Washington was the head? and sing hallelujahs to my administration?" To TJ's declaration that it was difficult to obtain correct information respecting candidates, "Brutus" responded: "Indeed while the ear of a President shall be opened only to one party, and this party containing individuals hungering 'for the loaves and fishes' of office, information will be incorrect" (Litchfield *Monitor,* 5 Aug. 1801).

List of Inoculations

Inoculns

Aug. 7.   Burwell
          Joe
          <Brown>
          <Jamy>
          <Critta>
          <Thenia> Melinda. taken

---

13.   Brown
      Jamy 21. taken
      Critta. 21. q.
      <Thenia> Thenia.
      Lavinia. 21. taken

16.	Nancy Jeff.	from Joe & Burw. 21. taken
	Elen.	Joe & Bur. 21. Joe's inflamd.
	Cornelia.	Bur. failed
	Priscilla.	Bur. 21. taken
	Wormely	Bur. 21. taken
	Edwin.	Bur. 21. taken
	Philip Ev.	Bur. & Joe 21. taken
	Thenia.	Joe & B. taken
	Ben	Joe & B.
	Cary	Joe & B.
	B. Davy	Joe & B. 21. taken
	B. Phill	Joe & B. 21. taken
	Bartlet	Joe. 21. taken
	John.	Joe & B. 21. taken
21.	mr Chisolm	
	Lewis	
	mrs Carr	
23.	Betsy	
	Sandy	
30.	Lilly's family	
Sep. 1.	*<Jame Hub.>*	from Betsy.
	Barnaby	do.
	Bedfd. John	do.
	Shepherd.	do.
	Moses.	do.

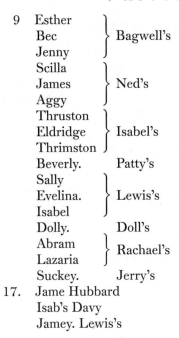

9   Esther
    Bec   } Bagwell's
    Jenny

    Scilla
    James   } Ned's
    Aggy

    Thruston
    Eldridge   } Isabel's
    Thrimston

    Beverly.   Patty's

    Sally
    Evelina.   } Lewis's
    Isabel

    Dolly.   Doll's

    Abram   } Rachael's
    Lazaria

    Suckey.   Jerry's
17.   Jame Hubbard
    Isab's Davy
    Jamey. Lewis's

MS (Roger W. Barrett, Chicago, 1947); partially dated; entirely in TJ's hand; on recto of a narrow sheet of paper with lists of vaccinations dated 1802, 1816, and 1826 on verso; written in several sittings; with canceled names shown in italics within angle brackets.

The information provided by this list supplements TJ's correspondence about his experiments with cowpox, or smallpox vaccine, at Monticello. He began by infecting six slaves with cowpox sent by Benjamin Waterhouse that arrived at Monticello on 6 and 13 Aug. 1801. On the 16th, William Wardlaw conducted arm-to-arm inoculations using matter from the first two successful subjects, Burwell Colbert and Joe Fossett. TJ documented the effectiveness of the 16 Aug. procedure on day five, the 21st, and wrote to Waterhouse the same day. Thereafter TJ kept up a "succession of cases" with vaccine drawn on the eighth day, as urged by Waterhouse in his letter to TJ of 4 Sep. (Waterhouse to TJ, 24, 26 July, 1 Aug; TJ to Waterhouse, 14, 21 Aug.).

For the ages and occupations of slaves on the list, see Stanton, *Free Some Day*; Betts, *Farm Book*, especially 58a; and Vols. 29 and 32. Many of the young men vaccinated on the first three days and 1 Sep. worked in the nailery (Vol. 32:417-8).

Q: TJ typically wrote "q" to indicate "query." In the case above, he probably meant that the success of Critta's vaccination was questionable.

To James Madison

Monticello Aug. 7. 1801.

Th: Jefferson presents his affectionate salutations to mr Madison & sends him the inclosed which will explain itself. he hopes to see him & family at Monticello when most convenient to themselves; and observes for his information that the road through Shadwell is put into fine order, the right hand at issuing from the ford on this side to be greatly preferred to the left. the road by Milton is all but impassable. health & respect.

RC (Charles M. Storey, Boston, Massachusetts, 1958). Enclosure: George Helmbold to TJ, 30 July.

From Elijah Russell

RESPECTED SIR,   *Concord, N.H. August 7. 1801.*

Humanity, more than *self* interest, dictates this letter; I hope, therefore, you will excuse the freedom taken by a stranger occupying but an humble walk in the world—I write but because my respect for an aged, grey-headed Father, overpowers my diffidence in addressing the Chief Executive of the United States—My father (now about 70 years of age) was a *poor man;*—but he was not destitute of love to his country—He had a numerous family—they looked to him, many of them, for their support—But, when the tyranny of a British King, called for those who lov'd their country, and who valued their natural rights, to defend them—then did my Father *shoulder his musket, and march to the war*—he had Five Sons who also entered the service about the same time—leaving my mother, and four younger children—whose sole dependance was on *her industry* and the small pittance of his scanty wages—He returned from the war, as he went, a *poor man*—but I never heard that he dishonor'd the title of a *Soldier*—He is now principally dependant for the comforts of Old Age, upon my eldest Brother; who fought in the army by his side, as I have been informed—This Brother, on whom he rest his last hopes, has held the Office of *Inspector of the Revenue at Burlington, in Vermont*—and, as he is a *Federalist*, it is probable application will be made to have some other person appointed to said office—I believe his *integrity* has never been doubted—and, as I believe him a wrongly prejudiced, but *true Friend to his Country*, and prefers its interest to that of any other country whatever—and as my aged Parents

[36]

are so much dependant on him, to render the evening of their lives calm and comfortable—and as this office has considerably assisted him to administer to their necessities—In *their* behalf, I humbly plead, that he may be continued in said Office, if it is consistent with the honor and interest of the Government—and provided he shall discharge its duties with honest fidelity—

With the utmost deference and respect, I am Sir, your most humble servt.—   ELIJAH RUSSELL

RC (DNA: RG 59, LAR); at foot of text: "Thomas Jefferson. Esq. Presd. of the U.S.—"; endorsed by TJ as received 27 Aug. and so recorded in SJL.

Elijah Russell (1769-1803) entered the printing business in 1792 in Concord, New Hampshire, where he worked sporadically over the next 11 years as a solo editor or in partnership on several New England newspapers. He established the *Gilmanton Rural Gazette* in late October 1799, served as the town postmaster from January through December 1800, and, in March 1800, printed Samuel G. Bishop's eulogy on the death of George Washington. His "true blue Jacobin paper," the *Republican Gazette,* which he established in Concord in February 1801, became the organ of the Republican party in New Hampshire. In May 1803, Russell was fined and sentenced in Connecticut for forging state certificates, but he jumped bond and absconded to his home state. He died at the age of 34 after a brief illness while returning from a visit to his parents in Burlington, Vermont (Brigham, *American Newspapers,* 1:201-2, 209, 442, 443, 445, 446, 447, 458; Stets, *Postmasters,* 161; James O. Lyford, ed., *History of Concord, New Hampshire,* 2 vols. [Concord, 1903], 1:295; Samuel G. Bishop,

An Eulogium on the Death of Gen. George Washington [Gilmanton, N.H., 1800; Evans, No. 36981]; Concord *Mirrour,* 6 Sep. 1792; *United States Oracle, and Portsmouth Advertiser,* 14 May 1803; Portsmouth *New Hampshire Gazette,* 7 June 1803; Worcester *National Aegis,* 15 June 1803).

MY FATHER: David Russell, with fellow printer Anthony Haswell, established the Bennington *Vermont Gazette* in 1783 and continued as partner until 1790. Either David Russell or his son by the same name was postmaster at Bennington from 1784 to 1797 (Brigham, *American Newspapers,* 2:1074; *Vermont Gazette,* 17 Oct. 1843; Stets, *Postmasters,* 242, 243).

MY ELDEST BROTHER: David Russell. After serving in the American Revolution the young man settled in Vermont in 1783, where he was associated with his father's newspaper in Bennington. He subsequently moved to Burlington, where he held a number of different offices. George Washington in 1797 nominated him as collector for the district of Vermont, a position he held until TJ replaced him with Jabez Penniman in 1803 (White, *Genealogical Abstracts,* 3:2983; JEP, 1:223, 441; Bennington *Vermont Gazette,* 17 Oct. 1843; Burlington *Vermont Centinel,* 5 May 1803; Vol. 33:125n, 672).

From Robert Smith

SIR,   Washington Aug. 7. 1801.

The chief Clerk of the department of State having this morning shewn to me a Letter from mr Thorton requesting the Executive to order the departure of the English Ship that has been brought into the port of Boston by certain French Citizens, I consider it proper to communicate to you my Opinion thereon. My numerous and pressing engagements will not allow me to go into an extensive discussion of the question.

Before the making of the Treaty with Great Brittain Citizens of France having made a prize, had a right to demand and we were obliged to give Shelter and refuge to them in our ports. This right they had under an existing Treaty, and it was known to the Brittish Government at the time of the making of their Treaty with us. The exception in the Brittish treaty stipulating that "nothing therein contained shall operate contrary to former and existing Treaties" must necessarily have reference to this privilege enjoyed by the French under a former Treaty *then* existing and it is the same in effect as if this privilege of the French had been expressly specified in the exception. After the Brittish treaty was concluded the French, as before, continued to enjoy this privilege. They enjoyed it as a Right. We were under an Obligation to allow it. And the Brittish had no ground of complaint against us for allowing it.

No change has been made in this State of things but by the Act of Congress which declared that the Treaty with France should not thenceforth be Obligatory on the Government or the Citizens of the United States. Under this Act France lost certain rights and the United States were relieved from certain Obligations. But it left all other Nations precisely where they had previously been. It did not give to Great Brittain any additional rights. It did not lay us under any additional obligations to her. Whence then does the Brittish Government deduce the right to exhibit this claim or our Obligation to allow it? Will it be urged that under the words "former and *existing* treaties" such a contingent right did accrue as soon as the French Treaty ceased to exist? Such a construction is not warranted by the prevailing rules of interpretation. On the Contrary, those rules declare that if such had been the intention or view of the Brittish Goverment, they ought to have provided for so important a contingent benefit by precise language, and especially as the idea could have been conveyed without the possibility of a doubt by the introduction of a few words of explanation. Not having disclosed such an intention, they cannot now insist upon so forced a construction.

There is an essential difference between the allowing French Citizens to do what may and what may not be done consistently with our Neutral Character. The Act complained of in this instance can be justified on our part upon principles of Neutrality and therefore may be allowed. But if it were forbidden by the Laws of Neutrality, although it had been allowed by our late Treaty with France we could not give it our sanction.

You will be pleased to consider these as mere hints that have suggested themselves upon the first view of the subject. I have not time to examine or digest them so as to satisfy myself. Accept assurances of my great respect and high consideration   RT SMITH

RC (DLC); at foot of text: "The President"; endorsed by TJ as received from the Navy Department on 13 Aug. concerning "French prizes" and so recorded in SJL.

SHEWN TO ME A LETTER: Jacob Wagner apparently showed Smith a letter to Madison of 1 Aug. from British chargé Edward Thornton. It followed up on a communication of 23 July, in which Thornton, who was in Philadelphia, said that he had learned from the newspapers that an English vessel from the West Indies had entered "one of the Eastern ports" after being seized by the French prisoners it was carrying. Saying that the ship was in effect a French prize, Thornton on the 23d asked the U.S. government "to order the immediate departure of the vessel from the port in which she has taken refuge." Wagner forwarded that letter to Madison on 3 Aug., and Madison passed it along to TJ at Monticello (see TJ to Madison, 13 Aug.). In his letter of 1 Aug., which Wagner forwarded

to Madison on the 10th, Thornton repeated his request that the ship be sent away, and he enclosed copies of documents he had received about the affair. The vessel was the snow *Windsor*, which had been carrying French, Swedish, and Danish prisoners of war. They had taken the ship to Boston after gaining control of it during a storm at sea (Madison, *Papers, Sec. of State Ser.*, 1:270, 463; 2:5, 12-13, 30-1).

In his opinion on the *Betsy Cathcart* case printed at 3 July above, Levi Lincoln also discussed Article 17 of the 1778 Treaty of Amity and Commerce, which enabled French warships and privateers to find SHELTER AND REFUGE for their prizes in American ports, and Article 25 of the Jay Treaty, which granted a similar privilege to Great Britain but was not to OPERATE CONTRARY to existing treaties with other nations.

The ACT OF CONGRESS that "freed and exonerated" the United States from its treaties with France was approved 7 July 1798 (U.S. Statutes at Large, 1:578).

From Joseph Yznardi, Sr.

[EXMO. SE]ÑOR   Baltimore 7 de Agosto 1801
Muy Señor mio, y de todo mi Respecto
Como dije á V.E en mi Ultima me puse en Camino el 27 del pasado, con el Ansia de Visitarlo, y despedirme, pero por mi delicadesa, u por Accidentes, no Conprehensibles Recay en esta muy Malo, donde Aviendome Visto, el General Smith me Inpuso de la reprehencible Conducta de mi Hijo, mas por estenso y de su Miserable Situasion, poniendome en la precision de pagar sus gastos, por el Honor de mi Nonbre, y decoro del Consulado
    dicho, G.S. me ha ensinado, la Apresiable de V.E de 25 del pasado,

qe me ha llenado de Consuelo, en ver la Opinion, qe Merese mi Conducta, y consequente, á ella, y al Contenido de mi Ultima de la Misma fecha á V.E me beo en la precision, de pedir, el Nonbramiento, del Consulado de Cadiz, qe Aseptaré por el tienpo que [. . .] [. . .]inasion de Asuntos pendientes [a mi Cargo] Cuyo Exequator, esperase si V.E lo tiene a bien asta mi Salida para España, permanesiendo aqui en Casa de Mr. Beraveu, H.C.M. Consul

tengo el Honor, con el Respecto, qe devo de repetir á V.E mi Obediencia

Exmo. Señor

JOSEF YZNARDY

E D I T O R S '   T R A N S L A T I O N

MOST EXCELLENT SIR   Baltimore, 7 August 1801

My Most Illustrious Sir and with all my respect

As I said to Your Excellency in my last letter, I departed on the 27th of last month with the desire to visit you and to say goodbye, but either because of my poor health or for unexpected illness I had a serious relapse. When General Smith saw me, he informed me in greater detail of the reprehensible conduct of my son as well as of his miserable situation, thus placing me under the obligation to pay his expenses, in order to save the honor of my name and the decorum of the consulate.

The above-mentioned General Smith has shown me your much appreciated letter of the 25th of last month, which gave me comfort when I saw the esteem that my behavior earned me, and as a result of that letter and what I wrote on the same date to Your Excellency, I find myself obliged to request to be named to the consulate of Cadiz, which I will accept for as long a time as [. . .] pending business for which I am responsible, whose execution is desirable if Your Excellency thinks it wise until my departure to Spain, while I remain here in the house of Mr. Bernabéu, His Catholic Majesty's consul.

I have the honor, with all the respect that is due you, to reiterate to Your Excellency my obedience.

Most Excellent Sir

JOSEF YZNARDY

RC (DNA: RG 59, LAR); torn; at foot of text: "Exmo. Sor. Dn. Thomas Jefferson Presidente de los E.U. &ca."; endorsed by TJ as received 13 Aug. and so recorded in SJL.

MI ULTIMA: Yznardi's letter of 25 July. DE 25 DEL PASADO: TJ to Samuel Smith, 25 July.

MR. BERAVEU: Juan Bautista Bernabéu, the Spanish consul at Baltimore (Miguel Gómez del Campillo, comp., *Relaciones Diplomáticas entre España y los Estados Unidos*, 2 vols. [Madrid, 1944-46], 1:214; 2:355, 490-1).

To William Duane

SIR   Monticello Aug. 8. 1801.

By a new arrangement of the post between Washington and Milton, Charlottesville &c it now leaves Washington Monday evening & reaches this neighborhood Thursday morning. consequently [. . .] the Philadelphia papers of Saturday morning arrive here the Thursday morning following, [say] in 4. days exclusive of Sunday. [. . .] they [would] before to be 9. days on the road. I recieved your paper of Saturday the 1st instant at this place on the morning of the 6th. I presume that in winter it would only be your Friday's paper which could get to Washington Monday evening in time to come by the post of that day for this neighborhood. this regulation has been affected by [making] the rider pass *direct* from Fredericksburg by Orange court house, to Milton & Charlottesville, where it arrives on the same day as formerly. I mention these things for your government as it enables you to send papers of several days later date to all your customers at & beyond this neighborhood. it is a considerable injury to your papers here that they have been [. . .] in their [news] by others. accept my salutations and best wishes.   TH: JEFFERSON

PrC (DLC); faint; at foot of text: "Mr. William Duane"; endorsed by TJ in ink on verso.

From Albert Gallatin

SIR,   Treasury Department August 8th. 1801

I have the honor to transmit sundry papers in relation to David Hopkins imprisoned at the suit of United States for non-payment of a penalty. and a copy of my letter on that subject to Mr. Freneau who transmitted them.

As he has mistaken the proper tribunal to whom he should have applied, & no relief can be obtained unless it be by a pardon, the papers are submitted to your consideration.

It is proper to add that the District Attorney opposed the remission, which probably was the cause of the late Secretary's decision. The penalty is for *not entering the Still*, although the duties seem to have been paid.

It is also alledged in favor of the Petititoner, that the suit was not commenced within the time limited by law, but that judgment was obtained by default. —

I have the honor to be with perfect respect Sir, Your obedient Servt.   ALBERT GALLATIN

RC (DLC); in a clerk's hand, signed by Gallatin; at foot of text: "The President of the United States"; endorsed by TJ as received 13 Aug. and "Hopkins's case" and so recorded in SJL. Enclosures not found, but see Peter Freneau to TJ, 11 Sep. 1801, and enclosure.

DISTRICT ATTORNEY: Thomas Parker, a Charleston attorney, who served in the position from 1792 until his death in 1820 (Washington, *Papers, Pres. Ser.*, 11:265; JEP, 1:126).

From Samuel Hanson

DEAR SIR,   George-Town 8th Augt. 1801.

Agreeably to your permission, I enclose a list of the Directors of the Bank of the U.S.—. In obtaining it, I found more difficulty than I expected; which is the reason of it's not having been forwarded by last mail. I have written to Philada. to engage the good-officers of the following Gentlemen, old Friends of 1777.[+] When I look over the list, however, and compare the *Politics* of my Rival Candidate with my own, I am not sanguine. yet I shall not decline any honourable means to obtain Success.

A few days after your departure your answer to the New-Haven Remonstrants made it's appearance here. I need not say that it gives great pleasure to the Democrats; and more particularly to a Sect of them who may be denominated *Sweepers*. They are greatly rejoiced to find that their ideas are to be adopted in part, if not *in toto*. As to the Aristocratic portion of the Federalists, it is not to be expected—I had almost said, *wished*—that they should be pleased with any Act of a Republican Chief-Magistrate. They, too, have their *Sweepers*, who maintain the propriety of a universal dismission of the Federal officers—but, whether they uphold this doctrine from an opinion of its soundness, or from a secret hope that an undiscriminating Sweep would render the administration unpopular, I am too well acquainted with their duplicity, and insidious practices, not to entertain some doubt. A passage in your answer to the Newhaveners is thought, by the Tories, to be singular, and almost ludicrous. They make you complain of the Federal Officers that they will neither "die nor resign." For my own part, were I not so well acquainted with the moderation of your temper, I should be induced to conclude that the passage in question was meant to be sarcastic. Some of the Officers doubtless

+ I forgot to insert them in the proper place. They are Wm. & Edw. Tilghman, Benja. Chew, Bishop White, Dr. Rush, Wm. Hamilton, Mr. Hans, Edw. Burd and others—

have no choice, not possessing any other means of Subsistence—but of those who *have*, what shall be said of the Spirit and consistency, in continuing in employments under an administration whose political principles they have publickly and uniformly reprobated and abused? what can equal their effrontery, and, at the same time, their meanness, in sustaining an Interview with a President whose private as well as political Character they have calumniated for years?

I had yesterday a glimpse of the majesty of the Supreme Federal Judiciary—of that all-important Corps, which, according to the declaration of one of them, is damned by Heaven to save these United States from the Horrors of Anarchy and confusion! To rescue their misguided Countrymen from the prevalence of Republicanism! to eradicate principles congenial with that form of Government expressly guaranteed to us by the Constitution!

In opposition to the Prophetic chase, permit me, Sir, to mention a tract of a Friend of mine. He is certainly what, in France, might be termed an *Immodere*. He is, of course, an inveterate *Sweeper*. His argument, if not conclusive, is short. He maintains that for an administration, decidedly and professedly Republican, to continue in office, in a Republican Government, any Person other than a Republican, is a manifest political solecism.

The doctrine asserted, or implied, by the Newhaveners respecting the indispensability of each officer's performance of the duties personally, is new. I mean that, while Charles Lee was Collector of Alexandria, he was not in that town half the year—& that, his Deputy being a very ignorant young Man, and the business of the Revenue suffering from the absence of his Principal, I, as Surveyor of the District, frequently remonstrated with Genl. Washington and Mr. Hamilton on the Subject, but without effect—

I have conversed with Mr. Gallatin on the probability of the Establishment of a Branch Bank here. He very obligingly promised to communicate to me, from time to time, the progress of the business.

A Friend of mine conversing a few days ago with a Federalist on the appointment of Mr. Gallatin, the former admitted that, had there been an American to be found equal to him on the subject of finance, he would have preferred him to a Foreigner. But this not being the case, the appointment was proper & commendable. The other, in order to rebut this argument, declared that you remarked last winter, while Vice-President, "that the Finances of the Country had been so well-managed, and so ably conducted by Hamilton and Wolcott, that a small portion of talents would be sufficient to continue them in their present prosperous train." My Friend denied your having said so.

The other maintained it; and, upon being pressed for his authority, said that the declaration was made by you at Genl. Forrest's the day you dined with him. All who know Forrest will want no other proof of its being a lie than his asserting it—Knowing, as they do, if he even speaks the truth it is by accident—and that he is incapable of quoting "the truth, the whole truth, and nothing but the truth."

You have never, I believe, Sir, received a letter so full of "Brimborion." My excuse is, the constant access you have always allowed me—and the hope that you will be equally indulgent to me on paper as in person.

Encouraged by this hope, I venture to continue my Letter, though it has already run into thrice the length that I at first intended.

Permit me, Sir, to apprise you that my contest with Forrest, in which the Bank must be, eventually, implicated, will necessarily have the effect of exciting against me the Enmity of all his connexions and those of his *Brother Directors*. Among them (the connexions) are some very respectable Characters. I expected to be traduced and vilified. What I have to beg of you is to listen to their accounts of me with the proper allowance—and to take my real character from some of the best men upon whom the Sun ever shone—from Men who have been my fast Friends for more than 20 years. You will be told, perhaps, that I am a man of a turbulent temper, and addicted to quarrels. In proof of this, they will refer to a notorious disagreement with the Aristocrats of Alexandria 9 years ago. But I should have no objection to rest my character upon the representations of the Inhabitants of Alexandria, including my then Adversaries, who have long ceased to be so. I am charged by a Hypocritical Friend with "disturbing the peace of Society." The proper expression would have been, "the peace of the Board of Directors." He forgets the quiet of families, disturbed by Forrest's Swindlings—He forgets the peace of my own family, destroyed for many years, by the constant dread of this man's power at the Board, and his exercise of it to deprive me of my scanty support. In making the charges against Forrest, I declare to Heaven that I was less activated by a spirit of resentment for his long secret designs to injure me, than by a sense of duty in exposing him and his abettors and Co-Adjutors to the World. This purpose I have long been determined to effect, as soon as I could do it with impunity. I conceived that this period was now arrived—but I have lately found that I have made an egregious miscalculation as to the cashiership of the Branch-Bank. Had the appointment been in the Directors of it, I should have entertained no doubt of obtaining it. As the matter stands, [there] is very great. Confident, as I am of my own existence, that a Branch-Bank here will supersede the ne[. . .], at any rate, the existence, of any other Bank on the Maryland Side of the District, I fear[1] my situation will be deplorable, should the Directors of the Bank of U.S. reject my application. It is from this gloomy view of that Subject that I am constrained to entreat you not to suffer your present Good-Opinion of me to be impaired by the malice of my Enemies, or, more properly of the Friends of U. Forrest and his Abettors & *Peers*. You already know why I would prefer the Cashiership to an appointment under the Government—because I conceive it would be more lucrative, upon the whole—Should I be unsuccessful in that attempt, I must again, as a *dernier ressort*, throw myself upon your favour.

From some passages in this letter, you may be inclined to suspect that I am myself of the Sect of *Sweepers*. But it is not so. As I might be eventually benefitted by that operative stroke, I dare not trust my Judgment with it, knowing that "the heart is deceitful above all things."

I felicitate you on the daily accession of Strength to the Republican Side. The State of Parties may be expressed by the following division:

1st.   The Monarchickal Federalists
2   The Aristocratic   Do.
3   The conscientious do.
4   The Democrats

Of the 1st. class there are no hopes. They are inexorable. Nothing but a King will satisfy them—of course, they are doomed to everlasting discontent

=

The 2d. must, from the nature of their principles, come over, in appearance at least, to the Republican Side. Their maxim is that pious one—"Reverence the powers that be"—and their practice is, finally to be on the Side of the Court for the time being.

=

The 3d., having been duped by the artifices & calumnies of the other two, will, like all other honest men, recant their past Errors as soon as they perceive them. The accession from this quarter will, of course, be immense

=

Of the 4th. it is sufficient to say that, from that large class there will be no defection. They are unchanged and unchangeable

=

I take no account of the Trimmers; because, being of no real Strength to any Party, they ought not to be taken into the Estimate—

except it be to designate them as more contemptible, if possible, than the Monarchists themselves.

I cannot conclude this long and farraginous Epistle without begging the favour of you to employ me, during your absence, in any way in which I can be serviceable or convenient to you—. I shall be always solicitous of every opportunity of obeying your Commands, and of evincing the perfect respect and esteem with which I am,

Dear Sir, Your much obliged and grateful Servant

S. HANSON OF SAML

RC (DLC); endorsed by TJ as received 13 Aug. and so recorded in SJL. Enclosure: undated list of 25 directors of the Bank of the U.S., in Hanson's hand, including Thomas Willing, Elias Boudinot, Samuel Breck, William Bingham, Isaac Wharton, Robert Smith, James C. Fisher, Abijah Dawes, Joseph Sims, Archibald McCall, F. G. Wacksmuth, Andrew Bayard, Samuel Coates, Jeremiah Parker, John Miller, Jr., William Chancellor; Harrison G. Otis of Massachusetts; John Charlton, Abijah Hammond, Matthew Clarkson, John G. Leake, William Rutherford of New York; James McLurg of Virginia; Samuel Johnston of North Carolina; and Jacob Read of South Carolina (MS in same).

SWEEPERS: i.e., those who believed that all Federalists should be removed from office. In his letter to Wilson Cary Nicholas of 11 June, TJ referred to the need for a "general sweep" in Connecticut.

TJ's ANSWER TO THE NEW-HAVEN REMONSTRANTS of 12 July appeared in the National Intelligencer on 29 July and in the Alexandria Advertiser and Commercial Intelligencer on 30 July.

SUPREME FEDERAL JUDICIARY: John Marshall was in Washington from 4 to 12 Aug. for a session of the U.S. Supreme Court. In his first case as chief justice, he delivered the Court's opinion in Talbot v. Seeman. The Court also heard arguments on another case, Wilson v. Mason, on 8 and 10 Aug. (Marshall, Papers, 6:xliii, 267n, 538; Washington Federalist, 5 Aug.; New York Daily Advertiser, 24 Aug.).

As surveyor of customs, Hanson had served under collector CHARLES LEE,

whose DEPUTY was Vincent Gray. Despite Hanson's repeated complaints to George WASHINGTON and Alexander HAMILTON in 1791 and 1792 about the collector's neglect of duty and absences, Lee retained his office until April 1793 (JEP, 1:11, 14; Syrett, Hamilton, 10:522-3; Washington, Papers, Pres. Series, 9:80-2; 10:80-3).

BRIMBORION: a thing with little value or use (OED).

CONTEST WITH FORREST: Uriah Forrest brought charges against Hanson for calling him a liar and a swindler. The case, which came to trial before the circuit court in the District of Columbia on 30 Sep., was decided in favor of Forrest, who was awarded one cent in damages (Charleston City Gazette and Daily Advertiser, 17 July 1801; National Intelligencer, 12 Oct. 1801; TJ to Thomas Willing, 6 Oct. 1801).

BROTHER DIRECTORS: the directors of the Bank of Columbia and the District of Columbia commissioners had many overlapping interests. William Thornton, Alexander White, and Tristram Dalton were the District of Columbia commissioners in 1801. The Bank of Columbia facilitated the business of Washington and was deliberately organized to handle the papers of the commissioners as well as of the lot buyers. The Bank of Columbia's first three presidents were Samuel Blodget, Jr., Benjamin Stoddert, and John Mason, and its incorporators included William Deakins, Jr. (the treasurer of the commissioners), Uriah Forrest, John Mason, James M. Lingan, William B. Magruder, and Thomas Peter. Tristram Dalton, one of the commissioners, was also elected a director of the Washington branch of the Bank of the United States in

October 1801 (Walsh, *Early Banks in D.C.*, 68-9; Bryan, *National Capital*, 1:145, 223; *Alexandria Advertiser and Commercial Intelligencer*, 10 Oct. 1801; Vol. 33:481).

ARISTOCRATS OF ALEXANDRIA: see Samuel Hanson to TJ, 6 Apr. 1801.

[1] Preceding two words interlined.

To Benjamin Waterhouse

DEAR SIR   Monticello Aug. 8. 1801.

I had the pleasure of writing you on the 25th. of July and of acknoleging the receipt of yours of July 17. with the vaccine matter which was immediately delivered to Doctr. Gantt. your favors of the 24th. & 26th. came to me at this place on the 6th. inst. and the matter accompanying them was, by a skilful physician of the neighborhood, Dr. Wardlaw, immediately inserted into six persons of my own family. we shall thus stand a chance of planting the disease here where I imagine it will be as salutary as any where in the union. our laws indeed have permitted inoculation of the small pox, but under such conditions of consent of the neighborhood as have admitted not much use of the permission. that disease therefore is almost a stranger here, and extremely dreaded. I will take care to inform you of the result of our operation. accept my esteem and respect.

TH: JEFFERSON

RC (MBCo); at foot of text: "Doctr. Benjamin Waterhouse." PrC (DLC).

MY OWN FAMILY: see TJ to John Shore of 12 Sep. and List of Inoculations, printed at 7 Aug.

From Alexander White

SIR   Washington 8th. August 1801

To enable me to comply with your request respecting Samuel Davidsons claim, I have re-examined all the papers in the Commissioners Office relative to that case, and find that his claim rests solely on a supposition that L'Enfants Plan is the proper Plan of the City; that it received its confirmation by the transmission thereof to Congress; In respect to which President Washington, in his letter dated 20th February 1797 in answer to the Commissioners letter, enclosing Mr. Davidsons memorial says "That many alterations have been made from Major L'Enfants Plan by Major Ellicott (with the approbation of the Executive) is not denied, that some were deemed essential, is avowed" Again "Mr Davidson is mistaken if he supposes that

[47]

the transmission of Major L'Enfant's Plan of the City to Congress was the completion thereof; so far from it, it will appear by the message which accompanied the same, that it was given as matter of information to show what state the business was in, and the return of it requested; that neither House of Congress passed any Act consequent thereupon; that it remained, as before, under the controul of the Executive; that afterwards several errors were discovered and corrected, many alterations made, and the appropriations (except as to the Capitol and Presidents house) struck out, before it went to the Engraver, intending that work and the promulgation thereof were to give it the final and regulating stamp" Although the words "Presidents House" were retained in the engraved Plan, the square was laid down differently from that of L'Enfant, and the President in his Act appropriating the same, has described it as delineated on the engraved Plan, on the same principle Mr Davidson has been paid for his Land within the square—These circumstances appear to me conclusive; the Land thus described is vested in the U. States; and the President cannot restore it, or any part of it to the Original Proprietor. I therefore deem it unnecessary to detail the desultory matter which Mr. Davidson has introduced in his various applications; but I would observe, that if Mr L'Enfants Plan is to be admitted, as a matter of right, in one instance, it must be so in the whole; that this would set the City property afloat; the Streets, public appropriations, and building lots being laid out without any reference to that Plan; but generally corresponding with the engraved Plan, as nearly as the same could be adapted by actual Survey, to the surface of the earth—This letter, I expect, will be considered as a private communication only—The Board if called upon will answer Mr. Davidsons Complaint

I am with Sentiments of the highest respect Sir Your most Obedt Servant   ALEX WHITE

RC (DLC); at foot of text: "President of the U. States"; endorsed by TJ as received 13 Aug. and so recorded in SJL.

Samuel Davidson had asked TJ to consider his CLAIM to property in President's Square in a letter of 27 July.

The letter of George WASHINGTON to the District of Columbia commissioners of 20 Feb. 1797 is printed in full in RCHS, 17 (1914), 186-8. Davidson made VARIOUS APPLICATIONS about his claim to Presidents Washington, Adams, and Jefferson, but without result (Bryan, *National Capital*, 1:296-7n).

To Andrew Moore

DEAR SIR   Monticello Aug. 9. 1801.

I recieved yesterday your favor of the 5th. and am much gratified by your accepting the commission of Marshal. immediately on reciept of your letter I filled up the commission but shall not forward it till Thursday, being the next post day, when it shall be deposited in the post office at Staunton, under cover to you, & endorsed 'to be delivered to yourself or your order.' in the mean time I shall send this present letter by such casual opportunity as may occur from Charlottesville in hopes it may get to you in time to notify you where your commission will be lodged. I must pray you to make the census of your district the very first object of your attention because it must be returned to the Secretary of state (now at his seat in Orange) before the 1st. day of the next month. no doubt the former marshal of the whole district of Virginia, mr D. M. Randolph had compleated the census, as he had no notice of the appointment of his successor till some time in April, within which month the work was to be completed. I trust therefore you have only the formality of the return of your part of the former district[1] to execute; but it should be seen to without a day's delay. accept assurances of my esteem & respect.

                                                    TH: JEFFERSON

PrC (DLC); at foot of text: "Colo Andrew Moore."

FILLED UP THE COMMISSION: in a list of appointments, TJ noted that Moore was appointed 16 July, with the commission dated 8 Aug. (Vol 33:677).

[1] Preceding seven words interlined.

From John Barnes

SIR   George Town (Potomac) 10th. Augst 1801.

I have already dispatched Original & duplicates each, of the inclosed letters & a/c in Philada. and transmitted duplicate thereof for your [government?].

—Some few days since both the plaisterers called on me, respecting their intended Journey. the small Man (for I do not recollect his Name) was very urgent to set out immediately ℔ land. the other proposed—going ℔ water to Richmond—in the course of last week I asked if they required any money in advance & to what amot. the former proposed $15 each. the latter replied he could do without any advance. I desired them to fix the time and boat, and to call on me the day before to receive my letter to Messrs. G & J—in Case they should go ℔ water to Richmond, on Friday—the small man called to inform me, his Partner had engaged a Job & declined going. (which I very much questioned. supposing he wd: not do any such thing without acquainting me with his particular reasons, so a difference between them I presume and withal—I suspect, his Objections might arise from a dislike to the intended partner of the Journey, for, at both interviews *this man* appeared to be in liquor however—I told him if he should go by himself—I should require a security for the $15. to which he readily assented—and I expected he would *have* calld on saturday but I have not seen him—of *this man* I have but a very slender opinion as to his sobriety or promise.—

the other I look upon to be a prudent sedate man. and I cannot yet suppose he would be so deficient (if he realy declined going—) not to make me acquainted with his determination & reasons for postponing. or refusal of his engagement—in Case then, you should be disappointed in One or both, shall I look out, to engage any Other;—still, I think it not improbable, that the same small plaisterer—notwithstand:g he has not called with *his* security—may—(thro the want of *him*.) be on his way Journeying—towards Monticello— and still as likely his Companion—a decent looking man who Accompanied him the last time he called on me, if so (and a few days will determine so) it may confirm that a difference between him & his former Companion did exist.

I have this moment seen, Mr Rapin—who informs me—that Mr LeMaire is engaged to be here. early the insuing [mo]   Mr. Rapin writes to you ℔ this days mail—

waiting your further Commands I am Sir your most obed. H Servt

JOHN BARNES

inclosed Also—a packet recd from Mr Hanson.—

RC (ViU: Edgehill-Randolph Papers); words illegible from bleeding of ink; addressed: "Thomas Jefferson Esquire President U States Monticello"; endorsed by TJ as received 13 Aug. and so recorded in SJL. Enclosures: (1) Barnes to Tadeusz Kosciuszko, 3 Aug., acknowledging receipt of Kosciuszko's letter from Paris of 30 Floréal (20 May), which Barnes "presented" to TJ "for his perusal," and assuring Kosciuszko that he will be given the interest and dividend on his stock "as they are received" (Tr in same; in Barnes's hand and signed by him; at head of text: "Copy"; at foot of text: "Genl: Kosciuszko—Paris"). (2) Barnes to William Short, 3 Aug., acknowledging Short's letter of 19 Apr. from Paris, received 25 July, enclosing a statement of Short's account with a credit balance of $1,844, and stating his intent to make a second purchase of public stock (Tr in same; in Barnes's hand and signed by him; at head of text: "Copy"; at foot of text: "William Short Esqr—Paris"). (3) Statement of Barnes's account with

William Short, 31 July, noting transactions from 16 Jan. to 25 July 1801 (Tr in same; in Barnes's hand and signed by him; at head of text: "Copy").

Barnes wrote again about the PLAISTERERS, Mr. King and Martin Wanscher, on 17 Aug.

From David Fergusson

Baltimore Monday 10th. August 1801.

With regard to the tittle of addressing you, I am from the wood of diffidence at a loss—but I hope the plain apology—will plead & operate as an excuse, unto a Mind impress'd with just sentiments of Honour, and susceptible of the tender feelings of humanity—.

Fraught with an ardency, unto a Country, from which I have participated, it's friendship & favor, I shou'd be wanting in my small scale of ability & penetration—not to aid it's movement—from the most hospitable breath of a Heart, bent fully upon the agrandizement—of it's Strengths, it's Morality, it's happiness—, it's quite, it's tranquility—from that spring, my intention springs—and as far as the mind can suggest—or the liabillity of the Heart to bestow—I shall endeavour to express a few words—which appears to my mind & feeling—(& which I've seen wh. disgust).

Upon the last session of Congress, I wrote about 3 Years ago, about Taxes & a general list I sent—to J. Adams then Predt. under the tittle of 7. Friends—Mr. Wolcott, I wrote at the same time under my real name—not wishing to be Known as a publick writter—I write this, to take the liberty, to ask you the favour of Your Time—in reading a paquett of Taxes for the approaching Assembly of Congress—which appear to be salutary & in their operation, will be light—& can't admit of any wry thought, or useless grumbling, (common[1] phrase).

A list of the Taxes, which I shall send on—with my remarks—about the offspring of their utillity—I shall direct to you at the City of Washington—& I expect to be their in a few days—where, perhaps I may have the Honour to see thee—my name I subscribe to this & unto the Inclosure—with the papers thus *Seven Friends.*—

I have been troubled with the Rheumatism & just from the south—in Carolina—I live at the Eastern Shore of Virginia—& have been in the Country 31 Years—(Scotch). Annexed I quote a list of The Taxes & wherever this finds thee—I wish you every happiness—which your goodness of Heart is able to afford—& alongst with the aid of the Supreme Being, the Heart of the Land & the Bosom of the Sea, is able to bestow. And under the hope—that what I have aimed at to express, may meet the approbation—of a Mind which I have before expressed is the wish of one, who is with a high Esteem, not to be refused, & not less with High Regard   DAVID FERGUSSON

RC (DLC); endorsed by TJ as received 20 Aug. and so recorded in SJL. Enclosure: List of nine taxes, ranging from a post office tax to taxes on public stages, receipts, bills of lading, and vessels in quarantine, dated 10 Aug. 1801 (MS in same; in Fergusson's hand, signed "Seven Friends").

In 1787, David Fergusson, a merchant from Great Britain, opened a store with John Tennent, in Blandford, near Petersburg, Virginia. Tennent, a naturalized citizen, obtained the license for the establishment and paid the £5 tax required of citizens, instead of the £20 tax required of aliens. Because the store was called "David Fergusson's," although the license was not in his name, the court fined him £40. In 1789, Fergusson petitioned Virginia state authorities for a remission of the fine (CVSP, 4:626; Fergusson to Washington, 25 Apr. 1783, RC in DLC: Washington Papers).

Between 30 Apr. and 4 May 1783, Fergusson, writing from London, composed a GENERAL LIST of 15 taxes "for raising a Revenue, for the Support of the Government; of the thirteen United Provinces of North America," signed it "Thirteen Friends," and sent it to George Washington (MS in DLC: Washington Papers). Fergusson explained to Washington, in a letter of 6 May 1783, that he would probably come to America and reside in some part of Virginia or Maryland. In that case, he noted, the recommended taxes "would be chearfully paid on my part; from the sense of that utility to which they are pointed" (RC in same).

PAQUETT OF TAXES: see Fergusson to TJ, 22 Sep. 1801.

TROUBLED WITH THE RHEUMATISM: on 18 Aug., Fergusson wrote Gallatin from Georgetown, noting his health problem and requesting some "eligible employ, where Ability, Integrity & Secrecy are required" (Gallatin, *Papers*, 5:598-9).

[1] Fergusson placed check marks above the preceding three words.

From Albert Gallatin

DR SIR   City of Washington 10th August 1800 [i.e. 1801]

I have the honor to enclose the following papers vizt.

1st. Extract of a letter from the Collector of Sag harbour Long Island on the application of hospital money. The same complaints have occasionally been made by other collectors in those small ports from whence the money has heretofore been drawn to the principal port. It might be a good rule to permit the Collectors of those small ports to expend when necessary a sum not exceeding one half of the monies there collected, reserving the other half to assist the ports of the same State, when from any extraordinary cause the expence[1] would be greater in any one year than the receipts, to purchase stocks or to erect hospitals. But, as mentioned in a former letter, an exception is necessary in relation to Charleston S.C. & principally Norfolk on account of the public hospital there. I have as yet no answer to the permission requested to apply in relation to those two ports part of the money collected in the adjoining States.

2d. Mr Page's letter recommending Mount Ed. Chisman for Collector of Hampton instead of William Kerby to be removed for delinquency as pr. your answer to my official report on that subject. Two months have elapsed since I had applied to Mr Page for a recommendation & if you approve One of the blank commissions may be filled accordingly.

3d. Govr. Jackson's, of Georgia, recommendation in favor of T. De Mottos Johnson for Collector Savannah instead of Powell to be removed for the same cause as Kerby. The port of Savannah being of great importance & the accounts much deranged, render it essential that a perfectly suitable & very[2] *active* man should be appointed. From Messrs. Taliafero, Millege & Baldwin to whom I had writen on the subject no answer is yet received. You will be pleased to decide whether a commission should issue also in this case.

4th Letters from Watson Collect. of Plymouth & Gen. Lincoln Collector of Boston in relation to the enquiry into Watson's conduct & its result. It is presumable that the liberality displayed in this instance had a good effect

5th A letter from Charles Pinckney on the propriety of removals there & one from Simmons showing his compliance with a former *circular* in rendering his accounts. The letter from Mr Pinckney, who has since sailed, was received the next day after I had written to you on the same subject & had enclosed St. Th. Mason's letter. It shows that I was not mistaken in what I had understood to be Mr Pinckney's opinion. But it shows also that Mr Doyley who was Gen. Mason's correspondent & said that a removal after the meeting of Congress should be too late, is the candidate for the office. There is something mysterious in that & in your having recieved such different impressions on that subject from what I had. It is necessary that the true situation of affairs there should be known, & it is desirable that it may not be necessary to remove the Collector. He is the only active officer who has yet been obtained there. His predecessor Holmes had left every thing in immense confusion. Much has been recovered through Simmons's exertions, & although the general relaxation, which pervaded[3] the internal administration of this & every other department during the reign of energy, had produced the delay of his accounts, you see with what rapidity he has regained the time lost.

6th. Letters from Mr Lincoln atty. general on present aspect in Massachusets—from Gov. Langdon wishing for more removals & enclosing a letter from Judge Burke S.C. wishing also for some & recommending Ths. Burke to the office in Savannah for which Gov. Jackson recommends Johnson—& from Mr Osgood of thanks.

7th. return of Warrants issued last week amounting to Dlrs. 90,804.12 At the beginning of the week 3d. August the balance of cash in the Treasury was 2,520,228.42. On the 25th May which was the first regular return I could obtain the balance was 1,926,263.05. The surplus money, for we have got more than we want in the Treasury, is applied as fast as we can procure good bills to purchase remittances for Holland where we have to pay 1,900,000 dollars next year, & if we do not take care to be beforehand, will necessarily raise the exchange by purchasing large sums at once. But this place is unfavorable on account of the distance from Philada. & New-York. You must altogether depend on Banks or private agents. I have not been able to purchase since beginning of July more than about 300,000 dollars worth, the whole at 39 cents. Exchange is now at 40 & I must stop; otherwise Governt. continuing to purchase would raise it above par.

Jonas Clark Collector of Kennebunk was it seems appointed Inspector of *external* revenue by the late Presidt. & Senate, but through some mistake notice not given to the Dept. of State & no commission issued. In all the ports where there is a surveyor, he receives also a commission of inspector which is necessary in the performance of some of his duties in relation to imported teas & spirits. In the ports where, as Kennebunk, there is no Surveyor, the Collector receives the same commission. Considering it as a matter of course, I have filled one of the blank commissions with his name for that office, which, I hope, will meet your approbation.

Govr. Drayton has communicated that Ed. Darrel had accepted the place of Commissr. of direct tax for the first division of South Carolina, for which he had received a blank commission; Mr Darrel has also written & hopes to complete the assessment in Nover. That of N. Carolina is completed. No answer yet on that subject from Georgia.

The answer to New Haven seems to have had a greater effect than had been calculated upon. The republicans hope for a greater number of removals; the federals also expect it. I have already received several letters from Philada. applying for the offices of customs upon the ground that it is generally understood that the officers there are to be removed. There is no doubt that the federal leaders are making a powerful effort to rally their party on the same ground. Although some mistakes may have been made, as to the proper objects both of removal & appointment, it does not appear that less than what has been done could have been done without injustice to the republicans. But ought much more to be done? It is so important for the permanent establishment of those republican principles of limitation of power & public economy, for which we have successfully contended, that they should rest on the broad basis of the people & not on a fluctuating party majority, that it would be better to displease many of our political friends than to give an opportunity to the irreconcilable enemies of a free government of inducing the mass of the federal citizens to make a common cause with them. The sooner we can stop the ferment the better, and at all events it is not desirable that it should affect the eastern & Southern parts of the Union. I fear less from the importunity for obtaining offices, than from the arts of those men whose political existence depends on that of party. Office hunters cannot have much influence; but the other class may easily persuade the warmest of our friends that more ought to be done for them. Upon the whole although a few more changes may be necessary, I hope there will be but few. The number of removals is not great, but in importance they are beyond their number. The Supervisors of all the violent party States embrace all the Collectors. Add to that the intended change in the Post-office & you have in fact every man in office out of the sea-ports. Whilst on that subject, is it not proper that the suppression of the 19 offices of inspectors worth 20,000 dollars should be known & understood? If you approve, I would send to the press the Order itself which you signed for that purpose.

Duane is here & applies for two appointments in favor of Gardner a native of Pennsylvania & Campbell an united Irishman the two clerks who gave him the transcript of the accounts of Dayton Pickering &c. The last was suspected & turned out; the first was not suspected but resigned. He wants Gardner to be made Agent with the Choctaw Indians & Campbell to have a commission in the army. Whatever impropriety there might be in their conduct, I have reason to believe Gardner to be a man of honor. Campbell is very impudent but as enthusiastic as his friends (the U. Ir. I mean)[4] commonly are.

Mr Thornton presses for a decision in the question of admission of French privateers & their prizes. I can give no opinion having never considered the subject; but unless it is much clearer than I expect, it seems that delay is desirable, at least until after the ratification of the French Convention. I know that you must at last meet the question; but Thornton would not speak if he was not instructed, & the importance of a decision is too great to be risked on any but the strongest grounds.

Hoping to hear soon from you, I remain with great respect Dear Sir Your most obt. Servt ALBERT GALLATIN

RC (DLC); at foot of text: "Thomas Jefferson President United States"; endorsed by TJ as received from the Treasury Department on 13 Aug. and so recorded in SJL with notation "multifarious." Enclosures: (1) John Page to Gallatin, 31 July 1801 (not found, but see Page to Gallatin, 18 Aug., in Gallatin, *Papers*, 5:601). (2) Benjamin Lincoln to Gallatin, Boston, 31 July, stating that he was pleased with the decision in the case of William Watson, because "it relieved the Mind of an old public servant, whose Character through life has hardly been shaded with a blemish, from a state of perplexing anxiety," and concluding that "through the whole investigation there appeared a firmness ornamental in the chief Majistrate, and a Candour which cannot fail of inspiring confidence & esteem." (3) Levi Lincoln to Gallatin, Worcester, 29 July, noting that except for Federalist newspapers and "the exertions of some violent people to keep it alive," the spirit of opposition was subsiding in Massachusetts and "misrepresentations & slander" were "losing ground and yielding to truth, and candid explanations," with TJ's answer to the New Haven merchants having had a good effect and leaving "our Boston friends . . . in a preposterous situation" because "their conduct is changed but their principles are unaltered," and concluding with a recommendation of Samuel Flagg, Jr., to serve as an officer on the *Boston* under Captain Daniel McNeill. (4) John Langdon to Gallatin, Portsmouth, New Hampshire, 30 July, enclosing Aedanus Burke to Langdon, undated, recommend-

ing Langdon's friend Thomas Burke, who had firmly adhered to his republican principles during the system of terror in 1798 and 1799, as collector at Savannah and describing him as a merchant with property there who until recently had resided in Charleston, where he had many influential friends. (5) Samuel Osgood to Gallatin, New York, 4 Aug., thanking Gallatin and the president for his appointment as supervisor of New York, an office more valuable than he had contemplated, and promising to give "steady attention" to the business (RCs in NHi: Gallatin Papers; Gallatin, *Papers*, 5:469, 478, 484, 512). (6) "Weekly return of Warrants issued on the Treasurer for the week ending 8th August 1801," listing seven warrants, Nos. 105 to 111, for a total of $90,804.12, including two for the civil list, one being an appropriation under courts and prisons to Daniel C. Brent for $99.76; one miscellaneous, under appropriations for unclaimed merchandise, in favor of Paul Coulon, attorney, for the ship *Betsy Cathcart*, for $34,038.48; two for the War Department, both in favor of Samuel Meredith, one for the army for $25,000 and one for the purchase of arms for $25,000; one for intercourse with foreign nations for $203.75 for the protection of seamen; and two for the public debt, being interest on the domestic debt in favor of the Bank of Columbia for $4,431.35; leaving a balance of specie in the Treasury at the end of the week of $2,477,387.16 (MS in DLC: TJ Papers, 115:19803; in Gallatin's hand and initialed by him). (7) John Drayton to TJ, 29 July 1801. Other enclosures not found.

COLLECTOR OF SAG HARBOUR: Henry P. Dering (Gallatin, *Papers*, 6:258). For Gallatin's FORMER LETTER on funds collected for marine hospitals, see his first letter to the president on 29 July.

MY OFFICIAL REPORT: see Gallatin's Report on Delinquent Collectors, 9 June. TJ's answer to the report may have been given verbally, for no response has been found or recorded in SJL.

President Adams nominated JONAS CLARK as COLLECTOR OF KENNEBUNK on 9 May 1800, but he did not include the office of inspector in the appointment. Clark appears on TJ's lists of appointments at 4 Aug., under his additional position as inspector (JEP, 1:353; Vol. 33:671, 677).

LETTERS FROM PHILADA.: William Duane, Alexander J. Dallas, and Moses Levy brought Gallatin several applications from friends in Philadelphia requesting that the Treasury secretary use his influence with the president to help them gain federal appointments. Citing "some recent Information & the Presidents answer to the merchants of new Haven," Anthony Butler wrote Gallatin on 29 July, applying for the customs collectorship in place of George Latimer. On the same date John M. Taylor requested that Gallatin keep him in mind if changes were made "in the Customshouse here." Alexander Boyd recommended James Gamble as naval officer at the port, and Blair McClenachan applied for the position of purveyor of public supplies in place of Israel Whelen (Gallatin, *Papers*, 5:460-1, 472-4, 504, 510; JEP, 1:352).

I WOULD SEND TO THE PRESS THE ORDER: see note to Executive Order on Revenue Districts, printed at 29 July.

For the plight of William P. GARDNER and Anthony CAMPBELL, see William Duane to TJ, 1 Mch. 1801.

QUESTION OF ADMISSION OF FRENCH PRIVATEERS: in a letter to Madison of 24 July, Edward Thornton made several complaints of U.S. neutrality violations, one being that the French armed ship *Beguine*, under the guise of regular commerce, had remained at Boston and "equipped herself in that harbour in a hostile manner in order to cruize against His Majesty's Subjects." As with the *Windsor*, Thornton noted that he had gathered the information from the newspapers. On 3 Aug., Wagner brought Thornton's charge to Gallatin's attention. The next day Gallatin sent Benjamin Lincoln a copy of the paragraph from Thornton's letter regarding the French vessel and requested that the Boston collector "take immediate measures for ascertaining whether the facts," as stated by Thornton, were correct and called for the implementation of the Treasury Department circular of 4 Aug. 1793, which forbade the arming of privateers at U.S. ports (Gallatin, *Papers*, 5:507-8; Madison, *Papers, Sec. of State Ser.*, 1:270-1, 473-4, 2:12-14, 57-8; Syrett, *Hamilton*, 15:178-81).

¹ Word interlined in place of "demand."
² Word interlined.
³ Word interlined in place of "marred."
⁴ Phrase in parentheses interlined.

From Benjamin Homans

SIR   Bordeaux 10th August 1801.

In the great occupations to which your important station calls you, permit me Sir to request a few moments of your attention to the Subject of this Letter. I feel it incumbent on me to make an Apology for the freedom I take. I am aware even that I may offend in what you may judge an improper interference; yet the Zeal I feel for my Country, the sentiments of republicanism which I profess, my respect for your talents, my gratitude for your services and my veneration for your patriotism & political Conduct, all inspire me with a confidence in approaching you as a Son to a Father.

You have been induced Sir to nominate a Person to succeed Isaac Cox Barnet at Bordeaux. I must presume that neither of the Characters are known to you, or have not been represented in their even merits; I know intimately both, and in a Competition for an Appointment of so much consequence to the Commercial relations of the United States, Mr Barnet has qualifications which Mr Lee has not, nor ever will attain. pardon me if I am presumptuous in offering my opinion. I know the respect due to your dignified station, but I feel more forcible a respect for your Person & Abilities. I was nursed in the Lap of Liberty, and my mind has ever imbibed pure republican principles. I would anticipate your indulgence, I would save you the regret of doing a double injustice, that of displacing an honest deserving Man, by one who can have no just pretentions to the patronage of our Goverment, (tho' he is my friend.) I have known Mr Barnet intimately in all his Conduct since at Bordx. if he was known to you Sir, he would be honoured with your highest confidence; of all the List nominated by Mr Adams as Consuls for foreign ports, he is the most worthy. Mr Barnet is perfect in the french language, in the routine of Duties of his Office, in a knowledge of the Country & conversant with the constituted Authorities, his natural abilities are good, his judgement & experience have matured them, his probity is above all proof, his patriotism is unequivocal, his political sentiments are just & such as you approve, but his modesty has ever prevented his making them conspicuous in party disputes, he is a real republican, a true American, a friend to his Country and to those principles which do honour to you; he is married in france, he has an encreasing family to Support, he has been at great expence in removing here under a promise of having the Appointment, he never obtained that promise by servility or collusion, he never deviated from his Duty or compromitted his honour & public Character for the sake of interest, You cannot investigate the Conduct of Mr Barnet but to his advantage. if he has had ennimies to calumniate him, they are the ennimies of virtue & merit, or they are the ignorant Agents of malignity. The withdrawing the Confidence of the Goverment from Mr Barnet, is ruinous to him & to his family, it is his only resource, he has devoted five years of his youthfull Life to the Service of his Country which has prevented his forming Connections & making an establishment. Condescend Sir to consider these circumstances, appreciate a Man who deserves your confidence, & submit to listen to the representations of his friends in his behalf. his family & local connections in America can best furnish the testimony of his origin and of his father's Services in the War which established our Independance, in the Course of the War a valuable part of his patrimonial Estate was devasted by the british, which obliges him now to solicit employment from the Goverment, he has fulfilled an arduous task in the most critical & difficult times in france, to render Services to his fellow Citizens; while doing his Duty here, others have intrigued to his prejudice, have deceived you as much in the Character of Mr Lee as of Mr Barnet.—with this reflection, I would not insult One of the worthiest Characters in America, James Munroe Esqr. it is possible that a transient Superficial knowledge of Mr Lee at Paris, may have induced Mr Munroe from his usual benevolence of heart, to recommend Mr Lee; I am this moment informed so, and I will profit of the circumstance to write to Mr. Munroe. he is deceived in the qualities & principles of Mr Lee; he does not know him as well as I do, he came to france with me in 1796. he was then a warm advocate for our *lamentable british Treaty.* he is closely allied with your most violent Ennimies in Boston, he is not a *native Citizen.* he was born & educated in Nova Scotia, where his Father & family now reside; he has no fixed political opinion but what hangs on the Springs of imediate interest. he has no Credit, no reputation, no property & no public Spirit. he has no discretion & less judgement to conduct the ordinary Affairs of business. he is ignorant of the french language & never will be able to Speak it, these are all perhaps bold assertions, but they are extorted from me by the idea of an honest respectable Citizen being superceded by such a Man.

If my Zeal has carried me too far, I implore your forgiveness. I loose sight for a moment of the respect due to the President of the United States, in considering that I am writing to Thomas Jefferson Esqr. the Man whom my heart teaches me to love and admire. yet Sir, your judgement is compromitted in this appointment, if it is confirmed you will have cause to regret it, and I am certain you would regret injuring an innocent Man in Mr Barnet;—it was the height of presumption it was *meaness* in Mr Lee to apply for the place of Bordeaux where he knew there was a prior claim, and after having been named to so important a place as Marseilles, a ridiculous vanity alone could prompt him to apply for Bordeaux, he ought to have been satisfied with the humblest appointment you could bestow on him, & without prejudice to a native Citizen whose father & family have supported our Revolution with their Lives & property.

I now descend to myself, You ought to know who it is who dare to address you upon so delicate a Subject as that of executing the Office of first Majestrate of an enlightened independent Nation. I am a humble native Citizen of Boston, and known for the fervour of my political sentiments. I reside in Bordeaux since the sedition Law deprived me of the liberty of Speech at home, my heart is always in my native Country, and my Life devoted to it's interests & wellfare. I have learnt to appreciate the merits of Mr Barnet, and I cannot resist the desire of serving him, if I am worthy your notice, I pledge myself for what I have written, and I confess that I am a friend to Mr Wm. Lee, but that I do not consider him to be worthy of Succeeding to Mr Barnet.—

I beg leave to offer you the hommage of my greatest respect, may your life be long preserved for the good of our Country, and may every good Man ever bless your Memory.

I am Sir most respectfully Your devoted Obedient fellow Citizen and most humble Servant   BENJAMIN HOMANS

RC (DNA: RG 59, LAR); at foot of text: "Thomas Jefferson Esqr President of the United states Washington"; endorsed by TJ as received 20 Oct. and so recorded in SJL; also endorsed by TJ "Barnet" and "Lee."

Benjamin Homans (1765-1823) was a merchant sea captain. When William Lee left Boston for France early in 1796, Homans was the master of the ship on which Lee traveled, the *Mary*. Pounded by a storm, the ship, which carried whale oil and provisions, broke up along the French coast. Praising Homans's skill in getting the *Mary* close to land before abandoning the ship, Lee called the captain "a man of good sense and information, and well acquainted with his business." During Madison's presidency, Homans became the chief clerk of the Navy Department (Mary Lee Mann, ed., *A Yankee Jeffersonian: Selections from the Diary and Letters of William Lee of Massachusetts, Written from 1796 to 1840* [Cambridge, Mass., 1958], 2-9, 253; Madison, *Papers, Sec. of State Ser.*, 2:28n).

MUNROE: Homans wrote to James Monroe and also to James Madison to argue against the substitution of Lee for Isaac Cox Barnet as the commercial agent at Bordeaux. "I venerate Mr Jefferson," Homans declared in his 10 Aug. letter to Madison (Madison, *Papers, Sec. of State Ser.*, 2:26-8; Preston, *Catalogue*, 116).

From Philippe de Létombe

MONSIEUR LE PRÉSIDENT,   Philadelphie, 10 aoust 1801. (v. st.)

La bonté avec laquelle Vous avez bien voulu Vous enquérir, par la lettre dont Vous m'avez honoré le 15 ulto., de l'issue de ma conférence avec Monsieur Livingston, relativement à mon passage sur la fregate qui le portera en France, me fait un devoir de Vous informer qu'il m'en a écrit, de la maniére la plus obligeante, aussitot aprés son retour à New york, et que sa lettre m'a été remise, par Monsieur son frere Edward allant à Washington où il s'est Chargé d'en parler à Monsieur le Sécrétaire de la Marine à l'effet d'en obtenir votre Agrément.

Monsieur Gerry m'a aussi écrit, à ce sujet, avant hier: "Having called twice on Mr. Edward Livingston, without seeing him, & hearing yesterday the Chancellor was in town, I saw him and conferred on the subject of your passage with him for France. He is well disposed to the measure, has written to you thereon & desired his brother to confer with you on the best means of accomplishing it.   I remain Your Friend . . . . ."

Rien au monde ne me sera plus cher, Monsieur le Président, que la continuation des bontés dont Vous daignez m'honorer depuis dix sept années.

Je Vous supplie, Monsieur le Président, de agréér l'hommage de mon profond Respect.   LÉTOMBE

EDITORS' TRANSLATION

MISTER PRESIDENT,   Philadelphia, 10 Aug. 1801 (old style)
The kindness with which you deigned to inquire, in the letter with which you honored me on the 15th of last month, concerning the outcome of my meeting with Mr. Livingston about my passage on the frigate that will bear him to France, obliges me to advise you that he wrote to me about it in the most obliging manner immediately after his return to New York, and that his letter was delivered to me by his brother Edward on his way to Washington, where he took it upon himself to mention it to the secretary of the navy in order to obtain your consent to it.

Mr. Gerry also wrote to me on this subject the day before yesterday: "Having called twice on Mr. Edward Livingston, without seeing him, and hearing yesterday the Chancellor was in town, I saw him and conferred on the subject of your passage with him for France. He is well disposed to the measure, has written to you thereon and desired his brother to confer with you on the best means of accomplishing it.   I remain Your Friend . . . . ."

Nothing in the world will be dearer to me, Mr. President, than the continuation of the kindnesses with which you have deigned to honor me for seventeen years.

I beg you, Mister President, to accept the homage of my profound respect.
                                                                              LÉTOMBE

RC (DLC); ellipses in original; extraneous quotation marks removed; endorsed by TJ as received 20 Aug.; recorded in SJL as a letter of 20 Aug. received on that day.

From Robert R. Livingston

DEAR SIR   ClerMont 10th. Augt 1801

I some time since had the honor to write to you on the subject of some of the appointments in New York on which you had requested my opinion. I apprehended from what you then said, that Bailey had voluntarily withdrawn, which I now find is not the case but that he still retains some expectations of the office, & is supported in his pretentions by Armstrong. which renders what I now have to offer somewhat delicate & which I therefore trust will be considered as perfectly confidential. The removal of Rogers is so much expected, & he falls so clearly within the description of those that you have thought it improper to continue that I think you can hardly avoid displacing him. He is an Englishman, was the whole war within the british lines, a professed & open Royalist, & of no such standing in life as to reflect any honor on the station or the government. Jenkins who I had considered as well-qualified, will be controuler of this State So that two candidates only remain. Baily, the objections to whom you have heard, & which I believe are generally thought to be well founded, & for which I presume you considered him as withdrawn, & Davis. In the appointment of the latter there are the most weighty objections. His present station (that of runner to the bank) his want of that standing in society which reflects honor upon a government. But above all his being absolutely under the influence of   who is considered as having made all the appointments in this State & Connecticut those of any importance being from the most devoted of his friends. The appointment of Davis would be a confirmation of this sentiment, & very disagreeable, not only to the whole mercantile interest, but to the public, the men of all parties would consider it as conclusive evidence of an influence that they are unwilling to see in our councils.

Permit me now Sir to offer to your notice a new candidate that I know to be capable of the duties of the office and who I have reason to believe would be peculiarly agreeable to the mercantile interest, & the old inhabitants of this State. Philip Livingston whom you knew in Congress, & who died at York town was always at the head of the mercantile interest here, & represented it for the greater part of his life in the legislature. His memory is much cherished by the most respectable men among us. With a veiw to this circumstance, he directed that one of his grandsons should be brought up a merchant. Edward Philip Livingston, was accordingly (after obtaining his accademical honors at a very early period in life) sent to England where he continued for some years in the counting house of an eminent merchant, & acquired a knowledge and habit of business without suffering his political prinples to be at all corrupted by it. On his return to America he married my eldest daughter, And as he will inherit with her a considerable landed estate, I thought it improper to permit him to embark it in the hazard of commerce. I wish him however to be employed, and meant to bring him forward in a political line in this State. My compliance with your wishes in going abroad, puts this out of my power, & I propose in case you should not think him useful upon this occasion, to take him with me to France, but as he has already travelled, it would be more pleasing to me to see him esstablished in business at home. I merely submit this hint to your consideration, without pressing, if lyable to the smallest objection, or without designing by it to oppose Mr. Baileys pretentions if you have not already decided on them. I will vouch for the young gents capacity & honor, & I persuade myself that a more unexceptionable appointment can hardly be made in this state, & the more so as it may be offered as a tribute of respect that you have been induced voluntarily to pay to the memory of his grandfather. I will only ask the favor of you to inform me of your determination on this subject as soon as you have come to any. as his remaining here or going with me will depend solely upon it. No person whatever is Acquainted with the subject of this letter, should you be so obliging as to comply with my wishes, I would pray you to make the offer to him directly, by a letter in which

RC (DNA: RG 59, LAR); incomplete. Recorded in SJL as received 27 Aug. with notation "Edwd. Phil. Livingston to Off."

For Livingston's opinions on APPOINTMENTS IN NEW YORK, see Notes on a Conversation with Robert R. Livingston, printed at 4 June, and Livingston to TJ, 5 June. He may also have discussed appointments in a letter to TJ of 16 June, recorded in SJL as received from New York on the 19th, but not found.

BAILEY HAD VOLUNTARILY WITHDRAWN: on 23 July, Theodorus Bailey wrote John Armstrong that he was surprised to learn it had been represented at Washington that he had relinquished any thought of a federal appointment in New York. He asserted that he had "neither directly nor indirectly given authority" to anyone to withdraw his name from consideration. Bailey entreated Armstrong to try "to discover the source of this misrepresentation" and adopt measures to counteract it (RC in DNA: RG 59, LAR). On 28 July, Armstrong wrote TJ and may have enclosed Bailey's letter. According to SJL, TJ received Armstrong's letter, now missing, from New York on 6 Aug. and noted that it regarded "Bayley for office." Armstrong was Livingston's brother-in-law (Kline, *Burr*, 1:577n). For the OBJECTIONS to Bailey, see Burr to TJ, 21 Apr., TJ to George Clinton, 17 May, and Gallatin to TJ, [21 May 1801].

Matthew L. DAVIS was UNDER THE

INFLUENCE OF Aaron Burr (Kline, *Burr*, 2:602-3; Vol. 32:219n; Memorandum from Aaron Burr, printed at 17 Mch. 1801).

On 17 Nov. 1799, EDWARD PHILIP LIV- INGSTON married Elizabeth, Robert R. Livingston's ELDEST DAUGHTER. They accompanied Chancellor Livingston to France (Dangerfield, *Livingston*, 281, 309).

From Thomas McKean

DEAR SIR,   Philadelphia. August 10th. 1801.

Your esteemed letter of the 24th. last month I received, and I confess the sentiments therein expressed coeincide with my own: The hearts of our opponent leaders I do not expect to gain, but those of the persons lead by them may be secured by the measures you suggest, and when the principals discover the desertion, prudence & self-interest will induce at least a cessation of their hostilities, but I rest assured from long and attentive experience, that no measures Your Excellency or myself can adopt will ever obtain their cordial approbation, and that whenever a favorable opportunity shall occur they will exhibit their accustomed enmity against the true & firm friends of the American Revolution & of our present happy form of Republican Government.

Your answer to the impudent & ill-written remonstrance of the Tory merchants of Newhaven has been read with avidity and pleasure by all the Gentlemen with whom I converse; one Gentleman of higher mettle observed, that you honored them too much by giving them any answer whatsoever, but soon after acknowledged it might be proper, as it applied to every other of the like kind, and developed to the world the wise and just principles by which you were actuated.

When ever any party are notoriously predominant they will split; this is in nature, it has been the case time immemorial, and will be so until mankind become wiser & better—The Outs envy the Inns—The struggle in such a situation is only for the loaves & fishes.

In this State as well as Delaware it has manifested itself on account of what I have just mentioned, but by cautious & well-advised measures I can assure you, as much as a circumstance of the kind can be assured, that in Pennsylvania the division will be healed, and I flatter myself it will also be effected in Delaware.

The thirst for office is immoderate, it has become an object of serious attention, and I wish I knew how to check it.

Permit me now, Sir, to inclose a lre. I received on Saturday from Mr; Charles D. Coxe, as it will save me some time & trouble in going into detail; I beleive the contents are true. Mr; Coxe's parents have been well known to me upwards of forty years, his mother died about four months ago, he has a sister married to Mr; Tench Coxe and another to Mr; Chamont, son of a considerable Banker in Paris, who was an Intimate acquaintance of Doctor Franklin and probably not unknown to you. Colo. Jones (member of Congress for this city) and Messrs. Girard, Vasse and Vanuxem, three French merchants here (the last a native of Dunkirk) all sincere Republican citizens, together with a great number of other respectable citizen-merchants have recommended him to your Excellency, and I can add my opinion in his favor.

Accept the assurance of the most sincere respect and friendship of, dear Sir, Your Excellency's Most obedient humble servt

THO M:KEAN

RC (DLC); addressed: "His Excellency Thomas Jefferson Esq; President of the United States At Monticello"; endorsed by TJ as received 20 Aug. and so recorded in SJL. Enclosure: Charles D. Coxe to McKean, Philadelphia, 7 Aug., reminding the governor of his promise to send a letter of recommendation for him to the president; recalling his active pursuit of mercantile interests, primarily with "French possessions in the old and new world," where he "acquired a knowledge of the language and an enlarged acquaintance with the particular modes of Commerce peculiar to the French" and was twice plundered by British cruisers "& cruelly stript of the fruits of several years application to business"; therefore seeking a position as consul at the ports of Dunkirk and Calais, which could be managed by one consul, or Île de France, where he resided for more than six months and became acquainted with the "Trade and principal inhabitants"; and finally noting that he had solicited the consulate at Île de France under the Adams administration, but had been "totally disregarded" (RC in DNA: RG 59, LAR).

COXE'S PARENTS: Charles and Rebecca Wells Coxe, who for decades lived at Sidney, a few miles from Flemington, New Jersey. In 1782, Charles D. Coxe's SISTER, Rebecca, married her first

cousin Tench Coxe. Another sister, Grace, married Jacques Le Ray de Chaumont, whose father, Jacques Donatien Le Ray de Chaumont, had corresponded with TJ (Cooke, Coxe, 54, 406; Leonard W. Labaree and others, eds., The Papers of Benjamin Franklin, 38 vols. to date [1959-], 28:239; Vol. 13:286-7).

William JONES, Stephen GIRARD, Ambrose VASSE, and James VANUXEM were among the 78 Philadelphians who signed a petition addressed to TJ, on 20 July, recommending Charles D. Coxe as consul for the United States at Dunkirk or Île de France. Clement Biddle headed the list of signers (MS in DNA: RG 59, LAR, in an unidentified hand, at head of text: "To His Excellency The President of The United States of America"; Tr in same). The petition may have been enclosed in a short letter from Coxe to TJ, dated 7 Aug., at Philadelphia, in which he put himself forward as a candidate for consul at Dunkirk or Île de France and forwarded recommendations (RC in same; at foot of text: "His Excellency Thomas Jefferson Esq. President of the Unite[d States]"; endorsed by TJ as received 20 Aug. and so recorded in SJL with notation "Off.").

TJ appointed Coxe the U.S. commercial agent at Dunkirk, signing a temporary commission, dated 16 Oct. 1801, and another commission, after Senate confirmation, dated 26 Jan. 1802. In his lists of appointments, TJ noted that Coxe was appointed on 17 Oct. in place of James H. Hooe, a midnight appointment (FCs in DNA: RG 59, PTCC; JEP, 1:402, 405; Vol. 33:672, 677). In 1806, Coxe began serving as chargé d'affaires in Tunis. He became consul there in 1824. The next year he was transferred to Tripoli, where he died in 1830 or 1831 (JEP, 3:357, 449; 4:151; NDBW, 6:491-2, 520).

From Joseph Rapin

VOTRE EXELENCE   de washinton le 10 Aousts 1801

je prand la Libertee de vous infformer que je Sui de Retour de philadelphie en Cas que vous eussiez qu'elque ordre a me Comuniquer. Jai Convercé avec Mr. Le Maire il est charmé de Bientot avoir L'honneur de vous appartenir il fut immediattement après la Reception de la lettre que je lui Ecrivis avant votre depart; faire les arrengement avec Monsieur Létombe qui lui accordat trente dolare par mois Cest ce qu'il demandat il me dit que quand il demandat les dit trente dolare il Croyoit que vous donniez chaque année deux habillement Complet a votre Maitre d'hotel je lui dit qu'il avoit été mal informé et que trente dolare etoient tres emple parfaitement des genereux Gage et qu a ce prix la vous pouvez avoir un homme et Sa fame qui Rempliroit L'office de feme de charge et que dailleur Son Linge Se trouvoit Blanchi dans la Maison allors il me dit qu'il etoit parfaitement Satisfai de ce prix et qu'il Se flatoit que vous Seriz Satisfait de Son Service et qu'il Se Rendras ici les premiers jours de Septembre et je Remetrais toute chose en Sa charge; et je Laisserais Mes Comptes en ordre dans votre Cabinet.

il ny a Rien de nouveaux n'y dEtrange dans votre Maison. on travill avec activitée a votre chambre a Couché la charpente est prete a Recevoir le Lattage et le Sallon de Compagni est debarracé des charpentiers et des platreurs et le tapissier est a L'ammeubler; Rien autre a vous informer et Suis le Respectueux Sujet &c de votre Exelence

JOSEPH RAPIN

EDITORS' TRANSLATION

YOUR EXCELLENCY   Washington 10 August 1801

I am taking the liberty of informing you that I am back from Philadelphia in case you should have some order to communicate to me. I spoke with Mr. Lemaire, and he is delighted to have the honor to be in your service soon. Immediately after receiving the letter that I wrote to him before your departure, he went to make the arrangements with Mr. Létombe, who granted him thirty dollars per month. That is what he was asking for, and he said that when he requested the aforesaid thirty dollars per month, he thought that you gave your maître d'hôtel two new sets of clothing every year. I told him that he had been ill informed and that thirty dollars were perfectly ample and generous wages, and that for that price you can have a man and his wife who would fulfill the function of housekeeper, and besides his linen would be laundered in the house. Then he told me that he was perfectly satisfied with the price and that he was certain you would be satisfied with his service, and that he will arrive here during the first days of September and that I would put him in charge of everything, and that I would leave my accounts in order in your office.

There is nothing new or strange in your house. They are actively working on your bedroom, the framework is ready to receive the lathing and the drawing room is emptied of the carpenters and plasterers, and the upholsterer is furnishing it. Nothing else to inform you, and I am Your Excellency's respectful subject, etc.,   JOSEPH RAPIN

RC (MHi); endorsed by TJ as received 13 Aug. and so recorded in SJL.

PHILADELPHIE: TJ's settlement of accounts with Rapin included a reimbursement of $32 for expenses of a trip by the steward to Philadelphia and back (MB, 2:1054; TJ to Philippe de Létombe, 29 July).

From John Thomson

No 102 Pearl Street.

RESPECTED SIR,   New York 10th. August 1801.

If amidst the numerous and important duties of the high station to which you have been called by the voice of your country, you should ever find leasure to peruse the Pamphlet herewith sent; it will be a circumstance highly gratifying to me: But infinitely more so, should the sentiments which it contains meet with your approbation.

With the most profound respect, I am, Sir, Your Most Obdt. Humble Servant   JOHN THOMSON

RC (MoSHi: Jefferson Papers); at foot of text: "His Excellency Thomas Jefferson President of the United States"; endorsed by TJ as received 28 Nov. and so recorded in SJL with notation "on Liberty of the press." Enclosure: John Thomson, *An Enquiry, Concerning the Liberty, and Licentiousness of the Press, and the Uncontroulable Nature of the Human Mind: Containing an Investigation of the Right Which Government have to Controul the Free Expression of Public Opinion, Addressed to the People of the U. States* (New York, 1801). See Sowerby, Nos. 3280, 3533.

John Thomson, a New York lawyer, held strong and distinctive views in support of freedom of speech and of the press. He believed that opinion, being involuntary, should be protected from prosecution (Donna Lee Dickerson, *The Course of Tolerance: Freedom of the Press in Nineteenth-Century America* [Westport, Conn., 1990], 6-9; Leonard W. Levy, *Freedom of the Press from Zenger to Jefferson: Early American Libertarian Theories* [Indianapolis, 1966], 284).

TJ replied to Thomson on 2 Dec., and expressed "thanks for his book on the freedom of the press, which he shall peruse with pleasure. the subject is one of the most interesting to man, and it is hoped that the attentions of those who are able to elucidate it by doing away all protests for it's suppression, will force it's enemies to avow that their object in wishing it done, is sheer tyranny" (PrC in MoSHi: Jefferson Papers; endorsed by TJ in ink on verso).

From Jean Xavier Bureaux de Pusy

Monsieur le Président,   New York, août, 11. 1801

Le Signataire du Memoire ci joint m'a prié de Vous le faire parvenir et de l'appuyer auprès de vous. Je ne me Connais aucun Droit à vous recommander Personne, Et de plus, je Croirais autant manquer à la Vénération que je vous dois, en Cherchant à capter Votre bienveillance, même en faveur d'un de mes amis, dont les prétentions ou les Droits seraient bien fondès, comme je crois l'être ceux de Mr. Poirey, qu'en essayant de vous interesser pour une Cause injuste. Je crois donc remplir Suffisamment toutes les intentions du Petitionnaire, en vous transmettant Son Mémoire Et les pieces qui y Sont annexèes. Il parait mettre un grand prix à la lettre de Mr. Washington, qu'il regarde comme un reconnaissance de Ses Services Et il me charge de la lui Conserver: J'ose donc vous prier de me renvoyer Cette lettre, lorsque vous estimeres qu'elle ne vous est plus nècessaire.

Veuillez recevoir avec bonté, Monsieur le Président, l'hommage de mon Profond respect.   JX. Bureaux-Pusy

EDITORS' TRANSLATION

Mister President,   New York, August 11, 1801

The writer of the attached memorandum begged me to transmit it to you with my recommendation. I recognize in myself no right to recommend anyone to you, and moreover, I would feel that I derogated as much from the reverence that I owe you in seeking to gain your favorable consideration, even in favor of one of my friends whose claims and rights were solidly founded—as I believe Mr. Poirey's are—as if I were trying to interest you in an unjust cause. I feel therefore that I am sufficiently fulfilling all the petitioner's intentions by transmitting to you his memorandum and the attached documents. He appears to lay great store by Mr. Washington's letter, which he considers to be recognition for his services, and he charges me to keep it for him; I make bold, therefore, to beg you to send me back that letter, when you judge that it is no longer necessary for you.

Please receive with kindness, Mister President, the homage of my profound respect.   JX. Bureaux-Pusy

RC (privately owned, New York City, 1949); endorsed by TJ as received 20 Aug. and so recorded in SJL. Enclosures: (1) Joseph Léonard Poirey to TJ, 15 Apr.

1801, and enclosure. (2) George Washington to the Marquise de Lafayette, 3 June 1790 (Washington, *Papers*, *Pres. Ser.*, 4:572-3n). (3) Certificate of the Marquis de Lafayette, not found, probably relating to Poirey's service during the American Revolution (see TJ to Bureaux de Pusy, 3 Sep. 1801).

At the request of Madame de Lafayette, George WASHINGTON in 1790 nominated Poirey, who had "served in the American Army" as the Marquis de Lafayette's secretary during the Revolutionary War, to receive the brevet rank of captain. The Senate approved the brevet commission, which qualified Poirey for membership in the Society of the Cincinnati and made him, according to Lafayette, "the Happiest Man in the World." For Poirey's efforts to obtain compensation for his American war service, see his 15 Apr. letter to TJ (Washington, *Papers*, *Pres. Ser.*, 4:571-4; 5:446; 7:520; 12:229-30).

From Caesar A. Rodney

HONORED & DEAR SIR,   Wilmington August 11th. 1801.

Some time after my return home I wrote a letter to Mr. Madison on the subject of the late appointment in this State, in which I gave a pretty full account of what had occurred relative thereto. I shall not trouble you therefore on that head. I will only observe that every day furnishes us with new proofs of the propriety of the opinions contained therein for I really do scarcely know of a dissenting voice among the Republicans here.

On tuesday I returned from a tour to Kent County, the middle one in this state & which holds the scales. The Republicans are very sanguine of success & appear determined to exert every nerve, for that purpose. Among many with whom I conversed, I found some who on most occasions are not apt to be too sanguine, extremely confident on this. I do most anxiously hope that our flattering prospects may be realized. In order to excite the most active exertions, I stated to them that a Senator of the United States was more important to us, than a Governor, & that it was essential to complete the column of your administration. I shall pay another visit to that county in September, after they have formed their ticket, which they mean to do of the best & most popular characters.

Some of our prominent *Feds* have taken great umbrage at your dignified answer to the New-Haven merchants, whilst our Republicans to a man have been delighted with the sentiments which it breathes. It will have no doubt a very happy effect on the approaching elections throughout the United States. It is not to be wondered at that those who had ascended high on the ladder of preferment should embrace every opportunity of venting those feelings to which disappointment has given birth. The smile of ridicule is perhaps the severest answer to their mortifical ambition. The rash intemperate language of such men is a volume in favour of our cause with considerate minds.

I cannot but calculate with great confidence on the support of a large majority[1] of those who have heretofore opposed us, before the end of four years. As to the leaders of the *Federal Party*, as they styled themselves, I have no hopes of them they are activated by motives of ambition to persevere. The principal actors in the late tragic comedy will continue to perform in the public theatre in their true characters. But I trust all[2] the thinking men in the community will ere long array themselves under the banners of administration.

When they cast their eyes back & review the [. . .] thro' which we have past, when they reflect on the principles which have been mantained & the consequences to which they lead, they must rejoice at the political salvation which has been wrought for this country: But when they see instead of a system espionage & persecution, one of impartiality & equal justice; in the place of political proscription & intolerance, a manly liberality as to opinions & a due participation in office; in lieu of plans of expence & taxation, measures of retrenchment & economy; the encouragement of commerce & manufactures in preference to schemes of speculation & avarice,[3] the sincere cultivations of peace & moderation in opposition to war & violence, I believe the most reluctant & unwilling will be compelled to yeild & that those considerations will flash conviction at once on the minds of all better disposed.

It will be a subject of admiration (if that be not inconsistent with the deepest regret) if the change in our administration does not make a difference of fifty votes in the Kent Election which is all we want. With great esteem & with due impressions of the many marks of attention I have received from you I remain very sincerely yours

C. A. RODNEY

RC (DLC); endorsed by TJ as received 20 Aug. and so recorded in SJL.

For Rodney's LETTER TO MR. MADISON of 17 July, see the third letter from Albert Gallatin to TJ, 29 July.
THE REPUBLICANS ARE VERY SANGUINE OF SUCCESS: for the results of the elections, see Dr. John Vaughan to TJ, 10 Oct. 1801.

[1] Preceding two words interlined in place of "great part."
[2] Word interlined.
[3] Preceding word, ampersand, and comma interlined.

From Philo Andrews

New Haven August 12th 1801

Sir   It is with great defference that I address Your Excellency on the present occasion but impelled by a wish to serve my Country as well promote My own prosperity & happiness I humbly beg leave to offer myself as a Candidate for a Consular Appointment on the Coast of Barbary—My pretensions are as follow—I was born in the Town of Wallingford of reputable Parents my Education is such as to enable me to discharge the duties of the Office which I solicit honorably to myself and beneficialy to my Country, My profession is that of the Law to the practice of Which I have been regularly admitted in the States of Connecticut New York and North Carolina for more than two years My age twenty three My political principles purely republican. for the truth of the above statement I refer Your Excellency to Peirpont Edwards Ephraim Kirby and Gideon Granger Esquire.—If any vacancy now exists or should happen on said Coast by death resignation or otherwise I am authorised to say that I can procure the necessary recommendations from the Above Named Gentlemen to whom I request Your Excellency to write for a confirmation of the statements herein containd and hope from Your Excellency's Condescention an Answer to this Letter—when Convenient—

I am Sir with sentiments of respect and Esteem Your Excellency's Very Huml. Sevant—   PHILO ANDREWS

RC (DNA: RG 59, LAR); at head of text: "To his Excellency Thomas Jefferson Esquire President of the United States"; endorsed by TJ as received 20 Aug. and so recorded in SJL with notation "Off."

Philo Andrews (b. 24 June 1778) was the youngest son of the six children born to Episcopal minister and Yale graduate Samuel Andrews and his wife Hannah Shelton Andrews of Wallingford, Connecticut. He was a member of the masonic lodge of St. John's, in New Bern, North Carolina, in 1800 (Dexter, *Yale*, 2:568-9; 4:378; Donald Lines Jacobus, comp., *Families of Ancient New Haven*, 3 vols. [Baltimore, 1981], 1:51; Gertrude S. Carraway, *Years of Light: History of St. John's Lodge, No. 3 A. F. & A. M. New Bern, North Carolina 1772-1944* [New Bern, N.C., 1944], 223).

From Abraham Baldwin

DEAR SIR   Athens Augst. 12th 1801

I have been, for several weeks, in one of the western counties of this state near the mountains, where we are building a college. It is so seldom I have had opportunities to send to Augusta for my letters, that yours of the 13th ult has not reached me till this morning. My colleagues Jackson and Taliaferro are almost on the other opposite extremes of the state, it is now so late that I cannot obtain their opinion on the subject of your letter in season to be communicated to you. They have both been members of the state legislature whenever this question of our western boundary has been under consideration and are much more minutely acquainted with it than I am: for my information I am almost entirely indebted to your instructions to our ministers appointed to treat with Spain. Whether those principles extend to the part below the mouth of the Yazoo or not, I have supposed would make very little difference in the negotiation the quantity of land in either case, at the most trifling valuation, would go far beyond any sum that has ever been mentioned in our negotiation. It is not my opinion, neither has it yet appeared to be the opinion of either of my colleagues, or of our best informed citizens generally that it is desirable to obtain a large sum of money in our treasury.

It was not till very late under the articles of confederation that congress would agree to be at the expence of holding treaties, or doing any thing for the protection of this part of the frontier. The Creeks had taken sides so strongly with Britain that they were very hostile for several years after the peace, and this state was under the necessity of incurring a heavy debt for Indian treaties and militia guards, which is still upon them, and they have never yet been able to raise their certificates to more than five or six shillings in the pound. In the resolutions of our assembly which you may probably have seen among the papers of the commissioners on the part of the United States, this sum is estimated a million and a half dollars it is probably taken from the returns in our treasury. If the United States should agree to the principle, that this burden should not be left on the state, after the land is ceded to the united States, I am persuaded there will be found no great difficulty in detailing it so as to render it agreeable. The United States might undertake to liquidate these accounts, and agree before hand that the amount should be receivable at the land office when it should be opened for the sale of those lands, or that the state should be reimbursed that sum out of the first proceeds of that land office. The principle appears so reasonable that there can be no difficulty but in devising a mode to render it practicable. I have made these remarks to convey my opinion that there is not at present any unreasonable expectation on the part of this state, from which you need apprehend much embarrassment in proceeding as you propose, and making it a part of your present negotiation with the Creeks.

Though the opinion of my colleagues can not be obtained, yet these are considerations which I trust will be conclusive with you to instruct the commissioners to obtain if possible the Tallassee county and the Oakmulgee fork. This state has for many years considered itself as having all the right to expect it that can be derived from the acts of the government of the United States, independent of its connection with the negotiation respecting its western territory. Three commissioners of the United States who examined into all the evidence on the spot reported it to have been fairly purchased and to be the right of the state. Messrs. Venable Pinckney & Smith the committee on the memorial and remonstrance of the state legislature, and the almost unanimous act of congress on that report, and making the appropriation to repurchase that county was also to the same effect. I do not hesitate to give it as my opinion, that its being already done by the United States, will have a more favorable effect on our negotiations than could be given to any present stipulation which should regard it as future. The state by their act limited us so precisely on that head, that it was the principal embarrassment in our former attempt to negotiate. The commrs of U.S. objected to the expence and delay of holding an Indian treaty for this sole object, but tendered to us the strongest assurances that it should be done as soon as possible; the present is so fit an occasion I hope and trust that obstacle may now be removed. With great respect I have the honor to be your obt sert

ABR BALDWIN

There is nothing new on this frontier, and no opportunity of knowing the news of any other place—

RC (DLC); at foot of first page: "Thos. Jefferson President of the United States"; endorsed by TJ as received 3 Sep. and so recorded in SJL.

WE ARE BUILDING A COLLEGE: Baldwin was one of the original trustees of what became the University of Georgia. The institution, chartered by the legislature in January 1785, received its first students in 1801 (E. Merton Coulter, *Abraham Baldwin: Patriot, Educator, and Founding Father* [Arlington, Va., 1987], 52-4, 76).

INSTRUCTIONS TO OUR MINISTERS:

apparently TJ's March 1792 Report on Negotiations with Spain, which served as instructions to William Carmichael and William Short (Vol. 23:296-9, 313-14n).

Benjamin Lincoln, David Humphreys, and Cyrus Griffin were the THREE COMMISSIONERS who had looked into Georgia's claim to Tallassee County. Baldwin's and Benjamin Taliaferro's letter to TJ of 5 Mch. 1801 mentioned the commissioners, Georgia's MEMORIAL AND REMONSTRANCE, and the 1799 ACT OF CONGRESS pertaining to the recovery of Tallassee County or an equivalent tract of land for the state.

From Henry Dearborn

SIR,—   Pittston August 12th. 1801

I have been honoured with your note of the twenty eighth ulto. enclosing a letter from Mr. Dupont, I have it in contemplation to authorise Mr. Dupont's Son, to make an experiment on a small quantity, say one hundred weight, of the impure salt petre, by which he will be enabled to set his price for clarifying, pr. hundred, and we shall be better able to decide on the propriety of incuring the expence of clarifying any considerable quantity;—to ingage him to purify any large quantity, on the conditions proposed by his father, might lead to some dispute in settleing the business, when a satisfactory experiment shall have been made, we may probably agree on a price, and sell the whole of the impure salt petre to Mr Dupont in its present state.—

The *apparent*, pacific and even friendly, disposition of the British Government towards our Mediterranean Squadron, is a pleasing circumstance, the use of the harbour of Malta is really important. it is possible that I may be detained here longer than I had contemplated, but I hope not, on my arrival, one of my daughters who had been in a feble state for several months, (having a child about six months, old) was too abruptly informed of my arrival, after a few minutes[1] of the livelyest expressions of joy fell into a violent convulsive fitt which left her in a deranged state of mind which in the course of four days became too much like a real madness. within the last two days we are flattered with simtoms of returning reason.—

be pleascd to accept Sir assurances of the most respectfull esteem from Your very Huml Servt.   H, DEARBORN

RC (DLC); below dateline: "To the President of the United States"; endorsed by TJ as received 3 Sep. and so recorded in SJL.

[1] MS: "munites."

From Matthew Lyon

                    Eddyville Ky 40 Miles up the Cumberland River
Sir.   August 12th. 1801

In this remote Situation I can have but a very imperfect view of the affairs of the great part of the United States, yet I read enough to give me infinite pleasure to see your popularity increases even beyond my very sanguine expectations. In this Country you have always stood without a Rival; those that I have seen on my way from the Seat of Goverment to this place who formerly adheared to Mr Adams & his Administration have universally expressed their confidence in yours.

Haveing a great deal of bussness on the way I did not arrive here until the 15th. of June, I found my affairs in a prosperous condition but our being on the water in some of the hottest weather made all my family more or less sick after their arrival, with some the disorder was very light all have recovered except a Weakly Girl of between 4 & 5 years old to whom it proved fatal—

This Country increases fast in population in industry & in Riches & I am pleased to see in this County particularly (which was first Settled mostly with a kind of Arabs from the back part of the Carolinas) that civilization is fast gaining ground, many of the Idle & dissolute have gone to the Spanish dominions & their places have been filled up by people of more property & more industry; people possessed of some knoledge of the Comforts of civilized life & the benefit of Commerce, since I have been acquainted with this Country the population of this County has five folded altho it is a frontier on two sides. It is said to be scare Seven miles from my house to the Tennessee river & the Indian boundary is about half way between here & there. This rapid population is partly owing to the tranquility between the people of this Country & the Indians and partly owing to a croud of people's coming to this edge in order to be ready to settle between Tennessee & Ohio the moment the Country opens—

This tranquility has been attributed in some measure to the posts on the Ohio below the mouth of these rivers & the constant comunication between them & the posts above. General Wilkison spent a night with me A few days ago on his way from Wilkisonville to the treaty near Knoxville, I had an acquaintance with the General at the retreat from Ticonderoga & at the takeing of Burgoine, then I thought him the likeliest young man I ever saw, the acquaintance has been dormant yet I have watched for his fame & have been pleased to see him prosperous & happy, he is industrious to an extreme, Zealous for the public service, Eocenimical as a duty because his Superiors are so; Altho he had been as it were on a race ever since he left the Federal City I could not perswade him to stay one day here to rest. He was the first who informed me who were the Commissioners to treat with the Indians, The Selection appears very proper, General Davie is an exalted Character his conduct in France probably deserved the earliest notice of the new administration, Mr Hawkins's appointment I suppose saved the expence of one Commissioner as perhaps his attendance would be necessary, The Generals appointment I conclude was necessary to keep up his consequence with the Indians & he wants the Perquisite—

I have been much alarmed by something General Dearbourne said to me, as well as Mr Gallatins Idea that the Treaty was to be held merely for the sake of the North Carolina applicants, & General Wilkisons Idea of confineing the present purchases of the Indians to this Side the Tennessee, I did hope & have encouraged the people of this Vicinity to hope that the little neck of Land between the Missisipi & the Tennesee belonging to Kentucky would be Cleared of the Indian Claim by this Commission and it will be an amazeing disappointment to the people of this part of the State if that does not take place.

The lands have been cheifly located by the Officers & Soldiers of the Virginia Line & as I understood have been considerd as clearly belonging to that State without any acknoledged Indian claim before the Treaty of New York, for my part I can see no pretention the Claimants under North Carolina can have to a treaty to clear their lands more than the Kentucky Claimants save that a few persons (& I believe it was but very few) have petitioned Congress, we can easily get a number to petition, but I suppose when Goverment are takeing Steps to do right to one part of the Comunity, Honour, Justice, & Consistency would lead them to extend that Justice to a Neighbouring State in similar circumstances, I hope & wish that my fears on this score may prove without foundation & that the Commissioners are or will be instructed to obtain a Cession of the Indian claim to the Lands in question.

Some thing General Dearbourn said in Conversation on the subject before I left the seat of Goverment has made me fear that some time erelong the Troops below these two rivers on the Ohio would all be orderd away, General Wilkison seems unable to solve my doubts on this Subject & from his Conversation I have grown more apprehensive on the Subject & I have even fear'd that they would be ordered away directly, A Regiment is now on the move up this river toward Nashville to commence cutting the road to Natchez & the General tells me that as soon as leave is given by the Indians an other Regiment will Assend the Tennessee to commence the Work on the South Side of that River, this is an Excellent disposition of the Surplus Troops, should the road be well laid out & the Work well executed it will be of Infinite advantage to this part of the World & should the Indian claim be removed to our wish we will soon have a Road from here to intersect that before it crosses the Tennese & settlements all along upon that road—I never saw any use in bringing all the Troops to the Spot they are leaveing, but I dread the total evacuation of it—the Indians are often insolent & troublesome now when they are kept very much in awe by that post, should it be evacuated we may expect it Worse & worse, within the last three months they Burned a new house hansomely furnished for Major Gist about three miles below the Mouth of this river it is not long since they Killed a man a small distance above the Mouth of Trade water on the Ohio. The General informed me a Company was to be moved to St Vincent, I should suppose the same reasons which cause a company to be orderd there would be in favor of keeping a few Companies at Wilkisonville or Massac, beside which the Keeping up a Communication from St Vincent's, from up the Mississipi, the Ohio, the Cumberland & the Tennessee would justifie our expectation of a Military post's being kept up there. I have not been able to spare time to go to Wilksonville yet, but the information I get from every one is that it is well Situated on a large high flat of Good land; I am told likewise that the Troops have many of them been sick there this year, that all are subject to, by way of Seasoning especially those who come from a High Country, Soldiers are not apt to keep themselves clean, and in such a detached Station to have all the Comforts which are to be Obtained by Country people, I am told the Army are on the gain & that three quarters of the sick list are convalasent & many are on the sick list merely for want of Cloathing, many of them had Received no pay for many months before the General came & there was a loud complaint on that Score, so that they have not been able with their own money to buy comforts for themselves. I who came from the low sickly neighboorhood of Ticonderoga have had to go through a Seasoning here last year the fatigue of travelling kept me down until your decisive election since which time I have (thank god) enjoyed the best Health.

I have been urged by many people to write to the seat of Goverment on the subject of the posts below this. Official rotine would have led me to the War office but I had promised myself the pleasure of once in a while writeing to you from this Obscure Corner & I beleived you would hear my opinions, & my wishes with kindness

I say obscure corner because it is so not only by real distance from the Seat of Goverment but for want of direct communication with rest of the World, much has been done by Law to facilitate this communication, some thing has been done by the Post Master General, I do not mean to complain of him far from it, I have but lately given him a

detail of the proceedings of those who have carried the mail or undertaken it in these parts & pointed out improvements & accomodations
consistent with law which I wish, A Word even by way of enquiry
however indirect from the great house might hasten on those accomodations, this letter will go from this in the Mail on tuesday the 18th. of
August the time of its arrival will be sufficient to comment upon

I might easily find matter for praise & Adulation to lenghten out a
letter those things I leave to Scycophantic Legislatures, I have seen,
enjoyed, & dispised the Address from Rhode Island. Vermont will be
next, I give you Joy on the Republican accession to the Senate from
Island, Vt will follow in that also I expect you are in, or have trouble
before you respecting the Barbarian powers, Brittain has surely set
them on & our own ill policy & profusion will make it a hard job for
you—I congratulate you on the accession of the Services of the Good
& the Wise Mr Langdon to your Councils I heartily regretted his former refusal to accept the Office of Secretary of the Navy, & I rejoice'd
when I saw it announced in the news paper that he had accepted the
Office, he is pure Gold without Alloy he has passed through the fire
times without number without the loss of a single hair—

I will finish this letter as the Yankee preachers do their prayers by
asking pardon for what ever I have said amiss & by praying that if I
have asked for too much or that which is improper it may be denied
me after which I will not say as they "do more & better for us than we
can ask speak or think"

Accept Sir the most sincere wishes for your domestic Happiness as
well as pleasure & Satisfaction in your public Carrier of your Sincere
friend & humble Scrvt   M LYON

RC (DLC); at foot of text: "The Presi-
dent of the United States"; endorsed by
TJ as received 12 Oct. but recorded in
SJL as received 1 Oct. with notation "W."

Earlier, Lyon had moved some members of his family to EDDYVILLE in
western Kentucky. In 1801 he finished
transplanting the remainder of his extended family, and ten other families,
west from Vermont (J. Fairfax McLaugh-
lin, Matthew Lyon, The Hampden of Congress: A Biography [New York, 1900],
407-14; Aleine Austin, Matthew Lyon:
"New Man" of the Democratic Revolution,
1749-1822 [University Park, Penn.,
1981], 132-3).

WILKISONVILLE: James Wilkinson,
who had embarked down the Ohio River
from Pittsburgh, spent a few days at
Cantonment Wilkinsonville at the end of
July and beginning of August (Wilkin-
son to the secretary of war, 2 Aug. 1801,
DNA: RG 107, RLRMS; Norman W.
Caldwell, "Cantonment Wilkinsonville,"
Mid-America: An Historical Review, 31
[1949], 21).

TREATY NEAR KNOXVILLE: the intended negotiation with the Cherokees.
Wilkinson arrived at Southwest Point,
the meeting site, on 14 Aug. (Foster,
Hawkins, 361-3).

Claims to the Kentucky region by some
Indian tribes and the colony of VIRGINIA
had been the subject of a 1768 treaty at
Fort Stanwix, NEW YORK (Anthony F. C.

Wallace, *Jefferson and the Indians: The Tragic Fate of the First Americans* [Cambridge, Mass., 1999], 35-6, 39).
THAN WE CAN ASK SPEAK OR THINK: a

prayer in Ephesians 3:20 refers to a divine power with capabilities far beyond "all that we ask or think."

From James Madison

DEAR SIR   [12 August 1801]

Doctr. Rose being about to call at Monticello I prefer a conveyance by him to the mail, for the papers herewith inclosed, as I shall thereby be saved the necessity of having a messenger at the Ct. House in time to catch the arrival of the post. I have recd. yours of the 7th. inst. Having been before applied to by a letter from Hembold, on the subject of printing the laws in his German newspaper, I had authorized Mr Wagner to have it done, with an understanding that the preference was not to influence a future decision on the place & the press most eligible for the purpose. I was not at the time acquainted with the character or principles of the man, & it had been suggested that Lancaster or Reading, as more central might be more proper sources of publication.   Among the papers sent for perusal you will find the letter from Thornton as to the quoad prize carried into Boston. I send Wagner's sketch of an answer. If you think it proper to meet the pretension under the British Treaty, now rather than to wait the result of depending questions, you will please to signify it: as well as whether the ground taken by Wagner be *substantially* approved. Perhaps a more *concise* reply in the first instance might be better. Perhaps also the advantage of silence under present circumstances may balance the objection of its fostering an inadmissible claim. You will find also a letter from N. Webster. It is observable that he does not directly combat the principle of distribution laid down in your reply to the Remonstrance. You will be so good as to return his letter with such of the other papers as would encumber your files, or be more properly placed in mine. Mrs. M. offers her affectionate complits to the ladies of your family and looks with pleasure to the opportunity of visiting them, which cannot at present be fixt to a day or even to a week, but will probably be pretty soon. She also joins in the best respects we can both offer to yourself.

Yrs. with respectful attachment   JAMES MADISON

RC (DLC); undated; endorsed by TJ as received from the State Department on 12 Aug. and so recorded in SJL. Enclosures: (1) Edward Thornton to Madison, Philadelphia, 23 July, regarding the *Windsor* (Madison, *Papers, Sec. of State*

Ser., 1:463; see also Robert Smith to TJ, 7 Aug.). (2) Thornton to Madison, Philadelphia, 24 July (first letter), regarding the *Beguine* at Boston (Madison, *Papers, Sec. of State Ser.*, 1:473-4; see also Gallatin to TJ, 10 Aug.). (3) Thornton to Madison, Philadelphia, 24 July (second letter), forwarding Governor George Beckwith's papers (Madison, *Papers, Sec. of State Ser.*, 1:475). (4) Noah Webster to Madison, New Haven, 18 July, protesting Elizur Goodrich's displacement by Samuel Bishop as the collector at New Haven; with a long addendum attacking TJ's justifications of Bishop's appointment, dated 20 July, and written after Webster had seen TJ's reply to the New

Haven merchants (Madison, *Papers, Sec. of State Ser.*, 1:436-41). Other enclosures not found.

BEFORE APPLIED TO: George Helmbold to Madison, 30 July (not found, but see Madison, *Papers, Sec. of State Ser.*, 1:488). For the decision on PRINTING THE LAWS in German, see Helmbold to TJ, 30 July. HIS GERMAN NEWSPAPER: *Neue Philadelphische Correspondenz* (Vol. 33:529n).

Madison sent for TJ's PERUSAL the papers that Jacob Wagner had forwarded to the secretary of state on 3 Aug. (Madison, *Papers, Sec. of State Ser.*, 2:12-14).

To James Madison

DEAR SIR   Monticello Aug. 13. 1801.

Doctr. Rose delivered me last night the letter with which you charged him, and I have thought it better to attend to it's contents at once before the arrival of the load of other business which this morning's post will bring. Pinckney's, Orr's, Livermore's, Howell's, Webster's, Murray's, Otis's, Graham's & Thornton's letters, with Wagner's sketch of an answer to the latter are all returned herewith. Reed's papers being voluminous have not yet been read.—I thought a commission as District attorney had been forwarded to Howell: if so, his letter is not intelligible to me where he says he is prepared to quit his office when a more deserving person shall be thought of. that he would have preferred himself to Barnes as judge is evident enough.—tho' I view Webster as a mere pedagogue of very limited understanding and very strong prejudices & party passions, yet as editor of a paper & as of the Newhaven association, he may be worth stroking. his letter leaves two very fair points whereon to answer him. 1. the justice of making vacancies in order to introduce a participation of office. 2. that admitted, the propriety of preventing men indecently appointed & not yet warm in the seat of office from continuing, rather than to remove those fairly appointed & long in possession. as to Goodrich & Bishop it would be like talking to the deaf to say any thing to a man as immoveably biassed as he is.—Thornton's letter is the same I had seen before I left Washington. when we consider that our minister has to wait months & years for an answer to the most trifling or most urgent application to his government, there would be no indecency to decline answering so crude an application as this respecting the prize, which he does not know if it be prize or not, brought into Boston *as the newspapers say.* I think it better to avoid determining, with foreign ministers, hypothetical cases. they may by stating possible cases, so employ us as to leave no time for those which are actual. the actual furnish occupation enough for our whole time. perhaps the case of giving or refusing asylum for prizes may never arise. yet if we predetermine it, we shall be led into all the altercation & discussion which would be necessary were we obliged to decide it. I think therefore the answer to Thornton might be that his letter being hypothetical presents two questions, calling for very different considerations, both of which it cannot now be necessary to determine. that both are founded on newspaper information only, which is too uncertain ground for the government to act on: and that so soon as certain information shall be recieved that any such case has happened & what the exact nature of the case is, we will do on it what shall be right.—I have been reading Schlegel's pamphlet with great attention. it contains a great deal of sound information. he does not however prove that in cases uncontrouled by treaty, the nations of Europe (or a single one of them in a single case) have practised on the principle, as a principle of natural law, that free bottoms make free goods. his own facts shew that the principle practised on in the earliest times was that an enemy's goods in a friend's bottom are lawful prize: that on an attempt by the Dutch to introduce the other principle, it was overborne by Lewis XIV. and by England, and the old principle adhered to. still it does not follow but that a sound principle may have been smothered by powerful states acting on a temporary interest: and that we have always a right to correct antient errors, and to establish what is more conformable to reason & convenience. this is the ground we must take.—I shall rejoice to see mrs Madison, yourself & the Chess heroine here. observe that the governor is at Richmond every other Saturday. he goes down this day, & will be back on Tuesday. accept assurances of my affectionate friendship—   TH: JEFFERSON

RC (DLC: Madison Papers, Rives Collection); at foot of first page: "The Secretary of state"; recorded in SJL as a letter of 12 Aug. PrC (DLC).

LETTER WITH WHICH YOU CHARGED HIM: see the letter printed above.

REED'S PAPERS: possibly those associated with Dr. John K. Read, quarantine inspector and alderman at Norfolk, whose involvement in the 1799 surrender of a seaman suspected of being a British deserter led to quo warranto proceedings in district court against Read and an attempt to remove him from his post for overstepping his authority (see Madison, *Papers, Sec. of State Ser.*, 1:396n; James Monroe to TJ, 22 May).

Madison sent David HOWELL his commission as U.S. district attorney for Rhode Island on 2 June and Howell acknowledged its receipt on 15 June (Madison, *Papers, Sec. of State Ser.*, 1:318-19).

SCHLEGEL'S PAMPHLET: Johan Frederik Wilhelm Schlegel wrote a pamphlet published in Philadelphia in 1801, *Neutral Rights; or, An Impartial Examination of the Right of Search of Neutral Vessels Under Convoy, and of a Judgment Pronounced by the English Court of Admiralty, the 11th June, 1799, in the Case of the Swedish Convoy* (Sowerby, No. 2128).

CHESS HEROINE: Anna Payne, Dolley Madison's younger sister (Lucia B. Cutts, *Memoirs and Letters of Dolly Madison,* [Boston, 1887], 17, 39).

From Elizabeth House Trist

DEAR SIR   Birdwood August 13th 1801

Among the numerous recommendations which you daily receive for appointments I beg leave to Step forward in favor of my friend Mr David Easton whose Merits are I know equal to his Misfortunes, and whose talents and integrity are fully commensurate to the duties of the Office he solicits. His necessities have been occasion'd by the late Merciless captures, but notwithstanding by Sacraficeing every species of his property as well as that of which his Wife was possess'd, his character has been unimpeach'd.

Mrs Easton is the Daughter of the late Colonel Harrison who you may remember as Secretary to General Washington, Mr Easton is a native of Scotland a resident of this Country Sixteen Years, a Citizen fourteen and being a Commercial Character his object is a Consulship The Gentleman that has been appointed to that Situation at Hamburgh he understands declines accepting the Office, shou'd that be the case it wou'd be a situation most desireable if not, that of Glasgow or any other wou'd be acceptable—He has been offerd recommendations for this appointment particularly by Governor Stone of Maryland who no doubt will Authenticate what I have above written—.

Was I not affraid of being too prolix I wou'd unfold to you the sensations of my heart the emotions of which have on this occasion been particularly excited—therefore conclude with a request that you will peruse the inclosed letters—In truth believe me

Your obliged friend   E. TRIST

RC (DNA: RG 59, LAR); endorsed by TJ as received 14 Aug. and "David Easton to be Consul" and so recorded in SJL.

DAVID EASTON was an Alexandria merchant and importer of rum and citrus from Grenada. LATE MERCILESS CAPTURES: Easton, along with William Wilson and John Potts, suffered losses in August 1793 when their brigantine *Jessie* and its cargo were captured by the French privateer *Sans Pareille* and sold

at Charleston (Miller, *Alexandria Artisans*, 1:123; JHR, 4:291; 5:315).

MRS. EASTON: Sarah Easton was the widow of Captain John Jordon and the daughter of Robert Hanson HARRISON, a native of Charles County, Maryland, who served as one of George Washington's aides-de-camp during the Revolution (George T. Ness, Jr., "A Lost Man of Maryland," *Maryland Historical Magazine*, 35 [1940], 315-36).

Trist was under the impression that Benjamin Grayson Orr, who had hoped for a CONSULSHIP at Bordeaux, had been offered a consulship at Hamburg, and had until October to determine if he would accept it (Madison, *Papers, Sec. of State Ser.*, 2:235; Trist to TJ, 24 Oct. 1801).

To John Barnes

DEAR SIR   Monticello Aug. 14. 1801.

Your favor of the 10th. came to hand in the morning of the 13th. I shall be glad if the plaisterers arrive soon. it would be too late to engage others, as I should wish the work done under my eye. if they are not set out, and will come off immediately, they may still accomplish the work. or even if one will come we might get him an aid. the plaister of Paris arrived two days ago, and all the packages of groceries &c which accompanied it, except No. 8. a barrel containing 15. loaves sugar & 60. ℔ coffee. this had not been delivered to the boatman, as his reciept corresponded with the packages he delivered. it was probably omitted at Richmond by mistake. I have written there to have it sought into, and trust we shall find it there. I am very much pleased to learn from Mr Le Tombe & M. Rapin that they have engaged Le Maire to take the place of Rapin. Please accept assurances of my sincere esteem.   TH: JEFFERSON

PrC (CSmH); at foot of text: "Mr. Barnes"; endorsed by TJ in ink on verso.

To Henry Dearborn

DEAR SIR   Monticello Aug. 14. 1801.

I inclose you a letter from a mr Quarrier of this state asking a military commission. I know little of him, but that he is young, and ought to expect to be merely a commissioned officer. those who recommend him are persons of the first respectability.

the abuses in the military & naval departments seem to have been so great, that it will doubtless be indispensable that we bring them in some way, directly or indirectly, under the eye of the legislature. I inclose you a note of one instance, which merits enquiry. I strongly suspect it will be found to have originated[1] with the engineer. I hardly believe that the Secretary could have given such orders. I write to my informant to furnish me with the particulars so exactly as to be absolutely relied on, & the names of witnesses. in the mean time you may have some opportunities of learning something about it without exciting alarm.

I propose that we shall all rendezvous in Washington on the last day of September if there be no pressing obstacle to it. I shall be there on or before that day myself. Accept assurances of my affectionate esteem & high respect. Th: Jefferson

PrC (DLC); at foot of text: "Genl. Dearborne." Enclosures: (1) Samuel Quarrier to TJ, 4 Aug. 1801, not found, but recorded in SJL as received from Washington on 13 Aug., with notation "Off. W." (2) Extract from "Nicholas Geffroy" to TJ, 1 Aug. (see TJ to Madison, 14 Aug.). Enclosed in TJ to Robert Smith, 14 Aug.

hath been promoted to some office, which he shall be found qualified to execute" (RC in NNPM; endorsed by TJ as received 29 July and so recorded in SJL). Alexander Quarrier, a Richmond coach dealer, was captain of the city's militia guard. His son Samuel wrote to TJ again on 21 Aug. (Marshall, *Papers*, 2:266; Preston, *Catalogue*, 1:109-10; Vol. 30:116, 235; Vol. 31:376-7).

those who recommend him: in a brief note to TJ on 4 July, George Wythe wrote, "The friends of Alexander Quarrier will be not a little gratified by hearing that his son, of whom they think well,

[1] TJ first wrote "it will originate" before interlining and altering the passage to read as above.

To Albert Gallatin

Dear Sir   Monticello Aug. 14. 1801.

Your favors of the 8th. & 10th. came to hand yesterday. with respect to Hopkins's case, which is the subject of the former, my opinion is generally that when a case is exactly that which the law meant to punish, it is one for which the power of pardon was not intended. but when a case is not that which the law meant to make criminal, & yet happens to be within it's letter, there is proper ground to exercise the power of pardon. ignorance of the law in the case of Hopkins, together with his having paid every thing the treasury had a right to, & gained nothing by the non-entry of his still, appear to bring him within the scope of the pardoning power. if you think so, & will have a pardon forwarded to me, I will sign it.

I inclose you the resignation of Anthony W. White as Surveyor of the port of New Brunswick. if this be the person I suppose, it will be no loss to the public.

The case of the expenditure of the hospital money, partly from the defects of the law, partly the difficulty of the subject, is very perplexing. how would it answer to get along as we have done till the meeting of the legislature, & then to endeavor to establish a systematic plan legislatively?

I know nothing of Chisman, proposed as Collector of Hampton; and our friend mr Page, from the benevolent & unsuspicious cast of his mind, is the most unsafe recommender we can possibly follow. he never sees but the good qualities of a man, & those through the largest magnifiers. as the case will I suppose admit of some delay, I will write to persons of the neighborhood for further information; & will communicate the result. but if it admits no delay, then we may appoint Chisman; but be assured it will be at considerable risk.—for the Collectorship of Savannah I should prefer the recommendation of Jackson who is of the state, to that of Burke who is out of it. will it not await the answers you expect from Baldwin, Milledge & Taliaferro? if not, let us name Johnson.—I shall have great reluctance indeed at removing Simmons; & especially as he promises the same support to this which he gave to the preceding administration. this removes the only reason urged by mr Pinckney for depriving him of his place, to wit his electioneering influence & energy. at any rate we must take time & have more information on the subject.—the removals desired by mr Langdon are on better ground. but they also may wait awhile.—is Jonas Clark proposed as Collector of Kennebunk, a republican? his having been nominated by our predecessors excites a presumption against it; & if he is not, we must be inflexible against appointing federalists till there be a due portion of republicans introduced into office. it gives just offence to those who have been constantly excluded heretofore, to be still excluded by those who have been brought in to correct the system.—the answer to Newhaven does not work harder than I expected. it gives mortal offence to the Monarchical federalists who were mortally offended before. I do not believe it is thought unreasonable by the Republican federalists. in one point the effect is not exactly what I expected. it has given more expectation to the *Sweeping* republicans than I think it's terms justify. to the moderate & genuine republicans it seems to have given perfect satisfaction. I am satisfied it was indispensably necessary in order to rally round one point all the shades of republicanism & federalism, exclusive of the Monarchical: and I am in hopes it will do it. at any event while we push the patience of our friends to the utmost it will bear in order that we may gather into the same fold all the republican federalists possible, we must not, even for this object, absolutely revolt our tried[1] friends. it would be a poor maneuvre to exchange them for[2] new converts.

I have no doubt of the expediency of publishing the suppression of the inspectorships, with an explanation of the grounds of it.—with respect to Gardner as agent with the Choctaws, is one wanting, & has he the fitnesses for the place? if not, I should wish to make some other provision for him. with respect to Campbell a restoration to the same office would seem the best & safest redress.—I have no doubt we have a right to put the French & English on the same footing, by either recieving or excluding the prizes of both nations. the latter is our best policy. but I would never permit a foreign minister, on the foundation of a mere newspaper paragraph, before the character of a fact be known, or even that it is a fact, to draw the government into the discussion & decision of the gravest and most difficult questions. I am clear therefore for giving no answer till the transaction and it's whole character be authentically defined. from mr Thornton's court we can never get a decision after a fact has happened. why should we be so complaisant as to decide for them beforehand? in a letter of this day to Genl. Dearborne I have proposed our general rendezvous at Washington on the last day of September. present my best respects to mrs Gallatin, & be assured yourself of my sincere & friendly attachment & respect.   TH: JEFFERSON

P.S. all your papers are returned except the report of warrants issued.

RC (NHi: Gallatin Papers); at foot of first page: "The Secretary of the Treasury"; endorsed by Gallatin. PrC (DLC). Enclosure: Anthony W. White to TJ, 1 Aug. 1801 (recorded in SJL as received from New Brunswick on 13 Aug. with notation "T." but not found).

HAVE A PARDON FORWARDED TO ME: on 19 Aug., Gallatin enclosed a pardon for David Hopkins, of the same date, to Jacob Wagner, requesting him to forward it to the secretary of state for his signature and then on to the president (RC in DLC; endorsed by TJ: "Departmt. of Treasury"; FC of pardon in Lb in DNA: RG 59, GPR). Wagner enclosed the pardon in his letter to Madison of 24 Aug. (Madison, *Papers, Sec. of State Ser.*, 2:63-5).

ANTHONY W. WHITE had served as surveyor and inspector of the port at New Brunswick, New Jersey, since March 1797. He received an appointment as brigadier general in the provisional army in July 1798 (JEP, 1:232, 292-3).

I WILL WRITE: TJ wrote Wilson Cary

Nicholas and Thomas Newton requesting information on Mount Edward Chisman (TJ to Newton, 14 Aug.).

GREAT RELUCTANCE INDEED AT REMOVING SIMMONS: TJ may have been influenced by two pamphlets sent by Charleston collector James Simons to the War Department with the request that the secretary "would do him the honor to present them with his best respects to the President." In Dearborn's absence, John Newman, on 8 Aug., sent the pamphlets, which have not been identified, to Meriwether Lewis (RC in DLC; endorsed by TJ as received from Newman at the "War Office" on 14 Aug. and so recorded in SJL; also endorsed by TJ: "with pamphlets"). Months earlier, Charles PINCKNEY had sent TJ a pamphlet by Simons, in which the collector praised the administrations of Washington and Adams (see Pinckney to TJ, 26 May 1801).

[1] Word interlined in place of "own."
[2] Several illegible words canceled.

To "Nicholas Geffroy"

SIR   Monticello Aug. 14. 1801.

Your favor of the 1st. inst. came to hand here yesterday. no apologies are necessary from my fellow citizens for addressing to me either facts or opinions. on the contrary I am always glad to recieve them, claiming the indulgence of not being required to write special answers (which would be really impossible) except where they require something further to be done. your letter mentions an abuse which I would wish to ascertain; to wit that the timber, bricks & lime used in building the fort at Newport were brought from Maine; & that lands, for the mere accomodation of the garrison were bought at an unexampled price. the bringing timber from Maine might be justifiable: but none of the other articles appear so. will you be pleased to satisfy yourself of the particulars of these abuses, & to communicate to me what on more particular enquiry, you find to have been the exact[1] truth, & to give me the names of the persons on whom we may call to prove them. the source of my information shall be known to nobody but myself unless you chuse to permit it expressly. it is to avoid suspicion that I shall not frank this letter. accept my thanks for the information as well as the obliging expressions of your letter, together with my best wishes for your health & happiness.   TH: JEFFERSON

PrC (DLC); at foot of text: "Mr Nicholas Geffroy. Newport." Tr (DLC: TJ Papers, 115:19845); entirely in Christopher Ellery's hand; at head of text: "(Copy Nov. 3)"; at foot of text: "President's letter to Nicholas Geffroy Recd. from Geffroy by C. Ellery Aug. 28th. 1801." Enclosed in Ellery to TJ, 28 Aug.

[1] Word interlined.

To George Jefferson

DEAR SIR   Monticello Aug. 14. 1801.

On the day of your departure we recieved the packages of our groceries, towit from 1. to 7. and from 9. to 12. No. 8. is wanting being a barrel containing 15. loaves of sugar & 60. ℔ of coffee. the receipt given by the boatman expresses only 11. packages, which he delivered. I presume therefore the other one is still with you or has been delivered to some other boatman. it may be forwarded either by water or waggon as first occurs. or perhaps better by water with the other things you have to send. accept assurances of my sincere friendship.

                                                TH: JEFFERSON

PrC (MHi); at foot of text: "Mr. George Jefferson"; endorsed by TJ in ink on verso.

From Levi Lincoln

Sir   Worcester August 14th 1801.

Since my last by a letter from Brown the Navy agent in Boston I have his accont of the condemnation, sale & repairs of the Berceau, excepting the cost which, at present, he is not able to furnish but which he will forward as soon as it is in his power—The words of the instruction are different from what I supposed they were. I supposed them to have been expressed, as Brown considered the meaning to have been—For that I understood to have been the design of Government. The inclosed extract from his letter shew the transaction, respecting the Berceau in the town of Boston—

It is perceived by the papers that your answer to the N.H. remonstrance produced great excitements for the moment. The remarks on it were pitiful, the expressions of deep mortification & disappointment. They are dying away—and its beneficial effects discovering themselves, in more caution & prudence on the part of the federalist. On my return from Boston where I expect to be in a day or two, I shall trouble you with further communications—Accept Sir assurances of my highest esteem & respect   LEVI LINCOLN

RC (DLC); at head of text: "President of the United States"; endorsed by TJ as received 27 Aug. and so recorded in SJL. Enclosure: Extract from Samuel Brown to Lincoln, [4 Aug. 1801], two paragraphs, one giving a sequence of events from the capture of the *Berceau* on 12 Oct. 1800 to its sale at Boston on 15 Jan. 1801, and the second paragraph explaining the instructions that Brown received from the Navy Department, which called for the vessel to be repaired to "the state she was in at the time of her capture"; Brown declaring that he "presumed it was the meaning of the instructions, 'tho not fully expressed, that the Corvette should be restored, in all respects, to the condition she was in, immediately anterior to the Commencement of the action with the Boston"; he noting also that strict adherence to that rule "was soon found impracticable," since the new rigging, sails, masts, spars, and other items installed during the restoration of the ship were worth more than the fittings on the ship before the battle with the *Boston* (Tr in DLC: TJ Papers, 117:20146-7, in a clerk's hand, except at head of text in Lincoln's hand: "Extract from Brown's letter," undated, but date mentioned in Brown to Lincoln, 16 Oct. 1801, in DLC; printed in ASP, *Foreign Relations*, 2:436).

MY LAST: Lincoln to TJ, 28 July.

To James Madison

DEAR SIR   Monticello Aug. 14. 1801.

I wrote yesterday to you, before the arrival of the post. that brought some blank commissions which I have signed & now forward. mr Wagner's note will explain them.

The abuses & waste of public money in the military & naval departments have been so gross, that I do not think we can avoid laying some of them before Congress. I inclose you information of one which is not to be neglected. I have desired further information. I expect it will be found to have originated in Toussard who was a protegé of Knox's.—of 6. patients inoculated with the kine pox on the 7th. inst. one shews considerable symptoms of having taken the disease. we yesterday performed 6. more inoculations from matter recieved from Boston & some from England viâ Boston. I learn that Dr. Gant's efforts have all failed. health & affectionate attachment.

TH: JEFFERSON

RC (Charles M. Storey, Boston, 1958); addressed: "James Madison Secretary of State at his seat near Orange court house." PrC (DLC). Enclosure: "Nicholas Geffroy" to TJ, 1 Aug. (see PrC of extract).

WAGNER'S NOTE has not been found.

To Thomas Newton

DEAR SIR   Monticello Aug 14. 1801.

A collector for the port of Hampton is wanting in the room of mr Kirby, removed for gross delinquency. Mount E. Chisman has been proposed. can you inform me of his character & circumstances? or can you recommend any better person? I must ask your answer without any delay, as I believe the case presses. indeed I am not certain if it's pressure may not oblige the Secretary of the Treasury to issue a commission before we can be fully advised. pardon the free use I make of you for public as well as private purposes, which proceeds from my confidence in you. accept assurances of my sincere esteem & high consideration.   TH: JEFFERSON

PrC (DLC); at foot of text: "Colo. Thomas Newton."

To Joseph Rapin

DEAR SIR   Monticello Aug. 14. 1801.

Your letter of the 10th. came to hand yesterday. I am very glad indeed that Le Maire is engaged for me. still this does not suppress my regret at losing you: your conduct having given me the most perfect satisfaction. I am very sensible to the interest you have taken in procuring me a good successor. you will impress on him that while I wish to have every thing good in it's kind, and handsome in stile, I am a great enemy to waste and useless extravagance, and see them with real pain. you will recieve from mr Barnes on account any portion you may call for of what shall be due to you, so as to experience no inconvenience from my absence. having nothing in particular to give in charge respecting the affairs of the house & family, I offer you my best wishes & friendly attachment.   TH: JEFFERSON

PrC (MHi); at foot of text: "Mr. Joseph Rapin"; endorsed by TJ in ink on verso.

To Robert Smith

DEAR SIR   Monticello Aug. 14. 1801.

I recieved yesterday mr Thomas's favor covering the list of warrants for the week, and your's of the 7th. inst. I am very glad to learn your opinion on the question of admitting French & English prizes into our ports, & that it coincides with my own. indeed it is the opinion of every member of the administration. I consider that we are free to recieve, or to refuse the prizes of both nations, & that our best policy will be to reject both: treating them with exact equality. still I have urged to mr Madison not to permit a foreign minister to suppose that he may on the simple foundation of a newspaper paragraph call on the government to determine questions of the first interest. let it be known that a fact is authentic, & what is it's exact character, & then we may act on real & not hypothetical ground. the real facts arising will occupy all our time. if we spend any in hypothetical discussions, we shall want time for real business.

Not knowing what precise portion of Genl. Dearborne's business you undertake to execute, I inclose open to you a letter addressed to him. I would wish not only yourself but mr Gallatin to see the *extract*. you will probably think it well to seal & forward it to Genl. Dearborne, as, before his return, he may have some opportunities of enquiry. it is necessary we should all know all the facts of this nature, & reflect on them; as we have to determine the question whether we can avoid laying them before Congress consistently with our duty. accept assurances of my sincere attachment & high consideration.

                                        TH: JEFFERSON

PrC (DLC); at foot of text: "Robert Smith Secretary of the navy." Enclosure: TJ to Henry Dearborn, 14 Aug., with enclosure.

MR THOMAS'S FAVOR: Abishai Thomas to TJ, 10 Aug., transmitting an abstract of warrants on the Treasury related to the Navy Department for the week ending 8

Aug. (RC in DLC, endorsed by TJ as re-
ceived from the Navy Department on 13
Aug. and "Warrants" and so recorded in
SJL; FC in Lb in DNA: RG 45, LSP).

To Benjamin Waterhouse

DEAR SIR   Monticello Aug. 14. 1801.
I wrote you on the 8th. inst. that your favors of July 24. & 26. had
come to me here. Doctr. Wardlaw on the 7th. inoculated two persons
with the matter of the 24th. & 4. with that of the 26th. the latter has
no effect, but the two former shew inflammation & matter. one of them
complains of pain under the arm pit, & yesterday was a little feverish.
the matter is of this size & form. ⦚ the inflammation about $\frac{1}{2}$ an inch
all round from the pustule. we have considerable hopes he has the true
infection. yesterday I recieved your favor of the 1st. inst. Dr. Wardlaw
immediately inoculated 5. of the former subjects with it, & one other.
he also inoculated one from the pustule above described. you shall
be regularly informed of the progress & success of this business. I
learn from Washington indirectly that Doctr. Gantt's essays have all
failed. should ours succeed he shall be supplied hence. I am very anxious to obtain the disease here. accept my best esteem & respectful
salutations.   TH: JEFFERSON

RC (MBCo); at foot of text: "Doctr. Benjamin Waterhouse." PrC (DLC).

From Albert Gallatin

SIR   Treasury Department Augt. 15th 1801
I have the honor to enclose a letter from the Commissioner of the
revenue accompanying proposals for erecting a light house on
Falkner's Island. There are two applicants, Mr Woodward of Con-
necticut & Mr M'Comb of New York. For the reasons stated in the
Commissioner's & Gen. Huntingdon's letters, the first named gentle-
man seems to merit the preference. By the Act of 3d March last, the
Secretary is authorized to provide by Contract, to be approved by the
President of the United States, for the building the said light house.
The proposals are now submitted to your consideration, and, if ap-
proved by you, a contract will be made in conformity thereto.
I have the honor to be with great respect Sir Your most obt. Servt.
                                    ALBERT GALLATIN

RC (DLC); at foot of text: "The President of the United States"; endorsed by TJ as received 20 Aug. and "Lighthouse Faulkner's isld." and so recorded in SJL with notation "lighthouse." Enclosure: William Miller to Gallatin, Revenue Office, Treasury Department, 13 Aug., stating that a site had been selected for the proposed lighthouse on Falkner Island in Long Island Sound, a plan agreed upon for the building, and bids for construction advertised in New York and New London newspapers, but "none offered to undertake & complete the whole work" for less than $7,000, while the appropriation allowed only $6,000, making it necessary to alter the plan in ways "not likely to lessen its usefulness, and to notify the persons who had come forward" that their proposals would be considered "if their terms were reasonably reduced and brought within the appropriation," which was the case with Abishai Woodward and John McComb, Jr., both agreeing to complete the lighthouse for $5,500; Miller, considering both men of "good reputation and equal experience in constructing buildings of this kind," recommended Woodward because he offered to "face with *hewn stone*" and "it is well known that facings of hewn or hammer dressed stone, are preferable to common stone walls—The circumstance of his not compleating the whole workmanship untill the spring, will add to its strength, and it ought not to be considered a material ob-jection, if it is delayed a short time" (RC in ViU, endorsed and signed by Gallatin: "Approved provided the President shall consent," with note by TJ: "this proposition is approved. Th: Jefferson Aug. 21. 1801"; FC in Lb in DNA: RG 26, LDC). Other enclosures not found.

The TWO APPLICANTS had experience in the construction of lighthouses. Abishai Woodward, a carpenter in New London, Connecticut, had worked on a lighthouse at Bald Head in North Carolina in 1793. John McComb, Jr., a New York City architect, had contracts for the construction of several lighthouses in the 1790s, including Montauk and Eaton's Neck, New York. In 1802 he was appointed architect for the building of New York City Hall (ANB, s.v. "McComb, John, Jr."; Syrett, *Hamilton*, 14:230-1, 311, 323-4; Washington, *Papers, Pres. Ser.*, 7:183-5; 12:445-6).

By the ACT of 3 Mch. 1801, Congress appropriated $6,000 for construction of a lighthouse on Falkner Island. The lighthouse contract and the appointment of the lighthouse keeper had to be approved by the president (U.S. Statutes at Large, 2:125).

CONTRACT WILL BE MADE: on 2 Sep. 1801, Huntington and Woodward signed an agreement at New London for the construction of the "lighthouse and other buildings," on Falkner Island, which included detailed specifications for the work (Lb in DNA: RG 26, LDC).

To Wilson Cary Nicholas

DEAR SIR   Monticello Aug. 15. 1801

A collector for the port of Hampton is wanting in the room of one Kirby removed for gross delinquency. Mount E. Chisman has been recommended. can you give me his character, & circumstances? can you recommend any body better, or advise me to any person whose judgment may be relied on to recommend, and who is acquainted with the characters of the neighborhood? I believe the case presses so that I must ask your answer by the post if no conveyance occurs sooner. health & sincere affection.   TH: JEFFERSON

PrC (DLC); at foot of text: "W. C. Nicholas."

From Jacob Nixon

SIR Norfolk Augt. 15, 1801

As a total stranger to you an apology is necessary, for intruding with this letter, this I hope you will excuse when I mention I am an Irish Exile. Henry Jackson who probably has the happiness of your acquaintance, formerly of Dublin is my freind, & formerly in Coercisien with me.—

I have been bred a Surgeon, If you will, so as its not disagreeable to you, to allow me, either, in Army, or Navy, the same situation I will not do less than render much service

It wd. be wrong to say any thing without trial.—I am with very good *wish*. Yr. truly Obt Servant JACOB NIXON

RC (DNA: RG 59, LAR); endorsed by TJ as received 27 Aug. and "to be Surgeon" and so recorded in SJL.

Jacob Nixon, a "physician, surgeon and man-midwife," lived at 125 Main Street in Norfolk (*Simmons's Norfolk Directory* [Norfolk, 1801], 25).

HENRY JACKSON was an ironfounder in Dublin and a prominent member of the Society of United Irishmen when he was imprisoned by the British during the Irish rebellion of 1798. Following his release from Kilmainham prison in 1799, Jackson emigrated to the United States (Jane Hayter Hames, *Arthur O'Connor, United Irishman* [Doughcloyne, Ireland, 2001], 188; David A. Wilson, *United Irishmen, United States: Immigrant Radicals in the Early Republic* [Ithaca, 1998], 19, 29; William Adamson to TJ, 28 Dec. 1801; Edward Hudson to Henry Jackson, 20 Jan. 1803, enclosed in Adamson to TJ, 30 Jan. 1803).

From James Currie

SIR Richmond Augt. 16th 1801

I had the pleasure, t'other day to read in the News paper you had left the seat of Goverment for Monticello—permit me to congratulate you on your good health & that you have leisure to pay this Visit, to your friends in Virginia & Enjoy for a moment retirement, & the Salubrious air of your Elevated & charming seat in Albemarle; where if I can possibly leave Richmond—I intend myself the honor of paying you a Visit before you return to the seat of Government—I wrote you a note last Spring addressed to you at Monticello—. I never had any notice of its being received by you—The purport of it was to inform that I had submitted the Papers of yours and Mr D Ross to the referees.—I now have the pleasure to inform you that the matter is brought to a conclusion, how settled I am not yet apprised—as soon as I am you will immediately have an account of it—in the mean time, please read the underwritten note to me of this day from Philip N.

Nicholas Esqr—who presents his respects to Dr Currie & informs him that, upon looking into the report made, by Mr Robinson to whom the accts. between Mr Jefferson & Mr Ross were referred, to state an Account of the ballance due, he finds he cannot begin the award, without comparing the account rendred by Mr Robinson with the Documents & as he is obliged to sett off for GoochLand to day he cannot compleat the business till his return, which will be on Thursday next—and will certainly look over the papers so as to inable Dr Currie to write to Mr Jefferson by Tuesday Sennights Post, as soon as I receive the award—& the papers deposited wt. the Referees. I shall return to Mr Ross as you have requested Colo T M Randolph's order on Mr Ross & the Other papers will take care of till a proper oppty offers of transmitting them to you Safely—with the award, & shall if this finds you at Monticello be glad of hearing from you how long youll probably remain at home & whether you wish them forwarded immediately to you there &

I am Sir —with Sentiments of the most respectfull Esteem—Your Very Hble servt   JAMES CURRIE

RC (MHi); addressed: "To His Excellency Thomas Jefferson Esquire President of the United States now at Monticello"; franked and postmarked; endorsed by TJ as received 20 Aug. and so recorded in SJL.

I WROTE YOU A NOTE: see Currie to TJ, 15 Apr. For the settlement of TJ's dispute with David ROSS, see Vol. 31:209-10n.

From James Madison

DEAR SIR   Augst 16. 1801

Mrs. Tudor (the lady of Judge Tudor of Boston) with her son, intending to be at Monticello this evening or tomorrow, I entrust to them the inclosed papers, which will thus reach you a little earlier, than if detained for the mail, by which I shall again write to you. In the mean time I remain

Yours most respectfully & affy.   JAMES MADISON

RC (ViU); endorsed by TJ as received 16 Aug. and so recorded in SJL as from the State Department with notation "inclosing papers & ad legendum." Enclosure: Joel Roberts Poinsett to TJ, 24 July. Other enclosures not found.

Delia Jarvis TUDOR, the wife of Massachusetts state senator William Tudor, traveled with her SON, William Tudor, Jr. (George Clinton to TJ, 29 July 1801).

From John Barnes

The suspected—*King*, have absconded, After being taken by the Constable for debt. it also Appears by his plaistering—lately at Mr Dorseys he was—but a very indifft. Workman.—Mr Martin Wanscher the other Plaisterer—his detention has been Occasioned by a disputed a/c with his late employer a Mr Hugh Densley—who unable to pay.—of course unwilling to adjust his a/c Obliged—W. to sue him—and by persuasion Afterwards—to an Arbitration the Award $56. in favr of W—and when demanded offered him his Note Only—at 90 days. which I advised him not to accept, but to indorse, & leave it with me. in consequence, of this Arrangement, I have advanced him $30.—ten of which—he leaves with his *New Wife*—at Alexand. and I expect forward from thence on Wednesday 19th ℞ packet to Norfolk—also takes charge—of your Case of dry fruits—& almonds—your 2 Books—including—a small Box, containing 22. best Glass—barrel shape—Tumblers the only ones—to be met with in Alexanda. & recd late last Eveng.—together with his Chest Clothes & tools: He has, moreover—from the Capt. of the—Abigail & Rebecca; an Order, to pick up at Norfolk one bbl: of your plaister of Paris—delivered there by Mistake of his Boy—in lieu of a bbl flour— if he secured this—and meet with no other Obstruction—by the way—I still hope He may reach you—with the Need full in Season— by what I can learn of Mr W. He is a quiet sober, steady, & industrious—man—& understands his business—and Assured me, that with proper assistance He had rather do without *Mr King* who he knows to be a Bad Man—

—it seems, almost every incident that have reference to this & my late dispatch.—meets with *opposition*—the *times* are so.   why then ought I to complain—of these trifling incidents.—Andrews, a week since—wanted to send to Mr Rapin the Box of Doric Ornaments. I desired Mr Rapin to send them here—not coming, I sent for them.—there was still some thing wanting—to compleat them— I rather suppose—Mr Andrews—has parted with that *something*— for the Precious Metal—and is now proceeding to replace that deficiency—

Be that as it may, I shall not, be possessed of the Box—this week— and for the want of it—the loss—of this days favorable Opportunity— of Conveyance. your glass & Other Articles—Mr Richards—Phila to Richmond—I trust—are on their way. altho—no particular a/c.

I have reason to expect it by an early post.— your friend Mr Higginbotham presentd. your letter to me—in his favr.—late. the Eveng. before he left town for Baltimore—his Numerous letters addressed to the first Houses—in Baltimore—Philada. and New York, left me—a mere Shadow—to guide him by. the Caution I gave him—was not making particular engagemts—to any great amt. in this his first assay—but to try several in separate distinct parcels—might be of Use in his future Choice—& Selection—and Begged of him to do me, the Honor of calling—on his return thro Geo. Town—

I cannot yet meet with a pair of Glass—suitable—to present Mr Conrad with—neither have I yet drawn your last months Compensation—purposing—holding out—as long—as my Bank is tenantable.—

I am sir most Respectfully your Obed. & very H St.

JOHN BARNES

Mr Rapin writes you by this post—
Doct Bache arrived last Eveng at Washington—

RC (ViU: Edgehill-Randolph Papers); at foot of text: "Thomas Jefferson Esqr. Monticello"; endorsed by TJ as received 20 Aug. and so recorded in SJL.

Plasterer MARTIN WANSCHER left Washington on 17 Aug. for Monticello, where he was employed intermittently until 1804 (MB, 2:1053). Barnes recorded payment of a $30 advance to Wanscher at 15 Aug. (statement of private account from John Barnes, 30 Sep. 1801, in ViU). In a statement of account dated 3 May 1802, Wanscher recorded a total of 181 workdays between 17 Aug. 1801 and 29 Apr. 1802, with time off in December, January, and early February, at a rate of 7 shillings and 6 pence a day. Wanscher described only the work he performed over 20 days in the winter: preparing lime for finishing the dining room, pouring "th palastring stone," plastering a cellar room and "aberth th arch" in the dining room, and clearing lime from woodwork (MS in MHi, in Wanscher's hand and signed by

him, addressed: "Mr Tómas Jefferson esqire Mounteselle Albemarle County virginia state," endorsed by TJ on verso: "Wañscher Martin his acct. from Aug. 15. 1801 to Apr. 29. 1802"; MB, 2:1073).

HUGH DENSLEY did plasterwork in the President's House in 1799 (Seale, The President's House, 1:76, 78).

In an invoice to TJ dated 17 Aug. at Georgetown, Barnes recorded the value and freight charges of YOUR CASE containing dried fruits, almonds, and "22. double flint barl shape Tumblers," sent via Alexandria, Norfolk, and Richmond in the care of Martin Wanscher, totaling $22.52 (MS in ViU; in Barnes's hand and signed by him). For TJ's grocery order, see TJ to Barnes, printed at 20 July, and Barnes to TJ, 3 Aug. TJ requested tumblers in a letter to Barnes of 7 Aug.

HIGGINBOTHAM PRESENTD. YOUR LETTER: see TJ to Barnes, 6 Aug.

RAPIN WRITES YOU BY THIS POST: letter not recorded in SJL.

From the District of Columbia Commissioners

SIR,   Washington 17th. August 1801

On taking a view of the Business entrusted to us, we are of opinion that with the Money now on hand and the Sums which we may depend on receiving, we shall be able to compleat the several works recommended to us, and to pay the current Expenses of the Year, provided no more than four thousand Dollars shall be expended on the Streets, and no more laid out on the temporary House of Representatives than the Contract calls for:—

But without further Payments, there will be an arrear of Interest due to the State of Maryland on the first of October next, to the amount of ten thousand five hundred Dollars.—We cannot rely on voluntary Payments to answer this Sum;—we therefore submit to the President of the United-States whether we shall proceed to enforce further Payments, particularly from those who are bound to the State of Maryland for the re-payment of fifty thousand Dollars United-States six per cent Stock, (Resolution of the Assembly of that State A) and whose Debts to the City funds originated in purchases of Property resold for default in payment by the first purchasers at public Sales in the Years 1799 & 1800 on the Terms enclosed (B) and for which, the following notes have since been given, payable 4th. February 1801. vizt.

One note drawn by Uriah Forrest, and endorsed by Gustavus Scott for	$6,269.92
Ditto—endorsed by Benjamin Stoddert for	16 407.04.
Ditto—endorsed by John Templeman & Ben: Stoddert for	6 641.00.
Ditto—endorsed by the same for	4 485.00.
Ditto—drawn by William Thornton & endorsed by Samuel Blodget	1 675.68
Amounting to Dollars	35,478.64

We understand that the Right of the Commissioners to enforce the payment of these Sums will be disputed, should a Sale be proposed; and we think it improper to risk involving the affairs of the City in a Dispute, without acquainting the President with the Grounds thereof and receiving his sanction to the Measures to be pursued—The facts of the case are, that on the application of Gustavus Scott & William Thornton two of the Commissioners, the Legislature of Maryland authorised the Loan of fifty thousand Dollars, six per cent Stock, on the Terms mentioned in the aforesaid Resolution—that the said Gustavus Scott and William Thornton with Uriah Forrest and James M Lingan as their Sureties, entered into Bond to the State of Maryland, and Uriah Forrest executed a Mortgage on four hundred and twenty acres of Land, for securing the payment of the said fifty thousand Dollars Stock, on the first of November 1802; with Interest quarter-yearly; agreeably to the Terms of the said Resolution—The said Gustavus Scott and William Thornton having engaged by Letter to hold all the City Property (except that pledged by Act of Congress to secure the Payment of three hundred thousand Dollars) as a Security for the re-payment of the said Stock, and to sell the said Property or such part thereof as might be necessary, on notice from the said Forrest and Lingan, and to pay over the Notes or money arising therefrom, to the State, in discharge of that Debt. The Correspondence on this Subject is enclosed (C)—Gustavus Scott has since deceased, and it is supposed that he was interested in this Property, and that it has descended to his infant Children—The Questions arising from these facts are—First—Whether the Commissioners had a Right to pledge the public Property in the manner stipulated by the aforesaid Correspondence, and what effect will it have on the right of enforcing the Payment of Debts either from the Sureties or others, although the Debts from the Sureties were not due, and although it appeared evident that the Commissioners were incapable of obtaining by legal process or otherwise, the Money then due to the City—Therefore, without this Loan the public Buildings could not be so far compleated as to accommodate the several Departments of Government? Note—We must add that the monies received, as well from the Sureties to the State of Maryland, as from others, have been indiscriminately applied to the general Expenditures on the Seat of Government, except that a preference has been given in the Payment of one quarter's Interest of the said Loan of fifty thousand Dollars—2d.—Whether Infants are entitled to any privilege in Proceedings under the Act of Assembly; an Extract of which is enclosed (D)?—And 3d.—Whether property sold under that Act can be resold for default of payment by the second Purchaser?—

It may be proper to observe, that between seven and eight thousand Dollars have been paid by General Forrest, and the Endorsers of the Notes drawn by him, and that Mr Stoddert purchased property at the public Sale in May last, to the amount of upwards of ten thousand Dollars; for which, by the Articles of Sale, he was entitled to a credit of nine Months; but he has paid the Money, in expectation of Indulgence for the same Time, in the payment of an equal Sum on the Note endorsed by him.—We would likewise submit to the President's consideration whether it is necessary to enforce payments beyond the Interest to the State of Maryland, having, as we suppose, already the means of accomplishing the other objects contemplated for the present Year, the Debts being well secured, and bearing Interest can be called in as the exigencies of the City may require.

We are, with sentiments of the highest respect, Sir, Yr. mo: Obedient Servts.

WILLIAM THORNTON
ALEX WHITE
TRISTRAM DALTON

P.S. Doctor Thornton has always observed that he would give no opposition to any measures which the President may think proper to direct, respecting the Debts due from him.

ALEX WHITE
TRISTRAM DALTON

RC (DLC); in William Brent's hand, signed by Thornton, White, and Dalton; above postscript: "President of the United-States"; endorsed by TJ as received 20 Aug. and so recorded in SJL. FC (DNA: RG 42, DCLB). Enclosures not found, but see below.

TEMPORARY HOUSE OF REPRESENTATIVES: TJ to the District of Columbia Commissioners, 2 June.

INTEREST DUE TO THE STATE OF MARYLAND: a total of $10,500 was due on 1 Oct. 1801 for the interest on the loans of $200,000 and $50,000 by the state of Maryland to the commission (see enclosure at the District of Columbia Commissioners to TJ, 3 Oct.; Vol. 33:481n).

RESOLUTION OF THE ASSEMBLY OF THAT STATE A: a resolution passed by the Maryland legislature in December 1799 authorized a $50,000 loan to the District of Columbia Commissioners. The principal was due 1 Nov. 1802, and if the interest due quarterly was "at any time 30 days in arrear, the whole principal to be sued for and recovered" (Laws of Maryland, Made and Passed at a Session of Assembly, Begun and held at the city of Annapolis on Monday the fourth of November, in the year of our Lord one thousand seven hundred and ninety-nine [Annapolis, 1800], Evans No. 37893; Vol. 33:510-11n).

By an ACT OF CONGRESS in May 1796 "authorizing a Loan for the Use of the City of Washington, in the District of Columbia," the commissioners, under the direction of the president, were authorized to borrow up to $300,000 to develop the city of Washington. Money raised by the sale of lots held in trust by the commissioners or trustees of the original proprietors, except lots appropriated to public use, was to be applied toward payment of the loan or loans. Failing this, the U.S. government guaranteed the repayment of authorized loans: "if the product of the sales of all the said lots shall prove inadequate to the payment of the principal and interest of the sums borrowed under this act, then the deficiency shall be paid by the United States" (U.S. Statutes at Large, 1:461; Vol. 29:11n).

The ACT OF ASSEMBLY of Maryland, an extract of which the commissioners sent as enclosure "D," was passed on 28 Dec. 1793. It allowed the District of Columbia commissioners to resell lots at public sale if the original purchaser had not paid the entire purchase price and interest, if any, within 30 days of coming due (*Laws of Maryland, Made and Passed at a Session of Assembly, Begun and held at the city of Annapolis, on Monday the fourth of November, in the year of our Lord one thousand seven hundred and ninety-three* [Annapolis, 1794], chap. 58, Evans No. 27268; TJ to District of Columbia Commissioners, 24 Aug.).

From Albert Gallatin

DR SIR   City of Washington 17th August 1801

Your favor of the 7th instt. was received on the 11th, the day after the mail had closed. It arrives here on Tuesday, departs on Monday. You may answer by same mail, but cannot receive answers in less than fortnight.

You will receive enclosed, as usual, the list of Warrants; & I also enclose a letter from Mr Doyley & one from W. Jones member of Congress for Philada.

The first letter is not written in as explicit a language as might have been wished; but may not this be inferred from his & Mr Pinckney's letters?—that not only there is some danger of a federal Senator being elected; which indeed I have uniformly apprehended; but that Mr Doyley & his friends fear, in case of a republican succeeding, that he may have personal views different from theirs, & favour appointments of different persons. And is not this the reason why Mr Doyley & friends wish the appointments to take place before the meeting of Congress? I have invited Mr Doyley to a free communication of his sentiments—

You will find by the other letter that the Republicans expect a change in Philada.; this expectation is owing partly to the removal of the collector of New York, & partly to the answer to New Haven which, as I mentioned before, has had a greater, if not a better effect than was expected. Of the four persons he recommends, the *name* of Bache would be most popular; but he wants industry; Clay is certainly the most capable, unless Conolly, who is highly respected by all who know him, should be supposed to understand that particular business better. Upon the whole, in that also, it is much better to wait the meeting of Congress. Dallas who was here agrees with me. Yet it must be allowed that the warm republicans will be displeased; it is the same in New York in regard to Rogers who, though the most capable, was the most obnoxious to the zealous republicans. Duane has been here, & I have taken an opportunity of showing the impropriety of numerous removals. He may think the reasons good; but his feelings will be at war with any argument on the subject. Clay has also been here; the number of young men of true merit & some scientific knowledge is so small in our middle States, that I cannot help being very desirous that something for which he may be fit might be done for him. His father has, excluding him, placed his younger brother in an eligible commercial situation, & the Bank of N. America will never promote him beyond his 1000 dollars salary. What do you think of the Lisbon or one of the Barbary Consulships? I do not know that either would suit him, but wish only to be acquaintted with your intentions generally.

I had understood that a Commission of Marshal New Jersey had been directed to issue in favour of General John Heard; & I believe he had understood as much. An application has in fact been made for the commission on a supposition that it had been lost. I have told Wagner to send you a blank one that, if it was intended, it may be filled. The present Marshal is Thomas Lowry; he has been in since 26 Sept. 1789; his commission expires 28 Jany. 1802.

Mr Miller has put in my hands the enclosed from Mr Fish. It may be difficult to answer; yet he has been uniformly considered as the mere tool of Hamilton, & was, with Giles & Watson, the most active electioneering officer of Govt. in New York. I must say something to Miller about it. E. Livingston said that the removal of Fish was not expected so long as Rogers was permitted to continue. By the bye it seems to me that Fish intends that letter for publication.

I have heard that Fenwick had received a letter of late date from Bourdeaux stating the ratification of our Convention with France & Dawson being on his way back, but have not been able to ascertain whether true or not.

I am with sincere respect & attachment Dr Sir Your most obt. Servt.   ALBERT GALLATIN

RC (DLC); at foot of text: "President of the United States"; endorsed by TJ as received 20 Aug. and so recorded in SJL. Enclosures: (1) "Weekly List of Warrants issued on Treasurer for the Week ending 15th August 1801," listing fourteen warrants, Nos. 112 to 125, including five under the civil list, for a total of $895; four under intercourse with foreign nations, including $3,000 for Charles Pinckney's outfit, for a total of $6,332.87; two for the military establishment, for a total of $2,079.33; one for the naval establishment, for a total of $50,000; and two under the public debt, being a purchase of guilders for the payment of the Dutch debt, for a total of $91,845; for a grand total of $151,152.20, and leaving a balance of specie in the Treasury at the end of the week of $2,716,629.71 (MS in DLC: TJ Papers, 115:19847; entirely in Gallatin's hand, and endorsed by him on verso). (2) Daniel D'Oyley to Gallatin, Charleston, 29 July 1801, thanking Gallatin for information on banks, which will be useful in establishing a state bank in South Carolina, and for providing political news on events leading to the election of a U.S. senator in November, noting that unless precautionary measures are adopted he fears a split betweeen votes for Thomas Sumter, the favorite of most

Republicans, and Judge Aedanus Burke, whose friends' activities ought to be "particularly known at Washington," because a Republican division could lead to the victory of John Ward, the Federalist candidate; D'Oyley declaring that the Federalists wanted to "preserve their old influence in all its extent," while the Republicans felt disappointed that they were neither "cherished" nor supported by the administration after the insults and sufferings they had endured (RC in DNA: RG 59, LAR; endorsed by TJ: "Doyley Danl. to mr Gallatin"). (3) William Jones to Alexander J. Dallas, Philadelphia, 3 Aug. 1801, recommending four candidates for customs collector at Philadelphia—although the mercantile list was "extremely barren of Republicans"—Richard Bache, known as a respectable merchant and highly esteemed as a gentleman, whose "connection with the family of our beloved Franklin" would add weight to the appointment; John Shee, who already has "a handsome state appointment"; Joseph Clay, clerk at the Bank of North America, who, while he may lack weight of character, has "merit, talents and integrity" and has adhered to republicanism "from principle" even though "a contrary course would have gratified his nearest connections and advanced his interest and standing in society"; and John Connelly, "a man of business, of understanding & principle and a steady republican"; Jones observing that the appointment of a collector was of great importance and should not be made hurriedly, but recommending that the "Dunwoody Secretary"—identified by Gallatin as William Jackson—should be dismissed "without delay," with Major

Jonas Simonds appointed as surveyor in his place; Jones concluding that perhaps it would be "expedient to spare" William McPherson, the naval officer, who was undoubtedly a zealous Federalist but "displayed less of the spirit of intolerance than most of them" and was "always a gentleman in his deportment" (RC in NHi: Gallatin Papers; addressed: "A. J. Dallas Esquire Washington"; with a mark in Gallatin's hand after "Dunwoody Secretary" and a note on verso: "meaning Major Jackson present surveyor AG"; endorsed by TJ: "William Jones recommends Richard Bache, John Shee Joseph Clay & John Connolly for Collector Philada."). Other enclosure not found.

Gallatin sent Charles PINCKNEY's letter on patronage in South Carolina to TJ on 10 Aug., but it has not been found. REPUBLICANS EXPECT A CHANGE IN PHILADA.: for the political activities of Federalists George Latimer, William McPherson, and William Jackson, the three top customs officials in Philadelphia, see Prince, *Federalists*, 85-94. Jonas Simonds, a Republican customs inspector, had refrained from political activities to retain his position at the port (same, 86; Simonds to TJ, 14 Apr. 1801). For the FOUR PERSONS recommended by William Jones, see Enclosure No. 3, above.

For the confusion and delay in the appointment of John Heard as MARSHAL for NEW JERSEY, see Vol. 33:183-4.

In late June, Samuel Osgood replaced Nicholas FISH as supervisor of the revenue in New York (Vol. 33:673; Notes on a Conversation with Robert R. Livingston, [4 June 1801]).

From Edward Gantt

SIR   George Town August 17th. 1801.

When I last saw you, I informed you that I had succeeded in communicating the vaccine Pox to one of my Patients. The Day after, I found the Inflammation had entirely disappeared, & that the Matter had in every Instance proved inactive. I hope the Gentleman who inoculated your Family has been successful, and that we may get supplied with recent Matter from him. I daily expect some from New-York—Should the Matter you have received from Doctor Waterhouse prove as inert, as those Portions of it which you was so obliging to furnish me with; and the Matter I receive from New York prove efficient, I will take the earliest opportunity of furnishing you with it recent. Your Family in Washington were all well, at twelve OClock this day. I am Sir,

with sincere Respect your much obliged & most obedt. Servt.

EDWARD GANTT

RC (DLC); endorsed by TJ as received 20 Aug. and so recorded in SJL.

Edward Gantt (c. 1741-1837), a native of Prince George's County, Maryland, was the attending physician at the President's House from 1801 to about 1806, when he moved to Kentucky. A graduate of the College of New Jersey, Gantt obtained medical training at the University of Edinburgh and a medical degree at the University of Leiden. Gantt worked with TJ to introduce smallpox vaccination in Washington (MB, 2:1118-9, 1144; Papenfuse, *Maryland Legislature*, 1:342; McLachlan, *Princetonians, 1748-1768*, 377-8; Washington, *Papers, Ret. Ser.*, 2:569; Madison, *Papers, Pres. Ser.*, 4:196).

GENTLEMAN WHO INOCULATED YOUR FAMILY: William Wardlaw.

Gantt may have been expecting smallpox vaccine (cowpox) from A. Bainbridge, who on 20 Aug. wrote to TJ from NEW YORK, hoping that TJ would pardon the liberty he took in writing to him. It was "at the request of my old intimate friend, Doctor Edward Gantt—the inclosed letter to him contains some of the Vaccine matter—he says the most certain conveyance will be to inclose it to you, and you would send it to him" (RC in MHi; endorsed by TJ as received 3 Sep. and so recorded in SJL; enclosure not found.) The author was probably Absalom Bainbridge, a classmate of Gantt's at college and a physician in New York (McLachlan, *Princetonians, 1748-1768*, 367, 372-5; *Longworth's American Almanac, New-York Register, and City Directory, for the twenty-sixth year of American Independence* [New York, 1801], 111).

From George Jefferson

DEAR SIR   Richmond 17th. Augt. 1801

Your favor of the 14th. is duly received; the mistake of one package which you mention, happened before their arrival here—Mr. G however thought it was a barrel of plaister of paris which was missing—No. 5, & not No. 8, as you suppose—this I hope may still be the case—as the delay in getting *that* would be less material.

The Capt. informed Mr. G. that he received the things from on board another Vessel, and that he must either have left the one barrel on board that Vessel, or else in Norfolk. we received no bill of lading.

Mr. G. had previous to my return paid Mr. Ast the amot. of his demand against you, both of principal & Interest—the latter being $:26.49, charged from 1st. Septr. '96; the policies are not yet received, but will probably be forwarded by next post.

Mr. G. was induced to pay this without your instruction as several persons had lately been compelled *by law* to pay it, and A— refused to receive the principal without it.

I am Dear Sir Your Very humble servt.   GEO. JEFFERSON

Wheat is down to 7/6 & 8/—

RC (MHi); endorsed by TJ as received 20 Aug. and so recorded in SJL; with note by TJ below postscript, in pencil: "powder wh sug. & coffee 200. D."

MR. G: Patrick Gibson, of Gibson & Jefferson. For the payment to William Frederick AST for insurance on the buildings at Monticello, see TJ to George Jefferson, 29 July. TJ received five POLICIES from the Mutual Assurance Society, numbered 970 through 974, all dated 4 Aug. 1801, and prepared according to the information provided in his Declaration for the Mutual Assurance Society, 16 Aug. 1800, which is cited in the policies as declaration No. 389 (see Vol. 32:104-7). On the

verso of policy No. 970, TJ listed in a column the sums due on the policies, respectively, including the stamp tax: $63, $5.80, $4.60, $10.60, $5.80, with a total of $89.80. On that policy, TJ paid $60 for the premium on the main dwelling house at Monticello and $3 in tax. On the other four, TJ paid a tax of $1 each (MSS in MHi; printed forms, each signed by William F. Ast, Robert Whitehill, William DuVal, and Jacob J. Cohen; with blanks filled by an unidentified hand using information provided in TJ's declaration of 16 Aug. 1800; at head of text, around insignia: "Mutual Assurance Society against Fire in Virginia"; indented; sealed).

From Robert Smith

SIR   Navy Dept. 17th Augt. 1801

I have the honor to transmit herewith Abstracts of the Warrants on the Treasury issued by me for the use of the Departments of War and Navy, and the balances remaining on hand, for the Week ending the 15th Inst.

I have the honor to be Sir with the highest Consideration & respect your most obt. Servt.   RT SMITH

RC (DLC); in clerk's hand, signed by Smith; at foot of text: "The President"; endorsed by TJ as received 20 Aug. and "Warrants" and so recorded in SJL. FC (Lb in DNA: RG 45, LSP). Enclosures not found.

On 24 Aug., Abishai Thomas sent TJ a letter covering abstracts of Treasury war-

rants drawn by the Navy and War Departments for the week ending 22 Aug. (RC in DLC, in clerk's hand, signed by Thomas, at foot of text: "The President," endorsed by TJ as received from the Navy Department on 27 Aug. and "Warrants" and so recorded in SJL; FC in Lb in DNA: RG 45, LSP).

From John Dawson

MY DEAR SIR.   Paris August 18 1801.

My letters to the Secretary of State will give all the political information which I have, and what I deem it prudent to write.

I inclose to you a letter from Mr. Volney on a subject interesting to our country—had I funds I coud acquire Some things which woud be beneficial—that gentleman, and some others have been friendly and usefull—they remember you, who have many friends in this country.

With truth and Esteem Your freind   J DAWSON

RC (DLC); endorsed by TJ as received 5 Nov. and so recorded in SJL. Enclosure: Volney to Dawson, Paris, 19 Thermidor Year 9 [i.e. 7 Aug. 1801], about the potential importation of useful plants and animals from the Old World to the New; he recommends Corsican olive trees rather than those of Provençal as better suited to the Virginia climate; for the same reason he advises importing sheep directly from Spain rather than Spanish sheep bred in France, noting also that sheep from Spain would be pure-blooded; he praises the improvement of English horse breeds by the introduction of Arabian bloodlines, but recommends obtaining Arabian horses from the bedouins or other direct sources, such as Basra on the Persian Gulf, for horses from the plains of the Euphrates, or Syria; even more useful than horses would be donkeys, for the breeding of mules, with Malta producing the finest donkeys and Egypt the greatest quantity; he discounts the assertion of the Abbé Raynal, who claimed that an attempt to introduce camels in Florida failed—Raynal was an orator and a writer, Volney asserts, but he was not a historian; camels could be useful in the sandy regions of Virginia and the Carolinas, but it would be necessary to find a species resistant to cold and humidity, such as the Turkoman camel, with long hair and short legs, or the two-humped Bactrian camel of northern China; he suggests offering large bonuses to encourage the importation of useful plants and animals, or sending expeditions to find items of utility; how much better it would be if Magellan and Bougainville had sought practical products, such as camels, on their voyages rather than luxury goods; on a smaller scale, Volney also urges the importation to America of the nightingale, and that a new attempt be made to send American redbirds to France, which Franklin tried to do more than once without success (RC in same; in French).

Dawson had addressed letters to the SECRETARY OF STATE on 5 Aug., 25 June, and 27 May 1801. Those communications have not been found. In the one of 5 Aug., he stated that the French government had ratified the revised Convention of 1800, which William Vans Murray also reported in a dispatch to Madison on 3 Aug. 1801. Bonaparte approved the ratification on 31 July, accepting the eight-year limit on duration of the convention imposed by the U.S. Senate. He also agreed to expunge the second article, leaving the status of previous treaties between the United States and France unresolved but closing off indemnity claims. Dawson wrote private letters to Madison on 25 June and 5 Aug. in addition to his official communications to the State Department. Hinting that Murray may have been responsible for the delay in ratification, Dawson indicated that he would have more to say on that subject in person after his return. Dawson, who hoped to visit England before returning to the United States, forwarded the documents pertaining to the ratification of the convention (Madison, *Papers, Sec. of State Ser.*, 1:233, 350-1; 2:11-12, 17-18; Parry, *Consolidated Treaty Series*, 55:346-7, 369-70; Stephen Thorn to TJ, 19 Feb. 1801).

From Andrew Ellicott

DEAR SIR   Philadelphia August 18th. 1801

Immediately upon my return from the City of Washington I began the reduction of my Charts to a scale of 8 inches to a mile, which I find will be as small as they can be reduced, and at the same time retain all the waters, and the bends, or crooks of the rivers.—The Mississippi river, and the line will now make one map of about 6 feet, by 5., to which will be added a Chart of the coast of the gulf of Mexico, from the mouth of the Mississippi, to Fort St. Marks.—I have not yet spent less than 10 hours a day on this work, and have some hopes of rendering it sufficiently interesting to obtain a recompence from one, or other, of our Secretaries.—It will be accompanied with a discription of the navigable waters rising in the United States, and falling into the gulf of Mexico.—The whole will be completed about the beginning of October next if I should be so fortunate as to retain my health.—I can already see that west Florida, or that part of it which falls to his Catholic Majesty, will be a small narrow strip, and not worth holding upon any other principle than to cramp our trade on those rivers, which pass thro it into the gulf of Mexico, and consequently impede the settlement of our southern country, and this can only be prevented by our possessing the strip of country above mentioned.—

In speaking of west Florida, I would not be understood to comprehend the City of New Orleans, nor any of that tract which lies between the Mississippi, the bayou Manchac, and the lakes Merapaus and Pontchatrain, which has if my information be correct, been generally considered a part of Louisiana and held by France as such till exchanged with Spain after the peace of 1763—: Exclusive of that tract on which New Orleans stands, and which is an island at the time of every annual inundation his Catholic Majesty has no subjects east of the Mississippi, except those on the bank of that river, and in the towns of Mobile, and Pensacola:—with those exceptions the whole country does not afford ten Planters or Farmers; and yet for its protection the King of Spain is at the expence of paying, and supporting one regiment of infantry, four companies of artillery, and one company of dragoons!

His Catholic Majesty's holding east Florida is but of little consequence to our country at present, as none of its navigable waters rise within our limits:—And it is clearly my opinion, that it is our interest for New Orleans to remain with its present master for some years

to come.—I shall be more full on those points when I have the pleasure of shewing you the Chart.

Mr. Peale writes that he has obtained almost the whole of the skeleton of the Mamoth,—I suspect it will be found to be a variety of the
Elephant tribe,—a similarity is observed in many of their parts, particularly in their feet; but at the same time, some striking differences
may be seen,—such as in their grinders,—and the tusks of the non-
discript are much more curved than in the Elephant,—another essential difference is in the ribs, which in the non-discript stand like
sickles, with their broad surfaces in a contrary direction to that of all
other known animals, except in a variety of the Sloth.—

I have the honour to be with great esteem your friend and Hbl.
Servt.   ANDW; ELLICOTT.

RC (DLC); at foot of text: "Thos. Jef-
ferson President of the U.S. and of the
A.P.S."; endorsed by TJ as received 27
Aug. and so recorded in SJL.

The CHARTS were for Ellicott's record
of the southern boundary survey, published in 1803. In the finished work, the
maps of the Mississippi River and Gulf
Coast were printed at a SCALE of 15 miles
to an inch, and the charts of the boundary
were at one mile or one-half mile to the
inch, depending on the section of the
boundary (*The Journal of Andrew Ellicott, Late Commissioner on Behalf of the*

*United States during Part of the Year
1796, the Years 1797, 1798, 1799, and Part
of the Year 1800: for Determining the
Boundary between the United States and
the Possessions of His Catholic Majesty in
America* [Philadelphia, 1803]).

On 12 July, when Ellicott was in Washington, Charles Willson PEALE wrote to
inform him of Peale's acquisition of the
mastodon bones found at Shawangunk,
New York, and his intention to excavate
the remainder of the skeleton (Peale, *Papers*, v. 2, pt. 1:342-5; Peale to TJ, 29
June 1801).

From Albert Gallatin

DEAR SIR   City of Washington August 18th 1801

I am this moment favored with your letter of the 14th instt. & although I have little to add to mine of yesterday, will send a few lines
by Doctr. Bache.

I saw Clay last night; he spoke to me for the first time about office;
I threw some general hints about Consulship; but he at once told me
that he was not fond of commercial pursuits without which a place of
Consul could not be accepted; indeed that he was too obnoxious to
merchants, to hope any thing from that quarter—   I do not
know very well to whom to apply to fill the vacancy caused by Gen.
White's resignation. That business was, I think, perfectly correct,
but it was a transaction altogether of Mr Steele.—It will be very diffi-

cult to go on this summer at Norfolk & Charleston, in respect to the Marine hospitals, unless you permit the application of money from adjacent States. Yet I confess it as under the present system a very embarrassing subject.

It is very difficult to obtain a proper collector at Hampton & Mr Page had taken a long time to consider. In this & Savannah, it is very desirable that the places should be filled. They remain the only chasm in our present collectors-arrangement. *All* the other collectors to whom the circular was written have, rendered their accounts for 1800 except Mr Gerry of Marblehead to whom I have written a very pressing letter; & I have no doubt that hereafter we will make them settle regularly every quarter. The Supervisors of the Southern & Western States will be much more difficult to manage.

I dare say that Jonas Clark of Kennebunk is a federal; but you mistook my meaning. He is Collector & the commission he wanted is that of Inspector of revenue which in small ports Collectors ought to have in order to enable them to do certain duties in relation to distilled spirits. His not having it would not prevent his being collector but might injure the revenue, or interrupt commerce, there being no person to grant certificates of transportation.

Campbell wants to be restored. The Auditor turned him out because he had given the accounts of Dayton & others to Duane. He was 70 dollars in debt to Treasury which had been advanced to him beyond his wages for the purpose of defraying his expenses to Washington. He was sued for the money & Duane had to pay it. He has no employment. The Auditor appoints his own clerks. Can I or ought I to interfere in this case? Gardner who is in the same situation, except that he was not suspected & resigned was also desirous to be restored. His fitness to be a Choctaw agent is not known to me. Duane alone recommends him. I understood a clerk had been appointed by the War Depart. who has resigned & that has suggested the idea to Gardner to apply.

I do not understand on what ground you think that we are free to exclude the prizes of both French & English. That it is our policy cannot be doubted; but it seems to me that we are prevented from pursuing it by our treaties with both nations.

The report of a letter received by Fenwick was unfounded. We have none but flying reports from Egypt, & suggestions on the terms of peace with Portugal & its probable ratification. From Eaton's last dispatches, & O'Brian's letter announcing that the Dey of Algiers had written to Tripoli, I am apt to think that there will be no fighting in the Mediterranean, & that the sight of our Frigates will be sufficient to arrange matters there.

Wagner has been requested to forward for signature a pardon in the case of Hopkins. The city is rather sickly, my family has their share, & they are extremely anxious on that account to move on Capitol hill. I think it will be necessary to indulge them, & I do not foresee any inconvenience from it. It is substituting precisely 20 minutes ride to ten.

With sincere respect & attachment Your most obt. Servt.

ALBERT GALLATIN

RC (DLC); at foot of text: "The President of the United States"; endorsed by TJ as received 27 Aug. and so recorded in SJL. Enclosed in Gallatin to TJ, 24 Aug.

For the financial predicament of the MARINE HOSPITALS at Charleston and Norfolk, see Gallatin's first and second letters to TJ of 29 July. COLLECTORS TO WHOM THE CIRCULAR WAS WRITTEN: Gallatin probably referred to a letter, dated 9 June 1801, addressed to collectors who had "not rendered their quarterly accounts, with the regularity prescribed by Law and the regulations" of the Treasury Department. The only example of the circular found is that addressed to Robert Guerard, collector at Beaufort, South Carolina, whose last quarterly account extended through 30 Sep. 1800. Gallatin observed: "There can be no good reason given why that & similar delays have taken place. Officers appointed to enforce the laws should be particularly strict in obeying their instructions." The Treasury secretary concluded: "The President requires that hereafter a strict adherence to the regulations of rendering each quarterly account before the expiration of the next ensuing quarter, be observed indispensibly" (Gallatin, *Papers*, 5:117; in a clerk's hand,

signed by Gallatin). Neither a list of the collectors to whom the circular was sent nor Gallatin's PRESSING LETTER to Samuel R. Gerry has been found.

In May, Richard O'Brien, the American consul at ALGIERS, wrote William Loughton Smith in Lisbon to report that the dey of Algiers had sent "a very strong letter" to the bashaw of TRIPOLI. O'Brien hoped that war between the United States and Tripoli might be averted. Smith sent a copy of O'Brien's letter to the State Department on 30 June. Jacob Wagner received Smith's dispatch with its enclosure on 14 Aug. and forwarded them to Madison on the 17th, along with dispatches that William Eaton, the U.S. consul at Tunis, had written in April about the situation in the Mediterranean (Smith to the secretary of state, 30 June 1801, enclosing O'Brien to Smith, 24 May, in DNA: RG 59, DD; Madison, *Papers, Sec. of State Ser.*, 1:78-82, 104, 346, 365; 2:50, 52, 53n).

MOVE ON CAPITOL HILL: the Gallatin family moved to a house northeast of the Capitol on the road to Bladensburg. The location soon made Gallatin's residence a gathering place for congressmen (Raymond Walters, Jr., *Albert Gallatin: Jeffersonian Financier and Diplomat* [New York, 1957], 143).

From James Madison

Dear Sir   Aug: 18. 1801.

Inclosed herewith are several letters & papers for perusal. Among the former you are troubled with another from Thornton. You will observe that the Declaration of the Master of the British vessel carried into Boston, states only that the Prisoners were French Spanish Danish &c &c. without saying whether they were taken in the French service, or that of their respective countries. This circumstance, and the distinction between a prize of such a description and one made by a Ship of war or privateer, or even a letter of Marque, seem to admit an easy reply to Thornton, in general terms that the case is not considered as within the purview of the Treaty, but will be attended to on the principles applicable to it. What these may require deserve both enquiry & consideration. The Books which I have & have looked into take no specific notice of such a capture. In whatever light it be regarded, it cannot, if out of the stipulation in the British treaty, fall within that of the French either antient or recent. We seem to be free therefore to permit the vessel to continue or to order her away as may be expedient, unless the law of nations prescribe one or the other course, or the instructions of 1793. impose one or the other, on our consistency. The law of nations, as far as I recollect, prescribes nothing more than an equality in the Neutral towards the beligerent nations. The instructions of 1793. have the same object, as far as antecedent Treaties would allow. The question results, whether the late order for the departure of the Spanish prize, be not sufficiently analogous to require a like one in the present case, even if it be ascertained that the prize was made by French Prisoners only. Should this be your determination, and it be deemed of importance to avoid the delay of a week, you can drop a line to the Secretary of the Treasury, directing him to give the proper order to the Collector at Boston; or in case the delay be not of importance, I can on receiving your determination transmit it to Mr. G. by the ensuing mail. you will find under cover to Mr. Wagner an answer to the Danish Resident, which if approved you will please to forward.

We cannot yet fix the time which is to give us the pleasure of seeing Monticello. We have been in expectation of a visit from some of our distant friends which has not yet been executed, and we are without information when it will be, or whether it has been laid aside. It is probable we shall know more on the subject in a few days, and we shall then decide, having regard to your hint as to the periods observed by the Governour in dividing his time between Richmond & Albemarle.

Always & Affecty. yours

JAMES MADISON

RC (DLC); endorsed by TJ as received from the State Department on 20 Aug. and so recorded in SJL. Enclosures: (1) Edward Thornton to Madison, Philadelphia, 1 Aug., regarding the British snow *Windsor* and enclosing the declaration of William Jones, master, dated 13 July, describing events which led to the capture of his vessel by prisoners of war on board, including "Blacks and Whites, of whom as I believe some were French, some Swedes, some Dutch, Some Danes, some Spaniards and one American"; also enclosing Thomas MacDonogh, British consul in Boston, to Massachusetts Governor Caleb Strong, 13 July, calling upon the governor to enforce immediately the Jay Treaty provisions regarding prizes taken by an enemy and brought into British or American ports; and also enclosing Strong to MacDonogh, 14 July, stating that he knew of "no law of the United States or request of the Executive of the General Government that could justify" his "interference in the case" (Lb in DNA: RG 59, NL; Madison, *Papers, Sec. of State Ser.*, 2:5). (2) Madison to Peder Blicher Olsen, 15 Aug., assuring the Danish diplomat, who arrived in Washington just after TJ had left for Monticello, that the president would be back at the seat of government about 1 Oct. and ready to receive the letters Blicher Olsen wanted to present from Christian VII (Madison, *Papers, Sec. of State Ser.*, 2:44). Other enclosures not found.

In 1793, TJ, Alexander Hamilton, and the other members of Washington's cabinet framed a set of rules to stop infractions of American neutrality. In most respects the directives, which were issued in the form of INSTRUCTIONS to customs collectors, placed all "belligerent parties" on an equal footing. In accordance with the 1778 Treaty of Amity and Commerce with France, however, an exception to the regulations blocked ships that captured French prizes from U.S. ports, and treaties then in effect with France, the Netherlands, and Prussia allowed warships in distress to enter American harbors (Alexander DeConde, *Entangling Alliance: Politics & Diplomacy under George Washington* [Durham, N.C., 1958], 223-4; Syrett, *Hamilton*, 15:178-81; Madison, *Papers, Sec. of State Ser.*, 1:269; Vol. 26:608-10).

LATE ORDER FOR THE DEPARTURE OF THE SPANISH PRIZE: the armed Spanish vessel, *Santa Escolastica*, along with her British prize entered the Delaware River in late May and was permitted to land cargo at Philadelphia. Edward Thornton requested orders for the immediate exclusion of the vessel and its prize from American ports on the grounds that by the act of capturing an enemy vessel the ship had assumed the character of a privateer and was subject to the penalty of expulsion. TJ decided that the prize should not be able to continue within the United States. Thornton called for the departure of the *Santa Escolastica* as well, while the Spanish minister Carlos Martínez de Irujo claimed that the damaged vessel was eligible for safe harbor. The vessel was permitted to unload the American-owned cargo and to conduct nonmilitary repairs only (Madison, *Papers, Sec. of State Ser.*, 1:270, 271-2, 307, 328-9, 404-5).

From Wilson Cary Nicholas

DEAR SIR   Warren Aug. 18. 1801

I wish it was in my power to give you the information you want, as to a proper person for collector at the port of Hampton; there has been an entire change of inhabitants in that part of the country since I was there. the person that you mention I am unacquainted with. Col. George Booker of that neighbourhood, is the most influential republican in the County of E. City; I shou'd think his recommendation might be relied on; you may however with perfect safety confide the nomination of the collector to Mr. Samuel Shields of York county and to Mr. Booker, I have no doubt that a person that they wou'd concur in recommending wou'd be worthy of the trust, and I am sure they wou'd be much gratified by this evidence of your confidence in them. The enclosed was forwarded to me by my brother Norborne, I know nothing of Capt. Eddins except that he was a capt. of artillery in our army during the war with G. Britain.

I am Dear Sir with the greatest respect your hum. Serv.

WILSON C NICHOLAS

RC (DLC); endorsed by TJ as received 20 Aug. and so recorded in SJL. Enclosure: Samuel Eddins to Philip Norborne Nicholas, Richmond, 29 July 1801, seeking appointment as keeper of the lighthouse being constructed at Old Point Comfort, Virginia, and requesting Nicholas to intercede with his brother "to personally mention to the President whatever you can with propriety say in my favour" (RC in same).

PERSON THAT YOU MENTION: Mount Edward Chisman (TJ to Thomas Newton, 14 Aug.). GEORGE BOOKER, Samuel Sheild (SHIELDS), and Nicholas served together as members of the Republican coalition in the Virginia House of Delegates from 1797 through 1799 (Leonard, *General Assembly*, 207, 209, 211, 213, 215, 217; Richard R. Beeman, *The Old Dominion and the New Nation, 1788-1801* [Lexington, Ky., 1972], 262-3, 265).

In the enclosure described above, Samuel EDDINS explained his recent service in the army. Believing that the country was on the "eve of a War" and "being in some measure rather poor," he entered the "service, but with a determin'd resolution not to continue any longer than there appear'd to be a general Peace in our Country." In May 1798, Eddins received an appointment as a captain of the second regiment of artillerists and engineers and continued to serve into 1800 (Syrett, *Hamilton*, 23:494-5; 24:200-1, 241-2; JEP, 1:277). On 21 July 1801, Eddins wrote the president about the lighthouse appointment (recorded in SJL as received from Richmond on 24 July, but not found). On 28 July, Meriwether Jones also wrote TJ in favor of Eddins's appointment (letter now missing, but recorded in SJL as received 6 Aug. with notation "Eddins to keep lighthouse"). TJ probably had this letter in mind when he recommended Eddins for the position at Old Point Comfort in January 1803, noting that 18 months before he had received powerful recommendations in his favor (TJ to Gallatin, 13 Jan. 1803).

From Benjamin Stoddert

SIR   Geo Town 18 August 1801.

Knowing that the Comrs. of Washington, were about addressing you on a subject in which I have an Interest, I sent to them a letter, the copy of which I take the liberty to lay before you; as I find they had made up their dispatches before the rect. of the letter.

Mr White, the Comr. alluded to, as not Joining in the engagement to the State of Maryland, informs me, that I have mistated his motive for the refusal.—that it was not the apprehension of pecuniary loss, but a doubt of the power of the Comrs. to pledge the lots to the State, which with-held him.—Be it so—My object was to prove some little merit, & no crime in those, who notwithstanding such doubts would risk themselves to obtain money for the City, at a time when it could be got by no other means, and when it was known the necessary ac-comodations for the Govt could not be prepared without it.

I have the honor to be with great respect Sir Yr. most Obed Servt
                                             BEN STODDERT.

RC (DLC); endorsed by TJ as received 27 Aug. and so recorded in SJL. Enclosure: Stoddert to the "Commissioners of the City of Washington," 17 Aug., pointing out inaccuracies in their account sent to the president of payments made on notes given by Uriah Forrest for the purchase of lots, which included payments made by Stoddert of "something more than 1000 Drs."; these lots had previously been mortgaged by Robert Morris and John Nicholson to Stoddert, Forrest, and Gustavus Scott, and were purchased at public sale to prevent losing the debt due them by Morris and Nicholson and not "with views to speculation"; Stoddert also wishes it known to the president that Scott's estate owes more than one-third of the debt remaining on the notes, but that the trustees have yet to authorize the sale of any part of the estate; much of the property belonging to Forrest and Scott is bound to the state of Maryland for its loan of $50,000 to the commissioners, a loan of such risk that "one of the Comrs. equal to any in zeal for the advancement of the City, refused to be a party in it"; Stoddert

claims that considerable sums have already been paid to the commissioners as payments on the Maryland loan, but that "little or none of it, has been so applied"; Stoddert cannot sell his lots because they are tied up in the Maryland loan and he questions the justice of directing "coercive measures to enforce payment from persons circumstanced as the Debtors in these notes are"; if the lots bound to Maryland were released for sale, Stoddert believes that all of the debt would be repaid within one month except that due from Scott's estate; in the meantime Stoddert will work to pay "every dollar in which I have any concern" and reminds the commissioners that he has already caused around $17,000 to be paid them, almost one half of it on account of Forrest's notes, and that the remainder is not due for another eight months (Tr in same; in Stoddert's hand).

ADDRESSING YOU ON A SUBJECT: District of Columbia Commissioners to TJ, 17 Aug.

From John Drayton

South Carolina
Charleston Augt: 20th: 1801.

Sir.

I have the honor to inform you, that on Sunday last, the Spanish Consul presented & introduced to me, Citizen Simon Jude Chancognie; as Agent of the Commissary General's Department of Commercial Relations, on the part of the French Republic, to this State. The Citizen at the same time presented me, Credentials from Citizen Pichon; copies of which are enclosed, regularly certified under the Seal of this State.   I enquired of him, whether he had any recognition from you; his answer was, no.

Thus circumstanced, I felt myself rather unpleasantly situated: for, while on the one side, I was desirous of respecting a public Functionary from the French Republic; on the other side, I was fearful that by acknowleging him as Agent, I should unintentionally interfere, with those powers, which the Constitution of the United States, has particularly vested in you.   From this dilemma, however, I was some what releaved, by recurring to your letter of the 17th. June: by which you inform me, that "Mr Pichon" was the successor of Mr Le Tombe: and "tho' we have no reason to doubt his immediate attention to the subject, yet it may not be amiss to urge the French Consul (or Commercial Agent) at Charleston at proper times, to hasten their discharge."

As we have been at variance, with the French Government lately, I was unwilling to throw cold water, on this first re-commencement of friendship: & I therefore have recognized the said Agent; as appears by my proclamation enclosed.   In this, I hope, I have acted for the best: but, I should be happy to be honored with your opinion respecting it; as well as respecting any future occasions of the kind, which may occur. And request I may be informed, in what cases, I am to wait for your recognition of Public Functionaries to the United States, before, I shall receive or know them here as such.

In consequence of my recognizing the said Agent, I forthwith commenced a correspondence with him, respecting the french prisoners; concerning whom, I had the honor of writing you.   And, I beg leave to enclose to you, so much of the Correspondence, as has already taken place.   I should be glad to know, in what manner, the expences of the said prisoners are to be defrayed: whether by the United States, or the French Republic. For as they were brought in here in a prize, to one of the United States vessels of war, it is a national business altogether: and one, in which this State has only taken apart, to forward, the more extensive operations of the Union—

I avail myself of this opportunity to assure you, that I shall at all times be happy to arrange any matters of public concern in this part of the Union, which you may think proper to refer to me. And, that with sentiments of high respect and consideration I have the honor to be

Sir Yr: most Obt: Sevt. JOHN DRAYTON.

RC (DLC); at foot of text: "Thomas Jefferson Esq. President of the United States of America"; endorsed by TJ as received 10 Sep. and so recorded in SJL. Enclosures not found, but see below.

SPANISH CONSUL: Diego Morphy (*Nelson's Charleston Directory, and Strangers Guide, for the Year of Our Lord, 1801* [Charleston, 1800], 99).

SIMON JUDE CHANCOGNIE was commissioned "*Agent du Commissariat*

Général" at Charleston by Louis André Pichon on 1 July. On 17 Aug., Drayton issued a PROCLAMATION recognizing Chancognie's appointment (Madison, *Papers, Sec. of State Ser.*, 1:450, 451n; Charleston *City Gazette and Daily Advertiser,* 18 Aug. 1801).

For previous correspondence regarding the FRENCH PRISONERS at Charleston, see Drayton to TJ, 21 May, 29 July 1801; TJ to Drayton, 17 June 1801.

From Enoch Edwards

DEAR SIR— Frankford 20 Augt. 1801

Since the Receipt of your last favor I have delayed Mr: Hanse all I could in the finishing of your Carriage. as I prefered its being in his hands untill near the Time of your return, it may now however be sent for, as soon as you please—in Order that you may receive it spotless, & beautiful as it really now is, I shall direct the outside cover to be tacked under in a way to prevent the Eyes & the Fingers of the curious from doing it an Injury, on it's Journey—the Harness must be put up neatly in coarse Canvass—& confined by Straps at the Bottom within so as nothing must be sullied—you will see therefore the Necessity—of old Harness being sent with the Horses or purchased here to take it to the federal City—

A Friend of mine at N York has made the Enquiry you suggested of Mr: Savage—he has a Portrait of Mr: Samuel Adams. unfinished and for sale. the price when done will be one hundred Dollars. he will complete it immediately on being contracted for. I will attend to, & have executed any further Direction about this you will please to give—

I wish you may not be deceived about the Expence of your Turnpike at Washington—We are about geting one on foot from Philada.

to Trenton—and we do not calculate its costing less than four thousand dollars pr: mile. altho' to run on the bed of the old Road made to our hands near a century past. & the Bridges already built. it is a disagreable Reflection to think how prone all Undertakers are to make Jobs out of every thing entreprised by the public—

My next will contain an Answer about the Landau, I have not been too feirce with Mr: Hanse about it—let Us see the End of this, & then as you say I should like him to *tempt* Us instead of we him—

I will examine the Bill for you before it is forwarded—

With the greatest Respect I am your obedt Sevt.

ENO. EDWARDS

RC (DLC); addressed: "Thomas Jefferson President of the United States—Monticello Virginia"; franked; postmarked 21 Aug.; endorsed by TJ as received 27 Aug. and so recorded in SJL.

LAST FAVOR: TJ to Edwards, 9 July.
In an undated note to Edwards, Conrad Hanse estimated the cost of a LANDAU, or, "a dubble body with a Top to fall Each way," at $220, plus $120 for plating, and cautioned, "I dont think it will due to hang Such a body on the Chariot Carriage as the front Springs Stand three or four Inchis Closer then the Hind wons due there for it wont hang well with out the Body is made on a Taper that is wider be Hind than be fore" (MS in DLC: TJ Papers, 116:19942; entirely in Hanse's hand).

To Henry Dearborn

DEAR SIR   Monticello Aug. 21. 1801.

I think I once before sent you an application from the same person from whom the inclosed is, with some notes on the subject of his application to me before the 4th. of March. his recollection of a promise *on my word & honour*, is a proof that he recollects too much with those who know me. a much greater occasion would have been requisite to draw such a pledge from me. I do not recollect the particulars of what passed, but in giving the impressions of my mind at that day, I shall give limits out of which I could not have gone. I was & am impressed with the expediency of having a good stock of arms: but what the stock was at that time was unknown to me. I may have given assurance that contracts should be fulfilled; that as to what were wanting those who worked well might expect to be employed, and perhaps I may have found his musket well made: I do not remember: but as to any thing like a *specific promise*, that is impossible. in consideration however that these people *say* they have recieved encouragement from me personally, I would only wish that so far as they offer good arms & it is expedient for the public to take them, they may have a preference over those who have no better grounds of claim: and this merely lest I should have used any expression which they have given greater extent to than was intended. I will ask the favor of you to drop them a line, ascertaining what they may expect.—I wrote you on the 14th. inst.   Accept assurances of my affectionate esteem & high respect.   TH: JEFFERSON

RC (MB); at foot of text: "The Secretary at War." PrC (DLC). Enclosure: Amos Stillman and Ethan Stillman to TJ, 4 Aug. 1801, not found, but recorded in SJL as received from Farmington on 20 Aug.

A letter from Amos Stillman to TJ of 2 June 1801, which is recorded in SJL as received on 8 June but has not been found, apparently involved an APPLICATION to extend a contract granted to Stillman and his brother Ethan during the Adams administration for the fabrication of muskets at their forge in Farmington, Connecticut. In September 1801, before Dearborn could write to the Stillmans, they delivered 100 guns to the U.S. arsenal at Springfield, Massachusetts, citing

"verbal authority" from the president. Conceding "all reasonable indulgence," Dearborn authorized them to make more guns. He told them, however, that TJ's "recollection of the circumstances of your conversation with him at the seat of Government will not justify so great an extension of your Contract as you wish to take," and in 1802 he stopped extending their contract (Amos and Ethan Stillman to the War Department, 23 Sep. 1801, 29 Mch., 9 June 1802, DNA: RG 107, RLRMS; Dearborn to the Stillmans, 19 Oct. 1801, 16 June, 12 Aug. 1802, DNA: RG 107, MLS; Arcadi Gluckman, *United States Muskets, Rifles and Carbines* [Harrisburg, Penn., 1959], 77, 112; Christopher P. Bickford, *Farmington in Connecticut* [Canaan, N.H., 1982], 230).

To Albert Gallatin

DEAR SIR   Monticello Aug. 21. 1801.

Your favors of the 15th. & 17th. are recieved. you will find an approbation signed at the foot of mr Millar's letter. all the papers inclosed to me, are re-inclosed except the list of warrants.—I do not with very great certainty recollect the particulars as to Genl. Herd. but I think we at first intended him the place afterwards given to Lynn: that it was after that suggested he would accept the Marshal's office, & some of us at least thought it fortunate. but I do not remember that it was decided finally. as far as I see of the matter I should approve of his appointment; but I rather think it was concluded there should be no more removals till we should meet again. this is still my opinion; for however this gradual proceeding may in some respects be disagreeable, yet I have no doubt it offers greater advantage than evil. on this ground, as well as that specially noted in a former letter, nothing should be immediately done in S. Carolina. the Dunwooddy Secretary stands on a mass of family interest not to be thought little of. we should make a great many enemies for one friend. I sincerely wish judge Burke could be fully impressed with the fatal consequences of a division on the election of a Senator for S.C.—I like much the idea of giving Clay the consulship of Lisbon. I deem it the most important consulship in our gift. I will write to mr Madison on the subject & ask his opinion.—the letter of Fish is certainly not to be answered. the answer to N. Haven was called for by great motives: but it must not lead us into the lists with every individual. we have nothing to fear from Fish's publication. I presume somebody will answer him for us, by reminding him of his carrying his official influence into elections &c. accept assurances of my affectionate esteem & high consideration.

TH: JEFFERSON

RC (NHi: Gallatin Papers); at foot of text: "The Secretary of the Treasury."; endorsed by Gallatin. PrC (DLC).

For TJ's APPROBATION of the selection of Abishai Woodward to construct a lighthouse on Falkner Island, see the enclosure described at Gallatin to TJ, 15 Aug. 1801. John Heard (HERD) was designated to be the collector at Perth Amboy, but Daniel Marsh, not James Linn, AFTERWARDS received the appointment (see Notes on New Jersey Patronage, printed at 5 Mch. 1801). FORMER LETTER: see TJ to Gallatin, 7 Aug.

DUNWOODDY SECRETARY: identified by Gallatin as William Jackson (see Enclosure No. 3, listed at Gallatin to TJ, 17 Aug.). Philadelphia Federalists regularly held their meetings at Dunwoody's tavern (*Philadelphia Gazette*, 28 July 1800; *Gazette of the United States*, 29 July, 7 Aug., 24 Sep., 7 Oct., 5 Nov. 1800, 7 Oct. 1801; Philadelphia *Aurora*, 10, 17 Nov. 1800). MASS OF FAMILY INTEREST: Jackson was married to Elizabeth Willing, daughter of Philadelphia merchant and banker Thomas Willing. Her sisters, Anne, Mary, Dorothy, and Abigail, married William Bingham, Henry Clymer, Thomas Willing Francis, and Richard Peters, respectively (ANB; Alberts, *Golden Voyage*, 360). For the DIVISION in Republican ranks ON THE ELECTION OF A SENATOR in South Carolina, see Enclosure No. 2, listed at Gallatin to TJ, 17 Aug.

To George Jefferson

DEAR SIR   Monticello Aug. 21. 1801

Your's of the 17th came to hand yesterday. there being little prospect of recovering my cask of white sugar & coffee (which contained 15 loaves of sugar & 60. ℔ coffee) or at any rate in time for my use here, I must ask the favor of you to send me by the first boats 8. loaves of single refined sugar, and 30. ℔ coffee; to which be pleased to add a cask of about 50. ℔ of good gunpowder.— I am in hourly hopes of recieving the porter & syrop of punch &c. given you in memorandum when here. we are all well, except as to the Cowpox which is going on well also, and unequivocal as to it's genuineness. we have about 25. of my family now under the disease. a little fever, headache, kernels under the arm, take place in those who have [it wo]rst. some have no complaint but the inoculated pustule. accept assurances of my affectionate esteem & attachment.   TH: JEFFERSON

PrC (MHi); faint; at foot of text: "Mr. George Jefferson"; endorsed by TJ in ink on verso.

For the articles ordered in the MEMO-RANDUM (not found), see George Jefferson to TJ, 24 Aug.

From Samuel Quarrier

RESPECTED SIR   City of Washington, Augt. 21st. 1801—
    I hope You'l Excuse me for thus intruedeing on You this Second Letter as it arises intirely from A Report that's circulated in this place of Your beeing taken[1] exstreemly ill on Your Way to Monticello, insomuch that You Where not abel to proseede at all on Your Way, in traceing the fabricated Report I found it Came from Docr. Wiemes of George town, Ive made frequent enquirey's to find out the truth of the Report, but had the agreeable Satisfaction to understand that You'd arived at Your seat in good health—Believe me Sir it's one of the first Wishes of my life to heere of your health and happiness, not only mine but the wish of Millions—
    Receive dear Sir my best Wishes for Your prosperity and every other blessing this life affords, Respectfully

SAML. QUARRIER

RC (DLC); at head of text: "Thomas Jefferson Esqre. President of the United States"; endorsed by TJ as received 3 Sep. and so recorded in SJL.

Samuel Quarrier was one of thirteen children of Alexander Quarrier who survived to adulthood. In 1811, when Alexander Quarrier relocated from Richmond to the Kanawha Valley, his offspring moved west with him (Jim Comstock,

ed., *West Virginia Heritage Encyclopedia: Supplemental Series*, 25 vols. [Richwood, W. Va., 1974], 4:79; 21:41).
    For Quarrier's earlier LETTER, see TJ to Henry Dearborn, 14 Aug.
    DOCR. WIEMES: John Weems was a physician in Georgetown (Bryan, *National Capital*, 1:324n).

[1] MS: "takeinging."

To Samuel Sheild

SIR   Monticello Aug. 21. 1801.
    A collector for the port of Hampton is wanting in the room of a mr Kerby, removed for delinquency. a person of the name of Mount E. Chisman has been recommended. can you favor me with his character, or recommend any person more fit? you will much oblige me in

doing so; fully & freely, under an assurance that no use shall be made of it which shall bring you into question. indeed I must even ask that nothing may be said of this application to you; because it is possible the case may have been so pressing as to have obliged the Secretary of the Treasury to make the appointment, and in that case I would not chuse that false hopes should have been excited in others. this will also apologize for my asking the favor of an answer by return of post, addressed to this place. accept assurances of my perfect respect & consideration.

Th: Jefferson

RC (CSmH: Brock Collection); addressed: "Colo. Samuel Shields of York County near Williamsburg"; franked and postmarked. PrC (MHi); endorsed by TJ in ink of verso.

Probably the clergyman and planter Samuel Sheild (d. 1803), a Republican who represented York County in the Virginia House of Delegates for eight terms between 1794 and his death (Madison, *Papers, Sec. of State Ser.*, 3:518; Leonard, *General Assembly*, 197, 201, 209, 213, 217, 221, 225, 229; Richard R. Beeman, *The Old Dominion and the New Nation, 1788-1801* [Lexington, Ky., 1972], 265).

TJ sent a similarly worded communication to George Booker on this date (PrC in DLC; at foot of text: "Colo George Booker; endorsed by TJ in ink on verso). Booker, a planter, represented Elizabeth City County in the Virginia House of Delegates for a number of terms beginning in 1782 and continuously from 1797 through 1804. Booker's response of 29 Aug., recorded in SJL as received from "Backriver" on 3 Sep., has not been found (Leonard, *General Assembly*, 145, 149, 160, 164, 168, 175, 179, 183, 187, 207, 211, 215, 219, 223, 227, 231; Beeman, *Old Dominion*, 263).

To Benjamin Waterhouse

Dear Sir   Monticello Aug. 21. 1801.

I had the pleasure of informing you on the 14th. inst. that I supposed the inoculation of the kine pox to have taken effect in two subjects. these were from the matter you were kind enough to send July 24. that of July 26. succeeded with 2. others. that of Aug. 1. with 4. on the 16th. inst. we inoculated from the 2. first subjects 15. others, 14. of whom very evidently have the infection, so that we have 20. now of my family on whom the disease has taken, besides some recent inoculations. some of them have slight fevers, headache, kernels under the arms, & one only has a very sore arm. most however experience no inconvenience; and have nothing but the inoculated pustule, well defined, moderately[1] filled with matter, & hollow in the center. I have this day impregnated some thread, & half a dozen toothpicks, which I forward to Doctr. Gantt, who writes me that his inoculations all failed. Doctr. Wardlaw of this neighborhood has so much other business that he has been able to be with us only twice. however I expect that the extent of my experiment will encourage the neighborhood generally to engage him to introduce it in their families. to you they will be indebted for it, and I am sure they will be sensible of the obligation. accept assurances of my great esteem & respect. TH: JEFFERSON

RC (MBCo); at foot of text: "Doctr. Benjamin Waterhouse." PrC (DLC).

I FORWARD TO DOCTR. GANTT: in a letter to Edward Gantt of the same day, TJ acknowledged receipt of Gantt's letter of 17 Aug. and gave a similar report on smallpox vaccination at Monticello, adding to his description of an "inoculated pustule" that it had a "narrow margin of inflammation." TJ continued, "I send you herewith a vial in which are a needle & thread which have been drawn through a pustule in a proper state & the thread well moistened with the fluid, as also half a dozen toothpicks, the point of each of which was stuck into the pustule, turned around in the matter, & then suffered to remain in the open [air] about 5 minutes to dry before they were put into the vial." TJ closed the letter, "I will send fresh matter again tomorrow week" (PrC in DLC; faint; at foot of text: "Doctr. Edward Gantt").

[1] Word interlined.

From William Dunbar

DEAR SIR   Natchez 22d August 1801

I have delayed untill the present moment acknowledging the honor of your letter of the 12th Jan. last, from a conviction of the impropriety of all trivial intrusion upon your time, always precious, but now dedicated to duties of the highest importance. However anxious I may be to express a due sense of your condescension, I shall ever guard myself against so impardonable an error. I shall therefore confine my communications solely to such objects as you have been pleased to introduce into our correspondence and such matters as have naturally sprung from them.

By the present occasion I have the honor of transmitting you a monthly recapitulation of meteorological Observations for the year 1800; to which I have subjoined remarks calculated to convey some idea of the nature of our climate.—I have also attended to a hint dropt in one of your letters respecting the Missisippi, by preparing a short account of that river, but my copist having fallen sick, I am obliged to defer transmitting it untill next post.

I have some time since received notices of fossil bones discovered to the west of the Missisippi, and lately an intelligent french Gentleman, Commandant of the Opelousas, informs me, that at three different places of that Country, bones have been found which are supposed to resemble those of the big-bone-lick near the Ohio, and at another place he is well assured that in digging a well, a set of human teeth (la denture d'un homme) have been found at the depth of 30 or 35 feet. I have recommended to that Gentleman to set on foot a diligent investigation of those objects and if practicable to transmit me specimens of the bones, particularly a jawbone with its included teeth as little mutilated as possible. Shou'd I prove so fortunate as to acquire the possession of any object worthy the attention of the Society, I shall take an early opportunity of presenting it. Mr. Nolan has formerly given me some intimation of fossil bones of great magnitude being found in various parts of new Mexico, but we have lately been cut off from our usual communication with that country by the imprudence of Mr. Nolan who persisted in hunting wild horses without a regular permission; the consequence of which has been, that a party being sent against him, he was the only man of his company who was killed by a random shot.—I am much concerned for the loss of this man. Altho' his excentricities were many and great, yet he was not destitute of romantic principles of honor united to the highest personal courage, with energy of mind not sufficiently cultivated by education, but which under the guidance of a little more prudence might have conducted him to enterprises of the first magnitude. We hope the usual intercourse will be renewed, and I shall endeavour to prosecute our researches into the western continent.

I have received some imperfect account from Mr. Nolan and his man who instructed us in the signs, of an uncommon Animal having been seen by the Natives in a considerable lake in a sequestered situation in New Mexico. It is compared when somewhat elevated in the water, to the upper part of the body of a Spaniard with his broad brimmed hat, & that it is often hear'd to breathe or blow heavily. The Indians who are often superstitious express a dislike or abhorrence of the place, seldom going near it, and assert that the departed spirits of the first Spaniards who conquered their Country dwell in the lake. Mr. Nolan informed me that he was once very near that lake, but knew nothing of it untill some time after, when he was told the above circumstances. Whether we are to suppose this a fable invented by the Indians—or that there really exists an Animal, perhaps the hippopotamus or a non-descript, will remain the discovery of a future time.

In my last I gave you an extract from an old book in my possession, containing Dor. Hooks scheme of a telegraph in the year 1684, wondering that the invention of their country man had not been claimed by the English, but I now find I have been anticipated in that communication by a paper in the 1st. Vol. of the Philosophical Magazine p. 312 London.

Your observation of a Lunar rain-bow is entirely new to me, but I have often observed a Phœnomenon which seems to have been overlooked by Philosophers; it is slightly noticed in Brydone's tour through Sicily and Malta Vol. 1. p. 356 2d Edit. London. This curious and beautiful phœnomenon may be seen every fine summer's evening in this and perhaps in all other countries, where serenity is united to a cloudless sky. It is caused by the prismatic effect of the atmosphere upon the sun's departing rays. Soon after sun-set a belt of a yellowish orange color is seen to extend itself along the eastern horizon; this belt ascends in the same proportion as the sun descends, being about one degree in breadth; in contact with the first appears a second belt below, of a dark blue color & about the same breadth as the first, both belts being tollerably well defined and of an uniform color throughout: when the double belt has risen a little above the horizon, the azure sky may be seen below, and as they continue to ascend the belts become fainter, untill at length the prismatic rays meeting with no vapors sufficiently dense to reflect their colors, the whole phœnomenon disolves into pale celestial light; the belts disappear at about 6 or 7° of altitude. This phœnomenon merits some attention; it exhibits as upon a skreen that species of light, which after a greater angular dispersion, arriving at the moon's orbit, faintly illumines her disk during the time of a total eclipse.

It would seem to result from the above appearances, that if a prism were formed of atmospheric air, the solar ray wou'd be separated thereby into two colors only, a yellow orange and a blue: it is known to Opticians that the compound Color of orange and yellow and the color which Newton calls indigo, comprise within themselves the seven primitive colors, that is, united they ought to form White. we ought not therefore to reject this effect of atmospheric air, because dissimilar to the prismatic powers of such diaphanous bodies as are best known to us: modern experiments have shewn that refracting bodies possess very different dispersive powers; and when we reflect upon the heterogeneous nature of our atmosphere, composed of at least three permanently elastic fluids, with the adventitious mixture of perhaps a hundred others, subject from chemical afinity to perpetual resolution and composition, disolving at all times a great proportion of aqueous fluid, and the whole pervaded by the electric fluid; shall we then presume to doubt that Nature has it in her power to compose a refracting body, whose dispersive powers are equal with respect to the red, orange, yellow & green making rays, and tho' greater with regard to the three remaining primitive colors yet perfectly equal among themselves.

I have the honor to be with the highest respect and consideration Your most humble and most Obedient Servant

WILLIAM DUNBAR

RC (DLC); with square brackets added to enclose two passages, one consisting of the second paragraph and the beginning of the third paragraph through "various parts of New Mexico," and the other containing the two paragraphs beginning "Your observation of a Lunar rain-bow," those passages appearing as an extract of the letter in APS, *Transactions*, 6 [1809], 40-2; endorsed by TJ as received 8 Oct. and so recorded in SJL. Enclosure: "Monthly Recapitulation" of Dunbar's observations of temperature, barometric pressure, and rainfall during 1800, consisting of a table supplemented by remarks about each month and general remarks; submitted to the American Philosophical Society, 18 Dec. 1801, and referred to Robert Patterson and James Woodhouse, who on 16 Apr. 1802 reported the paper worthy of publication; printed in the Society's *Transactions* (APS, *Proceedings*, 22, pt. 3 [1884], 319, 323; APS, *Transactions*, 6 [1809], 43-55).

For Dunbar's SHORT ACCOUNT of the Mississippi River, see Vol. 31:138 and Vol. 32:54-5.

Martin Milony Duralde sent Dunbar a description of various FOSSIL BONES found in the Opelousas area. The account, written in French, was presented to the APS on 4 Mch. 1803. The society published an abstract in English. Duralde, a Basque by birth, had lived in the Opelousas district since at least the early

1780s, and he became the military commandant there in 1795. One of his daughters married W. C. C. Claiborne in 1806 (APS, *Proceedings*, 22, pt. 3 [1884], 334-5, 339; APS, *Transactions*, 6 [1809], 55-8; Glenn R. Conrad, ed., *A Dictionary of Louisiana Biography*, 2 vols. [New Orleans, 1988], 1:273; Jack D. L. Holmes, "Martin Duralde Observes Louisiana in 1802," *Revue de Louisiane*, 9 [1980], 69-84; ANB).

INSTRUCTED US IN THE SIGNS: an associate of Philip Nolan had been the source of information about a sign language that Dunbar sent to TJ in 1800 and TJ conveyed to the APS. Nolan was killed while gathering horses in Texas in March 1801 (Vol. 30:425-6n; Vol. 32:35-7).

Among other papers that Dunbar sent to TJ on 14 July 1800 was an account he had found of a TELEGRAPH invented by Robert Hooke. The APS declined to publish the description, since it had already appeared in print and was mentioned in a history of the Royal Society (APS, *Transactions*, 6 [1809], 25n; Vol. 32:55n).

In his letter of 12 Jan. 1801, TJ reported seeing LUNAR rainbows (Vol. 32:449). Patrick Brydone had briefly described seeing, at MALTA, the eastern sky filled with "a fine deep purple" after sunset (Patrick Brydone, *A Tour through Sicily and Malta*, new ed., 2 vols. [London, 1790], 1:356-7).

To James Madison

DEAR SIR   Monticello Aug. 22. 1801.

Your's of the 18th. is recieved, and I now return all the papers which accompanied it, (except those in Bingham's case) and also the papers inclosed in that of the 16th.—The case of the British Snow Windsor taken by the prisoners she was carrying & brought into Boston is new in some circumstances. yet I think she must fairly be considered as a prize made on Great Britain, to which no shelter or

refuge is to be given in our ports, according to our treaty. a vessel may
be made prize of by persons attacking from another vessel, or from
the shore, or from within itself. it is true the masters declaration is
that the prisoners were French, Swedes, Dutch, Danes, Spaniards &
one American, without saying in the French service; but the French,
Dutch & Spaniards were enemies, and the others must have been in
enemy's service or they were pirates. the case of the Spanish prize
sent away may be urged on us, & I see no reason why we should attempt an exception to the general rule for this singular & small description of cases. I hardly imagine Pichon will object to it, further
than to strengthen the force of a precedent which is in the long run to
be so much in favor of France & Spain, who are captured ten times
where they are once captors. still, wishing you to revise this opinion
of mine, I refer it back to yourself to give the order for departure, or
any other answer you think best.—Toussaint's offence at our sending
no letters of credence with mr Lear is not regular. such letters are
never sent with a Consul, nor to a subordinate officer. the latter point,
I doubt not, is that of the offence.—Poinsette's application requires
attention as a precedent. a frigate is going on public service. we give
a passage to our own minister & his suite. that is in rule. a French
chargé (Le Tombe) asks a passage. he is allowed it with the consent
of mr Livingston. this too is in rule as a matter of comity, and a return
for similar civilities from that nation. in 1782-3. I was to have gone in
the Romulus, on the offer of the French minister. they actually went
to the expence of building a round house for my sole accomodation.
but have we a right to give passages generally to private individuals
whenever a public vessel is passing from one place to another? what
would the public vessels become in that case? it is true I have given
Thomas Paine a passage in the Maryland: but there is a clear enough
line between Thomas Paine & citizens in general. if mr Poinsette
could get mr Livingston to recieve him as one of his suite, there
would be no inconvenience in the precedent. these are my hasty
thoughts on the subject. be so good as to weigh & correct them, & do
in it what you think right.—do you know if mr Dallas has commenced another prosecution against Duane on behalf of the Senate?
either this should be done, or an official opinion given against it. perhaps it would be best to do it, & leave to juries & judges to decide
against it's being sustainable.—what would you think of Clay of
Philadelphia for the Consulship of Lisbon? it has been suggested that
he might perhaps accept it. we cannot expect a man of better talents.
if you have no reason in opposition to it, I will have it proposed to
him privately through the channel which suggested it.—is it not wor-

thy of consideration whether we should not, through mr Livingston, propose to Prussia to exchange the new articles inserted in our late treaty for the old ones of the former omitted in it? the change was excessively against her will, & places us in a disgraceful position as to interesting principles of public law.—there is a Charles D. Coxe (brother in law of Tenche) so well recommended for a Consulship that I wish he could be gratified.—Bingham's case shall be the subject of the next letter. respect & attachment to mrs Madison & miss Payne; affectionate friendship to yourself.   TH: JEFFERSON

RC (DLC: Madison Papers); at foot of first page: "The Secretary of State." PrC (DLC).

For BINGHAM'S CASE, see TJ to Levi Lincoln, 28 Aug.

MASTERS DECLARATION: see Enclosure No. 1, listed at Madison to TJ, 18 Aug.

TOUSSAINT'S OFFENCE: the July 1801 constitution for Saint-Domingue made Toussaint-Louverture governor for life. When Tobias Lear arrived on the island that month, Toussaint initially refused to look at Lear's commission as U.S. commercial agent. Taking offense that TJ had not formally addressed him as head of state, the governor said "that his Colour was the cause of his being neglected, and not thought worthy of the Usual attentions." Lear convinced Toussaint that his mission did not require a formal letter of credence from the president, and the governor then received Lear with the appropriate protections in the execution of his office (National Intelligencer, 12 Aug. 1801; Madison, Papers, Sec. of State Ser., 1:243-4, 427-8; Ray Brighton, The Checkered Career of Tobias Lear

[Portsmouth, N.H., 1985], 183; Lear to TJ, 25 July 1801).

In the winter of 1782-83, TJ accepted from French minister La Luzerne an offer of transport on the frigate ROMULUS, bound for France where TJ was to assume ministerial duties. Ice in the Baltimore port postponed his departure, which was later canceled altogether when news reached Congress that the provisional treaty of peace had already been ratified (Vol. 6:210-11).

TJ extended an offer to THOMAS PAINE of return passage from France on the Maryland (which Paine declined), but the offer to a private citizen of the use of a public vessel spurred an outcry in the Federalist press (Jerry W. Knudson, Jefferson and the Press [Columbia, S.C., 2006], 68-74; Vol. 32:185, 191; TJ to Paine, 18 Mch. 1801, and Paine to TJ, 9 June).

For Joel Roberts Poinsett's APPLICATION for passage to France with Robert R. Livingston, see Poinsett to TJ, 24 July.

ANOTHER PROSECUTION AGAINST DUANE ON BEHALF OF THE SENATE: see TJ to William Duane, 23 May 1801, and Madison to TJ, on or before 17 July.

From Thomas Newton

DR SIR   Norfolk 22 Augt 1801

Your favor of the 14th I recd. yesterday afternoon, being unacquainted with a proper person to fill the place of Mr Kirby, I applyd to Capt. Robt. Baron, who informd me that mr David Brodie living there, Hampton[1] was a man fitting for the place, mr Brodie I have often noticed as a serious steady man, & from Mr. Barons assurance believe him to be a good man for the purpose. Mr Chisman I know not. I pray you command me whenever you think proper, it will give me pleasure to serve you & the public & be assured, that I shall be faithful in any trust reposed in me, I have my Countrys good at heart & am the same now as in 1776 I am respectfully Yr.

T NEWTON

RC (DLC); endorsed by TJ as received 27 Aug. and so recorded in SJL with notation "David Brodie to office." Probably enclosed in letter below.

Robert Barron (BARON), an officer in the Virginia navy during the American Revolution, was a member of the Norfolk common council for several years. In 1792, he expressed interest in becoming the lighthouse keeper at Cape Henry, Virginia. After the death of Mount E. Chisman in 1804, Newton again recommended DAVID BRODIE for the collectorship at Hampton, and he received the appointment (Washington, *Papers, Pres. Ser.*, 11:164-5; Gallatin, *Papers*, 9:942; JEP, 1:471).

¹ Word interlined.

From Thomas Newton

DR SIR   Augt 22. 1801

The post just going off and appearances of the seal being rather suspicious of having been opend I have inclosed it; this place at present is remarkably healthy, the frequent thunder & rains I believe in a great measure contributes to it. we have no late arivals therefore no news from Europe, the trade is dull & I think will continue for some time, freights are much falling & provisions not worth sending from this to any market. accept my best wishes   THOS NEWTON

RC (DLC); endorsed by TJ as received 27 Aug. and so recorded in SJL. Enclosure: probably Newton's letter printed above.

From John Barnes

SIR   Geo: Town 24th. Augt 1801—

Mr Andrews after two Messages—sent his Assistant to inform me, the ornaments were securely packed up. in one large Case & 3. middle size Boxes. I prevailed with him to go with them—that very Eveng. (Friday.) or early next morning from the point—to Alexandria in order—if possible—to meet Mr. Wanscher who perhaps had not yet left that port, or—in Case he had left it, to see them shipped on board: the 1st. vessel bound to Norfolk or Richmond. I made out two Bills Lading for that purpose—and addressed them, to Messrs.

G. & J. leaving the Blank parts to be filled up—for the Vessel & masters names—to return me One of them—and to make his report to me immediately—on his return to Town—I have not yet seen him.—On the 18th Inst. Messrs: G. & J. advised me of their having rec'd on that day from, the James River Canal Compy. Principal £74.5 with Int. on 1st July £2.4.1. is £76.9.1. Virg. Cury. equal to $254.85 on Mr Shorts a/c. subject to my order—if then you should have Occasion for this sum at Richmond—you will please make use of it—and I have only to debit your a/c. therefor—

—If nothing extra should intervene I purpose setting out for Philada. abt. the middle Sept. expect to be—absent from G: Town abt. 12 days: in which Case—I shall leave in Columbia Bank, $1000. at least—subject—to your Orders on me—here—as usual. of which Mr Hanson shall have previous Notice—to take up for me as well— Mr Rapin—or Mr LeMaire & Mr Dougherty—be supplied—with Cash—as usual:—and possibly something may Occur to you, that I could Attend too while at Philadelphia respecting your Carriage—or Portrait. whatever it may be. your letters to my address here—or at Philada. will be readily recd. there, via Post Office—at all events,—I shall not set out, before I am favd. with an Ans. to this.

—I shall inquire minutely into the prices of Stocks. particular 6 pts. late deferred—if not to make an Aditional purchase of $2000— in the Name of Wm. Short Esqr. whose last $1500—8 pts. is now transferred too—(heretofore in my name.)

I most ardently wish sir—you would suffer me to make the purchases—on your Own a/c every two or 3,000.00 at most—it would Accumulate—a handsome Principal—in a few years—or, should this scale—be thought—too large, even *one half* would produce a—very desireable sum:—you will I hope pardon me for the liberty I have taken in making you any such proposition—but the present Occurrence—struck me too forcibly,—not to risque—the Mentioning of it here—

excuse—and Believe me to be, sir most Respectfully—your Obedt. hb Sevt: JOHN BARNES

PS. I wrote immediately on recpt. of your favr. 14 recd the 18th—to Mr Wanscher then at Alexandria to see after the bbl of loaf sugar & Coffee (instead of P. Paris.) which I hope will correct the mistake—

RC (ViU: Edgehill-Randolph Papers); above postscript: "Thomas Jefferson Esqr."; endorsed by TJ as received 27 Aug. and so recorded in SJL.

To the District of Columbia
Commissioners

GENTLEMEN   Monticello Aug. 24. 1801.

Your favor of the 17th. came to hand on the 20th. but as it's contents required greater consideration and time than the stay of the post and pressure of other business permitted I have been obliged to take another post for it's answer. the questions indeed which it proposes are so much blended with law that I should have been glad to have had the opinion of the Attorney general for my government: but his distance & the urgency of the case rendering this impracticable, I must venture to form opinions myself; which I shall do the more readily as such of the questions as it is now necessary to determine do not present great difficulties. you state that for the works contemplated now to be done, & the current expences of the year you have a prospect of money sufficient; but that without further paiments there will be a deficiency in the paiment of interest to the state of Maryland on the 1st. of Oct. next to the amount of 10,500. D. & that you cannot rely on voluntary paiments for that sum. when we consider that by the terms of the loan a failure in the paiment of interest gives the state a right to recover the whole principal *immediately*, and the ruinous distress on the funds of the city which this would induce, duty leaves us but one alternative, to *enforce paiments*. but as you observe, at the close of the letter, that you have the means of accomplishing the other objects contemplated for the present year, and it is desireable to produce no unnecessary distress, we should limit ourselves to enforce paiment only *to the extent of the interest* due to Maryland. that a contribution towards this should be required from the sureties to the state of Maryland as well as others, seems both just & lawful. the case as to the principal of these is shortly this. General Forrest being indebted to the city about 33,800. D paiable at short days, becomes security for the city for 50,000. D. payable at a long day. this is no legal payment of his 33,800. D. the contracts have no connection. it is possible that if by *subsequent events* the affairs of the city were verging to evident bankruptcy, the Chancery might stay his paiment till counter security should be given. but that is not our case. and were he to propose it to the Chancery, we would save them the question by saying, pay the money into the treasury of Maryland & all purposes will be answered, ours of the payment of interest, & his of lessening his responsibility by exactly as much as should be paid. I have heard it suggested that he might object to payment till he is countersecured as to the amount of securityship beyond his debt. but I think no lawyer will say this.—the advance of 10,000. D. by mr Stoddart 9. months before it was due seems justly to entitle him to an equal delay of an equal portion of the note endorsed by him & Genl. Forrest.

To the question whether property sold under the act of Maryland of Dec. 28. 1793. can be resold on default of payment? I should say that act in all cases of sale *on credit*, authorises a re-sale. it is true that it allows the resale to be for *ready money*, but if it be *on credit*, then a 3d. sale for default of paiment is within the very words as well as the purview of the act. and I should extremely doubt whether the purview as well as the letter of this act will not be understood to have, so far as it extends, repealed, in these cases, the general principle which saves the rights of infants till they come of age. but will not all these questions be saved by a voluntary assessment by the debtors themselves, in proportion to their debts respectively, to the amount of the sum we want? less than 5/ in the pound would probably make it up. but if they consent to this, it should be in such a way as to render disappointment impossible.

My idea of the functions of the Board of commissioners is that they are to form resolutions, on which the President has an affirmative or negative. had I been at Washington I would have asked of them to resolve first on what they themselves should think right & have reserved my own opinion for a simple approval or disapproval. it is at their request only, & to avoid the delay which a reference back to them might occasion, that I have presumed to originate propositions, which I do however on the express condition that they shall be deemed of no effect until approved by a vote of the commissioners. as such of them as shall be so approved will then include their opinion as well as that of the President, it will be of less importance which opinion was first given.

I pray you to accept assurances of my high consideration & respect.

TH: JEFFERSON

RC (DLC: District of Columbia Papers); at foot of first page: "The Commissioners of Washington." PrC (DLC).

From the District of Columbia Commissioners

SIR,   Washington 24th. August 1801.

We should think an apology very necessary for intruding on your retirement, were we not convinced that your solicitude for the advancement of the City authorizes this Liberty.—

In reviewing the objects you were pleased to recommend to our attention, and calculating what has been done, and what is yet to accomplish, we find our means will be inadequate to fulfil the whole of your intentions respecting the Roads, within the Estimate. We therefore thought it proper to state what has been executed, and the Expenditures.—

For work executed

		Dolls Cts
The former Expenses on Pennsylvania Avenue and the Capitol-Hill, since the Month of June inclusive	}	2130.00
The work on the President's Square, and on 15th. Street west, gravelled principally, has cost	}	693.00
The work on new-Jersey Avenue, including a good Road up the Hill, and a free-Stone Bridge, has cost	}	872.99
	Dolls	3,695.99

For work to be done of necessity.

The Road between the upper end of Pennsylvania Avenue and the upper Bridge on Rock Creek, has been calculated, and the work by mensuration to make an easy Passage, will cost $800—The people of George Town have taken and will require as much Sand &c, as will lessen the Expense—Dolls 100— } 700.00

Work Contemplated

The circular Road on the west of the Capitol continued into A Street north, and A Street South, also 1st. Street east on the Capitol Square, between the two above mentioned Streets; but particularly A Street, north now commenced, and 1st. Street east in front of Mr. Carroll's Buildings— } =

To round Pennsylvania Avenue from the President's Square, to 26th Street west, ready to receive the Gravel.— } =

To continue from the new Bridge down new-Jersey Avenue, rounding it, so as to receive the Gravel } =

These last objects are unprovided for, and as we cannot execute the whole, we solicit your Determination respecting the choice, should we be enabled to expend a few hundred Dollars more than the Sum calculated.

We have the satisfaction of informing you that the Brick-work of the chamber of Representatives advances with such rapidity, that the whole will be finished ready for the Roof by the end of next Week, & the Roof is in forwardness.

Previous to the departure of our Colleague, Mr White, for Winchester, some Days ago, he joined in our opinion respecting the propriety of making this statement, as soon as the proper returns were collected.

We have the honor to be, Sir, with sentiments of the highest respect and consideration, Yr. Mo. Obt. Servts.

WILLIAM THORNTON
TRISTRAM DALTON

RC (DLC); at foot of text: "President of the United-States"; in William Brent's hand, signed by Thornton and Dalton; endorsed by TJ as received 27 Aug. and so recorded in SJL. FC (DNA: RG 42, DCLB).

In a letter to TJ of 20 Aug., Alexander White announced his imminent DEPARTURE for Winchester for "particular business" and his anticipated return on 5 or 6 Sep. (RC in DLC; at foot of text: "President of the U. States"; endorsed by TJ as received 27 Aug. and so recorded in SJL).

From Albert Gallatin

DR SIR   City of Washington 24th August 1801

The letter I had the pleasure to write to you the other day, & intended to send by Dr Bache will accompany this. I have little to add & only enclose some papers vizt

No. 1 is the answer of Presidt. Bank U.S. to mine enclosing a list of names proposed for Directors here, and the order of the board in relation to the intended establishment of a branch here.

No. 2 is the answer of the Collector of Boston on the subject of Mr Thornton's supposed French privateer evincing the [worth?][1] of your position that no official discussions should be permitted until the facts are ascertained

No. 3 is a letter from the Collector at Wilmington N.C. in relation to a Spanish privateer and british prize having entered that port, together with my answer. Can a part of the cargo of sd. prize be sold to defray the expense of necessary repairs to the privateer? This is the only new question & not included in the instructions of 1793 & 1796 which is presented by this case. I incline for the negative.

No. 4 consists of a correspondence between the Auditor and myself commenced on my part[2] in order to try to induce him to forward the settlement of accounts in his office. They are most shamefully in arrears; which he ascribes to the removal of the seat of Govt. & death or resignation of his best clerks. You will see that the Revenue accounts are on an average about 15 months in arrears; that is to say 15 months in his hands behind the Collectors themselves. I am afraid it will take a long time before it will be possible to gain so much upon current business, which, I think with confidence, will now come regularly from the Collectors on him.

No. 5 is the usual list of Warrants issued during the week.

No. 6 copy of a letter from Comr. of the revenue. Your approbation is by law requisite to place the superintendence of light houses in the hands of the new collectors.

If no answer shall be received this week from any of the delegation of Georgia, it will be, I think, necessary to commission the person recommended by Gov. Jackson, for collector of Savannah. As the present Collector has never settled a single account his continuance is a public evil.

We have been alarmed by a report of your being sick—I hope to morrow's mail will relieve our apprehensions. Anxiety for the health of my family has induced me to take a house on Capitol hill. It may be prejudice; but I think, & this summmer's experience confirms it, that it is a more healthy situation.

With respect & attachment Your most obt. Servt.

ALBERT GALLATIN

RC (DLC); endorsed by TJ as received from the Treasury Department on 27 Aug. and so recorded in SJL. Enclosures: (1) Thomas Willing to Gallatin, 19 Aug., thanking him for his letter of 11 Aug., with the list of names of possible directors enclosed "and particularly for the caution and candour manifested, in the account given of their qualifications," noting that he presented the letter and enclosure to the board of directors of the Bank of the United States at the 18 Aug. meeting, and a resolution was passed to establish an office of discount and deposit at Washington "which, we flatter ourselves, will answer the objects of Government, without being in any way injurious, or inconven-ient to the parent Institution," and informing Gallatin that 15 Sep. was the date set for the election of nine directors "if such a number of suitable characters," can be found, and promising to use their "best endeavours to find out such men as, we think, may best be confided in; and if we find they are not Stockholders at that day, which the law requires them to be," to let their names be known and allow them to purchase the necessary stock (Tr in DLC; in a clerk's hand; on verso in Gallatin's hand: "No. 1"). (2) Resolution passed by the president and directors of the Bank of the United States, 18 Aug., "That it is expedient from the relative situation this Bank stands in with the Government of the United States, in its pecuniary operations, to establish an office of Discount & Deposit at the City of Washington" and that as the city is in "its infancy and not *at this period*, in a capacity to furnish" the 13 directors called for by the resolution of the board of 6 Feb. 1792, that requirement is rescinded, and instead 9 directors will be elected to manage the office of discount and deposit and $75,000 appropriated as capital (Tr in same, in same clerk's hand, including signature of Thomas Willing as president and attestation by George Simpson, cashier; enclosed in No. 1, above). (3) Benjamin Lincoln to Gallatin, collector's office, Boston, 12 Aug., informing the Treasury secretary that the French armed schooner *Beguine* arrived at Boston on 8 May with six guns and twelve men and departed for Guadeloupe on 4 June with the same number, noting that the paperwork for the vessel was completed 24 hours after departure because British vessels bound for Halifax left at the same time, but he had no complaints from the agent of the British vessels or anyone else that the *Beguine* had increased her crew or number of guns while in port; and enclosing two documents, one dated 8 May, indicating that the *Beguine*, master Raymond Colles, entered Boston with a cargo of sugar, molasses, and coffee from Guadeloupe, the other, dated 4 June, indicating that Colles cleared his vessel for a return trip to Guadeloupe, with a cargo including candles, codfish, herring, oil, and soap (Trs in same; in a clerk's hand; on verso of second enclosure in Gallatin's hand: "No. 2"). (4) Griffith J. McRee, collector's office, Wilmington, North Carolina, 10 Aug., reporting that on 8 Aug. a Spanish privateer entered the port in distress with a British prize, the brig *Eagle*, John McKee, master, and sought permission to sell part of the prize's cargo to defray expenses for the repair of the privateer and the prize; with the collector refusing permission until he obtains instructions from Gallatin (Tr in same). (5) Gallatin to McRee, 22 Aug., noting that Articles 24 and 25 of the Jay Treaty and the 26 Nov. 1796 circular from the Treasury Department applied equally to Spanish and French privateers and required the imme-

diate departure of the prize unless repairs were absolutely necessary; with Gallatin observing that "there exists a general tendency in owners & Masters of Privateers to attempt an evasion of our regulations by a sale of the Cargoes of their prizes" and recommending that McRee make "a strict survey of the two Vessels in order to enforce and hasten" their departure; and informing McRee that while certain that a part of the prize's cargo may be sold to defray the expence of her own repairs, he was submitting McRee's letter to the president to obtain TJ's opinion on "whether a part may be sold to defray the necessary repairs of the Privateer" (Tr in same; endorsed in Gallatin's hand: "No. 3"). (6) Gallatin to Richard Harrison, auditor of the Treasury, 19 Aug., enclosing a list of accounts of collectors, which were rendered but not yet settled at the auditor's office (see Enclosure No. 8), noting that the accumulation was "easily accounted for from the great number of those accounts, which were in arrears and have very lately been rendered" but reminding Harrison that all of the accounts for 1800 needed to be settled early to enable Gallatin to include them in his report to the House of Representatives due during the first week of the session, and observing that the time "is short, and that strictness of examination and correctness must not, under any possible circumstance be sacrificed to dispatch," and consequently authorizing "any reasonable extra expense which you may think necessary for the completion of the Settlement within the time" (Tr in same). (7) "List of Collectors at Customs Accompts in the Auditor's Office remaining to be adjusted," 19 Aug. 1801, in columns, with the districts listed alphabetically (70 in all), the collectors, and the years 1800 and 1801, subdivided into quarters, with a mark at each quarter where accounts had been received but not adjusted (MS in same: TJ Papers, 115:19869; in a clerk's hand, with emendation in Gallatin's hand). (8) Harrison to Gallatin, auditor's office, Treasury Department, 20 Aug., acknowledging Gallatin's letter of 19 Aug., Harrison accepts Gallatin's offer to "take immediate measures to procure all the extra aid that can be usefully or safely employed; by means of which I hope to have the accounts of 1800 ready, or nearly so, at the time desired," and expresses a desire to contribute "to the order & regularity of the business of the Department" (Tr in same). (9) Elias Boudinot to Gallatin, Mint of the United States, Philadelphia, 18 Aug., alerting Gallatin that although the accounts of the treasurer of the Mint were forwarded to the auditor's office regularly every quarter "yet we have had no account of their having passed later than to the 30th of June last year," noting that "if any errors should be discovered in them, it will be difficult to have them rectified," and requesting that the Treasury secretary have them examined as soon as possible (Tr in same). (10) Gallatin to Harrison, auditor of the Treasury, 21 Aug., responding to Boudinot's letter (see preceding enclosure) and urging "the necessity of settling without delay the accounts of public officers," observing, "I am satisfied that whatever blame may be deserved, cannot attach to you personally and that the delay must be owing either to some defect in the general system, or to want of proper assistance in your office— whatever the cause may be, the effect however, is the same: it should be removed, and you may in your endeavours towards it, rely on every assistance which it is in my power to give," and requesting that Harrison transmit a list of all the accounts rendered for settlement now in his office (Tr in same). (11) Harrison to Gallatin, 21 Aug., promising to provide the Treasury secretary with the list as requested in a day or two and stating that the accounts of the treasurer of the Mint from the 1 July 1800 to 31 Mch. 1801 were adjusted on 27 June and those of the quarter ending 30 June 1801, on 15 Aug., and noting that the delay in settling the accounts was "occasioned solely by the want (during a considerable time) of proper assistance, being deprived of the services of some of his best Clerks by Death, resignation and sickness" (Tr in same). (12) "Weekly List of Warrants issued by the Treasurer during the Week ending 22d Augt. 1801," dated 24 Aug., reporting eight warrants, Nos. 126 to 133, for a total of $24,231.10 (MS in same; entirely in Gallatin's hand; with

note at foot of text: "Specie balance in Treasury at end of the week—Dollars— Not rendered"; endorsed by Gallatin on verso: "No. 5"). (13) William Miller to Gallatin, Revenue Office, Treasury Department, 21 Aug. 1801, informing the Treasury secretary that the lighthouses and other establishments for the protection of navigation at Portsmouth, New Hampshire, and New York have been under the superintendance of the collectors of those ports and as Joseph Whipple and David Gelston have replaced Thomas Martin and Joshua Sands, respectively, "the present Superintendants consider it proper to hand over the business which is connected with the Light House establishment also," and if Gallatin approves of the arrangement, he will "notify the parties and instruct Mr. Whipple and Mr. Gelston in relation to the charge assigned to them" (Tr in same; in Gallatin's hand on verso: "No. 6").

For the LETTER Gallatin wrote THE OTHER DAY, see Gallatin to TJ, 18 Aug.

Gallatin's letter of 11 Aug. to Thomas Willing, enclosing the LIST OF NAMES PROPOSED FOR DIRECTORS, has not been found, but in a 9 June letter to the president of the Bank of the United States, presented at the 18 Aug. board of directors meeting at which the resolution for the establishment of an office of discount and deposit at Washington was passed, Gallatin made his case for the establishment of the branch bank. He observed: "It is extremely unpleasant to be obliged to have your money transactions passing through hands of an Institution in which you have not full confidence. I repose no confidence in the Bank of Columbia." Yet necessity compelled the Treasury secretary to place large sums at the bank. Gallatin urged the Bank of the United States to set up an office in Washington even if it would not be lucrative for the bank. Gallatin argued: "the establishment itself cannot be expensive. It will require no other capital than the deposits of Government with the Bank of Columbia, and if it is to be only an office of deposit, the expense would be confined to that of a Cashier and one or two clerks." Gallatin concluded that it was "equally the interest" of the Treasury Department and the Bank of the United States "mutually to observe the most liberal Spirit of accommodation towards each other," and while he felt disposed to show on every occasion the sincerity of his wishes "for the prosperity & advantage of the institution over which you preside, I have not the least doubt of the present Administration meeting with every support and accommodation from the Bank which public good may require and their situation justify." In a postscript Gallatin cautioned that the letter was "perfectly confidential" (RC in NHi: Gallatin Papers; at foot of text: "Private Thomas Willing Esqr President of the Bank of the United States"; endorsed: "To minutes 18 Augst 1801"). On 12 Oct. the *National Intelli-*

gencer published the names of the newly elected directors, including Tristram Dalton, Thomas Tingey, and Thomas Peter of Washington; John Thomson Mason, Joseph Carleton, and William H. Dorsey of Georgetown; and John Dunlop, William Oxley, and John C. Vowell of Alexandria.

YOUR POSITION: see TJ to Gallatin, 14 Aug.

For the INSTRUCTIONS to customs collectors of 1793 and 1796, see Syrett, *Hamilton*, 15:178-81; 20:348-9n.

DELEGATION OF GEORGIA: see Gallatin to TJ, 10 Aug.

[1] Word written over illegible word.
[2] Preceding four words interlined.

From George Hay

SIR,   Richmond. August 24. 1801

I now send you the book, which you were so good as to lend me; for which you will be pleased to accept my thanks. It would have been returned at an earlier day, had I not put it into the hands of Mr. Wythe.

This book has been the occasion of my Committing three faults. I borrowed it without being authorised to ask such a favor: I lent it to a third person, (sed, clarum et venerabile nomen!) without the permission of the owner: and I have once more endeavored to investigate a Subject, which, experience ought to have taught me is placed beyond the reach of my understanding.—I will not commit a fourth by giving you the trouble of reading another Sentence.

I am with great respect, Your mo: ob. Svt.   GEO: HAY.

RC (MHi); endorsed by TJ as received 27 Aug. and so recorded in SJL.

George Hay (1765-1830) was a Williamsburg native and political writer who practiced law in Petersburg and actively campaigned on TJ's behalf in the election of 1800. Relocating to Virginia's capital shortly thereafter, he practiced in the state's superior courts and became a supporter of James Monroe, who appointed him to minor offices and whose

daughter he later married. Under the pseudonym "Hortensius," Hay published *An Essay on the Liberty of the Press*, in 1799 in Philadelphia (Evans, No. 35605). He represented James Thomson Callender in the seditious libel case against him in federal circuit court in 1800 and prosecuted Aaron Burr for treason in 1807 (ANB).

SED, CLARUM ET VENERABILE NOMEN: but, with an illustrious and venerable name.

From George Jefferson

DEAR SIR   Richmond 24th. Augt. 1801

I sent you a few days ago by Thomas Kindred the articles contained in the memorandum which I brought down with me—together with 4 dozen chairs which came from Philadelphia.

I have received of the James River company on acct. of Mr. Short £76.9.1, of which I have informed Mr. Barnes as usual.

The Gunpowder you mention shall be forwarded by the first opportunity.

I am Dear Sir Your Very humble servt.   GEO. JEFFERSON

I am sorry to inform you that Mr. Purdie of Smithfield has not been able to procure any Hams for you; as he could not meet with such as he approved of.   G. J.

RC (MHi); at foot of text: "Thomas Jefferson esqr."; endorsed by TJ as received 27 Aug. and so recorded in SJL.

On 21 Aug., George Jefferson provided Thomas Kindred with a receipt for the goods he had received from Gibson & Jefferson "to deliver in good order to Thomas Jefferson esquire at Milton he paying the freight." The items included "four dozen Chairs, one barrel, one keg, and two small boxes." A note indicated that the bottom of one chair was split. A list of charges for 14 gallons of brandy, 1 cask of porter, 1 dozen bottles of syrup punch, 1 dozen tumblers, and a cask for brandy for a total of £19.3.3 was provided on the bottom half of the sheet (MS in MHi; entirely in George Jefferson's hand, including Edward Kindred's mark as received for Thomas Kindred; endorsed by TJ as received from George Jefferson on 27 Aug.). On 29 Aug., TJ paid Thomas Kindred $14.75 for "water carriage" (MB, 2:1050).

GUNPOWDER YOU MENTION: see TJ to George Jefferson, 21 Aug.

From Ignatius Palyart

Washington 24 Aoust 1801—

Le Consul General de S.A.R. Le Prince Regent de Portugal a eu l'honneur de se rendre chez le president des Etats Unis pour presenter ses hommages—Il se propose de se rendre a Lisbonne par congé dans le Cours du mois proxain—S'il peut être utile a quelque chose il será enchanté de recevoir les ordres du President à Philadelphie—

E D I T O R S '   T R A N S L A T I O N

Washington 24 Aug. 1801.

The consul general of His Royal Highness the Prince Regent of Portugal has had the honor to call at the house of the president of the United States to present his respects. He intends to go to Lisbon on leave of absence in the course of the next month. If he can be useful in any way, he will be delighted to receive the president's orders in Philadelphia.

RC (ViW); endorsed by TJ as a letter of the consul general of Portugal received 3 Sep. and so recorded in SJL.

A merchant with connections in Havana as well as the United States, Palyart had been the CONSUL GENERAL of Portugal, based in Philadelphia, since 1790 (Madison, *Papers, Sec. of State Ser.*, 2:294; NDQW, Apr.-July 1799, 144; Vol. 17:571; Vol. 19:314).

From David Austin

RESPECTED SIR.   Washington Augt. 25th. 1801.

Fully pursuaded of your natural benevolence, & having no cause to doubt of your readiness to put forth your hand to any enterprize that promises well to the interest of the nation, & of mankind; & knowing that evidence of the truth of the things I have offered to you, & may offer, arrises from an accurate regard to the *tendency of the measures suggested*, & also to the *counter effect of counter proceedings*; you will not deem it unpardonable in me, that I take the liberty of recalling your attention to things happening.

The neglect of the matter of the proclamation, previous to the 4th. of July last, hath left the Executive, without object & without nerve. The waters are unsetled, & the winds blow from every quarter.

Failing to give opportunity for the principles of Universal pacification to open their design upon the European theatre; all the smoke respecting the Mission existing, took occasion to rise.—

Giving way to *very illegitimate address*, in the matter of New Haven, the President became involved in discussions, needless, on the ground of former recommendation. This paragraph needs explications not proper to be placed on paper. (Matters very plausible may be represented on paper from abroad, & enforced by considerations *irresistable*, which, however, have not the peace & ho-[1] of the Executive, nor the good of the Nation for their main spring.)— Untoutched, the State of Connect: would have yielded its whole revenue to Executive emolument. The means of revolution pressed, there, amount but to a pressure against the object the Executive would promote.

The matter of the Barbary powers, is as a broken cake. The forces the President hath passed by, will yet be needful to place this matter upon its proper footing.

In respect to the place of Rufus King, & the equitable adjustment of our National concerns with that power; it is enough to say; fair as the face of things may appear; there is an Engine playing, that means to take advantage of existing turmoil.—

The President relies too much upon the force of Republican principles. They form an excellent drumhead; but the design of the Drummer is, but to beat himself into National employt. & pay.

The President feels too high an obligation towards these Drummers. They demand higher pay, than their sound is worth. The same principles continued would rock the Ship forever, & give no peace to the Helmsman, nor quiet to the Crew. The President must walk his own quarter deck, & with the Ship's trumpet keep the men in their places. The severity of a Ship's discipline is but a Copy for the National Mariner! Speak with kindness & indulgence to the Boatswain's Mate, & he will but insult you the more!

The fact is the President, whether he knows it or not, is born at the opening of a new state of things. He is *cast forth upon the waters*, & every wind takes the liberty to assail his bark. You have Sir a task, that needs powers of more than usual strength. National force is stormed down, or discharged. Nought but Mental powers & personal prowess remains. You have to sail upon the waters of the people. Their tumultuous passions, wishes & objects form the waves. To split these waves to advantage, & to disperse the storm requires good Nautical abilities.

The President needs a Compass whose needle is untoutched by the unhallowed fires of the present moment. The Executive is surrounded by these fires. Many have their censers, ready to receive fire from the National Altar; & they are ready to enkindle the fire & to make it blaze, still more & more, no way to the honor, or emolument of the Chief Minister, in the National sanctuary.

Suffer me to hint at a few things, already past. In the first place; at whose solicitation, did the President depart from the principles of the Inaugural Speech? How elegantly, might the Chief Pilot, have moved off "Wing & Wing" to the pointings of his own Compass, had no intruding Mariner been suffered to bejostle the Pilot from his station!

Secondly: Would not a little recollection of the circumstances of the Election have been highly useful in the maintenance of the doctrine of "Wing & Wing?"—

Thirdly, Would it not be policy to preserve the existance of such national energies, as the state of things placed in the hands of the Commander in Chief?—

Fourthly; Hath the Chief Mariner, consented to alter his course to *oblige himself*, or to *oblige others*?

Fifthly, If the roarings of a tumultuous sea, to the ear of the Pilot, became *intollerable*; where was the speaking trumpet, & the prerogative of the Admiral at the time?—

Sixtly If the sails of the National Ship, by their flapping about, augur too great negligence; will it not be useful, that the sails be sheeted to their tasks, with a heavier hand, in time to come?—This may be done in the stile & manner of the opening speech at the next session of Congress.—

I know the President will receive this communication with the sentiments, to wh. it may be entitled; & at once believe, that the words of one speaking the truth, in soberness, in the ears of his Prince, are of higher worth, than the words of those who flatter, but to destroy.—

From motives of delicacy the signature is waved, if the Communication, be worth a recollection, the Prest. will not be at a loss for a supposition, as to the quarter from whence it comes.—

The winds will blow, both in Europe & America, until the American Ship catches & carries off that breeze appointed of God, to shew to the Nations the course of permanent peace.—

P.S. I have become permanent, in the City, & shall have no objection to dine with the Prest: when he comes to Town: & if, as Joseph in the house of Pharaoh, I may be instrumental, in increasing the Corn of the land; there will be no loss on the whole.

RC (DNA: RG 59, LAR); addressed: "Thomas Jefferson, Prest. United States Monticello Virginia"; endorsed by TJ as received 3 Sep. and so recorded in SJL.

In the first of two letters written to TJ on 16 June, Austin had enclosed an eight-page PROCLAMATION regarding his plan of UNIVERSAL PACIFICATION and commerical federalism.

TJ received another letter from Austin on 3 Sep., dated 26 Aug., which enclosed a three-page address that Austin hoped the president would present at the opening of Congress. The address congratulated the nation on the peace and prosperity it enjoyed and invited Congress to give thanks "to the wise & munificent Disposer of all things" for bestowing such blessings. Only Barbary affairs required legislative action, and it was now up to the administration to decide whether the nation remained bound by treaty stipulations with the Barbary powers in light of their recent "unlawful depredations." Similar attacks suffered by European nations might induce them to join the United States in a "system of defence" for mutual protection, which in turn could inspire a positive change in the "Commercial relations of the European powers." In his letter covering the proposed address, Austin explained that looking toward a "general & fraternal estate" in Europe would lessen "the fears of a Republican estate of things," while an emphasis on Barbary would bring the nation together in a "common channel, through which their united waters may be sent abroad!" To unite the county further, Austin noted that his address deliberately avoided the terms "revolutionary" and "antirevolutionary" as well as the use of party names. He explained, "It is enough that the revolutionary waves have cast the President into the chair. His policy, now is, to lay his hand upon the revolutionary waters & say, 'hitherto shall ye come, but no farther!'" (RC in DNA: RG 59, LAR; at foot of text: "Th: Jefferson Prest: U:States"; endorsed by TJ as received 3 Sep. and so recorded in SJL).

[1] Thus in MS. Austin failed to complete the hyphenated word.

From Joel Barlow

DEAR SIR,   Paris 25 Aug. 1801—

I have recieved your kind letter by Mr. Dawson, and be assured no man in America rejoices more sincerely than I do at the change of political measures & the happy reconciliation of parties of which it speaks. I do not congratulate you, but my country, on the event of your election. I now indulge myself in the hope that we are not to lose the fruits of former labors, but that we may be wise enough to improve the unspeakable advantages which we possess, and that other nations may have at least an opportunity of profiting by our example. I feel a certain elevation of thought which nothing else can inspire when I contemplate the immensity of the field in which the present & the rising generation in America have to labor. It depends much on you & your present friends to put them in the right way & so familiarise them with sound principles that they will not afterwards go wrong.

I am now determined to come to America as soon as possible, either this autumn or early in the spring. And I wish to mention to you in confidence that my private concerns being placed on such a footing as to give me no more avocations from objects which I have much more at heart, my intention is to devote the remainder of my life (as far as there is a chance of success) to the promotion of the solid improvements of that country, moral, political & economical. Governments & nations would certainly pursue their own happiness much better than they do if they knew how. Some instruction is doubtless to be dirived from precept, but more from example. We are probably the nation the most free from prejudice, and on that account the most capable of setting good examples & of commanding respect. I know your administration will be directed to these objects; and as it is one of the first administrations that ever was so directed, I hope you will meet from all your friends the aid which that circumstance renders necessary.

I forbear to entertain you with the present state of France or of Europe. The return of Mr. Dawson by whom I write makes it unnecessary, besides I apprehend that your own views of things here, even at your distance, will not be very erroneous.

I am, Dear Sir, with every sentiment of respect, yr. obt. sert.

JOEL BARLOW

RC (DLC); addressed: "Thomas Jefferson President of the United States"; mistakenly endorsed by TJ as a letter of 25 Aug. 1802 received 27 Mch. 1802 and so recorded in SJL.

YOUR KIND LETTER: TJ to Barlow, 14 Mch. 1801.

From Samuel Broome

New Haven State of

SIR   Connecticut Aug. 25 1801.

Sometime past I took the liberty to address a line to your Excellency, advising that I would gladly Accept, an office under the Government of the United States, provided there was a Vacancy which in the opinion of my friends I might be Capable of filling; I have now to inform your Excellency that I am about removing to Greenfield Twenty five miles Westerd from hence on a Small estate I have lately purchased there. If the office of Post Master for this district should become Vacant I beg leave to mention my Brother in Law Mr Jeremiah Platt resident here, to said office, who is as good Accomptant, as any in the United States of America, and in every respect qualified to discharge the duties of Said office.—With regard to myself I shall only add that through the Vicissitudes of the late War I have been reduced from Affluence to a limited State in point of property. Any appointment, in Any part of the United States, which I might be capable of filling, I would with pleasure Accept.

My Character and principles are Well known to the Vice President, Governor Clinton, the Hon'ble Elbridge Gerry, and others I could mention. If your Excellency [could?] aid me Consistent with the duty we owe our Country I shall be happy. My Son in Law Mr Joseph Fay, together with other Similar Characters in New york would Come forward, and give the most Ample and satisfactory Security for the just fulfilment of any trust reposed in me; I had the Honor of being frequently at your seat near Paris twelve years past, but I believe I am not of your Excellency's recollection, A line directed to me either at this City or Greenfield Connecticut will Come to hand, I am with Sincere regard and ardent wishes for your health and length of days, your Excellencys Most Assured friend

SAMUEL BROOME

RC (DNA: RG 59, LAR); with ink smudges; at foot of text: "His Excellency President of the United States"; endorsed by TJ as received 3 Sep. and so recorded in SJL.

I TOOK THE LIBERTY TO ADDRESS A LINE: Broome to TJ, 8 Apr. 1801, Vol. 33:571-2.

From Henry Remsen

SIR   New York August 25th. 1801

At the request of Mr. Matthew L. Davis, I take the liberty to state certain facts & circumstances relative to his employment, conduct and character.—

When the Manhattan Company determined to employ a part of their capital in Banking operations, they appointed this gentleman to an Office in their Bank, on the recommendation of several respectable citizens. Being of good capacity and ready apprehension, he very soon after entering on the execution of the duties of the said Office, which were trust-worthy & laborious, accommodated himself to his situation, and to the present moment has performed those duties, reputably to himself and satisfactorily to the Company. His conduct in other respects has likewise entitled him to the approbation of the Company. His character among his fellow-citizens and in the institution stands fair; and I myself believe him to be a man of strict integrity.—

I have the honor to be with perfect respect, Sir Your most obt. & h'ble servt.

HENRY REMSEN

RC (DNA: RG 59, LAR); at foot of text: "The President of the U.S."; endorsed by TJ as received 17 Sep. but recorded in SJL at 18 Sep. and connected by a brace with eight other letters, including the subscription described below, received on that date with the notation: "Davis to be Naval officer"; also endorsed by TJ: "Davis."

For the candidacy of MATTHEW L. DAVIS as naval officer at New York, see Gallatin to TJ, 21 May.

TJ also received a subscription from New York, dated 26 Aug. 1801, and

signed by Daniel Ludlow, John Broome, Brockholst Livingston, and John B. Prevost, recommending Davis as qualified to discharge the duties of naval officer. They concluded that his appointment "would be satisfactory to the Republicans" of the city (RC in DNA: RG 59, LAR; in unidentified hand; at head of text: "To the President of the United States"; endorsed by TJ as received 18 Sep. and so recorded in SJL). Ludlow served as president; Prevost, Aaron Burr's stepson, as secretary; and Broome and Livingston as directors of the Manhattan Company. Remsen was cashier at the bank (*Longworth's*

American Almanac, New-York Register, and City Directory, for the Twenty-Sixth Year of American Independence [New York, 1801], 69; Kline, Burr, 1:180; 2:741n).

From Josiah Tattnall, Jr.

DEAR SIR,   New York. 25th. August 1801

Mr. Clarke the Son of the late General Clarke of Georgia, an old & celebrated Officer of the late Revolutionary War, being Solicitous of the honor of an introduction to the Chief Majistrate of the Union, in which character he participates with his fellow Citizens of Georgia in viewing you Sir with unfeigned Satisfaction; I take the liberty of recommending him to your attention as a gentleman of Science & merit—Mr. Clarke having graduated at Yale College in Connecticut is now on his way to the City of Washington, where he contemplates engaging in the Study of Law: Mr. Baldwin had recommended Mr. C. to Mr. Jno. T. Mason, but he has since found that the Office of that gentleman is already too much thronged: If it will not be encroaching too much on your time & goodness you will Sir very much oblige me by assisting Mr. C with your advice as to a Suitable character under whom to pursue his Studies—With every Sincere wish for your health & happiness, I have the Honor to be very Respectfully

Dr Sir; Your obedt. Humle. St.   JOSIAH TATTNALL JUNR.
                                          of the State of Georgia

RC (MHi); at foot of text: "Thos. Jefferson Esquire President of the United States"; endorsed by TJ as received 5 Oct. and so recorded in SJL with notation "by mr Clarke."

Josiah Tattnall, Jr. (1764-1803) was a prominent militia leader in Georgia and a political ally of James Jackson. In 1796 he was elected to fill the U.S. Senate seat vacated by Jackson and served until 1799, when he was replaced by Abraham Baldwin. TJ approved of the change, noting that Tattnall's "want of firmness" in the Senate "had produced the effect of a change of sides." Tattnall became governor of Georgia in November 1801, but poor health forced his resignation the following year (Kenneth Coleman and Charles Stephen Gurr, eds., Dictionary of Georgia Biography, 2 vols. [Athens, 1983], 2:960-2; Vol. 31:10).

Elijah CLARKE, Jr., graduated from Yale in 1801. Returning to Georgia, he was recommended to TJ by John Milledge for the office of secretary of legation in London, but did not receive the appointment. He served briefly in the state legislature and as a solicitor general before relocating to Louisiana. His father, Elijah Clarke (d. 1799), earned fame as a partisan fighter during the American Revolution and as a controversial postwar militia and political leader on the Georgia frontier (Dexter, Yale, 5:434-5; Louise Frederick Hays, Hero of Hornet's Nest, A Biography of Elijah Clark, 1733 to 1799 [New York, 1946], 301-2, 366; Dictionary of Georgia Biography, 1:190-2; Milledge to TJ, 25 Nov. 1802; Elijah Clarke to TJ, 10 Oct. 1803).

To Pierce Butler

DEAR SIR   Monticello Aug. 26. 1801.

Your favor of the 14th. came to hand on the 20th. I thank you for the information it contained. it is of that kind which I am anxious to recieve. after so long and complete an exclusion from office as republicans have suffered insomuch that every place is filled with their opponents justice as well as principle requires that they should have some participation. I believe they will be contented with less than [their] just share for the sake of peace & conciliation. this latter motive [has] weighed powerfully with me to do as little in the way of removal [as cir]cumstances will admit: for after the bloody severance of the nation into two parts which our predecessors affected, the first duty of every patriot is to reunite & heal the severed parts. exclusive possession [moves] one party; removal the other. yet both must be brought together. the [moderat]ion of the Southern republicans has been really magnanimous. in Maryland little has been asked. in Virginia N. Cara. Georgia nothing. as to S. C[ara.] I do not think we are yet well enough informed to do any thing. but I am extremely happy to find you disapprove of much removal. you say 'there are [perhaps] two or three at most, who, it appears to you should be [removed] that [there is one] in particular, whose continuance in office will disgust every Republican in the state.' may I ask of you who is the *one*, & who the two or [three]? I do it under the seal of confidence & with no earthly view but to [use it for the?] best purpose of the common cause. our views are to do little [more in the way?] of removal. we [shall] get through it in the course of the year, after [which the] measures we shall pursue & propose will I hope have the effect of making into one body all except the Monarchical federalis[ts who] are incurable & hopeless. accept assurances of my friendly attachment and [high] respect.

PrC (DLC); faint; at foot of text: "Pierce Butler esq."

YOUR FAVOR OF THE 14TH: not found, but recorded in SJL as received from Philadelphia on 20 Aug.

To Levi Lincoln

DEAR SIR   Monticello Aug. 26. 1801.

Your favor of July 28. was recieved here on the 20th. instant. the superscription of my letter of July 11. by another hand was to prevent danger to it from the curious. your statement respecting the Berceau, coincides with my own recollections in the circumstances recollected by me, and I concur with you in supposing it may not now be necessary to give any explanations on the subject in the papers. the purchase was made by our predecessors & the repairs begun by them. had she been to continue ours we were authorized to put & keep her in good order out of the fund of the naval contingencies, & when in good order, we obeyed a law of the land, the treaty in giving her up. it is true the treaty was not ratified; but when ratified it is validated retrospectively. we took on ourselves this risk, but France had put more into our hands on the same risk.—I do not know whether the clamour as to the allowance to the French officers of their regular pay has been rectified by a statement that it was on the request of the French Consul & his promise to repay it. so that they cost the US. on this arrangement, nothing.—I am glad to learn from you that the answer to Newhaven had a good effect in Massachusets on the republicans, & no ill effect on the sincere federalists. I had foreseen, years ago, that the first republican president who should come into office after all the places in the government had become exclusively occupied by federalists, would have a dreadful operation to perform. that the republicans would consent to a continuation of every thing in federal hands was not to be expected, because neither just nor politic. on him then was to devolve the office of an executioner, that of lopping of. I cannot say that it has worked harder than I expected. you know the moderation of our views in this business, and that we all concurred in them. we determined to proceed with deliberation. this produced impatience in the republicans & a belief we meant to do nothing. some occasion of public explanation was eagerly desired, when the Newhaven remonstrance offered us that occasion. the answer was meant as an explanation to our friends. it has had on them every where the most wholsome effect. appearances of schismatising from us have been entirely done away. I own I expected it would check the current with which the republican federalists were returning to their brethren the republicans. I extremely lamented this effect. for the moment which would convince me that a healing of the nation into one is impracticable would be the last moment of my wishing to remain where I am. (of the monarchical federalists I have no expectations. they are incurables, to be taken care of in a madhouse if necessary & on motives of charity.) I am much pleased therefore with your information that the republican federalists are still coming in to the desired union. the Eastern newspapers had given me a different impression, because I supposed the printers knew the taste of their customers & cooked their dishes to their palates. the palladium is understood to be the *Clerical* paper, & from the clergy I expect no mercy. they crucified their Saviour who preached that their kingdom was not of this world, and all who practise on that precept must expect the extreme of their wrath. the laws of the present day withold their hands from blood. but lies and slander still remain to them. I am satisfied that the heaping of abuse on me personally has been with the design & the hope of provoking me to make a general sweep of all federalists out of office. but as I have carried no passion into the execution of this disagreeable duty, I shall suffer none to be excited. the clamour which has been raised will not provoke me to remove one more, nor deter me to remove one less than if not a word had been said on the subject. in Massachusets you may be assured great moderation will be used. indeed Connecticut, New York, New Jersey, Pensylva & Delaware are the only states where any thing considerable is desired. in the course of the summer all which is necessary will be done; and we may hope that this cause of offence being at an end, the measures we shall pursue & propose for the amelioration of the public affairs will be so confessedly salutary as to unite all men not monarchists in principle.—we have considerable hopes of republican Senators from S. Carolina, Maryland & Delaware, & some as to Vermont. in any event we are secure of a majority in the Senate; and consequently that there will be a concert of action between the legislative & executive. the removal of excrescences from the Judiciary is the universal demand.—We propose to reassemble at Washington on the last day of September. accept assurances of my affectionate esteem & high respect.   TH: JEFFERSON

RC (MHi: Levi Lincoln Papers); at foot of first page: "Mr. Lincoln"; endorsed by Lincoln. PrC (DLC).

RECTIFIED BY A STATEMENT: during the spring of 1801, the Federalist *Columbian Centinel* of Boston made an issue of payments to the officers of the *Berceau* in addition to the cost of repairs to the ship. In August, writing as "A Farmer" in the *Massachusetts Spy* of Worcester, Lincoln defended various actions of TJ's administration, including the advance of money to the French officers in lieu of their pay "on security by the agent for the French government for its repayment in France." The officers had been boarded in private homes, and in arranging for the advance to allow them to meet their expenses, the United States was "but copying the examples of other civilized nations." For Lincoln's use of the "Farmer" pseudonym, see his letter to TJ of 16 Sep. (*Massachusetts Spy, or Worcester Gazette*, 19 Aug. 1801; *Columbian Centinel*, 29 Apr., 9 May; Lincoln to TJ, 28 July 1801).

From James Madison

Dear Sir   Aug. 26. 1801

I have duly recd. yours of Aug. 22. with the papers sent with it. I have heard nothing from Dallas on the subject of another prosecution agst. Duane. It is to be presumed that he will either commence it, or let us know his reasons for not doing so. Should further silence take place, I will jog his attention. I know nothing of Clay personally. All I know thro' others is in his favor, and speak him well adapted to the station you have thought of for him. C. D. Coxe can have Madeira, if you determine against Pintard. No other place occurs as so clearly disposeable.

I inclose herewith the communications brought me by the last mail. I have signed the exequatur requested by Mr. Olsen, that if a grant of it should be decided, there may be no delay. He seems to have had in view something less formal. It is odd that Soderstrom should still proceed in Danish Business, knowing as he must the presence of Olsen, and being himself too, without any regular authority from that Govt.

Consul Eaton you will find has taken another extraordinary step. Wagner's explanation of it with his own letter, leaves me nothing to add on the subject, farther than that I have signified my opinion that under the choice of difficulties, the least will be to ship the powder & ball requested by the Dey of Algiers. As there is little room for doubting his continuance at peace, it may not be amiss to take the oppy. to make another payment to him; and there will be less trouble & loss in doing it in these articles than any other. I have also signified that the contract of Eaton must as the lesser evil be fulfilled, but that it ought to be done in a way if possible, that may throw the expence on himself, if hereafter so determined. The private commission as to the Timber, and the equivocal one as to the Cattle, I have desired Mr. Wagner not to meddle with.

Can you give me any information towards an answer to the letter from Mr. Starke. I recollect nothing on the subject.

I have desired Mr. Wagner to send you copy of the last letters from the Dept. of State to Mr. Eaton with such other information so he might enable you to give your answer to the Bey of Tunis with care & precision. It is probable you may find it convenient to attend to the jewels preparing for him in London. Yours respectfully & Affecy.

James Madison

RC (DLC); at foot of text: "The President of the U States"; endorsed by TJ as received from the State Department on 27 Aug. and so recorded in SJL. Enclosures: (1) Jacob Wagner to Madison, 17 Aug., enclosing various communications as described in his covering letter (Madison, *Papers, Sec. of State Ser.*, 2:49-54). (2) Peder Blicher Olsen to Madison, 9 Aug., forwarding two letters confided to him before he left Europe for delivery to the president and requesting permission to announce his arrival in America unofficially in the newspapers before he is formally received (same, 2:25). (3) Richard Söderström, consul general of Sweden, to Madison, 10 Aug., requesting speedy justice in the American judicial system for Danish claims, especially regarding the case of the *William* (same, 2:29-30). (4) William Eaton to Madison, 10 Apr., enclosing a packet of 12 communications, including a letter from the Bey of Tunis to TJ, 15 Apr. requesting larger cannon, informing the secretary of state he had chartered a Ragusan brig for $8,000 to bring dispatches from Tunis, and expressing

hope the brig on its return voyage could bring timber, as part of a private business transaction and cattle that he had promised the Tunisian prime minister (same, 1:78-82). (5) Eaton to Madison, 18 Apr., reporting that contrary winds had delayed the vessel and enclosing a copy of the captain's instructions, inadvertently omitted in his previous letter (same, 1:104). (6) Theodore Stark to Madison, 4 Aug., inquiring about the status of his application for Mississippi territorial attorney (same, 2:68).

For the MADEIRA consulship, see TJ to Pierce Butler, 27 July 1801, and TJ to Madison, 22 Aug.

For Eaton's EXTRAORDINARY STEP, see enclosure No. 4, and for Wagner's criticism of Eaton's actions, see Madison, *Papers, Sec. of State Ser.*, 2:51-2.

From James Blair

DEAR SIR   Vermont, Jerico Augt. 27th. 1801

As Names and titles is but Empty sounds to a philosipher and he whos soul is naturaly great for in my opinion there is no name so great as man—for we find by record that he that was Posesed of all the arts of friendship and love did not assume The name but only the son of Man and as a desendent of That root I shall adress you—
Sir About eight years ago I began to be Distrustfull of myself my fathers and bretherin respecting what we beleived and the more I tryed to find the cause of my distrust the more confirmed I was that there was a deception some where. and this naturaly led me to the acount given of a Saviour. and my own feelings with all the visable evidence that I could find in the world gave this acount the lie. and here I was in a strait between two for I found myself with all created nature in a State of imperfection and that it was imposable for any being or thing to Judge what was right as what was wrong where imperfection had the rule. And my anxiety increased—I wanted a certainty for an uncertainty But these agitations increased dayly and produced the result that the acount peradventer might be true. as it began to be reasonable to me if it was a perfect rule that it was imposable for imperfection to understand or beleive it. I therefore imbraced it in contridiction to every impulse of natural reason; and Was not long in suspence after entering upon this Determination for I found every

suggesion, and every thought raryfied and brightened. and an internal war that comenced confirmed me that I had enterd in at the straight gate. But the greatness of the sience was too powerfull for me. I therefore was some times in hopes some times in Dispair and in this way I continued for the space of two years through manyfold trials which is not uterable. when it terminated in the result of the acount given of a Saviour being true. and this Discovery turned every thing that was practised by mankind in all shapes and places into the abomination of Desolation spoaken of by him standing where it ought not. pretty soon after this I saw a publication in the news paper by Cornelious Davis of New York and Editor of the theological magazine. that he would receive and publish impartialy all candid esays of every religious Denomination and that every mater would be thankfully received. And I had not foresight enough at that time to perceive that I was not comprehended in that Declaration. I therefore imbraced it as a door opened to me that I might expose my Discoverys to public view. But To my greate Disapointment I found the door to shut whenever I apeared in sight. for after writing the result of my discoverys I sent The esays to New York. But the editor after perusal hesitated and Called for the advice of his orthodox friends who all with one consent Agreed that the esays ware candedly and injeniously written but they ware hetrodox. therefore could not be admited into the magazine, Altho both these names ware excluded by the publication. and I should not have known what had Become of the esays had it not been for as I supose one of the council who posesed a firm and liberal spirit who by way of letter to his friend on free Discussion made the Above Statements in the third. no. & 2d vol. of that magazine under the Name of Menander. I then used my indevour to obtain the esays from mr. Davis but never could. and about this time the Sedition Law Under the late administration came in force and as I expected that an undue advantage would be taken by it I therefore posponed trying to have it published untill March last when I Sent the esays to mr. Smith Editor of the national Inteligencer with this advice that after perusal if he found any thing in them worthy of public Discussion to publish it in any way he chose. if not to send it imediately back to me I waited a reasonable time but no answer which made me feel uneasy and impatient whereupon I wrote him an other letter Stating to him my uneaseyness and Desiaring him to send them as soon as he receivd that information if he was not going to publish them. and as soon As transmission could be had both ways I received them. and in the Corse of time that mr. Smith had them their was a printer set up his business not far from this place. and from some feeble incouragement I expected to be able to have it printed there but when it came to the test I found my confidence was misplaced however the Editor was willing to print it if I would pay him and the amount for the Number of Coppys that he was willing to print was more than I was able to pay. but I made him aproposal on which I have receivd. no answer. and know not wheather he intends printing them or not. mr Smiths Delicacy with respect to the station that he fills was the only reason that he Did not publish it. for I beleive his modesty would Suffer insult rather than give offence. now sir as an elder and father I requaist your fostering care and this is my petetion that my Discovery may be brought onto the publick Stage eposed and Defended that the merits of it may be asertained. and if the evidence Given Show that it is not worthy of cultivation then let it sink into oblivion. But if no such evidence can be produced then let it have that place It merits and that confidence that it deserves in society. but I am fully aware of the Dificulty that atends its having aplace for the gender of this Science stands in all places exactly in opesition to the suggesions and Persutes of human reson. therefore the mind long habituated to a different way of think-ing, is not prepaired to receive it and the essence is lost before it even gets into an embryo state. and no idea can be Drawn of its shape or figure. people in speaking of me. some say he is fancysick. others he is an Anarch. others if he is not right there is no Right. and I am of opinion, sir, when you come to read the esays and compair them with the standard that the Saviour gave to mankind to walk by and then look at the traditions and persutes of mankind and you would Doubt of its being safe to publish it. yea I know if it is published that my life is in Jepherdy. for so far as the Divel has power to influence the minde. which I beleive will Go so far as to think that in taking my life they will do God service. but my life is a willing and a living Sacrifice for I am confident that the way must be prepaired by some one of the race of Adam in the way the Saviour has pointed out. and if it falls to my lot I chearfuly under take it altho it is asevair trial to human na-ture now Sir, Grant me my requaist, and hesitate not at my petetion. and your Servant will ever pray to the sarcher of all hearts that you may be directed in the paths of virtue and truth. that you may be able to conduct wisely in the midst of an imperfect people—After the pe-rusal of this as it is altho I feel confident you would excuse the blun-dering manner in which it is wrote if I had time to explain it if you have adesiar to see the esays I think by aplying to the Editor above mentioned at washington city who from existing circumstances has preserved acoppy in his own hands. if not if you will signify it to me

I will imediately send them printed or unprinted. and if your condesestion will give an answer to this I shall think myself happy.
From your obediant Sert.,   JAMES BLAIR.

RC (MHi); endorsed by TJ as a letter of 29 Aug. and so recorded in SJL. Recorded in SJL as received 17 Sep.

Cornelius DAVIS OF NEW YORK was a religiously inclined publisher and bookseller who published, from 1795 to 1799, his *Theological Magazine, or Synopsis of Modern Religious Sentiment, on a New Plan*, which was succeeded by his *New-York Missionary Magazine, and Repository of Religious Intelligence* from 1800 to 1803 (Gaylord P. Albaugh, *History and Annotated Bibliography of American Religious Periodicals and Newspapers Established from 1730 through 1830*, 2 vols. [Worcester, Mass., 1994], 1:325, 687-8).

From Thomas Claxton

HONOR'D SIR   City of Washington August 27, 1801.

Some time prior to your departure from this place, I think you informed me that your return would take place about the first of October, which is about a month hence—a space of time not sufficient to have the six Sophas made and forwarded to Monticello before you leave it—As I have concluded they could be of no service during your present visit, and knowing the difficulty of explaining to many mechanics by letter any thing out of their common line, I have thought it advisable to consult you on the propriety of letting the order remain until your return, about which time I have it in contemplation to go to Philadelphia to see some of my Children, when it would be in my power to explain verbally any directions you may be pleased to give— If you should not think proper to let the matter lie, Sir, you will please to inform me by your answer, whether you wish the cushions to be made for one or two Sophas—if each has a cushion, it will be a handsomer piece of furniture in a room, but when two are placed together for the purpose of sleeping on, one cushion covering both, would, perhaps be more convenient—

I have hopes, that in the course of two weeks I shall be able to have every thing completed in the President's house, (except the grates) which was in hand when you left this—I shall then close the accounts, and get them settled in the Treasury, if possible, before the first of the next month, in order that you may know the exact state of the furnishing fund on your return—

The partition in your bed room is going on, and will be done, it is said in about two weeks

I have a handsome carpet ready to place on the floor[1] as soon as done—The circular room is furnished with its drapery, and carpet, girandols, and chandelier—it looks well indeed, considering that all its furniture is common—The sophas are now in the hands of the Up-holsterer, who is deliberate with all his work. As soon as the different mechanics are out of the house, I shall have all put in order as soon as possible—

The walls of the chamber of the house of Representatives are up to the window heads, above which I believe they have to go about 3 feet—

I should be happy to learn, Sir, whether the trunk with the plated ware went safe, and without being defaced, and also how the chairs look, which I think might have arrived

In your letter, Sir, which you did me the honor of writing last, you was pleased to mention some thing about the trouble you had given me—I flatter myself, Sir, that you will believe me when I say, that what you deem trouble I consider as a real pleasure, and that your approbation of my conduct in the little commissions which I have had the honor of executing for you, is a reward the value of which no one can estimate except those who have been so fortunate as to have the honor of a personal intercourse with you

With the most sincere esteem I have the honor to be Sir Your most obt. Svt   THOS CLAXTON

RC (MHi); endorsed by TJ as received 3 Sep. and so recorded in SJL.

YOUR LETTER: TJ to Claxton, 18 Aug., recorded in SJL but not found.

[1] MS: "foor."

From James Madison

DEAR SIR   Aug. 27. 1801

I sent you yesterday by Docr. Bache a packet recd. by the mail of last week, that it might the less interfere with what you receive directly. I avail myself of another private opportunity to forward the communications recd. by the mail of yesterday, by which means the further advantage will be obtained, of gaining a week in those cases which require your sanction, and which need not go back thro' my hands.

Among the communications you will find Thornton again on our hands, and with a case that seems to compel us to meet the question whether the British Treaty is to operate agst. French Ships with prizes, as well as those of other nations. It is more than probable that[1] another privateer which has arrived in N. Carolina with a British prize, though called in the newspapers Spanish will be found to be French and will soon double the demand for a decision of that question. Will it be best to give in the first instance a particular & argumentative, or a more general & categorical answer to Mr Thornton. It may be a consideration in favor of the latter that we have no reason to suppose, that his Govt. enters into his construction of the Treaty of 1794.

Yours truly &c.   JAMES MADISON

I forgot to mention St. Petersburg as vacant for a Consul. If Coxe will go there, it would be more convenient than to give him Madeira, which may be eligible for other[2]

RC (DLC); addressed: "The President of the United States"; endorsed by TJ as received from the State Department on 28 Aug. and so recorded in SJL. Enclosure: Edward Thornton to Madison, 16 Aug., regarding news of a French privateer, *L'Experience*, and her prize, *British Queen,* that had anchored in Portland, Maine, as described in an enclosed extract from the *Gazette of the United States* of 12 Aug., and expressing concern for the injury done to British commerce by asylum granted to vessels "which ought to be im-

mediately excluded from the American harbours" (Madison, *Papers, Sec. of State Ser.,* 2:47-8). Other enclosures not identified.

For the PRIVATEER that arrived in Wilmington, North Carolina, see Gallatin to TJ, 24 Aug.

[1] MS: "than."
[2] Postscript written perpendicular to text in left margin.

From Thomas T. Davis

SIR   Danville Kentucky [28 Aug. 1801]

I have been informed that Mr W. Claiborn does not accept his appointment as Govenor of the Mississippi Territory: Should this be the case I would be pleased with the appointment. A Residence of thirteen years among the Western people & a frequent intercourse with every part of the Western Country enables me to form Just notions of them & their policy. Whether my character as a man authorise me to ask this or not you will be able to form some opinion from the large majorities by which I have been Elected to Congress from this State. Whether I am friendly to our Constitution or not can be decided by my Conduct since I have been in Congress. Frequent & long absences from home while attending my publick duty in Congress is disagreeable & unprofitable. Being considerably under middle life, with a growing family, my exertions are necessary for their support in some way & the practice of the Law irksome & Bar, in this Country crowded. I am with respect

your obt Sert. THO. T. DAVIS

The appointment of Colo. Jos. Crockett meets with universal approbation. Mr Fowler is Elected by a majority of near five thousand & I by a majority of 6.501.

RC (DNA: RG 59, LAR); mutilated, with date supplied from SJL; endorsed by TJ as received 15 Sep. and so recorded in SJL; also endorsed by TJ, in part, "to be Govr. of Missisip[i]."

TJ appointed Joseph CROCKETT the marshal for the district of Kentucky in June 1801 (Vol. 32:592). Davis and John FOWLER had represented Kentucky in the House of Representatives since the Fifth Congress (*Biog. Dir. Cong.*).

To Enoch Edwards

DEAR SIR Monticello Aug. 28. 1801.

I recieved yesterday your favor of the 20th. informing me that the carriage made for me is now ready to be delivered. I recieved at the same time from mr Barnes of Georgetown information that he was going on in a few days to Philadelphia. I have therefore this day written to him and committed to him the charge of recieving & forwarding it on to Washington, & of paying for it, he being my universal agent in money matters. I have so often had occasion to thank you for your attentions & trouble in this business that a repetition offers nothing new, altho' it be just. under that conviction they are sincerely rendered.

You think our estimate of turnpike road may be deceptive. there was a mile of it at Washington finished, when I came away[1] 30. feet wide, and compleatly well done. it was all gravel. &, made under some disadvantages, had cost under 1200. D. we expect on good grounds to do the residue for 1000. D. per mile. I saw nothing better done in England. in Massachusets they have done upwards of 100. miles. having no gravel, they use common stone broken into small pieces. the cost has been regularly 1000. D. per mile. accept the tender of my sincere esteem & respect. TH: JEFFERSON

PrC (DLC); at foot of text: "Doctr. Edwards"; endorsed by TJ in ink on verso.

THIS DAY WRITTEN TO HIM: TJ to John Barnes, 28 Aug., recorded in SJL but not found.

[1] Preceding four words interlined.

From Christopher Ellery

Sir.   Newport August 28th. 1801—

Conscious of a want of the *talents* which should grace the station to which I am appointed I shall endeavor to supply the deficiency by *fidelity* in discharging the duties imposed on me by my acceptance of the important trust—During your administration Sir I well know that honesty will be esteemed above brilliancy—and on this ground I hope to merit your approbation and that of my constituents—The communication which I am about to make will be received as irresistable evidence of *faithfulness* when its nature is considered—for to an honorable mind the disclosure of the crime of forgery—and perhaps treachery—must be ever painful in the extreme—But feelings aside, allow me to state facts—   On the 3d. & 4th. inst. the communications of which I enclose a copy (No. 1) were made to me and on the 8th. inst those of which No. 2 is a copy—these copies are exact from the memoranda penned & filed by me on the said days, with the endorsments then made—This day the postmaster has handed me your letter, of which No. 3. is a copy—Mr. Richardson informs me that this letter was given to him by Mr. Geffroy, *who knew not what to make of it*—I waited on Mr. Geffroy, who makes & deals in watches & jewelery on a pretty large scale and with whom I have frequently done business to our mutual satisfaction, and enjoined silence—He could not believe that the letter actually came from the President and indeed was wholly at a loss for conjecture after having exhibited it to two or three persons for explanation—

Mr. Geffroy was born in France—has lived in Newport 10 or 20 years, owns real estate here— married the daughter of a worthy mechanic, by whom he has children—and supports the character of industry & honesty, attending closely to his trade and not taking a part in politics—He is sensible to the injury done him by the scandalous assumption of his name—   It is probable that one of these persons who gained knowledge of the letter may speak of it—

I ought not to pass over the conduct of the postmaster and his assistant silently convinced as I am that they have acted from the most pure motives and that they deserve the fullest approbation—The father has ever been and is now as he was in '75 a republican—the son follows in the steps of his father—and I declare freely my satisfaction in the confidence they have reposed in me, flattering myself they are entitled to your favorable opinion and that no injury can result from the part taken in this affair through a desire to detect villany—

Ever ready to throw my mite into the measure of public happiness

I beg you Sir to afford me the opportunity whenever circumstances shall permit—And pardon me Sir for indulging the strongest indignation towards the wretch who aims his blows against the public happiness in gross attempts to impose on the Chief Magistrate by feigned signatures—

That you may discover and defeat the detestable designs of the foes to our Country and its First Friend is my fervent prayer—

CHRIST. ELLERY

John Rutledge representative from S. Carolina spends his summers in Newport—I have the letter to N. Geffroy in my possession—There may be *some* truth in the fortification story &c, as you have undoubtedly learned from pure sources— C. E.

RC (DLC); addressed: "Thomas Jefferson—President of United States"; endorsed by TJ as received 10 Sep. and so recorded in SJL. Enclosures: (1) Depositions by postmaster Jacob Richardson and assistant postmaster Jacob Richardson, Jr., 3 and 4 Aug. 1801, claiming that the post office received letters for TJ that appeared to be in John Rutledge's hand although disguised (Tr in DLC: TJ Papers, 115:19767; entirely in Ellery's hand; at head of text:"Copy No. 1"; at foot of text: "Memoranda—of Rutledge's letter"). (2) Depositions by Jacob Richardson and Jacob Richardson, Jr., 8 Aug.

1801, regarding another letter presumably in Rutledge's hand, with Ellery's commitment to render his future services to the country by exposing the wickedness of the presumed forgery (Tr in DLC: TJ Papers, 115:19768; entirely in Ellery's hand; at head of text: "Copy No. 2"; at foot of text: "Memo. Rutledge's letter"). (3) See TJ to "Nicholas Geffroy," 14 Aug. 1801.

Ellery also wrote to TJ on 1 July, 1 and 4 Aug. (all recorded in SJL as received 20 Aug. from Newport, but not found).

To Albert Gallatin

DEAR SIR   Monticello Aug. 28. 1801.

Your favors of the 18th. & 24th. came by yesterday's post. I am sorry mr Clay declines a Consulship. it would have been very pleasing to us to replace our Minister at Lisbon[1] by such a Consul as Clay. perhaps reconsideration and enquiry into the advantages of the situation may reconcile it to him. I have not here my bundle of claims for office, & therefore cannot propose a successor for Colo. White in Jersey. your acquaintance in the state will better enable you to do it.—I have written to three gentlemen of great discretion one at Norfolk the others[2] near Hampton on the subject of Chisman. I have an answer from the one at Norfolk who has never heard of him. I shall hear from the others before the next post. I have known mr Page from the time we were boys & classmates together, & love him as a brother. but I have always known him the worst judge of man existing. he has fallen a sacrifice to the ease with which he gives his confidence to those who deserve it not. still if we hear nothing against Chisman we may venture to do what will be agreeable to mr Page. I am very anxious to do something useful for him: and so universally is he esteemed in this country that no man's promotion would be more generally approved. he has not an enemy in the world. but we have but one officer here whom the *general* voice, whig & tory,[3] marks for removal; & I am not well enough acquainted with it's duties to be certain that they are adapted to mr Page's talents. the explanation you give of the nature of the office proposed for Jonas Clarke silences my doubts, and I agree to the appointment. I think we should do justice to Campbell & Gardner, & cannot suppose the Auditor will think hard of[4] replacing them in their former births. he has seen us restore officers where we thought their removal unjust, and cannot therefore view it in this case as meant to censure himself specially. specific restitution is the particular measure of justice which the case calls for.

The doctrine as to the admission of prizes, maintained by the government, from the commencement of the war between England, France &c to this day has been this. the treaties give a right to armed vessels *with their prizes* to go where they please (consequently into our ports) & that these prizes shall not be detained, siezed nor adjudicated; but that the armed vessel may depart as *speedily as may be, with her prize*, to the place of her commission: and we are not to suffer their enemies to sell in our ports the prizes taken by their privateers. before the British treaty no stipulation stood in the way of permitting France to sell her prizes here; & we did permit it; but expressly as a favor, not as a right. see letter of Aug. 16. 1793. to Gouv. Morris §. 4. and other letters in that correspondence which I cannot now turn to. these stipulations admit the prizes to put into our ports in cases of necessity, or perhaps of convenience, but no right to remain, if disagreeable to us; & absolutely not to be sold. we have accordingly lately ordered away a British vessel brought in by a Spanish armed ship, and I have given it as my opinion to mr Madison that the British snow Windsor lately brought in by the prisoners she was carrying, ought to be sent away. my opinion is that whatever we are free to do, we ought to do, to throw difficulties in the way of the depredations committed on commerce, & chiefly our own commerce.

In the case of the Spanish privateer at Wilmington N.C. who wants to sell as much of his prize as will refit the privateer, it is absolutely forbidden. the directions you have already given as to the prize herself coincide perfectly with what I think right.—no pardon has come to me from mr Wagner for Hopkins. I consent to the transfer you propose of the superintendance of the lighthouses of Portsmouth & N. York to the present collectors of those ports; and to the appointment of the Collector for Savanna recommended by Genl. Jackson, if you learn nothing to the contrary from the delegates. accept assurances of my affectionate esteem & high respect.   TH: JEFFERSON

RC (NHi: Gallatin Papers); at foot of first page: "The Secretary of the Treasury"; endorsed by Gallatin. PrC (DLC).

REPLACE OUR MINISTER AT LISBON: for the recall of William Loughton Smith, the closure of the U.S. legation in Portugal, and TJ's search for a qualified, trusted consul to replace Thomas Bulkeley at Lisbon, see Vol. 34:129-31, 176, 429-30.

I HAVE WRITTEN: see TJ to Thomas Newton, 14 Aug., and TJ to Samuel Sheild, 21 Aug.

For TJ's view as expressed in the fourth point of his 16 Aug. 1793 letter to Gouverneur MORRIS, see Vol. 26:705-6.

MY OPINION TO MR MADISON: see TJ to Madison, 22 Aug. Gallatin received instructions from Madison, on 29 Aug., to issue orders to Benjamin Lincoln to expel the BRITISH SNOW WINDSOR from the port (Madison, *Papers, Sec. of State Ser.*, 2:73). On 3 Sep. Gallatin wrote Lincoln that the president "thought it proper on general grounds, though not required by the Treaty with Great Britain," that the vessel should depart from U.S. jurisdiction and requested that the collector "take prompt & efficient measures for carrying it into immediate effect." Gallatin explained the general grounds of the president's decision, noting that although treaties may have given several nations a right to send prizes to U.S. ports without being "detained siezed or adjudicated, no right exists for them to remain beyond a reasonable time if disagreeable to us, and

that it is neither our duty nor our interest to grant to prizes principally made on our coast, & which can hardly be considered in any better light than indirect depradations on our commerce, any further indulgence than is strictly enjoined by the obligations of treaties & of the law of nations or by the dictates of humanity" (Gallatin, *Papers*, 5:680-1).

For Gallatin's DIRECTIONS to Griffith J. McRee regarding the Spanish privateer at Wilmington, see Enclosure No. 5, listed at Gallatin to TJ, 24 Aug. On 13 Sep., the collector wrote Gallatin that the commander "finding that He could not succeed in disposing of his prize or part thereof under any pretence, made all reasonable haste in refitting his privateer and put to Sea again with both Vessels" (Gallatin, *Papers*, 5:732).

On 5 Sep., Gallatin wrote William Miller, the commissioner of the revenue, that the president had authorized the transfer of the superintendence of the LIGHTHOUSES from Thomas Martin and Joshua Sands, former collectors at Portsmouth, New Hampshire, and New York City "to the present collectors of those two ports respectively" (Gallatin, *Papers*, 47:405-6).

[1] Preceding two words interlined in place of "there."
[2] Preceding five words interlined.
[3] TJ here canceled "designates."
[4] Remainder of sentence interlined in place of "it."

To Levi Lincoln

DEAR SIR   Monticello Aug. 28. 1801.

Your favor of the 14th. came to hand yesterday. having written to you two days ago only, I have but to acknolege the reciept of the letter before mentioned and to refer to you a case in which the US. seem threatened with the danger of having a considerable sum to pay, contrary to law & justice, and if the inclosed statements are right, merely by the negligence of their district-attorney. the printed pamphlet, & mr Bingham's letter inclosed will explain to you the transaction, and I must pray you to take into serious consideration the best steps to be taken for warding off this loss from the public, and that you will undertake the direction & superintendence of the proceedings. accept assurances of my sincere & affectionate esteem & respect

TH: JEFFERSON

RC (MHi: Levi Lincoln Papers); at foot of text: "Levi Lincoln esq."; endorsed by Lincoln: "respecting Bingham's action"; with notation in SJL: "Bingham's case." PrC (DLC). Enclosure: [William Bingham], *Proceedings Relative to the Danish Brig Hope, and Cargo* (Philadelphia, 1801?), a synopsis of Bingham's view of the case with printed texts of documents, prepared by Bingham before leaving for England in 1801 (see Alberts, *Golden Voyage*, 417; Evans, No. 38328). Other enclosure not found.

Lincoln had already seen, in June or earlier, some papers relating to William Bingham's CASE, which stemmed from the taking of the brigantine *Hope* by the Massachusetts privateer *Pilgrim* during the American Revolution. Bingham was the agent of the Continental Congress at Martinique when the *Hope* put in there in January 1779 after the capture. Convinced that neither the vessel nor its cargo of barreled flour were British, Bingham and the governor of the island released the ship and sold the flour, holding the proceeds in escrow. A consortium of merchants that owned the *Pilgrim*, including members of the Cabot family, brought suit against Bingham, first in a Massachusetts court and later in federal court. Contending that the cargo had been British property, making the *Hope* a valid prize, the plaintiffs obtained liens on

Bingham's assets in Pennsylvania and Massachusetts, including his land in the district of Maine. In a U.S. circuit court they won a judgment for more than $30,000. Despite two appeals to the Supreme Court, Bingham was unable to have the judgment reversed before he left the United States for England in 1801 (Madison, *Papers, Sec. of State Ser.*, 1:310; DHSC, 6:554-63; Alberts, *Golden Voyage*, 78-9, 365-7; Lincoln to Madison, 21 Jan. 1802, in DNA: RG 59, LOAG).

NEGLIGENCE OF THEIR DISTRICT-ATTORNEY: in 1793, when the plaintiffs filed their case in federal court, Bingham asked the U.S. government to defend the suit. Attorney General Edmund Randolph, Alexander Hamilton, and TJ, who was then secretary of state, concurred in advising George Washington that the United States did have responsibility in the case. Christopher Gore, the U.S. attorney for the district of Massachusetts, worked on the case with Bingham's attorneys, but Gore's successor, John Davis, did not. In 1799, after the circuit court issued the judgment against Bingham, Timothy Pickering instructed Davis to join the case on Bingham's behalf (Dorothy Twohig, ed., *The Journal of the Proceedings of the President, 1793-1797* [Charlottesville, 1981], 106n; Syrett, *Hamilton*, 14:154-7, 226, 239-40; Alberts, *Golden Voyage*, 366).

To Robert R. Livingston

DEAR SIR   Monticello Aug. 28. 1801.

Your favor of the 10th. inst. came to hand yesterday, and I recieve it with the respect & attention with which I do every thing coming from you. nothing can be done on the subject of it till after my return to Washington which will probably be after your departure for France. whatever may be determined by the gentlemen of the administration on the subject of mr Davis, other candidates have been brought forward on grounds so respectable that the prospects of any new candidate cannot but be very doubtful. on this view of the subject I could not undertake to recommend the changing the destination of mr Edward P. Livingston in his intended voyage with you.

We are in hourly expectation of recieving information that the treaty with France is ratified. the only letter from Dawson supposes it unquestionable & that it will be without delay. I am afraid that government may have ideas of sending either La Forest or Otto here. I believe them both unprincipled men, entirely antirevolutionary, & so much in sentiment with the monarchical federalists here, that I should expect nothing less than their betraying to them every transaction which should pass with the Executive. under this impression we could never say a word to either which we should not be willing to publish at once.[1] whether our suspicions are just or not, their effect would defeat whatever should depend on confidential communications. should no appointment be made before your arrival at Paris, it would be important that that government should be apprised in some delicate way that however confidential these men might be with the opposition, they cannot be so with any[2] administration here which shall be republican. I shall trouble you with another letter before your departure. health & happiness.

TH: JEFFERSON

RC (NNMus); addressed: "Robert R. Livingston Chancellor of New York"; franked; endorsed by Livingston. PrC (DLC).

ONLY LETTER FROM DAWSON: probably John Dawson's letter to Madison of 27 May, which has not been found (see Madison, *Papers, Sec. of State Ser.*, 1:233).

LA FOREST served as the interim French consul general to the United States and consul for the states of Pennsylvania and Delaware from 1785 until 1792, when he received a new commission for a permanent appointment. At that time, TJ questioned whether La Forest was to become consul general to the states of New York, New Jersey, Pennsylvania, and Delaware only, or to the United States as a whole. The French government recalled La Forest in November 1792 (Vol. 24:530-1). Louis Guillaume OTTO served as French chargé d'affaires in the United States from 1785 to 1788 and 1789 to 1791. TJ first became acquainted with him in 1783. In late 1790

[161]

and early 1791, Otto presented France's complaints against U.S. commercial policies—specifically the tonnage acts—to TJ. In April 1790, TJ witnessed Otto's marriage to the daughter of St. John de

Crèvecoeur (Vol. 18:516, 528-77; Vol. 26:479; Vol. 27:781).

[1] TJ here canceled "you may judge."
[2] Word interlined in place of "this."

To James Madison

DEAR SIR   Monticello Aug. 28. 1801.

Your's of the 26th. by Doctr. Bache came duly to hand: and I now return you all the papers you inclosed except the commission for the Marshal of New Jersey, which I retain till I see you, which Dr. Bache gives me hopes will be the ensuing week, & I suppose will of course be the day after tomorrow, as you will then be free from the pressure of the post. I inclose with those papers, for perusal, a letter & memorial from a mr Joseph Allen Smith, of whom I know nothing more than these papers inform me. you will be sensible that in his assumption of diplomatic functions he has not shewn much diplomatic subtlety. he seems not afraid of Logan's law in our hands. of mr Starke's application for the attorney's place of Missisipi I recollect nothing; and not having here my bundle of applications for office I can ascertain nothing. but I am persuaded he has not applied to me; & consequently it must have been to our predecessors. this would afford a reason the more for enquiries concerning him before we decide about him. this shall be reserved for conversation when we meet.—I feel a scruple at signing the recital of a falshood in the Exequatur for Olsen, to wit, 'the having seen his commission'. it would bind us to admit his credentials let them be what they will; and be an useless departure from fact. I think with you that he desires much less, & what is perfectly admissible; & consequently that it would be better to write him a very civil letter yielding exactly what he asks.

What are the delays in the performance of our stipulations of which the Bey of Tunis, & Eaton complain? I thought we had not only complied with the treaty, but were doing considerably more. I have read Eaton's correspondence, and form a very respectable opinion of his understanding. I should be disposed to do so too of his honesty: but how, to these two qualities, can we reconcile his extraordinary mission of this vessel? if nothing sinister appears on the enquiry mr Wagner is making, he should be made to understand that the administration will not admit such unauthorised & useless waste of the public money. as to the cattle & timber, I would leave them to be sent or not by those charged with them. I am an enemy to all these douceurs, tributes & humiliations. what the laws impose on us let us execute faithfully; but nothing more. I think it would be well to engage mr Wagner (who is fully competent to it) to make up, for the eye of Congress a full statement of every expence which our transactions with the Barbary powers has occasioned, & of what we still owe, that they may be enabled to decide, on a full view of the subject, what course they will pursue. I know that nothing will stop the eternal increase of demand from these pirates but the presence of an armed force, and it will be more economical & more honorable to use the same means at once for suppressing their insolencies.—I think with you we had better send by Eaton's vessel the powder & ball wanting for Algiers.—I have recieved information through a single hand [from one of Bainbridge's lieutenants, that Bainbridge himself connived at] the pretended [impressment] of [the George Washington,] & perhaps [recieved a douceur.] as soon [as we hear] of any [actual] hostility by [Tripoli], I think [Cathcart] should be sent to [Algiers, & Obrian permitted to retire.] these two men have completely shewn themselves to be what I concieved of them on a pretty full acquaintance in Philadelphia.—would it not be well to instruct our agents resident where there have been British admiralty courts to collect all the cases, which can be authenticated, of the enormities of those courts? I am persuaded it must be the groundwork of a demand on our part of stipulations from that country entirely novel in their nature, and which nothing but the disgrace of their proceedings can extort from them. but they are indispensably necessary for us. we are surely never more to submit to such ruinous degradations again. in hopes of seeing you soon I conclude with assurances of sincere & affectionate friendship   TH: JEFFERSON

P.S. I send Bingham's case to mr Lincoln.

RC (DLC: Madison Papers); at foot of first page: "The Secretary of State"; words in brackets, canceled heavily in RC, supplied from PrC. PrC (DLC). Enclosure: Joseph Allen Smith to TJ, 22 Mch. 1801; see Vol. 33:404-6.

LOGAN'S LAW: the 1799 act preventing private citizens such as Smith from acting as diplomats (U.S. Statutes at Large, 1:613).

TJ approved a letter of EXEQUATUR dated 13 Oct. for Blicher Olsen after he produced his letter of appointment as consul general for the king of Denmark (Tr in DNA: RG 59, Exequaturs).

IMPRESSMENT OF THE GEORGE WASHINGTON: in September 1800, after the U.S. frigate George Washington arrived in Algiers carrying goods for the annuity, the dey demanded that the ship transport his ambassador and presents, under an Algerian flag, to the sultan at Constantinople. William Bainbridge, the ship's captain, and Richard O'Brien, the U.S. consul, protested, but as Bainbridge reported to the secretary of the navy, he had "no alternative but compliance or war." The ship made the trip to Constantinople without incident and arrived back in the United States in April 1801. In a letter to O'Brien in May, Madison deemed the episode an "indignity" that had "deeply affected the sensibility not only of the President, but of the people of the United States" (NDBW, 1:361-2, 365-6, 375-80, 385, 401, 436; Madison, *Papers, Sec. of State Ser.*, 1:214; 2:51).

From Timothy Matlack

SIR,   Lancaster August 28. 1801.

The knowledge of political characters is at all times of importance to the Chief Magistrate of the Union, and at no time was it more so than at the present moment. In Pennsylvania it is peculiarly so from the extreme Violence of those who have taken a lead among the Federalists; and [in] no part of the state has this violence been so outragious & insulting as in this borough and county. The Address of their last years committee with the additions by General Hand and Secretary Charles Smith⁰ having fallen into my hands, I have had it transcribed, and herewith enclose it, as a specimen of the Sentiments language & measures of the party, and a list of its leading men.

The respect which is due to your high Station, may require an apology for encroaching on your time, and it is an honest one to say, that I feel it to be my duty to express to you the Sentiments I entertain respecting the appointing of over zealous Federal men to offices which give them weight and influence in the county. It is by this means that they have for several years back, obtained a majority at our Elections, and if such appointments are continued, there is much reason to fear that they will continue to carry their men into our legislature, and keep us involved in many and great difficulties.

There is in this county, more wealth & less knowledge than many other within the state; and perhaps it is equally true that there is more of the old leaven of Toryism working among us here, than there is even in our great cities. This affords the fatal opportunity to those who these [ill]–informed men consider as their old friends, not only to impress on their min[ions] whatever sentiments they find convenient to their purposes, but effectually to exclude every communication which might tend to open the eyes of those men to their real situation.

It is said that eight thousand copies of the inclosed address were printed, and yet it was with great difficulty that a compleat copy could be obtained by any democratic republican.

I have the honor to be with the highest respect Sir, Your most obedient servant   T MATLACK

⁰ Son of the reverend Dr. W Smith of Philada.

RC (DNA: RG 59, LAR); torn at right margin; endorsed by TJ as received 10 Sep. and so recorded in SJL. Enclosure not found, but see below.

As a clerk for the Continental Congress, Timothy Matlack (ca. 1736-1829) is believed to have penned the parchment copy of the Declaration of Independence. He was also a member and former secretary of the American Philosophical Society and held a variety of government posts during his public career, including clerk of the Pennsylvania senate from 1790 to 1800. He relocated from Philadelphia to Lancaster in 1799 and was appointed state master of the rolls the following year (ANB; Vol. 1:433n; Vol. 4:544, 545n).

ADDRESS OF THEIR LAST YEARS COMMITTEE: a broadside circulated by the "Committee for promoting the Election of Federal Republicans in the County of Lancaster" presented a list of Federalist candidates for federal, state, and local office, headed by congressional candidate Thomas Boude and state senate candidate Matthias Barton. The broadside urged Federal electors not to "strike out or change the name of any Federal candidates," warning that, "at a time when all our dearest rights are deeply concerned," any division among Federalists could lead to the election of persons who "ought not to be trusted in the public councils" ("To the Federal Electors of Lancaster County" [Lancaster?, 1800]; Evans, No. 38650).

Edward HAND was an inspector of the revenue for Pennsylvania, a former major general in the provisional army, and a well-known Federalist partisan (Vol. 32:308, 309n; William Findley to TJ, 12 May). The son of educator and clergyman William Smith, CHARLES SMITH was a rising Lancaster attorney and ardent Federalist, who subsequently enjoyed a distinguished career as a state legislator, jurist, and legal scholar (David Hackett Fischer, *The Revolution of American Conservatism, The Federalist Party in the Era of Jeffersonian Democracy* [New York, 1965], 351-2; Alexander Harris, *A Biographical History of Lancaster County* [Lancaster, 1872], 544; PMHB, 4 [1880], 380-1).

To James Taylor, Jr.

SIR   Monticello Aug. 28. 1801.

The term of payment for the two last pipes of wine being now at hand I have desired mr John Barnes of Georgetown to remit you in the first week of the month now about to enter seven hundred dollars: which if my memory serves me (for I have not my papers here) is the sum due. if you have now remaining on hand any of *the same* quality I would gladly take two pipes more, payable at 90. days. accept assurances of my respect.   TH: JEFFERSON

PrC (MHi); at foot of text: "Mr. James Taylor. Norfolk"; endorsed by TJ in ink on verso.

TWO LAST PIPES OF WINE: Brazil quality Madeira that arrived in Washington in June (Taylor to TJ, 4 June).

According to his financial memoranda, TJ on this day requested John Barnes to pay Taylor $700 for two pipes of wine (MB, 2:1050).

From Benjamin Waterhouse

Sir   Boston August 28th. 1801

I have this moment taken your letter of the 14th. inst. from the Post-office, and have step'd into the first house to write a line, and pray you to excuse me untill I return home before I can answer it properly.

I congratulate you, Sir, in having produced the true disease, of which I have little or indeed *no doubt*. I hope Dr. Wardlow will inoculate from the part affected as soon as he finds a drop of clear, pellucid fluid, that is to say on the 8th. day, or even the seventh and where the inoculated part is affected at no greater distance from the incision than this 𝆔 . or if a simple scratch or puncture be made, as in case of using the recent fluid when it is of no greater size than this ✹ , or even less. I believe there is an art in inserting the matter which Dr. Gantt had not acquired, & which Dr. Wardlow has. I hope he will inoculate from patient to patient, and never trust to the thread when he has a recent pustule to take it from. Excuse this hasty scrawl, and accept of my profound respects.   B. WATERHOUSE

RC (DLC); frayed; endorsed by TJ.   DR. WARDLOW: William Wardlaw.
Recorded in SJL as received 10 Sep.

To Thomas Willing

DEAR SIR   Monticello Aug. 28. 1801.

I have been requested by a very worthy man to bear testimony in his favor to some one of the Directors of the bank of the US. and being not in habits of acquaintance with any member but yourself, I take the liberty of addressing this to you. I do it the more willingly because I think you will be more able to make the distinction I wish between my private & public character, a distinction I ask indispensably on this occasion as nothing less would admit me to say a word. in truth, speaking of facts only it is only as a private individual I can bear testimony to them. you propose the establishment of a branch bank at Washington. mr Samuel Hanson is the cashier of the Georgetown bank. he has got into a dispute with Genl. U. Forrest, which, from the known talents for intrigue of that gentleman, every one foresees will end in getting mr Hanson out of his present birth. the influence of Forrest with that board is irresistable almost. mr Hanson therefore has much at heart to obtain the same birth in the new bank.

were it to depend on [any?] directors who will be appointed at the place, he would be confident of obtaining it, as being known to them. but he is not known to your board. I know the appointment is highly confidential. but as far as integrity, talents & a perfect knolege of the ground can qualify any man, I believe every one would vouch for this gentleman. believing conscientiously in this truth, I have thought myself in duty bound to bear witness to it, wishing at the same time it may be used for your own satisfaction only. I should fear to be named to others, lest something more than my personal character should enter into their consideration. accept assurances of my perfect esteem & respect.   TH: JEFFERSON

PrC (MoSHi: Jefferson Papers); blurred; at foot of text: "Thomas Willing esquire"; endorsed by TJ in ink on verso.

To the District of Columbia Commissioners

GENTLEMEN   Monticello Aug. 29. 1801.
    Your favor of the 24th. is duly recieved. I consider the erection of the Representatives chamber, and the making a good gravel road from the New bridge on Rock creek along the Pensylva & Jersey avenues to the Eastern branch as the most important objects for ensuring the destinies of the city which can be undertaken. all others appear to me entirely subordinate and to rest on considerations quite distinct from these. for the first of these works the ordinary funds of the city are understood to be competent; but not for the second. tho' according to rigorous law, the price of the site of the Marine barracks (pledged to Congress) should only have been credited by them to the city, I ventured to have 4000. D. part of it advanced from the treasury to be applied to the sole purpose of making the road abovementioned. I supposed that Congress in consideration of the utility of the object & the ampleness [of the] rest of the grounds pledged to them as a security would[1] [relax] the rigor of their rights and approve what has been done. 4000. D. for 4 miles of road were then estimated to be sufficient. but from your statement 3695.99 D have been expended, and half the distance (tho not half the work) remains to be finished. in this situation I should think it adviseable to postpone the circular street round the Capitol, because we have already a very practicable road ascending the Capitol hill at the North end of the building: then to apply what remains of the 4000. D. and any funds the city can

spare to rounding the Pensylva avenue from the President's square to Rock creek & on to the upper bridge; & then to round the Jersey avenue from the work already done to the Eastern branch. I write by this post to the Secretary of the Navy to know whether any more & how much can be spared from the 20,000. D. appropriated by Congress for the Marine barracks beyond the 4000. D. already paid the Commissioners. I fear it will be little. but if any thing remain of that fund, I will venture to direct a further portion of the price of the Site to be paid you for compleating this road, on the same principles & presumption on which the 4000. D. were advanced from the treasury. in the mean time will you have the goodness to forward to me by post as just a statement as possible of what it will cost to accomplish these portions of the road I have designated, over and above the remains of the 4000. D. & the city funds which can be spared for this object? I shall at the same time recieve an answer from the Secretary of the navy, & on a view of the whole decide on the further aid which can be given. Accept assurances of my high consideration & respect.   TH: JEFFERSON

RC (DLC: District of Columbia Papers); torn, with words in brackets supplied from PrC; at foot of first page: "The Commrs. of Washington." PrC (DLC).

Congress appropriated $20,000 for marine barracks in Washington, $4,000 of which was to be paid to the District of Columbia Commissioners for land (Benjamin Bryen to TJ, 16 Mch.; Samuel Smith to TJ, 13 June). In a letter to Henry Dearborn of 23 June, the commissioners informed him that, "in consequence of an agreement made by General Smith acting by direction of the President," the commissioners executed a deed to the United States for a lot and requested $4,000 to be paid to them (FC in DNA: RG 42, DCLB).

I WRITE BY THIS POST TO THE SECRETARY OF THE NAVY: TJ to Robert Smith, 29 Aug.

On an undated sheet, in an unidentified hand, appears an estimate that pavement 8,250 feet long, 12 feet wide, and 3 inches deep required 3,988 barrels of gravel. On the same sheet, TJ calculated the number of cubic inches in $1\frac{1}{4}$ cubic feet (2,160) and wrote down this figure alongside "10,720," the number of cubic inches covered by one barrel of gravel according to the estimate (MS in DLC: District of Columbia Papers; with additional figures on verso in TJ's hand).

[1] Canceled: "excuse."

From Albert Gallatin

DR SIR   City of Washington 29 Augt. 1801

My child continuing very unwell, I sent him with Miss Nicholson about 16 miles out of town, mean to go there this evening, perhaps will take them as far as Frederick town & may not be back till Tuesday—therefore write a few lines to day.

Enclosed you will find the list of Warrants, copy of a late circular to the collectors, application from E. Sproat late inspector to be supervisor of N. West district, and a letter from Mr Newton. On receiving the last I wrote to Mr Wagner to issue a commission to Chisman. Sproat lives not in the proper place & has been, I believe, but an indifferent officer. I have written for information for a proper officer for that district.

Mr Meredith returned about a fortnight ago. From various petty circumstances, I judged it better to let him take his course & not to run the risk of offering him any thing in Philada. He has this day communicated a letter he writes to you, declaring his intention to resign latter end of October taking time to settle this quarter's accounts, which is proper. Will it not be more gracious, that the offer of the office to Mr Habersham should come direct from you, instead of going through my channel? If you think so, you may write him at once by return of mail without waiting for his asking for it. If you think differently, please to write to me and I will act as you may direct. At all events I will not do nor say any thing till I hear from you.

Nothing new this week. I enclose a letter from Gen. Dearborn whose family situation is distressing. A Mr Tisdall, firm & leading republican from Hartford Connect. says that your answer to New Haven has done much good & that next months election will show that they have gained ground. The Maryld. Election of electors is next Monday week—the prospect favourable but not certain

With sincere respect & attachment Your very obt. Servt.

ALBERT GALLATIN

RC (DLC); at foot of text: "Thomas Jefferson. President of the United States"; endorsed by TJ as received from the Treasury Department on 3 Sep. and so recorded in SJL. Enclosures: (1) "Weekly list of Warrants issued on the Treasurer for the week ending 29th August 1801," reporting 10 warrants, Nos. 134 to 143, for a total of $62,424.38, the largest being issued to Samuel Meredith for $50,000 for the army; with a balance in the Treasury at the beginning of the week of $3,081,736.45 and that at the close "not yet returned" (MS in DLC; entirely in Gallatin's hand). (2) Treasury Department circular to customs collectors, 20 Aug., reminding them of the requirement of transmitting their accounts punctually and noting that the president directed him to say that "a rigid adher-

ence to the regulation of rendering each quarterly account, previously to the expiration of the next ensuing quarter, shall, hereafter, be considered as indispensably necessary," with Gallatin explaining what was to be forwarded to the Treasury, by some collectors on a weekly and others on a monthly basis, and inviting them "to communicate, from time to time, whatever your observations and experience may suggest, in relation to any defects, improvements, or evasions of the revenue laws" (printed copy in DNA: RG 36, LFT, with several blanks filled by clerk, signed by Gallatin, at foot of text: "Benjamin Lincoln Esqr. Collector of Boston"; see Gallatin, *Papers*, 5:607-8, for the list of collectors to whom the circular was sent, with the names of those who were requested to submit weekly reports in the first column, and with those who were to submit theirs monthly in the second column). (3) Henry Dearborn to Gallatin, Pittston, Maine, 8 Aug., giving news of his daughter who appeared to be in a state of "fixed madness" (Gallatin, *Papers*, 5:525). Other enclosures not found.

Gallatin's CHILD who continued VERY UNWELL was his second son, Albert Rolaz, about 19 months old. On 14 Aug., Gallatin wrote James Witter Nicholson, his brother-in-law, that after being ill for seven weeks Albert Rolaz was reduced to a skeleton and could neither eat nor walk. Gallatin feared for his life. Hannah Gallatin gave birth to a daughter, Catherine, on 22 Aug. Immediately afterwards, Gallatin took Albert Rolaz, who was slowly recovering, and his aunt Maria NICHOLSON, Hannah's sister, to Montgomery County, Maryland (Gallatin, *Papers*, 5:534, 569, 650; Raymond Walters, Jr., *Albert Gallatin: Jeffersonian Financier and Diplomat* [New York, 1957], 140, 218).

I HAVE WRITTEN FOR INFORMATION: on 7 Aug., Gallatin wrote Thomas Worthington, register of the land office at Chillicothe, requesting recommendations for several offices, including supervisor of the new revenue district. Gallatin explained that until Congress provided a salary for the supervisor, the appointee would receive a commission as inspector, along with a $500 salary, a $200 allowance for clerks, and "the usual commission on duties collected & allowance for books & stationary." Even though he initially would not have the title of supervisor, Gallatin wanted him to act as such and "be entirely independant from the Supervisor in Kentucky & correspond directly with the Treasury Department." He noted that Samuel Finley, receiver of public monies at Chillicothe, had been strongly recommended, with the suggestion that he could hold both positions. Gallatin observed: "Perhaps I am mistaken; but if the two offices may be blended, may not yours & that also be held together? Can either you or he do your duty in both offices connected; if so will you accept of it? If you think that one office is enough for one man, can you recommend any other person?" (Gallatin, *Papers*, 5:520).

COMMUNICATED A LETTER: Samuel Meredith to TJ, 29 Aug.

To Edward Gantt

DEAR SIR   Monticello Aug. 29. 1801.

I send you a fresh supply of vaccine matter. the toothpicks are perhaps feebly impregnated; the thread well soaked. they are from pustules in a very proper state; but it is now 3. or 4. days since they were impregnated. we happen at this time to have no subjects in a proper state for communication. by the next post I hope we shall have some who may furnish matter on the morning of the departure of the post. the similarity of the disease from the matter sent by Doctr. Jenner (& which succeeded in two patients) with that furnished from Dr. Waterhouse's patients encourages me to have great confidence in the genuineness of our matter. indeed every appearance confirms this confidence. a very few have slight fevers, & one only a very bad arm, occasioned by too deep an incision, and by scratching it when enflamed. as soon as it has taken with you be so good as to inform me. accept of my best wishes & high respect.   TH: JEFFERSON

PrC (DLC); at foot of text: "Dr. Gantt."

MATTER SENT BY DOCTR. JENNER: see Benjamin Waterhouse to TJ, 1 Aug.

To George Jefferson

DEAR SIR   Monticello Aug. 29. 1801.

Yours of the 24th is recieved and the articles [forwarded partly] brought here & the [rest] at Milton. the money recieved for mr Short must be remitted to mr Barnes as he is just about making an [investment] for him. I must still pray you to [avail] yourself of any opportunity which may offer of purchasing hams for me. the money for my last crop of tobo. became due on the [24th.] inst. and I presume is at your command. I must pray you to send me immediately a state of my account, as I have occasion to make an appropriation of what I can command. will you [also] inform me whether the sellers of coal will suffer it to be [picked?] for a large quantity such as 1000. or 2000. bushels, & what will be the [price]. accept assurance of my constant & high esteem.   TH: JEFFERSON

PrC (MHi); faint; at foot of text: "Mr. George Jefferson"; endorsed by TJ in ink on verso.

On 31 Aug., George Jefferson wrote TJ that he had received his letter of the 24th and promised to forward the account statement by the next post. He informed TJ that the money from the last tobacco crop "is in our hands, and is of course ready to be paid to your order" (RC in MHi; at foot of text: "Thos. Jefferson esqr."; endorsed by TJ as received 3 Sep. and so recorded in SJL).

MY LAST CROP: on 12 May 1801, TJ noted in his financial accounts that Gibson & Jefferson had sold his tobacco for a total of $2,974.09, payable 24 Aug. (MB, 2:1041; George Jefferson to TJ, 7 May).

From George Jefferson

DEAR SIR   Richmond 29th. Augt 1801

I have paid Mr. Wanscher who will hand you this $:10. on yr. a/c. he takes with him the barrel of plaister of Paris which was left, & a box from Mr. Barnes—I likewise send under his care in one of Henderson's boats the 50 ℔. of Powder, together with a small box from Philada.

I am Dear Sir Yr. very humble servt.   GEO. JEFFERSON

2 Casks 50 ℔. Gun Powder ℱ @ 4/6 £11.5.—

RC (MHi); at foot of text: "Thomas Jefferson esqr."; endorsed by TJ as received 3 Sep. and so recorded in SJL.

From Samuel Meredith

SIR,   Washington August 29th. 1801

The precarious state of Mrs. Meredith's health, which has been injured by change of situation, the anxious desire she and the family have to be with their Friends & relations, as well as the necessary attention to my private affairs, which are suffering by my absence from Philada.; have induced me to offer you my resignation, to take place if you think proper about the last of October, or beginning of November, which I think will give me time to receive returns from the most distant Banks, make up my Quarterly Accounts to the 30th: September, and hand them to the Auditor for settlement: And for you Sir, to fix on a successor, to whom I may deliver over the funds in my hands, giving him every information I am capable of;

With offers of service, & thanks for your polite attention;

I am Sir, with perfect respect Your Mo: huml Servt.

SAM MEREDITH Tres
of the United States

RC (DLC); in a clerk's hand, signed by Meredith; at foot of text: "The President of the United States"; endorsed by TJ as received 3 Sep. and so recorded in SJL. FC (PWbH); in same clerk's hand; lacks signature.

Philadelphia merchant Samuel Meredith (1741-1817) was appointed the first treasurer of the United States in 1789 and retained the post until his retirement in 1801. A veteran of the American Revolution, he served in the Pennsylvania legis- lature and Confederation Congress prior to his appointment, and was also among the initial directors of the Bank of North America. Following his departure from the Treasury Department, Meredith retired from public life and spent most of his remaining years at his rural estate in Wayne County, Pennsylvania (ANB).

MRS. MEREDITH: in 1772, Meredith married Margaret Cadwalader, who survived her husband and died in 1820 (ANB; *New-York Evening Post*, 3 Oct. 1820).

To Robert Smith

DEAR SIR   Monticello Aug. 29. 1801.

Congress appropriated 20,000 D. to effecting the Marine hospital. the Site purchased of the Commissioners cost between 8. & 9000 Dollars. but it was thought that 4000 D. only of that in cash[1] would be requisite for their purposes & that the balance might be applied to their credit in account of the sum guaranteed by Congress: consequently that there remained 16,000. D. of the appropriation free to be expended in building the barracks.[2] the important object of compleating the gravel road from Georgetown to the Eastern branch, the

Commissioners now find cannot be effected without a further sum. is it possible to spare any more of the 16000 Dollars from the building? your brother thought he could throw the cost of the *Births*, (Bunks I believe they are called) on the contingencies of the naval department, considering them as furniture rather than a part of the building. perhaps some other articles of the expence may be taken from the 20,000. D. fund & thrown on the Contingent or some other fund. perhaps some part of the building may be left unfinished, or unexecuted, without violating the engagements made, and without much injury. the object of the present is to pray you to see what economies can be practised on the 20,000. D. fund, and how much more of it could be spared to be advanced to the Commissioners on account of the Site, & to be applied exclusively to the accomplishment of this road. be so good as to give me an answer by the mail which is made up on the 7th. Sep. for Milton; as by the same I shall recieve an estimate from the Commissioners. Accept assurances of my friendly attachment & high consideration.   TH: JEFFERSON

PrC (DLC); at foot of text: "The Secretary of the Navy."

¹ Preceding two words interlined.
² Preceding two words interlined.

MARINE HOSPITAL: that is, marine barracks.

From Samuel Smith

SIR/   Baltimore 29th. Augt. 1801

The Maryland arrived last Night & this Morning, Mr. Purviance the Bearer of her Dispatches proceeded to Washington—The inclosed Letter from Capt. Barney will Aid in explaining the Causes why no Exchange of Ratification had taken effect—and will shew, that Federalists Can not be trusted with the Objects of Government. I Confess that I highly approved of the Delicacy of your Conduct towards Mr: Elsworth & Mr. Murray. the former would not have Committed his Character—the latter is so trifling a Creature, that I fear he is Acting under Instructions from this Side of the Water—I am sir—
with the greatest Respect your Friend & servt: S. SMITH

RC (DLC); endorsed by TJ as received 10 Sep. and so recorded in SJL. Enclosure: Joshua Barney to Smith, Paris, 11 July 1801, expressing his wish that Smith had been named U.S. minister to France and declaring that the ratification of the Convention of 1800 is "very uncertain" because its negotiation is in William Vans Murray's hands rather than John Dawson's; Murray, from his "attachment to the British," probably wants reconciliation with

France to fail, and has appointed as his secretary James C. Mountflorence, who is despised by every "publick Officer in france from the first Consul, down"; under the pretense of being "the only *Official Commercial Character* in france," Mountflorence charges commissions to issue papers for ships and cargoes, a practice that he knows will come to an end if normal relations between the U.S. and France are restored; perhaps Dawson, who "does honour to the US," will be able to bring about ratification; and Barney, believing that his "Exile" in France is at an end, states his readiness to serve the United States (RC in same).

On the return voyage of the *Maryland* to the United States, John H. PURVIANCE, who in Dawson's opinion was worthy of "entire confidence," carried Dawson's and Murray's official dispatches (Madison, *Papers, Sec. of State Ser.,* 1:350; William Short to TJ, 9 June 1801).

Joshua BARNEY had also written directly to TJ, but not on the subject of the ratification of the convention (Barney to TJ, 5 June 1801).

To James Currie

DEAR SIR   Monticello Aug. 30. 1801.

Since my arrival at home I have two or three times recieved Vaccine matter from Dr. Waterhouse at Boston & through him from Dr. Jenner of London, which has been inoculated directly or by succession[1] into 30. or 40. of my family, & 20. or 30. of mr Randolph's with perfect success. many of them are through the disease. a few had slight fevers, and one only a bad arm, produced by too deep an incision & scratching the [pustule?]. the matter from England & Boston produced exactly the same appearances & I have entire confidence in it's genuineness. understanding that from spurious matter or some other cause you have failed in introducing the genuine disease into Richmond, I send you by judge Stuart a phial in which is a needle & thread & half a dozen tooth picks impregnated yesterday from a pustule of the 7th. day in a very proper state. the thread was drawn through several times till stiff with matter: the tooth picks inserted into the pustule and well moistened at their points, about an eighth to a quarter of an inch.   I thank you for your attention to the arbitration & shall be glad to recieve the award as soon as delivered. I shall remain here to the last week of the ensuing month & shall be very happy to see you here at any time & all times. accept assurances of my constant esteem & respect.   TH: JEFFERSON

PrC (DLC); faint; at foot of text: "Doctr. Currie."

YOUR ATTENTION TO THE ARBITRATION: see Currie to TJ, 16 Aug.

TJ wrote a similar letter to William Foushee on this day; see Foushee to TJ, 13 Sep.

[1] Preceding three words interlined.

From George Izard

Sir, Baltimore. August 30th 1801.

Mr. Barbé Marbois whom I had the pleasure to see at Paris charged me with one of the enclosed Letters for You; the other was sent to my Lodgings by a person whom I do not know. I profit of the oppertunity the circumstance of forwarding them affords me of presenting my Respects to You and have the Honor to be,

Sir, Your very obedient humble Servt

GEO. IZARD,
Capt. 1 Regt Art. & Engrs.

RC (NNPM); at foot of text: "His Excellency Thos. Jefferson"; endorsed by TJ as received 10 Sep. and so recorded in SJL. Enclosures: (1) François Barbé de Marbois to TJ, 24 June. (2) Probably Charles Louis Clérisseau to TJ, 29 Apr. (recorded in SJL as received from Paris on 10 Sep., but not found).

George Izard (1776-1828) returned to America as a passenger in the *Maryland*, after serving as secretary to his brother-in-law, the U.S. minister to Portugal, William Loughton Smith. A son of former U.S. Senator Ralph Izard of South Carolina, George Izard subsequently enjoyed a distinguished public career, which included service as a major general during the War of 1812 and an appointment as governor of the Arkansas Territory (ANB; *South Carolina Historical and Genealogical Magazine,* 2 [1901], 223; *Federal Gazette & Baltimore Daily Advertiser,* 29 Aug. 1801).

To Benjamin Stoddert

SIR Monticello Aug. 30. 1801.

Your favor of the 18th. is duly recieved. before it's reciept however, the letter from the Commrs. to which it referred had been recieved and answered. it contains some facts I had not been before informed of, and which I am glad to learn; but on a review of the subject I do not percieve that a previous knowlege of them could have changed the general answers I gave to the general questions proposed. the Commissioners stated that without further paiments than they had reason to depend on voluntarily[1] there would be a failure of 10,500 D. for paying interest which would be due on the 1st. of Oct. to the state of Maryland; and they asked whether they should proceed to enforce paiments, & particularly from those bound as sureties to the state of Maryland? it appeared also from a paper they inclosed, that on failure to pay interest, the state of Maryland would have a right to demand the principal instantly. the sum of my answer was that such a demand would be so ruinous to the city, that duty left us but one alternative, to enforce paiments. but to avoid all unnecessary distress, they should limit themselves to enforce only to the extent of the Maryland interest: & that a contribution towards this appeared justly & lawfully due from the sureties as well as others; except that as to yourself an equivalent indulgence in time and sum should be admitted for the sum you had advanced before it became due: & I expressed a hope that the debtors considering the necessity & moderation of the demand would by voluntary contributions bring in the sum necessary. though a somewhat further sum would be of immense value to the city, I did not propose any thing further. a sum which I wished, not a dollar of it to be laid out on the public buildings, from which (after the partial structure of the Representatives chamber now on hand) the funds of the city ought forever to be relieved. but on the gravelling other streets (in the manner of the Pensylva & Jersey avenues) as the buildings extend along them, and opening two or three roads very necessary for facilitating a communication with the country. to render the city a convenient & comfortable place of sojournment for those on whom it's destinies depend, is an object of the very first interest to those who hold lots in it; and this would be in a great measure affected could the debts due to the institution be recieved during this & the ensuing summer. two or three thousand dollars beyond the demands of the interest, for the present summer, could do what would be considerable for the ensuing winter. however it is the want of the interest alone which threatens entire ruin. in urging these things it is the furthest from my wish to distress one living mortal beyond what is absolutely necessary to save the trust committed to us. my anxiety for any thing further flows merely from a wish to secure the fortunes of the city, a wish which is sincere and divested of every personal interest. accept assurances of my high consideration & respect.   TH: JEFFERSON

PrC (DLC); at foot of first page: [1] Word interlined.
"Benj. Stoddert esq."

From David Austin

RESPECTED SIR.   Washington August 31st. 1801
    Hearing that the Treaty with France, was not, at the sailing of the Maryland ratified, I beg liberty to lay before the President a few things in respect to this instrument, & to the appending circumstances of our relations with France.
    Please to understand that the total operation of what is stiled *Rev-*

olution is, in the design of the Great Supreme, *deadly & destructive*. It is as a pioniering system. It is an ax, a saw, or a rod. In the hand of the Chief performers, it is as a firebrand.—

Buoneparte now holds the torch. He is all eye, all action; all fire. His Commission leads to the destruction of Nations, "not a few!" The removal of the [fa]tal fabric of Antichristian domination is his design; & he has countenance in what he does: but it is as the countenance of one on the dark side of things.

His policy is piercing like lightening: & the burthen he lays is weighty.—Let us come nearer home. Read, Sir, the instrument that the Commissioners signed in Paris: read with impartial eye. The features of a Parisian policy are interwoven in every texture of the instrument. We surrender all & receive nothing. The real business of the Envoys is hove into the back-ground. "We will speak to that another day"—

The policy of France, only waits a good opportunity to present to the United States a demand, that would make every heart to quake had she power to make good her design. I say this, Sir, that you may be on your guard agaist the opening of any door, for the planting of the foot of that Nation upon the toes of the Executive. The reactings of the tide of Revolution will give us a back stroke, if the shield is not well poised. The whole Ocean is yet in a tremulous situation. The waters still boil, & the repast is not yet upon the table.

I could give a sketch of the mind of the French Executive in regard to us; but I choose not to put it upon paper. I can see the clouds that are charged with fluid; but there are none so heavy but they may be broken.

Our American fabric is the first building that hath arrisen from the tumultuous state of things. All other nations, have the fire of revolution, still, in their bowells. The indignation of Heaven is still amongst them. It is not to be quenched so easily as some may imagine. It will give our Executive full employment to watch the tides and counter-tides that still bejostle the Ark, & to look out for breakers ahead! The National Ship must stand upon her own legs:—Leaning to any falacious prospect, will prove but the dependance of a broken reed. It will pierce the hand of him that leaneth thereon.

The Prest. will survey, at leisure, the system of things falling from my pen: he will find that the system looks towards a state of things like unto *seventy six*, in its second edition.—On this ground alone, can the Peace of the Nation & honor of the Executive be obtained. The more you lean to the proppings of foreign things, the more will your wings be encompassed by the bird-lime of their policy; & in proportion as you receive the firebrand from their hand; in the same degree, will the hand of the Executive be burned.

If Impediments arise, on the subject of the instrument in hand; be not too hasty *in desire*; or *in measures* to accommodate the difference. Let their waters boil; let our National strength increase.

If the Prest. should find, on his return, any place in his family, where a person, as Sec'y; as Assist. Sec'y, or private Chaplain might be useful (Sundays to himself) the Prest will not be ignorant of one ready to serve him.

Of stipends he will not speak.—A corn[er of] the House, & place at table shall be his reward.

with all due esteem

RC (DNA: RG 59, LAR); torn at seal; addressed: "Thomas Jefferson Esqr Monticello Virginia"; franked and postmarked; endorsed by TJ as received 3 Sep. and so recorded in SJL.

Austin followed up the above letter with another to TJ dated 4 Sep., in which he suggested that TJ appoint him in place of Rufus King as minister to Great Britain. Austin asserted that any envoy TJ sent to Europe would "answer no solid purpose" and that a "general pacifi-cation" could only be obtained "through means springing from the Portals of our National Edifice." Had the president appointed Austin instead of John Dawson to convey the ratified Convention of 1800 to France, "he should have heard a different report from his treatybearer than the one, now presented" (RC in DNA: RG 59, LAR; unsigned; at foot of text: "Pres: U:States"; endorsed by TJ as a letter from David Austin received 10 Sep. and so recorded in SJL).

From John Barnes

SIR—   George Town 31st Augt. 1801—

Your two favrs 21. & 22d. are at hand. and I hope the plaisterer—as well the missing bbl. plaister are also Arrived with you.—that your experiments on the New tried matter of the Cow pox, meet your most sanguine wishes, must of course (—from its happy & most extray. effects.) become generally—to be practised, for the Benefit of the present, & future generations.—Mr Rapin, expects Mr Le Mair daily, purposes paying the servants wages—this week &c say 100 or $150. I told him he should have what money he wanted. and hoped he would tarry a few days extra. in order to give Mr Le Mair every necessary information—Another Wedding! have been Consumated. at the mansion—Frederick—versus—Molly—at this Rate—or Ratio, your next years Census. may be expected to increase considerable; abt. the 7 or 8 Sept. I purpose receiving your 2 mos Compensation $1000 of which, I shall have to pay—on your a/c at B of C—another

$1000. on like a/c for Mr. M. with $1000 to be left there for your Use. the remaining $1000. I purpose to take with me to Philada where I expect a further supply. should it become needful there—

Waiting your Commands I am most Respectfully, Sir—Your Obedt. Hble Servant   JOHN BARNES

Doctr. Gantt, I expect, writes you ℔ this mail—

RC (ViU: Edgehill-Randolph Papers); at foot of text: "Thomas Jefferson Esqr. President U States Monticello"; endorsed by TJ as received 3 Sep. and so recorded in SJL.

YOUR TWO FAVRS: a letter from TJ to Barnes of 21 Aug. is recorded in SJL but has not been found. No letter to Barnes of the 22nd has been located or is recorded in SJL.

PLAISTERER: Martin Wanscher.

On the expected payment of $4,000 for TJ's COMPENSATION, see note at Barnes to TJ, 3 Aug.

B OF C: Bank of Columbia.

A/C FOR MR. M.: Barnes may have been trying to cover a note for $1,000 from the Bank of Columbia that he negotiated for Madison, for which payment was due from Madison in September (Madison, *Papers, Sec. of State Ser.*, 2:78-9).

FOR YOUR USE: Barnes intended to have $1,000 available at the Bank of Columbia for TJ's use while Barnes was out of town (Barnes to TJ, 24 Aug.)

FURTHER SUPPLY: TJ apparently misunderstood this phrase as a request for funds and, on 12 Sep., TJ ordered Gibson & Jefferson to send Barnes $1,000 "instantly" by way of Philadelphia (TJ to Barnes, 12 Sep.; TJ to George Jefferson, 12 Sep.). Barnes, in his letter of 21 Sep., suggested that delivery of the sum was unexpected.

From John Davis

SIR,   Colchester,[1] Virginia, August 31, 1801.

Having lately visited that Scene which you have pronounced one of the most stupendous in Nature, & purposing to return to Philadelphia in a Month, where I shall publish my Travels under the title of A Journey from New York to the Passage of the Potomac through the Blue Ridge Mountains,—I take the liberty to entreat permission to dedicate my Work to you. If Gadienus travelled from the remote parts of Spain to behold the Historian of Rome, I can affirm from the very bottom of my heart that I would have gone much further to see the Author of the Notes on Virginia,—the first & greatest Work that ever taught me to reflect; but the etiquette of a refined Age would not allow me this honor at Washington; and I can now only hope for your sanction to my literary undertakings by epistolary intercourse.

Chastellux is, perhaps, the most interesting Traveller through the United States. His volumes enlivened with anecdote, & abounding with remark, seldom fail to hold the mind in pleasing captivity. Indeed from so great a personage much was expected. He was a

Member of the French Academy, the Correspondent of Voltaire, the Companion of Princes, & a General officer in the French Army. On military subjects he could not be otherwise than *au fait*; and he stalks over the field of battle with the grace & dignity of a soldier.

Hic Dolopum manus: hic soevics tendebat Achilles:
Classibus hic locus: hic acies certare solebant.

I have rather made Chastellux than Brissot the model of my Tour. The narrative of the one yields flowers & fragrance, transporting the reader on fairy ground; while that of the other inspires no emotion of pleasure, but casts a gloom over every scene.

I have, perhaps, Sir, the honor of being slightly known to you. You may possibly have seen a Translation of General Buonaparte's Campaign in Italy; and Mr Gallatin informed me at Washington that he had presented you, pursuant to my entreaty, with a small Collection of my Lyric Poems. A mistake of Mr Burr, to whom I have the honor of being personally known, was the occasion of my coming to Virginia; but having been a Traveller from my childhood, having visited China, & resided both on the Coast of Malabar & Coromandel, I rather rejoice at, than deplore an event, that has caused me to gratify my disposition for roving

I conclude with repeating my entreaty that you will allow me the honor of inscribing to you my Journey; or at least flatter myself you will not withold an answer from me *studiis florentem ignobilis otii;* an *Otium* which would be rendered *Nobile* by your condescension.

I am, Sir, Your most obedient, humble Servant,

JOHN DAVIS.

RC (DLC); addressed: "Thomas Jefferson Esqr. President of the United States, Monticello"; franked; postmarked 1 Sep.; endorsed by TJ as received 3 Sep. and so recorded in SJL.

John Davis (1774-1854) was a British seaman and man of letters whose translation of the *Campaign of General Buonaparte in Italy* (New York, 1798) brought him to the attention of Aaron Burr, who suggested that Davis study law with him. Davis traveled extensively in the South, thereafter became a tutor to the children of Daniel Ludlow, and published two books, *Poems Written at Coosohatchie, in South-Carolina* in Charleston in 1799, and *The Farmer of New Jersey; or, A Picture of Domestic Life* in New York in 1800 (Kline, *Burr,* 1:592-3).

THAT SCENE: a reference to the Natural Bridge, which TJ described as "the most sublime of Nature's works" in *Notes on the State of Virginia* (*Notes,* ed. Peden, 24).

Davis did not publish his TRAVELS until 1803 from London, under the title, *Travels of Four Years and a Half in the United States of America; During 1798, 1799, 1800, 1801, and 1802.* Dedicated to the third president, Davis's work included his recollections of the inauguration and also the text of the first inaugural address.

HISTORIAN OF ROME: probably the Roman historian Livy (59 B.C.-17 A.D.). According to Pliny the Younger, a citizen from Cadiz ("the Spaniard from Gades") came all the way to Rome from "his far corner of the earth to have "one look" at the famous man and then went home again (*Epistles*, 2:3).

HIC DOLOPUM MANUS: Davis here quotes Virgil, which translates as: "Here the Dolopian bands encamped, here cruel Achilles; here lay the fleet; here they used to meet us in battle" (*Aeneid*, 2.29-30).

A MISTAKE OF MR BURR: Davis went to Washington thinking that Burr had recommended him to the Treasury secretary for a government position. Apparently Burr failed to make clear to Gallatin that

this Davis was a British man with literary pursuits, not a member of the large New York family of the same name (Gallatin, *Papers*, 5:114, 268; Kline, *Burr,* 1:592-3).

STUDIIS FLORENTEM IGNOBILIS OTII: "and rejoiced in the arts of inglorious ease," Virgil, *Georgics*, 4.564.

OTIUM: "leisure."

[1] In front of preceding word Davis canceled "(Occoquan Mills, Two Miles from)."

From Enoch Edwards

DEAR SIR   Frankford 31 August 1801.

In my last I informed you that your Chariot was finished. and I now inclose you Mr: Hanse's Account. you will see he has adhered exactly to the original terms. by allowing the eighty four Dollars. the work is well executed and he has shewn every disposition to put into it the best of materials.

He will lend Us a Set of old harness to take it to the City of Washington, which he says can be thrown in a Barrell & sent home to him by water.—At his earnest Solicitation I have sent your harness also by water. The bulk I saw was too great to go within, without damaging the Carriage—& so I gratified him—

I hope you will take out the slip lining pretty soon in the Autumn you cannot see how beatifully it is trimed within untill you do. it is just stitched in. a Seamstress can do it in half an hour—all that, together with the Color—is Mrs: Edwards Taste. The having the Body made without a Scrole behind is mine and I think you will approve it—as that gives a very heavy Appearance—but as it is now finished it is universally admired—Perhaps you will think it would have been better if the wheels had been a shaving lighter—I think I would have had them so, but they were made at a distance from the Body which I most attended to.—however it is a Carriage for four horses, and has rough as well as smooth Roads to go. and on the whole they are better if not handsomer—they are rather lighter than the common run of Carriages for this City—

You are now at the Place where you spoke of sending Directions from, for Carpets &c—your directions for any thing you wish shall be most chearfully complied with. I shall be much gratified to render any Service you will please to put it in my power to do—it can be no

Inconvenience to Me—I have nothing to do in this world but to take care of the small Stack of Health I have yet left to me. and a few Rides now & then to oblige a Friend is one of the most agreable Means I could use for that Purpose. I am with the utmost Respect

your obedt st—   ENO. EDWARDS

The sooner the Carriage is sent for the more agreable it will be to Mr: Hanse—as he is very anxious it should get driven during the fine weather.

RC (DLC); addressed: "Thomas Jefferson. President of the United States. Monticello Virginia"; franked; postmarked 1 Sep.; endorsed by TJ. Recorded in SJL as received 10 Sep.

Conrad Hanse's Account

THOMAS JEFFERSON, ESQUIRE,
1801.   To Conrad Hanse   Dr.
Augt. 29.   To a new plain, well-finished Chariot, with plated   Dolls.
            Harness for 4 Horses, and 2 postillion Saddles.   1206

MS (DLC); in unknown hand.

In a statement of TJ's account, John Barnes entered at 18 Sep. a payment to Hanse of $1,000 for the CHARIOT (statement of private account from John Barnes, 30 Sep., in ViU; Barnes to TJ, 21 Sep.). While Barnes was in Philadelphia, he paid the remaining $206 to Hanse on 19 Oct. (statement of private account from Barnes, 4 Nov., in ViU). On the same day, Hanse wrote a receipt of payment in full of $1,206 by John Barnes, with a bill on Walker & Kennedy for $1,000 and a check for $206 by Barnes, "for a Chariot and Harness for four Horses Built for the Honarable Thomas Jefferson Presidant of the United States" (MS in ViU; in Hanse's hand and signed by him; endorsed by TJ: "Conrad & Hans"; endorsed by Barnes).

From John Hurt

DEAR SIR   Green Springs 31st Augst. 1801

I do myself the pleasure to make you acquainted with Doctor Baynham—he & his brother (who I have not the pleasure of being acquainted with) are travailing up to your healthy country for the benefit of a pure air—happening to hear them say they wished to pay their respects to you but was not furnished with letters of introduction I make use of the opportunity of Congratulating you on what has happened since I saw you—& to say that my worthy friend Doctor Baynham is one of your warmest friends—this I experienced last summer in his own neighborhood where he was encircled with a hot bed of Aristocrats—Colo. New his half brother you know very well & therefore I know there was no occasion of any introduction of the Doctor to you but I could not resist the opportunity of laying you under an obligation in so doing.—

As to my health I am almost gone & never expect to see you or Mr Madison again—but never was a poor wretch more completely gratified in their political wishes than I am at seeing you—Mr. Madn. & Gallatin at the head of the Government—& if I could be gratified in another wish it would be that you three might be transposed round those departments till every one had served in every place about 4 or 8 years each—May the great Jehovah prosper you, & that it may terminate in your honor & the peace & happiness our Country is the prayer of your dying friend   JOHN HURT

RC (DLC); at foot of text: "Thos. Jefferson President of the U.S."; endorsed by TJ as received 3 Sep. and so recorded in SJL.

Virginia clergyman John Hurt served as a brigade chaplain during the American Revolution and as a chaplain in the U.S. Army from 1791 to 1794. He was TJ's acquaintance and an infrequent correspondent of James Madison during the 1790s (Heitman, *Register*, 311; Madison, *Papers*, 16:7-8; 17:388n; Vol. 29:309; Vol. 30:608-9; Vol. 31:579).

A highly regarded surgeon and anatomist, Dr. William BAYNHAM of Essex County had considered purchasing land in Albemarle County in 1799 (Vol. 30:612, 613n, 658; Vol. 31:92). His BROTHER was Richard Baynham of Gloucester County (Washington, *Papers, Ret. Ser.*, 4:263, 264n). His HALF BROTHER was probably Anthony New of Caroline County, a Republican who represented Virginia in Congress from 1793 to 1805 before relocating to Kentucky (*Biog. Dir. Cong.*; Madison, *Papers*, 13:150n; Vol. 25:463; Vol. 29:382n, 573; Vol. 30:388, 430).

From Meriwether Lewis

DEAR SIR,   Staunton, August 31st. 1801.

I was a few minutes since with Mr. Glendy: on saturday last he was attacked with a violent bilious disorder which has since confined him to his bed: he laments much that his indisposition prevents his keeping the appointment he had made to preach in Charlottsville on Thursday next: he requested me to give you this information as early as possible, and to offer the violence of disorder, as his apology for not writing himself.—

I received from Mr. T. Bates of Pittsburgh the other day a letter containing the following paragraph relative to Genl. Alexr. Fowler, in answer to my inquiry with regard to the character of that gentleman "As to Genl. Alexander Fowler, it might seem improper for a young man like me to speak, yet as you ask, and as blindness itself could not missrepresent him, I presume to say—His intimate, or reather near connections, speak of him as unprincipled in the extreme. His acquaintances, all of them at least with whom I am acquainted, concur in opinion. He has heretofore made great exertions to get into the Assembly without success. He was for Govenor McKean, on whose election Judge Brackenridge because there was much dearth of proper materials, procured him the appointment of Brigadier Genl., and of a Justice of the Peace. Getting these he was indignant; he was solicitious for the office of associate Judge, bestowed on Lucas (a man of firmness talents and integrity), but was refused it. He has since done all he could to divide and distract the party and their plans. They have discarded him, altho Mr. Brackenridge stood by him as long as it was possible to do so without ruining the cause, and now at the instigation of one or two ex-feds, he has declared for Congress with the confidence of being carried by the federal interest, but he is absolutely so dispised that I am persuaded he can not get more than fifty votes, and them upon the interest of oald Genl. Nevill. He is in the *last stages* of *inebiety*, so much so that it is considered as a novelty to see him sober, and to crown all he is insolvent, and could not get credit or security for 2/6.—His Brigade Majr. did give him his uniform on credit, but they have split on politics. Of all things he ought not to touch money."

These strictures seem harsh, however you can allow them Sir, what credit you think, I know of no personal difference between Mr. B. and the Genl.—

I am sir, with sinceer regard Your very obt. Sert.

MERIWETHER LEWIS.

RC (DLC); at foot of text: "Thos. Jefferson. President. of the U.S."; endorsed by TJ as received 3 Sep. and so recorded in SJL.

Presbyterian clergyman John GLENDY, who at this time was a minister in Augusta County, Virginia, had immigrated from Ulster in 1799 (Sprague, *American Pulpit*, 4:229-30).

OALD GENL. NEVILL: John Neville had been an influential resident of western Pennsylvania since the 1770s. He was the center of what was called the "Neville connection," a group of men linked by marriage or blood, who among them held several important positions. In 1794, when Neville was the region's inspector of the revenue, an attack on his house by excise resisters became a key event of the Whiskey Rebellion (Syrett, *Hamilton*, 17:2-6; DAB).

From Samuel Sheild

S<small>IR</small>   York County August 31st. 1801.

Your much respected Favor of the 21st. Augt. reached me yesterday. Permit me, Sir, to embrace this unlooked for Opportunity of assuring you that one of the most ardent Wishes of my Heart has been
realized in seeing a republican Administration established in The
United States under your Auspices and that I largely participated
that heart-felt Satisfaction, which pervaded a Majority of the Community at the Issue of the late Election. One of the first Objects of
such an administration, as I have believed, would be to select the
most proper Characters to fill the subordinate as well as the higher
offices in the different Departments of the Government. Was I therefore to refuse the small Aid which it is in my Power to afford, in
furthering this important End, I should consider myself equally deficient in Respect to you and in Duty to my Country. As to the Subject
of your particular Inquiry—Mr. Mount E. Chisman—he was born
of respectable Parents in the County of York, was raised there and
has supported an upright Character. I cannot speak with equal
Confidence of his Prudence in the Management of his private affairs.
His first Essay in Life was in the mercantile Line, in which he was totally unsuccessful, and sunk, I believe, the greater Part of his small
Capital—He then retired to Hampton and he lived there for several
years, last past in the Capacity of a Tavern-keeper, with what Success
in Point of Profit I am not informed.—but his Conduct, I believe, has
been such as to gain him the Esteem of his Neighbors and Acquaintance. These are the principal Facts which have come to my Knowledge respecting either the Character of Mr. Chisman or his Situation
in Life.

As you have been pleased to desire me to write freely on this Subject, I cannot forbear to suggest a Difficulty, which is likely to present
the most judicious Disposal of the office, for which Mr. Chisman is an
Applicant. It is this—The Emoluments are, as I suspect, too inconsiderable to excite a Competition or to induce Gentlemen of the first
Respectability to solicit the Appointment. If this was not the Case, I
must confess that there are several Gentlemen in that Neighborhood,
whom I should prefer to Mr. Chisman. The Possession of a decent
Property and a permanent Residence are great additional securities
to the Government for a faithful discharge of Duty in its officers. If,
for Instance, Major George Wray or Mr. Thomas Jones would accept
the office, in either Case these Securities would be had, but as I am
not authorized to propose one or the other of those Gentlemen as a

Candidate for the Office, and as a Refusal on their Part might be attended with Inconvenience to you, I cannot venture to go further than merely to make these observations for your Consideration.

I am much obliged to you for the Assurance that no Use shall be made of this which shall bring me into Question, and you may rely upon it, that the Silence desired of me shall be observed.   With the greatest Respect and the most sincere wishes for your Health and Happiness

I am, Sir, your very obdt. Servt.   SAM. SHEILD

RC (NHi: Gallatin Papers); endorsed by TJ as received 10 Sep. and so recorded in SJL.

MAJOR GEORGE WRAY: Jacob Wray, a merchant, served as collector of customs at Hampton from August 1789 until March 1790, when his son George Wray, Jr., assumed the position, although the young Wray's commission was at first made out so as to confuse him with his uncle, of the same name, surveyor of the port. In 1794 both Sheild and George Wray, Sr., served in the Virginia House of Delegates. THOMAS JONES, former postmaster at Hampton, served as collector at the port from 1794 until 1796, when William Kirby was appointed (Washington, *Papers, Pres. Ser.*, 5:276-7, 352-3; 11:111-12; Syrett, *Hamilton*, 16:354; Stets, *Postmasters*, 259; Leonard, *General Assembly*, 195, 197; JEP, 1:11, 43, 165, 216).

From Robert Smith

SIR,   Washington Augt. 31. 1801

From the dispatches received by Captain Rodgers, which will be transmitted by this post from the department of State to you and to mr Madison, we have the unhappiness to perceive that the French Government have not appeared disposed to accede to the terms of ratification proposed by us. Apprehensive that at some future day claims respecting indemnities might be revived, they, it seems, have signified their wish that all the objects of the 2nd. Article Indemnities as well as Treaties be for ever abandoned by both parties. But mr Murray, not considering himself authorised, has not subscribed to such an abandonment.

It is impossible for us to ascertain in this instance the real Object of the first Consul or in what manner this negotiation will terminate. Be this, however, as it may, from a view of this new state of things certain questions present themselves that deserve immediate consideration.

If we should not be informed of the exchange of ratifications at the time the Frigate Boston be ready to sail, ought she to remain here in port without further orders until the ultimate determination of the French Government be communicated to us? or Ought she to proceed directly to the Mediterranean without the Minister? or ought mr Livingston to be sent to France in aid of mr Murray with suitable instructions?

Is it not necessary to be prepared to decide, as soon as the Boston shall be equipped for sea, what course is to be taken? To detain this Vessel in port at so great an expence and upon so uncertain an event would be attended with unpleasant circumstances. To dispatch her directly for the Mediterranean to join the squadron would in my opinion be adviseable, until it should be considered that mr Livingston could be at Paris *in time* and when there, that he could materially assist mr Murray.

It is probable that in the Course of this Week I shall receive a Letter from Captain McNeill informing me that the Boston is equipped and that agreeably to instructions some time since sent to him, he is about proceeding to New-York.

The enclosed Letters are upon subjects that merit attention. But as I was not in Office at the time the improvements of the Navy Yard and the Barracks were first projected, I have to ask the favor of your advice upon the propriety of these additional buildings.

Accept the assurances of my great respect & high Consideration

RT. SMITH

RC (DLC); endorsed by TJ as received from the Navy Department on 3 Sep. and so recorded in SJL with notation "the Boston." Enclosures: (1) Captain Thomas Tingey to Smith, 29 Aug., from the Washington Navy Yard, advising the construction of a warehouse for the storage of rigging, sails, stores, and other materials from ships docked at the yard so that their holds may be properly ventilated; the new building would also save costs of renting storage space in Georgetown, where some naval stores are kept now for $200 rent and $400 paid to a storekeeper each year; reporting that he has an estimate of $9,000 to build a warehouse of 100 feet by 40 feet, Tingey notes that a timely authorization for the construction might enable him to save money in the acquisition of materials for the building and would allow for bricks to be made "while the weather remains fine" (RC in same). (2) William W. Burrows, lieutenant colonel commandant of the Marine Corps, to Smith, 31 Aug., stating that the barracks under construction should have a unit built at each end to protect the building

from the elements and to save rent that will otherwise have to be paid for the housing of stores; noting also that privies were not provided for in the plans but are necessary for sanitation; and declaring that this required new construction will not exceed $4,000, which, added to the contracted cost of $16,000 for the main part of the building already in progress, will reach the amount of $20,000 appropriated by Congress (RC in same; with diagram, a simple outline plan identifying the main sections of the building, marked "now to be finished," and the proposed "Ends required to be finished").

DISPATCHES RECEIVED BY CAPTAIN RODGERS: that is, communications that reached Smith through John Rodgers, the commander of the *Maryland*. The papers probably included six dispatches from William Vans Murray to the secretary of state, ranging in date from 23 June to 9 July and enclosing copies of Murray's written exchanges with the French commissioners, and a letter from John Dawson to Madison dated 25 June. Early in

July, the French had proposed an explicit renunciation of claims in the form of a statement agreed to by both parties and incorporated into the exchange of ratifications. Murray replied that he was "not authorised to enter into such an Engagement for his Government" (Charles Pierre Claret Fleurieu and Pierre Louis Roederer to Murray, 3 July, Murray to Joseph Bonaparte, Fleurieu, and Roederer, 5 July, in DNA: RG 59, DD, Netherlands; Madison, *Papers, Sec. of State Ser.*, 1:340-1, 345, 353, 369, 375-6, 390-1; 2:77n; NDQW, Dec. 1800-Dec. 1801, 148, 279).

Preparations had been underway for the BOSTON to deliver Robert R. Livingston to France and then join the squadron that had been sent to the Mediterranean under Richard Dale's command. Daniel MCNEILL received command of the *Boston* in July, and on 14 Aug. Smith authorized him to take the frigate from Boston to New York, where Livingston would embark. The ship's cabin had been enlarged to accommodate Livingston's party (NDQW, Dec. 1800-Dec. 1801, 246, 266, 272, 274-5, 285; Notes on a Cabinet Meeting, 15 May 1801).

From Jacob Wagner

SIR   Department of State:—Washington, 31 Augt. 1801.

On Saturday evening arrived in this city Capt. Rogers of the Maryland, accompanied by Mr. Purviance, the bearers of dispatches from Messrs. Murray and Dawson. I have forwarded them to the Secretary of State, after they were perused by the Secretary of the Navy, the Secretary of the Treasury being absent in the country with his sick child. The latest letter from Mr. Murray is dated 9th. July, and the vessel left Havre the 15th. of the same month.

The treaty had not been ratified on the part of France, her Ministers insisting upon the formal renunciation of our claims for captures, and offering the renunciation of the validity of the old treaties, in return. Mr. Murray had offered an article, subject to the approbation of the Senate, whereby the second article of the Convention should be reinstated. This offer was rejected. No objection was made to the clause of limitation superadded by the Senate. Mr. Murray says he does not despair of obtaining our terms or nearly so. This probably is no more than a conjecture.

The Bashaw of Tripoli ordered our flag-staff to be cut down on the 14th. May and declared war against the U. States. Mr. Cathcart has arrived at Leghorn.

As the Secretary will not have an opportunity of communicating the dispatches to you, Sir, by the same mail by which he receives them, I have supposed the above information would not be unacceptable to you.

I have also the honor of informing you, that I forward by this mail a packet addressed to you in Mr. Short's hand writing and another packet in which I have enclosed a number of letters for you, the whole received by the Maryland. She brought no newspapers for the Department of State.

With the most perfect respect, I have the honor, Sir, to be your most obed. servt.   JACOB WAGNER

P.S. The Secretary of State directed me to send you the recent letters written to Mr. Eaton, to enable you to answer the letter of the Bey of Tunis, demanding cannon:—they are accordingly enclosed. Mr. Graham, whom you intend to appoint Secretary of the Legation to Spain, being now here, his commission is transmitted to you for signature.

RC (DLC); addressed: "The President of the United States Monticello"; franked and postmarked; endorsed by TJ as received 3 Sep. and so recorded in SJL. Enclosures: see below.

According to the instructions that William Vans Murray received from TJ and Levi Lincoln in March, if the suppression of the SECOND ARTICLE of the convention met with enough resistance from the French to put implementation of the convention into jeopardy, he could offer to retain that article, with the proviso that ratification would then have to come before the Senate again. Murray offered that proposal, which he considered to be his "last Resort," to the French commissioners on 27 June. On 3 July they came back with their suggestion of making a mutual renunciation of claims part of the instrument of ratification. Murray did not detect any opposition by the French to the addition of an article to provide a LIMITATION on the duration of the convention. "My Object is yet to obtain a simple Exchange on our Terms," Murray wrote to Madison on 9 July, "and even yet I do not dispair of obtaining it, or Something very near it" (Madison, Papers, Sec. of State Ser., 1:390; Murray to Madison, 23 June, Murray to French commissioners, 27 June, Charles Pierre Claret Fleurieu and Pierre Louis Roederer to Murray, 3 July, in DNA: RG 59, DD, Netherlands; TJ to Oliver Ellsworth and Murray, with Lincoln, 18 Mch. 1801).

TRIPOLI: the removal of the flagpole at the U.S. consulate was the symbolic confirmation of a declaration of war by

Yusuf, the bey. A circular letter by James L. Cathcart, consul at Tripoli, dated 15 May, informing U.S. agents and consuls in France and Spain that "our flag staff was chopped down," was printed in the National Intelligencer on 31 Aug. Cathcart originally intended to evacuate himself and his family to Tunis, but decided to go to Leghorn (Livorno, Italy) instead. Before leaving Tripoli, he asked the Danish consul general to watch over any Americans who might be brought there as prisoners (NDBW, 1:453-60; Madison, Papers, Sec. of State Ser., 1:262).

The PACKET from William Short included Short's letter of 9 June and its enclosures, which were a communication from Cardinal Dugnani to TJ of 30 Mch. and letters from Short to John Barnes and Peyton Short. The other letters from France that TJ received on 3 Sep., perhaps all of which were contained in the second packet mentioned by Wagner, were from Madame de Corny, 19 May; Thomas Paine, 9 June, 25 June, and the description of a means of mechanical power noted at 25 June; Paul Richard Randall, [11 June]; Stephen Cathalan, Jr., 14 June; Madame de Tessé, 14 June; Stephen Drayton, 20 June; Lafayette, 21 June; Pierre Auguste Adet, 24 June; Francis Rotch, two letters of 24 June and one of 9 July, none of which have been found; Volney, 24, [25] June; A. H. Homberg, 7 July, noted at Volney to TJ, [25 June]; and Daniel Parker, 10 July.

SEND YOU THE RECENT LETTERS: probably copies of Madison to William Eaton, 20 May and 17 July 1801, regarding a cargo to complete the payment of the "Regalia" to the bey of Tunis, including the "extortionate" requirement of jewels worth $40,000, to be obtained in London and sent directly to Tunis (Madison, *Papers, Sec. of State Ser.*, 1:200, 423).

The commission for John GRAHAM as secretary of the U.S. legation to Spain is dated 31 Aug. (FC in Lb in DNA: RG 59, Credences). TJ informed Charles Pinckney in March that Graham would be the legation secretary. Graham, a Virginian who graduated from Columbia College in 1790 and subsequently moved to Kentucky, remained in Europe until 1804. Shortly after he returned to the United States, TJ appointed him secretary of Orleans Territory (ANB; Madison, *Papers, Sec. of State Ser.*, 1:279; 7:158n, 612n; Vol. 33:677; TJ to Pinckney, 17 Mch. 1801; TJ to Graham, 1 Dec. 1804).

John Thomson Mason's Notes on Candidates for Bank Director

[ca. August 1801]

James Dunlop. A merchant of good character, not much understanding, in good circumstances, clear of debt, but a tool to U.F.

Thos. Beall of Geo. A man clear of debt, of good estate, and character, of no understanding, and a tool to F. & S.

John Laird A merchant of fair character, exceeding good understanding, of considerable property clear of Debt, and a tool to no man.

These men reside in George Town and are violent and bitter Federalists.

Daniel Carroll of Dudlington ⎫
Notley Young ⎬ Two wealthy honest men, unacquaintcd with business, but very attentive to their own interest, moderate Federalists ⎭

Thomas Law A man by no means deficient in either genius or knowledge, but totally unfit for any kind of business, and perhaps of all men the least fit for a Bank Director.

John Oakely. A very honest upright man, of very good understanding, *very eccentrick*, he would be perfectly regardless of his own money, if he had any, and for that reason I think it might not be altogether safe to trust him with the management of that which belongs to others.

Daniel Carroll Brent. A very honest man, entirely unacquainted with Banking or mercantile business, but joined with others who had a competent knowledge of those subjects, would make a very good director.

John Mason A man of very fair character, I believe very deservedly so, and as he is a man of very good understanding, and has been long engaged in business of this kind, I presume he would make a very good director.

It does not occur to me that there is any other man in the County of Washington who would be thought of as a Bank director by any person who knew him. I have endeavoured to give you some idea of the character of those I have named, how far they or any them are proper persons to be trusted in that way, you will determine, if men tollerably well quallified could be found, there are only five of them that I should be willing to trust, Carroll, Young, Laird Brent & Mason. Every man that I have named on the other side, except Brent & Oakely, are I believe very large Stock holders in the Bank of Columbia.

MS (DNA: RG 59, LAR); undated, but see below; entirely in Mason's hand; endorsed by TJ: "Mason J. T. for Bank directors."

TJ may have asked John T. Mason for his recommendations for the board of directors of the Bank of the United States's office of discount and deposit at Washington as early as June, when Gallatin wrote Thomas Willing, arguing for the establishment of a branch in the city to be used for the deposit of government funds instead of the Bank of Columbia. TJ and Gallatin probably discussed who should be included on a list of proposed candidates for directors (now missing), which Gallatin submitted to Willing in a letter of 11 Aug. Whether TJ had gathered information on the subject by that time, or waited until after the Bank of the United States agreed to establish the branch on 18 Aug., is not clear. The election of the directors took place in early October. None of the candidates described above were elected, but John T. Mason became a director (see Gallatin to TJ, 24 Aug., especially Enclosure No. 2, and note).

u.f.: Uriah Forrest. f. & s.: Forrest and Benjamin Stoddert. Forrest, Stoddert, Beall, Young, and Carroll were among the early property holders in the federal district. In 1793, Forrest, Stoddert, John Mason, and several others founded the Bank of Columbia. By 1798, Dunlop, Laird, and Law had joined the board of directors. John Mason served as president of the Bank from 1798 to 1816. TJ appointed John Oakley (Oakely) collector of customs at Georgetown in October 1801. He had earlier appointed Daniel Carroll Brent marshal of the District of Columbia (Bryan, *National Capital*, 1:135, 223; Walsh, *Early Banks in D.C.*, 68, 76-7; Vol. 33:203n, 231n, 345, 670, 671, 675, 677). For TJ's appointment of John T. Mason as U.S. attorney for the District of Columbia, see Vol. 33:380n, 671, 675.

From Thomas Paine

DEAR SIR   [August 1801]

The ratification of the treaty at last gives me another opportunity of writing to you. The coalition of the North has vanished almost to nothing. There is no certain News from Egypt either in france or England. Admiral Gantheame is returned without being able to land in Egypt the reinforcement he took with him. He has taken the Swift-sure an English 74—and another 74 the Hanibal has been taken in the bay of Algesiras; but afterwards, two Spanish Ships of the line attacked each other in the Night by mistake and both perished. The general talk is now a descent upon England, and the english Government has some alarms upon the Case. Preparations for this ought to have been made last year immediately after signing the peace with Austria. In the Memoir I sent to B—— in answer to the question he sent to me at that time (a copy of which you have) I endeavoured to press this point strongly upon him. Had the preparation been set about then neither the expedition of the English to the Baltic, nor to Egypt could have taken place. They could not have left their Coast unfurnished, nor sent their best troops abroad as they have done. I believe the peace with Portugal is not ratified by france, but be it, or be it not, if france does not make preparations for a descent, I feel perswaded the English will send an expedition against the portugese settlements in S America. A 1000 Gun-boats proper for a descent would not cost more than four or five ships of the line would cost, and they would hold england more in Check than 100 Ships of the line would do. Boats do not require to be manned by Sailors as Ships do, and need no other kind of Naval Stores than are produced in france. The Secretary General of Marine who speaks English ask me, a few days ago, to give a Memoir on the descent which himself would translate for the Minister, which I did. But from the short interview I had with the Minister he did not appear to me much disposed to promote a descent by Boats. He is a Naval Architect, and reckoned capital in his line, and I suppose would rather build Ships than boats. I think the french governt. would do well were it to divide the Marine office into two parts and separate the construction and direction of the boat-marine from that of Ships, The boat-marine, it is probable, would then be carried on with Ambition and energy, which, I see, will not be the case while the two are blended together. If preparation for a descent go forward, it will of consequence hold England in check and alarm, perhaps more so than the Coalition of the North did, and in that case she will be cautious how she conducts herself towards America.

I have been observing for some days past the manner of finishing the out-side of houses in Paris. They appear to be stone fronts, but are not so; and except some costly Buildings the walls are built of rough Stone and plaistered or stuccoed. In America no plaistered or

stuccoed work will stand the breaking up of the frost. In Paris it
stands perfectly, and I have seen some winters nearly as severe here
as in America. The difference is in the material and not in the work-
manship. In America the plaister or stucco is made of lime Mortar. In
Paris it is made of Plaister of Paris which has not any quality of lime
stone in it. I know not if you have observed it, but about a third of
this stone in its natural state is Water in a fixed state. When it is
burnt, or rather roasted, about 10 or 12 hours in a large heap, the watery part is expelled. It is then pounded, for it will not, after being
burnt, dissolve in water like lime, nor produce any heat. It is then
sifted, and mixed with water to about the thickness of white-wash
which in a few Minutes will become fixed, In this state, that is, before
it becomes hard, it is plaistered upon the rough stone and marked
into squares resembling stone. It is then white washed with the same
Material sifted finer. I observe they throw the first coating on, after it
is a little stiff, with the hand. to make it adhere the better, and smooth
it with the trowel. They begin at the top. The Cornish is made of this
plaister. They finish as they go. When they have plaistered about four
or five feet downward and before the plaister is got hard, they draw
the lines with a tool like a graver which cuts out the joints resembling
stone. To make the lines strait they use a long rule, and they put the
last washing on before the first coating is dry. These fronts resist wet
and are not injured by frost, but Bricks absorb a great quantity of
wet. If a pint of water be thrown against a brick wall in a hot day
scarcely any of it will reach the ground; and as to plaistered fronts in
America made of lime Mortar they fall to pieces with the breaking up
of the frost. There is plenty of this Stone in Nova Scotia, and I think
it would be a useful material in houses in America.—Were I to build
a brick house in America I would have the bricks made large and of
the shape of the capital letter ⌐⌐ There would then be so many hol-
lows from the top to the bottom of the Wall that I question if the wet
would get thro'. I know not why we follow the english statute measure of 9 Inches by 4.

The priests begin again to put up their heads, as you will see by the
enclosed publication of the Minister of Police.—   T—

RC (DLC); undated; endorsed by TJ
as received 4 Nov. and so recorded in
SJL. Enclosure: Joseph Fouché to prefects of France, 20 July 1801 (see below).

Paine's reference to the RATIFICATION
of the convention between the United
States and France indicates that he composed this letter after 31 July. He could
have written it no later than early October, when the French government announced the signing of preliminary articles of peace with Great Britain. It seems
likely, given the events mentioned in the
letter, that Paine wrote it in August. TJ
received John Dawson's letter of 18 Aug.

on 5 Nov., the day after he got this one from Paine, which suggests that the two communications may have crossed the Atlantic in the same ship. Paine certainly missed the opportunity of sending his letter with the ratification, since the letter reached TJ over two months after John H. Purviance, the courier of the ratification papers, arrived in the United States. The only other letter that TJ received from France on 4 Nov. was the one from Jacques Joseph Ducarne de Blangy of 3 July 1801.

On his return from EGYPT, where he had been unable to land French reinforcements, Admiral Honoré Joseph Ganteaume captured the British 74-gun ship SWIFTSURE in the Mediterranean. The French brought the warship into Toulon harbor on 22 July. Earlier that month, Spanish and French ships operating in concert fought two battles against a British squadron on the southern coast of Spain, near Gibraltar and Algeciras. Approximately 1,700 men were lost when two large Spanish warships sank in the confusion of a night battle (William Laird Clowes, *The Royal Navy: A History from the Earliest Times to the Present*, 7 vols. [London, 1897-1903; repr. 1996-97], 4:452-3, 458-70; John D. Grainger, *The Amiens Truce: Britain and Bonaparte, 1801-1803* [Rochester, N.Y., 2004], 44; Tulard, *Dictionnaire Napoléon*, 773).

MEMOIR I SENT TO B—: in October 1800, Paine sent TJ a copy of a memorandum that Paine had written in response to a query from Napoleon Bonaparte. In that document, Paine argued that political, social, and economic factors made Britain vulnerable to invasion, and he proposed a scheme for an attack across the English Channel using rowed gunboats (Vol. 32:188, 191n).

Dissatisfied with the terms of PEACE WITH PORTUGAL signed in June, Bonaparte demanded a new treaty. The new compact required Portugal to close its ports to the British, open them to the French, provide no aid to the enemies of France, and pay a large indemnity. Portugal also had to cede a portion of Brazil to French Guiana. The treaty was signed in Madrid on 29 Sep. (Parry, *Consolidated Treaty Series*, 56:77-92, 207-9; H. V. Livermore, *A History of Portugal* [Cambridge, 1947], 390-1).

MARINE: the French naval department. Pierre Alexandre Forfait was minister of the department from 1799 until the fall of 1801. As an engineer for the navy beginning in the 1770s, Forfait designed or supervised the construction of various ships (Tulard, *Dictionnaire Napoléon*, 745).

The STATUTE MEASURE of an English brick from the sixteenth to the eighteenth centuries was nine inches in length, a little more than four inches in width, and a little more than two inches thick. After 1776 the prescribed size was 8.5 by 4 by 2.5 inches (Nathaniel Lloyd, *A History of English Brickwork* [London, 1925], 12).

PRIESTS BEGIN AGAIN TO PUT UP THEIR HEADS: France and the Vatican severed official connections in 1790, when the French government brought the ecclesiastical structure of the church under state control. In mid-July 1801, after months of negotiation, French and papal representatives signed a concordat in Paris that recognized the Roman Catholic church in France and established roles for both the secular government and the pope in the governance of religious affairs. The MINISTER OF POLICE, Joseph Fouché, disliked the new arrangement, and on 20 July he issued a circular letter to the prefects of France's *départements* opposing the reinstatement of priests who had not cooperated with the republic's control over religion. The action brought Fouché a reprimand from Bonaparte, who wanted ed a restoration of good relations with the pope. The concordat was ratified in September (Hubert Cole, *Fouché: The Unprincipled Patriot* [New York, 1971], 133; Margaret M. O'Dwyer, *The Papacy in the Age of Napoleon and the Restoration: Pius VII, 1800-1823* [Lanham, Md., 1985], 49-57; Alfred Boulay de la Meurthe, *Documents sur la négociation du concordat et sur les autres rapports de la France avec le Saint-Siège en 1800 et 1801*, 6 vols. [Paris, 1891-1905], 3:445-7; Parry, *Consolidated Treaty Series*, 56:161-5; Stewart, *French Revolution*, 167-90).

From Henry Dearborn

SIR   Pittston Septemr. 1t. 1801

I was last evening honour'd with your letter of the 14th. ulto. with the enclosed papers relative to Mr. Quarrier, &c.

There has undoubtedly been very improper management at Newport. on my way home I visited & examined the public works at that place & shall call there on my return, and make some further enquiries.

In a former letter I took the liberty of mentioning the unhappy situation of one of my daughters. she has in a great measure recovered her reason, but not perfectly, I doubt whether I shall be able to leave home sooner than the twenty fourth or[1] fifth, inst. Mrs. Dearborn with our son & one daughter will accompany me.   Mr. Benja. Jarvis has been induced (by a liberal offer from Genl Lincoln) to decline the appointment of Collector at Penobscut.—A Mr. Josiah Hook, a Gentleman of education & unblemished charactor, and who lives on Penobscut river at a place called Orrington is perhaps the most suitable charractor to fill that office that will be found in that quarter, he is a sound Republican & in all respects well suited to the office, he is under thirty years of age, has a family, & would like the appointment. I have mentioned him to Mr. Gallatin.—Mr John Lee's removal is generally popular, & his brother Silas Lee, is highly pleased with his appointment as District Attorney and promises to do well.

with sentiments of respectfull esteem I am Sir Your Obedt. Huml. Servt.   HENRY DEARBORN

RC (DLC); at foot of text: "The President. of the U.S."; endorsed by TJ as received from the War Department on 24 Sep. and so recorded in SJL.

Dearborn suspended the construction of harbor fortifications at NEWPORT, Rhode Island, in March. Since then he had learned that the land for the project had apparently been purchased on the basis of "verbal or implied orders" when James McHenry was secretary of war. In August, TJ received an accusation that Henry Knox had benefited from the project. Dearborn's visit to Newport that month may have fostered rumors that additional fortifications would be built (Louis Tousard to Dearborn, 4 May, 27 May 1801, summaries in DNA: RG 107,

RLRMS; Henry Dearborn's Report on the War Department, [12 May 1801]; "Nicholas Geffroy" to TJ, 1 Aug. 1801).

FORMER LETTER: Dearborn to TJ, 12 Aug.

Benjamin JARVIS had been the original choice to replace John Lee as collector of customs at Penobscot, Maine. Lee had, in TJ's assessment, "very violent" and obnoxious political sentiments. Dearborn recommended JOSIAH HOOK in a letter of 1 Sep. to Gallatin. Hook received the appointment in November (Gallatin, *Papers*, 5:672; Madison, *Papers, Sec. of State Ser.*, 1:479; Vol. 33:219, 669, 673, 677; Hook to TJ, 24 Dec. 1801).

[1] MS: "of."

From James Wilkinson and
Benjamin Hawkins

South West point September 1st. 1801

Understanding from the public prints, that you are at Monticello, we avail ourselves of the direct conveyance to intrude on you our communications of the 25th ult, and of this day, to the secretary of War; and we hope you may approve of this deviation from the regular course of our correspondence, which we hazard, with the intent to secure time, for the seasonable arrival of any order you may think proper to issue, respecting the place for holding the proposed conference with the Choctaws.

Our letter of the 25th. was intended to be sent on the day it was written by a Mr. Watson of Alexandria who informed us, of his being on the road and that he should pass near your residence, but as we found afterwards that he would be detained we took it back and send it by the mail.—Our colleague General Pickins arrived last evening.

With the highest consideration and most respectful attachment we have the honour to be sir, Your most obedient servants.

JA WILKINSON
BENJAMIN HAWKINS

RC (DLC); at foot of text: "Thomas Jefferson President of the United States"; in Hawkins's hand, signed by him and Wilkinson; endorsed by TJ as received 15 Sep. and so recorded in SJL. Enclosures: see below.

COMMUNICATIONS OF THE 25TH ULT: Wilkinson and Hawkins were at Southwest Point as commissioners for talks with the Cherokees. Writing to the secretary of war on 25 Aug., they enclosed a copy of a message they had received from The Glass, who with some other Cherokee chiefs wanted to move the conference to Tellico. Wilkinson and Hawkins refused the request, saying that the meeting site could not be changed in time. The Cherokees were also upset about the recent murder of a Cherokee woman by a white man, and the commissioners reported to Dearborn that the killer had probably "escaped from the country." Hawkins and Wilkinson expected to meet with at least two prominent Cherokee chiefs at Southwest Point and then pro-

ceed to Chickasaw Bluffs, where, according to Dearborn's instructions of 24 June, they were to confer with the Chickasaws. The commissioners asked that the third stop on their tour of negotiations, at Natchez to meet with the Choctaws, be changed, since holding the conference at Natchez would "expose the inhabitants to much unavoidable vexation and abuse of property, and the Indians to the debauchery inseperable from our frontier villages." AND OF THIS DAY: in their letter of 1 Sep. to Dearborn, Wilkinson and Hawkins related that the Cherokees seemed "indisposed to any conference at this time," from a fear of more encroachment on their lands and the failure of the United States to capture the murderer. The commissioners also informed Dearborn that "The Glass has illy requited the courtesies he experienced at the seat of government," having instigated "several violent propositions" in the Cherokees' councils. Hawkins and Wilkinson, if unable to complete a negotiation with the Cherokees, expected to go immediately to

Chickasaw Bluffs. In their communication of 1 Sep. to Dearborn they enclosed a copy of their letter to TJ printed above (Foster, *Hawkins*, 371-7; the War Department's correspondence registers in DNA: RG 107, RLRMS, record the commissioners' letters to Dearborn as received 15 Sep. 1801; ASP, *Indian Affairs*, 1:649-50;

Editorial Note to Reply to a Cherokee Delegation, printed at 3 July 1801).

GENERAL PICKINS: Andrew Pickens replaced William R. Davie, who declined to serve as one of the commissioners for the talks with the Indian tribes (TJ to Abraham Baldwin, 13 July).

From William Gardiner

SIR.   Baltimore Pitt Street Sepr 2d 1801.

The undersign'd could not have assum'd the exercise of the present Freedom, had he not been convinc'd Mr Jeffersons private Virtues added the brightest Splendor to his Title of President.—

To the cold Systemist or Machine of inherited prejudice, this Application would be spurn'd with reprehensions of contempt. But seduc'd by the true Lustre of Humanity and Fame, a Young Man, without a Friend, dares to sollicit the first Magistrate of a free People, for some inferior employ, in the various Departments, that, might suit his Talents.

The undersign'd is the Son of an English Gentleman of decay'd Fortunes, has been near 5 Years in Baltimore, in the Capacity of Tutor, and can produce good recommendations as ℈ Enclos'd.—

His Abilities embrace most what a liberal Education confers, a thorough Knowledge of Accompts (from his connexions in Business) the Translation of French readily, the Spanish, Italian & Portugueze with the Aid of a Dictionary and a general Reading of Ancient and Modern History

He thinks it proper to add when an Infant, he had the Misfortune to lose the Sight of an Eye, is a married Man, and about Thirty Years of Age.—

If the undersign'd should succeed, the pride of his Heart dictates this expression, he ever will be deserving—If otherwise the disappointment will never chill, that Respect, ever warm in his Breast, for the illustrious Character of Mr. Jefferson.   WM. GARDINER.

RC (DLC); at head of text: "To his Excellency the President of the United States"; endorsed by TJ as received 10 Sep. and so recorded in SJL. Enclosures not found.

From Benjamin Waterhouse

SIR   Cambridge Sepr. 2d. 1801.

I know not if I acknowledged the receipt of your letter of the 8th. ulto. in the hasty scrawl I lately wrote from Boston. That of the 14th. gave me pleasure inexpressible, as it informed me that you had succeeded in planting the benign remedy against the small pox in the vast region of Virginia. I have written to Dr. Wardlaw on the important subject of preserving the active fluid-virus for inoculation, in constant succession from patient to patient. I wish he had inoculated as many as he possibly could, from the pustule, and not trusted to the thread, as the fresh fluid never, or very rarely fails communicating the infection, even when no other instrument is used than a cambric:needle.

I have referred Dr. Wardlaw to the letter I wrote to you at Washington for more minute directions. I have repeated to him, and hope to be excused for re-iterating it here, to take the matter on the 8th. day, nay the 7th. if possible, and never later than the 9th. The efflorescence is a sign that the absorption has commenced, and the nicety of the business is to take the virus just before that period. I have watched this process with a microscope in a number of persons whom I had taken into my house for this express purpose, and experience has now taught me a sure procedure, somewhat different from my early theory, which was to take the matter at the very acme of the inflammation. I now take it before the virus is so far absorbed as to affect the lymphatics in the arm-pit with pain; and by so doing I always succeed. In consequence of the hint in your letter just on your departure from Washington, I sent Dr Gantt the virus in a phial of water, but have not heard of its reception. This matter I took on a cool & rainy day and put it up with great care, and can hardly conceive that it should fail. The weather has been oppressively hot,—98 in the shade! an occurrence not easily accounted for in this northern latitude, and in our situation. On a journey this time 12 months, I found it as hot an hundred miles east of us, and more like a *sirocco* than any thing I ever felt. "There is something in this which our philosophy has never dreamt of."—I carefully avoided taking matter for transportation during such hot days, for I presume the mercury must have risen to 106, in the open fields

I may be mistaken, but I at present believe that my thus sending the vaccine matter to President Jefferson has forwarded the practice in Virginia at least a year, if not two. The rivalship of physicians, the desire of taking, and keeping the lead in this new inoculation have retarded the advancement of the *true* inoculation, while it has diffused the *spurious* far & wide. I therefore presume that a number of decidedly perfect cases in the neighborhood of Monticello will give the genuine disease a currency through Virginia. The vaccine inoculation is progressing at Newfoundland. The physician general at Halifax has just written to me on the subject of introducing it there. At Geneva it is now the custom with the ministers of religion to impress on the minds of every parent, who presents a child for baptism the duty of giving it this newly discovered disease. The minister of the interior, directed Professor Odier to make him a report of the state of *vaccinism* in France. But the most eloquent production I have yet seen on the subject, is by a physician at Hamburgh, so that the practice is becoming universal in Europe. What a blessing will this discovery be to the inhabitants of the African side of the mediterranean where the small-pox has always raged with a peculiar malignity! We already know that the kine-pox has preserved its characteristic mildness at Minorca.

I have had a number of communications from different parts of New England, tending to induce a belief, that this disease has been found among the kine of our own country. I am not, however, entirely convinced of it. I gave full credence to one account transmitted to me by our Attorney General. I even sent the history to London, which may possibly be already published. I communicated it also to the Massachusetts Medical society as a proff of the domestic origin of the kine pox. And it is not many days since I discovered that the cow was inoculated by a mischevous medical-pupil, who took this method to convince an old, unbelieving country practitioner that there really did exist such a disease. This rustic physician's daughters were his milk maids. They being soon disabled from milking the diseased cow, their mother performed that office and took the disorder also In the height of the disorder they were seen by Chief Justice Dana, Judge Sulivan, and some other gentlemen who had seen the disease in their own families. I gave more credit to this account coming from gentlemen belonging to that order whose very essence is *evidence*, than if it were related by physicians, yet my account sent to England must be followed by this explanation.

There appeared in almost all the news-papers in the Union a paragraph saying that a Dr. Lacci had discovered the vaccine virus among the *Leaves* in Switzerland, to which the printers added three notes of admiration!!!—I wrote to one of the Boston printers that he might change the *L.* into a *B.* and then erase the three notes of admiration.

This epizootic distemper has existed so long in Ireland as to be known there by a *Celtic* name, viz. "*Shinnaugh*"; which word is found on dissection to mean "*a Cow's. teat.*" To a knowledge of this disease has been connected an opinion that persons once affected with the *Shinnaugh* could never take the small pox. But Dr. Jenner a learned, skillful, and philanthropic physician was the first who took this knowledge so long vaguely floating on the breath of the vulgar and impressed upon it the stable form of science. He, with a Franklian sagacity first transferred it from the brute to the human kind, and demonstrated it to be a perfect security against the small pox. This extraordinary fact came forth from his masterly hands in so perfect a form, that were all other writings on the Cow-pox but his, destroyed, posterity would have a clear & unconfused idea of this singular disease & its saluteferous consequences.

I am preparing a second pamphlet, being "Observations on the local appearance, symptoms, & mode of treating the Variola Vaccinæ, with some rules for determining the *true* pustule from the *spurious*," but my collegiate duties will scarcely allow me to publish it very soon, my course on Natural History having just commenced, and when that terminates my medical Lectures begin

In the course of my researches, I have learnt that the pustular disease denominated *Chicken pox* originated in those domestic birds, which having no specific name in the english language are called by the general one of *fowls*, or by the still more vague one of *Cocks* & *Hens*. It originated in Hyndostan. The small pox and that disease in the poultry having, with the natives, the same denomination viz. "*gooty.*"

With the highest respect for your station and character I remain your very humble servt.   Benjn. Waterhouse

RC (DLC); endorsed by TJ as received 17 Sep. and so recorded in SJL.

OUR PHILOSOPHY HAS NEVER DREAMT OF: possibly an allusion to Hamlet's words to Horatio, "There are more things in heaven and earth, Horatio, than are dreamt of in your philosophy" (Shakespeare, *Hamlet*, 1.5).
THE LETTER I WROTE TO YOU AT WASHINGTON: Waterhouse to TJ, 8 June.

In 1802, Waterhouse published a SECOND PAMPHLET on smallpox vaccination, titled *A Prospect of Exterminating the Small Pox, Part II, Being a Continuation of a Narrative of Facts Concerning the Progress of the New Inoculation in America* (Cambridge, Mass.; Sowerby, No. 946).

To Jean Xavier Bureaux de Pusy

DEAR SIR   Monticello Sep. 3. 1801.
I have duly recieved your favor of Aug. 11. with the letter from Mr.
Poirey to myself & his Memoire to Congress. I should be glad to render mr Poirey any service I could in this, wishing him sincerely well.
but the rules of communication with Congress forbid me to be the
channel of a petition for a particular individual. I will take for mr
Poirey the only step I can. I will put his memoir into the hands of
some member of Congress to be brought forward in his place. it is in
this way all petitions come before this body. for this purpose it will be
necessary to deliver with the petition, the letter of Genl. Washington
to Made. de la Fayette & M. de la Fayette's certificate. Accept assurances of my high consideration & respect.   TH: JEFFERSON

RC (privately owned, New York City, 1949); at foot of text: "M. Bureaux Pusy." PrC
(DLC). Tr (same).

From Pierce Butler

DEAR SIR   Philada. September the 3d. 1801—
I am just now favoured with Your letter of the 26th of August—
Whatever removal I might recommend in So. Carolina can never
have in view the strengthening of any personal Interest; yet If I was
guided by such considerations the encrease of personal Interest woud
be used only in support of the present State of things as regards the
General Governmt. The truth is I have no personal object in So. Carolina or else where—I can not place myself, nor allow of being placed
among Ear Wiggs who always hang about Men in power—I know
there are some Characters in or of So. Carolina who have sent forward a list of removals, and Successors—I have seen them. Of the
motive in trying to lead the Executive into a wrong direction I shall
say nothing in this letter—
The person to whom I had allusion is Mr Danl. Stevens the Supervisor—he has been represented to me as having, previous to the
late Election, written circular letters through the State, propagating
the grossest falsehoods of the present Chief Magistrate of the US—
as having sent all the petty Excise Officers posting through the State,
to try to prevent the Election of such Men to the State Legislature as
were of Republican principles—If my information was correct, and I
believe it was, such Corruption shoud not have power—I have been

assured that himself and his Sattelites influenc'd One hundred Votes in Charleston only—I have no objection to his being informd that he is removed by my recommendation—At this moment I woud not recommend one other removal—the two others I mentiond are inferior Excise Officers of no Note

Offering, respectfully, my opinion on the general principle of Removal; it appears to me prudent to do it sparingly; and where only Corruption in Office stares Us in the face, 'till it is ascertaind who are to Compose the Senate at the next meeting—The line of Conduct of Govr McKean, as to removals, can not have Your approbation; and yet I believe he woud lead You into it if he coud—

View me not I pray You, as one Courting a Correspondence with the Chief Magistrate of the Union—

In Publick or in private life You have had the highest esteem, respect, and regard of   P. BUTLER

RC (DNA: RG 59, LAR); endorsed by TJ as received 10 Sep. and so recorded in SJL; also endorsed by TJ: "Stevens to be removed."

Charleston merchant Daniel STEVENS had served as SUPERVISOR of the revenue in South Carolina since 1791. He subsequently secured additional federal appointments as a revenue inspector, superintendent of the lighthouse, and procurement agent for the War Department (JEP, 1:81; S.C. Biographical Directory, Senate, 3:1546-7).

To John Carroll

SIR   Monticello Sep. 3. 1801.

I have recieved at this place the application signed by yourself and several respectable inhabitants of Washington on the purchase of a site for a Roman Catholic church from the Commissioners. as the regulation of price rests very much with them, I have referred the paper to them, recommending to them all the favor which the object of the purchase would urge, the advantages of every kind which it would promise, and their duties permit. I shall be happy on this and on every other occasion of shewing my respect & concern for the religious society over which you preside in these states and in tendering to yourself assurances of my high esteem and consideration.

TH: JEFFERSON

PrC (DLC); at foot of text: "Bishop Carrol Baltimore."

Born in Maryland and educated in Europe, John Carroll (1736-1815) became America's first Roman Catholic bishop in 1789, when he was named bishop of the new diocese of Baltimore. A strong supporter of Catholic education, he was instrumental in the creation of a number of

TJ = Thomas Jefferson; SJL

To Jean Chas

institutions of higher learning in America, including St. Mary's Seminary in Baltimore (the nation's first Catholic seminary) and Georgetown College in the District of Columbia (ANB).

THE APPLICATION: on 13 Aug., TJ recorded in SJL the receipt of an undated letter from Bishop Carroll and others, which has not been found. The plan related to what became St. Mary's Church, a small Catholic church erected between O and P streets near the navy yard. It was more commonly known as Barry's Chapel in honor of the project's primary supporter, Washington merchant James Barry (Bryan, *National Capital*, 1:602-3; RCHS, 15 [1912], 48-9; 42-3 [1942], 13-15;

Thomas O'Brien Hanley, ed., *The John Carroll Papers*, 3 vols. [Notre Dame, 1976], 2:355-6, 363, 366).

Forwarding Carroll's application to the District of Columbia Commissioners, TJ covered it with a brief letter dated 3 Sep., which noted that "none can better than yourselves estimate the considerations of propriety & even of advantage which would urge a just attention to the application, nor better judge of the degree of favor to it which your duties would admit" (RC in DLC; bottom of page removed. PrC in DLC; at foot of text: "The Commissioners of Washington"; endorsed by TJ in ink on verso).

To Jean Chas

SIR   Monticello Sep. 3. 1801.

I have safely recieved the copy of your history of the American revolution, of your smaller work on the Premier Consul of France, & of the Synonimes of Dalembert, Diderot & Jaucourt which you have been pleased to send me, and for which accept my respectful thanks, & the assurances of my sensibility at this mark of attention. it is a happy circumstance for our country that it's fortunes interest the eloquent writers of your country and through them find their way to the notice of the world. the scenes through which we have past were worthy of your pen, inasmuch as to they presented to mankind the first example in Modern times of a people asserting succesfully the right of self government, and establishing that government among themselves by common consent. the mighty concussions of the European nations have not been unfelt here; they have on the contrary strongly interested the feelings of our citizens in different directions, and given us an example of the force with which the wave of popular opinion may bear upon the constituted authorities of the government. in so doing they have furnished an opportunity of estimating the stability of our edifice which fills with hopes and confidence the sincere friends of human liberty. Accept I pray you assurances of my high consideration & respect.   TH: JEFFERSON

PrC (DLC); at foot of text: "M. Chas."

SAFELY RECIEVED: see Chas's letter of 1 Apr. 1801 concerning the books that he

sent to TJ. Chas had written again from Paris on 29 Aug. 1801 to ask if TJ had received the books, which on 13 Apr. he had entrusted to Mr. Petit, a Baltimore merchant who sailed from Le Havre aboard the *Benjamin Franklin*. Chas wished that his situation would allow him to visit the United States, a people worthy of the attention, high regard, and respect of other nations, but he was a poor man whose fortune consisted only of nearly sterile talents ("talens presque steriles") at a time when France still felt the up-

heavals of its revolution. Wishing TJ a long life, Chas hoped that Heaven would watch over the people whom TJ governed so wisely, and in whom prosperity, morals, and virtue were so comfortingly merged (RC in DLC; in French; endorsed by TJ as received 27 Mch. 1802 and so recorded in SJL; endorsed by TJ as a letter of 29 Aug. 1802).

From Aaron Burr

DEAR SIR   N York 4 Septr. 1801

The enclosed belongs properly to you. The writer is now representative in Congress and was many Years member of the Senate of the U.S. I have no personal knowledge of the persons Named.

Some time since, I gave you my opinion against the expediency of appointing [Davis] to the office of Supervisor—Hence I learn it has been inferred as his competency or fitness to discharge the duties of Naval officer—No such thing was intended, nor will any respectable person deny the ability of Mr [Davis] to discharge the duties of either office;—but the office of Supervisor being an independent one, I thought that an elderly Man would be more in Conformity with public opinion especially as there was an elderly Man of Suitable character & talents who had rendered very eminent services to this Country both in Civil and Military life & who desired the office; and again, it appeared to me that there was a peculiar aptitude in the habits & talents of Davis to the duties of Naval officer.

I should not have troubled you with any thing further on this subject, but for the Misapprehension which had taken place—

with great Respect & attachment I am Dr Sir Your friend & st

A; BURR

RC (DNA: RG 59, LAR); cut, removing the name in brackets; at foot of text: "Thos Jefferson The Prest. of the U.S"; endorsed by TJ. Recorded in SJL as received 17 Sep. with notation "Off." Enclosure not identified (see Kline, *Burr*, 2:620n).

To Thomas Claxton

DEAR SIR   Monticello Sep. 4. 1801.

Your favor of Aug. 27. came to hand yesterday. I am sensible the settees could not be here till long after I shall have left this place, & that it will be better they should await your going to Philadelphia.

the mattrasses were intended to be single, and to have a decent furniture cover. I shall be at Washington on or before the last day of this month, barring sickness & accidents on the road. I hope the arrangements in the house will be compleated before that time. accept assurances of my esteem & good wishes.   TH: JEFFERSON

PrC (MHi); at foot of text: "Mr. Claxton"; endorsed by TJ in ink on verso.

From Tench Coxe

SIR   Lancaster Pa. Septr. 4. 1801.

In the Course of public business it has been my lot and duty to meet a gentleman, who held a quadrennial situation on the first Wednesday in Decembr.—He had been recently in the army and is, as you will perceive, in the Senate. The inclosed voluntary letter (from the original on *public* file,) will prove how little calculation is to be made upon that determined hostility to me, which rival and ungenerous spirits have dextriously insinuated to the principal officers of the general government. I have the honor to request that after perusal it may be destroyed, as it may be misinterpreted into ostentation that I have communicated it to you. As to secrecy, on its proper principles, there is none in the case, for the original is a public record from the nature of my office.

I have recd. incidentally to my official duty, in another most important public Case, a letter of the most strong and decided cast, in which an eminent federal character concerned, in behalf of himself and a number of others, declares to me that my official and extra official conduct has placed me upon a footing *"with those from whom I have been widely separated, which must have with them the most important and most permanent effects."*

I have recd. other letters from persons in the same interest, which embraces at least 100 of the weightiest federalists in Pennsa. of the same tenor.

The testimonials from our own side, with the exception of *one* person, whom *duty commands*, but prudence forbids me to explain to you, are higher than I ever claimed. But they have been unsollicited, unexpected, and unknown, till they occurred.

The offer of an office of 700 Drs. which I then thought, and now conceive ought to have been abolished, would not have been well received by the public, so impressed, and informed as they are concerning me. Conscienciously believing so, I declined from duty to you to the standing of my family in life, and to the republican cause of which I had been, in the state & national scale, a conspicuous agent. The additional office would have been considered as a degradation of one who had been a Commr. of a convention with Madison, Dickinson, & Hamilton, who had been a member of Congress, assistant secy of the Treasury, nominated and approved as a foreign Commr. in a case of 14 Millions of Dollars, Commr. of the Revenue of the US. and Secretary of the land office of Pennsa.—I felt that this would be perverted against you, by the skill of your enemies personally, your enemies upon public principle. I feel that I ought to have declined, on every ground, but that of mere pecuniary amelioration—that I owed it particularly to the cause, which cannot afford to lose any of that small number of men, who risked every thing from 1797 to 1801.

I knew that it would be reflected, that there are in Office men who have perverted *military power* to the invasion of a private dwelling and the public outrage of a fellow citizen, or civil power to the destruction of the right of suffrage, and that men, circumstanced as I have been, should not be placed in the humblest scenes of duty, while they were suffered to retain more respectable situations. It would have appeared manifest too that I must have been refused my former station.

Affecting as my situation has been, I have kept my sorrows to myself, tho weekly and daily disturbed by the malicious taunts of illiberal enemies, or embarrassed by observations of candid and generous opponents, at the expence of our cause and of our government. It is now above half a year since your mind has been engaged in the duty of official arrangements. I can say that it has been expected by *eminent* republicans of 1776 & 1798, that I should go into some confidential Situation at Washington: and it has been the universal sense of all parties that I should receive my station of Commr., at least, without delay. Suffer me to say, Sir, that the public appearance of its being with-held from me by you after repeated requests, after your avowing the principle of restoration, after filling so many other offices, is to me an afflicting disgrace, and is considered as such by the wise and good of both parties. I have recd. information from Philada. that proves too many to be acquainted that the lowest station in the public service has been, by some persons, desired for me. I am called thither by public business, and shall remain there some days. I know not how to treat my case, or conduct myself in the unavoidable addresses to me that will occur from individuals, of every sentiment, in regard to my situation. If the Government at Washington conceives that nothing can or is to be done by it for me, and if I am not to receive from it my old office, or something more respectable at Washington, or something decent at Philadelphia, it will be kind to have me informed. I wish before I return to take some arrangement of private employment to maintain my family there, if I am to drop other expectations.

Whether the government has filled its stations and will fill them with men who, after fifteen years of various public services & trusts have shewn more of the necessary qualities, and who are better prepared to continue the struggles of the friends of liberty in the new and the old world, are questions of importance. But it is of much more importance to determine, whether the respectability of those, who have endured so much for our form of government and for distributive justice among the middle & southern States against an heretical & geographic[1] combination, is to be diminished by throwing them into disgraceful situations or private life, when there is *every certainty* that Justice *&* *Freedom* will have yet long to struggle against domestic & foreign powers.

I am very much afraid that I shall appear to you to urge my case without due consideration for you or in a manner derogatory from myself. But I mean nothing wrong. I am in a situation unlike any other person in this country, with the duties that a numerous family impose upon me. Was I a *single* man, I would have made no direct or indirect movement upon the subject from the Hour of your election; but the simple justice to which I have long confined my views are deeply important to a most interesting family. My case too is otherwise attended with circumstances to give concern to any man of spirit, or who has a due Sense of Character. Perhaps even these things may not justify all I have written. I can only say I have wished to restrain my sensibilities and to lay before you considerations, wch. while they have a strong relation to myself are far from being irrelative to you, to the prosperity of our country or to the credit of the friends of our Form of Government.

I have the honor to be with the most respectful Consideration yr. obedt. hble Servant   Tench Coxe

RC (DNA: RG 59, LAR); endorsed by TJ as received 17 Sep. and so recorded in SJL with notation "Off." Enclosure: Samuel White to Coxe, 24 Aug. 1801, thanking Coxe for enabling him to accomplish his work at the Pennsylvania Land Office for the state of Delaware in preparation for a Chesapeake and Delaware canal and noting "To you Sir, especially, I am infinitely indebted, your perfect acquaintance with the records, the friendly information you early gave me on the subject, and your unremitting endeavours since to facilitate me in every stage of this laborious business, have contributed in a high degree to the advanced state in which I at present see it" (Tr in same).

QUADRENNIAL SITUATION: Samuel White, a Delaware Federalist attorney, served as a presidential elector in 1800. Previously he had sought and received a commission as a captain in the provisional army, serving from 1799 to 1800. In February 1801, Delaware Governor Richard Bassett appointed White to the U.S. Senate, a position he held until his death in 1809, often opposing TJ's policies (DAB; Syrett, *Hamilton*, 22:282; 24:250-1; JEP, 1:299).

For the OFFER OF AN OFFICE, see TJ to

Coxe, 17 June, and for Coxe's refusal, see Coxe to TJ, 24 and 25 June 1801.

COMMR. OF A CONVENTION: Coxe represented Pennsylvania at the Annapolis Convention in 1786 (Syrett, *Hamilton*, 3:686, 690).

[1] MS: "geograhic."

From the District of Columbia Commissioners

SIR, Washington 4th. September 1801.

We have had the honor of your Letters of the 24th. 29th. ulto., which we take the earliest opportunity of answering.— We presume the impression you were under respecting our subjection to the payment of the whole debt of 250,000 Dollars to the State of Maryland might have weight in your decision relative to the part we were to pursue in enforcing payment from the Debtors, and we perceive that we have been deficient in our information on that subject.—

The State of Maryland have the power of subjecting us to the payment of only the last Loan on default of payment of the Interest, but the Debt of 200,000 Dollars not being subject to the same procedure raises a doubt regarding your instructions to us.—

We have not only conceived that the Law of Maryland authorised us to resell the property in default of payment, but to repeat the sales, and we have thus uniformly proceeded:—It therefore gives us great satisfaction to find that we have the indirect approbation of such high authority: The titles being still in us as Trustees and Agents for the Public, we imagine would diminish the doubt of our power to sell the property to whomsoever it belonged, otherwise the spirit of the Act for the accommodation of Government might be defeated by common process.—We are in hopes that nothing will be left undone by the Debtors to raise such a sum as will be necessary, and when we can have their assurances of what they expect and intend to do we shall not fail to communicate them to you, with our opinions, which we acknowledge with sensibility ought rather to have been submitted than required to meet your decision.— To the objects stated in your Letter of the 29th. we have paid particular attention, and shall expedite them as much as possible—. The returns that have lately been made are less favorable to our progress than we had supposed—The very dry and hot weather that we have so long experienced, diminished much the progress of our Labourers, and we have now changed entirely our mode of operating, by which we can execute as much in one day as we have done in two—We have got strong ploughs, and two thousand Dollars will finish, we hope, the roads you have recommended to our attention in such a manner as will make them convenient and good—Half this sum will finish rounding the road to Rock creek bridge, from the Presidents house, including the cut through the hill—the other thousand will round the road in New Jersey Avenue, and first street east on the Capitol Square.—The road is compleated to the seven buildings on square No. 118, and A street north, on the Capitol hill. The whole expense incurred on the roads till the 1t. Instant amounts to 4,018 Dollars—Our present expenses on Pennsylvania and New Jersey Avenues amount to fifty Dollars ₩ day; but, on a review of our funds we cannot proceed much further in the roads, unless we obtain resources upon which we cannot at present calculate, or presume on a favorable answer from the Secretary of the Navy.—We have the honor to be

Sir, with the highest respect and Consideration, Your mo: Obt. Servts.   WILLIAM THORNTON
                                   TRISTRAM DALTON

RC (DLC); in Thomas Munroe's hand, signed by Thornton and Dalton; at foot of text: "President of the United States"; endorsed by TJ as received 17 Sep. and so recorded in SJL. FC (DNA: RG 42, DCLB).

To Joseph Habersham

DEAR SIR   Monticello Sep. 4. 1801.

Mr. Madison happened to be with me here at the arrival of our yesterday's post, and read to me a letter he then recieved from you, expressing a wish to decline accepting a judiciary appointment in Georgia which had been the subject of some previous communications. I recieved at the same time a letter from mr Meredith resigning the office of Treasurer after the last day of October next. having the most entire confidence in your integrity, & accuracy in business, I am persuaded I cannot serve the public better than by availing them of your services in that office, if you think proper to accept it. I make the proposition therefore to you with real satisfaction, and tender you assurances of my high esteem & consideration.

TH: JEFFERSON

RC (GHi); addressed: "Colo. Habersham Post office Washington Cola." PrC (DLC).

For Habersham's letter to Madison of 31 Aug. declining the JUDICIARY APPOINTMENT, see Madison, *Papers, Sec. of State Ser.,* 2:75. Samuel MEREDITH wrote his letter of resignation on 29 Aug.

To George Jefferson

DEAR SIR   Monticello Sep. 4. 1801.

Your favors of the 29th. & 31st. are recieved, and the articles sent under the care of mr Wanscher are said to be safely arrived at Milton. I will thank you to send me by the first boats a gross of bottled porter. the last sent is good & came very safely, but will hardly last the arrival of the next. be assured of my sincere and affectionate esteem & attachment.   TH: JEFFERSON

PrC (MHi); at foot of text: "Mr. George Jefferson."; endorsed by TJ in ink on verso.

To Samuel Meredith

DEAR SIR   Monticello Sep. 4. 1801.

I recieved yesterday your favor of Aug. 29. resigning your office of Treasurer of the US. after the last day of Octob. next. I am sorry for the circumstances which dictate this measure to you; but from their nature, and the deliberate consideration of which it seems to be the result I presume that dissuasives on my part would be without effect. my time in office has not been such as to bring me into an intimate insight of the proceedings in the several departments; but I am sure I hazard nothing when I testify in your favor that you have conducted yourself with perfect integrity & propriety in the duties of the office you have filled; and I pray you to be assured of my high esteem & consideration.   TH: JEFFERSON

PrC (DLC); at foot of text: "Mr. Meredith."

From Robert Smith

SIR,   Washington Sep. 4. 1801

I cannot find that any of the 20,000 Dol fund can be spared for the purpose mentioned in your Letter of the 29h. Ult. The Report made to me by Col Burrows which was inclosed in my Letter to you of the 31st. Ult has no doubt satisfied you that this fund, instead of lending, would willingly borrow money for the purpose of completing the Barracks. This letter was put into the post-Office the day before I had the honor of receiving your favor of the 29h.—

In my last letter which accompanied the dispatches brought by Captain Rodgers I hazarded an intimation that it was impossible for us to ascertain the real Object of the first Consul in the pending negotiation. I then and yet do suspect that he is not cordially disposed to ratify the treaty. My suspicions proceed from the great change in the political views of France since the time of the projecting of the Treaty; and these suspicions have almost grown into an Opinion from a consideration that the Objection insisted on by the French Government is utterly unimportant. For if the second Article should be expunged the effect of the treaty with respect to France would be precisely the same whether the proposed abandonment of indemnities be or be not expressly declared. Nothing is better established than that a Treaty of peace necessarily implies a dereliction of all claims for antecedent damages which either produced the war or were caused during the war and which are not mentioned in such Treaty. The Commissioners on the part of the French Government could not but have known this. And had they been sincerely desirous of having such a Treaty with us, they doubtless would not have resorted to so captious an Objection. Besides, the declining of the proposition of Mr. Murray to re-establish the second Article upon the Original ground is a further manifestation of their aversion at this time to the Treaty itself. They are not willing to adopt it either with or without the second Article. The times are changed and, it seems, they must change with the times.

Upon reflection I am yet inclined to the opinion, in case we be not informed of the ratification of the treaty, that the Boston frigate, as soon as she is equipped, ought to proceed without the Minister to the Mediterranean. In a conversation yesterday with Mr Gallatin he expressed the same Opinion. If this course of proceeding should acquire your approbation, it would be agreeable to me to be so informed in order that I might without delay send the Orders for her sailing as soon as I may be assured of her being ready for Sea.

If Mr Murray and the French Commissioners should not agree, we will probably notwithstanding glide into a state of peace and into all the advantages of a commercial intercourse without a Treaty.

Accept the assurances of my great esteem and high Consideration.

Rt Smith

RC (DLC); first endorsed by TJ as a letter from Smith, then canceled and endorsed as from the Navy Department received 10 Sep. and so recorded in SJL.

TO RE-ESTABLISH THE SECOND ARTICLE: see Jacob Wagner to TJ, 31 Aug.

From Samuel Harrison Smith

Sir   Washington City Sep. 4. 1801

I would not take the liberty of trespassing upon your retirement, did not the subject on wch. I write warmly interest my feelings and did it not also seem to require from me immediate attention

Thos: P. Smith, from his extensive life, has not ceased to possess my friendship, wch. has been yearly invigorated by the exhibition of growing talents, and of a spirit of independence.

The prospects wch. took him to Europe have proved in a great degree, if not altogether abortive, and the period of his contemplated return has arrived. But owing to the state of his affairs, wch. are in the hands of administrators that may take an age to settle them, he will return without any definite views.—At Moulins he has received the most flattering offers, in case he will undertake the superintendance of manufactories there, connected with late clerical improvements— He is offered 6000 livres a year certain, and the probability of 12,000 in case he agrees to stay some years. On these offers he observes: "These are I am convinced more advantageous than any that can be made me in America. But much less there wd. better satisfy me. Tis to our land of freedom that all my hopes and wishes tend. There I think I could be much more useful than here. During my excursion in Europe I shall collect a small quantity of knowledge wch. I think I could employ usefully with you. I shall bring with me a collection of minerals and substances relating to the arts and manufactures wch. wd. enable me to give instruction in mineralogy, chemistry, and technology, in I think a more interesting and instructive manner than we have yet had in America. If therefore such a chair could be had in any Institution, I would at once sacrifice my expectations here to much less with you.

It is the particular will of my friend that I should consult you generally on the subject, but particularly in relation to an existing or contemplated chemical chair in the University of Wm. & Mary. It may not be improper to state that more than a year ago, when the same object engaged the thoughts of Mr. Smith, Mr. Patterson, whose judgement and talents cannot be too highly respected, unequivocally declared him equal to the professorship of Nat. Phil. then and still held by Dr. Ewing, and suggested with circumspection the propriety of the latter's resigning—But, were that event to take place, or should the Dr. die, I should entertain little hopes of the election of Mr. Smith, as the complexion of the board would be probably hostile to any ma[. . .] politics.

If it be not too much trouble, I will ask the favor of an early answer to this letter, containing any knowledge you may now possess on the subject, and your opinion of any favorable prospect.

I am with sentiments of the most respectful Esteem

SAM. H. SMITH.

RC (DLC); torn; addressed: "The President of the U. States Monticello Milton (Va.)"; franked; postmarked 7 Sep.; endorsed by TJ as received 10 Sep. and so recorded in SJL.

WM. & MARY: for the problems in establishing a professorship of chemistry at the college and the failure to name

Thomas Peters Smith to a post, see Vol. 31:291, 316, 472.

John EWING, a Presbyterian clergyman and vice president of the American Philosophical Society, was provost as well as professor of natural philosophy at the University of Pennsylvania from 1779 until his death in 1802 (DAB).

From Benjamin Waterhouse

SIR   Cambridge Sepr. 4th. 1801.

Since closing the letter I had the honor of writing to you yesterday, yours of the 21st. ult. came to hand. I think it quite unnecessary to send you any more matter, being thoroughly convinced that you have planted the genuine disease in your family. I cannot, however, too emphatically recommend to all concerned in this new inoculation to keep up a *succession* of *cases*, from which matter may be taken on the 8th. day. I should be gratified could any of your physicians have sent me some on a tooth-pick, and some on a little cotton thread, secured with some of the sheet lead. I have found the advantage of such an exchange, and should wish to propose it to Dr. Wardlaw or any other physician in your quarter. They shall have some in return from this neighbourhood. I should be pleased likewise to prove that your cases were, what I am well convinced they are, genuine. I increased the bulk of the packet I sent you yesterday by one or two printed papers, of be

sure very little consequence, excepting indeed that on the new manufactory of paper. It is deplorable that one of the first manufactures of
paper in this State, sent to Hamburgh for a Ship load of rags. Accept
sentiments of the highest respect   BENJN. WATERHOUSE

RC (DLC); endorsed by TJ as received   YESTERDAY: Waterhouse's letter is
17 Sep. and so recorded in SJL.   dated 2 Sep.

From Turner Richardson Whitlock

HOND. SIR.   Hanover 4th. Sepr. 1801.
My presumption in writing you, I hope should it meet your disap-
probation will by you be looked over, as it is Sir my knowing your as-
sendency and Interest, that Induces me to write.

I have been in writing business for Some time, and am anxious to
be Still engaged in that line of Business.

I have Served five years in an office, but am Induced to believe that
I can receive much Instruction at the Federal City, and on this account business will be acceptable, in that City;

Letters of Recommendation will if required be produced from
Messrs Meriwether Jones, & Edmond Randolph and from the representatives from this County, as also from John Clopton esqr. our representative to Congress.

Should your Honor take upon yourself the Trouble of procureing
me a birth the favor will forever be acknowledged.

I beg you will be so good as to write me Pr. Post by way of Rich-
mond, and Should you procure me a birth in the Federal City, I will
Immediately on the reception of your letter be up
I am Sir Yr. Mo: Obt.   TURNER RICHARDSON WHITLOCK

RC (DNA: RG 59, LAR); endorsed by
TJ as received 17 Sep. and so recorded in
SJL with notation "Off."; also endorsed
by TJ: "to be a clerk."

Turner Richardson Whitlock was born
in St. Paul's Parish, Hanover, Virginia.
Upon his father's death in 1798, he inherited land in Randolph County. He died

sometime between 1801 and 1825, un-
married and without children (William
Ronald Cocke, III, *Hanover County
Chancery Wills and Notes* [Baltimore,
1978], 167, 168, 169).

A letter from Edmund RANDOLPH to
TJ, 7 Sep., recorded in SJL as received 10
Sep., has not been found.

To Henry Dearborn

DEAR SIR   Monticello Sep. 5. 1801.

I inclose for your consideration a paper addressed to me from Lieutt. Landais of the Artillery, to consider & decide whether any thing & what should be done in consequence of it.—I formerly referred to your consideration the petition of John Rowe, confined in jail for having counselled or procured a souldier to desert. he was sentenced to 3. months imprisonmt. & to paiment of costs. his 3. months expired near 2. months ago, and he is detained & likely to be so for costs. you will be pleased to consider the expediency of pardoning him. but there is one circumstance meriting attention. he says the bill of costs is 88. D. when the bill of costs against a prisoner amounts to such a sum the probability is either that the fee bill authorised by law is monstrous, or that there is extortion. in the latter case we should have it punished; in the former make it the occasion of referring to Congress to review their fee-bill. I will pray you to have a copy of this bill forwarded to me. perhaps the one given in to the prisoner will be considered as the best evidence.—I have duly recieved your favor of Aug. 12. and sincerely sympathise with you on the condition of your daughter. I hope the signs of amelioration have continued and ended in perfect re-establishment. where the cause has been so momentary & every subsequent impression tending to recall the mind to it's former state, I should hope the first effect could not be a permanent one. letters written to me after your reciept of this will find me at Washington where I shall be punctually on the last day of the month. accept assurances of my sincere esteem & high consideration.

TH: JEFFERSON

RC (J. M. Fox, Philadelphia, 1946); at foot of text: "The Secretary at War"; endorsed by Dearborn. PrC (DLC). Enclosure not found, but see below.

Philip LANDAIS, a lieutenant of artillerists and engineers since December 1796, had written to TJ from Albany on 17 Aug. Neither that letter nor another that Landais wrote on 14 Dec. has been found, but the lieutenant also wrote to the secretary of war during August. That correspondence was about Landais's pay and accounts for traveling expenses. One of those letters elicited a reply from Robert Smith, as the acting secretary of war, that severely rebuked the officer for the "illib-

erality" of his comments about the accountant of the War Department: "Your representations of him," Smith wrote, "want alike the recommendations of truth, and the grace of decorum." In December 1801, Dearborn refused a request by Landais for a paid leave of absence of unlimited duration to attend to private business in the West Indies. Turning down a second such request a few weeks later, this time for a leave of one year, the secretary referred to the improper tone of Landais's correspondence and stated that the lieutenant, who had already received "unusual indulgence," could "certainly have no claim for such extra favor." Meriwether Lewis, in his assessment of the army's officers, marked Landais as politically apathetic and of the "second class" in terms of ability. In June 1802, Landais, a native of France, received an honorable discharge from the army (Heitman, *Dictionary*, 1:613; Landais to secretary of war, 1, 26 Aug., 3 Nov., 14 Dec. 1801, 4 Jan. 1802, recorded in DNA: RG 107, RLRMS; Smith to Landais, 3 Sep., Dearborn to Landais, 23 Dec. 1801, 12 Jan. 1802, in DNA: RG 107, LSMA; Meriwether Lewis's Classification of Army Officers, [after 24 July 1801], and War Department list of officers, 24 July, cited there).

JOHN ROWE had written to TJ from Boston on 18 May, 15 June, 27 July, and 24 Aug. 1801. None of those communications has been found. Rowe also wrote to the secretary of war on 5 Oct. On the 23d of that month TJ signed a pardon for Rowe, who was identified in the clemency as a "Yeoman" from Massachusetts (MS in Ct, in a clerk's hand, signed by TJ and by Madison; FC in DNA: RG 59, GPR, in a clerk's hand; DNA: RG 107, RLRMS).

Enticing a soldier to desert could result in a fine of up to $300 or imprisonment for up to a year. Under a 1792 "Act for Regulating Processes in the Courts," a judge could require a defendant convicted in a noncapital case to pay the COSTS of prosecution (U.S. Statutes at Large, 1:277, 432, 485).

To Albert Gallatin

DEAR SIR   Monticello Sep. 5. 1801.

Your favor of Aug. 29. came to hand on the 3d. but no commission for Chisman is come to hand from mr Wagner. it shall be signed as soon as recieved, as my information relative to him is favorable. I return you all the papers recieved in your last except the list of warrants. with respect to Sproat you will do what you find best. the Circular letter has my entire approbation. I have written by this post both to mr Meredith & Colo. Habersham fixing the translation of the latter to the last day of October.

Mr. Madison happened to be with me on the arrival of our last post, & had directed his mail to be brought here. but it has failed. consequently he has not yet recieved his letters by the Maryland, and we are as yet uninformed of the points on which the ratification is suspended. but we both conclude it improper to delay either the Boston or mr Livingston. he gives notice by this post that the departure of both must be prepared, and hopes to recieve his letters in time to prepare & forward mr Livingston's ultimate instructions by the next. I wish Murray may not trust himself with any important modifications. if the treaty should never be ratified it will only begin the work of placing us clear of treaty with all nations.

I learn with sincere regret the continued illness of your child. my sympathies with you in that distress flow from great trials in the same school at a former period of my life. Genl. Dearborne's situation is peculiarly afflicting. my health has been uninterrupted as well as that of my family. so also has been mr Madison's. no letter written by you after your reciept of this can be answered sooner than by myself in person, as I shall be with you on the 30th. accept assurances of my sincere esteem and high respect.   TH: JEFFERSON

RC (NHi: Gallatin Papers); at foot of text: "The Secretary of the Treasury"; endorsed by Gallatin. PrC (DLC).

TJ wrote Samuel MEREDITH and Joseph HABERSHAM on 4 Sep.

HE GIVES NOTICE: Madison wrote Robert R. Livingston on 4 Sep., advising him to embark for France as soon as the *Boston* was ready. On 2 Oct., Jacob Wagner sent Livingston his commission, a letter of credence, and Madison's INSTRUCTIONS of 28 Sep. (Madison, *Papers, Sec. of State Ser.*, 2:82-3, 142-7, 154-5n).

To Robert Smith

DEAR SIR   Monticello Sep. 5. 1801.

Your favors of Aug. 27. 31. 31. are received. the last one requires only to be acknoleged. the commissions, which are the subject of the first, are signed & forwarded herewith. with respect to the Boston she may get ready for departure as soon as possible. we do not consider it as proper to delay either the vessel or mr Livingston. the delay under which the treaty is may possibly be perpetual; and if it be so, I see no great misfortune in it. perhaps the best footing with every nation would be that of no treaty. in the mean time the minister should take his place, and relieve mr Murray from attendance at Paris. mr Madison happened to be with me on the arrival of our mail the day before yesterday; and by some unlucky accident his letters were not brought here as he had directed at the post office of Orange court house. so that we have not yet seen the letters from mr Dawson or mr Murray, nor have any information as to the points of difficulty. he will go home tomorrow, and as we hope, find his letters at Orange C.H. unless they have been detained at Fredericksburg or some earlier stage.

My letter of the last week informed you I wished any remnant there might be of the 16,000. D. approprian for the marine barracks might be applied towards paying for the site in addition to the 4000. D. I think this object more important than the compleating the [. . .]; besides that there can be no remnant competent to that, and we must not go beyond appropriations in a case to which the legislature manifestly did not mean to extend. surely the end of the building may be so closed or finished as not to be injured by the weather.—with respect to the other magazine proposed to be built, the reasons urged by capt Tingey appear very cogent. before undertaking it, you will of course have an exact estimate of the cost, and examine the particular appropriation of money from which it's cost is to be drawn, and that it does not overrun that. in the plan of the building attention should be paid to beauty, because a handsome form costs no more than an ugly one.

After your reciept of this (which I suppose will be on the 8th. after the departure of the post of the 7th.) no letter which you can write me can be answered much[1] sooner than by myself in person. a letter of the 21st. for instance could only recieve an answer on the 29th. & I shall be with you on the 30th. there is one only consideration, the possibility of sickness which may render it worth your while to write on the 21st.

accept assurances of my friendly & high consideration & respect.

TH: JEFFERSON

P.S. You will of course acquaint mr Livingston of the movements of the Boston. mr Graham is to have his passage in her. we suppose Bourdeaux the most convenient port for the Boston, having regard to her further destination.

PrC (DLC); faint; at foot of first page: "The Secretary of the Navy."

FAVORS OF AUG. 27. 31. 31: in addition to his letter of the 31st discussing the dispatches from France, Smith wrote a note on that day to cover abstracts of War Department and navy warrants on the Treasury for the week ending 29 Aug. (RC in DLC, at foot of text: "The President," endorsed by TJ as received from the Navy Department on 3 Sep. and "Warrants" and so recorded in SJL; FC in Lb in DNA: RG 45, LSP). Smith's letter of 27 Aug. enclosed, for TJ's signature, COMMISSIONS for five Marine Corps lieutenants who had been "long since appointed & acting." The commissions were probably for Edward Hall, John Hall, James R. Middleton, Michael Reynolds, and Samuel Llewellin. Reynolds was one of the officers who publicly accosted John Randolph in Philadelphia in January 1800 after Randolph made disparaging remarks about the military on the floor of the House of Representatives (RC in DLC, in a clerk's hand, signed by Smith, at foot of text: "Prest. U: States," endorsed by TJ as received from the Navy Department on 3 Sep. and "Commissions" and so recorded in SJL; FC in Lb in DNA: RG 45, LSP; NDQW, Dec. 1800–Dec. 1801, 360-1; NDBW, *Register*, 64-6; Vol. 31:305-7).

DETAINED AT FREDERICKSBURG OR SOME EARLIER STAGE: the letters had been detained at the Georgetown post office by the mistake of the postmaster (Madison, *Papers, Sec. of State Ser.*, 2:106-7).

LETTER OF THE LAST WEEK: TJ to Smith, 29 Aug.

[1] Word interlined.

From Samuel Smith

SIR/   Balte. 5 Septr. 1801

My Brother has Come up to Attend to his Business in Court. I first to meet him with the distressing Account of the Death of his Eldest son (a Charming Boy) his Distress is great, that of his family will be greater, he will of course be detained some time at home—

Our squadron had arrived—The Essex had gone to Tunis having under Convoy the ship for that Regency—The Philadelphia was seen Cruizing off Gibraltar. the Tripolitan Admiral & a Brig being in that Port, It is probable the President Could not have been far distant. I am sir/

With the greatest Respect your freind & servt   S. SMITH

RC (DLC); endorsed by TJ as received 17 Sep. and so recorded in SJL.

On 2 July, Commodore Richard Dale wrote the secretary of the navy, informing him that the American SQUADRON HAD ARRIVED the previous day at Gibraltar. There, Dale found two armed Tripolitan vessels at anchor under the command of Peter Lisle, a Scotsman and deserter from the British navy who converted to Islam in 1794 and took the name Murad Rais. He was appointed ADMIRAL of the Tripolitan navy the following year. Queried by Dale, Murad declared that Tripoli was not at war with the United States. Sources on shore, however, led Dale to believe the opposite and that Murad was intent on capturing American merchant vessels. He therefore ordered the frigate *Philadelphia* to remain near Gibraltar and keep watch on Murad's vessels, while the frigate *Essex* was directed to convoy the ship *Grand Turk*, which carried a cargo of regalia for the bey of Tunis, and the brig *Hope*, a Baltimore vessel bound for Trieste. The remainder of the American squadron, the frigate *President* and the schooner *Enterprize*, departed for Algiers on 4 July (NDBW, 1:497-501; Madison, *Papers, Sec. of State Ser.*, 1:160n). A copy of Dale's letter was enclosed by John Gavino, the U.S. consul at Gibraltar, in his letter to the secretary of state of 4 July. It arrived at the State Department on 7 Sep., along with Gavino's letter to the secretary of 18 July, which reported that the *Philadelphia* "was off this port" (Madison, *Papers, Sec. of State Ser.*, 1:379-81, 441). Extracts from Gavino's dispatches appeared in the *National Intelligencer* on 7 Sep.

From St. George Tucker

DEAR SIR   Northumberland Court House, Sept. 5th. 1801

I have this moment received a Letter from my much valued friend Doctor Barraud, of Norfolk, stating, that the "Collector on the 24th. ulto, received notice that arrangements are making to place a navy-surgeon & mate at the head of the marine hospital at that port, and that his services will not be required, after the first day of October next."

Believing, Sir, that I can never render a service more acceptable to you, than in assisting you to discriminate men of the most deserving Character, from those of a different Complexion, I hesitate not to address this Letter to you in behalf of a Gentleman, whom an Intimacy of twelve years has enabled me to judge of in the various Characters of a Man, a physician and a Friend. And when I assure you that during that period, I have never known a man of more genuine moral virtue; more unbounded liberality, & feeling for the miseries & distresses of his fellow men; or more extensive Charity, benevolence, tenderness, and attention, to their sufferings; or so *punctual*[1] to the duties of his profession, I beg leave to add that I shall have drawn but a faint Sketch of the virtues of my friend.—

His dismission from the office that he holds, would give the most painful impression to all who are acquainted with him, and with the Circumstances under which he was prevailed upon to quit a most desirable establishment in Williamsburg, and an Extensive practice in the neighbourhood to remove to Norfolk for the express purpose of taking charge of that hospital, then under the direction of a gentleman, in no respect his equal, as I have the best reason to believe. He was promised the warmest support to procure for him the final establishment, if he would accept the temporary provision, and from my personal knowledge of him, I will venture to pledge myself that no man ever was, or will be, found more punctual; and that none *can* be found more equal, to the duties of his office than Doctor Barraud.—

If the insufficiency of the hospital funds, and the want of provision by the late Congress, for its support, should be the Inducement to an œconomical arrangement, permit me to observe, that the proposed arrangement contemplates a provision for the pay of a navy-surgeon, & mate, and that Doctor Barraud has never been allowed more, than a navy-surgeons pay & subsistence which at least, must be extended to his successor, if he be removed. And if actual services rendered be the foundation of the pretensions of any Gentleman of that grade, will not two years actual services performed in this department itself, plead most powerfully against the removal of the person who has rendered them, to make way for one whose pretensions stand upon no better ground?

I believe I owe it to that liberality of Sentiment which I know you to possess, to say nothing of Doctor Barrauds political Character & Conduct; but I should accuse myself of Injustice to him, were I not to assure you upon the word of a man of honor, that at no period of political heat, did he ever discover the smallest trait of that bitterness or intollerance which characterised the Conduct of almost every man employed or hoping to be employed by the then administration. Whatever difference of opinion existed between him & those whose opinions have at length prevailed, he never on any Occasion, betrayed a sentiment which his adversaries would not have respected as that of an honest well-meaning, candid and moderate man.—

Permit me then, Sir, most earnestly to sollicit you in behalf of my friend, that he may not be removed from his office, to make room for any other. He will be Content with the present emoluments thereof if the purposes of Œconomy forbid their Enlargement: and if permitted to Continue until Congress may act finally upon the subject, either by discontinuing, or finally establishing the office, he will discharge the duties that he now does, with punctuality, without receiving until that Period any Emolument from the time that his dismissal is now intended to take place.—

I can not prevail upon myself to offer an apology for a Letter, which nothing but the most unbounded Confidence in your Liberality of sentiments could have induced me to address to you.

I am with due respect & sincere good wishes, Sir, Your Obedt. hble. Servt   S: G: Tucker

RC (ViW); at foot of text: "Thomas Jefferson Esqr. President of the United States." Recorded in SJL as received 10 Sep.

Tucker also wrote James Madison on 5 Sep., urging that Philip BARRAUD be retained as director of the MARINE HOSPITAL at Norfolk (Madison, *Papers, Sec. of State Ser.*, 2:88). For earlier discussions regarding Barraud's removal and subsequent replacement with George Balfour, see TJ to Bishop James Madison, 9 May, and Gallatin to TJ, 29 July.

In his reply to Tucker dated 11 Sep., TJ wrote, "Your letter of Sep. 5. has been

recieved & is this day forwarded to the Secretary of the Navy, who will doubtless pay just attention to it. my absence from the seat of government has prevented my being informed of the arrangements to which the letter refers, and the grounds on which they are proposed. I shall probably hear from the Secretary of the navy on the subject. health & respect" (RC in ViW, addressed: "Judge Tucker Williamsburg," franked; PrC in DLC, endorsed by TJ in ink on verso).

[1] Preceding six words and semicolon written in left margin and keyed for insertion here.

From James Warren

Sir,   Plymouth (Mass) Sep: 5th. 1801.

I did myself the honour to write to you, under date of May 31st. last, and to cover a letter of compliment and congratulation from Mrs Warren, who has taken a large share in the joy and triumph of the second, as she did in the first revolution in this country.—But such are the prevailing complaints of frauds in the Post-Offices that I cannot calculate with any certainty of its reaching you.—My design was to give you some information of the state of parties here, & of political objects that might possibly be useful.—

I did not intend again very soon to trouble you with another letter, lest I should be thought intrusive & officious:—but my local situation seems to impose it as a duty to you and the publick, to represent to you the character and conduct of the Collector of this port.—Naturally indolent and incapable of business a considerable paternal inheritance did not preserve a family he *then* had, from becoming objects of charity, which induced me to procure for him before the general constitution, the Naval Office of this port.—an office of little consequence, but of some little emolument.—With watching and management, this small business was tolerably executed, but not without complaint.—

This office brought him under a rule established by President Washington, (with very good intentions, but very erroneous in the general application) and he was appointed the Collector &c. of this port.—Every body wondered, but the celebrity of the then President, hushed into silence the ridicule attached to the appointment.—His particular connections, some of them the principal *importers*, step'd in and assisted in the execution of the office, to save him, and as is generally supposed their own interest.—

A dupe to party, his officious servility preserved him in office during the imperious circumstances of the last administration, while it is the general opinion prevailing here (and I have good reason to suppose it well-founded) that more goods are run in this district than in any other in the State.—

I will not trouble you with details of his mismanagement—the instances are numerous and well-known here;—nor will you expect me to come forward with formal evidences to prove his deliquency.—It is sufficient to state to you the universal expectation, that he would be immediately dismissed from office.—His own party have been alarmed, and while they abuse Mr Gallatin every day in the grossest manner, have had (I am told,) the impudence, to write to him in his favour.—

I know that the unsullied reputation, activity and adroitness for business, of my son Henry Warren, has engaged the public opinion to mark him out as a very suitable person for an office of importance, and that the publick mind and conversation in the district of this port, have pointed to him, as the successor to the present Collector here.

But be assured, Sir, the publick good is my sole object, and that no personal views, or private interest ever did, or ever shall lead me so far to a dereliction of a boasted trait in my character, as to misrepresent characters and facts, to any person to whom I profess personal regards, and certainly not to you.—

I have the honor to be, with the greatest esteem and respect, Your obedient, Humble Servant.   JAS: WARREN

RC (DNA: RG 59, LAR); endorsed by TJ as received 1 Oct. and so recorded in SJL; also endorsed by TJ "his son to be Collector."

CHARACTER AND CONDUCT OF THE COLLECTOR OF THIS PORT: for the investigation of William Watson of Plymouth, see Vol. 34:531-4. In March 1803, Henry Warren replaced Watson, who was dismissed for "malpractice" (JEP, 1:453; Vol. 33:673; James Warren to TJ, 25 Apr. 1803).

From John Thomson Mason

DEAR SIR   George Town 6th Sep. 1801.

We have learned here that the Treasurer of the U.S. has determined to resign his appointment. My friend and relation Mr. John Mason, who has been suddenly called to Phida., has authorized and requested me to mention to you that he would thankfully accept this appointment, if you thought him quallified to fill it, and no person more acceptable to you should be thought of.

But Mr Mason has reason to beleive that this appointment would be very acceptable to my friend Sam. Hanson, and supposes he may be thought of by you as a proper person to succeed Mr Meredith. Should this be the case, he has charged me to request of you that he may not be considered as an applicant. Mr Hanson has a large family, and is an indigent needy man. to him, should he be thought of by you, the object is highly important. Mr Mason who is truly his[1] friend (tho' Mr Hanson perhaps does not think so) would upon no consideration stand in the way of his preferment, or inter[est.] Be the result as it may I hope this application will be known only to yourself.

To morrow is the day of our election. The time which has elapsed since your departure from this place has given to the republicans great confidence, we entertain no doubt of success. We now consider Fredk. as sure a County as any in the State, of Calvert we entertain very little doubt—of Prince Georges we have great hopes.

Wishing you health and happiness I have the honor to be with sincere esteem and high respect Your Obedt Servt   J. T. MASON

RC (DNA: RG 59, LAR); torn; endorsed by TJ as received 17 Sep. and so recorded in SJL, where TJ canceled his notation "Off." and added "J. Mason to be Tr."; he also emended the endorsement.

MY FRIEND AND RELATION: John Thomson Mason, son of Thomson Mason

of Raspberry Plain, and John Mason, son of George Mason of Gunston Hall, were cousins (Robert A. Rutland, ed., *The Papers of George Mason 1725-1792*, 3 vols. [Chapel Hill, 1970], 1:lvii, lxxvii; Vol. 30:13n; Vol. 33:380n).

[1] MS: "is."

From John Barnes

SIR   George Town 7th. Sept 1801.

Your esteemed favr. 28th. Ulto., recd the 1st Instant—with the several paymts. to be made at Norfolk, Alexandria and Philada. together—with the few remaining debits here, including the Necessary disbursemts. of Househd: &c. *see—sketch.* inclosed [. . .] shall be pointedly Attended to.

—of course, on a present View of my Finances, I find, it will be Absolutely Necessary for me—to defer my setting out for Philada. untill after the ensuing Qr. say 6–8 Octr. I shall then be inabled to fullfill every engagemt: both on yours, as well my Own Acct.—

—Doctr. Edwards has favd: me, with a Letter & Bill Lading of your Chariots Harness & expects handing me Mr Hanses a/c while the latter have Offered to lent him, a sett of Harness for the Use of your Carriage to Washington and doubtless, I could, with his Assistance, engage a pair of Steady Horses & sober driver—to undertake the Conducting it here.—Or I should you think it adviseable—as Mr Dougherty it seems is very Anxious, for the safety of the Carriage—and wishes to be employed in that particular service—as well to see a Brother of his who is in business at Philada.—I promised him to state to you his desire—and moreover what in that Case, provided it met with your Approbation, would be adviseable, viz. for Mr Dougherty to take with him to Philadelphia your present market waggon *Horse*, and to hire a suitable one there for the Journey—the Harness, to be returned by water—as proposed by Mr Hanse, to Doctr Edwards, the only remaining inconvenience would be to return the hired Horse, which I do not Apprehend would be Attended with much difficulty. Mr Dougherty would undoubtedly take all possible Care—and I would see that nothing should be wanting to retard,—or injure, its safety: and the Approaching equinoctial gale, would then be passed over. which—at an earlier season might risque its safety. via the ferry,—either at Wrights via Lancaster—the quietest rout, or the Susquehannah, via Havre de Grace. whichever, road you should prefer him to take—my only objection, to take passage in it would be *Contrasting*—the inelegance of the passengers, to the superbness of the Carriage! that provided the Covering will admit of an Entrance, without taken it off I should Console myself—with having the Honor, as well convenience of being Conveyed—at my Ease, from Philadelphia to the seat of Government, &c. &c.—but of this, you will please give me further directions. I must also inform you, that I took the liberty of intimating to Doctr. Edwards, your wish respecting Mr Stewart abt. your Portrait; & request, of having a suitable frame, & to consult him thereupon—in order, not only to secure the picture—but (Knowing him to be careless in these matters) to hasten the shipping of it: and that I should do myself the pleasure to wait upon him at Frankford immediately on my Arrival at Philada.   Mr Taylors remittance—of $700. will be transmitted to him ℔ tomorrows mail.

—Mr. Richards I find has at length shipped your sundries (but omitted sending on the particulars) [Amt] $42.5.
together with sundry extra charges [Coms] &c. on ⎫
the former 6 Boxes sirup & pay:mts [&c] on   ⎬   7.20
your a/c postage &c. which I think a little extray: ⎪
—but however adjusted with him—   ⎭   49.75
of his intended removal. to Richmond to settle there. He also informs that he could not possibly procure neither the window glass. (the most material) nor sheeting—to your pattern. the former I have already desired, him to Apply for to Mr. Donath. who used to procure it for me, of the nearest size, and to have it cut to the particular size ordered, and to prevail on him to ship it—by the earliest opporty. as to the sheeting I can see to it myself. when on the spot,

Mr Richards I presume have forwarded the particulars of your Inv. to Messrs. G & J—at Richmond—

—Nothing further at present occur to my recollection for your particular information—

but, to Assure you, I am Sir, your most Obedt: & very Hble servant
JOHN BARNES

I have the satisfaction of informing you of Mr Lemaire's Arrival Friday Eveng. [4th.] inst. and that on my return from the Treasury with your [wages] for $4000. this very day dined with him & Mr Rapin. I am much prejudiced in his favr. and I hope deservedly so. Mr Rapin talks of leaving Town friday next—

RC (ViU: Edgehill-Randolph Papers); at foot of text: "Thomas Jefferson Esqr. President U States"; endorsed by TJ as received 10 Sep. and so recorded in SJL. Enclosure not found.

YOUR ESTEEMED FAVR.: TJ to Barnes, 28 Aug., recorded in SJL but not found. According to his financial memoranda, TJ on 28 Aug. ordered Barnes to pay $700 to James Taylor, Jr., $553.80 to Henry Sheaff, both for wine, and $268.12 to Roberts & Jones for nailrod (MB, 2:1050). In statements of TJ's account, Barnes entered payment in full to Taylor at 8 Sep., to Roberts & Jones at 16 Sep., and to Sheaff on 17 Oct. (statements of private account from John Barnes, 30 Sep., 4 Nov., in ViU). Barnes recorded a separate payment of $218.82 to Roberts & Jones of Philadelphia at 9 Nov. (statement of household and private account from John Barnes, 4 Dec., in ViU).

In 1800, TJ sat for Gilbert Stuart (STEWART) for a PORTRAIT that TJ never obtained (Vol. 31:xliv-xlv, 587n).

YOUR WAGES: on this day, Barnes received TJ's salary for the months of July and August (Barnes to TJ, 3 Aug. 1801).

From Albert Gallatin

DEAR SIR   Washington 7th Septer. 1801

I duly received your favor of the 28th ulto.—In the case of the intended successor of Gen. White as surveyor at Brunswick, I applied to the printer S. H. Smith who married there, & who after ten days deliberation, told me that he had in vain tried to find a republican there fitted for the office, but mentioned the name of John Nelson as a very respectable & moderate federal character there. If that will not do, might it not be well to apply for information to Gen. Heard who lives within ten miles of Brunswick?—I received a letter from Mr Millege of Georgia recommending, without any remarks, four persons as proper to succeed Mr Powell the collector of Savannah. One of the four, though not the first in order, is the same person whom Gov. Jackson recommended. The office is so important that I have thought it best to delay filling the commission for one week longer, in order, if possible to receive answers from Messrs. Taliaferro & Baldwin; and I have also written on the subject to Colo. Few at New York. As you have acquaintances in the vicinity of Norfolk, it is very desirable that information should be obtained from them on the subject of a proper successor for Nat. Wilkins collector of Cherry Stone, (Eastern shore Virga.) who is the worst delinquent on the list, his last account rendered being to 31 Dec. 1796. I have written to Mr Page & young Mr Newton, but neither can recommend any person. The successor should have integrity, keenness & firmness. There is much smuggling in that district, & the people being in the habit of favouring it, it will require some exertions to put an end to it.

The two enclosed from Mr Brent, & from Mr Steele, the last covering one from Mr Simmons, require no comment.

You will see by that of Mr Jarvis, that he declines accepting the collectorship of Penobscott. This leaves us in a very awkward situation, as in the mean while, Lee being superceded, we have no collector there. Mr Jarvis recommends his brother. On the other hand I have a recommendation for P. D. Serjeant which I enclose. It was given me at the time by Gen. Dearborn, who spoke favourably of the applicant, but on the whole preferred Mr. Jarvis, him who declines. Of this last gentleman's brother I did not hear Gen. Dearborn speak, though he must have known that he resided on the spot, whilst the brother whom he recommended was established at Boston.

In respect to the appointment of an inspector of int. revenue for the new district N. West of Ohio, I enclose Mr Worthington's letter, but have not time to wait for an answer from you, as the person must receive his appointment by 1st of Octer.—Upon the whole, it has appeared to me most eligible to fill the blank commission you left for that object with the name of Ths. Worthington, leaving him a reasonable time to resign either that or the place of Register of the land office. I had much rather he would keep the last, which is of more importance to the revenue, & of far more to the people than the other, because I consider him as being, upon the whole, the most respectable character in the North West Territory; but a decision of the Atty. general in relation to his fees has, I apprehend, somewhat disgusted him. It had been my intention to fill the commission with the name of Samuel Finley the receiver at Chilicothe, as the two offices seemed more compatible & the commission on that of receiver (1 p% on monies received) is not equal to the risk & trouble: but he has now upwards of 100,000 dollars in hand, & is not as regular in making his returns as he ought to be. If upon investigation, it will appear that it was owing only to the pressure of business, & Mr Worthington will keep the register's place, I would still incline for that arrangement; but the temporary appointment of Mr W. will give us time to examine. You will be able to appreciate the weight of his recommendations in favor of two persons as collectors at Cayuga and *Cincinnati*. I do not expect any further information in relation to those two posts, & will of course wait for your instructions.

The list of warrants is, as usual, enclosed. Payments go on very well. After making the payment of interest due for this quarter at the end of this month, we will have 2 millions & half at least in the Treasury. We had but two at the end of last quarter. My only embarrassment proceeds from the difficulty of purchasing good bills on Amsterdam, in which we ought to have had 500,000 dollars more invested by 1st. of Octer. next. We have paid heretofore but 39; but must now give 40 cents pr guilder.

I was absent when the dispatches from France arrived, & cannot form any precise opinion of the result. I have uniformly thought, that, the modification proposed by the Senate having put it in the power of France to act as they pleased; that consistency was not, in the situation of Bonaparte, to be expected, which a government solely actuated by the permanent & solid interest of its nation would be likely to preserve. If, for any reasons connected with foreign policy, or their own domestic concerns, they do not think it their interest to ratify at the moment when the negociation takes place, I think that they will take hold of the alteration proposed. Yet, I had thought that peace with America was so popular in France that they would not run the risk of a rejection, & that that cause would preponderate over any other. On the other hand, it is clear that the signing of the convention was at least hastened by the wish[1] to operate favorably on the northern powers, and that this motive has now ceased. If they intend to make peace with Great Britain, may they not think that they will be likely to make a more advantageous treaty with us after that event, or rather after the expiration of the British treaty than now? If they are really sincere in their objections to the omission &, it seems also, to the restoration of the second Article, and insist on a positive renunciation of indemnities & treaties, not with a view of defeating the treaty, but because they actually want such renunciation, may it be that they intend to occupy not only Louisiana but also the Floridas, & wish therefore an explicit annullation of the Treaty of 1777? I hope these delays will not be attended with any real change in the relative situation of the two countries; but I fear the effect on the public mind here.   Commodore Dale has arrived almost in the nick of time in the Mediterranean; yet it is to be wished that he had met the Tripolitan at sea instead of Gibralter.

With great respect & sincere attachment Your very obt. Servt.

ALBERT GALLATIN

RC (DLC); at foot of first page: "President of the United States"; endorsed by TJ as received 17 Sep. and so recorded in SJL. Enclosures: (1) Richard Brent to Gallatin, 24 Aug., noting that Osburn Sprigg, a Maryland native now representing Hampshire County in the Virginia House of Delegates, wished to recommend John Burbridge, a merchant, for postmaster at Oldtown, Maryland, because Daniel Fetter, the appointed postmaster, has moved, leaving his brother George Fetter in charge; Brent asks Gallatin to speak to the postmaster general about the situation; he also hopes that the president will make no further dismissals from office on the basis of "political opinion for nothing is more odious to the people and nothing more anxiously wished for by those who wish to render the Administration odious" (Gallatin, *Papers*, 5:636; Stets, *Postmasters*, 140; Leonard, *General Assembly*, 220, 224, 228). (2) William Hull to Henry Dearborn, Newton, Massachusetts, 15 July 1801, expressing Paul Dudley Sargent's desire to become collector at Penobscot in place of John Lee, who would likely be removed "for his violence agt. the present Administration," but also remarking that "You are doubtless well acquainted with both the Characters, and will use your influence, as your Judgment shall dictate" (Gallatin, *Papers*, 5:380). (3) Thomas Worthington to Gallatin, Chillicothe, 21 Aug., noting that if offered to him he "would accept the office of Inspector under the expectation of being appointed the supervisor," as described in Gallatin's letter of 7 Aug., but not wishing to combine it with his present position as register of public lands he would resign it as soon as his books were put in order, finding the business of the land office so confining as to be injurious to his health and the compensation "inadequate to the services rendered"; recommending Winn Winship, a former resident of Berkeley County, Virginia, as an excellent accountant qualified to fill the office of inspector or either land office position at Chillicothe, Charles Kilgore of Cincinnati, who acted as clerk to the territorial legislature, as a worthy young man capable of filling the office of collector at that port, and John Edwards, son of Pierpont Edwards, as "very capable of discharging the duties of collector" in the district of Erie; and acknowledging receipt of Gallatin's second letter of 7 Aug., enclosing the attorney general's opinion on land office fees (Gallatin, *Papers*, 5:621-3; endorsed by Gallatin with notation: "on proper persons for the several offices of Supervisor N.W. Territory, Collectors at Cincinnati & Erie" and "*Private*"). (4) "Weekly list of Warrants issued on the Treasurer for the week ending 5th Septer. 1801," reporting 13 warrants, Nos. 144 to 156, for a total of $121,798.50, including No. 147 for Jonathan Burrall, cashier at the New

York branch of the Bank of the United States, for $26,325, in payment of bills on Amsterdam "at 39 cts. Principal & interest" and No. 155 for Smith & Buchanan in payment "of 60,000 Guild. bills on Holland at 39 cts. Diplomatic"; with a balance in the Treasury at the beginning of the week of $3,271,305.60 and at the end of the week of $3,442,058.68 (MS in DLC, entirely in Gallatin's hand; Syrett, *Hamilton*, 20:450n). For the letter from James Simons to John Steele, see below. Other enclosures not found.

In his letter to Gallatin, dated 21 Aug., Congressman John Milledge listed FOUR PERSONS he found "after enquiry and consideration" he could recommend "as qualified to discharge the duties of Collector" at Savannah. They were, in the order listed, James Alger, Thomas de Mattos Johnson, Archibald Bullock, and Richard Wylly (Gallatin, *Papers*, 5:620). WORST DELINQUENT ON THE LIST: Gallatin's Report on Delinquent Collectors is printed at 9 June.

John STEELE forwarded the letter of 24 July that James Simons (SIMMONS) sent from the custom house at Charleston, enclosing an issue of Benjamin F. Timothy's *South-Carolina State Gazette, and Timothy's Daily Advertiser* of the same date, in which appeared a letter addressed to the president and signed "Americanus," being the second of the series printed in the South Carolina newspaper and reprinted in many other papers. The other two in the series were dated 17 July and 1 Aug. Simons was concerned because in his second letter, "Americanus" argued against unwarranted dismissals from office and urged TJ to "beware, sir, how you attend to the busy whispers of slander." "Americanus" cautioned TJ: "A man distinguished for his services during the American revolution; one of the most punctual and valuable officers under our present government, who has actually reclaimed the office he holds, and made it extremely lucrative, has been grossly misrepresented to you. Who, sir, are the persons who traduced him, and aimed at his removal? They are principally public defaulters; persons who were miscreant during our struggles for independence, or newly imported patriots who have no importance in society, but what they derive from disgraceful intrigues. It is true they were your advocates; but they are not entitled to your confidence." Evidently Simons believed that the administration would know "Americanus" was referring to efforts to have him removed. Simons wrote Steele that he immediately called on the printer, requesting the name of "Americanus." When the printer would not reveal the source, Simons urged him to inform the author "That I regretted exceedingly that I should be introduced in the publication, for that I had reasons to believe, that I possessed the confidence of the President, and that as any communication which may have been made to him had not been acted upon by him to injure me I could have wished that the circumstance he mentioned had not been published; that the public mind appeared to me disposed to conciliation, and that I hoped the administration would be supported—towards which my best efforts should be exerted." Simons asserted that he believed that the president and the heads of departments were making "every proper effort" to uphold the national interest. He urged "Americanus" to unite with him "to effect an union of parties" for the public good. If the opportunity arose, Simons requested that Steele "communicate what I now say to you as my friend, to the President, towards whom I shall so act, as to merit both his confidence and friendship" (RC in NHi: Gallatin Papers, see Gallatin, *Papers*, 5:432-3; Concord *Courier of New Hampshire*, 20, 27 Aug.; *Norwich Packet*, 25 Aug.; *Philadelphia Gazette*, 14 Sep.).

RECOMMENDATION FOR P. D. SERJEANT: see Enclosure No. 2. On 6 July, Sargent also applied directly to Gallatin for the position at Penobscot. In a short

letter, he assured the Treasury secretary that he would support "the character of the Republican United States of America" (Gallatin, *Papers*, 5:311).

For Gallatin's 7 Aug. letter to Thomas Worthington on the APPOINTMENT OF AN INSPECTOR and collectorships, see Gallatin to TJ, 29 Aug. BLANK COMMISSION YOU LEFT: see Gallatin to TJ, 29 July (second letter). In another letter to Worthington dated 7 Aug., Gallatin enclosed Levi Lincoln's DECISION that FEES should not be collected by the register at the land office for lands purchased at public sale. On 15 Aug., Gallatin informed Worthington that Lincoln's opinion did not "accord precisely" with his own and that "it is not to be considered as binding but merely as advice." Gallatin added that a decision from a court "would settle the point." A suit had already been brought against Worthington for the collection of fees and the court of common pleas had found in his favor. Worthington believed the judges of the general court, where the case was being decided, would do the same. On 29 Oct., Worthington informed Gallatin that although the court had done so, Governor Arthur St. Clair threatened to renew the prosecution of the case (Gallatin, *Papers*, 5:519, 574, 621-3; *Terr. Papers*, 3:156-7, 183). For the disagreement over the collection of fees at Chillicothe, see also *Terr. Papers*, 3:133-5, 139-40, 148-50, 154-5.

EXPIRATION OF THE BRITISH TREATY: according to Article 28, only the first ten articles of Jay's Treaty were permanent. Article 12 expired at the end of two years, and the others were limited in duration to twelve years (Miller, *Treaties*, 2:264).

[1] Preceding six words interlined in place of "with an intent."

From Edward Gantt

DEAR SIR   Septr. 7th. 1801

I have the Pleasure of informing you, that I have at last succeeded in communicating the Vaccine Disease to several Patients. The first Matter you sent me, infected three Persons, who were inoculated with it. Before the Receipt of your next Favour of the 29th. of August, I had made Use of the Virus from the Arms of those inoculated, & found it did not fail in a single Instance. I have several in Town who are desirous of Inoculation, and will every sixth or eighth Day during the Continuance of the warm weather inoculate some of them, by which Means there will be a certainty of preserving the Virus among us. A few Day previous to the Receipt of your first Favour, I received by Post some of the Vaccine Matter, in Tooth Picks, & some also in Thread, inclosed in a Swan Quill, sealed at both Ends, wrapped up in thin Sheet Lead & put into a Phial of water—when I opened it, I found the Quills filled with water, & the Matter totally dissolved. The Letter which accompanied it, contains those Observations which perhaps may not have been communicated to you.

"Should any of your Inoculations appear to fester, or in other words, have a fiery Inflammation before the eighth Day, & the inoculated Part have yellow Matter instead of the pellucid, I pray you not to take Matter from such a Pustle for the Purpose of Inoculation— The true Disease is, a circular or oval Pustle appearing on the 6th. or 7th. Day, sometimes as late as the 8th. though rarely. This Pustle contains a perfectly transparent fluid from which you must inoculate, & that never later than the 9th Day, unless it should come on with more than common Tardiness. The Efflorescence comes on about the 10th Day & then the Habit is affected, & the Virus in the inoculated Part is weakened. Sometimes there is an abundant Effusion from the Pustule of Lymph in Consequence of the Inflammation; but this is not the genuine Virus. The true Virus rises from the punctured Pustule in a shining Globule, in Size no larger than the Head of a Pin. I am now able to say, on pricking a Pustle, this is Lymph, & that is the virus, but the Distinction cannot be conveyed by the Pen or the Pencil—"

In one of the late London Papers it is said, that the Officers of the British Navy on the Home Station have presented Doctr. Jenner with a Gold Medal with this Device.—Apollo presenting Britania with a young Sailor, recovered from the Kine Pox. Britania extends a Laurel on which is written *Jenner*. The Motto is *Alba Nautis Stella refulsit*. In their written Address they say, that vaccine Inoculation is the greatest Blessing ever extended to the British Navy—Accept Sir the sincere Acknowledgments of respect & Esteem of

your most obedt. Servt   EDWD GANTT

RC (DLC); closing quotation mark supplied; endorsed by TJ as received 10 Sep. and so recorded in SJL.

Edward JENNER received a medal from medical OFFICERS OF THE BRITISH NAVY in February 1801. For a history and draw-

ing of the medal, see K. Bryn Thomas, "A
Jenner Letter," *Journal of the History of
Medicine and Allied Sciences*, 12 (1957),

453-5. ALBA NAUTIS STELLA REFULSIT:
"white stars shine brightly for sailors"
(Horace, *Odes*, 1.12.27-8).

From George Jefferson

DEAR SIR   Richmond 7th. Septr. 1801

Previous to the receipt of your letter I was applied to by Mr. Heth
respecting Coal; he had been informed by a Mr. Davidson of Washington that you would require a supply, and who recommended his
furnishing you—which he appears anxious to do. he readily consented to let you have large pick'd coal, and that, at his usual price of
1/. delivered at the landing. I am sorry however to add that from his
apparently compliant, and *really*[1] heedless disposition, he is generally
apt to make almost any promise that may be required of him, without
afterwards paying much regard to its performance—and to which I
fear he would in the present instance be further stimulated, from his
necessitous situation, & consequent eagerness to make sales. for these
reasons I made application to Mr. Graham who might be depended
on, and whose Coal is equal to Heth's; but he would not on any terms
consent to pick it. there are several other Coal-dealers here, but none
who have it of equal quality to these two—there is a person in Manchester whose Coal is *altogether* large; but so very inferior in quality
that he cannot sell it, nothwithstanding the partiality of almost every
one for that which is large: indeed I am told, (and it appears to be
reasonable) that the best Coal is most apt to be fine; as that which is
rich and good is most subject to be broken.

I am inclined to think, taking every thing into consideration, that
your best plan will be to get Davidson, who is Heths agent, to deliver
you Coal in Washington—*stipulating if* it is not such as you approve
of when you see it, that you are not to be bound to receive it. if you
cannot do this, and think proper to run the risk here, I will of course
do as well as I can.

I inclose your acct. by which you will find there is a balance due
you of £599.8.10. You will observe that we have charged freight on
some Tobo. from Milton contrary to custom—this was owing to our
having been directed to pay it by Mr. Garrett who sent it down. there
is likewise I notice a charge for freight of two Casks to Milton, which
I suppose was paid in consequence of some particular circumstance.

The freight of the chairs I imagine you will think with me is enormous! I think it would be better if you have many things sent round in future, to direct your correspondents to agree on the freight, instead of filling up the bills of lading to be paid "as customary" as they generally do; for if they were to fix on the freight, the Captains would always be glad to engage at what it was really worth—and sometimes indeed when it was scarce, even at less; whereas if it is left to be settled here they almost universally charge too much, calculating that sooner than have a noise, or perhaps a law suit, the merchant will submit to the imposition.

You will find a charge of 48/. paid M. Jones which he promises to return, as he says that you paid it to his collector without his knowledge.

I am Dear Sir Your Very humble servt.   GEO. JEFFERSON

RC (MHi); addressed: "Thomas Jefferson esquire Monticello"; endorsed by TJ as received 10 Sep. and so recorded in SJL. Enclosure not found.

YOUR LETTER: TJ to George Jefferson, 29 Aug. Henry HETH, who had a large plantation outside of Richmond, also founded Black Heath Pits, a coal mining operation located in Chesterfield County near Manchester. (Ronald L. Lewis, *Coal, Iron, and Slaves: Industrial Slavery in Maryland and Virginia, 1715-1865*

[Westport, Conn., 1979], 52, 64-5; Sean Patrick Adams, *Old Dominion, Industrial Commonwealth* [Baltimore, 2004], 36-7; VMHB, 42 [1934], 277). For TJ's decision to purchase coal from John DAVIDSON, Heth's agent in Washington, see TJ to George Jefferson, 19 Oct.

On 17 Apr. 1801 (first letter), TJ requested that George Jefferson pay Meriwether JONES to continue his subscription for the Richmond *Examiner*.

¹ Word interlined.

From Isaac Ledyard

SIR   N York 7th. Septr. 1801

I have been solicited by several respectable gentlemen to avail myself of the very little knowledge which your Excellency can be supposed to retain of me, to recommend Mr. Mathw. L. Davis for the Office of Naval Officer of this port. The respect which I owe to these Gentlemen urges me to trouble your Excellency with this rather unwarrantable Letter—

Mr. Davis is one of those active Citizens, who have been instrumental in the late triumphant Elections of N York. He has very considerable talent, deciciveness of mind, & promptitude of action, & I doubt not would fill the office in question with integrity & ability. His not being known as a mercantile character, & how far that may deduct from his pretentions, will be for your Excellencies consideration

I have the honor to be with the most entire respect Your Excellencies Obedt. & most humble servant   ISAAC LEDYARD

Health Establishment
Staten Island 7th. Septr. 1801

RC (DNA: RG 59, LAR); at foot of text: "His Excellency Thos. Jefferson"; endorsed by TJ as received 17 Sep. but recorded in SJL at 18 Sep. and connected by a brace with eight other letters received from New York on that date with notation: "Davis to be Naval officer"; also endorsed by TJ: "Davis."

KNOWLEDGE WHICH YOUR EXCELLENCY CAN BE SUPPOSED TO RETAIN OF ME: Ledyard, a physician, wrote TJ in March 1798 about the publication of the papers of his cousin, John Ledyard. TJ had earlier given Dr. Ledyard his correspondence with the world traveler. Ledyard also served as a Republican elector in 1800 (Kline, *Burr*, 1:453-4; Vol. 30:226-7).

On this day Ledyard wrote TJ another short letter, noting that it was the "earnest wish" of the collector (David Gelston) "to have Mr. Davis for his Colleague" and enclosing an oration "that you may know something of the talents of Mr. Davis" (RC in DNA: RG 59, LAR; at foot of text: "His Excellency Thos. Jefferson"; endorsed by TJ as received 18 Sep. and "Davis" and recorded in SJL along with Ledyard's letter printed above). Ledyard probably enclosed Davis's *Oration, Delivered in St. Paul's Church, on The Fourth of July, 1800: Being the Twenty-Fourth Anniversary of our Independence; before the General Society of Mechanics & Tradesmen, Tammany Society or Columbian Order, and other Associations and Citizens* (New York, 1800). See Sowerby, No. 3232.

From Anthony Lispenard

SIR   New york 7th Septemr. 1801—

Having understood that Mr Mathew L. Davis is a Candidate for the place of Naval Officer of this Port, I chearfully add my opinion in favor of his talents and character to that of his numerous and respectable friends. He is much esteemed in this City and wherever he is known, for his Candor, his Integrity, his Patriotism, and the purity of his life and manners, as far as my knowlege extends, and I mingle much with my fellow Citizens; his appointment would be highly grateful. The Person now holding that Office is paticularly obnoxious to our Republicans on account of his avowed political sentiments, his removal and the appointment of Mr Davis has been long expected and much desired. I might add that Mr Davis is one of our first Writers and public Speakers.   I ought perhaps to apologize for this intrusion, but I am emboldened to the freedom by a knowlege of your character and particularly by the sentiments expressed in your justly admired answer to the remonstrance of the New Haven Merchants. Having no other View but that of contributing my mite to the pros-

perity and popularity of Your administration, I have the honor to subscribe myself with entire respect.

Your sincere admirer and very humble Servant

ANTHONY LISPENARD

RC (DNA: RG 59, LAR); endorsed by TJ as received 18 Sep. and so recorded in SJL and connected by a brace with eight other letters received from New York on that date with notation: "Davis to be Naval officer"; also endorsed by TJ: "Davis."

Anthony Lispenard (1740-1806) owned a brewery on Greenwich Road and extensive property in New York City between Canal Street and the Hudson River. He chaired Republican meetings in the sixth ward in the spring of 1800 and on 6 Nov. was chosen to serve as the presidential elector for the city and county of New York. In February 1801, he presided over a meeting of Republicans that approved the nomination of George Clinton for governor and became a mem-

ber of the committee of correspondence, serving with James Nicholson, Marinus Willett, Samuel L. Mitchill, and other New York City Republicans (New York *Mercantile Advertiser,* 21, 28 Apr. 1800; New York *Daily Advertiser,* 3 Mch. 1801; *Longworth's American Almanac, New-York Register, and City Directory, for the Twenty-Fifth Year of American Independence* [New York, 1800], 258; *New York Genealogical and Biographical Record,* 106 [1975], 234; *Minutes of the Common Council of the City of New York, 1784-1831,* 19 vols. [New York, 1917], 5:6-7, 263, 273; *Journal of the Assembly of the State of New-York: At Their Twenty-Fourth Session, Began and Held at the City of Albany, the Fourth Day of November, 1800* [Albany, 1801], 9, 13).

From William Stephens Smith

SIR.   Surveyors office new york Septr. 7th. 1801.

Your goodness will pardon the Liberty I take in addressing a Letter particularly to you, at the moment perhaps, in which you are,
more importantly engaged than to attend to my individual wishes
and pursuits—The veneration however, that I have for you as the
Cheif majestrate of my Country, connected with the particular respect
I have for your private Virtues derived from the acquaintance I formerly had the honor of enjoying with you in Europe, emboldens me
to present myself to you, in the first instance soliciting your confirmation of the office I now hold under your administration

It cannot be necessary for me to represent to you, Sir, the active
and early part I took in the defence of the Liberties of my Country—
or to state, that the greatest part of my Life, has been devoted to its
Service—But I feel no diffidence in concluding from your personal
knowledge of my sentiments and the Springs of my action, you will
rely upon the duties required of me being discharged with a consien-
tious impartiallity and true Republican fidelity—.

I am flattered with the assurance, that the duties of the office I at present fill, are discharged, to the Satisfaction of my fellow Citizens, who are disposed to regulate their Commerce, by the established laws of our Country, the applause of the other description, I shall not Seek for—Should you think my pretensions equal to others who may be solicitous to occupy the station I fill, and think proper to continue me in it, I shall think myself vastly obliged

But should you view me thro' a more favourable medium, and compliment me with promotion in the department of The Customs, I shall esteem myself highly honoured, and particularly complimented,—I have been pointedly interferred with by the past administrations, they first became hostile to me in consequence of a Letter I wrote to Mr. Jay when secretary of foreign affairs under date of the 6th. of Decbr. 1785—when I returned from Berlin & Vienna to London and gave him a detail of my tour thro. Germany in which was this sentence—"In the first place Sir permit me to breathe a Serious wish, that my Countrymen had a proper Idea of the happiness within their grasp; and the benefits arising to society from Virtuous republican establishments.—The very fact of nature here speaks for itself, and as you pass this variegated Country and Government bears in strong lines the different degrees of toleration and indulgence they enjoy; I will not prostitute the term of Liberty by using it, when speaking of any of them: and as for myself, if it were possible for an addition to be made to my enthusiam in that Subject, I am now a most perfect devotee"—for this sentence I was never forgiven by those, who under the mask of republican systems, perpetrated acts of tyranny, and advocated the principles of monarchical Establishments—

But I will refer you to the letter itself in the files of the secretary of State, and feel myself emboldened to say, if the pure preservation of the Principles of the earliest part of our revolution would be considered of moment—I can boast of their most pointed cultivation and support—and my enemies cannot charge me with the Shaddow of changing.

I hope I may not be considered as overstepping the bounds of propriety, in Stating to you, Sir, that there does not, neither do I believe there can exist, that Cordiallity between the Collector and the present naval officer, which the good of the Service requires—The Principles of the Collector you are well acquainted with, those of the Naval officer, are in the highest scale of toryism, with an evident prejudice against our present establishment—a case lately occured relative to the Brigg Rainbow, which I reported to the Collector as a Vessel sailing under false papers, and of course subject to seizure—the hesitation and delays which the Collector experienced from the Naval officer, were such that he finally took counsel of The Attorney General whose opinion was prompt and decissive, and an order consequently issued to me to seize her, but the Brigg having then cleared out, had got under way, & tho' I sent the Custom House boat in pursuit of her, she made her escape—

It being the received opinion in society here that the Naval officer will be removed—the Bearer Mr. Mathew L. Davis, a very deserving Citizen, and whose name cannot be unknown to you, has been flattered by his friends with the expectation of receiving the appointment, I am highly sensible, that he is entitled to notice, and the countenance and protection of administration. his indefatigable assiduity, his talents and influence in society, ought to be cultivated, and nourished It cannot however be expected I should advocate his promotion to a Station in office above me I have had a friendly conversation with him on the subject, and should it be the determination of The President to remove the present naval officer, and appoint Mr. Davis in his place I shall like a good Citizen, bow with respect to his arrangement—But should he Compliment the present Surveyor with the appointment of Naval officer and make Mr. Davis Surveyor The attention will be gratefully received, and most pointedly acknowledged, by strict attention to the discharge of the duties of the office

By Sir—Your most obedt and Very Humble Servt.

W. S. SMITH

RC (DNA: RG 59, LAR); with closing quotation mark supplied; at head of text: "To The President of The United States"; endorsed by TJ as received 17 Sep. but recorded in SJL at 18 Sep. and connected by a brace with eight other letters received from New York on that date with notation: "Davis to be Naval officer"; also endorsed by TJ: "Davis."

ACQUAINTANCE I FORMERLY HAD THE HONOR OF ENJOYING WITH YOU: Smith arrived in London to serve as secretary of the U.S. legation in May 1785. In the fall he toured Europe, visiting Potsdam, Leipzig, Dresden, Vienna, and Paris, where TJ entertained him. After Smith's return to London, TJ wrote Abigail Adams and commented upon the "extreme worth of his character." On 12 June 1786, Smith informed TJ of his impending marriage to the Adams's daughter, Abigail. TJ and Smith communicated

regularly until Smith's return to the United States in May 1788 (ANB; Vol. 8:249-50, 541-2; Vol. 9:47-9, 634-5; Vol. 12:484-5; Vol. 13:315).

OFFICE I NOW HOLD: for the Senate debate over the appointment of Smith as surveyor and inspector of customs at New York in December 1800, see Vol. 32:351-2. The opinion relating to the brig RAINBOW has not been found and may have been given by the U.S. district attorney rather than the attorney general. David Gelston later reported that shortly after he took office in 1801 he found that many ships, the real property of persons residing in Europe, had fraudulently obtained American registers. On 2 Oct. 1801, Edward Livington, as U.S. district attorney, wrote on the New York surveyor's report, which recommended the seizure of *Liberty* and *Two Marys*, two ships registered as American vessels but believed to be owned by British subjects: "I think the

Circumstances related of these two Ships well warrant a Seizure and that the expectation of more complete proofs on the vessels is reasonable." Additional proof, however, was not obtained and the seizures ended in suits brought against the collector (Gallatin, *Papers*, 13:662-5, 672).

From Marinus Willett

SIR   New York, 7th September 1801

The republicans of this City have been much Gratified by the Removal of several persons from office and Replacing them with good republicans.

There remains however two offices in the hands of persons equally obnoxious to the friends of the present administration, Those are the Naval office occupied by Mr Rogers and the agency of the war Department in the posession of Col. Stevens—Excuse my obtruding this Information upon you. It arises from a Conviction of the Justise and propriety of the measure of such Removals—

This will be handed you by Mr Davis whose exertions have been such as to merit attention and whose abilities by the best Judges are deemed amply sufficient to fill with reputation the office at present enjoyed by Mr Rogers whose state of health & temper as well as avowed tory principals unfit him for the discharge of the duties, and render him odious—The appointment of Mr Davis will I am of opinion should it take place give great satisfaction—

With the greatest respect I am Sir Your very obedient servant

MARINUS WILLETT

RC (DNA: RG 59, LAR); at foot of text: "Thomas Jefferson Esq"; endorsed by TJ as received 17 Sep. but recorded in SJL at 18 Sep. and connected by a brace with eight other letters received from New York on that date with notation: "Davis to be Naval officer"; also endorsed by TJ: "Davis."

GRATIFIED BY THE REMOVAL: for Willett's previous assessment of appointments in New York, including remarks on Davis as a candidate, see his letter to TJ of 4 May 1801.

A New York merchant and founding member of the Tammany Society, Ebenezer STEVENS began serving in 1794 as U.S. agent for erecting the fortifications at New York. In October and November 1801, he continued to superintend the construction of fortifications on Governor's Island (Kline, *Burr*, 1:523n; Washington, *Papers, Pres. Ser.*, 3:228; Syrett, *Hamilton*, 21:465-6).

From Charles Pinckney

DEAR SIR   September 8: 1801 Helder (Holland)

In pursuance of my promise I have the honour to inform you that as soon as I recieved my instructions I sailed for Europe & had almost the whole way Eastwardly Winds—by which means the ship in which I arrived two hours agoe at Helder in Holland has had upwards of fifty six days passage—five of which we have been off the Texel & unable from the Winds to get in.—I propose to set out to morrow for Amsterdam, & proceed on to Madrid as fast as I can, by the way of Paris, as you advised me to take that rout.—I had very clear & pleasant Weather in the English Channel & went so near to the whole Western Coast of England as to see it almost as well as if I was on shore, but I carefully avoided going into an English Port as I was going to Countries in hostility with them.—Being so long at sea & this moment arrived I am unable to send you any intelligence but such as you must have heard.—the Peace between the Northern Powers & England—& the intelligence from Egypt as well as the naval engagement between the English & Spaniards were all new to me—& at this little remote town of pilots & fishermen I can hear nothing to be relied upon—but meeting a ship to sail in a few days for Philadelphia I thought it my duty to announce my arrival in Europe.—at Amsterdam I shall be probably able to hear more & will write you from thence.—There is a report here of a probability of Peace but the American agent's Brother here, the agent being absent, thinks the report is not to be relied on.—I will thank you to have the inclosed put into the Post-office & to do me the honour to remember me to Mr Madison, Mr Gallatin & the gentlemen with you.—

I am dear Sir with profound attachment & respectful Esteem & regard Yours truly   CHARLES PINCKNEY

RC (DLC); endorsed by TJ as received 14 Dec. Enclosure not found.

Pinckney's INSTRUCTIONS as minister to Spain were dated 6 June; see Pinckney to TJ, 12 Mch. 1801.

INTELLIGENCE FROM EGYPT: on his arrival in Europe, Pinckney apparently learned that the British had begun a siege of Alexandria, Egypt, in mid-August. He would also have been aware of reports confirming the surrender of Cairo to British and Turkish forces on 27 June, but he did not yet know that the French had surrendered Alexandria on 30 Aug. That capitulation forced the end of the French occupation of Egypt (Smith, *Napoleonic Wars*, 196-7; Parry, *Consolidated Treaty Series*, 56:195-204; Madison, *Papers, Sec. of State Ser.*, 2:95, 112).

To Hammuda Pasha, Bey of Tunis

GREAT AND GOOD FRIEND,

The letter which you addressed to the President of the United State of America on the 15th. of April, has been received, and has conveyed us the assurances, always welcome, that your friendly dispositions towards these States still continue firm and unimpaired. We feel deep regret that the regalia and other tokens of our esteem for you had not, at that date, reached their destination. These delays proceed from the distance of our situation, and from the circumstance that some of the articles acceptable to you, are not fabricated here, but are to be sought for in foreign countries, where also they require time to be prepared. We trust they will all have been received before this reaches you. We are a nation not practising the difficult arts, but employed in agriculture, and transportation of its produce for commercial exchange with others. Peace therefore with all nations is essentially our pursuit, so long as it can be obtained on just and equal grounds. Of this desire on our part we have given to the States bordering on the Mediterranean the same manifestations of which Europe had set the example. Like them, we consented to give a price for friendships, which would have been properly requited by our own. So long as we have been met with moderation and good faith we have preferred these means of peace, rather than to seek it through our own strength. At length, however, the inadmissible demands of the Bashaw of Tripoli and our determination to owe to our own energies, and not to dishonorable condescensions the protection of our right to navigate the Ocean freely, have induced us to send a squadron into the Mediterranean sea, for the protection of our commerce against the Bashaw of Tripoli. We gave, illustrious friend, in strict charge to our Officer, chief in command, to respect, and treat with particular friendship, your flags, your vessels and your subjects, and to take an early occasion after his arrival in those seas, to testify his respect to you; to assure you of our adherence to the peace and friendship established with you, and of our orders to him to cultivate them with assiduity: and we trusted you would yield him that hospitable reception, and those accommodations in the ports of your dominions, which his necessities require. We did this with the greater confidence, as knowing the liberality of your mind, and being ourselves in the habit of rendering similar good offices to all nations in friendship with us.

Trusting, good Friend, that our Consul will have received and delivered those evidences of our good will, which circumstances permit us to offer for your acceptance, we ask the continuance of your friendship in return for that which we sincerely bear to you; and pray to God that he may long preserve your life, and have you under the safeguard of his holy keeping.

Done in the United States of America this ninth day of September one thousand eight hundred and one.　　　　　　Th: Jefferson

FC (DNA: RG 233, PM, 7th Cong., 1st sess.); in a clerk's hand; at head of text: "Thomas Jefferson President of the United States of America To Hamouda Pacha Bey of Tunis"; transmitted to Congress, 22 Dec. 1801 (ASP, *Foreign Relations*, 2:358). PrC (DNA: RG 46, EPFR, 7th Cong., 1st sess.). FC (Lb in DNA: RG 59, Credences); in a clerk's hand. Tr (CSmH); in Italian; with note by William Eaton in English at foot of text, 9 Oct. 1802. Not recorded in SJL. Enclosed in TJ to Madison, 11 Sep.

OFFICER, CHIEF IN COMMAND: Richard Dale. In May, when TJ and Samuel Smith gave Dale his orders, he also received a draft of a letter that he could use to TESTIFY HIS RESPECT to the dey of Algiers and to Hammuda if they were still at peace with the United States when he reached the Mediterranean. The letter identified Dale's force as "a squadron of observation" that would support American commerce and serve as a training exercise. It expressed "the profound respect which is due to your Excellency's dignity and character," the "friendly dispositions of the United States," and "the reliance of the President on similar dispositions on your part" (Lb in DNA: RG 59, Credences; NDBW, 1:465-71, 508). The "Form" of Dale's letter was among the documents that TJ communicated to Congress in December (ASP, *Foreign Relations*, 2:349; *National Intelligencer*, 4 Jan. 1802).

OUR CONSUL: William Eaton.

To Robert R. Livingston

Dear Sir　　　　　　　　　　　　Monticello Sep. 9. 1801.

You will recieve, probably by this post, from the Secretary of State, the final instructions for your mission to France. we have not thought it necessary to say any thing in them on the great question of the Maritime law of nations, which at present agitates Europe, that is to say, Whether free ships shall make free goods? because we do not mean to take any side in it during the war. but, as I had before communicated to you some loose thoughts on that subject, and have since considered it with somewhat more attention, I have thought it might not be unuseful that you should possess my ideas in a more matured form than that in which they were before given. unforeseen circumstances may perhaps oblige you to hazard an opinion, on some occasion or other, on this subject, and it is better that it should not be at variance with ours. I write this too myself, that it may not be considered as official, but merely my individual opinion, unadvised by those official counsellors, whose opinions I deem my safest guide, & should unquestionably take in form were circumstances to call for a solemn decision of the question.

When Europe assumed the general form in which it is occupied by the nations now composing it, and turned it's attention to maritime commerce, we find, among it's earliest practices, that of taking the goods of an enemy from the ship of a friend: and that into this practice every maritime state went, sooner or later, as it appeared on the theatre of the ocean. if therefore we were to consider the practice of nations as the sole & sufficient evidence of the law of nature among nations, we should unquestionably place this principle among those of Natural law. but it's inconveniences, as they affected Neutral nations peaceably pursuing their commerce, and it's tendency to embroil with them the powers happening to be at war, and thus to extend the flames of war, induced nations to introduce, by special compacts from time to time, a more convenient rule that 'free ships should make free goods' and this latter principle has, by every maritime nation of Europe, been established, to a greater or less degree, in it's treaties with other nations: insomuch that all of them have, more or less frequently, assented to it as a rule of action in particular cases. indeed, it is now urged, and I think with great appearance of reason, that this is the genuine principle dictated by National morality; & that the first practice arose from accident & the particular convenience of the* states[1] which first figured on the water, rather than from well digested reflections on the relations of friend & enemy, on the rights of territorial jurisdiction, & on the dictates of Moral law applied to these. thus, it had never been supposed lawful, in the territory of a friend, to sieze the goods of an enemy. on an element which nature has not subjected to the jurisdiction of any particular nation, but has made common to all, for the purposes to which it is fitted, it would seem that the particular portion of it which happens to be occupied by the vessel of any nation, in the course of it's voyage, is, for the moment, the exclusive property of that nation, and, with the vessel, is exempt from intrusion by any other, & from it's jurisdiction, as much as if it were lying in the harbour of it's sovereign. in no country we believe is the rule otherwise, as to the subjects of property common to all. thus the place occupied by an individual in a highway, a church, a theater, or other public assembly, cannot be intruded on, while it's occupant holds it for the purposes of it's institution. the persons on board a vessel traversing the ocean, carry with them the laws of their nation, have among themselves a jurisdiction, a police, not established by their individual will, but by the authority of their nation, of whose territory their vessel still seems to compose a part, so long as it does not enter the exclusive territory of another. no nation ever pretended a right to govern by their laws the ship of another nation navigating the ocean. by what law then can it enter that ship while in peaceable & orderly use of the common element? we recognize no natural precept for submission to such a right; & percieve no distinction between the moveable & immoveable jurisdiction of a friend, which would authorise the entering the one, & not the other, to sieze the property of an enemy.

It may be objected that this proves too much, as it proves you cannot enter the ship of a friend to search for Contraband of war. but this is not proving too much. we believe the practice of seising what is called Contraband of war is an abusive practice, not founded in natural right. war between two nations cannot diminish the rights of the rest of the world remaining at peace. the doctrine that the rights of nations remaining quietly under the exercise of moral & social duties, are to give way to the convenience of those who prefer plundering & murdering one another, is a monstrous doctrine, and ought to yield to the more rational law that 'the wrongs which two nations endeavor to inflict on each other, must not infringe on the rights or conveniences of those remaining at peace.' and what is *contraband* by the law of nature? either every thing which may aid or comfort an enemy, or nothing. either all commerce which would accomodate him is unlawful, or none is. the difference between articles of one or another description, is a difference in degree only. no line between them can be drawn. either all intercourse must cease between neutrals & belligerents, or all be permitted. can the world hesitate to say which shall be the rule? shall two nations, turning tygers, break up in one instant the peaceable relations of the whole world? reason & nature clearly pronounce that the Neutral is to go on in the enjoyment of all it's rights, that it's commerce remains free, not subject to the jurisdiction of another, nor consequently it's vessels to search, or to enquiries whether their contents are the property of an enemy, or are of those which have been called Contraband of war.

Nor does this doctrine contravene that right of preventing vessels from entering a blockaded port. this right stands on other ground. when the fleet of any nation actually beleaguers the port of it's enemy, no other has a right to enter their line, any more than their line of battle in the open sea, or their lines of circumvallation, or of encampment, or of battle array, on land. the space included within their lines in any of those cases, is either the property of it's enemy, or it is common property, assumed and possessed for the moment, which cannot

be intruded on, even by a Neutral, without committing the very trespass we are now condemning, that of intruding into the lawful possession of a friend.

Although I consider the observance of these principles as of great
importance to the interests of peaceable nations, among whom I hope
the US. will ever place themselves, yet, in the present state of things,
they are not worth a war. nor do I believe war the most certain means
of enforcing them. those peaceable coercions, which are in the power
of every nation, if undertaken in concert, & in time of peace, are more
likely to produce the desired effect.

The opinions I have here given are those which have generally
been sanctioned by our government. in our treaties with France, the
United Netherlands Sweden & Prussia the principle of free bottoms
free goods was uniformly maintained. in the instructions of 1784.
given by Congress to their ministers appointed to treat with the nations of Europe generally, the same principle, and the doing away
Contraband of war, were enjoined, and were acceded to in the treaty
signed with Portugal. in the late treaty with England indeed, that
power perseveringly refused the principle of free bottoms free goods;
and it was avoided, in the late treaty with Prussia, at the instance of
our then administration, lest it should seem to take side in a question
then threatening decision by the sword. At the commencement of the
war between France & England, the representative of the French republic then residing in the US. complaining that the British armed
ships captured French property in American bottoms, insisted that
the principle of 'free bottoms free goods' was of the acknoleged law of
nations, that the violation of that principle by the British was a
wrong committed on us, and such an one as we ought to repel by
joining in the war against that country. we denied his position, and
appealed to the universal practice of Europe in proof that the principles of 'free bottoms free goods' was not acknoleged as of the Natural
law of Nations, but only of it's Conventional law. and I believe we
may safely affirm that not a single instance can be produced where
any nation of Europe, acting professedly under the Law of nations
alone, unrestrained by treaty, has, either by it's Executive or Judiciary organs, decided on the principle of 'free bottoms free goods.'
judging of the Law of nations by what has been *practised* among nations, we were authorised to say that the contrary principle was their
rule, and this but an exception to it, introduced by special treaties in
special cases only: that having no treaty with England substituting
this instead of the ordinary rule, we had neither the right nor the disposition to go to war for it's establishment.   But tho' we would

not then, nor will we now, engage in war to establish this principle, we are nevertheless sincerely friendly to it. we think that the nations of Europe have originally set out in error; that experience has proved the error oppressive to the rights & interests of the peaceable part of mankind; that every nation but one has acknoleged this by consenting to the change, & that one has consented in particular cases; that nations have a right to correct an erroneous principle, & to establish that which is right as their rule of action; and if they should adopt measures for effecting this in a peaceable way, we shall wish them success, and not stand in their way to it. but should it become at any time expedient for us to co-operate in the establishment of this principle, the opinion of the Executive, on the advice of it's constitutional counsellors, must then be given; & that of the Legislature, an independant & essential organ in the operation, must also be expressed; in forming which they will be governed, every man by his own judgment, & may very possibly judge differently from the Executive. with the same honest views, the most honest men often form different conclusions. as far however as we can judge, the principle of 'free bottoms free goods' is that which would carry the wishes of our nation.

Wishing you smooth seas & prosperous gales, with the enjoyment of good health, I tender you the assurance of my constant friendship & high consideration & respect.   Th: Jefferson

RC (NNMus); at foot of first page: "Robert R. Livingston. M.P. of the US. to France"; endorsed by Livingston. PrC (DLC); in ink in TJ's hand at foot of first page: "Rob. R. Livingston." Enclosed in TJ to Madison, 11 Sep.

When Madison wrote to Livingston on 4 Sep. he asked him to depart for France right away, even though the convention between France and the United States was apparently still unratified. Madison's FINAL INSTRUCTIONS to Livingston were dated 28 Sep., by which time news of the ratification had arrived in the United States (Madison, *Papers, Sec. of State Ser.*, 2:82-3, 142-7; TJ to Gallatin, 5 Sep.). SOME LOOSE THOUGHTS ON THAT SUBJECT: for TJ's observations on the law of nations and neutral rights, see his letter to Livingston of 4 June 1801, the memorandum he enclosed with that letter, and Livingston's reply of the same day. SANCTIONED BY OUR GOVERNMENT:

in treaties of amity and commerce between the United States and other nations, the principle that free ships made free goods was incorporated in Article 25 (Article 23 as ratified) of the 1778 treaty with France, Article 11 of the 1782 treaty with the Netherlands, Article 7 of the 1783 treaty with Sweden, and Article 12 of the 1785 treaty with Prussia (Miller, *Treaties*, 2:21, 70, 128-9, 170-1).

The Instructions to the Commissioners for Negotiating Treaties of Amity and Commerce were adopted by CONGRESS on 7 May 1784 and subsequently transmitted to Benjamin Franklin, John Adams, and TJ, who were the commissioners for the negotiations (Vol. 7:267-8, 271n). Beginning in Paris in 1784 and concluding in London in 1786, TJ and Adams negotiated a treaty with diplomats from PORTUGAL. The Americans' proposed treaty was based on a model by TJ that declared that "free vessels" made "free goods." It contained an article stating that in case of war between one of the contracting nations and another country,

"to prevent all the difficulties and misunderstandings that usually arise respecting the merchandize heretofore called Contraband such as arms, ammunition and military stores of every kind, no such articles carried in the vessels or by the subjects or citizens of one of the parties to the enemies of the other shall be deemed contraband so as to induce confiscation or condemnation and a loss of property to individuals." Luís Pinto de Sousa Coutinho, who at the time was Portugal's minister to Great Britain, insisted on replacing that article with one that defined weapons and military equipment as contraband of war and made them subject to confiscation. TJ and Adams signed the treaty, but the Portuguese government never approved it (Vol. 7:419-20, 482-3, 490, 492n, 551; Vol. 9:410-12, 415-16, 423n, 425, 430-1, 432, 448; Vol. 10:61, 106, 179, 241-2; Vol. 11:35, 65-6, 78, 513n; Vol. 12:146).
LATE TREATY WITH ENGLAND: the Jay Treaty. LATE TREATY WITH PRUSSIA: a

treaty with Prussia, signed in 1799 and ratified the following year, conceded that the principle that *"free ships make free goods,"* embodied in the 1785 treaty between the two nations, "has not been sufficiently respected during the two last Wars, and especially in that which still continues." Prussia and the United States pledged "to concert with the great maritime Powers of Europe" upon the restoration of peace and to institute "such arrangements, and such permanent principles as may serve to consolidate the liberty and the safety of the neutral Navigation and Commerce in future Wars" (Miller, *Treaties*, 2:441-2).

Edmond Charles Genet was the unnamed REPRESENTATIVE OF THE FRENCH REPUBLIC; see the enclosure to TJ's letter of 4 June.

[1] In margin TJ wrote: "*Venice & Genoa."

From Anonymous

SIR   [before 10 Sep. 1801]
As the Writer wishes the following to meet your attention only in proportion to their merit they are submited to your consideration without comment—

first Melitia—   Every man ought to serve under penalty of paying fine in proportion to his Riches.—He that owns 100000 is more indebted to Society for protection than he who owns 100—each man ought to be considered as a Capital of $4000— at 5 ⅌ cent—which might be the data for proportioning the fines

2d. Eligibility   No man should hold a place of Honor or profit in the Government, who has received a fee or Sallary as a Lawyer, or Clergyman; within four Years—There ought a Check to be given to the increase of unproductive professions—Professions ought to be honorable in proportion as they promote the happiness of man

3d Sallaries   Sallaries of Officers in the Government ought to be reduced 50 ℔ Cent during the time the Nation is in War—

4 Congress   No Senate—but the Representatives to form two houses—of equal numbers, divided by lot, and all questions to be decided by a *majority* of *both* Houses

5 Agriculture   No Toll ought to be levied on Dung or manure passing allong any Turnpike or Canal nor Wharfage on vessels loading these articles

7 Marine policy   A Neutral State ought to prohibit from entering its ports All vessels that had been the property of said Neutral State but been captured by some Belligerant nation—no matter on what account the vessell had been taken—Excepting only from the operation of this law such vessells as were bought in, by their original owners at the sale made by the Captors

8—Quarantine—   There is nothing of more importance to a Country than Health—and if Congress do not make general regulation for—Commerce; a Quarantine law for the whole Union—the Country will be perpetualy exposed to the introduction of Cotageous Maladies, and the respective states at variance on acct of mutial Jealousies one state admiting vessels with less ceremony than another

RC (DLC: TJ Papers, 235:42165); undated; endorsed by TJ as received 10 Sep. and "Phila. post mark" and so recorded in SJL.

From Isaac Cox Barnet

SIR,   Bordeaux September 10th. 1801.

Although it may appear presumptuous in me to adress myself directly to the first magistrate of my Country, particularly when my duty points out one of your executive departments as the regular chanel through which all public communications should be made, yet I hope sir, that the liberty I now take, may not be construed as an informality wanting in respectfull deference to the established usages of our Government.

I have already written to the secretary of state on the subject of my removal from the Consulate of Bordeaux; but feeling as I do, with the keen sensibility, naturally resulting from a disapointment, in an event which immediatly deprives me of the means of support, and might remotely affect my reputation, I have resolved to leave no expedient untried, to obviate the evil.

I have hesitated in the propriety of adressing you in person, but I have determined on this measure from the counsels of Mr. Benjamin Homans, a worthy & respectable Citizen of Boston, who has ever venerated your public & private character & has served with zealous patriotism, the principles which have clothed you with the confidence of your Countrymen. His good sense and experience have taught me to listen to his advice, which he has communicated to me in the language of an honnest and upright man. "Write to the president *direct*: he will not refuse to hear a just complaint: he knows the laws of nature, reason and justice better; his ear is, and will be the organ of truth justice and recompense. Adress him as the friend of evry individual citizen of America; convince him that you are amongst the number of those who have the best right to claim his protection and confidence. That the loss of your paternal estate in our Contest for liberty & independence now obliges you to seek a compensation by serving your Country in an employment for which your talents are adequate & your experience entitles you to, before those who are ignorant of its functions: ignorant of the language and ignorant of political distinctions. The president does not know you: he must know you, and he will hear you as well as your insidious ennemies."

Thus, sir, in the language of my friend, I have stated the object of this letter: May you find in it my opology.

Apreciating fully the value & importance of your time, I will be as concise as possible, on the subject to which I respectfully beg leave to sollicit your attention.

I have learnt by a paragraph in an American News paper that it has pleased you to superceede me as Consul for this port by Mr. William Lee: but having received no official advice, I hope the appointment is not definitively made, and if it should be the case, that on hearing me, justice will prevail. An animating confidence in the rectitude of my Cause & justice of My pretentions induces me to submit them to you, with Candour & truth.

I am the son of Doct. Wm. M. Barnet of Elizabeth town, New Jersey, whose Ancestors to the third generation were natives of that peacefull land of retreat, which my father & grand father aided in rendering free and independant states; a Cause in whose support your memorable services will be handed down to posterity by a gratefull people.

After serving in the Jersey line from the commencement of the war: after having his proprety & hereditary expectations devastated by British & Refugee incendiaries, my father remained faithfull to the Cause of Liberty and his Country. Anxious to repair his losses & provide a support for his family, he embarked in a letter of marque, in 1782, for L'orient, to which place he conducted me, when about nine years of age, and by the intercession of a friend at Nantz, left me with him during twenty months to acquire a knowledge of the language.

On his return to America, my father, though happy in the termination of a war which secured freedom & independence to his Country, had many private calamities to regret.

In August 1783 (soon after his return) a sudden illness deprived him of his existence, and his family of their only hope for protection & support. On this melancholy event, I returned to my afflicted widow mother, her eldest & only son.

I was educated at Elizabeth town, by a tutor who had bravely defended the liberties of his Country, and who instilled into his pupils, that spirit of freedom which so generaly pervaded our happy land.

In 1789, I was four months with Mr. Andrew Elicott, in Upper Canada: but my eyes proved too feeble for the exercise of his proffession, which I was consequently forced to abandon. I am happy in this opportunity to express my gratitude for his paternal care, and proud to say that he honoured me with his good opinion.

My pecuniary faculties being very limited, I found much difficulty in procuring an elligible situation to exericse my industry: at length a daughter of the Unfortunate parson Cadwell (my father's friend & neighbour, a man whose memory will ever be respected, and whose fate will ever be deplored as long as British perfidy stands on record,) procured me a place in the Coumpting house of a respectable merchant in New York, where I remained four years, and made myself acquainted with Commerce.

In 1794 I came to France, charged with the management of a Cargo belonging to Mr. John R. Livingston of New York. On my arrival at Paris, I was honoured with the notice of our worthy minister, Mr. Munroe who will ever be remembered with gratitude by the Citizens of America who have had occasion to claim his protection and assistance.—his natural benevolence, and perhaps some partiality for the son of a fellow soldier, recommended me to his friendly attention, & paternal sollicitude. I was advised in the Autumn of 1796, to apply for the Consulship of Brest, which I declined on account of my youth & inexperience; but the invitation being repeated and approved by Mr. Munroe, I thought proper to accept it. Mr. Munroe's printed correspondence shews the honourable manner in which he recommended me. Mr. Skipwith was also pleased to favour me with his support: I feel conscious of having justified their good opinion, which I believe is undiminished & unimpaired.

My Commission as Consul at Brest was under date of the 20th. of february 1797.

The circumstances, both political & local, under which I acted there during three years, were fully stated to our secretary of state, in my letter of the fifth of october last, and I hope are known and apreciated by our government who have hitherto found no fault with my Conduct. I brought with me from Brest Ample & honourable Testimonies of local approbation.

I removed to this place by order of Government, and with the promise of being confirmed in the Consulate if my Agency was aproved of. On this head, my conscience dictates the fullest security, and I appeal to the Archives of the department of state for more material proofs, and am willing to be judged by my own works. They will shew that I have always been actuated by an honnest zeal; to acquit myself well of the important trust: that I have relieved my distressed fellow citizens and succoured suffering humanity.

If I thought there could be a doubt of my being agreeable to the citizens & authorities of this place, I would offer you sir, Vouchers unequivocal of their approbation and esteem: I have them as well as the testimony of my fellow Citizens: but I can not submit to anticipate a justification, without having any motive, even to suspect a charge.

I beseech you then, Sir, to cause an investigation of my conduct to be made: it will prove as satisfactory to you sir, as honourable to me.

I speak the language as a French man: I write it with almost equal facility as my own: the routine of the office is familiar to me: my abilities, I conceive are adequate to all its duties. My experience during more than five years, compensates & is equivalent to brighter talents. Since my official establishmt I have done no other business: I gave up several commercial prospects to serve my Country, and with the hope, by deserving the confidence of government, and esteem of my fellow Citizens to form a respectable establishment.

I have not made in all the time, by the emoluments of the office, the expences of it (though I am to expect a compensation as Agent for Prisoners.)

I am not richer than I was six years ago: that is, I am still poor: for I never would enrich myself at the risk of my reputation, and at the expense of our national honour.

My removal from Brest, was attended with considerable expense and since the first of May last, in the confidence of receiving a Commission my present establishment has occasioned me heavy disbursments.

In consequence of the intercourse being opened, the duties of my office have engrossed all my attention, and occupied all my time:—its emoluments have about met my economical expences.

I have an encreasing family, and at my instigation, founded upon the auspices of my late appointment my mother & sister left their peacefull abode & embarked at New York to join me: they will soon arrive. Their only hope for protection & support is in me, & to deprive me of my official resources will expose us all, to great distress.

In withdrawing from me your confidence, sir, you withdraw that of the American public, and expose me to forfeit that of the European.

Suffer me, I conjure you Sir, to submit these reflextions to your consideration.

Let my competitor content himself with the appointment to Marseilles: his removal there, from America, will cost him no more than to come to Bordeaux

It is a matter of surprise with many, how he could have acquired the preference in the opinion of the most enlightened man in America. Is it by himself, alone? I do not believe it, or the reputation I have heard of him is false. has it been through friends of influence? they have misled you Sir.

Mr. Lee has no founded pretentions over mine. my prior claim is established by birth right, services & principles which have ever been those of an American Republican. Mr. Lee, I am assured, is a *Native of Nova Scotia*, where his father's family now reside. he went to Boston, when a youth, and there compleated his education. of his late political principles, I will say nothing: nor repeat what I have heard of his Commercial & personal difficulties. It is not my wish to strengthen my cause in depreciating him: but I must observe that the very application he made to supplant me was illiberal, and supports the reports I heard & may appoligize for the little I have just said.

I know that Colonel Palfrey was an active & valuable character in our struggle for liberty: That he lost his life in the Service of his Country: but if his memory gives his *son in Law* any rights, mine are at least equal.

I have said above, that my conduct never has, that I know of, been complained of, and I challenge my detractors (for such no doubt I have,) to bring forward, any proof against me.

My moral principles, and my private conduct are, and ever have been open to the investigation of the world. I am ready to appear before my judges.

And as to my political sentiments (Though I have never espoused any party, so I have never given umbrage to any) They can bear your strictest scrutiny.

My love of Country, my respect for the authors of our independence: for our happy constitution: the interest I feel in the prosperity and the happiness of United America, and my confidence in the talents of the present Administration, are co-equal with your sentiments and deserve your patronage. And I believe Sir, that your being called to preside over the interests of our Republic is a guarantée of our Civil Liberty (Late too *"chancelant"*). That your talents, experience, & patriotism, of which your important services have given so many proofs, were necessary, and indispensable to our Union.

To expatiate, would expose me to the suspicion of flattery, and flattery is degrading to the manly feelings of a republican.

Returning then to the subject of my letter, and addressing you sir, "as the friend of evry individual, Citizen of America." suffer me to sollicit of your Justice, my Confirmation in this office.

Accept the assurance of my profound respect, and of my wishes for your public & private happiness   I, COX BARNET

Dupl (DNA: RG 59, LAR); at head of text: "Duplicate"; addressed: "Thomas Jefferson President of the United States"; endorsed by TJ as received 23 Nov. Recorded in SJL as a letter of September 1801 received 22 Nov. Probably enclosed in Peter Muhlenberg to TJ, Philadelphia, 19 Nov. 1801: "The enclosed Letter was this Morning presented to me, by a French Gentleman direct from Bordeaux, with the request that I would forward it imediately. I have the Honor to be with the highest Respect Sir Your Most Obedt P. Muhlenberg" (RC in MHi; at foot of text: "The President of The United States"; endorsed by TJ as received 22 Nov. and so recorded in SJL).

Isaac Cox Barnet (1773-1833) was born in Elizabeth, New Jersey, where his father, William M. Barnet, and grandfather, William Barnet, were both physicians. Elias Boudinot, a friend of Barnet's father, lent his influence to aid Barnet's advancement. According to Boudinot, George Washington considered Barnet to be, during his tenure as consul at Brest, "a very promising Officer of Government and among the best in France." Charles Pinckney heard that Barnet was one of the best U.S. consuls in Europe, although James Monroe thought that Barnet owed much to his connections in New Jersey. TJ classified John Adams's late-term appointment of Barnet to be commercial agent at Bordeaux as a "midnight" appointment, and named William Lee to the place at Lee's request. In 1802, TJ appointed Barnet commercial agent at Antwerp. Barnet left Antwerp in 1803 when TJ and Madison offered him the position of commercial agent at Le Havre. That year Monroe and Robert R. Livingston also named Barnet a commissioner of U.S. claims in France. In 1816, Madison appointed him to the consulship at Paris (Charles Coleman Sellers, "The Barnet Franklin," *Antiques*, 70 [1956],

354; Kline, *Burr*, 2:617n; Madison, *Papers, Sec. of State Ser.*, 3:64-5, 123-4, 235, 309n, 352, 402-3, 567; 4:117, 137-82, 280-1, 426n, 570; Marshall, *Papers*, 4:251; Vol. 33:225-6, 666, 671, 676).

ALREADY WRITTEN TO THE SECRETARY OF STATE: in a letter of 5 Aug. to Madison on consular business, Barnet argued against his replacement by Lee, calling himself a "true republican" and stating his belief that the president had been misled. Barnet also solicited statements of support from American ship captains, merchants, French officials, Charles Pinckney, and William R. Davie (Madison, *Papers, Sec. of State Ser.*, 2:18-19, 289n; 3:235, 402).

Barnet's MOTHER, Elizabeth Barnet, had written to TJ on 20 Apr. 1801.

To ascertain the western boundary of New York in 1789-90, a surveying party headed by Andrew Ellicott had to enter territory under British control in CANADA (Mathews, *Ellicott*, 70-6).

UNFORTUNATE PARSON: in 1781, James Caldwell, a Presbyterian minister at Elizabeth and an ardent supporter of the American Revolution, was killed by an American sentry. Loyalists or the British were thought to be behind the shooting. Caldwell's wife had been killed the previous year by a bullet fired into a house, apparently by a British soldier, during fighting between American and British troops. Elias Boudinot oversaw the upbringing of the Caldwells' orphaned children, one of whom, John Edwards Caldwell, received part of his education in France under Lafayette's patronage. In June 1801, on the recommendation of Boudinot and Benjamin Rush, TJ appointed John E. Caldwell to a consular position at Santo Domingo. In

the middle of the nineteenth century, a monument to James and Hannah Caldwell was erected in Elizabeth's Presbyterian cemetery (Theodore Thayer, *As We Were: The Story of Old Elizabethtown*, vol. 13 of *The Collections of the New Jersey Historical Society* [Elizabeth, N.J., 1964], 110-11, 117, 127, 136, 149-50; Edwin F. Hatfield, *History of Elizabeth, New Jersey; Including the Early History of Union County* [New York, 1868], 523-36; Vol. 33:189-90, 663-4, 666-7, 676).

MR. MUNROE: in a letter to the secretary of state on 24 July 1796, James Monroe recommended Barnet's appointment as consul at Brest. Monroe wrote that Barnet "is well recommended to me in point of morality; appears to possess adequate talents, and from what I hear, is industrious." Monroe's acquaintance with Barnet was not extensive. Monroe, who for other reasons included that letter in his *View of the Conduct of the Executive*, also indicated that Brest was an important port that at the time lacked a U.S. consul (James Monroe, *A View of the Conduct of the Executive, in the Foreign Affairs of the United States, Connected with the Mission to the French Republic, During the Years 1794, 5, & 6* [Philadelphia, 1797], 354-5; Madison, *Papers, Sec. of State Ser.*, 3:123-4).

Barnet advanced funds for American seamen in need and to help Americans who were held by the French as PRISONERS of war after being captured on British ships (Marshall, *Papers*, 3:326-7; Madison, *Papers, Sec. of State Ser.*, 1:32, 258, 312; 2:211, 337; 3:352, 564-5; 4:19, 415).

Lee was the son-in-law of the deceased William PALFREY (Vol. 33:226n).

CHANCELANT: wavering.

From Robert Brent

SIR   Washington Sepr. 10th 1801.

Having understood that Mr. Meredith has resigned the office of Treasurer of the United States I take the liberty of informing you that I beg leave to be considered as a Candidate to fill this vacancy.

[253]

In imparting this wish to you, I cannot forbear assureing you that If I should be honored with the appointment, nothing shall be wanting on my part towards a proper discharge of it's duties—fully to justify your confidence and to meet with credit the utmost responsibility of the Station. But if the superior Claims of some other person, (and I am by no means sanguine, myself,) eventually shall induce you to prefer him for the appointment in question, be assured, Sir, that this Circumstance will not in the smallest degree diminish my attachment for your person, or lessen my zeal in your Administration: for on this, as on all other occasions you will have done, I am persuaded, what you think most conducive to the advantage of your Country. If however you should think favorably of my application, I would in that case procure abundant and the most respectable Testimonials in my favor if required.   In the mean time it may not be amiss to inform you that during the greater part of my life I have been much employed in the detail of Accts. having been trained to them from my Youth, and that I am at this time, & have long been a Director of the Bank of Columbia

I have the Honor to be, with great and respectful attachment, Sir, Your Most Obt Servt   ROBERT BRENT

RC (DNA: RG 59, LAR); endorsed by TJ as received 17 Sep. and so recorded in SJL with notation "Off."; also endorsed by TJ: "to be Treasurer."

Robert Brent (1764-1819), son of Robert and Anne Carroll Brent of Aquia, Virginia, had been a director of the Bank of Columbia since at least 1798. Brent resided with his father-in-law, Notley Young, in Washington, D.C., and was a justice of the peace in Washington County. In 1802, TJ appointed Brent to be the first mayor of Washington. TJ and his successor, James Madison, appointed Brent annually until this position became an elective office in 1812. In 1806, TJ appointed Brent to be a judge of the Orphan's Court for Washington County (Washington, *Papers, Pres. Ser.*, 9:20; *Washington Gazette*, 17-24 Mch. 1798; Bryan, *National Capital*, 1:467, 573; JEP, 1:388, 404, 2:33; RS, 1:12n).

From Henry Dearborn

SIR   Pittston Septr. 10th. 1801—

I have been honoured with your letter of the 21st. ulto. enclosing Mr. Stilmans long story concerning small armes.

He discovers a disposition to give you a specimen of Connecticut Ingenuity. I am not sufficiently aquainted with the perticular circumstancies relative to his contract, to be able to write to him until I arrive at the Seat of Government. I presume there will be no difficulty in settling the business.—I hope not to fail of seting out with my family for Washington by the 25th. inst.—

with sentiments of the highest respect I am Sir, Your Obedt. Huml. Servt. HENRY DEARBORN

RC (DLC); at foot of text: "The President of the U.S."; endorsed by TJ as received from the War Department on 1 Oct. and "Stilman's application" and so recorded in SJL.

From Andrew Moore

SIR   Rockbridge Cy. Augt. [i.e. Sep.] 10th. 1801

I receiv'd your Letter Informing me of the Marshals Commission being forwarded for me to Staunton—Within a few days past I however was Inform'd of it—And have taken the Oath requir'd—The returns of the Census were so imperfectly made—That I have been constantly employ'd in Correcting Errors—And have not been able to form a Genl. return before this day—Which I have forwarded by Post

I am Sir With Respt & Estm Yours &c   ANDREW MOORE

The Amount in this district Including Negroes is 282,368

RC (ViW); at foot of text: "Thos Jefferson Esq President of the U: States"; endorsed by TJ as received 15 Sep. and so recorded in SJL.   YOUR LETTER: TJ to Andrew Moore, 9 Aug. 1801.

From James Taylor, Jr.

SIR   Norfolk Sept: 10. 1801

Your letter of the 28th. August is received. Mr. Barnes will no doubt make the remittance you have directed; I had disposed of the two pipes which I informed you some time since were reserved for you, but the friend to whom they were sold, has consented to let me have them back, & they shall be forwarded by the first careful Skipper for Georgetown, to the care of Mr. Barnes, who, I presume, will take care of them—

I am respectfully Yr: ob: Servt.   JAS TAYLOR, JR.

RC (MHi); endorsed by TJ as received 24 Sep. and so recorded in SJL.

From "Tru Federalist"

SIR,   N.Y. Va. Sept. 10th. 1801

I the most unfortenate Hatter of all hatters Existing in this world have thought proper to inform You of my Grievences. Knowing my lord you are Compashioned to all men in distress, therefore I Hope you will Relieve me as I have but few friends in this County and the are like myself not able to relieve themselves of there many afflictions. Sir my Distemper is this I a your Election thought that Mr. Jno. Adams wold be Reelected and for me to give my vote To you wold be injurious to me there fore I Voted for Mr. adams. but Sir, I found my mistake on the forth of march. I was Calld. a federalist and go by that name Even my very hatt blocks go by that the will not answer to make a single Republickan Hatt what hatts I have blockd. on them Remains on hand my stock is out I have no money to purches a new and Even if I Had, I wold be at the needsesity of applying To the Republickan turner for new fashioned Republickan blocks and perhaps pay the price of a good bever hatt for Every block what an immens sum one gross wold amount to & then Sir, I wold be oblidge to Commit my old ones to The flames which has Cost me upward of fifty Dollars. Dredfull those Reflection are to me—I Hope Sir, you will investigate into my Situation and find how hard it is that I by one Single mistake am to be Reducd. to poverty my trade is undone money out and to beg I am afraid for I Shold make a poor hand of begging in a Republick nation I say no one can Relieve me but you alone if you wold but take Compashion on me and grant me a small office of profit for one year that I might Establish myself anew and Keep my Politick Sentiments under a Republick Cloak I then Shold Regain my Prior Customers & Resine my Commission for a worthy Demacrat to hold Sir I hope the Period is not yet arive when the awfull question is to be pronounced is he Honest is he Capable is he faithfull to the Constitution if that has Commenced there will be no Remedy for my loss which has alredy amounted to [14]01 Hatt blocks & keeps increasing there are but 99 more to Spend & then I must bid adieu to my honest Respective trade & seek Refuge in some Distant Place where I may enjoy some happy hours under so good a President

from your Humble Ser [P, Oblgendre]

           G H. TRU FEDERALIST

RC (DLC); endorsed by TJ as received 15 Sep. and so recorded in SJL.

From Hugh Williamson

SIR   New York 10th Septr. 1801.

This will be handed you by my brother John Williamson who now for the first Time has expressed a desire of being introduced to the President of the United States, for it is but a short Time since a system of government has been abdicated which for many years he has zealously opposed. Not that he is a bad citizen or pleased with controversy but he served his native country in arms during the revolution war and he does not forget that he had an Enemy who since the war has given too many proofs of hollow friendship.

My brother settled as a merchant, in Charleston, South Carolina, at the End of the war. That city as you know had been some years in the Possession of the Enemy and its commerce after the war was chiefly managed by British agents. Their first representative in Congress was little Wm Smith, himself warm from England & warmly supported by British influence. The Treaty, called Jay's, was uniformly supported by the same Influence and the same men. Parties were soon formed in Charleston; They were government or anti government men; Treaty or antitreaty men. Captn: Williamson chanced to be one of the very few American merchants in Charleston whose commercial capital placed him above the necessity of seeking British credit. He spoke and acted with perfect freedom. As he could not be suspected of sinister or selfish views and was by all who knew him of blameless Integrity his influence at elections was the greater, for he had embraced many opportunities of serving his fellow Citizens. He has now the satisfaction to find that a great and decided majority through the State have embraced the same political opinions with himself.

If there is any individual in Charleston of whose integrity or political opinions you may wish to be informed I think my brother will tell you what he knows of him or them with truth and sincerity.

I have the honour to be with the utmost consideration & Respect Your most obedient and very humble Servant

HU WILLIAMSON

RC (DLC); at foot of text: "The President of the United States"; endorsed by TJ as received 2 Nov. and so recorded in SJL.

A younger brother of Hugh Williamson, JOHN WILLIAMSON was the senior partner in the Charleston mercantile firm of Williamson & Stoney. After Hugh returned to America in 1776, he and John undertook a mercantile venture in Charleston, importing supplies from the West Indies for Continental forces. John also served as a captain in the First South

Carolina infantry during the Revolutionary War (ANB, s.v. "Williamson, Hugh"; South Carolina Historical and Genealogical Magazine, 47 [1946], 67; Heitman, Register, 597; Charleston City Gazette and Daily Advertiser, 19 Aug. 1805).

To John Davis

SIR   Monticello Sep. 11. 1801.

I have duly recieved your favor of Aug. 31. and am sensible of the honor you do me in proposing to dedicate to me the work you are about to publish. such a testimony of respect from an enlightened fellow citizen cannot but be flattering to me, and I have only to lament that the choice of the patron will be little likely to give circulation to the work. it's own merit however will supply this defect. should your journeyings have led you to observe on the same places or subjects on which I gave crude notes some years ago, I shall be happy to see them either corrected or confirmed by a more accurate observer. I pray you to accept assurances of my consideration & respect.

TH: JEFFERSON

PrC (DLC); at foot of text: "Mr. John Davis." Enclosed in TJ to Burr, 19 Nov.

In THE WORK that Davis dedicated to TJ, he included the above letter, with some variation, printing it under a date of 9 Sep. 1801, and substituting "enlightened Foreigner" for ENLIGHTENED FEL-

LOW CITIZEN. In a letter to TJ written in 1805, Davis acknowledged that inscribing his work to the third president made him "a hundred pounds richer" and helped him to return to Philadelphia and become a bookseller (Davis to TJ, 16 Feb. 1805, in DLC).

To John Drayton

SIR   Monticello Sep. 11. 1801.

Your favor of Aug. 20. was recieved yesterday. the commissions of Consuls or Commercial agents should regularly[1] be signed by the Executive of their state. none such having been commissioned as yet from France, mr Pichon their Commercial agent general & Chargé des affaires asked permission to name special agents himself to act till commissions in due form should be recieved. this was agreed to by us, but as no Exaquatur could be ratified in the usual way, on an agency of this kind mr Pichon thought it proper to inform the Governors of the states of his appointments. the credence you have given him therefore has been just. it is hardly probable another occasion will arise of authorising such a procedure. your enquiry relative to the expence of the French prisoners calling for a greater knowledge of detail than I possess here, I have forwarded it to the Secretary of the Navy & desired him to give you the information desired.

I recieve with great pleasure the assurance of your cooperation in our proceedings. it behoves us, as friends of the constitution, to avail our country of the powers they have confided to us, by doing whatsoever may give strength to the rights of the states reserved to them, & the rights of the general government in those matters granted to that, which constitute the excellence & the security of our political situation. be assured nothing on my part shall be wanting to do this, and that it will be my principal endeavor to settle such precedents for all proceedings as shall tend to keep the Executive within a safe & proper line. Accept assurances of my great esteem & high consideration & respect.   Th: Jefferson

PrC (DLC); at foot of text: "Governor Drayton."

FORWARDED IT TO THE SECRETARY: on 23 Sep., Robert Smith wrote Drayton, notifying him that the president had forwarded Drayton's letter "on the subject of the French prisoners at Charleston." Smith explained that L. A. Pichon had informed him that measures were under-

way to send them to Saint-Domingue. Regarding payment for the expenses incurred for their maintenance, Smith wrote that the new navy agent at Charleston "will have directions to take upon himself the settlement of that business" (Lb in DNA: RG 45, MLS).

[1] Word interlined.

From Pierpont Edwards

SIR,   Hartford Sept 11th 1801

Mr Jackson Browne, whom I took the liberty to mention in a former letter, woud be highly gratified should he be appointed Consul at some place, at which the people of the United States carry on an extensive commerce—At his desire I report to you his wishes in this regard—I shoud be pleased to see him placed in some office in which he woud be useful to himself and to our Country. I am with respect and esteem

Your most Obed Servt   P Edwards

RC (DNA: RG 59, LAR); at foot of text: "His Excellency Thomas Jefferson"; endorsed by TJ as received 1 Oct. and "Jackson Browne to some office" and so recorded in SJL. Enclosure: Browne to Edwards, 6 June, requesting to be brought to the president's attention as an applicant for an office (RC in same).

JACKSON BROWNE was an educated West Indian Creole from Barbados who relocated to Connecticut about 1789. He had amassed a sizable fortune before falling on hard times, including near bankruptcy and a fatal house fire on 13 Apr. 1801 in which he lost a daughter as well as all of his papers and apparel.

Browne appealed to his friend Alexander J. Dallas on 6 June, after learning of a possible vacancy in the Middletown collectorship and Dallas forwarded his request to Albert Gallatin (Gallatin, *Papers*, 5:125-7; Hartford *American Mer-*

cury, 28 May; Norwich *Courier,* 23 Sep.).

FORMER LETTER: probably Edwards to TJ, 15 June, not found but recorded by TJ in SJL as received 26 June with notation "N. Haven [Brown]."

To Theodore Foster

DEAR SIR   Monticello Sep. 11. 1801.

I am very tardy in acknoleging the reciept of your favor of July 25. because being obliged to conduct here, the same business which would occur at Washington, I have often long letters to write here, where a few words there would do the business; so that in truth I am much more pressed here than there. that it is very desireable that a periodical work of the kind you describe should be undertaken there can be no doubt. it would indeed be valuable if at the close of every year, when truth has been able to rise to the surface & separate itself from the lies of the day, a judicious person would set himself to work to select & record the truths & to contradict the lies. when I read the newspapers & see what a mass of falshood & what an atom of truth they contain, I am mortified with the consideration that $\frac{99}{100}$ths. of mankind pass through life imagining they have known what was going forward when they would have been nearer to truth had they heard nothing. I have as little doubt that you will well execute this charge. I know your industry, your accuracy and your attachment to truth, and that your opportunities of coming at the true springs & motives of transactions will be far better than most others possess. I shall willingly assure you of every service I can render the undertaking: not with the pen, for it is a sacred rule with me to write nothing I do not put my name to, but by communicating to you verbally whatever may enable you to decide between falshood & truth, and to give to posterity a genuine view of the transactions of the day. I am sure my fellow labourers will do the same. I pray you to accept assurances of my friendly esteem & high consideration.   TH: JEFFERSON

PrC (DLC); at foot of text: "The honble Theodore Foster."

PERIODICAL WORK: in his 25 July letter to TJ, Foster described his plans for "an *annual Publication,* intended to give a *correct* Historical View of the great Na-

tional Measures, adopted by the Government, *illustrative of the Reasons and Motives of the Public Counsels more especially those of the Executive Power, so far as they may be known and it may be proper to publish them.*"

From Peter Freneau

SIR   Charleston, September 11th. 1801.

I do myself the honor of inclosing you a letter from Col. David Hopkins, a citizen of this State who has been confined for a considerable time past in gaol, for the non-payment of a penalty incurred under one of the revenue laws of the United States.   Before Mr Pinckney left this for Spain, he was kind enough to write a letter in behalf of Hopkins to Mr Gallatin. Since his departure Mr Gallatin has informed me that he is precluded from granting relief, the case having been decided on by the late Secretary Mr Wolcott, but that he would transmit the papers to you who alone could extend it. In consequence of this information Col. Hopkins has written the inclosed letter and requested me to forward it to you, nothing but a wish to serve an unfortunate man, who I really believe has erred through ignorance, could induce me to trespass on your time, I trust Sir, that this plea will be a sufficient excuse for my intrusion.

With the most perfect respect, I have the honor to be, Sir, your most obedient & Very humble Servant   PETER FRENEAU

RC (DLC); endorsed by TJ as received 1 Oct. and so recorded in SJL with notation "Hopkins pardon"; also endorsed by TJ: "refd. to the Secy. of the Treasury. Th:J Oct. 3 1801"; notation by Gallatin: "A pardon has been signed by the President & transmitted to Mr Freneau— A.G."

On 4 June, Charles PINCKNEY had written Gallatin IN BEHALF OF David Hopkins, enclosing correspondence between Hopkins and Freneau and requesting that the secretary exercise his "humane interference in favor of an aged sufferer under the excise" (Gallatin, *Papers*, 5:96).

ENCLOSURE

From David Hopkins

SIR,   Chester Court House. S,C. 31st. August. 1801—

I have been here ever since last February confin'd within the bounds of this prison on a Ca, Sa. under the Authority of the United States for making default in the Revenue law respecting Stills &Ca. (as is said) the propriety of which I doubt—I have ever since been trying by myself and friends to find some proper method of getting released without paying the money, but all unfortunately seems to appear ineffectual and here I remain still in a very disagreeable situation—every effort that I tho't necessary to bring the matter to a right understanding has been laid before the Secretary, but all to no purpose—Mr. Gallitan I think has paid every attention in his power to my situation, but don't appear to possess the means required. He has very politely promised to transmit the documents to you, which I humbly trust will meet your attention, & serious consideration, and let me know your determination thereon.—A similar circumstance transpired in this district some time passed—A Mr. Gaston was cited to attend the Federal Court in Charleston as a defaulter in this Law, Gaston fortunately attended and there proved to the Satisfaction of the Court that Mr. Davie who was the prosecutor of both me and Gaston, during the time he was Collector never kept an Office in the district, on which grounds he was acquitted—If I am not wrong informed these are facts now remaining of Record—I also see a clause in the first Act passed on this Subject making provisions that where a man Occupies only one Still for his own use under the Capacity of 50 Gallons shall not be liable to the penalties, or words tantamount—but whether this clause has been repealed or not, I am not able to say—My Still never was gaged till of late, that is, after Mr. Davie resigned, and that at 35 Gallons & only occupied for my own family use. For any further particular facts I refer you to the documents which I expect will be transmitted to you by Mr. Gallitan—I am now an old man, near 70 years of age. I bore an oppressive part in our Revolution—My own exertions were never wanting in that business—My property harrased, and also partly lost the use of one of my Arms by a Wound in the field of Action; I have always been willing to Submit to just Laws when rightly administred; I have now a large family to command my attention & should also be better employed looking forward after things unseen than to be here tortur'd in this manner. it appears as tho' it might be a happy change, if the Wise disposer of events would remove me off this transitory stage, if nothing else can be done for me

If Sir you can think it will comport with your elivated station in life to condescend to take my case into consideration & if you can do any thing for me by remitting the fine &c. I should be very glad—If you may think a Petition in my behalf would be requisite, I can have one forwarded under the Signature of some hundreds of influential and respectable characters in this country. I hope to receive an Answer by the earliest conveyances as my situation demands it. Your attention to this business will confer a real Obligation on Sir One of Your constituents And Most Obedient Servant

DD. HOPKINS

RC (DLC); endorsed by TJ as received 1 Oct. and so recorded in SJL.

A native of Virginia, David Hopkins (1737-1816) migrated to South Carolina before the American Revolution and eventually settled in the area that became Chester District. A large landholder, he attained the rank of lieutenant colonel during the war and served in the General Assembly twice during the 1780s (*S.C. Biographical Directory, House of Representatives*, 3:343-4).

CA SA: *ca. sa.*, the abbreviation for *capias ad satisfaciendum*, "that you take to satisfy," or a writ ordering the sheriff to hold the defendant until the judgment is satisfied.

DOCUMENTS WHICH I EXPECT WILL BE TRANSMITTED TO YOU: Hopkins also wrote Gallatin on 31 Aug., requesting that "you will forward the documents in my behalf to the President as soon as may be, As also my Letter to him accompanying this, Soliciting his determination" (Gallatin, *Papers*, 5:666).

After learning that his fine had been remitted, Hopkins wrote TJ a brief letter on 14 Nov., expressing gratitude "for the favor conferred upon me" and offering "my most sincere & unfeigned thanks" (RC in DLC; endorsed by TJ as received 21 Dec. and so recorded in SJL).

To Albert Gallatin

DEAR SIR   Monticello Sep. 11. 1801.

I inclose you a note, which tho' it came unsigned, as you see it, I know by the handwriting came from Tenche Coxe. you will judge whether it contains any thing calling for attention. it was accompanied by an Aurora of Aug. 22. in which was a piece signed A Pensylvanian with numerous corrections with the pen. it is the way in which he usually made known to me the pieces he wrote.   I also inclose a letter in answer to one of mine on the subject of *Chisholm.*ˣ it is merely to shew that from the state of his affairs, he is one of those who should be held to punctuality.   this mail is also come without bringing me any thing relative to the public dispatches which came by the Maryland. Mr. Madison left me on Monday, not very well, & I have no letter from him by the post. possibly he has recieved the dispatches by the Maryland, & will forward them by special conveyance. Accept assurances of my affectionate esteem & high consideration.   TH: JEFFERSON

Sep. 12. since writing this the French dispatches are recd by express from Mr. Madison who is recovered.

ˣ*Chisman* is meant.

RC (NHi: Gallatin Papers); addressed: "Albert Gallatin Secretary of the Treasury Washington Columbia"; endorsed by Gallatin. PrC (DLC); lacks author's note and postscript. Enclosure: Samuel Sheild to TJ, 31 Aug. 1801. Other enclosure printed below.

The author of the article signed "A Pennsylvanian" in the Philadelphia AURORA of 22 Aug. defended TJ against charges that he had removed several officeholders because of their political opinions. The author observed that the late John Wilkes Kittera was not removed by TJ, because he was never "invested with the office of attorney of the United States." Henry Miller was not removed on account of his political opinions, but because he did not settle his accounts or pay his balance. In New Hampshire, William Gardner and Joseph Whipple were well educated, "punctual, regular, upright and excellent officers," who were understood to have been dismissed by Adams "soon after refusing to sign a very strong, and (to them) unsatisfactory address to President Adams, the contents of which were against their judgments." TJ restored Gardner and Whipple to the offices they had lost, and in the process John Pierce and Thomas Martin, their successors, were dismissed. "A Pennsylvanian" noted that he had unsuccessfully attempted to have his article printed in the *Lancaster Journal.* When the "essay was refused a place on a plea of want of candor," he submitted it without changes to William Duane. The piece as sent by Coxe to TJ WITH NUMEROUS CORRECTIONS WITH THE PEN has not been found. For TJ's assessment of the removals, see Vol. 33:669, 671-6.

Memorandum from Tench Coxe

[before 10 Sep.]

Note on the act of the President of the United States of the — of — 1801. relative to the internal Revenues.

By the constitution of the United States (Sect. 8 art. 1) it is ordained, that all duties imposts and excises shall be uniform throughout the U.S. All the internal revenues have been collected in the N.W. Territory, as well as in Virginia, Pennsa. or Massachusetts. It was discovered, that the act of the President of the U.S of 1791, made while the Secy. of the Treasury superintended that service, did not provide for the collection of those duties in the Northwestern territory. Tho inconsiderable, the constitution was against the omission. It is submitted whether the Mississippi Territory is not at this time in the same situation

MS (NHi: Gallatin Papers); undated; in Coxe's hand; endorsed by TJ: "Cox Tench." Recorded in SJL as received 10 Sep.

TJ signed the order RELATIVE TO THE INTERNAL REVENUES on 29 July. In the executive order of 15 Mch. 1791, Washington set up the surveys in the 13 states, each being a separate district, appointed the officers, and established their compensation. TJ's order of 29 July established the Northwest revenue district (Washington, *Papers, Pres. Ser.*, 7:568-74; Gallatin to TJ, 28 July; Executive Order on Revenue Districts, 29 July 1801).

To William Gardiner

SIR   Monticello Sep. 11. 1801.

The nomination of the principal officers of the government only resting with me, and all subordinate places being in the gift of those immediately superintending them, I return you the letters you were pleased to inclose me as they may be useful to you should you propose to make application to those directly who have the appointment in their several lines. if any vacancy be to be found it is less likely to be in the principal offices at Washington (which I know to be overflowing) than in the seaports & other distant places. it would have given me real pleasure to have been able to answer your friendly letter more to your satisfaction. accept my salutations & good wishes.

TH: JEFFERSON

PrC (DLC); at foot of text: "Mr. William Gardiner. Baltimore."; endorsed by TJ in ink on verso.

YOUR FRIENDLY LETTER: Gardiner to TJ, 2 Sep.

To Anthony Haswell

SIR   Monticello Sep. 11. 1801.

Your favor of July 20. came to me at this place. I am sorry to learn from that that the officers in the public employment still use the influence and the business of their offices to encourage presses which disseminate principles contrary to those on which our constitution is built. this evil will be remedied. we proceed with circumspection to avoid doing any wrong. your press having been in the habit of inculcating the genuine principles of our constitution, and your sufferings for those principles, entitle you to any favors in your line which the public servants can give you; and those who do not give them, act against their duty. should you continue in the business you will have the publication of the laws in your state, & probably whatever else of business any of the offices within your state can give. accept my salutations & best wishes.   TH: JEFFERSON

PrC (DLC); at foot of text: "Mr. Anthony Haswell. Bennington."

YOU WILL HAVE THE PUBLICATION OF THE LAWS: in 1802, Anthony Haswell & Co. published the *Acts and Laws Passed by the Legislature of the State of Vermont, at Their Session at Burlington.* Alden Spooner, printer of the weekly *Vermont Journal* in Windsor, who had published the acts and laws for the state in 1801, received the contract again in 1803, 1804, and 1805. From his Bennington office in the western district, Haswell vied with Spooner, who identified himself as the "Printer to the State of Vermont, for the Eastern District" for the annual printing of the journals of the general assembly (Shaw-Shoemaker, Nos. 1578, 1579, 1580, 3458, 3460, 5501, 5502, 7658, 7659, 9655, 9656; Haswell to TJ, 10 May 1801).

To James Madison

DEAR SIR   Monticello Sep. 11. 1801.

I have no letter from you by the mail, whence I conclude I may possibly recieve something by private conveyance. a letter from miss Paine to Virginia Randolph saying nothing of your health makes me hope it is reestablished. I inclose you a letter from Genl. Saml. Smith with Barney's letter to him. it contains matters worthy of some attention. I do not believe that Murray would endeavor to defeat the treaty. on the contrary I believe he would be anxious to get it through. however the more I reflect on it the more I am satisfied it's non-¹ratification is unimportant, and will give us all the benefits of peace & commercial relations without the embarrasments of a treaty.—you will recieve by this post my letter to the Bey of Tunis, &

one to Rob. R. Livingston on Neutral rights; both open, & to be forwarded. I have recieved no letter by this post from mr Gallatin which augurs ill of the situation of his family, as he has had occasion to write me weekly on a great variety of matter. Accept assurances of my constant & affectionate esteem & great respect.　　Th: Jefferson

RC (NjP); at foot of text: "The Secretary of state." PrC (DLC). Enclosures: (1) Samuel Smith to TJ, 29 Aug., enclosing Joshua Barney to Smith, 11 July. (2) TJ to Hammuda Pasha, Bey of Tunis, 9 Sep. (3) TJ to Robert R. Livingston, 9 Sep.

Virginia Randolph: a sister-in-law of Martha Jefferson Randolph and the youngest child of Anne Cary Randolph and Thomas Mann Randolph, Sr. Commonly known as "Jenny," she became a permanent resident at Monticello until her marriage in 1805 to her cousin, Wilson Jefferson Cary. TJ's granddaughter named Virginia Randolph was born at Monticello on 22 Aug. 1801 (Daniels, *Randolphs of Virginia*, xii, xiii, 133, 134, 214, 240; Malone, *Jefferson*, 4:160).

[1] Prefix and hyphen interlined.

From James Madison

Dear Sir　　　　　　　　　　　　　　Sepr. 11. 1801

The mail of wednesday brought the despatches from France which ought to have come in the preceding one. I enclose them with sundry other letters &c. They would have been sent yesterday but an express could not readily be procured. I have engaged the Bearer a free negro of good character to deliver them to you as early today as he can accomplish the ride. He is to receive a dollar & a half per day, counting a day for going, the like for returning, and adding the time he may be detained. As it may not be convenient for you to read the papers in time to return them, with any directions you may wish, by the post of tomorrow, you can keep him as long as may be necessary. I shall be glad to have the letters back which require answers that may be prepared for the mail in course.

The complaint I brought with me from Monticello proved more slight than I apprehended. It has kept me however little fit for business since my return, and I do not yet find myself in the state to be desired. I shall nevertheless take up the subject of instructions for Mr. L that no delay may happen. Be so good as to let me know when the Boston will be ready, and any account if any you have as to Mr. Livingstons forwardness for embarking. I have not yet recd. from Wagner some papers required to assist my agency in the case, nor do I recollect that the Commission & letters of Credence were signed before we left Washington. Perhaps these may have gone on to you yesterday. As it has been objected to Murray, that he had no *special* commission, it might not be amiss to add one to Mr. L. if it could be done without delay.

Bishop Madison & Doctor Jones being with me, & understanding that I am sending a Messenger to Monticello, charge me to tender you their particular respects.

With the sincerest attachment I am Dear Sir yours

JAMES MADISON

RC (DLC); at foot of text: "The President of the U. States"; endorsed by TJ as received from the State Department on 11 Sep. and so recorded in SJL. Enclosures: see below.

For the dispatches FROM FRANCE, see Robert Smith to TJ, 31 Aug. OTHER LETTERS: see TJ to Madison, 12 Sep.

INSTRUCTIONS FOR MR. L: for the papers Madison awaited from Wagner, relating to instructions for Robert R. Livingston, see Madison, *Papers, Sec. of State Ser.*, 2:76-7. Around 17 Sep., Madison prepared a draft of instructions for Livingston, which were abandoned in favor of his final instructions of 28 Sep. (same, 2:120-22, 142-7).

To Ignatius Palyart

Monticello. Sep. 11. 1801.

Th: Jefferson presents his respects to the Consul General of his R.H. the Prince Regent of Portugal; regrets that he was not at Washington when he visited that place, thanks him for the kind offer of services proposed, and having nothing to trouble him with, wishes him a pleasant voyage & happy sight of his friends.

PrC (ViW); endorsed by TJ in ink on verso.

To Joseph T. Scott

SIR   Monticello Sep. 11. 1801.

Your favor dated June 13. came to me at this place only one week ago. it is probable that mr Cummings has deposited for me at Washington the copy of your geographical dictionary which you have been so kind as to send me, for which I pray you to accept my thanks. I anticipate with pleasure the satisfaction I shall recieve from it, and am happy that we are to see at length contradicted the miserable libels which have been published on the Southern states. I pray you to accept assurances of my esteem & high consideration.

TH: JEFFERSON

PrC (DLC); at foot of text: "Mr. Joseph Scott Philadelphia"; endorsed by TJ in ink on verso.

To Robert Smith

DEAR SIR   Monticello Sep. 11. 1801.

I have just recieved from Govr. Drayton a letter [on] the subject of the French prisoners there, with copies of those which had passed between him and the French agent, which I inclose you. in his letter to me is this passage. 'I should be glad to know in what manner the expences of the said prisoners are to be defrayed: whether by the US. or the French republic. for as they were brought in here in a prize to one of the US. vessels of war it is a national business altogether, & one in which this state has only taken a part to forward the more extensive operations of the union.' I have said to him that you will be so good as to write [to] him on this subject.

I also inclose you a letter from Judge Tucker of this state on the subject of Doctr. Barraud. being unacquainted with the circumstances I can only add that Barraud is a man very much respected. I recieved some time ago a letter in his favor from Bishop Madison, which is at Washington where I can communicate it to you for [consi]deration.

I have duly recieved your favor of the 4th. I know not what may be the policy of France in declining the ratification of the treaty, but the more I reflect on it, the more I consider it's ratification as very uninteresting. [the] restoration of prizes might be provided for by [a sin]gle sentence. we [shall] then [. . .] all the relations of peace & commerce, without the embarrasment [of a] treaty, on which footing I wish we stood with every nation. the public letters by the Maryland had not come to mr Madison's hands on the 7th. when he left us. I have no letter from him by this post, so that I do not know whether it has brought him those dispatches. in the mean time mr Livingston is notified to be in readiness, as the Boston should also be. Accept my sincere esteem & high respect.

                                                   TH: JEFFERSON

PrC (DLC); faint; at foot of text: "The Secretary of the Navy." Enclosures: (1) John Drayton to TJ, 20 Aug. (2) St. George Tucker to TJ, 5 Sep.

The letter from BISHOP James Madison about Philip Barraud was probably one of 19 Apr. 1801 that has not been found; see note to TJ to Bishop Madison, 9 May.

Not until 18 Sep. did the Navy Department have word that the BOSTON had reached New York. Abishai Thomas immediately sent instructions to complete preparations for the transatlantic voyage, anticipating that the order for the frigate to sail would come "in a very few days." The departure had to await preparation of Livingston's final instructions, and then on 1 Oct. Smith ordered Daniel McNeill, the ship's commander, to sail as soon as he had the minister's party on board (Thomas to Daniel Ludlow, 17, 18 Sep. 1801, in Lb in DNA: RG 45, MLS; Smith to McNeill, 22 Sep., in Lb in same, LSO; NDBW, 1:587-8).

From Robert Smith

SIR,   Baltimore Sep. 11. 1801

I have great satisfaction in informing you that the Elections in the State of Maryland for Electors of the State Senate have terminated in favor of the Republicans. I hasten to give you this information from the knowledge that you are sensible of its great importance in the national Councils. We have retained our ground in all the Counties in which we had succeeded in the last Election and we have prevailed in Counties in which we had failed in the last election. This so far denotes the progress of republicanism. It is, besides, a proof that the recent illiberal and abusive clamor about certain trivial proceedings has not produced in this State any injurious impressions.

A mournful event in my family, the death of my eldest son, has detained me here some days.

Accept the assurances of my great regard & esteem

RT SMITH

RC (DLC); endorsed by TJ as received from the Navy Department. Recorded in SJL as received 17 Sep.

Republicans in Maryland carried the elections for ELECTORS OF THE STATE SENATE by a wide margin. Convening in Annapolis on 21 Sep. to choose a new state senate, the electors carried the entire Republican ticket into office, filling all fifteen senate seats and assuring that a Republican would be chosen at the next election for U.S. senator. In November the Maryland senate replaced Federalist Senator William Hindman with Robert Wright, a Republican (*National Intelligencer,* 11, 16, 21, 25 Sep. 1801; *Biog. Dir. Cong.*).

To Samuel Harrison Smith

DEAR SIR   Monticello Sep. 11. 1801.

Your favor of the 4th. is recieved. I formerly, at the desire of mr T. P. Smith wrote to Bishop Madison, President of Wm. & Mary college in Williamsburg to know whether there was room for him in that institution as professor of Chemistry. the answer was communicated to mr Smith. from it's tenor, and from the course of that institution since I do not suppose it in a situation to offer him any thing which ought to attract his attention, & certainly not to make him forego the offers made him in France. his continuance there, till something useful may turn up here, will in my opinion be advantageous to himself, & increase his qualifications to be useful here whenever he shall return. accept my best wishes & assurances of esteem.

TH: JEFFERSON

RC (DLC: J. Henley Smith Papers); addressed: "Samuel Harrison Smith Washington. Col."; franked; endorsed by Smith. PrC (DLC).

TJ wrote to Bishop James MADISON on the subject of Thomas Peters Smith on 6 Jan. 1800 (Vol. 31:291-2).

To John Barnes

DEAR SIR   Monticello Sep. 12. 1801.

Your favor of the 7th came to hand on the 10th. by the delay of your journey to Philadelphia I am afraid my arrearages are inconvenient to you. I write to Gibson & Jefferson by this day's post to forward you a thousand dollars instantly. they will recieve my letter on the same day you recieve this, and if they can procure good paper immediately, it may be with you by the time you originally fixed for your journey. mr Hanse I presume will be contented to recieve his money the first week of Oct. when further funds will come in, or perhaps half then & half the first week in Nov. which will be an accomodation. his whole bill is 1206. Dol. I should have no objection to Daugherty's going personally for the carriage; but by no means to take one of my horses. the one he proposes particularly is 15. years old, and entirely unequal to such a journey. it would unquestionably destroy him, & he would leave the carriage on the road. I know his strength exactly, & that it is only equal to moderate service at home. a pair of good horses must be hired, as before proposed, and I presume the owner will not hire his horses without himself. the road by Baltimore & Havre de grace is the best, and [. . .] miles shorter than by Lancaster. the former order for the sheeting may as well lie, to be executed in the course of the winter with a supply of counterpanes, feathers &c. I am very glad to hear of the arrival of mr LeMaire. I shall be in Washington without fail on the 30th. inst. if not a day or two sooner. accept assurances of my sincere & affectionate esteem.   TH: JEFFERSON

PrC (CSmH); faint; at foot of text: "Mr. J. Barnes"; endorsed by TJ in ink on verso.

To Napoleon Bonaparte

CITIZEN FIRST CONSUL,

I have made choice of Robert R. Livingston, one of our distinguished citizens, to reside near the French Republic in quality of Minister Plenipotentiary of the United States of America. He is well apprized of the friendship which we bear to your Republic, and of our desire to cultivate the harmony and good correspondence so happily subsisting between us. From a knowledge of his fidelity, probity and good conduct, I have entire confidence that he will render himself acceptable to you, and give effect to our desire of preserving and advancing on all occasions the interest and happiness of the two nations. I beseech you, therefore, Citizen First Consul to give full credence to whatever he shall say on the part of the United States, and most of all when he shall assure you of their friendship and wishes for the prosperity of the French Republic: and I pray God to have you, Citizen First Consul, in his safe and holy keeping.

Written at the City of Washington the twelfth day of September, in the year of our Lord one thousand Eight hundred and one.

Th: Jefferson

FC (Lb in DNA: RG 59, Credences); in a clerk's hand; at head of text: "Thomas Jefferson, President of the United States of America, To the First Consul of the French Republic"; at foot of text: "By the President James Madison, Secretary of State." Tr (NHi: Robert R. Livingston Papers); in hand of Thomas Sumter, Jr.; at head of text: "Copy of letter of credence"; endorsed by Sumter as a copy of the letter delivered to Bonaparte on 6 Dec. 1801. Tr in Lb (same).

Livingston presented the letter of credence to Bonaparte in a public audience on 6 Dec., a few days after Livingston's arrival in Paris. Livingston reported that in accordance with the "present etiquette" of the French government, the letter was not read on that occasion but was handed to Talleyrand (Madison, *Papers, Sec. of State Ser.*, 2:302-3). TJ's formal letter of appointment of Livingston as minister plenipotentiary to the Republic of France, authorizing him "to do and perform all such matters and things, as to the said place or office do appertain, or as may be duly given you in charge hereafter," was dated at Washington, 2 Oct. 1801 (RC in NHi: Gilder Lehrman Collection at the Gilder Lehrman Institute of American History, in a clerk's hand, signed by TJ and countersigned by Madison, with seal of the United States; FC in Lb in DNA: RG 59, Credences, in a clerk's hand; Tr in Lb in NHi: Robert R. Livingston Papers).

To Henry Dearborn

Dear Sir   Monticello Sep. 12. 1801

In my letter of the 14th. of August I inclosed you a note respecting some abuses said to have been committed in the works at Newport. tho' I am since informed that the facts are possibly or even probably true, yet I find they were sent to me under a forged name. this may render circumspection necessary, as it certainly lessens the probability of the truth of the information. I thought it proper to put you on your guard, that you might shape your enquiries accordingly. be pleased to speak with mr Christopher Ellery, Senator for R.I. on the subject, if you meet with him. I shall leave this place this day fortnight for Washington. accept assurances of my sincere esteem & high respect. Th: Jefferson

PrC (DLC); at foot of text: "Genl. Dearborne."

From Albert Gallatin

Dear Sir City of Washington Septer. 12th 1801

This will be handed by Mr M. L. Davies of New York, the candidate for the naval office. I used my endeavours to prevent his proceeding to Monticello; but he had left New York with that intention & is not easily diverted from his purpose. The reason he gives for his anxiety is that, immediately after the adjournt. of Congress, E. Livingston & others mentioned to him that a positive arrangement was made by the administration by which he was to be appointed to that office; that he was so perfectly confident, till some time in June, that such was the fact, as to refuse advantageous proposals of a permanent establishment; & that the general belief on that subject has placed him in a very awkward situation at New York.

He presses me much on the ground of my personal knowledge both of him & of the local politics of N. York, to give you my opinion in a decided manner on that subject; which to him I declined; both, because in one respect it was not made up, & because my own opinion even if decided neither ought nor would decide yours. The propriety of removing Rogers remains with me the doubtful point; after Fish's removal & that of others, they, in N.Y., seem to suppose that the dismission of Rogers is, on account of antirevolutionary adherence to enemies, unavoidable; the answer to New Haven appears to have left no doubt on their mind on that subject; and I apprehend that the numerous removals already made by you there, & the almost general sweep by their State Government have only encreased the anxiety & expectation of a total change. In relation to Rogers himself, though he is a good officer, I would feel but little regret at his being dismissed, because he has no claim detached from having fulfilled his official duties, has made an independent fortune by that office, & having no personal popularity cannot lose us one friend nor make us one enemy. But I feel a great reluctance in yielding to that general spirit of persecution which, in that State particularly, disgraces our cause & sinks us on a level with our predecessors. Whether policy must yield to principle, by going farther into those removals, than justice to our political friends & the public welfare seem to require, is a question on which I do not feel myself, at present, capable of deciding. I have used the word "persecution" & I think with propriety; for the Council of appointts. have extended their removals to almost every auctioneer, &, that not being a political office, the two parties ought certainly to have an equal chance in such appointments.

As to the other point; if Rogers shall be removed, I have no hesitation in saying that I do not know a man whom I would prefer to Mr Davis for that office. This may, however, be owing to my knowing him better than I do others who may be[1] equally well qualified. I believe Davis to be a man of talents, (particularly quickness & correctness) suited for the office, of strict integrity, untainted[2] reputation, & pure republican principles. Nor am I deterred from saying so far in his favour on account of any personal connection with any other individual; because I am convinced that his political principles stand not on the frail basis of *persons*, but are exclusively bottomed on his conviction of their truth, & will ever govern his political conduct. So far, as I think a prejudice against him in that respect existed, I consider myself, in justice to him, bound to declare as my sincere opinion. Farther I cannot go.

As the mail will reach you only one day later than Mr Davis, I will defer writing on business till Monday. The elections of Maryland are decisively in our favour—26 to 14 is the probable result—a majority certain.

I feel in better health & better spirits since the change of weather which, together with change of air, seems to have had a favorable effect on my child's health. Mrs Gallatin & her daughter 3 weeks old are very well. Robert Smith is & will continue absent for some time longer. On his arriving home last Saturday, he found his eldest son dead; & his wife expects daily to be confined. S. Smith who wrote me on the subject that this ought to hasten Mr Madison's return, & that friends & foes begin to complain of long *absences*. I wish earnestly we may all meet as early as possible; yet do not apprehend any inconvenience to have yet resulted for the public service from your absence.

I am with sincere respect & attachment Your obt. Servt.

ALBERT GALLATIN

I enclose recommendations sent to me in favr. of Davis

RC (DLC); addressed: "Thomas Jefferson President of the United States"; endorsed by TJ as received from the Treasury Department on 17 Sep. and so recorded in SJL. Enclosures: (1) John Swartwout to Gallatin, New York, 1

Sep., noting that Matthew L. Davis had received information from Edward Livingston in April "that he had been favorably mentioned to the President, for the office of Naval officer of this Port," and with that expectation Davis had declined a position with a salary of $1,500 per year and had kept his friends from seeking a state appointment for him, and while the government could not be held responsible for Livingston's indiscretion, it placed Davis in an "unpleasant Situation"; also noting that the removal of Richard Rogers, "Independent of his disaffection to the Revolution," would give general satisfaction because "his Manners, his gross and Unaccomodating temper, Renders him disgusting (as an officer) to a very great proportion of our Citizens of both interests"; recommending Davis for his industry and integrity, Swartwout predicts that his appointment "would gratify the Public as much as any appointment that has been Made by the administration" (RC in DNA: RG 59, LAR; endorsed by TJ: "Swartwout. to mr Gallatin" and "Davis"). (2) David Gelston to Gallatin, New York, 4 Sep., contradicting reports "industriously propagated, with a view to injure" Davis, the New York customs collector notes that Davis is a 30-year-old New Yorker, married seven years, and of respectable parentage, with a father who died of wounds received in defense of his country; Davis's "knowlege in accounts, and his uncommon assiduity, and peculiar talent of dispatch in business," Gelston concludes, "qualify him eminently for a complete discharge of the duties of the office, which public report has long since assigned to him" (RC in same; endorsed by TJ: "Gelston David. to mr Gallatin. Davis to be Naval officer"). (3) Ezekiel Robins to Gallatin, New York, 6 Sep., recommending Davis as of "excellent Moral Character" and as "a firm and decided Republican" who "has uniformly exerted himself at all our Elections in favour of the Republican Interest," and noting that in case of the removal of Rogers, "which would be highly gratifying to the Republicans," the appointment of Davis "would meet the general Approbation of our Republican fellow Citi-

zens" (RC in same; endorsed by TJ: "Robins Ezekl. to mr Gallatin" and "Davis"). (4) Tunis Wortman to Gallatin, New York, 4 Sep., arguing for the propriety of removing Rogers, observing that not only were his principles "peculiarly hostile to our revolution," but his manners were "rigid and austere, and his conduct marked with bitterness and asperity towards the Republicans," thus giving him "no pretentions whatsoever to the patronage of government"; while believing it "presumptious of him to give any recommendation," Wortman informed Gallatin that it was long the prevailing belief that Davis had been selected for the position, and he could testify that "in the worst of times he was an advocate of public liberty" and a man of business and respectable talents (RC in same; endorsed by TJ: "Wortman to mr Gallatin" and "Davis"). (5) Henry Rutgers to Gallatin, New York, 7 Sep., recommending Davis as a person well qualified to serve as naval officer, knowing that the public service "will be strictly attended to" (RC in same; endorsed by TJ: "Rutgers Henry to mr Gallatin" and "Davis").

Matthew L. Davis probably HANDED TJ a 6 Sep. letter from John Rathbone to Gallatin as well. Writing from New York, Rathbone supported the appointment of a U.S. consul at Newry in Ireland, owing to the great increase of commercial intercourse between the United States and the Irish port in recent years. He recommended Trevor Corey, a partner at the house of Isaac Corey & Sons at Newry, as a person of "talents and unimpeachable integrity" capable of filling the position. Rathbone indicated that Davis could give Gallatin information about the applicant (RC in DNA: RG 59, LAR; endorsed by TJ: "Rathbone to mr Gallatin to be Consul at Newry").

Edward LIVINGSTON wrote TJ a brief, undated letter of introduction for Davis, who was about to pay his respects to TJ at Monticello. Livingston observed that "he is a gentleman whose principles and talents have commanded my Esteem & will I think justify the introduction I have presumed to give" (RC in MHi; at foot of text: "Thos Jefferson President of the US."; endorsed by TJ. Recorded in SJL as received 17 Sep.).

EXTENDED THEIR REMOVALS: for the power of the Council of Appointment in New York, which included the governor and four state senators, see Vol. 32:304n. When George Clinton succeeded John Jay as governor in August 1801, the impediment to the removal of Federalist officeholders was dissolved. The council, dominated by the Livingstons and Clintonians, also determined that Burr and his followers should receive no patronage. The governor and Robert R. Livingston had misgivings about the extreme measures against Burr, but George Clinton would not defy DeWitt Clinton and other members of the council who were hostile to the vice president (Dangerfield, *Livingston*, 305-6).

On 11 Sep., the *Washington Federalist* reprinted an article that pointed to the LONG ABSENCES of heads of departments, commenting that "the Secretary of State, the Attorney General, and the Secretary of War, find it easy and convenient to have a recess from the duties of office, during the summer months." The author compared them unfavorably with their counterparts in former administrations, who "never found time to make long visits to distant parts of the country, for the purpose of pleasure or business." The writer questioned: "How then can these Secretaries, just introduced to office, without a previous knowledge of the details & arrangements of their several departments, find so much leisure for amuse-

ment or unofficial business?" Levi Lincoln and Henry Dearborn were charged with conducting political campaigns. On 14 Sep., a notice appeared in the same newspaper declaring that during his stay in Maryland in early September, Gallatin was "busily engaged in electioneering, instead of attending to his duty at the seat of government" (*Washington Federalist*, 11, 14, 21 Sep.; Gallatin to TJ, 29 Aug.).

Prominent New York City Republicans sent Gallatin RECOMMENDATIONS in favor of Davis (see enclosures listed above). David Gelston, Tunis Wortman, and Henry Rutgers served as officers of the Democratic Society of the City of New-York in the 1790s, and John Swartwout, Ezekiel Robins, and Rutgers represented New York City Republicans in the state assembly in 1800. Gelston and Swartwout had already received federal appointments, as customs collector and U.S. marshal, respectively (*Journal of the Assembly of the State of New-York: at Their Twenty-Fourth Session, Began and Held at the City of Albany, the Fourth Day of November, 1800* [Albany, 1801], 3; Philip S. Foner, ed., *The Democratic-Republican Societies, 1790-1800* [Westport, Conn., 1976], 171, 183-4, 425n; Alfred F. Young, *The Democratic Republicans of New York: The Origins, 1763-1797* [Chapel Hill, 1967], 393-4, 491, 567; Vol. 33:668-9, 672-3, 675-6).

[1] Preceding two words interlined in place of "are."

[2] Gallatin here canceled "character."

To George Jefferson

DEAR SIR   Monticello Sep. 12. 1801.

I recieved by the last post your favor of the 7th. covering a copy of my account with you. I have occasion for a thousand dollars to be immediately remitted to mr Barnes, who proposed setting out to Philadelphia in a few days, and it is material he should recieve it before his departure. a good draught on Philadelphia, or notes of the proper banks will be the best form of remittance. I shall remain here one fortnight longer only. I will determine with respect to the coal after my return to Washington. accept my affectionate salutations and best wishes.   TH: JEFFERSON

PrC (MHi); at foot of text: "Mr. George Jefferson"; endorsed by TJ in ink on verso.

On 14 Sep., George Jefferson wrote TJ that he had received his letter of 12 Sep. and had remitted $1,000 to John Barnes with a bill on Philadelphia, according to

TJ's direction. Referring to his letter on coal of 7 Sep., George Jefferson noted that the usual freight charge was six pence per bushel (RC in MHi; at foot of text: "Thos. Jefferson esqr."; endorsed by TJ as received 17 Sep. and so recorded in SJL).

To James Madison

DEAR SIR   Monticello Sep. 12. 1801.

Your's of yesterday was delivered by your express about 5. aclock in the evening. my occupations for the departing post have prevented my answering instantly.

No commission, nor letter of credence was signed for mr Livingston before we left Washington. I think the Boston has not yet left Boston for New York. I presume therefore that we can sign those papers in time after our return to Washington. I suspect, on view of Murray's letters, that the real obstacle to the ratification is nothing more than a desire to obtain an express renunciation of the demand of indemnities. if this be the case it will probably be ratified on that condition. on the established principle that every thing is abandoned which is not provided for in a treaty of peace, the express abandonment would not be necessary if the 2d. article is expunged. suppose we were to instruct Livingston, in case he finds on arrival at Paris that the ratification is witheld, that he propose the single article for the restitution of prizes, and say to them that with every disposition towards them of perfect friendliness & free commerce, we are willing to trust, without a treaty, to the mutual interests of the two countries for dictating the terms of our commercial relations, not doubting that each will give the best terms in practice to the other, that on the expiration of the British treaty we shall probably do the same with that nation, & so with others. unless indeed events should render it practicable to sign a short formula merely explanatory or amendatory of the L. of Nations in a few special articles. the being in freedom to refuse entrance in time of war to armed ships, or prizes, to refuse or send off ministers & consuls[1] in time of war, is a most desireable situation in my judgment.—I wonder to see such an arrearage from the departmt. of state to our bankers in Holland. our predecessors seem to have levied immense sums from their constituents merely to feed favorites by large advances, & thus to purchase by corruption an extension of their influence & power. their just debts appear to have been left in the background. I understood that the advance to Genl. Lloyd was to relieve his distress, and the contract a mere cover for letting him have the benefit of the 5000. D. what would you think of agreeing to annul the contract on his previous *actual reimbursement* of the money?—I think we may conclude with tolerable certainty that the Tripolitans had not taken any of our vessels before Dale's arrival at Gibraltar. what a pity he did not know of the war, that he might have taken their admiral & his ship.

mr Church does not exactly ask for a restoration of his consulship of Lisbon; but I am inclined to think it the very best step we can take. however this may be a subject of conversation when we meet. I am happy to hear your complaint has been so slight. I hope the great change in the weather since last night will secure us against the return of any more very hot weather. my respects to the ladies, & sincere and affectionate esteem to yourself.   TH: JEFFERSON

P.S. all the papers are returned except Davis's letter recommending a collector for the Ohio district.

RC (DLC: Madison Papers). PrC (DLC); in ink at foot of first page: "The Secretary of State."

ADVANCE TO GENL. LLOYD: in March 1799, the Navy Department contracted with Maryland Federalist Senator James Lloyd to provide barrel staves, for which he was to receive a $1,500 advance. After Lloyd cut timber from his own property and discovered that it was not suitable for staves, he proposed that the contract be canceled and returned the advance, with interest, in May 1802 in the amount of $1,786.03 (Madison, *Papers, Sec. of State Ser.*, 2:91; *Biog. Dir. Cong.*).

Edward CHURCH wrote Madison from Paris on 23 June, protesting his dismissal

as American consul in Lisbon by the Adams administration. He hoped the new administration would recognize and make restitution for the injustice he had suffered. Church had served as consul at Lisbon from 1792 until his replacement in 1797 by Thomas Bulkeley (Madison, *Papers, Sec. of State Ser.*, 1:340; 2:106). The Church letter was undoubtedly one of those forwarded by Madison on 11 Sep.

DAVIS'S LETTER: probably a letter, now missing, from Kentucky Congressman Thomas Terry Davis, an ally of Thomas Worthington (same, 2:106).

[1] Preceding word and ampersand interlined.

To John Shore

SIR   Monticello Sep. 12. 1801.

I recieved about a month ago some vaccine matter from Dr. Waterhouse at Boston, and by a second conveyance some which he had just recieved from Doctr. Jenner of London. both have succeeded perfectly. they were inserted into different arms of the same subjects, and exhibited precisely the same appearances. I have inoculated about 50. of my family, and mr Randolph & mr Eppes about 60. or 70. of theirs. we have had in the whole one instance of a little delirium, two of considerably sore arms from too large incisions,[1] about one third have had slight fevers, & the greater part have intermitted labour 1. 2. or 3. days on account of kernels under their arms. none changed their diet or occupation previously. it is now disseminating through this part of the country, & has taken in Georgetown from matter I sent there. understanding that a former trial had failed in Richmond, I have sent some matter there, & presuming it might be acceptable to you also, now inclose a phial in which are half a dozen tooth picks, the points impregnated with virus, and a thread well soaked. by Doctr. Waterhouse's advice we have confined ourselves to inoculate from a subject on[2] the day sennight from his inoculation, or the day after. later than this there is danger of communicating the disease in a spurious form, & one which is not preventative of the small pox. this seems to be the only danger attending this inoculation, & renders it necessary to be rigorously attentive neither to inoculate from the mere lymph which the pustule yields in it's first stage, nor the ripened pus of the latter. the matter at the time prescribed is a thin pellucid liquid, & is said to be then only proper. we barely draw a speck of blood. the pustule is of this size **𝟬** & form **𝟬** generally, the middle depressed, the edges well defined. perhaps larger than I have drawn it. accept assurances of my high consideration & respect.   TH: JEFFERSON

PrC (DLC); at foot of text: "Doctr. Shore."

Dr. John Shore of Petersburg graduated from the University of Edinburgh in 1777. John Wayles Eppes negotiated with him the purchase of a pair of horses for TJ in March and April 1801. In 1802, TJ gave Shore a recess appointment as customs collector of Petersburg to replace William Heth. Shore held the office until he died in 1811 (Blanton, *Medicine in Virginia*, 87; JEP, 1:433, 2:192; Vol. 33:349-50, 460, 610-11, 672).

[1] Preceding four words interlined.
[2] TJ here canceled five or six illegible words.

From William Foushee

DEAR SIR   Richmond Sept. 13th. 1801

Judge Stewart politely handed me your obliging favor of the 30. ulto. with a vial containing recent matter of the *Kine-Pox* & for which attention I beg leave to make my acknowledgments—I hope with you, for the general benefit of mankind, this discovery may answer the description given of it & that we may not be disappointed in our expectations therein; or of the genuiness of the infection; for I am extremely unwilling, however greatly we have hitherto been foiled here, to believe that, Practioners of Reputation who have spoken so positively respecting this Discovery, can have been mistaken; but that some accidental casualty must have produced in this quarter of the Globe a delay in extending security from one of the most violent Pests the human system can undergo.—The present being the most dangerous Season for attacks of the Fall Complaints, I have thought proper not to commence immediately any experiments, being unwilling to excite fever just now; but as soon as the period for the usual Autumnal diseases is past, I shall proceed with this matter & afterwards with the Variolus, in such Patients as can be prevailed on to submit to it—: & will beg permission to trouble you with some account of the result—.

with great esteem & respect am Dr. Sir Yours.   W: FOUSHEE

Dr. Currie has received his Packet also.

RC (DLC); postscript on verso; endorsed by TJ as received 15 Sep. and so recorded in SJL.

William Foushee (1749-1824), a native of Virginia, studied medicine at the University of Edinburgh before serving as a physician and surgeon for the American army in the Revolutionary War. Foushee represented Richmond in the Virginia Assembly in 1791 and 1797-99, then served on the governor's council of state before returning to the assembly as a representative of Henrico County in 1806-1808. According to an advertisement in Richmond's *Virginia Argus* on 2 Sep. 1800, Foushee and John H. Foushee were licensed by Henrico County to inoculate patients with smallpox at a location outside of Richmond. On 7 Aug. 1802 in the same newspaper, the Foushees advertised the option of inoculation with cowpox or smallpox (Blanton, *Medicine in Virginia,* 87, 327-8, 404; Leonard, *General Assembly,* 185, 209, 213, 244, 248).

YOUR OBLIGING FAVOR OF THE 30. ULTO.: TJ's letter to Foushee of 30 Aug. was similar to the letter he wrote to James Currie that day and included a postscript in which TJ informed Foushee that a vial of smallpox vaccine was sent to Currie (PrC in DLC; faint and blurred; at foot of text: "Doctr. Foushee").

From David Meade Randolph

SIR,   Richmond 13th September 1801

I received your favor of the 14th Ult. in due course of the Mail, and shou'd have answered the same at the moment, if I had recollected the place of my friend's birth; Nor can I, with certainty ascertain that point now—but, it is beleived by those who were his intimate friends during his residence at Petersburg, that he was born at Dunkirk—this also is my own conviction—to which I will add, as you have done me the honor to ask, that Mr. John Gregorie prosecuted his profession as a merchant in this Country; and supported the Character of an honest, enlightened and very much respected Citizen—which character, I have no doubt, he has sustained since his return to Europe. In France, where he possessed an Estate, he has been greatly reduced by the revolution—His present circumstances are said to require aid.

I am, with respect, your Huml. Sevt.   D M RANDOLPH

RC (DNA: RG 59, LAR); endorsed by TJ as received 15 Sep. but recorded in SJL at 17 Sep. with notation "Gregory to be Consul."

I RECEIVED YOUR FAVOR: TJ's letter to Randolph, recorded in SJL at 14 Aug., has not been found, but it regarded John Gregorie's 25 Mch. application to TJ for a consular appointment. Randolph had forwarded the letter from Gregorie, "a particular acquaintance residing in Europe," to the president on 8 Aug. (RC in DNA: RG 59, LAR; at foot of text: "Thomas Jefferson Esqr."; endorsed by TJ as received 13 Aug. and so recorded in SJL).

From Thomas Auldjo

HONBLE SIR   Cowes 14 Septemr 1801

Having had the honor & advantage of your friendship & protection now for a considerable number of years it would very ill become me to be indifferent to your concerns whether publick or private—

Your late elevation to the highest Station in the United States has given me the greatest satisfaction & as I am certain the publick good will be always in your view & intention so I trust that will receive the gratefull cooperation & assistance of all well disposed men in the execution of your arduous undertaking at this perilous moment—

The navigation of the United States had been for a considerable time uninterrupted in these parts; lately it has received a little check in my neighbourhood here by the detention & sending into port of sundry ships from the U.S. with valuable Cargoes going into Havre de Grace the Blockade of which has been overlooked by the Merchants with you—I gave immediate information of this business to Mr King & I hope the representation made by him in consequence will procure the release of the Ships detained—

We have had an abundant crop of all grain this season, but the effects have hitherto not been felt in the beneficial manner expected— the reduction of the price of wheat has only reached 14/ the Winchester bushel & altho we may think from the abundance of the crop well saved that we have a right to expect a greater reduction in price, yet I am of opinion that from the Old Stock having been quite exhausted, the price for the year will not go Under 12/ ℔ bushel

I beg leave to add my best wishes for your health & prosperity & that I am with great truth

Honble Sir Your much obliged & very obedient Servt

THOMAS AULDJO

RC (MHi); at foot of text: "Honble Thos Jefferson &c &c &c"; endorsed by TJ as received 31 Oct. and so recorded in SJL.

ADVANTAGE OF YOUR FRIENDSHIP: Thomas Auldjo, appointed vice consul at Poole in 1791 by George Washington, was a merchant of distinction in Cowes, England (JEP, 1:76; Vol. 27:95; Vol. 29:583-4).

INFORMATION OF THIS BUSINESS TO MR KING: on 29 Aug., Rufus King wrote the British foreign secretary, Lord Hawkesbury, that the blockade of Le Havre was not well known in America and cited the case of the American ship *Frederick*, which had been detained off the port of Le Havre and sent into Portsmouth. King inquired which French ports were blockaded by the British so that he could send notice to America. He also wanted to renew the instructions that they turn away rather than detain American vessels met on passage to such ports (King, *Life*, 3:505-7).

From David Austin

RESPECTED SIR/ Washington Sepr. 14th. 1801—

Will you forgive a second address on the subject of the place left by Mr Meredith?—

The considerations, by which this application is supported, are

1. The openings of providence in favor of the General Objects of my many addresses—
2. No Injury will be done to any man should the President comply with this request.—
3. No man can bring more intrinsic worth into the Councils of the Presidt.
4. It will aid to favor the Impression, that the Executive is not unfriendly to things tinged with Moral rectitude.
5—The duties of the Office are easy; & I will presume to say, will be punctually & faithfully discharged.—
6.—The emoluments of the Office would mightily relieve many good Citizens of the City, from the burthen of Gospel service: & they would accept this Office *as a bequest from the President in this view.*—
7. The Book keeper of the Department is of my acquaintance; I have passed my eye carelessly through the rotine of Official

duty, & nothing would please me more, than the Presidents Authority to enter upon its course—

8—I have a degree of influence over the Editors of the Washington Federalist; & think I could easily bring them, fully, to accord with the subsequent proceedings of Government; & thereby add one wheel more to the Machine of National Influence.—

Submitting, with all Cheerfulness to the Presidts. decision, subscribe with all esteem— D: AUSTIN

RC (DNA: RG 59, LAR); endorsed by TJ as received 24 Sep. and so recorded in SJL.

SECOND ADDRESS: Austin first wrote TJ on the subject of the treasurer's office on 12 Sep., suggesting that "all former petitions" for office would be "buried" if he were made Samuel Meredith's successor. Austin added that "if there be any thing of moment in the general strain of former communications worthy of notice; or even any thing likely to arise, from wh. the President might make selections use-

ful in the managment of the National Ship, would it not be useful to preserve this gift, to be had, in this view, without Expense?" (RC in DNA: RG 59, LAR; addressed: "His Ex'y Th: Jefferson Esqr Pres: U:States Monticello"; franked and postmarked; endorsed by TJ as received 17 Sep. and so recorded in SJL with notation "Off").

Beginning with the 9 Sep. 1801 issue, William A. Rind and Charles Prentiss served as EDITORS OF THE WASHINGTON FEDERALIST (Brigham, *American Newspapers*, 1:95-6).

From John Barnes

SIR George Town 14th Sepr 1801—

By not being favd: with a letter, last week, was probably owing—to my supposed Absence.—since my last of the 7th. (with inclosed sketch.) paymt: & receivals—the former have been reduced $2089.23. as at foot. that of Mr Gilpin was paid by Mr Rapin—at Alexandria on his own a/c last week: and the Liqueurs he took charge off.—

On the 10th I was favd: with a 2d letter from Doctr Edwards inclosing me Mr Hanses a/c $1206. the Box—with Harness—already Arrived, & Mr Dougherty have charge of it to Clean &c.—I have replied to Dr Edward & Assured him. that Order would be taken to discharge Mr Hanse's a/c—and to make sure (if possible) of the Picture: in time for me to secure & ship it. while in Philada. I wrote a Complimentary letter to Mr. Stewart. that my friend Doctr. Edwards—in his Neighbourhood—would wait on him—for the purpose of preparing a frame. & Case. for your Portrait against my expected Arrival. latter End of this month. in Order to its being shipped to Richmond & from thence conveyed to your seat at Monticello—as directed: that I. should pay him my personal respects &c. on my Arrival—Copy of which—I inclosed Doctr Edwards for his Govermt.—all which—I hope—may have the desired effect—

Of your Geo: Town debits—Only Carpenters, for $100—(who have not called.) exclusive of the Book binder and exten. househd: expenditures are Adjusted. and wait, your next particulars—for the Arranging & adjustmt. of them at Philada.

Suppose Robert & Jones for $268.12.
as well Mr Hanse on a/c say—   600—
                             $868.12.

I could very well send from hence before I set out, say. 8 or 10th Oct. Colum: drafts on B, US. dont seem so Currt: lately—as heretofore?

with perfect Esteem—I am Sir your most Obt. H St.

JOHN BARNES

RC (ViU: Edgehill-Randolph Papers); at foot of text: "Thomas Jefferson Esqr: Monticello"; endorsed by TJ as received 17 Sep. and so recorded in SJL.

According to his financial memoranda for 5 Oct., TJ asked Barnes to reimburse Joseph Rapin for the payment that Rapin made to George GILPIN for "liqueurs & preserves" sent to TJ by Tobias Lear from Saint-Domingue (MB, 2:1054; Lear to TJ, 25 July 1801). Barnes had paid $2 for the freight of the chariot HARNESS on 10 Sep., according to a statement of private account from Barnes of 30 Sep. (MS in ViU; Enoch Edwards to TJ, 31 Aug.).

CARPENTERS: on 15 Sep., tailor Thomas Carpenter signed his most recent statement of account, printed at 1 July 1801, in acknowledgment of receipt of $100 from Barnes. On a sheet of paper also dated 14 Sep., at Georgetown, Barnes listed the following "late payments": to James Taylor, Jr., $700; to a book subscription, $50; to Michael Roberts, $36.11; to Joseph Rapin "on wages a/c," $282; to Bank of Columbia, $1,000; and $21.12 to Rapin for reimbursing his payment to George Gilpin, for a total of $2,089.23 (MS in ViU; in Barnes's hand and signed by him).

From DeWitt Clinton

SIR   New York 14 September 1801.

In the event of a resignation of the Loan Officer of this State (which I am informed will be the case) I have taken the liberty to recommend James Nicholson Esquire of this City as his successor: His connection with the Secretary of the Treasury will I hope excuse my addressing this letter immediately to yourself.

Mr. Nicholson is I am persuaded fully adequate to the duties of the office; he is a man of inflexible integrity, a firm republican, of high consideration with the friends of the republican interest, and his appointment will unquestionably be very acceptable; His age, his standing in the community, and let me add his sincere and disinterested attachment to principles independent of all improper political & personal biases, impress the community very strongly in his favor.

I do not conceal that I have from my first acquaintance with Mr. Nicholson entertained a very great friendship for him—possibly I may in my recommendation be too much influenced by a sentiment of this kind—I have seen him in the day of proscription and peril as well as in the time of triumph & exultation—and in every scene he has received the confidence of your friends and the friends of the Country.

I have the honor to be, With every sentiment of sincere attachment and respect Your most Obedt. servt. DEWITT CLINTON

RC (NHi: Gallatin Papers); addressed: "The President of the United States Washington"; endorsed by Gallatin.

DeWitt Clinton (1769-1828) graduated from Columbia College in 1786 and was admitted to the bar in 1790, at the time serving as secretary for Governor George Clinton, his uncle. In 1797, he was elected to the state assembly and in 1798 to the state senate, where he served until appointed to the U.S. Senate in February 1802. In October 1803, he resigned to become mayor of New York City, a position he held for about ten years between 1803 and 1815. Clinton's unsuccessful bid for the presidency in 1812 led to his isolation from the Republican party and his removal as mayor. In 1817, Clinton won the special gubernatorial election held after Governor Daniel Tompkins became vice president. Popular for his advocacy of a waterway to connect the Hudson River with Lake Erie, Clinton won reelection as governor in 1820, 1824, and 1826. He did not run in 1822. In 1825 he led the celebration upon the completion of the Erie Canal (ANB).

RESIGNATION OF THE LOAN OFFICER:

on 12 Sep., Matthew Clarkson wrote TJ a short letter of resignation as commissioner of loans for New York. In conclusion he noted, "I shall continue Sir to execute the duties of the Office until it is perfectly convenient to you to appoint me a Successor" (RC in DNA: RG 59, RD, with second digit of date reworked to "12th," at foot of text: "The President of the United States," endorsed by TJ as a letter of 18 Sep. received the 24th and so recorded in SJL; Tr in NNC: Jay Papers, in Clarkson's hand, dated 12 Sep.). On 5 Nov. Clarkson again wrote TJ and enclosed a copy of the letter of 12 Sep., apprehending that the president might not have received it (RC in DLC, at foot of text: "Thomas Jefferson President of the United States," endorsed by TJ as received 9 Nov. and so recorded in SJL; Tr in NNC: Jay Papers, in Clarkson's hand).

HIS CONNECTION: Nicholson was Gallatin's father-in-law. At Gallatin's request, he consulted Republicans in New York City in May 1800 to recommend a candidate for vice president. TJ appointed Nicholson commissioner of loans in November 1801 (Vol. 31:556-7n; Vol. 33:670, 677).

From Albert Gallatin

DEAR SIR Washington 14th Sept. 1801

In relation to Gardner and Campbell formerly clerks in the Auditor's office, their case is not similar. Gardner voluntarily resigned about a year ago. As to Campbell, the Auditor states that when the public offices were about to be removed, the clerks, and he among the number, were supplied with an advance of money to defray their expenses to Washington; that Campbell remained behind without either explaining the cause of his delay or intimating his final intention, & that his place after being kept vacant a considerable time was at length necessarily supplied by another. Under those circumstances the Auditor thinks that, to make room for them by the removal of others, would be doing an Act of injustice, in which he cannot consent to have any Agency.

Mr Harrison seemed hurt at the supposition that he had been guilty of any act of wanton injustice or political intolerance; at the same time that he had no hesitation in saying that, although Campbell was not turned out, yet if he had returned here and it had appeared, that he was the person who had communicated official papers without his permission, it would have been considered as a breach of trust & a sufficient cause of removal. — He also represented that an interference of that nature was inadmissible; for, if C. & G. had been dismissed by him, no matter for what cause, how could he possibly submit to the indignity, or indeed be capable of performing his official duties & amongst others that of directing & controuling his clerks, if they were to be reinstated upon application by them to another than himself? — I am clearly of opinion that Campbell under all circumstances ought not to be restored, and I think also that, as a general principle, Mr Harrison's last observation is correct. But I must in candour add, that I made a blunder in this business: instead of speaking to Mr H. in my own name, I showed him what you had written to me, & he considered the whole as done with intention of hurting his feelings. I acted awkwardly, because acting against my own opinion in recommending Campbell's restoration. This is however only a trifling *family* controversy & will not be attended with any other effect abroad except giving some temporary offence to Duane, Beckley, Israel & some other very hot-headed, but, I believe, honest republicans. This leads me to a more important subject. Pennsylvania is, I think, fixed. Although we have there amongst our friends several office hunters, republicanism rests there on principle pretty generally; and it rests on the people at large, there not being, in the whole State a single individual whose influence could command even now one county, or whose defection could lose us one hundred votes at an election. It is ardently to be wished that the situation of New York was as favorable; but so much seems to depend in that State on certain individuals; the influence of a few is so great; & the majority in the city of New York (on which unfortunately the majority in the

State actually depends, that city making $\frac{1}{8}$th of the whole) is so artificial, that I much fear that we will eventually lose that State before next election of President. The most favorable event would certainly be the division of every State into districts for the election of electors; with that single point & only common sense in the Administration, republicanism would be established for one generation at least, beyond controversy: but if not obtainable as a general constitutional provision, I think that our friends, whilst they can, ought to introduce it immediately in New York. Davis's visit to Monticello has led me to that conclusion, by drawing my attention to that subject. There are also two points connected with this on which I wish the republicans throughout the Union would make up their mind. Do they eventually mean not to support Burr as your successor when you shall think fit to retire? Do they mean not to support him at next election for Vice President? These are serious questions; for although with Pennsylvania & [Maryd.] we can fear nothing so long as you will remain the object of contention with the federalists; yet the danger would be great, should any unfortunate event deprive the people of your services. Where is the man we could support with any reasonable prospect of success? Mr Madison is the only one, & his being a Virginian would be a considerable objection. But, if without thinking of events more distant or merely contingent, we confine ourselves to the next election which is near enough, the embarrassment is not less; for, even Mr Madison cannot on that occasion be supported with you: and it seems to me that there are but two ways, either to support Burr once more, or to give only one vote for President, scattering our votes for the other person to be voted for. If we do the first, we run, on the one hand, the risk of the federal party making B. president; & we seem, on the other, to give him an additional pledge of being eventually supported hereafter by the republicans for that office. If we embrace the last party, we not only lose the Vice President, but pave the way for the federal successful candidate to that office to become President. All this would be remedied by the amendt. of distinguishing the votes for the two offices; & by that of dividing the States into districts. But, as it is extremely uncertain whether such amendments will succeed, we must act on the ground of elections going on as heretofore. And here, I see the danger, but cannot discover the remedy; it is indeed but with reluctance, that I can even think of the policy necessary to counter-act intrigues & personal views, and wiser men than myself must devise the means. Yet, had I felt the same diffidence, I mean total want of confidence, which, during the course of last winter, I discovered in a large majority of the republicans towards Burr, I would have been wise enough never to give my consent in favor of his being supported last election as vice-president. In this our party, those at least who never could be reconciled to having him hereafter as President, have made a capital fault, for which there was no necessity at the time & which has produced & will produce us much embarrassment. I need not add that so far as your administration can influence any thing of that kind, it is impossible for us to act correctly, unless the ultimate object is ascertained. Yet I do not believe that *we* can do much; for I dislike much the idea of supporting a section of Republicans in New-York, & mistrusting the great majority, because that section is supposed to be hostile to Burr, & *he* is considered as the leader of that majority. A great reason against such policy is that the reputed leaders of that section, I mean the Livingstons generally, & some broken remnants of the Clintonian party who hate Burr (for Govr. Clinton is out of question & will not act) are so selfish & so uninfluential, that they never can obtain their great object, the state government, without the assistance of what is called Burr's party, & will not hesitate a moment to bargain for that object with him & his friends, granting in exchange their support for any thing he or they may want out of the State. I do not include in that number the Chancellor nor Mr Armstrong, but the first is, in that State, only a name, & there is something which will for ever prevent the last having any direct influence with the people. I said before that I was led to that train of ideas by Davis's personal application; for although in writing to you by him, I said, as I sincerely believe it, that he never would or could be influenced by B. or any other person to do an improper act or any thing which could hurt the general republican principle, yet it is not to be doubted that after all that has been said on the subject, his refusal will, by Burr, be considered as a declaration of war. The federalists have been busy on the occasion; Tillotson also has said many things which might not have been said with equal propriety, and I do know that there is hardly a man who meddles with politics in New York, who does not believe that Davis's rejection is owing to Burr's recommendation. On that as well as on many other accounts, I was anxious to prevent Davis's journey; but to want of early education & mixing with the world, I ascribe his want of sense of propriety on this occasion; and his going is the worst thing I have known of him.

I leave this subject with pleasure, & yet find that I have in a hurry thrown my ideas on it in such a confused manner as would require a revision, but I trust in your indulgence & candour.

I enclose Mr. Millege's & Mr. Few's letters, & will in pursuance with your last letter but one, direct a commission for Mr Thomas Johnson the person recommended by Govr. Jackson.

A Mr Richard Parrot called this morning on me to tell me that the office of collector at Georgetown was vacant, and that he had been formerly recommended to you.   Mr Habersham has not communicated any thing to me.

I have not seen the dispatches from France, & do not know on what ground you have determined to send the Minister to France at present; but it will at least afford an argument to those who have attacked the sending Mr Dawson. Why not send Mr Livingston at first? and if that was improper then, why is it proper now? An answer to this should be ready to go to the public, when his departure shall be announced.

The list of Warrants is enclosed as usual.

Believe me to be with great and sincere respect and attachment Your obt. Servt.   ALBERT GALLATIN

Mr Smith is still absent. Several of the more decent fed. papers begin to attack the absence of so many members of the administn.

RC (DLC); at foot of first page: "President of the U. States"; endorsed by TJ as received from the Treasury Department on 17 Sep. and so recorded in SJL. Enclosures: (1) John Milledge to Gallatin, Savannah, 24 Aug., enclosing a letter from Charles Harris, an attorney, "whose principles are correct, and whose friendship and esteem I highly value," requesting that Gallatin show it to Madison and noting that he concurs fully with what Harris "observes of the Marshal" (RC in DNA: RG 59, LAR; endorsed by TJ: "Milledge John to mr Gallatin. the Marshal of Georgia to be removd. but the District attorney not"). (2) Harris to Milledge, Savannah, 20 Aug., advising against the removal of the U.S. attorney of Georgia (George Woodruff) and noting that although a Federalist, Woodruff's "Disposition, equanimity and kindness make him an Exception to the high toned and over-bearing patricians of that Class," and "his legal talents place him at the Head of the Bar"; observing that Woodruff is "esteemed and loved by all parties" and connected, by marriage, "with a highly respectable *native* family, many of whom are determined Republicans," Har-

ris reports that his dismissal would displease most Republicans and "may be creating unnecessary Ennemies to Mr. Jefferson"; on the other hand, Harris supports the removal of the U.S. marshal (Ambrose Gordon), noting that he was appointed "from a Superior Claim to the federalism of 1797 & 1798" and would "Glide into obscurity . . . unpitied" (same, endorsed by TJ: "Harris Charles to John Milledge"; James Jackson to TJ, 18 July 1801). (3) "Weekly list of Warrants issued on the Treasurer during the week ending 12th Septer. 1801," reporting 14 warrants, Nos. 157 to 170, including No. 160, on John Barnes for $4,000, being payment of the president's salary; 3 warrants, totaling $37,080.82, for the purchase of bills on Holland for the payment of the Dutch debt; and 3 warrants, totaling $13,766.81, for the payment of the expenses of the census in North and South Carolina and Connecticut; for a total $62,678.85 for all warrants (MS in DLC; entirely in Gallatin's hand). Other enclosure not found.

For the final list of clerks from the auditor's office who received reimbursement for THEIR EXPENSES for moving TO WASHINGTON, see ASP, *Finance*, 1:811. William P. Gardner received $175, but Anthony Campbell was not on the list, probably because he did not leave Philadelphia. Campbell observed that some weeks before the proposed move, he was asked how much he would require for moving expenses. He replied that he needed only his salary and was given a check for $200. Upon his dismissal, Campbell was ordered to repay $80, the sum over his regular salary included in the check. Israel Israel gave him the money to discharge the debt. Treasury Department accounts indicate that during the quarter ending 31 Dec. 1800, Campbell repaid $78, "which had been advanced him to defray his expences in removing from Philadelphia to Washington, with the Government" (Gallatin, *Papers*, 5:374-5; 6:168). COMMUNICATED OFFICIAL PAPERS WITHOUT HIS PERMISSION: see William Duane to TJ, 1 Mch. 1801. WHAT YOU HAD WRITTEN TO ME: TJ to Gallatin, 28 Aug.

WRITING TO YOU BY HIM: Gallatin's letter to TJ of 12 Sep. was carried to Monticello by Matthew L. Davis. On 10 Aug., Thomas TILLOTSON, a physician who was married to Margaret Livingston, sister of Robert R. and Edward Livingston, resigned his congressional seat, before ever serving, to accept appointment as secretary of state of New York (Dangerfield, *Livingston*, 189; *Biog. Dir. Cong.*; Kline, *Burr*, 1:577).

LAST LETTER BUT ONE: Gallatin refers to TJ's letter of 28 Aug.

AMENDT: for congressional efforts to pass a constitutional amendment in early 1802 that called for the district elections of presidential electors and the designation of candidates for president or vice president, see Tadahisa Kuroda, *The Origins of the Twelfth Amendment* (Westport, Conn., 1994), 118-23.

On this date, RICHARD Parrott (PARROT) also wrote TJ, informing the president that James M. Lingan had resigned the collectorship at Georgetown and adding that he was reapplying for the position for which he had earlier received the recommendation of merchants in Georgetown (RC in DNA: RG 59, LAR; at head of text: "Ths, Jefferson Esquire President United States"; endorsed by TJ as received 17 Sep. and "to be Collector Geo. T." and so recorded in SJL with notation "Off."). FORMERLY RECOMMENDED TO YOU: see Parrott to TJ, 14 Mch. 1801. On 16 Sep., Parrott reiterated his application in a letter to Gallatin, observing that he wished the Treasury secretary to be aware of the earlier address in his favor made to the president by the "Merchants Generally, the Mayor, some of the Majistrates & others" at Georgetown, and hoping that he would receive the approbation of Gallatin and the executive (RC in DNA: RG 59, LAR; endorsed by TJ: "Parrott Richd to mr Gallatin" and "to be made Collector of Geo. T.").

From Edward Gantt

DEAR SIR,   Septr. 14th. 1801

When I wrote to you last I informed you that the Vaccine Matter you supplied me with had proved effectual. I then had one of Mr. Mason's Boys under the Disease, and from his Arm had inoculated two Patients, who had also taken the Infection. I was called on the sixth Day to visit a Lady in Prince George's County about sixteen Miles from George Town from whence I did not return until the Evening—I visited my Patients early on the seventh Day, expecting to be furnished with a Sufficiency of good Matter, but found a very considerable Efflorescence had come on. However I got what Matter I could, & with it inoculated immediately three other Patients, neither of whom were infected by it. I then tried the Remainder of the Matter you had sent me, but had the Misfortune to find it effete— When I wrote to you, I expected from your Letter of the 29 of August to have received a fresh supply by that Post, which I was in hopes I should not have wanted. I must now request a fresh Supply, & promise that no Avocation shall prevent my taking it again in the proper Time. Doctr. Worthington also took Matter the 7th. Day from Mr. Mason's Boy, which was the Day after I used it with Success, which proved totally ineffectual. What could have brought on the Inflammation or Efflorescence so much sooner, than the Time mentioned by Doctr. Waterhouse? Must it not have been accelerated by the violent Heat of the atmosphere which then prevailed?—

The remaining Part of this Letter needs an Apology—I hope you will not impute it to Presumption in me, or even think it a voluntary Act of mine—This Morning Mr. Parrott who has always supported the Character of a good Republican, & a decided Friend to Mr. Jefferson, came & informed me that General Lingham had resigned his Office, that the Merchants of this Place with the two Mr. Masons had applied to you in his Favour soon after Mr. Lingham had been appointed Marshall, expecting that Office would have become vacant— That Mr. John Mason was now in Philadelphia, & Mr. J. T. Mason at Prince George's County Court, by which Means he was deprived of their Intercession in his Favour, and begged that I would mention those Circumstances to you—I evaded it as long as I could, but at last was constrained to promise that I would write to you on the Subject. He immediately waited on Mr. Gallatin since which Time I have not seen him—

I am Dear Sir with every Sentiment of Esteem & Respect your most obedt. Servt.   EDWD GANTT

RC (DLC); endorsed by TJ as received 17 Sep. and so recorded in SJL.

WROTE TO YOU LAST: Gantt to TJ, 7 Sep.

For the application of Richard PARROTT, see the preceding document. Gantt had supported Parrott's earlier application for the same position (Parrott to TJ, 14 Mch. 1801).

From Joseph Habersham

Washington City
DEAR SIR/   14th. Septr. 1801.
Your favor of the 4th came duly to hand tendering me the office of
Treasurer—
For your kindness in making that offer as well as the obliging man-
ner in which it was expressed, I beg you to accept of my thanks. Cer-
tain circumstances require that I should consider further on the
subject before I make a definitive reply I must therefore request your
indulgence until the next Post.
I am, with great respect, Yr mo. obed svt   JOS HABERSHAM

RC (DLC); at foot of text: "Thomas Jefferson President of the United States Monticello"; endorsed by TJ as received 17 Sep. and so recorded in SJL.

From Robert R. Livingston

DEAR SIR   ClerMont 14th. Sepr 1801
I am just favoured by your note without date covering two letters
for Paris. I conclude from this circumstance that you have recd advices of the ratification of the treaty, & have determined upon my
departure. but I have yet heard nothing on the subject from the Secretary of State. I presume however that the next post will bring me
my commission & instructions, immediatly after which I will proceed
to New York, & embark as soon as I can provide stores, & other articles which the new arrangment of the secretary of the navy renders
necessary. As this will bring us to the equinox the capt. will probably
chuse to permit that to pass, so that I suppose we shall take our departure about the begining of Octr. Any further commands that you
may honor me with will find me at New York.
I should not have taken the liberty to mention a new candidate for
the naval office, had I not imagined from what you were pleased to
communicate to me at Washington, that none were brought forward,
but those you then mentioned, one of whom you considered as withdrawn (tho as I since find not by himself or his friends) & had I not
thought it duty I owed to you, in return for the marks I had recd of
your confidence, to mention what I know to be the sentiment of the
influenceal characters among the republicans of this State relative to
the others. The office of collector having fallen into the hands of a
good republican, but one very limited in his circumstances & stand-

ing among the merchants, they are the more solicitous about that of the naval officer. I am pleased to hear that candidates are brought forward upon such respectable ground as you intimate, & tho I am at a loss to judge who they are, or of the interest that has brought them forward, yet I am far from wishing to oppose the gentlemen, I mentioned to them. I am only solicitous that the subject of my letter may remain unknown to the gent. of the administration.

I shall be very attentive to your instructions of the subject of La forest, & Otto, of the first of these, from long acquaintance & observation I am induced to think exactly as you do. But I believe as he stands on very high ground with the ruling party in France, & has the most decided aversion to this country, that he will not accept the mission, which indeed I have been told he has actualy refused. Of the second I think more favorably, But I shall govern myself by your judgment of him, & shall be the more attentive to your hint, since I have reason to believe that he will make the appointment an object.

From Mr. Sumpter I have not yet received a single line, or message, tho I am told at second hand, that he is at Baltimore & intends to take his passage with me.

I have the honor to be Dear Sir with the most perfect attachment Your Most Obt hm: Servt   ROBT R LIVINGSTON

RC (DLC); at foot of text: "Thomas Jefferson Esqr pres: of the United States"; endorsed by TJ as received 1 Oct. and so recorded in SJL.

The NOTE WITHOUT DATE has not been found. TJ to Jean Chas, 3 Sep., may have been one of the TWO LETTERS FOR PARIS; the other has not been identified.

Livingston and Aaron Burr had asked the SECRETARY OF THE NAVY to allow Nathalie Delage de Volude, a young Frenchwoman whom Burr treated as a foster daughter, and her governess to travel to France with Livingston's party on the *Boston*. Robert Smith agreed, but made clear that the navy could furnish only passage, not provisions, for Livingston's entourage. Smith authorized an enlargement of the frigate's cabin to accommodate the group, which in the end included, in addition to Livingston and five members of his family, Delage, the governess, several other French citizens, some servants, and Thomas Sumter, Jr.— who later married Mademoiselle Delage (Kline, *Burr*, 1:280n, 559, 560n; 2:618-19; Dangerfield, *Livingston*, 309, 382; Smith to Livingston, 28 Aug. 1801, in Lb in DNA: RG 45, MLS).

From Arnold Oelrichs

RIGHT HONORABLE SIR!   Bremen the 14th. Septbr. 1801.

Presuming that the Subject of this Letter, will neither be wholly uninterresting nor[1] unacceptable, I am therefore encouraged to address myself to your Excellency!

Some Time ago, I heard from an Acquaintance of mine that an

American Merchant traveling in this part of the World, had an Order from the Right-honorable Congress of the United States, to make all possible Search after an Artist, who had spent some Years in America, and executed a Bust of a very striking Likeness of the late immortal President & General Washington! which was very much admired, and universally approved of. That the Right-Honorable Congress had agreed upon a very Considerable Sum of money to be paid this Artist for the Accomplishment of 15 Busts, one of each to be erected in the different respective Provinces of North America. That this Artist was no where to be met with, tho every pains, were taken to find him out.

As I have been most Zealously attached to the Interests of North-America ever since the memorable & glorious Revolution. I took every pains possible to discover this man, and Kept this Matter quite private. I have succeeded at last in discovering, that probably this Man, was a Certain unfortunate person of the Name of Cerrachi, who was an Italian Emigrant probably a native of Rome and being concerned in the late plot against Bonaparte, was soon after taken into Custody & suffered Death.

I hope your Excellency! will take it as a particular mark of my Attachment to the United States, and Veneration for the names[2] of the late by all the World admired Washington, when I make bold to offer the Services of an Artist, of peculiar Merit, who was a Pupil of the late unfortunate Cerachi, when he was in London, where he lived with him for 4 Years, and made a most rapid Improvement. This Artist whose Name is G: G: Wessell a native German Lived 16 Years in London, has received at different Times the first Præmiums at the Exhibitions in that Metropolis has finished the following Works to general Satisfaction

The Bust of the Imperial Ambassador Count de Belgiojoso
    "   do. of General Paoli
    "   do. of Sir Josuah Reynholds President of the Royal Academy
          of Arts & Sciences in London
    "   do. of Admiral Keppel, Three Times, and
    "   do. of Prince Lewis Ferdinand of Prussia, and Several Statues; in particular two which are placed in the Front of Sommerseth-house in London, which are of Carrarian Marble, much larger than Life or Colossial Size. Afterwards he worked under an Italian of the Name of J: B Locatelly where he made & finished to very great Satisfaction! several large Groupes of 3 & more Figures also of a Colossial Size, and remain'd with this Artist for 5 Years, and acquitted himself always with strict Sobriety & Integrity. He was also em-

ployed for many Years successfully in the celebrated Manufactory of Messrs. Wedgewood, Bentley & Compy in the most principal Parts of their highly finished Works, which alone signalized him as a man of great Merit.

I beg leave to Transmit your Excellency Three Boxes, containing an Original finished Venus Urania of Carrarian marble, the Second an Original model of burned Clay, of the Bust of the late famous Mr. Möser a Man of great distinction in the Litterary World, and the Statue of Aeolus in the Same Manner, of which Scientifick Men, and Connoisseurs of the fine Arts are best enabled to form their Judgment of the Capacity of the Artist.

I hope your Excellency will have the Goodness to permit me by this Opportunity, to refer myself to the Contents of a letter you'll be pleased to receive from My Friend Mr. James Zwisler of Baltimore, which contains the Utmost Wish of my Ambition and believe me to retain a Grateful Sense of what ever Favors you will be pleased, to Confer on

Right Honorable Sir your Excellency's most devoted & most obedt. humble. Servant ARNOLD OELRICHS

RC (DLC); at foot of text: "His Excellency the Right Honorable T. Jefferson President of the United States"; endorsed by TJ as received 2 Dec. and so recorded in SJL. Quadruplicate (DLC); at head of text: "Copÿ Quadruplicate No. 3"; enclosed in Oelrichs to TJ, 28 Dec. 1802 (Dupl and Tripl mentioned by Oelrichs in that letter have not been found). Enclosed in George Latimer to TJ, 28 Nov. 1801.

Arnold Oelrichs was presumably a member of the Oelrichs family that was prominent in Bremen from the fifteenth to the early twentieth centuries (*Neue Deutsche Biographie*, 22 vols. to date [Berlin, 1953-], 19:440). For Giuseppe Ceracchi's busts of WASHINGTON, see Ulysse Desportes, "Giuseppe Ceracchi in America and his Busts of George Washington," *Art Quarterly*, 26 [1963], 141-79. Ceracchi's last correspondence with TJ was in July 1800, a few months before the artist was arrested for conspiring to kill Bonaparte (Vol. 32:61-2).

G: G: WESSELL: Gerhard George Wessel studied in Berlin, then went to England in 1773 under George III's patron-

age. Wessel studied at the Royal Academy and exhibited there, but left Britain in 1787 for Osnabrück, where some of the work he did was for a palace owned by the British monarchs. According to what Oelrichs says above, Wessel apparently performed finishing work on Ceracchi's busts of Count Ludovico Barbiano di Belgioioso, Pasquale Paoli, Sir Joshua Reynolds, and Augustus Keppel, and other works by Ceracchi, including sculptures for the facade of Somerset House. LOCATELLY: John Baptist Locatelli, a native of Verona, worked in Britain from about 1775 to 1796. After that he lived in Milan, where he received a pension for life through Bonaparte's patronage (Rupert Gunnis, *Dictionary of British Sculptors, 1660-1851*, new rev. ed. [London, 1968], 89-90, 240-1, 420; *Giuseppe Ceracchi: Scultore Giacobino, 1751-1801* [Rome, 1989], 45).

When the THREE BOXES containing examples of Wessel's work arrived in Philadelphia, TJ declined to receive them, explaining that "it is inconsistent with the law he has laid down for himself to accept presents while in public office" (Oelrichs to TJ, 28 Dec. 1802, and TJ's

Dft of letter from Lewis Harvie to Oelrichs, 9 June 1803, both in DLC). Justus
MÖSER, who died in 1794, was an Osnabrück attorney and administrator who
wrote several works on history and other
topics (Henry Garland and Mary Gar-

land, *The Oxford Companion to German
Literature* [Oxford, 1976], 607-8).

[1] MS: "not."
[2] MS: "manes."

From Charles Pinckney

DEAR SIR   September 14: 1801 In Amsterdam

I had the honour to acquaint you that I arrived in Holland on the
10th of this month & yesterday reached Amsterdam—the fatigue &
length of my very long sea Voyage & a desire to examine this store-
house of Batavia will keep me here a few days & then I mean to proceed by the way of the Hague & Brussells as rapidly as I can to Paris
& from thence to Madrid—To you who are so well acquainted with
Europe any Description of mine would be superfluous—to me Holland is one of the most extraordinary spectacles that could be exhibited & as my stay can be but short in it, I am incessantly engaged all
day & some times half the night in seeing & examining every thing
I can—My route from the Texel Mouth at Helder through North
Holland & by the Hague will give me a View of the whole of it & I am
hopeful my health will improve by the route, as riding generally
agrees with me—I inclose you the Leyden Gazettes of the 8 & 4th
September—they will inform you that the report of a Peace is unfounded—nor is it likely as Great Britain insists, if she is obliged to
return her colonial acquisitions that France shall restore her continental ones—this she will never do while she can hold them—besides
it is said from authority which appears almost unquestionable, that
one of the secret articles of the Luneville treaty is that *the Stadht-
holder shall be indemnified by being made* Elector *of Hanover*—the
intelligence respecting Egypt, Portugal & the serious differences
likely to arise from the recent death of the Elector of Cologne, as well
as the late attempt of Lord Nelson on the coasts of this country, are
detailed in the Gazettes inclosed—from those you will think with me,
that Peace between France & Great Britain is not at present very
likely.—the conferences through Mr Otto & Mr Merry are kept up
but it is considered here as more matter of form than any thing else—
in the meantime all the small powers will be compelled to take their
sides as the larger shall decide—in short I still hold my opinion that
no lasting or permanent peace will take place, until the great Question is completely decided, whether Europe shall be republican or

Monarchical—if a Peace could be patched up it would soon be broken—If the European republics new model their Governments & give to their citizens, such a Government as the American, or such a one as will ensure to them their public & private rights particularly the rights of property & the trial by Jury there can be no Question as to the result—the Batavian Government are now seriously engaged in preparing a plan to be hereafter submitted to a Convention for reforming their Constitution, but it is pretty clear they do not understand the nature & principles of republican Systems as well as we do & I suspect the new one of Batavia will, under some other name, be very much like that of France.—I propose in a short time to go to the Hague in my way to Paris & from thence to write you again whatever I shall suppose worthy your Notice.—I request my best respects to my friends Mr Madison, Mr Galletin & the gentlemen at Washington & with the Most affectionate respect & regard I am Dear Sir

Yours Truly   CHARLES PINCKNEY

I take the liberty of inclosing a Letter covering for my little Daughter which I will be much obliged to you to have the goodness to let one of your servants put in the Post office.—

Since writing the above I have the Leyden Gazette of yesterday which I also inclose: by this you will percieve the train of politics in Europe & also that Menou is determined to bury himself under the ruins of Alexandria rather than submit.—I have just seen some gentlemen from Paris arrived last night—notwithstanding the great secrecy with which General Buonoparte conducts every thing & the silence that is particularly observed on the subject of a Descent, there is little doubt this is his grand object, & that he will keep in preparation for striking, & not with a palsied hand, whenever opportunities shall occur to render it probable of success—I am hopeful to be in Paris by the 24th.—

RC (DLC); endorsed by TJ as received 28 Dec. and so recorded in SJL. Enclosure: Issues of *Nouvelles Politiques* of Leiden. Other enclosure not found.

LEYDEN GAZETTES: *Gazette de Leide* was the name commonly used for a French-language newspaper published in Leiden. In 1801 the newspaper's formal title was *Nouvelles Politiques*. Earlier, TJ considered the *Gazette* to be the best source of European news. On occasion he had sent items for publication in its columns or supplied American newspapers with translated extracts from the Leiden publication (Eugène Hatin, *Les Gazettes de Hollande et la Presse Clandestine aux XVIIe et XVIIIe Siècles* [Paris, 1865], 146-55; MB, 1:561n; Vol. 7:540-5; Vol. 13:246-7; Vol. 16:239-40; Vol. 25:394, 439, 535; Vol. 27:117).

There was no article in the Lunéville treaty making the former Dutch stadtholder, William of Orange, the ELECTOR OF HANOVER (Parry, *Consolidated Treaty Series*, 55:475-95).

The death in July 1801 of the archbishop and ELECTOR OF COLOGNE, Maximilian Franz, created friction between Prussia and the Holy Roman Empire, since the treaty of Lunéville called for vacant ecclesiastical principalities to become indemnification for territory lost to France. Max Franz—the youngest son of Maria Theresa of Austria, a brother of Marie Antoinette, and an early patron of Ludwig van Beethoven—had been a vigorous promoter of social and political reform, arguing against the empire's participation in the wars against revolutionary France (Madison, *Papers, Sec. of State Ser.*, 2:113n; *Nouvelles Politiques, Supplement*, 8 Sep.; Friedrich Heer, *The Holy Roman Empire*, trans. Janet Sondheimer [New York, 1968], 271, 279-81).

LORD NELSON had attacked French ships at Boulogne, where a potential invasion flotilla was gathering, and a portion of the British fleet also kept watch on the Dutch coast (Grainger, *Amiens Truce*, 45; William Laird Clowes, *The Royal Navy: A History from the Earliest Times to the Present*, 7 vols. [London, 1897-1903; repr. 1996-97], 4:444-6; *Nouvelles Politiques*, 8 Sep., and *Supplement*).

Louis Guillaume OTTO, who went to London as the French commissioner for prisoners of war in 1799, was the conduit through which the French government, in 1800, broached the idea of a naval armistice. In March 1801, Lord Hawkesbury, the British foreign secretary, opened new discussions with Otto about terms of a peace agreement. The exchanges between Hawkesbury and Otto, which centered on the status of places that had been occupied by Britain and France during the war, dragged on, and

in July Hawkesbury sent Anthony MERRY to Paris—nominally, like Otto, as a commissioner of prisoners—to act as another channel of communication between Hawkesbury and Talleyrand (Grainger, *Amiens Truce*, 7-42; Vol. 32:192n).

The CONSTITUTION of the Batavian Republic was not supposed to be revised until 1803, but in March 1801 the government called for a new constitution. Under the new frame of government, implemented in September, executive powers were held by a newly created 12-member body called the Staatsbewind, the executive directory ceased to exist, and the role of the legislature was to approve or reject laws handed down by the executive (Louis Legrand, *La Révolution Française en Hollande: La République Batave* [Paris, 1895], 270-8; Tulard, *Dictionnaire Napoléon*, 885).

MY LITTLE DAUGHTER: Pinckney had two daughters, Frances Henrietta Pinckney (b. 1790) and Mary Eleanor Pinckney (b. 1792). He also had a son. Pinckney, a widower, did not take the children with him to Europe, and he is known to have written on at least one occasion to his elder daughter (Marty D. Matthews, *Forgotten Founder: The Life and Times of Charles Pinckney* [Columbia, 2004], 72, 82-3, 86, 110).

Knowing that his government was discussing peace terms with the British, the French commander in Egypt, the Baron de Menou, attempted to delay the surrender of ALEXANDRIA as long as possible. He did not die in the siege (Grainger, *Amiens Truce*, 44-5; Tulard, *Dictionnaire Napoléon*, 1163-5).

From Alexander White

SIR   Washington 14th. September 1801

I returned on the 6th. instant a good deal indisposed. Although my disease (a diarrhoea) is in some measure checked, yet my health is not so far restored as to enable me to take an active part in business

My Colleagues having answered your letters of the 24th. and 29th. Ulo. before my arrival I have nothing to say on the subjects of them, except to observe that it has been the practice of this Office when a legal difficulty occurred to state the case to the President, not for his individual opinion, but for the opinion of his Law Officer; which opinion when transmitted to the Board has been considered as the instruction of the Executive. I expected the present business would have taken the same course, and altho' I had myself no doubt on any of the points stated, yet I thought the sanction of the Goverment absolutely necessary to enable us to carry into effect any coercive measures with respect to the Parties concerned. I am with sentiments of the highest respect

Sir Your most Obt. Servant   ALEXR WHITE

RC (DLC); at foot of text: "President of the U. States"; endorsed by TJ as received 17 Sep. and so recorded in SJL.

MY COLLEAGUES: the District of Columbia Commissioners.

From Solomon Bartlett

September the 15 day 1801

to the father or perteckter of a meracea i as a unwise son do beg to your exlence to for give and excuse my forrodness. i must acknolledg to my sham that my discovery when broug in to completness it did not answer to my expecttation and grat astoneshment in which i shall be ever coud in my own a perences everry thing answered com plet but the spring of my fountain has failed i must beleve that it was a judgment on me from the Lord so my good will and prayer to you

SOLOMON BARTLETT

RC (MHi); addressed: "to the present of the unniteed States of amarycea"; franked; postmarked at Easton, Maryland, 6 Oct.; recorded in SJL as received 9 Oct. with notation "postmarkd Boston."

From Tench Coxe

[ca. 15 Sep. 1801]

This letter is transmitted, respectfully, as the only information I possess of the Gentleman, tho I should rely on the recommendation of Mr. le Ray (de Chaumont) Junr. had he given one.   T. C.

RC (DNA: RG 59, LAR); undated; on same sheet as James Anderson to Coxe, Paris, 9 June 1801, requesting a consular post in France, Spain, or Italy, and naming Jacques Donatien Le Ray de Chaumont as a reference; at foot of text:

"Tench Cox Esquire Philadelphia"; endorsed by TJ: "Anderson James of S.C. to Tench Coxe to be Consul."

On 8 June, James Anderson also wrote James Monroe a letter from Paris requesting a consular post (RC in DNA: RG 59, LAR; endorsed by TJ as received 15 Sep. and "Anderson Jas. of S.C. to Govr. Monroe} to be Consul in France"). Monroe probably brought the letter to TJ. Anderson first addressed TJ about an appointment in September 1792. In June 1802, TJ appointed him vice commercial agent at Sète (Cette), in France, and the next year the Senate confirmed his appointment as commercial agent there (FC in Lb in DNA: RG 59, PTCC; JEP, 1:433, 440; Vol. 24:423-4).

From Levi Lincoln

SIR   Worcester Sept 15—1801

Since my last, has been received your's of the 26th & 28 of August. The former was read with great pleasure, and the subject matter of the latter had been previously attended to—I lately spent several days in Boston, find the sentiments and feelings of the opposition, much as I have heretofore stated. The republicans in spirits, the federalists depressed, and the lower classes of them, are little more sharpened, from an idea that their railings will have no effect, unless it be to produce more firmness in the measures of Government. The tone of the public papers more feeble in the matter, & a little more bitter in the manner of the abuse. I met with the late President, at a meeting of the academy of arts & sciences, he appeared pleasant, treated me with politeness, but nothing very particular took place between us.—The first time, I was in Boston after my return from the Southward, I had a consultation with Otis and Ames on the Bingham cause, Mr Davis was with us a part of the time, but was obliged to leave us for the Plymouth court. As he had, the most knowledge of the cause, from having been in it from the first, we agreed to attend further to it, at a then future time when he could be present. Lately I went through the cause, with him, & Mr Blake, to whom Mr Otis had delivered over the business of the United States, examined all the papers, & the existing state of the action,—and am sorry to say, I can see no prospect of preventing a judgment for a considerable sum of money, from any situation into which, the action can now be placed. It is unnecessary to state the various measures which have been gone through with, in reference to this controversy—Many of them are so now fixed, by some means or another, as to admit of no alteration. The action now is, for money had & received the object to reverse a judgment recovered on a default, for the proceeds of the sale of the cargo of the Brig Hope. There has been a condemnation of the Brig & Cargo, in the Circuit court by a default, on a regular process. This condemnation is binding on all the world, in favour of the libellents. It cannot now be altered. A monition had been proposed, & conceded to, by the opposite party, as securing some advantages to Mr Bingham. I can see none from changing the shape of the action, or, even the court, in the situation of the remaining merits of the cause—It is already agreed, that all special matters shall be given in evidence, under the general issue in the present action. As it respects the United States I am decided, it is not best for them, to make any further agreements about the action, but to let it take its legal course. If Mr. Bingham in receiving the property, acted as Agent for the United States, and can make it appear to the purposes of charging them, independent of their resolves for that purposes, he can make it appear, to the purposes, of defeating this action. For this would be a good bar, and can be given in evidence under the agreement. If he did not act as Agent, It will be a question, how far Govt have bound themselves by their past acts. If Mr. Bingham is entitled, to deductions for use charges & monies expended, out of the proceeds of the cargo, in his care and attentions to the business, it will be as regular, to make those deductions, in the equitable action, now pending as under a monition—At any rate, I think Cabot ought not to recover interest, untill after the condemnation—After a full consultation both Mr Davis & Blake agreed, with me, it was not best to alter the shape of the action—Mr. Ames, who had been engaged, both by the late Secretary of the treasury, & Mr Bingham, and who was present on the former consultation was absent on account of the escape of Fairbanks from the Dedham Gaol—It was determined, on the trial, to state all the points to the Court without changing the nature of the action, & principally to urge the agency of Bingham, in Bar; and a deduction of the cost charges & expences, & a limitation of the interest, from the time of the condemnation, in mitigation of damages. I shall see the Gentlemen again, before the trial, But if no further instructions are received, the cause will take the above described course. The letter of the resolve of June 20 1780 does not necessarily go to indemnify for any thing further, than the cost & expences of the suits, perhaps however its intent might extend to the debt or damage—

Accept Sir assurances of my highest friendship & respect—

LEVI LINCOLN

RC (DLC); at head of text: "President of the United States"; endorsed by TJ as received 1 Oct. and so recorded in SJL with notation "S."

MY LAST: Lincoln to TJ, 14 Aug.

Harrison Gray OTIS and Fisher AMES were William Bingham's legal counsel in the case pertaining to the *Hope* and its cargo. In July, TJ made Boston attorney George BLAKE the U.S. attorney for the district of Massachusetts in place of Otis, whom John Adams had appointed to the position late in his term (Alberts, *Golden Voyage*, 366; Kline, *Burr*, 1:443n; Vol. 33:219, 245n, 672, 677).

LET IT TAKE ITS LEGAL COURSE: in January 1802, in response to a query from Madison prompted by a letter from Bingham's agent, Charles Willing Hare, Lincoln stated his opinion that "the U.S. ought not to be any farther concerned in lawsuits on this subject." Lincoln argued that the judgment against Bingham in circuit court was "a legal proof, that he had not sufficient authority from the U.S. to take the property as their agent," and that the government was "not in strictness bound" to pay the judgment. Ames may have held a similar opinion, since he advised Bingham that he would probably have to pay the judgment. Following Bingham's death in 1804, Hare paid the plaintiffs from Bingham's estate (Lincoln to Madison, 21 Jan. 1802, in DNA: RG 59, LOAG; Alberts, *Golden Voyage*, 415, 417, 430).

RESOLVES: at Bingham's request, Congress had passed two resolutions relating to the *Hope* affair. The second one, dated 20 June 1780, sanctioned what he had done, authorized the reimbursement of his legal expenses, and pledged to pay any judgment found against him in the case of the *Hope*. The United States was "ulti-mately responsible" for Bingham's actions in the matter "by virtue of resolution of the Congress under the Confederation," Timothy Pickering attested in 1799 (DHSC, 6:556; Alberts, *Golden Voyage*, 366).

John CABOT was the lead plaintiff in the suit against Bingham (Syrett, *Hamilton*, 14:156n; DHSC, 6:554n).

In August 1801, Jason FAIRBANKS, a young man of Dedham, Massachusetts, was convicted of murdering his love interest, Elizabeth Fales. They were both reported to be of "respectable families" of Dedham, and according to one account almost 2,000 people attended Fales's burial. Otis was one of Fairbanks's court-appointed attorneys. Fairbanks received a sentence of death, but on the night of 17-18 Aug. a party of men freed him from jail. Captured before he could reach Canada, he was brought back to Massachusetts and hanged on 10 Sep. 1801. Newspapers outside Massachusetts reprinted news of the murder, trial, jailbreak, and execution (Dale H. Freeman, "'Melancholy Catastrophe!' The Story of Jason Fairbanks and Elizabeth Fales," *Historical Journal of Massachusetts*, 26 [1998], 1-25; *Alexandria Advertiser and Commercial Intelligencer*, 1 June; *Washington Federalist*, 12 June, 19 Aug.; Alexandria *Times*, 27 Aug., 21 Sep. 1801).

From Beriah Norton

SIR/ Edgartown on Marthas Vineyard Sepr. 15th. 1801.

With the most Perfect Deference and respect, Permit me to Address a Line to your Excellency, and to Acquaint you that not Long after I arived home to my family from the Seat of Government I recd. a Line from my worthy friend Mr. Dolton informing me that he had wrot to Judge Paterson, and that his answer Could not tend to the Success of my applycation, which was inexpressably heavy news to me and the rest of his friends,—more Especially to his wife my Precious Daughter, who I found when I returned home but just able to set up. She has not been out of the House for Six Months Past. I much fear that she is or soon will be in a *Dangerous Decline*. God forbid.

Directly after I recd. the said Letter I took Passeg for New York and went over to Brounswick to see the Judge, (I took a Letter to him from my Good friend Colo. Ogden,) the Judge informed me that he had seen Mr. Dolton, and it did appear to me that the Judge wished that the President would Discharge Marchant, and obsearved that the President had full Power to do it. I informed him that I had no Doubt of it. But that I supposed it had been Practised to have a Certificate from the Judge Implying that he had no Objection to it. I am in hopes that before this reaches you that there will be a Line from the Judge, Lodged in the Department of State, if not I hope and Pray that the President will from the Conversation which Mr. Dolton may inform the President that he had with the Judge, & from other Circumstances, Grant in Marcy & in Pity to the innocent & Virtuous that a Discharge may be Granted as soon a Possible, Especially when it is Considered that it is the first fault, that he is young, that he was Drawn away by Capt. Sheffield, that he has been a Long while alredy Confined, that it is the Prayer in the Memorial, of a Great Number of the most Prinsiple Charectors in two Counties in the Massachusetts, as well as a Great Number of others that I have Convarsed with in New England that the President will Extend Marcy in this Perticular.—I have not upon my Honor the Least Doubt that from the Conversation I was Honord. with by the President, & with his Worthy Minister of State, but that they feel for us & will Discharge the Prisoner as soon as Expedient.

I remane Sir your Most obedent Huml. Sert.

BERIAH NORTON

RC (ViU); at foot of text: "President of the U.S."; endorsed by TJ as received 6 Oct. and so recorded in SJL.

A militia colonel during the Revolution, Beriah Norton (ca. 1733-1820) was a prominent resident of Martha's Vineyard and postmaster at Edgartown. He had traveled to Washington the previous June seeking a presidential pardon for his son-in-law, Elihu Marchant, who was convicted of absconding with the armed brig *Ranger* (Charles Edward Banks, *The History of Martha's Vineyard Dukes County Massachusetts*, 3 vols. [Boston, 1911-25; repr. Edgartown, Mass., 1966], 2:186; 3:379; James Monroe to TJ, 16 June 1801; William Rose to TJ, 16 June 1801).

William PATERSON had presided over the November 1800 session of the U.S. circuit court at Richmond that convicted Marchant (DHSC, 3:456).

MY PRECIOUS DAUGHTER: Sarah Norton Marchant (Vol. 34:364n).

From Samuel Smith

SIR/   Baltimore 15. septr. 1801
I Congratulate you on the Compleat Success of the Republican
Candidates for Electors of the senate of Maryland—this Secures us a
Majority in the senate of the U.S.—
I have a Letter from Mr. Dent mentioning that Mr. Merideth will
resign the office of Treasurer, & requesting that I would mention to
you his Wish to fill that office—from my knowledge of Mr. Dent, I
believe no Man more worthy of an appointment than he is—He is
honest upright & of a Character unimpeached—He has been in public Life from 21 Years & is fully equal to the Post of Treasurer. the appointment would gratify Maryland & would reward him for the
firmness of his Conduct on the late trying Occasion
The arrival of our squadron at the Critical Moment in the Mediterranean has silenced the Bablers on that subject—The Philadelphia
will keep the Tripolitan Admiral in Port until the Boston shall arrive—I believe the Treaty is ratified in France—I am sir
with real Esteem Your friend & servt.   S. SMITH

RC (DNA: RG 59, LAR); endorsed by
TJ as received 24 Sep. and so recorded in
SJL; also endorsed by TJ: "Dent to be
Treasurer."

FIRMNESS OF HIS CONDUCT ON THE
LATE TRYING OCCASION: George Dent
helped deliver the Maryland vote for TJ
in the election of the president in the
House of Representatives (TJ to Madison, 18 Feb. 1801). Dent also applied to

Gallatin for the treasurer's position (see
Enclosure No. 2, listed at Gallatin to TJ,
21 Sep.).
On an undated scrap of paper, in an
unidentified hand, TJ received notice that
Dent was available for another position:
"Should a Postmaster Genl be wanted, I
am requested to say that Mr George Dent
would except that Appointment" (MS in
DNA: RG 59, LAR, 3:0197; unsigned;
endorsed by TJ: "Postmaster Genl.").

From Thomas Willing

HONOURED SIR   Phila. Septr. 15th. 1801
I rec'd by the Post your favor of the 28th of August, on the
Subject of Mr. C. H— whose general Character, supported as it is
by your testimony and warm recommendation, wou'd have had full
weight with me, & a great majority of our Direction, if there had
been room left consistently with our, Plighted, faith to have put him
in Nomination—
From particular circumstances, I was not only pledg'd myself, to
Mr. Jas. Davidson, the first Teller of the bank US; but the Case was
the same, with every Gentleman of our Direction

The fact is, that Mr. Davidsons abilities, correct behaviour, & long Services as an Officer of the Bank, had well intitled him to any Office or preferment we cou'd give him—

When an Agent was wanted at Washington to negociate any business wh. might occur between the Government, & Us, he applied for that Station, but we cou'd not then, supply his place here as Teller, quite to our satisfaction; and therefore we passed him by—One of his brother's with his family, having removed to Washington, he was particularly anxious for the Appointment, which wou'd have given him a residence there; and felt greatly disappointed that the Agency was given to Mr. Dalton—havg. a strong attachment to him myself; not only from his Services & general good conduct, but also from his Manly behavior in the time of the Sickness of 1797 & 1798. *At that time*, when Our Cashier & the Assistant Cashier were both extreemly Ill, & when we had buried full half our people belongg. to the Institution, he was, at his Post, my faithfull assistant, with but four others, thro: the whole of those dismal Scenes—Under the Impression excited, by such usefull services; I obtain'd leave from a full board of the Directors, to assure him, that whenever Government shou'd find it essentially necessary for us to open an Office at Washington, & it shou'd be found practicable to do so, that in such case, he shoud be Our Cashier—Mr. Davidson has been accordingly appointed this day, to the Office of Cashier—

I beg Sir, that you will be fully persuaded of the high satisfaction it wou'd have given me, to have promoted your Wishes in the present, as it will be on every future Occasion, where I shall feel myself unrestrained by an Imperious necessity like the present—

I hope Sir, the reason's which I have now detaild & given you the trouble to read, will be fully satisfactory to you, as well as to the Gentleman you have so highly honoured with your kind & friendly recommendation—

Your Letter, I shall consider as you desire it may be, perfectly a private & confidential one, & am Sir

with the most sincere respect & esteem Yr. Obedt.

THOS. WILLING

RC (MoSHi: Jefferson Papers); at foot of text: "Thos. Jefferson Esqr."; endorsed by TJ as received 24 Sep. and so recorded in SJL.

MR. C. H—: that is, Samuel Hanson. James DAVIDSON, Jr., of 77 Union Street in Philadelphia, was a cashier of the Bank of the United States. In the summer of 1801 when the bank's directors decided to establish a branch office in Washington, they appointed Davidson cashier of the office of discount and deposit. Later that year they built a two-story office for the bank at the northeast corner of 13th and F Streets, N.W., with a three-story building for its cashier (Stafford, *Philadelphia Directory, for 1801,*

100; *National Intelligencer,* 23 Sep.; *Poulson's American Daily Advertiser,* 16 Oct.; RCHS, 46-47 [1947], 272).

To Benjamin Hawkins

DEAR SIR   Monticello. Sep 16. 18[01.]

Mrs. Trist who is here brought me her letter to inclose after I had [sent off my public] one to the post office: [. . .] I give it a special cover, which she thinks will render it safer than if committed to the post uncovered. she had neither sealed nor directed: but it [goes as I] [. . .] [prying] into [. . .] between [. . .] & to lie. I forgot to say in my public letter that I shall be with the heads of departments at Washington on the last day of the month, [&] continue there to the last day of July next; our plan being [to] [. . .] the two bilious months of Aug. & Sep. to seek health at home or elsewhere. this is for your general government in the direction of your letters. accept assurances of my constant esteem & respect   TH: JEFFERSON

PrC (DLC); faint; at foot of text: "Colo. Hawkins"; endorsed by TJ in ink on verso.

TJ's PUBLIC letter was the one of this date to James Wilkinson, Hawkins, and Andrew Pickens as Indian commissioners, printed below.

From Levi Lincoln

SIR   Worcester Sept. 16. 1801

you will have learnt before this reaches you, that we have failed in electing a republican member for the next Congress. The defeat was occasioned by the grossest misrepresentations & the basest arts. Emissaries were sent round the district to propagate slander in a way which could not be detected untill it was too late—Both the Worcester papers have been devoted to the federal party. The pieces under the signature of the farmer & the federal republican, are the first which for years they have published of that complexion for years— The latter altho they did not go to the press, in my hand writing, are charged by public suspicion on me—From a fear on your seeing, the animadversions in the public papers on these numbers, you might be apprehensive of more improprieties, than they in fact contain—I have prevailed on myself, however, apparently indelicate, to forward them,

The farmer's numbers will be continued so long as they are thought to be useful—any hints will be gratefully acknowledged—We are about establishing a republican paper in this town from, which we promise ourselves pleasing effects—

accept sir of my most sincere assurances of the highest esteem & respect—   Levi Lincoln

RC (DLC); at head of text: "To the President of the United States"; endorsed by TJ as received 1 Oct. and so recorded in SJL.

WE HAVE FAILED: General John Whiting, Lincoln's ally, lost to Federalist Seth Hastings in the contest for the seat that Lincoln had vacated in the House of Representatives (Worcester *Independent Gazetteer*, 8 Sep. 1801; *Biog. Dir. Cong.*; Paul Goodman, *The Democratic-Republicans of Massachusetts: Politics in a Young Republic* [Cambridge, Mass., 1964], 225).

In August, before the election to fill his former congressional seat, Lincoln began using the pen name FARMER for a series of essays that argued for Republican principles and was addressed "To the People." Isaiah Thomas's *Massachusetts Spy* published the first two installments on 19 Aug., and the other Worcester newspaper, the *Independent Gazetteer*, reprinted them on 1 Sep. The series continued after the election, with numbers 3 through 9 running in the *Spy* from 9 Sep. well into

November. Another numbered series of commentaries, this one signed by someone calling himself the FEDERAL REPUBLICAN, began in the *Spy* a week before the "Farmer" essays opened. The first item from the "Federal Republican" declared the author's intention to present "some arguments in favor of political charity, forbearance and toleration." In 1802, Lincoln's "Farmer" essays, 14 in all, were published as a collection (*Massachusetts Spy*, 12, 19, 26 Aug., 9, 16, 23 Sep., 7, 21, 28 Oct., 11, 18, 25 Nov. 1801; *Letters to the People. By a Farmer* [Salem, Mass., 1802]; Sowerby, No. 3442; ANB).

REPUBLICAN PAPER: Lincoln was the key force behind the establishment of the *National Aegis*, which began publication in Worcester early in December. Its first issue included the tenth of the "Farmer" essays, which stopped appearing in the *Massachusetts Spy*. The "Federal Republican" series continued in the *Spy* (Pasley, *Tyranny of Printers*, 206; *National Aegis*, 2 Dec.; *Massachusetts Spy*, 16, 23, 30 Dec. 1801, 6, 13 Jan. 1802).

From James Madison

DEAR SIR,   Sepr. 16. 1801

The Messenger delivered me about 9 OC. on saturday evening the packet with your letters of Sepr. 11 & 12. I join in your opinion that the suspicions of Murray in the letters inclosed in the former are too harsh to be probable. Still his situation may produce feelings & views not coincident with ours, and strengthens the policy of getting the Chancellor on the ground as soon as possible. I hear nothing of the Boston frigate. Perhaps the mail of day may bring some account of her movements. I shall take care that no delay shall be chargeable on me; though I have been very little in a condition since I got home for close application of any sort. I have not been under the necessity of lying up, or renouncing current attentions, but have felt too much of the "Malaise" for any thing beyond them. I return the letters from S. Smith & B. and forward a letter from Dr. Thornton. I have one from him myself, which I shall answer by saying that on the receipt of M's resignation you had fixt on a successor, and closed the door to further applications. I find that the idea of H's appointment had leaked out, and that his pretensions were not regarded by the Docr. as a bar to his own. I inclose also a letter from F. Preston which speaks itself, the object of the Writer. I believe him to be a man of worth, of good understanding, and in a position to have some knowledge of Indian affairs. With these qualifications he might be a fit Associate of Hawkins & Wilkinson, should Pickens decline & his being a Virginian be no objection. I have with me Mr. Davis of N.Y. whom I presume to be the candidate for an office in that City. As he has but just arrived I have not had conversation eno' with him to find out whether he means to visit Monticello. I conjecture that to be his primary object. He brings me an introduction from Ed. Livingston & from him only.

Yours always most affectionately & respectfully

JAMES MADISON

RC (DLC); at foot of text: "The President of the U.S."; endorsed by TJ as received 17 Sep. and so recorded in SJL. Enclosures: (1) Samuel Harrison Smith to TJ, 4 Sep. (2) Aaron Burr to TJ, 4 Sep. (3) William Thornton to TJ, 8 Sep. (recorded in SJL as received 17 Sep. with notation "Off," but not found), which was enclosed in Thornton to Madison, also of the 8th, soliciting an appointment as U.S. treasurer in the wake of Samuel Meredith's resignation (Madison, *Papers, Sec. of State Ser.*, 2:92-3). (4) Francis Preston to Madison, 2 Sep., learning that William R. Davie has declined an appointment to negotiate with the southern Indians, he offers himself for the job in the event that Andrew Pickens also declines the appointment and a more qualified candidate fails to apply (same, 2:80).

To James Wilkinson, Benjamin Hawkins, and Andrew Pickens

GENTLEMEN   Monticello Sep. 16. 1801

Your favor of the 1st. inst. covering letters to the Secretary at war, left open for my perusal, came to hand yesterday. General Dearborne being at present at his own house in the province of Maine, were we to await an answer from him, the object of your application would be passed by before you could recieve it. to prevent the public from recieving injury therefore from this circumstance I shall undertake to answer for him. the reasons which you urge for changing the place of meeting the Choctaws from the Natchez, appear solid. that it might be disagreeable to the inhabitants, and injurious also, to recieve such a number of Indians among them, and that it might produce incidents disagreeable to the Indians themselves is very possible. confiding therefore in your judgment on this subject I approve of your proposition to remove the meeting to some other place free from those objections, convenient still to the Indians and to the reception of the provisions & stores provided for you.

I am sincerely sorry the Cherokees shew an indisposition to meet us: being very desirous of keeping on good terms with them, and of [attending] & serving them by every act of friendship & liberality. if the murderer of the [woman] cannot be found I refer to yourselves to consider whether it would not be proper to satisfy her relations by presents as is practised among themselves, and as we [do by] compact with some of the tribes of Indians. still assuring the nation however that if the murderer [can] be found he shall be punished.—I am disappointed in [the conduct] of the Glass. percieving that he was a man of strong mind, no attention [. . .]ed at Washington to conciliate his friendship; and we believed he had [left us with the best] dispositions. Accept assurances of my high consideration & respect, and my best wishes for the success of your negociations.

TH: JEFFERSON

PrC (DLC); faint; at foot of text: "The Commissioners for treating with the Southern Indians."

CHANGING THE PLACE OF MEETING: Wilkinson, Hawkins, and Pickens changed the location of their meeting with the Choctaws to Fort Adams on the Mississippi River. The negotiation took place in December 1801 (ASP, *Indian Affairs*, 1:658-63).

The commissioners met with a few chiefs of the CHEROKEES at Southwest Point on 4 and 5 Sep., conveying the government's wish to improve roads between Natchez, Nashville, and South Carolina, and to build houses of accommodation and ferries along the roads. The commissioners declared that there was no intention by the United States to take more of the Cherokees' land. In reply, the Cherokees said no to any further improvement of routes through their country. They also referred to the eagerness of land speculators to acquire their lands, asked for the removal of settlers who had encroached on Cherokee territory, and complained that the state of Tennessee did not abide by agreements made between the Indians and the United States (same, 656-7; Foster, *Hawkins*, 377-84).

To Enoch Edwards

DEAR SIR   Monticello Sep. 17. 1801

I recieved by our last post your favor of Aug. 31. and immediately wrote to mr Barnes, who was soon to set out for Philadelphia, to have measures taken for recieving & bringing on the carriage, & for paying mr Hanse's bill. I am glad you had no scroll put behind it, as I think them unhandsome. I have no doubt of entire satisfaction with the whole business and have to give you many thanks for the attentions yourself and mrs Edwards have been so good as to bestow on it. the favor respecting the carpets I will in due time ask of you. I expect within a week from this time to return to Washington, and suppose mr Barnes will by that time have got back from Philadelphia, or very soon after. I pray you to present me respectfully to mrs Edwards and to be assured of my sensibility to your kindness and my high esteem & respect.   TH: JEFFERSON

P.S. Govr. Monroe is at present with his family in my neighborhood, is well, & presents his respects to you.

PrC (DLC); at foot of text: "Doctr. Edwards"; endorsed by TJ in ink on verso.

To Christopher Ellery

SIR   Monticello Sep. 17. 1801.

Your favor of Aug. 28. came to my hands by our last post. mr Geffroy's declaration is sufficient proof that he did not write the letters addressed to me in his name. on recurring to them I percieve that it is a constrained hand such as a person would write who desired to disguise his own. but with what view it could be done is difficult to conjecture. the facts stated are such as none but a friend to this administration should wish to bring forward. and why should such an one conceal his own name? but whether the information comes from friend or foe, it is my duty to have the facts enquired into. they are stated in my letter to mr Geffroy which I am glad to hear is in your hands. I have desired Genl. Dearborne to look into the subject with the proper caution, and particularly to speak with yourself on the subject if he should see you on his return to Washington: and I should hope from your attachment to the public interest that you would be so good as to communicate either to him or myself what you can find to be the truth as to those facts. if the information really came from an enemy, I shall always thank them for such information. the opinions & expressions of sentiment which make up the rest of the letters I give to the air. Accept assurances of my high consideration & respect.   TH: JEFFERSON

PrC (DLC); at foot of text: "The honble Christopher Ellery."

MY LETTER TO MR GEFFROY: TJ to "Nicholas Geffroy," 14 Aug.

I HAVE DESIRED: see TJ to Henry Dearborn, 12 Sep.

To James Hopkins

DEAR SIR   Monticello Sep. 17. 1801.

Your favor of July 16. was recd. about 10. days ago only. I have examined my papers, and am still in possession of a copy of the deed for the Hardware limestone lands, in your handwriting, which you were so kind as to send me before you sent the original. but the original itself I unquestionably delivered to the clerk, on a court day, at his table, where I presented it to be recorded. after looking at it he told me the act was expired which permitted the recording lost deeds. I desired him then to keep it as his office was the proper place, until measures could be taken for placing it legally on the records. I have been only twice to Charlottesville since I came home, both times on court days, when I could not have an opportunity of speaking with mr Carr. if I am able to go there before I leave this (which will be in a week) I will look into it.—having no longer occasion to go to Philadelphia, I ceased to answer to mr Duanc & others, the commissions which I had formerly been charged by my friends to execute there. hence it was that I did not pay him for your papers the last winter as I had before done. your commission for the purchase of the journals of the old¹ Congress is in a course of execution. the old edition was exhausted & a new one in the press. I had recieved 3. vols for you before I left Washington, and expect by the time I return the remaining volumes will be ready. I sincerely join with you in congratulations on the recovery of our fellow citizens from the phantasms of 1798 which had been conjured up to turn their minds from their natural course. I hope they will not be again so disturbed. accept assurances of my high esteem & respect   TH: JEFFERSON

PrC (DLC); at foot of text: "Doctr. James Hopkins."

For the LIMESTONE LANDS, see Vol. 28:570-1.

3 VOLS: for TJ's subscription to Richard Folwell's edition of the *Journals of Congress*, see Vol. 31 :392n.

¹ Preceding two words interlined.

From James Madison

DEAR SIR   Sepr. 17. 1801

I make use of the oppy. by Mr. Davis to forward you the contents of the weekly packet recd yesterday from the Office of State. Having had time scarcely to read some of the communications, I am unable, if there were occasion, to submit comments on them. Mr. Wagner writes that Mr. Graham left Washington on saturday last with the papers relating to the Mission of Mr. Livingston, and was to be with me on monday evening past. As he is not yet arrived, I think it not unprobable that he may have gone by to Monticello with an intention to take me in his way back. I inclose a letter from Genl. Gates, concurring in the recommendations of Mr. Davis.

Mr. Graham has this moment arrived, and has brought me sundry documents some of which I am obliged to sign without reading, as they will be subject to your revision, and I shd. otherwise lose the oppy. by Mr. Davis. Mr. Graham declines proceeding further than Orange. The inclosed very confidential letter from DW. Clinton was brought by Mr. G. very apropos to be forwarded to you. Adieu

Yrs. most affy. & repy.   JAMES MADISON

I send a newspaper copy of the French Convention

RC (DLC); with postscript written in left margin perpendicular to text; endorsed by TJ as received from the State Department on 17 Sep. and so recorded in SJL. Enclosures: (1) Jacob Wagner to Madison, 14 Sep., stating that State Department clerk Daniel Brent set out for Dumfries on 12 Sep. with papers relating to the mission of Robert R. Livingston, which he was to convey to John Graham for delivery to TJ (Madison, *Sec. of State Ser.*, 2:113-14). (2) DeWitt Clinton to Madison, 3 Sep., advising TJ against appointing Matthew L. Davis as naval officer of New York (same, 2:81). Other enclosures not found.

To Benjamin Waterhouse

SIR   Monticello Sep. 17. 1801.

I recieved by the last post your favor of Aug. 28. and by the same a letter from Doctr. Gantt informing me that the matter I first sent him from hence had taken in three of the subjects into whom it had been inserted, that from these he had inoculated others, so that they are now in full possession of the disease at Washington. I have also sent matter to Richmond, Petersburg, and several other parts of this state so that I have no doubt it will be generally spread through it, notwithstanding the incredulity which had been produced by the ineffectual experiments of Richmond & Norfolk. the first letter you were so kind as to write to me on the subject, & which contained a great deal of useful information, I put into the hands of Doctr. Gantt, and we concluded it would be useful to publish it as soon as the public should be possessed of the disease. it is still in his hands, and as you have been so kind as to permit us to make any use of it which the general good may require, I shall propose to him to have it published immediately on my return to Washington, which will be within a week from this time. it is just our countrymen should know to whose philanthropic attentions they will be indebted for relief from a disease which has always been the terror of this country. Accept my particular thanks for this great good, and assurances of my high esteem & respect.   TH: JEFFERSON

RC (MBCo); at foot of text: "Doctr. Waterhouse." PrC (DLC).

LETTER FROM DOCTR. GANTT: Edward Gantt to TJ, 7 Sep.

TJ sent smallpox vaccine to James Cur-

rie and William Foushee, both of RICH-MOND, with letters dated 30 Aug., and to John Shore of PETERSBURG with a letter of 12 Sep.

FIRST LETTER: Waterhouse to TJ, 8 June.

From Bartholomew Dandridge, Jr.

SIR,   Cap françois 18 Sep: 1801.

I have the honor to inform you that I arrived at this city from Aux Cayes the day before yesterday, for the purpose of conferring with my friend Colo. Lear; as well respecting the situation of this island in relation to the United States and to obtain from him some information which it would have been imprudent to commit to writing, as also to fix a plan of Commercial business between us. To the information which has been so fully given by Colo. Lear respecting the state of things here I will only add that the greatest tranquillity & order prevail in the South department of the island. The cultivation of Coffee, Sugar &c. is beginning to be well attended to, & a very abundant crop, especially of Coffee, is now growing & will shortly be gathered.

A few days before I left Aux Cayes I recd. information from Mr. Ritchie, our consul at Port Republican, that he intended soon to embark for Philada. & that he shd. be absent two or three months. When I arrived at Port Republican, on my way hither, Mr. Ritchie had saild, & from all the intelligence I obtained there, he went away with no great expectation of being continued in his office, having understood that a change was contemplated. Should this be really the case & a successor to Mr. Ritchie shd. not have been already appointed, I take the liberty, Sir, to ask the Agency of the United States at Port Republican, both on account of its superior commercial advantages to the agency at Aux Cayes, & the satisfaction I shd. derive in being placed near my friend Colo. Lear. Whether I am so fortunate as to be thought worthy of the agency at Port Republican, or whether I am continued in my present station, my best abilities shall be used for the benefit of my Country, & to forward the honest views of my Countrymen trading to this island.

The seat of the Govt. of the island being fixed at Port Republican, it is however probable that it may become necessary for Colo Lear to remove there, which will cause a vacancy here; in that case I take the further liberty to solicit the Agency at this Port.—As an evidence that my appointment either to Port Republican or this place wou'd be satisfactory to Colo. Lear, he is so good as to write to you upon the subject, as he has already done to the Secy. of State.

With sentiments of the highest Respect & sincere Esteem, I have the honor to be, Sir, Yr. mo: obdt. Sert.   BEW. DANDRIDGE

RC (DNA: RG 59, LAR); at foot of first page: "Thos. Jefferson Esqe. &c. &c. &c."; endorsed by TJ as received 23 Oct. and so recorded in SJL; also endorsed by TJ: "to be Commercl. Agent at Cap. Francois vice Lear or Port Republicain vice Ritchie." Enclosed in Tobias Lear to TJ, 19 Sep.

By appointment from John Adams in 1800, Dandridge was consul for the southern district of the island of Saint-Domingue. Born about 1772, he had been a secretary for George Washington, William Vans Murray at the Hague, and Rufus King in London, and Tobias LEAR recommended him to TJ in March 1801. Dandridge's previous correspondence with TJ, all of it in 1793 when Dandridge worked for Washington, consisted of brief communications transmitting papers or requests from the president to the secretary of state (Washington, *Papers, Pres. Ser.*, 8:234-5n; *Ret. Ser.*, 1:23-4n; Vol. 26:319-20, 578; Vol. 27:481, 503, 620, 629; Vol. 33:448).

Robert RITCHIE was the American consul for Port-au-Prince, which during the Saint-Domingue revolution received the new name Port Républicain. Toussaint-Louverture announced in August that he was moving the SEAT of government there (Madison, *Papers, Sec. of State Ser.*, 1:162n; 2:65; Laurent Dubois, *Avengers of the New World: The Story of the Haitian Revolution* [Cambridge, Mass., 2004], 167).

AS HE HAS ALREADY DONE: Lear wrote to Madison on 15 Sep. to suggest that Dandridge succeed Ritchie as consul at Port Républicain, or succeed Lear at Cap-Français if Lear, the consul general, moved to Port Républicain to be near the government. In November, after Ritchie formally resigned from his position, TJ named Dandridge the commercial agent at Port Républicain, with the proviso that he might be moved to a different location depending on where Lear ended up (Madison, *Papers, Sec. of State Ser.*, 2:115, 257, 404, 490; Vol. 33:677, 678).

To Albert Gallatin

Dear Sir   Monticello Sep. 18. 1801.

Your favors of the 7th. 12th. & 14th. inst. came to hand yesterday. consequently that of the 7th. must have slept a week somewhere. mr Davis is now with me. he has not opened himself. when he does I shall inform him that nothing is decided, nor can be till we get together at Washington. I keep all the letters of recommendn of him which you inclosed me, as also Milledge's letter, & return you all your other papers. I approve of your intended application to Genl. Herd for a successor to White; and wish you to appoint any one whom his recommendation or other better evidence shall place in your view as the best. as to the successor to Powell of Savanna I should think the person on whom Milledge & Jackson both unite, might be safely appointed. I will write to enquire for a substitute for Wilkins of Cherrystone.—as to Jarvis's successor, will it not be better to wait for Genl. Dearborne, who, I suppose will be at Washington as early as I shall or nearly so. not however that I know this, but only presume it. I am glad you have yourself settled Worthington's appointment, as I possess no knowlege which could have aided you. in the case of Cayuga & Cincinnati, where you seem to be without information, it is probable Capt Lewis can help us out. he is well acquainted there. being absent at this time I have not an opportunity of asking him, but he will be on with me at Washington on or before the last day of the month. with respect to Gardner & Campbell I must leave them to yourself. I think we are bound to take care of them. could we not procure them as good births as their former at least in some of the custom houses? one part of the subject of one of your letters is of a nature which forbids my interference altogether. the amendment to the constitution of which you speak would be a remedy to a certain degree. so will a different amendment which I know will be proposed, to wit, to have no electors, but let the people vote directly, and the ticket which has a plurality of the votes of any state, to be considered as recieving thereby the whole vote of the state.—our motions with respect to Livingston are easily explained. it was impossible for him to go off in the instant he was named, or on shorter warning than two or three months. in the mean time Bingham & others, mercantile men, complained in Congress that we were losing so many thousand dollars every day till the ratificn of the treaty. a vessel to carry it was prepared by our predecessors & all the preparatory expences of her mission incurred. this is the reason why mr L. did not go then. the

reason why he must go now is that difficulties have arisen unexpectedly in the ratificn of the treaty, which we believe him more capable
of getting over than mr Murray. we think that the state of the treaty
there calls earnestly for the presence of a person of talents &
confidence. we would rather trust him than Murray in shaping any
new modification.

I sincerely congratulate you on the better health of your son, as well
as on the new addition to your family, and mrs Gallatin's convales-
cence. I consider it as a trying experiment for a person from the
mountains to pass the two bilious months on the tidewaters. I have
not done it these 40. years, and nothing should induce me to do it.
as it is not possible but that the administration must take some portion of time for their own affairs, I think it best they should select
that season for absence. Genl. Washington set the example of those
2. months. mr Adams extended them to 8. months. I should not
suppose our bringing it back to 2. months a ground for grumbling.
but grumble who will, I will never pass those months on tide
water.   Accept assurances of my constant & sincere esteem &
respect.   TH: JEFFERSON

RC (NHi: Gallatin Papers); at foot of
first page: "Secretary of the Treasury";
endorsed by Gallatin. PrC (DLC).

I WILL WRITE: see TJ to Thomas New-
ton of this date.
SUBJECT OF ONE OF YOUR LETTERS:
Gallatin to TJ, 14 Sep.

From William Heath

SIR   Roxbury (Massachusetts) September 18th. 1801

While I have been enjoying, with grateful satisfaction, your Judicious administration of the Government of the United States.—and
its daily increasing estimation with the real friends of our Country in
this quarter,—I have carefully avoided giving you interruption in
your important duties by any epistles or applications of mine, and I
pray you to excuse my doing of it at this time,—Colonel Lee of Marblehead in this state who will either do me the Honour of handing
this to you, or forward it by some other hand,—wishes to act in the
revenue department in the County of Essex and as Collector at the
Port of Salem, where it seems to be conjectured, that a vacancy may
happen,—I therefore beg leave to observe, that Colonel Lee is a Gentleman well qualified for any office, or trust to which he may be appointed.—he was an early able and faithful officer in the American

Army during the revolutionary war, is a Uniform and Staunch republican, a man of integrity ability and good information in the commercial world,—permit me therefore most heartily to recommend him to your notice, and employment.

Wishing you every felicity I have the honour to be with the highest respect Sir Your most humble Servant   W HEATH

RC (DNA: RG 59, LAR); at foot of text: "President Jefferson"; endorsed by TJ as received 3 Oct. and so recorded in SJL, where it is connected by a brace with Elbridge Gerry to TJ, 18 Sep. (not found), with notation "Wm. Lee to be collectr Salem"; also endorsed by TJ: "Colo. Wm. Lee of Marblehead to be Collector of Salem."

To James Madison

DEAR SIR   Monticello Sep. 18. 1801.

Your favor of the 16th. by post & 17th. by mr Davis have been duly recieved. he has not yet opened himself to me; but I shall assure him that nothing can [be] said here on the subject, nor determined on but when we shall be together at Washington. I have a letter from mr Gallatin whose only doubt is whether Rogers should be removed. if he is, he seems clear Davis had better have the appointment.—I think it will be better to postpone an answer to Govr. Clinton on Brant's proposition till we can be together at Washington. in fact [it] belongs to the War department.—Genl. Pickens is arrived at S.W. [point] which [answers] mr Preston's application.—I wrote to the Secretary of the [Navy] Sep. 5. to have the Boston expedited. I have a letter from him dated Baltimore Sep. 11. he had not then recieved mine. he had just lost his eldest son. it is pretty [evident] we shall be at Washington in time to dispatch papers for the Chancellor. for that reason I retain the several commissions signed by you and forwarded yesterday, not being satisfied which we had better use. I am satisfied we ought not to keep Murray there [. . .] on so slender a business. I count fully myself the 1st Consul will ratify on condn. of an abandonment of spoliations on our part. if he does not, would it not be better to give the Chancellor a power [. . .] to execute the article for the [restitution] of prizes, and leave to the Senate whether any new [modifications] shall be agreed to? you know my opinion [as to] the importance of the ratificn. but all this shall be the subject [of consultation] when we meet. I return all your papers except [those] applying for offices, which I imagine had better be in my bundle. I shall see you on Saturday or Sunday if you be not gone. my respects to the ladies & affectionate attachment to yourself.   TH: JEFFERSON

PrC (DLC); faint; at foot of text: "The Secy. of State"; words in brackets supplied from Tr. Tr (MHi); in unidentified hand.

LETTER FROM MR GALLATIN: Gallatin to TJ, 12 Sep.

AN ANSWER TO GOVR. CLINTON ON

BRANT'S PROPOSITION: in the summer of 1801, Joseph Brant wrote New York Governor George Clinton, inquiring whether Iroquois settlement all in one place in the West would meet with the protection and approbation of the U.S. government (Madison, *Papers, Sec. of State Ser.*, 2:123n).

To Thomas Newton

DEAR SIR   Monticello Sep. 18. 1801.

The Secretary of the Treasury informs me that he is obliged to remove mr Wilkins the collector at Cherrystone's on the Eastern shore, having never rendered any account of his collection since Dec. 1796. and that he can get no information whom to put in his place. he says 'the successor should have integrity, keenness & firmness. there is much smuggling in that district, & the people being in the habit of favouring it, it will require some exertions to put an end to it.' to increase our difficulties I am afraid it is not easy to find a republican there, and yet after so many years exclusion justice calls aloud for their being introduced into the offices falling [vacant.] accustomed to repose myself on your zeal for the public good, I take the liberty of solliciting your enquiries for a proper character to give this appointment to, which I presume will be practicable from Norfolk. I have no republican acquaintance on the Eastern shore to whom I could apply.   Mr. Barnes, whom I had desired to pay 700. D. to mr Taylor the first week of this month, informs he has done it, & I wrote some time ago to mr Taylor to know if he could let me have any more of the same qualitied Madeira. Accept assurances of my constant esteem & respect.   TH: JEFFERSON

PrC (DLC); faint and blurred; at foot of text: "Colo. Thos. Newton."

SECRETARY OF THE TREASURY INFORMS ME: see Gallatin to TJ, 7 Sep.

TJ WROTE James Taylor, Jr., on 28 Aug.

From John Shore

SIR   Petersburg. Septemb. 18th. 1801.

The vaccine matter which you have been so obliging as to send me, I have received, & for which I beg leave to offer you my best thanks—

Your observations, deduced from late experiments under your own eye, are important, inasmuch as they will tend to remove any prejudice against this invaluable discovery, in consequence of its failure in many parts of this state. I had received some from this same stock, which I believe was sent by Dr. Waterhouse to Dr. Spence of Dumfries, but would not use it, until I had received some assurance of its activity.

Our autumnal diseases are about to pay us their annual visit, as soon as they disappear, probably early in November, I shall avail myself of the Opportunity, which your kindness has furnished me with, of witnessing the several phenomena of this formidable rival of the Small Pox.

With every sentiment of the highest respect I am Sir, Your obedt. servt.   JNO. SHORE

RC (PPCP); endorsed by TJ as received on 24 Sep. and so recorded in SJL.

MATTER WHICH YOU HAVE BEEN SO OBLIGING AS TO SEND ME: TJ enclosed vaccine matter with his letter to Shore of 12 Sep.

From John Syme

DEAR SIR,   Rockey Mills 18th Sepr. 1801.

I did write you sometime Since, but hear it miscarry'd. Bestow one of your precious Momts. on a Very Aged Republican, always Your Friend; Depress'd indeed 4 yrs. ago; But rejoic'd (perhaps) in the Extreme, last Congress. I perceve the Dust Kick'd up, whenever You Dismiss a Federal culprit. One & all your well wishers, are Clearly of Opinion wth. Abraham Bishop, that you possibly may halt too long at Capua. The Buisness being done in a General Way, They will have time, to digest it, & their Stomachs properly come Down. How[ever] that may be, beleive Me My good Sir, it is of no consequence, My Opinion is, these Wretches, will always Oppose You. We want them Not. If We had them, We should be wrong. If I am travelling North, & fall in, wth. one of these Men, instantly I Turn to the South, as to go their Road is Death & Destruction.

I am told Yourself & Friends, are not quite supply'd wth. Horses. I have a pair, Superior to any, I ever saw. They are full 19 hands, Young, Sound & Well Broke. Mr. Randolph could Call and visit them. Meantime, pray Deliver Him the Inclos'd, wth. My Compts. to all the Family, wch. Concludes Me for present, My Dear Sir,

With the Highest Consideration, Your Old Friend & Obedt. Servt.

J SYME

Please make my Respects to Mr. Madison & Lady.

RC (MoSHi: Jefferson Papers); torn; endorsed by TJ as received 24 Sep. and so recorded in SJL. Enclosure not found.

John Syme (1728-1805) served with TJ in the Virginia legislature during the 1770s and early 1780s, and as a colonel of militia and county lieutenant during the Revolution, he corresponded frequently with TJ in early 1781 on military matters. The two men also shared an interest in fine horses, with TJ attempting to purchase one from Syme in 1792 (Washington, *Papers, Col. Ser.*, 7:274n; *Rev. War Ser.*, 1:177n; Leonard, *General Assembly*, 102-3, 105-6, 109-10, 112, 114-15, 122-3, 125-6, 129-30, 141-2; Robert Bolling Lancaster, *A Sketch of the Early History of Hanover County Virginia and Its Large and Important Contributions to The American Revolution* [Richmond, 1976], 16; Vol. 24:340-1, 387-8).

In the preface to his published 11 Mch. address on TJ's election, ABRAHAM BISH-OP warned that the freedoms gained by "Our revolution" were in danger of being lost, "if, like Hannibal's army in Capua, we regaled on luxuries and reposed on down; if we committed all the spoils of our triumphs, our military chest and weapons of warfare to that class of men, who know no treasury nor arsenal, except their own" (Abraham Bishop, *Oration Delivered in Wallingford, On the 11th of March 1801, Before the Republicans of the State of Connecticut, at Their General Thanksgiving, For the Election Of Thomas Jefferson to the Presidency, And of Aaron Burr to the Vice-Presidency, Of the United States of America* [Bennington, Vt., 1801], iv). The Roman historian Livy asserted that the Carthaginians under Hannibal squandered their triumph at Cannae by wintering at Capua and indulging in that city's vices, rather than pushing on for final victory against Rome (Livy, *The History of Rome*, 6 vols. [London, 1921-37], 3:147).

From Pierce Butler

DEAR SIR   Philada. Septbr. the 19th. 1801

It will not be amiss for You to read the inclosed, which I recd yesterday. please to destroy it when read—It was not very prudent, nor very dignified in Mr. P. to assail You through another person. If he felt true independence of mind he woud unreservedly have stated to You any measure that he consider'd adviseable to be adopted in the State he represented. It might be well for himself if he had a more correct sense of personal Character. I anex my answer to the inclosed

With the highest esteem Yr Sincere friend   P. B—

I purpose being at the Federal City the middle of October

RC (DLC); with Enclosure No. 2 subjoined on same sheet below postscript;
endorsed by TJ as received 1 Oct. and so
recorded in SJL. Enclosures: (1) Aaron
Burr to Butler, New York, 16 Sep. 1801,
writing that following conversations with
Charles Pinckney the previous March in
Washington "respecting some Changes
which he wished to take place in certain
offices in S.C.," he had presented Pinckney's recommendations to the president,
but could not learn that any of the proposed changes have been made nor recall
any of the persons recommended except
Daniel D'Oyley; Burr has heard from several South Carolina "gentlemen" that
only Butler can "successfully oppose
General Pinckney as federal Senator"
(RC in DLC; see also Vol. 33:332n). (2)

Butler to Burr, 19 Sep. 1801, declaring
that removals "should be done sparingly
and only where necessary"; while many
appointments by Washington and Adams
were undoubtedly "partial," it would be
imprudent to follow their example because "Every man removed adds twenty
enemies to republicanism and the present
administration, while it adds nothing to
our friends"; moderation will prove to the
"great body of the landed interest, the
true support of good government, that the
present administration are the friends of
an equal, mild, economical, and just government"; Butler's offering for the Senate
is "out of the question, but I am not, nor
shall I be inactive on that occasion" (Tr in
same; in unidentified hand).

To William Fleming

DEAR SIR   Monticello Sep. 19. 1801.

I am called on to answer Gilliam's bill against mr Wayles's [Exrs
by] B. Skelton's representatives. there are some facts to the recollection of which you can perhaps aid me. you remember we had a meeting in Richmond with M. Skelton, and I believe, J. Baker acting as
his atty. when was it? did not J. Baker act for M. Skelton & in his
presence? I have our account which I think he compared with the
vouchers and marked thus v the articles he passed, which marks are
on the papers. do you remember his passing them? did we enter on
your account & what progress did we make in it? what prevented our
going through the whole business? can you be so good as to furnish
me with a copy of the account of Colo. J. Fleming's admin. of B. Skelton's estate, with any additional articles of account of his exrs relating
to that estate? I should be extremely obliged to you for it, [not] only
[as necessary] for the statement of my proceedings as exr on the right
of mrs Jefferson to that estate, but as it may assist in harmonizing our
answers. have you answered the bill? I shall be at Washington on the
last day of this month, and will therefore ask you [to address] your
answer to these queries to that place. accept assurances of my constant & affectionate esteem & respect.   TH: JEFFERSON

PrC (MHi); faint; at foot of text: "The
honble Judge Fleming"; endorsed by TJ
in ink on verso.

GILLIAM'S BILL: Robert Gilliam had
filed a chancery suit against the estate
of TJ's father-in-law, John Wayles

(d. 1773), on behalf of the estate of TJ's wife's first husband, Bathurst Skelton (d. 1768). Gilliam was the husband of Skelton's sister Lucy. The suit concerned arrangements between Wayles and Skelton over certain lands, including Elk Island. The long-standing controversy involved TJ in multiple ways: as one of the executors of Wayles's estate, as a former administrator of Skelton's estate, by his wife's dower right, and by her interest in her first husband's estate. The suit was not resolved before 1813. Fleming, whose

brother had been the administrator of Skelton's father's estate, was also the object of chancery action by Gilliam (MB, 1:286, 349n; 2:1051, 1248n, 1290; RS, 1:305n; Shackelford, *Jefferson's Adoptive Son*, 8-9; Malone, *Jefferson*, 1:156, 161; Vol. 7:17-18, 43; Vol. 15:659-60, 661; Fleming to TJ, 13 Oct.).

M. SKELTON: Bathurst Skelton's brother Meriwether, who died about 1778 (WMQ, 1st ser., 12 [1903], 62-4; 2d ser., 9 [1929], 212).

To Edward Gantt

DEAR SIR   Monticello Sep 19. 1801.

I have duly recieved your favor of the 14th and am sorry I have no subject at present in such a stage of vaccination as to yield the matter in it's proper state. on the 24th I shall have some, which will be in time to forward by the post which will reach you on the 29th as well as to carry on myself, as I shall be with you about the same time. it is now very much spread in this part of the country, but I am afraid that under so many operators not acquainted with the proper time of taking the matter, it will immediately become spurious. I very much doubt whether it is at all to be depended on after eight times 24. hours from the hour of innoculation. I observe that immediately after that the matter begins to be yellowish, to thicken, & to shew that absorption has begun. Accept assurances of my esteem & high respect.   TH: JEFFERSON

PrC (DLC); at foot of text: "Doctr. Gantt"; endorsed by TJ in ink on verso.

To Samuel Hanson

DEAR SIR   Monticello Sep. 19. 1801

Your favor of the 14th is recieved by the last post. by the one preceding I had recieved mr Meredith's resignation in future, and had sent an appointment to another, according to arrangements [settled] before I left Washington. there were circumstances attending that which absolutely controuled us.

Not having any other acquaintance among the Directors of the bank of the US. at Philadelphia, I wrote to the President mr Willing, with the delicacy which the case required[. until] I recieve his answer I shall not consider your appointment as desperate however respectable the grounds on which mr Tilghman contends the contrary. my having recieved no answer as yet, is favorable. I return you mr Tilghman's letter, and shall within not many days be with you myself. accept assurances of my best wishes & high respect.

TH: JEFFERSON

PrC (DLC); faint; at foot of text: "Saml Hanson esq"; endorsed by TJ in ink on verso.

YOUR FAVOR OF THE 14TH: Hanson's letter was dated 14 Sep. 1800, but endorsed by TJ and recorded in SJL as a letter of 14 Sep. 1801, received 17 Sep.; printed at 14 Sep. 1800 (Vol. 32:139-40).

I WROTE TO THE PRESIDENT MR WILLING: TJ to Thomas Willing, 28 Aug.

From Tobias Lear

SIR,   Cape François, September 19th: 1801.

The enclosed letter from Mr. Dandridge, who is now in this City, will express to you his wish to be appointed Commercial Agent for the United States, either at Port Republican or here.—

In a letter to the Secretary of State, under date of the 24th of August, I informed him of the determination of the Governor to fix his residence at Port Republican, and of his expressing a wish that I might be instructed by my Government to establish myself at the same place.—

In my own part I have no wish to remove from hence, unless the interest of the United States should require it; and, in any event, I could not think of relinquishing the emoluments which are attached by the Agency of a particular port for the sake of residing near the Governor. But whether my residence be here or there, in the Character of General Commercial Agent, I should expect the Agency of the port to be attached to it.—

Should the Agency of Port Republican become vacant, and my personal residence not be necessary at that place, as the seat of Government, I should feel highly gratified by the appointment of Mr. Dandridge thereto; or, if it is thought proper for me to establish myself at Port Republican, and the particular agency of this place thereby become vacant it would afford me the greatest satisfaction to see it filled by Mr. Dandridge; and certain I am that no person would discharge the public duties with more fidelity.—

I have written so frequently and so fully to the Secretary of State on the Affairs of this Island, since my arrival, that I shall forbear troubling you with any detail on the subject, presuming that my communications, or such parts of them as may be worth your notice, have been laid before you.—

I pray that God may preserve your valuable life for the good of our Country, and give you happiness in the enjoyment of it.—

Accept, I pray you, the assurances of my highest respect, and most sincere attachment.   Tobias Lear.

RC (DNA: RG 59, LAR); at foot of text: "The President of the United States"; endorsed by TJ as received 23 Oct. and so recorded in SJL. PrC (DNA: RG 59, CD, Cap Haitien). Enclosure: Bartholomew Dandridge to TJ, 18 Sep.

In a letter to Madison on 24 Aug., Lear enclosed a communication from Toussaint-Louverture, the GOVERNOR of Saint-Domingue, about the relocation of the colony's government to Port Républicain (Madison, *Papers, Sec. of State Ser.*, 2:65-6).

From Levi McKeen

SIR   New York the 19th Septembr 1801

The Republicans of the district which Mr Theodorus Bailey has represented in Congress was encouraged to believe, that Mr Bailey would have been appointed either Supervisor or Naval officer for the state[1] of New York, when a vacancy should happen in those offices, by resignation or otherwise. The first of those offices has however been otherwise filled and I am Just now informed that it is not the Pleasure of the Government that the latter officer should be removed.

I have this moment Learned that the office of Commissioner of Loans for this district has become vacant by resignation, and as Mr Bailey's Friends have reason to believe that the President of the United States is well acquainted with Mr Bailey's Merits, they Hope that He will be appointed to that office as a Compensation for His long and faithful Service in our Republican Cause.

Mr Bailey has for many years been a Loan-officer in the County in which He resides under the Government of this State, and would be a very acceptable officer, should He be Appointed to this office. I would further observe that the Republican Citizens of Dutchess County believe they have a Claim to at least one of the respectable offices to be filled in this State.

In presuming to address this to You Sir (as I have not Honor to be known[2] to You) I have been governed by a desire to serve my country, as well as Mr Bailey who is my Neighbor and Friend, and who is

[323]

not Yet advised that the office of Commissioner of Loans is vacant. I am also induced to believe, that as soon as it was known that the office was vacant there would be other aplications and that it was only necessary to mention Mr Bailey, and for You to know He would accept of the office, to ensure His appointment, I Shall Set off from this City this afternoon and hope to See Mr Bailey in a day or two

I am Sir Your Most obedient Humble servant

LEVI MCKEEN

RC (DNA: RG 59, LAR); at foot of text: "His Excellency The President of the United States"; endorsed by TJ as received 1 Oct. from Levi McKeen and so recorded in SJL with notation "Theod. Bailey to be commr loans"; TJ later canceled McKeen's name and added "Theo. Bailey" to the endorsement.

A Quaker merchant at Poughkeepsie, Levi McKeen was active in local Republican politics. He replaced Nicholas Power, the avid Federalist printer of the *Poughkeepsie Journal*, as postmaster in January 1802, after receiving the recommendation of Gilbert Livingston and other Poughkeepsie Republicans. McKeen supported Burr in the 1804 New York gubernatorial race. He supported Andrew Jackson in the election of 1824 (Kline, *Burr*, 1:543; 2:636-7, 830, 1190-1; Prince, *Federalists*, 219-20; Stets, *Postmasters*, 186; Memorandum from Aaron Burr, printed at 17 Mch. 1801).

OTHER APPLICATIONS: see DeWitt Clinton to TJ, 14 Sep.

On this date McKeen addressed a letter to Gallatin, almost identical to the one printed above (RC in DNA: RG 59, LAR; endorsed by TJ: "Mc.kean Levi to mr Gallatin" and "Theod. Bailey to be Commr. of loans").

¹ MS: "sate."
² MS: "kown."

To Robert Smith

DEAR SIR   Monticello Sep. 19. 1801.

The letters of the 7th. 8th. 11th. & [14]th. inst. from yourself and your chief clerk came to hand the day before yesterday. consequently that of the 7th. must have slept a week by the way somewhere. I now return the warrants for the midshipmen signed. I rejoice at the event of your election. it gives solidity to the Union by gaining a legislative & ensuring an Executive ascendancy to republicans, from Georgia to Rhode island inclusive; for I have considerable hopes of a like issue in Delaware. it's most important consequence is a federal Senator which [assures] us an equality in the Senate, even if the elections of SC. Delaware & Vermont should all go against us. I inclose a letter for Genl. Dearborne but his distance and the pressure of time obliged me to answer to the Indian commrs. myself by acceding to their proposition to change the place of meeting with the Choctaws.—we learn that Dale's squadron sailed from Gibraltar on the 4th of July,

produc'd an equal unlook'd for one in my future views respecting my
situation in life.—At the above time, I sollicited of you an appointment in the City of Philada. having reasons to believe that the cares
of my Family render'd such a Situation the most eligible—I have
lately reciev'd letters from the Missisippi which have given me a
strong desire of being settle'd in that Country: perticularly too, as I
am confident I can again serve the United States in many essentials
in the Spanish Government provided I was once more fix'd there in
my Old Official Character—On this Subject, I address you with
much diffidence, knowing through the medium of the Public Papers
that you have already nominated Mr Daniel Clark to fill that Station—but, perhaps there is a way still open through which I may be
indulg'd—The Senate have yet to confirm Mr Clark's nomination;
permit me to request that you will be so good as to lay this application with your own Statement before them—those, through so good
a channel, with my Personal attendance; flatter me with success—

Had there been any Person nominated from the United States,
which would have cost him the expence &c of a Voyage, I should not
have made this Application; but as Mr Clark is there establish'd in
Commerce as an Inhabitant of that Country, and of course this Appointment of no great consiquence to him, and perticularly he having
in fact no pretentions to any Services render'd to the United States at
any period whatever to my knowledge; he nor the Public can be disappointed or surpriss'd at my being placed in a Situation that first
originated in myself—Salary Offices are most sollicited, and it is often
difficult to find suitable Characters to fill an appointment in a foriegn
Country without some emolument—but under my present circumstance relative to that Country, and the Change that is likely to take
place in that Government; my Presence there, or any other well
known character immediately from that Country, may become essentially useful to the United States—Should I be so unfortunate as not
to succeed in this or some other Appointment on the Missisippi, I
beg leave to refer you to my first application—In addition to the Documents I had the pleasure of presenting you with, I beg leave to add
the incloss'd which will serve to refresh your memory with past occurrences—I expect to do myself the pleasure of waiting on you Personally at the next ensuing Session of Congress, and in the mean time
subscribe myself with the highest respect,

Your most faithful Humbl Servt.   OLR. POLLOCK

PS. It may be proper for me to explain to you how the incloss'd letter from yourself to Genl De Galvez came into my Hands. At the

period it was written and during the whole revolutionary War with Great Britain, I was the perticular Confident of that Gentleman and in all Translations of english Letters into the Spanish language, including all those reciev'd Officially from America as well as those intercepted from the Enemy; notwithstanding He had Persons in the Capacity of the Kings Interpreters—

After I had given him the Translation of your letter, I requested permission to keep a Copy of it, which He readily granted, and I have preserv'd it to this day—   OLR. POLLOCK

RC (DNA, RG 59, LAR); at foot of text: "Thomas Jefferson. President of the United States"; endorsed by TJ as received 1 Oct. and "to be Consul at N. Orleans" and so recorded in SJL. Enclosures: (1) *Oliver Pollock, Most Respectfully Submits to the Consideration of the Members of Congress, the Following Documents, in Explanation of his Claim, Now Depending before Them*, a printed pamphlet, without date or place of publication (copy in same; contains six documents from the 1780s testifying to Pollock's actions as agent at New Orleans for the United States and Virginia). (2) Probably a copy of TJ's letter as governor of Virginia to Bernardo de Gálvez,

the Spanish governor of Louisiana, 8 Nov. 1779, requesting financial support for Virginia's military efforts in the west and referring to hardships incurred by Pollock; this and a short follow-up letter were apparently the only letters TJ ever addressed to Gálvez (Vol. 3:167-70; see also Vol. 27:688).

Prior to the meeting he evidently had with TJ in the spring, Pollock had written on 4 Apr. to solicit an APPOINTMENT to any suitable office (Vol. 33:537-8).

MY OLD OFFICIAL CHARACTER: from 1777 to 1781, Pollock was commercial agent at New Orleans for the Continental Congress (ANB).

From John Barnes

SIR   Geo: Town 21st Sept. 1801

By the time this reaches you, 24th-25th I flatter myself, your Chariot, is nearly at Havre de Grace, on its way to Washington—As, on receipt of your favr. 12th recd the 15th. I instantly set ab: the means of procuring, an Able & steady pair of horses.—which we effected late on the 16th. *shod* & prepared on Thursday and on Friday morning early. Mr Dougherty set off from your stables with letter—and instructions to Mr Hanse—who I had previously noticed by Wednesys: Evening Mail, to be in readiness against Mr Doughertys expected Arrival Sunday Evening 20th. Urging him to leave Philada. if possible Monday so as to reach Darby. all which I persuade myself have or will be nearly Accomplished—And whereas you had—judged it expedient to reimburse me $1000, (which I could have made a reel of without, troubling your friends at Richmond—via Messrs. G & J) from whom I recd by Thursdays mail, viz: Brown, Rivers, & Co.

draft at[1] ten days After sight on Walker & Kennedy: I thought it best to forward it ℔ that Evening Mail, to Mr Hanse, on a/c—I had already remitted Roberts & Jones—as well discharged Mr Carpenters Balla. $100; so that, of your late lists either here, or at Philada. there remains only, Sheaffs $553.80. unadjusted—and that, shall be closed by the middle of Octr:—In the course of our inquiries After a pair suitable horses & driver—they would not engage under $60. beside paying ferriages—Such is the busy season for horses—that by engaging their Horses Only and the time Allowed, being barely sufft: for the return of Mr Dougherty before your expected Arrival—I thought my self fortunate in closing—with this pair of Approved Horses at $30. to be allowed Eleven days in Case of unforeseen Accident or delay or Bad Weather &c. and withal, prefering Mr. Doughertys Care—in point of preserving every thing Appertaining thereto—with strict charge, not to suffer any one to Enter the Carriage—that these several expectations may be realized and *your* safe Arrival is the Ardent wish,

of, Sir, your most Respectfull Obedt & very huml Servt:

JOHN BARNES

PS. in a late letter received from Dr. Edwards—who I am sorry to inform—is much indisposed—He had paid a visit to German town—but could not see Mr Stewart—from his engagemts—but intended writing him a line—on the subject of my letter—in order to prepare him against my expected Arrival—

RC (ViU: Edgehill-Randolph Papers); addressed: "Thomas Jefferson Esqr. President. U States. Monticello Virginia"; franked; postmarked 20 Sep.; endorsed by TJ as received 20 Oct. and so recorded in SJL. Tr (same); in Barnes's hand; at head of text: "Copy"; endorsed by Barnes: "original not recd."; endorsed by TJ: "copy of Sep. 21. 1801."

On FRIDAY, 18 Sep., Joseph DOUGHERTY SET OFF for Philadelphia to pick up

TJ's chariot. He returned to Washington by 26 Sep., when Barnes paid him $25.18 for "travelling expns. to & from Philadelphia." On that date, Barnes also paid Mr. Cromwell $30 for the pair of APPROVED HORSES, giving a total of $55.18 in expenses for the trip (statement of household account from John Barnes, 30 Sep. 1801, in ViU).

[1] MS: "A."

From Albert Gallatin

DEAR SIR   Washington Sept. 21st 1801

I have nothing new to communicate; expecting to see you in a few days, and being much engaged this day, I only enclose the list of

Warrants & two letters, one from Mr Dent applying for the Treasurer's office, & one from Doctr. Bache, to which last I am at a loss how to answer. Mr Habersham seems embittered and determined not to accept the office of Treasurer.

I can go on with the routine of this Department; but I have not been used to be so long left to myself for every thing &, besides the pleasure I will feel in seeing you, am on public account extremely anxious for your arrival. Robt. Smith returned only last night. Gen. Dearborne expects to leave home the 24th.

With great respect & attachment Your obt. Servt.

ALBERT GALLATIN

RC (DLC); at foot of text: "The President of the United States"; endorsed by TJ as received from the Treasury Department. Recorded in SJL as received 24 Sep. Enclosures: (1) "Weekly list of Warrants issued on Treasurer for week ending 19th Septer. 1801," reporting 28 warrants, Nos. 171 to 198, inclusive, for a total of $526,418.16, including 6 for "Intercourse with foreign nations," totaling $68,747.96; 8 on commissioners of loans for interest and reimbursement of the domestic debt, totaling $378,284; and 5 for the purchase of bills on Holland at 40 cents, totaling $68,852; with a balance in the Treasury at the beginning of the week of $3,717,381.05, and a closing balance of $3,423,888.66 (MS in DLC; entirely in Gallatin's hand; endorsed by Gallatin on verso). (2) George Dent to Gallatin, Port Tobacco, 14 Sep., applying for the office of treasurer, being informed that it is vacant (RC in DLC). (3) William Bache to Gallatin, 11 Sep., writing as a friend, he notes that his Albemarle establishment has not been as profitable as expected and inquires about a position in the federal government at Washington or Philadelphia, "which, from the knowledge you may have of me, as well as my connections, it may not be improper to employ me in" and asking especially about "new arrangements in the Post office"; requesting that Gallatin answer him as soon as possible "as my arrangments depend entirely upon its tenor" (same).

From Joseph Habersham

SIR/ Washington City 21st Septr. 1801.

Soon after I resigned the Office of Post Master General I made some observations to Mr. Madison relative to a judicial appointment rather hastily—my letter declining that appointment having reached you at the same time with Mr. Merediths resignation may have induced you to suppose that I knew of that circumstance and intended it as a hint that I was desirous to succeed him—this was however by no means the case as I did not hear that he had resigned until after my Letter was sent away. Upon a retrospect of the several communications which have taken place between us directly and through Mr. Madison I found that I could not consistent with that respect which I owed to myself accept of any appointment under the present administration and it was in consequence of that retrospect that the judicial appointment was declined—Office is desirable to me, to commence a new business at my time of Life is disagreable and it is not a small sacrifice that is made in leaving my children behind when I return to Georgia a thing necessary on account of their education, but having through life endeavored to support a proper spirit and independence of character I cannot now sacrifice it by accepting the office of Treasurer—Admitting that office was equally important and respectable what assurance could I have that I should not be crowded out by the same unauthorised means which compelled me to resign the office of Post Master General—Sincerity I have always considered to be one of the essential virtues and I should have had no occasion to make this explanation if my observations to Mr. Madison and the circumstance of the Letter had not occurrd

It is due to the former administration's to mention in this place that I had their cordial support and that the officers of the government left the entire management of the department where the Law places it, in its head; without any interference—it has never been made neither has the former administration ever attempted to make it an engine of Party

In retiring from Office I carry no resentments with me and I hope your administration will prove beneficial to the community and honorable to yourself.

I am with great respect Sir yr mo obedt. svt

JOS HABERSHAM

I sent your letter to Mr. Dawson by the first Post for Hancock after I recieved.

RC (DLC); addressed: "Thomas Jefferson President of the United States Monticello near Milton Va."; franked; postmarked 22 Sep.; endorsed by TJ as received 24 Sep. and so recorded in SJL.

LETTER DECLINING THAT APPOINT-MENT: see TJ to Habersham, 4 Sep., for a reference to the letter that Habersham wrote Madison on 31 Aug. On the use of post office appointments as an ENGINE OF PARTY by the Federalists, despite Habersham's statement to the contrary, see Prince, *Federalists*, 17-18, 186-8, 212, 231-2.

From Levi McKeen

SIR   Poughkeepsie 21st September 1801

Before I left New York I presumed to state to you what had been the expectations of the Republican Citizens of Dutchess County in favor of their Friend and beloved Citizen General Bailey, and what they now hoped from the Federal Goverment in His favor. That we had been encouraged to believe that He would have been appointed supervisor of this district. And indeed we were greatly disapointed that He did not obtain that place.

We however acquiessed under the impression that our President was influenced by the best of reasons to Appoint Mr Osgood to that office. And it was then understood that the Naval office Had been Suggested to the Goverment, as a Compensation to Mr Bailey, for His sacrifices in the republican Cause, and as a compliment to His Friends for their Ardent and unweared exertions to Effect those Arangements in the Legislature of this state, which has made the Man of our Choice the Chief Magestrate of the United States.

And we were the more Strongly induced to put confidence in this Arangement, as we could not believe that a Republican Goverment would retain in office a Foreigner, who was a Petty officer in one of the Piratical Governments in the West Indies during our revolution-ary Strugle, And has perhaps never been Naturalized—whose Ap-pointment to the Naval office has always been considered one of the strange things of the late administrations. We further understood that General Bailey's Friends in Applying for the Naval office for Him would meet with no Competitor but Mr Matthew L Davis of New York who is undoubtedly a republican; But who will place Mr Davises Merits in compitition with Mr Bailey's! General Bailey's Pretention I need not to mention to You, to whom they must be well known already.

Since my arrival from New York I have conversed with my friends, who think it would not be proper for them to give up their strong Claims in favor of their Friend General Bailey, to the Naval office, And they *will* yet Hope from the Justice of the President and His constant disposition to favor Revolutionary Characters that they will succeed in their Aplication, to obtain that office for a Man who has spent the best part of His life in Public Service to the very great in-jury of His professional avocation's.

On my Arrival from New York I made Known to Genral Baileys Friends in this Place the subject of my letter to You from New York, they approved of the measure but recollecting that although the office of Commissioner of Loans was an honorable and confidential place Yet the Salary was two small to aford such a living as we thought[1] Mr Bailey's deserved as a reward for His past and future services. We then determined to communicate the subject of my corespondence to General Bailey Himself, who said he should always consider it His duty to serve His Country to the utmost of His abilities, but observed that He was the father of a large family, who on account of His having been employed in public Business, were yet unprovided for and who looked up to Him for such a living as could not be expected from the office of Commissioner of Loans. Under all these Circumstances, it appear'd most prudent that His Friends should withdraw their application for the Commissioner of Loans office and rest our Claim to the Naval officers Place on the known Justice and Patriotizm of our *Beloved President, who will* not refuse to the Republican Citizens of Dutchess County a Just participation of the offices in His Gift, nor will He refuse to General Bailey this Just reward of His Long and faithful services

I am Sir Your Excellencies Most obedient Humble Servant

LEVI MCKEEN

RC (DNA: RG 59, LAR); at foot of text: "The President of the United States"; endorsed by TJ as received 1 Oct. and so recorded in SJL with notation Theodorus Bailey "to be Naval Officer"; also endorsed by TJ: "Bailey."

On this date McKeen addressed a letter to Gallatin in almost the same words as the one printed above (RC in same; endorsed by Gallatin: "L. McKeen withdraws his recommendn. of Mr Bailey as Cm. of Loans"; endorsed by TJ: "Mc.keen Levi to mr Gallatin" and "Theod. Bailey to be Naval officer" with TJ then canceling the first part of the endorsement). TJ also saw the letter that Theodorus Bailey addressed to Madison and Gallatin, from Poughkeepsie, on 22 Sep., immediately after he learned that his neighbor McKeen, while in New York City, had written the Treasury secretary soliciting the office of commissioner of loans for him. Observing that the office could only be performed in New York City, Bailey concluded that the compensation would be inadequate to support his young family there. Bailey also recalled that a few days before Congress adjourned in March, several of his Republican friends had interceded with the president-elect to obtain his appointment as naval officer, and he was given to understand when he left Washington "that I might expect that office in the course of the summer." Bailey later learned that Matthew L. Davis was also a candidate for the appointment. He believed that McKeen, an honest Republican, but whose "acquaintance with some of our public men, and their views, is rather limited," had been encouraged by Davis's supporters to write Gallatin and thus remove him as a rival. This provided an additional reason for declining the office of commissioner of loans (RC in same; at foot of text: "The honorable James Madison & Albert Gallatin Esquires"; endorsed by TJ: "Bailey Theod. to mr Madison to be naval officer"). In his letter, Bailey indicated twice that he was responding to McKeen's correspondence with Gallatin. He perhaps did not realize that McKeen had also written the president (see McKeen to TJ, 19 Sep.).

PIRATICAL GOVERNMENTS: in his letter to Gallatin of this date, McKeen wrote "Piratical Courts of Admiralty." Richard Rogers served as a clerk in the New York naval office before Washington appointed him naval officer for the district of New York in early 1797. Hamilton described him as "a remarkably accurate accountant" with long experience in the office (Syrett, *Hamilton*, 20:498-9).

MY LETTER TO YOU: McKeen to TJ, 19 Sep.

[1] MS: "though."

From William Barton

SIR,   Lancaster, Pennsylva. Septr. 22d. 1801.

When I did myself the honor of addressing a letter to You, in May last—in which I took the liberty of offering myself a candidate from some appointment under the United States,—I deemed it proper, from motives of delicacy, not to designate any particular station, as the object of my wishes.—A vacancy is now announced in the public prints, to have recently taken place in an office, to which my attention has been directed; and which some of my friends had early recommended to me to keep in view—I allude to the office of Postmaster General.—

The object, then, of the present letter, is only to present myself in the most respectful manner to Your consideration, when You shall think proper to appoint a successor to Mr. Habersham; and to observe, that, should I be so fortunate as to be honoured with the appointment, I shall earnestly endeavour to justify so distinguished a mark of the confidence of the Executive, by a faithful attention to the duties of the department.—It is, Sir, I trust, unnecessary to say any thing further on the occasion knowing, as I presume You do, what are my qualifications and character,—than merely to add, that a sense of duty to my Country, and of the greatest obligation to You, personally, would stimulate me to exert my best faculties in the public service.—

I pray You, Sir, to pardon the intrusion of this address.—

With sentiments of the highest Respect And all due Consideration, I have the Honor to be, Sir, Your most obedient servant

W. BARTON

RC (DNA: RG 59, LAR); at foot of text: "The President of the United States"; endorsed by TJ as received 1 Oct. and "to be Postmaster Genl." and so recorded in SJL.

LETTER TO YOU, IN MAY LAST: Barton to TJ, 26 May 1801.

From David Fergusson

RESPECTED SIR,   Geo: Town 22d. Septemr. 1801.

Having had the Rheumatism a good while, and thereby from another cause, *a rupture*, has delay'd the papers I wrote you of before,—the result of them will be known in the approaching Session,—I hand You a Petition—which if you think proper to sign and send me I will be much oblidged to you for—if not, any aid you can give me, being much in need of help at this time, and which I am sorry on this occasion goes with the Papers—as it looks unpleasant, unto a retrospect of the circumstances attending on a press of imperious Necessity.

With great Esteem, &c. &c. DAVID FERGUSSON

N.B. I called at the House & Mr. [Romaye] told me you wouldn't be up till 1st Novr.—

RC (DLC); faint; endorsed by TJ as received 1 Oct. and so recorded in SJL.

I WROTE YOU: see Fergusson to TJ, 10 Aug., for the papers Fergusson promised to send. The five separate proposals— all dated September 1801 and signed "Seven Friends"—called for raising revenues through a variety of taxes, including a post office tax; an additional tax on seamen to support lighthouses and marine hospitals; an additional duty on rum; a receipt tax on bank notes, ranging from 12½ cents on $20 to $50 notes to $1 on notes of $2,000 or more; and a fine of $1,000 per year on counties with churches, especially along the main roads, in disrepair, as they

"ought to be either removed or repaired, it being necessary for the Worship of the Supreme Being, and tending to promote Virtue and Morality, and suppress Vice and licentiousness" (MSS in DLC; in Fergusson's hand; endorsed and numbered by Fergusson on verso).

I HAND YOU A PETITION: in his brief request, also dated 22 Sep., Fergusson entreated: "Having the Rheumatism & a rupture, and at the present time in distress for aid—your subscription unto this will much oblidge, and not injure a generous and humane Heart" (MS in DLC; in Fergusson's hand and signed by him; endorsed by Fergusson on verso: "Petition").

Petition from Henry Roberts

City of Baltimore Sept. 22d. 1801.

The Petition of Henry Roberts Humbly Sheweth.

that your Petitioner was formerly a Soldier in the Virginia, line, in the third regment of Dragoons Commanded by Colonels George Baylor and William Washington, which the muster roles of the fourth troop of said Regment will testify. your Petitioner further Sheweth that at the Close of the late war he went to the City of Philadelphia where he Commenced the Study of the law, but the want of means prevented him from Completeing his Study at that time. Since which time your Petitioner has devoted great part of his leasure time in reading law, and attending the Courts in the State of Maryland. your Petitioner having from time to time as he was able to spare money purchased law Books, which in so many years brought into his possession a sufficient number to enable him to Complete his Study. your Petitioner further Sheweth that for several years last Past he has devoted his time in pursuit of legal information, and being Confident that he possessed Sufficient to intitle him to permission to practice in any of the Courts of law in the State of Maryland. your Petitioner made application to three attorney's who were in practice, who Certified in writing that they were acquainted with your Petitioner several years, that to their knowledge he had in his Possession a good Law Libra, and that for several years last past he had been very assiduous in acquireing legal information, and that they were of Opinion your Petitioner was Competent to the Management of Business in the Courts of Law. your Petitioner made application to the Judges of one of the County Courts in Maryland, who refused to grant permission. your Petitioner further Sheweth that on the first Day of September in the year Eighteen hundred and one, he made application to the Judge of the District Court of the United States, which Court was then Sitting at the City of Baltimore. the Judge of said Court refused to admit him to practice. your Petitioner being of Opinion that the Proceedings of the District Judge in this respect was Contrary to the Laws of the United States, and rights of the Citizens, as well as to the manifest injury and oppression of your Petitioner. wherefore he Prays your Excellency would take his Case into Consideration and grant him such relief as to your Excellency may seem meet. and your Petitioner as in duty bound will ever Pray.

HENRY ROBERTS

September 3d. 1801 I Called upon General Swan, who has Certified in the words following to wit, The Bearer Mr. Henry Roberts to the best of my recolection served in the 3d. Regment of Light Dragoons from the year 1777 to 1780 when he Claim,d his Discharge, the period for which he had inlisted being Expired. Signed

J. SWAN
formerly a Captn. 3d. Regt L Dragoons
Baltimore Septemb. 23d. 1801

Should your Excellency Condesend to Consider my Case, and any information respecting my Moral or Political Character be necessary, I Can send or bring such accounts of my Conduct as will be satisfactory.

RC (DLC); in an unidentified hand, signed by Roberts; with postscripts in Roberts's hand; at head of text: "To His Excellency the President of the United States"; endorsed by TJ as a letter of 23 Sep. received 1 Oct. and so recorded in SJL.

A Henry Roberts appears in the 1803 Baltimore directory as a conveyancer residing at 52 Green St., Old Town (Cornelius William Stafford, *The Baltimore Directory, for 1803* [Baltimore, 1803], 111).

James Winchester had served as JUDGE OF THE DISTRICT COURT OF THE UNITED STATES for Maryland since December 1799 (JEP, 1:325, 327).

From Aaron Burr

DEAR SIR   NYork 23 Septr. 1801

Several Valuable Men, of our friends in this City who are much attached to Mr. K[eteltas], have requested that I would, in this Way, make him Known to you: a duty which I perform with pleasure.

William Ke[teltas] is the son of a Clergyman, now deceased, who was eminent for his piety and learning and for his zeal and uniform attachment to the principles of our revolution. on the british invasion, he fled with the patriots of that Day and suffered all those losses and inconveniencies which are incident to a state of exile. His son, the subject of this letter, now about 35 or 36 Yrs. of age, was some Years ago admitted to our bar. His ardor in the Cause of republicanism seemed to engross every other passion, and, possessing great boldness and firmness, he became particularly obnoxious to the party lately in power and has suffered every species of persecution and indignity; so that, with a large family, he is left without business and without property. He writes with ease and correctness, is active and industrious, has been very useful during our political contests and, under severe trials and singular distresses, has merited and preserved a character of irreproachable integrity. Mr. K. was, by our present Council of appointment, recommended to the newly appointed Justices of a court for the trial of small Causes in this City, for the office of Clerk to that Court; a place worth about three thousand dolrs. per ann. but I am told it is probable that those justices are disposed to regard their personal attachments, more than the Merits of Mr. K. or the recommendations of the Council—If he should have any Views under the general Govt. I have advised him to explain them himself—

I persuade myself that you will pardon this intrusion from the Motives which have produced it, and I beg you to be assured of the very great respect and Esteem with which I have the honor to be Your friend & Obt st   A; BURR

RC (DNA: RG 59, LAR); cut, with missing letters supplied in brackets; at foot of text: "Th. Jefferson. Prest. of the U.S"; endorsed by TJ as received 1 Oct. and "Keteltas to be Commr. of loans" and so recorded in SJL.

Abraham Keteltas, a CLERGYMAN in Queens County, New York, was active in the REVOLUTION as chair of the Jamaica Committee of Safety and an elected delegate to the Provincial Congress of New York in 1776. The family fled to Connecticut when the British won the battle of Long Island in August 1776 (Alfred F. Young, *The Democratic Republicans of New York: The Origins, 1763-1797* [Chapel Hill, 1967], 480; Dexter, *Yale*, 2:289-91).

COURT FOR THE TRIAL OF SMALL

CAUSES: the New York Council of Appointments named five justices to the "Ten Pounds Court" on 26 Aug. (New York *American Citizen and General Advertiser*, 31 Aug.).

From Connecticut Officers and Soldiers of the 12th Regiment

SIR   Lebanon 23rd September 1801

While the Friends of Civil & Religious Liberty in the Old & new world, are rejoicing at the elavation of their ablest Advocate to the summit of human Glory—the first Magistrate of a Free & enlightened people—Permit the Officers & Soldiers of the 12th Regiment of Militia of Connecticut to present a respectfull testimonial of Attachment to the Constitution of our Country "the worlds best hope" and to our beloved Chief the Friend of Man—

We have long viewed with anxious salicitude the conflict of contending principles—We have seen with regret Republicanism *ridiculed & dispised*—its votaries stigmatised and denounced as the *enemies of God & Man*—and we have felt with grief & indignation the degrading influence of the reign of *terror & delusion*—But thanks to an Overruling Providence—Virtue & patriotism have burst "the Lilliputian ties"—revived the Creed of Seventy Six—and consecrated to Liberty a new era in the Annals of our Country—Henceforth the *political* Anathemas of a profaned Pulpit are as little to be dreaded as the Thunders of the Vatican—and the Malignant invectives of a prostituted Press (like the wounded Serpent poisoning its self) are to us harmless as legendary tales—

Whatever may be the Opinion of some of our fellow Citizens who have not yet forgotten "the Flesh Pots of Eygpt" we contemplate with pleasure the prospect before us—Peace abroad tranquility at home a Republican Government faithfully executed & firmly supported by the confidence of the people Armed for defence but never for Offence—Such Sir are our sentiments and such will the sentiments of the Citizens of Connecticut as soon as the rays of a Mild & genial Administration shall dissipate the delusive mists which political intrigue artifice & design have diffused over their Minds—

Accept Sir the assurance of our Affectionate esteem and cordial support. in full confidence that your practice will illustrat your Theory—

in behalf of the Regiment   DANIEL TILDEN
                                                  Leiutt Col. Commadant

RC (DLC); at head of text: "To Thomas Jefferson President of the United States"; endorsed by TJ as received 20 Oct. and so recorded in SJL.

A captain during the American Revolution, Daniel Tilden (1743-1833) of Lebanon also served as a town selectman and representative in the Connecticut legislature. In May 1801 the legislature denied his promotion to brigadier general in the Connecticut militia due to his Republican sympathies (Heitman, *Register*, 543; Orlo D. Hine, *Early Lebanon. An Historical Address Delivered in Lebanon, Conn., On The National Centennial, July 4, 1876* [Hartford, 1880], 116-17, 126-8; White, *Genealogical Abstracts*, 3:3499; *Connecticut Courant*, 13 Jan. 1834; Kline, *Burr*, 1:585-7; Aaron Burr to TJ, 4 June 1801).

From James Currie

DEAR SIR   Richmond Sepr. 23d. 1801

I was honored with the reception of your favor of the 30th ulto. sent by Judge Stewart, accompanied by a Vial containing a Needle & thread, & half a dozen Tooth Picks, impregnated on the 29th. of Augt. & in a very proper manner. I am Satisfied; you have not observd. the heat of the atmosphere the day you took the matter from the Patients, which I Should have wished to have been informed of as in a very hot state of the Air—it is supposed or known soon to lose, its infective quality. the Sp Vin, stood in my Therm, at 3 o'clock PM. on that day[1] at 91°—with you I presume not so much, there has been no chance as yet afforded of trying it—Should the Inoculation be again introduced here, it shall have a fair trial, either by myself or under my immediate Inspection, by some Respectable Practitioner & you shall be faithfully informed of the result,—In regard to the trial here with the Vaccine matter last Spring, I send you the result, inclosed from my friend Dr. Trent a young Gentleman of promising hopes & very considerable talents & practice here

I have this day only & with much difficulty at last Obtained the Award of the referees in your matters & Mr. Ross's—which I inclose, with the Papers A & B containing a statement of the accts. by Anthony Robison, & the principles on which the award is founded, all your Other papers will this Evening be delivered to Mr Geo Jefferson to be transmitted in due time & safely.—Mr Ross's papers including Col TMR's order on him will be rendred back to him, & this last by your particular request to me in One of your Letters. Robison's fee is 15$ for each, to him the Professional Gentn. have not said what they[2] expect. I expect they intend, to make no charge particularly but mean to leave it to the Principals DR has paid AR his fee— if youll be pleased to signify to me your pleasure in regard to those, fees to be offered the referees & paid to A Robison Special attention Shall be paid to it. I am sorry I have been so long in bringing about this much wished for award, but glad it is now finished—I have Only to add it will ever give me real pleasure to render you any service, in every way in my power & with tenders of my warmest wishes for your health & happiness. I am

Always Dr Sir—with much Truth Your Very Hble Serv.

JAMES CURRIE

RC (MHi); endorsed by TJ as received 26 Sep. and so recorded in SJL. Enclosure: P. Trent to James Currie, Richmond, 20 Sep., describing trials performed in Richmond with cowpox obtained from Norfolk that Trent concluded was spurious (RC in MHi; endorsed by TJ: "Trent to Dr Currie"). Other enclosures not found.

[1] Previous three words interlined.
[2] MS: "the."

From James Madison

DEAR SIR   Sepr. 23. 1801

Having sent you by Mr. Davis the communications recd. by the mail of last week, I have none to make you at present. You will find me at home, on saturday or sunday, when I hope to be able to fix the day for following you to Washington. The despatches for Mr Livingston will be ready by the time I shall have the pleasure of seeing you. My conversation with Mr. Graham who staid a day or two with me, & appears to be a sensible & steady young man, has suggested some ideas for enlarging the instructions to Mr. Pinkney on the subject of Louisiana, which I will also put in form by the time of your arrival.

With the most respectful attachment I remain Dear Sir, Yrs.

JAMES MADISON

RC (DLC); at foot of text: "The President of the U. States"; endorsed by TJ as received from the State Department on 23 Sep. and so recorded in SJL.

ON THE SUBJECT OF LOUISIANA: Madison wrote to Charles Pinckney on 25 Sep. enlarging the instructions of 9 June accompanying Pinckney's commission and including the counterpart to a common cipher to be used in Pinckney's correspondence with Robert R. Livingston (Madison, *Papers, Sec. of State Ser.,* 1:273-9; 2:131-2).

From James Mease

SIR   Philadelphia Sept 23d. 1801.—
   I have the honor to acknowledge the receipt of your letter in answer to my communication by Mr le Tombe—
   In pursuance of my intention to deliver a course of lectures upon Æconomicks, I applied to the Trustees of our university to establish a professorship to countenance my exertions and to extend the utility of my labours, but owing to the opposition of the professor of Chemistry, I am disposed to believe that the request I made will not be granted. I am however resolved to Carry the plan into effect, but for the present I must suspend it, and as other prospects have lately opened which promise such advantages, as I do not think myself authorised to neglect, I am determined to embrace them. I allude to a voyage to Constantinople. But as considerable advantages would attend my going there as a public agent, at the same time that I might have it in my power to render very important advantages to my Country, by forming permanent Commercial regulations, I take the liberty of solliciting the appointment of Commercial agent from the U. States, at the above port, without salary.—
   I need not tell you Sir who are so perfectly well acquainted with the trade of the whole world, how important that of the Levant is, and how many vessels are employed therein belonging to various European nations, neither need I tell you of how much consequence a participation of that trade will be to the Citizens of the U States, after a peace, when the powers for whom they are the carriers, will have their commerce revived, and when they will confine the advantages it affords to their own subjects, but I may mention what it has been within my province to know, that hitherto the prices of the many useful medicinal and dye drugs have been considerably increased in consequence of our merchants being obliged to purchase them at second or third hand, in Leghorn, or from the monopolizers in London. A direct trade from the U States to Constantinople, Smyrna, Salonica, and to Alexandria, regulated by known rules and protected by accredited public agents, would save an immense sum annually to our Country, as well as give employment to the active disposition, of our Citizens, who will require new sources of trade to employ their shipping, whenever the tranquillity of the European world shall be restored.—
   I am well aware of the genius and character of the people, with whom I shall have to treat, and of the influence of the British Government with those in power, but I am prepared to Manage the one, and to avoid the other, and should I be honored with the commission

no address or exertions on my part shall be wanting to effect the important object in view.—   I will not trouble you at present with any further observations upon the subject, of which I have fully informed myself, and shall only add, that I have mentioned my plan to my friend Mr Butler, who authorizes me to say, that it meets with his approbation.—

I am with sentiments of high respect Sir, your most obedient

JAMES MEASE

RC (DLC); at foot of text: "The President of the U States"; endorsed by TJ as received 6 Oct. and so recorded in SJL.

YOUR LETTER: TJ to Mease, 29 June. PROFESSOR OF CHEMISTRY: James Woodhouse (Vol. 33:648n).

MR BUTLER: probably Pierce Butler, Mease's father-in-law (Vol. 33:381n).

Declaration of Trust with Craven Peyton

This indenture made between Thomas Jefferson of Monticello in Albemarle and Craven Peyton of the same county witnesseth that whereas the said Craven hath purchased from John R. Kerr & Sarah his wife, James L. Henderson, Isham Henderson & Charles Henderson (which said Sarah, James L. Isham and Charles are children & co-heirs with six others to Bennet Henderson late of Albemarle aforesd) their undivided portions of the lands in the same county which descended on them from their said father, and now holds their several obligations to convey to him a title in fee simple, with certain exceptions in the said obligations specified, Now the said Craven doth declare that he holds the said obligations in trust only for the said Thomas & his heirs, that one hundred & eighty pounds already paid for the purchase of the said lands was of the proper monies of the said Thomas, and that three hundred and thirty four pounds the residue of the said purchase money is to be paid by him with interest thereon from the 14th. day of July last past, of which sums making £494. one hundred and fifty pounds were for the portion of the sd John R. Kerr & Sarah his wife £140. for that of the said James L. £102. for that of the sd Isham, and £102. for that of the sd Charles: and that the conveyances which are to be made to the said Craven will be in trust for the said Thomas & his heirs and are so to ensure without any claims or pretensions of title of him the sd Craven or any person claiming under him as absolutely to all intents & purposes as if the legal estate in fee simple were conveyed directly from the said vendors to the said Thomas: & the said Craven for himself & his heirs covenants with the said Thomas & his heirs that he will convey the said title in fee simple to the sd Thomas, whensoever, after the same shall have been conveyed to him the sd Craven, a demand shall be made by the sd Thomas or his heirs, in witness whereof he has hereto set his hand and seal this 25th day of September 1801. Signed sealed & delivered in presence of   CRAVEN PEYTON

MS (ViU); entirely in TJ's hand except for signatures and day of month, which Peyton inserted in blank left by TJ; signed by Peyton and by David Anderson and M. Camder as witnesses; indented and sealed; endorsed by TJ: "Peyton to Jefferson." PrC (same); lacks date and signatures. Probably enclosed in Peyton to TJ, 3 Oct. 1801.

Bennett HENDERSON died in 1793, leaving a widow and 11 children, most of whom were minors. Henderson had set out to acquire and develop property around the town of Milton, at the falls of the Rivanna River in Albemarle County. That project, particularly the development of a water mill, was incomplete when Henderson died. The family was left with debts and was, by TJ's description, "absolutely pennyless" in terms of liquid capital, although they did hold title to the land surrounding Milton. In 1795, TJ filed suit against Henderson's estate in the Virginia High Court of Chancery, arguing that the Henderson milldam on the Rivanna had not been authorized by the county court and raised the water level upstream enough to interfere with the mill TJ wanted to develop at Shadwell. TJ won the lawsuit, but delayed tearing down the Hendersons' dam while work proceeded on the excavation of the mill canal at Shadwell (Vol. 28:471-4, 479-85, 520; Vol. 30:621-2; Vol. 31:165-6, 176, 190, 193, 205-8, 217).

HOLDS THEIR SEVERAL OBLIGATIONS: Bennett Henderson left no will. Under Virginia law, his estate would go to his children, distributed among them by partition "per capita" with each of the heirs receiving an equal share. In January 1801, TJ arranged for Craven Peyton, the

husband of one of his nieces, to begin buying Henderson family members' portions of the estate. By that time there were ten Henderson children, one of the older brothers, William, having died. The transactions were to be in Peyton's name and TJ's role kept secret. Peyton first acquired the shares of Sarah (Sally) Henderson Kerr and her brothers James, Charles, and Isham. Apart from the oldest of the offspring, a son named John who continued his father's business activities, Sarah, James, Charles, and Isham were, in that order, the oldest of the heirs (William Waller Hening, ed., *The Statutes at Large; Being a Collection of All the Laws of Virginia*, 13 vols. [Richmond, 1809-23], 12:138, 139, 146; Craven Peyton, amended bill in chancery, 2 June 1804, in Tr of TJ v. Michie, ViU: Carr Papers; Robert Haggard, "Thomas Jefferson v. The Heirs of Bennett Henderson, 1795-1818: A Case Study in Caveat Emptor," *Magazine of Albemarle County History*, 63 [2005], 1-29; Vol. 31:199; Vol. 32:469-70, 558-9).

ONE HUNDRED & EIGHTY POUNDS ALREADY PAID: see Peyton to TJ, 10 July 1801, and TJ to Peyton, 14 July, for TJ's first payment for land from the Hendersons. That remittance, $600 in gold and bills carried by Thomas Walker, was the first entry in a statement that TJ later drew up of his account with Peyton for the Henderson purchases. In that statement TJ also included, under the general date of 1801, £140 (or $500) for Sarah Henderson Kerr's share of the estate, £140 ($466.67) for James L. Henderson's part, and £128.18.6 ($429.75) each for Isham and Charles. By the rate of conversion TJ used in recording those transactions, his initial payment of $600, which he recorded in the account statement only in dollars, equaled £180 (statement of account with Peyton "for Hender- son's lands," 1801-1809, in DLC, enclosed in TJ to Peyton, 28 Oct. 1812).

From William Branch Giles

SIR   Petersburg September 25th. *1801*
   This letter will probably be presented to you by Mr. Tubuffe.—He is the son of a gentleman of that name, who, some years ago, came from France to the United states, with a view of establishing himself in some parts of the western country, but in making the attempt, was unfortunately murdered by the Indians.—It is represented to me, that after the death of the father, and during the minority of the son, the family was put on the list of emigrants by the then government of France. Mr. Tubuffe having received assurances that their names will now be erased from the emigrant list, proposes to visit his native country, with a view of making his respects to his Mother, who is still living, and as far as may be practicable of reclaiming his estate,—Mr. Tubuffe sensible of the High consideration attached to your name in France, conceives, that letters from you of his good conduct here, will essentially facilitate the execution of his objects, and for this purpose has applyed to me through a friend for a letter of recommendation to you.—I comply with Mr. Tubuffe's request with the greater pleasure both from the consideration of his own good conduct in this place; and the irreparable misfortune he has sustained in this country in the loss of his father.—Mr. Tubuffe, connected with his elder brother, has been for some time doing business in this place in the mercantile line,—Their house is in good credit, and as far as I am informed, their conduct individually unexceptionable.—under these circumstances, I have no doubt, that as far as propriety will admit, you will render to Mr. Tubuffe the services he solicits.—
Be pleased Sir to accept assurances of my High consideration and Respect &c   WM. B GILES

RC (NHi: Robert R. Livingston Papers); at foot of first page and foot of text: "Mr. Jefferson"; endorsed by TJ as received 1 Oct. and so recorded in SJL; also endorsed by TJ: "by Tubuffe." Enclosed in TJ to Robert R. Livingston, 3 Oct. 1801.

MR. TUBUFFE: Alexandre Tubeuf, born in 1779, was the younger son of

Pierre François Tubeuf of France, who had acquired a large tract of land on the Clinch River in Russell County, Virginia, where he hoped to settle a number of French immigrants. The elder Tubeuf moved to Virginia to establish the settlement in 1791, writing to TJ, George Washington, and Patrick Henry after his arrival and citing Lafayette in his support, but the enterprise did not develop very far before the entrepreneur was murdered in 1795. Although some accounts attributed the killing to INDIANS, Tubeuf was the victim of a conspiracy of local inhabitants who had robbery as their motive and who started a rumor to put the blame on Native Americans. Earlier, Tubeuf had obtained concessions for the development of coal deposits in France, but his widow, who had remained there, could not assert that claim until 1801, when the family's name was removed from the list of banned émigrés. Alexandre and his brother François (Pierre François, or Peter Francis) were by then merchants in Petersburg, Virginia, specializing in wine and spirits and branching into trade with Saint-Domingue. Alexandre went to France in November 1801 to help press the family's claim to mines in the Alès region. The brothers also attempted to secure their father's Virginia tract, which contained ore-bearing lands but was subject to foreclosure as security for a loan from the state (Gwynne Lewis, *The Advent of Modern Capitalism in France, 1770-1840: The Contribution of Pierre-François Tubeuf* [Oxford, 1993], 19-20, 158-63, 175-6, 198-201, 232-6; James William Hagy, "The Frontier Dreams of François Pierre de Tubeuf," VMHB, 77 [1969], 329-35; CVSP, 8:241, 364-5; 9:359, 363; Washington, *Papers, Pres. Ser.*, 8:518-20; Vol. 22:141-2, 195).

From William Keteltas

DR SIR   New York 25th September 1801—

Being informed that Gnl. Clarkson of this City has sent in his Resignation as Loan Officer—And Also Advised by some friends to Apply to fill that Vacancy, You will therefore please to Consider me a Candidate for that office, Not without first Assuring You, that I Consider it the Most unfortunate occurrence in My Life, politically Speaking, to think that a Sincere and Consiencious Endeavour to Support the Constitution under our Infant Republic, Should have been attended with such runious Consequences to my Family, by the Tyranny of the late Administration, as to be Obliged to look to the *New* in the way of an Office for their support—The Obtaining an Office is A Consideration that never Soild. My Motives for Acting in favour of the people, Concieving that when Men are Stimulated from such Impure Views, they are unworthy the character of patriots— The Enclosed publication is a feeble production of My own, which I submit to Your Superior wisdom, and Information for Correction, Being a fixed Rule with me, to Give full force and Effect in practice to the Theories I adopt, as A Proof of the sincerity of My Professions, therefore wish to be Correct if possible in their Adoption to Avoid Error. Your answer to my letter of the 4th of July I Received and duly Apreciate Its Value—Believe me sincere when I say Should their be any other Applicant for the said Office Who in Your Opinion will Add More Weight to the Republican Cause, Hesitate Not a Moment to Give him the preference.

With Respect & Consideration   WM. KETELTAS

RC (DNA: RG 59, LAR); at foot of text: "Thomas Jefferson President Of the United States"; endorsed by TJ as received 1 Oct. and "to be Commr. of loans" and so recorded in SJL. Enclosure not found.

From Charles Lewis

DEAR SIR,   Monteagle 25th. Sept. 1801

It has been my wish for some time past to place myself in a situation for reading. in my endeavours to do this, I have ever found a difficulty in not having that scholastic knowledge necessary, but having devoted some time past to that purpose, and feeling myself as to that, in some degree prepared to prosecute my end; another difficulty arises, the want of books, to remove which, I am induced from necessity, though with gratitude in full recollection of your past endeavours to promote my interest, which perhaps ought to forbid it, to request your favor in the loan of such as I cannot otherwise procure. The delicacy I feel in making this request, knowing the abuse to which borrowed books are some times exposed is great indeed, but should you be disposed to favor, and lend me such, or any part of the enclosed list, I promise particular care shall be taken of them whilst in my possession.

I have the honor to be Sir yr Obt. Servt.   CH LEWIS

RC (MHi); at foot of text: "Mr. Thomas Jefferson." Enclosure: list of 16 books, including works by Edward Gibbon, Thomas Paine, John Locke, Jean Jacques Rousseau, Adam Smith, and William Godwin (MS in same).

TJ's nephew, Charles Lewis, was the third son of TJ's sister Lucy and her husband, Charles Lilburne Lewis of Monteagle, who was also TJ's first cousin. The young man had planned to marry his first cousin Nancy Jefferson in 1800 but the marriage never occurred. About that time, young Charles fathered a mulatto girl, Matilda, who was owned by his old-est brother Randolph. In 1806, TJ gave young Charles a commission as a lieutenant in the army, but the artillery soldier died from a severe head inflammation later that summer while in Opelousas (Boynton Merrill, Jr., *Jefferson's Nephews: A Frontier Tragedy* [Princeton, 1976], 48, 76, 84-6, 339, 344, 347).

On 27 Sep., Lewis wrote a letter to Thomas Mann Randolph explaining that the president had sent word by Lewis's brother that in TJ's absence his son-in-law would "look over his library, and send by the boy such as are inserted in the list" (RC in MHi; endorsed by TJ: "Lewis Charles to TMR. to borrow books").

From Nathaniel Macon

SIR   Warrenton 25 Septr. 1801

I have been requested to name Col John Pugh Williams to you for an appointment either in the collection of the revenue or as a Consul at some foreign port; I only write now to inform you that such a request has been made, but shall delay saying any thing on the subject untill I see you at Washington in December, I wish to make some enquiries before I undertake to recommend, and hope to do it, before the meeting of Congress, although the blame of improper appointments will in a great measure constitutionally attach to you; In justice & equity, those who recommend, should have a share of the responsibility, I am with the utmost respect

Sir yr. most obt. sert   NATHL MACON

RC (DNA: RG 59, LAR); endorsed by TJ as received 1 Oct. and "John Pugh Williams to some office" and so recorded in SJL.

JOHN PUGH WILLIAMS had been recommended for office in a 30 June letter from former U.S. Senator Timothy Bloodworth to TJ, suggesting that additional information about Williams could be obtained from Macon, "who is wel Acquainted with his Charrecter." Macon wrote TJ regarding an appointment for Williams again on 9 Oct., reporting that "I am not by any means convinced, that I ought to recommend him, I have not been informed, that he is well qualified for one, Indeed I have some reason to believe, that he is too fond of ardent spirits." Macon promised to continue his investigation and report in person to TJ upon his arrival in Washington (RC in DNA: RG 59, LAR; endorsed by TJ as received 15 Oct. and so recorded in SJL; also endorsed by TJ: "concerning John Pugh Williams").

From Thomas Newton

Dr SIR   Norfolk 25th Septr 1801—

I Received your favor of the 18th I most sincerely wish I had it in my power to recommend to you a person, to fill the place of Mr Wilkins at Cherrystone, but I am so little acquainted, that I have it not in my power.—The Eastern shore, I apprehend contains but few republicans & those I am acquainted with, I have reason to beleive if Mr. Peter Bowdoin would accept the office, he would faithfully execute it, being a man esteemd for his integrety. he lives on Hungars, a convinient situation for preventing smugling & near the Court house where the public business is done. I have made inquiry of several, who are well acquainted & could get no recommendation, that I could safely rely on, a Mr. Nathl. Holland & Mr Caleb Fisher were mentioned to me, but I am unacquainted with them. I have had several conversations with many Gentlemen from the Eastern Shore, they all say they are determind to support the present administration & submit to the choice of a majority. it is my wish to see republicans in all offices falling vacant & be assured I shall give you every information in my power whenever you shall please to require it. I am sorry to inform you that Coll Davies our Collector lies very ill with a paryleitic or an appoplectic affection in the head; but has not had a fitt as the Doctr expressed it to me—I apprehend he will not recover, tho I hope he may, as he is the best collector we have had at this place. Mr. Barnes has pd. Mr Taylor & two more pipes of the same quality of wines are forwarded for you, which I obtaind from a Gentleman that had bought them; Mr. Taylor has left some very fine London Particular wines three years old & very little differance between it & the Brazil & fifty Dollars lower in price. I can safely recommend it as good wine & very few would know any differance in the taste. I expect more Brasil quality if the Brittish will permit it to come from Madeira & shall be glad to supply you. Accept my best wishes & believe me to be respectfully yr.   THOS NEWTON

RC (DLC); endorsed by TJ as received 13 Oct. and so recorded in SJL.

With a note to John BARNES dated 19 Sep., wine merchant James TAYLOR, Jr., sent a "Receipt for Two pipes Wine for the President of the US" (RC in MHi; endorsed by TJ: "Taylor James to mr Barnes"). In his financial memoranda at an entry dated 28 Sep., TJ recorded the arrival at Washington of two pipes of Brazil quality Madeira wine from "Taylor & Newton" (MB, 2:1115).

From James Barry

City of Washington. September 26th. 1801

The subscriber being interrested in property in this City and the regulations belonging thereto; & finding some deviations from the conduct heretofore observed by the Commissioners, He has to complain that in the compact formed between the Proprietors when they gave up half their property to the United States, it was considered, the City was to be laid off, & their lotts & squares surveyed out of the fund arising from that property given up, & the residue to be appropriated to the Public buildings &ca., altho not materially concerned in this part, He considers what property he bought from the Public, that the Commissioners had a right to have the Lotts measured & bounded for him, in fact it has been the practice heretofore, as it is also the practice [with other] [. . .] of Lands & Lotts, that they allways survey & convey the sold lands to the purchasers, at their own expence, the Subscriber considered it the duty of the Commissioners, to mark out his Lotts at the public expence, but from the enclosed papers, it appears the Commissioners refuse doing so—He wrote them on the subject enclosing Mr King's account receiving from them no satisfaction or inclination to do what he thinks just, He takes the liberty to transmit the same to the President of the United States for his decision—   JAMES BARRY

RC (DLC); top of sheet clipped, including TJ's endorsement; at head of text: "Thomas Jefferson Esqr. President of the United States." Recorded in SJL as received 1 Oct. Enclosure: Gustavus Scott, William Thornton, and Alexander White to James Barry, Commissioners' Office, 12 Dec. 1800, acknowledging that they had seen King's statement of lots surveyed for Barry; the commissioners explaining to Barry that while it had been their practice not to charge for the survey of lots "purchased of the public" when two surveyors were in the commission's employ, "the Affairs of the City" now required that only one surveyor be kept in its employ, and by powers vested in them by President John Adams, the commissioners allowed King to charge "reasonable compensation" for his work (RC in DLC; in William Brent's hand, signed by Scott, Thornton, and White; addressed: "James Barry Esqr"). Other enclosures not found.

James Barry (1755?-1808), a merchant born in Ireland, lived in India, Portugal, and Baltimore before moving to Washington around 1800. He began investing

in real estate in the capital in the 1790s, and by 1801 he had constructed a wharf on the Anacostia River. Since 1791, Barry had been vice consul for Portugal in Maryland and Virginia. In December 1801, Madison acknowledged Barry as acting consul general of Portugal. Barry, his wife, Joanna Gould, and their two daughters were buried at St. Mary's Church in Washington (Allen C. Clark, "Captain James Barry," RCHS, 42-43 [1942], 1-16; Carrie Rebora Barratt and Ellen G. Miles, *Gilbert Stuart* [New Haven, 2004], 268-9; Madison, *Papers, Sec. of State Ser.*, 2:294; TJ to John Carroll, 3 Sep.).

COMPACT FORMED BETWEEN THE PROPRIETORS: for the 1791 agreement by which proprietors of land in the newly created District of Columbia conveyed land to trustees, see Opinion on George Walker's Case, 14 June.

The principal surveyor of the city of Washington from 1797 to 1802 was Robert King, Sr. He was the father of Nicholas King (Ralph E. Ehrenberg, "Nicholas King: First Surveyor of the City of Washington, 1803-1812," RCHS, 69-70 [1971], 45-6; Vol. 34:199-200).

To Gibson & Jefferson

GENTLEMEN   Monticello Sep. 26. 1801.

This serves to advise you that on the 20th. inst. I desired you to pay to Joel Yancey or order three hundred & eighty two dollars fifty two cents, on [. . .] paper, not being able to get a stamp. I am now [. . .] you to pay to Alexander Garrett five hundred and twenty seven dollars & thirty eight cents.

I have this day drawn on you in favor of Bowling Clarke for £144.19.2 payable the 1st. day of November ensuing.

I set out tomorrow morning for Washington. accept assurances of my esteem.

527.38 D.

TH: JEFFERSON

PrC (MHi); faint; at foot of text: "Messrs. Gibson & Jefferson"; endorsed by TJ in ink on verso.

TJ's payment to JOEL YANCEY included $11.15 for federal taxes on his land at Shadwell in Fredericksville Parish, Albemarle County. The remaining $371.37 was for cash TJ had received from Yancey on 29 Aug. and 20 Sep., which was to be repaid at Richmond. The payment to ALEXANDER GARRETT included $408.24 for cash received from him on 21, 26, and 27 Aug. and 26 Sep., $10.24 for taxes on William Short's land, $12.97 for taxes on TJ's land in St. Anne's Parish, and various other payments (MB, 1:40; 2:1023-4n, 1050-2).

TJ had settled his account with Bowling Clark (CLARKE), who had served as overseer at Poplar Forest since the early 1790s, on 31 Oct. 1800. At that time TJ owed him £136.15.1. TJ's payment due on 1 Nov., for $483.21, included £8.4.1 in interest (same, 2:878, 1052, 1067).

In a second letter to Gibson & Jefferson of this date TJ reiterated that the firm was to pay Clark £144.19.2 for him on 1 Nov. TJ also enclosed a letter to Clark (recorded in SJL at 26 Sep. but not found) and described his first letter to Gibson & Jefferson, printed above, as that carried "by mr Garrett" (PrC in MHi; at foot of text: "Messrs. Gibson & Jefferson"; endorsed by TJ in ink on verso; with notation in SJL "by Bowling Clarke £144.19.2").

From Thomas Newton

DEAR SIR   26. Septr. 1801—

Since writing yesterday I have heard of a Mr Mathew Bryant at Northampton Court house, who has been recommended as Collector, Mr Bryant I am informd is a reformd man, & well approved of, but I am of opinion, that few fully reform who have been dissipated, and as most of the inhabitants on that Shore are of the same opinions I think the most respectable will make the best officer & Mr Bowdoin I think a worthy character & is generally esteemd. Coll Davies still lies ill, but hope he will recover—Our Town is remarkably healthy as to the inhabitants but many strangers have died, especially Irish who arive in indigent circumstances drink hard & expose themselves to the Sun & dews—health &C attend you are the wishes of   T NEWTON

RC (DLC); endorsed by TJ as received 13 Oct. and so recorded in SJL.

To Samuel Smith

DEAR SIR   Monticello Sep. 26. 1801.

Mr. Glendye a presbyterian clergyman from Ireland, who settled two or three years ago at Staunton about 40. miles from this place, understanding that there is or will be a vacancy at Baltimore, proposes to go there to offer himself. my personal acquaintance with him is small, but I have had abundant attestations of his character from others. he is a man of excellent character, goodhumoured, sociable, and the most eloquent preacher of the living clergy whom I have heard. in this he is really great, and without disparaging any other, I may safely say he is unrivalled. he is a good republican, & on that account having become obnoxious to government he left Ireland. he speaks with the emphasis of an eyewitness of the worse than Robespierrian enormities committed in that country. he wishes to go to Baltimore as a place more congenial with the habits & manners of himself and family. being desirous that I should say to you what I can with justice, I do it with great satisfaction persuaded you will be uncommonly pleased with such an acquisition to your city. I send this letter by post. he will go on himself in about a fortnight. accept assurances of my high esteem & respect.   Th: Jefferson

PrC (DLC); at foot of text: "Genl. Samuel Smith"; endorsed by TJ in ink on verso.

From Mathias Kin

Sir   Philaa. Septr. 28. 1801.
    Mr Professor Harmer of Strasburgh on the Rhine requested me to bear the enclosed to your Excellency. the season for collecting seeds being pretty far advanced and as I wish to go to the western part of this State and return hither in time to send to Europe before winter I am debar'd the pleasure of presenting it.—if my memory does not deceive me I saw in the neighbourhood of Monte Cello some trees of the Paccan or Illinois nut. the impossibility of procuring some of the Nuts from any other place that I know soon enough to send to Europe this Autumn will I hope excuse me with your Excellency for intruding so far as to request the favor of you to send me a few by the end of November, any seeds or Plants you may wish to obtain from Europe will be procured with the greatest pleasure by your most obedient humble Sevt.   Matthias King.

RC (MH); below signature: "Botanist No. 423 North Second Street Philadelphia"; endorsed by TJ as received 1 Oct. and so recorded in SJL. Enclosure: Frédéric L. Hammer to TJ, 12 May 1801.

Mathias Kin, also known as Matthias King, made a specialty of locating seeds and plants. He was originally from Strasbourg. On a recent trip to Europe, he had carried to Frédéric Hammer a new edition of *Notes on the State of Virginia* that included TJ's appendix of 1800. Hammer was one of Kin's clients, and

Kin, under a charge from François André Michaux, also collected seeds from American forests for the French government. Kin traveled widely in the United States and made at least one journey to Asia, although on the return voyage he lost his specimens to "cruizers at sea." He collected over 60 varieties of American oaks. During the nineteenth century, Germantown, Pennsylvania, where Kin had friends, boasted impressive magnolias, pecan trees, yews, and other trees that were the products of his travels (Henry Savage, Jr., and Elizabeth J. Savage, *André and François André Michaux* [Charlottesville, 1986], 215, 262, 283; Edwin C. Jellett, *Germantown Gardens and Gardeners* [Philadelphia, 1914], 74-6; Townsend Ward, "The Germantown Road and its Associations," PMHB, 6 [1882], 396-8, 401; *Bartonia: Proceedings of the Philadelphia Botanical Club*, 9 [1926], 38-9; Hammer to TJ, 12 May 1801; Kin to TJ, 24 Dec. 1805, in MH; TJ to Kin, 15 Jan. 1806, in DLC).

From William R. Lee

SIR   Marblehead Sept 28. 1801

Being informed that the Collectorship for the port of Salem & Beverly are to be changed— should that event take place I have to offer my self a candidate for that Office with a full conviction of my abilities to execute the duties in every respect

Conceiving it of the first importance your Excellency should be informed of the characters of those who apply for places of trust under your administration—I have requested the favour of Friends in this quarter to furnish you with information requisite

in addition to those I beg leave to refer you to the Honbl. Levi Lincoln Esqr. to whome I have the honour of being known—also Genl. Dearborn and Doctr Eustace for further information—with my most ardent wishes for you health & happiness, I have the honour to be with the highes Respect

Sir. Your Most Obd Servt   WILLIAM R. LEE

RC (DNA: RG 59, LAR); at foot of text: "His Exclly Thomas Jefferson Esqr"; endorsed by TJ as received 12 Oct. and so recorded in SJL; also endorsed by TJ: "to be collector of Salem & Beverley."

William R. Lee (1745-1824) of Marblehead attained the rank of colonel during the American Revolution, but resigned from the army in 1778 and returned to his lucrative commercial ventures. Around 1802, however, a series of financial reversals, including losses from his Yazoo land speculations, led to his retirement from business. TJ appointed him collector for Salem and Beverly in July 1802 (Thomas Amory Lee, "The Lee Family of Marblehead," *Essex Institute Historical Collections*, 53 [1917], 155-68; JEP, 1:432; Vol. 33:670).

From Philip Mazzei

28 7bre, 1801.

In molte lettere, posteriori alla sua del 24 Aprile 1796 (l'ultima pervenutami) ò desiderato di sapere, se gradirebbe ch'io Le mandassi alcune piante di frutte, e se per l'acquisto di nuove specie vorrebbe mandare per la cassa che le conterrebbe al porto ove giungesse il bastimento che la portasse, e in tal caso quali sarebbero i porti a Lei più convenienti. Aspetto tuttavia la sua risposta per saper come contenermi, e intanto mi prendo la libertà di mandarle 40 noccioli di Pesche della Vaga Loggia, 12 di Pesche Mele, 4 di Pesche della Maddalena, et 4 di Pesche Poppe di Venere, ogni qualità involta separatamente in carta col nome sopra, e il tutto in un sacchetto cucito. Le prime 2 qualità non l'ò vedute nè in Francia, nè in America, nè in verun'altro paese fuori di questo. Le Pesche Mele maturano conservando la buccia verdacchia pendente alquanto in giallo; si staccano dal nocciolo; si fondono in bocca come le Poppe di Venere; e conservano anche nella massima maturità una piccola pòrzione d'acidetto, che le rende gustosissime. Le Pesche che della V.L. maturano colla buccia rossa e gialla; la polpa è consistente come quella delle megliori che abbiamo in Virginia, e che qua si chiamano Cotogne; il gusto è diverso, ma ottimo; e per renderle più grate al palato bisogna levarne la buccia con un coltello bene affilato, poichè la parte più accosto alla buccia è la megliore. Delle altre 2 qualità, Ella ne avrà probabilmente portati seco i noccioli di Francia; ma ò voluto non ostante mandarne 4 noccioli d'ognuna, perchè qua sono molto megliori, e oltre di ciò quelle della maddalena maturano sì presto, che l'ultime precedono le prime d'ogni altra qualità, e le Poppe di V. son tanto più grosse di quelle di Francia, che ne ò avute nel mio orto di 11 oncie. I noccioli son provati, cioè tutti buoni, onde consiglierei di piantargli al posto per non fargli subire la traspiantazione, e conseguentemente la perdita del un'anno; e se alcuni non nascono il primo anno, a motivo d'esser prosciugati, nasceranno il secondo.

EDITORS' TRANSLATION

28 September 1801

In many letters subsequent to yours of 24 April 1796 (the last one I received) I have expressed the wish you would let me know if you would like me to send you some fruit plants and if to acquire new varieties you would send for the trunk to contain them to the port of arrival of the boat bringing it. And, in that case, if you would, please name what ports would be most convenient for you. I shall wait for your answer in order to learn what I should do and meanwhile I take the liberty of sending you 40 pits of Vaga

Loggia peaches, 12 of apple peaches, 4 of Maddalena peaches and 4 of Breasts-of-Venus peaches, each variety wrapped up separately in paper and labeled, and all of them sewn up in a pouch. I did not see the first two varieties either in France or America, or in any other place outside of here. The apple peaches ripen with their greenish skin turning slightly yellow; they are free-stone, melt in your mouth like the Breasts-of-Venus variety, and even when very ripe retain a bit of tartness that makes them very tasty. The Vaga Loggia Peaches, when ripe, have a red and yellow skin and their pulp is firm like that of the best in Virginia, and here they are called quinces (cotogne). Their taste is different but very fine, and to make them more palatable they must be peeled with a very sharp knife, for the part closest to the skin is the best. You probably took some stones of the other two varieties with you when you left France; just the same I have decided to send you four pits of each variety because here they are much better. Furthermore the Maddalena variety ripen so early that the last of them precede the first of any other variety, and the Breasts-of-Venus variety are so much larger here than in those in France that in my orchard I have picked some weighing 11 ounces. The pits are tested, that is, they are all good, therefore I would suggest you plant them where they will not have to be transplanted and suffer thereby the loss of a year's growth. If some do not come up the first year because of their being dried up, they will the next.

Dft (Archivio Filippo Mazzei, Pisa, Italy); in Mazzei's hand. RC (not found) recorded in SJL as received from Pisa on 5 May 1802. Dupl (not found) recorded in SJL as received 5 Mch. 1805.

PESCHE: in 1794, TJ planted 1,157 peach trees in his north orchard and as a boundary fence at Monticello. The harvested fruits were used for peach liqueurs and hog feed. TJ's collection of European and local peaches included 38 varieties grown at Monticello. Several of the varieties Mazzei sent to TJ, including the Vaga Loggia, Maddelena, and Apple peach, were introduced into the United States by TJ. Mazzei sent stones and cuttings of Poppa di Venere to TJ at Monticello and in Washington, where nurseryman Alexander Hepburn custom propagated trees for the president. In a 26 May 1802 entry in his garden book, TJ recorded, "planted in the upper row of the Nursery beginning at the N.E. end the following peach stones, sent me by Mazzei from Pisa. see his letter. 4. stones of the Maddelena peach. then 4. of the poppe de Venere. then 12 Melon peaches. then 40. Vaga loggia" (Peter J. Hatch, *The Fruits and Fruit Trees of Monticello* [Charlottesville, 1998], 79, 85, 86, 89, 90; Betts, *Garden Book*, 277).

From James Monroe

DEAR SIR   Richmond Sepr. 28. 1801

At the request of Mr. Arthur Lee of Norfolk I have given him an introduction to you, but not knowing his object, think proper to mention that I do not, as the contrary might otherwise be inferrd. He is in my opinion a young man of merit, tho it is not founded on much acquaintance with him. He deliver'd an oration not long since which was well spoken of, and is a republican. He is however young;

I have heard him spoken of as gay; and if his object is the attainment of an office, you ought to have much better information of him than I can give. What I here state does not derogate from what I state in my other letter; it is intended only to prevent an inference from it wh. might be drawn without this intimation—Sincerely I am yr. fnd. & servt   JAS. MONROE

RC (DLC); endorsed by TJ as received 3 Oct. and so recorded in SJL.

In 1799, a friend commented that ARTHUR LEE had apparently "carried his Democratic principles so far as to make the common mechanicks & apprentices of Norfolk his intimate Friends." Not long before that, in 1797-98, Lee attended the College of William and Mary. He was elected to the Virginia House of Delegates from Norfolk County in May 1801 for the session that was to begin in December (WMQ, 1st ser., 4 [1895], 108; VMHB, 29 [1921], 259-60; *The History of the College of William and Mary (Including the General Catalogue) from its Foundation, 1660, to 1874* [Richmond, 1874], 101; *Alexandria Advertiser*, 2 May 1801; Leonard, *General Assembly*, 224).

Monroe's letter of INTRODUCTION, which like the letter above was dated Richmond, 28 Sep., read: "Mr. Arthur Lee of Norfolk has requested me to make him known to you, with which I readily comply. He is the son of R. Evers Lee of that borough who is perhaps known to you. Mr. A. Lee is a young man of merit, of wh. his election as a delegate to our assembly by his county is an ample testimonial. I beg to recommend him to yr. civilities & am with great respect & esteem yr. fnd. & servt" (RC in DLC; endorsed by TJ as received 6 Oct. and so recorded in SJL). Arthur Lee's father was evidently Richard Evers Lee, a Norfolk attorney, borough officeholder, and banker (Madison, *Papers, Sec. of State Ser.*, 5:587-8n; Vol. 15:556; Arthur Lee to TJ, 5 Apr. 1804, in MHi).

Statement of Account with John March

Georgetown, Potomac

1801	To John March	
May 25	To 12 Paper Cases for Lrs: &c.	$ 4.00
30	Binding Cookery Book, 12mo:	0.50
June 24	Sewing & Covering 3 Manuscripts, Post 4o.	3.00
July 21	Binding Blackstone, &c. 8vo. S. lettered	0.62½
"	Furbishing & lettering 2 vols. Baltimore Advertiser	1.50
"	Making, &c. 8 Post. 4o: Cases for Writings	16.00
24	½ Binding Nautical Almanack, 8vo.	0.50
Sept: 29	½ Binding 17 vols. Demy folio Music Books, lettd. &c.	34.00
"	½ Binding 19 vols. folio News Papers, & *arranging* Do.	55.00

"   ½ Binding in Calf St. Domingue,
        par Moreau, 2 vols. 4o: 3.00
"   Binding in Calf 26 vols.
     Encyclopedie Methodique,
     Demy 4o: tooled & lettered at $2.25   58.50
                                                    _____
                                                    $176.62½

MS (CSmH); in March's hand; at head of text: "Thomas Jefferson, Esqr:"; endorsed by TJ: "March John"; with order in TJ's hand on verso: "Nov. 7. 1801. Mr. Barnes will be pleased to pay the within Th: Jefferson"; signed by March acknowledging payment on 7 Nov.; endorsed by Barnes on 7 Nov.

John March (d. 1804), formerly of Norwich, England, was a stationer, bookseller, and bookbinder in Georgetown (David Stoker, "The Norwich Book Trades Before 1800," *Transactions of the Cambridge Bibliographical Society,* 8 [1986], 109; *Washington Federalist,* 4 June 1804; MB, 2:1057).

BALTIMORE ADVERTISER: the Baltimore *American and Daily Advertiser,* a Republican daily newspaper to which TJ subscribed. TJ owned issues from 1799 and 1800 bound in two volumes, according to an 1815 catalogue of his library (Sowerby, No. 597; MB, 2:1070, 1123, 1215).

DEMY FOLIO: demi-folio, or half the size of folio pages.

NAUTICAL ALMANACK: *The Nautical Almanac and Astronomical Ephemeris,* an annual London imprint (see Vol. 31:592n).

ST. DOMINGUE: *Description topographique, physique, civile, politique et historique de la partie française de l'isle Saint-Domingue,* by Médéric Louis Elie Moreau de St. Méry, published in Philadelphia in 1796 (Sowerby, No. 4155).

Since 1783, TJ had been a subscriber to the ENCYCLOPEDIE METHODIQUE, a serial work published in Paris (Sowerby, No. 4889; Vol. 6:258).

In his financial memoranda, TJ recorded at 7 Nov. his order on John Barnes to pay March, "the bookbinder," $176.625. Barnes also recorded the transaction under TJ's private expenditures at 7 Nov. in a statement of account with TJ (MB, 2:1057; statement of household and private account from John Barnes, 4 Dec. 1801, in ViU).

From James Patton Preston

Smithfield Sepr 29th 1801

Being informed that there will be a vacancy in the Sixth Survey Virginia, or a Consolidation of the present Inspection Districts, and a Supervisor appointed in the place of the present Inspectors of Revenue, I am desirous of becoming a Candidate for the appointment.

not having a personal acquaintance with you, and being assured that you must be satisfyed of the Integrity, and Capacity, of a person making such application (In case of this new arrangement) I should be compelled to rely on the recommendation of such friends as I suppose you would confide in—James Monroe Esquire, Colo Wilson Nicholas, Judge Alexr. Stuart, Colo. Andw. Moore, and others would join in the nomination. I have written to Capt. M. Lewis on this subject with whom I am acquainted—Your determination on this head will be communicated to me by him whenever you may think proper to inform him of it—

I am with respect   JAMES PATTON PRESTON

RC (DLC); endorsed by TJ as received 11 Oct. and so recorded in SJL.

James Patton Preston (1774-1843) of Smithfield, Montgomery County, Virginia, graduated from the College of William and Mary in 1795, and served several terms in both the Virginia Senate and the House of Delegates. Promoted to infantry colonel in the War of 1812, during which he suffered crippling wounds, he also served as governor of Virginia from 1816 to 1819 and became postmaster of Richmond before retiring to his estate in Montgomery County (Robert Sobel and John Raimo, *Biographical Directory of the Governors of the United States 1789-1978*, 4 vols. [Westport, Conn., 1978], 4:1632).

Preston wrote to James MONROE on 28 Sep. asking to be recommended for the revenue position (Gallatin, *Papers*, 5:802). On the same day, Preston wrote Meriwether LEWIS a similar letter on the subject (RC in DLC).

From Thomas Newton

DEAR SIR   Norfolk Sept. 30. 1801—

I have the pleasure of informing you that Coll Davies is on the recovery & in fair way of soon being well. the Emigrants, especially from Ireland have suffered greatly, many have died; the inhabitants are generally healthy who have been used to our climate & except late setlers I know of none that have been ill & very few have the common fall complaint as yet, & I hope the setting in of the NE wind will put a stop to all sicknesses. this place contains 2398 tithables above 16 years old, the Census taken, I think falls very short of our numbers, as in the list of tithables no seamen are taken in & I suppose there are not less than 1200 belonging to this place, by which you can calculate the No. of inhabitants. I hope something will be done to put the Marine Hospital in repair next Congress, it is realy a valuable building but getting much out of repair, a small tax on sailors, would support it handsomely, a leave for admittance of foreign seamen, on paying customary board wages would greatly assist in maintaining it; the Courthouse & Prison of Norfolk County, is adjoining the hospital lotts, (except a street) which will be sold, these would make a very great addition & will sell very low, not at half the Cost of building them, & in Cases of Contagious sickness among the seamen, they could be kept in separate houses & be a means of saving many lives.

I pray you excuse for troubling you with this, but it is of so much consequence to the poor sailors that I could not refrain. I am wishing you health & happiness

respectfully yr   THOS NEWTON

RC (DLC); endorsed by TJ as received 13 Oct. and so recorded in SJL with notation "N."

From Robert Smith

SIR,   Navy Department Sep. 30th. 1801

The case of Doctor Barraud brought to your attention by Judge Tucker was acted upon before I came into Office. To enable you to give to Judge Tucker a view of the proceedings that lead to the removal of this Gentleman, I herewith send to you enclosed copies of the Letters upon the subject. The high pretensions of Doctor Barraud were probably not known to either Mr Gallatin or Genl Dearborne—

Be pleased to accept the assurances of my great Esteem & high Consideration   RT SMITH

RC (DLC); endorsed by TJ as received from the Navy Department on 1 Oct. and "Barraud & Balfour" and so recorded in SJL. Enclosures: (1) Extract of Albert Gallatin to Henry Dearborn, 20 June 1801, reporting that navy surgeon George Balfour, who is still on full pay though not assigned to any vessel, has offered to attend the marine hospital at Norfolk without an assistant; accepting the offer would save the $1,400 spent for the current surgeon and assistant; if approved by Dearborn, Gallatin will "take Measures to have the present Surgeon discharged." (2) Extract of Dearborn to Gallatin, 9 July 1801, agreeing that placing Balfour in charge of the marine hospital would be "very agreeable to this department" and that orders will be sent to Balfour as soon as Gallatin makes the arrangements. (3) George Balfour to Gallatin, 27 July 1801, requesting that a surgeon's mate be sent to assist at the marine hospital, understanding that several of them are still on full pay and not attached to any ship. (4) Gallatin to Robert Smith, 18 Aug. 1801, requesting that Balfour be ordered to take charge of the marine hospital at Norfolk "after the 30th. Sept. next" and that similar orders be given to one of the surgeon's mates still in service but not attached to any vessel. (5) Smith to Balfour, 19 Aug. 1801, directing Balfour to take charge of the marine hospital at Norfolk after 30 Sep. and authorizing him to offer the place of surgeon's mate to "Doctor Starke late of the Navy, who is now at Norfolk"; if Starke declines, then Balfour may choose another and inform Smith so that he may be commissioned as a surgeon's mate in the navy (Trs in DLC; in clerk's hand).

From "Philopoemen"

Dear Sir,   September 1801.

The exalted situation in which the suffrages of your fellow-countrymen has placed you, probably prevents your knowing, and I have therefore thought it might be proper to apprize you of the ruinous effects which *certain* dismissals and appointments of Officers have had, on the minds not only of people in general, but even of your best friends and warmest advocates.

It is not necessary for me to use any individual name in explaining the thing; a single statement of a case in point will serve fully to illustrate it, in which I will be candid enough to appeal to your own judgment and feelings for a decision—Give me leave therefore to ask, If it is not peculiarly ungratefull, ungenerous, distressing, and I may add oppressive, that the venerable grey haired veteran who has suffered and bled in the cause of establishing a government in his native soil, free from tyrannical abuses, should without any allegation whatever be dismissed from an Office meritoriously obtained; as a reward justly due for the toilsome hazardous and important services rendered to his country, and without which he could not, from age and infirmity obtain the necessary comforts of this life—The conclusions natural for people to draw, in such cases you can easily conceive of.

When the Offices of our government become a mere article of merchandize, as they already have; time only can determine the consequences that will result from such an alarming traffic as that of buying votes and selling Offices.

These measures may answer your *present purposes*, but they cannot secure to you a lasting confidence of the people of the United States.

PHILOPOEMEN

RC (DLC); at head of text: "Private"; at foot of text: "Thomas Jefferson Esqr. President U. States"; endorsed by TJ as received 26 Oct. from "Anonimous" and so recorded in SJL.

Form of Deeds for Henderson Purchases

[September? 1801]

The deeds to be in the following form.

This indenture made on the   day of   1801. between John R. Kerr and   his wife on the one part and Craven Peyton on the other part, all of the county of Albemarle, witnesseth that the

[359]

said John R. Kerr and   his wife in consideration of the sum
of   to them in hand actually paid, have given granted bargained and sold unto the said Craven [here insert the description of
the land as stated hereafter] To have & to hold the said lands and appurtenances (conveyed as aforesaid to the sd Craven) to him the said
Craven & his heirs: and the said John R. Kerr &   his wife their
heirs, executors & administrators. the said lands & appurtenances
(conveyed as aforesaid to the said Craven) to him the said Craven &
his heirs will for ever warrant & defend, in witness whereof the said
John R. Kerr &   his wife have hereto set their hands & seals
on the day & year above written.
signed sealed & delivered   John R. Kerr
in presence of   Kerr
   3 witnesses

———————

the description to be inserted in John R. Kerr's deed
   "all the undivided portion of the lands of the late Bennet Henderson deceased in the county of Albemarle which descended on the
said   Kerr wife of the said John R. as one of the children & coheirs of the sd Bennet, meaning to include as well the reversion of
those now held in dower as those vested in possession, with all their
appurtenances, but excepting thereout the lots in the town of Milton,
the tobacco warehouses, the distillery & the mill reserved to the said
John R. Kerr"

———————

   Description for the deed of James L. Henderson.
   "all the undivided portion of the lands and lots of the late Bennet
Henderson decd. in the county of Alb. which descended on the said
James L. Henderson as one of his children & coheirs, meaning to include as well the reversion of those now held in dower as those vested
in possession, with all their appurtenances but excepting thereout a
mill which is now erected and standing on a part of the abovemen-
tioned land which with it's perquisites is reserved to the said James
L. & excepting also his portion in the house & lot in the town of Milton now occupied by Henderson & Connard reserved to the said
James L."

———————

   Description for the deed of Isham Henderson.
   "all the undivided portion of the lands & lots of the late Bennet
Henderson decd. in the county of Alb. which descended on the said
Isham as one of his children & coheirs, meaning to include as well the

reversion of those now held in dower as those vested in possession with all their appurtenances: but excepting thereout the mill standing theron, and the right to continue it in tobacco warehouse & lot, & a store house and lot in the town of Milton now occupied by Henderson & Connard, and reserved to the said Isham"

Description for the deed of Charles Henderson.

"all the undivided portion of the lands & lots of the late Bennet Henderson decd. in the county of Alb. which descended on the said Charles as one of his children and coheirs, meaning to include as well the reversion of those now held in dower as those vested in possession with all their appurtenances but excepting thereout the mill and seat beside [. . .] mill, a tobacco warehouse & lot, the store house and lot in the town of Milton now occupied by Henderson & Connard & the undivided lots in the town of Milton, reserved to the said Charles"

PrC (ViU); faint; entirely in TJ's hand, with hand-drawn facsimile seals beside signatures.

This form was for DEEDS to be executed with the heirs of the Bennett Henderson estate from whom Craven Peyton had made purchases earlier in 1801. TJ may have prepared this document while at Monticello during August and September 1801, very likely leaving the paper with Peyton before departing for Washington (see Declaration of Trust with Craven Peyton, 25 Sep.; Peyton to TJ, 3 Oct.; TJ to Peyton, 8 Oct.).

The references to each heir's UNDIVIDED PORTION of the Henderson family's property confirm that TJ made out this form for the deeds before the Henderson estate was partitioned. In that division of the estate, carried out on the 1st of October 1801 by commissioners appointed by the county court, a drawing by lots determined which parcels of land would go to each of the Henderson brothers and sisters. John Henderson, the oldest sibling, had pressed for the division for months, hoping to acquire control over a piece of land that might be developed as a site for a new mill that would not require the use of the milldam condemned through TJ's lawsuit (Vol. 32:558; Vol. 33:18; Peyton to TJ, 10 July, 3 Oct.; TJ to Peyton, 14 July). For the form the deeds took after the division of the estate among the heirs, see TJ to Peyton, 8 Oct., and the deed printed at 29 Nov.

For the DOWER share of the estate reserved for the use of Bennett Henderson's widow, Elizabeth Lewis Henderson, see the next document.

HENDERSON & CONNARD: John Henderson, continuing a business begun by his father, operated boats that transported goods on the rivers between Milton and Richmond. More than once, George Jefferson sent items to Monticello for TJ by Henderson's boats (Vol. 28:8; Vol. 32:37, 286; Vol. 33:542; George Jefferson to TJ, 29 Aug. 1801).

Valuation of Henderson Property
for Dower

[before 1 Oct. 1801]

Valuation of the property of Bennet Henderson in which dower was assigned.

	£
1. house occupied at present by mr John Henderson	325. 0.0
1. do. by mrs Henderson	120. 0.0
1. still house & lot	120. 0.0
1. field lying on the upper part of the land 69. as. @ 30/	103.10.0
1. do of Low grounds below Milton 37½ as. @ £ 3.	112.10.0
1. do of high do. to the right of the Low grounds	
16. acres @ 17/6	14. 8.6
the lands lying below the mill supposed to be	
3. acres @ £4.3.4	12.10.0
Store house & lot occupied by mr Snelson	350.
15. acres to run in a direct line from mr Sheffield's	
shop to the river & above the mill so as to give it	
above the mill	33. 9.6
	1191. 8.

Mrs. Henderson's dower ⅓ to wit	£	
the 2 story house	325	
the 15 acres	33.9.6	358. 9.6

⅓ of the profits of the mill
⅓ of the rents of the ware house
⅓ of the back lands valued @ 8/ per acre.

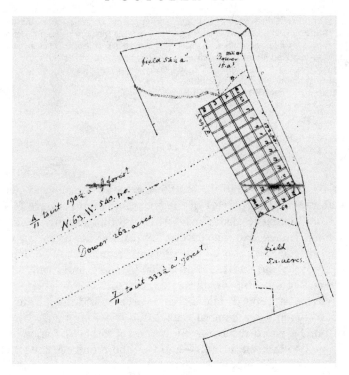

MS (ViU); entirely in TJ's hand, including diagram, which is on verso of "Valuation"; undated, but see below.

Bennett Henderson's children inherited his estate, but by DOWER, a principle that came from English common law, their mother received the use of one third of the land during her lifetime (William Waller Hening, ed., *The Statutes at Large; Being a Collection of All the Laws of Virginia*, 13 vols. [Richmond, 1809-23], 12:138, 139, 146, 162-5; William F. Fratcher, "Protection of the Family against Disinheritance in American Law," *International and Comparative Law Quarterly*, 14 [1965], 294).

MRS HENDERSON: Henderson's widow, Elizabeth Lewis Henderson, was TJ's cousin. The dwelling house and 15 acres of land allotted to her as part of her dower were not included in the 1 Oct. partition of the estate among the heirs. The Hendersons' MILL stood on that parcel of land. In 1801, she moved with her

younger children to Kentucky, where her husband had also acquired property (Craven Peyton, amended bill in chancery, 2 June 1804, in Tr of TJ v. Michie, ViU: Carr Papers; Vol. 28:474n).

TJ made this valuation and diagram before 1 Oct. 1801, when the commissioners partitioned the estate. The sizes and designations of the tracts of land in the valuation do not match the results of the partition that Craven Peyton sent on 3 Oct., and when TJ made his diagram he thought the Henderson property would be allocated in eleven rather than ten shares. Moreover, when TJ made his diagram, he thought that the Hendersons' unimproved woodlands (which in the diagram are to the left of the rectangular grid of the town of Milton) contained a total of 786 acres, with one-third of that, 262 acres, allotted to the widow's dower. The 786-acre figure used for the county court's assignment of the dower was probably only an estimate of the tract's size. A survey made in conjunction with the partition revealed that the estate's BACK LANDS actually included 1,020 acres, as TJ learned when Peyton sent him information about the partition. For his diagram, TJ also supposed that the dower portion would be excluded from the partitioning of the back lands, whereas the commissioners divided that entire tract into ten parcels for allocation to the heirs (Craven Peyton, amended bill in chancery, cited above; Vol. 28:520; plat enclosed by Peyton to TJ, 6 Nov.).

From Anonymous

October 1st. 1801

A report prevails, that the auditor general, Postmaster-general, Treasurer, and other officers of the general government are about to retire from their several stations—Altho unknown to the president of the United States; He will pardon my calling his attention to Mr. George Biscoe Collector of the Port of Nottingham on Patuxent river; an early, and steady friend to his Country, and firmly attach'd to correct Republican principles—Mr. Biscoe is a gentleman of stubborn virtue, approved talents, and great assiduity; from those qualifications and his general knowledge of fiscal affairs, I have no doubt but he woud discharge the duties of either the above offices with honor to himself, usefulness to the Community & reflect credit on the patron who appointed him.

No thought is entertained by the person who presumes thus to address the chief majestrate of the Union, but Mr. Biscoe's being appointed wou'd gratify a great part of the citizens of Maryland particularly the friends to the present administration—

Doct. Gant of George Town can more particularly inform the President of this Gentlemans, private & publick charecter—The returns from his little office may give as well some idea of his correctness.

with all deference

RC (DNA: RG 59, LAR); addressed: "Thomas Jefferson Esqr. President of the United States"; franked; postmarked: "Uppr. Marlbro 13th Octr."; endorsed by TJ as received 16 Oct. and so recorded in SJL with notation "Biscoe to be Treasurer or P.M.G."; also endorsed by TJ: "George Biscoe, collector of Nottingham on Patuxent to be Treasurer or Post M.G."

Appointed collector of customs at Nottingham, Maryland, by President Washington in 1789, GEORGE BISCOE continued to serve in that post throughout TJ's presidency. On 1 Jan. 1807, the anonymous author of this letter again recommended Biscoe to TJ, this time for the Baltimore collectorship (RC in DNA: RG 59, LAR; Washington, *Papers, Pres. Ser.*, 2:145-6; Gallatin, *Papers*, 20:712, 716).

From Little Egg Harbor, New Jersey, Republican Citizens

District of Little Egg-harbour.

Tuckerton October 1. 1801

The Memorial & Representation of the subscribers in behalf of themselves & other Republican cittizens of the District of Little-Egg-Harbour in the State of New-Jersey, Respectfully Sheweth.

That in consequence of a cruel persecution and an unjust & unfounded complaint encouraged by the late Secretary of the Treasury against Ebenezer Tucker Esquire a republican late Collector of the [. . .] [. . .]s'd. he was induced (by the advice of his friends) to [. . .] said Office. And in his place was appointed by the late [admin]istration a young man by the name of Wm. Watson a native residentor of Burlington, fifty miles distant from the district aforsd. an entire stranger in the district and had not, nor yet hath, any property in the place either real or personal, and we further represent that in the late contested Elections for President, Congress, & State Legislature, he has Strenuously opposed the republican Interest, a specimen of his modesty will be seen by a recurrence to the New-Jersey Federalist annexed. Not only so he has repeatedly absented himself from the district and from the duties of his Office from three to six weeks at a time, to the great inconvenience of the commercial interest of the place. Not only so he has taken the men out of the revenue Boat Patterson employed on this station, to go after his private business while they were paid by the public, & further he does not pay the boatmen he employs their wages, except by his notes and several good men have left the service for that reason, For all those reasons the citizens in General & in Particular the republican citizens of this district wish him removed, & that our late Collector may be reinstated, or that Capt. Silas Crane (a firm republican) a man of respectability & property may be appointed to succeed Mr. Watson, and we as in duty bound will every pray.— SAMUEL ROSE

RC (DNA: RG 59, LAR); torn; at head of text: "To the President of the United States"; in Samuel Rose's hand and signed by him and fourteen others; endorsed by TJ: "Little Egg harbor N.J. [. . .]ved. [. . .]mmended."

EBENEZER TUCKER, a shipbuilder, merchant, and judge, of Burlington County, New Jersey, was appointed surveyor of the port of Little Egg Harbor in 1789. He became its collector and inspector of the revenue in 1796 and later postmaster at Tuckerton and a member of Congress. He was heavily involved in the partisan battles in New Jersey politics in 1801 (JEP, 1:212-13; *Biog. Dir. Cong.*; Washington, *Papers, Pres. Ser.*, 5:61;

Carl E. Prince, *New Jersey's Jeffersonian Republicans: The Genesis of an Early Party Machine 1789-1817* [Chapel Hill, N.C., 1967], 105).
In April 1802, TJ nominated SILAS CRANE as the successor to William Watson, who was removed for absence and neglect of office (JEP, 1:422; Vol. 33:669, 673, 679).

From Lewis Osmont

Brunswick, Glynn County,

SIR.   State of Georgia October 1st. 1801.

Presumption, I acknowledge, may readily be adjudged to be my Guilt to pretend from my obscure Cabbin to trouble your Excellency; still, Sir, please to permit me to recollect that I once had the gratifying oportunity of admiring (tho' I was not able to apreciate) your merits both private, political & public; then no doubt you will grant it to be an irresistible impulsion I should expatiate on the happiness I felt at the intelligence received last spring of the Justice done you by the people of the United States. Be pleased, Sir, indulge your natural Goodness and let for an Instant your Excellency descend from its summit of sublime honor (for I dare not even in imagination aproach it) to receive the humble and heartfelt Congratulations of one whom you have formerly been so Good as to take pains, concerns & pleasure to protect.

Had I follow'd the heat of my imagination as I might have done in times of blooming and uninterrupted happiness, long since had I filled Sheets to express my Joy: but crowded as you were with addresses I could not expect that you would in any shape notice mine; I would wait some time that I might have Grounds to hope you would bestow a perusal over my feeble expressions. Could even Sobriety prevail at public *Fêtes* I had surely been Conspicuous in all such as I could have reached to, in celebrating not only the promotion confered on your Excellency, but also the amendment which my fellow Citizens had been making to the opinion they Gave abroad on their Judgement by not making at the first oportunity, diplomatic accomplishments & Virtue succeed the military hero; and thereby disapointing the Sanguine hopes of the Sensible and true feeling part of the World.

May God now crown his instrument of liberty by Granting duration to your Administration, as well as success in bringing to an indissoluble friendship two Nations of both of which Nature and law give me the title of Citizen!

May it in the Course of things please your Excellency to take some notice of this remote spott as a District, and after an official information of the several Violations Committed in it of the laws of the United States, redress the Grievances! Such for Instance as the non residense of the Collector of the revenue at Brunswick, whereby our Coasters are put to much trouble: Such also as the non attendence to the prevention of Smuggling, the Post office filled by an openly acknowledged British Subject and the want of a single sheet of stamped paper by which the Citizen is exposed & the revenue neglected.

Conscious that the fatal events which have removed from me those elegant prospects I once beheld (the Circumstance of British Spoils on my Infant fortune, as yourself were pleased to term it, being one of them) have alarmed your ear & thoughts whether or not I had been deserving of your Good opinion or now do merit your Sympathy; at the same time Convinced that profound wisdom & genuine Virtue do reign in you hand in hand with Christianlike charity, of Course that you will allow that uprightness is often the Victim of frownsome fortune, and that with me propriety of Conduct is soothing to the sorrows of snapping disapointments, I do hope you may not disdain my homage on this Solemn occasion; nor even a Sketch of my present situation with the Causes of alteration in my former ones; Which in order to insure the Welcome of to your Excellent and pure hands I accompany with Sundry Vauchures hereto subjoined —

In Consequense of divers heavy losses, I made a general surrender to the full Satisfaction of a Very numerous body of Creditors on the first day of April 1796. during the two ensuing Years my upright heart still undismay'd by the burthen of Calamities which attended it and which my inexperienced youth so unexpectedly encountered, I did warmly and diligently prosecute recoveries, and towards the latter end of '97 receiving intelligence of an award being at last Granted in my favor by the British Admiralty, I had the happiness Voluntarily to accomplish my total devestment by waiting on the assignees I had apointed on the 1st. of April 1796. making out the proper accounts and authorising them to receive the amo[unts.] lastly after melting even the plate I brought from my parents to pay such as could not afford to wait the slow motions of assignees, I proceeded to Georgia destitute of a Capital, but with a fresh credit to a small amount for which I have wholly remitted. The dreads of Town expenses have induced me to live in the Country and latterly finding that trade in a new place requires credits to be given which I Cannot afford, I am withdrawing from the mercantile World; Owning no negroes I do not plant, but possessed of some knowledge of Conveyancing & Common Law, as well as intrusted with the direction of the property of several distant proprietors, (even all the way from

Philadelphia) With Industry and strict economy I am enabled to maintain, still genteely, an affectionate and Virtuous Wife and a promising child.

Be it your pleasure to believe me to be sincerely With the most profound respect

Sir Your Excellency's Most obedient Servant

LEWIS OSMONT

RC (MoSHi: Jefferson Papers); torn; addressed: "To his Excellency Thomas Jefferson President of the United States at the City Washington"; endorsed by TJ as received 25 Nov. and so recorded in SJL. Enclosures: (1) Certificate of Montmollin & Herron and three others, Savannah, 22 Apr. 1801, stating that they have known Osmont since early 1798, have found him "punctual" in his dealings, and consider him a man of "integrity and uprightness"; they know of no adverse reasons for his departure from Savannah and that he left "with the consent of those with whom he had dealings." (2) Certificate of William Hunter, Savannah, 25 Apr. 1801, stating that he has transacted Osmont's business since his removal to Brunswick and that he has been "just and honorable" in his dealings and has never abused the confidence placed in him. (3) Certificate of J. B. Goupy, "Island of Jakil," 9 Sep. 1801, certifying the "undisputable reputation" of the authors of the above two letters and the authenticity of their signatures. (4) Certificate of Samuel Burnett, clerk's office, Glynn County, 29 Oct. 1801, that the above are true copies of originals recorded in the clerk's office of Glynn County (all Trs in same; written on recto and verso of single sheet). (5) Certificate of Leighton Wilson and John Burnett, Brunswick, 15 Sep. 1801, stating that Osmont has resided in Brunswick for "upwards of two years," during which time he has gained "the esteem of the respectable class of his fellow Citizens as a person of Good principles both political and private"; they understand that his conduct while residing in Savannah

was "as proper as it has been at this place." (6) Certificate of Samuel Burnett, clerk's office, Glynn County, 29 Oct. 1801, stating that Wilson and Burnett are justices of the inferior court of Glynn County and that "True faith ought to be Considered" on their certificate (both Trs in same; written on single sheet).

Lewis (Louis) Osmont (d. 1802) was a young Frenchman of straitened circumstances who came to America in 1791 with recommendations from William Short and others. TJ assisted Osmont in his efforts to recover lands in upstate New York, describing him as "a young man of extraordinary merit and talents." Osmont subsequently engaged in mercantile pursuits in Philadelphia before relocating to Georgia (Margaret Davis Cate, *Our Todays and Yesterdays, A Story of Brunswick and the Coastal Islands*, rev. ed. [Brunswick, 1930; repr. Spartanburg, S.C., 1972], 259; James Hardie, *Philadelphia Directory and Register* [Philadelphia, 1794], 110; Vol. 18:30-1; Vol. 20:617-18; Vol. 22:101-2; Vol. 28:5-6).

Claud Thompson served as COLLECTOR OF THE REVENUE for the district of Brunswick since December 1800 (JEP, 1:357). The POST OFFICE at Brunswick was filled by Adam Mackay on 17 Nov. 1800 (Stets, *Postmasters*, 109).

AS YOURSELF WERE PLEASED TO TERM IT: writing on Osmont's behalf to George Hammond on 3 Jan. 1794, TJ thanked the British minister for any act he might take "which may prevent the wreck of his infant fortunes, which he seems to apprehend" (Vol. 28:5-6).

From Benjamin Waterhouse

SIR   Cambridge October 1st. 1801.

Yesterday I was honored with your letter of Sepr. 17th. from Monticello informing me that the Vaccine inoculation was effectually planted at Washington, as well as at and near your own residence, and that you had sent the matter to several parts of the State of Virginia. I rejoice, beyond what a person less zealous than myself can realize at this intelligence, being convinced that the matter commences its career in Virginia & Columbia under more favorable circumstances than it has in any other State in the Union. Avarice, rivalship, and mistrust have accompanied its incipient practice in most parts of the Eastern States. These unworthy passions have prevented that cool & deliberate train of experiments which I presume has taken place under your auspices. Before I had determined on sending the matter to President Jefferson, I perceived symptoms of a similar disposition in Virginia, for I had not a few letters from different parts of the State, in which the practitioners held out what they conceived luring baites to send them the matter & instructions to the exclusion of their bretheren. Several practitioners rode night & day from the extreme parts of Connecticut & Vermont to Cambridge to get before hand of their neighbours. Sometimes the two rival Doctors of the same town were at my house at the same time, each wishing to outbid the other! An association of six practitioners in New Hampshire absolutely new districted the State, and then applied to me for the matter, and offering me their conjoint bonds to give me a fourth part of all that were inoculated by them & their subordinates! so that before I well knew the spirit & extent of the plan, I found myself the centre of a vile speculation. Some went through Vermont & Connecticut calling themselves my agents, commissioned from me to sell the *matter* & spreading a spurious disease & endangering the lives of the people by the abominable cheat. The keenest apostles in this new doctrine went out from Connecticut. I checked, however, this vile traffic in that quarter, by exposing the trick in a letter to the President of Yale-College, which he published, with a suitable introduction in his own name. I believe that such speculations would not be so apt to show themselves in the southern States, I however perceived by letters from that part of the union that some wished to monopolize the practice within certain circles, but the mode I adopted has effectually checked that disposition, and has at the same time given the practice a dignity, which it has never acquired in some parts of the Union.

I here enclose a few unpublished pages by Dr Jenner, on the origin

1 OCTOBER 1801

of the inoculation. He has also sent me two or three fine representations of the Disease in all its stages, and these contrasted with the small-pox; one of which I here send for your acceptance. From a letter I received from the worthy Dr dated London July 18th. I transcribe the following paragraph,—"I don't care what British laws the americans discard so that they stick to this.—*never to take the virus from a Vaccine pustule for the purpose of inoculation after the efflorescence is formed around it.* I wish this Efflorescence to be considered as a sacred boundary over which the lancet should never pass." My own experience entirely corresponds with the above injunction of Dr Jenner. I never take the matter *after* the 8th. day as represented in the coloured plate, never so late as[1] the 10th.—I should be still pleased to hear of the progress of this new inoculation among our bretheren of the south, and should I receive any thing further of importance to the practice, from England, I will transmit it.

With the highest respect for your character & station, I remain your very humble servt.　　　　　　　　BENJN. WATERHOUSE

P.S. The paper on which this letter is written is made from *old paper, written* or *printed on*; the ink being discharged by a process which is cheap, & easily performed. This paper is six shillings sterling the ream, cheaper than that if the same quality made from rags.

　　　　　　　　　　　　　　　　　　　　　　BW.

RC (DLC); addressed: "President Jefferson"; endorsed by TJ. Recorded in SJL as received 8 Oct. Enclosures not found.

A letter on vaccination from Waterhouse to Timothy Dwight, the PRESIDENT of Yale College, was printed in the New Haven *Connecticut Journal* on 29 Apr.

REPRESENTATIONS OF THE DISEASE IN ALL ITS STAGES: in his 1802 treatise on smallpox vaccination, Waterhouse referred to colored engravings that he had received from Jenner and distributed to TJ and others showing cowpox at different stages (Waterhouse, *A Prospect of Exterminating the Small-Pox, Part II* [Cambridge, Mass., 1802], 78; Waterhouse to TJ, 2 Sep.).

[1] Preceding three words interlined in place of "on."

To Jacob Wagner

Oct. 2. 1801.

Th: Jefferson, with his compliments to mr Wagner returns him Forman's & Chancellor Livingston's letters. the moment the gentleman returns who went express to the Secretary of state, the ultimate dispatches for Chancellor Livingston may go off. there seems to be an enquiry in his letter, as to the person to whom he is to address himself in pecuniary matters, which it is important to answer, & probably mr Wagner can answer it to him.   mr Wagner can also inform him that a mr Gantt is appointed Commercial Agent at Nantes, but that the agency of L'Orient is still vacant, & that the Secretary of State shall be reminded of the Chancellor's recommendation of mr Patterson.

Th: Jefferson asks the favr. of mr Wagner to make him out a list of all commissions given out since the 29th. of July, as he has not noted them himself since that date. the Commission of Marshal for the Western district of Virginia was filled up for Andrew Moore Aug. 8.

RC (DNA: RG 59, MLR). PrC (DLC); at foot of text in ink: "Mr. Wagner." Enclosure: Robert R. Livingston to Madison, 16 Sep. (Madison, *Papers, Sec. of State Ser.*, 2:117-19). Other enclosure not found.

GENTLEMAN RETURNS: Hazen Kimball (see Madison to TJ, 3 Oct.).

MR WAGNER CAN ANSWER IT: on 2 Oct., Wagner wrote Livingston, responding to the queries in Livingston's letter to Madison of 16 Sep. and transmitting his "commission and instructions as Minister Plenipotentiary to the French Republic" and other papers. Wagner noted that Madison had not yet returned to Washington and that he was writing under the "President's directions." Wagner informed Livingston that his accounts were "to be regularly and punctually transmitted by duplicate for settlement with the Treasury at the end of every quarter" and that he could draw upon the secretary of state for the whole or any part of his outfit—set at $9,000, his salary for one year—before he departed. In France, Liv-

ingston was to draw on the bankers at Amsterdam for his salary and authorized expenditures. Wagner enclosed a letter of credit for that purpose directed to Willink, Van Staphorst, & Hubbard (RC in NHi: Robert R. Livingston Papers; in an unidentified hand, with closing, signature as chief clerk, and address in Wagner's hand; endorsed by Livingston as from Wagner in the absence of the secretary, "relative to accounts &c.").

TJ appointed Thomas T. GANTT of Maryland as commercial agent at the French port of Nantes in place of John J. Waldo, a late-term appointment. The commission is dated 20 July, but TJ recorded the appointment on his lists at 7 Nov. CHANCELLOR'S RECOMMENDATION: William Patterson of New York received the appointment as commercial agent at the French port of L'Orient with a commission dated 16 Oct. The appointment appears on TJ's lists at that date with the note that he was replacing Turell Tufts, a late-term appointment (both commissions in Lb in DNA: RG 59, PTCC; Vol. 33:173n, 672, 677).

From the District of Columbia Commissioners

SIR   Commissioners Office 3d Octobr. 1801.

We inclose an estimate of the sums which we consider as necessary to carry on the operations of the season, and to pay the interest to the State of Maryland to the end of this year—   This estimate we do not consider as perfectly accurate, but think it may be so far relied on, as to enable the President to determine whether the sum stated, as necessary to complete the Streets, or what other sum shall be expended thereon.—

This work which has been recommended by the President we are very desirous of accomplishing, but wish to have his sanction for the necessary expenditures.—

We are with the highest respect Sir, Your most obdt. Servants

WILLIAM THORNTON
ALEXR WHITE
TRISTRAM DALTON

RC (DLC); in a clerk's hand, signed by Thornton, White, and Dalton; at foot of text: "President of the U.S."; endorsed by TJ as received 3 Oct. and so recorded in SJL. FC (DNA: RG 42, DCLB).

In a memorial to Maryland's House of Delegates dated 17 Oct., the commission expressed its "regret" for late payments on the total interest due to the state in 1801, noting that they had insufficient

funds to execute the work requested by the president and to pay the interest. The commissioners asked the state assembly to renegotiate the terms of the loans and their repayment with Congress. The commission sent the memorial to TJ, who endorsed the cover letter as received on 21 Oct. (Trs in DLC, in William Brent's hand, including signatures of Thornton, White, and Dalton). For the memorial, see Gallatin to TJ, 10 Jan. 1802.

ENCLOSURE

District of Columbia Commissioners' Estimate of Debts

Commissioners Office, Washington 2d October 1801
Estimate of Debts due, and becoming due from the Commissioncrs prior to the 1t January 1802—

Eliptical room at the Capitol, due on Contract	$1626.00	
additional work	650.00	2276.00
Presidents house, Carpenters work	600.00	
Painters work	350.00	
Ornament work, whole cost $1796.67. balc. due	386.21	
Fence, Ice house &c.	350.00	1686.21
Roads—roll Labourers for September	1,300.00	
October	1500.00	
November	1500.00	
plank, iron work &c.	100.00	4,400.00
Salaries of the Commissioners, their Clerks, Surveyor and the Superintendent of the public buildings Balance due 1t. October	1,700.00	
Ditto—becoming due 31 Decem 1801	2770.50	4470.50
Interest on Debt to State of Maryland, on $200,000 from 1 January 1801 to 1. Octo. 1801	9000.00	

on $50,000 from 1 April 1801 to Ditto	1500.00	
on $200,000 from 1 Octo. to 1 Jany 1802	3000.00	
on $50,000 for Ditto	750.00	14250.00

Patrick Whelan awarded to him on acct of digging
        Canal from Tiber to James's creek,
        exclusive of Costs of a suit   678.30

Covered way from north wing of the Capitol to the $27,761.01
Eliptical room & other Contingencies during the year 1801
of which no Estimate is made

Funds, exclusive of what may be raised by the sale of Lots
on 8th. December next, advertised this day, and payments wch
may be previously made on those Lots, and on Lots which
may be sold at private sale viz

Cash in hand	$975.24	
Ditto, promised to be paid by Mr. Stoddert in		
the months of October & November 1801	5000.00	
Ditto—becoming due from Michael Nourse	280.70	6255.94
Deficiency exclusive of Contingencies		Ds. 21,505.07

Thomas Munroe Clk Coms.

Tr (DLC); in Munroe's hand.

From John Wayles Eppes

Dear Sir,   Monticello Oct: 3. 1801.

Our little one continues in good health and I feel no apprehensions about Maria. The hardness in her breasts has gone off entirely and as the milk flows freely there can be no danger of return. We have considerable apprehensions about the whooping cough which rages in every part of this neighbourhood. At Charlottesville & Milton we know that they certainly have it, & I have just learnt that Rogers, Colo Harveys tenant has it in his family. This brings it so near Edgehill that it will scarcely be possible for them to escape.

Your plaisterers have put on the first coat on the room adjoining the one finished before you left us, & also on the Octagon down stairs— They begin with the second coat on the square room above this morning. The masons go on badly not a single stone has been laid since you left us. Their first load of lime arrived yesterday evening. The Waggon got back from Augusta yesterday morning with lime for the plaisterers—I have passed your horse in review this morning—He is mending rapidly in flesh and his lameness considerably lessened—

Maria joins me in affectionate wishes for your happiness.

Yours sincerely   Jno: W: Eppes

RC (MHi); endorsed by TJ as received 6 Oct. and so recorded in SJL.

OUR LITTLE ONE: Francis Eppes, born 20 Sep. at Monticello (Malone, *Jefferson*, 4:160).

THE OCTAGON DOWN STAIRS at Monticello was the north octagonal chamber just off the North Piazza, served as a bedroom or possibly a sitting room, and was used frequently by James and Dolley Madison (Stein, *Worlds*, 113).

To Albert Gallatin

TH:JEFFERSON [TO MR] GALLATIN   Oct. 3. 1801.

The inducement which you propose in order to engage Powell to bring up his accounts is approved.—so is also the idea of collecting men of talents about us, even in offices which do not need them. upon the principle of distribution also I doubt if the treasury should be given to Maryland.

With respect to Doctr. Bache I must have conversation with you. as to the office of Post M. G. he might be told that an arrangement made as soon as the resignation took place, binds us up from any change.   health & respect.

RC (NHi: Gallatin Papers); torn at seal, with words in brackets supplied from PrC; addressed: "The Secretary of the Treasury"; endorsed. PrC (DLC); faint.

To encourage James POWELL TO BRING UP HIS ACCOUNTS, Gallatin invoked Section 4 of the act passed in 1799 regarding the compensation of collectors, which allowed the equal division of commissions to which the collector leaving office "would have been entitled, on the receipt of all duties bonded by him," with his successor, "whose duty it shall be to collect them." Gallatin wrote Thomas de Mattos Johnson on 6 Oct. notifying him of the arrangement, as "directed by the President." Gallatin informed the new collector at Savannah that the accounts of his predecessor remained unsettled from the first quarter of 1800 and assured Johnson, "Should it become necessary on account of any further delay on his part that you should settle the accounts yourself, the half commission, which in this case is considered as a matter of accommodation would be differently applied" (Gallatin, *Papers*, 5:823; U.S. Statutes at Large, 1:704, 709).

George Dent from MARYLAND applied for the office of treasurer (see enclosure No. 2, listed at Gallatin to TJ, 21 Sep.). WITH RESPECT TO DOCTR. BACHE: see enclosure No. 3, listed at same.

On this date, Gallatin sent TJ the "Half weekly list of Warrants" drawn on the treasurer from 1 to 3 Oct. Of the warrants listed, Nos. 1 through 48, 41 were under the civil list for the payment of salaries of officers and clerks in the executive departments, the judiciary, commissioners of loans, and others, for a total of $56,584.32. Three warrants were on banks in Baltimore and Philadelphia for the purchase of bills on Holland at 40 cents per guilder for the payment of interest and principle on the Dutch debt, for a total of $79,260.80. All the warrants totaled $137,392.82 (MS in DLC: TJ Papers, 116:20103; entirely in Gallatin's hand; endorsed by Gallatin; endorsed by TJ as a document of 3 Oct. from the Treasury Department and "Warrants" and so recorded in SJL at 3 Oct.). Perhaps at the same time, Gallatin sent TJ the list of 35 warrants, Nos. 199 through 233, issued from 20 to 30 Sep., the close of the quarter. Under the civil list, five warrants, including a payment to Benjamin Rush of $2,650 to cover the quarterly salaries of the Mint officers, totaled $5,065. Seventeen miscellaneous warrants totaled $14,121.22, including payments to three marshals for the census, totaling $10,846.81, and eleven warrants for lighthouses and navigation, totaling $2,598.34. Two warrants were issued, one for the army, the other for the navy, each for $50,000. Three warrants were issued for the payment of interest on the public debt, totaling $502,194.61; five were issued to banks in New York, Boston, and Baltimore for bills on Holland at 40 cents for the payment of principle and interest on the Dutch debt, totaling $111,212.28; one was issued for $63,540.26, for reimbursement of domestic debt; and two were issued, each for $250,000, for reimbursement of temporary loans; for a grand total of

$1,296,133.37. Below the list of warrants, Gallatin included a "Recapitulation of the whole Quarter," where he noted payments totaling $93,182.51, for the civil list; $84,467.40, for miscellaneous; $124,277.24, for foreign intercourse; $302,079.33, for the military; $285,000, for the navy; $1,147,689.66, for payment of interest on the public debt; and $1,002,631.37, for the reduction of the public debt; for a grand total of $3,039,327.51. In a note written perpendicular to the account summary, Gallatin observed: "Receipts of the Quarter not yet ascertained, but exceed the expenditures" (MS in DLC: TJ Papers, 116:20086; entirely in Gallatin's hand; endorsed by Gallatin; endorsed by TJ: "Departmt of Treasury. Sep. 30. 1801. Warrants").

To George Jefferson

DEAR SIR,   Washington Oct. 3. 1801.

In my letter by mr Garrett I informed you of my draug[hts in] favr. of Yancey, Garrett, & Clarke. after that I drew on you in favor of John Sneed for 50. D. and of Anthony Robinson for 15. D.—I have not yet had an opportunity of applying to mr Davidson agent of Heth for coal, [but] if practicable, shall prefer getting my coal here from him, rather than from Richmond.—the arbitrators between mr Ross & myself have settled my balance to him at 12. Hhds. tobo & interest, to be of the upper inspections of Jas. or Appomattox rivers. I presume this will be cheapest. I have not yet had time to [look into] the [. . .] in order to direct paiment if there be no objection; but in the [mean] time I will ask the favor of you to inform me the present price of Petersburg tobo. & your opinion whether it will be cheaper [. . .] the new crop begins to come in & when that will be, so that as [soon] as I can go through the papers I may be able to take [. . .] measures at once for having [the tobo.] [. . .] paid. accept assurances of my constant esteem.   TH: JEFFERSON

PrC (MHi); faint; at foot of text: "Mr. George Jefferson"; endorsed by TJ in ink on verso.

LETTER BY MR GARRETT: TJ to Gibson & Jefferson, 26 Sep. TJ's payment to

JOHN SNEED was for the purchase of a "Chickasaw colt." TJ paid ANTHONY ROBINSON for his services in the arbitration of the dispute with David Ross (MB, 2:1052).

From David Ker

SIR Natchez October 3d 1801

As a citizen of this Territory warmly attached to its interest & anxious for the success of your administration I take the liberty of offering you my services. The difficulty of finding men of information in this country free from the influence of violent party spirit has suggested to me the idea that I might be of use in public life. It is believed here that the office of one of the judges of the Supreme Court is vacant by the resignation of Judge Tilton. Should that or any other reputable office the duties of which I could perform be offered me I would accept it. I am conscious of possessing integrity suited to the discharge of public duties where it is most difficult among violent contending views & interests. It would give me pleasure to avail myself of the oppertunity which a public station affords of spreading information & cultivating the love of Republican governments.

I am so sensible of the value of your time to the public that I have felt reluctance in attempting to engage it for a moment. I have lived in North Carolina from the year 1788 until last year when I removed from it on my way hither. From the gentlemen of that State to most of whom I am known information may be easily obtained concerning me. Mr Stone & Mr Henderson both Lawyers are somewhat acquainted with my professional abilities. Mr Grove with whom as a neighbour tho differing in political sentiments I have lived in habits of intimacy can say what he knows of my integrity sobriety & uniform attachment to the principles of liberty.

I have only to add that the smallness of the salaries annexed to the offices in this territory considering the expensiveness of labour here will remove from me the suspicion of interested views in my present application.

Of all the public events which have happened since the revolution in this country none has given me so much pleasure as the prospect which the friends of liberty in the United states now enjoy of the prevalence of honesty & common sense in the public councils. Please to accept in that view the ardent wishes for your happiness & success of your Humble Servant DAVID KER.

RC (DNA: RG 59, LAR); endorsed by TJ as received 28 Dec. and "to be judge of Missisipi vice Tilton" and so recorded in SJL. Enclosed in David Stone to TJ, 28 Dec. 1801.

A native of Ireland, David Ker (1758-1805) was educated at Trinity College, Dublin, before immigrating to North Carolina. He worked as a Presbyterian minister and educator for several years before being appointed to the faculty of the University of North Carolina in 1794. He left the school two years later, due in part to his diminishing Christian faith and growing Republicanism. Settling at Lumberton, he directed an academy and studied law before removing to Mississippi. TJ appointed Ker a judge of the Mississippi Territory in 1802 in place of Daniel Tilton, who had abandoned the office. His nomination was approved by the Senate in January 1803, and Ker retained the position until his death (William S. Powell, ed., *Dictionary of North Carolina Biography*, 6 vols. [Chapel Hill, 1979-96], 3:353-4; Dunbar Rowland, *Courts, Judges, and Lawyers of Mississippi, 1798-1935* [Jackson, 1935], 11-12, 18-19; JEP, 1:433, 437).

To Robert R. Livingston

DEAR SIR   Washington Oct. 3. 1801.

The bearer hereof, mr Tubeuffe, is the son of a gentleman of that name from France who settled in Virginia some years ago, and was unhappily murdered by some ruffians who made their escape. I was not acquainted personally with him or any of his family, but heard much of them from time to time, and always favorably. the inclosed letter from mr Giles however, as personally acquainted with their situation & conduct will supply the defects of my information. mr Tubeuffe the bearer now goes to France in the hope of getting restitution of his patrimonial possessions. being a citizen of the US. I beg the favor of you to lend him any aid you can consistently with the duties of your station. Accept assurances of my high consideration & respect.   TH: JEFFERSON

RC (NHi: Robert R. Livingston Papers); addressed: "Robert R. Livingston Min. Pleny. of the US. of America at Paris by mr Tubeuffe"; endorsed by Livingston. PrC (DLC); endorsed by TJ in ink on verso. Enclosure: William Branch Giles to TJ, 25 Sep. TJ sent an identical-ly worded letter to Fulwar Skipwith (PrC in DLC; dated Washington, 3 Oct.; in Meriwether Lewis's hand, signed by TJ; at foot of text, probably by TJ: "Fulwar Skipwith esq. Paris"; endorsed by TJ in ink on verso).

To Robert R. Livingston

DEAR SIR   Washington Oct. 3. 1801.

This is probably the last time I shall address you on this side the water. the occasion is furnished by a desire that you will be so good as to deliver the inclosed letter to my eleve and friend mr Short. I recommend him at the same time to your patronage and attentions. you will find him a man of great natural ability, compleatly read, and better acquainted with the world than most in it. he is at the same time of pure honor & integrity. he began with the French as a perfect revolutionist; on their deflection from justice & patriotism, he separated from them; and the murder of his friend La Rochefoucault anti-revolutionized him. he became soured & embittered; but has with great prudence acquiesced in the events which have passed & taken no part in them. this conduct has ensured to him the protection of the government in the worst of times; nor has any thing which has past there lessened his attachment to genuine republicanism, such as he knew it in America, & now recognises here. the extent of his aberration has only been a conviction that the French nation are not ripe for a genuine republic. I have given you his character fully that you may know him at once, and his real opinions. in society you will find him very amiable. he is tolerably rich here, and in a very easy situation there, which you will better understand after being there awhile. mr Sumpter had gone on to join you before I arrived. you will find him a perfectly good creature, the only son & solace of a most respectable father. wishing you calm seas, prosperous gales, and good health I tender you my last & affectionate assurances of esteem & respect. TH: JEFFERSON

RC (NNMus); addressed: "Chancellor Livingston New York"; franked; postmarked 5 Oct.; endorsed by Livingston: "Mr. Short char." PrC (DLC); endorsed by TJ in ink on verso. Enclosure: TJ to William Short, 3 Oct.

ELEVE: "élève" in French, meaning a pupil or follower.

From James Madison

DEAR SIR   Orange Octobr. 3. 1801

Mr. Kemble followed you on tuesday afternoon, with the despatches for Mr. Livingston & Mr. Pinkney, & I hope arrived in time to get them to N. York before the frigate could sail. By detaining him no time was lost as he was employed in making fair copies, otherwise to be made in the office, & as by reposing himself & his horse he could return the more expeditiously. The distribution of the slaves among the Legatees & the subsequent interchanges among them for the accomodation of both have consumed the whole of this week. The sales of personal estate &c. will begin on monday, & I had hoped would have ended on the same day. It is now understood that it will employ two days. I shall not lose a moment in hastening thereafter my departure & journey. The delay would give me much concern if it were not unavoidable, & if I did not flatter myself that no public inconvenience would flow from it.

With the most respectful attachment I am ever yours

JAMES MADISON

RC (DLC: Madison Papers); endorsed by TJ as received 6 Oct. and so recorded in SJL.

MR. KEMBLE: State Department clerk Hazen Kimball. He was paid 50 dollars on 23 Oct. "for going from Washington to Orange County, Virginia, with dispatches for the Secretary of State" (Madison, Pa-

pers, Sec. of State Ser., 2:155; Vol. 33:512, 513n).

SALES OF PERSONAL ESTATE: the sale of items from the personal estate of Madison's father occurred on 9 Sep., 5 Oct., and 20 Nov., with a few remaining items sold in May 1802 (Madison, Papers, Sec. of State Ser., 2:155).

From Craven Peyton

DEAR SIR   Shadwell 3d October 1801

from the Inclosd papars you will see how very fortunate you have been on balloting for the different Lots as they were laid of by the Commissioners. No 9. drawn by J L. Henderson most certainly includes the Mill seat. but in drawing no difference was made by the Commissioners, the House of Thorpe you will observe is likewise drawn. & leaves a ballance due the Legatees of £84.0.0. in laying of this Land no part of yours was interferd with as on a former survey. the instruments which you give me will not answer as deeds may be had but for your own safety have inclosd the instrument agreeable to request. As henderson is disappointed in getting the Mill seat I think he may be baught out. I wish you to say how far I may bid. there has been several applications for the Houses which are occupied by Thorp & Faris togethar with the four lots of Land, whatevar you wish done with them & will let me no by next mail I will do with pleasure, I am in hopes you will considar it so much more to your interest to improve the Mill seat at Milton in preference to this, that you will decline hear, the expence from this time would not amount to more than One third, you will please let me no how you approve of the proceedings.

I am with much Respt. Yr. Mst. Obt.   C PEYTON

RC (ViU); endorsed by TJ as received 6 Oct. and so recorded in SJL. Enclosures: (1) Report of division of lands among Henderson family heirs, 1 Oct. 1801, listing four tracts, the "Upper Field Lands of Bennett Henderson Desd" (49 acres), "Back Lands" (1,020 acres), "Lower Field" (58.25 acres), and "Lands below the Town" (20 acres); dividing each tract into ten allotments of equal or near-equal acreage; and listing the name of the family member who received each numbered parcel, with each of the ten children of Bennett Henderson receiving one parcel in each tract (Tr in ViU, entirely in Peyton's hand, including names of David Anderson, David Higginbotham, and John Sneed, the commissioners who performed the division, endorsed by TJ: "Henderson's partition. a copy of the report of the Commissioners as returned to court"; MS in same, in an unidentified hand, signed by Anderson, Higginbotham, and Sneed, with emendations in TJ's hand, giving the total acreage beside the heading of each tract). (2) Declaration of Trust with Craven Peyton, 25 Sep. 1801.

MILL SEAT: in the "Lands below the Town," a strip of two-acre plots between the edge of the town of Milton and the bank of the Rivanna River, James Henderson received lot No. 9. That parcel was the potential location for a mill, as mentioned in TJ's and Peyton's letters of 8 and 16 Oct., respectively. TJ wrote "mill seat" by that lot on the plat of the Henderson land division he received from Peyton (plat listed as enclosure, Peyton to TJ, 6 Nov., and see illustration).

NO PART OF YOURS WAS INTERFERD WITH: TJ already owned property that bordered on the "Back Lands" and "Upper Field" tracts of the Henderson lands (same).

INSTRUMENTS WHICH YOU GIVE ME: the Form of Deeds for Henderson Purchases, printed at the end of September. The INSTRUMENT enclosed by Peyton in the letter above seems most likely to have been the 25 Sep. indenture between him and TJ.

John Henderson was the family member DISAPPOINTED in his hope of obtaining the prospective mill site.

HOUSES WHICH ARE OCCUPIED BY THORP & FARIS: in the division of the estate, Sarah Henderson Kerr received both a five-acre parcel in the "Upper Field," upriver from Milton, which had "Thorps House valued to £140.0.0," and a six-acre parcel in the "Lower Field," downstream from the town, where the "Farras House" stood (Enclosure No. 1, above).

To William Short

DEAR SIR   Washington Oct. 3. 1801.

Since my letter of Mar. 17. by mr Dawson I have recieved your favors of Apr. 19. & June 9. the vouchers accompanying the last I yesterday deposited in the Secretary of state's office, sealed as they came, and desired a reciept to be made out & sent to me. whenever a settlement of your accounts shall take place, I will take care that the explanations of your last & other letters shall be given. with respect to the article furnished mr J. Cutting, your only resource is in the public responsibility, he being compleatly bankrupt in reputation & property. the last I heard of him was that he was in jail in the West Indies. E.R. has[1] still got the trial of his suit postponed, till which trial no further part of the 9. M̶. D. can be touched. But the sum of 8. M̶. D. was invested by our predecessors in 8. pr. cent stock in the name of one of their officers, which is held in trust to he delivered you on the event of the suit. in the mean time the government has recieved what monies Pendleton & Lyon were ready to pay for E.R. on his order in your favor, which I transferred to the government immediately on their purchasing the stock. with respect to the investiture of your monies, as they come in, mr Barnes will keep you informed. whenever they amount to a respectable sum he invests them.

I trusted to mr Dawson to have given you a full explanation verbally on a subject which I find he has but slightly mentioned to you. I shall therefore now do it. When I returned from France, after an absence of 6. or 7. years, I was astonished at the change which I found had taken place in the US. in that time. no more like the same people; their notions, their habits & manners, the course of their commerce, so totally changed that I, who stood in those of 1784. found myself not at all qualified to speak their sentiments, or forward their views in 1790. very soon therefore after entering on the office of Secy. of state I recommended to Genl. Washington to establish as a rule of practice that no person should be continued on a foreign mission beyond an absence of 6. 7. or 8. years. he approved it. on the only subsequent missions which took place in my time the persons appointed were notified that they would not be continued beyond that period. all returned within it except Humphreys. his term was not quite out when Genl. Washington went out of office. the succeeding administration had no rule for any thing. so he continued. immediately on my coming to the administration I wrote to him myself, reminded him of the rule I had communicated to him on his departure, that he had then been absent 11. years, and consequently must return. on this ground solely he was superceded. under these circumstances your appointment was impossible after an absence of 17. years. under any others, I should never fail to give to yourself & the world proofs of my friendship for you, & of my confidence in you. whenever you shall return, you will be sensible in a greater of what I was in a smaller degree, of the change in this nation from what it was when we both left it in 1784. we return like foreigners & like them require a considerable residence here to become Americanized.

The state of political opinion continues to return steadily towards republicanism. to judge from the Opposition papers, a stranger would suppose that a considerable check to it had been produced by certain removals of public officers. but this is not the case. all offices were in the hands of the Federalists. the injustice of having totally excluded Republicans was acknoleged by every man. to have removed one half & to have placed republicans in their stead would have been rigorously just, when it was known that these composed a very great majority of the nation. yet such was their moderation in most of the states that they did not desire it. in these therefore no removals took place but for malversation. in the middle states the contention had been higher, spirits were more sharpened & less accomodating. it was necessary in these to practice a different treatment, and to make a few changes to tranquilize the injured party. a few have been made there & a very few still remain to be made. when this painful operation shall be over, I see nothing else ahead of us which can give uneasiness to any of our citizens or retard that consolidation of sentiment so essential to our happiness & our strength. the tory papers will still find fault with every thing. but these papers are sinking daily from their dissonance with the sentiments of their subscribers, & very few will shortly remain to keep up a solitary & ineffectual barking.

There is no point in which an American long absent from his country wanders so widely from it's sentiments as on the subject of it's foreign affairs. we have a perfect horror at every thing like connecting ourselves with the politics of Europe. it would indeed be advantageous to us to have neutral rights established on a broad ground; but no dependence can be placed in any European coalition for that. they have so many other bye-interests of greater weight, that some one or other will always be bought off. to be entangled with them would be a much greater evil than a temporary acquiescence in the false principles which have prevailed. peace is our most important interest, and a recovery from debt. we feel ourselves strong, & daily growing stronger. the census just now concluded shews we have added to our population a third of what it was 10. years ago. this will be a duplication in 23. or 24. years. if we can delay but for a few years the necessity of vindicating the laws of nature on the ocean, we shall be the more sure of doing it with effect. the day is within my time as well as yours when we may say by what laws other nations shall treat us on the sea. and we will say it. in the mean time we wish to let every treaty we have drop off, without renewal. we call in our diplomatic missions, barely keeping up those to the most important nations. there is a strong disposition in our countrymen to discontinue even these; and very possibly it may be done. Consuls will be continued as usual. the interest which European nations feel as well as ourselves in the mutual patronage of commercial intercourse is a sufficient stimulus on both sides to ensure that patronage. a treaty contrary to that interest renders war necessary to get rid of it.

I send this by Chancellor Livingston, named to the Senate the day after I came into office, as our M.P. to France. I have taken care to impress him with the value of your society. you will find him an able and honorable man; unfortunately so deaf that he will have to transact all his business by writing.—you will have known long ago that mr Skipwith is reinstated in his Consulship, as well as some others who

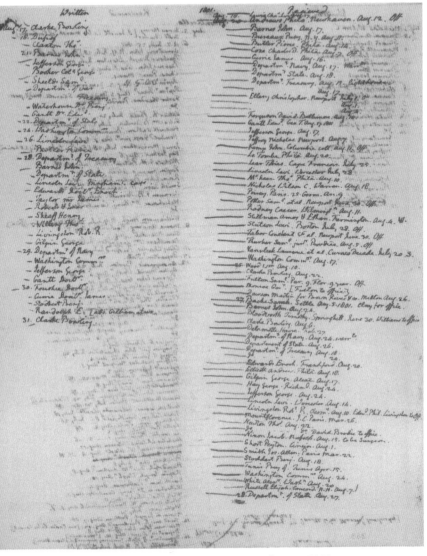

Summary Journal of Letters, 17-31 August 1801

Carlos Martínez de Irujo

Sarah McKean Irujo

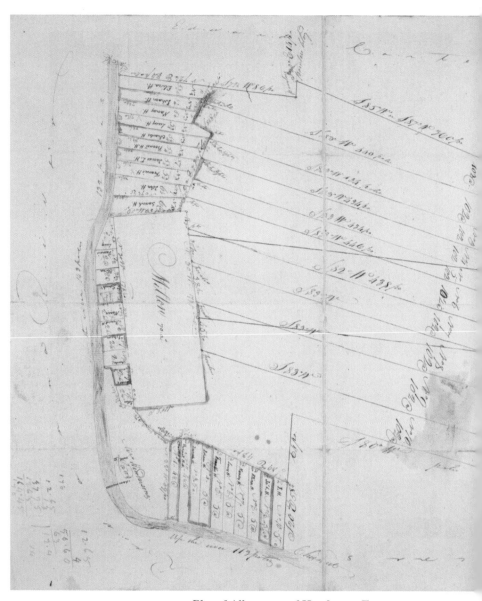

Plat of Allotments of Henderson Estate

162
94
256

A Copy of the Plat of the
Land belonging to the Legatees of
Bennett Henderson dec'd in Albemarle
County
Copied for Craven Peyton
by Wm Woods

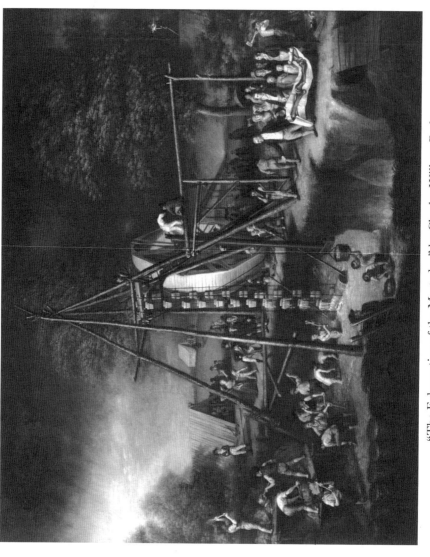

"The Exhumation of the Mastodon" by Charles Willson Peale

Teton de Vénus

Breast of Venus Peach

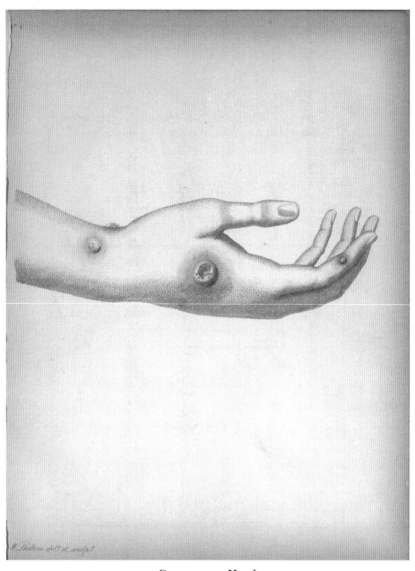

Cowpox on a Hand

had been set aside. I recollect no domestic news interesting to you. your letters to your brother have been regularly transmitted, & I lately forwarded one from him, to be carried you by mr Livingston. present my best respects to our amiable & mutual friend, and accept yourself assurances of my sincere & constant affection.

TH: JEFFERSON

P.S. I inclose the reciept from the Secretary of state's office for your vouchers.

RC (ViW); at foot of first page: "Mr. Short." PrC (DLC). Enclosure: Statement by Jacob Wagner, 2 Oct. 1801, certifying that on that day TJ "deposited in the office of the department of State of the U. States a sealed package containing vouchers and papers relative to the accounts of William Short with the United States" (MS in ViW; entirely in Wagner's hand).

For the money Short advanced to John B. CUTTING in 1791, see Short's letter of 9 June 1801. Cutting had written to TJ from Antigua on 20 Apr., although TJ did not receive that letter until January 1802 (Madison, *Papers, Sec. of State Ser.*, 2:301-2).

E.R.: Edmund Randolph, whose accounts as secretary of state were still unsettled, had asked that money owed him by Peter Lyons and Edmund PENDLETON be paid to Short, who wanted payment for back salary for diplomatic service (Vol. 29:574; Vol. 31:497-9).

I FIND HE HAS BUT SLIGHTLY MENTIONED: see Short to TJ, 9 June.

WROTE TO HIM MYSELF: TJ composed, for Levi Lincoln's signature as act-

ing secretary of state, the letter to David Humphreys of [17] Mch. 1801 that cited the practice regarding diplomatic appointments (Vol. 33:321-3).

For the letter from Short's BROTHER forwarded by TJ, see Peyton Short to TJ, 1 Aug. 1801.

OUR AMIABLE & MUTUAL FRIEND: the Duchesse de La Rochefoucauld.

On 21 Sep. 1801, TJ made a note on a slip of paper about a legal action involving Short's Albemarle County property: "William Short v. Richard Meeks William Meeks & Charles Reynolds. desired D. Carr to issue writ in Trespass for cutting timber for a boat. G. Haden gives me information of it. at same time told D.C. that if they would pay for the timber & pay costs he might dismiss" (MS in DLC: Short Papers; entirely in TJ's hand, dated but not signed; endorsed by TJ: "Short, Wm. v. Meeks et al."). TJ sometimes hired his nephew Dabney Carr as an attorney. George Haden was one of Short's tenants (MB, 2:1027, 1106; Vol. 28:354, 356n; Vol. 31:514).

¹ TJ here canceled "continued."

From John Tyler

SIR Frederick Town. October 3d 1801.

At the request of Doctor Gantt of George Town I have examined the eyes of a young man, said now to be in your service, and am of the opinion that it would be improper to attempt the operation for the removal of the Cataract at this time. It appears to me, from the best view of the case, that there is a partial paralysis of the Optic nerves in both eyes, an entire opacity in the *Chrystalline lens* of the right eye, a small opacity in the lens of the other, that the nervous affection is the primary disease, and that when the Cataract is removed, vision will be very imperfect untill the energy of the nerves can be fully restored.

I have therefore thought it most adviseable to defer the operation untill the next spring, when the Cataract will probably acquire a firmer consistence more favourable to it's removal and when the ensuing warm season will enable us to pursue an alterative mercurial course for the removal of the paralytic affection with more safety and a greater prospect of success.

I have the honour to be with very great respect your most obedient Servant   JOHN TYLER

RC (DLC); endorsed by TJ as received 5 Oct. and so recorded in SJL.

John Tyler (1763-1841) of Frederick, Maryland, was a founding member of the Medical and Chirurgical Faculty of the State of Maryland, incorporated in 1799. Tyler was a republican candidate for elector in the presidential elections of 1800 and 1804. In 1801 and 1802, he served in the Maryland Senate (Eugene Fauntleroy Cordell, *The Medical Annals of Maryland* *1799-1899* [Baltimore, 1903], 601; Elizabethtown *Maryland Herald*, 5 June 1800, 19 Jan. 1803, 19 Sep. 1804; *Votes and Proceedings of the Senate of the State of Maryland, November session, one thousand eight hundred and one* [Annapolis, 1802; Shaw-Shoemaker, No. 2603], 4; *Votes and Proceedings of the Senate of the State of Maryland, November session, one thousand eight hundred and two* [Annapolis, 1803; Shaw-Shoemaker, No. 4589], 3).

Notes on the District of Columbia Commissioners' Accounts

[after 3 Oct. 1801]

Elliptical room	2276.	
Pr's house	1686	
Board	1700	
September labour	1300	
Interest paid	1500	
	8462[1]	

whole funds	6255.94
present deficiency	2206.06[2]
	6962.

	D.
debts due to the Commissioners	130,000
due on Morris & Nicholson's lots 1000.	80,000

3000. f. front of water property @ 10. D.	30,000
4600. lots of 5265. sq. f. each	460,000
no lot ever sold for less than 105. D	
due from them	
debts guaranteed	300,000
unguaranteed	50,000
price of site	6247.18
paid	4000
	2247.18

MS (DLC: TJ Papers, District of Columbia Miscellany); undated, but see
below; entirely in TJ's hand.

TJ probably composed these notes
sometime after his receipt of the District
of Columbia Commissioners' Estimate of
Debts dated 2 Oct. enclosed in their letter
to him of 3 Oct. Several of the words and
figures, from "Elliptical room" to "whole
funds," correspond to the information
given in the 2 Oct. statement. See also the

memorial from the commissioners to TJ
of 4 Dec.

[1] After TJ totaled the first four items
above, making $6,962, he added the line
for "Interest paid" of $1,500, overwriting
the original total of $6,962, and provided
the new total of $8,462.

[2] TJ first wrote "706.06" before he revised the total above to include the $1,500
for "Interest paid." He then recalculated
the "present deficiency" and altered the
figure to $2,206.06.

From Joel Barlow

DEAR SIR,   Paris 4 Oct. 1801—

I wrote you some time ago by Mr. Dawson and mentioned my intention of returning to America early in the spring. I still adhere to
this intention, and am happy to learn by every letter from that country that the violence of party spirit is abated & that all honest men
seem cordially united in support of your administration. I am persuaded that your election was the only means of uniting them and of
bringing a great proportion of our citizens back to the principles of
liberty and of social improvement on which our revolution was
founded.—Your inaugural speech has had a general run in Europe &
will have a good effect. I enclose you here a polyglotte or tetraglotte
of it as printed here & distributed to all the ambassadors & other persons from foreign countries, as likewise an American copy printed for
the use of the Americans here.—The preliminary treaty of peace with
England was proclaimed here last night to the great joy of the french

nation. We shall now see what talents the present rulers have for government in peace.—But it seems that Europe must still look to America for lessons on this subject.—

I am dear Sir—with great respect—yr. obt. sert—

JOEL BARLOW

RC (DLC); at foot of text: "Mr. Jefferson"; endorsed by TJ as received 25 Dec. and so recorded in SJL. Enclosures: (1) *Speech of Thomas Jefferson, President of the United States, Delivered at his Instalment, March 4, 1801, at the City of Washington. With Translations into the French, Italian, and German Tongues*, printed at the English Press, Paris, [1801]; see Noble E. Cunningham, Jr., *The Inaugural Addresses of President Thomas Jefferson, 1801 and 1805* (Columbia, Mo., 2001), 53, 64-7; Shaw-Shoemaker, No. 732. (2) Possibly *Speech of Thomas Jefferson, President of the United States: Delivered at his Instalment, March 4, 1801, at the City of Washington*, a broadside, also by the English Press, Paris, [1801]; copy at Carl A. Kroch Library, Division of

Rare and Manuscript Collections, Cornell University.

Barlow last WROTE on 25 Aug.

PRELIMINARY TREATY OF PEACE: in London late on the last day of September, Louis Guillaume Otto and Lord Hawkesbury reached agreement on preliminary articles of peace between France and Great Britain. The document, which was formally dated 1 Oct., was PROCLAIMED in the streets of Paris on Saturday evening, 3 Oct., heralded by cannon shots, announcements in the theaters, and the illumination of buildings (*Gazette Nationale ou le Moniteur Universel*, 13 Vendémiaire Year 10 [5 Oct. 1801]; Grainger, *Amiens Truce*, 42-3, 45-6).

From Daniel Carroll Brent

D[EAR] SIR/   [on or before 4 Oct. 1801]

It is not perhaps for me to intrude upon you. Yet as I believe to *men* of your *mind*, placed in your elevated Station, information from all quarters is acceptable, I will under these impressions address you.

The Office of Treasurer of the United States is now vacant, to fill such an office I know *one* man who I *believe* has every *necessary* qualification—his character is *pure* & *chaste*; to which no censure is attached, or against which calumny dare not to dart its tongue—he has always been in private life, is of moderate fortune & therefore not *much* known in the political world, is a *pure* Republican, has always, (even in the worst of times) been firm & steady—no change of men or circumstances has made him deviate—the gentleman I mean is Col. John Cooke of Stafford County Virginia, he is *well* known to John T Mason, who is his *friend*, & to whom I will refer you for a confirmation of what I have stated—this application is unknown to this Gentn. yet I *know* the appointment will be acceptable

I will not apologize for addressing you as I can conceive it is the duty of us all to give you information—yet Sir whatever may be your determination on this subject I shall consider it as made for the public good & rest content.

With sentiments of high respect I am yrs &c

DANIEL CARROLL BRENT

RC (DNA: RG 59, LAR); undated; endorsed by TJ as received 4 Mch. but recorded in SJL at 4 Oct. with notation "John Cocke of Virga to be treasurer"; TJ canceled "Brent Daniel" and added "Capt John Cocke of Staffd. Virga to be treasurer" to the endorsement.

Perhaps Brent was recommending John COOKE of West Farms in Stafford County who married Mary Thomson Mason, George Mason's daughter, at Gunston Hall in 1784 (Robert A. Rutland, ed., *The Papers of George Mason 1725-1792*, 3 vols. [Chapel Hill, 1970], 1:xliv; Washington, *Papers, Pres. Ser.*, 1:369; George H. S. King, comp., *The Register of Overwharton Parish Stafford County Virginia, 1723-1758* [Fredericksburg, 1961], 224).

From Samuel Harrison Smith

Oct. 4. 1801.

Samuel H. Smith presents his respectful compliments to Mr. Jefferson, to whom he encloses the within Letter. It was thought too unimportant to notice during Mr. Jeffersons absence, and is still presumed to respect some trifling circumstance. But as it *may* be connected with something of interest, it is submitted.

RC (MoSHi: Jefferson Papers); torn; addressed: "The Preside[nt]"; endorsed by TJ as received 6 Oct. and so recorded in SJL. Enclosure not identified.

From John Thomson Mason

DEAR SIR   Georgetown 5th Octo. 1801.

The inclosed letter from the Revd. Mr Knox a very Republican Minister and the Head of an accademy in Frederick town, was sent to me with a view I presume of its being laid before you. Mr Polk the subject is I beleive personally known to you, he is a limner by profession.

Mr Knox is I beleive mistaken as to the hopes of Mr Kilty's doing anything for him. There is not like to be any vacancy in that County, which Mr Kilty has power to fill, and he well knows the discontent that would be produced by filling up a vacancy in any other County with a man not residing therein.

With the highest respect & esteem I am D Sir Your Obedt Servt
JOHN T. MASON

Mr Polk talks of calling on you this after noon in person

RC (DNA: RG 59, LAR); endorsed by TJ as received 5 Oct. and so recorded in SJL with notation: "Polke to office"; TJ canceled "Mason J. T." and added "Charles P. Polke for office" to the endorsement. Enclosure: Samuel Knox to John T. Mason, Frederick Academy, 30 Sept. 1801, providing information on the financial distress experienced by Polk and his family, assuring Mason that Polk "would not Disappoint the Expectations of those who would Introduce Him to Any thing by which He Could Make a Sustenance for his family," and noting that John Kilty of Baltimore "would employ Him in the Revenue, if He thought that the Appointment would be approved," but for want of influential recommendations Polk despairs "of success in that quarter, And goes once more down to the City to enquire of Any place suited to His Talents might offer" (RC in DNA: RG 59, LAR).

Presbyterian clergyman and educator Samuel KNOX served as principal of Frederick Academy in Maryland from 1797 to 1803 and again from 1823 to 1827. Knox wrote A Vindication of the Religion of Mr. Jefferson and a Statement of his Services in the Cause of Religious Liberty, which he signed "By a Friend to Real Religion" and had published in Baltimore in 1800. He defended a strict separation of church and state in his sermons and writings (ANB; RS, 2:174n).

PERSONALLY KNOWN TO YOU: Charles Peale Polk painted TJ's portrait at Monticello in 1799. On 12 Apr. 1801, Mason forwarded Levi Lincoln a letter recommending Polk for a revenue inspectorship in Maryland. Mason described Polk as "a man of real merit and cleverness, he has a large and promising family to support, and his means to do it are very precarious and still more scanty" (RC in DNA: RG 59, LAR; Vol. 31:xliii, 231-2). For Polk's appeals to Madison for a position in the federal government in 1801 and 1802, see Madison, Papers, Sec. of State Ser., 1:65-6; 2:234; 3:399. Polk observed that the wealthy in Maryland had not encouraged him as a painter because of his Republican principles. In 1806 he received employment as a clerk in the comptroller's office at the Treasury Department (Gallatin, Papers, 13:651).

John KILTY, supervisor of the revenue for the district of Maryland, was a Washington appointee and noted Federalist who feared for his position under the new administration (Prince, Federalists, 144-5; JEP, 1:179).

On 10 Oct., Mason wrote TJ from Alexandria introducing his friend Robert Young, a respectable merchant from that town, who wished to have a personal interview with the president (RC in DNA: RG 59, LAR; endorsed by TJ as received 10 Oct. and "Robert Young to be Consul at Havanna" and so recorded in SJL). Two days later, Young informed Daniel C. Brent that he had learned that John Morton, consul at Havana, was resigning for health reasons, and that he had mentioned the fact to TJ. In recognition of their many years of friendship, Young requested that Brent give the president a character reference for him. Young received the appointment as consul at the port of Havana with a commission dated 4 Feb. 1802 (RC in same, endorsed by TJ: "Young Robert to Danl. Carrol Brent to be Consul at Havanna"; commission in Lb in DNA: RG 59, PTCC).

To Elizabeth House Trist

TH: JEFFERSON TO MRS TRIST   [5 Oct. 1801]

Can you tell me, my good friend, how I came by the enclosed letter? it is more than I can. on my unpacking here I found it in a bundle of papers which I had carried to Monticello & had not occasion to open there. I suspect it was given me here in the moment of departure in July, & put into the bundle for safe keeping: where indeed it has been very safely kept, if not so speedily delivered as ought to have been. I cry peccavi & in obedience to the maxim of 'better late than never' now send it. we have nothing new here but that the Tripolitan vessels have escaped from Gibraltar. it will be mortifying if they escape all our frigates and get back to Tripoli. mrs Brown's family is well, which I know from having seen one of the young gentlemen. mr & mrs Madison not yet arrived here. health, happiness & fraternity.

TH: JEFFERSON

RC (ViHan); undated, with date supplied from TJ's endorsement on PrC; salutation clipped, supplied from PrC; at foot of text: "Mrs. Trist." PrC (MHi); endorsed by TJ in ink on verso. Recorded in SJL at 5 Oct.

ENCLOSED LETTER: presumably Lucy Brown to Trist; see Trist to TJ, 24 Oct.

From Timothy Bloodworth

DEAR SIR   Spring Hill October 6th 1801

Permit me to acquaint You of the Death, of Mr; Griffith John McRee, Collecter of the Port of Wilmington, who departed on the 3d Instant. by this Circumstance the office becomes Vacant. at the request of Mr John Pue Williams, I mention his desire to fill the Vacancy. Also my son Samuel Bloodworth, who is in the 27th Year of his Age, Active in Business, & has the hand of a ready writer. at this time Inspector of Navel stores in Wilmington, & does the Business of Collector, & Surveyor of Revenue, in that Town. in Adition to the above, suffer me to make a tender of my own Services in that, or any other office the President may Pleas to bestow, & should his Indulgence favour an appointment to Merrit his Confidence, will Awaken my Ambition, & excite to Vigelence, & Punctuality, in discharge of the Duties incumbant on the Station. nor do I entertain a Doubt, that the persons above Mentioned, should they be favoured with the appointment, would conduct themselves with equal fidellity.

In my last Address I mentioned the probability of a favorable

Change of political Sintiments, in this County this opinion was not unfounded, but fully Verifyed by the event of the last Election of Members, for the ensuing Assembly of this State, the Federalist made every exertion in their power to prevent my Election, but prov'd Unsuccessfull. the Republican Ticket prevaild by a decided Majority. & such was the Case in the County of Brunswick, where Genrl. Benjamin Smith, was ousted by a Republican. I am inform'd that boath that Gentleman, & Dunkin Moore, offers in place of Mr. Hill for Congress. I presume that Gillispie, or Major Ashe, will oppose them. I mention this Circumstance from Report, & not Certain Knowledge.

Since I began this Address, one other application has been Made, Requesting to be Mentioned as A Candidate, by Mr: Thomas Robinson, a Young Man who has for some time don the business of the office, his Character is Unimpeach'd, & I have no doubt of his Abillities. I am also press'd to acquaint the President, that a Mr Callender who applies for the appointment, by a Petition Sign'd by a Number of Federalist, was an Active Enemy to Youre Election. I mention this Circumstance with reluctance, as the fact does not come Under my Certain knowledge, Yet I have no doubt of the assertion, being founded in truth.

I hope You will excuse the freedom I have taken in this address, I have Mentioned all the applicants, Agreeably to their request, Many More I presume will apply. the public Interest I am persuaded will Govern Youre Choice, should the Indulgence of the President favoure my application, I shall accept the appointment with gratefull remembrance, if not, I shall rest fully contented with Youre pleasure, believing that a discovery of disquallification, forbid the Indulgence.

With sentiments of perfect Esteem, & Sincear Respect, I have the Honor to be, Dr Sir. Youre Very Humble Servant.

TIMOTHY BLOODWORTH

RC (DNA: RG 59, LAR); addressed: "Thomas Jefferson Esqr. President of the United States Washington"; endorsed by TJ as received 17 Oct. and so recorded in SJL.

After the death of Griffith John McRee,

TJ appointed Bloodworth to the vacant collectorship of the PORT of Wilmington, North Carolina (Vol. 33:670, 678).

MY LAST ADDRESS: Bloodworth to TJ, 30 June 1801.

THOMAS ROBINSON: that is, Thomas Robeson (Gallatin to TJ, [19 Oct.]).

Statement of Account from Thomas Claxton

Oct. 6th 1801

Statement of Cash, drawn for the purpose of
furnishing the Presidents House—

By Gen Lee, as reported by the Treasury, to compensate
    him for the portrait of Gen. Washington,   800.

By Thos. Claxton,

Aug. 27, 1800	4500
Nov. 9	1459.38
May 19, 1801	3500
July 2	1500
Oct. 6 called for, to settle every demand, excepting for grates	1755.55
	13,514.93

The Balance of the 15,000 dollars is   1485. 7

This balance is increased by discounts &c   215.76

                          1700.83

To this sum is added the proceeds of
    the Sale of Carriages, horses &c.   about 1600.

The balance, of an appropriation made
    in 1797, and deposited in the treasury   1102.
    by Mr Adams

Total not expended, and in the Treasury   4402.83

MS (MHi); entirely in Claxton's hand; endorsed by TJ. For an earlier account submitted by Claxton for FURNISHING the President's House, see Vol. 33:153n.

From Albert Gallatin

Treasury Department Octer. 6th 1801

The Secretary of the Treasury wishes to know where the Commrs., appointed to decide on the claims under judge Symme's purchase, reside, in order to send the commisions. There is no time to be lost.

A pardon has already been signed in favor of Hopkins & transmitted to Mr P. Freneau.

The situation of the revenue district of Massac renders an appointment necessary. The resignation of Mr Irwin shows the difficulty of finding a proper character to reside there. Mr Chribbs had been recommended by Mr Claibourne next to Mr Irwin. The two enclosed letters are also in his favour. No other application has been made—

Respectfully submitted by ALBERT GALLATIN

RC (DLC); at foot of text: "The President of the United States"; endorsed by TJ as received 7 Oct. and "Commrs. Symmes. Hopkins Chribbs." Enclosures not found.

On 3 Oct., TJ APPOINTED William Goforth of Columbia and John Reily of Cincinnati to serve as commissioners under Section 4 of "An Act giving a right of pre-emption to certain persons who have contracted with John Cleves Symmes, or his Associates, for lands lying between the Miami rivers, in the Territory of the United States northwest of the Ohio," passed by Congress on 3 Mch. 1801 (U.S. Statutes at Large, 2:112-14; Vol. 33:671, 677). William McMillan, former delegate to Congress from the Northwest Territory, recommended Goforth and Reily in a 15 June letter to Madison. McMillan noted that Kentucky Senator John Brown agreed with the recommendation and requested that Madison show the letter to the president. TJ wrote on the second page of the letter: "I have in their proper place the names of Goforth & Reily: but they are not to act till Nov. 1. therefore we need not appoint till Oct. 1. this will give time to hear more about them" (RC in DNA: RG 59, LAR, 10:0376-8). TJ also received an undated memorandum in Brown's hand, regarding appointments

in the Northwest Territory. Brown may have given TJ the document before he left Washington in the spring. As well as recommending Goforth and Reily, Brown supported McMillan for district attorney and James Smith for marshal. Below the recommendations, TJ added: "James H. Stewart of Kentucky. printer of the Herald. to print the laws" (MS in same, 10:0379-80; endorsed by TJ on verso: "N.W. territory. mr Brown's memm. Commrs. on Symmes's purchase Atty. McMillan Marshall. James Smith"). Goforth and McMillan represented Hamilton County at the territory's first general assembly in 1800 and Reily served as clerk of the House. Gallatin wrote Goforth and Reily on 9 Oct. and enclosed their commissions. He sent the letters to James Findlay, land office receiver at Cincinnati, with the request that Findlay immediately forward them to the newly appointed commissioners (*Journal of the House of Representatives of the Territory of the United States, North-west of the river Ohio, at the Second Session of the First General Assembly* [Chillicothe, 1800], 3, 5, 100; *Terr. Papers*, 3:177-9).

For the appointment of James IRWIN as collector at Massac, see William C. C. Claiborne to TJ, 17 Apr. 1801. Recommendations for William CHRIBBS by Claiborne and others have not been found.

From Carlos Martínez de Irujo

DEAR SIR   Philadelphia 6 of Octr. 1801

After the friendly interest you have been pleas'd to take on my continuance in this Country I flatter myself you will hear with pleasure that, by the Dispatches *just* receiv'd from my Court, I am inform'd, that your demand on this head has been readily acquiesc'd to by the King my Master, on terms as flattering to myself, as they show all the weight & consideration given to your respectable interference—I have at the same time receiv'd the particular & agreable[1] commission to compliment you on your last Election, & to assure this Governement of friendly disposition of the King my Master towards this Country, & I'll fullfill this pleasant duty personally & immediatly after my arrival to Washington—

I am going then to enter again on the laberinthe of setting up a house! the adquisition of furniture will Keep me hither ten or twelve days longer. Immediatly after that, I'll proceed down to the Federal City & I'll not neglect a situation, from which I may easily & frequently have the honor to present you my respects.

Mme. d'Irujo, the Governor & all the Family join themselves to me to thank you, for your friendly offices towards me, & they are all animated by the same sentiment of affection & gratitude than your most obt. & respl. Servt.　　　　　　　　　　Le Chevalier d'Irujo

RC (MoSHi: Jefferson Papers); at head of text: "Private"; at foot of text: "H. Ex. Ths. Jefferson Presidt. of the U States"; as with other letters written by Irujo in English, his accents and diacritical marks have been omitted; endorsed by TJ as received 9 Oct. and so recorded in SJL.

your demand on this head: through David Humphreys as minister to Spain and less formally through Joseph Yznardi, Sr., TJ had asked the Spanish government to reverse its recall of Irujo as its minister to the United States. The recall had been requested by the Adams administration, and late in July the Spanish agreed to retain Irujo in the position. He had not received word by 4 Sep., when, unsure if he was to take his family to Spain or remain in America, he wrote to ask Madison if the State Department had heard anything about the decision (enclosure to Humphreys to the secretary of state, 21 Aug. 1801, in DNA: RG 59, DD; Madison, *Papers, Sec. of State Ser.*, 2:84-5; Vol. 33:269n, 322, 430, 453, 457).

mme. d'irujo: Sally McKean Irujo, the daughter of Governor Thomas McKean (Vol. 33:230, 269n, 392).

[1] Preceding word and ampersand interlined.

From Robert R. Livingston

Dear Sir　　　　　　　　　　　　　　New York 6th. Octr. 1801

I feel myself extremely obliged by your favor of Sepr. not only on account of the friendly wishes it contains but because of the elucidation that it affords to your former communications on that very interesting subject the rights of commerce.

Your arguments leave no doubt of the principles you endeavour to establish, it is however much to be lamented that the favourable moment for establishing them is past for the present. The jealousy however that the maritime power of Britain, & the harsh use she makes of it keeps alive, can not fail to present others that we may probably embrace with advantage. An idea has occurred to me on this subject which I beg leave to submit to your consideration. The difficulty of eradicating old prejudices may however render it necessary for some time to come to consent to consider certain articles as contraband, & to limmit the list to such as are soly applicable to the purposes of war. But as this will carry wth. it (as the law is now construed) the right of search, & as such right will, as now, be liable to abuse, may not some substitute be found for it, more effectual as to the nations at war, & at the same time, less vexatious to neutrals? Let the bellegerent powers have Consuls or other agents (which indeed they usualy have) resident with the neutral nation. Let the Ship owners & Capts. enter into bond with very severe penalties for their carrying any of the enumerated contraband articles to the nations at war, or either of them. In case of forfeiture let such bond be assigned to the Consul of the nation injured, for the benefit of such nation who may give him a personal interest therein. I am satisfied that this wd be a much more effectual check to what is at present considered as an improper commerce, than the right of search, & would take away one very common source of uneasiness between nations who delight in war, & those at peace. I have been ever since the arrival of the Maryland in a very unsettled State & on the arrival of the Boston broke up my family, & kept a vessel in waiting to bring them here where we have been for some time in lodging expecting impatiently our final orders.

Accept Sir my adieus, & my sincere assurances of the highest respect & most perfect attachment.

I have the honor to be D Sir Your Most Obt hum. Servt

ROBT R LIVINGSTON

RC (DLC); at foot of text: "Thomas Jefferson Esqr pres: United States"; endorsed by TJ as received 10 Oct. and so recorded in SJL.

YOUR FAVOR: TJ's letter of 9 Sep.

Order on John Barnes

Oct. 6. 1801.

Mr. Barnes is desired to pay to Capt Lewis or order seventy two dollars for six months wages of his servant Abram on account of his humble servt. TH: JEFFERSON

also twenty seven dollars in lieu of a suit of clothes. TH:J.

MS (PWacD: Feinstone Collection on deposit PPAmP); in TJ's hand; in a column to the left of his signature, TJ added the figures "72. D." and "27." for the sum of "99"; at foot of text: "Mr. Barnes"; on verso in Meriwether Lewis's hand and signed by him: "Received of Mr. John Barnes ninty nine dollars agreeably to the within order—Oct. 7th. 1801"; acknowledgment of receipt on 8 Oct. "for Capt. Lewis" written by Barnes and signed in an unknown hand: "for Abrahm golden"; endorsed by TJ: "Gaulding Abram"; endorsed by Barnes.

ABRAM: Abraham Golden was a personal servant for Meriwether Lewis and later for Lewis's successor as TJ's private secretary. TJ wrote this order a day after he reviewed accounts for his Washington household from the period since his departure for Monticello, including servants' wages. In his personal financial memoranda, TJ recorded on 6 Oct. that he gave "Abraham Gaulding" an order on Barnes for $99 (Lucia Stanton, "'A Well-Ordered Household': Domestic Servants in Jefferson's White House," *White House History*, 17 [2006], 8, 21n; MB, 2:1053-4).

From Charles Pinckney

DEAR SIR   October 6: 1801 In Paris

I wrote you from Brussells that I had by accident met with a gentleman at that place who had from some private communications convinced me a peace would be immediately made between France & England.—that particular reasons would induce France at this time to give up to England points she would not at any other concede & that the force of popular opinion would compell her (England) to a Peace against the Opinions or Wishes of Mr: Pitt & his friends who still *actually* directed their affairs.—I have now to inform you that his information has proved correct & that Peace has been this Evening announced in all the public places at Paris.—the particulars are not published, but as far as I can hear or gather from those I suppose to be best informed it is as follows—Martinique restored to the french.—Egypt to the Porte.—Malta to it's knights.—The Cape of Good Hope is[1] open to the Trade of both nations.—France retains all her acquisitions in Europe & Great Britain retains the Spice Islands—all her acquisitions in India & Trinidad.—I could not hear certainly with respect to Surinam, but from the authority I recieved it, I have little doubt that these are the Outlines of the treaty—as soon as it is published I will send it to you.—it will perhaps surprise you that such a peace has been made, leaving Great Britain so much the means of extending her commerce & maintaning her superiority at sea.—My own Opinion is that the conduct of Toussaint, & important movements intended *at home* have hastened this Event.—there can be no Question that this Government intends sending out a large force to the Island of Saint Domingo to replace things in their former

[395]

situation & that this will be done immediately.—indeed it is suspected there is a secret article in the treaty to this Effect & that in case of necessity Great Britain will cooperate as she is now seriously alarmed about her own Islands.—the Peace happening at the time I was in Paris, & there being no diplomatic man from our country here at this moment who would mix in those circles from which intelligence alone is to be drawn I considered it my duty to remain at this centre of politics a few days longer than I should otherwise have done, & shall be able whenever I meet with a safe opportunity of some individual I can trust to furnish you with interesting details.— at present I am not quite satisfied of the safety of the conveyance of the post & shall only say that from the most undoubted authority you may be assured that notwithstanding the peace or however quiet or secure things may be *no change²* *either in the Constitution or Government of this country is soon intended, that will make them approach nearer our own.—the present System is intended to continue.*—You may also be assured that the occupation of Louisiana is with them a favourite object & that the cession has been absolutely made by Spain.—I have however reason to believe that Bonaparte himself, his Brother Joseph, Marbois (now Minister of Finance & the public Treasure), La Forest, Otto & others are highly friendly to us.—I have been frequently asked & sometimes in a pointed manner since my arrival what is the Opinion of our Government respecting the change in France & their existing constitution but had always answered, Our country wishes peace, friendship & a liberal commerce with all the World—She interferes not in the Governments of others, nor sees the necessity of giving any opinions on them.—these are questions that rest with themselves.—

I think it will be difficult for the best informed men in Europe to calculate upon what will be the changes in this Quarter of the World in six years to come.—the state of things is entirely altered by the War just concluded.—England however powerful at sea has lost for the present her influence in continental affairs.—the Empire of Germany will undergo a serious alteration without her having any opinion, or interference on the subject—the influence & power of the King of Prussia, of France & Russia which were unknown in the last age in the diets of the Empire, now determine nearly every thing & it seems to me that the Time is not very distant when those powers in conjunction with Austria will mix all the little principalities & minor states of Europe into five or six large Governments, the forms or principles of which it will be, or rather as I have observed, it is at present extremely difficult to calculate on.—notwithstanding the late change of Government in France & the *military aristocratic* aspect every thing bears here, it is to be remembered that in the struggle the people of France have gained some thing—they have made some progress towards that state which they will probably one day arrive at.—they have gained some idea of what a Jury is in criminal cases.— they have destroyed the privileged Orders & the power of the Clergy.—industry is more extended & better rewarded & merchants & tradesmen are in more repute.—however unmeaning & misapplied at present it may appear, yet the very existence & use of the term of *"Citizen"* will have an effect, & the uncommon rise & happiness *of our own country*, will be to them an Example too powerful to be un-attended to.—I have no doubt the corruption, outrage & cruelty of the former Systems in France, have under the name of Liberty, done a great deal to injure the cause of *true republicanism*, but I still think that so powerful & iresistible are it's principles, that when the *reign of Terror & it's cruelties* come to be a little forgotten the true Light will yet shine in France & dissipate all the Mists that may obscure it.—although the general opinion here is against it, I must confess I cannot but have some hope from Bonaparte.—his pursuit & passion is Glory—in his military career he has attained the summit of fame.— he has by his Valour & talents saved France from the grasp of it's ex-ternal Enemies.—if, when *she is in a condition to receive it*, he adds to this, the true Glory of giving her a constitution something like our own his fame will be without a rival.—he will still continue unques-tionably her Executive & with substantially the same power or nearly the same he possesses at present but held by a different & more palat-able tenure—his then fellow citizens will rejoice in the recollection of his Virtue & talents & like our President he will have occasion for *no Guards* but the hearts & affections of his countrymen.—Feeling great respect for the character of Buonaparte I cannot, but continue to have this confidence in him.—I was introduced to him yesterday & judg-ing as I always do a great deal by the countenance of celebrated men, I am much mistaken, if he lives, if he does not at a proper time & when it is safe to do so take the road which alone leads to true glory.—his countenance is a good one—all the portraits you have seen are unlike him—Marbois is now Minister of Finance—La For-est at the head of the Post office. & Otto, as you already know, goes to America.—it is singular I found the only three french men I inti-mately knew in our own country, all high in power here.—My time has been incessantly & laboriously employed since my arrival in Eu-rope in examining & searching into every thing respecting the Arts, agriculture modes of life & government of the countries I have passed

& in comparing them with our own.—my notes already amount to Volumes & the description of the places & things I have seen form a little Library.—if I have time when I get a little settled to form a Journal of what I have seen in Holland, the low Countries & France & hope to see in Spain, I trust it will not be unentertaining to you.— I arrived at the Hague just after their Directory had closed the Door of their Legislature & was in Paris when Peace was concluded—two interesting periods for these countries.—you will do me a favour to make my affectionate compliments to my good friend Mr Madison & Mr Gallatin: Mr Nicholas Mrs: Baldwin & Brown & General Mason & to believe me with the most sincere & profound Esteem regard & Respect Dear Sir Yours Truly   CHARLES PINCKNEY

I propose to leave this in a very few days for Madrid.—

RC (DLC); endorsed by TJ as received 20 Jan. 1802 and so recorded in SJL. Enclosed in Hary Grant to TJ, 16 Oct. 1801.

I WROTE YOU: no letter to TJ from Pinckney at Brussels, and none written between 14 Sep. and this date, has been found or is recorded in SJL. Pinckney wrote to both TJ and Madison from Amsterdam on the 14th, and to Madison from The Hague on 22 Sep. At least one letter that Pinckney wrote to Madison after his arrival in Europe never reached its destination (Madison, *Papers, Sec. of State Ser.*, 2:94, 112, 126).

By the preliminary articles of PEACE between Great Britain and France, Britain gave up all French, Spanish, and Dutch possessions it had occupied during the war except Trinidad and Ceylon. The Ottoman Empire would have control over EGYPT. British forces were to withdraw from ports and islands in the Mediterranean and the Adriatic. Reflecting an initial reluctance on the part of the British to accept a Russian protectorate over MALTA, the preliminary articles of peace stated only that the restoration of the island to the Order of Knights of St. John of Jerusalem would be under the protection of a country to be designated in the definitive peace treaty. Although the published articles affirmed the integrity of Portugal's territory and possessions, a secret article acknowledged the concessions that Spain and France had forced on Por-

tugal earlier in the year (Parry, *Consolidated Treaty Series*, 56:211-16; Grainger, *Amiens Truce*, 40-1, 46).

SENDING OUT A LARGE FORCE: during October and November, the French assembled troops and ships at several harbors for an expedition to reassert control over Saint-Domingue. Bonaparte named his brother-in-law, General Victoire Emmanuel Leclerc, to command the venture and be captain general of the pacified colony. Leclerc and the primary element of the invasion force sailed from Brest in December and reached the island late in January 1802. There was no secret article about Saint-Domingue in the peace agreement, but Otto and Hawkesbury discussed the matter and the British did not interfere with the expedition. Bonaparte and Talleyrand also believed, from Louis André Pichon's representation of a conversation with TJ in July, that the United States favored the suppression of Toussaint's regime and could assist in the provisioning of an expedition to keep Saint-Domingue from becoming an "Algiers" in American waters (Thomas O. Ott, *The Haitian Revolution, 1789-1804* [Knoxville, Tenn., 1973], 139, 141-2, 147-8; Tulard, *Dictionnaire Napoléon*, 1046; Henri Mézière, *Le Général Leclerc (1772-1802) et l'Expédition de Saint-Domingue* [Paris, 1990], 126, 164-71; Carl Ludwig Lokke, "Jefferson and the Leclerc Expedition," *American Historical Review*, 33 [1928], 322-8; Malone, *Jefferson*, 4:251-3).

[1] Remainder of sentence interlined in place of "made a free Port."

[2] Pinckney double-underlined the preceding two words.

To John Syme

DEAR SIR   Washington Oct. 6. 1801.

Your favor of Sep. 18. was handed me just as I was preparing to leave Monticello, when a press of preparation put it out of my power to answer it. I thank you for this instance of attention and should have availed myself of your offer but that my wants in that line have been supplied. I concur with you in believing that whatever I do will meet the censure of the Federal brawlers. my anxiety is only to disabuse their followers, and [once] more consolidate our nation in social intercourse as well as [rally] them all to the pure principles of republicanism. to do this requires a different treatment of the case in different states according to the temper existing in each. their leaders & printers are incurables. perhaps they may even be useful to put us [in] mind of our errors & our faults. I pray you to accept my best wishes and friendly recollections.   TH: JEFFERSON

PrC (MoSHi: Jefferson Papers); faint; at foot of text: "Colo. John Syme"; endorsed by TJ in ink on verso.

To Thomas Willing

DEAR SIR   Washington Oct. 6. 1801.

Your favor of the 15th. Sep. reached me in due time, and I think it my duty to express my entire satisfaction with the reasons given in favor of mr Davidson. besides these, I knew the place to require such confidence as little short of personal knowlege could inspire. the quarrel between Forest & mr Hanson, which threatened to the latter the danger which occasioned my application, is now in discussion at the bar: and will end in good to none, ruin to several, & injury to many. an imprudent charge made by mr Hanson in a moment of warmth:[1] obliges him to bring such facts for his justification as will displease his employers & produce pretty certainly his dismission. but in all probability it will destroy their bank. Accept assurances of my high respect & consideration.   TH: JEFFERSON

PrC (MoSHi: Jefferson Papers); endorsed by TJ in ink on verso.

Samuel HANSON was removed on 13 Oct. from his position as cashier of the

Bank of Columbia after seven and a half years of service. An airing of his grievances in the newspaper, fulfilling his CHARGE to disclose "bank secrets," included his assertion that the bank directors and Benjamin Stoddert owed more than half the debt of the bank, amounting to seven-eighths of the bank's capital, and that Uriah Forrest was not without flaw despite the recent verdict in his favor (Walsh, *Early Banks in D.C.*, 75; Wilmington *Mirror of the Times*, 7 Nov. 1801).

[1] TJ canceled "however supported."

From John Barnes

SIR   Geo: Town 7th Oct 1801—

By favr Mr Claxton I have the pleasure to hand you, the inclosed five post Notes—

the most eligible I could procure for the purpose of remittance—I decided Mr Peytons—on the supposition of their being more convenient—in passing.—their Notes I find are quite Currt. at Richmond Mr Davison tells me—he makes Constant remittance on them to Mr Heath—

I am Sir your very Obedt servt: JOHN BARNES

NB. I have already taken register—viz

No 2298—favr D Higgenbotham		500
2299—	John Watson	143.73
2300	Craven Peyton 500.	
2301	do	500.
2302	do	240.27
		1240.27
		$1884.

RC (ViU); at foot of text: "Thomas Jefferson Esqr."; endorsed by TJ as received 7 Oct.

John Davidson (DAVISON) of Washington was an agent of Henry Heth (HEATH); George Jefferson to TJ, 7 Sep.

TJ enclosed the three notes for Craven Peyton in his letter to Peyton of 8 Oct.

TJ's letters to David Higginbotham and John Watson on 8 Oct., noted in SJL, have not been found. In his financial memoranda under that date, TJ recorded the payment to Higginbotham as "to David Higginbotham for Brown Rives & co." (MB, 2:1055). On TJ's debt to Watson, see TJ to Watson, 2 June.

From Sylvanus Bourne

Consular Office of the Ud. States

SIR—   Amsterdam Octo 7h 1801—

As the preliminaries of a peace between Great Britain & France were signed at London on the night of the 2d Instant, we now approach that period when with the war will cease the necessity which that occasioned of having many Certificates of divers kinds from the Consular office & will of course reduce the income of this one to a mere trifle—In this position of the case may I be permitted Respectfully to submit to your Consideration whether the importance of the Consular Establishment here (which now Constitutes the *only* representation of our Country to this, either in the political or commercial departs.) is not sufficient to claim the patronage or support of our Govt. by the allowance of a moderate annual compensation say 2000 to 2500 Dolls. towards the payt of which Sum the fees still receivable in the Office can be credited—in order to make it bear as little as possible on the publick—

The Value of this arrangment would be enhanced to me by the Consideration of the heavy expences & losses to Which I have been subjected for some years past. as my first & unsuccessfull mission to the Island of Hispaniola I was at the Charge of 1000 Dolls—since then the British have robbed me of 8000 Dolls more—I suffered by the failure of Mssr Morris Nicholson & Greenleaf to an equal amount these repeated misfortunes have fallen hard upon me on the eve of my establishment here & under the increasing expences of my family— thro every scene I [however?] uniformly attended to the various objects comprised in my Official duty & if not with ability—my heart will uphold me in saying that [this] has been with integrity & fidelity to those interests which have been Committed to my charge—& I hope that I shall continue to merit the confidence & approbation of my Country & its Goverment which I esteem to be among the most gratefull rewards attached to public Employ &

I have the honor to be With the greatest Respect Your Ob & devoted Sert.   S BOURNE

PS The Contents of the preliminary Articles of Peace between E & F are as yet unknown here—

RC (DNA: RG 59, CD); at head of text: "The President the United States." Enclosed in Bourne to James Madison, 7 Oct., commenting on the future support of the consular establishment in Amster-dam and enclosing "a letter for the President" (RC in same; see also Madison, *Papers, Sec. of State Ser.*, 2:162).

For Bourne's previous attempts to

obtain consular COMPENSATION, see Vol. 32:133.

HEAVY EXPENCES & LOSSES: Bourne, who had resigned in December 1791 as U.S. consul for Saint-Domingue and complained to TJ of his accumulated expenses and sacrifice of fortune, was named vice consul for Amsterdam in 1794 and continued in consular service in the Netherlands for almost 23 years. In March 1797, a British admiralty court condemned a ship that he owned and rejected the idea that his mercantile property was protected by virtue of his consular position. Bourne also experienced some financial setbacks resulting from the bankruptcy of the consortium of Robert Morris, John Nicholson, and James Greenleaf, whose real estate schemes in the new federal city were unsuccessful (Helen Bourne Joy Lee, *The Bourne Genealogy* [Chester, Conn., 1972], 89; JEP, 1:158; Madison, *Papers, Sec. of State Ser.*, 2:418-19; Bryan, *National Capital*, 1:234-5; Vol. 22:386-7, 468).

Bourne had sent TJ a letter from Amsterdam on 2 Oct. (not found), which TJ recorded in SJL on 4 Jan. 1802 with the notation "S."

From William C. C. Claiborne

DEAR SIR,   Nashville October 7th 1801.

I am sorry that I have remained thus long from my Post; But it really was not in my power sooner to have left Tennessee;—On tomorrow however, I shall certainly take my departure for the Missisippi Territory:—The Western Waters are uncommonly low, and I anticipate a long Voyage, but the season of the year, is favorable, and if the health of myself, and family should be preserved, my passage will (probably) be agreeable.

I do myself the honor to inclose for your perusal, a copy of the Letters which passed between Governor Sevier and myself, upon my declining a Seat in Congress, together with a Resolution of the House of Representatives of this State, approbating my late public Conduct.

An Election will be holden on the last thursday in this Month, to supply my Vacancy; there are four candidates, and all avowed Republicans.

The Objects of the late Negociation with the Cherokee Indians, as far as they have been known, appear to have been very pleasing to the Citizens of Tennessee, and the failure which ensued, is greatly regret'ed—The Commissioners (I believe) forwarded your Wishes with great zeal, but they had many difficulties to encounter, of which, no doubt, you have been made acquainted.—

I fear Sir, you will find the Southern Indians very unaccommodating;—The Cherokees have been taught to view the New President as their Enemy, and to expect the worse from his Administration; There is good reason to believe, that these Impressions have been made by Men, whose duty would have dictated a contrary Conduct; It is not improbable, but the Chiccasaws and perhaps, the Choctaws have been tampered with, in the same way.

The removal of the late Agent for the Cherokees, must be approved of by every person, who had any knowledge of his Conduct; his Successor Colo: Meggs is at present much esteemed by the Frontier Citizens, and will, in all probability, soon have considerable weight with the Indians; He is a temperate, prudent Man, and very attentive to Business;—If similar Characters were Agents for the Chiccasaws and Choctaws, I am sure Sir, the policy of the Executive in respect to the Indians, would be more zealously promoted, and your Instructions observed with better faith;—With the exception of Colo: Hawkins and Colo: Meggs, the Southern Indians profit little, either by the precept or example of the present Agents.

Most of the young Men, who are sent among the Indians, very soon form Indian Connections, and become highly dissipated; A loss of Influence and Respect immediately *follows.*

I have supposed, that an Agent residing upon the Frontiers, & visiting the Indians once in three Months, or oftener, if the occasion demanded, would be most likely to command Respect & acquire Influence; From time to time, he might receive information from his Interpreters, & thro them, (who might reside in the Nation) he could make his Communications to the Indians.

The Chiccasaws were once managed in this way, under the direction of General James Robertson, a respectable Citizen of this District, and I believe better managed, than they since have been. I do not know, that an Agency of this kind, would again be pleasing to General Robertson, but I rather think he would Act, and I with pleasure, name him, as a Man of great Merit, & one in Whom, you might place, great confidence.

I hope Sir, you will excuse the liberty I have taken in this Letter;—my sincere friendship for your person, and great solicitude for the happiness & usefulness of your Administration, have induced me to say this much on the subject of Indian affairs.—

I pray you sir, to accept assurances of my very sincere & respectful Attachment.

I have the honor to be Dr Sir, Your Mo. ob: hble servt

WILLIAM C. C. CLAIBORNE.

RC (DLC); at foot of text: "The President of the United States"; endorsed by TJ as received 11 Nov. and so recorded in SJL. Enclosures: (1) John Sevier to Claiborne and Claiborne's reply, both dated Knoxville, 22 Sep. 1801; Sevier notifying Claiborne of his reelection as representative in Congress from Tennessee;

Claiborne returning his thanks, but declining the seat, stating that he received official word of his appointment as governor of Mississippi Territory too late to withdraw his name from the congressional election, and declaring that the welfare of Tennessee "will always be dear to my heart" (printed broadside; Shaw-Shoemaker, No. 1310). (2) Resolution of the Tennessee House of Representatives, 24 Sep., thanking Claiborne unanimously for the "faithful discharge" of the trust given him as congressman and particularly for his firm action during the "glorious struggle" of the late presidential contest (*Journal of the House of Representatives at the First Session of the Fourth General Assembly of the State of Tennessee* [Knoxville, 1801], 25).

LATE AGENT FOR THE CHEROKEES: Thomas Lewis, removed from that position in March 1801. In May, TJ and Dearborn had appointed Return Jonathan Meigs as Lewis's SUCCESSOR (Henry Dearborn's Report on the War Department, [12 May 1801]).

In March 1801, Joseph Anderson and William Cocke, the U.S. senators from Tennessee, had called James ROBERTSON to TJ's attention as a potential commissioner for treaty talks with Indian tribes (Vol. 33:175).

From Albert Gallatin

T. Dt. 7 Oct. 1801

It is requested by Mr Hancock, if not impracticable, that he should obtain this afternoon the intended letter for the Collector of Philada. in relation to prize vessel "Harmony." At all events he wishes for an answer before he leaves the city. The messenger of the Secry. of the Treasury is directed to call at six o'Clock this afternoon for the President's answer which he will bring to his lodgings.

Respectfully   ALBERT GALLATIN

RC (DLC); at foot of text: "The President of the U. States"; endorsed by TJ as a letter of "Oct. 7. for 8." received from the Treasury Department on 8 Oct. and "the Harmony" and so recorded in SJL, but as a letter of 7 Oct.

Mr. HANCOCK, a U.S. citizen from Petersburg, Virginia, owned part of the cargo on the British sloop *Harmony*, which had been brought into Philadelphia by a French privateer. Hancock sought permission to unload the cargo before the prize vessel was ordered to leave the port (Madison, *Papers, Sec. of State Ser.*, 2:173-4; Gallatin to TJ, 8 Oct.).

To Gideon Granger

DEAR SIR   Washington Oct. 7. 1801.

The office either of Auditor or Treasurer of the US. will either the one or the other be vacant after this month. I do not as yet know which. their salaries are equal, 3000. D. each; their rank equal. I shall be happy to have the vacancy supplied by yourself; and shall consider it as fortunate for the public. I therefore take the liberty of proposing to you to accept whichever of the two shall be vacant, and to give me an answer with as little delay as you can, the applications from other quarters being urgent. as the less said on these occasions the better, until the appointment is actually made, I will pray you to let it remain unknown till then.

Accept assurances of my friendly esteem & respect.

TH: JEFFERSON

RC (DLC: Granger Papers); at foot of text: "Gideon Granger esq."; endorsed. PrC (DLC).

OFFICE EITHER OF AUDITOR OR TREASURER: after Joseph Habersham declined the office of treasurer, it was offered to Richard Harrison, auditor at the Treasury Department. On 12 Oct., Harrison wrote John Steele, declining the offer. He noted that the office of treasurer was "equal in point of respectability and emolument" to the one he held, but the security required for treasurer was much greater and he could procure it only by putting himself "under obligations of a very unpleasant kind." Although grateful for the confidence the president expressed in him, Harrison wrote: "I do not see how I can, consistently with prudence, venture to accept; and I must therefore beg permission, (however contrary to my wish to

accomodate) to decline the honor intended me." Steele forwarded Harrison's response to Gallatin the same day it was written (Gallatin, *Papers*, 5:847; Habersham to TJ, 21 Sep.).

On 18 Oct., Granger wrote TJ a brief letter from Suffield, Connecticut, acknowledging that he had received with "high Pleasure" that morning the president's letter of 7 Oct., as he was "on the point of setting off a Journey to New hampshire" from which he would return in eight days. "As I never contemplated an Office of the kind it struck me unexpectedly," he confided, "& I ask a little time to determine my Answer." He also promised to forward speedily "pretty correct Information respecting Connecticut" (RC in DLC; at foot of text: "Thos: Jefferson. Presidt: United States"; endorsed by TJ as received 23 Oct. and so recorded in SJL).

From George Jefferson

DEAR SIR   Richmond 7th. Octr. 1801

I received last night your favor of the 3d. and have in reply to inform you that the present price of Petersburg Tobacco is 4$:, to which it has risen within this week or two from 22/. As I understand the present growing crop will be a very short one, I do not suppose that it will be so low when it comes to market as the article is at this time; and I am therefore inclined to think that this would be the best time for you to make a settlement with Ross. it is not improbable however that although the *growing crop* may be above 24/.—yet that the *old crop* may go below it when the new comes in—owing to the very inferior quality of the old, of which you have doubtless heard— for if the new should be as good as usual the shippers perhaps would not purchase any other, except at a reduced price—indeed I should think this almost certain if I did not calculate upon the planters holding up very much in expectation of a rise in consequence of the short crop. They generally begin to bring it to market about the first of Novr., but as this depends very much upon *seasons* & other casualties no great regularity can be expected.

I desired our correspondent in Norfolk soon after I left Monticello to purchase & forward you 12 dozen hams; he informed us they were high & very scarce, but that he would endeavour to procure them.

I am Dear Sir Your Very humble servt.   GEO. JEFFERSON

Richmond Tobo. 31/6.

RC (MHi); at foot of text: "Thomas Jefferson esq."; endorsed by TJ as received 10 Oct. and so recorded in SJL.

CORRESPONDENT IN NORFOLK: Warren Ashley (George Jefferson to TJ, 26 May 1801).

From Samuel Smith

DR. SIR/   Baltimore 7th. Octr. 1801

I have shewn your letter recommending a clergyman to some of my particular friends, they laugh at the Idea of my being written to on that Subject, however your Recommendation will have great Weight—There is no positive Vacancy here yet, but there must be, for Doctr. Allison's situation is little short of Lunacy, Nor is there any Appearance of his recovery—There has been a young Gentleman of some Talents on trial from N: York, a Mr Mc.Knight who has given satisfaction, whether this will prevent your friends success I know not—

The Spaniards had declared (a L'Anglais) the Blockade of Gibraltar & our ships Avoided going there—but since the sailing of our ships of War—almost every Vessel had Orders to touch there for convoy & Information, a Number of those have Actually been Captured, bound to Leghorn Smyrma &c &c & carried to Algezira—The losses are tremendous & will be reported to the Departmt. of State by the Insurance companies—something I hope will be done—If C. Pinckney can stop this Infamous Conduct—& Recover for those latter Captures—It will be another successful Attempt in favor of our Commerce—I am sir with Truth your freind   S. SMITH

P.S—I have opened this Letter to Inform you that Capt. Rogers has sent a Box to my Care with a Mark Containing Books, which he believes to be for you. He delivered me two large Boxes sometime past which I forwarded—I have recd. a present of a Box of Old Hock from the Consul at Bremen Mr. Wichelhausen for myself & another for your Acceptance, shall I forward it

RC (DLC); endorsed by TJ as received 9 Oct. and so recorded in SJL.

YOUR LETTER: TJ to Smith, 26 Sep., regarding John Glendy. Patrick Allison, D.D., had been the pastor of a Presbyterian church in Baltimore since the 1760s. For several years before his death in 1802, he suffered from disease that erratically impaired his mental functions. Washington McKnight, the son of a New York City minister, was licensed to preach by the Presbytery of New York in October 1800 (Sprague, *American Pulpit*, 3:257-9, 373-4).

On 21 Aug., David Humphreys reported from Madrid the "disagreeable intelligence" that five ships owned by Americans had been brought into the port of Algeciras for violation of a Spanish BLOCKADE OF GIBRALTAR, "altho' they were most, if not all of them, destined to ports up the Mediterranean." Another American vessel that had been detained in the bay at Algeciras was sunk during the naval battles between the Spanish and the British in the area. On 25 Oct., Madison sent Charles PINCKNEY copies of letters and memorials from Americans about "the predatory cruizers from the port of Algeciras." Madison explained the U.S. government's position on the issue, argu-

ing that the Spanish blockade of Gibraltar, based on a proclamation of February 1800, had never been properly announced or enforced. "Among the abuses committed under pretext of War," Madison wrote, "none seem to have been carried to greater extravagance or to threaten greater mischief to neutral commerce, than the attempts to substitute fictitious blockades by proclamation, for real blockades formed according to the law of nations." Smith blamed that practice on the British with his phrase "a L'Anglais" in the letter above. Lafayette, writing to TJ in 1799, called Britain's imposition of sweeping blockades by proclamation a "Contrivance" (Humphreys to the secretary of state, 21 Aug., in DNA: RG 59, DD; Madison, *Papers, Sec. of State Ser.*, 2:199-203; Vol. 31:94). TJ sent papers relating to the Algeciras seizures and other spoliations involving Spain to the House of Representatives on 20 Apr. 1802 (ASP, *Foreign Relations*, 2:440-58).

The U.S. CONSUL AT BREMEN, Frederick Jacob Wichelhausen, had written to Madison on 31 July congratulating Madison and praising TJ. That letter was received at the State Department on 7 Oct. (Madison, *Papers, Sec. of State Ser.*, 1:410).

From the Danbury Baptist Association

SIR, [after 7 Oct. 1801]

Among the many millions in America and Europe who rejoice in your Election to office; we embrace the first opportunity which we have enjoy'd in our collective capacity, since your Inauguration, to express our great satisfaction, in your appointment to the chief Magistracy in the United States: And though our mode of expression may be less courtly and pompious than what many others clothe their addresses with, we beg you, Sir to believe, that none are more sincere.

Our Sentiments are uniformly on the side of Religious Liberty—That Religion is at all times and places a Matter between God and Individuals—That no man aught to suffer in Name, person or effects on account of his religious Opinions—That the legetimate Power of civil Goverment extends no further than to punish the man *who works ill to his neighbour*: But Sir, our constitution of goverment is not specific. Our antient charter, together with the Laws made coincident therewith, were adopted as the Basis of our goverment, At the time of our revolution; and such had been our Laws & usages, & such still are; that religion is consider'd as the first object of Legislation; & therefore what religious privileges we enjoy (as a minor part of the State) we enjoy as favors granted, and not as inalienable rights: and these favors we receive at the expence of such degrading acknowledgements as are inconsistant with the rights of freemen. It is not to be wondred at therefore; if those, who seek after *power* & *gain* under the pretence *of goverment* & *Religion* should reproach their fellow men—should reproach their chief Magistrate, as an enemy of religion Law & good order because he will not, dares not assume the prerogative of Jehovah and make Laws to govern the Kingdom of Christ.

Sir, we are sensible that the President of the united States, is not the national Legislator, & also sensible that the national goverment cannot destroy the Laws of each State; but our hopes are strong that the sentiments of our beloved President, which have had such genial Effect already, like the radiant beams of the Sun, will shine & prevail through all these States and all the world till Hierarchy and tyranny be destroyed from the Earth. Sir when we reflect on your past services, and see a glow of philanthropy and good will shining forth in a course of more than thirty years we have reason to believe that America's God has raised you up to fill the chair of State out of that good will which he bears to the Millions which you preside over. May God strengthen you for the arduous task which providence & the voice of the people have cal'd you to sustain and support you in your Administration against all the predetermin'd opposition of those who wish to rise to wealth & importance on the poverty and subjection of the people

And may the Lord preserve you safe from every evil and bring you at last to his Heavenly Kingdom throug Jesus Christ our Glorious Mediator.

Signed in behalf of the Association

NEHH. DODGE
EPHM. ROBBINS   } The Committee
STEPHEN S NELSON

RC (DLC); in Dodge's hand, signed by all; at head of text: "The address of the Danbury Baptist Association, in the State of Connecticut; assembled October 7th. 1801. To *Thomas Jefferson* Esqr: President of the united States of America";

endorsed by TJ as received 30 Dec. and so recorded in SJL.

A Baptist elder in Connecticut, Nehemiah Dodge began his career in the ministry in Hampton in 1788 before moving on to Southington. He published many tracts and orations and fought for disestablishment. About 1820, upon becoming a Universalist, he served as pastor of the Universalist Church in New London. Stephen S. Nelson was a graduate of Rhode Island College and moved from Hartford to Mt. Pleasant, New York, in 1801 to become principal of an academy (William G. McLoughlin, *New England Dissent 1630-1833: The Baptists and the Separation of Church and State*, 2 vols. [Cambridge, Mass., 1971], 2:930, 987, 1008).

OUR COLLECTIVE CAPACITY: the Danbury Baptist Association was organized in 1790 and consisted of twenty-six churches, mostly in western Connecticut, but including three churches in eastern New York. At its October 1800 meeting, the association initiated a petition movement to redress the grievances of the dissenting minority against the Congregationalist majority in the region. Although disestablishment had not been an issue in the 1800 election in Connecticut, the movement was a call for the statewide repeal of all laws that could be understood as supporting an established religion. In 1801, the petition movement tried to remain above partisan politics and cultivated support of some Congregationalists, Episcopalians, and other dissenters who might be sympathetic to their cause. On 8 Oct. 1801, the Danbury Baptist Association, meeting at Colebrook, Connecticut, voted that Elders Stephen Royce (Stratfield), Daniel Wildman (Wolcott and Bristol), Nehemiah Dodge (Southington and Farmington), Stephen S. Nelson (Hartford), and Deacons Jared Mills (Simsbury) and Ephraim Robbins (Hartford) "be a committee to prepare an address to the President of the United States, in behalf of this association." The address and the president's reply of 1 Jan. 1802 were reprinted in newspapers across the country, including Denniston and Cheetham's *American Citizen* on 18 Jan. 1802 (*Minutes of the Danbury Baptist Association, Holden at Colebrook, October 7 and 8, 1801; Together with Their Circular and Corresponding Letters* [Hartford, 1801]; Shaw-Shoemaker, No. 109; McLoughlin, *New England Dissent*, 2:920, 985-8, 1004-5; *Connecticut Courant*, 25 May 1801).

To John Coalter

DEAR SIR   Washington Oct. 8. 1801.

I have recieved your favor of Sep. 25. informing me you have obtained a judgment against mr Clarke on my behalf. this I presume is a lien on his moveable property and renders me secure, if there be not others on similiar ground beyond the amount of that property. I therefore do not wish to distress mr Clarke, or by prematurely pressing the sale of his property to lessen his resources. I will leave it with yourself, who are on the spot, to give mr Clarke all the time which may be of service to him, & to await any reasonable prospect he may have of raising the money in any way most accomodating to himself, and consistent with the ultimate security of the debt.

Accept assurances of my friendly esteem & respect.

TH: JEFFERSON

PrC (MHi); at foot of text: "Mr. Coalter"; endorsed by TJ in ink on verso.

Coalter's FAVOR OF 25 Sep., recorded in SJL as received from Staunton on 6 Oct., has not been found. In July, Coalter wrote TJ that he thought he would receive a judgment against Samuel CLARKE during the court's August term. Clarke owed TJ almost £100 for nails (MB, 2:939; Coalter to TJ, 3 July).

From Albert Gallatin

SIR   Treasy. Depart. 8 Oct. 1801

The enclosed letter from Mr Dallas, received this morning, showeth that the Brit. Consul has not agreed to the restoration in the case of the prize vessel "Harmony." The instructions sent yesterday to the Collector do not, however, seem to require any alteration.

Mr D. seems to have supposed that, had the capture been made before the exchange of ratifications, a restoration might have been claimed under the law of nations, which, in that case, would have protected American property on board an English vessel. It is so difficult to define with precision what was the political relation of the U. States & France from the date of the treaty to that of the exchange, that a decision on that ground would have, perhaps, been inexpedient.

Mr Hancock hinted something of the kind: my answer was that our interference in his favour went no farther than to permit a restoration if all the parties were agreed & the Brit. Consul did not object; but, that if he thought he had a legal claim, we meant not to bar his pursuing it before the courts in such manner as his counsel might advise, nor, on the other hand, to interfere by an exercise of executive authority. He asked whether we considered the French convention as ratified; my answer was in the affirmative.

With great respect   ALBERT GALLATIN

RC (DLC); at foot of text: "The President of the United States"; endorsed by TJ as received 9 Oct. and "the Fame & Harmony" and so recorded in SJL. Enclosure not found.

Phineas Bond served as British CONSUL general for the middle and southern states, but the surviving correspondence on the case of the *Harmony* is between Edward Thornton, the acting British chargé d'affaires, and Madison (Madison, *Papers, Sec. of State Ser.*, 2:173-4, 234-5; Vol. 26:398; Vol. 33:190). INSTRUCTIONS SENT YESTERDAY: Gallatin's letter to George Latimer, customs collector at Philadelphia, has not been found, but eight days later the Treasury secretary wrote Madison: "By direction of the President, I had written to the Collector that without pretending to decide on the application of treaties to this specific case, he might admit to an entry such part of the cargo owned by Mr Hancock an american citizen as the captors were willing to restore, provided the British Consul made no objection to it" (Madison, *Papers, Sec. of State Ser.*, 2:177). On 12 Oct., Thornton wrote Madison from Philadelphia that he had been informed only an hour earlier that Hancock had "made such terms with the captors as to be enabled to recover his property without great loss, and that there will be a permission granted by the Government of the United States for the landing of that part of the cargo, provided no objection shall be made on my part." Thornton agreed to the request with the stipulation that as soon as Hancock's property was landed, the *Harmony* and the remainder of her cargo would be ordered to sea. On 15 Oct., Gallatin received a letter from Latimer with the news that Thornton would allow the restoration of the cargo as long as the case was not used as a precedent. With that information Gallatin thought Latimer "would have been justifiable in suffering Mr Hancock's property to be re-stored" (same, 2:173-4, 177-8). Later that day, Gallatin wrote the Philadelphia collector: "The President being satisfied, from the assent of Mr Thornton, in the case of the prize vessel 'Harmony,' that there is no collusion, directs me to instruct you, to admit to an entry & to permit to be landed & delivered to Mr Hancock, or to his agent, such part of the cargo of the said vessel, as has been stated to be his property, and as the captors may be willing to restore; the same being, under those circumstances, considered, by the President, as bona fide american property." Latimer informed Gallatin, on 20 Oct., that the *Harmony* had sailed before he received the instructions (Gallatin, *Papers*, 5:859, 899).

From Dennis Griffith

SIR   Elk Ridge Landing October 8th. 1801

An Idea has occured to me, that it is possible to ascertain the Longitude of places in the Northern Hemisphere, when the necessary preparatory Tables are formed, in as simple manner, (or nearly so) as the Latitude. It appears to me that if the nightly positions of the pointers, in their revolution round the north Star, can be accurately fixed, & a Table formed thereof similar to that of the Sun's daily declination, as used in the Seaman's assistant, the desired effect might be obtained by observation with a Quadrant. It will perhaps be necessary to ascertain the relative distances of the pointers to the polar Star & of the same to each other, & to combine the nightly observation of them, with the last preceeding daily observation for the Latitude; hence, something more will depend upon reckoning & calculation, than in taking the Latitude & the operation, perhaps, from other circumstances will be a little more complex.

I have observed that the Sun's declination on the meridian is the source of our Latitude & an Idea of a revolutionary body round a fixed (or nearly so) object would give as just an Idea from observation of our easting & westing, as the other does of our northing & southing (when the observations are combined). Relying upon your character I have been emboldened to write to you on the subject, with full confidence that if there is any thing in the suggestion worth attention, that it will not be lost. I am not master of a sufficient degree of Science to pursue the investigation, if worthy, you will put it into possession of some person that is. If not I am well assured in my mind that you will pardon the intrusion, that the perusal of this may make upon your public functions.

I am with the most sincere respect yr. obt.   D GRIFFITH

RC (PPAmP); endorsed by TJ as received 15 Oct. and so recorded in SJL; endorsed in an unknown hand: "Non est inventor"; also endorsed for the American Philosophical Society.

Dennis Griffith exchanged letters with TJ in 1793, shortly before publishing a map of Maryland (Vol. 26:798; Vol.

27:53-4). After being read at the APS on 7 May 1802, Griffith's communication was referred to a committee made up of Robert Patterson and Benjamin Henry Latrobe. The committee was discharged on 18 June (APS, *Proceedings,* 22, pt. 3 [1884], 323, 325; John Vaughan to TJ, 8 May 1802).

To Craven Peyton

DEAR SIR   Washington Oct. 8. 1801.

I recieved the day before yesterday your favor of the 3d. inst. the post leaving this always the day before the return of the post of the preceding week prevents our neighborhood from recieving an answer from hence till the Thursday sennight after they have sent off their letter. I do not perfectly understand your statement of the additions on account of a greater quantity of forest land than was expected; and therefore I inclose you a sum in postnotes of this bank which I was able to obtain from a particular person, divided for convenience into those of 500. 500. & 240.27 amounting in the whole to 1240. D. 27 c which will be near the sum probably remaining due, & any difference may remain in account between us. I am assured these notes are gladly exchanged for cash in Richmond. probably the Collector there is peculiarly accomodated by them, as well as the merchants. I will pray you to have them disposed of immediately, because the establishment of an US. bank here will possibly oblige the other to discontinue their business; in which event the less delay in exchanging these notes, the safer against any delay of paiment which the discontinuance of that institution might occasion. I will pray you by return of post to send me an exact statement of the whole amount of the price[1] of my four shares. I must also ask for a plat of the manner in which each of the fields, or different lots of property, were divided into 10. parts, so that I may see exactly which are mine, and what others it would be most advantageous to me to acquire. for instance No. 9. in the lands below the town comprehending the mill seat, it would be proper for me to see who owns the divisions on the river above that, through which the canal must pass, and for them I might go beyond the valuation price. in the mean time I shall be glad to get J. Henderson's parts, every where, at the valuation price, and any others on the river[2] which will consolidate with my parts above the mill seat or any of the forest lands above the dower tract which will consolidate with my former possessions. I wish you still to do everything in your own name, & as you would for yourself; and particularly to lease Thorp's & Faris's houses as you think best. the forms I left with you for the deeds will still do if you will strike out the words 'undivided portion' and insert instead of them 'part or property divided or undivided' and then it will be 'all the part or property divided or undivided of the lands of the late Bennett Henderson deceased in the county of Albemarle which descended on the said' A. B. &c.   I would pray you to get the deeds executed the moment the parties are of age to execute them, and to furnish me immediately with the plat of the division as before desired, each parcel numbered in it, or marked with the name of the person who drew it. Accept assurances of my friendly esteem & attachment   TH: JEFFERSON

PrC (ViU); endorsed by TJ in ink on verso. Enclosures not found.

The listing of the division of the Henderson estate that Peyton sent on 3 Oct. showed that there was a GREATER QUANTITY OF FOREST LAND making up the "Back Lands" portion of the estate than TJ and Peyton had previously thought (Valuation of Henderson Property for Dower, [before 1 Oct. 1801]).

TJ recorded in his financial memoranda for 8 Oct. the payment of $1,240.27 to Peyton "for Henderson's land." The notes were from the BANK of Columbia. TJ also recorded the remittance in a statement he later drew up of his purchases of property from the Hendersons (MB, 2:1055; John Barnes to TJ, 7 Oct.; TJ to Peyton, 1 Nov.; statement of account with Peyton, 1801-1809, in DLC, enclosed in TJ to Peyton, 28 Oct. 1812).

MY FOUR SHARES: the rights of Sarah Henderson Kerr and her brothers James, Charles, and Isham Henderson, already purchased by Peyton for TJ (Declaration of Trust with Craven Peyton, 25 Sep.).

The undeveloped MILL SEAT that would require construction of a CANAL was on the parcel of the "below the Town" tract that had fallen to James Henderson in the partition of the estate (Peyton to TJ, 3 Oct.).

J. HENDERSON'S PARTS: TJ and Peyton had not acquired rights from John Henderson, the member of the Henderson family most interested in carrying on the father's development of the land. In the partitioning of the estate, John received the number 10 lot of the "Lands below the Town," which was adjacent on the upstream side to the number 9 lot, the one with the potential mill site allotted to John's brother James. The land upstream from John's parcel of the "Lands below the Town" was the 15-acre piece that was part of Elizabeth Lewis Henderson's dower. The two lots on the downriver side of number 9 went to Charles and Isham Henderson (Vol. 32:558; Valuation of Henderson Property for Dower, [before 1 Oct. 1801]; Enclosure No. 1 listed at Peyton to TJ, 3 Oct.; Peyton to TJ, 16 Oct.; enclosure listed at Peyton to TJ, 6 Nov.).

TJ meant by FORMER POSSESSIONS the nearby land that he owned before beginning the acquisition of Henderson properties.

FORMS I LEFT WITH YOU: see the Form of Deeds for Henderson Purchases, [September? 1801]; for the alteration of language, see the deed from James Henderson and his wife at 29 Nov.

THE MOMENT THE PARTIES ARE OF AGE: see Peyton to TJ, 16 Oct.

[1] Preceding three words interlined.
[2] Preceding three words interlined.

To Thomas Mann Randolph

DEAR SIR   Washington Oct. 8. 1801.

In a letter written to you (the last fall, I believe) I took occasion to mention to you that should a certain event take place it would be in my power to aid you in the course of the present year; and the paiment to Gibson & Jefferson of 450. D. in February was intended only in part of what I had further meditated. the event has happened; and yet such are the extraordinary expences of an outfit here, while the current expences must be going on that I am not only unable to do any thing in the pecuniary way at present, but am so far in anticipation that were any accident to happen to me for some time to come, it would leave my private fortune under serious embarrasment. wishing very anxiously to do any thing I can to make your situation & that of mr Eppes easy, I have contemplated to do it in a way which may be permanent. I have desired Bowling Clarke, who is perfectly well acquainted with the Poplar Forest lands, is an honest & judicious man, to lay off for each of you a parcel of that tract of 6 or 800 or 1000. as. as the convenience of the tract will admit, making the two as equal in value as he can. I expect daily to learn that he has done it. then I will propose that each of you shall hire 10. laboring men for the ensuing year, to be employed solely in clearing the lands, and I will pay the hire and maintenance of the hands. I presume that at the end of the year you would each of you have a fresh farm opened of 300. as. which you could either occupy or rent as might suit your own convenience. — as soon as I hear from Clarke, I will communicate to you what he has done, but in the mean time you may safely take any measures for the execution of the plan, which opportunity may offer you. from an actual survey of the plantation I occupy there (which you will see in one of the desk drawers in my study) which was made this last summer, it appears that one of these parcels must be laid off on the Southeast side of mine and the other to the North, adjoining your's. I am afraid the land in the S.E. end is not as rich as to the North. in that case I have directed Clarke to equalize the two by a difference in quantity. but how the fact is, I am not intimate enough with the land to say. it may require a difference in the size of the clearing also to produce in inferior lands a rent equal to what those of superior quality may command. but when the exact state of the thing shall be known, some modification of arrangement may be formed to produce equality.

We have nothing new & to be depended on from Europe. it is impossible to judge of what has past in Egypt. lying on that subject has been so shamelessly established into system, that the names of a Tooke or an Elgin seem nothing more than the badges of a lie.—I am afraid the two Tripolitan vessels have escaped from Gibraltar. perhaps some of our vessels may pick them up in the Mediterranean. by the course of our post letters going from here to you can be acknoleged in a week, but coming from you here require a fortnight. my tenderest affections to my dear Martha, kisses to the little ones, and sincere esteem & attachment to yourself.   TH: JEFFERSON

P.S. I write to mr Eppes on this subject.

RC (DLC); endorsed by Randolph. PrC (CSmH); postscript added by TJ in ink; at foot of first page in ink: "T M Randolph"; endorsed by TJ in ink on verso.

LETTER WRITTEN TO YOU: TJ to Randolph, 7 May 1800. For TJ's payment to GIBSON & JEFFERSON on Randolph's behalf, see Vol. 32:499, 534-5, 557-8.

ADJOINING YOUR'S: TJ gave his daughter Martha 1,000 acres of the Poplar Forest tract when she married Randolph in 1790 (Vol. 16:154-5). For TJ's plat survey of Poplar Forest that year, see Vol. 16:190.

On 7 Oct., an article taken from the Boston *Independent Chronicle* appeared in the Philadelphia *Aurora*, which noted that London papers had reported "with so much confidence" the fall of Cairo to British and Turkish forces. The information had come through letters from Constantinople by Peter TOOKE, agent of the East India Company, and Lord ELGIN, British ambassador to Turkey. The essay pointed out that in numerous instances official accounts from Constantinople had "turned out to be *mere Eastern tales*" and noted discrepancies in the accounts by Tooke and Lord Elgin (*An East-India Register and Directory, for 1803; Corrected to the 12th July, 1803,* 2d ed. [London, 1803], xxvii; DNB, 8:329-31).

I WRITE TO MR EPPES: TJ to John Wayles Eppes, 9 Oct.

From Benjamin Rittenhouse

SIR

Montgomery Couty. State of Pensylvania Ocr. 8th 1801

Powerfully impress'd with the apparent impropriety of personal importunity, and perfectly sensible of the great work and important duties of the Executive of a great nation, Were it not for the urgent perswasion of a number of Gentlemen of Character in this State who originally induc'd me to make application, and whose friendship perhaps have much overated my claim to your patronage, I shou'd not again presume to Trouble you with further solicitation being perfectly convinc'd of your inclination to do what you concieve will most tend to promote the common Interest of our country. But shoud a leasure hour Occur to bestow attention to my application and shou'd you be pleas'd to honour me with an appointment worth acceptance, you may depend on my unremited indeavours to merit your favor, and it will be receiv'd with gratitude by Sir

    Your Devoted Humble Servant   BENJN. RITTENHOUSE

RC (NHi: Gallatin Papers); at foot of text: "His Excellency, Thomas Jefferson"; endorsed by TJ as received 14 Oct. and so recorded in SJL. Enclosed in TJ to Gallatin, 15 Oct. (see below).

ORIGINALLY INDUC'D ME TO MAKE APPLICATION: see Rittenhouse to TJ, 17 Mch. 1801. In support of Rittenhouse's application, TJ received an undated recommendation signed by all of the Montgomery County members of the Pennsylvania General Assembly in 1801, including Isaiah Davis, Nathaniel B. Boileau, Frederic Conrad, and Samuel Henderson, representatives; John Richards, the state senator and former congressman; Pennsylvania Republicans Jacob Morgan and William Barton; and seven others. They noted Rittenhouse's service during the Revolution and his uniform Republican principles. His well-known mechanical and mathematical abilities designated him as "a suitable

person to an appointment in the Mint department" or whatever office the president thought proper (RC in DNA: RG 59, LAR, in an unidentified hand; *Journal of the First Session of the Twelfth House of Representatives of the Commonwealth of Pennsylvania* [Lancaster, 1801, i.e., 1802], 4; *Journal of the Senate of the Commonwealth of Pennsylvania* [same], 4; *Biog. Dir. Cong.*; Harry Marlin Tinkcom, *The Republicans and Federalists in Pennsylvania 1790-1801: A Study in National Stimulus and Local Response* [Harrisburg, 1950], 201, 231).

On 15 Oct., TJ sent Rittenhouse's letter to Gallatin with a covering note: "You best know the writer of the inclosed, what he is fit for, and if any thing may probably arise fit for him. I inclose it merely to have him in mind. his name & family possess the public respect" (RC in NHi: Gallatin Papers; addressed: "The Secretary of the Treasury").

From Stephen Sayre

SIR.   Philadelphia 8th octor. 1801.

    Supposing the secretary of State is not yet return'd to Washington, I trust you will pardon me the liberty I now take.   On the 15th Inst. I shall be call'd upon to pay the Sum of £420 sterling, money lent me in 1777. & 1778—while I was actually in the public service. My freinds, who advanced me this sum, have employ'd an agent, now here, & he has given me indulgence, to this period. If I had any assurances from the executive, that I should be provided for, in a short time, he might be persuaded to wait still longer. My freinds who have mentioned my name to you, deeming me entitled to your patronage have given me reason to beleive I may expect it.

I shall not trouble you with argument, or observation—the object of this letter is, simply, to inform you, that if it is intended by the administration to employ me, in any shape under the government, they may, *by doing it now*, prevent my ruin & disgrace—will you do me the singular favour to consider, for a moment, how my fall must glut the malignant feelings, & wishes of your enimies & mine. As soon as Congress are assembled you will have the joint request of the Members of New Jersey, pressing, too late, that somthing may be done for me—Let me then have your pardon for this attempt to prevent such extensive mischiff—the mortification will not be confined to myself & family—it will touch every man who loves his country—I am respectfully &c   STEPHEN SAYRE

RC (DNA: RG 59, LAR); torn; endorsed by TJ as received 10 Oct. and so recorded in SJL; also endorsed by TJ: "refd. to Secy. State Th:J." and "qu. if to be ansd."

Sayre was indebted to Bordeaux men while he was IN THE PUBLIC SERVICE, for money lent him to pay an obligation to Isaac Panchaud. Throughout TJ's terms in office, Sayre repeatedly and unsuccessfully sent employment requests to the president and his ADMINISTRATION (John R. Alden, *Stephen Sayre, American Revolutionary Adventurer* [Baton Rouge, 1983], 171, 189-91).

From Robert Smith

SIR,   Oct. 8. 1801.

I have Seen Col Burrows and I have arranged with him to be at the Barracks at half after 9 OClock tomorrow morning. I have taken the liberty of fixing this time as I shall thus have more time for the business of my department, and it will not, I trust, be an inconvenient time to you

Be pleased to accept the assurance of my Respect

RT SMITH

RC (DLC); endorsed by TJ as received 8 Oct. from the Navy Department and so recorded in SJL.

Marine Corps Commandant William Ward BURROWS had expressed concerns to Smith regarding the quality of the work completed on the marine BARRACKS in Washington. On 28 Sep., Smith ordered Burrows to have the work surveyed in order to determine whether it had been carried out according to contract (FC in Lb in DNA: RG 45, MLS). On 9 Oct., Smith addressed a letter to Francis Deakins, Francis Lowndes, Daniel Carroll, Thomas Law, and Thomas Tingey, informing them that "the president is desirous" that they inspect the brickwork completed by Lawrence Pearson and Robert Brown and report on whether the barracks should be accepted by the government (same).

From John Barnes

Washington 9th. Octr 1801

It appears the following are the remaining a/c for which JB. have not recd Orders upon viz.

Order I presume in favr of Mr Rapin—   286.98.

Capt. Lewis last 3 mos. Compensation
presume may be passed to his Ct   } 150.
with JB. and charged you for

probably there will be a Mr Andrews for
    Composition Ornaments a/c
Also Mr March's Book binders a/c

Those at Philada—JB have minute of Accts to   958.62

If any other—or Later to Dr Edwards or Mr Stewart &c.—JB purpose to wait on you early Sunday Morng

RC (ViU); at foot of text: "for The President: UStates"; endorsed by TJ.

According to TJ's financial memoranda, TJ gave George ANDREWS two orders on Barnes—one on 12 Oct. for $20.50 for making composition ornaments for the dining room at Monticello, the other on 7 Nov. for $2.49 for packing the "Doric composition ornaments." In a statement of TJ's accounts, Barnes recorded a payment of $22.99 to Andrews at 7 Nov. TJ emended the entry to clarify that there were two payments, the one at 7 Nov. for $2.49, the other for $20.50 (MB, 2:1055, 1057; statement of private and household account from John Barnes, 4 Dec. 1801, in ViU).

MR STEWART: Gilbert Stuart.

To John Wayles Eppes

DEAR SIR   Washington Oct. 9. 1801

Understanding that you thought of building some time ere long on the upper Pantops, I mentioned to Maria (I do not recollect whether
I did to you) that I thought it indispensable that the ground should be first levelled as that of Monticello is, and that if you would be at the trouble of hiring hands, & having the work done, I would pay their hire: and this I recommend to you: desirous of doing any thing which my circumstances will admit for the ease & comfort of Maria & yourself, I have contemplated, as a permanent addition to your income, the having a farm laid off for you in the Poplar forest tract. I accordingly had a survey made this summer of the plantation

[418]

I occupy there, and it's relative position in the tract. this you will find in the desk drawer in my Cabinet. and I sometime since wrote to Bowling Clarke, who is honest, judicious & intimately acquainted with the tract to have two parcels of 800. or 1000. as. laid off for yourself & mr Randolph. one of these (from the shape of the tract) must be at it's South East end; the other North of my plantation & adjoining mr Randolph's. I apprehend the land to the South East is not absolutely equal in quality to that North; but by adding to the quantity, it may be made of equal value, & this I directed Bowling Clarke to observe. it will be certainly more convenient that mr Randolph should take the lot adjoining his own, & your being thus fixed at opposite ends will make it easy hereafter by a proper division of the middle part to equalize the division of the whole tract. I now therefore propose to yourself & mr Randolph, if you will undertake to hire 10. laboring men each for the next year, & employ them in clearing lands within your respective parts, I will pay their hire & maintenance. they will probably clear 300. acres for each of you, so that at the end of the year you will have a fresh farm of 300. acres open for occupation or rent. should there be a difference in the fertility of the land, it would require a greater quantity to be cleared of that which is inferior, to make up an equal rent to that of superior quality. of this I should suppose Bowling Clarke a perfect judge, and should authorize him to settle how much additional ground should be opened in the one parcel to make it equal to the other, and a proportional increase of hands should be hired at my expence. I should have proposed this matter to you sooner but that I was in hourly expectation, as I still am, of hearing from him. in the mean while however you may be making any arrangements you think proper towards carrying it into execution. I have written to mr Randolph on the same subject. perhaps it might be best for you both to visit the place and see the allotment Clarke has made, for certainly it is done before now.　　　this business & Pantops would give you so much to do in the upper country that I should think you & Maria had better make Monticello your head quarters for the next year as Central to all your concerns. the resources of the smokehouse, cellar, servants &c should be all at your command, & it will give me great pleasure that you should be there.

I recieved by the last post your's of the 3d. & am happy to hear that Maria and the child are so well. I hope they will continue so. present me affectionately to my sister Marks: my tenderest love to my ever dear Maria, and sincere esteem & attachment to yourself.

TH: JEFFERSON

Pantops is I think naturally shaped thus.
all the earth dug within the level line which you should run
round it, should be carried into the hollow at A. to fill that
up & bring the ground to a regular shape.

RC (NHi); addressed: "John W. Eppes   I HAVE WRITTEN TO MR RANDOLPH
Monticello near Milton"; franked. PrC   ON THE SAME SUBJECT: TJ to Thomas
(CSmH); endorsed by TJ in ink on verso.   Mann Randolph, 8 Oct.

To Albert Gallatin

DEAR SIR   Washington Oct. 9. 1801.
    I return you mr Dallas's opinion on the question whether the goods
of a citizen taken by one belligerent in the bottom of another may be
recieved here, with the consent of the Captor, by the owner. his idea
that, by the principle established with France, that enemy bottoms
make enemy goods, these goods are assimilated to the real enemy
goods which were on board, is imposing at first view; but yields, in
my opinion, to further consideration. for whose benefit was that principle established? clearly for the benefit of the Captor; and how can a
third party, not interested in the question, prevent him from relinquishing his benefit in favor of our citizen. ransom or fraud may make
another question of it; but while it is stated as a bona fide relinquish-
ment of the benefit which the treaty between France & us had introduced for the Captor, I cannot concieve that the owner of the bottom
has a right to object. suppose the British owner had ransomed his
vessel; or that the captor had ceded to him the benefit which the laws
of war had given him[1] by making capture a transfer of property;
could we, who have no interest nor right embarked in the question,
controul their transaction? it would really be hard that the goods of
our own citizen, relinquished to him by the captor, should be prohibited *by us* from our own ports. yet as we have no atty genl. here, I
would not proceed against mr Dallas's opinion. I wish it may go off
on your first letter supposing a consent of all parties; or if the British
minister objects, I wish mr Hancock could find some means of carrying it into court. whether this can be done by Mandamus, I am not
satisfied. if it could it would be a prompt trial of the question. should
the case come back to us on the dissent of the British minister, it is
so important as a first precedent, that great consideration must be
bestowed on it.   health & respect.   TH: JEFFERSON

RC (NHi: Gallatin Papers); addressed: "The Secretary of the Treasury." PrC (DLC). Recorded in SJL with the notation "Fame & Harmony."

[1] Preceding two words interlined in place of "established."

From Conrad Hanse

DEAR SIR   Philadelphia October 9th 1801

At the tim your Coachman Cald for your Chariot he informed me that the Links of the Ames of the wheel horse Harness apeard to Short and prest the Collars to Close to the Horses necks I then told him I wold have a pair of Longer wons made and sende them on as sune as poseble I hope those In Closed will Answer better then them that whent ferst with the Harness

I am with Respect your Huml Servent   CONRAD HANSE

RC (MHi); at foot of text: "Thomas Jefferson Esq. President of the United Stats;" endorsed by TJ as received 12 Oct. and so recorded in SJL.

AMES: "hames" (OED).

From Edward Maher

[9 Oct. 1801]

Sir as you Cant a ford me more weages I must See and[1] beter my Self I am sorrey to leave you   EDWARD MAHER

RC (MHi); endorsed by TJ as a letter of 9 Oct. 1801.

Edward Maher began work at the President's House on 12 Mch. 1801. His pay was $12 each month, plus an additional $2 "for drink" that was a routine gratuity for some members of the household staff. He was also to receive two suits of clothes. Maher, who held the job of porter, apparently thought that the range of duties associated with that position should be narrowly defined, whereas TJ and the stewards wanted him to work on any tasks that might need attention. In April, Maher was dismayed when TJ had John Freeman, rather than Maher, accompany him to Virginia.

Maher also grumbled about his livery outfit, objecting to wearing the same uniform as a black man. In the spring of 1802, Maher's successor as porter left abruptly, but TJ refused to take Maher back. Citing Maher's apparent inability to stay with any employer very long, TJ called him "fickle." TJ wanted "servants who will do every thing they are wanted to do," and Maher, though "capable," did not meet that standard. TJ also confided to Étienne Lemaire that Maher had been in the habit of reading papers on TJ's desk when TJ was out of the room. Joseph Dougherty, the coachman, found Maher "a verry Disagreeable Man in a family although he is a good Servant" (MB, 2:1035, 1036, 1040, 1042, 1045;

Vol. 33:504n, 530-1, 605; Étienne
Lemaire to TJ, 10 May 1802; Joseph
Dougherty to TJ, 11 May 1802; TJ to
Lemaire, 14, 20 May 1802).

[1] MS: "Seeand."

Order on John Barnes

[9 Oct. 1801]

Mr. Barnes will be pleased to pay to the bearer Edward 7. Dollars in lieu of a jacket which he claims 5. Doll. for 9. days wages,[1] & to furnish him such a hat as was furnished to the other servants say 12. D. & a hat.   TH: JEFFERSON

MS (ViU: Edgehill-Randolph Papers); in TJ's hand; at foot of text: "Mr. Barnes"; endorsed by Barnes, who wrote the acknowledgment of receipt "for Edward" by Étienne Lemaire, who signed for the payment on 9 Oct.; also endorsed by Barnes on verso: "Edwd Maher 9 Oct. 1801 $12."

In his financial memoranda on 9 Oct., TJ recorded writing this order on Barnes for EDWARD Maher and added, "He goes away." Maher had previously received wages for the period 4 Sep. to 4 Oct. along with other employees of the president's household (MB, 2:1054, 1055).

[1] Preceding four words and two figures interlined.

To Robert Smith

TH:J. TO MR SMITH.   Octor. 9 1801.

Capt Truxton's idea of a [gradual] relief of our frigates [presents] advantages. in addition to what he [mentions], the frigate going out [might] always carry supplies; the frigate relieved may always be any particular one which may have got damaged & need repairs. it puts it in our power to shift the officers at our will & without offence. [it] might, on the arrival of the one & before the departure of the other, enable the Commodore to undertake an enterprize with 4. frigates to which 3. would be incompetent, it would enable him to send home from time to time[1] such men as were become permanently sick or disabled. perhaps the intervals from 4. months to 4. months may be rather long.

PrC (DLC); faint, with words in brackets supplied from Tr. Tr (MHi).

On 9 Oct., Secretary of the Navy Smith wrote another letter, enclosing warrants for Richard B. Brandt, James Lawrence,

and Morris Newman as sailing masters. The enclosed documents (not found) required TJ's signature (RC in DLC, in a clerk's hand, signed by Smith, at foot of text: "Ths. Jefferson Esqr Prest. UStates," endorsed by TJ as received from the Navy Department on 10 Oct. and "Commissions" and so recorded in SJL; FC in Lb in DNA: RG 45, LSP).

[1] Preceding four words interlined.

From William Barton

SIR, Lancaster (Pennsylva.) Oct. 10. 1801.

In a letter, sent herewith, to my friend Mr. Saml. H. Smith, editor of the National Intelligencer, I have stated the cause of my taking the liberty of addressing to You the foregoing Duplicate of my late letter. —

I have requested Mr. Smith to explain to You my motives: — they are of a very delicate nature, — important, in a public point of view, — and such as I trust, Sir, will be a satisfactory apology for me, on this occasion. —

I have the Honor to be, with the mo. perfect considn. and Respect, Sir, Your faithful and obedt. Servt. W. BARTON

RC (MHi); addressed: "The President of the United States"; endorsed by TJ as received 24 Oct. and so recorded in SJL. Enclosure not found.

From Andrew Ellicott

DEAR SIR Lancaster October 10th. 1801

I have enclosed the observations made by Mr. Patterson and myself on the lunar eclipse of september last, — if you think them of sufficient importance you are at liberty to communicate them to the American Philosophical Society. —

The Map on which I informed you some time ago I was engaged is completed: — it comprehends the Mississippi from the mouth of the Ohio down to the Gulf of Mexico, the provence of West Florida and the whole southern boundary of the United States accompanied with thirty two pages, (in folio), of manuscript remarks on the navigation of the rivers, proper positions for military works &c. — I have endeavoured to make it interesting both as a geographical, and national document: — it cost me more than forty days labour, and I intended, to hand it to you myself, immediately on your return to Washington; but have been prevented by accepting an appointment under the State Government. I intend nevertheless to be at Washington before the commencement of the next year; but could not with any propriety leave the Office at present, owing to a dangerous indisposition of the first Clerk, whose life was for some time despaired of, and whose duties have in part devolved upon myself.—To which may be added a resolution of the republican officers of this State, to suffer no arreages of business to accrue in their offices during the administration of Govr. McKean, which would be unavoidable in mine should I be absent before the first clerk is able to attend to his duty.—From this I would not wish it to be inferred that I have any desire to retain the map and remarks till I go to Washington myself,—on the contrary I am anxious to have them forwarded as soon as possible;—but from the size of the map, being upwards of six feet north, and south, and the same east and west, I fear it would be difficult to find a person willing to take charge of it,[1] unless it was made his perticular business.—If therefore any person in the employ of the United States, who might be going on to the seat of government[2] thro this place, and directed by either of the departments to[3] receive the Chart, and remarks, they shall be delivered to him.—

Every leisure hour which I can spare from the labourious duties of a complicated, and intricate office, I am devoting to the arrangement of my journal, and other papers for publication.—

With sentiments of the most perfect respect, and esteem I am sir your Hbl. Servt.   ANDW; ELLICOTT

RC (DLC); at foot of text: "Thos. Jefferson President of the U.S. and of the American Philosophical Society"; endorsed by TJ as received 14 Oct. and so recorded in SJL. Enclosure: Robert Patterson and Andrew Ellicott, "Observations made on a Lunar Eclipse at the Observatory in the City of Philadelphia on the 21st, of September 1801," a brief report on the time when total darkness ended during the eclipse; read at a meeting of the APS on 18 Dec. 1801 and referred to a committee (APS, *Proceedings*, 22, pt. 3 [1884], 319); printed in APS, *Transactions*, 6 (1809), 59.

OFFICE: Ellicott had become secretary of the Pennsylvania Land Office in Lancaster, succeeding Tench Coxe in that position. In the summer of 1801, Ellicott declined an offer from TJ to be surveyor general of the U.S., a job that would have required him to move nearer to the western territories and carried, in Ellicott's opinion, other disadvantages (Mathews, *Ellicott*, 204-6; Rowe, *McKean*, 344).

[1] MS: "take charge it."
[2] MS: "seat government."
[3] Ellicott here canceled "take charge of it."

From John Coakley Lettsom

London Oct. 10. 1801.

Although unknown to the President of the United States of America, I could not be ignorant of his high character, even before Dr. Thornton introduced it to me; and from his account of the President's condescension, as well as of his love to, and encouragement of, the Arts, I am induced to request his acceptance of a performance, which I have printed with a view to promote a practice of great national importance; and, which of course, is patronized[1] by the distinguished character addressed by   JOHN COAKLEY LETTSOM

RC (DLC); endorsed by TJ as received 6 Feb. 1802 and so recorded in SJL. Enclosure: John Coakley Lettsom, *Observations on the Cow-Pock* (London, 1801; Sowerby, No. 949).

Physician and philanthropist John Coakley Lettsom (1744-1815) was educated in England and at the universities of Edinburgh and Leiden. In addition to having a successful medical practice in London, Lettsom was a prolific author and promoter of institutions for the improvement of public health and education. Benjamin Waterhouse credited

Lettsom, a supporter of vaccination, for sending to him a copy of Edward Jenner's *Inquiry into the Causes and Effects of the Variolæ Vaccinæ, a Disease . . . Known by the Name of the Cow Pox*, published in London in 1798 (DNB; Waterhouse, *A Prospect of Exterminating the Small-Pox* [Cambridge, 1800], 3).

DR. THORNTON: William Thornton was a friend and relative of Lettsom's. Both were born into Quaker families in the British Virgin Islands (Harris, *Thornton*, 1:xxxv, xxxix).

[1] MS: "pratronized."

From the Philadelphia Chamber of Commerce

Philadelphia, 10 October 1801. The memorial of the Chamber of Commerce represents that ships "cruizing under Spanish Colors" threaten the extinction of American trade with Mediterranean ports. According to recent information, a number of American-owned ships have been captured and taken into the port of Algeciras, including three vessels from Philadelphia and one from Baltimore with a combined value of more than $400,000. Even if the courts free the ships, the captors have taken "a considerable amount" of property from the vessels and "grossly abused and ill-treated" the crews and passengers. Americans do little trade at Gibraltar, but the United States has advised the masters of merchant vessels to assemble at that port to sail in convoy under protection from "the Barbary Corsairs." The merchants of Philadelphia have received no notice of a blockade of Gibraltar "as is usually given, by Nations acting with good faith to each other." Ships that do not put into that port except in distress or to meet their convoys, and which have "fair & clear" papers, should not be molested. The merchants hope that the president "will take such Measures thereon, as the nature and Importance of the Case, may, in his opinion, require."

RC (DNA: RG 76, Claims against Spain); 4 p.; at head of text: "To Thomas Jefferson, President of the United States"; in a clerk's hand, signed by Thomas FitzSimons as president of the Chamber of Commerce. Tr (DNA: RG 233, PM, 7th Cong., 1st sess.); in a clerk's hand; ASP, *Foreign Relations*, 2:441. Enclosed in a letter from FitzSimons to Madison, 10 Oct. 1801, discussing the problems caused by the seizures of American ships; FitzSimons enclosed letters from owners of captured vessels and asked Madison to bring the papers to TJ's attention (Madison, *Papers, Sec. of State Ser.*, 2:168-9).

To Samuel Smith

Dear Sir   Washington Oct. 10. 1801

Your favor of the 7th: came to hand last night. I do not recollect having recieved advice of any books delivered Capt. Rogers for me. if you have no other way of discovering for whom they are, I should think you had better open them, & a [very superficial] note of the contents would satisfy me whether they were intended for me. if they are they should come here. the two former boxes you were so kind as to forward [were], one of them for the Secretary of states office, containing a model of a ship with some nautical improvement: the other from a friend containing a model of one of the Pyramids of Egypt.

Mr. Glendye will probably be with you in a very few days. if he can enter into competition *on equal terms* with any clergyman whatever, I have no doubt of the issue. a man rarely sees as eloquent a preacher twice in his life.

With respect to the present of hock from mr Wichelhauser. I pray you to make my [excuses] to him on the general rule that I accept presents while in public office from nobody. I would wish this to be stated to him so as to give no offence, & that you will dispose of the wine for his benefit or by his order.

I some time ago recieved a letter from you proposing mr Dent for one of the offices soon to become vacant. I have the highest regard for mr Dent, and should shew it in any case where it was admissible. but the fact is that Maryland as well as Virginia has such an overproportion of the general offices that on the just principle of distribution, it is impossible that any person of either [of] those States can be appointed. the present state of the offices, with respect to distribution, gives me great uneasiness, & anxiety to advance towards something like equilibrium. it is true at the same time that but one officer in either state is of my appointment, to wit, the Secretaries of state & navy, in which appointments peculiar indulgence is a right.   Accept my sincere esteem & attachment.

Th: Jefferson

PrC (DLC); faint; at foot of text: "Genl. Saml. Smith"; endorsed by TJ in ink on verso.

Since the MODEL OF A SHIP went to the State Department, it was probably associated with a patent application. The MODEL OF ONE OF THE PYRAMIDS was sent by Volney to TJ; see Volney's letter of 25 June 1801.

Smith's letter concerning George DENT was that of 15 Sep.

From Dr. John Vaughan

Esteemed Sir,   Wilmington October 10th 1801.

The anxieties expressed, in your much valued favour of the 17th. of July, for our political welfare, induce me to assume the privilege & enjoy the pleasure of informing you, that we have succeeded in electing a republican Governor: but, we have lost the Legislature, &, of course, the choice of a federal senator. As it respects our local politics, the great point is gained. If we had succeeded in the Legislature & lost the Governor, we should have reverted to our old condition in another year. Now, Delaware may be classed among the *republics* of America—toryism has received its death-wound. Some of the infuriate partizans observed during the contest—"That if we failed we would persevere, but, if they failed, they were *dead* & *d—d*"!

You, Sir, would be greatly astonished, if informed of the manoeuvres & pitiful artifices employed by the expiring faction to preserve the tyranny of this state—forgery, fabrication, bribery & every species of seduction ever tried, in the last struggle for life. But, the great desideratum in their electioneering distress, was to divide the republican interest & destroy the system adopted for promoting free inquiry & arousing the people to a sense of their condition: and when they conceived the foundation of this grand overture to be laid (by the temporary dissention of which you are informed) they met on the first of August in grand conclave & vowed eternal hostility to the present national administration, with as much fervour, as the fallen angels abjured their allegiance to heaven; & like their infuriate predecessors, exerted their evil genius to devise new plans for disturbing the public peace & abridging their misfortunes; by perpetuating the vestige of federalism in Delaware—For a short time the republican spirit of this county appeared to be paralysed—the exfederalists became more clamorous every day—the forced combination of republicans, or rather deluded association, was dissolved; the individuals of which began to suspect each other, & the leading partizans of the federalists began to triumph[1] in our dissention. During this transition of things, a number of honest men who had been duped into an acquiescence in the late proceedings, discovered their delusion, & acknowleged they were deceived & willing to make retribution—but the evil was done—it could not be recalled, & as jealousies of this sort usually cease when passion subsides, it wore out in the course of incidental events. Social harmony succeeded & political concert took place by such imperceptible degrees, that our opponents did not perceive it until we were in complete co-operation. Being in possession of some important documents respecting the official conduct of Govr. Bassatt, including his inconsistent & tyrannical disposal of the office of sheriff, I published them at this juncture—it was a dispassionate appeal to the understandings of the people, under the signature of the disappointed candidate. The effect was more happy than could have been anticipated—the people aroused into immediate action against the common enemy, & previous jealousies were forgotten. The exfedt. now became alarmed, & Bayard, chief justice Johns, & the whole host of federal lawyers set out to convoke meetings of the people & harrangue them into their measures—but they were foiled—we opposed them on every occasion & out-reasoned & out-numbered them. Mr. Read, our District Attorny, came forward & shewed himself the avowed, but calm & firm advocate of republicanism.—We had the largest election that has been for many years, & tho at the previous election Bassatt had a majority of 18 votes in this county, Hall had, this year a majority of 783, over Mitchel his fedl. antagonist. This number was barely sufficient. In Sussex Mitchel had a majority of 704, & in Kent 60, leaving Hall but 19 of an ultimate majority out of 7,000 votes.

I hope this detail of [circum]stances will not be altogether uninteresting to you, & that [you] will excuse my prolixity, as it is probably the last time I shall take the liberty of addressing you.—Cicero says, there are certain times & certain occasions which privilege a man to speak of himself, & I think the situation in which I was lately placed was one of those. There are few, if any, individuals in my condition of life that have shared more liberaly of federal[2] persecution than I have done; but I disregard all, save the unwarrantable attack lately made in the disguise of republicanism. However, for the sake of the republican character, I shall submit to time & the ordinary course of events—justice will unfold itself sooner or later: But I shall endeavour to secure myself in future, by renouncing every thing like popular agency in politics, & confine myself to the exercise of my professional functions & those individual duties, which no wish of mine, no art of *theirs*, can absolve me from.

If the representations lately made to you thro & by the late association should unfortunately have left any unfavourable impressions on your mind, respecting my conduct, I beg, most earnestly, to have an opportunity of removing them. My fellow citizens are now doing me justice, & my final wish is—to know you to be satisfied. Be pleased to accept the homage of my esteem & devotion thro life—

JOHN VAUGHAN.

RC (DLC); torn at seal; addressed: "Thomas Jefferson President U.S. America"; also on address sheet in Vaughan's hand: "Mr. Patterson"; endorsed by TJ as received 14 Oct. and so recorded in SJL.

WE HAVE SUCCEEDED IN ELECTING A REPUBLICAN GOVERNOR: Republican nominee David Hall of Lewes, a veteran officer from the Delaware Regiment in the Revolutionary War, was opposed by the Federalist Nathaniel Mitchell, a professed deist. The Federalist majorities in Kent and Sussex counties were not large enough to overcome Hall's margin of 783 in New Castle. Hall was elected on 6 Oct. by a plurality of 18 votes. The Federalists contested the narrow Republican victory, and more than 700 petitioners requested that the legislature investigate the legality of the balloting. The Federalists, who continued to maintain control of the legislature, ultimately dropped the battle and the first Republican governor in the state was inaugurated in 1802 (John A. Munroe, *Federalist Delaware 1775-1815* [New Brunswick, N.J., 1954], 209-10; Wilmington *Mirror of the Times*, 10, 24 Oct.; Vol. 33:629).

DISPOSAL OF THE OFFICE OF SHERIFF: by law, every three years the Delaware governor chose a county sheriff from the two candidates selected by popular vote. Former governor Richard Bassett received criticism for trying to maintain Federalist supremacy in his appointment of Joseph Israel over Charles Anderson, the popular choice for sheriff. A handbill circulating prior to the state election quoted from a letter threatening Israel in the execution of his duties as presiding officer of county elections. Israel promised to discover the identity of the author and expressed confidence that the people of New Castle County would defend him against the hand of an assassin (Munroe, *Federalist Delaware*, 196-7; Wilmington *Mirror of the Times*, 19, 23, 30 Sep.; *Gazette of the United States*, 3 Oct.; Vol. 32:442-3).

CERTAIN OCCASIONS WHICH PRIVILEGE A MAN TO SPEAK OF HIMSELF: Vaughan may be referring to Cicero's *De Senectute* (On Old Age), which, loosely translated, would read, "I need say nothing of myself in this connexion, though to do so is an old man's privilege and permitted to one of my age" (Marcus Tullius Cicero, *Cicero: De Senectute, De Amicitia, De Divinatione*, trans. William A. Falconer [Cambridge, Mass., 1964], 39).

¹ MS: "Triump."
² Deleted: "abuse."

To Enoch Edwards

DEAR SIR   Washington Oct. 11. 1801.

On my return to this place I found my chariot arrived in perfect good order. it is in every respect exactly the thing I wished for, as great as it can possibly be without any tawdriness; and all the work to appearance good, substantial & well finished. I cannot be too thankful to you for the trouble you have been so good as to take in it. this letter will probably be handed you by mr Barnes. his business here has retarded his departure much beyond what we had expected. it is probable he will do himself the pleasure of waiting on you at Frankford. the other commission with which I had threatened mrs Edwards and yourself will possibly be for the next spring only. bc pleased to present her my respectful compliments, & accept yourself my best wishes and friendly esteem   TH: JEFFERSON

PrC (DLC); at foot of text: "Doctr Edwards"; endorsed by TJ in ink on verso.

From Edward Gantt

DEAR SIR   Octr. 11th. 1801

You mentioned toDay that you had furnished Mr. Smith with Dr. Jenner's Observations on the Origen of the Vaccine Virus. As Doctr. Mitchell requests in the inclosed, that You may be informed that the Virus may be obtained in this Country, I have sent you his Memorandum; which perhaps you may think a necessary Communication, to accompany what may be inserted in the Washington Intelligencer.

I am Sir Your most obedt. Servt   EDWD. GANTT

RC (DLC); endorsed by TJ as received 1 Oct. but recorded in SJL at 10 Oct. Enclosure: "Memorandum on the Vaccine Disease" by Samuel Latham Mitchill, sent from New York and dated 2 Aug. 1801, which concludes, "Dr. Mitchill wishes the President of the U.S. to be informed, that he has correct information that the Vaccine Poison has been discovered both at Danbury in Connecticut and Sheffield in Massachusetts among the Cows of this Country. The mode of obtaining and perpetuating it will therefore be speedily established so as to render its' importation from Europe unnecessary" (MS in same; entirely in Mitchill's hand; addressed on verso: "Dr. Bainbridge").

The following day, Samuel Harrison SMITH reprinted in the *National Intelligencer* Edward JENNER's pamphlet, *The Origin of the Vaccine Inoculation*, which had been published in London the previous May. Smith did not print Mitchill's memorandum (Richard B. Fisher, *Edward Jenner 1749-1823* [London, 1991], 113).

Gantt probably obtained Mitchill's memorandum as part of the communication from Absalom Bainbridge to TJ of 20 Aug. (see Edward Gantt to TJ, 17 Aug.).

From Charles Willson Peale

DEAR SIR   Museum Octr 11th. 1801.

Your favour of the 29th. July I did not receive until I had reached the place of bones, when I should have been pleased to have answered it, had it been possible or proper to have taken my attentions from engagments so earnest & constant. The use of a powerful Pump might have saved me 50 or 60 Dollars expence, but perhaps the obligation to return one belonging to the Public in a limited time, might not have been altogather convenient—for, contrary to my expectation my stay was longer, and labours much greater than I had contemplated when I planed the Journey. Accept my thanks for your intention to serve me, and permit me to give a short account of my progress and success.

I carried with me up the north river one common Pump and contemplated getting others, or devising such other means, on a review of the grounds ajacent to the Morass, as might then appear best.

The field bordering on the Morass where the Bones were found, being covered with Grain on my former Visit, prevented me from seeing a Bason which seemed to be formed exactly for my purpose; Sufficiently large to receive all the water in the ponds where the Bones lay, not more than 100 feet distant. When I ascended a nole of the stubble field and discovered the Bason, The Idea instantly occured of a chain of Buckets carried round an axis, pouring the lifted Water into a Trough communicating to the Bason.

The Power of raising the weight of which, Obtained by a wheel of 20 feet diameter, of a width for men to walk within, as a Squirril in a Cage.[1]

This design was soon executed in the simplest manner, the Buckets made of boards nailed togather, suspended between two ropes tyed into a great number of knots, to prevent their sliping in the Pully—a strong Rope served as a band to drive the axis, for carrying the Buckets. This[2] Machinery, when mooved by 2 or 3 men walking slowly, raised, according to a moderate calculation, 1440 Gallons of Water every hour, and thus I was enabled to emty the Ponds and keep them free of Water, while the men remooved the Mud.

This we conceived was an important object, as the Water came from powerful springs, so intensely cold, as rendered it almost impossible for men to bear the effect of it for any length of time.

Having accomplished this part of the labour, we supposed on remooving the Mud and uncovering the Bones, we should see how they lay, and take them up leisurely—however the task was not so easy, and other difficulties came upon us; the banks, after the support of the Water was remooved, cracked and mooved forward, and obliged us to drive Piles &c.

The obtaining all the bones belonging to one Animal was an important object and therefore I neither spared labour nor expence, yet the great debth of the Morass, with a bottom descending in an Angle of 45 degrees, some of the large Bones after being disjointed by the farmers when they made their rude attemps to pull them up, have as I suppose slid forward into the deep parts of the Morass—for I could not get the second Tusk and a *Femur*. Yet I was so fortunate as to find so many pieces of the Tusk which was broken and part of it taken up before, that the size and form is accurately assertained—the length nearly eleven feet, very much curved; nearly to a semi-circle, with a moderate spiral—The form beautiful as infinite varied circles & spirals can make it. Although I could not get all the Bones of the feet, yet with the number in possession, and carving some counter parts, I have now nearly compleated them before and behind—by which a knowledge of its feet is now obtained. Several pieces which I got of the under Jaw, prooved that it[3] was broken so much as to loose its Value, and although I got many pieces of the upper head, and shall put all togather in the most careful manner, yet the form of the skull will be deficient. I obtained a part of the *Sternum* or breast bone; all the Vertebraes, and part of the *os Sacrum*, all the ribs—a *Tibia* & *fibula* or lower part of the hind leggs which was wanting before—besides many small pieces of bones, which carfully put togather, with some inconsiderable additions of Carved pieces, will render this a tolerable compleat Skeleton. Being disappointed of getting all I wanted of this first Skeleton, I determined to try some other morasses, where some few bones had before been found, I went to[4] a Morass 16 miles distant, from this, only three Ribs had been taken up—Here I obtained 43 bones of the feet, 10 tail bones, 2 Tusks, many Ribs, some Vertebres, and a Blade bone.

I found these bones scattered in every direction, and some of them buried between large stones, & even under them, tho' the Stones that covered them were not large. After diging about 40 feet square, and spending about 8 or 9 days of several mens labour—I went to another Morass, 5 miles furthur where several bones had been taken up—but as no part of the Head had been found, my hopes were particularly to obtain that part. Here I found the Bones more scattered than at the last place—This part of the Morass was not so deep as those I had explored before. After finding a number of ribs and some few bones of the feet—and having dug up manure to a very considerable distance round, in the moment when dispairing of getting any more bones, and thinking to discharge the labourers—By means of a spear which we used, we luckily discovered other Bones—which uncovered prooved to be a fore leg, beneath which was an intire under Jaw not a part deficient, except one of the lesser grinders, which appears to have been lost while the Animal lived. here also we found part of a foot. from this spot to where we found the heal of the hind foot measured 82 feet. After exploring in every direction, at last found the upper head, but in such total decay, that no part would hold togather except the enamel of the Grinders, and that part which joins the neck. The place the Skull once occupied appeared to be a little blacker than other parts of the mud—The *form* in part was discoverable, although all was converted into manure—yet it would seperate & shew the rounded parts.

All the Morasses where these Bones have been found, have marly Bottoms. Bones found in the whitest shell-marle, are most perfect, those parts found in a bluesh coloured marle, less so, and bones found in the black marles, generally in total decay.

The experience I have had, enables me to judge with certainty; several bones we have found, exhibits these facts in the clearest point of view. The Shell-marle it is probable possesses much anticeptic qualities—The Spring water is also essential to the preservation of the bones—I have brought specimens of the several strata where these Bones are found, and Doctr Woodhouse has promised to analize them for me.

When I undertook this journey, I was under considerable apprehension of subjecting myself to putrid or bilious fever—by exposing to a hot Sun, a great quantity of rotten Vegetables, also with the addition of much stagnant Water—and although the weather was extremely hot, and some of the morasses and Ponds were surrounded by woods that prevented the passage of the winds, yet we enjoyed good health, perhaps the precautions I used in a great measure guarded our health— but I am much inclined to beleive, that those morasses are not so unhealthy as many people have immagined—For many Gentlemen of that Country marveled how I could enjoy health undergoing such fateague. The Bones found in that country are not petrefied like many found on the ohio, yet in the vicinity of those morasses we found immense quantities of Petrefactions of Shells and even nuts—and what I thought extraordinary near the last place we explored, we found a considerable quantity of petrefied corals, some of which are large. I do not find any Saltness in the taste of substances found in these morasses, but on the contrary, the Water which we took from the Springs was the most pure and agreable that I ever meet with; it was so clear as not to impede the sight of the bottom of the deepest Vessel that held it.

When we take a view of the mountains through which the north River passes, the Idea naturally occurs, that probably once those waters were damed up by those Mountains, and thuse formed a great Lake from thence to the Shawangunk mountain, such I find has been the oppinion of many.

As my wheel buckets and other Machinery excited the curiosity of all the people of that part of the country, I was visited by crouds of all sexes and ages. Among the croud one day I observed a venerable old man, upon enquiry I found he was a native & Inhabitant of the neighbourhood, that he was also inteligent, and a man of[5] veracity—He told me that he was well aquainted with the Indians before they left that part of the Country—That those Indians had a tradition among them, which was particularly told him in 1754 by an Inteligent Indian (John Paulen) about 50 or 60 years of age—That formerly the whole of the land between the Shawangunt mountain and the north River, was covered with Water, that when the water subsided, it left large Ponds in many places, and that these Ponds gradually dried up and became morasses. The general appearance of the lands in the neighbourhood of these morasses favour such an opinion, they are in small round hills, as if thrown into those forms by the agitation of Waters.

But to leave conjectures, and return to the Bones, The quantity we collected at the two last explored Morasses, with those that had been before taken, which we have also obtained, will enable my son Rembrandt by the aid of his Chizil to carve in wood all the deficiences in order to compleat a second Skeleton, with which he hopes to pay his expences of traveling into Europe. He has long wished to improve his talents in painting, and I am happy to have it in[6] my power to aid him, more especially as by the Exhibition of it, there is a chance of his making something handsome and at the same time to make an exchange of the duplicate subjects I possess, for those of Europe, yet wanting in my Museum, besides settling a good and sure correspondence for a reciprocal exchange of Natural Subjects—It is supposed that a great deal of money may be made in London & Paris with such a Skeleton, but I am taught not to be so sanguine in my expectations—If he can meet all his expences, and take the Portraits of distinguished charactors in the large Cities of Europe, and gain more knowledge with a small addition to his Purse, it will be well. The first Skeleton might soon be erected in the Museum, but the necessity of keeping it apart until my Son has made up the deficiences of the 2d Skeleton, will be a cause of some delay.

Doctr Wistar has been so obliging as to aid me with his knowledge in the disposition of the bones, and he is now determining the enalegy of the feet of this Animal & the Elephant.

Having now given a detail of what I conceive to be the most interesting on this occasion, I shall only add, that it is my intention to explore other places, as soon as I have leisure, and season and opportunity shall be most favorable. Having borrowed some money from the Philosophical Society, which with what I collected elsewhere, was sufficient to pay all my expences, this I am fully satisfied, will be returned to me as soon as the exhibition of this Skeleton is opened, when I shall be enabled to fulfill all my engagments. Therefore with the present prospect it is not necessary to gain other pecuniary aid— my Museum under its present Visitations, supplies the common exigences of the family, and a little more by our frugality, to enable me to pursue some of my plans of improvements that are not very expensive, therefore permit me to return you my most cordial thanks for your kind intention of serving your much obliged friend and Humble Servant   C W PEALE

PS. Having made a Petition to Spain, some months ago, for liberty to collect subjects of Natural History in South America. The Spanish Minister called on me yesterday, to inform me that he had his orders to permit me to explore *all South America*, and also to defray the expence of Cariage of those articles intended for the Cabinet of Madrid.[7]

RC (DLC); lacks last page, containing final words of text (see note 7 below); endorsed by TJ as received 15 Oct. and so recorded in SJL. Dft (Lb in PPAmP: Peale-Sellers Papers).

TJ's letter of 29 July had offered to loan Peale a PUMP from the navy and tents from the War Department. Peale borrowed a pump from a ship chandler as he passed through New York City on his way up the Hudson (or NORTH RIVER) to Newburgh. In June, he had purchased the mastodon bones found in the MORASS on John Masten's farm at Shawangunk, along with the right to look for more of the skeleton. Early in August he had a millwright build the large WHEEL at Masten's. People walking inside the wheel powered a chain of buckets to lift water out of the pit. Peale hired 25 laborers for the work at Masten's farm, and most of their effort was spent on drainage and shoring up the collapsing mud walls of the excavation. When he decided that digging there was no longer productive, Peale excavated at two other locations in the area. One was the MORASS 16 MILES DISTANT—actually 11 miles from Masten's, according to Peale's diary and his son's account—on a farm owned by Joseph Barber. Five miles beyond Barber's was the third site worked by Peale, a place where Peter

Millspaw had found bones a few years before. It was at Millspaw's that Peale's helpers successfully probed the ground with a rod or SPEAR. At the second and third morasses, as at Masten's farm, the initial task was to remove water from marl pits or other low areas to begin the search for more mastodon remains, which were usually discovered in that region when farm workers dug out shell marl for fertilizer (the "manure" of Peale's letter above). Peale hired fewer workers at Barber's and Millspaw's farms than at Shawangunk and did not need a large treadmill wheel at either of those locations. Peale and his son Rembrandt also visited other morasses where mastodon remains had been found, but the Peales only conducted their own drainage and excavation operations at Masten's, Barber's, and Millspaw's (Peale, *Papers*, v. 2, pt. 1:351, 354, 356-69, 550-7; Peale to TJ, 29 June, 24 July 1801).

When Peale traveled from Philadelphia late in July to begin work at Shawangunk, James WOODHOUSE accompanied him. Woodhouse was interested in scientific research and had sent TJ, in April, one of Georges Cuvier's scholarly papers on paleontology (Peale, *Papers*, v. 2, pt. 1:350; Vol. 33:647-8).

VENERABLE OLD MAN: Peale's informant was William Graham, who had lived his entire life in the vicinity of Shawangunk (Peale, *Papers*, v. 2, pt. 1:365).

For the loan from the American PHILOSOPHICAL SOCIETY, see Peale to TJ, 24 July 1801. The Peales used wood and papier-mâché to reproduce missing elements from the Shawangunk skeleton and mounted it in the APS's Philosophical Hall in Philadelphia, where Peale also had his museum. Opening the "Mammoth" exhibit on 24 Dec. 1801, Peale charged 50 cents to see the skeleton. It brought in more than $7,000 in admissions from 1802 to 1811 in addition to the museum's separate admissions revenue. Peale estimated the cost of acquiring and mounting the two skeletons to be $2,000. His sons Rembrandt and Rubens exhibited the second skeleton in New York and then took it to Britain. The renewal of war between Britain and France in 1803 prohibited them from taking the bones to the Continent, and they returned with the skeleton to the United States (Peale, *Papers*, v. 2, pt. 1:376, 378; Charles Coleman Sellers, *Mr. Peale's Museum: Charles Willson Peale and the First Popular Museum of Natural Science and Art* [New York, 1980], 142-7, 156-7; Paul Semonin, *American Monster: How the Nation's First Prehistoric Creature Became a Symbol of National Identity* [New York, 2000], 328-40).

PETITION TO SPAIN: through Carlos Martínez de Irujo, Peale had requested permission to go to South America to collect natural history specimens. He offered to send duplicate specimens to the royal CABINET or collection of natural history in Spain. Earlier, TJ had put Peale in contact with Louis of Parma, a son-in-law of the king of Spain who had sought to augment the Spanish collections (Peale, *Papers*, v. 2, pt. 1:376n; Vol. 28:517-18; Vol. 29:121, 136, 286-7, 389-91; Vol. 30:232-4; Vol. 31:61-2).

[1] Peale first wrote "as Squirrils in Cages" before altering the phrase to read as above. Dft: "as Squirrils moove in Cages."

[2] Here in Dft Peale canceled "Simple rough made."

[3] MS: "is."

[4] Here in Dft Peale canceled "Captain Barbers."

[5] Word omitted in MS, supplied from Dft.

[6] Word omitted in MS, supplied from Dft.

[7] Preceding two words and period supplied from Dft. RC ends with "Cabinet," positioned as a catchword at the foot of the page. Alongside it TJ wrote "Cabinet of Madrid." It seems likely that Peale finished the sentence with those three words on another page, and that TJ took that sheet for another use.

To Joseph Rapin

DEAR SIR   Washington Oct. 11. 1801.

On my arrival here I recieved your account: which I found to be all perfectly right & just, and mr Barnes, who is now going on to Philadelphia will pay you the balance. it is my duty to declare to you that I have been entirely satisfied with the integrity, diligence and skill, with which you have conducted yourself in my service, and that I very much regretted the circumstances which obliged you to leave me; however if they were for your benefit it will be a consolation, as I shall be happy always to hear of your success in life. mr LeMaire conducts himself & my affairs here extremely well, and I am in hopes we shall be perfectly satisfied with each other. accept my best wishes for your prosperity and happiness and assurances of my esteem & attachment. Th: Jefferson

PrC (MHi); at foot of text: "M. Rapin"; endorsed by TJ in ink on verso.

YOUR ACCOUNT: on 5 Oct., after reviewing the "accounts left by Rapin" as steward of the President's House, TJ asked John BARNES to pay Rapin $286.98. That amount included $68.74 for household expenses in the period 26-31 July; $150.21 for household expenses, 1 Aug. to 6 Sep.; $32 for the expenses of Rapin's trip to Philadelphia and back; $13.45 "for tinning vessels"; and $22.58 paid to George Gilpin for the items sent by Tobias Lear (MB, 2:1054).

On 5 Oct., TJ also wrote an order on Barnes to pay $376.17 to Étienne LEMAIRE, Rapin's successor as steward. That sum, according to the "Analysis" or summary that TJ recorded in his financial memoranda, included £6.15.0 for Lemaire's journey from Philadelphia and £4.15.0 for articles he obtained in that city, plus weekly household expenditures at the President's House from 6 Sep. to 3 Oct., for a total of £85.4.6 or $227.17. The payment to Lemaire on 5 Oct. also included $139 for wages of the household staff, including the steward, from 4 Sep. to 4 Oct., and $10 for Lemaire's wages from 25 Aug. to 4 Sep. On 11 Oct., TJ gave Lemaire another order on Barnes for $51.66 (which TJ also rendered as £19.7.5) for expenditures during the week of 4-10 Oct., consisting of $48.66 for provisions, $2 for servants' clothes, and $1 for "Miscellanies." In his financial memoranda, TJ divided the cost of that week's provisions by 34, which was apparently the number of main meals served at the President's House during the week. By his calculation, the cost per dinner was $1.43 (MB, 2:1053-5).

From Anthony Campbell

SIR   No. 297 Arch Street Philadelphia October 12, 1801

I am sorry a combination of circumstances, which I neither could foresee nor expect compels me to address you; but I feel convinced, when you are informed, that necessity and self defence urge the measure, you will excuse the liberty. Had my communications to Mr Gallatin upon an interesting subject, been treated with that politeness and attention, which from his character, I had a right to expect, I most certainly would not have troubled you.

It is painful for me to relate after upwards of sixteen months disappointments and difficulties, that the exposition of the defalcations and peculations which took place under the former administration originated with me. As a clerk in the office of the Auditor of the Treasury of the United States; on a review of the different accounts presented for adjustment, but particularly those of a Messrs. Pickering and Dayton, I felt that indignation which I suppose every honest man does, on becomeing acquainted with a breach of trust, either public or private.—not bound by oath of office, or any other moral obligation to secresy, I did consider it an imperious duty to make the

people of the United States acquainted with the fraudulent conduct
of their agents. Accordingly early in the month of June 1800, I called
on Mr Isreal Isreal, and informed him that I was in possession of information, which I intended to publish, and I trusted the publication
would be the happy means of turning the current of public opinion,
against a party whose measures were in open hostility, against republicanism, and whose removal from power was my most ardent
wish. I then handed him six copies of the accounts of Mr Pickering,
in whose hands at that time, an unaccounted[1] balance of upwards of
half a million of dollars remained, and one copy of the account of Mr
Dayton, as agent for paying the compensation due to members of the
house of representatives, upon which, at that time, a large unaccounted balance remained in his hands from different sessions of
Congress. I requested the editor of the Aurora might be sent for;
consequently, that afternoon, an interview took place, when the aforesaid seven copies of the Auditor's reports on the accounts of Messrs.
Pickering and Dayton, were put in the hands of Mr Duane, for the
purpose of publication. Soon after this part of the transaction, in consequence of the removal of government to Washington, all the clerks,
another and myself excepted, were sent to that place. At that time of
almost general suspension of public bussiness, I had more leisure
than usual, which I employed taking cursory reviews of the accounts
of individuals in public service, and found that delinquints were
numerous, and consisted of influential characters in the departments
of finance.

Some doubts remaining on the mind of Mr Isreal, as to the authenticity of the reports, on the accounts of Pickering and Dayton, and
being apprehensive, that Mr Duane, might be led into error by publishing them, in order to do away every doubt, and to be able by respectable testimony to refute all attempts that might be made to
invalidate the intended publications, I did voluntarily, and without
the previous knowledge of any person whatever, convey the Book containing these accounts to Mr Isreal's house, where in the presence of
John Beckly, Isreal Isreal, Saml. Isreal, auctioneer, William Duane,
and myself, the former copies were compared, and others equally as
important were taken off, part of which were afterwards published in
the Aurora.—

Previous to the publications appearing, hints and queries were inserted in the Aurora, relative to public defaulters; which alarmed
those of the party acquainted with the nefarious measures pursued,
and as the accounts had lately been transmitted from the auditor's

office, I miraculously being the only Jacobin acquainted with any part of them, was immediately suspected. Two confidential persons belonging to the Departments of State & Treasury, waited on me, and offered bribes for supressing the publication of the Accounts of Mr Pickering, which I did not accept. I was soon after dismissed from the office!

During the agitation and discussions produced by those publications in the Aurora, American Citizen &c &c, and the fortunate change that consequently took place in the public mind, some claimed the merit, while I remained silent, and was sacrificed. But, Sir, I solemnly assure you no other person had any share in exposeing those delinquincies, but myself, except some assistance afforded me by William P. Gardner, an honest man, and a genuine republican, then a Clerk in the Auditor's office. For the truth of this assertion, I refer to Mr Gallatin, having sent him certificates to substantiate that fact, and to prove the rectitude of my moral character, some time ago.

It is not the neglect I have experienced, nor the sacrifices I have made that grieve me, but an unworthy attempt to cast an odium on my moral character. Whence has this arisen? Surely no republican will say that exposeing, the delinquincies of Federalist is a breach of moral duty. I was bound to no secresy,—I took no oath on admission as a Clerk into the auditor's office but simply to support the constitution of the United States. If the obtainment of wealth had been my governing principle, I might to day be in easy circumstances. Had I concealed the delinquincies of those who made an improper use of the public money, I most certainly would have considered it a crime against the state.

The cruelty of the Federalists, the neglect and injustice of the Republicans, and the state of my finances, almost overwhelm me. When it was in my power to obtain a handsome competency by a direliction of principle, I spurned the ignominious bribe; I would spurn it again; Yet where is my reward? Am I to be despised by one party,—and neglected by the other,—to whom I have rendered the most important services. To whom shall I look for the reward of principle; most certainly, Sir, it is to you. I pray pardon my freedom. I feel the injustice I have received, and to whom, in a political view, can I with equal propriety apply as to Mr. Jefferson.

With sentiments of the greatest respect, Sir, I have the honor to be from principle Your most Obedient Servant

ANTHONY CAMPBELL

RC (NHi: Gallatin Papers); addressed: "His Excellency Thomas Jefferson President of the United States"; endorsed by TJ as received 13 Oct. and so recorded in SJL with notation "T."

Forced to leave his native Ireland, Anthony Campbell renewed several acquaintances when he emigrated to the United States and took up residence in Philadelphia. Dr. James Reynolds, local leader of the United Irishmen, and the geographer Joseph Scott both knew his family and him since birth. Campbell probably became a clerk in the auditor's office at the Treasury Department in early 1799. He and fellow clerk William P. Gardner delivered copies of Treasury Department records relating to the accounts of Timothy Pickering, Jonathan Dayton, and others to William Duane, who published them in the *Aurora*, with comments, between 17 June and 15 July 1800. Duane charged that the delinquent accounts indicated that public funds were used for "Private Speculations." According to the auditor, Campbell was officially dismissed as a clerk because he did not move with the department to Washington in the summer of 1800. On 25 Mch. 1802, Dearborn recommended Campbell for a military appointment as ensign in the First Regiment of Infantry. He was promoted to second lieutenant in April 1803 (JEP, 1:415, 457; Philadelphia *Aurora*, 17-18, 20-1, 23 June, 3 July 1800; Kline, *Burr*, 1:458, 530n; Gallatin, *Papers*, 5:708; 6:937; Gallatin to TJ, 14 Sep. 1801; Campbell to TJ, 26 Feb. 1802). For another view of the delivery of the Treasury Department accounts to Duane for publication, see Gardner to TJ, 20 Nov.

COMMUNICATIONS TO MR GALLATIN: Campbell's earliest letter to Gallatin, of 26 May 1801, has not been found. On 4 June, he wrote a short letter to the Treasury secretary from New York, which was carried to Washington by William Few, Gallatin's brother-in-law. Campbell observed that Congressman William Jones, Joseph Clay, and Joseph Scott would provide character references for him, in addition to those already supplied (Gallatin, *Papers*, 5:93). Campbell wrote Gallatin from Philadelphia on 14 July, after "hav-

ing learned that reports were in circulation at Washington, injurious" to his moral character. Describing himself as a "republican and United Irishman," Campbell defended his role in the publication of the Treasury Department accounts, arguing that he considered it "criminal to conceal, and a duty to publish all accurate information that would promote the cause of republicanism, and destroy the influence of the desperate aristocractic faction." Campbell described WILLIAM P. GARDNER as "equally concerned with myself in the aurora Publications" and noted that Doyle Sweeny was the only other Treasury Department clerk who had the courage to defend republican principles (same, 5:374-5).

In a letter to Gallatin dated 20 Sep., Campbell referred to two CERTIFICATES he had recently sent the Treasury secretary. Because Gallatin had not replied to his letters, Campbell feared they had been intercepted by one of his "rancorous enemies in the different departments." Campbell had sent the documents after learning that Gallatin had expressed "unfavorable sentiments" respecting his moral conduct and he argued: "I felt it a duty due to myself to have the false impressions removed from your mind, as well as to refute the Slanders of my enemies, so far as the testimony of many respectable Citizens could have any influence." (Gallatin, *Papers*, 5:768). Israel Israel, James Reynolds, John Beckley, Joseph Scott, William Priestman, James Kerr, and one other Philadelphian signed an affidavit dated 7 Aug., recommending Campbell as always "regular, sober and orderly," with a character that in every respect stood "fair and irreproachable." He was not "guilty of gaming, drinking or Swearing," as was common "to young men in large cities." The signers of the affidavits observed: "his politicks and principles are republican, and we believe that in consequence of them he has been persecuted." Below the signatures, seven others, including John Smith, Michael Leib, William Jones, Mahlon Dickerson, John Shee, and Mathew Carey, wrote and signed short testimonials agreeing with the affidavit (Tr in NHi: Gallatin Papers, certified and signed by Joseph Scott and

William Priestman as a "true copy of the original which we have carefully examined," at foot of text: "Original transmitted to Mr Gallatin Secretary of the Treasury on the 3rd. September 1801"; see Gallatin, *Papers*, 5:518). On 10 Aug., Beckley, Israel Israel, and Samuel Israel signed an affidavit testifying that Campbell was the person who voluntarily made known to them and to William Duane the delinquencies of Pickering, Dayton, and others, whose accounts were published in the *Aurora*. They concluded: "we believe that Mr Campbell in making this communication to us was actuated by a pure regard to the public good, and thereby rendered an essential service to the United States" (Tr in same, certified and signed by Scott and Priestman, at foot of text: "Original transmitted to Albert Gallatin Secretary of the treasury on the 3rd of September 1801"; see Gallatin, *Papers*, 5:527). On 12 Oct., Campbell wrote Gallatin: "As you have not returned my certificates, and having this day written to the President of the United States, in which I referred to them in your possession, I have to request you will be so good as to shew them to him" (same, 5:846).

[1] MS: "uaccounted."

To João, Prince Regent of Portugal

To our Great and Good Friend, His Royal Highness the Prince Regent of Portugal and the two Algarves, on this side and on that of the sea, in Africa of Guinea, and of the conquest, Navigation and Commerce of Æthiopia, Arabia, Persia and of India &ca.

I have received with the deepest concern the letter of your Royal Highness, dated on the 12th of June last, wherein you announce to me the decease of your much beloved son, the most serene Prince of Beira, Don Antonio, which took place on the preceding evening. A Prince who even at his tender years afforded such flattering expectations of future virtues and greatness snatched from the hopes of your Royal Highness and his country, is justly considered as an irreparable bereavement, and claims our sincere sympathy. Whilst under this mournful visitation we mingle our affliction with that of your Royal Family, and the Portuguese nation, we pray you to be assured of the continuance of those friendly sentiments, founded on mutual interest, which have hitherto united the two nations in an harmonious and beneficial intercourse. May the Lord have you, Great and Good Friend, in his most holy keeping.

Written at the City of Washington on this 12th. day of October in the Year of Our Lord One thousand eight hundred & one.

Your Good Friend. TH: JEFFERSON.

FC (Lb in DNA: RG 59, Credences); in a clerk's hand; at head of text: "Thomas Jefferson, President of the U. States of America"; below signature: "By the President" and "James Madison Secy. of State." Enclosed in Madison to the Portuguese minister of foreign affairs, 16 Oct. 1801, asking him to give TJ's letter to the prince regent; the secretary of state for foreign affairs and war was João de Almeida de Mello e Castro, formerly Portugal's minister to Great Britain (Madison, *Papers, Sec. of State Ser.*, 2:179; José Calvet de Magalhães, *História das Relaçoes Diplomáticas entre Portugal e os Estados Unidos da América (1776-1911)* [Mem Martins, Portugal, 1991], 55, 62; A. H. de Oliveira Marques, *História de Portugal*, 13th ed., 3 vols. [Lisbon, 1997-98], 2:464).

João (1767-1826) ruled in the place of his mother, Queen Maria I, who because of mental problems was unable to act as head of state after 1792. João had the title prince regent from 1799 until 1816, when his mother died and he became king. His coronation took place in Brazil, where the royal family migrated upon the invasion of Portugal by France in 1807. Known as João "the Clement," he moved back to Portugal in 1821 (José Correia do Souto, *Dicionário de História de Portugal*, 6 vols. [Lisbon, 1985], 4:78-83; Douglas L. Wheeler, *Historical Dictionary of Portugal* [Metuchen, N.J., 1993], 122-3).

In the LETTER of 12 June 1801, João announced the death of his son António the day before. As João's oldest son, António, who was six years old when he died, had been next in line for the throne after his father and was the PRINCE OF BEIRA. João's letter, addressed to the United States of America rather than to the president or to TJ personally, conveyed an expectation that the U.S. would make a reciprocal expression of sentiment (RC in DNA: RG 59, Ceremonial Letters, addressed: "Aos Estados Unidos da America que muito amo e prezo" ["To the United States of America, which I much

love and esteem"], in Portuguese, in a clerk's hand, signed by João as prince of Brazil and countersigned by Mello e Castro, endorsed by Jacob Wagner; Souto, *Dicionário*, 1:232; 4:83).

João had written again on 4 July 1801, this time to announce the birth of a daughter on that day. The baby received the name Isabel Maria. In the letter, João referred to his wife, Carlota Joaquina, by her title, the princess of Brazil. She was a daughter of King Carlos IV of Spain (RC in DNA: RG 59, Ceremonial Letters, addressed to the United States, in Portuguese, in a clerk's hand, signed by João, countersigned by Mello e Castro, endorsed by Wagner; Souto, *Dicionário*, 2:178-9; 3:310). On 10 Nov. 1801, TJ wrote to acknowledge that letter, "in which you communicate to me the pleasing intelligence, that on the same day your very dear Spouse, the most serene Princess of Brazil, had happily encreased your royal family with another daughter: An event which whilst it fills your paternal heart with joy, confirms the loyal hopes of your subjects, that they will long continue to be governed by the virtues which distinguish your illustrious house, has not failed to excite in us a lively interest. On the auspicious occasion receive our cordial congratulations and at the same time our prayers that the Lord may keep you, Great and Good Friend and your royal Family under his most holy protection" (FC in Lb in DNA: RG 59, Credences; in a clerk's hand, including signatures by TJ and Madison; enclosed in Madison to Mello e Castro, 13 Nov. 1801, requesting him to present the letter to the prince regent "in suitable time" [Madison, *Papers, Sec. of State Ser.*, 2:239]).

From Andrew Marshall

DR. SIR   St Clairsville Octr, 12th. 1801.

It is on a subject of the Utmost Importance, I wish to lay before you, (But I, with many of my fellow Citizens, may[1] Lament my ability) But knowing that a free Goverment is your greatest pleasure I rest ashured that you will be willing to give a hearing to any person,

or thing, that may appear to be of Use to the Community at Large.
I at the present live in an Infant state, Whare I have Not it in my
power to Elect for my states men, which appears to be Universally
Lamented with my self. The people here appears to be Much dissat-
isfyed with the proceedings of Arthur St Clair as a Governor thinking that he rather takes power out of the Lejuslature respecting the
Division of Countys and placing County seats. he has of late, Divided
Jefferson County and placed the seat of Justice at a place Contrary to
the Voice of the people. about one year past the people sent a petition
to him praying the division of the County with about 500 Subscribers, and for the seat of Justice of the new County to be placed at
St Clairsville. but this had no effect. he put it off till there went a petition to him for the seat to be placed on the River Which could not
be done without disoblidgeing a great part of the County, as the river
was the line between Virginia and the new state it throwed the seat
of Justice on an extremity, and back from the place there can be no
settlement nearer than 6 Miles The people after they[2] saw the proclamation drew a remonstrance against his proceedings and out of the
County I believe they will Get three fourths of the free holders to sign
the Remonstrance against the new seat. this is to be laid before him,
and if it has no effect, (as I do not expect it will) what will the Con-
sequenses be. he will not suffer the Lejuslature to do any thing in it
as he says agreeable to the ordinance of Congress the whole power is
invested in him It is not this County alone he has put into Bondage
but several others; Dr. Sir from the regard [. . .] to a Republican
Goverment and the wish to promote peace and Fr[aterni]ty in our Infant Country. I Implore you to lay some Method before us for the
remedy of the bondage We lie Under. I Must say that I am very Jeal-
ous of St Clairs zeal to wards his Country. If there had been no former evidences of this to me and my Country It might perhaps be two
rash an expression.
You do not know me, but I must desire the favour of you to write to
me What would be the most best way for us to get quit of our griev-
eances Whether it would be of any use for us to lay the Busnys before
Congress or not, or what steps might appear most prudent. If it was a
thing Consistent with your will to remove him from his office I think
it would be a pleasing thing to the people he rules over, as I would
hope his Successor would Join in favour of a Republican Goverment
If you think proper to write to me you will please to direct to Andrew
Marshall. Post Master St Clairsville N.W. Territory.
    I am Sir with due Respect your Most obedient and Humble Servant
ANDREW MARSHALL

[443]

RC (ViW); damaged at seal; at foot of text: "Thos Jefferson President of the U States"; endorsed by TJ as received 26 Oct. and so recorded in SJL with notation "S."

Andrew Marshall was the postmaster at St. Clairsville and served as treasurer of Belmont County, Ohio, from 1804 to 1807 (Stets, *Postmasters*, 213; *Inventory of the County Archives of Ohio No. 7. Belmont County (St. Clairsville)* [Columbus, 1942], 296).

PROCEEDINGS OF ARTHUR ST CLAIR: on 7 Sep. 1801, a proclamation by territorial governor Arthur St. Clair created Belmont County from parts of Jefferson and Washington counties in Ohio. Pultney was designated the first county seat, but the site was relocated to St. Clairsville in 1804 (*Inventory of the County Archives of Ohio*, 5).

[1] MS: "Citizen, my."
[2] MS: "the."

From John Thomson Mason

DEAR SIR   George Town 12th Octo 1801

Inclosed I send you an estimate, from one of the Commissioners of the tax, of the taxes paid by that part of the District, which was formerly in the County of Prince Georges, to the State of Maryland.

I have not yet received the estimate for that part of the District which was in Montgomery County. It is prepared and I shall probably get it this week at Annapolis

Your Obedt Servt   J. T. MASON

RC (DNA: RG 59, LAR, 8:0232); frayed; endorsed by TJ as received 12 Oct. and so recorded in SJL; also endorsed by TJ: "[. . .] taxes." Enclosure: Samuel Hepburn to Mason, Upper Marlboro, 18 Aug., answering Mason's request for information on the county taxes for the last year, and enclosing a statement (not found) with "the amount of property now within the District of Columbia, but formerly assessed in this County," and separating the "property within the City from that without, because that within the City paid no part of the tax for building our Court House" (RC in DNA: RG 59, MCL; endorsed by TJ: "Hipburn to J. T. Mason").

COUNTY OF PRINCE GEORGES: Washington County, District of Columbia, included land from Prince George's and Montgomery counties in Maryland. Hepburn wrote from Upper Marlboro, in Prince George's County (see enclosure above). For the taxes formerly imposed by Virginia on Alexandria County, the other part of the District of Columbia, see Francis Peyton to TJ, 30 July.

From John H. Purviance

SIR   Baltimore, October the 12th. 1801.

On my return here a few days ago after an absence of several weeks I was concerned to find that uncertainty as to the package of books which I received from Mr Short had prevented its being sent on as soon as I had directed—I have embraced the earliest opportunity of remedying this delay and I have now the honor to inclose the receit of a waterman who was to deliver it to Rob. Smith Esqr;—that gentleman's absence from Washington will I hope be my apology for troubling you with it.

I beg leave, Sir, to offer you the respectful assurances of my perfect respect & consideration   JOHN H. PURVIANCE

Tr (MHi); in an unidentified hand; at foot of text: "To The President of the United States." Recorded in SJL as received 14 Oct. Enclosure not found.

John H. Purviance (ca. 1772-1820) came from a Baltimore family prominent in shipping, distilling, and privateering. His father, Samuel Purviance, was captured by Indians on the frontier in 1788 and never heard from again. The next year John Purviance applied unsuccessfully to be the surveyor of customs for Baltimore, auditor, or register of the Treasury. In 1791, James McHenry recommended him for the position of comptroller. Purviance's uncle, Baltimore merchant Robert Purviance, and Samuel Smith supported his efforts to find public employment, and the young man became James Monroe's secretary when Monroe was minister to France. Purviance was in France in June 1801, when John Dawson selected him to carry dispatches to the United States on the *Maryland.* Monroe commended Purviance's abilities (see Monroe to TJ, 17 Nov.) and in correspondence with Madison, Monroe deemed Purviance "a man of great & rare merit." Monroe described Purviance as "a meek character," with a "delicate state of health" that imposed some limits on his employment. When Monroe went to London as minister in 1803, Purviance again became his secretary, and early in 1807, after Monroe and William Pinkney had negotiated a treaty with Britain, Purviance was the courier who brought the document to the United States. Later, he was a clerk in the State Department (New York *American,* 10 Nov. 1820; Madison, *Papers, Sec. of State Ser.,* 2:247, 375, 396; 3:10-11; 5:5-7, 535; Ammon, *Monroe,* 143, 196, 233; Washington, *Papers, Pres. Ser.,* 2:332-4; 3:369; W. W. Abbot, Dorothy Twohig, eds., *The Diaries of George Washington,* 6 vols. [Charlottesville, 1976-79], 5:407-8; Jerome R. Garitee, *The Republic's Private Navy: The American Privateering Business as Practiced by Baltimore during the War of 1812* [Middletown, Conn., 1977], 18, 43, 174-5; Gary Lawson Browne, *Baltimore in the Nation, 1789-1861* [Chapel Hill, 1980], 41; Vol. 20:226; William Short to TJ, 9 June 1801; Samuel Smith to TJ, 29 Apr. 1802; TJ to Monroe, 21 Mch. 1807).

William SHORT had not yet advised TJ that he had sent some books to the United States with Purviance; see Short to TJ, 18 Oct. Purviance had written to TJ on 31 Aug., soon after his arrival in the U.S., but that letter has not been found.

From William Fleming

DEAR SIR,   Richmond, 13th Octr. 1801.

I am just returned from Kentucky, and have recd. your favour from Monticello. I cannot at present answer your several queries with the precision I wish, but will endeavour to do so, as soon as I have leisure to examine, and reflect on the subject, more minutely.— From memory I can state that we had a meeting with mr. Skelton a short time before the commencement of the revolutionary war, in order to settle the accounts of my late brother's administration of Jas. Skelton's estate, not in Richmond but, at Mt. Pleasant. That Jerman Baker appeared as counsel for Skelton—that a considerable progress was made in the business, and further proceedings postponed, at the instance of mr. Skelton, who required time to procure certain documents from the vestry books of Abingdon parish, in which his father had undertaken to build a church, which was unfinished at the time of his death.—I also recollect that vouchers were wanting in several articles charged in my brother's account, which mr. Baker marked thus (v)—That those articles were not allowed, nor absolutely rejected, but were postponed for further consideration, at the next meeting, which, it was agreed, should be had, on proper notice, as soon as mr. Skelton should have procured the documents from Abingdon.—

I have not answered the bill, but intend to do so, soon after the rising of the court of appeals, which will probably be about the middle of next month. If I can, in the mean time, find leisure, will pay my respects to you in the city of Washington.

Accept assurances of my constant respect and esteem.

WM. FLEMING.

P.S. I left mr. Terrel's the 9th. of September; mrs. Terrel a little indisposed, but was to set out, with miss Carr, for Albemarle, about this time.—

RC (MHi); endorsed by TJ as received 19 Oct. and so recorded in SJL.

FAVOUR FROM MONTICELLO: TJ to Fleming, 19 Sep.

James Skelton was Bathurst Skelton's FATHER (MB, 1:349n; Vol. 31:162-3).

Fleming, an old friend of TJ's, had been a member of the Virginia COURT OF APPEALS since the creation of that court in 1789. Before that he was a judge of the Virginia General Court (Marshall, Papers, 5:xxviii, xxxii).

MRS. TERREL: TJ's niece, Lucy Carr Terrell, moved to Kentucky with her husband, Richard Terrell, in 1793 (Vol. 24:744; Vol. 25:297-8). MISS CARR was Lucy's sister Mary, who was called Polly (Vol. 28:166, 242; MB, 2:1085).

From Abishai Thomas

Tuesday evening October 13th

Ab Thomas has the honor & the satisfaction to inform the President that Letters are received from Capt. McNeill & the Navy Agent at New York, announcing that the Frigate Boston was got off the ledge of Rocks on which she had struck, at 10 OClock P.M. on the

9th inst.—previous to which all the water had been started and all the Guns, shot, provisions, anchors & heavy stores taken out of her—Capt. McNeill adds, "I do not find she has received any injury in her bottom as she is very tight"—and he hoped to have her again ready for sea by the next evening—

That the Secretary of the Navy may receive the good at the same time with the bad news A.T. has enclosed Cap McNeill's Letter to go by the same mail with the former

RC (DLC); at foot of text: "The President"; endorsed by TJ as received 13 Oct. from the Navy Department and so recorded in SJL with notation "Boston."

Abishai Thomas served as a deputy quartermaster general in the Continental army during the Revolution and as an agent of North Carolina for settling its claims against the U.S. during the early 1790s. In the summer of 1799, he was appointed principal clerk of the Navy Department, serving until he was replaced by Charles W. Goldsborough on 1 Apr. 1802 (Palmer, *Stoddert's War*, 126; Syrett, *Hamilton*, 15:450; Washington, *Papers, Pres. Ser.*, 6:182; NDBW, 2:102).

NAVY AGENT AT NEW YORK: Daniel Ludlow.

On the morning of 8 Oct., while entering the North (Hudson) River, the FRIGATE BOSTON struck a reef some two hundred rods from the Battery. The vessel received no significant damage and departed with Robert R. Livingston for France on 15 Oct. (New York *American Citizen and General Advertiser*, 9 Oct. 1801; New York *Daily Advertiser*, 10 Oct. 1801; Dangerfield, *Livingston*, 309).

On 12 Oct., Thomas sent TJ a letter covering an abstract of Treasury warrants drawn by the Navy Department and the balance on hand for the week ending 10 Oct. (RC in DLC, at foot of text: "President," endorsed by TJ as received from the Navy Department on 12 Oct. and so recorded in SJL with notation "Warrants"; FC in Lb in DNA: RG 45, LSP).

From George Clinton

SIR   Albany Octr. 14th. 1801

I have now the honor to transmit to the Office of the Secretary at war a plan for fortifying the Port of New York projected by Coll. De. Puzy under the direction of my Predecessor, accompanyed with surveys and Maps of the Harbor and an explanatory Memoir of the Engineer—If any other information on the subject should be deemed Necessary Coll. Willet who has been employed as my Agent in this business will be able to furnish it, and it is with this view I have thought proper to make him the bearer of this dispatch—Although it would appear to me that in order to have concerted an acceptable plan of this kind, the views of the general Government respecting the Nature of the defence, and the monies to be expended ought to have been previously Ascertained, As for the want of this knowledge the most perfect project may be rejected; Yet as Mr. Dexter late Secretary at War by his letter to Governor Jay of the 28th. of June 1800 A

Copy of which is inclosed, expressed a Contrary Opinion, the business was commenced and has been conducted according to his Ideas, at an expence little short of four thousand Dollars—It would be Difficult if not impracticable to calculate the expence which would attend the execution of the present plan tho' it is easy to determine that it would very far exceed the sums contemplated to be advanced by this State,[1] And it may be useful to remark that the Expenditure of them is expressly restricted to Fortifications to be erected on Lands within the State.

I have the honor to be with the highest respect & Esteem Your Most Obet. Servt—

GEO: CLINTON

RC (DLC); in a clerk's hand, signed by Clinton and with an insertion in his hand (see note 1); at foot of text: "Thomas Jefferson Esqe. President of the Ud: States"; endorsed by TJ as received 13 Nov. and so recorded in SJL. Enclosure: Samuel Dexter to John Jay, 28 June 1800, acknowledging a copy of an act by the legislature of New York concerning harbor fortifications for New York City; Dexter naming Jean Xavier Bureaux de Pusy to prepare a plan for submission to the president; suggesting, since Dexter himself was "so little of a Military Man," that it was "best to let a plan be taken without any particular instructions" from the War Department; cautioning, however, that foreign-trained engineers were inclined "to prepare their plans on too extensive a scale & with too little regard to Œconomy" (Tr in DLC; in a clerk's hand; at head of text: "Copy").

Under federal statutes, the state of New York could retire its debt to the United States by FORTIFYING THE PORT OF NEW YORK. In 1800, Jean Xavier Bureaux de Pusy, who had come to the U.S. as a member of Pierre Samuel Du Pont de Nemours's extended family and had training as a military engineer in France, obtained the appointment to draw up a plan for new harbor fortifications. His assessment, which Clinton sent to the War Department as indicated in the letter above, had an estimated cost of $3,968,658, far more than the state's $1,852,035 debt to the federal government. Bureaux de Pusy's plan also called for the primary fortifications to be at Sandy Hook, New Jersey—not WITHIN THE STATE of New York (ASP, *Military Affairs*, 1:193; Kline, *Burr*, 1:527-8; Vol. 31:265n; Vol. 32:56-7; Vol. 33:308-9).

On 17 Nov., Dearborn responded to Clinton about the submitted plan. Citing the projected cost as an "insuperable objection," Dearborn also expressed concerns about relying on the opinions of "any one or two Engineers" for such a large expenditure. It was "the wish of the President," Dearborn wrote, that Clinton should "select from five to seven Citizens of New York, who from their weight of Character in Society, their general information, and Knowledge of the subject may be able, on a full investigation, to make such a report as will be likely to afford good and sufficient grounds for commencing the Business as soon as the nature of the case will admit." The costs of whatever plan was recommended, the secretary of war added, would have to fall "within the means provided by law, it being very doubtful whether Congress will think proper to make any further provision at present" (Lb in DNA: RG 107, MLS).

[1] Remainder of paragraph interlined in Clinton's hand.

To Albert Gallatin

DEAR SIR   Washington Oct. 14. 1801.

I inclose you three letters from Colo. Newton of Norfolk on the subject of a successor to Wilkins at Cherrystone's. you will [see] also & duly estimate his proposition respecting the Marine [hospital] at Norfolk.—I think we ought to do something for Campbell, and indeed must do it. the general opinion will be greatly in his favor; and even those who may find something to [censure], will still be sensible of other motives for rewarding him. I [wish] we could provide for him in Philadelphia. health & affectionate respect.   TH: JEFFERSON

PrC (DLC); faint, with words in brackets supplied from Tr; at foot of text: "Secy of the Treasury." Tr (MHi). Enclosures: Thomas Newton to TJ, 25, 26, 30 Sep.

To Gideon Granger

DEAR SIR   Washington Oct. 14. 1801.

Since my letter of this day sennight, the question as to the public offices has taken a turn different from what was then expected. neither of the two then named is to be vacant, but instead thereof the Postmaster general's place. this being of equal grade, emolument, and importance, I propose it to your acceptance with the same satisfaction as either of the others. perhaps you will consider it as more eligible than the treasury, as that would have obliged you to call on your friends to become your sureties for 150,000 D. that being the sum fixed by law. judging of the feelings of others by my own, this would not have been pleasant. let me hear from you immediately, while the same reserve as to others is kept up. health and affectionate respect.   TH: JEFFERSON

RC (J. David Baker and Hugh J. Baker and Company, Indianapolis, Indiana, 1976); at foot of text: "Gideon Granger esq." PrC (DLC).

THIS DAY SENNIGHT: TJ to Granger, 7 Oct.

FIXED BY LAW: the "Act to Establish the Treasury Department," of 2 Sep. 1789, called for the treasurer of the United States, before entering office, to provide "sureties, to be approved by the Secretary of the Treasury and Comptroller, in the sum of one hundred and fifty thousand dollars" (U.S. Statutes at Large, 1:66)

From the District of Columbia Commissioners

SIR,   Commissioner's Office, 15th. Octo 1801

An application was this day made to us to grant Lots at a cash price, and permit the value to be laid out in improving F Street north from the President's Square to 11th. Street west, along E Street north to 8th Street west, and to Pennsylvania Avenue.

We are of opinion that the Improvement of F Street north as far as 11th Street west, and to the Avenue would be highly advantageous; but, while we contemplate and acknowledge the utility of this undertaking by the mode proposed, we however cannot forbear alluding to the specific purposes to which the funds arising from the property vested in the public, by the original proprietors, were defined; and, though in many instances the strict Letter of the original intention has been deviated from, these deviations have comprehended many general advantages to the public; and being peculiar in themselves, they could not lead as examples to general consequences. Yet, if the present application be admitted, we fear the danger of similar applications to an extent that would create many inconveniences by taking out of the public funds, the most favorable lots.

To the president however, we submit the decision with the great deference.

We are, with sentiments of the highest respect, Sir, Yr. mo: Obt. Servants

WILLIAM THORNTON
ALEXR WHITE
TRISTRAM DALTON

RC (DLC); at foot of text: "To the President of the United States"; in William Brent's hand, signed by Thornton, White, and Dalton; endorsed by TJ as received 15 Oct. and so recorded in SJL with notation "F. street." FC (DNA: RG 42, DCLB).

Peter Lenox, in an APPLICATION to the District of Columbia Commissioners dated 15 Oct. in Washington, cited the "Disadvantage" of "the Want of a good Carriage Way" in the area west of the President's House between F Street and Pennsylvania Avenue. If the commissioners were to sell him lots "at Cash price," Lenox proposed, he would contract for the improvement of F and 11th streets (RC in DNA: RG 42, LR).

From Richard Hutton

SIR   [on or before 15 Oct. 1801]

Please to forgive my forwardness in writing this to you, the opinion I and the World in general have of you emboldens me.

I am an Englishman, but have been in Principle a Repeblican from the beginning of the Revolution, by which I suffered much.

I am the Man who wrote the Letter to President Washington, requesting his attendance to view Mr. Pierce's Machienary, and was at the very handle the then President Turned, you will remember that circumstance

I wish to be heard,

and wish you all imaginable success in all your undertakings

RICHD. HUTTON

RC (DLC); undated; addressed: "The President"; endorsed by TJ as received 15 Oct. and so recorded in SJL.

MR. PIERCE'S MACHIENARY: on 5 June 1792, as a member of a distinguished party that included George Washington and Alexander Hamilton, TJ visited the Philadelphia cotton manufactory of William Pearce, an English artisan and inventor recently arrived in America (Washington, *Papers, Pres. Ser.*, 10:378n; Vol. 20:321-2; Vol. 24:805n).

From Richard Willson

SIR   City of Washington October 15th 1801.

Having had my fortune considerably impaired in the Revolutionary War, and a variety of unfavorable and imperious circumstances concurring to increase my embarrassments, I am impelled to solicit your Excellency for some appointment under Government.

On my arrival at this place from Queen Ann's County, my place of nativity and late residence, I found the sentiments of my few old friends and Acquaintances, and my own, not so congenial as formerly, when we were [. . .]ing together the dangers of battle, and having no other Acquaintances by whom I could be Presented to your Excellency, I take the liberty of addressing you by letter—

The last Public appointment I held, was, Register of Wills; for Queen Ann's County, and the emoluments of the Office being inadequate to the duty, occasioned my resignation. I beg leave to transmit herewith an acknowledgment of the Judges approbation of my conduct when in Office, and also to refer to a Baltimore paper, under the Easton head, for the Character there given of Colo. Arthur Emory, who was the presiding Justice of the Court.

I am fully sensible of the disadvantages resulting from want of friends here; but could so fortuitous an event happen, as the arrival of Mr. Joseph Nicholson of Centre Ville, I flatter myself every obstacle on that point would be removed, as that Gentleman favored me with letters recommendatory to Genrl. Dearborn some months past.

As it has always been my firm determination to perform the trusts reposed in me by the Public, to the utmost of my abilities, should you Sir, be pleased to [honor] me with an appointment it will be my great ambition to perform all the duties required, with Integrity, Promptitude and energy to merit your Confidence.

I remain with unfeigned and fervent wishes that the great Ruler of all human affairs may be pleased to Continue you in the full enjoyment of health, happiness and Public Confidence

your Excellency's most respectfull and Obdt Servt.

RICHARD WILLSON

RC (DNA: RG 59, LAR); torn; endorsed by TJ as received 17 Oct. and so recorded in SJL. Enclosures: (1) Certificate signed by Arthur Emory and Jacob Barnes, 27 June 1797, testifying that Willson, who served as register of wills in Queen Anne's County, Maryland, from 1792 to 1797, performed the duties "with ability, Industry and Integrity; And with the most Perfect Satisfaction to the Public—And the highest Honor & Credit to himself" (MS in same; with notation at brace connecting signatures: "The only surviving Justices of the Orphans Court for the above period of time"; certified and sealed by Samuel Wright, clerk of Queen Anne's County Court, 20 Apr. 1798, testifying that

Emory and Barnes were judges of the orphan's court for the county). (2) Obituary from the Baltimore *Federal Gazette*, 3 Sep. 1801, reporting the death of Arthur Emory, former judge of the orphan's court, after a fall from his horse on 13 Aug., and stating that as presiding judge he had discharged his duties with "promptitude, and ability rarely equalled."

In 1792, Richard Willson was appointed register of wills for Queen Anne's County in the place of Solomon Clayton, deceased (*Archives of Maryland: Journal and Correspondence of the Council of Maryland 1789-1793* [Baltimore, 1972], 72:248).

From Hary Grant

SIR   London 16 Ocr. 1801

The Enclosed Mr Pinckney desired I Would forward On my Arrivl: in England I Left Paris 7 days Ago. When Mr Livingstone Was hourly Expected and much Wisht for. You Will not Recollect me tho frequently With You through my particular friend Major Butler—

I have the honor to be Sir Your very Obd Sevt:

HARY GRANT
Consul U.S. for Scotland

RC (MHi); endorsed by TJ as received 20 Jan. 1802 and so recorded in SJL. Enclosure: Charles Pinckney to TJ, 6 Oct. 1801.

English native Hary Grant (ca. 1759-1814) arrived at Charleston, South Carolina, shortly after the end of the Revolutionary War. He was a business partner of James Simons in the mid-1780s and became Spain's agent in South Carolina in 1794. Although appointed U.S. consul at Leith, Scotland, in 1798, he reportedly spent most of his time in London and Paris (George C. Rogers, Jr., *Evolution of a Federalist: William Loughton Smith of Charleston (1758-1812)* [Columbia, 1962], 100-1, 186; *S.C. Biographical Directory, House of Representatives*, 3:649; New York *American Minerva*, 29 July 1794; JEP, 1:286; Madison, *Papers, Sec. of State Ser.*, 3:448; New York *National Advocate*, 20 Dec. 1814).

To Nicholas Lewis

DEAR SIR   Washington Oct. 16. 1801.

It has become considerably important, in the dispute between mr Ross & myself, to ascertain when the bonds taken at the Elkhill sale were payable. the sale was Feb. 1. 1785. Norris's & Selden's bonds were assigned to him, and as they are to be turned into tobacco at the time they were payable, & tobacco varied in it's price remarkably that year, the time of paiment is very interesting. your answer to this by return of post will greatly oblige Dear Sir

Your affectionate friend & servt   TH: JEFFERSON

PrC (MHi); at foot of text: "Colo. N. Lewis"; endorsed by TJ in ink on verso.

ELKHILL SALE: David Ross's purchase of TJ's Elkhill tobacco (MB, 2:1052-3; Vol. 31:209-10). During TJ's years in France, Lewis, a friend and neighbor, and Francis Eppes supervised his business and plantation affairs (MB, 1:23; Vol. 6:210; Vol. 7:239; Vol. 9:254-6).

From Thomas Newton

DR SIR   Norfolk Octr 16—1801—

A Vessel from New Orleans—putting in here in distress having some Shrubs & curiosities on board for you, on application of the Capt. I have taken them & now forward them by Capt Willis's Packet, they are, images dug up very high on the Missisipi & I hope will tend to some discoveries of the original settlement of this Country. the charges on them I have paid as below. it gives me pleasure to inform you that the decease which prevaild here among strangers has greatly abated, the settled inhabitants used to our climate are, generally very healthy. I have ingaged 4 barrels & more if it can be made by a Mr Caral of hughes crab cider for you, to be beat in Decr. it is to

be very fine as I am promised. my best wishes attend you
yrs respectfully   THOS NEWTON

Be pleased give directions to have the above articles recd at
Alexandria—

RC (DLC); endorsed by TJ as received 22 Oct. and so recorded in SJL. Enclosures: (1) Invoice, Captain Moses Tibbetts to Newton, 15 Oct. 1801, for $8 freight on two boxes and $12 freight on a box of trees, all sent to TJ from New Orleans on the brig *Sophia*, plus 75 cents for storage in Norfolk (MS in same; in a clerk's hand, with acknowledgment of receipt of payment from Newton signed by Tibbetts). (2) Receipt from Abel Willis, Norfolk, 16 Oct., for three boxes placed in his care by Newton to be delivered to TJ or his agent at Alexandria on payment of freight charges (MS in same, in Willis's hand and signed by him).

SHRUBS: young pecan and orange trees that Daniel Clark sent to TJ from New Orleans. The CURIOSITIES were two statues of Native American origin sent to TJ by Morgan Brown of Tennessee, plus castings of an Indian tobacco pipe Clark sent from Louisiana. Clark had dispatched the trees and antiquities in July on the *Sophia* with Philadelphia as the intended destination. Abel Willis regularly sailed between Norfolk and Alexandria in the sloop *Eliza* (*Simmons's Norfolk Directory* [Norfolk, 1801], 69; Vol. 31:195-6, 593; Daniel Clark to TJ, 20 July 1801).

MR. CARAL may have been John Carrel, a Norfolk house joiner (*Simmons's Norfolk Directory*, 12). For TJ's interest in obtaining cider made from the HUGHES crabapple, see his letter to Newton of 7 May and Newton's replies of 13 and 16 May.

From Craven Peyton

DEAR SIR   Shadwell 16th October 1801

Yours of the 8th Inst came safe to hand covering three post Notes amounting to 1240. D & 27 ¢ for which I am exceedingly Obligd. to you my motive for encloseing the statement of each legatees proportion was merely for your Own satisfaction & not from a wish for you to make any remittence as I can with much convenience pay them what may be due which will appear from the statement if I have been correct, although it does not affect you, my bargain with Carr. only in the two shears of Henderson, Kerr's shear including interest will cost me five pounds more than you gave me, owing to there being more land than was supposd., at the divition, woods promisd. to furnish me with a plat which was for you & shall be inclosd by the next mail. the lands which is above your Mill seat is undivided[1] as it is the dower land in which the Canal must pass, in a few Months J. Henderson may be bought on much more moderate terms then at present. his being liable for all his Farthars debts. shoud you have a claim agst the estate I think it woud be in my power to fix it in his shear, the Creditors are very pushing rest ashoard if it can be had no exertion on my part shall be wanting. the Deeds for those that are of age shall be executed immediately & the proparty rented for the extent of its value, you will oblige me greatly by saying what shall be done with Shadwell, my wish is to move in three weeks, James L. Henderson is about to return to the state of Kentuckey & as he is bound for the true performance of the two legatees that are under age, I shoud wish to hold him to security in this state if it coud be possible for fear of death or othar were the trouble woud be considerable to pursue him if Any Mode which may be pented Out by yourself shall be strictly attended to, was it immediately myself that was consernd. I shoud not be so anxious to secure the redress hear. as I am,

I am with real Respt.   C. PEYTON

RC (ViU); endorsed by TJ as received 20 Oct. and so recorded in SJL.

STATEMENT OF EACH LEGATEES PROPORTION: Enclosure No. 1 listed at Peyton to TJ, 3 Oct.

William WOODS was the Albemarle County surveyor from 1796 to 1828. He served briefly in the Virginia House of Delegates as the county's replacement for Wilson Cary Nicholas in December 1799, but lost a re-election bid in 1800 (Woods, *Albemarle*, 356; Vol. 29:322, 327-8; Vol. 31:241, 274, 542).

YOUR MILL SEAT: that is, lot number 9 of the "below the Town" tract of the Henderson estate. Peyton called the parcel TJ's because in the division of the Henderson estate it went to James Henderson, who had sold his share in the estate to Peyton, who was making the purchases for TJ.

For the 15-acre DOWER LAND that would have to be traversed by a CANAL for the prospective mill site, see the Valuation of Henderson Property for Dower, [before 1 Oct. 1801].

John Henderson was the administrator of his father's estate and thus LIABLE for its DEBTS (Vol. 28:482, 520n).

James L. Henderson, born in April 1779, was OF AGE, but his brothers Charles and Isham, born in January 1781 and November 1782, respectively, were not. James had sold his share in the estate to Tucker Woodson in October 1799, and Peyton purchased it from Woodson in April 1801. Charles and Isham sold their shares in the estate's Albemarle County lands to James in March 1801, and James immediately sold those rights to Peyton. Although James considered himself to be acting in behalf of his younger siblings, he had not been appointed their guardian. The county court had made John Henderson the guardian of all of his younger siblings in 1794 (order of court, 9 Oct. 1794, Craven Peyton's amended bill in chancery, 2 June 1804, and deposition of James L. Henderson, 15 Apr. 1805, all in Tr of TJ v. Michie, ViU: Carr Papers; Robert Haggard, "Thomas Jefferson v. The Heirs of Bennett Henderson, 1795-1818: A Case Study in Caveat Emptor," *Magazine of Albemarle County History*, 63 [2005], 3).

[1] MS: "undived."

From Johnson Cook

SIR   Maraetta 17th October 1801

the information I get by perusing the Urora Rivits your Excelency in my Esteem since the reins of goverment has ben Established in your Excelencys hands their seems to be A very Esentiel alteration in the affairs of government the Era has now opened for the first shew of an Republickan Goverment which asumes the aspeckt of good and holesom Laws takeng place in our country. the Former Pressedents has ben actuated by some unseen Motives in paying tribute to algiers in sinking large sums by Abusing the French Republick in maney instances—in Maintaining the warmist of Erestecrats in Ofice feasting them on the Exspence of real Republickans all Men must give in to Demockracy being the only governmnt wherein A nation can Exsist unless this is the prevaling sistem of A Country it must be exspeckted their will follow Revelutions commotions divisions Even to the sheding of blood of their Nearest relations and once friends this in many of the states has ben A subgeckt of conversation while goverment reald thus in the socket I have ben very Much Mortefyed with the Proceedings of goverment in their Neglecking the solgery who spent their best days in fighting for the Liberty of their Country I served seven years in prime of My days as A Serjiant in the army I suffered imprisenment in New york cruelly treated by the British almost starved for want of food I suffer:d by wounds I was in A number of actions in the field I was at taking of Stoney Point fort in the first squad that Enterd that garison I apeal to Coln Meigs to wittness the same after all the services I have receivd Nothing for the same John Shermon Pay Master to our Rigement fled from the Country with Eighteen thousand dollars belonging to the Connecticut line with about three Hundred Dollars which belonged to Me I have laid this Matter Before Jenl. Washington the year before he Resind his Presedency he did not think proper to answer me on the subgeckt I now am Confident I am about to lay this before A man of tender feelings that will [. . .] Rited out of the National Chest Sir in sinceerity and with afectinate Esteme

I Subscrbe My Self your Very humble Servant

JOHNSON COOK

Sir I would Likewise inform your Excelency that I had A son born the 21st day of July last and it being the first year of our Republickan goverment with your approbation I would Call his Name Thomas Jefferson.

I live in the thicket of your sworn enemys their is rarely a republickan in Marietta

RC (DLC); word obscured by tape; above second postscript: "To Thomas Jefferson Esqr Presedent of the United States"; endorsed by TJ on Cook's letter of 21 Oct. as one of three letters received from him on 9 Nov. and so recorded in SJL.

URORA: the Philadelphia *Aurora*.

In his letter to George WASHINGTON dated Marietta, Ohio, 1 Oct. 1796, Cook stated that he had enlisted as a private in 1777 at the age of 16. He saw extensive action during his service in the Connecticut line, received wounds on several occasions, and attained the rank of sergeant in 1782 (RC in DLC: Washington Papers). Cook filed pension applications in 1818 and 1833 while a resident of Ohio (White, *Genealogical Abstracts*, 1:746).

From Thomas Corcoran

the 17th of October 1801—

In the case of Thomas Leech, now in Confinement for an assault on myself, I have understood the Presedent of the United States, has expressed a determination not to pardon him, without my Consent expressed in writing. For which I feel myself much Obliged by the Presedent, Leech himself, has no claim to my Interference in his favour, but his Wife and Children, will need his assistance, perticularly as the Winter is approaching, Feeling for them, if by any means I could Contribute to their Happiness, If it Should please the Presedent, to remit the fine, and further Imprisonment, it will meet the approbation of his Obedient Servt   THOS. CORCORAN

RC (DLC); endorsed by TJ as received 21 Oct. from Georgetown and so recorded in SJL.

For the ASSAULT case against Thomas Leach, see Gean Leach to TJ, 17 July. TJ issued him a pardon on 21 Oct., ordering that all proceedings against Leach be halted upon his paying the costs of the prosecutions (FC in Lb in DNA: RG 59, GPR).

From Michael Fry and Nathan Coleman

SIR   Philada Oct 17 1801

The Victualers (Butchers) of Philadelphia have long been distinguished among their fellow Citizens, for their support of and attachment to Republican principles; and at the late election they have the satisfaction of seeing one of their own proffession elevated to the dignity of a representative in the State Assembly. This is indeed the triumph of republicanism

The Subscribers rejoiced at the downfall of a faction who wished to raise the rich & proud, over the humble and industrious Citizen; and we are now happy in being enabled to place confidence in the

Man who while a private citizen laboured with success to remove the European prejudice "That Animals were inferior & Degenerated in the New World"

As a further confirmation of the truths you have so well established we pray you to accept a hind Quarter of the largest Calf of her Age which we remember to have seen in this part of the Country. We have dressed it well and packed it in superfine flour; and as the weather is cool there is no doubt but it will be as good when it arrives in the City of Washington as if it had been dressed this day in Philada.

We hope that you will consider this as a small token of our Attachment and Gratitude—happy that we have lived to see the time, when we may, with sentiments of respect & Veneration, subscribe ourselves without giving Offence.

Your fellow Citizens
MICH FRY
NATHAN COLEMAN

The Calf weighed when Alive 438 1b. when dressed for the Market 315
Her age—115 Days

RC (DLC); closing quotation mark supplied; at foot of text: "To Thomas Jefferson President of the U.S."; endorsed by TJ as received 20 Oct. and so recorded in SJL with notation "veal 115 days old 438. ℔ alive 315. ℔ dressed."

Michael Fry was a victualler at 56 North Sixth Street, Philadelphia, in 1802 (James Robinson, *The Philadelphia Directory, City and County Register, for 1802* [Philadelphia, 1802], 94).

ONE OF THEIR OWN PROFFESSION: Philip Odenheimer, a Philadelphia butcher (*Journal of the First Session of the Twelfth House of Representatives of the Commonwealth of Pennsylvania* [Lancaster, 1801, i.e., 1802], 3; Stafford, *Philadelphia Directory, for 1801*, 80). TJ countered EUROPEAN PREJUDICE about the size of animals in North America in his *Notes on the State of Virginia* (*Notes*, ed. Peden, 43-58).

From Gabriel Phillips

SIR,   New York Octr 18th. 1801

Influenced by the Voice of Public Opinion so conspicuously evinced in the change of Political Sentiment I have taken the liberty to address you on a Subject connected with the most uncontrovertable Facts tho' some have contested & Even Denied their Existence
Some of the Disapointed & Clamorous Polititions of our Country have come forward with the utmost Virulence with Determined Opposition to the present Administration because it possesses an Independancy congenial with the Wishes of a large and increasing

Majority of the Citizens of these States. It has been asserted repeatedly that the former Councils never removed from Office a person whose political Sentiments were incompatible with their Own. This has been a Theme of continual Invective against some Removals which have taken. A Man under the fictitious Name of Marcus Junius Brutus in discenting on your Answer to the Merchants of New-Haven Asserts that no Collector of Duties under any particular State before the present Constitution but was continued in Office after the Collection of Duties was ceded to the United States.

Colonel Payne of Edenton North Carolina is a conspicuous Instance of the Contrary. Mr Payne at the commencment of the Revolution took a very Active Part in Defence of the Rights & Liberties of his Country. At the Expiration of the Contest he was by the Legislature of that State chosen Collector for the Port of Edenton. Upon the Adoption of the present Constitution of the United States Mr Samuel Jonston of that State was chosen one of the Senators in Congress. By his Exertions Mr Payne was removed & a Mr Samuel Tredwell a Young Man nephew of Mr. Jonstons apointed in his Room. Mr Tredwell was of a disafected Family in the state of New York (during the War with Great Britain) placed within the Enemies Lines. After the War Mr Tredwell became an Inhabitant of Edenton & connected to a Neece of Mr Jonstons. This may account for Mr Paynes Dissmission. While on the Other hand not a Single Objection could be attached to his Character. On the Contrary he was distinguished for his Activity in Defence of his Country against the Usurpation of a foreign Power. As a Collector he was Universally Esteemed and his Removal Lamented by all who well knew him. A Man of handsome Abilities & a Mind the Most Noble. I may Venture to assert no one who knows his Charecter but must Admire the Many Amiable Qualities he possesses. Two or three years after his Removal from Office as Collector he was Choshen Marshal of the District of North Carolina. His Apointment took place on the resignation of Col John Skinner the former Marshal and I presume apointed in his Room in consequence [of Mr] Skinners Recommendation to the President. Mr Payne was continued in Office between three & four Years. During that Period he was a zelous Advocate of the French Revolution and an Enthusust in their Successes believing its tendency would be the Emancipation from Slavery a large portion of the human Race Sunk in Ignorance & Despotism.

He was a Violent Opposer of the British Treaty and with Others Signed the largest Petition ever presented to the house of Representatives praying it might not be carried into Effect. Unfortunatly his Manly Resistance and Independent Mind caused his Dismission. Mr

Sedgraves the District Judge of that State could not think & act with Colonel Payne tho' in Offices connected a simelarity appeared necessary. How far this Effected Mr Paynes Situation I will not presume to determine but to these causes he attributes his fall. I hope Sir you will pardon the Liberty I have taken in this lengthy Degression tho' true Statment of Facts. Learning that Mr Habersham the Post Master General is about to retire from Office Could you think Colonel Payne worthy that Office or Another from what I have said from the knowledge you may heretofore possess of his Character or from Information from David Stone Esqr Senator in Congress and Charles Jonston Esqr Member of the house of Representatives both perfectly acquanted with Colonel Payne I cannot but flatter myself the Duties he may be entrusted with would meet the Aprobation of the President & his Country

Accept My Duty & Respects GABRL PHILLIPS

RC (DNA: RG 59, LAR); torn; addressed: "His Excellency Thomas Jefferson Esqr. Washington"; franked; postmarked 19 Oct.; endorsed by TJ as received 21 Oct. and so recorded in SJL; TJ later canceled "Philips Gabrl." and added "Colo. Payne of Edenton for office" to the endorsement.

FICTITIOUS NAME: *An Examination of the President's Reply to the New-Haven Remonstrance; with an Appendix, Containing the President's Inaugural Speech, the Remonstrance and Reply; Together with a List of Removals from Office, and New Appointments, Made Since the Fourth of March, 1801*, published in New York in September 1801, was signed Lucius Junius Brutus, the pseudonym used by William Coleman, a Federalist lawyer and ally of Alexander Hamilton, who became editor of the *New-York Evening Post* in November 1801. The author argued that eliminating the stability of tenure from public office destroys "a great inducement to enter into public service." He explained that "Previous to the adoption of the Federal Constitution, most of the individual States had their own particular laws of impost and excise, and consequently their several officers of the customs. These officers, deriving their authority from the respective States, lost of course their public characters, by the transfer to the general Government of the power under which they had acted." Washington, however, according to Brutus, appointed "all those officers who held analogous stations in the several States, and who were properly qualified, without any reference to their political opinions" (Brutus, *Examination*, 15, 23-4; Syrett, *Hamilton*, 25:419n).

During the Revolution, Michael PAYNE served as an officer in the Second North Carolina Regiment. In 1777 he became the naval officer, not COLLECTOR, at Edenton. Washington did appoint Thomas Benbury, state collector of customs for Albemarle Sound since 1784, collector at Edenton in 1790, which would support the contention by "Brutus." A naval officer was appointed only at Wilmington, North Carolina. SAMUEL TREDWELL became collector at Edenton in 1793, upon the death of Thomas Benbury. Payne did not receive an appointment under the Federal government until 1794, when John Skinner resigned as U.S. marshal for North Carolina and recommended him for the position. He accepted the appointment in a letter dated 19 Aug. 1794. When his term expired in 1798, Adams appointed John S. West in his stead (Washington, *Papers, Pres. Ser.*, 5:197; 12:59n; JEP, 1:37, 39, 129, 278). For evidence that the Washington administration listened primarily to Federalists in North Carolina and applied a political test to appointments at Edenton, including that of Tredwell, see Prince, *Federalists*, 120-4.

North Carolina's petition in opposition to the BRITISH TREATY was presented to the House of Representatives on 8 Mch. 1796 (JHR, 2:466). SEDGRAVES: John Sitgreaves.

From William Short

DEAR SIR   Paris Octob: 18. 1801.

I have just returned from Auvergne whither I informed you in my last of the 9th. of June I was going. We passed some time there near a considerable estate of a peculiar kind belonging to my friend—It consists entirely of mountain heights on which there is not a single house or a single tree, notwithstanding these heights extend for several leagues.—they are covered with snow one half of the year & at that time entirely uninhabited—these heights are rented out to different graziers & raisers of cattle, who send their stocks to pass the season—little huts of earth are erected there to lodge during that time, the persons who have charge of the cattle & make the cheese & butter wch. form a considerable part of the revenue. It is in the mountains of this estate that one of the divisions takes place between the waters of the Loire & the Garonne—for as you know there are several separate divisions between their branches.—Here on one part of the estate there is a little source which takes its course east to go & join the Allier—& on another part of the estate, at about a leagues distance, a small lake whose issue takes its course west to go & join the Dordogne. I have had a great deal of pleasure in climbing up the mountains of Auvergne—there is a something in the mountain air congenial to my constitution which I have always experienced, from the first time of my approaching them in Albemarle—It is an epoch which no circumstance of time or place will ever erase from my mind.—I have seen in this voyage also the effects of the mountain air on others—my friend who is remarkably weak in general & two other of her female friends not much stronger, & accustomed only to the walks of level ground, climbed up without a great deal of fatigue to the top of the Puy de Dome—the latter part of the route for about an hour and three quarters is made on foot, being too steep to admit of the *patache* a kind of little one horse cart in which the first part of the road is passed.—The Puy de Dome, overhangs Clermont, & is celebrated on account the first experiment made by Pascal with the barometer.—It is a mountain perfectly insulated & in the form of a sugar loaf—Its form frequently recalled to my mind your Monticello—but on an immense scale, its summit being eight hundred & twenty toises, above the level of the ocean, & five hundred & sixty toises above the level of the lower part of Clermont which stands at its foot—the level space on the summit of this mountain is smaller than that of the top of Monticello & the sides of the mountain all around more steep—the horizon all around without limits—& the view such as I believe it is impossible to form an idea of—Here is what the author of the Description of Auvergne, says of it & without exageration, "La magnificence & l'etendue du tableau qui se presente, (from this summit) vous ravit jusqu'a l'effroi; l'oeil intimidé semble hésiter, & n'ose d'abord parcourir un espace aussi vaste; on ne peut se defendre d'une emotion inconnue, mêlée de crainte & d'admiration; il faut quelque tems pour s'accoutumer à un spectacle si magnifique."—One of the objects which enters into this picture is the plain of the Limagne, which extends in length to right & left several leagues out of view, & varying in its breadth, but bounded—filled with populous cities such as Riom, Clermont. &c. & cultivated like a garden–square, in its whole extent. The Limagne is & has been from time immemorial one of the most fertile & enchanting spots of the earth—Sidonius Apollinarius & Gregoire de Tours have both celebrated it, & the former among other encomiums, says, that strangers who have once seen the Limagne, forget their country & can no more be prevailed on to quit it.—I do not perceive that it had altogether that effect on me—but it is certainly the most fertile the most highly cultivated & the most magnificent district that I have ever seen—I know nothing that can be compared with it as to the magnificence of its views—& only that small part of Valencia, called the Huerta, as to cultivation & fertility.—

But I have forgotten again that the person to whom I am writing has now less time than ever to lose, & that I have always taken up more of it than I ought to have done!—My excuse here must be the difficulty of passing over in silence a picture which has lately made so lively an impression on me, & which often recalled to my mind my first view of Monticello.—I more than once gave a loose to my imagination, & in order to assimilate the two objects pleased myself with forming a representation in Albemarle of what I had then under my view in Auvergne—To form one side of this, the situation of Monticello was perfectly adapted—I had only to increase the dimensions; and this costs nothing to the imagination—I gave Monticello therefore an elevation of more than three thousand feet, with a basis & circumference in proportion—Charlottesville became a city of twenty five thousand souls—& the valley between you & the blue ridge representing the Limagne in situation & form, I had only to give it the proper fertility & culture—I thus transported myself to my native soil & carried with me the Puy de Dome, Clermont & the Limagne.

In order not to repeat & take up your time I beg leave simply to refer you to my last by Mr. Purviance on the subject of my vouchers, which I sent by him, although I have no copy of them—I had always expected to be the bearer of these papers & therefore retained them from year to year until this opportunity—I hope they have long ago arrived safely to your hands—I endeavored in my letter to give such explanations as may be necessary & as I should have given if I were on the spot. I hope they will suffice & shall be happy to hear of this affair & that resulting from the 9. m. doll. of E Randolph being finally terminated, in order that I may cease giving you trouble, which I can assure you I feel more than ever, & which I will do every thing in my power to put an end to entirely as soon as possible.—

After having closed my last letter & left Paris I determined to make use of Mr Purviance & the frigate to send to America a box of books which I had left at Havre when I went there with Mr Gerry to embark—They are such as I had chosen out of my library to carry with me for the voyage—Not knowing whether I shall embark from Havre I thought it best to make use of so good a conveyance from thence, that I may have them in America, & wrote to beg Mr Purviance to take charge of them & deliver them to you—If there should be any which perchance you have not, they are of course at your service—I hope the others will not incommode you, but if so I beg you to charge Mr Barnes with them until my arrival in America, as I suppose he will have some room or magazine in which he can place them—I beg him however in that case to place them in a dry part & out of the way of the Sun.

Whilst on my late journey I recieved a letter from my brother on the address of which was expressed to your care—this letter was forwarded to me by Mr. Mountflorence who informed me he received it from Holland. I had formerly taken the liberty of authorizing my brother to make use of this means, as I had no other way on which I could rely—As he expressed an unwillingness to give you this trouble I had assured him you would not take it amiss & encouraged him that he might have no pretext for not writing.—Since being in correspondence with Mr Barnes I have desired my brother to send my letters to him & I repeat the same by that which I write him at present.

I have more than once in my former letters troubled you on subjects not merely relative to my affairs, & among them on the Spanish breed of sheep propagated here.—I know not what are your opinions on that subject, but take the liberty of inclosing you the last report of the Commissioners—Several Governments of Europe have made essays towards propagating this breed—It is ascertained that it will succeed in the climates from Sweden to this country inclusive. I wish to see the essay made in our climate. Your present situation would enable you to procure a permission to send out these animals both from here & from Spain, by means of the American Ministers. Otherwise it can be done only by clandestine means.—By my advice a person here who has an estate in New York, made an attempt this last spring to send there a Ram of this breed—he had three embarked which were recieved on board I believe as provisions—he has just recieved an account of the arrival of one of them only—the two others died on the passage probably from want of care. In order for the experiment to succeed fully a permission should be obtained for such a[1] number both of rams & ewes as would require the care of a man on purpose—& among the Shepherds yearly educated at Rambouillet, it would be easy to procure one to go out—He would be necessary not only to take care of the flock on the passage but after their arrival, & to instruct others in his art.—

The commissions which you mention in your last of the 17th. of March, have not yet got to me—I hope I need not add that I shall always take pleasure in employing my services for you in whatever way you may direct, & that I also consider you as having a right to command them.

I shall never again mention to you my intention or the time of my embarking for America;—not only because it has so often failed, but because I observe that what I have heretofore said on that subject has been always regarded as *non avenu*. It is true the event has thus far justified it, although it was not probable at the time.—I have never had an intention of ultimately abandoning my country, nor can any circumstance be considered as more painful by me than the idea of being regarded as estranged from her. I have been so far from feeling that my long absence had diminished in any degree my constant attachment to my country & my friends, or my zeal for their prosperity & happiness, that it would never have occurred to me to suppose such an idea could have existed.—

The present letter will be sent by Mr Dupont—I take the liberty of inclosing one for Mr Barnes, from whom I am surprized not to have heard conformably to his last of March.—With sentiments of the most perfect respect & attachment I have the honor to be Dear Sir; your most obedient srt   W: SHORT

RC (PHi); at foot of first page: "Thomas Jefferson President of the U.S."; endorsed by TJ as received 11 Feb. 1802 and so recorded in SJL. FC (DLC: Short Papers); a summary in Short's epistolary record. Enclosure: Short to John Barnes, 17 Oct., concerning Short's affairs in the U.S. (FC in same; a summary in Short's epistolary record).

CONSIDERABLE ESTATE: the Duchesse de La Rochefoucauld rented out much of her Auvergne estate for grazing (Shackelford, *Jefferson's Adoptive Son*, 218n).

In 1648, Blaise PASCAL directed experiments that involved simultaneous barometric readings at the top of the Puy de Dôme mountain and in the town of Clermont-Ferrand below. Scientists at the time, debating whether a vacuum could exist in nature, wanted to understand the effects of the weight of air (DSB, 10:333).

EIGHT HUNDRED & TWENTY TOISES: the *toise*, one of the French units of measure supplanted by the metric system beginning in 1793, was about $6\frac{1}{3}$ feet long (Stewart, *French Revolution*, 505).

In English, the passage from the DESCRIPTION OF AUVERGNE is: "The magnificence and the extent of the spectacle that unfolds (from this summit) transports you to a state of fright; your intimidated eye seems to hesitate, and at first doesn't dare encompass such a vast space; you cannot resist being overcome by an unknown emotion, mixed with fear and admiration; it takes some time to get used to such a magnificent spectacle."

The fifth-century poet SIDONIUS Apollinaris was from a French-Roman family. Born at Lyons, he held offices under the Roman empire and became bishop of Clermont. His writings included both verse and letters. Gregory (GREGOIRE) of Tours, also a bishop, lived in the sixth century. A native of Auvergne, he is best known for writing the *Historia Ecclesias-*

tica Francorum (Ludovic Lalanne, *Dictionnaire Historique de la France* [Paris, 1877], 938-9, 1663-4).

Short's last letter, carried by John H. PURVIANCE, was dated 9 June. It dealt, among other topics, with Short's claim for $9,000 in government salary from Edmund Randolph's tenure as secretary of state.

In the summer of 1798, Short intended to visit the United States and expected to make the transatlantic crossing with Elbridge GERRY. Before they sailed, Short changed his mind and stayed in France (Vol. 30:473-5).

According to Short's record of his correspondence, he wrote to his BROTHER Peyton on 14 Oct. acknowledging a letter of 15 Feb. (DLC: Short Papers).

SPANISH BREED OF SHEEP: in a letter to TJ of 18 Sep. 1800, Short had discussed the breeding of merino sheep in France. Each spring the science and mathematics division of the National Institute received and published a report on the state of the breeding program and the sale of sheep from the "national flock" on the experimental farms at RAMBOUILLET (Alexandre Henri Tessier and Jean Baptiste Huzard, *Compte Rendu . . . de la vente des laines et de l'accroissement du troupeau national de Rambouillet* [Paris, 1800]; Tessier and Huzard, *Compte Rendu . . . de la vente des laines et de cent soixante-une bêtes du troupeau national de Rambouillet* [Paris, 1801]; Vol. 29:333n; Vol. 32:147-9, 158-9n).

NON AVENU: void or canceled.

MR DUPONT: Victor M. du Pont, who had been in Europe seeking investors and financing for the family's business, left France to return to the United States late in 1801 (Saricks, *Du Pont*, 287; Pierre Samuel Du Pont de Nemours to TJ, 23 July 1801).

¹ MS: "for a such a."

From Thomas Claxton

HONORD SIR,   Philada Oct 19. 1801.

It gives me great mortification to be obliged to inform you that there is no prospect of being furnished with the grates I ordered in June—not even one is yet done, and I have stopped any farther progress being made by a man who has not only deceived me by repeated promises, but also falsely told half a dozen people who I had occasionally requested to call on him, that they were nearly completed—This, Sir, is the first time that any of my undertakings have failed, and, I flatter myself, when you consider the distance I was at from Philada. you will pardon me on this occasion—A Kitchen Grate I think may be procured here ready made, and as to the others I would propose to have a few temporary ones constructed for the ensuing winter—these may be executed in Washington in a few days—And in the course of next Summer proper ones may certainly be got—If it should please you, Sir, to agree to this proposition, the business can be executed in a few days, and, by taking a little extraordinary pains in fixing them in their places, they may appear tolerably decent—

I have been informed, since I came here, that altho I had chosen one of the best workmen in the city, he had lately taken to idle habits, from which circumstance the disappointment has taken place

I have the honor to be Sir With the most sincere respect Your Hble Svt.   THOS. CLAXTON

RC (MHi); endorsed by TJ as received 21 Oct. and so recorded in SJL.

To James Currie

DEAR SIR   Washington Oct. 19. 1801.

I recieved your favor accompanying the award of the Arbitrators in the case between mr Ross & myself, only on the eve of my departure from Monticello when it was impossible for me to take time even to read the papers. I have taken the first moment in my power, (after getting through the mass of business [accumulated] here) to examine the papers. I am perfectly satisfied with the correctness of the decision of the Arbitrators on every point which they have decided. [at] the commencement of the dispute I had supposed the law would justify a commutation of tobo. into money; but on reading not long since the decisions of the Chancery & Appeals I found them against a commutation. the principles therefore decided by the Arbitrators are exactly what I expected. but I think mr Robertson, in his settlement has embraced some matters which had never been in question & consequently not within the principles decided by the Arbitrators. I presume it is within [rule] for me to draw the attention of the arbitrators to what I [conceive] an erroneous execution of their award. I have accordingly made some notes on the subject, which I must pray you to hand to mr Wickham, who is first named in the submission, to be communicated to his colleagues. the questions I have made are so simple and trite, that I presume each of the gentlemen can make up his mind at once, so that they will have no further trouble than barely a short instruction to mr Robertson if they think my observations just. I send you all the papers recieved from you. when they shall be sent back to me I pray your attention to the note at the bottom of the last page of the inclosed paper. Accept assurances of my constant esteem & respect.   TH: JEFFERSON

PrC (MHi); faint; at foot of text: "Doctr. Currie"; endorsed by TJ in ink on verso. Enclosures not found.

YOUR FAVOR: Currie to TJ, 23 Sep. DECISIONS OF THE CHANCERY & APPEALS: George Wythe's *Decisions of Cases in Vir-* *ginia, By The High Court of Chancery, With Remarks upon Decrees By The Court of Appeals, Reversing some of those Decisions* (Richmond, 1795); see Vol. 28:332.

MR ROBERTSON: that is, Anthony Robinson (TJ to George Jefferson, 3 Oct.).

From Albert Gallatin

DR. SIR   [19 Oct. 1801]

I enclose the applications for the office of collector of customs at Wilmington. The office is worth at least 2000 dollars nett.

Colo. Read the former collector, recommended by Macon, Tatom & Robt. Williams, cannot be appointed. He was not removed on account of his politics, but dismissed for remissness in official duties upon an official report of the Secy. of the Treasury. He was removed in 1797, was pressed for years to settle, & is now delinquent for a balance of seven thousand dollars, for which, suit has been instituted in May last.

T. Bloodworth is not, it is presumed, the fittest person for the office & his son is recommended only by him

Carleton Walker naval officer & next in rank to the office of collector is not recommended by any person & does not seem to expect the office. He was very lately appointed on the resignation of his uncle who had held the office from the establisht. of this Government; & it is presumed that he considers the pretensions of the surveyor as superior to his own. His uncle has signed Callender's recommendn.

Thos. Callender surveyor seems to be considered generally, by right of promotion, as the proper successor of the late Collector. He is said by Mr Steele to be a good officer.

Ths. Robeson, deputy collector, was also deputy under Colo. Read, is supposed to be a man of integrity. He & Callender must be equally well qualified. Robeson is mentioned by Mr Bloodworth, but is not considered as having equal weight in the country with Callender, & seems hardly to expect the office. Yet I feel more inclined in his favour than in that of any other candidate.

An application for the Cherry Stone collectorship is also enclosed. With great respect.

ALBERT GALLATIN

RC (DLC); undated; endorsed by TJ as received from the Treasury Department on 19 Oct., also endorsed "Collector for Wilmington" and "for Cheryton's" and so recorded in SJL. Enclosures: (1) Nathaniel Macon to Gallatin, Warrenton, 11 Oct. 1801, recommending James Read to fill the vacancy of collector at Wilmington, North Carolina, noting that he had become acquainted with the former collector during the Revolutionary War and "always entertained a good opinion of him" and thought, in consultation with other local Republicans, that it would be advisable to restore him to office if there was "no good cause for turning him out," but promising to make the necessary enquiries if Gallatin had any doubts as to the propriety of the appointment, as his only wish was "that the most fit person should be appointed"; noting also that John Steele was acquainted with Read "and can doubtless inform you for what cause he was removed, there are those who believe it was for his political sentiments," and enclosing the letter from Absalom Tatom (Gallatin, *Papers*, 5:843-4; endorsed by Gallatin: "re giving office collector at Wilmington to Mr Read the former collector"). (2) Absalom Tatom to Nathaniel Macon, Hillsborough, 8 Oct., recommending Read as a man of integrity, whom he has known for almost 25 years, having served with him in the Revolution, for the vacancy, believing he was "removed by the late administration,

without any cause," and requesting that Macon write the proper officer in favor of Read (same, 5:844-5). (3) Robert Williams to TJ, 9 Oct., noting that upon receiving news of the death of the collector at Wilmington, he believes "it is the wish of most of respectable Character that the vacancy Should be fill'd by Col Read late Collector of that port, and who was removed by the late administration,—he was generally liked & said to be a good officer—My own acquaintance with Mr. Read & his character would authorise this opinion, besides being aided by the opinion of Maj. A Tatom (former Member of Congress) and others more acquainted with Mr. Read than I am" (RC in NHi: Gallatin Papers, at foot of text: "The President of the u States," addressed: "The Secretary of State of the united States City of Washington," postmarked and stamped, endorsed; see Gallatin, *Papers*, 5:841). (4) Timothy Bloodworth to Gallatin, Spring Hill, Fayetteville, North Carolina, 8 Oct., tendering his services for the collectorship at Wilmington and requesting that Gallatin mention him to the president; also recommending for the position: John P. Williams, whom he had formerly endorsed; his 27-year-old son Samuel Bloodworth, "active in Business, Now Inspector of Naval Stores in Wilmington, & does the Business of Collector, & surveyor of the Revenue"; and Thomas Robeson "who has Acted as Clerk in that office for some time, he supports a good Character, & I presume perfectly understands the Business, relating to the office" (Gallatin, *Papers*, 5:835). (5) Perhaps Isaac Smith to John Donnell, Northampton, 12 Oct., requesting that Donnell speak to Samuel or Robert Smith, who could recommend him to the president for the collectorship at Cherrystone, an office worth about $330 per year, noting, "I am perfectly well situated, and have a good office" and would conduct the business "with fidelity and care" (same, 5:850; endorsed by Gallatin: "Enclosed in a letter from Robt. Smith Secy. navy who may give information of the fitness of the applicant A.G.""). Recommendation for Thomas Callender not found.

REMISSNESS IN OFFICIAL DUTIES: after the dismissal of James Read, who had received his appointment from Washington in February 1790, John Steele, the comptroller of the Treasury, received enquiries from his home state of North Carolina. Steele replied that "appearances" were "very much against the vigilance if not the fidelity of the Custom house" at Wilmington and until these discrepancies were "better explained" the conduct of Read would "remain subject to the imputation of remissness at least." While some in Wilmington were transferring blame from the collector "to that of his deputy or some other person acting in a still more humble station," Steele reminded Edward Jones, soliciter general of North Carolina, that Read, as collector, would be held responsible at the Treasury Department (Wagstaff, *John Steele*, 1:154-8; Washington, *Papers, Pres. Ser.*, 4:430-1). For Read's role as a Federalist in Wilmington, his indebtedness, and his dismissal, see Prince, *Federalists*, 124-5.

On 11 Dec. 1800, Adams nominated CARLETON WALKER as naval officer at Wilmington in place of HIS UNCLE, John Walker, who had resigned. Thomas CALLENDER received his appointment as surveyor at the port in 1790, at the same time John Walker received his (JEP, 1:37, 39, 358-9).

Gallatin continued to send TJ the weekly list of warrants from the Treasury Department. The list for the week ending 10 Oct. included sixteen warrants, Nos. 49 to 64, for a total of $50,977.82. The nine warrants listed under the civil list, totaling $5,767.98, included No. 53, for $2,000, an installment on TJ's salary as president. Two warrants under miscellaneous were No. 55, for $1,755.55, issued to Thomas Claxton for "Furniture President's house" and No. 57, for $2,749.29, a payment to Marshal Thomas Lowry for the U.S. census in New Jersey. The largest warrant, No. 54, for $30,000, covered "Pay of the army." One warrant, No. 63, was issued for $2,000 for the purchase of "bills on Holland at 40 Cts." for the payment of principal and interest on the Dutch debt (MS in DLC; entirely in Gallatin's hand; endorsed by TJ as received from the Treasury Department on 10 Oct. and "Warrants" and so recorded in SJL). The list for the week ending 17 Oct. 1801 included twenty warrants, Nos. 65 to 84, for a total of $45,882.31. Fourteen warrants, totaling $10,461.46, appeared under the civil list, including No. 67, a payment of $225 to William Duane for printing and binding books for the "Surveying Dept." Three warrants, totaling $28,000, were issued for the purchase of "bills on Holland at 40 Cts.," for the payment of principal and interest on the Dutch debt. Gallatin reported an "Apparent" balance in the Treasury at the end of the week of $2,996,436.06 (MS in same; entirely in Gallatin's hand; endorsed by TJ as received from the Treasury Department on 19 Oct. and so recorded in SJL with notation "do." for "Warrants").

To George Jefferson

DEAR SIR   Washington Oct. 19. 1801.

I have been able at length to find time to look into the [account between] mr Ross & myself and am perfectly satisfied with it's correctness. but [I have] noted some errors (as I deem them) in mr Robertson's mode of statement, which I have resubmitted to the correction of the arbitrators, & I deem them so [justifiable] as not to doubt their correction. this reduces the sum awarded from [a total] of 12,000 ℔ tobo. to 9880, with interest from Oct. 15. 1790. say [. . .] by the time it is paid will be about 15,355. ℔. there is a question of [date] which I can not fix, but the arbitrators can. if this be in my favor it will reduce the [paiment?] to 3327. ℔. but I do not chuse to count on this, and will therefore ask the [favor of] you to purchase for me (either now or at any later time within a [. . .] think may be the cheapest) tobo. of the upper inspections of James river or Appomatox, which include Richmd & Petersburg, to the amount [. . .] as nearly as may be, provided it be inspected tobo. I do not care abo[ut the] quality, but wish that which is the very cheapest as I consider mr Ross as taking advantage of rigorous laws, in opposition to [. . .]. you [may?] purchase at either Richmond or Petersburg, whichever is cheapest at 60. days [credit] & I will take care to place funds in your hands in time. my observations to the Arbitrators go by this post, so their final decision [. . .] will give us some time. but still if it is the expectation with you [that] tobo. will rise immediately, we had better buy immediately.—we [have] contracted with mr Heth's agent here [. . .] for coal [. . .] his engagement, you will be relieved from that trouble. health & affectionate esteem   TH: JEFFERSON

PrC (MHi); faint; at foot of text: "Mr. George Jefferson"; endorsed by TJ in ink on verso.

On 23 Oct., TJ gave Joseph Dougherty an order on John Barnes for $21.80 for "cartage" of 1,000 bushels of COAL (MS in MHi, in TJ's hand and signed by him, signed by Dougherty acknowledging payment, endorsed by TJ and Barnes, also endorsed by Barnes: "Househd. Coal a/c"; MB, 2:1056). Barnes entered that payment to Dougherty for "hauling coal" in a statement of TJ's household account under 23 Oct. In the same statement of account, Barnes recorded payment on 29 Oct. of $250 to John Davidson, Henry Heth's agent at Washington, for the 1,000 bushels of coal at $.25 per bushel (statement of household account from John Barnes, 1 Oct.-4 Nov. 1801, in ViU).

From Kezia Norris

SIR,   Baltimore Oct 19th 1801.

    I had the honor of transmiting to you (in June last,) a plan of the Female Humane Charity School of this City; and likewise, a list of Doners and Annual subscribers to the same. I now inclose a note of Bishop Carrolls, for your perusal—, Which you will please to return by the next Mail, with the list above mentioned.

    Yll much Oblige Sir,   KEZIA NORRIS
                            Trustee, to the Female Humane
                            Charity School—No: 42 South S.

RC (MdHi); endorsed by TJ as received 19 Oct. and so recorded in SJL. Enclosure not found.

Norris's last letter to TJ was dated 24 JUNE. After the school became a legal corporation by an act of the Maryland legislature in December 1801, Bishop John Carroll was chosen to be president of the school's new, all-male board of trustees. Former female trustees were renamed "directors" and continued to operate the school (*A Brief Account of the Female Humane Association Charity School, of the City of Baltimore* [Baltimore, 1803], 4-6).

To Martha Jefferson Randolph

Washington Oct. 19. 1801.

    I am in hopes, my dear Martha, that I shall hear by the arrival of tomorrow morning's post, that you are all well. in the mean while the arrangement is such that my letter must go hence this evening. my last letter was from mr Eppes of Oct. 3. when all were well. I inclose a Crazy Jane for Anne, and a sweetheart for Ellen. the latter instead of the many coloured stories which she cannot yet read. from the resolution you had taken I imagine you are now at Edgehill surrounded by the cares and the comforts of your family. I wish they may be less interrupted than at Monticello. I set down this as a year of life lost to myself, having been crouded out of the enjoiment of the family during the only recess I can take in the year. I believe I must hereafter not let it be known when I intend to be at home, & make my visits by stealth. there is real disappointment felt here at neither of you coming with me. I promise them on your faith for the ensuing spring. I wish however that may be found as convenient a season of absence for mr Randolph. mr. Madison & family are with us for a few days, their house having been freshly plaistered & not yet dry enough to go into. such is the drought here that nobody can remember when it rained last. my sincere affections to mr Randolph[1] & mr Eppes. kisses to the young ones & my tenderest love to Maria & yourself.

TH: JEFFERSON

RC (NNPM); at foot of text: "Mrs. Randolph." PrC (CSmH); endorsed by TJ in ink on verso. Enclosures not found.

Matthew G. Lewis, the popular British author of gothic novels, wrote CRAZY JANE, a poem of seduction and abandonment, which included the lines "Henry fled!—With him, for ever, Fled the wits of Crazy Jane." The ballad was set to music by several composers and performed in concerts and theatrical productions frequently in the United States in 1800 and 1801. "Crazy Jane," and several sequels of unknown authorship, including "The Death of Crazy Jane" and "Henry's Return, the sequel to Crazy Jane," were reprinted in newspapers and published as songs sold in bookstores and music stores (Lewis F. Peck, *A Life of Matthew G. Lewis* [Cambridge, Mass., 1961], 46-7; *The Life and Correspondence of M. G. Lewis*, 2 vols. [London, 1839], 1:187-9;

New York *Mercantile Advertiser*, 11 June 1800; *New York Daily Advertiser*, 7 Aug. 1800; New York *Weekly Museum*, 6 Sep. 1800, 24 Jan. 1801; *Boston Gazette*, 23 Oct. 1800; Boston *Independent Chronicle and the Universal Advertiser*, 14 May 1801; *Newburyport Herald*, 6 Oct. 1801; *United States Chronicle*, 29 Oct. 1801; *New-York Evening Post*, 29 Dec. 1801). For another poem by Lewis, this one clipped by TJ from a literary magazine, see Jonathan Gross, ed., *Thomas Jefferson's Scrapbooks: Poems of Nation, Family, & Romantic Love Collected by America's Third President* (Hanover, N.H., 2006), 346, 380-1n.

THEIR HOUSE: the Madison family moved to 1333 F Street about 20 Oct. (see note to TJ to James and Dolley Madison and Anna Payne at 27 May 1801).

[1] Remainder of sentence interlined.

From Henry Rose

DEAR SIR   Alexandria 19th Octr. 1801

I observe it is stated in the Public Prints, that you have communicated to Doctr. Waterhouse the success of the Vaccine Matter in your family, and having been applyed to by my Medical friends of Kentucky and Tennassee for information on this subject, and for a supply of the infection,—I would be gratified in being informed whether you caused any of those persons who were inoculated with this matter to be exposed to the Variolous infection and the success of the experiment—Also where a supply of the first mentioned infection can be had—With every assurance of the highest respect & esteem I am Your Obt & very Huml. Sevt.   HENRY ROSE

RC (ViW); endorsed by TJ as received 21 Oct. and so recorded in SJL.

PUBLIC PRINTS: on 5 Oct., the *National Intelligencer,* citing a Boston newspaper, reported that "President Jefferson

has written to Dr. Waterhouse, that he is inoculating his domestics" with the kinepox and was "encouraging the neighborhood of Monticello to follow his example."

From Robert S. Coleman

D<small>R</small> <small>SR</small>   Fredrixbürg 20th October 1801

My friend Mr John Dawson wrote to you Last October for Information Respecting Lewis Littlepage, your Answer to him was handed to me, Carter Littlepage haveing a parte of Lewis'es property in possestion, And haveing disposd of a parte And attempting to dispose of the Hole of the Said property he being Insolvent as appears I haveing Lewis Littlepages will in my possestion I have Indeaverd to prevent the Destruction of the property—many Reports have arisin about the Return of Mr Lewis Littlepage And I have bean informd you have had Very Late Acpts of him—If So will Esteem It a Singlar faver to Communicate the Latest to me by a Line to Fredrixbürg, which will Give releaf to his Sincear friends, and may be a means of Saveing the property—

I am Dr sr Yr Hble sert   R<small>OBT</small>. S. C<small>OLEMAN</small>

RC (MHi); endorsed by TJ as received 22 Oct. and so recorded in SJL.

Robert Spilsbe Coleman was the brother-in-law of Lewis Littlepage. In court filings of 1798 and 1800 over the ownership of slaves, Coleman and his wife, Mary Littlepage Coleman, contended that Littlepage, who had seemingly disappeared in Europe for several years, was dead. The family had since learned that Littlepage was alive. Littlepage considered Coleman's lawsuits "unjustifiable" and deemed his brother-in-law the "shame &

plague of our family." Littlepage referred to Mary Coleman as his "unhappy, deluded Sister" (Curtis Carroll Davis, *The King's Chevalier: A Biography of Lewis Littlepage* [Indianapolis, 1965], 116, 362-3, 366-7, 387; Nell Holladay Boand, *Lewis Littlepage*, [Richmond, 1970], 270-6; Vol. 32:3-4, 40).

It is likely that the letter from J<small>OHN</small> D<small>AWSON</small> was one dated 30 Sep. 1800, and that TJ wrote his A<small>NSWER</small> a few days later, on 3 Oct. Neither communication has been found (Vol. 32:217n).

A<small>CPTS</small>: accounts.

From Johnson Cook

S<small>IR</small>   Maraetta 20th octobr 1801

in My first letter I dropt at the Close of the same some hints [concerning your] Enemys and the enemys to true rebubliccans in our first Election for A Reprisentative to the genaral assembly Coln Meigs was held up as A Candedate in oposition to the candedate above mentioned were Evry federal oficer then in publick service and they yousd Evry artifice that lay within their power to disgrace the man that had Merited better yousage from Evry American their Efforts were infectiel they were blasted in their desighn's and the blame thron upon an old Contenental Serjiant the Communications that I transmit to your Exelency are real and Can be attested to by hundreds in this County but I fear not the My Enemys which are but few in Comparison to My friends it is the farmers living out that out does the citysans in the County seats—

Sir I am perswaded your Excelency is not in dout who I have Aluded to one your Excelency has seen fit to deprive of govermental support and the Other it is the wish of Evry Rebublickan in this place that he Might share the same fate altho it would Cause A stagnation of Money in this place in Case the lot should not fall on some other person here his Overbaring influence with the Merchats on Acounts of his draughts on the bank of the united states Causes Eristecrassy to be the prevailing distemper raging in its direfull form on all those of that profession after A long seryes of insults unresented at the first but now openly profsions of My stedfastness has Excited their surprise and Ma[llace] to A high degree I and Evry American has reason to morn that their is such A party spirit hovering throughout the once united states but we have reason to believe that by your Excelencys good manegement of goverment that the unconvinced will find their Mistake and yet believe that your Exelenceys proceedings are Just and that they were in A reched Eror I find some of the greatest of your enemyes do give in that your shuting up algiers in stead of paying them tribute was the best peace of polycy Ever tranceacted in our goverment—

Sir I hope your Excellency will not take it amiss that A poor man as I am should attempt to rite upon politicks and Especilly to A man of your rank and station in the world for I must acnolege I am poor and lightly Esteemed besides being ignorant as to scribling My Maner of life Ever since I left the army in 83 has ben to labor Exsessively hard and by Meeting with some serios Misfortings I have acquired very little propperty notwithstand I have an independant Mind and A high Notion of suporting the Cause which I suffard amaisingly in the Contest with grat briton to gain Sir with sentements of Estem for the high notion of your Excelncys being the very man I wish for to hold the helm of goverment I reman your very humble Servant   JOHNSON COOK

RC (DLC); faint; addressed: "To Thomas Jefferson Esqr. Presedent of the united states Federal Citye" and "No 2"; endorsed by TJ on Cook's letter of 21 Oct. as one of three letters received from him on 9 Nov. and so recorded in SJL.

MY FIRST LETTER: Cook to TJ, 17 Oct. Return Jonathan MEIGS, Sr., represented Washington County in Ohio's first territorial legislature from 1799 to 1801 (ANB; Israel Ward Andrews, *Washington County, and the Early Settlement of Ohio* [Cincinnati, 1877], 20, 76).

To Kezia Norris

[MADAM]   Washington Oct. 20 1801

I have duly recieved your favor covering a Note of Bishop Carroll's which I now return according to your desire. [soon] after my coming to this place I recieved applications from different parts of the Union for contributions to churches, colleges, schools, bridges, & other useful institutions. I yielded to them until they became so numerous as to shew that either I must contribute to the useful institutions of e[. . .] or [confine] myself to the one with which I was associated by situation. beyond this, all had their equal claims. the first [alternative] being beyond the means of any individual, I was obliged to adopt the latter as the only remaining rule of my conduct. nobody applauds more than I do the institution which is the subject of your letter, nor the laudable [zeal] with which you espouse it's interests, nor can any one [hope] more sincerely for it's success. the wealth & public spirit of the city of Baltimore leaves us the less to fear on that subject, & the less to regret that it is out of the line of external aid. I beg you to accept assurances of my high consideration & respect.

TH: JEFFERSON

PrC (MdHi); faint; at foot of text: "Mrs Kesiah Norton," perhaps at the same time TJ endorsed the letter, he wrote, in ink, "Norris" in place of "Norton"; endorsed by TJ in ink on verso.

YOUR FAVOR: Norris to TJ, 19 Oct.

From Joseph Willcox

State of Connecticut

SIR   Killingworth Octr. 20th. 1801

My republican friends have solicited me to offer myself as a candidate for the office of Marshal of this State—and considering that the legislature has intolerantly driven me to the necessity of resigning all military rank, I am induced to waive those considerations of reserve, which might Otherwise have influenced me & to offer myself as a candidate for that Office,

However easy it might be to obtain a long list of respectable Names to sustain this Application, I prefer to rely on a direct statement, that my situation in the State is central, My habits of Attention to business established, and that my Ambition to discharge the duties of the Office (if conferred) will be equalled only by my respect for the administration, which has the power of conferring it.

I have the honor to be Sir—with the greatest respect yr very humble servant—   JOSEPH WILLCOX 2D

RC (DNA: RG 59, LAR); at head of text: "To the President of the United States"; endorsed by TJ as received 27 Oct. and so recorded in SJL; also endorsed by TJ: "to be Marshal of Connecticut."

Joseph Willcox (1757-1817), a Revolutionary War veteran from Killingworth, Connecticut, was a member of the Connecticut General Assembly in the 1790s. In June 1801, after thirty years' military duty, he resigned as brigadier general and commanding officer of Connecticut's second brigade militia upon learning that the state legislature promoted a subordinate officer ahead of him. TJ appointed him marshal of the district of Connecticut in December 1801 and re-newed him in this post in 1805. Willcox resigned as marshal in 1809 and subsequently settled in Marietta, Ohio (Heitman, *Register*, 593; *Roll of State Officers and Members of General Assembly of Connecticut, from 1776 to 1881* [Hartford, Conn., 1881], 96, 113; JEP, 1:397, 399; 2:5, 122; New Haven *Connecticut Journal*, 17 Aug. 1796; Boston *Constitutional Telegraphe*, 10 June 1801; Hartford *Connecticut Courant*, 5 July 1809 and 11 Feb. 1817; Vol. 33:671, 674n, 678).

MY REPUBLICAN FRIENDS: possibly Gideon Granger and Elisha Hyde, who along with Willcox were known as the "triumvirate of Connecticut" (Hartford *Connecticut Courant*, 16 Nov. 1801). See also Pierpont Edwards and Ephraim Kirby to TJ, 22 Oct.

From John Woodside

SIR   City of Washington Octr. 20th. 1801

The inclosed was lately received in a letter from Leghorn, but being unacquainted with Italian it is not for me to enjoy the pleasure of a perusal in that harmonious tongue.

Permit me Sir to say that the sentiments and principles therein expressed in Italian, as to their leading features have been, I trust, indelibly engraven on my heart in true republican characters, else why that unison, that glow & expansion of heart, and elevation of soul which with many was experienced on the memorable fourth of March last, when these sentiments flowed from the heart, and came in such manly patriotic accents from the lips, and such true republican dignity from the respected Citizen just about to be inaugurated with those constitutional powers, which the decidedly manifest, and previous confidence of "The People" his fellow Citizens wished him to possess.

Since that auspicious period many, very many, not only of the Citizens of these States, but of the World have participated in a degree of the same pleasure by its perusal in their several tongues and languages, and under favor of divine providence it is hoped that the principles of true republicanism thus happily disseminated, will in due time be productive of a portion of that "Peace, Liberty, and

Safety" which nothing but the diffusive light of the gospel of Jesus Christ and the universal prevalence of Christian motives, principles precepts and practice can increase and preserve to *All People.*

To Mr Cathcart who forwarded the inclosed had been sent in the language of the United States what is returned in Italian, the only acknowledgement of his having received the inaugural speech of the President of the United States, this has given occasion, and an individual though obscure, begs leave to present the inclosed *to you Sir,* as a token of that respect which I owe to the person who is the choice of that "*people,*" who, in opposition to the created hosts of dependents and all their influence, artifices and threatnings, evinced their firmness and patriotism, their discernment and good sense, in their choice.

Under these impressions and as it can be done in truth and sincerity I beg leave to subscribe myself, and

am Sir, very respectfully your Obedt. Servant

JNO WOODSIDE

RC (DLC); at foot of text: "To Thomas Jefferson President of the United States"; endorsed by TJ as received 21 Oct. and so recorded in SJL with notation: "Geo.T." Enclosure not found.

John Woodside (1749-1835) was a clerk in the comptroller's office of the Treasury Department and the father-in-law of James Leander Cathcart. A veteran of the Revolutionary War, Woodside was a second lieutenant in a Pennsylvania battalion when he was captured at Fort Washington in 1776 and imprisoned for a year and a half (Cunningham, *Process of Government*, 328; Madison, *Papers, Sec. of State Ser.*, 4:161, 163; Heitman, *Register*, 605; *Daily National Intelligencer*, 4 Aug. 1835; Robert Patterson to TJ, 8 June).

William Duane's 1801 evaluation of government clerks identified Woodside as a Republican (Gallatin, *Papers*, 6:354-5).

From Johnson Cook

SIR   Mareatta 21st October 1801

in my letter first I intimated something Respeckting your Enemys here and the Enemeys of true rebublickans god grant that they may be less or fewer of them their is some few of them got convinced within these few days their is not an Emegrant from Connecticut within this County but what is realy A friend to your honor and A true republickan the boston Emegrants are hauty Sovrin and overbaring arbitary in all our town affairs and wishing that your Excelency Might be beheaded within one year they are blind to all intents and purpeses they want their old adams to lead the band nothing Else will serve them in old scripter times they were wont to say among the Sirians &

babelonians that Jerusalem was formally A rebelyous Citye And we may say that bostonians are actially under the same discrption and ought to bare the same Curse from god and man as they did in those days My lord I pray you would not be discouriged at the Culumneys of New haven Merchants I know them all well or those bostonians which wants an adams or G Wtn or any other Eristicat at the helm of goverment the days will come that We and they shall know hoo direckts affairs best and hoo is just or unjust I wish your Excelency to Consider the Calumney as A blast of wind that will soon blow over and vanish as A scrall I wish[1] I could have the honer of knowing your Exelency persanly but I must content my self with knowing your honer and in out doing and out ving Evry leader before you god grant that you might long Continue in office treading down the haughty and lifting up those that is more diserving of publick Esteem and Suport that you Might hold out to the End doing good to the world pulling down the old bull works and Ereckting new ones more to the intrest and general weal of the States from Sentements of real Esteem and from the love I bare your Excelency I subscribe My Self your Excelencys very humble Servant   JOHNSON COOK

N.B. Sir I rite after I perform A hard days work in the field I wish to be Excused for the Badness of riting in concequence thereof

RC (DLC); addressed: "Thomas Jefferson Esqr Presaden of the United States Federal Citye" and "No 3"; endorsed by TJ as one of three letters (the others dated 17 and 20 Oct.) received from Cook on 9 Nov. and so recorded in SJL.

[1] MS: "I wish I wish."

From Samuel Smith

SIR/   Baltimore 21. Octr. 1801
    The Inclosed was sent to me by a Person now in Jail for Debt, He claims being introduced to me by Mr. Claiborne—I have no Recollections of that circumstance—nor have I any Knowledge of him or his character—He wishes me to release him from his present Confinement, but from his own Story I cannot See that he merits any Attention, if he has any claim on the Publick, his Father would Certainly not refuse him the small sum 75 Dolls. for which he is Confined—I take the Liberty to give this Information—he writes me that his Recommendations are from Mr. Wythe & Mr. Munroe, which ought certainly to have great Weight. Accept the Assurance of my most perfect Respect   S. SMITH

RC (DLC); endorsed by TJ as received 22 Oct. and so recorded in SJL. Enclosure: Samuel Quarrier to TJ, 19 Oct. 1801, not found, recorded in SJL as received from Baltimore on 22 Oct.

For the very brief note written by George WYTHE on 4 July on Samuel Quarrier's behalf, see TJ to Henry Dearborn, 14 Aug. 1801.

To John Beckley

[22 Oct. 1801]

I have this moment been called on by mr Saml. Hanson of Samuel of this place to write to you on the following subject. you have probably heard of the famous suit brought against him by Forrest for calling him a swindler, whereon the latter recovered one cent damage. but the bank of Columbia whose Cashier Hanson was, have removed him. there is not a worthier man on earth, nor one of more independant republican principles. he is [generally] called one of *the four* who alone preserved their political principles in this place through the late trying times. this removal leaves him without bread. we all take for granted you will be restored to your former office in the house of representatives. in that event mr Hanson asks to be one of your engrossing clerks which he says will subsist him till he can get under way in some other vocation. he is a man of literature, very much respected & beloved by the republican interest of this state. I have thought myself bound to bear this testimony to truth, leaving it's effect entirely to your own convenience or pre-arrangements.

I recieved from the persons to whom the inclosed is directed, a present of a quarter of a *Mammoth-veal* which at 115. days old weighed 438. ℔. [since] they are butchers, & not knowing their address I avail myself of your cover & of your friendship to have them sought, & the letter delivered them. mr Butler gave us hopes we should see you here shortly. accept assurances of my great esteem & attachment.   TH: JEFFERSON

P.S. I note the proceedings against mr Duane. my faculties whether public or private will be exercised for his support whenever I shall be informed that they are necessary.

PrC (DLC); top of sheet clipped and frayed, cutting off salutation and date; faint; torn; at foot of text in ink: "Beckley John"; endorsed by TJ in ink on verso as a letter of 22 Oct. and recorded in SJL under that date. Enclosure: TJ to Michael Fry and Nathan Coleman, 22 Oct.

YOUR FORMER OFFICE: Beckley served as the first clerk of the House of Representatives until removed by the Federalists in May 1797 (Vol. 29:374n).

To Thomas Claxton

SIR   Washington Oct. 22. 1801.

I have duly recieved your favor informing me of your disappointment as to the grates. I think with you we had better get common
cheap ones made here for this winter & perhaps order from England
proper ones for the next year. six will do for the house for this winter.
the one for the kitchen you will be pleased to get either in Philadelphia or here as you think best. accept my best wishes & esteem.

                                              TH: JEFFERSON

PrC (MHi); at foot of text: "Mr. Clax-   YOUR FAVOR: Claxton to TJ, 19 Oct.
ton"; endorsed by TJ in ink on verso.

From Denniston & Cheetham

SIR   New York October 22nd. 1801

Much noise has been made Concerning the report of your having
ordered Mr. Dallas to enter a *Nolle Prosequi* in the Suit against
Mr. Duane commenced by your predecessor on the behalf of the Senate of the United States. An inflamatory essay which appeared in the
gazette of the United States, on the unconstitutionality of the act,
under the Signature of *Juris Consultus* has been republished in most
of our federal prints and has excited a little disquietude even in the
minds of Some republicans not well acquainted with the nature of
such a proceeding. No defence of it has yet been made in our Republican prints, and our Silence has been Construed by many really
honest men into an acknowledgement that the act is neither Constitutional nor precedented. In both these points of view after a full
examination of the Subject, we are wholly satisfied, that if a *Nolle
Prosequi* was ordered by you to be entered it is neither unprecedented
nor in our opinion unconstitutional. We are Determined, however, to
defend your measures while they appear to us, as they have hitherto
done, not only Constitutional and Just, but highly Commendable.
We value the principle which raised you to the Chief Magistracy of
the Union, and on which you act, too highly not to exert ourselves in
the Defence of measures Compatible with it. We are Solicitous to
write a few essays on the subject here adverted to.—But we are wanting in information respecting it. We want to be informed Whether
the *Nolle Prosequi* was ordered to be entered by you in the Case mentioned, and if so on what ground? We are aware of the Delicacy of

asking this information from you. But we are persuaded that it Cannot come from a purer and more enlightened source. Should you think the request not incompatible with your high political station, the earlier you impart to us the information the more acceptable it will be. At all events we shall defend the act, but our Defence will not be so Complete without the information as with it.

We beg pardon for troubling you with so long a letter

We are Sincerely Your devouted freinds

DENNISTON & CHEETHAM

RC (DLC); in Denniston's hand and signed by him; addressed: "Thomas Jefferson President of the United States Washington"; endorsed by TJ as received 26 Oct. and so recorded in SJL.

On 3 Sep., the *Gazette of the United States* printed an essay signed JURIS CONSULTUS, which denounced TJ's decision to halt the federal prosecution against William Duane under the Sedition Act. Professing disbelief that "an expedient, so *fatal to the constitution*, has been adopted to screen a guilty *favourite* from the justice of the *law*," the author accused TJ of being "an *usurper,* that he has *broken the constitution*" and called upon public representatives to bring a bill of impeachment "for a HIGH CRIME against the *constitution* and *people* of the United States of America." Two additional essays under the same name appeared in the *Gazette of the United States* on 4 and 8 Sep. The first detailed Duane's history of "obscenity, calumny, and corruption" and again condemned TJ for wresting "from the hands of justice, a wretch, who having spared none himself, was less than any other entitled to the *extraordinary* interposition of presidential prerogative!" The final essay put forth a lengthy argument that "the power of granting *Nolle Prosequi's* to criminals is not, by the constitution of the United States, vested in the President."

On 22 Oct., Denniston & Cheetham also wrote Gallatin, forwarding documents respecting Richard Rogers, naval officer at the New York custom house, including a certificate written and signed by John Utt, Sr., dated New York, 20 Oct. 1801, with a 1782 bill of sale, in Rogers's hand, confirming that Rogers was "in the employ of the British" in New York during the Revolution. Utt concluded: "his Sentiments During the Revolution were monarchical and Still Remain so." Jacob Forsyth, clerk at the custom house, wrote and signed a statement, dated New York, 24 July 1801, describing an incident in which Rogers angrily refused to provide Denniston with commercial information on the arrival of a vessel for his newspaper. Denniston noted no impediments were "ever thrown in the way of federal printers." John Chapman, a Federalist merchant, signed a certificate dated New York, 19 June 1801, describing the difficulties he had in obtaining a register at New York for an American-built vessel. Denniston concluded that they were sending the documents to Gallatin as promised. He added: "though the removal of Mr. Rogers from office would gratify ourselves as well as every Republican in this City, Yet we shall be perfectly Satisfied with the determination of the executive on the point, whatever it may be—being Confident that all his measures are Guided by a love of Justice and a Sincere desire to promote the liberty of the Commonwealth" (RC in DNA: RG 59, LAR, 9:0854-6, in Denniston's hand and signed by him, endorsed by TJ: "Denniston & Chetham to mr Gallatin against Rogers"; enclosures in same, 9:0857-60).

From Nicolas Gouin Dufief

MONSIEUR, 22 d'octobre. 1801

J'ai remis suivant vos desirs à Mr. Barnes les livres dont vous m'avez envoyé la note—Le Remembrancer n'est pas celui dont il est fait mention dans mon Catalogue; il étoit vendu lorsque je reçus l'honneur de la votre, d'ailleurs plusieurs des volumes avoient été endommagés ce que j'avois oublié de mentioner.

J'ai ajouté depuis peu à ma Collection la portion de la Bibliotheque du Dr B. Franklin leguée par lui à son petit fils *Temple Franklin*. Sans l'entousiasme de nos Concitoyens a faire l'acquisition de ses livres J'aurois accompli mon dessein de vous en envoyer le catalogue manscript; mais en ayant une fois annoncé la vente dans les papiers publics il ne m'a pas été possible de me me refuser a l'empressement général à se les procurer—Il s'est trouvé parmi ces livres la fameuse lettre de *Trasibule* à *Leucippe* en Manuscript. peut étre plus correcte & plus complète que les Editions imprimées ce dont je n'ai pu m'assurer n'en ayant aucune pour en faire la comparaison—J'ai pensé que vous me feriez l'honneur de l'accepter; cela m'a enhardi a mettre cet ouvrage parmi vos livres—

Les livres suivans sont les principaux ouvrages qui me restent de cette Bibliotheque

			Dlrs	
The Parliamentary history in	24 V. 8o. neatly bd in calf		30	"
— Lords Protests from 1242=1767.	2 8	D	2	"
— — — during the Amer. war.	Do		1	"
the Journal of the house of Commons 15 V. folio (not complete)			40	"
Debates of	Do 22.	8	18	"

Je viens de recevoir de Londres un ouvrage curieux intitulé "Dictionnaire biographique & historique des hommes *marquans* de la fin du 18eme. siecle & plus particulierement de ceux qui ont figuré dans la Revolution francaise &ca" Je me propose de le garder quelque tems afin de le lire; ainsi s'il vous interesse il sera a votre disposition: prix six dollars les 3 V. 8vo.

Si vous desiriez faire l'acquisition de 2 beaux bustes de Voltaire & de Rousseau en marbre de *Carare*; J'en ai deux excellentes copies apportées de France par Mr. De Ternant, sculptés par Gèrrachy, d'après Pigal. J'ai fait faire deux colonnes à l'antique pour les supporter, elles font le plus bel effet du monde—Mr Barne a qui je les ai montrées pourra vous en donner une idée—le prix qui est de deux cents Gourdes est fort au dessous de ce qu'elles valent

J'ai l'honneur d'etre avec les sontimens les plus respectueux—&
l'estime la plus profonde Votre très devoué serviteur

N. G. DUFIEF

EDITORS' TRANSLATION

SIR,   22 October 1801

Following your desires, I have turned over to Mr. Barnes the books in
the note you sent to me. The *Remembrancer* is not the one mentioned in my
catalogue; it was sold at the time I had the honor of receiving your letter,
moreover, several of the volumes had been damaged, which I had forgotten
to mention.

Recently, I have added to my collection the portion of Dr. B. Franklin's library left by him to his grandson, *Temple Franklin*. Werc it not for the en-
thusiasm of our fellow citizens to acquire some of his books, I would have
fulfilled my plan of sending to you its manuscript catalogue; but, once having announced the sale in the public papers, it was not possible for me to
deny the general eagerness to acquire them. Among those books there was
the famous Letter from *Thrasybulus* to *Leucippus* in manuscript, perhaps
more correct and more complete than the printed editions, which I was not
able to ascertain, not having any to compare it with. I thought that you would
do me the honor of accepting it; that emboldened me to place that work
among your books.

The following books are the main works that I have left from that library:

			Dlrs	
The Parliamentary history in	24 V. 8o. neatly bd in calf		30	"
— Lords Protests from 1242=1767.	2 8	D	2	"
— — — during the Amer. war.	Do		1	"
the Journal of the house of Commons 15 V. folio (not complete)			40	"
Debates of	Do	22. 8	18	"

I have just received from London a curious work entitled "Biographical and
historical Dictionary of the *outstanding* men of the end of the 18th century,
and most especially of those who figured in the French Revolution, etc." I
propose to keep it for some time in order to read it; thus, if it interests you, it
will be at your disposal: price, six dollars for the three volumes in octavo.

If you should desire to acquire two fine busts of Voltaire and Rousseau in
Carrara marble, I have two excellent copies brought from France by Mr. de
Ternant, sculpted by Gèrrachy, after Pigalle. I had two antique-style columns
made for pedestals, which make the finest effect in the world. Mr. Barnes, to
whom I showed them, can give you an idea of them. The price of two hundred *gourdes* is far below what they are worth.

I have the honor to be, with the most respectful sentiments, and the deepest esteem, your very devoted servant   N. G. DUFIEF

RC (DLC; at head of text: "Thomas Jefferson. Esqre"; endorsed by TJ as received 26 Oct. and so recorded in SJL, but as a letter of 23 Oct.).

The NOTE may have been a communication from TJ to Dufief of 18 Aug., which is recorded in SJL but has not been found. The REMEMBRANCER that

Dufief sent was apparently *The Remembrancer, or Impartial Repository of Public Events*, compiled by John Almon and published in London in installments from 1775 to the end of the American Revolution (Sowerby, No. 3070).

In September and October 1801, Dufief advertised for sale "a considerable part of the select and valuable Library of the celebrated Philosopher and Statesman," Benjamin FRANKLIN. The offering attracted only a modest response, although the American Philosophical Society did buy several dozen volumes. In 1803, Dufief mounted a new effort to sell books from Franklin's collection, again with less success than he hoped (*Philadelphia Gazette*, 15 Sep. 1801; Madeleine B. Stern, *Nicholas Gouin Dufief of Philadelphia: Franco-American Bookseller, 1776-1834* [Philadelphia, 1988], 23-32; APS, *Proceedings*, 22, pt. 3 [1884], 314-17).

LA FAMEUSE LETTRE DE TRASIBULE À LEUCIPPE: the 155-leaf manuscript that Dufief gave TJ from Franklin's library was Nicolas Freret, "Lettre de Trasibule à Leucippe. Ouvrage critique, historique, metaphisique &c. Ou l'on nie la verité de toutes les Religions.—l'existence de Dieu, et l'immortalité de l'ame" ("a critical, historical, metaphysical, etc., work, in which is denied the truth of all religions, the existence of God, and the immortality of the soul"). Freret lived from 1688 to 1749. His authorship of the manuscript has been disputed (see Sowerby, No. 1291).

The PARLIAMENTARY HISTORY from Franklin's library was *The Parliamentary or Constitutional History of England; From the Earliest Times, to the Restoration of King Charles II. Collected . . . by Several Hands*, 2d ed., 24 vols. (London, 1761-63; Sowerby, No. 2925). The books pertaining to the House of Lords were *A Complete Collection of the Lords' Protests from the First upon Record, in the Reign of Henry the Third, to the Present Time*, 2 vols. (London, 1767), and *A Complete Collection of All the Protests of the Peers in Parliament Entered on their Journals, Since the Year 1774, on the Great Questions of the Cause and Issue of the War between Great-Britain and America, &c to the Present Time* (London, 1782).

DICTIONNAIRE BIOGRAPHIQUE: the *Dictionnaire biographique et historique des hommes marquans de la fin du dix-huitième siècle, et plus particulièrement de ceux qui ont figuré dans la Révolution Françoise*, 3 vols., 1800, with a London imprint but probably published in Hamburg. TJ described his copy as two books bound as a single volume. The work, credited in the publication itself as the product of a society of men of letters, has been attributed to Baron Coiffier de Verseux (Sowerby, No. 148).

The sculptor whom Dufief called GÈRRACHY may have been Giuseppe Ceracchi, who was executed in France in January 1801. Busts of Voltaire and Rousseau are not attributed to him, although the pieces mentioned by Dufief may not be well documented if they were copies of another artist's work. Jean Baptiste Pigalle made a famous statue of Voltaire and also a bust of him, but evidence is lacking of any Pigalle bust of Rousseau. One artist who did create notable busts of both Voltaire and Rousseau was Jean Antoine Houdon (Samuel Rocheblave, *Jean-Baptiste Pigalle* [Paris, 1919], 381-6; Dena Goodman, "Pigalle's *Voltaire nu*: The Republic of Letters Represents Itself to the World," *Representations*, 16 [1986], 86-109; Louis Réau, *Houdon: Sa Vie et son Œuvre*, 4 pts. in 2 vols. [Paris, 1964], 3:41, 44-5; Vol. 32:62n).

From Pierpont Edwards and Ephraim Kirby

SIR   New Haven Octr 22nd. 1801

It is with great diffidence that we make the communication, which forms the contents of this letter.—The subject has for a long time seriously engaged our attention, and that of our confidential republican friends—It is indeed of a very delicate nature.—Our troubles have been imbittered by the recollection that our own former measures have led us into the present dilemma.—A conviction, that we had been, by a wrong view of the subject, betrayed into an error, early took place.—To tread back our steps with honor seemed difficult—to suffer you to remain ignorant that we had wholly changed our opinion, untill it should be too late, would be little less than treason against you: but the honor and interest of our country; and faithfulness to our beloved President, were considerations superior to all others, and they demand of us to rescind our former nomination of a Marshall, and to state to you frankly, that we are perfectly convinced, that *Parsons* ought not to be appointed Marshall, and to name to you Genl Joseph Wilcox of Killingsworth in his place. General Wilcox is a Gentleman of a sound well informed mind, possesses a handsome property, and served thro' the whole revolutionary war in the American Army, and is very highly respected thro' out the State.

We have, however, in transacting this business also to discharge a duty which we owe to ourselves.—You will ask "why this change of opinion"? We foresaw that the question would occur; and altho' to us, the answer was obvious, and perfectly satisfactory, we were not without some solicitude, lest it should not appear so to you. Besides we were to apprehend, that you might imagine, that we had made our former nomination without due deliberation; but an impressive sense of its being our duty, rather to risque our character with you, in point of due deliberation than by our former nomination, to injure the interests of our country and hazard your honor, pointed us to an explicit acknowledgment that we had done wrong in nominating Parsons.

When we recommended him, we acted according to the knowledge we then possessed regarding his general and his political character. Since that time developements have been made which have totally destroyed all our confidence in him as a man and as a politician. We will mention one or two facts only.—He has already promised the office of Deputy Marshal to two persons, who have been and now are most violent Federalists.—The Federalists are all highly pleased with the idea, that he is to be Marshall, and some of their indiscreet ones have boasted that the democrats will be taken in by his being appointed.

He is a man of the most consummate art, and we can by no means give the smallest countenance to his appointment.

General Wilcox, is Joseph Wilcox the second; there being another man of the same name still living in the town of Killingworth.

This letter is written with the advice and approbation of Mr Granger and Mr Wolcott, and the appointment of Wilcox is a measure earnestly called for, by all the respectable republicans in Connecticut.

We are Sir, with the highest respect Your Obedt Servts

PIERPT EDWARDS
EPHM KIRBY

RC (DNA: RG 59, LAR); entirely in Edwards's hand and signed by him; at foot of text: "His Excy. Thomas Jefferson President of the U. States"; endorsed by TJ as received 27 Oct. and "Joseph Wilcox to be marshal" and so recorded in SJL.

OUR OWN FORMER MEASURES: for Connecticut Republicans' earlier recommendation of Enoch Parsons to TJ for the marshalship of Connecticut, see Vol. 33:590-1n.

To Michael Fry and Nathan Coleman

GENTLEMEN   Washington Oct. 22. 1801.

I recieved on the 20th. your favor of the 17th. and this morning arrived the quarter you were so kind as to send me of the Mammoth-veal. tho' so far advanced as to be condemned for the table, yet it retained all the beauty of it's appearance, it's fatness & enormous size. a repetition of such successful examples of enlarging the animal volume will do more towards correcting the erroneous opinions of European writers as to the effect of our climate on the size of animals, than any thing I have been able to do. I tender you my sincere thanks for this mark of your attention and recieve with very great satisfaction the expressions of your attachment to the form & principles of our government. as far as we can judge by the event of elections, these principles are resuming their empire over the minds of those who in a moment of alarm & terror had been made to doubt their practicability and safety. Accept I pray you assurances of my regard & best wishes.

TH: JEFFERSON

PrC (DLC); at foot of text: "Messrs. Fry & Coleman"; endorsed by TJ in ink on verso. Enclosed in TJ to John Beckley, 22 Oct.

According to his financial memoranda, on this day TJ paid John H. Barney, operator of a stage line between Philadelphia and Alexandria, for "portage" of the veal (MB, 2:1056; Vol. 33:415).

From George Jefferson

DEAR SIR   Richmond 22d. Octr. 1801

I duly received your favor of the 19th and have by to nights post written to our correspondent in Petersburg to make a purchase of the tobacco you require agreeably to your direction. for although it has got up there as I understand to 27/. yet I think it will more probably rise still higher than fall.

Mr. Ashley of Norfolk informs me that he has forwarded you some Hams, which I hope will arrive safe

I am Dear Sir Your Very humble servt.   GEO. JEFFERSON

RC (MHi); at foot of text: "Thos. Jefferson esqr."; endorsed by TJ as received 26 Oct. and so recorded in SJL.

From James Lyon

Oct. 22d—

The assistance which Mr. Jefferson has rendered to the Washington Printing & Bookselling Company, is thankfully acknowledged. The Agent has the pleasure to enclose him the Constitution of the Company; a prospectus of a Magazine, and the first number of the work; together with a copy of a letter explanatory of the Plan for Branch Offices. One of these last will be addressed to some Gentlemen, in Lynchburg, as soon as the agent can be informed of a proper character there, to receive subscriptions; and if one hundred and fifty can be obtained an office with a man to manage it will be sent to that place

RC (DLC); written on verso of second sheet of printed broadside of the constitution of the Washington Printing and Bookselling Company dated 1 Aug. 1801; endorsed by TJ as received 24 Oct. and so recorded in SJL. Enclosures: (1) Prospectus of the weekly *National Magazine, or Cabinet of the United States* and the biweekly *Franklin; or, A Political, Agricultural and Mechanical Gazette,* 17 Oct. 1801 (printed copy in same). (2) *National Magazine,* 22 Oct., the first issue of a publication that came out irregularly and was suspended with the 11 Jan. 1802 issue (Sowerby, No. 4899). (3) blank printed subscription forms with terms and conditions for the *Frank-* *lin Gazette* and subscription form for a gazette or weekly paper, 17 Oct. (printed copy in DLC).

For the ASSISTANCE TJ rendered to Lyon's previous printing endeavors, see MB, 2:1002, 1003; Vol. 32:305.

Lyon, as principal agent of the WASHINGTON PRINTING & BOOKSELLING COMPANY, superintended the business and subscriptions of the company as well as appointing agents in other parts of the country and serving on the board's pecuniary committee. Richard Dinmore was the publication's editor and served on the board's literary committee. By 11 Sep., enough shares of stock had been raised so that Lyon and ten others were appointed to a board of directors that met to commence the publication (*American Citizen and General Advertiser*, 23 Sep. 1801; Shaw-Shoemaker, No. 1612).

Lyon first presented his PLAN FOR BRANCH OFFICES, including one at Lynchburg, as well as a proposal for a weekly Washington paper in pamphlet form, in his letter to TJ of 23 July.

Notes on a Cabinet Meeting

Oct. 22. prest. 4. Secretaries. Captains of Navy reduced from 15.[1] to 9. by a vote on each man struck off. those struck off are Mc.Niel of Boston, Decatur of Pensva., Rogers of Maryld. Tingey of Columbia, *S. Barron of Virga, *Campbell from S. Cara. but a Northern man. the retained are Nicholson & Preble of Mass. Morris & Bainbridge of N.Y. Truxton of Jersey, Barry, Dale & Murray of Pensva. Jas Barron of Virga.

a state of the gallies to be called for and be ready for sale at meeting of Congress unless contrary determn.

Spain to be addressed in a firm but friendly tone on the depredns at Algesiras. not to order convoys for our vessels agt Spain

*on the resignation of Truxton S: Barron is retained, & on that of Preble, Campbell is retained. he is a S. Carolinian by birth[2]

MS (DLC: TJ Papers, 112:19297); entirely in TJ's hand; follows, on same sheet, Notes on a Cabinet Meeting of 13 June; TJ added the note, and the asterisks keying it to the text, in 1802 (see note 2 below).

SECRETARIES: Madison, Gallatin, Dearborn, and Robert Smith.

Probably in association with this meeting, TJ made a list of the 15 naval captains on a small slip of paper, grouping the officers by state. He STRUCK OFF the names of Daniel McNeill, Stephen Decatur, John Rodgers, Thomas Tingey, Samuel Barron, and Hugh George Campbell. He placed checkmarks next to Edward Preble's, William Bainbridge's, Thomas Truxtun's, and John Barry's names (MS in DLC: TJ Papers, 119:20566; entirely in TJ's hand; undated).

STATE OF THE GALLIES: in May 1798,

Congress appropriated $80,000 for the acquisition and outfitting of up to ten small vessels to be used as galleys. At least seven were built in North Carolina, South Carolina, and Georgia, where they were used for coastal defense. By early 1802, all seven had been either sold or transferred to the revenue cutter service (U.S. Statutes at Large, 1:556; NDQW, Aug. 1799-Dec. 1799, 484; Dec. 1800-Dec. 1801, 126, 364-5, 367-8, 371, 459-60).

According to Madison's letter of 25 Oct. to Charles Pinckney about the seizure of American ships for alleged blockade violations, TJ had "the strongest hopes" that SPAIN had already taken steps on its own to make redress for the captures and put a stop to the practice. If Pinckney found otherwise, he was to make "fair and frank representations" to the Spanish government (Madison, *Papers, Sec. of State Ser.*, 2:202).

[1] Figure altered by TJ from "16."

[2] TJ added this note on the same sheet, below his notes on cabinet meetings of 11 Nov. 1801 and 18 Jan. 1802 but preceding his notes on a meeting of 21 Oct. 1802. Robert Smith accepted Thomas Truxtun's resignation on 13 Mch. 1802. In April 1802, Smith granted Edward Preble a furlough for health reasons (NDBW, 2:76, 83, 123, 133).

From Rapine, Conrad & Co.

SIR,   Washington City Octr. 22, 1801

We are about to publish a new Law book of great merit; (as ℔ subscription paper inclosed) and as the sale of Law books is confined to a particular class of gentlemen, & consequently slow, we think it prudent to obtain as many subscribers as possible, to partly reimburse us soon after the publication of the work, which will be neatly executed & correctly printed. We therefore solicit your name as a sanction to the work, which will ever be remembered by

Sir, your Obt hble servts.   RAPINE, CONRAD & CO.

The bearer, our young man, will wait an answer

RC (MHi); in Daniel Rapine's hand and signed by him; at head of text: "The President of U.S."; endorsed by TJ as received 22 Oct. and so recorded in SJL. Enclosure not found.

In mid-November 1800, Rapine, Conrad & Co., formerly of Philadelphia, opened the new federal city's first bookstore and printing office, known as the Washington Book Store, at New Jersey Avenue and B Street, S.E. TJ was a regular customer who, on 10 July 1801, gave the booksellers an order on John Barnes for $76. On 6 Aug., Barnes entered in one of his statement of accounts with TJ the payment of another order in favor of Rapine, Conrad & Co., this one for $13.80. In October and November 1801, Rapine, Conrad & Co. advertised, in addition to the acts of the Sixth Congress, a "very handsome assortment of New Novels, of the first merit, with a good collection of law, and miscellaneous History, and a very elegant assortment of Ladies' and gentlemen's pocket books, of various prices and qualities" (MB, 2:1046, 1048; Bryan, National Capital, 1:383; National Intelligencer, 12 and 14 Oct., 6 Nov. 1801; statement of private account from John Barnes, 30 Sep. 1801, in ViU; Vol. 34:706, 708).

NEW LAW BOOK: TJ was one of the subscribers of Sir John Willes, *Reports of Adjudged Cases in the Court of Common Pleas. During the time Lord Chief Justice Willes presided in that Court; together with some few cases of the same period determined in the House of Lords, Court of Chancery, and Exchequer Chamber* (Philadelphia, 1802). The book, of which TJ received a copy on 7 Aug. 1802 for $4.50, was probably that referred to by the booksellers in their letter here (Sowerby, No. 2084; statement of account with Rapine, Conrad & Co., 4 May 1802-1 Jan. 1803, in MHi).

From John Vaughan

DEAR & RESPECTED SIR.   Philad: Oct. 22. 1801

I have been sir too many years acquainted with your Philanthropic Zeal, to concieve an apology necessary for addressing you on a Subject highly interesting to humanity

Since the Knowledge of the Vaccine Infection has become general, & its power of guarding against the Small Pox Contagion has been more Strongly Confirmed, than almost any discovery of like Standing; I have been extremely anxious to draw the attention of our Medical men towards it; & the more particularly, as thru' the medium of our Annual Lectures, This important discovery would Soon become familiar to the whole Continent—Many attempts have been made to introduce the Disorder here, but they have hitherto failed, as the Virus, brought here has in no Instance preserved its Power of Infecting—Dr J R Coxe has probably[1] been the most diligent in endeavoring to introduce it—Two packets recieved lately from England by him, have proved useless—Having accidentally heard, Sir, that you have introduced it into your family—I have hopes that you may have it in your power to enable D Coxe to make a more Successful experiment, by procuring (thro the medium of the Physician who may have attended your family)—the Virus.—It comes from England in Two ways, between Glass, Well covered with Gold beaters skin, or in Cotton thread in a small Ground Stopper Bottle—As the former may not easily be procured with you, I enclose a piece—Dr Valentine (One of the Members of our Phil: Sociy:) has informed us that the experiment has been generally, & Successfully tried in France.

A Mr Aikin of London, has published a Compendium of all that has been written upon the Subject—his Book has been reprinted at Boston, & as Soon as I can procure a Copy (which I have Sent for) I shall take the Liberty of forwarding it to you—

I remain with the greatest respect Your obedient Servant & friend

JN VAUGHAN

Should any Useful[2] important Ideas have Suggested themselves in the Course of the Experiments a communication of them will be thankfully recieved.

————

The *Limpid* liquor of the Pustule, not the Matter is recommended as the most efficacious

RC (DLC); at head of text: "His Exy. Thos. Jefferson Washington"; endorsed by TJ as received 24 Oct. and so recorded in SJL.

ANNUAL LECTURES: probably a reference to the lecture courses in medicine at the University of Pennsylvania that began each November (Joseph Carson, *A History of the Medical Department of the University of Pennsylvania* [Philadelphia, 1869], 95-6; *Poulson's American Daily Advertiser*, 15 Sep. 1801).

J R COXE: John Redman Coxe (Vol. 32:510n).

DR. VALENTINE: Louis Valentin, a French physician and surgeon and member of the American Philosophical Society since 1793. At a meeting on 16 Oct., the society recorded receipt from Valentin of a "pamphlet letter from the Comité Medical pour l'Inoculation, stating progress and soliciting the creation of similar establishments." The Comité Médical pour l'Inoculation de la Vaccine was founded in Paris in 1800 and supported by public subscriptions (Sowerby, No. 421; APS, *Proceedings*, 22, pt. 3 [1884], 212, 316); Elinor Meynell, "French Reactions to Jenner's Discovery of Smallpox Vaccination: The Primary Sources," *Social History of Medicine*, 8 [1995], 288).

An edition of *A Concise View of All the Most Important Facts which have Hitherto Appeared Concerning the Cowpox*, by Charles R. AIKIN, was published in Charlestown, Massachusetts, in April 1801. TJ already had a London edition sent by Benjamin Waterhouse (Shaw-Shoemaker, No. 24; Boston *Independent Chronicle*, 13-16 Apr.; Waterhouse to TJ, 8 June).

[1] Word interlined in place of "amongst others."
[2] Word interlined.

To Robert S. Coleman

SIR   Washington Oct. 23. 1801.

I recieved yesterday your favor of the 20. the last letter I have from Lewis Littlepage is dated at Altona Jan. 17. 1801. expressing his intention of coming to this country early the then ensuing spring. of this I gave notice to his brother mr Carter Littlepage. the latter further informed me that if any accident should happen to him he had deposited a will in England of which he had made Ld. Wycombe there, & myself here the executors. since the date of that letter I have heard nothing from him or of him. I think it probable he will endeavor to be here before the winter sets in. accept my respects & good wishes.

TH: JEFFERSON

PrC (MHi); at foot of text: "Mr. Robert S. Coleman"; endorsed by TJ in ink on verso.

LAST LETTER: TJ had not yet received Lewis Littlepage's 3 Aug. communication to him from London. On 8 May, after receiving Littlepage's January letter, TJ informed CARTER LITTLEPAGE that his brother's return to the United States seemed imminent.

Petition of William Hammell

New Haven Oct 23d 1801

The Petition of William Hammell of the City of New Haven in the State of Connecticutt, humbly sheweth—

That your Petitioner is informed that the United States are about to erect a Light House on Falkland Island in Long Island Sound; that there is to be appointed a keeper or overseer of said Light house— your Petr flatters himself that the certificate herewith sent will shew that he is well fitted to minster this office of Keeper or overseer of said Light house he therefore prays that he may be appointed Keeper or Overseer of said Light House whenever an appointment shall be made to said office   WILLIAM HAMMELL

RC (DNA: RG 26, MLR); at head of text: "To His Excellency Thomas Jefferson, President of the United States"; endorsed by clerk: "Falkner Island Lt house. Keeper recomd—this recomd. was handed by Mr Hillhouse of the Senate Jany 30, 1802." Enclosure: Certificate of Abraham Bradley and 35 others, New Haven, 21 Oct. 1801, stating that they are well acquainted with Hammell, that he is "an honest industrious, prudent, trusty man," and is "well fitted" to serve as keeper or overseer of the proposed lighthouse at Falkner Island (MS in same; in Hammell's hand, signed by Bradley and others).

For background on the construction of a lighthouse on Falkner (FALKLAND) ISLAND, see Albert Gallatin to TJ, 15 Aug. 1801. Joseph Griffing was appointed the first KEEPER of the Falkner Island lighthouse in 1802 (Harlan Hamilton, *Lights & Legends: A Historical Guide to Lighthouses of Long Island Sound, Fishers Island Sound and Block Island Sound* [Stamford, Conn., 1987], 116).

From Gouverneur Morris

DEAR SIR   Morrisania 23 Octr. 1801

I am asham'd at this late Day to reply to your Letter of the sixth of June. I waited at first for an opportunity to send round the Plate intending to let you have the whole on such Conditions as would have perfectly agreed with the State of the Funds which you was so kind as to communicate. I could meet with no Opportunity and lately the Chancellor being on his Way to France where a Service of Plate would be useful if not necessary I dispos'd of it to him on the same terms I had offered it to you.

I see by the public Papers that our modified Convention has been at length ratified. On this Event I heartily congratulate you. It will not, as many of the Gentlemen from your Quarter supposed it would, ruin the Price of Tobacco but it will have a remote Tendency to lower the extravagant Price of Labor and to bring Commerce more within the Circle of Oeconomic Calculation of Course to lower the Prices of foreign Productions which is in Effect the raising those of our own for Money you know is but the Counters by which the Game is scored and not the Stake played for.

I have the Honor to be with perfect Respect Dear Sir your obedient Servant   GOUV MORRIS

RC (DLC); at foot of text: "His Excellency Thomas Jefferson Esqr. President of the Unitd States"; endorsed by TJ as received 28 Oct. and so recorded in SJL. FC (Lb in DLC: Gouverneur Morris Papers).

From Henry Preble

SIR—   Bordeaux 23d. Octobr. 1801

I hope I shall be excused in addressing you when the cause of it so nearly regards my interest.

I had the honor to deliver to your Exy:, in Jany: last, a letter of introduction from Coln. Humphreys recommending me as a proper person to be appointed Consul of the U.S. at Cadiz.—Very contrary to my expectations I was appointed to that office by Mr Adams . . . for I had not the smallest promise of any thing of the kind;—but on the contrary, Mr Marshall told me, that he thought there would be no change in the Consulate at Cadiz at that time, but when there should be, as I was well recommended, no doubt I should have the appointment.—My commercial concerns obliged me to embark from the U.S. in March, soon after I heard of my appointment to the Consulship of Cadiz, otherwise, I should have waited on your Excy: and solicited a confirmation of that appointment, or some other, that might have been vacant. I wrote to the acting Secy: of State on the subject, but did not receive his answer 'till some time after my arrival in Europe.—

I flatter myself that your Exy. will believe me when I declare, that from the partiality I have always entertained for your sentiments & political opinions, I had more hopes of receiving an appointment from you, than from the former President of the U.S.; and I cannot but think, that had it been in my power to have visited Washington, before my departure from the U.S., I should have had the honor to receive some Consular appointment from your Excy.—

It was my intention to have embarked for the U.S. this Autumn, but understanding that the Consulship of Cadiz has been given to Mr

Forbes, great part of the object of my personal attendance there, no longer exists.—And as the person & property of any foreigner who may settle in a Port of Spain, who is not protected by a public office from his Govt:, or as a Roman Catholic, is not altogether secure, I have concluded not to settle in Spain, as I intended. I have therefore concluded to establish myself in France; and as it is, I believe, certain that the Government of France will not permit Mr Cathalan or Mr Dobree, as french citizens, to hold any employ in France under a foreign Govt:, there being a law to prevent it—I have humbly to solicit the appt: of Commercial Agent of the U.S. at Marseilles or Nantz, when your Exy. shall be officially assured that Mr Cathalan and Mr Dobree cannot hold any employ in France under the U.S.—

I flatter myself that my character is unimpeachable; and that there is in the Secy: of State's office a sufficient recommendation, from the Minister of the U.S. at Madrid, of my competent abilities to fill the office of Consul in any part of the World.—

With the highest consideration and respect I have the honor to be Your Exy. Mo: Obt. & Mo: huml Servt   HENRY PREBLE

RC (DNA: RG 59, LAR); at foot of text: "The President of the U.S. of America, &c &c &c Washington City"; ellipses in original; endorsed by TJ as received 21 Dec. and so recorded in SJL; also endorsed by TJ: "to be consul at Marseilles, Nantes, Cadiz."

Henry Preble (1770-1825), an American-born merchant in France, had been acting consul at Madrid and David Humphreys's secretary there. Preble, who was a younger brother of the naval officer Edward Preble, made "a general application" for a consulship by August 1800, hoping in particular for a position at Cadiz or Marseilles. In January 1801, he was in Washington and complained to then-Secretary of State John Marshall about the consul at Cadiz, Joseph Yznardi, Jr., in the case of a ship owned by Preble that had been captured by a Spanish privateer. On 18 Feb., John Adams appointed Preble to replace Yznardi as consul. The Senate, however, did not confirm the appointment in the closing days of the congressional session. In 1802 and after, Preble continued to seek a consular appointment. According to James Monroe in 1804, Preble was "not altogether in po-

litical sentiment" with TJ's administration. "M. says he is a federalist," TJ wrote in the filing endorsement of a letter from Preble to Monroe in January of that year. In 1819, Preble finally obtained a consular appointment at Palermo, Sicily, but he found the compensation inadequate and resigned the position (George Henry Preble, *Genealogical Sketch of the First Three Generations of Prebles in America* [Boston, 1868], 59, 265-71; Marshall, *Papers*, 4:241; 6:50, 55-6n, 517; Madison, *Papers, Sec. of State Ser.*, 3:342n; 6:531, 532n; Frank Landon Humphreys, *Life and Times of David Humphreys: Soldier–Statesman–Poet, 'Beloved of Washington'*, 2 vols. [New York, 1917], 2:279; Vol. 32:162-3; Humphreys to TJ, 8 May 1801; Preble to TJ, 26 Aug. 1802, Preble to Monroe, 2 Jan. 1804, and Preble to Madison, 19 June 1805, in DNA: RG 59, LAR).

The LETTER from Humphreys was dated 23 Sep. 1800 and received by TJ on 8 Jan. 1801 (Vol. 32:162).

WROTE TO THE ACTING SECY: OF STATE: on 31 Mch. 1801, Preble had written to the secretary of state from Boston, where he intended to embark for Europe, to ask if his commission as consul at Cadiz "would be forwarded to me or not" (DNA: RG 59, LAR). He apparently wrote on the previous day on that subject as well. At the time, Levi Lincoln was acting secretary of state.

Stephen CATHALAN, Jr., hoped to obtain U.S. citizenship to enable him to be a consul. Pierre Frédéric Dobrée, who died in 1801, had been appointed vice consul at Nantes in 1794. According to the December 1799 French constitution, acceptance of an appointment or pension from a foreign government meant a loss of French citizenship (Stewart, *French Revolution*, 769; Madison, *Papers, Sec. of State Ser.*, 1:351n; 2:19n, 211; Cathalan's letter to TJ of 14 June). On 5 Oct. 1801, William MacCreery, writing to [Robert?] Smith from Baltimore and unaware of Dobrée's death, recommended that Dobrée be reappointed as vice consul at Nantes. Smith passed MacCreery's letter along to TJ (RC in DNA: RG 59, LAR; torn; endorsed by TJ "Mcreery to mr Smith," which he canceled and endorsed "Dobree to be Consul Nantes."

MINISTER OF THE U.S. AT MADRID: that is, Humphreys, who had since been recalled.

To Henry Rose

DEAR SIR   Washington Oct. 23. 1801.

Your's of the 19th. is at hand. soon after my arrival at Monticello in Aug. I recieved from Dr. Waterhouse of Boston some vaccine matter of his own taking and some from Dr. Jenner of England just then come to hand. both of them took well, and exhibited the same identical appearances in the persons into whom they were inserted. I inoculated about 70 or 80 of my own family, my two sons in law as many, in Aug. & Sep. all had kernels under the arms, and a single pustule, to wit that made by the insertion. one or two of the whole number had very sore arms and 4. or 5 pustules on the arm. about 1 in 4. or 5. or 6. had slight feverish dispositions for an evening or two. none of them changed their regimen, & few intermitted their ordinary occupations. the inoculation of the mother in no instance gave it to the child which sucked her. being cautioned by Dr. Waterhouse to be particularly attentive to the state of the matter with which I inoculated, I was so & believe that I preserved the disease in it's genuine form. I found that taking the premature & the tardy cases of maturation, there was one day which both comprehended, to wit, the 8th. (say 8. times 24. hours) from the time of inoculation. at that point of time I do not know that I ever saw the matter in any patient either unformed, or shewing a commencement of maturation. I brought some matter to Dr. Gantt here who now inoculates from it, & means to try the variolous inoculation on some of his patients. I had no opportunity of doing that. I sent some matter to Doctr. Waterhouse, & I shall have his opinion in due time whether it had been continued genuine. from the trials I made, the Cowpox can hardly be called a

[495]

disease. it produces no more inconvenience than a burn or blister of a quarter of an inch diameter.

I propose some Saturday morning to ride & explore the road you described to me. if I knew on what Saturday I should find you at home, I would breakfast with you, and take your further directions to find it. Accept my best wishes for your health & happiness.

Th: Jefferson

PrC (ViW); at foot of text: "Doctr. Henry Rose"; endorsed by TJ in ink on verso.

To Samuel Smith

Dear Sir   Washington Oct. 23. 1801

Your of the 21st. came to hand last night. the father of the mr Quarrier, who is the subject of it, is a very estimable & zealous republican of Richmond. by profession a coachmaker, & at the same time commanding a regiment of Cavalry. the recommendations of mr Wythe & Govor. Monroe to me on behalf of the son, respected the father chiefly; they knew little of the son. his separation from his father, his extraordinary wanderings, and some eccentricities in what he says & writes, placed him on questionable ground with me. I know his father well. he would not abandon him if all were well. I write this entirely in confidence for yourself, & that you may not be committed for want of the little knowlege I have of the person. he is a candidate for a commission in the army, a clerkship or any thing else. health & affectionate respect.   Th: Jefferson

PrC (DLC); at foot of text: "Genl. Saml Smith."; endorsed by TJ in ink on verso.

From Albert Gallatin

Dear Sir   Washington 24 Oct. 1801

Enclosed is a letter of Mr Macon, & one from Mr Steele to whom I had communicated Mr Macon's, requesting his opinion as to any inconvenience which might arise from a postponement of the appointment of collector for Wilmington. Should you think this the most eligible mode, measures will be taken in conformity with Mr Steele's opinion.

I am still confined at home, more, however, from caution than real indisposition, as I feel much better & hope to be able to attend the office on Monday next.

With sincere respect & attachment Your obt. Servt.

ALBERT GALLATIN

RC (DLC); at foot of text: "Thomas Jefferson President of the United States"; endorsed by TJ as received from the Treasury Department on 24 Oct. and "Collectr. Wilmington N.C." and so recorded in SJL. Enclosure: Nathaniel Macon to Gallatin, Buck Spring, 15 Oct., informing the Treasury secretary that he has received several letters recommending persons for the vacancy at Wilmington and inquiring whether the appointment might be delayed, without detriment to the public service, until the meeting of Congress, by which time he would make inquiries and "use every endeavor to select the best person for the office," noting that he was not "anxious for any particular individual" but only wished "the best appointment to be made" (Gallatin, *Papers*, 5:862). For other enclosure, see below.

In a letter dated only "Friday morning," probably 23 Oct., Gallatin wrote John STEELE: "If you think that no inconvenience will arise from letting the dep. collector at Wilmington continue to act, & suspending the appointment of a collector till the meeting of Congress as requested by Mr. Macon, it would be the most eligible mode" (Wagstaff, *John Steele*, 1:238). No letter from Steele to Gallatin expressing an OPINION has been found.

From Levi Lincoln

PRESIDENT OF THE UNITED STATES— Worcester Octo 24. 1801—

Perceiving by a paper, just received, that Mr Madison had arrived at Washington, I am reminded of my own situation in reference to the Government. I have had no letter for a long time, which, is considered, as a proper, though, severe punishment for my neglect in not writing myself. I have no apology, unless the want of something of importance, enough to be communicated can be allowed, as such. The complexion of the public papers, are not much changed. This is undoubtedly owing to the labours of the editors, & a few other individuals. The tone of conversation, among the people, and even, among the federalist, with few exceptions, is much altered & is softening daily. The clergy in general are become silent, say but little & pray with caution. Some of them continue to write, Doct. Dwight the President of Yale College, & Smith, of a college in the jersey's, have lately been in Boston strengthening their brethern; but I am told, in public, they have been prudent, on politicks. The spirit of opposition is certainly enfeebled, & in time, with some intermediate struggles for life, will die away. The violent, having exhausted, & worn out their common place slander against[1] the General Government, will sink into a torpor, or attack the state Governments as they become republican, which they are every where doing. Accounts from New Hampshire are promising. The Yeomenry of Massachusetts are getting right. I am deceived, or our next legislature will be republican. I most heartily rejoice on the issue of the late elections, & congratulate you on the propitious aspect, they have to the general Government. I inclose you for the reasons heretofore assigned, two more papers. Public opinion having connected, the writer with an officer of your Government, it is proper you should know how far you may appear involved in the imputations thrown on him. They are written, with design, rather loosely, and with a preference, to the use of general terms, in many places. One object has been, to get the public attention, & prepare it for something more particular. Whether they have had any effect, is not for me to decide. Republican partiality, or perhaps, flatery, say they are doing good. The excitement, and the opponents, they have occasiond are favorable symptoms. Could I believe my services, or attendence, of any immediate importance to you, at the seat of Government, I should hurry on. Mrs. Lincoln is upstairs, with an addition to my family. The arrangements, which I have been revolving in my own mind, are to go to Boston in a few days, perhaps to Salem & Providence, for the sake of seeing some political friends, and to set out for Washington the fore part of next month. If it is your wish, that I hurry, a line on the subject will hasten the business. The enclosed letter, from Mr Brown, with the abstract of the expenditures for the repairs of the Berceu, I lately received. They are large, though I presumed supplied with care & economy by the agent—I understand that John M Forbes of New York is applying for a consular appointment at Lisbon, or Cadiz,—That John H Rogers of Newton is desirous of the Consulate for Alicant, and William Lee,—of the collector's office in Salem—At their request, I mention their names, am acquainted with them, particularly with Forbes & Lee, and should it, in the course of appointments, become important to know, the characters of those Gentlemen, I have no hisitancy in saying, they are persons of weight in society, of ability & respectability.[2] Forbes particularly a man of learning & strength of mind—

Accept Sir assurance of my highest esteem & respect

LEVI LINCOLN

RC (DNA: RG 59, LAR); addressed: "Thomas Jefferson Esq President of the United States Washington"; endorsed by TJ as received 31 Oct. and so recorded in SJL; also endorsed by TJ: "Lee to be collector Salem John H. Rogers of Newton. to be Consul Alicant." Enclosures: (1) Two of Lincoln's "Farmer" essays from Massachusetts newspapers; see Lincoln to TJ, 16 Sep. (2) Samuel

Brown to Lincoln, 16 Oct. 1801, regarding the cost of repairs and supplies for the *Berceau* and reporting the ship's departure (RC in DLC; endorsed by TJ: "Lincoln Levi. Brown's statement to him of the cost of the repairs of the Berceau").

Samuel Stanhope SMITH, an ordained Presbyterian minister, was president of the College of New Jersey (Princeton). In 1779, when Smith was rector of Hampden-Sydney Academy, he and TJ had corresponded about the education bill that TJ drafted for the revisal of Virginia laws (ANB; Vol. 2:246-9, 252-5).

ADDITION TO MY FAMILY: Lincoln married Martha Waldo in 1781. She bore ten children in the course of the marriage. The youngest, a son named William, was born 26 Sep. 1801 (Waldo Lincoln, *History of the Lincoln Family: An Account of the Descendants of Samuel Lincoln of Hingham, Massachusetts, 1637-1920* [Worcester, Mass., 1923], 162-4).

[1] MS: "against against."
[2] MS: "respectabity."

From John F. Mercer

DEAR SIR   Annapolis Oct. 24th. 1801—

It is with great regret that we have given up the hopes of seeing yourself & Mr. Madison at West River, but concluding at length that your promise had escaped yr. Memory, Mrs. Mercer took her departure to pay an annual visit to Balto. & I shall rejoin my better half in a day or two,—I shall however promise myself that before the session you find leisure to [seize?] a day or two with the oldest friend you have in state of Maryland, & certainly one not less sincere in his Attachment.—

With the highest respect yr Ob. Sr.   JOHN F. MERCER

RC (DLC); endorsed by TJ as received 27 Oct. and so recorded in SJL.

Mercer had invited TJ and James Madison to visit at Cedar Park, his estate on WEST RIVER Farm in Anne Arundel County, which he had inherited through his wife's grandparents and where he lived from 1785 until 1821 (*Biog. Dir. Cong.*; Papenfuse, *Maryland Legislature*, 2:594-5; Vol. 33:218).

From Elizabeth House Trist

DR SIR   24th October

I know your goodness will pardon the trouble I am about to give you: every sentiment, and feeling of My heart justifies me in the endeavour to erase the Slanderous aspersions which has been circulated against My friend Fowler. I therefore take the liberty to send you his letter to me, as also some extracts from the papers. I can readily believe that Mr Brackinridge has been the cause of promoting these

[499]

report I know him to be vindictive and hard in his epithets against those he is at variance with; The author of that letter you gave me to read, is a friend of Mr Brackinridge and is under obligations to him I am inform'd for the Office he holds,[1] and I can easily imagine that his opinion may have been fixd by the Prejudices and party spirit of Mr B. Mr Fowler may have his failings but that he shou'd turn out so base a character I never can credit, my only aim is that you shou'd not decide against him till you have further information and through another channel—I shou'd have sent this by the last Post but was too unwell in consiquence of a fall from my Horse which detain'd me a week at the Mountain and disabled me from writing a week after I got home—Your favor I recd. incloseing one from Lucy Brown. its detention was of no importance

I have one thing more that deeply interest me which is Mr Easton I have no doubt you have had other recommendation than mine in his favor knowing how much depends on his getting a Consular appointment I feel greatly interested. Mr Orr I understand had the appointment to Hamburg, and had till this Month to detirmine if he shou'd not go, I hope Mr Easton will succeed,—I shou'd be among the last that wou'd wish you to make an appointment that wou'd occasion you a single regret even if it was to advantage my own dear connections. I am therefore confidant that you will not forget him, for a more worthy man I dont know—Our Races seem to occupy all discription of people in this Neighbourhood. these deversions are productive of much Idleness. The countrey looks dreary in consiquence of the severe drouth and I am much afraid that the Influenza will visit us again   I hope you may continue to enjoy your health

    I am Dr Sir Your obliged   E. TRIST

RC (DNA: RG 59, LAR, 4:28-30); addressed: "The President"; endorsed by TJ as received 27 Oct. and so recorded in SJL with notation "Fowler & Eaton"; TJ later canceled "Trist Elizabeth" and added "Fowler to office Eaton to consulate" to the endorsement. Enclosure: Alexander Fowler to Trist, "Fowlers Glenn, near Pittsburgh," 25 Sep., regarding the involvement of Hugh Henry Brackenridge in the politics of the western Pennsylvania press (RC in same). Newspaper extracts not found.

On the day Alexander FOWLER wrote Trist (see enclosure listed above), he directed similar letters to Madison and Gallatin (Gallatin, *Papers*, 5:795; Madison, *Papers, Sec. of State Ser.*, 2:133-6).

YOUR FAVOR I RECD.: see TJ to Trist, 5 Oct.

[1] Trist here canceled "to his interest."

To Peter Carr

DEAR SIR   Washington Oct. 25. 1801.

I promised you one of the inclosed volumes, and one also for mr
Peter Johnston for whom you requested the perusal of my Parliamentary Commonplace. the inclosed contains every thing useful from
that, debarrassed of it's rubbish.—we have recieved the first Consul's
ratification of our Convention. it is with a 'bien entendu toujours that
the objects of the article suppressed are abandoned by both parties.'
as this abandonment of indemnifications for our spoliated merchants
was the work of a federal majority in the Senate, I shall leave to them
to accept the ratification before I proclaim it. in the mean time we
shall go on [with] the execution of it.—Govr. Sargeant has published
a pamphlet on my refusal to re-appoint him in which he makes
speeches for us both at a supposed interview which are entirely fabricated. we had an interview, but as his nonappointment had been decided by an unanimous vote in our cabinet & without a moment's
hesitation by any one, I took care to say not a word that could be
avoided, nor a word that could give him a probable expectation of
reappointment. knowing that I have never gone into the newspapers
he tells his lie boldly in order to patch up a broken reputation.—the
elections whether general or particular shew every where a wonderful progression in the republican spirit. if we are permitted to go on
as gradually in the removals called for by the republicans as not to
shock and revolt our well meaning citizens who are coming over to us
in a steady [. . .] we shall compleatly consolidate the nation in a short
time; excepting always the Royalists & Priests.—I will pray you
when on the assembly to [. . .] me from time to time information of
their proceedings. my affectionate respects to mrs Carr & sincere
wishes for health & happiness to yourself.

PrC (DLC); faint and blurred; at foot
of text: "Peter Carr." Enclosure: TJ's *A
Manual of Parliamentary Practice. For the
Use of the Senate of the United States*
(Washington, D.C., 1801); see Vol.
32:337, 405.

I PROMISED YOU: TJ last corresponded with Carr when he was preparing his
parliamentary manual for the press.
Carr's letter to TJ of 11 Nov. 1800, which
according to SJL was received from "Mt.
Warren" on the same day, and TJ's response of 13 Nov. have not been found.

Carr had probably visited TJ at Monticel-
lo during August and September as well.
PETER JOHNSTON began representing
Prince Edward County in the Virginia
General Assembly in 1793. He served as
speaker of the House of Delegates from
1805 to 1807. In 1801, Carr, representing
Albemarle County, also served in the
House (Leonard, *General Assembly*, xv,
192, 223, 225, 239, 243).

BIEN ENTENDU TOUJOURS: "always
understood," or "provided always." The
statement signed by Bonaparte on 31
July to ratify the convention reiterated

that both parties would be abandoning claims covered by the excised second article (Parry, *Consolidated Treaty Series*, 55:369-70).

PAMPHLET: *Political Intolerance, or The Violence of Party Spirit; Exemplified in a Recent Removal from Office: With a Comment upon Executive Conduct, and an Ample Refutation of Calumny; in a Sketch* of the Services and Sacrifices, of a Dismissed Officer by "One of the American People" (Boston, 1801). For TJ's INTERVIEW with the governor, see *Political Intolerance*, 30-2, and Winthrop Sargent to TJ, printed at 31 May. UNANIMOUS VOTE OF OUR CABINET: see Notes on a Cabinet Meeting, 16 May.

From Maria Digges

DEAR SIR   Williamsburg Octor. 25 1801

Permit me to Congratulate you on being Chose President of my Country I sencerely Pray every Blessing may Attend you I Intended to have done my Self this Honr. before this, but have been very Ill for ten weeks and have just lost my Dear and only Sister my Other Sister I lost about ten Months, Immagination cannot furnish Ideas Strong Enugh to Paint my Distrest Melancholy Situation, add to this My Dear only Brother in a Derainged State quite unable to Assist him Self on what I can do for him wch. is scarse enough to Exist on, Permit my Dear Freind to Arsk your Freindship and Attention I think I am to well Acquainted with the goodness of your Heart your tender Sensiblity to doubt your lending me a little Assistance that Being who is a Freind all will reward you, you will Pitty and frete whin I tell you my Dearest turned out a Volintear for is Country before he was sixtene, behaved so Well that he got a Captains Commisson at Eighteine, [. . .] Commanded the Garison at this Town with great Apptoi[tude] and Raised five Coates of Solders for his Countrey all our Old Freind were very fond of him, but an unlucky affair distrest him. Col Portefeild Struck one of his Solders wch my Brother resented so much that he gave the Col a Challenge wch Obliged him Ither to Arsk Pardon or *resine* Poor Dear Youth full of Fire, Chose the latter; but the Govr. and Counsilers gave him a Captains Comisions in Col Monroes Rigiment alass that was not filled before Peace so that this Young *Man*, had not only lost his time at College but spent his little in raiseing his Men he Parted with what he could in difence of Liberty and wee three Sisters distressed our Selves in lending him Expecting he would be an Honr. to his Country, I Sir have Mintained him for ten Years his Reson could not bare his Misfortunes to see us distrest and his Inabillity to Assist was too too much a Malencholy State he is now left to my Poor Exirtions A Word from you Sir

Perhaps may Git the Honble. Congress [to] do something to Assist
him he lost his half Pay and Land as allowed other Offirsers Endeed
wee have all Suffered by the late Revelution; a small Sum would assist him at Present he is very Sick and low brougt on by Cruel distress sometimes without the Common Necessaries of Life O Sir its
not in my Power to Tell you my Sufferings our Acquaintance in this
quater of the Globe only tell me that should it Please God to restore
my Brothers Reson he should have some Post but how am I to Assist
him without a Frd Pray Sir Assist your once happy Freind get something done I live in a Cottage that I feare, will Crush us, and have it
not in my Power to Mend one Hundred Dollars would mend it so as
to make it habitable but I feare being troublesom forgive and beleive
me your much obliged Frd with great Rispect and Warme Freindship your
Huml Sarvt   MARIA DIGGES

Hast let there be Musick all thrugh the land
Around your Home may Laurels twine
And every Voice be tuned to Love and *Peace*
[. . .] our Worthey President do me the Honr of an Epistle MD val-
ues her self on haveing Mr Jefferson her Freind and shall[1]

RC (DLC); torn; endorsed by TJ as received 31 Oct. and so recorded in SJL.

Maria Digges was appointed housekeeper of the College of William and
Mary in 1773 (WMQ, 1st ser., 1 [1893],
143-4; same, 14 [1905], 26). TJ referred
to her as "Molly" Digges in a 1776 letter.
Letters exchanged between them in late
1800 have not been found (Vol. 1:294;
Vol. 32:239).
Digges's BROTHER, Edward, was a

captain of Virginia troops from 1778 to
1780. He died in the public hospital for
the insane at Williamsburg (WMQ, 1st
ser., 1 [1893], 143-4; Heitman, *Register*,
197; E. M. Sanchez-Saavedra, *A Guide to
Virginia Military Organizations in the
American Revolution, 1774-1787* [Rich-
mond, 1978], 117, 122, 124; White,
Genealogical Abstracts, 1:976).

[1] MS ends here.

From John Wayles Eppes

DEAR SIR,   Monticello Oct: 25. 1801.
My being absent on a trip to the Hundred on the arrival of your letter has occasioned considerable delay in my answer. The arrangements proposed in it for my benefit, while I view them *only* as new
instances on your part of affectionate concern for the welfare of Maria
and myself give me great pleasure. When I consider however that
you have great and continued calls for money while I have none, &

that my limited income suffices me completely in the limited sphere in which I move, I cannot but regret that affection for us should induce you to lop off any part of your property which might be converted into additional income. Under this impression you will not I hope feel dissatisfaction if while grateful for your offer I decline accepting the part of the arrangement which relates to the hire of hands for clearing the Bedford Land—On the subject of Pant-ops I can only say that it has been & still continues to be my firm determination to build there as soon as I can without inconvenience—I have sown it this year in Bearded wheat so that nothing can be done until the next year. I consider with you that levelling the ground is essential. When you return the ensuing fall we will make an accurate examination of the spot and some estimate of the cost and if you find it not a heavier Job than you at present Suppose I will accept with pleasure of the offer you were kind enough to make—The levelling the ground has I confess had a serious operation on my mind & has almost at times induced me to abandon the spot & fix on some other not attended with this difficulty.

Maria has had for two days a pain in her Jaw—It is now tolerably easy, but considerably swelled—She is & has been except this in good health—Our son continues well & grows daily—Accept for your health & happiness the best wishes of yours sincerely

JNO: W: EPPES

P.S. I examined your Pecan Trees & can find only 33 remaining— These appear about Six inches high &[1] by no means in a thriving State—Mr. Lilly put hands about inclosing them the day after we received your letter—Your horse has recovered entirely from his lameness & may I think be sent for in safety whenever you think proper—

RC (ViU: Edgehill-Randolph Papers); addressed: "Thomas Jefferson President of the U States Washington City"; endorsed by TJ as received 27 Oct. and so recorded in SJL.

YOUR LETTER: TJ to Eppes, 9 Oct.

TJ's letters to Gabriel LILLY of 5 and 19 Oct. as well as Lilly's letter to TJ of 9 Oct., all recorded in SJL, have not been found.

[1] Preceding four words and ampersand interlined.

From Gideon Granger

DEAR SIR   Suffield Octr: 25th: 1801.
Upon my return from Newhampshire this morning I had the pleasure of receiving yours of the 14th. Instant. With diffidence I offer to

undertake the duties of Postmaster-General. my mind would be oppressed with great Solicitude and Anxiety, upon assuming to discharge any high and Important Office. even in that line of business, to a knowledge of which I have devoted a great part of my life, or in those, where legal Information would be of Importance—my Solicitude is much higher at the Thoughts of entering into an Office the duties of which I am wholly ignorant of.

My desire to reside with you, Sir, is very great. Improvement and pleasure are Inticing Objects—Yet to you, from whom I would not secrete, any Opinion I embrace, or any emotion of my heart, I cannot hesitate to declare that since the receipt of your Letter of the 7th. Instt. proposing my removal to Washington my mind has been overwhelmed with doubts and perplexities; owing to my personal Situation principally, tho' in a good measure to my Apprehensions respecting its effects upon Republicanism in Connecticut, and generally on Connecticut River. My Wife has lain more than Six years confined to her bed, for the Three last she has not walked, & for many months has not been able to turn in her bed. we have Three little Sons between 11 & 7 yrs. of Age—to remove my family is impossible—to leave them thus situated, and make my permanent Residence 400 Miles distant is very difficult & peculiarly trying. As it respects the effects it may have upon Republicanism—It will be recollected, that while for one of my years I stood without a Superiour in the estimations & Affections of the People, in the dark period of 1797. & 1798. almost alone I ventured to erect the standard of Republicanism & continued to fight under its Banners—you are not Ignorant of the evils which surrounded me—These Things gave me in the Estimation of Republicans an Ideal Importance in this State, far beyond a just estimate of my Character, or my real Strength of Talents. Tho, I blush while I declare it, yet it is beleived by my friends & my Enemies that my personal Services & actual Residence are for the present of much Importance possibly as much so as that of All most any Other person. In this Situation, I am free to declare, that if it did, or probably would, at the End of some Months comport as well with the Interest of the Govermt to appoint me a Commissioner under the 6th. Article of the British Treaty, or to notice me in Judicial Appointments, or in any Other manner consistent with my partial Residce. in Connecticut to restore me to that rank which I should have enjoyed had I not embarked all to defend our common Liberties, I should not wish to accept the Office of Postmaster-General. Tho whenever these reasons shall cease to operate, There is nothing I should so ardently wish as to reside at the Seat of Goverment in an honorable Station.—

yet if noticing me in the Manner I have Stated will be inconsistent with the Interest of the Goverment—I think it due to my Character to accept the Honorable Post you have been pleased to Assign me, & will accordingly accept the same.—Our complete Victory in Vermont adds to the Catalogue of Our Triumphs & secures us from the Captious folly of Aristocracy. By a prudent Management in Two Years I think we shall carry evry State—In Connecticut we have gaind more than 80 pr Ct in five Months—& tho we used evry exertion to propagate the faith—yet we did not to bring the Republicans to vote—from this till Spring the highest exertions will be made—we shall then be again defeated—But they must soon cease their opposition or perish in their Attempt to Support it. In the Course of a few Weeks a decent & cool answer to the Various Charges against the Executive will be circulated through the state.—I shall make a visit to Washington about the middle of December, if I am not previously calld. to discharge the duties of the proposed Office, if called for that purpose, I shall wish to know how soon I must attend—having fairly stated my situation, Opinions, feelings & wishes—to You I most cheerfully Submit the same with a mind prepared to accord to Your Wishes—

Accept, Dear Sir, Assurances of my real Esteem & Sincere friendship   GIDN: GRANGER

RC (DLC); at foot of text: "Thos. Jefferson Esq Presidt. of United States"; endorsed by TJ as received 30 Oct. and so recorded in SJL.

MY WIFE: Granger married Mindwell Pease in 1790. Their three SONS, Ralph, Francis, and John Albert, were born in 1790, 1792, and 1795, respectively. During Granger's years in Washington, his family remained in Suffield, Connecticut (ANB; Arthur S. Hamlin, *Gideon Granger* [Canandaigua, N.Y., 1982], vi, 10, 18).

To Wilson Cary Nicholas

DEAR SIR   Washington Oct. 25. 1801.

I take the benefit of your cover to get a safe conveyance for the inclosed. a copy of the ratification by the first Consul, of our convention, is arrived. it is expressed to be with an 'understanding always that the matters which were the subject of the suppressed article are abandoned on both sides.' altho' I consider this as a superfluous caution, nothing being more settled than that things not provided for on a treaty of peace are abandoned, yet, as it is a sore circumstance to the merchants, I shall not proclaim the treaty, but leave it on the shoulders of the Senate to accept.—I think it probable mr King has signed a convention with England commuting the VIth. article of that treaty with £600,000. sterl. payable at 10. annual instalments. this however, being not yet certain, is for your own ear only. spoliations are still to be compensated to us. the banditti boats of Algesiras have lately committed very unwarrantable depredations on our commerce, which we are representing duly to their government. our suppression of the Portuguese mission arrived there fortunately 3. or 4. days only before a minister was to have come here. he was of course stopped. I begin to hope the transfer of Louisiana to France has not been definitively decided. the new census proves our increase to be in the compound ratio of $3\frac{1}{6}$ per cent annually & consequently that we double in 22. years 3. months. Accept my best affections & wishes for your health & happiness.   TH: JEFFERSON

RC (NjP: Andre De Coppet Collection); at foot of text: "Colo. W. C. Nicholas"; endorsed. PrC (DLC). Enclosure: TJ to Burgess Griffin, 25 Oct. 1801, recorded in SJL but not found; see Nicholas to TJ, 30 Oct.

Rufus KING had written to Madison from London on 24 Aug. to report progress in his discussions with Lord Hawkesbury about altering the means of settling British creditors' claims covered by Article 6 of the Jay Treaty. The British government had agreed to the American proposal of £600,000 as a lump-sum settlement, and Hawkesbury and King were negotiating a convention between the two countries that would resolve the issue. Not until January 1802, however, would that convention be agreed on and signed (King, *Life*, 3:502-4; Madison, *Papers, Sec. of State Ser.*, 2:65; Vol. 34:323-7).

PORTUGUESE MISSION: in a letter of 16 Aug. received by the State Department on 24 Oct., William Loughton Smith wrote to Madison that he had informed the Portuguese government of his recall and forestalled the sending of a new minister to the U.S. (Madison, *Papers, Sec. of State Ser.*, 2:48).

To Craven Peyton

DEAR SIR   Washington Oct. 25. 1801.

Your favor of the 16th. was recieved on the 20th. the post having departed the day before as usual. you ask what shall be done with Shadwell? there was a wish in mr Tom Esting Randolph to have rented it. mr T M Randolph can tell whether he now wishes it. if not, let it to some one tenant, if you please, subject to my approbation which can be asked in a fortnight always. I say to some one tenant, because I would not divide it into more than one tenement. I would much rather consolidate it into one with the residue of the tract. accept my best wishes for your health & happiness.

TH: JEFFERSON

PrC (ViU); at foot of text: "Mr. Craven Peyton"; endorsed by TJ in ink on verso.

TOM ESTING RANDOLPH: Thomas Eston Randolph was TJ's first cousin, the eldest son of TJ's uncle William. He married his cousin Jane Cary Randolph, the sister of TJ's son-in-law Thomas Mann Randolph, and became the father-in-law of TJ's grandson Francis Eppes. In 1803, he declined an offer by TJ to lease property at Shadwell and instead lived across the Rivanna River from Milton at Glenmore (Daniels, *Randolphs of Virginia,* xiii, xiv, 92, 93, 264; MB, 2:1156; Vol. 1:410n; Thomas Eston Randolph to TJ, 30 May 1803, in MHi).

To Samuel Harrison Smith

Oct. 25. 1801.

Th: Jefferson omitted to observe to mr Smith yesterday on the subject of mr Barton that as to the offices of the general governmt. Pensylva. Maryld. & Virga. are so overcharged, that, on a principle of distribution, no office[1] respecting the union generally can be given in those states till something more of an equilibrium has been obtained. offices exerciseable within a state are always filled within the state. mr Smith is at liberty to repeat this observation to mr Barton as it may be satisfactory to him.

RC (DLC: J. Henley Smith Papers); addressed: "Mr. Samuel H. Smith Washington"; endorsed by Smith with notation in his hand: "the substance of wch. communicated to Mr. Barton Oct. 27. 1801."

[1] TJ here canceled "of that."

From William Stuart

RESPECT'D SIR

HONE. THOMAS JEFFERSON   [on or before 25 Oct. 1801]

Confiding in your kinde patriotism. I deign to intrude on your tenderness. I deign to call fourth your humanity in my behalfe. I Know well, the reasonable conjectures which will arise in your minde; not alltogether in my favour. but Sir. I rely. I confide. I trust. mine will rise superior to them all. you will say Sir. why young man did you not bring proper recommendations? my reasons Sir are obvious. for my capitol will not admit any greate delay, and of course no greate expence. too be sure Sir. I have freinds that might introduce me, to those of whome I could get recommendations. but when I made applications to my freinds. theire answer was, you are too juvenile, and consiquently too unsettled, to be put in the army as a second Lieutenant. by, the, by, Sir. I do not thinke it exebited a singular instance of theire or his great superiority of understanding. apropo Sir. these freinds are not relation. no Sir. on these grounds. a destitute young

man, presumtively asks but small the meanes (through your goodness.) he presumes to raise them to his own honnor. to your greate
satisfaction. and to his Countrie's never ending glory!

With greate respect Sir I am Yr. Most Ob. Hb Servent

WILLIAM STUART

RC (DNA: RG 59, LAR); undated; endorsed by TJ as received 25 Oct. and so
recorded in SJL.

From Joel Barlow

DEAR SIR,   Paris 26 Oct. 1801—

Mr. Fulton's letter giving an account of his experiments in submarine navigation is to accompany this. In the present state of the naval
system of Europe every project for establishing the liberty of the seas
on a permanent basis seems to be attended with so many difficulties
that I am sometimes inclined to think the one he proposes may be
found the most simple as well as the most effectual that has hitherto
been devised. It seems to promise one advantage over mere conventions or agreements whether armed or unarmed, which is the physical certainty with which it may operate in putting the great military
navies at the mercy of the minor Powers whose interest in the liberty
of the seas is manifest. And if this project is adopted its execution will
not depend on the faith of treaties, nor on the caprice or corruption of
ministers. But if some such as this cannot be recieved, and no convention for an Armed or unarmed Neutrality can be relied on, the
prospect for civilization is frightful. We must all turn pirates abroad
& tax gatherers at home. England has now about 200 ships of the
line. France to cope with her must have about 300 as soon as possible. by that time England will encrease her number, & so on. Where
is this to end? If we mean to provide for our safety in the same way
how many ships must we have? And what is to become of political &
civil liberty under such a system.

It seems to me that this subject is among the first that the present
interval of peace ought to offer to the consideration of statesmen in all
countries, especially to those of the United States, where prejudice is
not yet so strong as to force us to reject a principle merely because it
is new, without examining whether it be right or wrong.

It is now probable that Louissiana is to belong to France. in this
case we are to be flanked on each wing by the two strongest Maritime Powers. This may furnish an additional motive to us to look

out for the most effectual as well as the most easy & pacific mode of defence.

I take the liberty of adding on this occasion that Mr. Fulton is not only a mechanical genius of great eminence, but he is well nourished in the principles of republican liberty, and those of political economy, and his talents are as disinterestedly devoted to public improvement as those of any man I know. I hope he will return to America with me in the spring.

I am, Dr. Sir, with great respect your obt. & very hume. Sert.

JOEL BARLOW

RC (DLC); addressed: "To Thomas Jefferson President of the United States"; endorsed by TJ as received 11 Feb. 1802 and so recorded in SJL.

Robert FULTON'S LETTER, dated 22 Oct. and recorded in SJL as received from Paris on 11 Feb. 1802, has not been found. Barlow had previously mentioned Fulton's experimentation in SUBMARINE NAVIGATION in a letter to TJ of 15 Sep. 1800 (Vol. 32:143, 144n).

To Mary Jefferson Eppes

MY EVER DEAR MARIA   Washington Oct. 26. 1801.

I have heard nothing of you since mr Eppes's letter dated the day sennight after I left home. the Milton mail[1] will be here tomorrow morning when I shall hope to recieve something. in the mean time this letter must go hence this evening. I trust it will still find you at Monticello, and that possibly mr Eppes may have concluded to take a journey to Bedford & still farther prolonged your stay. I am anxious to hear from you, lest you should have suffered in the same way now as on a former similar occasion. should any thing of that kind take place and the remedy which succeeded before fail now, I know nobody to whom I would so soon apply as mrs Suddarth. a little experience is worth a great deal of reading, and she has had great experience and a sound judgment to observe on it. I shall be glad to hear at the same time that the little boy[2] is well. if mr Eppes undertakes what I have proposed to him at Pantops & Poplar Forest the next year, I should think it indispensable that he should make Monticello his headquarters. you can be furnished with all plantation articles for the family from mr Craven who will be glad to pay his rent in that way. it would be a great satisfaction to me to find you fixed there in April. perhaps it might induce me to take flying trips by stealth, to have the enjoiment of family society for a few days undisturbed. nothing can repay me the loss of that society, the only one founded in affection and bosom confidence. I have here company enough, part of which is very friendly, part well enough disposed, part secretly hostile & a constant succession of strangers. but this only serves to get rid of life, not to enjoy it. it is in the love of one's family only that heartfelt happiness is known. I feel it when we are all together & alone beyond what can be imagined. present me affectionately to mr Eppes, mr Randolph & my dear Martha, & be assured yourself of my tenderest love.   TH: JEFFERSON

RC (ViU); addressed: "Mrs. Maria Eppes at Monticello near Milton"; franked; postmarked 27 Oct.

MR EPPES'S LETTER: John Wayles Eppes to TJ, 3 Oct.

A FORMER SIMILAR OCCASION: after losing a newborn daughter in early 1800, Maria suffered from an abscessed breast, fever, and inflammation. For her condition and its debated REMEDY, see Vol. 31:286n, 368, 389-90, 415, 440.

MRS SUDDARTH: Martha Suddarth, the wife of William Suddarth and the sister of General Thomas Sumter, was a respected midwife and nurse in Albemarle County. According to TJ's financial records, he ordered payment to her for medicine on 20 Sep., the day his grandson Francis Eppes was born (Woods, *Albemarle*, 323; MB, 2:1051).

[1] Word interlined in place of "post."
[2] TJ here interlined "x."

From Gideon Granger

DEAR SIR   Mond: Morning. Hartford Oct: 26, 1801.

In my Letter of Yesterday I designd to have mentiond: that Genl. Lyman had probably before this applied for the Office mentiond in your last. I saw him at New-haven—Mr Edwards & myself gave him a Letter to you stating that, any Recommendation from us, was unnecessary as you knew him & his Character & that We should feel happy in his having the Appointment. at that time I had no Idea of being selected for the Office, & had determind. never to solicit for any Office, tho, a few days before I had informd Mr. Edwards that if it was offered to Me I should probably accept the same.

When reflecting on the Subject it did not & does not appear to me that under the Circumstances it would be improper or unfair for me to accept the same, as offered without any Solicitation on my part. to you evry Thing respecting the business is cheerfully submitted—Yrs. Sincerely   GIDN. GRANGER

RC (DLC); at foot of text: "Thos. Jefferson Esq"; endorsed by TJ as received 30 Oct. and so recorded in SJL.

For an earlier query on an office for William LYMAN, see Vol. 34:548n. YOUR

LAST: TJ to Granger, 14 Oct. LETTER TO YOU: Granger and Pierpont Edwards to TJ, 10 Oct., recorded in SJL as received from New Haven on 16 Oct. and "Lyman to be P.M.G.," has not been found.

From Robert Smith

SIR, Navy Dept. Oct. 26. 1801

Before I make the proposed communication to Brown & Pearson I consider it proper to submit to your examination the enclosed Note. You will be pleased to make such alterations as to you may appear necessary.

Very respectfully Your Obed Sevt RT SMITH

RC (DLC); at foot of text: "The President"; endorsed by TJ as received 26 Oct. and "Marine barracks" and so recorded in SJL. Enclosure not found, but see below.

Writing on 26 Oct., Smith instructed Marine Corps commandant William Ward Burrows to inform contractors Robert BROWN and Lawrence PEARSON "that the president is of opinion that the Marine Barracks ought not to be received from them but on the following terms": that the south wing and center house be made good either by repairs or demolition; that the north wing be taken down, the "well burnt" bricks set apart, and the remaining bricks and bats "disposed of as they please"; that the walls and stone foundation be rebuilt, using the recently constructed navy arsenal as a model; that the price for bricks used in the north wing be the same as that paid for the navy arsenal (FC in Lb in DNA: RG 45, MLS). Writing in Smith's absence on 4 Nov., Abishai Thomas sent TJ a letter from Burrows enclosing "the form of an Obligation" to be entered into by Brown and Pearson to repair the barracks and requesting that TJ "signify whether it meets your approbation" (FC in Lb in DNA: RG 45, LSP). Writing later that day to Captain Thomas Tingey, Thomas informed him that TJ approved the proposed obligation as follows: "Mr. Smith being absent, and the season pressing, I will take the liberty of approving the within proposition for Mr. Smith, referring to Captn. Tingey, who made the agreement for the Marine Arsenal to fill up the Blank for the price ₱ thousand Bricks which was allowed in that instance, and also for the stone work proposed." Thomas closed by asking that Tingey fill in the blanks as requested by the president and conclude the remaining arrangements needed to execute the agreement (FC in Lb in DNA: RG 45, MLS).

On 2 Nov., Thomas sent TJ a letter covering an abstract of Treasury warrants drawn by the Navy Department and the balance on hand for the week ending 31 Oct. (RC in DLC, at foot of text: "The President," endorsed by TJ as received from the Navy Department on 2 Nov. and "Warrants" and so recorded in SJL; FC in Lb in DNA: RG 45, LSP).

From Robert Smith

SIR, Navy Dept. Oct. 26. 1801

The Enclosed has some relation to the Case of the Officer of the Marine Corps some days since submitted to your Consideration. His proposed bargain is an additional evidence of his meanness.

With great respect Your Mo. Obed Servt RT SMITH

RC (DLC); at foot of text: "The President"; endorsed by TJ as received 26 Oct. and "Lt. Church" and so recorded in SJL. Enclosures: (1) Jonathan Church to

William W. Burrows, Marine Camp, 24 Oct. 1801, in which Church understands that he has been "Unfavourably" represented to the secretary of the navy at the court-martial convened in the case of Captain George Little; Church requests an opportunity to defend himself, or, if Burrows thinks advisable, he will resign "on Receiving four months Advance pay." (2) Burrows to Church, 24 Oct. 1801, in which Burrows informs Church that "It is not in my Power to give away the publick money, but am willing to receive your Resignation" (both RCs in same).

Jonathan Church was a lieutenant of marines on the frigate *Boston* when it captured the French vessel the *Berceau* in late 1800 (NDQW, Dec. 1800-Dec. 1801, 359). For background on the mistreatment of the *Berceau*'s crew and subsequent court-martial of the *Boston*'s commander, George Little, see Samuel Smith to TJ, 18 July 1801.

Writing later on the same day as the above letter, Smith informed TJ that "To relieve you from any further consideration of the Case of Lieut. Church I hasten to inform you, that I have this instant received his Resignation" (RC in DLC, at foot of text: "The President," endorsed by TJ as received from the Navy Department on 26 Oct. and "Lt. Church" and so recorded in SJL; FC in Lb in DNA: RG 45, LSP).

From John Beckley

DEAR SIR,   Philadelphia 27th: October 1801.

A short but severe fit of the gout has delayed my acknowledgment of your favor of the 22d.—I sincerely regret the necessity that has occasioned Mr: Hansons reference to me, and in the just estimate of his Character and Merits, shall feel a twofold gratification in the possibility that I may afford him a temporary relief from political persecution and intolerance—If, in the event of my contemplated Success, the station he asks will be acceptable, he cannot receive it with half the pleasure I shall feel in that acceptance. No circumstance of pre-engagement interferes with the performance of this promise, and I only lament that a previous contingent arrangement, precludes my offering him, the more eligible station of principal Clerk.

I sought out and delivered your letter to Messrs. Fry and Chapman—they are Germans, and not understanding English, desired me to read it to one of their brethren to translate, which, being done, they requested that I would carry to you their high gratification and thankfulness, for so particular a Mark of your favor and attention.

In about ten days Mrs. Beckley and myself hope to be in Washington, when I shall have the pleasure to communicate to you, a singular overture to me, by letter, from a fœderal Senator, to place me in the station of Secretary of the Senate.   Mr: Duane desires me to express the deep sense he entertains of your favor, friendship and support—permit me to add a corresponding sentiment for myself, united with the most sincere esteem and attachment   JOHN BECKLEY

RC (MHi); endorsed by TJ as received 29 Oct. and so recorded in SJL.

YOUR LETTER: TJ to Michael Fry and Nathan Coleman, 22 Oct. The Federalist senator who supported Beckley as a candidate for SECRETARY OF THE SENATE in place of Samuel A. Otis has not been identified. On 12 Sep., however, Otis wrote Federalist Senator Jonathan Dayton that he had a "hint from pretty good authority" that plans were being made to turn him out of office and

"to introduce Mr. Beckley." Otis argued: "The Senate being a permanent body my office hath been considered permanent. Fairly in possession, I mean not to relinquish, as however small the provision, it is a chief dependence for the Support of my family; and it will be an odd measure to say the least of it, to elect a Secretary when one already holds the office, unless on a charge of malversation, which I defy" (Gerard W. Gawalt, *Justifying Jefferson: The Political Writings of John James Beckley* [Washington, D.C., 1995], 245n).

From Pierpont Edwards

SIR,   New Haven Octr. 27th 1801

This will be delivered to you by Mr Eli Whitney of this City; the gentleman who erected and carries on the celebrated manufactory of arms in this neighbourhood, and with whom the United States have formed a contract for manufacturing a large number of those impliments of death—Mr Whitney is the inventor and patentee of the machine for cleaning cotton, so much used in the Southern states; He is considered here as a gentleman of first respectability for talents, and particularly for mathematical and mechanical information, and I, with great pleasure, recommend him to your favorable notice—

I am with the highest respect and most sincere regard your Obed Servt   PIERPONT EDWARDS

RC (DLC); at foot of text: "Excellency Thomas Jefferson"; endorsed by TJ as received 9 Nov. and so recorded in SJL.

In 1798, inventor ELI WHITNEY, Edwards's son-in-law, received a contract to supply 10,000 muskets to the U.S. government, to be delivered in full by the end of September 1800. Produced at his Whitneyville factory near New Haven, the weapons were among the first items manufactured in America using the principle of interchangeable parts. Despite his advanced production techniques, however, Whitney did not deliver his first 500 muskets until September 1801 and would not complete the contract until January 1809 (ANB; McLachlan, *Princetonians,*

1748-1768, 638; Mirsky and Nevins, *Eli Whitney*, 143-6, 213, 218-19).

Whitney benefited little as the INVENTOR AND PATENTEE of the cotton gin, due to widespread pirating of the design and the lack of effective means to protect his patent. In the fall of 1801, he traveled to South Carolina to negotiate the sale of his patent right to that state's legislature, carrying with him an additional letter of introduction from Edwards to James Madison. Whitney spent a week in Washington, meeting with both TJ and Madison, before continuing his journey southward. In December he secured a payment of $50,000 from the South Carolina legislature, half the amount he had originally sought. Whitney and TJ had corresponded about the gin in

1793, when Whitney obtained his patent (ANB; Madison, *Papers, Sec. of State Ser.*, 2:206-7; Mirsky and Nevins, *Eli Whitney*, 150-4; Vol. 26:334; Vol. 27:240-51, 392-3, 433-5).

From Gideon Granger

DEAR SIR   Newhaven Octr: 27. 1801.

After writing you from Hartford yesterday morning I came to this City to attend the Legislature, and last Evning was at a Meeting of a Number of Republicans, a wish was expressed by many, who knew nothing of my Situation, to have at the Seat of Goverment some Citizen with whom they had an acquaintance, so that they might regularly correspond & thereby give and receive correct Information. reflecting on this & believing it would not disoblige you Or be Improper for me in a private & confidential Manner to consult our friend Edwards I went with him to his house & after gaining asurance of Secrecy—Informd. him of the Offer in the Letter of the 14th. & the Substance of my reply—he urged me strongly to *Accept* on the principle that it would give aid to the Cause & pressed so many Considerations to my mind as to Induce me to engage to write an unconditional Acceptance. I beg you to accept this as such, unless a Change of Circumstances has taken place or on Reflection the Interest of the Goverment will be better promoted by appointing another. I hope when all I have written is considered I shall not be considered as capricious & Unsteady—Your feelings will acknowledge a Strong reason for my Doubts.—

I Am, Sir, Your Sincere friend—   GIDN GRANGER

RC (DLC); at foot of text: "Thos: Jefferson Esq"; endorsed by TJ as received 31 Oct. and so recorded in SJL, but as a letter of 26 Oct.

From Isaac Story

                                    Marblehead Oct 27. 1801.
MOST RESPECTED SIRE,   Commonwealth of Massachusetts.

I had the happiness of being acquainted with your two worthy Predecessors. I have had the happiness of perusing the writings of Mr. Jefferson. They convinced me that he was a Gentleman of great Erudition, & of a most excellent taste. I hope he will shine with equal lustre as President of the united States. His inaugural speech filled me with rapture, it exceeds every thing of the kind I ever read. I drew up this Conclusion in my own mind, that if his public administrations quadrated with this speech, it would conciliate the affections of his Opposers, & make him the Pride & glory of America.

I am, by profession, a Clergyman; & was handsomely settled in 1771; & at the early age of twenty one. But by reason of the american war, & the war now in Europe, my salary, for a great part of the time, has been very inadequate. My applications for a permanent addition have been ineffectual, merely because I possess a private Income. Hence if I had a handsome public appointment, I should quit them, for nothing short of this will convince them of their folly & injustice.—

Capt. Michael Haskel of this town, who was formerly acquainted with you, speaks of you in the highest terms of veneration & respect. Indeed all the Inhabitants of this town, with a small exception, are Jeffersonians & Gerryites, which are synonimous terms. He has pressed me most ardently to pay you a visit, & has offered to defray the expences. But I have too independant a mind to accept the offer; nor do I think it prudent to be absent so long from my people, for my Parish is the largest in New England, containing 3,000 Souls.

I now send you, Sir, an Oration of my son; & should have sent it sooner, had it been in my power. He has wrote a book of poetry, which art he must have derived from his mother, who has a good taste that way, & she from her great grandmother, Governor Bradstreets Lady. He is a Lawyer in Sterling near Worcester. His brother Mr. Bradstreet Story is in England on Commercial business. I have spared neither for cost nor pains upon them, & they amply repay me.—

Possessing an active mind, I have not confined my attention to theological subjects; but have branched out into various Sciences. And have sent a number of Communications to the american Academy of Arts & Sciences. I inclose a Copy of one of them, & hope it will not be unacceptable to your philosophical mind.—

I subscribe myself with sentiments of the highest respect, your very humble Servant   ISAAC STORY

P.S. Two of your public Officers, Mr. Madison & Mr. Habersham were my Cotemporaries at College—

RC (MiU-C); endorsed by TJ as received 9 Nov. and so recorded in SJL. Enclosures: (1) Isaac Story, Jr., *An Oration, on the Anniversary of the Independence of the United States of America. Pronounced at Worcester, July 4, 1801* (Worcester, 1801); Sowerby, No. 3269. (2) Isaac Story, "The Metempsychosis doctrine, in a limited sense, defended," in which Story suggests that the transfer of a soul from one body to another, a notion condemned by most Christian theologians, might apply in cases where death occurred in those whose "spirits have never had a time of probation allotted them" (MS in same; entirely in Story's hand; at foot of text: "The Revd. Joseph Willard DD. Vice President of the american Academy of Arts & Sciences. penned in 1790").

Clergyman Isaac Story (1749-1816), a graduate of the College of New Jersey, became pastor of the Second Congregational Church of Marblehead in 1771. Shortly thereafter, he married Rebecca Bradstreet, the daughter of Story's recently deceased predecessor, the Reverend Simon Bradstreet. Although Story's tenure at Marblehead was lengthy, his relationship with the congregation became increasingly strained and he resigned his pastorate in 1802. Following his resignation, he wrote TJ sev-

eral times requesting a civil appointment. He was made a commissioner of bankruptcy in 1802, only to be informed by TJ that his appointment was a mistake and was intended for Joseph Story, his nephew (McLachlan, *Princetonians, 1748-1768*, 655-7; *Boston Post-Boy*, 6 Jan. 1772; Story to TJ, 8 May, 28 July, and 18 Aug. 1802; TJ to Story, 5 Aug. 1802).

MY SON: Isaac Story, Jr., the second of eleven children born to Isaac and Rebecca Story, was a lawyer, writer, and poet. A book of his poetry, *A Parnassian Shop, Opened in the Pindaric Stile*, was published in 1801 at Boston under the pseudonym Peter Quince (DAB).

GOVERNOR BRADSTREETS LADY: probably Anne Bradstreet, the seventeenth-century poet and first wife of Governor Simon Bradstreet of Massachusetts (ANB).

To Connecticut Officers and Soldiers of the 12th Regiment

SIR   Washington Oct. 28. 1801.

I accept with many thanks the kind expressions of the twelfth regiment of the militia of Connecticut towards myself personally, and with still greater satisfaction their declarations of attachment to our constitution. the principles you profess of peace abroad, tranquility at home, a faithful administration of the government, on it's genuine principles of republicanism, and arms for it's support in the hands of every citizen, are, I trust, those of the great body of our citizens, and steadily pursued will go far towards ensuring our happiness & freedom. I will ask the continuance of your approbation no longer than I make them the objects of my sollicitous attention. Accept I pray you for yourself, and the respectable regiment you command the assurances of my high esteem and consideration.   TH: JEFFERSON

PrC (DLC); at foot of text: "Colo. Daniel Tilden."

KIND EXPRESSIONS: see Connecticut Officers and Soldiers of the 12th Regiment to TJ, 23 Sep.

From Benjamin Hawkins

Chickasaw Bluffs 28th of October 1801.

I have had the honour to receive your favour of the 16th. of September covering a letter of my much esteemed and valuable friend Mrs. Trist; and availing myself of the permission heretofore given I take the liberty to enclose a letter for her to you. I find that her son has it in contemplation to move to the Mississippi territory to better his resources by the culture of cotton. The Agency South of Ohio, the Mississippi territory and Georgia is well suited to the raising of cotton; and the crop arising from a well chosen and cultivated field has produced from 3 to 500 dollars profit ℔ hand. One disagreeable circumstance attending this business is, the keen desire generated by such great profit to accumulate slaves by any and every mean in their power, regardless of future consequences: And it is more than probable that the period cannot be very distant when the black people of the North kidnaped and thrust into the severe labour of the South will make an effort to regain their Liberty.

I have communicated to my colleagues the information relative to the future direction of our letters and am with the sincerest wishes for your health and happiness

My dear sir, your obedient servant   BENJAMIN HAWKINS

RC (DLC); at foot of text: "Mr. Jefferson President of the US."; endorsed by TJ as received 11 Dec. and so recorded in SJL. Enclosure not found.

Hawkins and his COLLEAGUES in the negotiations with Indian tribes, James Wilkinson and Andrew Pickens, concluded a treaty with the Chickasaws at Chickasaw Bluffs on 24 Oct. The Chickasaws agreed to allow a road to be run between the Tennessee settlements and Mississippi Territory (ASP, *Indian Affairs*, 1:648-9).

From William Keteltas

DR SIR   New York Octr. 28th 1801

Since My Offering Myself as a Candidate for the Office of Loan Officer in the place of Gnl. Clarkson Resigned as I have been Informed, I have Provision Made for Me in one of the Inferior Courts of this state which took place on the 26th. Inst—Percieving such a desire for Office among Republicans, A Circumstance to be lamented, I withdraw my application should it so happen to be Considered in the way of some Other Candidate. As I think Offices should be distributed Equally among the deserving and not heaped on one Individual as is the Case under Monarchies, I beg leave to Recommend to

Your Consideration Theodorus Bailey Esqr. Representative to Congress for the district of Dutchess in this state, if not incompatable with the Principal I have laid Down. I know of but one Political Mishap of Mr. Bailys, which was his Voting for that disgracefull Instrument the *British Treaty*. This was owing I Concieve to a weekness of *Nerves* and not a defect of Republicanism, Men alike Virtuous are not alike firm under a Presure of Intilect Nor fited for the same Stations.

With Perfect Consideration　　　　　　　　　　Wm Keteltas

Ps. Written without the Knowledge of Mr. Bailey or knowing wether he is, or is not, a Candidate for the office

RC (DNA: RG 59, LAR); at foot of text: "Thomas Jefferson Pres— of the United States"; endorsed by TJ as received 30 Oct. and so recorded in SJL.

OFFERING MYSELF AS A CANDIDATE: see Keteltas to TJ, 25 Sep.

To Stevens Thomson Mason

Dear Sir　　　　　　　　　　　　　Washington Oct. 28. 1801.

Lest your rural tranquility should become insipid for want of a little seasoning, I have thought it might not be amiss to animate it from the pepper pots of the tories. their printers, when they have any thing very impudent, send it to me gratis. I will freely give therefore what I freely recieve. I this week send you a dish of the Monitor. the next perhaps it may be of the Palladium, or of Timothy of Charleston &c.

Our notice to mr Smith that we meant to discontinue the mission to Lisbon arrived opportunely two or three days before their minister was to have sailed for the U.S. it stopped him. Buonaparte's ratification of our convention is with a 'bien entendu toujours that the suppression of the 2d. article is considered as an abandonment by both parties of the objects it related to.' tho' this was perfectly so understood on our part, yet I shall send it to the Senate for acceptance that I may filch from them none of the popularity it gives them title to with the merchants. still we shall go on with the execution of it. we have reason to expect that the VIth. article of the British treaty has been amicably & not unconscionably adjusted. respects to mrs Mason, health & fraternity to yourself.　　　Th: Jefferson

PrC (DLC); at foot of text: "Genl. S. T. Mason."

Thomas Collier published the MONI-TOR, a weekly newspaper, at Litchfield, Connecticut. TJ may have received the issue of 16 Sep., which implored voters in the upcoming elections to cast their ballots for Federalists and resist the "Jacobin" intention of making Connecticut follow the "late revolution in the general government." Also in that issue, a long, unsigned address warned that the views of "leading Democrats," if unchecked, would "turn the Universe of God into one *common Brothel.*" The French Revolution proved that unless the "spirit of Democracy" could be resisted, "you will find no asylum, short of *Atheism.*" For the PALLADIUM, see Levi Lincoln to TJ, 5 July 1801. Benjamin F. TIMOTHY directed the *South-Carolina State Gazette* (Brigham, *American Newspapers,* 1:31; 2:1040).

MRS MASON: Mary Elizabeth Armistead Mason, originally of Louisa County, Virginia (DAB).

From Theodore Foster

DEAR SIR,   Providence Thursday Evening Oct. 29th. 1801

I most sincerely thank you for your Letter of the 11th. Ulto. and for the highly obliging Assurance you give Me of communicating *verbally* Such Information as may enable Me "*to give to Posterity a genuine Veiw of the Transactions of the Day*" in the Work, which I mentioned as contemplated, in my Letter of July 25. I feel the Arduousness of the Undertaking, which I should not have dared to think of was it not that I hope to possess "*Opportunities of coming to the True Springs and Motives of Transactions*" from those who could and who would give Me unadulterated Information, when they were convinced of the honest Sincerity of my Wishes to vindicate and Support, as much as in my Power, a Form of Government which I love and which I believe will, by the present Executive, be influenced and directed by the best of Motives.—I Recd. your Letter of the 11th on the 22d. Ult. and should have answered it earlier had I not fear'd intruding on your valuable Time, as I would by no Means abuse the High and honourable Privilege with which you condescend to favour Me, in allowing Me occasionally to make direct Epistolary Communications to you.

On Saturday last, I came from Brookfield, my native Town, in Massachusetts, where I had been to visit my aged Mother and my Brother Dwight who dwell there. Great Exertions have been made and are now making in that State and in Connecticut and indeed in all New England to mislead the Public Mind, by fabricating and spreading the most gross and wicked Falshoods calculated to *deceive* and *inflame,* and by distorting and misrepresenting your Expressions and Sentiment—But blessed be God! Righteousness and Truth will prevail. Falshoods are detected and exposed and the cool and dispassionate are more and more convinced *that Something has been wrong in the View of those who have been called High toned* Federalists. The Latter are of course losing the Ascendency they have had and more moder-

ate Men who love and will support a *Genuine* Republican Administration of the Government are every where gaining the public
Confidence and coming into Power, in so much that a Gentleman,* of
Brookfield, a Lawyer, and a Justice of the Peace, in that Town, and a
Man of Good Information assured Me, on Saturday Morning last that
he thought it was undoubtedly true that more than One Half the People of Massachusetts may now be considered as Friends and Supporters of *Jeffersonian Politicks*—[That was his Expression] and that it
will be evinced the next time an Occasion calls for a general Expression of the Feelings and Sentiments of the People at large.—

As a Specimen of the Shameful, *lying Spirit* prevalent, I here copy
verbatim a Paragraph from *the Providence Journal* published in this
Town on the 23d. Ult. inserted under the Providence Head, as an
original Article of the Printer of that Paper in these Words

"*The President of the United States has ordered a Removal of the
Arms*[1] *from Springfield* [Massachusetts] *to the Southward*"

A Similar Paragraph had previously appeared and had been contradicted in most of what are wrongly called the Federal Papers in
New England. The Editor of *the Providence Journal* however so far
from contradicting it in his Paper, did, on the 14th Instant republish
from the Stockbridge Paper, or rather under the Stockbridge Head,
the extraordinary "*Extract of a Letter* [*said to be*] *from a Gentleman in
Springfield to his Friend in that Town*," of which I inclose a Copy and
of which I intend to request a Contradiction to be inserted in the
Providence Journal to be published on Wednesday next, thinking it
a Duty I owe my Constituents to counteract the Tendency of a Publication so *inflamatory* and which has excited much Uneasiness where
it was not known to be false.—

There have been, in New England Two large Editions of *Mr.
Harper's last Letter to his Constituents*, dated Washington March
5th: 1801, published by Subscription and distributed *gratis* among
the People, to prove that "*those who had conducted the Government
had left an Easy Task to their Successors*"—"That every thing had
been done to their Hand, and in spite of thier constant and violent
Opposition"*—and I am told by a Clergyman of Massachusetts that
himself and most of the Clergy in that State are supplied with *the
Boston Palladium* in the same Way.—

But *true Republican Papers*, such as *the National Ægis*, and others
are about to be published by able Editors which it is hoped will

*Pliny Merrick Esq.
*Vide Providence Edition Page 16.

dispel the malignant² Vapours of Prejudice and Misrepresentation which have arisen in our political Atmosphere, and so much bewildered the Public Mind, that it has been hardly capable of discerning Truth from Falshood.—

The Time of the Assembling of Congress is fast approaching when I hope to have the Pleasure of seeing you in good Health and Spirits.—That the Session may be distinguished for Sincerity, in promoting the Public Good, with Cordiality and Unanimity, in Support of the Executive, in both Houses of Congress, in Measures which shall give general Satisfaction and increase the growing Confidence of the People in the Government, and that you may long enjoy the Heartfelt Pleasure of possessing the sincere Affections Gratitude and Support of *a great Majority* of this great and Flourishing Nation, is the Sincere Prayer of, Dear Sir,

Your much obliged Friend and obedient Servant

THEODORE FOSTER

RC (DLC); with brackets in Foster's hand; at head of text: "To the President of the United States"; endorsed by TJ as received 7 Nov. and so recorded in SJL. Enclosure: copy of a letter appearing in the *Providence Journal, and Town and Country Advertiser*, 14 Oct. 1801, under the dateline "Stockbridge, October 5," commenting on reports circulating that the president planned to remove all military stores from Springfield, Massachusetts, as well as all of New England, "*as the people of this district of country had shewn a spirit so hostile to the present administration, Mr. Jefferson was determined to put the public arms out of their reach*"; the author saw this as evidence of the administration's determination "*to bend and subjugate New England to Southern, or rather to Virginia politics and habits; and to do this, I beleive the government will go all lengths*" (Tr in same; entirely in Foster's hand).

Foster's MOTHER was Dorothy Dwight Foster (DAB, s.v. "Foster, Theodore"). His BROTHER, Dwight Foster, was a Federalist U.S. senator for Massachusetts (*Biog. Dir. Cong.*).

EDITOR OF THE PROVIDENCE JOUR-

NAL: John Carter, Jr., published the *Providence Journal, and Town and Country Advertiser* from 2 Jan. 1799 until 30 Dec. 1801, when the newspaper was discontinued. He was the son of John Carter, publisher of the *Providence Gazette* (Brigham, *American Newspapers*, 2:1007-8, 1012; *Rhode Island Historical Society Collections*, 11 [1918], 108).

At least three EDITIONS of *A Letter from Robert Goodloe Harper, of South Carolina, to His Constituents* were published in New England in 1801: by William Hilliard of Cambridge, Massachusetts; John Carter of Providence, Rhode Island; and Charles Peirce, editor of the Portsmouth, New Hampshire, *United States Oracle of the Day*. The title page of the Portsmouth edition included the declaration: "Presented gratis to the Respectable Patrons of The United States' Oracle of the Day, By The Editor" (Shaw-Shoemaker, Nos. 612, 613, 614; Portsmouth, N.H., *United States Oracle of the Day*, 16 May 1801). See also Gallatin to TJ, 20 Mch. 1801.

¹ MS: "Aarms."
² Canceled: "and noxious."

From Henry Rose

DEAR SIR   Fairfax 29th Octor 1801

Your esteemed favour of 23d Inst was regularly forwarded, had I been in place to receive it—The Facts stated in answer to my queries, are highly important, and as such shall endeavour to palliate the suffering of our fellow citizens, by forwarding the deductions from the communication, with such other documents as I can collect on the subject, (as early as Dr French of Fredg. will forward me the infection), to my Medical friends of Kentucky & Tennassee

It will afford me pleasure to accompany you on a view of the grounds over which I proposed *this new road* should pass, and will cause a Servant to meet you on the George Town road to conduct you to my House on next saturday morning or any other morning or day that you may find it convenient to yourself, during this or the ensuing week—I prescribe this time under an impression that it will not be in my power to be at home after that period untill the month of February.

With every assurance of the highest respect & esteem I am Your obt & Huml. Sert.   HENRY ROSE

RC (ViW); endorsed by TJ as received 31 Oct. and so recorded in SJL.

DR FRENCH: probably George French of Fredericksburg, Virginia (Blanton, *Medicine in Virginia*, 361).

From William Barton

SIR,   Lancaster, Oct. 30th. 1801—

Having been confined to my house with the gout, a considerable part of the past summer, I employed myself, during that time, in preparing for the press a work which is now compleated.—I have taken the liberty of sending a copy of the title and preface to You, by a Mr. Getz of this town, who set out to-day for Washington.

The subject—as You, Sir, will perceive,—is one of extensive concern; appearing to interest all maritime nations:—Yet its investigation unavoidably led to the introduction of observations, on some public transactions, which have an appropriate relation to the United States. Wherever this necessity occurred, I have endeavoured to render my strictures on those transactions, as conformable to candor and decorum,—as the nature of the subject, and a due regard to truth, would permit.—In the prosecution of this undertaking, it has been my wish to produce something that shall be useful:—And I flatter myself, that however defective the work may be, with regard to the manner of its execution in general,—it will be found to contain some valuable materials.—The whole will be comprized in about two hundred and eighty pages, in Octavo.—

I am ambitious, Sir, to have the honor of inscribing this treatise to You: and, therefore, the papers which were committed to the charge of Mr. Getz, for Your inspection, are now followed by my request, that You will be pleased to grant me that indulgence;—as I do not conceive myself at liberty to gratify my inclination in this respect, without having previously obtained Your permission for the purpose. Should there be no impropriety in my solicitation of this favor, Your compliance with it will be highly grateful to my feelings.—

With sentiments of the most perfect Respect, And great personal Consideration, I have the Honor to be, Sir, Your Obedt. Servt.

W. BARTON

RC (DLC); at foot of text: "The President"; endorsed by TJ as received 6 Nov. and so recorded in SJL. Enclosure: Title page, reading in part "A Dissertation on the maritime Rights of Neutrals, founded on the just principles of the Law of Na-tions: interspersed with Moral and political Reflexions, and historical Facts"; and preface of the work (MS in same; in Barton's hand, with some emendations in preface; endorsed by TJ: "Barton William on Neutral rights").

From Nicholas Lewis

DEAR SIR   Albemarle October 30th. 1801

Received Yours of 16th of the present month by the last post, and am very sorry to inform You that I have so far forgot the terms of the Elk-hill sale that I can not with Certainty give You the information You wish. Neither can I find a paper in my possession to assist me in recollecting, but I well remember that the Bonds of that sale are very particularly Entered in Capt. Ballows Book of Accounts, raising a seperate acct for every Bond, a Copy of those entries I am Satisfied would be perfectly satisfactory & if Mr. Randolph has the means of Coming at that Account Book, I will[1] send You on by the Next post Copy's of the Entries of the two Bonds You have mentioned.—Capt. Ballow was at that time Your Steward & Acted as Clerke at that sale. I am Dear Sr. with great respect

Your Humble Servt   NICHOLAS LEWIS

RC (MHi); endorsed by TJ as received 3 Nov. and so recorded in SJL.

CAPT. BALLOWS BOOK OF ACCOUNTS: Francis Eppes introduced Charles Bal-low as the new steward in a letter to TJ at Paris dated 11 Apr. 1786 (Vol. 15:625-6).

[1] MS: "will will."

From Wilson Cary Nicholas

DEAR SIR   Warren Octr. 30th. 1801

I have delivered your letter to Griffin, who has been to see your estate since you left Albemarle, from his account of Clarke's management, I am confident that you will be very much benefited by the change of men; you may expect an increase of crops and a great improvement of your estate, but to effect this you must allow Griffin two years.

It gives me great pleasure to hear that there is a probability of an accommodation of some of the points in dispute between England and this country, for I do not believe that any event wou'd produce more mischievous, consequences to the U.S. than a rupture with G.B. either in a political or pecuniary point of view. I suppose the general expectation in this country will be, that compensation for spoliations ought to be secured by the same instrument that provides for satisfying their claims against the United States. As a Senator I will most willingly bear my proportion of the responsibility of taking the French treaty with their understanding of it; indeed I consider the public welfare, as so much dependant upon your popularity that it wou'd give me very great concern to see it put to hazard upon any, but the most important occasions

I am Dear Sir your Humble Servant   WILSON C NICHOLAS

The inclosed letter is from a very respectable young man, who is a Senator in the State Legislature, for the district of Montgomery &c. I know the Gentn. who is in office, he is a man of great respectty. and I believe a good officer—his wife who is J. Preston's sister is as firm a democrat as any in the U.S.

RC (DLC); endorsed by TJ as received 9 Nov. and so recorded in SJL. Enclosure not found, but see below.

LETTER TO GRIFFIN: see enclosure listed at TJ to Nicholas, 25 Oct.

James P. Preston was the RESPECTABLE YOUNG MAN who applied for the position of inspector of the revenue for the sixth survey of the Virginia district

(Preston to TJ, 29 Sep.). GENTN. WHO IS IN OFFICE: James McDowell held that position. He was married to Sarah Preston (JEP, 1:208; ASP, *Miscellaneous*, 1:284; Robert Sobel and John Raimo, eds., *Biographical Directory of the Governors of the United States, 1789-1978*, 4 vols. [Westport, Conn., 1978], 4:1632, 1641).

From Fulwar Skipwith

I cannot let pass the opportunity by Mr. Dupont, of saying in this private manner some things which I am desirous of communicating to you, my dear Sir, but which I should feel an awkwardness in making the subject of a letter to the Department of State.—I shall in doing this expect your indulgence; perhaps, because I have so often experienced it.

In a sketch here inclosed I have hazarded, for your consideration, my ideas on the advantages which both the Government and the foreign trade of the U. States would derive from a regular exchange on Paris—to create this exchange, it is supposed, that the establishment of an American Bank in Paris must operate as the most effectual mean, and that the Government itself would see a motive of national policy as well as its own convenience in appearing at least to favour such an establishment—doubtless it would tend to increase our commercial relations with France, the greatest consuming Country of our produce, whilst it diminished those of other Countries who consume less; but who by lending us their Capitals, and supplying us almost exclusively with their manufactures, cause the most serious mischiefs among us. I suppose myself as the commercial Agent of the U. States, to be the most suitable character to commence such an establishment, and more actuated by my view of the public advantages, which I conceive would result, though I occupy a laborious station with little or no emolument and without the commercial advantages, which the sea ports offer to my Colleagues, I ask only the patronage of my Government, or, in other words, that they will confide to that establishment its money transactions in Europe.—If my plan should be approved by you in either a public or private sense, I should associate with me one or more Gentlemen of our Country whose talents and reputation in the commercial World would inspire confidence in our Merchants, and give weight to the establishment in Europe.

I have now to say a word on the subject of two of our Countrymen, who stood on the list of appointments made by your predecessor for this Country, the one, Mr. I. C. Barnet, to the commercial Agency at Bordeaux, and the other, Mr. J. J. Waldo, to that of Nantes: they are both I find soliciting appointments of a similar nature under your administration, and are both in my opinion deserving of the Offices they are endeavouring to obtain—from a long acquaintance with each of them, I can offer you with confidence my assurances of their being young men of intelligence and the strictest probity. they are equally attached to their Country and its Constitution, and though the latter was among those who supported our late Administration, I am positive that he did it from a belief that its measures were expedient and patriotic, and not from the foul motive of either personal interest or of weakening the glorious principles of Republican Governmt.—I am confident too, that there are few men who would serve under your Administration with greater Zeal and fidelity; because the veil of prejudices as it respects you, Sir, are from before his eyes.—The other Mr. Barnet has perhaps something more than an ordinary claim in his pretentions to the Office of a commercial Agency—at a very trying period in this Country he rendered the most disinterested Services to our suffering fellow Citizens at Brest, and has ever appeared to me to be one of your warmest admirers, and is in my belief a Republican. He is poor and has been consequently dependent on the trifling emoluments of his office for a subsistence, and to that circumstance do I attribute; a kind of complacency under men whose measures have not been tolerated in our blessed Country.

I have, in an official letter of this date to the Department of State, made some communications on the[1] points which appear to me immediately to concern the mercantile interests of the U. States. It remains for me to express my extreme desire of seeing Mr. Livingston at his post, for it is only under the weight of his Official character that we are left to hope to[2] see the Treaty carried, with any good faith, into execution, as it respects the trial and restitution of our captured Vessels. He would besides be able to ascertain many important facts singularly interesting to our Country, and which by him alone can be best made known to you.—Among others the possession of Louisiana, which, according to reports industriously circulated by men high in Office, for some days past, is to remain with the Spaniards—this I doubt myself exceedingly, or rather I am sure of the reverse, and that the possession of that Country, by this Government, is among its most favorite objects. Already, I have reason to believe, is a plan formed of peupling that Colony to an amazing extent, and already does this Government calculate on deriving in a few years from that Source, its principal supplies for its Islands, of Rice, Cotton, and Lumber, and above all, a deposit for that multitude of men, whose affections, habits, and principles in time of Peace, might render them a charge if not troublesome, if kept within the bosom of their Country.

The official paper, the Moniteur, it is remarked affects to speak well of Touissants conduct in St. Domingo and even to approve in most of its parts, the Constitution which has been adopted in that Island; at the same time it is observed that one of the greatest military armaments is preparing at Brest for the W. Indies that has ever been known. an army of 30,000 men is certainly appropriated for the Expedition, to be commanded by either Genl. Massena or Boudet. It is generally believed here that the french Government mean so to qualify the principles of emancipation in its Colonies, of its slaves, as to leave them but the name of being free.

With every sentiment of unshaken attattchment and respect, I remain, my dear Sir, Your mo. Ob. Servant   FULWAR SKIPWITH

N.B. It is a brother in law of the 1st. Consul, Genl. LeClerk, who is to command the expedition to St. Domingo

RC (DLC); endorsed by TJ as received 11 Feb. 1802 and so recorded in SJL. Enclosure: "A view of the advantages which the Merchants of the United States might derive from a regular course of Exchange on Paris, and other considerations of National importance for the improving, and extending our commercial Relations with France" (MS in same, TJ Papers, 117:20204-8, 9 p., in Skipwith's hand; Tr in same, 115:19858-61, 8 p., in an unidentified hand, lacks title, with variations in wording and paragraph breaks; printed, from MS, in Henry Bartholomew Cox, *The Parisian American: Fulwar Skipwith of Virginia* [Washington, D.C., 1964], 148-53).

Skipwith's OFFICIAL LETTER to the secretary of state was dated 29 Oct. He reported that the French government had granted him his exequatur and authorization to issue passports. He sent information pertaining to condemnations by the French Council of Prizes and advised that any commercial agents appointed for France be American citizens, since French citizens appointed as U.S. commercial agents had not received exequaturs (Madison, *Papers, Sec. of State Ser.*, 2:211).

[1] MS: "the the."
[2] MS: "hope see."

To Gideon Granger

DEAR SIR   Washington Oct. 31. 1801.

Your favors of the 25th. & 26th. inst. came to hand last night. I feel with great sensibility the domestic obstacles which embarras your mind on the subject of a removal to this place. but nobody knows better, because no one has encountered more steadfastly, the formidable phalanx opposed to the republican features of our constitution. to bear up against[1] this, the talents & virtue of our country must be formed into phalanx also. my wish is to collect in a mass round the administration all the abilities, & the respectability to which the offices exercised here can give employ. to give none of them to secondary characters. good principles, wisely & honestly administered cannot fail to attach our fellow citizens to the order of things which we espouse. under this view of the circumstances in which we are placed, we cannot dispense here with your aid. besides the preference which the general objects claim over those merely local, I cannot but believe that the rectification of public opinion even in Connecticut could be more promoted by you from hence, by disseminating correct information, than by your action there. you ask whether it would be necessary for you to come on immediately. the sooner the better certainly, because Colo. Habersham retires, I believe, this day. how far the principal deputy (a rank federalist of your state) can conduct the business by himself I know not. but I should think it better for you to come as soon as possible, qualify & possess yourself of the office and having obtained a sufficient view of it's business to judge how long you could be spared from it, return then for a while to make your ultimate arrangements at home. it is now 5. weeks to the meeting of Congress. it will occur to you as very desireable that you should be finally fixed here before their meeting. if you find it better to make your final arrangements before you come, be so good as to inform me. Accept assurances of my constant esteem & respect

Th: Jefferson

RC (DNDAR); addressed by TJ in a disguised hand: "Gideon Granger esqr. Suffield Connecticut"; stamped; postmarked 2 Nov.; endorsed. PrC (DLC).

PRINCIPAL DEPUTY: Abraham Bradley, Jr. (Richard R. John, *Spreading the*

News: The American Postal System from Franklin to Morse [Cambridge, Mass., 1995], 69-71).

[1] Preceding three words interlined in place of "oppose."

To John F. Mercer

DEAR SIR   Washington Oct. 31. 1801.

Your favor of the 24th. has been duly recieved. the promised visit to you had not escaped us; on the contrary mr Madison & myself conferring on the subject, it had been agreed that I should write to you to know when mrs Mercer & yourself would be at home. on further consideration however it occurred to us that such a jacobinical visit made at this time might have an influence of a character we could not foresee on the election which comes on the ensuing week at Annapolis. we knew how much the tories had tortured & perverted our own accidental visits in Virginia, and concluded it would be better to postpone this pleasure till it can do you no mischeif. claiming therefore the benefit of the French adage that 'tout ce qui est differé n'est pas perdu' we reserve ourselves for a more favorable moment. present my respectful compliments to mrs Mercer and accept yourself assurances of my constant & affectionate esteem.　　Th: Jefferson

RC (Harry Ackerman, Los Angeles, California, 1949); addressed: "John F. Mercer esq. Annapolis"; franked; postmarked 2 Nov. PrC (DLC).

TOUT CE QUI EST DIFFERÉ N'EST PAS PERDU: roughly translated, "all that is deferred is not lost."

To Thomas Tudor Tucker

DEAR SIR　　　　　　　　　　　　Washington Oct. 31. 1801.

I recieved a letter from you in March last which expressed a willingness to undertake the duties of an office in the General government should occasion arise. with whatever pleasure I recieved this information, and however much I was chagrined not to return an answer, yet I found myself obliged by a rigorous rule, under which it was absolutely necessary to lay myself, to pretermit that ceremony. the considerations which oblige me never to say, even to my bosom friends, that an office will, or will not be given, will readily suggest themselves to you: and to make it a justification to all, it must be acted on without exception. what is done, when the time for acting arrives, is the only answer affirmative or negative which is given. I had had my attention directed to the Mint, in the event of it's removal here & of the consequent resignation of the incumbent. but that institution will probably be suppressed & not removed. in the mean time I am happy that another vacancy happens wherein I can propose to avail the public of your integrity & talents, in a station of higher trust & respectability. the office of Treasurer of the US. is vacant by the resignation of mr Meredith, and I now propose it to your acceptance with assurances of the great satisfaction with which I shall see the public interest placed in hands so secure, and at the same time such an addition made to the mass of talents which I am anxious to concentrate in the administration of the government. mr Meredith proposes to retire from his office about the middle of November, if his successor is ready; but has politely offered to accomodate me by a further stay if necessary. I shall be anxious to recieve an answer as early as possible. I pray you to accept assurances of my high esteem & respect.　　　　　　　　　Th: Jefferson

PrC (DLC); at foot of text: "Doctr. Thomas Tudor Tucker." Enclosed in TJ to Philadelphia postmaster Robert Patton, 31 Oct., explaining that Tucker's "address in March last was No. 12 North 8th. street, Philada, or to the care of Messrs. E. & J. Perot," and as the letter was important and TJ wished "a speedy answer," urging Patton "to have him enquired for, & if he has left Philadelphia to have the enclosed addressed to the proper post office if you can discover it"; if Tucker was not in Philadelphia, TJ requested that Patton "be so good as to drop me a line of information" (PrC in DLC; at foot of text: "Mr. Patton. P.M. Phila."; endorsed by TJ in ink on verso).

Born in Port Royal, Bermuda, Thomas Tudor Tucker (1745-1828) received a degree in medicine from the University of Edinburgh in 1770. He settled in South Carolina where he practiced his profession and purchased land in Charleston, Camden, and Ninety Six districts. He served as physician and surgeon at a Continental army hospital during the Revolutionary War. In 1789 he was a founding member of the South Carolina Medical

Society. Active in South Carolina politics, Tucker served in the state assembly during the 1780s. He was elected to the Continental Congress in 1787 and served as a congressman from 1789 to 1793. He took office as treasurer of the United States on 1 Dec. 1801, a position he held until his death (*Biog. Dir. Cong.*; *S.C. Biographical Directory, House of Representatives*, 3:725-6).

LETTER FROM YOU: Tucker to TJ, 18 Mch., recorded in SJL as received from Philadelphia on the 21st, has not been found. For a recommendation of Tucker for director of the U.S. MINT, see Vol. 33:522-3. INCUMBENT: Washington appointed Elias Boudinot as director of the Mint in 1795, a position he continued to hold until 1805 (*Biog. Dir. Cong.*; JEP, 1:194-5; 2:7, 10).

Calculation of Population Increase

[October 1801]

the Census of 1791. was 3,929,326. wanting 70,474 of 4. millions
that   of 1801. is   5,366,786. includg. 10,000 for Maryld & 100,000. Tennessee

<calling the 1st. four millions & the last 5,000,000 in 10. years it is in the geometrical ratio of $2\frac{1}{4}$ per annum and would take[1] 31. years to double>

in a series of Geometrical progressionals
given the 1st. term   f. = 3,929,326
     the no. of terms t = 10
     the last term   l = 5,366,786
required the ratio   r
from the nature of geometrical progression we have this equation
$f \times r^t = l$. then $r^t = \frac{l}{f}$ and Log. r x t = Log. l.–Log. f

$$\text{Log. } r = \frac{\text{Log. l.–Log. f}}{t}$$

Log. l   6.7297142
Log. f.   6.5943180
       .1353962
÷10.   .0135396 = Log. r = Log. of 1.031667 = r

[531]

given $f = 3,929,326$

         $l = 3,929,326 \times 2 = 7,858,652$

         $r = 1.031667$

required t

$$f \times r^t = l \quad r^t = \tfrac{1}{f} \text{ Log } r. \times t = \text{Log. } l. - \text{Log. } f.$$
$$t = \frac{\text{Log. } l. - \text{Log. } f.}{\text{Log. } r}$$

Log. l. 6.8953480

Log. f <u>6.5943180</u>

        .3010300

which $\div$ by Log. r .0135396 gives 22.23 y

MS (DLC: TJ Papers, 232:41570); undated; entirely in TJ's hand; endorsed by TJ: "Census."

TJ apparently made these calculations sometime after 17 Sep. 1801, the day he received W. C. C. Claiborne's letter of 4 Aug., which included Claiborne's estimate of 100,000 for Tennessee's population. In December, when Madison conveyed the second CENSUS to TJ for transmittal to Congress, there was still no return for Tennessee. The return for part of Baltimore County, Maryland, was lacking until 19 Nov., which may account for TJ's addition of 10,000 people for Maryland along with the 100,000 for Tennessee in his calculations (Madison to TJ, 8 Dec.). TJ had not completed the computations printed above by 3 Oct., since in his letter to William Short on that day he forecast a "duplication" of the population "in 23. or 24. years." To Wilson Cary Nicholas on 25 Oct., TJ reported the doubling time of the population as 22 years and three months. That was the exact result of his figuring in the document printed above, which means he completed his computation by 25 Oct. 1801.

GEOMETRICAL PROGRESSION: in this document, TJ reckoned the growth of population as a geometric progression—the ratio of increase is considered to be constant, but the population grows by a greater number of individuals each successive year because the base population against which the rate of growth is multiplied grows larger. TJ used logarithms to perform those computations. The docu-

ment has three sections, separated by horizontal rules at the left margin. In the first section, TJ rounded the total for the 1790 census up to 4,000,000 and rounded his estimate for the 1800 census total down to 5,000,000. Without showing his arithmetic, he determined the annual rate of increase over ten years, using the rounded figures, to be 2.25%, which would result in a doubling of the population in 31 years. He subsequently voided that estimate, striking through it with three diagonal strokes. The middle and final sections of the document contain his calculations using specific figures for the two censuses, rather than the rounded totals. From the increase to 5,366,786 from 3,929,326 over ten years—ten TERMS in his figuring above—he computed an annual rate of growth of 3.1667% (each year the population was 1.031667 times what it had been the year before). In the final section, he used that rate of increase to calculate how long it would take the population to reach 7,858,652, or twice the total of the 1790 census. The result, by his analysis, was 22.23 years.

The idea that human populations increase by geometric progression gained widespread notice from Thomas Robert Malthus's *Essay on the Principle of Population*, first published in 1798. However, well before Malthus wrote that treatise, Leonhard Euler and others applied geometric progression, which had been used to figure compound interest and for other applications in commerce and finance, to the problem of calculating population growth. By the 1770s and 1780s the principle of geometrical increase of population had wide acceptance among people who wrote about and discussed demography. The arithmetical skills needed to calculate progressions, though, remained "a matter beyond most demographers and nearly all less specialized commentators on population" (James C. Riley, *Population Thought in the Age of the Demographic Revolution* [Durham, N.C., 1985], 131-5). In the 1750s, Benjamin Franklin stated in his *Observations Concerning the Increase of Mankind, Peopling of Countries, &c.* that the American population doubled every 25 years. European and British writers, including Malthus, fastened upon Franklin's period of doubling for North America, which was considerably shorter than the doubling period calculated for some regions of Europe. Franklin, however, based his estimate on a combination of suppositions rather than the computation of the actual rate of growth. Madison paid some notice to doubling rates in unsigned essays on emigration and population he wrote for Philip Freneau's *National Gazette* in 1791, but apparently got his figures from Franklin and other sources. That same year, William Barton wrote a long paper on population and longevity in the United States. Barton treated factors that affect population growth, such as birth and death rates, and like Franklin and Madison he did not venture into the mathematics of geometric increase. TJ apparently got the mathematical wherewithal to calculate geometric progressions from William Small, his professor at the College of William and Mary. Logarithms were among the practical skills of arithmetic that TJ, in 1799, deemed worthwhile to master (he classified mathematical functions beyond logarithms and quadratic equations as a "delicious," but mostly superfluous, "luxury"). Earlier, writing under Query VIII of his *Notes on the State of Virginia*, he did not refer specifically to the geometric progression of population, but took it for granted. Using data from the period 1654 to 1772—and employing the word "term," as in the document above—he computed that the population of Virginia was doubling every 27.25 years. Although he did not show his calculations, he must have worked out that geometric progression by a process similar to what he followed in the document above. In 1792, TJ wrote that the enslaved black population of the U.S. doubled "in about 25. years." He did not provide clues to indicate if he computed that rate himself or got the information by other means (Riley, *Population Thought*, 132-6; Thomas Robert Malthus, *An Essay on the Principle of Population*, ed. Patricia James, 2 vols. [Cambridge, 1989], 1:11-12, 295; Thomas Robert Malthus, *An Essay on the Principle of Population*, ed. Philip Appleman, 2d ed. [New York, 2004], 21; Patricia James, *Population Malthus: His Life and Times* [London, 1979], 103, 106-7, 380; Patricia Cline Cohen, *A Calculating People: The Spread of Numeracy in Early America* [Chicago, 1982], 112-15; Madison, *Papers*, 14:110-12, 114, 117-18; APS, *Transactions*, 3:25-62, 134-8; William Barton, *Observations on the Progress of Population, And the Probabilities of the Duration of Human Life, in the United States of America* [Philadelphia, 1791]; Sowerby, No. 667; William Petersen, *Malthus* [Cambridge, Mass., 1979], 61, 147-8; Malone, *Jefferson*, 1:54; Autobiography in Ford, 1:4; *Notes*, ed. Peden, 82-7; Vol. 19:584; Vol. 22:473; Vol. 24:98; Vol. 31:126-7).

Malthus's *Essay*, with its central assertion that the growth of population, increasing at a geometric rate, far outpaces the increase of resources needed to sustain life, appeared anonymously in 1798. TJ saw a review of the work and discussed its argument with Thomas Cooper, but he did not read that version of the *Essay*. Only after a revised and expanded second edition appeared in 1803, bearing its author's name, did TJ read Malthus. Later he acquired the book for his library (DNB; Drew R. McCoy, "Jefferson and Madison on Malthus: Population Growth in Jeffersonian Political Economy," VMHB, 88 [1980], 259-76; Sowerby, No. 2938; Thomas Cooper to TJ, 16 Feb. 1804; TJ to Cooper, 24 Feb. 1804).

[1] TJ here canceled "between."

Notes on John Morton

[October 1801]

John Morton. Consul at the Havana
he employed the US. Sloop Warren to go from the Hava to La Vera Cruz to bring up 102,000 Spanish money, & property[1] for which he was to recieve a commission. she went, lost 50. or 60. of her men by sickness. her absence occasioned many captures of American vessels by privateers: and a British frigate cruised to take her on her return. she escaped & got in with the money.
George Morton his brother is now acting as Consul.
Mr. Coffyn, a candidate for the office gives me this information.

MS (DNA: RG 59, MCL); entirely in TJ's hand; undated, but written before Morton's departure for Havana in late October 1801 (see below).

In June 1800, John Morton, the U.S. consul at HAVANA, persuaded the commander of the U.S. ship WARREN, Timothy Newman, to abandon temporarily his station and sail to Veracruz in order to collect a considerable sum of specie owned by American merchants. Shortly after departing for Veracruz, yellow fever broke out in the *Warren*, which claimed the lives of some 42 men, including Newman, by the time the ship returned to Havana in mid-August. The mission infuriated Secretary of the Navy Benjamin Stoddert, who ordered an investigation into Morton's role in the affair. Hastening to Washington in the fall of 1800, the Havana consul defended himself to the satisfaction of the Adams administration and he retained his appointment. He remained in Washington, however, to defend himself to the new administration. In a 4 June 1801 letter to James Madison, Morton justified his conduct by claiming that the *Warren*'s term of service was

nearly expired, that the Havana station had already been cleared of French vessels, that another American navy ship was soon expected to relieve the *Warren*, and that Secretary Stoddert had previously expressed a willingness to accommodate American merchants in transporting their property from Veracruz. The explanation apparently satisfied Madison and TJ, and Morton was permitted to return to his post. The illness and death of a relative, Dr. David Jackson, delayed his departure until late October, prompting Morton to offer his resignation if the president desired. In a 30 Oct. letter to Madison, Morton expressed his gratitude for the "indulgent accommodation of the President." He resumed his post at Havana in December, but resigned shortly thereafter (Palmer, *Stoddert's War*, 228-9; NDQW, June to Nov. 1800, 345-6, 385-6; Dec. 1800 to Dec. 1801, 244-5; Madison, *Papers, Sec. of State Ser.*, 1:263; 2:191, 212, 306; Morton to Madison, 17 Apr. 1805, in DNA: RG 59, LAR; JEP, 1:406; Vol. 32:544).

[1] Preceding three words and ampersand interlined.

From Charles Pinckney

DEAR SIR   October 1801. In Bourdeaux
My last to you was from Paris on the subject of the Peace. since this I have left that city & am now in Bourdeaux on my way to Spain

where I am hopeful to arrive in a few days.—as I informed You the Expedition to Saint Domingo will take place.—Benezech is appointed to the Civil Department with plenary powers & will go out as proconsul or Commissary.—this is fixed & it is said Rochambeau will command.—with respect to Louisiana the general opinion is, that the affair is dropped at least for the present.—it is a subject however on which it is difficult to decide what will be the issue as those who are best informed are extremely close & reserved whenever it is mentioned.—most of the men who are friends to America particularly Marbois, Laforest, Otto, Joseph Bonaparte & others are anxious it should not take place & as their interest is very great I rather think upon the whole it is not likely it will take place for some time, if at all—Mr Skipwith is fearful from a conversation he says he accidentally overheard where he was not known that it will, but from alterations that have been made in the Disposition of a variety of articles originally intended for Louisiana & the Destination of Characters also originally intended for that place & who are now ordered elsewhere I am of Opinion it will not, (if at all), for some time—Mr: Livingston will be better able to judge when he arrives, for as it will depend altogether on France, whether she wishes to have it or not, it not being in the power of Spain to object to any thing France desires, so will it in some measure depend upon the influence of our friends at Paris to prevent it—fortunately America has some powerful ones there at present & if it is laid aside it will be greatly owing to them— sir there can be no doubt that the first Consul himself is friendly to the project—he has been induced to suppose that from thence large supplies of Rice & Cotton may be drawn & Timber & stores for the Marine & that it will be the best means of compensating their armies, by giving them lands in example of America.—The great objects with France at present are to restore her Marine & Commerce & to these Bonaparte gives unwearied attention.—his establishment of peace has given him great popularity & the idea of recovering their colonies & commerce makes them at least for the present forget to calculate what they have gained by the revolution.—They have undoubtedly increased the power & Consequence of France to an enormous extent.—the acquisition of Belgium, & the Department on the Rhine & other places making in the whole 115 & 34 millions of inhabitants give her an irresistible weight in the politics of Europe— nor is it possible at present to say into what their Government may settle down.—In having a senate for Life, to fill up their own Vacancies, & that senate to elect the Executive for 10 Years, & such Executive to have the sole proposition of Laws, which are silently to be rejected or recieved by Ballot, is not certainly in the American sense of the Word *a republic*.—but it is at present to be remembered that France did not perhaps possess those materials, for immediately recieving & forming a Republic *which our thrice happy Country does*.— it would be presumptuous in me who have been so short a time here to give an opinion, but our *own Americans* staunch Republicans themselves, & who have been long here, seem to doubt if the french character, of the present generation at least, is calculated to admit universal suffrage & the unlimited right of discussion to the extent that the American is.—they seem rather to think that these must be admitted slowly, & be gradually infused & the minds, & if possible the manners of the people prepared for it—& that until this is done, they must have what they call, a strong government to prevent the anarchy & divisions that would otherwise dismember the Empire[1]— Some of the most sanguine Republicans believe that it is the intention of Bonaparte hereafter to introduce Modifications of the present System & to extend the rights of the people—that he feels his character & particularly his true[2] glory concerned in doing so.—I am myself of this opinion & that not only his glory but perhaps his safety may depend upon it—You are to recollect that although the french have not by their revolution established what we call a republic, Yet that they have gained a great deal by the struggle & have made if I may use the Term; *some Lodgements* in the road to Republicanism of which it will not be easy to dispossess them.—they have abolished the long established hereditary monarchy.—the nobility & in short all their privileged orders.—the monstrous influence of the Clergy is destroyed.—they have in criminal cases some thing like a trial by Jury—not perfect but intended for a Jury.—the term Citizen is in common use with them.—they keep the name of Republic, & all their acts *profess* to be in the name of *the People*—let this people then be at peace a few Years & relieved from heavy exaction, & contributions— let them see & reflect on the happiness of America & be convinced by their Example that a people are able to govern themselves & that public & private rights are no where so secure as in the hands of those who enjoy & feel that they enjoy them & whose interest it is to secure them—let Education be extended as it is at present by the primary schools & other means adopted to improve & inform the people & the business is done—the generations now coming on, know nothing of the distinction of rank or hereditary consequence which it is so difficult to make their fathers forget, & as I have just observed, in times of peace & commerce & when they are in a situation to think they will be very apt to examine more minutely into the meaning of the Words "Citizen & Republic" & to enquire why those words do not mean the same thing here they do in our country[3]—it is for these reasons I judge that true Republicanism is not Yet lost in Europe & that there are lodgements made in its favour which will one day burst into Effect.—

I have my good sir had a long ride in Europe from the North of Holland—through the whole of it & Brabant or Belgium & from the north to the south of France—a Tour of upwards of 1000 Miles.—I staid 30 days in Paris & was laboriously employed day & night in examining what deserved my attention, & have as far as my powers of investigation enabled me, done the same wherever I have been—the notes I have made & the information I have obtained will I trust be one day, not unentertaining to You, or uninteresting to our friends.—

I feel myself particularly indebted to the gentlemen of the Diplomatic Corps at the Hague & those in power in Holland, Belgium & Paris for the agreeable Reception I met & the means of information they offered me.—I found that in Paris the idea left of our public men was that of a Stiffness & Reserve not pleasing to the French—Being at that time the only public man from our country on the continent I endeavoured to remove this impression by a conduct which appeared to me calculated to restore the confidence & affection which existed formerly, & if I am to believe the Report of our friends there, it was not without it's effect.—they considered me as the first of the *new order* of things who had arrived & the civilities & I believe the sincere Respect & attentions I recieved at Paris contributed very much to give me means of information I could not otherwise have obtained.—I have recieved a Letter within these few days from Admiral De Winter requesting my correspondence on the subject of the commerce of our two countries.—They lament extremely we have not a Minister at the Hague & while there, & at Paris I have had incessant applications to request You would send one there, I told them, it was impossible for me or for them to judge at this Distance; that You were the best & only[4] judge of the Situation of our country & it's foreign connexions— that Batavia had no Minister with us & certainly would have no right to complain as they first withdrew their Minister.—I thought however I would mention it to You, as the men who intimated it to me are among our warmest friends in Holland & France.—

As this letter will go by a safe opportunity I take the Liberty of mentioning to You *in confidence* my wish to remain in Europe for two Years.—As I have had the trouble to cross the Atlantic & am here & as I believe a View & Examination of Europe in the manner I examine it will make me much more useful to my country than I should otherwise be & as I am eager to investigate it thoroughly, I will thank You to continue me in Europe for two Years from this Time.—I am hopeful my nomination to Spain will be confirmed—but should it be impracticable, I rely upon your goodness & friendship for me, not to submit me to the Dangerous affront of a rejection but to alter my Destination to some other place to which You may be inclined to send a Minister.—I would prefer Madrid certainly, if it can be confirmed, but I am afraid, some of *our own* friends want to go there & it may Be difficult.—if it is impracticable I should like to go to Florence, or to any respectable situation in Europe for two Years, as I am apprehensive if I am obliged to return in so short a time it may be injurious to my future influence or public situation in our own country, a circumstance which I am sure Your friendship for me will wish to prevent.— You see how I unbosom myself to You as among my best friends & how I rely on that affection which my best exertions shall be used always to merit.—

I send You a work just published which I have not Yet read but which the author requested me to send to You & Mr Gallatin.—I have directed to be sent to You from Paris, the account of the grand collections of Antiques & of Modern Paintings in the Louvre collected from every Part of Europe.—the antique marbles are deposited in six different Salles, called, the Salle of the Seasons—of the Romans—of the Muses—of Laocoon—of Apollo (Belvidere) & of illustrious men.—

The Paintings are collected in one grand Gallery & divided into the four schools of Lombardy: Bologne Belgium. & France & contain a collection of 942 Paintings of the first Masters in Europe.—the whole are originals.—

The monuments of merit are collected from all the Cathedrals & deposited in different Salles according to the different ages: Egyptian & athenian & roman & the Modern ones beginning with the Time *of Clovis.*—

In these different salles of Marbles—paintings & Monuments I spent nearly a Week at different times.—I should like to be able to return to Paris before I reembark for America—but this will depend upon the Arrangements Your Goodness may have in View for me & I now remain with profound attachment & with the most affectionate respect & obliged

Dear Sir Yours Truly   CHARLES PINCKNEY

My best Compliments to Mr Madison.—
I wrote him a long Letter from Paris & to Mr Gallatin also to my good friends Generals Mason, Mr Baldwin Mr Nicholas & Mr. Brown.—I

trust the intelligence we have had of the death of Colonel Burrs daughter is not true.—please remember me particularly to him.

RC (DLC); at head of text: "Private"; endorsed by TJ as received 28 Dec. and so recorded in SJL.

Pinckney's LAST letter to TJ was the one of 6 Oct. Pinckney arrived in PARIS no earlier than the latter part of September, since he wrote to Madison from The Hague on the 22d of that month and stopped in both Antwerp and Brussels on his way between The Hague and Paris, according to the document that follows and the 6 Oct. letter. If he stayed in Paris thirty days, as stated in the letter above, then he wrote this letter and the one that follows—which he also dated "October 1801" in Bordeaux—late in the month (Madison, *Papers, Sec. of State Ser.,* 2:126).

BENEZECH: the French government named Pierre Bénézech, who had held various administrative positions in France, to be colonial prefect at Cap-Français. He died of yellow fever soon after his arrival in Saint-Domingue in 1802 (*Dictionnaire,* 5:1407-9).

The Vicomte de ROCHAMBEAU, son of the Comte de Rochambeau who commanded French troops in the American Revolution, was, like his father, an army officer. He had experience in the West Indies and was named governor general of Saint-Domingue in 1796, although the civil authorities on the island would not let him exercise that office and dispatched him back to France under arrest. Rochambeau went with the expedition that sailed late in 1801, and took command after General Leclerc died of yellow fever in November 1802 (Tulard, *Dictionnaire Napoléon,* 1047, 1470).

BELGIUM had been incorporated into France under a French decree of October 1795. The Treaty of Lunéville, between Emperor Francis II and France in February 1801, confirmed that cession and put the left bank of the RHINE under French control (same, 184, 1461; John B. Duvergier and others, eds., *Collection Complète des Lois, Décrets, Ordonnances, Réglemens, avis du Conseil-d'État,* 108 vols.

[Paris, 1834-1908], 8:300-1; Parry, *Consolidated Treaty Series,* 55:478-9).

ADMIRAL DE WINTER: Jan Willem de Winter was a senior officer of the navy of the Batavian Republic (Simon Schama, *Patriots and Liberators: Revolution in the Netherlands 1780–1813* [New York, 1977], 278, 282, 292, 343, 408; Tulard, *Dictionnaire Napoléon,* 1752).

TJ submitted Pinckney's NOMINATION as minister plenipotentiary to Spain to the Senate on 6 Jan. 1802. The Senate approved the appointment on 26 Jan. (JEP, 1:404, 405).

The six exhibition rooms of antique marble statuary Pinckney saw at the LOUVRE opened to the public in November 1800. Featured in two of the halls ("salles" in French) were the *Laocoon,* a Greek statue depicting a father and two sons beset by serpents, which had been the subject of attention by artists and writers since the 16th century, and the *Apollo Belvedere.* Both sculptures were among the works of art brought back from Italy under armistice terms that Bonaparte imposed on the Vatican in 1796 (Andrew McClellan, *Inventing the Louvre: Art, Politics, and the Origins of the Modern Museum in Eighteenth-Century Paris* [Cambridge, 1994], 119, 152-4, 259; Sylvain Laveissière and others, *Napoléon et le Louvre* [Paris, 2004], 175, 182; Margarete Bieber, *Laocoon: The Influence of the Group Since Its Rediscovery,* rev. and enlarged ed. [Detroit, 1967], 11-12, 26-7; Tulard, *Dictionnaire Napoléon,* 1210; Parry, *Consolidated Treaty Series,* 53:128, 489).

Aaron Burr's DAUGHTER, Theodosia Burr Alston, lived until 1812 (Kline, *Burr,* 2:1146).

[1] Word interlined in place of "government."

[2] Word interlined.

[3] Pinckney first wrote "other countries" before altering the phrase to read as above.

[4] Preceding word and ampersand interlined.

From Charles Pinckney

Dear Sir   October 1801 In Bourdeaux.

I wrote You two days since by a Vessel from hence—& as another goes in a short time I thought I would send You a Line to say I had written you & delivered Your Letters to Mr Lee our Consul at this port.—it seems to be the general opinion in France that their government will at an early day adopt some thing like the Navigation act of Great Britain, but that at present such is the Want of merchant ships in all their ports, it is probable they will allow the purchase of American ships & the navigation of them by french citizens under certain limitations.—it is with great pleasure I tell you that I found through all France a very great disposition to be upon the most intimate terms with us & to forget that it had been ever possible for *any thing* to bring us to the situation we were in.—this disposition to consider us as their friends prevails generally—all parties in France agree in it & We have at present such powerful friends in Paris that I cannot but think if the affair *is delicately* & adroitly managed, some thing may be advantageously done towards paving the way for our hereafter obtaining Louisiana upon tolerable terms.—This port will be a very considerable commercial one indeed, if Antwerp is not completely opened & fostered by the french consul.—if it is, both Amsterdam & Bourdeaux will suffer considerably.— while I staid at Antwerp they were in high Spirits & Lots & houses had taken a rise on the idea of their becoming again one of the great marts of Europe.—while I was there seeing their neglected Exchange, their streets in Grass, their noble harbour empty & the melancholy aspect of every thing, it gave rise to such reflections as ought for ever to spring in the minds of a republican, at seeing a place destined probably by the Creator to be among the most considerable in Europe for supplying the Wants & *ministering* to the conveniences of its inhabitants stripped by the lawless hand of Power of all its natural advantages & consigned for ages to penury & insignificance.—

I wrote you before of my having recieved Letters from several distinguished men requesting my correspondence on the politics & intercourse of our several countries, *but in the present* state of Europe I have declined, generally correspondences on politics.—on commerce I have no objection, as far as my means of information will extend— but on politics I have declined it on obvious grounds & desired them, particularly such as have been in America, to remember we were not *now there.*—indeed my dear sir when I reflect on the present state of Europe as it respects *private rights* & compare it with our own country there is scarcely an hour in the day that I do not burst as it were into a secret exclamation, "how happy are our citizens[1]—how dearly ought they to cherish a situation more precious than any other Spot on the Globe possesses."—if I know myself, I believe I am sincere in saying that I would rather possess a cot within our *own Bounds*, than a palace within the Dominions of any power in Europe.—In order to enable our citizens fully to appreciate their rights & never suffer a Violation of them, I have been & am now laboriously employed in possessing myself of all the information I can collect respecting Europe.—in my public character I have access to all the public characters & places as I pass & ample means of information.—I believe that I knew Paris, when I left it better than $\frac{2}{3}$ds of the inhabitants who have always lived there.—the notes & information I have collected & mean to collect will be voluminous & I am hopeful to live one day at home & where it can be done with leisure to digest & throw the whole on paper for the use of our citizens.—to enable them to compare their own with other nations & to make them love & cherish those rights which can alone make any country truly happy.—it is for this Reason I wish very much to remain in Europe two Years as a *public man* & as I am here & I trust you know my immutable principles I am hopeful it will be in Your power to confirm me in the one I have or to give me such a situation elsewhere as will enable me to fulfill the valuable Ends I have in View by my coming here.—wishing you all the happiness & honour Your Virtues so well deserve, with profound attachment & regard Esteem & affection I remain dear sir

Your's Truly   CHARLES PINCKNEY

I am particularly requested by *our own* friends in Paris & here to mention to you Mr: Cox Barnet, the late Consul here who has Wife & mother & a large family here, as a very deserving man indeed.—if Lisbon or Leghorn should be Vacant I think it will be well bestowed, or any other consulate to some place of Trade.—

RC (DLC); addressed: "To The President of the United States of America Washington"; with unrelated writing by Pinckney, "Vous Et Mon Ami," on verso of last page of text; endorsed by TJ as received 11 Feb. and so recorded in SJL.

No letter from TJ to William LEE from the period before Pinckney's departure from the United States is recorded in SJL. What Pinckney delivered was probably Lee's commission as U.S. commercial agent at Bordeaux, dated 3 June. Lee apparently assumed the duties of that office on 22 Oct., replacing Isaac Cox Barnet (Madison, *Papers, Sec. of State Ser.*, 2:211; Stephen Cathalan, Jr., to TJ, 14 June 1801).

[1] Pinckney originally closed his quotation here.

To Nicolas Gouin Dufief

SIR   Washington Nov. 1. 1801.

Among the books mentioned in the letter of Oct. 22. with which you favored me is one only which I would wish to acquire: it is the Parliamentary history 24. vols 8vo. price 30. D. should it not be disposed of before you recieve this I will thank you to send it. perhaps the vessel may still be not departed which was to bring the others.—I have the Dictionnaire des hommes Marquans. judging of it's merit by turning to the characters I personally know, it is the work of a zealous partizan of the ancien regime. still it is useful to possess. the busts you are pleased to propose to me are not within the line of my acquisitions. accept my thanks for the lettre de Trasybule a Leucippe, and my best wishes for your health & happiness.   TH: JEFFERSON

PrC (DLC); at foot of text: "M. du Fief"; endorsed by TJ in ink on verso.

Dufief wrote TJ a brief letter on 13 Nov., stating that on the 12th he put on board the sloop *Highland*, bound for Alexandria and Georgetown, the 24-volume PARLIAMENTARY HISTORY, addressed to John Barnes for TJ. Dufief hoped that the shipment would arrive without damage, expressed his wishes for TJ's good health, and offered assurances of his respectful devotion. In endorsing

the letter, TJ noted other books that he wanted, an edition of Homer's *Odyssey* by the Foulis publishing firm and a work on chemistry by Jean Antoine Chaptal. TJ conveyed those requests to the bookseller in February 1802 (RC in DLC, in French, at head of text: "Le Président des Etats Unis," endorsed by TJ as received 16 Nov. and so recorded in SJL, also endorsed by TJ: "Homer. Od. Foul. 12mo. Chymie de Chaptal"; Sowerby, Nos. 831, 4270; TJ to Dufief, 19 Feb. 1802).

To William Evans

DEAR SIR   Washington Nov. 1. 1801.

I recieved some days ago a very fine rock fish by the stage which, by a card of address accompanying it I percieved to have come from you. It was indeed a remarkeably fine one and I pray you to accept my thanks for it. a report has come here through some connection of one of my servants that James Hemings my former cook has committed an act of suicide. as this whether true or founded will give uneasiness to his friends, will you be so good as to ascertain the truth & communicate it to me. Accept my best wishes for your health & happiness.   TH: JEFFERSON

PrC (MHi); at foot of text: "Mr. William Evans"; endorsed by TJ in ink on verso.

JAMES HEMINGS, who had accompanied TJ to France to learn the "art of cookery," served as TJ's chef from 1787 until 1796, when TJ signed his deed of manumission. Hemings was working as a cook in Baltimore in February 1801 when TJ contacted Evans, requesting that he urge Hemings to go immediately to Washington to serve as chef at the President's House. Hemings did not pursue the invitation, perhaps because TJ did not ask him directly. Hemings did, however, run the kitchen at Monticello while TJ was at home during August and September. On 19 Sep., TJ paid him $30, "a month & a half's wages" (Stanton, *Free Some Day*, 125-9; MB, 2:1051; Vol. 27:119-20; Vol. 28:605; Vol. 33:38-9, 53-4, 91-2, 505).

From John Gardiner

SIR   Pensylvania Avenue 1st Novr 1801

The only Apology I have to offer for presuming to trouble your Excellency with the inclosd, is my full persuasion of your Excellencys wishes for the prosperity & population of this City—

From my own experience I am convinced that were there direct conveyances from Gt Brittain here, the Tide of emigration woud run this Way

I saild last Year from Dublin, in a Brittish Vessell calld the Washington Packett bound hither; & intended for a constant Trader—At same time several ships were bound from same port to different Ports in the United States, but we had more passengers than *all* the other vessells—

In consequence of being Wreckd near New York the passengers remaind there—had they landed here they woud probably have continued here—

Shoud your Excellency approve of those proposals & countenance them with a Subscription they will doubtless succeed, & be the first step to Foreign Commerce from the Fedral City—

I have the Honor to be most Respectfully Your Excellencys most obedt Servt   JOHN GARDINER

RC (DLC); endorsed by TJ as received 4 Nov. and so recorded in SJL. Enclosure not found, but see below.

For Gardiner's PROPOSALS to establish a ship company in Washington, D.C., see Gardiner to TJ, 12 Jan. 1802.

To Edward Livingston

DEAR SIR   Washington Nov. 1. 1801.

I some days ago recieved a letter from Messrs. Denniston & Chetham of the most friendly kind, asking the general grounds on which the Nolle prosequi in Duane's case ought to be presented to the public, which they proposed to do. you are sensible I must avoid committing myself in that channel of justification, & that were I to do it in this case I might be called on by other printers in other cases where it might be inexpedient to say any thing. yet to so civil an application I cannot reconcile myself to the incivility of giving no answer. I have thought therefore of laying your friendship under contribution & asking you to take the trouble of seeing them, & of saying to them, that the question being in the line of the law I had desired you to give them the explanation necessary. my text of explanation would be this. the President is to have[1] the laws executed. he may order an offence then to be prosecuted. if he sees a prosecution put into a train which is not lawful, he may order it to be discontinued and put into legal train. I found a prosecution going on against Duane for an offence against the Senate, founded on the Sedition act. I affirm that act to be no law, because in opposition to the Constitution; and I shall treat it as a nullity wherever it comes in the way of my functions. I therefore directed that prosecution to be discontinued & a new one to be commenced, founded on whatsoever other law might be in existence against the offence. this was done & the Grand jury finding no other law against it, declined doing any thing under the bill. there appears to me to be no weak part in any of these positions or inferences. there is however in the application to you to trouble yourself with the question. for this I owe apology, & build it on your goodness & friendship. health & happiness cum caeteris votis.

Th: Jefferson

RC (Victor B. Levit, San Francisco, California, 1966); addressed: "Edward Livingston esq. Mayor of New York"; franked; postmarked 2 Nov. PrC (DLC).

SOME DAYS AGO RECIEVED A LETTER: Denniston & Cheetham to TJ, 22 Oct.

CUM CAETERIS VOTIS: and other good wishes.

Livingston was appointed mayor of New York City in mid-August 1801 (New York *American Citizen and General Advertiser*, 14 Aug. 1801).

[1] Word interlined in place of "see."

To Gouverneur Morris

DEAR SIR   Washington Nov. 1. 1801.

Your favor of Oct. 28. is duly recieved, and I am very glad you have disposed of the service of plate which had been the subject of our correspondence. the purchase of indispensable articles of furniture for the house had gone so much deeper into the funds remaining on hand that they would not have been equal to what I had proposed to you. in fact the only articles of plate really wanting are a half dozen Casseroles. these I must have imported.

The ratification of our convention with France, & the expected arrangement of the VIth. article of the British treaty with the new modifications of their courts of Admiralty will I hope place our foreign affairs in a state of greater tranquility. the Spanish depredations at Algesiras will doubtless yield to proper remonstrances.

The new Census shews our increase to be in the geometrical ratio of $3\frac{1}{6}$ pr. cent annually which gives a duplication in 22 y—3 m equal to the most sanguine of our calculations. we are already about the 7th. of the Christian nations in population, but holding a higher place in substantial abilities. if we can keep at peace for our time the next generation will have nothing to fear but from their own[1] want of moderation in the use of their strength. health & happiness cum caeteris votis.   TH: JEFFERSON

PrC (DLC); at foot of text: "Gouverneur Morris esq."   [1] Word interlined.

To Craven Peyton

DEAR SIR   Washington Nov. 1. 1801.

In my letter of Oct. 8 covering a Columbia bank note for 1240 D. 27 c I recommended to you to dispose of it without delay. I had more reasons for this than would have been proper then to mention. that bank is now in a crisis which may end mortally. if that note is still in your hands or any where else so as not to have cleared us of all responsibility for it, if it be sent to me by return of the 1st. or 2d post after you recieve this, I shall be able to secure it. otherwise it will not be in my power. if you are entirely clear of it, let it go unless it be in Colo. C. L. Lewis's hands on whose account I would meet the inconvenience it would cost me to get it saved. I shall be glad to hear from you on this subject by return of post, as I have considerable anxiety about it. health happiness & my best wishes   TH: JEFFERSON

RC (facsimile in Profiles in History, Catalogue No. 9, September 1989). PrC (ViU); in ink at foot of text: "Mr. Craven Peyton"; endorsed by TJ in ink on verso.

THAT BANK IS NOW IN A CRISIS: Gallatin feared that if the run on the Bank of Columbia continued, the bank would have to stop payments. The Treasury secretary conversed with Comptroller John Steele, a stockholder in the institution, over measures to be pursued to restore the bank's credit, including the "resignation of so many directors as will secure a majority in the direction, on whom reliance may be placed for the execution of any measures which may be recommended." On 3 Nov., Gallatin reiterated the points in a letter to Steele. Gallatin questioned: "If there is an actual danger of a stoppage of payment, can the shopkeepers of George town alone, prevent it by their deposits & encouraging the circulation of notes?" Believing that a loss of confidence in the bank notes in circulation would "be injurious to the revenue, commerce & wealth of the U. States," Gallatin pledged: "Upon the whole, I feel willing to go certain lengths towards the support of the Columbia Bank; greater certainly than they expected from me; greater than will be pleasing to most of my friends; but not greater than a sense of my duty may impel." The officers at the Bank of Columbia contended that the bank's credit had been injured by "malicious reports lately circulated and published in handbills, and in some of the newspapers." To

restore confidence, the bank allowed "a few intelligent Stockholders" to examine the bank's transactions. On 4 Nov., Steele and four others issued a statement indicating that they had minutely examined the affairs of the bank and found "that the Specie funds compared with the amount of Notes in circulation and all claims of every nature on the Bank" completely confirmed "the safety and stability of the institution" (Wagstaff, *John Steele*, 1:230-3; *Washington Federalist*, 9 Nov. 1801).

COLO. C. L. LEWIS'S HANDS: Charles Lilburne Lewis was Peyton's father-in-law and one of TJ's brothers-in-law. He was also TJ's cousin and the brother of Bennett Henderson's widow, Elizabeth Lewis Henderson (Vol. 28:474n; Vol. 31:199n).

From Ledyard Seymour

HONORD SIR;   Havana November 1st. 1801.

With sentiments of Respect, and esteem, I humbly hasten to the dwelling of the first Magistrate, of the Republick of America, for by this name, have I been taught, to Address, that part of the Western world, over which he presides. in attemptinng a Task, so novel, what emotions do I feel, much like the bewildered traveller, happening to approach the distant Thunders of great Niagara. beholds the refulgent Arc uprising from its troubld Bosom.—or so the Western Children of the sun, filled with a mingled horror, at the impending, hollow, bursting storm; now darkening hovering oer their devoted heads, led on by their ferocious manners, dare e'n the Spirits of the air—When I left my native Country in the year 1800, every circumstance of regret was present to me. Enfranchised Liberty, allegiance; and the protection of her laws, after remaining sixteen days in New Providence, from the Capture of several American Vessels, among which was one of a Brother in law—the Brigantine Aurora of New York. it may seem pardonable to have remained thus long in a place, whose very air, is infected with the vapours of Circean poison—No Exertions of mine do I pretend were effectual in releasing the Aurora—. she sailed the third day after her arrival, and the noted firm of then Hamilton & Wilkinson, Seton and others paid her pi-

lotage from the port of Nassau.—from a casual fortunate management of this case, I was addressed at the same time by five American
Captains, which prevented my immediate departure for the Havana,
I could do no more than refer them to Mr. John Armstrong high at
this time in the mistaken opinion of my Friends, and countrymen—
tho compelld to resort as they unfortunately discovered soon after to
mock, Law and the forms of justice—. how could his pleadings have
effect with the great digest—the Honble. Judge Kelsall; here the law
was marriageable nor did I hear a more salutary decision from
the learned [Sack?], than that his honor also had the misfortune to
be born in America, had the modest Mr. Armstrong continued his
pleadings forever, they would have been fruitless, nay impotent;
after the plaintive response of the Accomplished Mr. Mathews; an
Advocate of the inner temple bar: how might we have expended
weeks in listening to the language of Alehouse Pimps—or more
agreeably amused with the latent honesty of Pearl Fishermen—. the
cases of two of those Gentleman, who suffered at this time are hard
indeed—. and native feelings dictate a hope; that measures may have
been pursued for a revisal of their Claims—
Arriving the 8th September; I departed the 25th. inst. from this
apostate land of Law, reason and justice, together with William Stoddert Bond of Baltimore, Captain of the Schooner Americanus, with a
Cargo, bona fide American property, and the 1st of October was
suffered to come within the firm protection of the Moro Castle at the
entrance of the port of the Havana—here Sir have I since remained
rendering to my fellow Citizens, such assistance as the laws and usages of an allied nation allow, cultivating with my best wishes the
friendship of the inhabitants of this place, nor can I belive better
laws; more wholesome institutions; or more refined honor; could
have existed, since the days of Ferdinand and Isabella—. I sometimes
think this a Godly City; trifling breaches of eather Civil or Military
laws; little quarrelling; or disturbance; and but few dark Assasina-
tions; I have never known but one, Assassin; one George C Morton;
who attempted to kill a young Man, with his sword Cane, on the 18th
October last, they had some difference respecting the disposal of
some property, tis certain this Morton; defamed this man in the hearing of his Friends; without assigning reasons: then first struck, and
collard; *me*: that in defence of Person only; I warded off his blows, a
few nights after returning from my Friend's, house; he would even
murder me: thrice he attempted, thrice did my throbbing heart just
feel the approach of fate; with my naked hands at length I hurled the

shuddering sword; from the fell murtherer's hands; thanks to Great St. Dominic; and all the Choir of Guardian Spirits else; I yet survive the wounds inflicted by a Brother; a fellow Citizen; the marks I bear; the memory of the man, that gave them; will soon have faded;—

His addiction was to courses vain &c.

With every mark of esteem for my Country, and unfeigned Respect and esteem for the first Magistrate; of the United States; I subscribe myself their; and Your;

Excellency's Hble. Servt.   LEDIARD SEYMOUR

RC (MoSHi: Jefferson Papers); at head of text: "To Thomas Jefferson President of the United of America"; endorsed by TJ as received 8 Jan. 1802 and so recorded in SJL.

Ledyard (Lediard) Seymour (1771-1848) was a native of Hartford, Connecticut. After graduating from Yale College in 1792, he entered the mercantile business in New York with the support of his wife's family. Losses to British spoliations forced him into bankruptcy by 1797. He removed to Havana in 1800, where he remained for three years before returning to Hartford. In 1805, he wrote TJ seeking a post in "any one of the Spanish Colonies," but did not receive an appointment (Dexter, *Yale*, 5:37-8; Seymour to TJ, 14 June 1805, in DNA: RG 59, LAR).

Seymour's BROTHER IN LAW was New York merchant Nathaniel G. Ingraham, whose vessel, the BRIGANTINE AURORA, was among 12 merchant ships that sailed from Havana in late June 1800 under convoy with the frigate *General Greene* (NDQW, June-Nov. 1800, 88, 92; Seymour to TJ, 14 June 1805).

JOHN ARMSTRONG may have been the lawyer who was solicitor general of the Bahamas in 1813 (Sandra Riley, *Homeward Bound, A History of the Bahama Islands to 1850 with a Definitive Study of Abaco in the American Loyalist Plantation Period* [Miami, 1983], 253, 270).

John KELSALL was a judge of the vice-admiralty court of the Bahamas (Michael Craton and Gail Saunders, *Islanders in the Stream: A History of the Bahamian People*, 2 vols. [Athens, Ga., 1992-98], 1:233).

GEORGE C. MORTON was the acting U.S. consul at Havana (Madison, *Papers, Sec. of State Ser.*, 1:107-8).

HIS ADDICTION WAS TO COURSES VAIN: Shakespeare, *Henry V*, 1.1.

From Andrew Ellicott

DEAR SIR   Lancaster Novbr. 2. 1801

I have forwarded by the bearer Mr. Brown the notes to accompany the map which I informed you some weeks ago was finished:—from these notes you will be able to judge in some degree of the value of the map, and whether it will be worth sending on to Washington;— I have it enclosed in a tin case Six feet 2 inches long.—

I have the honour to be with great esteem your Hbl. Servt

ANDW. ELLICOTT.

P.S. I intend observing the occultation of ε♓ on the 16th. if not prevented by clouds.   A. E.

RC (DLC); above postscript: "President of the United States"; endorsed by TJ as received 16 Nov. and so recorded in SJL; also endorsed by TJ: "referred to the Secretary at war to be answered as he thinks proper Th:J."

MR. BROWN was probably a relative of Ellicott's wife, Sarah Brown Ellicott, originally of Newton, Pennsylvania (ANB).

Ellicott hoped to observe the OCCULTATION of the star Epsilon Piscium (that is, the fifth-brightest star of the constellation Pisces) by the moon, which was in that constellation in the middle of No-

vember. Ellicott made various astronomical observations during his residence at Lancaster, Pennsylvania, with the particular intention of determining the town's longitude. Earlier in the year he sent TJ details of his observation of another star's occultation, which Ellicott used along with other data to find the longitude of Washington, D.C. (*An Almanack, for the Year 1801; Containing, Besides the Usual Astronomical Calculations, the Gardener's Calendar* [Frankfort, Ky., 1800?]; Evans, No. 36804; APS, *Transactions*, 6 [1809], 61-9, 113-19; APS, *Proceedings*, 22, pt. 3 [1884], 321; Vol. 33:580-2).

From John Devereux DeLacy

SIR   Pennsacola Novembr. the 3d. 1801

Convinced as I am that information relative to the situation of any empire now under your particular charge will be always welcome to you, (especially if such place be remote,) let such information come from whatever person or through whatsoever channel it may; I therefore take the liberty of making the following statement of facts to you, on the perusal and confirmation of which I am convinced that some mode will be adobted to avert the mischeivous consequences of the evil. In the first place Sir persons resident in america long previous to the passing the acts of naturalization have had their Boats Stopped at fort Adams when Returning from N Orleans to the M.T. Loaden & have been obliged to pay the duties imposed on foreign Bottoms which they consider an extreme hardship.—2ndly. Persons Resident in America for very many years some of them there during the Revolutionary war have had protections denied to them by the Consuls for want of certificates of Naturalization. My opinion having been taken in some measure on one occasion, & having Returned it to me after he had shewn it to the Consul or Vice Consul, I take the liberty of inclosing it to you Sir for your perusal—Indeed Sir Mr Jones the present Consul in Orleans is by no means fit for, nor adabted to the office, The trade via Orleans is Certainly the most badly arranged of any trade or market the Americans frequent or have a right to, and it is beyond a question a place of the greatest importance to america of any she knows and is growing into importance every day insomuch as to very nearly double annually the quantity of Produce she sends to this market, and ships to foreign ports from hence, this Sir I am enabled to say with certainty having procured from the Custom house in N. Ors. the Gross amt. of the produce Brought down the River in the two last years whether sold here or shipped and also the amt. of the importations for the same time from America and elsewhere, but allmost all are either directly from America or imported in american Bottoms, And all things considered the Balance of trade to this Country is more in favr. of america than at a first or cursory veiw could be expected by the most sanguine American, Indeed Sir when every thing[1] is taken into veiw connected with the trade of the place it must be admitted to be of the utmost importance and advantage to america and that its commercial advantages are sensibly and forcibly felt in all the atlantic ports of the U.S. but its more beneficial influence is felt in the ports of New York & Philada: & Baltimore as they afford the greater quantity of goods and adventures to the Western Country the Returns for all which are either made through this port or drawn from it. Yet notwithstanding all those advantages there is describing the many and innumerable difficulties that the American trade to and through this port labours under, and that owing to the americans themselves, for the Spaniards in their mode of doing business are liberal in the extreme and with that freindly kind and attentive to the discharging of every little of[2] civility that may be necessary, while the Americans themselves from that desire to get rich at all hazards that predominates in the Bosom of every one of them here together with a malicious envy by which they are actuated at the seeing of any person succeeding in his enterprises or prospering in his Business added to the extreme bad Policy not to give it an harsher name by which all the Officers of the U.S. having any communication with this place or neighbourhood have overwhelmed the trade with confusion perplexity trouble and embarrassment—from which it will certainly Require the fostering aid of the executive to extricate it.

As connected with the trade of Orleans I will beg leave to say a few words to you Sir about the M.T A Country Rich and fruitful, abounding in Rich Soil good water fine timber some extremely Rich and valuable ores and very contiguous to a Market, The Planter here possesses probably more advantages and labours under more disadvantages than in any country in the World, the Port at fort Adams can answer no one purpose of Real utility and convenience except for the time present to the present collector; who being stationary surgeon at fort Adams can thereby hold both appointments, and here I must state to you Sir as a fact that the conduct of the whole of the Governmental and U.S. officers in that Territory with the exception of Judge McGuire has been execrable the military especially with some few very few exceptions insomuch that should they attempt to discharge the Guns at Ft. Adams they will surely emit nothing but scandal lies murders and assassinations, even the murder of the Brave but unfortunate Kersey a Majr in the service, and to perpetrate which deed a sword was Borrowed has to this hour gone unpunished, and the offender escaped—But I must state to you sir that I do not include the officers arrived there since the departure of Genl. W. for as I do not know them nor what their conduct has been I can not pretend to bestow praise or dispraise, but that as some of them have been at S.W. Pt. I beleive they will be liked as all the officers there were generally esteemed, nor can I omit mentioning the amiable and good Majr Pike who differing widely in Politics with his Protean general and indeed almost all the officers and who dared be honest in the worst of times has been withdrawn from there tho universally beloved & Majr. Guion Universally hated and detested put in his Room, but Guion is the privy Counsellor & confidant of the General a hopeful pair! before I dismiss this part of the subject I will give you Sir a short acct. of two attempts made to assassinate Mr David Fero formerly a Leiut. in the service but, muleted through the management of Guion, the whole of which would fully appear but for the loss of the papers in the department of War, Fero went on the Business from Natchez to Philada. and after making his arrangmts. Smarting with the injuries done him by Guion he returned and expressed his detestation of and Resentmt to Guion, the consequence of which was that a number of the³ officers assembled where he lodged for the purpose of and did headed by Guion immediately attack him and left him for dead, tho he acquited himself with so much intrepidity as to wound some of them desperately also tho alone. Here I can not help mentioning the conduct of the immaculate Judge Bruen who tho' a lodger in the house and knowing the young mans life to be despaired of together with the atrocity of the attempt upon him nevertheless left town the next day for his own house without taking any steps whatsoever to ensure peace and tranquility and prevent Bloodshed—the unfortunate young man had occasion some time after his Recovery (which contrary to general expectation took place) to go to new Orleans, on Returning from thence his Road and the only one to Natchez lay by Ft. Adams. he had letters for the Noble General who was then there which he sent to him and went to the public tavern from whence without provocation he was taken by those Gallant officers and a party of soldiers devoted to their will and carried to the Guard House and there kept untill between the Hours of 12 & 1

oclock at night when by special order of the officer of the day and ad-
jutant the Brave and honest Serjeant of the Guard Refusing otherwise as he suspected their intentions the unfortunate young man was
again delivered to the Serjaent Major and a party of Soldiers who
took him a little distance from the guard house and commenced the
tragedy, and beat and wounded the young man untill they considered
him dead and then left him for such weltring in his Blood on the
ground from which situation he was releived by the humanity of the
honest Sergeant before mentioned and the guard but nevertheless
they were obliged as soon as they restored him a little to carry him
off the public ground by order of those good officers and there leave
him to his fate. these Sir are stubborn facts alive in the memory of
every Body in that part of the country but the dread of a similar fate
is such that few are hardy enough to speak about it. I will here add
what I beleive many of the officers would be honest enough to confirm, that the noble protean Genl. wrote to the principal actor in the
tragedy approving and in a measure applauding his conduct at the
very same time that he wrote to Governor Sargeant and the Wise
Judge Bruen, in terms the most strongly Reprehensible of their conduct add to which that the Sergeant Majr has been since restored to
his Rank—

And now Sir I will beg leave to mention the Federal Bench (which it
truly is) in the territory, and the Judicial arrangments there, which I
do assure you Sir are in a very lame state indeed, and its present situation disgraceful to the American Goverment. P. B. Bruen a man
without law knowledge and possessing strong passions, and no Resolution is by no means fit for nor adabted to the office and it is in fact
a doing an injury to society the continuing a man so utterly unfit for
that office[4] particularly to fill it at a time that men of sound legal
knowledge and information are wanting on the Bench to give the
proper tone to the proceedings of the courts and Reduce their practice to system. for it will take a length of time to undo what will now
be done, so that the united States giving a liberal Salary to a Gentleman of known Celebrity in his profession and procuring such a one to
come down as cheif Justice would be productive of very happy
effects, indeed there is but one man in all that Territory that is fit for
an associate Judge in the Supreme Court, and that is Majr. Roger
Dickson a native of Winchester and who studied the Law under his
Brother but never practised, a Gentleman of Great natural talents
highly improved by Reading and extremely independent in Sentiment as well as in property—and tolerably good and petulant county
court Atty will generally make but a bad Judge—

The appointments of sheriffs especially in the County of Adams together with Attorney general by Governor Sargeant (who was himself an honest man perhaps too rigidly so and firm his only faults) were very unfortunate, for they are men agreeable to the general opinion totally unfit for and incapable of their respective offices, being men of bad and dishonest principles, and I confess that to be my opinion upon a perfect knowledge of them, Evans the high Sheriff is in mine and the general opinion capable of any thing however bad, as one instance witness the number of atrocious murderers that have escaped,—And there have been many other appointments equally as unhappy—

Indeed the Country but especially the town of Natchez was so completely ruled by them and the military, (Wilkinson being in the Neighbourhood at his house) that I being the only person who appearred openly a McKeanite & Republican and have suffered every thing from their intemperate party zeal and spirit that their utmost malevolence could suggest or ingenuity devise, they did not proceed to actual personal violence for they found that I possessed spirit enough to[5] resent it, but the grossest Slanders were invented and circulated to injure me, especially by the Brave officers who occasionally travel to Orleans to spend time to amuse themselves, even when the Joyful issue of that Election to which we had all looked with such anxious solicitude was known to me and that I mentioned I was flatly contradicted by a brave son of mars one of those officers, and I beleive would with pleasure have been sacrificed by them to their fury—But Sir as I should exhaust your patience by detailing the many other greivances complained of and Justly in the Territory, I shall here close my acct. of them for the present, and beg your attention to the following for which I beg you Sir not to deem me impertinent. The above being intended but as private information for yourself sir (unless you should deem it necessary to shew it to Genl. Stephen T Mason Esqr. who knows me a little) but the subsequent you are welcome to make any use you please of—

Having travelled through the greater part of the province of Louisiana up to near the frontiers of Mexico I submit the following Remarks to you sir that I have made, first to speak of the soil S.W. of the Missouri and the salt Mountain and Plains it is rich, the Missouri divides and the S.W Branch runs a long way into New Leon—the Misso' runs through or rather is precipitated through immense large plains of Sand strongly impregnated with Saline particles which it carries down with it with incredible velocity to the Mississippi and mingling with its waters thus discolours them. there are volcanos on the Margin of the Missouri or in its neighbourhood for though I could not ascertain precisely where yet the quantity of lava on its Banks which is generally but erroneously taken for pumice, but from which it is essentially different, it being apparent that it has undergone a calcination from some very violent effort of fire yet it has that specific lightness and porosity that characterises pumice but not that flexibility being extremely hard brittle and sandy or rather gritty, answering in every thing the description of the vesuvian lava—tho' I explored the River for a considerable distance yet I am obliged to depend upon best information I could collect, The lava I personally examind as also set some of the water by In a tin vessel in which it deposited a gritty sedimt. strongly impregnated with Saline particles. One of the finest countries in the world probably presents itself from St. Geneveivre all the way back as far as I have been or could hear of with any certainty, but to speak of, what I have seen The ground is broken at a distance from the Mississippi Bank Westward across the Head Waters of the Rivers St. Francis which interlock with some small Branches that empty into the Missouri on the S. Side, and from thence all the way to the Sea, The Indians here near and on the Missouri are quite uncivilised some had never seen a white before, but they are all hospitable—

and with whom it would be easy to establish a trade could some mode be adobted to prevent impositions on them similar to those so shamefully practised by the American licensed traders on the unfortunate Cherokees, Creeks Chocktaws &c, &c, indeed an excursion up the Missouri well planned would more than Repay every charge attending it and leave the adventurers a very great reward for their labour—No Country in the World is better Watered and several fine Navigable Rivers intersect the way downwards the cheif of which are the St. Francis, the White River the Osark which has an inland communication with the white River, The Red River, which by means of the Black River that empties into it and which is formed by the Junction of the Tennesaw, the Ouachita and the Catahoola 20 Leagues above its confluence with the Red River. In the back parts of this Country the forts which have been such a length of time the subject of vague and uncertain conjecture with the learned and the curious are in high preservation, one in particular above the Codoque Nation on the Bayu or Rivulet Naasch which is amazingly Rough Rapid and its Banks high Sterile and Rocky and about which they have a tradition that a nation came there and lived and being strangers made that but that about two or three Generations or centuries for centuries it must be, they went away back Westward and that since they have moved farther westward between the big lands and the great water, whether they mean by that the mountains and the Pacific or the Mountains and the great River of the W. which the Iatan Indians are well acquainted with I can not say but this one principle I state as an absolute fact that from ocean to ocean there is an intercourse kept up by the Indians and an Intelligence that is incredible notwithstanding their continual wars with and predatory excursions on each others towns and territorys Yet the free and warlike tribes of St. Bernard as they are called will know what passes at the opposite sea or Bay sooner than can be imagined indeed from the Bay of St. Bernards in the Gulph of Mexico on the Vast Atlantic to the opposite coast of the great Pacific the chain of Indians is complete, and formidable, first comes in the St. Bernards Bay indians, next the Alibama Indians who, emigrated thither and sacrificed their Lands to preserve their liberty, next to them are the Codoques, next to them are the Iatans whose settlements extend up to the head waters of the Missouri, there is another nation settled in the forks of the Missouri whom I have seen none of and forget their names with some small tribes intermixed with the above all so powerful and warlike that all his catholic M. forces could make no impression on them nor has any spanish enterprise against them ever succeeded tho they have hardly any fire arms among them and are in a measure wholly unused to And unknowing of them such is the spanish policy—

And here Sir I will mention A few facts to you and solicit your opinion on them, In the first place the Western parts of the Country I am speaking about as in a measure overstocked with horses, insomuch that their extensive meadows or prairies are overstocked and the indians possess abundance of them, and where the indians take care of them they are a handsome and serviceable horse; one of the best of which can be bought from the upper Cado;s or Iatans for a good Handkercheif. those horses are difft. in their colour make and form from either the Spanish or english horses, and their whole appearrance exhibits indubitable proofs of a specific difference with those I have mentioned added to which that those indians appear to have been acquainted with Horses previous to their importation into S.A. by the Spaniards, and an easy calculation will shew that it was impossible for the Spaniards to have brot. over a sufft. number to produce the myriads within the time with which this country abounds added to which that many of those tribes to the westward have no intercourse whatsoever with the Spaniards tho they possess immense numbers as does all the Indians however far W and N.W. as I have been told and also that they bring many horses from the Westward

And N.W. occasionally—I must also Remark to you Sir that the saddles that are in use among them are precisely the same as those said to be in use among the tartars that Horn before, that raised back open in the middle a wooden socket or step suspended by a peice of raw Hide serves for a stirrup and is preferred by them for Galloping or driving through the woods, all this induces me to beleive that there has been a communication heretofore with the opposite continent—

two other remarks I beg leave to subjoin, first that[6] the women are entirely destitute of Hair except upon their Heads nor have the men, those are also characterestics of the Asiatics, and the Lama which is a native of Asia has been undubitably been at least a resident or sojourner in this, And to these I will add one General Remark that all the Indians N.W. and here from what I can learn and observation I can make worship the sun and pay considerable adoration, to every new moon—

I will also take the liberty of stating one other fact to you Sir to wit that the weapons of defence of all Savages have a wonderful resemblance—those of the Indians both in N:A. and here that I have seen being precisely the same With those known to and in use among the africans of the parts of africa that I have travelled on and visited namely, Cape Coast, Seirra Leon, Anamaboo, Cape Formosa, River Sombrero on which New Callebar is situate and which River I travelled a long way, Bonny, Bennin, Penantapo-o, Cape Lopez & Cape three points, and except the Tomohawk and the taking of the scalp on the Indian part, and the taking and selling the prisoners taken in War by the Negroes, I have observed nor can I hear of any essential difference in their modes of Waging war—In Benin many of them are christians of the Roman catholic persuasion that have been converted by Spanish missionaries as there have been some in all the portuguese territories—and I can not help saying here Sir that as far as my observation has enabled me to form an opinion on the subject that opinion is hostile to the general doctrine of the employing religious missionaries to effect the civilization or even conversion of people in a state of nature, for the missionaries but too commonly inflamed by a desire of working miracles tho this is not an age of canonization are in general actuated by a zeal and Bigotry bordering on if not all out intemperate and thus endeavour to cram down the throats of these innocent creatures a belief of the mysteries as they are pleased to term them of the Christian faith, mysteries which they can hardly explain themselves with any degree of satisfaction a proof that they do not understand them perfectly themselves—in place of those a few settled steady mechanics that would have encouragement from government to settle among, intermarry with and teach them the useful would have I am convinced a very happy effect that and the introduction of schools to the keeping of which some of the old invalids and pensioners[7] would be well adabted—of this Place I can only say that it is going to Ruin fast and is only the skeleton of what it has been, the very elegant Barracks and other Buildings Remnants and monuments of the British industry are crumbling to Ruins, nor do I wonder at it for the keeping this place can answer no one good Political purpose but that of entailing a heavy Bill of expence on the holders, the only thing that can be said for it is that it is healthy and that says all as it has neither commercial nor political advantages—

There is a Leut. or Captn. Scott appointed to the command of the American post at Mobile who has I am told given the Spanish Government considerable dissatisfaction by his having taken up and imprisoned as he not[8] a passport I can not vouch for the veracity of the report but this I know that Mr Scott is one of General Wilkinsons favorites and is to the full as firm as constant and as honourable as his magnanimous General, and I know that the creed for some time has been, to make the Army necessary and keep great men in their places, so that I should not wonder, (to speak in their own language) if there was a row kicked up here on the frontiers—

As I propose setting out in 3 months on an excursion to the W. and N.W. in which I mean to penetrate into the country as far as possible I will beg of you Sir to point out to me the objects that you would wish most immediately attended to and investigated, as the most gratifying to you and most beneficial to society being in want of the instructions of some gentleman of talents and reflection to guide my attention and researches to those objects most immediately conducive to public good in the choice of which objects I might most probably from my youth fail myself—

If you should be so good as to favour me with your Sentiments on that head which I take the liberty of soliciting please to direct for me to the care of Danl. Clark Esqr. or Captn. Walsh New Orleans—

And here Sir I must beg your permission to state a transaction to you that equals the story of inkle and Yarico and that calls aloud for humane and energetic interference, at the House of Joseph Andrews on the District of Appeluchia and Province of Louisiana I met a poor Mulatto or Quadroon Girl who was born free near knoxville in Tennessee, and her father and mother are also free when at the age of 15 or 16 years (she is still very young) and about 3 years ago a young man a farmer and horse Jockey living in that neighbourhood seduced her under a promise of keeping her, and prevailed on her to accompany him on a Journey he was about taking to Natchez and to return with him which the poor fond Creature agreed to, and they arrived in Natchez where the monster sold her and the matter from the poor creatures making the story known made a stir tho there was none to be found disinterested or Philantrophic enough to take the part of a poor creature of colour, however the noise it made induced the purchaser to send her off to appaluchia and there sell her where the poor creature now is a slave without the means of Redress and to mend the matter the all wise and virtuous Atty General of the Mississippi Territory is said to be securely for the validity of the title to her and the right of the vendor to sell her some doubts being expressed by the purchaser I arrived (soon after she had been sent away) at Natchez determined to interfere but she was gone nor could I learn where they had Sent her to untill I by chance met with her in my travels almost in despair nor has she the means of extricating herself unless the Government of the U.S. demands her as a Citizen which they should certainly do as also punish all the persons (principals as well as abettors) in this infamous business which is becoming to common in this part of the world—before I had left Tennessee the Business had been mentioned to me by William Blount Esqr. and Jenkin Whitesides Esqr. Atty at Law who will give the names of those concerned which I forget, and many others spoke to me on the subject, which I promised to interfere in, but she was gone ere I arrived and I could do nothing as an individual to releive her, if your Excellency will but transmit me any power or authority however limitted or special I will exert myself to the utmost without fee or reward to procure her enlargment which can not be denied or refused, The poor unfortunate wretch is of colour and poor, of course she is freindless, and notwithstanding her being a free born American may by the infamous arts of the designing drag[9] out a miserable life in slavery unless extricated through the interference of Government—

I must not omit mentioning to you Sir that at the Ouachita 300 miles or thereabouts from the Mouth of the Red River I saw the Chevalier Daunemour formerly consul General from france to the U.S. who resides there quite in Philosophic ease and retirement his Garden an eden in Miniature and his house a little Palace or rather The epitome of a Museum Gallery of Paintings &c, and laid out with the most exquisite taste, such a place breaking in upon the sight in the midst of the woods has an effect on the senses not easily described he behaved with a freindly politeness, and then did & has always been very particular in his enquiries about you Sir and desired me to present his Respects to you, The Chevr. lives temperate and is healthy heal[10] vigorous and Robust tho 75. and talks of travelling in that country on foot—Longevity there is near the ouachita a man named Peirre Olivo who is upwards of an Hundred and goes out to Hunt with his Grandsons at this heal vigorous & Robust—There is also on the Homochito near Ellis Landing one McHoy an Highlander aged an 112. some say 140 but I could only trace it to 112. he has lived there between twenty & thirty years—There are numbers west of the Mississippi who are upwards of 80 Years, so that the country must be healthy, which I think it to be in a high degree

With the most unbounded Respect I have the Honour to subscribe myself Sir Your truly devoted Servant   JOHN DEVX DELACY

You will Sir I hope Pardon my presumption on thus addressing you—

As the Courier for Savannah is going of from here instantly I will beg of you Sir to pardon any errors or inaccuracies there may be in the orthography or stile, the Hurry I have written and made up this letter in precluding the possibility of Revisal or correction[11]—

RC (DLC); endorsed by TJ as received 10 Mar. 1802 and so recorded in SJL. Enclosure: DeLacy to Luke Walpole, written at New Orleans 11 July 1801, stating that there is no U.S. law authorizing officers of the government to administer oaths attesting to a person's citizenship, referring also to a circular to customs collectors by Oliver Wolcott, Jr., and to the Constitution, but noting that he has no books to consult on the question since he has been "for some time retired from the practice of my profession" (RC in same).

John Devereux DeLacy (d. 1837) was, according to Benjamin H. Latrobe's estimation, about 40 years old in 1815. Born in Ireland, DeLacy immigrated to the United States at the age of 14. He stated to TJ in 1821 that when he was "a Boy" he had received the "notice" of George Washington, although he did not explain the circumstances of his contact with Washington. In 1801, DeLacy, who was trained as a lawyer, acted as an agent for business interests in the Bahamas. British mercantile firms at Nassau in the Bahamas traded with Indians through West Florida, and on behalf of some of those firms DeLacy hoped to break the domination of Panton, Leslie & Company over the trade. That company enjoyed a favorable relationship with Spanish colonial officials, so DeLacy sought to ally himself with William Augustus Bowles, who had a long history of challenging the Panton, Leslie firm and defying Spanish authority. To the United States government and to Spanish officials, DeLacy depicted himself as independent of Bowles or even working against him, but DeLacy and Bowles met by December 1801 and discussed DeLacy's plans to displace the Panton, Leslie company. The Spanish arrested DeLacy in 1802, seized his papers, and held him at New Orleans until William C. C. Claiborne arranged his release two years later. Writing about DeLacy from New Orleans, Claiborne informed James Madison that "fame gives him a bad name, and his confinement here, did not seem to excite a great share of the public sympathy." DeLacy wrote to Madison in October 1803 seeking, without success, an appointment as an agent to persuade the Creeks, Choctaws, Cherokees, and Chickasaws to move west of the Mississippi River. The next spring

DeLacy asked TJ to help him retrieve some of his papers from the Spanish. According to SJL, TJ did not answer any of DeLacy's communications before 1813, when they corresponded briefly about Robert Fulton's efforts to develop steamboat navigation in the south. DeLacy began working as an agent for Fulton in 1812, collecting subscriptions for new steamboat lines, lobbying Congress and state legislatures, filing patent applications, and examining southern waterways. Two years later Fulton concluded that DeLacy was a "rogue" and a "busy and bold intriguer." They parted company, DeLacy allying himself with Nicholas Roosevelt, one of Fulton's rivals, and Fulton wanting DeLacy jailed for nonpayment of some funds. In 1821, DeLacy was in Raleigh, North Carolina, and asked TJ's assistance in obtaining an appointment as the U.S. attorney for East Florida. At some point after his employment by Fulton, DeLacy was so short of assets that he was put in jail for buying a coat on credit without intending to pay for it. Latrobe, who for a time was involved with DeLacy in Fulton's steamboat projects, commended DeLacy's "perseverance in all he undertakes," although he was marked by "manners the most extraordinary" and was "as indiscreet as any man I know, with a great opinion of his talents for business and intrigue." According to Latrobe, DeLacy was for a time the agent of "a gang of Land speculators, in whose services it was necessary to do and say many things, which were not very advantageous to his character" (John C. Van Horne, ed., *The Correspondence and Miscellaneous Papers of Benjamin Henry Latrobe*, 3 vols. [New Haven, 1984-88], 3:390n, 488n, 613n, 615n, 621-2, 624-6; J. Leitch Wright, Jr., *William Augustus Bowles: Director General of the Creek Nation* [Athens, Ga., 1967], 142-8, 151-4; William S. Coker and Thomas D. Watson, *Indian Traders of the Southeastern Spanish Borderlands: Panton, Leslie & Company and John Forbes & Company, 1783-1847* [Pensacola, Fla., 1986], 235-7; David Hart White, *Vicente Folch, Governor in Spanish Florida, 1787-1811* [Washington, D.C., 1981], 63; Cynthia Owen Philip, *Robert Fulton: A Biography* [New

York, 1985], 285-6, 293-4, 296, 306, 323, 335-8, 353; Robert Fulton and John D. DeLacy, *Report on the Practicability of Navigating with Steam Boats on the Southern Waters of the United States from the Chesapeak to the River St. Mary's* [New York, 1813]; Madison, *Papers, Sec. of State Ser.*, 5:520-4; 7:373-4, 542-3; Vol. 32:50-2, 548; TJ to DeLacy, 10 Apr., 23 July 1813, DeLacy to TJ, 18 Dec. 1801, 19 Dec. 1813, 16 Apr. 1821, all in DLC).

M.T.: Mississippi Territory. In July, TJ replaced Evan JONES with Daniel Clark as consul at New Orleans (TJ to William C. C. Claiborne, 13 July 1801).

William MCGUIRE of Virginia became the chief judge of Mississippi Territory in 1798 (*Terr. Papers*, 5:39-40; Vol. 30:281n).

The army officer who killed Major William KERSEY in an altercation at Fort Adams was Peter S. Marks, who had a family connection to TJ; see Marks to TJ, 20 May 1801.

GENL. W.: James Wilkinson.

Zebulon PIKE was for a time commandant of Fort Massac on the Ohio River. However, Piercy Smith Pope was the officer who preceded Isaac GUION in command of the military district along the east side of the Mississippi River that included Natchez and Fort Adams. DAVID FERO, Jr., received a commission as an ensign in the army in 1794, was promoted to lieutenant in 1798, and resigned in July 1799 (*Terr. Papers*, 5:9n, 16-17n, 73; Heitman, *Dictionary*, 1:417, 483, 792, 798; *Annual Report of the Mississippi Department of Archives and History*, 7 [1908-09], 26, 44-6, 56-7; Mathews, *Ellicott*, 141).

JUDGE BRUEN: Peter Bryan Bruin, one of the judges of Mississippi Territory. He became the presiding judge, but resigned that position in 1808 after the territorial legislature instructed the Mississippi delegate to Congress to initiate impeachment proceedings for neglect of duty and drunkenness and a committee of the U.S. House of Representatives began to investigate his conduct (*Terr. Papers*, 5:615-16, 626-7, 650; Vol. 30:281n).

Roger Dixon (DICKSON) was a member of a "Permanent Committee" that represented inhabitants of the Natchez area in 1797, before the creation of Mississippi Territory. Dixon, who was from Virginia, had two brothers (*Terr. Papers*, 5:11, 15; VMHB, 19 [1911], 286).

Lewis EVANS was sheriff of Adams County, Mississippi Territory (*Terr. Papers*, 5:254).

NEW LEON: DeLacy was using the name of the province of Nuevo León, which had its administrative center at Monterrey, to refer to Spanish territory in the plains west of the Mississippi River. At the time it was established in 1596, Nuevo León was the only *gobierno* or governorship on Mexico's northeastern frontier, and during the seventeenth century the province had, in practical terms, no limits to the north and northeast. By well before 1801, however, the northern boundary of Nuevo León was located south of the Rio Grande River (Peter Gerhard, *The North Frontier of New Spain*, rev. ed. [Norman, Okla., 1993], 14, 16, 344, 347, 349-50; Peter Gerhard, *A Guide to the Historical Geography of New Spain*, rev. ed. [Norman, Okla., 1993], 11, 213).

IATAN INDIANS: a variant of a French name for the Comanches. The French called a large inlet on the Texas coast, where the Sieur de La Salle landed in 1685, ST. BERNARD Bay. It is now known as Matagorda Bay. The Karankawa tribe lived in that region. By the 1780s, communities of the Alabama (ALIBAMA) and Koasati tribes moved west from their earlier homeland to cross the Mississippi River and establish towns in east Texas and western Louisiana. CODOQUES: the Caddo Indians, centered in what is now east Texas, northwestern Louisiana, and parts of Arkansas and Oklahoma (Sturtevant, *Handbook*, v. 13, pt. 2:ix, 903; 14:ix, 407-8, 616-17, 630; Charmion Clair Shelby, "Projected French Attacks upon the North-Eastern Frontier of New Spain, 1719-1721," *Hispanic American Historical Review*, 13 [1933], 459, 465; James E. Bruseth and Toni S. Turner, *From a Watery Grave: The Discovery and Excavation of La Salle's Shipwreck, La Belle* [College Station, Tex., 2005], 34-5; Kelly F. Himmel, *The Conquest of the Karankawas and the Tonkawas* [College Station, Tex.,

1999], 6-7; Richard P. Schaedel, "The Karankawa of the Texas Gulf Coast," *Southwestern Journal of Anthropology*, 5 [1949], 119; ASP, *Indian Affairs*, 1:755-6).

The places in AFRICA listed by DeLacy beginning with CAPE COAST were all in West Africa, particularly along the northern and eastern coast of the Gulf of Guinea where European activity and the slave trade were concentrated. The Dutch put a trading house at Anomabo (ANAMABOO), a town on the coast of Ghana, in the mid-seventeenth century, and the British subsequently built forts there. SOMBRERO and New Calabar were among a confusing array of names that outsiders gave to two of the many mouths of the Niger River. New Calabar (Elem Kalabari) was also the name of a community in the Niger River delta. PENANTAPO-O: perhaps the island of Fernando Póo, also spelled Fernando Po (David Owusu-Ansah, *Historical Dictionary of Ghana*, 3d ed. [Lanham, Md., 2005], 38-9; William Balfour Baikie, *Narrative of an Exploring Voyage up the Rivers Kwóra and Bínue, Commonly Known as the Niger and Tsádda, in 1854* [London, 1856; repr. London, 1966], 426-7; Christopher Lloyd, *The Search for the Niger* [London, 1973], 15-17; B. A. Ogot, ed., *Africa from the Sixteenth to the Eighteenth Century*, vol. 5 of *UNESCO General History of Africa* [Paris, 1992], 105, 447; Anthony Oyewole and John Lucas, *Historical Dictionary of Nigeria*, 2d ed. [Lanham, Md., 2000], 214; Harold Bindloss, *In the Niger Country* [Edinburgh, 1898; repr. London, 1968], maps facing 1, 338).

William SCOTT of Maryland, an officer of the army since 1795, was promoted from first lieutenant to captain in November 1800 (Heitman, *Dictionary*, 1:870). The AMERICAN POST AT MOBILE was Fort Stoddert, located on the border between U.S. and Spanish territory. The Americans built the outpost, which stood on the Mobile River upriver from the Spanish settlements on Mobile Bay, after Andrew Ellicott's survey of the late 1790s established the boundary line (Richmond F. Brown, "Colonial Mobile, 1712-1813," in Michael V. R. Thomason, ed., *Mobile: The New History of Alabama's First*

City [Tuscaloosa, Ala., 2001], 58-60; Theodore J. Crackel, *Mr. Jefferson's Army: Political and Social Reform of the Military Establishment, 1801-1809* [New York, 1987], 99-100).

In 1798, the governor of Spanish Louisiana gave Antonio Patricio WALSH the command of a vessel protecting the entrance to the Mississippi (Jack D. L. Holmes, *Gayoso: The Life of a Spanish Governor in the Mississippi Valley, 1789-1799* [Baton Rouge, 1965], 246, 255).

STORY OF INKLE AND YARICO: Richard Steele wrote a story for his *Spectator* in 1711 in which an Englishman stranded on a Caribbean island, Thomas Inkle, is saved by "an *Indian* maid," Yarico. After they make their way to Barbados, Inkle sells the devoted Yarico into slavery, and when she informs him that she is pregnant with his child, hoping to persuade him to change his mind, he not only goes ahead with the sale, but uses the news of her pregnancy to raise the price he puts on her. Steele's tale, which he based on an anecdote in a book about Barbados, was recast many times in the eighteenth century, including a very popular musical play (Frank Felsenstein, ed., *English Trader, Indian Maid: Representing Gen-* *der, Race, and Slavery in the New World. An Inkle and Yarico Reader* [Baltimore, 1999], 1-2, 18, 55-7, 81-2, 86-8, 167-72).

DeLacy was acquainted with WILLIAM BLOUNT and apparently handled some business relating to his estate after Blount's death in 1800 (Madison, *Papers, Sec. of State Ser.,* 5:521; Wright, *William Augustus Bowles,* 154).

CHEVALIER DAUNEMOUR: the Chevalier d'Anmours was French consul for Virginia and Maryland for several years beginning in 1779 (Vol. 3:162, 164; Vol. 14:64n; Vol. 23:455-6).

[1] MS: "when it every thing."

[2] MS: "of of." DeLacy evidently omitted a word before the "of."

[3] MS: "of the of the."

[4] Word interlined in place of "station."

[5] MS: "enough to enough to."

[6] MS: "that that."

[7] Someone, probably not TJ, drew a pointing hand in the margin alongside the preceding phrase.

[8] Thus in MS.

[9] MS: "drg."

[10] That is, "hale."

[11] DeLacy added this paragraph in the margin.

From Pierre Charles L'Enfant

SER.   City of Washington November 3d—1801

The peculiarity of my position and the embarrassement answering from the conduct of the Board of the Commissionaires of the City of Washington in regard to requests and communications made to them rendering the freedome of a direct address to you unavoidable—I hope the necessity will plead my excuse, and seeing the time near approaches when it is presumable you will wish to call Congress attention to the state of things relative to this new seat of Government; I now with great dependance on your goodness beg your consideration of the circumstance with me.

Noticing that my object with the board of Commissionaires was to have obtained through thier mediation a Compensation for services and for Injuries experienced at the hands of the Jealousers of the reputation and of the fortune which the planing and Executing of the city of washington promised to me? it would be usless for me to relate how I became charged of the entreprise and to what extant my agency was servicible to it—my plans orriginally met your approval and the zeal the Integrity and impartiallity of my management being generally acknowleged especially of those whose property the opperations affected, assures me the service still must be fresh to memory and be remimbered as deserving—therefore passing over my Endeavours to promote the public object, the difficulties subdued, the contrarieties met and all the reasons for the resignation of my agency: the treatment experienced being likewise reminded of by letter to the Board of Commissionaires (August 1800) and by tow subsequent memorial to Congress (december same year and febuary 1801 Inst.) the latter together with papers accompaging[1] it remaining with other business of the committee of claim not reported upon I believe I may spare the recital of any the contents?—but Attributing the repulse of my prayer, by the first petition, to misconception of the manner of my engagement and connexion of agency with the Commissionaires, finding they have deceived the dependance I placed in them for Explanation of matters to the Committee of claim, and—unable to account way that Board elluded answering the request and communication to them, and on what principle having themselves advised, and offered thier aide to, the petition to Congress, they can have deneyed to the committee my having any cause for the call on Government I presume the Inclosed paper (A) may with propriety be here offered in explanation of certain transactions the Injuries from which answing, gave me some right to the expectation but the Board of Commissrs. would have proved more earnest to help an obtainment of the redress and compensation prayed for.

deeming it to be here manifest that the conduct of the Board forbided the possibility of further call on them about the pending business exciting at the Same time a mistruest of the end, and, making my difficulties the greater by thus discouraging what assistance it has been my unhappy lot for many years past to have had to recur to for Sustainance, I forbear more to animadvert upon the proceeding wishing but by this plain exposure of to Shew the necessity of the appeal to your and the Equity of Government.

Ensuring thus the exact state of thing will be known to you which it seem were kept from former administrations to an hinderance of the hearing of my call on different departments—what ever be those Interests the Jealousies and machinations, of which I have been dup and victime they will not be feared where your power is extant.— and allowing the private animosities, as of late years were fostered by parties politique, may yet stimule opposition to affording me a compensation commensurate to the greatness of objects of national import in which I had a principal primary and essential agency.— possible as it is too for some minds not to feel the obligation to repay voluntary sacrifices or compensate the deprivation of great promises and of Employements of great Expectancy—I nevertheless trust but upon the whole the propriety will be generally acknowleged, of an honorable return being due to honorable acts and for the liberal use I have made of my talents and fortune particularly in the business of the city of washington as also in other, services constantly volunteered to this country for these twenty five years past both in a military and civil employement to which I might add the merite of wounds of painfull captivity and of exertions, in a mission abroad too, at the close of the revolution war the succes of which obtained at a great personal cost to me first of all embarrassed my affairs and never has been redeemed.

about these military matters: I have, in Jun last given in a statement to the Secretary at war *Genal Dearborn* claiming particular dues and respecting the manner of the eventual cessation of my services as the habituate[2] Engineer to the United States; of which having beged the representation to be made to you, I only remind here to bring together to your view every circumstance, which Joined to the absolut destruction of family fortune in Europe concured at almost the same Instant to reduce me from a state of ease and of content, to one the most distressed and helpless? and the only raisonable hope I can maintain of relief from—being in the Justice and liberality with which Government may reward my long services I will own deed urged me to more minute Enumeration of performance, to my own praise and with more reflection perhaps upon the treatment experienced than is congenial to my habit and disposition to have done. and, having thus out of necessity explained upon transactions the most Injurious to the reputation dear to all artists and also upon the most hurtfull to my fortune.

Now Ser, permit me to observe as before expressed by the petitions above reffered to—that none of the related by me flowed from wish of disgracing any one, not even those who acted the most unfriendly to me, being with much reluctancy that I related particular proceedings and yelded to the suggestion by the board of Commissionaires of the propriety of the petition, to the late Congress.—and although the sum stated by those petitions as the loss by me sustained be an exact nay moderate compute of the value of the maps taken from me and of other benefit expected and of Right for a first year of the opperation of my plan.—observing that I mean not to dictate what should the Compensation be for all that. but mearly by the Enumeration of what my expectancy and right were, to invite the consideration of the hardship of the reverse of my fortune: to render that reverse more sensible I gave the contrast of the riches I would have now necessarily been accumulating and how these were werested from me by those Speculations and Jealousies which having left nothing posible to have pursued but with dishonor, it is well known made me resigne all the concerns.

believing the honesty and greatness of the sacrifices I have made of Enticing prospects universally acknowleged, as that also my care to have Ensured first the public advantage in all the bargain and schem, by me brought within power of effecting carried me to a disregard of myself.—an Impossibility then being that in the hurry of so extansive business, whilst Endeavouring my best in all thing I could have watched the usage made of my plans &&a—or have thought of procuring surety to the promised to me so as to be able as in Ordinary business to have produced those and made up accounts for settlement.—I cannot Imagine possible that any thing the like be demanded nor expected from me. and—to speak openly—were this in my power to do, I would not think of offering other support to the claim profered than what I have offered—a Comprehensive view, and general sum up, of the Interest in the business in which I was Employed—conceiving best consistant with the liberality of unconditional services and with the confidence I place in the propriety of my system of plans and of opperation altogether to wait from the Public sense of the merite of performance the Government award of the Compensation due for all the Injuries of the end.

Agreable to these Impressions and sentiments I confine, Ser, to sollicite your kind consideration of the misfortune depriving me of the necessary to Existance.—the small remain of hope, till very lately Indulged in, of regaining at least in part, some stock's of Bank, my only having in the country being now vanished away—by reason of *Rt Morris* taking the benefit of the bankrupt act and the property on which he made me believe to have been secured being found absorbed by treble previous mortgage for sum each far excedant the worth of that property.—thus for a generous friendly assistance afforded him (on request for only three or four days)—for these seven years past, both Capital and Interest, were inhumanly retained and I necessitated all the while to live upon Borrowed bread the obligations for which at this time to repay comming with Imperious call and the addition of exorbitant charges for the advance, I must be excused for bringing to notice in this address being indeed what has been determining me to the disagreable disclosure of my situation and Confidently to request your permission now absolutly to leave the adjustment of the matters of the subject of this address, to your Benevollance and Justice.—

Doing this I will no more than express—that I after many heavy pecuniary sacrifices occasioned by variety of situations during the revolution war—I since the peace of 1787 was also differently Encouraged, and Invited by many commissions to the free spending of my own, dependant upon promises of regular reappointment with promotion all which ended to my loss and absolut ruin.—that on the particular Instance of my agency to the Entreprise of the city of washington I have received no renumeration what ever that—no kind of preconvention were for the service—no price agreed upon for plans, nor the copy right conceded to the commissionaires nor to any ones else, and that—extanded as was my concerns and agency beyond the usual to Architects, although by the grand combination of new schems I contributed eminently to the ensurance of the city establishment by which, numbers, of Individuals and the Country to an immense distance derive a increasing of their wealth—I deed by no one opperations nor transactions worked to my own profit.

Acquainted Ser as you necessarily must have became with managements of the city affairs in which my free exertions were not the least usefull to the promotion of the national object—the merite, and that of the orriginating of the plan you, doubtless, will readily allow to me and certain I am that—for all what I suffered, the only reproach to which I may be liable (in this and business of military description) is my having been more faithfull to principle than ambitious—too zealous in my pursuits—and too hazardous on a dependance on mouth friends—admitting I would deserve reproach if I had Imagined every man actuated by liberal honorable views—I nevertheless believe my Conduct in all Instance stand well applauded and Justified by all who knew the Spirite of the oppositions I met and the personages in whom I confided and—since seeing you, ser, occupying the same heigh station as the chief under whose order I acted as a military and at whose Invitation my services were engaged and by whose Instructions I Conducted in the affairs of the city now become the seat of Government.—esteeming your dispositions equally as I esteemed his, to be to redress Injuries and to recompense active honest services—knowing your power is all commensurate to—I for all the reasons I have to lament the decease of that chief, feel reassured that the loss of his good testimonial and promised support shall not opperate any way detrimentally to my present expectancy and that in all respect your Justice will grant me the prayer made.

with great respect I have the honor to be Ser your most humble and obedient Servant   P. CHARLES L'ENFANT.

RC (DLC); L'Enfant possibly altered the date from 1 Nov.; at foot of text: "To Thomas Jefferson Peresidint of the united States"; endorsed by TJ as received 3 Nov. and so recorded in SJL. Dft (DLC: Digges-L'Enfant-Morgan Papers); incomplete; dated 1 Nov.; at head of text: "Copie." Enclosure not found.

CITY OF WASHINGTON: TJ last wrote to L'Enfant, an engineer and architect, in 1792, when TJ was secretary of state in George Washington's administration. Washington had personally engaged L'Enfant the previous year to survey and plan the new federal city. No contract was made and no compensation agreed to at the time of hire. TJ consulted with L'Enfant as the work progressed. After L'Enfant failed to complete the map by October 1791, his relations with President Washington and the commissioners of the District of Columbia deteriorated. L'Enfant refused to submit to the commissioners' authority, claiming, with some justice, that he was engaged by the president. In February 1792, TJ informed L'Enfant of his dismissal (Vol. 20:9-13, 33-5, 39-53; Vol. 23:161).

L'Enfant's REQUESTS AND COMMUNICATIONS to the District of Columbia commissioners regarding compensation for his service in planning the city of Washington began as early as 1792. The board, at President Washington's direction, offered L'Enfant 500 guineas and a city lot. L'Enfant rejected the offer. Another exchange occurred in 1795 (Kenneth R. Bowling, *Vision, Honor and Male Friendship: Peter Charles L'Enfant in the Early American Republic* [Washington, D.C., 2002], 33, 34; Vol. 23:280n, 352).

LETTER TO THE BOARD: according to board minutes, the District of Columbia commissioners received a letter from L'Enfant, presumably the letter of AUGUST referred to above and now lost, on 3 Sep. 1800 (DNA: RG 42, PC). In a reply dated 16 Oct., the board suggested that

L'Enfant petition Congress (DNA: RG 42, DCLB).

SUBSEQUENT MEMORIAL: L'Enfant wrote to TJ on 7 Dec. 1800, asking TJ, in his capacity as vice president and president of the Senate, to present L'Enfant's petition to the Senate (RC in MeHi: J. S. H. Fogg Autograph Collection). Senator John Langdon presented the petition to that body on 11 December. Six days later, the Committee of Claims of the House of Representatives issued a report, and the House voted not to grant L'Enfant's petition. He presented a second, more detailed, memorial to Congress in February 1801. The committee issued a report on the second memorial on 15 April, when Congress was out of session. According to a committee report dated 24 Dec. 1802, L'Enfant claimed a total of $95,500 in compensation for a year of labor and revenue from map sales. L'Enfant continued to petition Congress until 1813 (JS, 3:112; JHR, 3:741; 4:259; Shaw-Shoemaker, No. 3386; Bowling, *Vision, Honor and Male Friendship*, 47, 55).

L'Enfant's STATEMENT to Henry DEARBORN has not been found. In 1794, Henry Knox, then the secretary of war, appointed L'Enfant a temporary engineer to plan fortifications for the protection of Philadelphia and Wilmington, Delaware. L'Enfant's designs for the defenses were too expensive, and the War Department replaced him with another engineer. Knox wrote to Dearborn from Maine on 16 Oct. 1801 about pay due to L'Enfant as engineer (DNA: RG 107, RLRMS; ASP, *Military Affairs*, 1:82-7; ANB).

DESTRUCTION OF FAMILY FORTUNE IN EUROPE: L'Enfant lost his right to an unspecified amount of property in his native country during the French Revolution, when he was working in the U.S. and could not assert his claim in France (H. Paul Caemmerer, *The Life of Pierre Charles L'Enfant: Planner of the City Beautiful, the City of Washington* [Washington, D.C., 1950], 377, 445).

THE VALUE OF THE MAPS TAKEN FROM ME: L'Enfant's name did not appear on the first published map (Vol. 20:64, 68-9).

The bankruptcy of Robert MORRIS was among L'Enfant's misfortunes, for L'Enfant had loaned bank shares to Morris. To help L'Enfant, Morris gave him a claim to speculated land in New York State and supported his petition on the subject of land to New York's city council (Bowling, *Vision, Honor and Male Friendship*, 41, 48-50).

[1] Dft: "accompagning."
[2] MS: "abituate."

From Thomas Newton

DR SIR   Norfolk. Novr. 4. 1801—

This will be deliverd you by my friend Mr. Newsam, member of Assembly from Princess Ann County, I beg leave to introduce him to you, as a worthy good republican—I sent you some images & Orange shrubs, brought in from the Missisipi. I hope they got safe to your hands, also the two pipes of wine sent to the care of Mr Barnes, by Mr. Taylor. I have sent a pipe of L P. to Mr Madison by your recommendation, which I am much obliged to you for, & shall be glad to hear of its being approved of.[1] it is much esteemd here & nearly 4 years old & cheap at $300. Health & Happiness attend you is the wish of yr. obt Serv   THOS NEWTON

RC (DLC); endorsed by TJ.

NEWSAM: William Newsum, a member of the Virginia assembly from December 1800 to January 1803 (Leonard, *General Assembly*, 221, 225, 229). A letter from Newsum to TJ of 13 Nov., recorded in SJL as received the same day, has not been found.

[1] MS: "off."

To Henry Rose

DEAR SIR   Washington Nov. 4. 1801

I promised you the stages & distances of the route from your house by Slate & Elkrun churches to Charlottesville. they are as follows

to Songster's	10.	
Bull run	5.	
Gaines's tavern	5	
Slate run church	5	
Elkrun church	15	a tolerable tavern
Norman's ford	9.	
Stevensburg	9.	
Somerville's mill	8	

Downey's ford	3.	
Clark's	2.	
Orange courthouse	7.	78. miles. by Fredericksburg this distance is 108. miles. difference 30.
Gordon's	10	
Charlottesville	24	
	112. miles	

Altho' I have long been sensible how advantageous & desireable for the public would be a direct road Southwardly through Virginia, and that the only part where there is now a difficulty is that portion of it over which we passed yesterday yet I would not wish it to be supposed that I mean to take any part personally in obtaining it, much less to institute measures for forcing it. I have certainly no idea of disturbing the quiet of any one on the subject of roads. I shall only for myself & my family ask from the mr Fitzhugh's the indulgence which I observe they extend to others generally, of passing three or four times a year along their private road, leaving gates & fences exactly open or shut as we find them. my watch obliged me to stretch your distance from the [ox]road to Thomas's a good half mile at least. a little more would have been still nearer the truth. Accept my best wishes for your health & happiness & assurances of respect.

TH: JEFFERSON

PrC (ViW); blurred; at foot of text: "Doctr. Henry Rose"; endorsed by TJ in ink on verso.

THE MR FITZHUGH'S: divided among five sons of Henry Fitzhugh and their uncle, William Fitzhugh, was a tract called Ravensworth in Fairfax County, Virginia, that totaled nearly 22,000 acres. TJ sometimes stopped at the houses of Nicholas and Richard Fitzhugh, sons of Henry, while traveling between Washing-

ton and Monticello. William, formerly of Stafford County, moved to Alexandria and a residence in Fairfax County in the late 1790s (VMHB, 7 [1899-1900], 425; 8 [1900] 94-5; Washington, Papers, Ret. Ser., 1:521; 2:616; MB, 2:1071-2, 1123).

THOMAS'S: probably a reference to "Thomas's x roads," an entry between Georgetown and Falls Church, Fairfax County, in TJ's Table of Mileages of 30 Sep. 1807 (DLC: TJ Papers, 233:41688).

From William Evans

SIR/   Baltimore Novr. 5th. 1801

I received your favour of the 1st Instant, and am sorry to inform you that the report respecting James Hennings Having commited an act of Suicide is true. I made every enquiry at the time this melancholy circumstance took place, the result of which was, that he had been delirious for Some days previous to his having commited the act, and it was the General opinion that drinking too freely was the cause, I am Sir

Your obedient Servant   WILLIAM EVANS

RC (MHi); at foot of text: "Thos. Jefferson Esqr."; endorsed by TJ as received 6 Nov. and so recorded in SJL.

From Albert Gallatin

DEAR SIR   Treas. Dep. Nov. 5 1801

The Commr. of Loans Georgia is dead and Mr Millege recommends a Mr Alger for successor.

Shall Mr Peter Bowdoin be made Collector for Cherry Stone? Mr Lee of Norfolk says that he is a violent federal partizan & that a republican may be obtained. But it is necessary that an appointment should take place before the meeting of Congress.

Respectfully your obt. Servt   ALBERT GALLATIN

RC (DLC); at foot of text: "The President of the United States"; endorsed by TJ as received 5 Nov. and "Commr loans Georgia. Collector Cherrystone's" and so recorded in SJL.

Congressman John Milledge wrote Gallatin from Savannah on 15 Oct., informing him of the death of Richard Wylly, Georgia's commissioner of loans, and recommending James ALGER as his SUCCESSOR, describing him as a man of "industry, talents, and integrity" (Gallatin, *Papers*, 5:864). Alger received the appointment (JEP, 1:401, 405; Vol. 33:670, 677).

Gallatin sent TJ two lists of warrants after his last letter of 24 Oct. In the first list for the week ending 24 Oct., Gallatin reported 16 warrants, Nos. 85 to 100, including No. 95, a sum of $2,131.18 to Andrew Moore, marshal of the western district of Virginia, for conducting the census. Two warrants were listed under the military establishment, one for $10,000 for arms, the other for $40,000 for "Ordinance & clothing" for the army. One warrant, No. 88, under the naval establishment totaled $50,000. Three warrants, totaling $85,000, were issued for

the purchase of bills on Holland at 40 cents per guilder for the payment of the Dutch debt. The total for the week was $191,834.25 (MS in DLC, TJ Papers, 117:20175; entirely in Gallatin's hand; endorsed by Gallatin: "Weekly list of Warrants ending 24th Octer."; endorsed by TJ as received from the Treasury Department on 26 Oct. and so recorded in SJL). In the "Weekly List of Warrants for week ending 31st Oct. 1801," Gallatin reported 13 warrants, Nos. 101 to 113. Five were recorded under the civil list, including No. 111 for $1,220.45 to Samuel Harrison Smith for printing for the State Department. Three warrants were recorded under miscellaneous, including No. 108 to John Woodside, clerk in the comptroller's office, for $300, reimbursement of expenses for his move to Washington. Two warrants were issued under "Intercourse with foreign nations," No. 104, for $9,000, to Robert R. Livingston for his outfit as minister to France, and No. 105, for $650, to Thomas Sumter, for his salary as secretary of the legation. One warrant for $10,000 was recorded under the military establishment for payment of the army. Two warrants, totaling $17,000, were issued for the purchase of bills on Holland at 40 cents per guilder for the payment of the Dutch debt. The warrants for the last week of October totaled $44,178.45 (MS in same, TJ Papers, 117:20213; entirely in Gallatin's hand; endorsed by TJ as received from the Treasury Department on 31 Oct. and "Warrants" and so recorded in SJL).

To James Madison

Tн:J. то J.M.   Nov. 5. 1801.

Will you consider whether a copy of the inclosed sent to each head of department would be best, or to avail myself of your kind offer to speak to them. my only fear as to the latter is that they might infer a want of confidence on my part. but you can decide on sounder views of the subject than my position may admit. [if] you prefer the letter, modify any expressions which you may think need it. health & affection.

RC (DLC: Madison Papers, Rives Collection); torn; endorsed by Madison. Enclosure: see Circular to the Heads of Departments, 6 Nov.

From Thomas Tudor Tucker

DEAR SIR   New York Novr. 5th. 1801.—

The Letter of the 31st. Octo. with which you have honor'd me has been just now put into my hands, & I beg you to accept my hearty acknowledgments for the polite & friendly terms in which it is conceiv'd, as well as for the confidence you evince by the offer to my acceptance of a respectable & important station in the Government of the United States. The office is agreeable to me & I accept it with pleasure, but with diffidence; for I am sensible that my little experience in business will give me an awkwardness in any office for a considerable time. But it will be my earnest endeavour to acquire as early as possible the due qualifications & expertness in business, & I trust that my fidelity to the public interests will never be liable to impeachment. I was about to engage my passage this day for Charleston, where I have business of consequence, but the call you have made on me, renders it necessary for me to put it into other hands, & as some little time will be required for the proper arrangements, I will request of you a short indulgence, especially as Mr. Meredith's politeness will induce him to favor the accomodation. By the end of this month at farthest it will be in my power to receive your commands at the seat of government, & I shall, if possible, shorten the time.

With perfect respect I have the honor to be Sir Your obedt. Servt.

THOS. TUD. TUCKER

RC (DLC); endorsed by TJ as received 9 Nov. and so recorded in SJL.

JUST NOW PUT INTO MY HANDS: on 4 Nov., Robert Patton, writing from the post office in Philadelphia, notified TJ that Tucker had left Philadelphia for New York "a few days since." He forwarded the president's 31 Oct. letter to the New York postmaster, therefore, with instructions to inquire for Tucker at "No 18 William street" (RC in DLC; at foot of text: "The President U.S."; endorsed by TJ as received 8 Nov. but recorded in SJL at 7 Nov.).

In response to the SHORT INDULGENCE Tucker requested, TJ wrote Samuel Meredith on 9 Nov., informing him that Tucker had accepted the appointment but would not be able to assume the duties until the last of the month. The president thus apprised Meredith of the "time when he can probably be relieved from his continuance here in consequence of his obliging offer to Th:J." (RC in NN: Clymer-Meredith-Read Papers, addressed: "Mr. Meredith"; Meredith to TJ, 29 Aug.).

To John Vaughan

DEAR SIR   Washington Nov. 5. 1801.

I recieved on the 24th. Ult. your favor of the 22d. but it is not till this day that I am enabled to comply with your request of forwarding some of the vaccine matter for Doctr. Coxe. on my arrival at Monticello in July I recieved from Dr. Waterhouse of Cambridge some vaccine matter taken by himself, and some which he at the same time recieved from Dr. Jenner of London. both of them succeeded, and exhibited precisely the same aspect and affections. in the course of July and August I inoculated about 70. or 80. of my own family, my sons in law about as many of theirs, and including our neighbors who wished to avail themselves of the opportunity our whole experiment extended to about 200. persons. one only case was attended with much fever, & some delirium, & two or three with sore arms which required common dressings. all these were from accidents too palpable to be ascribed to the simple disease. about one in 5. or 6. had slight feverish dispositions, more perhaps had a little headach, and all of them had swellings of the axillary glands, which in the case of adults disabled them from labour 1. 2. or 3. days. two or three only had from 2. to half a dozen pustules on the inoculated arm & no where else, and all the rest only the single pustule where the matter was inserted, something less than a coffee bean, depressed in the middle, fuller at the edges & well defined. as far as my observation went the most premature cases presented a pellucid liquor the 6th. day, which continued in that form the 6th. 7th. & 8th. days, when it began to thicken, appear yellowish, & to be environed with inflammation. the most tardy cases offered matter on the 8th. day which continued thin & limpid the 8th. 9th. & 10th. days. percieving therefore that the most premature as well as the tardiest cases embraced the 8th. day, I made that the constant day for taking matter for inoculation: say 8. times 24. hours from the hour of it's previous insertion. in this way it failed to infect in not more I think than 3. or 4. out of the 200. cases. I have great confidence therefore that I preserved the matter genuine, & in that state brought it to Doctr. Gantt of this place on my return, from whom I obtain the matter I now send you, taken yesterday from a patient of the 8th. day. he has observed this rule as well as myself. in my neighborhood we had no opportunity of obtaining variolous matter to try by that test the genuineness of our vaccine matter; nor can any be had here, or Dr. Gantt would have tried it on some of those on whom the vaccination has been performed. we are very anxious to try this experiment for the satisfaction of those here, and also those in the neighborhood of Monticello, from whom the matter here having been transferred, the establishment of it's genuineness here will satisfy them. I am therefore induced to ask the favor of you to send me in exchange some fresh variolous matter, so carefully taken and done up as that we may rely on it. you are sensible of the dangerous security which a trial with effete matter might induce. I should add that we never changed the regimen nor occupations of those we inoculated. a smiter at the anvil continued in his place without a moment's intermission, or indisposition. generally it gives no more of disease than a blister as large as a coffee bean, produced by burning, would occasion. sucking children did not take the disease from the inoculated mother. these I think are the most material of the observations I made in the limited experiment of my own family. in Aikin's book, which I have, you will find a great deal more. I pray you to accept assurances of my esteem & respect.

Th: Jefferson

RC (PPAmP); at foot of first page: "Mr. J. Vaughan"; endorsed by Vaughan. PrC (DLC).

From the Vermont
House of Representatives

SIR, [5 Nov. 1801]

Although we are by no means fond of formal Addresses, to any of our rulers, yet, as the practice has already obtained, our silence on the present auspicious occasion might be falsely interpreted into an indifference toward your person, your political opinions, or your Administration. We take, therefore, this earliest opportunity to assure you, that we love and admire the federal constitution, not merely because it is the result and display of the collected wisdom of our own country; but especially, because its principles are the principles of liberty, both civil and religious, and of the rights of Man. We contemplate the general government as "the sheet anchor of our peace at home, and safety abroad." We sincerely respect all the constituted authorities of our country. We regard the Presidency with a cordial attachment, and profound respect. But, Sir, we do not regard you, merely, as the dignified functionary of this august office. That you are an American, both in birth, and principle, excites in us sensations of more exalted pleasure. We revere your talents—are assured of your patriotism, and rely on your fidelity. More than this,—our hearts, in unison with your own, reverberate the political opinions you have been pleased to announce in your inaugural Speech.—Having said this, we need not add that you may assure yourself of our constant and faithful support, while you carry into effect your own rules of government.

Your disposition expressed in plainly delineating, in your inaugural[1] Address, and in a particular instance of a more recent date, the chart by which you propose to direct the course of the political ship, on board of which we have embarked the best of our temporal interests, invites a reciprocity of communication. Under this indulgence, we are constrained to express some of our most ardent wishes.—May the general government draw around the whole nation, such lines of defence, as shall prove forever impassable to any foreign foe; may it secure to the several States, as well the *reality*, as the *form* of republican Government; may it ever respect those Governments as the most "competent for our domestic concerns, and cherish them as the surest bulwarks against anti republican tendencies"; and effectually protect them against any possible encroachments on each other. may it effectually extend to us, and to every Individual of our fellow citizens, all that protection to which the state governments may be found incompetent. While it thus defends us, against ourselves, and all the world, may it leave every Individual to the free pursuit of his own object, in his own way. May the means of defraying the expence necessarily incurred by these measures, be drawn from all the Inhabitants, in as just proportion to their respective ability, as is possible. May your administration be found, on experiment, to be effectually instrumental in adapting all the subordinate offices of government to the real accommodation of the great public; and, of annexing such a specific compensation to the discharge of every trust, as shall invite the ready acceptance of modest ability, and distinguished merit,—while the avaricious, the ambitious, and the luxurious, shall see in it, no allurement; and may no one description of citizens be ever favoured at the expense of any other.

Liberty herself demands these restrictions,—and these indulgencies are all she asks.

Thus administered, our government will stand fast, on the surest basis—that of public opinion,—nor will it need the mercenary support of any privileged class of men, however influencial they may be. May He whose Kingdom ruleth over all, direct, and bless your whole Administration, and yourself.

Signed on behalf, & by order.   Amos Marsh Speaker

RC (DLC); undated; in an unidentified hand, signed by Marsh; at head of text: "The House of Representatives of the Freemen of the State of Vermont. To Thomas Jefferson, President of the United States." Enclosed in Marsh to TJ, Newbury, 5 Nov. 1801, stating: "I execute with pleasure the duties of my Office in transmitting to you the enclosed Address agreeably to the order of the Genl Assembly" (RC in DLC; at foot of text: "Thomas Jefferson, Esq. President of the United States"; endorsed by TJ as received 18 Nov. and so recorded in SJL; also endorsed by TJ: "Address of legislature of Vermont").

Amos Marsh (d. 1811), an attorney and Federalist from Vergennes, graduated from the College of New Jersey in 1786. He served as U.S. attorney for Vermont from 1794 to 1796 and speaker of the state House of Representatives from 1799 to 1801 (Ruth L. Woodward and Wesley Frank Craven, *Princetonians, 1784-1790, A Biographical Dictionary* [Princeton, 1991], 141-3; JEP, 1:161-2, 219).

A PARTICULAR INSTANCE OF A MORE RECENT DATE: TJ to the New Haven Merchants, 12 July 1801.

[1] MS: "inagural."

From "The Voice of A Sybil"

GREAT SIR,   [before Nov. 6. 1801]

In my travels, through several countys of the state of Pennsylvania, three different, political sentiments obtruded themeselvs upon my observations. the first was a very impatient desire to see *Your* speak,

to the insuing Congress—the scecond was, an Extreem apprehen-
tion, least federalism, and the Constitution should fall together—and
a new one be formed by the present government—And the third was,
that, an absolite Equality is the only Object of Democracy. those prevail, in general, among the people in the Country, who voted for a
continuation, of the former administeration—
Those only can speak to all!—
Who are at the head of Mankind!—
    The tyranical Pride of the Roman Tarquin instigated him to treat
the greater part of the Sybilline Books with contempt, And drive the
sacred Maid away—
    But You are no tyrant! No Tarquin!   THE VOICE OF A SYBIL

RC (DLC); undated; endorsed by TJ
as received from "Anonymous" on 6 Nov.
and so recorded in SJL.

PRIDE OF THE ROMAN TARQUIN: Tarquin the Proud (Lucius Tarquinius Su-
perbus), sixth century B.C., said by tradition to be the seventh and last king of
Rome, was offered nine books of prophecy by a sibyl (prophetess). When Tarquin
refused to pay the exorbitant price she demanded, the sibyl burned three of the
books, then offered the remaining six to
the king at the same price. He again refused, and the prophetess burned three
more books before Tarquin relented and
purchased the surviving three books at

the original price (*The Roman Antiquities
of Dionysius Halicarnassensis*, Edward
Spelman, trans., 4 vols. [London, 1758],
2:228-9, 261-2; H. W. Parke, *Sibyls and
Sibylline Prophecy in Classical Antiquity*
[New York, 1988], 76-8).
    TJ would receive at least two more
communications from the author of the
above letter. On 13 May 1802, he received
an undated letter from "A Sybilline
Voice," reporting complaints over reductions in the military establishment. Another undated letter, signed "A Sybill
leafe" and received on 5 Oct. 1802,
warned the president not to meddle in religious and other concerns that might
jeopardize his impartiality.

Circular to the Heads of Departments

DEAR SIR   Washington Nov. 6. 1801
    Coming all of us into Executive office new, and unfamiliar with the
course of business previously practised, it was not to be expected we
should in the first outset adopt, in every part a line of proceeding so
perfect as to admit no amendment. the mode & degrees of communication particularly between the President & heads of departments
have not been practised exactly on the same scale in all of them. yet it
would certainly be more safe & satisfactory for ourselves as well as
the public, that not only the best, but also an uniform course of proceeding, as to manner & degree, should be observed. having been a
member of the first administration under Genl. Washington, I can
state with exactness what our course then was. letters of business

came addressed sometimes to the President, but most frequently to
the heads of departments. if addressed to himself, he referred them to
the proper department to be acted on: if to one of the Secretaries, the
letter, if it required no answer, was communicated to the President
simply for his information. if an answer was requisite, the Secretary
of the department communicated[1] the letter & his proposed answer to
the President. generally they were simply sent back, after perusal,
which signified his approbation. sometimes he returned them with an
informal note, suggesting an alteration or a query. if a doubt of any
importance arose, he reserved it for conference. by this means he was
always in accurate possession of all facts & proceedings in every part
of the Union, & to whatsoever department they related; he formed a
central point for the different branches, preserved an unity of object
and action[2] among them, exercised that participation in the gestion of
affairs which his office made incumbent on him, and met himself the
due responsibility for whatever was done.   during mr Adams's
administration, his long & habitual absences from the seat of government rendered this kind of communication impracticable, removed
him from any share in the transaction of affairs, & parcelled out[3] the
government in fact among four independant heads, drawing sometimes in opposite directions. that the former is preferable to the latter
course cannot be doubted. it gave indeed to the heads of departments
the trouble of making up, once a day, a packet of all their communications for the perusal of the President; it commonly also retarded
one day their dispatches by mail: but, in pressing cases, this injury
was prevented by presenting that case singly for immediate attention[4] and it produced us in return the benefit of his sanction for every
act we did. whether any change of circumstances may render a
change in this procedure necessary, a little experience will shew us.
but I cannot withold recommending to the heads of departments that
we should adopt this course for the present, leaving any necessary
modifications of it to time & trial.   I am sure my conduct must
have proved, better than a thousand declarations would, that my
confidence in those whom I am so happy as to have associated with
me, is unlimited, unqualified, & unabated. I am well satisfied that
every thing goes on with a wisdom & rectitude which I could not improve. if I had the Universe to chuse from, I could not change one of
my associates to my better satisfaction. my sole motives are those before expressed as governing the first administration in chalking out
the rules of their proceeding; adding to them only a sense of obligation imposed on me by the public will, to meet personally the duties
to which they have appointed me. if this mode of proceeding shall

meet the approbation of the heads of departments, it may go into execution without giving them the trouble of an answer: if any other can be suggested which would answer our views, and add less to their labours,[5] that will be a sufficient reason for my preferring it to my own proposition, to the substance of which only, & not the form, I attach any importance.

Accept for yourself particularly, my dear Sir, assurances of my constant & sincere affection & respect. TH: JEFFERSON

RC (NHi: Gallatin Papers); at head of text: "Circular to the heads of departments, *and Private*"; addressed: "The Secretary of the Treasury" and "Private"; franked; endorsed by a clerk as a letter of 5 Nov. PrC (DLC: Madison Papers); endorsed. RC (MeHi). Dft (DLC). Dft apparently enclosed in TJ to Madison, 5 Nov.

[1] In Dft TJ here canceled "at the same time."

[2] Dft: word interlined in place of "procedure."

[3] Dft: preceding two words interlined in place of "partitioned."

[4] Remainder of sentence interlined in Dft.

[5] In Dft TJ began this sentence "if any other mode can be suggested which would answer our views and give less to the [trouble] of the heads of departments," before altering and expanding the passage to read as above.

From John Wayles Eppes

DEAR SIR, Monticello Novr. 6. 1801.

I postponed writing by the last post from a hope that a cough with which our little infant had been attacked a few days before might prove only a common cold—There is no longer room for indulging so pleasing an idea as it most certainly is the hooping-cough—The violent symptoms which in general attend the commencement of the disease such as fever & difficulty of breathing have disappeared for some days—His cough however is extremely violent—If his strength is sufficient to bear that it is all he has now to contend with—He sucks well and after the most violent paroxisms of coughing in which he becomes almost lifeless will take the breast—The total absence of fever, the continuance of his apetite and above all a variety of instances of which I have recently heard of children of his age passing safely thro' the disease inspire me with hope—Change of air and gentle exercise have been so strongly recommended to me that I think in 8 or 10 days I shall try carrying him down the country by short journeys of 18 or 20 miles—The chicken pox which has appeared at Edge-hill strengthens me in this determination as any new complaint added to the hooping cough would render the recovery of our child quite hopeless—

The plaisterers have finished the rooms above & below on the right & put the first coat on the nursery & appendix—The Masons have done little—Morland undertook work in Milton & had all his hands there for some time—Until last Monday they have done no work here for more than a fortnight—There is not the least chance for your shop & indeed I doubt very much whether the walls for your offices will be completed—.

Accept for your health & happiness the best wishes of yours sincerly

JNO: W: EPPES

RC (MHi); endorsed by TJ as received 11 Nov. and so recorded in SJL.

MORLAND UNDERTOOK WORK IN MILTON: probably Joseph Moran, a stone mason who worked on the new nailery and the L-shaped wings of Monticello in 1801 and 1802 (Bear, *Family Letters*, 213; MB, 2:1050n).

From Mary Jefferson Eppes

Monticello November the 6th

I did not write to you last week my dear Papa, I had discover'd my little Francis had the hooping cough & my apprehensions about him were so great that I could not at that time write. he has now struggled with it eleven days & tho' he coughs most violently so as to become perfectly black with it in the face[1] he is so little affected by it otherwise that my hopes are great that he will go through with it, he has as yet lost no flesh & has had only one fever we shall endeavour to travel with him the last of next week if he is not worse. I have borrow'd Crity as a nurse for this winter, Betsys ill health was such that I could depend on her as one & we shall return with Crity in the spring to meet you. the children at Edgehill stand the disorder very well, Cornelia suffers most with it but she still looks very well, (Mr Eppes says who saw her yesterday). Ellen next to her is most unwell the other three are better, Virginia particularly. I have not seen my Sister since her return to Edgehill she remain'd here four weeks after you left us during which time except a few days we were entirely alone, how much did we wish for you then my dear Papa, but I am afraid that except in the spring we shall never enjoy the happiness of being alone with you. nothing would give me greater pleasure could Mr Eppes so arrange it as to spend the next summer here, the hope of a flying visit sometimes from you, would alone make it most desirable independent of every thing else. Adieu dear Papa believe me most tenderly yours

M EPPES

RC (MHi); endorsed by TJ as received 11 Nov. and so recorded in SJL.

CRITY AS A NURSE: Critta Hemings, daughter of TJ's slave Betty Hemings and sister of Sally Hemings, was a thirty-two-year-old housemaid at Monticello who temporarily served as nurse to Francis Wayles Eppes. In 1827 after the death of his grandfather, Eppes purchased his former nursemaid's freedom so that she could join her husband Zachariah

Bowles, a free black farmer and landholder living north of Charlottesville (Stanton, *Free Some Day*, 156; Vol. 26:65).

BETSYS ILL HEALTH: Betsy Hemings, daughter of Mary Hemings and niece of Sally Hemings, was a slave given by TJ to John Wayles Eppes and Maria Jefferson Eppes upon their marriage in October 1797 (RS, 1:321n; Vol. 29:532).

[1] Preceding three words interlined.

To Albert Gallatin

TH: JEFFERSON TO MR GALLATIN   Nov. 6. 1801.

The appointment of mr Alger, recommended by mr Milledge, as Commr. of loans, in the room of the one who is dead, is approved. extreme reluctance to appoint a violent federalist at Cherrystone's induces a wish to defer it as long as can be admitted in the hope of hearing of some good republican to invest with it.

RC (NHi: Gallatin Papers); addressed: "The Secretary of the Treasury."

From Craven Peyton

DEAR SIR   Shadwell 6th November 1801

Those notes which you mention was disposd of immediately aftar they were receivd & in case of failure in the bank it appears that the holder of the Note must be the sufferer, it was requisite for me to put my Name on them. Mr. Randolph does not take shadwell as supposd. William Davenport has made application shoud you approve of him you will please let me no. Aftar Constant Application Wood has furnish the plat which is inclosd. I am about to engage with a numbar of the Miltonians for fire Wood they prefer getting of me to Henderson & was I not to contract with them Henderson woud receave the pay. & in all probability one half woud cut of & pillage your land more than it is & you receave no pay. therefore I thought it to your interest to encourage them & wish your centiments. from the manner which it is laid of it will be difficult to confine persons to one lott.

with much Respt   C. PEYTON

RC (ViU); endorsed by TJ as received 11 Nov. and so recorded in SJL; also endorsed by TJ: "Henderson's land." Enclosure: Plat of the lands in Albemarle

County belonging to the heirs of Bennett Henderson, locating the property in relationship to the Rivanna River, the town of Milton, and surrounding lands owned by Edward Carter, Kemp Catlett, a member of the Reynolds family, and TJ; the lands being divided into four tracts—property below the town, the back lands, and the upper and lower fields—and each partitioned into ten allotments; with dower rights of Elizabeth Lewis Henderson also marked (MS in same; undated; originally on two conjoined pieces; in William Woods's hand, with later emendations in TJ's hand assigning the names of individual Henderson legatees to the allotments, indicating the acreage of Milton and of portions of some allotments in the back lands, and marking other features including the Henderson dam and mill and a prospective mill site between Milton and the Rivanna River; TJ also outlining in red ink the allotments to the Henderson heirs Sarah, James, Isham, and Charles; attested by Woods: "A Copy of the Plat of the Land belonging to the Legatees of Bennett Henderson decd. in Albemarle County—Copied for Craven Peyton by Wm. Woods SAC"; endorsed by Woods; endorsed by TJ: "Henderson's. Plat of division"; with notation on verso in TJ's hand:

"back lands   1020
Lower field   58¼
Upper field   49. ?
below the town   20.
Dower lands   15
                   1162¼
Milton   70
                   1232¼";

other figures and calculations by TJ in pencil and ink on recto and verso).

For the NOTES written on the Bank of Columbia, see TJ to Peyton, 1 Nov. and John Barnes to TJ, 7 Oct.

MR. RANDOLPH: Thomas Eston Randolph; see TJ to Craven Peyton, 25 Oct.

From Henry Rose

DEAR SIR   Fairfax 6th Novr. 1801

Your esteemed favour of the 4th, containing the route from this to Charlottville, by Elk & Slate run Churches, is to hand, for which please accept my acknoledgements

On Yesterday the Mr Fitzhughs, dined with me, which afforded me an opporty of anticipating you in a wish, that these Gentlemen should understand your true intention in riding Over their grounds, in assuring them, that your only view was to learn a more convenient & direct rout from the City to Monticello, than the one, you have hitherto travelled, and as you had thought the rout over their Lands more convenient & direct, than any you had met with, you would be pleased that the privilege of using this road, should be extended to yourself, as well as to others To which there was an unanimous consent I went so far, as to suggest to them, that this, Bye way could be made a public convenience & would eventually reflect value on their Lands, by affording them a more convenient market for their produce &c, to which they appeared willing to accede, on condition that they were compensated in, an usual way—You may rest satisfied that nothing has or will fall from me on this subject or any other intentionally that shall in any shape affect the quiet of private or public repose

I am with every assurance of the highest respect & esteem Your Most Obt. & very hul Sert   HENRY ROSE

RC (ViW); endorsed by TJ as received 7 Nov. and so recorded in SJL.

From Tench Coxe

SIR   Philada. Novr. 8. 1801.

As I had the honor to receive from you some remarks on the office I now hold from Genl. M, I trust it will not be improper to give you some information on the subject, and I take this liberty the more freely, because I cannot deprive myself of the satisfaction of believing, that my situation, as an Individual and as connected with the sufferings & exertions in the cause of American & human liberty are not indifferent to you.

I have abstracted from the accots. of Mr. Ash for the latest year (1800) the following sum total of quarterly emoluments, which you will be pleased to observe are gross, and not net—

March quarter 1800		438.33
June do.		778.97
Septemr. do.		631.30
Decemr. do.		882.76
	Drs.	2731.36
He paid one constant indoor clerk		
& Book keeper	500.0	
also one out door assistant for the inspection		
of distilleries, marking & other business	300.0	
Office rent, office furniture not allowed, fuel, law books &c. culled by him, I think	200.0	1000.0
	Drs.	1731.36

The prices of fuel, cabinet work for furniture, books relative to the public service, which cannot be expected from the Government, horse keeping & a horse for country services not allowed, and the actual charges beyond the Government allowances, convince me that if the business is fully and comfortably executed & conducted the sum total of Mr. Ash's estimate of expences would be consumed.

I cannot form an estimate of the value of the office during the Time I may hold it, but tho I have been busily engaged with one Clerk, an apprentice & my two oldest Sons in opening, conducting & reforming the business, the *whole* emoluments of the office in October fell short of 50. Drs. This is in a great measure owing to my predecessor's collecting, after Septr. and charging Comms. on Bonds payable in that month. On this point the necessary controul of the Supervisor & the Treasury department will be resorted to, & no doubt with all proper success.

I am sorry to observe, Sir, that my applications in relation to certain offices, if they should become vacant, have become publicly known at Washington and Philadelphia, particularly in regard to the naval office & the office of Comm. of the Revenue. I never meant the addresses, I took the liberty to make, as to the President; but wished them to be deemed the most frank communications to a respected friend, who, I doubted not, was desirous to combine the power of his station with his personal convictions & wishes. Being placed on your files, it is probable, that these circumstances have inadvertently become known. Believe me, Sir, I only mention it, because I suppose you are unacquainted with the circumstance of their contents having gone abroad. It is certain, however, that good men among the friends of our Government, & unworthy men among its enemies have treated, in a manner to be regretted, my appearance, under such circumstances in such an office as this, not held from you. It was from a sure anticipation of such things, that I declined the office in June. It was only from the deep importance of my return to Philadelphia, from the extreme difficulty of my continuing to be deprived of income for my family, and from the Judgment on my prospects, which foes, and friends & pretended friends concurd in pronouncing, that I consented to accept this office on the first of October. It was openly said in Washington, in the presence of my successor that my hopes of his or any other office from you were quashed forever, since you had been applied to for it, and had not given it, and since the various other offices I was as willing to accept had been reserved to or given to others. An income of £1000 here was necessary for my family. I *thought* this office gave it—and, tho I sacrificed *my standing* in public life, and in society, and much of my utility in that *great and certain struggle* to which Republicanism is *yet destined* in America & Europe, the *interests* and comforts of my family *obliged* to take, in the sight of republicans and antirepublicans, an office not given by you, and, wch. with my property in money, *I never* would have thought of. The Inspectorship was well abolished, and was too useless and inconsiderable an affair for me to receive at your hands.

Excuse me, Sir, for this private, confidential communication of my situation, calculations, & feelings. Let no part, if you please, of this or any other letter I have had the honor to write be extended beyond Mr. Madison & Mr. Gallatin a confidence in whose friendship & esteem, with yours, I yet cherrish. I do not doubt the Justice and kindness of one, nor of several other Gentlemen, but I should wish my case, so far as I have written on it, known to those alone whom I have mentioned. Tho considerations relative to your interests, or happiness or to the public good will always induce me to the liberty of a communication to you, it is my intention after all I have said to be sparing of letters relating to myself. My having dismissed objects of great emolument & of an honourable & respectable nature, and my desire to enjoy, in peace here, a decent competency, as a compensation for business, office, and tranquility sacrificed is now well known to you & my friends at Washington. I trust I shall be rescued from my present degradation, for such it is universally considered.[1]

I devoutly wish the success of your administration in all its parts & in all its[2] objects being, Sir,

in truth one of your most sincere friends   TENCH COXE

RC (DNA: RG 59, LAR); endorsed by TJ as received 11 Nov. and so recorded in SJL.

For TJ's REMARKS ON THE OFFICE, see his letter to Coxe of 17 June. GENL. M: Peter Muhlenberg, supervisor of internal revenues for the district of Pennsylvania (Vol. 33:29, 219). Muhlenberg appointed Coxe revenue collector at Philadelphia in place of James Ash. For the arrangement of the appointment and Gallatin's estimate of the worth of the position, see Gallatin to TJ, printed at 16 June (first letter).

Coxe's TWO OLDEST SONS who worked with him in the office were Tench Coxe,

Jr., born in 1784, and Francis Sidney Coxe, born in 1789 (Cooke, *Coxe*, 83, 236n).

For Coxe's APPLICATIONS, see Vol. 33:237-8, 410-11, 612-14. DECLINED THE OFFICE: see Coxe to TJ, 24 and 25 June. William Miller was Coxe's SUCCESSOR as commissioner of the revenue (Vol. 33:411n; Coxe to TJ, 25 June). INSPECTORSHIP WAS WELL ABOLISHED: for Coxe's criticism of the position of inspector, see Vol. 34:655n. The office was abolished by the Executive Order on Revenue Districts, printed at 29 July.

[1] Preceding sentence interlined.
[2] MS: "is."

From Gideon Granger

DR SIR   Suffield Novr: 8th: 1801.

Yours of 31st. Ultimo arrived last Evening

In Conformity to Your Wishes within Ten days I will sett off for Washington and tarry with you untill such time as I can return without Injury to the Public on any ground—you being Judge. when that period arrives I must claim the priviledge of returning to arange my private concerns, which are very numerous and extensive. evry Exertion in my power shall allways be made to bear up against the Aristocratic phalanx.

Your Sincere friend   GIDN: GRANGER

RC (DLC); at foot of text: "Thos: Jefferson Esq Presidt. of the United States"; endorsed by TJ as received 14 Nov. and so recorded in SJL.

From Joseph Yznardi, Sr.

EXMO. SEÑOR   Philadelphia 8 Nobe. de 1801
Muy Señor mio, y de mi Aprecio Mayor
    Aora qe me allo Capas de Cumplir mi dever presento á V.E mis respectos, y doy gracias por los Singulares favores y distinciones con qe me ha Honrrado, y le Comunico he dado punto á mis Comiciones, qe pienso Realisar en el resto del Año, y enbarcarme para mi destino Infaliblemente á principios del Año proximo á Cuyo Intento oy mismo Escribo á Madrid esta mi Resolusion, y Consequente a lo qe Ofrecy á V.E quando tubo la vondad de Consederme el Nonbramiento de Consul, que pasare á desempeñar con el Celo Acreditado, teniendo la vondad de no dudar, lo Cumpliré assy mras tengo el Honor de Repetir á V.E mis Respetos, y Ruego á Dios gue su Vida ms. as.
    Exmo. Sor BLM de V.E su Obte. Servr   JOSEF YZNARDY

E D I T O R S '   T R A N S L A T I O N

MOST EXCELLENT SIR   Philadelphia 8 Nov. 1801
My most illustrious sir and with my utmost appreciation
    Now that I find myself capable of fulfilling my duty, I present to Your Excellency my respects, and I thank you for the special favors and distinctions with which you have honored me. And I tell you that I have finished the assignments I planned to complete this year, and that I will definitely leave for my post at the beginning of next year, a decision about which I am writing to Madrid today. Consistant with what I offered Your Excellency when you had the kindness to grant me the position of consul, which I will begin to perform with utmost care, your having the kindness not to doubt me, I will thus fulfill my duties. Meanwhile, I have the honor to repeat to Your Excellency my respects, and pray that God be with you many years.
    Most excellent sir your obedient servant kisses Your Excellency's hand.
                                                JOSEF YZNARDY

RC (DLC); at foot of text: "Exmo. Sor. Dn. Thomas Jefferson"; endorsed by TJ as received 15 Nov. and so recorded in SJL.

On 14 Oct., TJ signed a commission for Yznardi as U.S. CONSUL at Cadiz (FC in Lb in DNA: RG 59, PTCC).

From Albert Gallatin

Dᴇᴀʀ Sɪʀ   Nover. 9th 1801

Enclosed you will find the letters received by last mail. (one excepted from Survr. gen. on which I have not yet formed an opinion) I would suggest the propriety of my not sending those which require certain previous enquiries, such as those of Th. Worthington, E. Boudinot, J. Ingersol, until after the enquiries have been made and an opinion formed, when the whole subject may be laid before you. I also enclose two drafts of letters, one on Mr Pichon's application & the other in relation to an apparently delinquent collector.

I send along with this a bundle of what we call "public letters" also received by this mail. The greater part of these are endorsed so as to be distinguishable & are opened by the principal clerk. They consist principally of the weekly Statement &c. of collectors, never require any answer except when at the end of a quarter the result does not agree with the quarterly accounts, or they exhibit too much money in hands of a collector. I never look at them. but they are entered in a book, which has been prepared under my direction, by one of the clerks so as to exhibit weekly a general view of all the transactions. From that book a weekly sheet is made out exhibiting the balance in hands of collectors &c. subject to drafts of the Treasury and that general view enables to draw upon them, to call on them, when necessary, for more regular returns, & sometimes to institute enquiries as in Mr Gerry's case. I do not suppose you want to see those letters, but have sent them as a sample & will confine myself hereafter to letters on which it is necessary for me to act, unless you shall otherwise direct.

The whole of my correspondence is generally very insipid, consisting of petty details &c.; and, I have as much as possible, abridged it. It will, by no means, convey just ideas of the real business of this Department; this, as well as the object you have generally in view, & which is of primary importance, can, in my opinion, be obtained only[1] by regular meetings. It seems to me that a general conference once a week, to which might be added private conferences of the President with each of the Secretaries respectively once or twice a week, is a necessary measure; but those conferences should be fixed on certain days & hours, otherwise, they will be only occasional, &, as we have already experienced, often omitted.   Feeling, as I do, the necessity of concert, I make no apology for the suggestion.

I have the honor to be With sincere respect & attachment Your most obed. Servt.   ALBERT GALLATIN

RC (DLC); at foot of text: "The President of the United States"; endorsed by TJ as received from the Treasury Department on 9 Nov. and so recorded in SJL. Enclosures: (1) Elias Boudinot to Gallatin, U.S. Mint, 5 Nov. 1801, noting that he has with great difficulty obtained fifty tons of copper from England on credit for four months at a cost of about $16,000; being entitled to draw $10,000 from the Treasury, he requests a warrant for that amount; also proposing that "If you can lend the Mint Four thousand more, I am confident I can repay it in Cents within eight or nine weeks," and concluding "By this means I shall save as much interest to the U. States, preserve our credit, and take advantage of the present state of exchange, which will probably rise during the winter" (Gallatin, Papers, 5:924, 967). (2) Probably the Dft of Gallatin to Benjamin Lincoln, 10 Nov. (see below). Other enclosures not found.

ONE EXCEPTED: Rufus Putnam to Gallatin, Marietta, Ohio, 15 Oct., posing questions about the land surveys as prescribed under the land act of 10 May 1800. Gallatin endorsed the letter and wrote the following OPINION: "Note. His arguments are by no means conclusive. But the subject, on account of incorrect original surveys, is difficult. It is best to write him, to suspend the subdivn. of the townships partly sold before the Act of 10th May 1800 for the reasons stated in letter of 24th Sept. & lay the subject before Congress—A.G." Gallatin also noted that the letter was answered on 12 Nov. (Gallatin, Papers, 5:866-9). At that time TJ probably saw both Putnam's letter and Gallatin's response. The Treasury secretary's reply directed the surveyor general "to suspend the Subdivision of the Townships partly sold" before the Act of 1800 "in order that the subject may be submitted to Congress, at the approaching Sessions" (Gallatin, Papers, 6:15; Malcolm J. Rohrbough, The Land Office Business: The Settlement and Ad-

ministration of American Public Lands, 1789-1837 [New York, 1968], 34).

Louis André PICHON'S APPLICATION probably concerned the French chargé's request for a refund of the duties he was required to pay on shoes and silk stockings that arrived on the Maryland. On 7 Nov., Gallatin informed Robert Purviance, the collector of Baltimore, of the president's decision that Pichon should receive the same exemption afforded a foreign minister residing in the United States. Gallatin requested that Purviance repay William Barney, Pichon's agent, $8.80, "being the amount of the duties received by you on the articles" (Gallatin, Papers, 5:974).

APPARENTLY DELINQUENT COLLECTOR: probably the draft of a letter Gallatin addressed to Benjamin Lincoln on 10 Nov., requesting that the Boston collector appoint a qualified person, preferably the deputy collector or "an intelligent clerk" in his office, to proceed immediately to Marblehead, Massachusetts, and make an inquiry into Samuel R. Gerry's official transactions. Gallatin directed the investigator to determine the "amount of specie, bonds and other public papers" that were in the hands of the Marblehead collector; to ascertain the cause "of the variation between the weekly Returns & quarterly accounts Current and the reason of their long continuance"; and to discover "the causes of the delays in rendering the accounts, and if practicable, what was the true balance of cash on hand at the end of the three first quarters of the present year respectively." Gallatin also requested that Lincoln provide information, which would be kept confidential, "respecting the general character, qualifications, and age" of Gerry (Gallatin, Papers, 6:3). On 24 Oct. and 7 Nov., Gallatin wrote John Steele seeking his advice regarding the delinquency and discrepancies in Gerry's accounts (same, 5:894-5, 975).

On 7 Nov., Gallatin sent TJ the weekly list of warrants on the Treasury for the week ending 7 Nov., recording 14 warrants, Nos. 114 to 127, including No. 126, for $2,000, the periodic payment of TJ's salary as president. One of four warrants under miscellaneous, No. 121, for $800, was issued to Thomas Claxton for furniture at the "President's house." One warrant appeared under the military establishment, for $50,000 for the army, and two warrants under the Dutch debt for a total of $14,000, for the purchase of bills on Holland at 40 cents per guilder. The warrants for the week totaled $75,101.16 (MS in DLC; in Gallatin's hand; endorsed by TJ as received from the Treasury Department on 7 Nov. and "Warrants" and so recorded in SJL).

¹ Word interlined.

To Thomas Newton

DEAR SIR   Washington Nov. 9. 1801.

An extraordinary press of business has prevented my sooner acknoleging the reciept of your favor of Oct. 16. the articles from New Orleans were safely recieved, and I now with thankfulness inclose the 20 D. 75 c you had been so kind as to pay on that account. a few days before my return to this place two other pipes of Brazil wine had come to hand. this is the first occasion I have had to acknolege their reciept.   I am particularly obliged to you for having thought of me in the article of cyder. nothing is more desired generally than fine Hughes's crab cyder. about 60. doz. bottles would probably be about a year's supply. if you have in Norfolk, as they have in Philadelphia, persons who make a trade of bottling, perhaps it might be safer to have it bottled there & moved in bottles. but if it will come without fermentation or injury in the casks, and as safe from being drank & watered, we can have it bottled here. this would give us earlier use of it. I much wish mr Carrol may be able to furnish the whole quantity.

Though we have nothing but the newspaper account of Sterritt's having captured the Tripolitan, yet it comes under hopeful appearances. I wish it true the rather as it may encourage the legislature to throw off the whole of that Barbary yoke. we could easily confederate 3. or 4. other nations who, dividing the cruising season with us, would relieve us from a great portion, & yet keep that sea under constant guard. a few years would destroy every vessel those states have, & they have no materials within themselves for building a single one. Accept my best wishes & affectionate esteem & respect.

TH: JEFFERSON

PrC (DLC); at foot of text: "Colo. Thomas Newton"; endorsed by TJ in ink on verso. Enclosure not found, but see below.

In his personal financial memoranda on this day, TJ recorded his enclosure of $20.75 to reimburse Newton for freight charges (MB, 2:1058). On the recent delivery of Brazil quality Madeira WINE to TJ in Washington, see Newton to TJ, 25 Sep.

On 6 Nov., the *National Intelligencer* printed an ACCOUNT, published in New York's *American Citizen and General Advertiser* on 3 Nov., that Lieutenant Andrew Sterett, commander of the American schooner *Enterprize*, captured a Tripolitan corsair. After a three-hour battle near Malta on 1 Aug., more than half of the Tripolitan crew was killed or wounded, while the *Enterprize* did not sustain a single casualty. After taking possession, Sterett dismantled the corsair, then returned it to Tripoli. The *Enterprize* arrived 15 Nov. at Baltimore. In recognition of the victory, Congress authorized the presentation of a sword to Sterett and one month's extra pay for his crew (NDBW, 1:537-40; *Federal Gazette & Baltimore Daily Advertiser*, 16 Nov.).

From Ellen Wayles Randolph

[before 10 Nov. 1801]

How do you do my dear Grand papa I thank you for the picture You sent me. All my Sisters have got the Hooping cough, Virginia has got a very bad cold. I hope you will bring me some books my dear grand papa I thank you. when I was writing the children made such a noise I could not write well.   your affectionate Grand daughter

ELLENANORA W. RANDOLPH

Make haste & come home to see us. & all our books [are in?] the press

RC (MHi); undated; endorsed by TJ as received 10 Nov. and so recorded in SJL.

Ellen Wayles Randolph (1796-1876) was the second surviving daughter of Martha Jefferson Randolph and Thomas Mann Randolph, and she often accompanied TJ to Poplar Forest. She read widely and studied languages, especially French. In 1825, she married Boston merchant Joseph Coolidge, Jr., in a ceremony at Monticello. They settled in Boston and had six children, four sons and two daughters. After her husband took an extended business trip to China, Ellen met him in London in June 1838, where they remained about one year. Ellen then spent two years in Macao, while her husband was in China, and in the 1840s, she spent several years with her family in Europe, before returning to Boston (Bear, *Family Letters*, 268, 293, 324, 333, 341, 418-19; Monticello Association, *Collected Papers*, ed. George G. Shackelford, 2 vols. [Princeton and Charlottesville, 1965-84], 1:89-99).

OUR BOOKS: perhaps a reference to the scrapbook being compiled at this time from the poems and clippings sent by TJ to his granddaughters. THE PRESS: a cabinet where letters were stored (Jonathan Gross, ed., *Thomas Jefferson's Scrapbooks: Poems of Nation, Family, & Romantic Love Collected by America's Third President* [Hanover, N.H., 2006], 499-501; RS, 3:xlvii).

From Martha Jefferson Randolph

[before 10 Nov. 1801]

I am doomed to write you, in a hurry allways My Dearest Father. Abraham who will be the bearer of this has arrived [. . .] I began my letter, and it will not be proper to make him wait [longer] than I can possibly help it. my children are doing generally well except Ellen and Cornelia the latter has had fevers for three days & with triffling intermissions morning and evening tho very short. we have reason to fear they have worms in which case the worst consequences are to be apprehended unless they can be destroyed before the disorder weakens them too much to resist. That we are told has generally been the fate of those who have died of it. Francis is doing well. his cough is extremely violent but he continues to thrive—in which case I apprehend the danger not to be great. Virginia is in the same state, coughing most violently so as to endanger strangling but evidently gaining strength to contend with it I have been very unwell my self from cold taken by frequent getting up in the night & want of sleep but am infinitely better to day however I have no reason to expect to be well again untill the fatigue of nursing is over adieu Dearest Father believe me with tender affection yours   M Randolph

RC (ViU: Edgehill-Randolph Papers); undated; frayed at margin; endorsed by TJ as received 10 Nov. and so recorded in SJL.

On 3 Nov., TJ paid ABRAHAM Golden's passage on the Georgetown ferry and gave him $12 for expences for a trip that included stops at Monticello and Edge- hill. Golden returned to Washington by 10 Nov., when TJ recorded in his financial records that he had received $1.60 "back from Abram Galdin" (MB, 2:1057, 1058). According to SJL on 10 Nov., TJ also received undated letters from Gabriel Lilly at Monticello and Thomas Mann Randolph, presumably delivered to him by Golden. Both are missing.

From Joseph Bloomfield

MOST RESPECTED SIR,   Trenton November 10th 1801.

It is my misfortune to feel the necessity of addressing you this letter, without being personally known to you. I must rely on your adherence to Republican principles and men, as the ground on which its propriety may rest.

The same spirit which has lately pervaded the union and changed the Administration of the general government, has had its proportionate effects in the State of New-Jersey. Men of like principle, who resisted the progress of dangerous innovations and who have by firmness and temperate means, placed you in the seat of our federal government, have bestowed on me the responsible office I now hold.

Presuming you must feel pleasure in the recollection of those characters, who have contributed by their exertions and influence in turning the tide of public opinion; induces me, to request your attention, to the services of Mr. Stephen Sayre. He was active for several months before the general election of the last year, on which we conceived depended the salvation of our beloved country, in the choice of a President; the majority in the Legislature, who choose Electors, were against us:—We however continued, by all means in our power, to give information to the People, and succeeded in the Congressional election; it is impossible to say what the vote of this State would have been, on the most solemn occasion, had not the sentiments of the people of New-Jersey been declared, before that important day.

Mr Sayre's past services, in support of the rights of Man, his Republican principles, integrity and capacity, entitle him to public notice. I have nothing in my gift, that I could ask him to take; but the President of the Union, may possibly bestow some thing worthy Mr. Sayre's acceptance.

I cannot add to the high respect & esteem, with which, I am, most truly and sincerely, Your friend & Fellow Citizen

JOSEPH BLOOMFIELD.

RC (DLC); in an unidentified hand, with closing and signature in Bloomfield's hand; at foot of text: "The President of the United States"; endorsed by TJ as received 13 Nov. and so recorded in SJL with notation "Govr. Trenton."

Joseph Bloomfield (1753-1823), born in Woodbridge, New Jersey, was a lawyer and veteran of the Revolutionary War who became attorney general for his state, achieved prominence as one of its Federalist leaders, and served as a presidential elector for George Washington in 1792. After growing disillusioned with Federalist policies under John Adams, he declared himself a Republican in 1797, although lingering suspicions of his Federalist ties haunted him for the rest of his life. As chairman of New Jersey's Republican nominating convention in 1800, he became a spokesman for his state party to the Jefferson administration, expressing his opinion on patronage appointments.

Bloomfield became the state's first Republican governor in 1801 (Paul A. Stellhorn and Michael J. Birkner, eds., *The Governors of New Jersey 1664-1974: Biographical Essays* [Trenton, 1982], 85-8; ANB; Vol. 33:184n).

PROPORTIONATE EFFECTS IN THE STATE OF NEW-JERSEY: in 1801 the Republicans gained ascendancy in New Jersey as the result of the introduction of the caucus system early in the year and the election of a Republican governor and a majority in the legislature in October (Carl E. Prince, *New Jersey's Jeffersonian Republicans: The Genesis of an Early Party Machine, 1789-1817* [Chapel Hill, 1967], 89, 98-100).

STEPHEN SAYRE: see Sayre to TJ, 8 Oct., and Sayre to James Madison, 30 Oct., requesting him to remind TJ that his services had still gone unrewarded (Madison, *Papers, Sec. of State Ser.,* 2:213).

From Cornelius Coningham

S<small>IR</small>   City of Washington Nov. 10th. 1801.

Having rented a Brewery in Alexandria about two years ago, and having entrusted an English-Man with the superintendance of it; I unfortunately, thro' his conduct, sunk almost the whole of my active stock: Since that time, I have not been able to carry on my business to any advantage.

But can I despair under an administration I have ardently wished for? I have been long opposed, almost alone, to the Demagogues who *led* the City, and from whom I also suffered, not only personal abuse, but by introducing beer from other places in opposition to mine.   Now the political current is changed. I have it not in my power to take advantage of it unless I get some assistance.   I therefore address you as a man of feeling, not as President of the United States; and should you think it reasonable for the Government to lend me fifteen hundred dollars, I will secure it by a Mortgage on my property which is worth double that sum. With this assistance I could free myself from the debts I owe in a short time, & be enabled to pursue my business to some advantage, hoping for a favourable answer I am Sir with the greatest regard

    Your obedient Servant   C<small>ORN</small>. C<small>ONINGHAM</small>

RC (MHi); endorsed by TJ as received 10 Nov.

Irish native Cornelius Coningham (ca. 1746-1820) was a physician and veteran of the Revolutionary War, serving primarily as a hospital surgeon. He entered the brewing business in Washington in 1796 in partnership with James Greenleaf, then opened a second brewery in Alexandria in late 1798. TJ appointed him a justice of the peace for Washington County in March 1801. Coningham offered his Washington brewery for sale in 1805, then unsuccessfully sought appointment as librarian of Congress in 1807, citing his "past services & sufferings." He reentered the military in 1810 as a surgeon's mate in the U.S. Army, then as surgeon at Fort Trumbull in New London, Connecticut, from 1816 to 1820 (Heitman, *Dictionary*, 1:320; Bryan, *National Capital*, 1:291; J<small>EP</small>, 2:163; *Alexandria Advertiser*, 25 Dec. 1798; *National Intelligencer*, 2 Sep. 1805; Boston *Columbian Centinel*, 30 Sep. 1820; Benjamin Tinkham Marshall, ed., *A Modern History of New London County Connecticut*, 3 vols. [New York, 1922], 1:390; Vol. 33:674; Coningham to TJ, 8 June 1807).

A letter from Coningham dated Washington, 13 Oct. 1801, is recorded in SJL as received the same day with the notation "N," but has not been found.

From Samuel Elam

Newport Rhode Island Novr. 10th 1801.

The Newport Insurance Company in Rhode Island, think it a duty they owe to themselves and those of their fellow citizens who are immediately concerned in trade, respectfully to represent to the Chief Magistrate of the Union, that great spoliations have been, during the present year, committed upon their lawful commerce by vessels acting under authority from the Government of Spain.

As Underwriters we have been unexpectedly injured by these spoliations, and are apprehensive of sustaining further and great losses by a continuance of them; we therefore beg leave to remonstrate against them.

The differences, between the United States and France, having been terminated by their late Treaty, and the Treaty subsisting between this Country and *Spain*, expressly allowing our Citizens the liberty of trading to and from the ports of the enemies of the *latter*, it was presumed, that vessels of the United States destined to ports in the Mediterranean sea, would not be *by being cleared for or ordered to touch at a British port* rendered liable to be captured and condemned by the French or Spaniards.

War with several of the Barbary States having been apprehended for some months previous to the declaration of it by the Government of Tripoli, the Merchants of the United States had deemed it prudent, for nearly a year past, to have their vessels when bound to any port in the Mediterranean Sea, *cleared for or ordered to touch at Gibraltar* to obtain information that might lead them to avoid, or to procure convoy to protect them against the Barbary Corsairs. And it has not been unusual for American vessels, in times of the greatest security to touch at Gibraltar merely for the purpose of gaining commercial intelligence, always useful and sometimes absolutely necessary for the success of their Mediterranean voyages. But since the existence of the danger alluded to, it has been considered essential to the safety our Merchant vessels bound as before mentioned, that they should touch at Gibraltar. And when cleared for, or ordered to touch at, that port they have been insured at a lower rate than they otherwise would have been. It now appears however, that clearances and orders of this kind have exposed them to new dangers. They have been *avowedly in consequence of them*, taken near Gibraltar and carried into the port of Algeciras in Spain, by gun boats and other armed vessels, sailing under the flag and authority of Spain, but in company

as we are informed with French Privateers; and have there been condemned by a Spanish Tribunal. We have to regret the capture and
condemnation, under the circumstances and in the manner above re-
cited, of two vessels with valuable cargoes, owned wholly by Citizens
of the United States and not laded with any goods contraband of
War; in which as Underwriters, we were interested to the Amount of
thirty thousand dollars; that sum however comprising only a small
part of the whole value of them. The papers relating to, and proving
the Capture and condemnation of one of these ships called the Hercules Courtenay, of Newport, we are assured were transmitted by the
owners of her to the Secretary of State some months since; and the
facts respecting the case of the other, called the Molly of Philadelphia
have, we doubt not, been fully stated to the Secretary by the owners
of her, who are Merchants of that City. It is therefore unnecessary for
us, and we shall not presume, to lay before the President all the circumstances attending these two captures. We nevertheless think it
proper to mention, that it was alledged on the part of the Captors that
Gibraltar had been declared in a state of Blockade by the Government of Spain. This declaration was however not known here at the
time of the sailing, from the United States of the two vessels referred
to, and of many other vessels that have experienced a similar fate. It
can indeed be considered only as a pretext, for capturing defenceless
neutral vessels, when it is known that Gibraltar has not been actually
blockaded, for at least several years past, by any Spanish Naval force
capable of preventing a single British sloop of War from going into,
or coming out of that port.

The hostile disposition manifested by the Spaniards towards our
commerce in the Mediterranean Sea, and elsewhere excites in our
minds serious apprehensions for its safety, when we consider the
reduction that has lately taken place in our Navy and the present unarmed state of our Merchant vessels. But relying upon your assurances to the Legislature of this State, that "Commerce will be
cherished by you, both from principle and duty," we confidently
hope, that the powers vested in the President by the Constitution and
laws of the United States will be exerted to obtain indemnification for
the losses, and to prevent a repetition of the injuries of which we
complain.

By order and in behalf of the Newport Insurance Company

(signed)   SAMUEL ELAM. President

Attest

J DENNISON Secretary

Tr (DNA: RG 233, PM, 7th Cong., 1st sess.); ASP, *Foreign Relations*, 2:443. FC (RNHi: Lb of The Newport Insurance Company). Recorded in SJL as received 21 Nov.

Samuel Elam (ca. 1750-1813) emigrated to the United States from Leeds, England, and became a naturalized citizen of Rhode Island in 1789. A prominent business and civic leader residing in Portsmouth, he served terms in both houses of the Rhode Island legislature and played an active role in promoting the economic interests of his adopted state. He was unanimously elected the first president of the newly chartered Newport Insurance Company in 1799 (*Newport Mercury*, 2 Apr. 1799, 30 Oct. 1813; John Russell Bartlett, ed., *Records of the Colony of Rhode Island and Providence Plantations in New England*, 10 vols. [Providence, 1856-65], 10:317-18, 479; Peter J. Coleman, *The Transformation of Rhode Island 1790-1860* [Providence, 1963], 211).

In a 30 June 1801 letter to the secretary of state, Newport merchants George Gibbs and Walter Channing reported the capture of their ship, the HERCULES COURTENAY, by a "Spanish Gun boat and a french privateer" near the Barbary coast. Carried into Algeciras, the vessel was condemned for violating the alleged blockade of Gibraltar. Gibbs and Channing claimed that their vessel had not actually touched at that port, but was nevertheless taken because Gibraltar was mentioned in the ship's clearance and instructions (NDQW, Dec. 1800-Dec. 1801, 264-5; Madison, *Papers, Sec. of State Ser.*, 1:364). The ship MOLLY of Philadelphia was taken to Algeciras in late July, following a pitched battle near Gibraltar with gunboats flying French, Spanish, and Tripolitan colors. David Humphreys wrote several letters to the secretary of state detailing his negotiations with Spanish authorities to secure the vessel's release (*National Intelligencer*, 18 Nov. 1801; ASP, *Foreign Relations*, 2:441-2; Madison, *Papers, Sec. of State Ser.*, 2:256, 267, 321).

YOUR ASSURANCES TO THE LEGISLATURE: see TJ to the General Assembly of Rhode Island and Providence Plantations, 26 May 1801.

Jabez Denison had served as SECRETARY of the Newport Insurance Company since March 1799 (*Newport Mercury*, 2 Apr. 1799, 13 Jan. 1801).

To Albert Gallatin

DEAR SIR   Nov. 10. 1801.

A very little experience will probably shew us what description of letters &c. are worth perusal for the sake of information. among yesterday's communications the bundle of what you called public papers would hardly be worth sending me, because they contain nothing interesting but the balances in the hands of the collectors, which could be obtained by having barely a sight of the weekly sheet you mention in which a statement of these balances is presented in a single view: and this merely that I may have an idea of the existing state of things.   As to cases in the ordinary course of business, or depending on principles which are obvious, & on which consequently the head of the department & President can have no doubt, it would be a loss of time to make them the subject of conference with all the heads of departments. I doubt whether those out of the common line & presenting difficulty, are numerous enough to furnish subjects of conference weekly. at present there is a sufficiency of matter and I propose therefore a meeting for the day after tomorrow at 11. oclock.—your idea is precisely the one I meant to express, that when letters require an answer, they should be communicated with the proposed answer, & consequently not till that is ready, unless any difficulty in it presents grounds for previous conference.   the reappointments to the revenue cutters may be considered whenever you think it needful. I recieved yesterday from Dr. Tucker a letter accepting his appointment; he will be in place by the last of this month. accept assurances of my sincere & affectionate esteem.

TH: JEFFERSON

RC (NHi: Gallatin Papers); addressed: "The Secretary of the Treasury." PrC (DLC).

REAPPOINTMENTS TO THE REVENUE CUTTERS: on 14 Oct., Gallatin wrote Benjamin Lincoln and the collectors at New York, Philadelphia, Norfolk, Charleston, Savannah, and Portsmouth, New Hampshire, directing them to sell the large revenue cutters under their command and discharge the crews, except for the master and oldest commissioned mate. They were then to acquire new revenue cutters "built upon the best terms you can obtain, and of that particular construction which, in your opinion, is best calculated for the service, but not exceeding 45 tons." The collectors were also given the option to purchase a vessel if they found one that fit their requirements. The crews for the new revenue cutters were not to exceed the retained master and mate and six "seamen boys" (Gallatin, *Papers*, 5:857-8). For the plan to replace the large revenue cutters, which were "better calculated for War, than for the protection of the Revenue," see Gallatin to TJ, 16 June (second letter). TJ probably saw Lincoln's letter to Gallatin of 30 Oct. (not found), regarding a boat for the custom house at Boston. On 10 Nov., Gallatin wrote Lincoln that he approved of his employing the "Custom House boat in the manner suggested in your letter." Gallatin added in a postscript: "you are perfectly at liberty either to purchase a cutter or to have one built as you will think most advantageous for the public service" (Gallatin, *Papers*, 6:2).

Thomas Tudor Tucker's LETTER ACCEPTING HIS APPOINTMENT is printed at 5 Nov.

From Albert Gallatin

DEAR SIR   Nover. 10th 1801

Of the letters which accompany this, I request your attention to that which relates to the mint. I presume that those endorsed "no answer" and generally those on which it is not necessary to act need not be sent to you, unless they contain useful information. There is another description on which the decisions are uniform vizt. applications for monies due & for which an appropriation does exist. Such were that of Mr Boudinot of yesterday & that of Mr Simpson of this day. In those cases a Warrant uniformly issues, & the information reaches you weekly in the list of Warrants issued during the week. Those I will also omit sending; as I conceive the object is to communicate to you before a decision takes place every letter on which *judgment must be exercised*, and also every one which contains useful information.

Respectfully Your obedt. Servant ALBERT GALLATIN

It is necessary to fix the precise day on which Doctr. Tucker shall enter into office, in order that the Banks &c may be immediately notified.

RC (DLC); at foot of text: "The President of the United States"; endorsed by TJ as received from the Treasury Department on 10 Nov. Enclosures not found, but see below.

BOUDINOT OF YESTERDAY: see enclosure described at Gallatin to TJ, 9 Nov. The letter from George SIMPSON, cashier of the Bank of the United States, to Gallatin of 6 Nov., probably enclosed above, has not been found, but Gallatin replied on 10 Nov., acknowledging the receipt of two sets of bills of exchange, totaling 100,000 guilders, and instructing that they be paid out of the funds placed in the cashier's hands for that purpose. The Treasury secretary also requested that Simpson "continue the purchasing of

approv'd. bills, on Amsterdam, until otherwise instructed" and noted that the treasurer had been directed to remit $50,000 to him, for which he was to credit the United States (Gallatin, *Papers*, 6:4). Gallatin's "Weekly list of Warrants issued for the week ending 14th Nover 1801," describing six warrants, totaling $61,110.46, included No. 129 for $50,000, issued to Simpson "in advance for purchase of bills on Holland" and No. 130 for $10,000, to Benjamin Rush, treasurer of the Mint, for copper (MS in DLC: TJ Papers, 117:20286; in Gallatin's hand; endorsed by TJ as received from the Treasury Department on 14 Nov. and "Warrants" and so recorded in SJL).

From Ephraim Kirby

SIR   Litchfield Novemr 10th. 1801

I should not presume to trouble you with concerns subordinate to the duties of your important station, was not the subject of my communication really interesting to the people in this vicinity.

The Post Offices in this part of the United States have for years past been almost universally in the hands of violent political partizans—many of them insensible to the suggestions of honor, & regardless of the obligations of official duty. This department has been a monstrous engine of private abuse, and public deception. Correspondence between persons of known Republican character has been altogether unsafe. Republican News Papers conveyed by Mail—have been either suppressed, or ridiculed at the office of delivery, in such manner as to deter many from receiving them; while other papers calculated to poison the public mind, such as The New England Paladium &c have been circulated free of postage, among the ignorant and superstitious in every obscure corner. Many other inferior abuses of trust too[1] tedious to be enumerated, have been committed.— These things were submited to with patient expectation of eventual redress.

The Post Office in this Town, being the centre of a large County, and at the intersection of several Post roads, is of more importance than country Post Offices in general. The communication to and from the Supervisors office has increased its importance.

It was foreseen that Mr. Tallmadge, the Post Master, would be elected to a seat in Congress; and every one expec[ted] his place would be filled by a person of different cast.—A *partizan*, even of opposite politicks was not desired. But it was supposed, an honest, cool, principled republican might fairly be claimed.

As soon as the election of Mr. Tallmadge was ascertained, I wrote immediately to Mr Habersham. My letter reached him some days before Mr Tallmadges resignation.—It was however too late—This business had been all previously settled.—On the recommendation of *Oliver Wolcott, Uriah Tracy, John Allen* & *Tapping Reeve*, Mr. Habersham had anticipated the election of Tallmadge and appointed *Frederick Wolcott*, the brother of *Oliver*.—This man is a perfect *Tool* to the unprincipled leaders of the Federal party, a rancorous calumniator of the present administration, and in every respect the reverse of what he ought to be for that office.

I take the liberty to enclose my correspondence with Mr Habersham on this subject, and to entreat you to make such communications to his successor in office as you think proper. In doing this I am sensible that I am taking a great liberty, no less than to solicit your attention to a subordinate part of the administration of the general government; but sir I rely on the peculiar circumstances of the case for my justification.

With profound respect, I am, Sir, Your Obedt. Servt.

EPHM KIRBY

RC (DNA: RG 59, LAR); frayed at margin; at foot of text: "His Excy. Thomas Jefferson President of the United States"; endorsed by TJ as received [16] Nov. and so recorded in SJL. Enclosures: (1) Kirby to Joseph Habersham, 12 Oct. 1801, recommending Moses Seymour as postmaster at Litchfield (letter not found, but cited in Enclosure No. 2). (2) Habersham to Kirby, 20 Oct., noting that previous to the receipt of Kirby's letter he had appointed Frederick Wolcott as postmaster on the recommendation of several gentleman at Litchfield; defending the appointment, Habersham recalls that during his seven years in office he always acted independently and selected "men of integrity and good character without enquiring into their 'political faith'"; observing that men of both political parties continued "to hold post offices in every state," he argues that previous administrations "never made or attempted to make this department an engine of party or interfered at all in its management," but under Jefferson's administration he had found it expedient to apply to the president's friends for recommenda-

tions when vacancies occurred and had "conformed to them two or three instances excepted" (FC in Lb in DNA: RG 28, LPG).

SUPERVISORS OFFICE: TJ appointed Kirby supervisor for the collection of internal revenues in Connecticut in July 1801 (Vol. 33:672, 676). Benjamin TALL-MADGE, the newly elected Federalist congressman, had served as postmaster at Litchfield since 1792. FREDERICK WOL-COTT, who assumed the postal position in October, remained in office only a few months before being replaced by Moses Seymour, Kirby's nominee, in late January 1802 (*Biog. Dir. Cong.*; Stets, *Postmasters*, 99).

[1] Word supplied by Editors.

Notes on Actions for the War Department

1801.
Nov. 10. War. Monsr. Lorimier's conduct in procuring delivery of the two Delawares who murdd Harrison

Secy. of state to write letter of acknolmt to Chevr. Yrujo.

Secy. at war send copy of that to Lorimier with letter of thanks.

a talk & a medal to the chief of the Delawares (Loups) Takinowtha or Capt Allen.

write to Govr. Harrison

———

Eli Whitney's arms to be preferred.

MS (DLC: TJ Papers, 118:20350); entirely in TJ's hand; possibly noting a conversation with Henry Dearborn or topics that TJ intended to discuss with Dearborn or the cabinet; this is the first of a series of notes TJ wrote on both sides of one sheet, printed in this volume as Notes on the Bank of the United States and Internal Revenues, [10 Nov.]; Notes on Circuit Court Cases, 12 Nov.; Notes on a Consultation with Robert Smith, 15 Nov.;

and Notes on the Funded Debt, [15 Nov. 1801 or after].

MONSR. LORIMIER'S CONDUCT: Louis Lorimier, a French Canadian who had become a naturalized Spanish subject, was a trader, Indian agent, and militia commander at Cape Girardeau on the Mississippi River (Louis Houck, *A History of Missouri from the Earliest Explorations and Settlements until the Admission of the*

State into the Union, 3 vols. [Chicago, 1908; repr. New York, 1971], 2:170-79; Louis Houck, ed., *The Spanish Régime in Missouri*, 2 vols. [Chicago, 1909; repr. New York, 1971], 2:43, 47, 52, 322).

According to testimony in a trial held in Indiana Territory, Jesse HARRISON was robbed and killed after he encountered three Native Americans who were hunting near the Ohio River. Two of the Indians were caught, and one of them, Johnny, gave testimony that led to the conviction of the other, Wapikinamouk, who was hanged for the crime. LETTER OF THANKS: on 30 Nov., Henry Dearborn wrote to John H. Buell asking him to convey to Captain Lorimier the gratitude of the United States for his assistance in the apprehension of the two individuals. Dearborn praised "the prompt and persevering attention of his Catholic Majesty's Officer to the Political and friendly relations subsisting between his Majesty and the United States." Writing to William Henry Harrison, governor of the Indiana Territory, on 22 Dec., Dearborn asked the governor to inform the chief of the Delawares, "whose conduct appears to have been fair and honourable," that the president "has a high opinion of his integrity and good conduct." Dearborn suggested that Harrison might give the chief "some present as a token of our good opinion of him" (*New-York Herald*, 2 Jan. 1802; *Terr. Papers*, 7:37-8; Dearborn to Buell, 30 Nov. 1801, DNA: RG 75, LSIA; William Henry Harrison to Dearborn, 22 Oct., 3 Dec. 1801, noted in DNA: RG 107, RLRMS).

Following their migration to the Ohio Valley from the seaboard in the eighteenth century, the Algonquian tribes known in English as the Delawares, and groups associated with them such as the Mahicans and Munsees, were sometimes called LOUPS, a label the French had also given to other tribes in the colonial period (Sturtevant, *Handbook*, 15:71, 204-5, 213, 592).

TJ reportedly examined a sample of ELI WHITNEY'S ARMS and his system of interchangeable parts in January 1801, in the presence of the inventor and Congressman Elizur Goodrich of Connecticut. According to Goodrich, following a "very critical survey & examination," TJ declared that "he had in no instance seen any work or specimens equal to Mr. Whitney's." The only exception TJ offered was the factory of French gunmaker Honoré Blanc, which also employed interchangeable parts, but "Mr. Whitney equalled his specimens" (Mirsky and Nevins, *Eli Whitney*, 207-9; Vol. 8:455).

On 9 Nov., TJ received from Henry Dearborn an unsigned and undated memorandum giving numbers of noncommissioned and enlisted personnel of the army, based on the "last Genl. Return of the Army" in August 1801. Dearborn indicated that the number of noncommissioned officers, musicians, and privates, "including Artificers," was 4,195; the total authorized by law was 5,036; and "the proposed establishment," probably a figure that TJ and Dearborn had discussed as a goal, was 3,210. Dearborn also noted: "each company to consist of 72 rank & file.—exclusive of Sergeants & music" (MS in DLC: TJ Papers, 116:19957; entirely in Dearborn's hand; endorsed by TJ as received from the War Department on 9 Nov. with notation "Military establishment" and so recorded in SJL).

Notes on Patronage in
New Hampshire

1801.

Nov. 10.   Woodbury Langdon proposes the following changes.

Cilley the present Marshal to be removed. a violent, inveterate tory, appointed by the influence of Rogers, former
Marshal, has lately appointed a high toned federalist for
his deputy.

William Simmonds recommended in his place by John &
Woodb. Langdon.

Rogers the Supervisor to be removed. he was a violent
Revolutionary tory. he was the ringleader of the 16.
towns on Connecticut river, who were prevailed on to
join Vermont in going over to the British.

he has spent half his time in electioneering activity. still
mounts & glories in an enormous cockade

Nathanl. Folsome to be Naval officer vice Edwd. St. Loe
Livermore.

MS (DLC: TJ Papers, 108:18524); entirely in TJ's hand; on same sheet and follows Notes on Candidates for Public Office, 23 Dec. 1800.

For the appointment of WOODBURY LANGDON as navy agent at Portsmouth in May 1801, see John Langdon to TJ, 10 June.

Michael McClary was appointed marshal in April 1802 in place of Bradbury CILLEY, whose commission had expired. John Langdon recommended McClary at that time (Madison, *Papers, Sec. of State Ser.*, 3:106-7; JEP, 1:422-3).

Nathaniel ROGERS served as the federal marshal of New Hampshire from 1791 until 1798, when John Adams appointed him supervisor of the revenue for the New Hampshire district. He remained in office until accounts were settled after the repeal of the internal taxes in 1802 (JS, 1:89-90, 262; Gallatin, *Papers*, 7:261; 47:1026).

The Senate approved the appointment of Nathaniel Folsom (FOLSOME) as naval officer at Portsmouth in March 1802 (JS, 1:409-10).

Notes on the Bank of the United States

Treasury.   Bank statements. private. General result. [i.e. the bank US.]

Specie	5,000,000
due by banks, treasy. bills. & other bills immedly. convertible into specie	1,450,000
	6,450,000
Discounts	12,150,000
6 pr. cents & advances to govmt	5,460,000
	24,060,000

Revenues in 1800.

Excise	501,410.725
Auctions	51,646.63
Carriages	77,585.06
retail licenses	65,148.60
refined sugar	65,240.88
Stamps.	221,789.02
	982,820.92
exp. of collectn.	128,172.91
nett	854,648

An abstract of the last returns of the following banks.

	Specie	due by banks treasury &c. convertible in specie	Discounts	6 pr cents & advances to govmt
Bank of the US.	5,000,000	1,450,000	12,150,000.	5,460,000.
New York	581,819	809,894	2,718,736	562,563.
Boston	649,009	149,736	1,791,143	
Baltimore	554,933	232,583	1,575,766	
Norfolk	780,169	114,883	491,790	
Charleston	941,500	543,414	1,968,003	
	8,507,430	3,300,510	20,695,438	6,022,563

and Internal Revenues

bank notes in circuln		5,200,000
deposits. govmt	3,560,000	
Individuals	5,240,000	8,820,000
		14,020,000
demands against bank		
profits not yet divided		40,000
capital		10,000,000
		24,060,000

recommend to mr Gallatin to have a similar aggregate statement made for all the banks.

a mere apperçu, not accurate

Notes in circulation	deposits of govmt	deposits of individuals.	undivided profits	Capital.
5,200,000.	3,560,000.	5,240,000	40,000	10,000,000
1,027,000.	704,280.	1,390,046.		1,800,000.
767,360	955,365.	459,571.		700,000
938,025	487,446	435,249		600,000.
405,375	445,797	276,219		250,000
1,315,920	412,336	1,124,947		600,000.
9,653,680	6,565,224	8,926,032	40,000	13,950,000

MS (DLC: TJ Papers, 118:20350); entirely in TJ's hand, including brackets; undated, but follows, on same sheet, Notes on Actions for the War Department, 10 Nov., and apparently completed before TJ's letter to Gallatin of 11 Nov., at the head of which TJ copied the composite table with information from the branches of the Bank of the United States.

BANK STATEMENTS: the Bank of the United States and its branches, or offices of discount and deposit, furnished weekly balance sheets and regular consolidated balance statements. In making the notes printed above, TJ apparently drew on a statement of 5 Nov. 1801. He recorded the figures in the form of a balance sheet similar to the bank's regular statements, showing assets of $24,060,000 on the left matched by the same amount in obligations on the right. He expected to ask Gallatin to prepare A SIMILAR AGGREGATE STATEMENT that would include ALL THE BANKS, meaning the five offices of discount and deposit as well as the main bank in Philadelphia. After recording unrelated information about revenues, TJ used reports from the branches to draw up the comparative table that is the final component of the notes above. Although he called the table an *aperçu*—a quick overview—he apparently did not realize that the data he used for the balance sheet at the top of these notes, which he transposed to make the first line of his table

and labeled "Bank of the US.," actually already included figures from the branches as well as the bank in Philadelphia. This means that the assets and obligations of the primary bank alone, without the branches, were less than the figures appearing on each side of TJ's balance sheet. Also, the total for each column of TJ's table, with the obvious exception of the column for "undivided profits," is too high, in most cases by a significant amount. TJ finished the table no later than 11 Nov., since he copied it at the head of the letter he wrote to Gallatin on that day (James O. Wettereau, *Statistical Records of the First Bank of the United States* [New York, 1985], 3-5, 79-80, 114-15, 283-4, 288-9).

REVENUES IN 1800: in addition to the excise on distilled spirits, the country's internal revenues included a tax on AUCTIONS at the rate of a quarter dollar for every hundred dollars for land, farm equipment, farm stock, and ships, or a half dollar for every hundred dollars on anything else sold at auction; the tax on CARRIAGES; annual duties of five dollars each for LICENSES to sell wines or imported spirits at retail; a levy of two cents on every pound of SUGAR refined in the United States; and duties on the STAMPS the law required on several kinds of certificates and other documents (U.S. Statutes at Large, 1:373-5, 376-8, 384-90, 397-400, 527-32; ASP, *Finance*, 1:718-27).

From John Vaughan

DEAR SIR,   Philad: 10 Novr 1801—

Your very interesting letter of 5 Nov. I duely receivd & immediately gave into the hands of Dr Coxe, the Phial containing the Thread impregnated with the Vaccine Virus of which he has made immediate Use—The result will be communicated to you as soon as known—In Consequence of your request to procure Some of the Smallpox Virus—I applied to D Coxe, who has been fortunate enough to procure it from two patients of a very favorable kind—he Suggests, that it would add much to the Force of the Experiment, if Dr Gantt would inoculate some person who has not had either the Kine or the Small Pox—in order more fully to Satisfy as the quality of the Virus now Sent—& in order to be able to collect a larger quantity of it for Experiment, or for those who might still require Small Pox Innoculation—If Dr Gantt could without much Inconvenience send some of the Vaccine Virus in glass, as now sent, it would Dr Coxe says answer rather Better *for children*, than a thread—& will enable him to to extend the Innoculation which is very important at this Season, & particularly so, as the great number of medical Students here makes it desirable to familiarise them to it, in order the more Speedily to generalise its Introduction—

I have the pleasure of Sending you, by Directions of my Brother, a Copy of the Rural Socrates or Philosophic Farmer—You must be well acquainted with his Character, but will not yet have Seen So full an acct. of him—The Importance of the knowledge & Principles detailed in this Book, makes my Brother & myself desirous it should Circulate; it will be flattering to him to learn it meets with your approbation.

I remain with the highest respect Your ob. Serv.

Jn Vaughan

Altho' my brother Superintended the Publication he has avoided letting it be generally known, & has no kind of Interest in the Circulation, except his desire of promoting Useful knowledge

RC (DLC); at head of text: "His Excellency Thomas Jefferson"; in left margin of first page, perpendicular to text, in Vaughan's hand: "Dr Coxe is to furnish a further Supply to insure Success"; endorsed by TJ as received 13 Nov. and so recorded in SJL. For enclosure, see below.

Originally written in German by a Swiss man of letters, Hans Caspar Hirzel, THE RURAL SOCRATES was an account of the agricultural enthusiasms and practices of a Swiss peasant. Arthur Young prepared an English translation of the work from a French version, which he entitled "The Rural Socrates: Being Memoirs of A Country Philosopher" and published as an appendix to his *Rural Œconomy* (London, 1770). Benjamin Vaughan, John's brother, printed an American edition of the farmer's memoirs (*The Rural Socrates; or an Account of a Celebrated Philosophical Farmer, Lately Living in Switzerland, and Known by the Name of Kliyogg* [Hallowell, Maine, 1800]; Paul H. Johnstone, "The Rural Socrates," *Journal of the History of Ideas*, 5 [1944], 165-74; Sowerby, No. 705; Evans, No. 38923).

To Albert Gallatin

TH:J. TO MR GALLATIN   Nov. 11. 1801.

The bank statements are new to me and present curious information.
to obtain a general idea I have brought them together as above, very
inaccurately, omitting some items I did not understand, lumping others perhaps ill understood. but such an abstract accurately made
would be interesting. for this purpose it would require in the first
place a judicious form to be devised, and that sent to all the banks
with a request they would put their statements into that form. it
would then be easy to generalize every set of returns, & at the end of
the year to make an average from the whole: and why should not the
bottom line of the yearly average be presented to Congress? it would
give us the benefit of their & of the public observations, & betray no
secret as to any particular bank.

I inclose you a letter concerning Cherryston's of which I can make
little. the applications for monies due on appropriation may certainly
be omitted to be sent to me, as the effect appears in the weekly
abstract of warrants. those conveying information of *what is passing*,
or of *the state of things*, are the desireable. Dr. Tucker's coming into
office may be fixed for the 1st. day of December.   health & good
wishes.

RC (NHi: Gallatin Papers); with the
composite table of returns from the Bank
of the United States at head of text (see
below); addressed: "The Secretary of the
Treasury." PrC (DLC). Enclosure not
found.

I HAVE BROUGHT THEM TOGETHER AS
ABOVE: at the head of the text TJ reproduced the table he drew up from the
weekly balance sheets of the Bank of the
United States and its branches, the final
section of his Notes on the Bank of the
United States and Internal Revenues,
printed at 10 Nov.
On 14 Nov., Gallatin notified 11 banks
that the date of Thomas Tudor TUCKER'S

COMING INTO OFFICE had been set at 1
Dec. Gallatin ordered that on that date
the balance of the public monies in the
bank were to be transferred to the credit
of Tucker and "a Certificate, sign'd by the
Cashier, specifying the Amount of the
balance" was to be forwarded to the Treasury Department. Monies deposited with
the banks after 30 Nov. were to pass to the
credit of the new treasurer (Gallatin, *Papers*, 6:22). In printed circulars dated 16
Nov., Gallatin informed all revenue supervisors and customs collectors of Tucker's appointment and included instructions for implementing the change (same,
6:44-5).

From Edward Livingston

SIR   New York Novr. 11. 1801.

Immediately after the receipt of your letter I sent for the Gentlemen you mention and Stated to them the grounds of the proceeding alluded to; as being the result of some conversation with you on the Subject and now communicated to them at your request. I hope in this mode of answering their enquiries to have avoided the difficulty attending a direct communication on the Subject—

They had on Saturday commenced and are now continuing in their own way a series of papers on this Question which I think contain many more arguments than are necessary to its Solution. the Satisfactory answer could have been given in ten lines the substance of which they have promised me to introduce into some part of their reply—

The Charge however has not made the smallest impression in this quarter—and 'tho it has appeared in some paragraphs yet it is not insisted on as a topic even of party Declamations—

The opposition here calculate much more upon a Schism among us than on the Effect of any of their Attacks upon our measures—I am not quite free from apprehension on this Subject but yet have the fullest persuasion that the great mass of republicans will abandon the Leaders of defection the moment any connection or even intercourse with the fallen party should be discovered—

The appointment of Mr Tucker gives great Satisfaction here where he has been long known and[1] Esteemed—And that of Mr Granger can not fail to produce a good Effect in Connecticut while it gives an Excellent officer to a much neglected Department.

I beg you to believe Sir that I shall always Esteem myself favored by the Execution of any of your commands & that I am with the greatest personal attachment as well as the highest respect

Your Mo Obd Servt   EDWARD LIVINGSTON

RC (DLC); at foot of text: "The President of the United States"; endorsed by TJ as a letter of 4 Nov. received 15 Nov. and so recorded in SJL.

YOUR LETTER: TJ to Livingston, 1 Nov.

From 9 to 16 Nov., the *American Citizen and General Advertiser* published A SERIES OF PAPERS under the heading "Nolle Prosequi," which defended TJ's decision to halt the federal prosecution against William Duane. Countering the charges made by "Juris Consultus" in the *Gazette of the United States*, the articles in the *American Citizen* steadfastly upheld TJ's actions, asserting that "the president has a *constitutional right* to enter a Nolle Prosequi, by which a suit is suspended, *at discretion*" (New York *American Citizen and General Advertiser*, 9 Nov. 1801).

[1] MS: "an."

From Benjamin Nones

SIR,   Philadelphia 11th. November 1801.

I did myself the Honor of addressing you in March last, wherein I took the liberty of soliciting from you an Appointment under the General Governmt., shou'd I be so fortunate as to receive your Confidence and Attention. I enclosed you the Recommendation of some few of my Republican Friends, whose Esteem and Regard, I am happy to say, I have long been honor'd with. If it be necessary, I am ready to forward the Signatures, in my favour, of all the Republicans of the City of Philadelphia, to whom my Exertions and Sufferings in the common cause are not unknown. You will permit me, Sir, to observe, that, from a warm and ardent Attachment to the Rights and Liberties of America, I took an early and active part in that glorious revolution, which terminated in her Emancipation, and gave her rank among the independent Nations of the Earth. I entered into the American Army in the year 1776 and continued to serve untill the year 1780, when I was captured at Charleston in South Carolina.

I have been Nineteen Years settled with my family in Philadelphia. My principles have been uniform in the Cause of Republicanism. On account of my firm adherrence to these principles, during the political Changes which have taken place, my Interest has materially suffered. The commercial part of our Community to whose patronage I look for the Reward of my Industry in Business, have not been backward in declaring, that my political principles and Opposition to the Measures of Mr. Adams's Administration were such, that I shou'd never receive their Countenance or Support. Unable, from the Causes stated, to reap the just Rewards of my unremitted Industry, and urged by the Calls of my rising and extensive family, I feel persuaded that you will consider these as sufficient Apology for the Liberty I take of again addressing you upon the subject of my former Letter. It is with the most poignant pain I declare, that all my Exertions are almost incompetent to meet the present Expenses of my Family. If industry and Oeconomy and the Strictest attention to Business woul'd do, then indeed wou'd I feel myself completely happy.

Should you be pleased to bestow upon me any Appointment in which my services may be usefull to my Country, the Obligation will be acknowledg'd with the full force of Gratitude and I assure you, Sir, that I will use every Exertion, within the Limits of my power, to fulfill the Duties of the same with Credit to myself and Advantage to my Country.

Permit me again to refer you for a Knowledge of my Character and Conduct to my Friends Captain Wm. Jones and Doctor Leib, Representatives in Congress, to General John Shee, or the Governor of Pennsylvania.

Accept of my ardent Wishes for your Health and Happiness. I have the Honor to be with Sentiments of the higest Respect and Esteem,

Sir, Your most obt. hb. Servt.   BENJ. NONES

RC (DNA: RG 59, LAR); at foot of text: "The President of the United States"; endorsed by TJ as received 14 Nov. and so recorded in SJL; also endorsed by TJ: "to be in some office."

ADDRESSING YOU IN MARCH LAST: Nones to TJ, 18 Mch. 1801.

Notes on a Cabinet Meeting

Nov. 11. present the 4. Secretaries. qu. shall[1] Rogers be removd in N.Y.? unan. to let lie till Congress.

Qu. whether we shall proclaim the French treaty, or wait and lay it before the Senate? unan. not to proclaim but to say to Pichon we will go on with the exn.

MS (DLC: TJ Papers, 112:19297); entirely in TJ's hand; follows, on same sheet, Notes on a Cabinet Meeting of 22 Oct.

Louis André PICHON had written to Madison on 6 Nov., enclosing an extract of a communication from Talleyrand dated 4 Aug., which stated that the French government expected to name a minister to the United States when Robert R. Livingston appeared in France. Pichon, who was empowered to act as chargé d'affaires until a minister should arrive in the United States, was eager to inform his superiors of the U.S. government's intentions with regard to the execution of the Convention of 1800 (Madison, *Papers, Sec. of State Ser.,* 2:229-30).

[1] TJ here canceled "[Davies]."

To William Barton

DEAR SIR   Washington Nov. 12. 1801.

I have duly recieved your favor of Oct. 30. and the honour of your proposition to address to me your treatise on the law of nations. this proof of respect cannot but be flattering to one who entertains a sincere esteem for your person and character. the subject is important, involved in errors & contradictions, which, for the peace of the world, it[1] is very desireable to see rectified. but the want of a physical test whereby to try principles, and the passions & interests & power of the nations who are called to their bar, render that rectification very difficult. still every effort is laudable which goes to that object, and tends to promote it by increasing the mass of authorities which bear witness in it's favor. Accept my best wishes for the success of your work & assurances of my high esteem & respect. TH: JEFFERSON

RC (Sotheby's, 2008); at foot of text: "William Barton esq." PrC (DLC).

Barton's TREATISE was published in Philadelphia in 1802 with the title *A Dissertation on the Freedom of Navigation and Maritime Commerce, and Such Rights of States, Relative Thereto, as are Founded on the Law of Nations: Adapted More Particularly to the United States* (Sowerby, No. 2134; Shaw-Shoemaker, No. 1845). The dedication page reads: "To Thomas Jefferson, L.L.D. President of the United States of America; Eminently Distin-guished by his Talents and Virtues, and Rendered Still More Illustrious by the Approving Voice of his Country; the Following Dissertation is Inscribed, with Sentiments of the Highest Respect and the Greatest Personal Consideration, by The Author. Lancaster, in Pennsylvania; November, 1801." Barton sent TJ a copy of the book in February; see Barton to TJ, 20 Feb. 1802.

[1] TJ here canceled "were greatly to be."

From George Clymer

SIR/   Philadelphia Nov. 12. 1801

An inhabitant of this City, and of my own name, having made some important changes in the structure of the common forcing pump, proceeds with his invention, or improvement to Washington, where he will apply to the proper Officers, for a patent.

If he should presume, further, to offer his drawings, and specification to the inspection of the President, it will be, Sir, in Consequence of an Assurance I have ventured to give Mr. Clymer, from your philosophical taste, and the patronage you have always been ready to afford to the useful arts, that you will not be displeased with them, being, as they are thought here, the indications of a very considerable mechanical genius.—

I am, Sir, with the highest respect Your most obedt. servant

GEO CLYMER

RC (PHC); at foot of text: "President of the United States"; endorsed by TJ as received 21 Nov. and so recorded in SJL.

Clymer, a former merchant and a signer of the Declaration of Independence and of the Constitution, retired from public office after the Washington administration. Clymer's only previously recorded letter to TJ was dated 1 Sep. 1791 (ANB; Vol. 22:117).

Clymer wrote on behalf of inventor George E. Clymer, a native of Bucks County, Pennsylvania, who had recently moved to Philadelphia. On 22 Dec. 1801, the younger Clymer was awarded a U.S. PATENT for an "improvement in a ship's pump." Clymer created the device to clear cofferdams for the construction of the first permanent bridge across the Schuylkill River. Clymer is best known as the inventor of the Columbian printing press, a highly ornamented, cast-iron hand press introduced in England in 1817 (DAB; *List of Patents*, 26).

To Cornelius Coningham

SIR   Washington Nov. 12. 1801.

If the laws had permitted the application of the public money by way of loan to individuals suffering by unfortunate occurrences, I should have had great pleasure in administering relief against the untoward circumstances which render it desireable to yourself. but not a dollar can be applied but in conformity with an appropriation previously made by law, and rigorously exacted by the accounting officers. indeed your own good judgment will suggest to you how susceptable of abuse would be such a power of disposing of the public money, and how impossible to fix limits to the demands which would present themselves in that shape. these considerations will doubtless be a sufficient apology for the not doing in the present instance what you had deemed might be done. Accept my best wishes for your health & happiness.   TH: JEFFERSON

PrC (DLC); at foot of text: "Doctr. Cuningham."

Drafting the Annual Message to Congress

I. PRELIMINARY DRAFT: NATURALIZATION,
[BEFORE 12 NOV. 1801]

II. PARTIAL DRAFT: APPOINTMENTS AND POST OFFICE,
[BEFORE 12 NOV. 1801]

III. PARTIAL DRAFT: JUDICIARY, JURIES, AND NATURALIZATION,
[BEFORE 12 NOV. 1801]

IV. TO JAMES MADISON, 12 NOV. 1801

V. TO ALBERT GALLATIN, 14 NOV. 1801

VI. FROM ALBERT GALLATIN, [CA. 14-15 NOV. 1801]

VII. CALCULATION OF ANNUAL DEBT PAYMENT, [CA. 15 NOV. 1801]

VIII. FROM ALBERT GALLATIN, [ON OR BEFORE 16 NOV. 1801]

DRAFTING THE ANNUAL MESSAGE

EDITORIAL NOTE

Article 2, Section 3, of the Constitution specifies that the president "shall from time to time give to the Congress information of the state of the union." Washington and Adams performed the function by addressing Congress at the opening of the session in the fall. Adams gave his last such address on 22 Nov. 1800, soon after the convening of the second session of the Sixth Congress (Vol. 32:248). In the words of Noble Cunningham, Jefferson recognized that the annual communication to Congress was "a major vehicle of executive policymaking," both as a "principal means of influencing and directing legislative action" and as a policy statement to "the country at large." At the outset of his administration, however, Jefferson altered the form of the statement. Instead of appearing before both houses of Congress to deliver a speech, for his first annual report he determined to adopt the form of a written message, the mode used by Washington and Adams for communications to the legislative branch apart from the annual addresses. Jefferson abandoned the form of a "personal Address" in favor of reporting "by Message." When he asked Levi Lincoln to look over the message after more than two weeks of revision, he labeled it "the message on the state of the nation" (Cunningham, *Process of Government*, 72, 85; Malone, *Jefferson*, 4:92-3; TJ to the president of the Senate and the speaker of the House of Representatives, 8 Dec. 1801; Document XIV, below).

When Jefferson began writing the message is unknown. He may have had the annual report to Congress in mind when he wrote the middle part of the Notes on the Bank of the United States and Internal Revenues (printed at 10 Nov.). Other portions of that set of notes—the Notes on Circuit Court Cases, 12 Nov., the Notes on a Consultation with Robert Smith, 15 Nov., and the Notes on the Funded Debt, [15 Nov.]—appear to relate directly to the message (in the case of the tally of court cases) or might have played some role in its preparation. The earliest surviving remnant of his composition of the message appears to be a preliminary draft of the paragraph in which he suggested that Congress change the naturalization law (Document I). That draft is effectively an outline, consisting of notes of the sequence of an argument that he expected to develop. By the next stage of the drafting process of that paragraph—at least the next stage that is extant and known to us (see Document III)—he adopted a different line of argument and changed the language. There is overlap between the two versions only in the opening line, which in Document I is "recommend a revisal of the law respecting citizens" and in Document III is "I cannot omit recommendg. a revisal of the laws on the subject of Naturalization," which he retained as his final wording (Document XIII). He also found a place for the term "bona fide" in each version of the paragraph on naturalization.

Another undated draft in Jefferson's hand, Document II, lacks any overt tie to the 1801 annual message. The topics that Jefferson developed in Document II, an explanation of the situation regarding removals from office and a reference to "abusive conduct in the subordinate departments of the post office," do not appear in the finished annual message or in any of the cabinet members' remarks on the draft message. However, those subjects, which were relevant in 1801, were not pertinent to any subsequent annual message. It is likely, therefore, that Document II is an artifact of his early consideration of his first annual message. Two verbal clues, one at the beginning of the text and one at the end, suggest that he meant Document II to be part of a message to Congress. In the opening sentence, he addressed his "fellow citizens," a device that he employed in most of his annual messages (and an indication, perhaps, that he considered opening the message with Document II). The second clue is at the end of Document II, where he addressed Congress in the second person, referring to matters that "will probably be before you" and "will rest with you." Jefferson used similar diction several times in the 1801 message, such phrases for example as "to be laid before you," "that you may be enabled to judge," "occupy your attention," and "worthy your consideration" (Document XIII, sections on Economies; Fortifications; Agriculture, Manufactures, Commerce, Navigation; and Juries, respectively). He left a wide margin on Document II, allowing room for revisions, which is evidence that he considered it to be a draft, and he used several abbreviations in the text. The language of Document II also reflects an attempt to discover the right wording, as he experimented with such phrases as "claims of right," "temperature of mind," and "not unapprised," and tried different possibilities for "prevailed," "expediency" and "expedient," "exercise," and executive "will." The document's three paragraphs all end with incomplete sentences, each one stopping abruptly in the middle of a thought.

Document III is also a draft, with a broad margin and several changes of wording. Unlike Documents I and II, however, Document III has direct connections to the finished annual message of 1801. The topics covered by its three paragraphs—judiciary, juries, and the naturalization law—all appear in the annual message, in the same order, and much of the language of the draft appears in the later fair copy of the message (Document XIII). Although Document III is undated, it is on the verso of a page from Jefferson's draft of a message to the Senate about the prosecution of William Duane under the Sedition Act. When he sent that draft to Albert Gallatin on 12 Nov., he referred to "the sketches, on the back of it, of some paragraphs of the first message to Congress." This reference indicates that Jefferson drafted Document III by 12 Nov., and suggests that the contents of Document III were incorporated in the full text of the annual message that the president sent to James Madison on that day (see Document IV).

Although the contents of Documents I, II, and III, the surviving fragments of Jefferson's earliest drafting of the message, differ, they appear to illustrate stages of Jefferson's writing process. Document I is an outline, more concerned with the sequencing of ideas to make an argument than the development of specific phrasings. Development of particular language, on the other hand, was the function of Documents II and III. Those two drafts are similar, Jefferson structuring each of them with a wide margin and spending time over revisions of phrasing. Document II contains more abbreviations, and therefore appears more rudimentary than Document III, which includes the marginal headings that Jefferson used in the final version of the message (Document XIII).

For a model of participation by the cabinet in the creation of a president's annual communication to Congress, Jefferson could draw on his experience in George Washington's administration. In preparing his 1792 address, for example, Washington solicited advice from Jefferson as secretary of state, Alexander Hamilton as secretary of the Treasury, Henry Knox of the War Department, and Edmund Randolph as attorney general. Washington, however, asked for ideas even before beginning to draft the speech, and some of his advisers' suggestions included multiple paragraphs of proposed text. In 1792, also, Hamilton was the primary author of the address (Washington, *Papers, Pres. Ser.*, 11:342-51; Syrett, *Hamilton*, 12:558-66; Vol. 24:486, 552). Jefferson engaged his advisers in the creation of his message, but departed from Washington's example in significant ways. According to the surviving evidence, Jefferson composed his message himself, then asked his cabinet for suggestions to improve it. In his request to Madison on 12 Nov., he asked the secretary of state both to review the document and to begin the process of preparing the State Department's share of the supplementary papers they expected to send to Congress with the president's message. Unfortunately, no comments on the draft message by Madison, who was ill during some of the middle part of November, have survived. Jefferson's practice, at least in subsequent years, was to circulate the draft among the cabinet members in a particular order: first the State Department, then Treasury, War, and Navy (Cunningham, *Process of Government*, 74, 79). Jefferson sent the "rough draught" to Gallatin on 14 Nov. (Document V), but indicated that the sections dealing with the War Department were already "in unison" with Henry Dearborn's views. It may be that Jefferson still observed the formal sequence of referrals and had Dearborn look at the message sometime in the period from about 16 Nov. to about the 21st, which is to say between Gallatin's appraisal and that by Robert Smith of the Navy Department. Dearborn did supply some information relative to the message on the 17th (see note to Document X), which may mean that he saw a draft in that period, but no comments from him about the annual message have been found. Nor, in Dearborn's case, have we located any correspondence between him and Jefferson concerning a review of the text.

Since we have found no intermediate stages of the text between Document III, which existed by 12 Nov., and Document XIII, a revised fair copy that could date from as late as the 27th, it is not known if the text seen by Gallatin was identical to what Jefferson referred to Madison on the 12th. Nevertheless, Gallatin's comments on the text (Document IX) provide a shadow of the contents of an early state of the message. From Gallatin's remarks and Document III, one can infer that the structure of the annual message, arranged in sections on topics such as "Indians," "Finances," and "Judiciary," did not change during revisions. Keying his comments to Jefferson's text using extracts from the draft, Gallatin left evidence of a few instances in which Jefferson changed or deleted phrasing in subsequent revisions. Gallatin's remarks appear to echo language that Jefferson subsequently altered or dropped: "foreign powers friendly," "we may safely calculate on a certain augmentation," "calamities," "taxes on stamps &a. may be immediately suppressed," "Oeconomies in civil list," "foreign intercourse," "communicate an account of receipts &a also appropriations," and "few harbours in the U.S. offer &a." The president did not take up Gallatin's suggestion that he mention Rufus King's negotiations with the British over a lump-sum settlement of claims under the Jay Treaty or the talks in progress with Indian tribes. On the other hand, Jefferson's call in the message to "multiply barriers" against wasting money and to give the Treasury Department oversight of all expenditures surely resulted from Gallatin's study of the draft. It seems likely that Jefferson bolstered the "Tripoli" section in accordance with the Treasury secretary's suggestions (Document XIII).

Judging from the exchanges between Gallatin and Jefferson on the subjects of finance, appropriations, and economy measures (Documents VI through X), those portions of the message probably received heavy alteration and substantive changes between the earlier and later states of the text. In an undated letter received by Jefferson on 14 or 15 Nov. (Document VI), Gallatin informed the president that some of the supplementary documents on receipts and expenditures that Jefferson had expected to marry to his annual message would need to accompany, instead, the Treasury secretary's report to Congress. Gallatin also asked Jefferson how he would compute the annual payment required to eliminate a portion of the debt over eight years. Jefferson's calculations in response to that request are printed as Document VII. During the middle part of November, Gallatin labored to collect information, forecast revenues to be anticipated from import duties and internal taxes, and propose changes to the system of accounting for expenditures.

The placement of Document XI, an undated letter asking Madison to look over some revised version of the message, is by necessity conjectural. It could have been written anytime after the initial referral of the draft to the secretary of state on the 12th, and may have come at the end of the reviewing process, after Jefferson wrote out the fair copy. However, Jefferson's second request for an evaluation from Madison may have followed a reworking of the message based on the information and suggestions from Gallatin in the middle of the month, and for that reason the undated letter to Madison appears in the sequence below as Document XI. As noted above, there is no record of an analysis of the message by Dearborn, but the usual sequencing of the executive departments would put such a review between Gallatin's and Smith's, and there is a convenient time interval that would allow for consideration of the message by Dearborn before it went to Smith. The president received Smith's comments on 21 Nov. (Document XII), although no letter from Jefferson asking Smith for his comments, nor any note in return from Smith accompanying his remarks, has been found or is recorded in SJL. If Gallatin's remarks give a few clues about the early stages of the draft, Smith's reflect the middle state of the text. In keeping with what Jefferson asked of Madison, Gallatin, and later Lincoln (Documents IV, V, XI, and XIV), we can assume that he requested Smith not to write his remarks on the draft itself, and to separate substantive comments from those concerning grammar.

Smith complied, putting his comments into a form similar to what Gallatin, and later Lincoln, followed, keying his remarks and queries to particular spots in the text and setting apart those comments that were "*Verbal merely*" (Document XII).

Comparing Smith's page references to the pages of the fair copy makes evident that Smith saw a draft very similar to Document XIII in length, structure, and ordering of topics. It was not the same manuscript, though, for Smith's comments, like Gallatin's, refer to wording that disappeared before the text reached its final state. For example, Smith suggested that in one spot Jefferson should say "*weeks*" instead of "a few *days*," but neither term appears in the fair copy. The same is true of other phrasing Smith cited, including his suggestion of "*prevent*," apparently in place of "lessen" in "lessen like evils." In the end Jefferson eliminated the phrase. Yet in many respects the wording of Document XIII resembles what Smith saw, and the passage "especially that portion of it recently erected," in the section on the judiciary, remained intact from the first draft (see Document III) to the final version despite Smith's recommendation to remove it. The section on Tripoli in Document XIII reflects some of the language and sequencing of the passage at the beginning of Smith's remarks, although it is not clear if Smith was reworking a passage that was already in the draft or offering something entirely new. Similarly, in the "Finances" section of the fair copy, the expression "taxing the industry of our fellow citizens to accumulate treasure for wars to happen we know not when" may be Jefferson's moderate reworking of wording that was originally Smith's: "taxes for the purpose of accumulating a Treasure for wars to happen we know not when" (Documents XII, XIII).

Without the draft seen by Smith or any earlier version of the full message, it is difficult to know if the phrasing of those passages was all Smith's, or his suggested recasting of Jefferson's language. There can be little doubt, however, that the version of the text reviewed by Levi Lincoln was the fair copy, Document XIII. In Lincoln's remarks (Document XV), references to pages and lines correlate with the manuscript of the fair copy. Moreover, Jefferson clearly inserted a sentence about postage fees on newspapers in response to a suggestion from Lincoln (see Document XIII, note 1). Since Lincoln saw the fair copy, we know that it existed by 27 Nov., the day Jefferson asked for Lincoln's comments (Document XIV). The attorney general was not the head of a department or always in attendance at cabinet meetings. Lincoln was in Massachusetts on 24 Oct. and was probably not back in Washington during the early reviews of the draft message. The president referred the message to him late in the process, and although Jefferson made the request on the 27th, we do not know when he received Lincoln's remarks.

Jefferson intended Document XIII to be a finished copy. It lacks the roomy margin he left on Documents II and III in anticipation of potentially extensive revisions. He also wrote the fair copy in a careful script and made relatively frugal changes to it. Document XIII was, with those last revisions, the finished version of the annual message. It became the copy text for the message as it was sent to Congress, and for that purpose Jefferson, after the conclusion of the drafting process, signed it and added the date 8 Dec. 1801. The text he transmitted to Congress will be printed at that date in the next volume.

The fair copy contains one significant passage omitted from the message received by Congress. That deletion was the paragraph on the Sedition Act, in which Jefferson declared the law unconstitutional and twice called it a "nullity." He did not obliterate the paragraph in the fair copy, but simply made a marginal note about its excision (Document XIII, note 9). The most extensive change he made to the fair copy was a three-sentence insertion to the section on the Sedition Act (see Document XIII, note 11), which suggests that he did not decide to drop that paragraph until very late in the drafting process. Although early full drafts of the message have not survived, there is evidence of some evolution of the section on the Sedition Act during the cabinet members' assessments of the drafts. When Gallatin saw that section, it contained multiple paragraphs, including a "doubtful" one about "compensation to sufferers" under the act, and apparently Jefferson had suggested that there had not originally been a majority in the Senate in favor of the bill (see Document IX). Smith made no mention of the sedition law itself, but raised several questions about a passage in reference to nolle prosequi (see Document XII; since the manuscript Smith saw was similar to Document XIII in arrangement and length, his reference to nolle prosequi on page 6 of the draft he saw corresponds with the beginning of the Sedition Act section in Document XIII). There is no mention of nolle prosequi in the fair copy, and on 27 Nov., when Jefferson sent the message to Lincoln for review, he mentioned a distinct "message to the Senate respecting the Nolle prosequi" (Document XIV). Jefferson seems to have had a separate message to the Senate in mind on the 12th, when he sent Gallatin the draft of one, but only from Smith's queries do we know that the term nolle prosequi, presumably in relation to William Duane and the Sedition Act, appeared in the early states of the annual message. Jefferson evidently altered that part of the message throughout the revision process, and he continued to change it very late, as shown by his insertion in the fair copy. But in the end he removed the section on the Sedition Act. His doing so is the most prominent evidence of the serious consideration he gave his advisers' suggestions (Cunningham, *Process of Government*, 75-6).

The process of writing and revising the 1801 annual message began sometime before 12 Nov. and continued for more than fifteen days. It seems unlikely that the manuscript seen by Robert Smith, which differed from Document XIII, was the same document that Jefferson first referred to James Madison on the 12th. Plausibly, then, there were at least three major stages: the draft of 12 Nov., a revision several days later after Jefferson's intensive work with Gallatin, and the final version that Jefferson finished by the 27th, passed under Lincoln's eye, and then gave a last polishing. There could have been intermediate steps as well. Since the only surviving evidence of Jefferson's direct work on the annual message is the early drafting shown by Documents I through III and his changes to the fair copy, much must be left to inference. Fortunately Gallatin's, Smith's, and Lincoln's comments and the exchanges of very detailed information between Jefferson and Gallatin give impressions of the now-missing states of the text and display something of the revision process. From this record it appears that the president, although retaining to himself the principal authorship of the message, included all the heads of executive departments in the procedure and adopted some, but not all, suggestions offered by each adviser.

I. Preliminary Draft: Naturalization

[before 12 Nov. 1801]

recommend a revisal of the law respecting citizens.

every man has a right to live somewhere on the earth. and if somewhere, no one society has a greater right than another to exclude him.[1] becoming indeed a member of any society, he is bound to conform to the rules formed by the majority. but has the majority a right to subject him to unequal rules, to rules from which they exempt themselves. I hazard these suggestions[2] for the considn of Congress.

the only rightful line is between transient persons & bona fide citizens[3]

Dft (DLC: TJ Papers, 155:27102); entirely in TJ's hand; undated.

[1] TJ first wrote "no one nation has a greater right to exclude him than" before altering the passage to read as above.

[2] Preceding three words interlined in place of "suggest these considns."

[3] Above this word TJ interlined "residents" without canceling the original word.

II. Partial Draft: Appointments and Post Office

[before 12 Nov. 1801]

You are not unapprised, fel. cit, of the differences of opn which prevaild among our citizens as to the proceedings of the govmt, legislative & Exec; and that all offices were given exclusively to those who[1] thought with the govmt. when I was called to administer the Exve functions,[2] rigorous justice would have required that the proscribed party constituting in fact the bulk of the nation should have been restored to at least an equal participn of office. in the greater no of the states however, the desire to see[3] harmony & the friendly affections restored to society prevailed over a sense of injury,[4] & produced an acquiescence in the existing slate of office until the ordinary course of accidents might introduce them quietly into that participation of the honors & trusts of their country to which they were justly entitled. in these states few or no removals have taken place. in other parts of the union however where the conflict of opn had been higher, & the temperature of the public mind proportionably warmer, the claims of right were less yielding, & expediency as well as justice called on me to exercise this painful duty.[5] in order that there might be the less to do, I thought it expedient to refuse[6] office to the nomi-

nations made in the last moments[7] of the preceding admn. these comprehended nearly the whole ground of our foreign affairs, an important portion of the judiciary, besides other important offices. most of
these being[8] to enter into office at the same time with the new admn.
it was thought[9] but reasonable that the admn should appoint for itself. this was accdly done with the greater part of those who[10] depended on the Exve will. exclusive of these, the whole removals not
to be dispensed with have been[11] but of about   of the very numerous officers depending on the will of the Exve. moderate as this
exercise of the power appmt has been, I know it has given uneasiness
to some of[12] our best intentioned citizens, who residing in the parts
of the union where the passions had not
were not apprised that a different temperature of mind required in
other states a different treatmt. this opern being once performed it is
trusted that no other circumstance will arise to obstruct that concilia-
tory process which I am[13] sincerely desirous to
one thing indeed is still to be noted. the complaints of abusive conduct in the subordinate departments of the post office, are too multiplied, too well founded, not to command attention. great changes
must inevitably be made in that departmt. before the public confidce
can be restored. as the reguns of that office will probably be before
you; it will rest with you to consider whether

MS (DLC: TJ Papers, 233:41779);
entirely in TJ's hand, with a wide margin
for revisions; undated.

FEL. CIT: "fellow citizens." TJ addressed the Senate and House by this
phrase in all but one of his annual messages, omitting it only in 1805 (annual
messages of 15 Dec. 1802, 17 Oct. 1803, 8
Nov. 1804, 3 Dec. 1805, 2 Dec. 1806, 27
Oct. 1807, and 8 Nov. 1808; Document
XIII below).

The emphasis on REMOVALS and on
TJ's refusal to carry through with
Adams's late NOMINATIONS implies that
this partial draft is from 1801.

IT WILL REST WITH YOU TO CONSID-
ER: TJ repeatedly addressed Congress directly in the 1801 annual message, and
the wording he used in this partial draft is
resonant of such phrases as "that you may
judge of the additions still requisite" and
"as you shall think proper to adopt" (see
Document XIII).

[1] TJ here canceled "concurred."

[2] TJ here canceled "I was sensible."

[3] TJ first wrote "however, such was the
desire of our fel. cit. to see."

[4] Above the preceding three words TJ
interlined "the claim of right" without
canceling the original phrase.

[5] TJ here canceled "it has been done
to the least extent which circumstances
admitted."

[6] TJ here canceled "entrance into."

[7] TJ first wrote "the last nominations
of the preceding admn." before altering
the passage to read as above.

[8] Word interlined in place of "were."

[9] TJ here canceled "therefore."

[10] Word interlined in place of
"nominns which."

[11] TJ first wrote "removals have not
been" before altering the clause to read as
above.

[12] Preceding two words interlined.

[13] TJ here canceled "anxious to."

III. Partial Draft:
Judiciary, Juries, and Naturalization

[before 12 Nov. 1801]

Judiciary.   The Judiciary system of the US. and especially that portion of it recently erected will of course[1] present itself to the contemplation of Congress; and that they may judge[2] of the proportion which the institution bears to the business it has to perform, I have caused to be procured from the several states and now lay before Congress[3] an exact statement of all the cases decided since the first establishment of the courts, and of those which were depending when addnl courts & judges were brought in to their aid.[4]

And while on the Judiciary organization it will be worthy of your consideration[5] whether the protection of the inestimable instn[6] of juries has been extended to all the cases involving the security of our persons & property; and especially where fine & imprisonment are inflicted as a punishment, & the sum or time not precisely fixed by law, whether it's assesment by a jury may not be a necessary barrier against systematic obliquities, more dangerous to the genius of our government than the anomalous errors which juries may sometimes commit.

Naturalization laws.   I cannot omit recommendg. a revisal of the laws on the subject of Naturalization. considering the ordinary chances of human life, a denial[7] of citizenship under a residence of 14. years is a denial to the greater number. but this is directly opposite[8] to the fundamental policy of the great portion of these states from their first settlement. and shall we in times when[9] war and desolation are afflicting the other quarters of the earth refuse to their unhappy[10] fugitives that hospitality which the savages of the wilderness extended to our fathers arriving in this land. shall oppressed humanity find no asylum on this globe?[11] safety indeed may dictate[12] that, for admission to offices of important trust, a residence should be required long enough to develope character & design. some length of residence too may be necessary to guard against fraudulent usurpations of our flag. but the ordinary rights and capabilities of a citizen, & especially that of transmitting inheritance, might surely be extended without danger to every one manifesting a bona fide purpose of[13] embarking his life and fortunes permanently with us.

Dft (DLC: TJ Papers, 119:20569); entirely in TJ's hand, canceled with a single diagonal stroke; undated; first two paragraphs written with a wide margin for revisions; third paragraph written in a smaller hand and running across the width of the page to make full use of the available space; on verso of TJ's draft message to the Senate, [ca. 12 Nov. 1801], which was enclosed in TJ to Gallatin, 12 Nov.

The LAWS ON THE SUBJECT OF NATU-RALIZATION then in effect were "An Act to establish an uniform rule of Natural-ization" of January 1795 and a supple-mentary and amending act of 18 June 1798. The earlier act required a resi-dence of two years in the United States before an immigrant could become a cit-izen. The 1798 law, passed in the same session of Congress as the Alien Friends Act and Alien Enemies Act, imposed a residency requirement of 14 years before an alien could attain citizenship, allow-ing exceptions for people who had initi-ated the process under the older law (U.S. Statutes at Large, 1:414-15, 566-69; Vol. 30:301n, 324n).

FRAUDULENT USURPATIONS OF OUR FLAG: that is, misrepresentation of for-eign ships as American owned. TJ as sec-retary of state warned U.S. consular and diplomatic officers in March 1793 to guard against this problem in order "to preserve for our vessels all the rights of neutrality" in the event of the impending "very general war in Europe." "This usurpation," TJ advised, "tends to com-mit us with foreign nations, to subject those vessels truly ours to rigorous scruti-nies and delays to distinguish them from

counterfeits, and to take the business of transporation out of our hands" (Vol. 25:365, 415-16, 426-7, 435, 439).

[1] Preceding two words interlined in place "certainly."
[2] TJ first wrote "and in order that they may be able to judge" before altering the passage to read as above.
[3] Preceding five words interlined.
[4] TJ first wrote "in them on the day of last when the additional courts & judges it has been thought necessary to add other courts & judges <for> came in to their aid" before altering the passage to read as above.
[5] TJ first wrote "And while on the Ju-diciary functions, I recommend earnestly to their consideration the state of the laws on the subject of fines & imprisonments."
[6] Preceding five words interlined in place of "interposition," with "ines-timable" replacing "precious."
[7] Here and later in the sentence, TJ in-terlined "denial" in place of "refusal."
[8] TJ here reworked "in direct opposi-tion" to read as above.
[9] TJ here canceled "violence."
[10] Word interlined in place of "wretched."
[11] Question interlined.
[12] Word interlined in place of "re-quire."
[13] TJ here canceled "committing," and "bona fide" is interlined in place of "fixed."

IV. To James Madison

TH:J. TO J.M.   Nov. 12. 1801.

Will you give this inclosed a serious revisal, not only as to matter, but diction? where strictness of grammar does not weaken expres-sion, it should be attended to in complaisance to the purists of New England. but where by small grammatical negligences, the energy of an idea is condensed, or a word stand for a sentence, I hold gram-matical rigor in contempt. I will thank you to expedite it, and to con-sider, as you go along, in the documents promised, which of them go from your office, & to have them prepared in duplicate, with a press copy of one of the duplicates for me.

Genl. Hurd's commission is still wanting.

The inclosed letter &c. from Read was sent me by mr Gallatin. I inclose it[1] merely that you may have your eye on the establishment of those agents. be so good as to return it immediately to mr Gallatin.

PrC (DLC). Enclosure not found.   [1] TJ here canceled "for."

V. To Albert Gallatin

Nov. 14. 1801.

Th: Jefferson asks the favor of mr Gallatin to examine the inclosed rough draught of what is proposed for his first communication to Congress: not merely the part relating to finance but the whole. several[1] paragraphs are only provisionally drawn, to be altered or omitted according to further information. the whole respecting finance is predicated on a general view of the subject, presented according to what I wish, but subject to the particular consultation which Th:J. wishes to have with mr Gallatin, and especially to the calculation proposed to be made as to the adequacy of the impost to the support of govmt & discharge of the public debt, for which mr G. is to furnish correct materials for calculation. the part respecting the navy has not yet been opened to the Secretary of the Navy. what belongs to the deptmts of state & war, is in unison with the ideas of those gentlemen.   Th:J. asks the favor of mr Gallatin to devote the first moments he can spare to the inclosed, and to make notes on a separate paper with pencilled references at the passages noted on.   health & happiness.

RC (NHi: Gallatin Papers); addressed: "The Secretary of the Treasury"; endorsed by Gallatin, who also used the address sheet for calculations related to Document VII. PrC (DLC).

[1] TJ here canceled "articles."

VI. From Albert Gallatin

DEAR SIR   [ca. 14-15 Nov. 1801]

Mr Nourse acts, & has for ten years acted, as agent for the disbursements of this department for contingent expences amounting during that period to about 100,000 dollars. On settlement of his accounts there is a deficiency of 202 dollars, arising either from some expence not entered, or for which he had neglected to take a voucher, or from some voucher lost. He thinks it hard, as this was a kind of extra-duty that he should lose the money; and it is proposed that it should be allowed to him in a separate account, as a grant for his *trouble* in the business (not as compensation for monies lost or for a supposed expense for which he cannot account, as the precedent is considered as dangerous) to be paid out of the fund for unprovided claims. If I shall authorize the allowance the accounting officers will pass the account. It is not perfectly regular; yet I feel inclined to do it. Will you favour me with your opinion?

No letters received by last mail.

I have found so much difficulty in arranging or rather procuring correct statements amongst the Treasury documents, that I cannot yet give any probable[1] estimate of the revenue within half a million— of course cannot give any opinion of the propriety of[2] abolishing the internal revenues; but I am clearly of opinion they should all go or all remain. It would not be worth while to preserve the excise alone at such monstrous expence & inconvenience as the collection now costs. The two documents of "receipts & expenditures" for 1800 & of "estimates for 1802" cannot accompany your message, as they are directed by positive resolutions of the house to be laid yearly before them by the Secretary. But as they must be supposed to have been communicated by him to you, they may with propriety be referred to in the message. They are matters of form, prepared by the Register, & to which for the present year I have concluded to make no alteration in point of form.

If possible, I will on Tuesday lay before you general results sufficient to give you all the information you may want in relation to the general views you intend exhibiting in the message. But, in the mean while, could you calculate what will be the annual sum wanted to pay the interest on and pay off,[3] within eight years, a debt of 21,955,900 having an interest of $1,310,401.\frac{50}{100}$: it being promised that Dollars 6,481,700 part of the said debt bears an interest of 8 p% & must be paid the last, and that 950,965 dollars of the debt are already paid out of the Treasury, but without stopping the interest. If three millions will do, I think we can with the impost & lands, pay off *38* millions within the eight years 1802-1809. The total amount of unredeemed debt on 1st Jany. 1802 will be $77,866,402\frac{63}{100}$ of which we shall have already remitted to Holland the above stated sum of 950,965 dollars—The reduction or rather abolition of internal revenues will necessarily depend on the extent of the navy establisht.

I will give a first reading tomorrow to the sketch of the message & write some notes; but I cannot pay to it the proper attention till after

Tuesday & will of course return it Monday morning, with a wish to see it afterwards once more.

Respectfully Your most obedt. Servt.   ALBERT GALLATIN

You will be pleased to return the sheet of weekly balances.

RC (DLC); undated; addressed: "The President of the United States"; endorsed by TJ as received from the Treasury Department on 15 Nov. and "Nourse's accts. finance" and so recorded in SJL, but as a letter received 14 Nov.

ESTIMATES FOR 1802: in an undated, one-page document endorsed by Gallatin as a "Sketch of appropriations & expenditures for year 1802 other than those for public debt" and "also of intended savings & of intended annual expence resulting therefrom," the Treasury secretary indicated, in list form, how he proposed to reduce the annual expenditure of $3,700,000 to $2,450,000, the public debt excepted, for a savings of $1,250,000. Gallatin cut the civil list by $126,500, the army by $455,000, and the navy by $508,000, accounting for the major savings. Organizing the proposed expenditure of $2,450,000 for 1802 under "heads in round numbers," Gallatin allowed $490,000 for the civil list, $160,000 for miscellaneous, and $200,000 for foreign intercourse for a subtotal of $850,000; and $660,000 for the army, $270,000 for arms and fortifications, $70,000 for the Indian depart-

ment, and $600,000 for the navy for a subtotal of $1,600,000 for military and related expenditures. Below the endorsement, Gallatin wrote: "Mr G. requests the President to return this paper after he shall have examined it—It is only a rough sketch so far as relates to *savings*, but with the exception of the items 'Barbary powers' 'fabrication of arms' 'light houses' '2d census' & 'Quarantine laws' the estimate of appropriations is in conformity to existing laws & estimates furnished by the several departments" (MS in NHi: Gallatin Papers, entirely in Gallatin's hand, see Gallatin, *Papers*, 6:36; Tr in DLC: TJ Papers, 118:20417, in Meriwether Lewis's hand, lacks Gallatin's endorsement and notation). Gallatin increased the estimate of expenditures for 1802 to almost $3,500,000 in his 12 Dec. report, which was laid before the House of Representatives on the 14th (see Gallatin to TJ, 7 Dec. 1801).

[1] Preceding word interlined.
[2] Preceding two words interlined in place of "reduction."
[3] Preceding two words interlined in place of "redeem."

VII. Calculation of Annual Debt Payment

[ca. 15 Nov. 1801]

A debt of 21,955,900. D bearing an interest of 1,310,401.50 is to be paid in 8. years, by eql. annl. paimts.

what is the annual paiment?

if the interest were uniform, it would be of 6. pr. cent wanting an insensible fraction.

but   6,481,700. D. bears an interest of 8. p. cent, =   518,536.

then $\underline{15,474,200.}$ D. must be at $5\frac{117}{1000}$ p. cent $= \underline{791,865.50}$
       21,955,900.   1,310,401.50

in problems of this kind 4. things are material the annuity   a.

rate of int.   r.
time or no. of years. t.
amount to be paid   z.

any three of these being given, the 4th. can be found. but[1] from 2 only given, 2 cannt be found.

the present question divides itself into two. viz

what annual sum would pay 15,474,200. D @ $5\tfrac{117}{1000}$ p. cent so soon
> that

the same annual sum would pay 6,481,700. D @ 8 p. cent by the end of the 8th. year?

it is evident that here neither the time nor amount is fixed for either proposition.

in that form it is insoluble then. but we may solve it nearly enough for our purpose by assigning an uniform & equivalent interest, to wit, of 6. per cent to the whole, which gives us the time 8. years. and consequently we have then 3. things to wit the amount, rate, and time: required the 4th. which is the annual sum.

21,955,900. + 10,483,212. interest for 8. years at 6. p.c. makes the whole amt to be paid 32,439,112.

then   z. =   32,439,112.

        r   =   1.06

        t   =   8.

required a.

the equation of the case is that $a = \dfrac{z \times \overline{r-1}}{r^t-1}$ or by Logarithms Log.

a = Log. z + Log. $\overline{r-1}$ – Log. r^t–1

Log. of 32,439,112   is   7.5110686

Log. of r. or 1.06   is   0.0253059

Log of r–1 or 0.06   is   8.7781513

Log of r^t= Log. r x t = Log. r x 8 = 0.2024472 which is

Log. of   1.593848 = r^t
–1.
.593848 = r^t–1

Log. of r^t–1 or .593848 = 9.7736753

the Logarithms being stated the operation of the theorem is

Log. of z.   7.5110688

+ Log. of $\overline{r-1}$ 8.7781513

              16.2892201

– Log. of r^t–1   9.7736753

gives Log. a.   6.5155448 which is the Log. of 3,277,516. Dol.

the annual sum required.

[625]

it is stated that 950,965. D. of the 21,955,900. have been paid out of the treasury, but without stopping the interest: but for how long the interest has been unstopped is not mentioned: consequently we cannot say how much of 950,965 D. will be absorbed by the interest of the remainder, which remainder alone with 8. years interest should have been deducted from 32,439,112. at the commencement of the operation. but ascertaining how much of the 950,965. is absorbed as interest for the residuum of that sum, the following operation of the rule of three will give the effect it should have on the annual sum 3,277,516. above stated. to wit

As 32,439,112 : 3,277,516 :: 950,965 – the portion of it absorbed by interest + 8. years int. on that[2] : a 4th. number which will be the annual sum which the previous paiment of the 950,965 defalcates from the 3,277,516.

MS (NHi: Gallatin Papers); entirely in TJ's hand; undated, but likely written after TJ received Document VI and before Gallatin wrote Document VIII. PrC (DLC: TJ Papers, 118:20294).

TJ owned books that dealt with the problem of figuring an ANNUITY. One of them, by his friend Richard Price, devoted a chapter to "Public Credit, and the National Debt" (Richard Price, *Observations on Reversionary Payments*, 2d ed. [London, 1772], 135-65; Francis Maseres, *The Principles of the Doctrine of Life-Annuities* [London, 1783]; Sowerby, Nos. 3688, 3689).

[1] TJ here canceled "in the present [case]."

[2] TJ interlined "+ 8. years int. on that."

VIII. From Albert Gallatin

DEAR SIR   [on or before 16 Nov. 1801]
I enclose some hasty remarks on the message—
    The incorrectness of the documents of exports of foreign articles compels me after much labour to abandon the plan on which I had intended to calculate the impost and, as the next best, I will prepare one in the following form which rests on documents on which we may depend, being those of duties & drawbacks actually paid. For each of the ten years ending 31 Decr. 1800, I will take the quantity of each article paying specific duties, & the value of each class of articles, paying distinct duties ad valorem, on which duties were secured; deduct from each respective article & class the quantity & value respectively on which drawbacks have been allowed; and take the difference for the quantity & value of each article consumed in the U. States. On each of those articles, I will calculate the duties at the rate *now* estab-

lished by law. The result will give the revenue which would have been collected each year on each article, had the duties been the same as at present; and the total divided by ten, will show the average revenue of the ten years 1791-1800 at the present rate of duties. And, adding to this, $33\frac{1}{3}$ p%, the amt. of encrease of population in ten years as given by the census, the result will be assumed as the probable average revenue of the ten succeeding years 1801-1810 or 1802-1809; these being the eight years to which it is eligible that the calculations should apply. This will be but a rough estimate; and yet, I cannot perceive any way from our documents to render it more correct, unless it be to subtract from the total amount assumed as the consumption of the ten years 1791-1800, that part of the importations of 1800 not re-exported in the same year[1] which will, at first view, appear to be above the roughly estimated consumption of that year. The great defect of that mode arises from its including the duties on exported articles which, although not entitled to drawback, made no part of our consumption, and these might have been deducted, had the returns of actual foreign exports had[2] been correct & properly distinguished. A deduction at random might be made but then it would be as well to guess at the whole. Does any idea strike you which might lead to a better mode of making the calculation? Unless we have something precise, we never can with safety recommend a repeal of existing taxes.

Although I could not solve it, I thought that the problem of the annuity necessary to redeem the debt might be solved, because, although there were two unknown data vizt. the annuity & the time of redemption of *one of the classes* of debt (the time of the other class being 8–t) yet two equations might be formed, one term of each of which being the annuity, left an equation, with only the time, not given. At all events the approximation you have assumed is not sufficiently correct; for the annuity you fixed would, if I am not mistaken leave about one million & half unpaid at the end of the eight years. But the problem is, in fact, more complex than I had stated it, on account of the varieties & peculiar properties of the several kinds of debt, as you will judge by the enclosed statement.

If we cannot with the probable amount of impost & sale of lands pay the debt at the rate proposed & support the establishments on the proposed plans, one of three things must be done; either to continue the internal taxes—or to reduce the expenditure still more—or to discharge the debt with less rapidity. The last resource, to me, is the most objectionable, not only because I am firmly of opinion that, if the present administration & Congress do not take the most effective measures for that object, the debt will be entailed on us & the ensuing generations, together with all the systems which support it & which it supports; but also because any sinking fund operating in an increased ratio as it progresses, a very small deduction from an appropriation for that object would make a considerable difference in the ultimate term of redemption, which, provided we can, in some shape, manage the 3 p% without redeeming them at their nominal value, I think may be fixed at 14 or 15 years. On the other hand, if this administration shall not reduce taxes, they never will be permanently reduced; to strike at the root of the evil, & avert[3] the danger of encreasing taxes, encroaching government, temptations to offensive wars &a., nothing can be more effectual than a repeal of *all* internal taxes; but let them all go, & not one remain on which sister taxes may be hereafter engrafted. I agree most fully with you that pretended tax-preparations, treasury-preparations, & army preparations against contingent wars tend only to encourage wars; if the U. States shall unavoidably be drawn into a war, the people will submit to any necessary tax, & the system of internal taxation, which, *then*, shall be thought best adapted to the then situation of the country may be created, instead of being engrafted on the old or present plan; if there shall be no real necessity for them, their abolition by this administration will most powerfully deter any other from reviving them. A repeal now will attach as much unpopularity to them as the late direct tax has done to that mode of taxation. On those grounds, can I ask what, in your opinion, is the minimum of necessary[4] naval & foreign intercourse expenses, including in these last all those which are under the controul of the department of State?

You will perceive in one of the notes on the message that in giving general results, no provision appears for the British treaty vizt. for the St. 600,000 proposed to be paid in lieu of the 6th. Art.—This is a temporary demand which may be met by the four following temporary resources—1st the excess of specie in Treasury beyond the necessary sum to be kept there—2d the sale of the Bank shares belonging to the U. States—3d the surplus revenue arising from internal taxes beyond the expense, in case those int. taxes are [continued?], and if practicable to discontinue them, one nett year of their proceeds which is always due on them & will be due on the day when they may cease—4th the balance of the direct tax payable[5] after the present year.

You will also see that I lay less stress on savings on the civil list than you do: Some may be made, but the total amount cannot be great. The new judiciary, the Commissrs. of loans, the mint, the accountants of the navy & war departments seem to be the principal if not only objects of reforms. Of the clerks I cannot yet say much; those of the Comptroller & Auditor are less numerous & paid less in proportion than those of the Register & two accountants. Transcribing & common ones are easily obtained; good book-keepers are also every where to be found; but it is difficult to obtain faithful examining clerks on whose correctness & fidelity a just settlement of all the accounts depends; & still more difficult to find men of talents. My best clerk next to the principal & who had 1200 dollars has left me to take 1000 in Philadelphia. Under the present circumstances of this place we must calculate on paying higher all the inferior officers principally clerks, than in Philad. Coming all new in the administn., the heads of departt. must obtain a perfect knowledge of all the details before they can venture on a reform. The number of independent offices attached to the Treasury renders the task still more arduous for me. I can assure you that it will take me 12 months before I can thoroughly understand every detail of all those several offices. Current business & the more general & important duties of the office, do not permit to learn the lesser details but incidentally & by degrees. Until I know them all, I dare not touch the machine.

The most important reform I can suggest is that of specific appropriations, to which it would be desirable to add, by abolishing the accountants an immediate payment from the Treasury to the individuals who are to apply the money & an immediate accounting of those individuals to the Treasury; in short to place the War & Navy departments in relation to the expenditure of money[6] on the same footing on which, at Mr Madison's request, that of State has been placed. Enclosed is a short paper containing the principles I would propose, in which, you will perceive that the discretionary powers of those departments are intended to be checked by legal provisions & not by transferring any discretion to another department. What is called "illustration" in that paper is not correct.

The disappointment in the export documents will necessarily delay some days the proposed result of import; but I think it will be about Drs. 9,250,000.—The importance of correctness there renders it more eligible to wait a week longer for a more accurate estimate than to proceed now with what we have obtained—We have yet 3 weeks till the meeting of Congress—

With sincere respect Your most obedt. Servt.

ALBERT GALLATIN

The few letters received accompany this—A. G.

[629]

RC (DLC); undated; postscript written in left margin; at foot of text: "The President of the United States"; endorsed by TJ as received from the Treasury Department on 16 Nov. and "finance" and so recorded in SJL. Enclosures: Documents IX and X; other enclosure not found.

Gallatin ultimately used the years 1790 to 1792 and 1793 to 1798 to CALCULATE THE IMPOST and project revenues. See Gallatin's 18 Dec. report on the state of finances, especially statement L, for the estimate of revenues from duties, which Gallatin concluded would be at least $9,500,000 annually from 1802 to 1809 (ASP, *Finance*, 1:701-2, 713). See also Gallatin to TJ, [13 Dec. 1801].

ONE OF THE NOTES ON THE MESSAGE: see the first query of Document IX.

Edward Jones served as the chief clerk in the secretary of the Treasury's office with a salary of $1,500 per year. The BEST CLERK after Jones was probably Doyle Sweeny. As principal clerk in the office of the commissioner of the revenue, Sweeny had moved to Washington when the government relocated there in 1800, but then resigned, explaining that he had been treated unfairly because of his Republican "political sentiments." He rejoined the Treasury's staff on 10 June 1801, working in Gallatin's office, and served until the end of September, when he returned to Philadelphia. An experienced clerk, Sweeny had served in the Treasury Department for many years and was the examining clerk in the Auditor's Office who signed TJ's account statement when he left office as secretary of state in December 1793 (Gallatin, *Papers*, 4:917-19; 5:88, 287, 807; ASP, *Finance*, 1:811; Vol. 27:659).

MADISON'S REQUEST: in June, Madison arranged with the Treasury Department to have State Department funds "paid immediately by the treasury, to the agents or other individuals," instead of to the secretary of state. Under the new arrangement, Madison submitted a requisition designating the person or persons to whom payable, the precise amount to be paid, and the appropriation or account to be charged. The agents who received the funds were accountable to the Treasury, not to the secretary of state. The Treasury Department agreed to provide the secretary of state "with a balance sheet or quarterly statement of monies to be accounted for and by whom" (ASP, *Finance*, 1:756; Gallatin, *Papers*, 5:369, 372; Madison, *Papers, Sec. of State Ser.*, 1:413).

¹ Preceding six words interlined.
² Thus in MS.
³ Preceding word and ampersand interlined.
⁴ Preceding word interlined.
⁵ Preceding word interlined in place of "due."
⁶ Preceding seven words interlined.

IX. Albert Gallatin's Remarks on the Draft Message

[on or before 16 Nov. 1801]

foreign powers friendly—<u>effect</u> if redress is meant, it seems wrong to raise expectations which probably will be disappointed—*Quere* whether Mr King's negotiation should be hinted at?

Indians   Should not the attempt to treat be mentioned, stating also the determination not to press upon them any disagreeable demand? This to guard against any blame which the imprudence of the Commissrs. might occasion

Tripoly   more stress might be laid on the protection afforded by the frigates to our vessels which had been long blockaded & on the imminent peril from which our commerce in the Atlantic was preserved by the timely arrival of our squadron at the moment when the Tripolitans had already reached Gibraltar

this early &a–it will be said that the specimen had *already* been given by Truxton–

Finances   in nearly the same ratio &a–the revenue has increased more than in the same ratio with population–1st because our wealth has increased in a greater ratio than population–2dly. because the Sea-ports & towns which consume imported articles[1] much more than the country have encreased in a greater proportion (See census of New York, Philada. & Baltimore & compare their encrease with that of U. States) The greater encrease of wealth is due in part to our natural situation, but principally to our *neutrality* during the war–an evident proof of the advantages of peace notwithstanding the depredations of the belligerent powers

we may safely[2] calculate on a certain augmentation, & war indeed unfor. calamities may change &a

It appears perfectly correct to make our calculations & arrangements without any regard to alterations which might be produced by the possible tho' improbable event of the U.S. being involved in a war; but the alteration which may be produced by the restoration of peace in Europe should be taken into consideration. A reduction in the price of our exports would diminish our ability of paying & therefore of consuming imported articles, and it is perhaps as much as can be hoped for, if, taking an average of six or eight years immediately succeeding the peace, the natural encrease of population was sufficient to counterbalance the decrease of consumption arising from that cause. But supposing these to balance one another, there is still another cause of decrease of *revenue* arising from peace in Europe. Our enormous carrying trade of foreign articles, must be diminished by the peace. Having been much disappointed in the correctness of some of the custom house & Treasury documents on which I depended, I cannot ascertain with precision, but do not think far from the truth the following result vizt. that from $\frac{1}{8}$ to $\frac{1}{10}$th of our import revenue is raised on articles not consumed here, but exported without being entitled to drawbacks either because they have remained more than one year in the country, or are exported in too small parcels to be entitled, or for any other cause not ascertained. This item of revenue is not perhaps less at present than 1,200,000 dollars and as it does not rest on consumption but on an overgrown & accidental commerce, must be deducted from any calculation grounded on the gradual encrease of population & consumption. Could we depend only on a continuance of the present revenue from impost, we might at [once] dispense with all the int. taxes. For the *receipts* from that source for the year

ending 30th June 1801 were	9,550,500.56

to which must be added $\frac{7}{16}$ of the additional duties on sugar & $\frac{11}{12}$ of the addit. duties of $2\frac{1}{2}$ p% on merchandize which prior to 30th June 1800 paid only 10 p%; those addit. duties, on account of the credit given on duties, operated only in the proportion of $\frac{9}{16}$ on the sugar duty & of $\frac{1}{12}$ on the add. $2\frac{1}{2}$ p%, for the year ending 30th June 1801

These $\frac{7}{16}$ & $\frac{1}{12}$ of the respective addit. duties are equal to about	520,000.–
So that the *present* revenue from impost is not less than	10,000,000
But a permanent revenue from impost would be sufficient if amounting to	9,500,000
For adding to it Dollars 250,000 for lands & 50,000 for postage	300,000
	9,800,000
and deducting for interest & paymt. of the debt a yearly sum of	7,200,000
which will pay off about ˣ38 millions of the principal in 8 years leaves	2,600,000

for the expences of Government which I estimate in the gross as followeth Civil list 600,000—miscellaneous 200,000—

foreign intercourse 200,000	1,000,000
Military—the estimate for this year is 1,120,000—	
$\frac{3}{5}$ of which as per proposed reduction is *say*	672,000
Indian dept. 72,000—Fortific. 120,000—	
Arsenals & armouries 66,000	258,000
	1,930,000
leaving for the navy a sum equal to that for the army	670,000
	2,600,000

But for causes already assigned I dare not estimate the impost for

---

ˣ *Quere*—I think 150,000 dollars more a year will be necessary the eight years 1802-1809 at more than an average of 9,000,000 to 9,250,000 dollars. It must, however, be observed that our expenditures of navy & for. intercourse may be diminished when a general peace takes place

now laid before you—The statements & report of the Secy. of the T. are by resolutions & by law respectively laid before Congress by the Secy.—It would be better to say "which according to law & the orders of the two houses will be laid before you"

taxes on stamps &a. may be immediately suppressed   Although the Executive has a right to recommend the suppression of any one tax, yet, in ordinary cases, it seems more proper to recommend or suggest generally a reduction of taxes without designating particularly some of them. If the recommendation could be general as to a whole class of taxes, such as all internal taxes, it would not have so much the appearance of what may be attacked as an interference with legislation details.

Œconomies in civil list   These may be popular; but I am confident that no department is less susceptible of reform; it is by far that in which less abuse has been practised; it exceeds but little the original sum set a part for that object; the reason is that, it being the one to which the people are most attentive, it has been most closely watched & any encrease attempted but with caution & repelled with perseverance. At an early period, I examined it critically & the reductions which might be made appeared so trifling, that, the whole time I was in Congress, eager as we all were to propose popular measures, & to promote economy, I never proposed, nor do I remember to have seen a single reduction proposed—It seems to me that the subject may be mentioned, but less stress laid on it

expences of foreign intercourse   The diplomatic depart. forms but a small item of these; the expences attending the Barbary powers & principally those which are incurred by Consuls, for. ministers & agents, for prosecution of claims & relief of seamen abroad, deserve particular consideration. If any measure has been taken to check these, it might be mentioned; if the subject has not yet been attended to, I would prefer using the word diplomatic, or, foreign ministers, rather than the general words "foreign intercourse."

√ I communicate an account of receipts &a. also appropriations   All those documents, prepared & signed by the Register; are transmitted on the first week of the Session by the Secy. to Congress. By the law constituting the Treasury departt., it is enacted that the Secy. shall lay before Congress or either house[3] such reports, documents &a. as he may be directed from time to time. Hence, the invariable practice has been to call for financial information *directly* on the Treasy. de-part. except in the case of loans where the authority had been given to the Presidt.; and for information respecting army navy or state de-part. the application is always to the Presidt. requesting him to direct &a. The distinction, it is presumable, has been made in order to leave[4] to Congress a direct power, uncontrouled by the Executive, on financial documents & information, as connected with money & rev-enue subjects. It would, at present, be much more convenient to fol-low a different course; if, instead of six or seven reports called for by the standing orders of one or the other house, I could throw them all into one to be made to you, it would unite the advantages of simplic-ity & perspicuity to that of connection with the reports made by the other departments; as all might then be presented to Congress through you & by you; but, I fear that it would be attacked as an at-tempt to dispense with the orders of the houses or of Congress, if the usual reports were not made in the usual manner to them; and if these are still made, it becomes useless for you to communicate du-plicates. But the paragraph may be easily modified by saying "The accounts &a. will show &a." *Quere* whether this remarkable distinc-tion which will be found to pervade all the laws relative to the Treasy. Depart. was not introduced to that extent in order to give to Mr Hamilton a departt. independent of every executive controul? It may be remembered that he claimed under those laws the right of making reports & proposing reforms &a. without being called for the same by Congress. This was a Presidential power; for by the Constitution the President is to call on the departments for information, & has alone the power of recommending. But, in the present case, see the Act supplem. to the Act estab. the Tr. Dep. passed in 1800.

√ *Navy yards* Too much seems to be said in favour of the navy yards here. — Six appears too many & the legislature having heretofore au-thorized but two, it seems that a stronger recommendation to au-thorize a reduction of the number might be made, and a suggestion of the propricty of regulating by law to what kind of officers, their im-mediate superintendence should be committed.

Navy If possible, it would be better to avoid a direct recommenda-tion to continue in actual service a part of it; this subject should, as far as practicable, be treated generally, leaving the Legislat. to[5] decide exclusively upon it.

√ few harbours in the U.S. offer &a. Is that fact certain? Portsmouth, Philada. & even Boston are perfectly defensible — But, if true, should it be stated in a public speech? Will it not be charged as exposing the nakedness of the land?

Sedition Act   The idea contained in the[6] last paragraph had struck me; but to suggest its propriety to the legislature appears doubtful. Are we sure of a Senatorial majority originally opposed to that law? Quere as to Foster—

✓ *Juries*   A recommendation for a law, providing an impartial & uniform mode of summoning juries, & taking the power from the Marshals & clerks—from the judiciary & executive, would, if according with the sentiments of the Executive, come with propriety from him.

✓ *progress of opinion &a.*   is it perfectly right to touch on that subject? it appears to me more objectionable than the doubtful paragraph relative to compensation to sufferers under sedition act.

———

✓ There is but one subject not mentioned in the message[7] which I feel extremely anxious to see recommended; it is generally that Congress should adopt such measures as will effectually guard against misapplication of public monies—by making specific appropriations whenever practicable—by providing against the application of monies drawn from the treasury under an appropriation, to any other object, or to any greater amount, than that for which they have been drawn—by limiting discretionary powers in the application of that money whether by heads of depart. or by any other agents—& by rendering every person who receives public monies from the Treasury as immediately, promptly & effectually[8] accountable to the accounting officers (the Comptroller) as practicable. The great characteristic, the flagrant vice of the late administration has been total disregard of laws, & application of pub. monies by the Departments to objects for which they were not appropriated. Witness Pickering's account; but if you will see a palpable proof & an evidence of the necessity of a remedy, see the Quart. mast. gen. account for 500,000 drs. in the office of the Account. of the War depart.

MS (DLC: TJ Papers, 118:20295-7); in Gallatin's hand, words underscored by TJ in pencil underlined above; check marks added by TJ; undated; endorsed by Gallatin: "President's message." Enclosed in the preceding document.

MR KING'S NEGOTIATION: the proposal to give Britain a lump-sum settlement to resolve claims under Article 6 of the Jay Treaty (TJ to Wilson Cary Nicholas, 25 Oct.).

The September 1789 law CONSTITUTING THE TREASURY Department required the secretary "to make report, and give information to either branch of the legislature, in person or in writing (as he may be required), respecting all matters referred to him by the Senate or House of Representatives." The sole purpose of the supplementary act PASSED IN 1800 was to make it the "duty" of the secretary "to digest, prepare and lay before Congress at the commencement of every session, a report on the subject of finance, containing estimates of the public revenue and public expenditures, and plans for improving or increasing the revenues, from time to time, for the purpose of giving information to Congress in adopting modes of raising the money requisite to meet the public expenditures" (U.S. Statutes at Large, 1:66; 2:79-80).

In answer to a congressional inquiry, Gallatin reported on Timothy PICKER-ING'S ACCOUNT in March 1802, noting "although he drew the moneys from the treasury, under distinct appropriations, he did not sufficiently attend to these, in the application of the money, but has, in many instances, applied the sums drawn under one head, to another head of expenditure, and has, therefore, in some cases, spent less, and in others more, than was authorized by law" (ASP, *Finance*, 1:755, 757, 762).

QUART. MAST. GEN.: for Henry Dearborn's efforts to reduce expenditures of the army's quartermaster department,

and for the previous employment of funds from that department to build the large "Laboratory" storage depot near Philadelphia without appropriation by Congress, see Dearborn's Report on the War Department, [12 May 1801].

[1] Preceding two words interlined.
[2] Preceding word interlined.
[3] Preceding three words interlined.
[4] Preceding word interlined in place of "give."
[5] Gallatin here canceled "act altogether upon." He inserted this paragraph in the margin.
[6] Preceding four words interlined.
[7] Preceding five words interlined.
[8] Preceding two words and ampersand interlined.

X. Albert Gallatin's Memorandum on Reporting of Expenses

[on or before 16 Nov. 1801]

Outlines &a.

1. Specific appropriations—for each object of a distinct nature, and one to embrace for each department all contingencies including therein every *discretionary* expenditure
2. Each appropriation to refer to a calendar year, & the surplus remaining unexpended after having satisfied the demands on the appropriation from *that* year, to be carried to the surplus fund; that is to say, to cease.
3. Warrants to issue, on the requisition of the proper department, in favor of the person receiving the same, instead of issuing in the name of either the heads of Departt. or of the Treasurer of the U.S.
4. The Accountants to be abolished[1]
5. The head of each department to judge, previous to a settlement of accounts, of the propriety of making advances, & to make requsitions accordingly.
6. The head of each department to judge, on a settlement of accounts, of the propriety of making allowances of a discretionary nature in every case where discretion is not limited by law or uniform usage—in these last cases the Comptroller to judge.

Illustration—War Department

Appropriations for the Army for the year 1801 were includ. Fortif. 57,241.04 & fab. of arms 1,857242.4 which would be on above plan as followeth

Pay of army, subsistance & forage of officers	$ 488,076	to be paid by Warrants to Paymaster	
Subsistance	306,395	do.—	Contractors
Clothing	141,530	do.—	Purveyor or Contractors
Ordinance	100,000	do.—	Superintendents
Horses for cavalry[2]			
Bounties & premiums; indian, medical, hospital, & Quarter mast. departments; defensive protect. of frontiers, & contingt. expences of the departmt.	364,000	do.—	Agents, Quartermastr purveyor, paymaster, &c
Purchase of ammunit. & fabric. of arms	400,000	do.—	Contractors, purveyor, superintt.
Fortification of ports	57,241.04	do.—	
	1,857,242.04		

on requisitions of Secretary of War to the Secy of Treasy.

Specific appropns. for Navy

@ 400 dollars pr Seaman {	Pay incl. rations paid to officers calculated on the number of seamen & officers voted by Congress for the year—	pd. to Agent of the vessel or purser
	Provisions	pd. to contractors
	Medicine, hosp. stores, milit. stores & contingencies	pd. to purveyor or contractors
indefinite {	Completing Docks Navy yards, wharves includ. pay of superintend. store-keep. and all continginences in relat. to do.	pd. to Superintend. of navy yards or navy agents
	Building new vessels & repairs of old do.	pd. to do— do—
	Pay of marines	Pay master gen.
	Subsistance of do. on shore	Contractors
	Cloathing	Purveyor
	Contingencies	Contractors or purveyor—

MS (DLC: TJ Papers, 118:20298); entirely in Gallatin's hand; undated. Enclosed in Document VIII.

APPROPRIATIONS FOR THE ARMY: on 17 Nov., Dearborn furnished TJ with a statement of some of the War Department's appropriations and expenditures. The brief report showed $86,000 expended "for Cannon & small Arms, exclusive of the public Armories, up to the 1t. of Novr. 1801 and exclusive of what has been paid by the Treasury Department"; an appropriation of $400,000 "for the above object, for the year 1801"; $95,000 expended on fortifications to 1 Nov.; and $200,000 appropriated for fortifica-

tions for 1801, "exclusive of $30,000 appropriated for defensive protection of the frontiers" (MS in DLC: TJ Papers, 118:20303; entirely in Dearborn's hand; endorsed by TJ as received from the War Department on 17 Nov. and "Fortifications & arms. Expended to Nov. 1. 1801" and so recorded in SJL).

[1] Gallatin interlined this entry and corrected the renumbering of the two items below it.
[2] Gallatin here canceled a separate "5,000" appropriation for "Horses for cavalry," extended the brace, and altered the total appropriation for the category from "359,000" to "364,000."

XI. To James Madison

TH:J. TO J.M.   [16 Nov. 1801 or after?]

Will you be so good as once more to revise this? altho' I have not entirely obliterated all the passages which have been thought objectionable, yet I have very much reduced & smoothed them. still verbal & minor corrections of style or sentiment will be thankfully recieved & made.

RC (ViU); undated, but perhaps written after TJ saw Gallatin's remarks and made changes to the early draft. Enclosure not found, but apparently a second state of the draft message.

XII. Robert Smith's Remarks on the Draft Message

[on or before 21 Nov. 1801]

page 1st. I sent a small squadron of frigates into the Mediterranean with overtures of conciliation and with[1] instructions to assure the Bey of Tripoli of my cordial disposition to preserve with him a State of peace; but with orders at the same time, in case of a declaration of war by that Regency, to protect our Commerce against depradation and our Citizens against Captivity. The Measure was seasonable and salutary. The Bey had actually declared war in form against us[2] before the arrival of our Squadron. Some of his Corsairs were traversing the Mediterranean in quest of our vessels and two of them, destined for the Western Ocean, had arrived at Gibralter. Our Commerce in the Mediterranean had thus for a time been suspended and that of the Atlantic was³ endangered. The seasonable arrival of our squadron afforded however an effectual convoy and enabled our Citizens to prosecute their intended voyages.⁴

page. 3d—But it is submitted to your consideration whether the industry of our fellow Citizens ought to be burthened with taxes for the purpose of accumulating a Treasure for wars to happen we know not when and which perhaps would not so often happen but from the facility afforded by such Treasures.

page. 5—and for the frames of two extra Seventy four gun ships for the delivery of which contracts⁵ had been long since made.

page 6—a few *days*—better say—*weeks.*

page. 6—Would it not be well to omit the sentence mentioning the removal of the two other frigates? It will occur to practical men that such removal cannot be effected but at an expence of many thousand Dollars—besides the Law directs that they shall be laid up at *ports* not a port.

page. 3—Qu?—Is this government charged with nothing but "the external and mutual relations of these States"?

page. 8. Qu? Does not the *form* of the concluding sentence appear too much like party and⁶ *Self-Commendation?* Would not the purpose be equally answered in a form somewhat like the following?
—but I would willingly indulge the pleasing persuasion that all will cordially unite in honest and disinterested efforts to preserve the general and State governments in their &c &c &c

page. 7. Would the proposition respecting *Juries* be acceptable to any but the State of Virga. I am apprehensive such an innovation would alarm. It would be said that the powerful State of Virga. would impose her usages upon the other States.

page. 8. With respect to the Naturalisation-Laws, would it not be better to submit the subject generally without presenting in detail the modifications? The Opinions of Republicans upon this are various.

page. 6. Altho' I have no doubt of the power of the President to grant in the exercise of a sound discretion a Nolle-prosequi, yet I have very serious doubts respecting the ground stated. The prevailing Opinion among Constitutional Lawyers will I believe[7] be opposed to the principles set forth. But why make this communication? Does it give to Congress any information of the State of the Union or does it recommend to them any measure that requires legislative provision? Will it not be hazarding, without necessity, a division of our friends? The claim to such Executive prerogative will not be easily assented to.[8]
Verbal merely
page. 1—"effect"—qu? *retribution.*
          lessen like evils—*prevent*[9]

page 1st—"I receive"—*have received*

page 1st—[10]
page. 2. "to reduce"—to *make*

page. 5—"to be wanting"—*wanted*
id—"& be in readiness"—*may* be in readiness

page. 8. "Conclusion"—*investigation*

page. 8. "in having at length an oppy." qu? why *at length*?[11]
page 6—might not be omitted the detail respecting the fortifications—Vizt. from the words "*where important harbours*" to the words "*be found useful*" inclusive.

Qu? the prudence of saying any thing about the building of the 74's—as it is not proposed by the Executive and as no appropriation for it is submitted

page. 7—Would it not be as well to omit the sentence—"*and especially that portion of it recently erected*"

MS (DLC: TJ Papers, 118:20321-4); in Smith's hand; undated; endorsed by TJ as received from the Navy Department on 21 Nov. and so recorded in SJL.

PAGE 1ST: some of Smith's references to TJ's wording do not match the fair copy (Document XIII). However, there is some correlation between the page numbers he cited and the pages of the manuscript of Document XIII, which means that the draft he reviewed was similar to Document XIII in arrangement and length.

SEVENTY FOUR GUN SHIPS: as TJ mentioned in the "Navy" section of his message (see Document XIII), a February 1799 "Act for the augmentation of the Navy" called for the construction of six 74-gun ships. The navy's appropriation for 1801 contained funds for the ships. By the fall of that year construction was underway or completed on eight frames made of live oak—six for the ships required by the act plus two additional frames—but TJ postponed further work (U.S. Statutes at Large, 1:621; 2:123; ASP, *Naval Affairs*, 1:79; note to William Duane to TJ, 10 June 1801; Samuel Smith to TJ, 13 June 1801).

The Peace Establishment Act of March 1801 called for seven of the navy's frigates to be LAID UP in ports. As referred to by TJ at the end of the "Navy Yards" section of the annual message (see Document XIII), the act also called for the sale of several naval vessels (Vol. 33:250n; Samuel Smith to TJ, 4 May 1801).

In addition to these remarks, TJ received from Smith or his department a statement of "Expenditures on account of Navy yards Docks &c. to the 1st October 1801," reporting amounts paid for the land and improvements of the navy yards at Washington ($4,000 for land, $54,683.54 for improvements), Norfolk ($12,000 and $14,275.29, respectively), Philadelphia ($37,000 and $1,636.68), New York ($40,000 and $1,864.99), Boston ($40,000 and $3,643.41), and Portsmouth, New Hampshire ($5,500 and $26,304.07) for a total of $240,907.98 (MS in DLC; in Abishai Thomas's hand; at foot of text: "Navy department Nov. 21. 1801"). TJ

also received from Smith's department a statement of "Annual expense of maintaining a Frigate of 44 Guns, a Frigate of 36 Guns, & a Frigate of 32 Guns, in actual Service, & with their full complement of Men &c." The expense for a frigate of 44 guns with 400 men was $114,351.70; for one of 36 guns with 340 men, $96,836.65; and for one of 32 guns, 260 men, $73,719.74, for a total of $284,908.09 (MS in DLC: TJ Papers, 118:20300; undated; in Thomas's hand; endorsed by TJ as received from the Navy Department on 16 Nov. 1801 and "Annual expence of a frigate in service").

[1] Preceding five words interlined.

[2] Remainder of sentence interlined.

[3] Smith here canceled "indeed extensively."

[4] Below this paragraph Smith interlined and then canceled "page 2nd. bravery and [. . .]."

[5] Preceding six words interlined in place of "which."

[6] Preceding two words interlined.

[7] Preceding two words interlined.

[8] Sentence interlined.

[9] Line interlined.

[10] Canceled: "exception to a prospect. Qu if a correct figure."

[11] Smith left some space between this comment and the one that follows.

XIII. Fair Copy, First Annual Message

[by 27 Nov. 1801]

Fellow citizens of the Senate & House of Representatives.

It is a circumstance of sincere gratification to me, that on meeting Peace. the great council of our nation, I am able to announce to them, on grounds of reasonable certainty, that the wars & troubles, which have for so many years afflicted our sister-nations, have at length come to an end; & that the communications of peace & commerce are once more opening among them. whilst we devoutly return thanks to the beneficent being who has been pleased to breathe into them the spirit of conciliation & forgiveness, we are bound, with peculiar gratitude, to be thankful to him that our own peace has been preserved through so perilous a season, & ourselves permitted quietly to cultivate the earth, & to practise and improve those arts which tend to increase our comforts. the assurances indeed of friendly disposition recieved from all the powers, with whom we have principal relations, had inspired a confidence that our peace with them would not have been disturbed. but a cessation of the irregularities which had afflicted the commerce of neutral nations, & of the irritations & injuries produced by them, cannot but add to this confidence; and strengthens, at the same time, the hope that wrongs committed on unoffending friends, under a pressure of circumstances, will now be reviewed with candor, & will be considered as founding just claims of retribution for the past, & new assurance for the future.

Indians.   Among our Indian neighbors also a spirit of peace and friendship generally prevails; & I am happy to inform you that the continued efforts to introduce among them the implements & the practice of husbandry & of the houshold arts have not been without success: that they are becoming more & more sensible of the superiority of this dependance, for clothing & subsistence, over the precarious resources of hunting & fishing: & already we are able to announce that, instead of that constant diminution of numbers produced by their wars & their wants, some of them begin to experience an increase of population.

Tripoli.   To this state of general peace with which we have been blessed, one only exception exists. Tripoli, the least considerable of the Barbary states, had come forward with demands unfounded either in right or in compact, & had permitted itself to denounce war, on our failure to comply before a given day. the style of the demand admitted but one answer. I sent a small squadron of frigates into the Mediterranean, with assurances to that power of our sincere desire to remain in peace; but with orders to protect our commerce against the threatened attack. the measure was seasonable & salutary. the Bey had already declared war in form. his cruisers were out. two had arrived at Gibraltar. our commerce in the Mediterranean was blockaded: and that of the Atlantic in peril. the arrival of our squadron dispelled the danger. one of the Tripolitan cruisers having fallen in with, & engaged the small schooner Enterprize, commanded by Lieutt. Sterritt, which had gone as a tender to our larger vessels, was captured, after a heavy slaughter of her men, without the loss of a single one on our part. the bravery exhibited by our citizens on that element will, I trust, be a testimony to the world, that it is not a want of that virtue which makes us seek their peace; but a conscientious desire to direct the energies of our nation to the multiplication of the human race, & not to it's destruction. unauthorised by the constitution, without the sanction of Congress, to go beyond the line of defence, the vessel being disabled from committing further hostilities, was liberated with it's crew. the legislature will doubtless consider whether, by authorising measures of offence also, they will place our force on an equal footing with that of it's adversaries. I communicate all material information on this subject, that in the exercise of the important function, confided by the constitution to the legislature exclusively, their judgment may form itself on a knolege & consideration of every circumstance of weight.

I wish I could say that our situation with all the other Barbary states was entirely satisfactory. discovering that some delays had taken place in the performance of certain articles stipulated by us, I thought it my duty, by immediate measures for fulfilling them, to vindicate to ourselves the right of considering the effect of departure from stipulation on their side. from the papers which will be laid before you, you will be enabled to judge whether our treaties are regarded by them as fixing at all the measure of their demands; or as guarding from the exercise of force our vessels within their power: & to consider how far it will be safe and expedient to leave our affairs with them in their present posture. *Algiers. Tunis.*

I lay before you the result of the Census lately taken of our inhabitants, to a conformity with which we are now to reduce the ensuing ratio of representation & taxation. you will percieve that the increase of numbers during the last ten years, proceeding in geometrical ratio, promises a duplication in little more than twenty two years. we contemplate this rapid growth, & the prospect it holds up to us, not with a view to the injuries it may enable us to do to others in some future day, but to the settlement of the extensive country, still remaining vacant within our limits, to the multiplication of men, susceptible of happiness, educated in the love of order, habituated to self-government, & valuing it's blessings above all price. *Census.*

Other circumstances, combined with the increase of numbers, have produced an augmentation of revenue arising from consumption in a ratio far beyond that of population alone: and tho' the changes in foreign relations, now taking place so desireably for the whole world, may for a season affect this branch of revenue, yet weighing all probabilities of expence, as well as of income, there is reasonable ground of confidence that we may now safely dispense with all the internal taxes, comprehending excise, stamps, auctions, licenses, carriages & refined sugars; to which the postage on newspapers may be added to facilitate the progress of information:[1] and that the remaining sources of revenue will be sufficient to provide for the support of government, to pay the interest of the public debts, & to discharge the principals *Finances.*

within shorter periods than the laws, or the general expectation had contemplated. war indeed, & untoward events may change this prospect of things, & call for expences which the impost could not meet. but sound principles will not justify our taxing the industry of our fellow citizens to accumulate treasure for wars to happen we know not when, & which might not perhaps happen but from the temptations offered by that treasure.

Economies.   These views however of reducing our burthens, are formed on the expectation that a sensible, & at the same time a salutary reduction may take place in our habitual expenditures. for this purpose those of the civil government, the army & navy, will need revisal. when we consider that this government is charged with the external & mutual relations only of these states, that the states themselves have principal care of our persons, our property, & our reputation, constituting the great field of human concerns, we may well doubt whether our organisation is not too complicated, too expensive; whether offices & officers have not been multiplied unnecessarily, & sometimes injuriously to the service they were meant to promote. I will cause to be laid before you an essay towards a statement,[2] of those who, under public employment of various kinds, draw money from the treasury, or from our citizens. time has not permitted a perfect enumeration, the ramifications of office being too multiplied & remote to be completely traced in a first trial.[3] among those who are dependant on Executive discretion, I have begun the reduction of what was deemed unnecessary. the expences of diplomatic agency have been considerably diminished. the Inspectors of internal revenue, who were found to obstruct the accountability of the institution, have been discontinued. several agencies, created by Executive authority, on salaries fixed by that also, have been suppressed, and should suggest the expediency of regulating that power by law,[4] so as to subject it's exercises to legislative inspection & sanction. other reformations of the same kind will be pursued with that caution which is requisite, in removing useless things, not to injure what is retained. but the great mass of public offices is established by law, & therefore by law alone can be abolished. should the legislature think it expedient to pass this roll in review, and to try all it's parts by the test of public utility, they may be assured of every aid & light which Executive information can yield. considering the general tendency to multiply offices and dependancies, & to increase expence to the ultimate term of burthen which the citizen can bear, it behoves us to avail ourselves of every occasion which presents itself for taking off the surcharge; that it never may be seen here that, after leaving to labour the smallest portion of it's earnings on which it can subsist, government shall itself consume the whole residue of what it was instituted to guard.

In our care too of the public contributions entrusted to our direction, it would be prudent to multiply barriers against their dissipation, by appropriating specific sums to every specific purpose susceptible of definition; by disallowing all applications of money varying from the appropriation in object, or transcending it in amount; by reducing the undefined field of Contingencies, & thereby circumscribing discretionary powers over money; and by bringing back to a single department all accountabilities for money, where the examinations may be prompt, efficacious, & uniform. *Appropriations.*

An account of the reciepts & expenditures of the last year, as prepared by the Secretary of the treasury, will as usual be laid before you. the success which has attended the late sales of the public lands shews that, with attention, they may be made an important source of reciept. among the paiments, those made in discharge of the principal & interest of the national debt, will shew that the public faith has been exactly maintained. to these will be added an Estimate of appropriations necessary for the ensuing year. this last will of course be affected by such modifications of the system of expence as you shall think proper to adopt.

A statement has been formed by the Secretary at war, on mature consideration of all the forts & stations where garrisons will be expedient, & of the number of men requisite for each garrison. the whole amount is considerably short of the present military establishment. for the surplus, no particular use can be pointed out. for defence against invasion, their number is as nothing. nor is it concieved needful or safe that a standing army should be kept up, in time of peace, for that purpose. uncertain as we must ever be of the particular point in our circumference where an enemy may chuse to invade us, the only force which can be ready at every point, & competent to oppose them, is the body of neighboring citizens, as formed into a militia. on these, collected from the parts most convenient, in numbers proportioned to the invading force, it is best to rely, not only to meet the first attack, but, if it threatens to be permanent, to maintain the defence until regulars may be engaged to relieve them. these considerations render it important that we should, at every session continue to amend the defects, which from time to time shew themselves, in the laws for regulating the militia, until they are sufficiently perfect: nor should we now, or at any time, separate, until we can say we have done every thing for the militia which we could do were an enemy at our door. *Army.*

The provision of military stores on hand will be laid before you, that you may judge of the additions still requisite.

Navy. With respect to the extent to which our naval preparations should be carried some difference of opinion may be expected to[5] appear: but just attention to the circumstances of every part of the Union will doubtless reconcile all. a small force will probably continue to be wanted for actual service in the Mediterranean. whatever annual sum beyond that you may think proper to appropriate, to naval preparations, would perhaps be better employed in providing those articles which may be kept without waste or consumption, & be in readiness when any exigence calls them into use. Progress has been made, as will appear by papers now communicated, in providing materials for seventy-four-gun ships as directed by law.

Navy Yards. How far the authority given by the legislature for procuring & establishing sites for naval purposes, has been perfectly understood & pursued in the execution, admits of some doubt. a statement of the expences already incurred on that subject is now[6] laid before you. I have, in certain cases, suspended or slackened these expenditures, that the legislature might determine whether so many Yards are necessary as have been contemplated. the works at this place are among those permitted to go on; & five of the seven frigates directed to be laid up, have been brought and laid up here, where, besides the safety of their position, they are under the eye of the Executive administration, as well as of it's agents, and where yourselves also will be guided by your own view, in the legislative provisions respecting them, which may from time to time be necessary. they are preserved in such condition, as well the vessels as whatever belongs to them, as to be at all times ready for sea on a short warning. two others are yet to be laid up, so soon as they shall have recieved the repairs requisite to put them also into sound condition. As a superintending officer will be necessary at each yard, his duties & emoluments hitherto fixed by the Executive will be a more proper subject for legislation. a communication will also be made of our progress in the execution of the law respecting the vessels directed to be sold.

Fortifications. Fortifications. The fortifications of our harbours, more or less advanced, present considerations of great difficulty. while some of them are on a scale sufficiently proportioned to the advantages of their position, to the efficacy of their protection, & the importance of the points within it, others are so extensive, will cost so much in their first erection, so much in their maintenance, and require such a force to garrison them, as to make it questionable what is best now to be done. a statement of those commenced, or projected, of the expences already incurred, & estimates of their future cost, as far as can be foreseen, shall be laid before you, that you may be enabled to judge whether any alteration is necessary in the laws respecting this subject.

Agriculture, manufactures, commerce & navigation, the four pillars of our prosperity, are then most thriving when left most free to individual enterprize. protection from casual embarrasments however may sometimes be seasonably interposed. if, in the course of your observations or enquiries, they should appear to need any aid, within the limits of our constitutional powers, your sense of their importance is a sufficient assurance they will occupy your attention. we cannot indeed but all feel an anxious solicitude for the difficulties under which our carrying trade will soon be placed. how far[7] it can be relieved, otherwise than by time, is a subject for important[8] consideration.

Applications from different persons suffering prosecution under the act usually called the Sedition act, claimed my early attention to that instrument. our country has thought proper to distribute the powers of it's government among three equal & independant authorities, constituting each a check on one or both of the others, in all attempts to impair it's constitution. to make each an effectual check, it must have a right, in cases which arise[10] within the line of it's proper functions, where, equally with the others, it acts in the last resort & without appeal, to decide on the validity of an act according to it's own judgment, & uncontrouled by the opinions of any other department. we have accordingly, in more than one instance, seen the opinions of different departments in opposition to each other, & no ill ensue. the constitution moreover, as a further security for itself, against violation even by a concurrence of all the departments, has provided for it's own reintegration by a change of the persons exercising the functions of those departments. succeeding functionaries have the same right to judge of the conformity or non-conformity of an act with the constitution, as their predecessors who past it. for if it be against that instrument, it is a perpetual nullity. uniform decisions indeed, sanctioned by successive functionaries, by the public voice, and by repeated elections would so strengthen a construction as to render highly responsible a departure from it.[11]   On my accession to the administration, reclamations against the Sedition act were laid before me by individual citizens, claiming the protection of the constitution against the Sedition act. Called on by the position in which the nation had placed me, to exercise in their behalf my free & independant judgment, I took that act into consideration, compared it with the constitution, viewed it under every aspect of which I

Agriculture Manufactures Commerce Navigation.

Sedition act.[9]

[647]

thought it susceptible, and gave to it all the attention which the magnitude of the case demanded. on mature deliberation, in the presence of the nation, and under the tie of the solemn oath which binds me to them & to my duty, I do declare that I hold that act to be in palpable & unqualified contradiction to the constitution. considering it then as a nullity, I have relieved from oppression under it those of my fellow-citizens who were within the reach of the functions confided to me. in recalling our footsteps within the limits of the Constitution, I have been actuated by a zealous devotion to that instrument. it is the ligament which binds us into one nation. it is, to the national government, the law of it's existence, with which it began, and with which it is to end. infractions of it may sometimes be committed from inadvertence, sometimes from the panic, or passions of a moment. to correct these with good faith, as soon as discovered, will be an assurance to the states that, far from meaning to impair that sacred charter of it's authorities, the General government views it as the principle of it's own life.

Judiciary. The Judiciary system of the United states, & especially that portion of it recently erected, will of course present itself to the contemplation of Congress. and that they may be able to judge of the proportion which the institution bears to the business it has to perform, I have caused to be procured from the several states, and now lay before Congress, an exact statement of all the causes decided since the first establishment of the courts, & of those which were depending when additional courts & judges were brought in to their aid.

Juries. And while on the Judiciary organisation, it will be worthy your consideration whether the protection of the inestimable institution of juries has been extended to all the cases involving the security of our persons & property. Their impartial selection also being essential to their value, we ought further to consider whether that is sufficiently secured in those states where they are named by a marshal depending on Executive will, or designated by the court, or by officers dependant on them.

Naturalisation. I cannot omit recommending a revisal of the laws on the subject of naturalisation. considering the ordinary chances of human life, a denial of citizenship under a residence of fourteen years, is a denial to a great proportion of those who ask it: and controuls a policy pursued, from their first settlement, by many of these states, & still believed of consequence to their prosperity. and shall we refuse, to the unhappy fugitives from distress, that hospitality which the savages of the wilderness extended to our fathers arriving in this land? shall oppressed humanity find no asylum on this globe? the constitution indeed has wisely provided that, for admission to certain offices of important trust, a residence shall be required, sufficient to develope character & design. but might not the general character & capabilities of a citizen be safely communicated to everyone manifesting a bonâ fide purpose of embarking his life & fortunes permanently with us? with restrictions perhaps to guard against the fraudulent usurpation of our flag; an abuse which brings so much embarrasment & loss on the genuine citizen, and so much danger to the nation of being involved in war, that no endeavor should be spared to detect & suppress it.

These, fellow citizens, are the matters respecting the state of the nation which I have thought of importance to be submitted to your consideration at this time. some others of less moment, or not yet ready for communication, will be the subject of separate messages. I am happy in this opportunity of committing the arduous affairs of our government to the collected wisdom of the Union. nothing shall be wanting on my part to inform, as far as in my power, the legislative judgment; nor to carry that judgment into faithful execution. the prudence & temperance of your discussions will promote within your own walls that conciliation which so much befriends rational conclusion: and, by it's example, will encourage among our constitutents that progress of opinion which is tending to unite them in object and in will. that all should be satisfied with any one order of things is not to be expected: but I indulge the pleasing persuasion that the great body of our citizens will cordially concur in honest and disinterested efforts, which have for their object to preserve the general & state governments in their constitutional form & equilibrium; to maintain peace abroad, & order & obedience to the laws at home; to establish principles & practices of administration favorable to the security of liberty & property; & to reduce expences to what is necessary for the useful purposes of government.   TH: JEFFERSON

MS (DLC: TJ Papers, 118:20381-4); entirely in TJ's hand; a fair copy with emendations; signature, and below it "Dec. 8. 1801," both added after the completion of the drafting process.

POSTAGE ON NEWSPAPERS was one cent for a distance up to 100 miles, a cent and a half for any greater distance. On 2 Dec., TJ received a report indicating that from 1 July 1800 to 1 July 1801, postmasters had collected $21,296.48 in postage on newspapers. Of that amount, $10,645.91 remained in the hands of the local postmasters, being the fifty-percent commission allowed by the Post Office Act of 1794. During the same period, total receipts for the General Post Office amounted to $64,291.33. Allowing for miscellaneous income, expenses, and losses from small offices, the amount cleared annually from postage "exclusive of

Newspapers" would be $55,036.24 (MS in ViW, 1 p., undated, in an unidentified hand, at head of text: "Newspapers," endorsed by TJ as received 2 Dec. and "Post office"; MS in DLC: TJ Papers, 118:20413-14, undated, in Meriwether Lewis's hand, endorsed by Gallatin: "Postage—newspapers," with undated notation in Gallatin's hand: "I am clearly of opinion that unless the deputy Post-masters shall be paid by the persons who receive the news-papers that part of their duty will not be so well attended to. The part of the postage payable to the United States may clearly be given up. The people will not complain of the arrangement for they will understand it.—A.G."; U.S. Statutes at Large, 1:238, 354, 362).

Of the LAWS RESPECTING fortifica-tions, the primary one was an act "for the defence of certain Ports and Harbors" passed by the Third Congress in March 1794 (same, 1:345-6; ASP, *Military Affairs*, 1:153).

¹ TJ interlined the passage from "to which the postage" to this point. See Doc-ument XV.

² TJ here canceled "which further time

& enquiry will be requisite to compleat."

³ Preceding sentence interlined.

⁴ TJ here canceled "within."

⁵ Preceding five words interlined in place of "ideas may perhaps."

⁶ Preceding two words interlined in place of "shall be." TJ also made this change to the copies of the message sub-mitted to the House and Senate on 8 Dec. (see Document II of group of documents on annual message to Congress, 8 Dec. 1801).

⁷ Preceding two words interlined in place of "but whether."

⁸ Word interlined.

⁹ TJ added a long bracket alongside this paragraph and wrote in the margin: "this whole paragraph was omitted as <*being*> capable of being chicaned, and furnishing something to the opposition to make a handle of. it was thought better that the message should be clear of every thing which the public might be made to misunderstand."

¹⁰ Preceding four words interlined.

¹¹ TJ wrote the preceding three sen-tences in the margin, keyed for insertion at this spot in the text.

XIV. To Levi Lincoln

TH:J. TO MR LINCOLN.   Nov. 27. 1801.

I inclose you the message on the state of the nation to be sent to Congress on their meeting. I will ask the favor of you to give it serious perusal & to favor me with such observations, corrections & queries as you may think expedient: to observe also on any negligences of style, which may be corrected without weakening expression: for wherever by a small sacrifice of the rigorous rules of grammar, circumlocution may be saved, & expression condensed, I hold it right to give up gram-mar. but the habit of doing this has produced an inattention which occasions grammatical incorrectness sometimes where it is of no advantage. I require watching in this therefore.

The message to the Senate respecting the Nolle prosequi will shew you the footing on which I shall place that subject before them. you will then the better judge of the manner of presenting the Sedition law to both houses. health & affection.

RC (MHi); addressed: "The Attorney G," with remainder clipped; endorsed by Lincoln: "Mr Jefferson's Letter on his message respecting the State of the na- tion." Enclosures: (1) Document XIII. (2) A version of the draft message to the Senate about prosecution of William Duane (see TJ to Gallatin, 12 Nov.).

XV. Levi Lincoln's Remarks on the Message

[ca. 27 Nov.-8 Dec. 1801]

The Address.

relieved *from* the danger—2 page—3 line[1]

Quere—if the word *from* had not better be inserted as the word commerce understood is the object on which the verb seems immediately to operate

Quere, whether postage on newspapers had not better be added to the list of duties to be suspended. The means of instruction and of spreading knowledge are generally in all the States, not only exempted from duty, but in whole, or in part aided by a public support—The measure would be very popular with printers and both popular & useful with the people at large. The postage is too small to be of importance as an item of revenue, & yet so large as to prevent in some degree the circulation of papers— Page 3d.—

Quere If the ideas here expressed are not too valuable to be suppressed, and yet whether they will not be considered as too strong, or as expressing or implying too much, to be directly applicable, with their whole force, to the probable situation our Government may be in—Whether it would not be better to soften the application of the ideas, by changing the Phraseology in some such a manner as the following—viz Least we should see our Government approxamating to that state, which &c— 3 page 12 line—

Ideas against the building of the seventy-fours appear to me too important, to be omitted. It would be useful to change the public sentiment & expectation on this subject. I should doubt, could the U.S. now have a present of seven seventy fours, on the condition of their taking care of them & keeping them in repair for eight years, if they ought to accept of them. On the idea of our needing such ships eight years hence we could build them cheaper than we could preserve them. Smaller ships must be more useful to us. 5 page Navy

Considering the importance that agriculture and manufactures are to our Country, and the ideas, too prevalent in the nothern States, that the Administration & the Southern States, are hostile to our navigation & commerce, quere if it would not have a good effect, to add to the address some such general expressions as the following viz—It is with Congress to consider whether the Agriculture and manufactures of our Country require immediate attentions, beyound the private patronage of individuals, and whether any legislative efforts are necessary or practicable for the securing, encouraging, or preventing the abridgment of the carrying trade particularly important to the prosperity of the northern States—

MS (DLC: TJ Papers, 109:18686-7); entirely in Lincoln's hand; undated, but written after TJ asked Lincoln to review the annual message on 27 Nov. and before TJ gave it to Congress on 8 Dec.; endorsed by TJ: "Lincoln Levi."

2 PAGE—3 LINE: Lincoln referred to the second page of the MS of Document XIII, the passage in the "Tripoli" section of the message that reads: "our commerce in the Mediterranean was blockaded: and that of the Atlantic in peril. the arrival of our squadron dispelled the danger."

PAGE 3D.: the third page of the MS of

the fair copy, in the "Finances" section, where TJ inserted a sentence on newspaper postage in response to this suggestion from Lincoln (see Document XIII, note 1).

3 PAGE 12 LINE: "war indeed, & untoward events may change this prospect of things, & call for expences which the impost could not meet," in the "Finances" section (MS of Document XIII).

[1] Lincoln likely inserted this line, and the query below it, sometime after he wrote the subsequent queries.

From Albert Gallatin

DEAR SIR   [12 Nov. 1801]

Will you look at Mr Ingersoll's acct. & letters? It was objected to by this Departt. as being too high; but the point to which I request your attention is this. Does it not seem as if Mr Ingersol in concert with Mr Dallas dist. atty. acting under your positive instructions, had abandoned the senatorial prosecution against Duane under the sedition law, *because you thought this unconstitutional*? and had instituted it anew at common law, *because you did not think this mode unconstitutional*? What were the instructions to Dallas on that subject? How do you intend to introduce it to Congress? Is it necessary at present to take any notice of it either to Dallas or Ingersol? or must his account be passed without noticing that fact?

Mr Whipple's letters deserve also consideration. If those people act so, & you will change the Supervisor, I may withdraw all our public monies from the New Hamps. Bank, & make the payments of interest & for the navy,[1] out of the duties which will accumulate in hands of the collector & supervr.

The letter of T.C. is returned.

Respectfully Your obt. Servt   ALBERT GALLATIN

RC (DLC); undated; addressed: "The Presi[dent] of the," with remainder clipped; endorsed by TJ as received from the Treasury Department on 12 Nov. and so recorded in SJL; notations by TJ on verso: "I am ready to change the Supervisor of N.H.," "Duane's case," "Isaac Smith for Cherryston's," and "Reed's lre," all subjects included in TJ's letter to Gallatin of this date printed below. Enclosures: (1) Joseph Whipple to Gallatin, Portsmouth, New Hampshire, 27 Aug. 1801, reporting that the New Hampshire Bank was being used as "a depository for funds belonging to the United States" and describing the bank as a vehicle for the suppression of republicanism in the state, with the directors as the "chief calumniators of the Government—They are not merely the federalists of the character that supported generally the late administration, but they are of the ancient sect of Tories well known in this Country in 1775 & 76 and exert all their power & influence to bring into disrepute every measure of the Administration and all deposits placed in their hands increases in a degree their power & influence"; also noting that he places the funds he collects, at his own risk, in a bank, seeking a state charter, with John Langdon as its president (Gallatin, *Papers*, 5:646-7). (2) Probably Whipple to Gallatin, 27 Oct., enclosing a petition from Hopley Yeaton (Enclosure No. 3), who requested that it be transmitted to Gallatin, who would lay it before the president; with Whipple testifying to the truth of Yeaton's statement, but noting that he had observed the master of the revenue cutter as "intemperate" before his dismissal and had considered reporting it to the Treasury secretary; he had recently learned that Yeaton had "discontinued the habit of intemperance" and, therefore, could recommend him "with pleasure" (RC in same; at foot of text: "The Honble. Albert Gallatin Esquire";

endorsed by a clerk; with transmittal notes in Gallatin's hand and signed by him on verso of second sheet: "Orders have been given to sell the present cutter & either purchase or build a smaller one fit for the service, discharging at the same time the crew & officers (the master & one mate excepted) until a new one shall have been fitted" and "The propriety of re-appointing Capn. Yeaton rests of course with the President. He was dismissed at same time & for same cause with Messrs. Gardner & Whipple. The information heretofore received as to his habits from Mr Langdon, & Colo. Allen of Passamaquody was not favorable"; with TJ's undated response: "the reappointment to be decided on when Mr Gallatin shall think it needful. Th:J."). (3) Petition from Hopley Yeaton to TJ, 1 Aug. (printed below). (4) Tench Coxe to TJ, 8 Nov. 1801. Other enclosures not found.

INGERSOLL'S ACCT.: on 7 Sep., Jacob Wagner wrote Madison that the account submitted by Jared Ingersoll, the former U.S. attorney for Pennsylvania who had prosecuted the sedition case against William Duane, required the approval of the secretary of state. Wagner noted: "For my own part, altho' I think the charge is too high for his services in Duane's case, yet I do not know how to overrule Mr. Dallas' official certificate of its being reasonable." Ingersoll's bill for $300 was paid by the U.S. Treasury on 19 Nov. (Madison, *Papers, Sec. of State Ser.*, 2:90; Duane to TJ, 10 June 1801).

Madison sent instructions to Alexander J. DALLAS on 20 July, noting that the president wanted the U.S. attorney to "enter a nolle prosequi upon the indictment" against Duane in the U.S. circuit court "for an offence, by a seditious libel against the Senate." Madison observed, however, that the "interposition of the

President" was limited to the proceedings under the Sedition Act, and it was to be understood that the instruction to prosecute Duane "in pursuance of the resolution of the Senate" was still in force, for "prosecution in any other form or in any other Court" (Madison, *Papers, Sec. of*

State Ser., 1:442-3). See also Madison to TJ, printed at 17 July 1801.

T.C.: Tench Coxe (see Enclosure No. 4).

[1] Preceding three words and ampersand interlined.

ENCLOSURE

Petition from Hopley Yeaton

Portsmo. N.H.
August 1st. 1801

To the President of the United States—

Humbly shews, Hopley Yeaton of Portsmouth in the State of New Hampshire, that in the beginning of our revolutionary struggle, he served as third lieutenant on board the Raleigh frigate—that he was afterwards promoted to the first lieutenancy of the Deane frigate, in which capacity he served about five years—after which he became superintendent of the Navy yard at said Portsmouth, under the Honble. John Langdon Esqr., and so continued during the war—That on the establishment of revenue cutters, he was appointed by the late President Washington, to the command of the cutter Scammel, the first fitted out from this port and continued in that service, (to general approbation, so he flatters himself,) till removed by the late President Adams. This took place at the same time Mr Whipple & Mr. Gardner were dismiss'd from their offices—No reasons were assigned for the measure, nor can your petitioner conjecture any, unless it could be a steady adherence to republican principles, & a refusal to sign an address to Mr. Adams, expressing perfect satisfaction and entire confidence in his administration—

Your petitioner conceiving he has undeservedly suffered by this sudden & unexpected removal *therefore prays*, that the President would take into consideration the above statement of facts, and (if on enquiry found worthy) that your petitioner may be reinstated in his former office as commander of the revenue cutter in this station, *or* otherwise restored to public trust & confidence, as the President in his wisdom shall deem just & fit: And your petitioner as in duty bound shall ever pray—   HOPLEY YEATON

RC (NIIi: Gallatin Papers). Enclosed in Joseph Whipple to Gallatin, 27 Oct. 1801, listed as Enclosure No. 2 above.

Hopley Yeaton (1740-1812), of Portsmouth, New Hampshire, was a leader of the local Sons of Liberty before the American Revolution and, in 1776, received a commission as lieutenant in the American navy. In 1790, Washington appointed him commander of the *Scammell*, the New Hampshire revenue cutter. At the

urging of Federalists at Portsmouth, Adams dismissed Yeaton, along with other Republicans at the custom house, in June 1798. TJ appointed Yeaton master of the New Hampshire revenue cutter in September 1802. When Yeaton resigned in 1809 because of "age and infirmities," Whipple observed that he had been "a faithful Officer, prompt in executing and diligent in every part of his duty" (Gallatin, *Papers*, 19:875; Washington, *Papers, Pres. Ser.*, 4:395-6; 6:540-1;

Portsmouth *New-Hampshire Gazette*, 9 June 1812; Prince, *Federalists*, 46-56; Vol. 33:559-61; TJ to Gallatin, 17 Sep. 1802).

NO REASONS WERE ASSIGNED: Yeaton did not realize New Hampshire Federalists had informed the Adams administration that he was "well known to be a violent furious democrat, and abusive in the extreme." Federalist party leader Jeremiah Smith, the U.S. attorney and former New Hampshire congressman, described Yeaton as intemperate and "an open and decided Jacobin—he is a vehement railer against the government and of course a zealous partizan of France" (Prince, *Federalists*, 49, 52-6).

To Albert Gallatin

TH:J. TO MR GALLATIN   Nov. 12. 1801.

The supervisor of New hampshire (Rogers) was a revolutionary tory, I am therefore ready to change him.

If we are to appoint a federalist at Cherryton's, I have no doubt that Bowdoin is preferable to any other. his family has been among the most respectable on that shore for many generations. if however we have any means of enquiry we ought to avail ourselves of them.

Mr. Read's letter I forward to mr Madison merely to bring the establishment of those agents under his notice. he will return it to you.

The inclosed rough draught of a message I had prepared for the Senate will shew you the views in conformity with which were all the instructions which went from hence relative to the Senatorial complaint against Duane. my idea of the new prosecution was not that our atty should ever be heard to urge the Common law of England as in force otherwise than so far as adopted in any particular state. but that 1. he should renew it in the federal court if he supposed there was any Congressional statute which had provided for the case (other than the Sedition act) or if he thought he could shew that the Senate had made or adopted such a lex parliamentaria as might reach the case: or 2. that he should bring the prosecution in the state court of Pensylvania, if any statute of that state, or statutory adoption of the Common law of England had made the offence punishable. these were my views. they were not particularly given by way of instruction to the Attorney, because it was presumed they would occur to him, and we did not chuse by prescribing his line of procedure exactly, to take on ourselves an unnecessary responsability.—I will thank you to return the paper, as well for this message as the sketches, on the back of it, of some paragraphs of the first message to Congress, of which, in a day or two, I shall ask your revisal. in that the Sedition law will be presented under another view. health & good wishes.

RC (NHi: Gallatin Papers). PrC (DLC).

I FORWARD TO MR MADISON: the letter from James Read has not been found, but see TJ to Madison, 12 Nov., Document IV in Drafting the Annual Message to Congress, printed at this date. In 1792, two years after he became collector at Wilmington, North Carolina, Read received an appointment as inspector of excise with AGENTS UNDER HIS NOTICE (Madison, *Papers, Sec. of State Ser.*, 2:236-7; JEP, 1:102, 105-6; see also Gallatin to TJ, printed at 19 Oct.).

OUR ATTY: Alexander J. Dallas.

ENCLOSURE

Draft of Message to the Senate

GENT. OF THE SEN.   [before 12 Nov. 1801]

By a resoln of the Senate of the 14th. of May. 1800. the President was requested to instruct the proper law officer to prosecute William Duane editor of the newspaper called the Aurora for certain publications in that newspaper of the 19th. of Feb. 1800. learning[1] on my accession to the administration that the prosecution had been so instituted as to rest principally, if not solely, on the act called the Sedition act, I caused it to be discontinued, and another to be instituted under whatsoever [other] laws might be in existence against the offence alledged. if such other laws[2] did exist the object would be obtained which was desired by the Senate. but if the state of the laws before the passage of that act had[3] left the printer free to make the publication[4] complained of, then the Sedition act, abridging[5] that freedom was contrary to the very letter of the constitution which declares that Congress shall make no law abridging the freedom of the press[6] and consequently it was void. a new prosecution was accordingly instituted and brought forward with diligence, but the grand jury not finding the bill, it remains without effect. in this procedure I have endeavored to do the duty of my station between the Senate & Citizen; to pursue for the former that legal[7] vindication which was the object of their resolution; to cover the latter with whatsoever of protection the Constitution had guarded him, & to secure to the press that degree of freedom in which it remained under the authority of the states, with whom alone the power is left of abridging that freedom, the general government being expressly excluded from it.

The correspondence on this subject with the Atty of the district will shew more fully the details of the proceedings[8] in this case.

Dft (DLC: TJ Papers, 119:20569); entirely in TJ's hand, including set of brackets in the text; undated; written with wide margins for revisions; with partial first Dft of TJ's annual message to Congress on verso (see Document III in Drafting the Annual Message to Congress, printed at 12 Nov.).

RESOLN OF THE SENATE: realizing that William Duane would not be taken into custody and brought before them on contempt charges as ordered on 27 Mch. 1800, the Senate resolved, on 14 May, the last day of the session, "That the President of the United States be requested to instruct the proper law officer to commence and carry on a prosecution against William Duane, editor of the newspaper called the Aurora, for certain false, defamatory, scandalous, and malicious publications in the said newspaper, of the 19th of February last past, tending to defame the Senate of the United States, and to bring them into contempt and disrepute, and to excite against them the hatred of the good people of the United States" (JS, 3:60-1, 98). For the charges brought against Duane in March 1800 and TJ's involvement as president of the Senate, see Vol. 31:451-4, 466-7. TJ did not send this message to the Senate.

[1] Word interlined in place of "I learned."

[2] Preceding two words interlined.
[3] Preceding eleven words interlined in place of "[. . .] existing laws had."
[4] Preceding three words interlined in place of "do the act."
[5] Word interlined in place of "restraining."
[6] Preceding phrase from "which declares" to this point interlined.
[7] Word interlined.
[8] TJ first wrote "I send herewith a copy of the second bill & of the finding of the grand jury" before altering the sentence to read as above.

From Nicholas King

Washington 12th. Nov. 1801

Nicholas King's respects to Thomas Jefferson, and, begs his acceptance of the accompanying Drawing. Altho' inferior in execution, to the work of an Artist, he hopes it will not be thought the less of, as the tribute of esteem.

RC (DLC); endorsed by TJ as received 13 Nov. and so recorded in SJL. Enclosure not found, but see below.

The enclosed DRAWING has not been identified, but TJ's "Catalogue of Paintings &ca. at Monticello" includes, as item No. 85, "the President's House at Washington, in water colours by King." A week after sending this letter, the artist offered a proposal to publish, by subscription, "Two Views in the city of Washington," one of the President's House and executive offices and the other of the Capitol, "as they were in the Spring of the year 1801" (MS in ViU, undated, in TJ's hand; *National Magazine; or Cabinet of the United States* [Washington, D.C.], 19 Nov. 1801; Stein, *Worlds*, 84).

Notes on Circuit Court Cases

Nov. 12. State. Statement of causes in Circuit courts of US. from 1st. instn to 1801.

	institd.	decided	dependt.
N. Hampshire	111	99	12
R. Island	272	256	16
Mass.	284	248	36
Maine	7	7	
Conn.	358	320	38
Verm.	278	214	64
N. York	qu. 107	17	90
N. Jersey	101	90	11
Pennsylv.	980	796	184
Delaw.	130	100	30
Virginia	2063	1724	339
N. Carola	493	359	134
S. Carola	863	571	292
Georgia	898	751	147
W. Tenissee	188	112	76
	7133	5664	1469
Kentucky	670	445	225

MS (DLC: TJ Papers, 118:20350); entirely in TJ's hand; follows, on same sheet, Notes on the Bank of the United States and Internal Revenues, [10 Nov. 1801].

Early in June, James Madison sent a circular letter to U.S. district attorneys, indicating that he was "directed by the President" to collect information about cases instituted, decided, and still depending in the CIRCUIT COURTS as of 15 June. Madison asked the attorneys to have the information taken from the courts' dockets and to classify the cases "according to the nature of the suits" (Madison, *Papers, Sec. of State Ser.*, 1:256-7, 357; 2:42, 108, 123-4, 161). The figures collected for Maine, Kentucky, and Tennessee were for district, rather than circuit, courts. The data for New York included both the New York and the Albany districts, but the numbers obtained for Virginia and Pennsylvania included only the eastern district of each of those states. Madison apparently received information about the circuit court for Maryland after TJ made the tabulation above. Madison updated and corrected much of the information about the courts' cases up until 26 Feb. 1802, when TJ gave Congress detailed sets of tables from the State Department. TJ's figures for Vermont match those submitted to Congress. For the other courts, the totals incorporated in TJ's tally printed above differ, sometimes slightly, sometimes significantly, from the corrected results that Madison provided in February (same, 2:487-8; ASP, *Miscellaneous*, 1:319-25).

From Bowling Clark

Dear Sir   Poplar forist Novr. 13th. 1801

Yours of 26 Sept. & yours from Washinton came safe to hand, the Letter inclosed to Gipsen & Co. expect has answered my perpus in Richmond,—have delayed answering those two Letters in order to give you more sattisfactary acct. of your affairs hear—have layed of Mr Eppsis Land & Mr Randolphs the plats of which I inclose, am doutful you will not like the form of Mr Epps Land. I could not Lay it of aney other way so as to include Calliways & Rabartsons track & keep of[1] this plantation. to make it a tallirable track—not being willing to abide by my own Judgement alone in respect of the quallity of the Land I got the feaver of Mr Charles Clay & Mr Joshua Early. to ride with me over the Lands it was our appinions that the part sence laid of for Mr Randolph was worth double[2] that laid of for Mr Epps ℔ acre, being part of the prime of the old poplar forist track I think Mr Eppsis can be only called a midling track—have geathered & meashured the corn, make 466 Barrels. find my Judgement bad respecting the quantity mine & Whittinton shear of the above corn is 70 barrel which leaves you 396—so confident was I before the corn geathered that you would not have a nuf with my propotion, Whittinton not being willing to sell his that I ingaged 44 barrels in the neighberhood, which makes with my propotion (which is 48 barrels) added to yours 488 barrels, which is 38 barrels more then I think thay may do with unless the winter should prove vary hard, expect Mr Griffin may git of with some of this corn if hee thinks it to much 12 barrels of the corn that I have agreed for is to be delivered at Mr Pindexters Mill in Feby. to be takin away as its is wantin to eat which corn I gave 22/ ℔ barrle & paid for it with a Bond of Mr Bullocks due to your Est., I also agreed to give £20 for 20 barrles to be delive first decr. payable in Feby. 1802 & for the ballance 12 barrels I agreed to give 19/ payable in March 1802 for my own corn I shall charge you 19/ per barrel which I think is about avvirage price of corn selling hear—the Wheat I have sold to Brown & Co. with Mr Randolph & my own, for 6/6 certan & the best giniral price that shall be givin in Lynchburge for good crops betwix this & last of april—the quantity made 1090 bushels & 54 lb—

quantity sodded this fall	180
ground to eat	6
Ths. Whittintons shear	51.56
B. Clark shear	113.19
sold Brown & Co	739.39
	1090.54

in respect of pay for the corn & what debte your Est. my owe hear. I beleave your recource is to be full serfitiant I intend to drow as much money from Brown & Co as will pay me for my corn & what other ballances my be due me on the books for the present year, & beleave thare will be full serfitiant due you on black smiths acct. in good hands which Mr Griffin may cerlect to pay for the corn & what other nessisaryes hee may want for the use of the plantation. I doant recerlect of aney debt that your Est ows hear but what I mean to discharge before I gow away except that of the corn—the fall has bin so dry that thare has bin no chance to strip aney of our Tobacco that I cant say much about it only that it sorey but an in hopes that thare cant be less then twenty thousand weight—

have killed Ten Beaves & pickled them for you to be sent down. have put up Eighty hogs, midling good most of them as to sise, which provably may admit of a grater potion being sent you than useal—the wheat looks bad your Negrows has bin as helthy this fall as coman—I intind on your return to montisello to come down & bring my papers for a finell settlement unless I should hear of your intention of comeing to the forrist. should it be your intintion when you return home shall thenk to rite to me as it will save me a tiersom gerney expect to leave this in a few days an am

Dear sir your obt. sevt. &c   BOWLING CLARK

RC (ViU: Edgehill-Randolph Papers); addressed: "The Honourable Thomas Jefferson Esqr Preasident Washington"; franked; postmarked Lynchburg; endorsed by TJ as received 25 Nov. and so recorded in SJL with notation "Popl. for."; also endorsed by TJ: "on the lands laid off for J. W. Eppes and TMR." Enclosures not found.

YOURS OF 26 SEPT.: TJ's letters to Clark of 26 Sep. and 25 Oct., both recorded in SJL, have not been found.

1090 BUSHELS & 54 LB: sometimes bushels were reckoned not by volume but by weight—in this case, as shown by Clark's tallying, a bushel of wheat was 60 pounds (OED).

[1] MS: "of of."
[2] MS: "bubble."

From Gouverneur Morris

DEAR SIR   Morrisania 13 Novr. 1801

I have received your Favor of the first. Accept my Thanks for the Communications which it contains. Time will eventually give us whatever Great Britain may withhold in a commercial Treaty. It is probably fortunate for us that she had not the Good Sense to accede at an earlier Period to our reasonable Propositions. I am glad to find it is so clearly your Opinion that Spain will yield to proper Remonstrances respecting the Depredations at Algesiras. The rapid Encrease of our Population fosters the most pleasing Hopes. No Doubt can be reasonably entertained of the Prosperity Power and Glory of our Country if we preserve our Union and Form of Government. In a Word if we be not wanting to ourselves.

Accept I pray you Sir the Assurances of the Respect with which I have the Honor to be
your obedt Servt   GOUV MORRIS

RC (DLC); at foot of first page: "His Excellency Thomas Jefferson Esqr President of the United States"; endorsed by TJ as received 19 Nov. and so recorded in SJL. FC (Lb in DLC: Gouverneur Morris Papers; in Morris's hand).

From Robert Smith

SIR,   Navy Dept. Nov. 13. 1801

As it is probable that the frigate Boston may remain on the Mediterranean Station, and as Capt McNeill would in such case be improperly continued in service contrary to the determination of the Executive, I have conceived that some arrangement ought to be made to prevent such an impropriety. The enclosed letters have been prepared with that view and are submitted to your Consideration.

Be pleased to accept the assurances of my high Esteem—
RT SMITH

RC (DLC); endorsed by TJ as received from the Navy Department on 14 Nov. and so recorded in SJL with notation "McNeill & Barron"; also endorsed by TJ: "Barron to take place of McNiel." Enclosures: (1) Smith to James Barron, 13 Nov. 1801, informing Barron that "The President having the utmost confidence in your skill & Integrity" has appointed him to succeed Daniel McNeill as captain of the frigate *Boston*; Barron is therefore to assume command and follow whatever instructions he may receive from Commodore Richard Dale or the commanding officer of the Mediterranean station (FC in Lb in DNA: RG 45, LSO; notation in margin in unidentified hand: "not sent"). (2) Smith to Daniel McNeill, 13 Nov. 1801, informing him that under the terms of the Peace Establishment Act, the president must reduce the number of captains

in the navy to nine, and that he cannot retain McNeill in his commission "consistently with the principles of selection which have been adopted"; Smith orders McNeill to deliver command of the *Boston* to Barron, after which he is to consider himself out of the service and to take passage in the frigate Dale will send home (same; notation in margin in unidentified hand: "not sent").

Daniel MCNEILL remained in command of the *Boston* until August 1802, and was dismissed from the navy under the terms of the Peace Establishment Act the following October (NDBW, 2:232-3, 307).

THE DETERMINATION OF THE EXECUTIVE: see Notes on a Cabinet Meeting, 22 Oct.

From Willie Blount

S<small>IR</small>,   Knoxville November 14th. 1801

Being disengaged this evening from such pursuits as generally engage my attention, and it occuring to me that I might not be considered an intruder, since I am one of those who admire your doings and quite willing and desirous that you should continue to preside as President of the United States so long as you may feel disposed to act in that way, and feeling desirous you should know merely for my own gratification that there does exist within the limits of the United States a man of my name, have written you this letter to which I in language of the purest sincerity subscribe it, as

Your unfeigned and unalterable friend   W<small>ILLIE</small> B<small>LOUNT</small>

RC (DLC); at foot of text: "Thomas Jefferson Esquire President of the United States"; endorsed by TJ as received 18 Dec. and so recorded in SJL. Enclosed in Nathaniel Macon to TJ, 18 Dec.

Willie Blount (1768?-1835), a North Carolina lawyer educated at Columbia College and the College of New Jersey, moved to Knoxville in the 1790s and served as secretary to his half-brother William Blount (d. 1800), who was governor of the Southwest Territory. Willie Blount served one term in the state House of Representatives and became governor of Tennessee in 1809, holding that office for three consecutive terms. Blount wrote two other letters, not found, to TJ as president on 11 Jan. and 1 Feb. 1809 (A<small>NB</small>; D<small>AB</small>).

To James Monroe

D<small>EAR</small> S<small>IR</small>   Washington Nov. 14. 1801.

The bearer hereof is mr Whitney of Connecticut a mechanic of the first order of ingenuity, who invented the Cotton gin now so much used to the South; he is at the head of a considerable gun manufactory in Connecticut, and furnishes the US. with muskets, undoubtedly the best they recieve. he has invented moulds & machines for making all the peices of his locks so exactly equal, that take 100 locks to pieces & mingle their parts, and the hundred locks may be put together as well by taking the first pieces which come to hand. this is of importance in repairing, because out of 10. locks e.g. disabled for the want of different pieces, 9 good locks may be put together without employing a smith. Leblanc in France had invented a similar process in 1788. & had extended it to the barrel, mounting & stock. I endeavored to get the US. to bring him over, which he was ready for on moderate terms. I failed & I do not know what became of him.

mr Whitney has not yet extended his improvements beyond the lock. I think it possible he might be engaged in our manufactory of Richmd,[1] tho I have not asked him the question. I know nothing of his moral character. he is now on his way to S. Carola on the subject of his gin. health & happiness cum ceteris votis.

TH: JEFFERSON

RC (DLC: Monroe Papers); addressed: "Governour Monroe Richmond" and "favored by mr Whitney"; endorsed by Monroe. PrC (DLC).

LEBLANC: at varying times during TJ's tenure in France, he reported to John Jay, Patrick Henry, and Henry Knox on a system of interchangeable parts developed by French gunmaker Honoré Blanc (Bedini, *Statesman of Science*, 141-3; Vol. 8:455; Vol. 9:214; Vol. 15:421-3, 454-5).

In January 1798, the Virginia legislature authorized the establishment of an arms MANUFACTORY near Richmond. Designated the Virginia Manufactory of Arms, the site produced its first small arms (muskets and bayonets) in 1802 and turned out a variety of weaponry for the state's militia until operations ceased in 1821 (Giles Cromwell, *The Virginia Manufactory of Arms* [Charlottesville, 1975], 11, 43, 66, 133, 150).

CUM CETERIS VOTIS: "along with other good wishes."

[1] Preceding two words interlined.

From Samuel Smith

SIR/   Baltimore 14. Novr. 1801

I Congratulate you on the success & good Fortune of the Squadron under Commodore Dale—Lieut Sterett's success will Convince the Tripolitan & other Barbary Powers of the Truth of Mr. Cathcarts remark—(that they would not find the Americans like the Neopolitan Castratti) & I hope will tend to keep the other Powers in Peace with us—War having now Actually Commenced, It becomes a Duty to have a Force Constantly near Tripoli. this will be facilitated by having Malta open to us—they may be induced to go to Sea in the Winter Season & some of our Ships may be taken. this would Cause Censure especially as Six Ships are directed to be Constantly employed—and altho: I was formerly of opinion that the Second Squadron ought to remain untill the Middle of February—I now am unwilling to risque the Reputation the Administration has gained & I am (on Reflection) of Opinion that the Second Squadron ought to depart without Delay I consider the Boston as One & would recommend the Constitution & Chesapeake to Man & Join her—And (if Congress will permit) The Constellation, or Adams may proceed in March—There will then be four untill August when the times of the

Bostons Crew will have expired & she must return home—This perhaps will be the more necessary as Tunis demands what I presume will not be granted—Tunis you will remember has near 90 Boats Brigs Schooners Ships &c. and four Ports—and perhaps may make Common Cause with Tripoli—Her Demand of Cannon &c. not being Complied with, will perhaps be Considered by her as Cause of War— Our Commerce will now be pursued under the Idea of Security & may fall a Sacrifice to Tunis whose Cruizers (agreeably to Eaton) go to Sea at all Seasons of the Year, & if our Vessells are long absent may sieze this Moment most proper for Depredations—The Government knowing the Danger & not providing against, will be Subjected to Just Censure, for this War is a War of Slavery to our People that may be taken—

The appointment of William Paterson of N. York has distressed our Friends greatly—His Father was a Brittish Capt. made Collector of Philada. under the King—he went to England, an inveterate Tory[1] where this young Man was educated—on the Fathers Death the family returned. they have been Tories & are Invariably *violently Anglo Federalists*—The young Man your decided Enemy (for I am personally well Acquainted with him) and No Englishman ever had more decided prejudices against the French—His conversation respecting the Brittish, perfectly English—His family & that of Mr. Dallas are Intimate—I have been told that Mr. D. declined Interfering in his Behalf—He is related to the Chanceller—I was in favor of Mr. Lee— I am told both he & Mr. Irwin are the Sons of Refugees—I pray you to excuse my taking the liberty of offering my Opinions, & that you will believe that I am with sincerity—

your freind & Servt.   S. SMITH

RC (DLC); addressed: "Thomas Jefferson, Esqr. President of the U.S. Washington"; endorsed by TJ as received 15 Nov. and so recorded in SJL.

James Leander Cathcart's REMARK appeared in his 2 June 1801 letter to Thomas Appleton, the American consul at Leghorn, written shortly after Tripoli's declaration of war on the United States (NDBW, 1:483-5). Slightly different versions of the letter appeared in the *National Intelligencer* on 2 Sep. and in the *New-York Gazette* on 7 Sep.

For the estimates by William EATON of the marine force of Tunis, see Samuel Smith to TJ, 4 May 1801 (second letter).

William Patterson's FATHER was probably John Patterson (d. 1798), a former British army officer and the collector of customs at Philadelphia during the 1770s. He married Catharine Livingston, a daughter of Robert Livingston (1708-1790) and a distant cousin of Chancellor Robert R. Livingston (PMHB, 25 [1901], 576; 33 [1909], 124, 380-1; Edwin Brockholst Livingston, *The Livingstons of Livingston Manor* [New York, 1910], 545-6; Dangerfield, *Livingston*, genealogy table following p. 516; *Philadelphia Gazette*, 24 Feb. 1798).

[1] Preceding three words interlined.

From Samuel Smith

Sir/   Balto 14 Nov 1801

Since writing my Letter of this Morning, Mr. John Donnell (one of our Republican & most wealthy Merchts.) put into my hand the Inclosed Letter from his Father in Law Mr. Isaac Smith on whose subject I have already written Mr. Gallatin. Mr. Smith was Collector under the King, is a man of Business highly respectable & Invariably a Whig—Mr. Bowdon is also his son in Law—Mr. Savage the New Member of Congress is also Connected with him & I do really believe that his being appointed will have a very excellent effect in the Counties of Northampton & Accomack—the Federalism of those Counties is modest & means right. they only want Information

I had already written to Mr Gallatin on this subject & sincerely wish that the appointment of Mr. Smith, because I am Confident It will have an excellent effect—your friend & servt.   S SMITH

RC (NHi: Gallatin Papers); endorsed by TJ as received 15 Nov. and so recorded in SJL; also endorsed by a Treasury Department clerk. Enclosure: Extract of Isaac Smith to John Donnell, Northampton, 5 Nov., expressing his "wish to be appointed Collector of the Custom for the port of Cherryton" and noting that Peter Bowdoin had already been offered the position, according to James Taylor, son-in-law of Thomas Newton, and rejected it, recommending the writer instead (Tr in NHi: Gallatin Papers, in an undentified hand, with notation in Samuel Smith's hand: "NB—Mr Bowdoin is Son in Law to Mr. Smith"; Gallatin, *Papers*, 5:968). Enclosed in TJ to Gallatin, 16 Nov.

I HAVE ALREADY WRITTEN MR. GALLATIN: on 11 Nov., Samuel Smith wrote the Treasury secretary recommending Isaac Smith for the post at Cherrystone. He described Smith as an "honest upright Intelligent Man" who was "related to all the most respectable People" in the county. He was a Federalist, as were almost all men in Accomac and Northampton counties, "but their Federalism arose from their fear of the goverment being in

Danger, not of the Vicious kind that we have witnessed" (Gallatin, *Papers*, 6:13). On 17 Nov., Samuel Smith again wrote Gallatin recommending Isaac Smith. He enclosed a letter from Smith to John Donnell, of 9 Nov., confirming that Bowdoin had declined the office and had recommended Isaac Smith to James Taylor as a "proper person" for the position. Isaac Smith also thanked Donnell for offering to serve as his security. In closing, he noted, "I Shall be obliged to you to do the best you can for me in the business, and to lose no time, as there will be other applications" (same, 5:979; 6:51). SAVAGE THE NEW MEMBER OF CONGRESS: perhaps either Nathaniel L. or George Savage, who served as representatives of Northampton County in the Virginia House of Delegates in 1776, the same year Isaac Smith served as state senator representing Accomac and Northampton counties. Washington appointed George Savage customs collector at Cherrystone in 1789, a position he held until early 1790 (Leonard, *General Assembly*, 123-4; Washington, *Papers, Pres. Ser.*, 4:318).

[665]

From Philip Mazzei

Il 28 del[1] passato 7bre consegnai a Mr. Appleton un sacchettino, contenente dei noccioli di 4 qualità di Pesche, con un lettera cucitavi sopra e a Lei diretta, la quale non contenendo altro che la descrizione delle dette pesche, e ciò che riguarda La piantazione di quei noccioli, non ne mando copia, poichè sarebbe superflua senza i noccioli, e i noccioli non Le possono per venire senza la lettera, essendo cucita sul sacchettino che gli contiene.

Dopo quel tempo mi è per venuta una Lettera degli Amici N. & J. & R. Vanstaphorst d'Amsterdam, nella quale mi dicono: "Mr. John Barnes of Georgetown, Virginia, has remitted us for your account '*f* 1417:10 at 60 days sight, at the exchange of 40 Cts. per Guilder.'" Persuaso che questo denaro mi venga da Lei, e che Ella siasi degnato di darmene avviso, Le fo sapere che finora non ò avuto La sorta di ricever sue Lettere, dopo quella del 24 Aprile 1796, conforme Le significai in varie lettere, e più particularmente in quella del 6 xbre 1800. Non. Le posso esprimere quanto ciò mi rincresce. Spero che, quando ancora la moltiplicità dell'importantissime occupazioni pubbliche non Le permettessero scrivermi di proprio pugno, Ella si degnerebbe di darmi la sue nuove per terza mano, mettendovi la sua firma.

L'annesso foglio contiene, com'Ella vedrà, la 2da. copia della mia lettera del 2 Luglio, e l'aggiunta che feci alla prima copia il 30 dell'istesso mese, nella quale inclusi un'esemplare della traduzion toscana del suo discorso stampato alla macchia. Ora Le ne includo un'esemplare della 2da. edizione, della quale mi è riescito di correggerne le prove; e nella quale non trovo altro difetto che la mancanza d'un *che* alla p. 5, che ò messo nel margine.[2]

Ma se fosse creduto più opportuno l'averci un'Incaricato d'affari, o Ministro, con credenziali alla varie Corti, onde poter trattare gli affari direttamente, più prontamente, e con maggior probabilità d'efficacia, gradirei molto d'esser'io quello per i seguenti motivi. Sarebbe cosa molto consolante ed onorevole per me la dimostrazione di non esser dimenticato nella mia Patria adottiva. Un annuo salario di £.200 sterline, aggiunto alla mia tenue entrata, sarebbe un buon aiuto per me, e sufficiente per esercitarne le funzioni decorosamente; il doppio non basterebbe forse ad un'altro; e non vi sarebbe gran probablità, (il tutto considerato) di ottenerne un meglior servizio.

Per ora non La tedierò di vantaggio; e pieno di stima e di gratitudine per la continuazione dei suoi buoni officii, mi confermo di vero cuore,

Suo, &c &c

Dear, esteemed Friend,   15 Nov. 1801

On the 28th of last September I handed Mr. Appleton a small bag containing pits of four varieties of peaches with a letter addressed to you sewn on it. As the letter contained only the description of the peaches and directions for planting the pits, I am sending no copy herewith, for it would serve no purpose without the pits, and you cannot have received the pits without at the same time receiving the letter sewn on the bag containing them.

Later I received a letter from our Amsterdam friends N. & J. & R. Van Staphorst informing me that "Mr. John Barnes of Georgetown, Virginia, has remitted us for your account 1417.10 florins at 60 days sight, at the exchange of 4 Cts. per Guilder."

Since I am sure that the remittance comes from you and that you must have taken the trouble to so notify me, I will inform you that to date I have received no letter from you since the one dated April 24, 1796. I have so apprised you in several letters, especially in the one of December 6, 1800. I cannot tell you how much I regret the matter. I hope, however, that in case the many important duties of your office should prevent you from writing personally, you will be good enough to let me hear from you through a third person with only the signature in your own hand.

The enclosed paper contains, as you can see, the second copy of my letter of July 2 with the addition made on July 30. With the first copy I also enclosed a copy of my Tuscan translation of your inaugural address, printed clandestinely. Now I enclose a copy of the second edition, the proofs of which I was able to correct. The only error I find is the omission of a *che* on page five, which I have added on the margin.

However, should it be deemed more advisable to have a chargé d'affaires or a minister accredited to the various courts in order to negotiate directly, more expeditiously, and with greater probability of success, I would very much like to be it for the following reasons: it would be very comforting and honorable to me to have evidence that I have not been forgotten by my adoptive country; a yearly salary of £200 sterling added to my small income would be of great help to me and sufficient for me to fill the office decorously; double that amount would not perhaps be enough for someone else; and, all things considered, there would be no great likelihood that he would serve better.

Right now I shall trouble you no further. With great esteem and gratitude for your continued good offices, I again declare myself to be truly,

Yours, etc. etc.

Dft (Archivio Filippo Mazzei, Pisa, Italy); part of a conjoined series of Mazzei's drafts of letters to TJ, where it precedes Mazzei's letter of 10 Apr. 1802 (see Margherita Marchione and Barbara B. Oberg, eds., *Philip Mazzei: The Com-*

prehensive Microform Edition of his Papers, 9 reels [Millwood, N.Y., 1981], 6:905-7). RC recorded in SJL as received from Pisa on 12 Apr. 1802 but not found. Enclosure: (1) Dupl of Mazzei to TJ, 2 July, with 30 July addition (not found, but see below). (2) *Discorso del Signor Tommaso Jefferson*, rev. ed. (Pisa?, 1801), with marginal correction in ink in Mazzei's hand (same, 5:158-62; Sowerby, No. 3262).

UNA LETTERA DEGLI AMICI N. & J. & R. VANSTAPHORST: Mazzei answered a 25 Sep. letter from the Dutch bankers Van Staphorst & Hubbard on 23 Oct. He requested that they remit the money sent on his Virginia account. Mazzei wrote to

the firm again on 1 Jan. 1802, assuring it that the two bills they forwarded in a letter of 24 Nov. 1801 had been accepted and would be paid in due time (Margherita Marchione and others, eds., *Philip Mazzei: Selected Writings and Correspondence*, 3 vols. [Prato, Italy, 1983], 3:252, 254-5, 256; Vol. 33:329). LA 2DA. COPIA DELLA MIA LETTERA: for Mazzei's letter of 2 July see Mazzei to TJ, 30 July 1801.

[1] Mazzei here canceled "prossimo."

[2] Here follows a passage of two paragraphs, which Mazzei apparently decided to remove and send as a separate letter, dated 19 Nov. It is printed under that date.

Notes on a Consultation with Robert Smith

Nov. 15.   Navy departmt. settled with mr Smith the following arrangement for the Navy the ensuing year.

the Constitution now at Boston
Adams   N. York } to be employed in the Mediterranean.
Constellation Philada

Philadelphia }
Essex   } now in Mediterranean to come home ready for laying up if Congress so directs
Boston

President[1]   } to come here to be laid up.
Chesapeake now at Norfolk

Congress, J. Adams, United States, Genl. Greene, N. York to continue here laid up.

MS (DLC: TJ Papers, 118:20350); follows, on same sheet, Notes on Circuit Court Cases, 12 Nov. 1801.

On 17 Nov., TJ received a short letter from the Navy Department enclosing commissions for officers on board the schooner *Enterprize*, who had been acting "without regular Commissions & War-

rants" (RC in DLC; undated; unsigned, in a clerk's hand; endorsed by TJ as received 17 Nov. from the Navy Department and "Commissions for officers of Enterprize" and so recorded in SJL; enclosures not found).

[1] Word interlined in place of "G. Washington now in do."

From James Workman

Sir,   Alexandria, Novr. 15th. 1801—

This communication is addressed to you by one, who altho' not a citizen of the American Republic, is nevertheless desirous of promoting her just interests from a long formed prepossession in her favor, as well as for various reasons derived from the present moral & political State of the World.

To me it appears that an increase of her Power, if it could be justly & honorably obtained would at this time be expedient, from the enormous augmentation of the military resources of those States with which she may, at no distant period, be obliged to contend.

Should France get possession of Louisiana & the Floridas, & pursue there her usual policy towards the Negroes, the fatal consequences in respect to the only vulnerable part of this Commonwealth, are too obvious to be mentioned.

Were the United States to take those Countries, that danger would not only be for ever removed; but the Congress might, in virtue of the right of Conquest, make such beneficial regulations respecting the Slaves, there, and enforce such laws against the perpetuity of Slavery, as would in time annihilate that odious condition. This would necessarily lead to similar measures in the adjoining States, & consequently to the total abolition throughout the Empire of an Establishment by which it is enfeebled, Endangered, contaminated & disgraced.

Louisiana & the Floridas would afford abundant choice of Districts, suitable in every respect for the settlement of Emancipated Negroes.

The consequences of this conquest would, of course be the loss of much American[1] commercial property. The interest of merchants deserves, no doubt, considerable attention; but not to the detriment of all the rest of the community. A reduction in the price of grain, & the utmost losses that could arise from captures at Sea, could hardly be put in Estimation against the advantages derivable from the possession of these Territories.

But might not this lead to a breach with France?—Possibly it might. But such a breach, at all events, is not improbable. France will hardly forgive the past conduct of these States towards her; or forbear to resent it when a favorable opportunity offers. If you must quarrel with her, it is better to have your feeble flank defended. Most likely, however, the taking of Louisiana would prevent such a rupture, 'tho otherwise probable. France will by this time consider the Spanish Colonies as her own; She would therefore be unwilling to leave the richest of them in such peril as they would be in, when such an Enemy as the American Republic was in possession of Louisiana. She would therefore naturally be desirous of mediating betwen it & her Ally, to save him (that is herself) from any farther loss.

The authority of Congress over Louisiana would not easily be shaken; & the command of the Navigation of the Mississipi, would for ever secure to the Union the Western States; Whereas, if France were mistress of that river, their adherence to the Empire might, in critical times, become Exceedingly precarious.

I have the honor to be, Sir, With the greatest respect, Yr. Most Obedient Servant, JAMES WORKMAN.

RC (MoSHi: Jefferson Papers); at head of text: "Private"; at foot of text: "To His Excellency Thomas Jefferson, President of the United States of America"; endorsed by TJ as received 1 Dec. and so recorded in SJL. Enclosure: Workman's *Political Essays* (see below).

James Workman (d. 1832) was born in Ireland, probably in the 1770s. He studied law at the Middle Temple in London and may have had experience in the British army. In the 1790s, through such writings as *An Argument Against Continuing the War* and *A Letter to His Grace the Duke of Portland*, he advocated a cessation of Britain's war against France. Workman probably left England for the United States in 1799, and after spending time in several seaboard cities he took up residence in Charleston, South Carolina, in the winter of 1801-2. Workman's play *Liberty in Louisiana*, which praised the arrival of U.S. law in Louisiana, was staged and published in Charleston in 1804. That year he moved to New Orleans, where he worked as secretary to W. C. C. Claiborne, then the governor of Orleans Territory, and secretary of the territory's legislative council, in which capacity he drafted laws, assisted in the transition of Louisiana's legal system to accommodate the laws and practices of the United States, and earned some repute for his understanding of both systems of law. In 1805, Claiborne named

Workman a judge in Orleans County and probate judge of Orleans Territory. Politically, however, Workman became part of a faction opposed to Claiborne that included Daniel Clark and Edward Livingston. In the wake of the disclosure of the Burr conspiracy, James Wilkinson had Workman arrested for his role in the Mexican Association, a group that hoped to liberate Spain's North American colonies. Workman won acquittal at trial, but his dispute with Wilkinson and accusations of conspiracy further alienated him from Claiborne and made TJ suspicious of him. In 1808, Workman represented Livingston in a hearing in the Batture case, and a conflict with the U.S. attorney led to Workman's disbarment by the court. He left New Orleans in 1809 but returned in 1817, resumed the practice of law, and later won election to the Louisiana legislature. In 1821 he was elected a member of the American Philosophical Society. His wife had died of yellow fever not long after their arrival in Charleston, and he had no surviving spouse or children at the time of his death (Jared William Bradley, ed., *Interim Appointment: W. C. C. Claiborne Letter Book, 1804-1805* [Baton Rouge, 2002], 389-414, 596-603; James Workman, *An Argument Against Continuing the War* [London, 1795]; James Workman, *A Letter to His Grace the Duke of Portland*, 3d ed. [London, 1797]; James Workman, *Liberty in Louisiana; A Comedy*, 2d ed.

[Charleston, 1804]; APS, *Proceedings*, 22, pt. 3 [1884], 502, 531; Joseph C. Cabell to TJ, 13 Mch. 1807, in DLC; Claiborne to TJ, 1 June 1807, in same).

NOT A CITIZEN: Workman became a naturalized U.S. citizen in May 1804 (Bradley, *Interim Appointment*, 391).

With the letter printed above, Workman sent TJ a copy of his new pamphlet called *Political Essays*, which contained his *Argument Against Continuing the War*, his *Letter* to the Duke of Portland, and a previously unpublished memorial Workman had sent to the British government in 1800 proposing the seizure of Spanish possessions in the Americas and the settlement of Irish Catholics in the conquered territories. Published in Alexandria, Virginia, *Political Essays* bore the date 14 Nov. 1801 (James Workman, *Political Essays, Relative to the War*

of the French Revolution [Alexandria, Va., 1801]; Sowerby, No. 3272; Bradley, *Interim Appointment*, 392-3).

TJ answered Workman briefly on 4 Dec.: "Th: Jefferson presents his compliments to mr Workman and his thanks for the pamphlet sent him which he shall peruse with pleasure. the event of peace will leave territorial possessions in their present state until the men of Europe shall have recovered breath and strength enough to recommence their sanguinary conflicts which they seem to consider as the object for which they are brought into the world." No other correspondence between Workman and TJ has been found or is recorded in SJL (PrC in MoSHi: Jefferson Papers; endorsed by TJ in ink on verso).

[1] Word interlined.

Schedule of the funded debt of the US. Sep. 30. 1801.

	English	Dutch	Geneva Switzerland	all other foreigners
6. p. cents	3,961,104.43[1]	7,054,657.64	435,028.03[2]	451,174.25
3. pr. c.	6,454,044.23	4,337,094.83	523,571.46	287,810.45
Deferred 6.s	4,611,767.87	1,896,632.08	338,173.05	262,977.22
8. pr. cents	710,600.	71,600.	70,500	183,300
5$\frac{1}{2}$ pr. cent	727,500.	445,700	67,400.	30,000.
4$\frac{1}{2}$ pr. cent	41,600.		9,000.	
Navy 6. pr cents	3,400.	15,000.		1,500.
5. pr. cents				
	16,510,016.58	13,820,684.55	1,493,672.54	1,216,761.92

the Funded Debt

States	Incorporated bodies	Sinking fund	Domestic individuals	Total
2,298,251.65	5,236,840.34	1,884,680.22	8,669,246.28	30,040,982.89
1,739,360.49	885,789.17	620,365.61	4,816,310.23	19,664,346.47
1,549,418.98	1,234,572.54	973,204.66	3,723,091.15	14,589,837.55
	1,286,300.		4,113,100.	6,435,400.
	220,100.[3]	1,400.	354,800.	1,848,900.
	108,200.		17,200.	176,000.
2,000.	102,300.		584,900.	709,100.
		1,280,000.		1,280,000.
5,589,031.12	9,076,102.05	4,759,650.49	22,278,647.66	74,744,566.91

Add Georgia abstract not included	113,680.49
Certificates on their passage to and from the treasury	121,082.57
errors and fractions	1,005.32
	74,980,335.29

MS (DLC: TJ Papers, 118:20350);
entirely in TJ's hand; undated, but follows, on verso of same sheet, Notes on a
Consultation with Robert Smith, 15 Nov.

[1] For totals, this figure should be 3,961,104.48.

[2] This figure should be 485,028.03.

[3] This figure should be 222,100.

To Albert Gallatin

TH:J. TO MR GALLATIN.   Nov. 16. 1801.

I omitted in my last note to you to express my approbation of what you propose as to mr Nourse. his known integrity and every other circumstance of the case make it proper. it would seem by Genl. Smith's letter that Isaac Smith of Northampton has been *invariably a whig.* if so there need be no further hesitation to appoint him for Cherriton's, and the rather as he says that Bowdoin has declined on being spoken to by mr Taylor.

RC (NHi: Gallatin Papers); addressed: "The Secretary of the Treasury." Not recorded in SJL. Enclosure: Samuel Smith to TJ, 14 Nov. (second letter) and enclosure.

According to SJL, TJ's LAST letter to Gallatin was that of 14 Nov. (see Document v in Drafting the Annual Message to Congress, printed at 12 Nov.). WHAT YOU PROPOSE: see same, Document VI.

From Elisha Hinman

New London Novemr. 16th 1801

I beg leave to lay before his Excellency, Thomas Jefferson, President of the United States, some facts.

In the year 1775 I left the best employ in this town being called upon by Government to accept a lieutenant's commission in the navy—I raised 80 men and joined Commodore Hopkins in the Dellaware. He proceeded to New Providence, took possession of the Forts & town. Commodore Hopkins ordered me to take command of a sloop laden with Cannon and other war-like stores taken from the Forts. On our way home, by reason of a gale of wind in the night I lost sight of the fleet and came near being taken by two British ships of war. had that been the case at that time, my life would have been in great danger—On our arrival at New London the Commodore ordered me to take command of the Brig Cabbot; I proceeded on a cruise and captured five British ships from Jamaica laden with sugars & rum, and they arrived safe into ports. The Government then, had two thirds and the Captors one; my part lay in the hands of the agents 'till it was of but little value; and when recieved was employed in goods, in store, and burned by General Arnold. In 1777 I was commissioned a Capt. to command the Alfred, joined the Raleigh, Capt. Thompson, at Portsmouth. We proceeded on a cruise and captured one ship laden with sugars. she arrived in Massachusetts. Two large ships from Jamaica we carried to France with us, which were sold by the agents. I recieved my part and had it with me on my way home, was taken by two British ships and carried a prisoner to England, put in Fortune prison—some time after made my escape and got to France leaving all I had behind. At the close of the war Colol. Walker was appointed to settle with the navy officers. he settled my accounts without the least difficulty and found due to me 3000 dollars back wages; he gave me a Government note which I was obliged to sell for three shillings on the pound. When the Cutter was first established I was appointed to the command of the one I have now the command of; but being absent for a year knew not of it; and had made contracts in Hispaniola which honour bound me to comply with. Capt. Maltbie was then appointed—before his death I had met with great losses at sea: after his death I applied for the command and layed this statement before the President—believe I have been faithful, should I be displaced it will leave me and my family in distress: I beg his Excellence to take these things into consideration and continue my command. I have been and will be faithful to orders recieved.

I have the honour to be, with due respect, his Excellency's most obet. Humle. Sert.   ELISHA HINMAN

RC (DNA: RG 59, LAR); in an unidentified hand, signed by Hinman; addressed: "His Excely. Thomas Jefferson. President of the United States"; endorsed by TJ as received 10 Dec. and so recorded in SJL. Enclosed in John Langdon to Gideon Granger, 4 Dec. 1801, in which Langdon describes Hinman as "my old Acquaintance" and considers him to be "an honest man and a Republican," but admitting that Granger was probably a better judge as to "whether it would be proper to recommend him or not" (RC in DNA: RG 59, LAR; endorsed by TJ).

Elisha Hinman (d. 1807) of New London served with distinction during the American Revolution as an officer in the Continental navy and as a privateer commander. He received command of the federal revenue cutter *Argus* in 1798, following the death of the vessel's previous captain, Jonathan Maltbie. Concerns expressed about Hinman's advanced age were offset by the fact that he had been a steady Federalist and that the other candi-

date, first mate George House, was a firm Republican. TJ replaced Hinman with House in May 1803 (Louis F. Middlebrook, *History of Maritime Connecticut During the American Revolution, 1775-1783*, 2 vols. [Salem, Mass., 1925], 2:150-3; Prince, *Federalists*, 71-2; Madison, *Papers, Sec. of State Ser.*, 1:141, 193; *Connecticut Gazette and the Commercial Intelligencer*, 2 Sep. 1807; Vol. 33:673; Vol. 34:357n).

Commodore Esek HOPKINS, the first commander of the Continental navy, led a successful expedition against the Bahamas in 1776 (ANB).

Captain Thomas THOMPSON commanded the Continental frigate *Raleigh* from 1776 to 1778 (John A. McManemin, *Captains of the Continental Navy* [Ho-Ho-Kus, N.J., 1981], 423-36).

In 1786, the Confederation Congress appointed Benjamin WALKER, a former aide-de-camp to George Washington, a commissioner to settle the accounts of the hospital, marine, and clothing departments. He represented New York in Congress from 1801 to 1803 as a Federalist

(Washington, *Papers, Pres. Ser.*, 2:430-1; Syrett, *Hamilton*, 5:373-6; *Biog. Dir. Cong.*).

STATEMENT BEFORE THE PRESI-DENT: Hinman applied for command of the revenue cutter in a letter to John

Adams dated 18 Mch. 1798, citing his former service, good health, lack of further ambition, and a distressed financial situation that left his family in need of "a better support then what I am now able to give them" (DNA: RG 59, LAR).

From George Jefferson

DEAR SIR   Richmond 16th. Novr. 1801

The mad-man Stewart is again here. he has called on me for $:105—which I was obliged to let him have, or I supposed suffer him to go to Jail. The Captains a/c against him for six passages &C. was $:75.—& he could not he said do with less than 30 in addition. on my asking him if he had an order he informed me that you told him your former letter was sufficient.

Our friend in Petersburg has not yet made a purchase of the Tobacco; he informed us soon after the date of my last that he could not get any at what he thought it worth, and was of opinion that he could get it on better terms in the course of a few weeks—on which we desired that he would exercise his own judgment, but gave him notice that it would be required within two or three weeks. I expect daily to hear from him.

I am Dear Sir Your Very humble servt.   GEO. JEFFERSON

RC (MHi); at foot of text: "Thos. Jefferson esqr."; endorsed by TJ as received 20 Nov. and so recorded in SJL.

For TJ's previous letter regarding advances to William STEWART, see George Jefferson to TJ, 17 June.

SIX PASSAGES: Stewart now brought his wife, Mary, and children to Monticello. TJ noted in his financial records that George Jefferson paid Stewart $105 on 16 Nov. Before the Stewart family left Philadelphia, John Barnes advanced funds for the trip. On 20 Oct., Barnes gave Mary Stewart $30 "for Use of herself and Children's Clothing" and on 24 Oct. he gave Stewart $27 "as ₽ State-

ment." While in Philadelphia, Barnes also purchased various items for TJ which he gave to Stewart to deliver at Monticello, including $9.63 worth of glass purchased from Joseph Donath. TJ itemized all of the advances to Stewart in his financial memoranda at 22 Dec., including $6 furnished by Roberts & Jones, the Philadelphia ironmongers, on 24 Oct. The advances charged to Stewart's account totaled $168 (MB, 2:964, 1052, 1060; statement of private account from John Barnes, via Philadelphia, 4 Nov. 1801, in ViU; Vol. 34:407).

MY LAST: George Jefferson to TJ, 22 Oct.

From James Madison

Monday morning [16 Nov. 1801]

J. Madison presents his respects to the President with a letter from Col. Burr & another from Col. Humphreys, the latter is a duplicate, with an exception of the postscript. J.M. has been so much indisposed since saturday evening that he could not call on the President, as he wished, in order to consult his intentions as to Mr. Thornton's letter. If the President proposes to make it the subject of conversation among the heads of Depts. it is suggested whether it may not be best to hasten a meeting in order that no room may be given by delay, for inferring that hesitation existed as to the proper answer. A continuance of J.M's indisposition will deprive him & Mrs. M. of the pleasure of dining with the President today

RC (DLC); partially dated; endorsed by TJ as received from the State Department on 16 Nov. and "Thornton's lre" and so recorded in SJL. Enclosure: Burr to TJ, 10 Nov., recorded in SJL as received from New York on 13 Nov., but not found. Other enclosure not identified.

Thornton wrote to Madison from Philadelphia on 11 Nov. 1801, questioning TJ's opinion on the cases of the *Harmony* and the *Windsor* and seeking clarification on whether French armed vessels did or did not have the privilege of bringing British prizes into American ports (Madison, *Papers, Sec. of State Ser.*, 2:234-5).

MR. THORNTON'S LETTER: Edward

To Thomas Mann Randolph

DEAR SIR   Washington Nov. 16. 1801.

I am happy to hear that the children are likely to bear the attack of the whooping cough with vigour. it is a most unfortunate season for it to have come on; and I cannot but be anxious about them through the whole winter: consequently desirous to hear as often as possible how they are. my business I find will often prevent my writing by post. it is now got to a steady & uniform course. it keeps me from 10. to 12 & 13 hours aday at my writing table, giving me an interval of 4. hours for riding dining & a little unbending. pressing matters happening on our post day, of course[1] occasion me to miss a post. I inclose poems for Anne. if she takes care of all I send her, she may be able by & by to publish a volume of well selected poems. Ellen shall be answered the first vacant moment.—the proposition relative to Poplar Forest has been made on mature consideration, and will remain open for your acceptance when your own convenience shall determine it. it would have been made long ago, but that there were

[677]

sensible burthens of debt still on my shoulders. these are not yet cleared off; but I trust that the profits of my estate being now left entirely eased of any call towards my maintenance, they will discharge, while I am here, what remains still unpaid. to be entirely clear of debt is an object of great anxiety. that accomplished, I shall feel no uneasiness to accumulate property in my own hands. I foresee indeed that on my retirement, whenever that takes place, I may be subjected to an expence the more difficult to be controuled on account of the motives which will subject me to it. I must leave to the day to provide it's own remedy.—the Hessian fly is laying waste all the wheat in this quarter, the late as well as early sown. we are still suffering under drought.— I am informed Moran has neglected my work, to work elsewhere. if so, I ought to look elsewhere for the ensuing season, as it would seem he is not to be depended on. I should be glad of your opinion as to his conduct. my love to my ever dear Martha & the little ones, & affectionate esteem to yourself.   TH: JEFFERSON

RC (DLC); at foot of text: "T. M. Randolph"; endorsed by Randolph. Enclosures not identified.

PROPOSITION RELATIVE TO POPLAR FOREST: TJ to Randolph, 8 Oct. According to SJL, Randolph wrote TJ two letters after receiving the proposal, the first

on 31 Oct, received by TJ on 3 Nov., and the second, undated, received by TJ on 10 Nov. Both are missing.

I AM INFORMED: see John Wayles Eppes to TJ, 6 Nov., for the report on Joseph Moran.

[1] TJ here canceled "prevent my wri."

From David Turner

SIR   No Carolina Bertie County 16th Novr. 1801

I take the liberty to address you tho much in the rear of doing so,— I am not a person of Letters, and am in an Humble state, the deranged situation of my affairs has cast me so far to Leeward, that I do not know whither I shall be ever able to fetch up, which may perhaps disable me in what I now try to do—however this by the by—

Give me leave Sir to Congratulate you on your Appointment to the presidency of the United States, four years ago (or rather now five) I was for Jefferson, failing in my wish I considered as no inconsiderable disappointment, Your appointment now was my earnest wish, And your reappointment hereafter for many four Years yet to come is my most ardant wish, In such a length of time (tho not very long) I hope affairs may gain some Stability those who now are Children will arrive to manhood and those who now are 20 will be of age to take any seat in Goverment, and being acquainted with and bred in and used to our republican representative Goverment will the better know how to prize it, At the beginning dureing and at the end of our struggle with Britain for Liberty I had no Idea that those who Joined them against us, should after we gained our Independence, be our Revinue officers and agents in Goverment I have been and am now astonished at it. I wonder they[1] are not ashamed I have more than a crumb of hope, that their reproachfull scurillus & unmanly Language, will like the singing waves beating against the solid rock be all to froth and bubbles turn'd, I have not expected all such would Immediately be displaced, there being great difference between puting in and puting out of Office

I have great Confidence that under your Administration, our own Citizens as well as the Nations will respect our goverment. And I pray the Great Creator through his great bounty & redeeming Love will Guard us, And be pleased to give you strength of Body & mind; and finaly Cloath you with that inward Robe of Righteousness which fadeth not—

I beg you to accept my Highest Consideration and Esteem (and permit me to say) Dear sir I am

Your Most Obedient Humble Servant   DAVID TURNER

Please to catch at the sense rather than the words

Sir Please to suffer me to acquaint you, that as far as I can learn & I have reason to believe, that our standard half Bushel is larger than any in the neighbouring Countys or any in the United States, that of New York comes nearest to it, but is some smaller, we have no wine measures belonging to the standard, as to weights to try steelyards, I believe we have a 7th. a 14th., 28 & I believe 56.—

I am very sincerely As before   DAVID TURNER

RC (DLC); at foot of text: "Thomas Jefferson Esqr President of the United States"; endorsed by TJ as received 26 Dec. and so recorded in SJL.

David Turner represented Bertie County in the North Carolina House of Representatives from 1780 to 1783 and in 1790, and was also a delegate to the state ratification conventions of 1788 and 1789 (John L. Cheney, Jr., ed., *North Carolina Government, 1585-1979, A Narrative and Statistical History* [Raleigh, 1981], 765, 768, 1062).

[1] MS: "they they."

From Benjamin Waterhouse

Sir   Cambridge Novr. 16th. 1801.

The vaccine matter, which you were so good as to transmit to me 4 or 5 weeks ago, on quills & on thread, has been tried. I communicated the genuine disease with some from one of the tooth-picks, but am not absolutely certain that it ever took from the thread. This induces me to make an observation that may be useful to your inoculators.

I was, at first sight, suspicious of the goodness of the thread you sent me merely from its *quantity*; for if I understood you right, it was all taken from one patient. I think myself pretty fortunate if I obtain 2, or 3 inches of perfectly infected thread from one patient. Frequently I can procure not more than two inches, whereas the phial you sent me contained, perhaps, as many feet, and that two of very *fine* thread. I set more value on two inches of *coarser* thread repeatedly soaked in the fluid, so as to have acquired the stiffness of a wire; in which case, the contortions of the thread are nearly obliterated by the coat of matter, whereas that which I received scarcely agglutinated the fibrillæ of the cotton. My requesting a sample of the virus from your own cases, was with a view of demonstrating that your cases were genuine; and of judging if your physicians conducted the process of taking the virus (for transportation especially) in the manner, which we find by experience to be best. They will, therefore, I hope, excuse my observing that it is better to imbue repeatedly an inch or two *very well*, than merely to moisten ten times that quantity. By the first procedure they will very seldom, if ever be disappointed, by the latter frequently.

I have gone on inoculating with an almost undeviating success throughout the spring, summer, & this autumn. When I used the fresh virus, warm from the pustule, I *never failed*; but with the thread, I, in the very hot weather, was sometimes foiled.

The enemies of this new inoculation (for in this inferior walk, prejudice, envy, & other unworthy passions, will for a while hang heavily on the wheel destined to bring forth anything new in science) have lately rallied round one of our principal small:pox-inoculators, and gave a momentary check to the progress of truth & humanity, by publishing five cases (clearly spurious, except to the eye of ignorance) to whom he gave the small-pox. By placing a fact with it's wrong end foremost, some uneasiness was created in the public mind. Rumour generated from a simple fact, so placed, an apparently formidable structure, which on close examination was, however, discovered to have neither foundation, nor sides to it,—a mere illusion, calculated to deceive, & to retain a little while longer their old *friend*, the smallpox. Not but what there are still many unbelievers among that class of people, where we may not dispair of making them believe any thing but truth.

I have enclosed part of a News-paper containing some observations on this professional opposition. In the course of a few weeks, I propose to publish a *Report of the progress of the vaccine-inoculation during the year 1801*, a copy of which I will transmit to you: after which, as I have attained the ultimate object of my views, the planting the *true* Kine-pox in the most populous of the Southern-States, under the most favourable auspices, I shall have no further occasion to encroach on your valuable time, but conclude with wishing you long to possess the highest honor our country can bestow, with health to enjoy it.

BENJAMIN WATERHOUSE

RC (DLC); addressed: "President Jefferson"; endorsed by TJ as a letter of 10 Nov. received on 25 Nov. and so recorded in SJL. Enclosure not found.

TJ sent to Waterhouse a sample of VAC-CINE MATTER from Monticello by 23 Oct., according to his letter to Henry Rose of that day. Waterhouse requested the sample in his letter to TJ of 4 Sep.

ENEMIES OF THIS NEW INOCULATION: in October, a controversy erupted on the pages of the Boston newspaper *Independent Chronicle and the Universal Advertiser* over the effectiveness of cowpox in preventing smallpox. The 28 Sep.-1 Oct. issue carried an advertisement for Dr.

William Aspinwall's smallpox inoculations at a hospital in Brookline, Massachusetts. The advertisement claimed that FIVE out of six persons who had previously been inoculated with cowpox became infected with smallpox at the hospital. In the 12-15 Oct. issue, Waterhouse responded: "no Person I ever yet inoculated for the Kine-Pox has ever had the Small-Pox." Following statements defending Aspinwall in the 26-29 Oct. and 29 Oct.-2 Nov. issues, Waterhouse, in the 5-9 Nov. issue, cautioned the public to be aware of "spurious" cowpox and mentioned the success of cowpox inoculations at Monticello.

From Thomas Digges

SIR   Warburton (nr Piscataway) Nov. 17. 1801

I am very unwilling to trespass upon your time, but as my nephew Billy Carroll (a Clk. in the Auditors office) is going hence to the City and will wait upon you with this, I am inducd to solicit your reading the inclosd letter from Mr. Pinckney to me, and informing me whether you ever Rcd. the box and paper mentiond in His Lettr.

The Box contain some very fine specimens of Coins, medals, & provincial Copper money made at the famous manufactory of Messrs.

Boulton & Watt of Birmingham, which were obtaind by me for the purpose of presenting to you at the time when I understood you were at the head and engagd in establishing the mint of this Country.

At that time I was at Birmingham & Sheffield engagd in the pursuit & anxiously wishing to direct & get out to America some ten or a dozn. men of no small wealth & of celebrity in the manufacture of Iron founders, Nailors of the split cut sort, Smiths &c. &c.; and Mr. Pinckney knowing what I was about solicited what information I could obtain as to Dyesinkers and the value and prices of Copper, expences of Coinage &c. &c.

In these persuits I found out such a systematic villainy as to Forgings & Coinages of base money, that I added to the memoir or accot. given Mr P. a full description of the mode & process used by those Artists in the making false money: for they had been at the American Loan Office Certificates as well as at Dutch Ducats, Spanish Dollars, French Crowns, Pistereens &c. &c. &c. making a variety of each of these moneys Vizt. some plated & rimmd with Silver, & others of base mettal similar to Silver and of various grades as to the value of each—for instance they had orders (chiefly from London) to make such & such Dollars at the value of 1/10d each, some at 2/6d. & others as high as 3/- of actual value. I am sorry I have not now at hand the original descriptive account of this curious trafic or I would inclose it to you—The practice was not punishd in England tho it was connivd at.

In each of the three boxes I sent to yourself, Genl Washington and Mr Pinkney I inclosd a Copy of my memdms, and I had the pleasure of being informd by a letter from Colo. Fitzgerald that the information had arrived in time to detect a large quantity shippd to Chastown So Carolina, as well as an attempt to put some into the Bank at Alexandria while Colonel Fitzgerald was then a Director: For I had also inclosd one to Him and to Mr. Josa. Johnson then Consul in London.

It is very well known that many casks of this money coverd with nails & hardware were shippd to this Country and to the West Indies—The better sort of Dollrs. would deceive any one without close inspection.

I am Sir with great esteem and truth Yr. Obt. Servt.

Thos Digges

RC (MHi); endorsed by TJ as received 18 Nov. and so recorded in SJL. Enclosure not found, but possibly Thomas Pinckney to Digges, 22 Mch. 1793, acknowledging the receipt of letters dated 12 and 21 Mch. as well as "the Box of

Medals" for TJ, which would be "forwarded by the first Vessel sailing for Philadelphia" (Robert H. Elias and Eugene D. Finch, eds., *Letters of Thomas Attwood Digges (1742-1821)* [Columbia, S.C., 1982], 452).

For Digges's 1793 correspondence with TJ and Thomas PINCKNEY regarding coinage and counterfeiting, as well as the BOX of coins forwarded from Britain, see Vol. 25:347-50, 526-7; Vol. 26:191, 192-3, 779-82.

John FITZGERALD, Digges's brother-in-law and an aide-de-camp to George Washington during the American Revolution, served as collector at Alexandria from 1793 to 1799 (Elias and Finch, eds., *Digges*, xxvii; JEP, 1:142; Alexandria *Times; and District of Columbia Daily Advertiser*, 17 Aug., 5 Dec. 1799).

From James Monroe

DEAR SIR   Richmond Novr. 17. 1801.

The arrival of Mr. Purviance in the U States furnishes me with an occasion to make known to you his merit. He was a member of my family for sometime while I was in France, often present in my interviews with the French govt., and always in my confidence while I remain'd there, so that I speak of him without reserve, as a man of perfect integrity, excellent understanding & rare prudence. He is a man of delicacy & modesty, one with whom it is impossible to become acquainted & not interested in his fortune. What his views are I cannot say but whatever they may be I have felt it a duty I owed him to present him to you in the light in which he ought to be viewed.

You will not forget the answer I am to expect from you on my letter relative to the purchase of land for certain purposes. The legislature will expect a communication from me on that subject. with great respect

I am yr. fnd. & servant   JAS. MONROE

RC (DLC); endorsed by TJ as received 21 Nov. and so recorded in SJL.

Monroe's LETTER RELATIVE TO THE PURCHASE OF LAND was the first letter from him printed at 15 June 1801 (Vol. 34:345-7). At the request of the Virginia LEGISLATURE, Monroe consulted TJ about finding some location "without the limits of this state, to which persons obnoxious to the laws or dangerous to the peace of society may be removed." When TJ answered that letter on 21 July, he thought he might be able to discuss that "difficult" subject with Monroe in person during his visit to Virginia later in the summer.

From Moses Robinson

SIR,   Bennington Novr. 17th 1801

The Bearer doctor Benjamin Robinson is a native of this town and
a nephew of mine, Sustains a good moral Character, and has Acquired no inconsiderable knowledge in the Arts of Phisyck and
Surgery—in the latter Especially he has made Proficiency in Practice
he is Temperate, Sober, & Discreet in his General deportment, and I
Consider him a promising young man he is of an enterprising make
and wishes by Industry in his Calling to obtain property he has often
Expressd his desire of Going to the Southern States but has lately
had Information from a Gentleman living in Chesterfield County &
State of Virginia on the River Appamattox that there is at present a
Vacancy in that Vicinity for the Practice of Physick &c. he has therefore determind to Journey thither his informant also mentiond that a
letter from President Jefferson to his brother in law living in that
place would be of Service to Introduce him to practice he therefore
desires that favour from you Sir and I trust his future Conduct will
not Cause you to Regret your bestowment of such a favour—

The Return of Republicanism in this State is beyond our highest
Expectations there is a decided majority in both houses of the Legislature there was not a tryal in any Instance but the Republicans Carried there point, yet they believd it to be Good Policy not to Reject
the (Self Stiled) Federalist in every Instance the address to your Self
was Carried by a majority of thirty and the Reply to Governr.
Tichenors Speech which was a Severe Reprehension on his Past Conduct,[1] was nearly the Same which with Maryland Resolutions are
demonstrations beyond a doubt,—we have in Bennington labourd
Incessantly to Stem the Currant of Federalism (falsly Calld) in this
State but not without fear & trembling lest we should Fail we have
Gaind in a great measure our point and I believe the Progress of the
Cause of liberty through the United States Calls for Gratitude to that
being who Superintends the affairs of men, Governs the nation with
a nod, and has mercifully Crown'd their Efforts with Success—

I have Just now learnd. that Certain persons are doing all they Can
to Injure the Reputation of Mr. Willard the present Marshal in the
district of Vermont and to make or have made you Sir to beleive that
you had been misinformd as to his True Character. I therefore think
it my duty to give you some information on that Subject I have been
acquainted with Mr. Willard about Two years and Set in the Council
of Censors with him (he being a member) for nearly three month, he

appeard to be a person of Abilities a firm Republican and have never heard any thing unfavorible to his Charecter I this day have Calld on Col. David Fay District attorney to know of him how he the marshal performd the duties of his office he tells me he did it with dignity and Faithfulness and has had an oppertunity to Look into his Conduct in Relation to the discharge of his duty in taking a Prisoner in a Civil Suit or in Execution that had Caused some talk by the Federalist but it was Settld or rather there never was any difficulty between the marshal and the Prisoner to wit mr Hatheway—that mr Fay Considers him as Competent to Execute the office of Marshal well with honor to himself and the Government—

This I think ought to have more weight in as much as many persons who wish to Supplant mr Willard have mentiond my Brother David Robinson the present Sheriff of Bennington County as a Candidate to Succeed him in the office of Marshal and Say he had the best Right to it however I may Respect my Brother and may Beleive him to be Sufficiently Capable to Execute that office yet I beleive mr Willard to be so too and ought not to be Supplanted by him or any other person—unless there appears Sufficient Cause—

Accept Sir my best wishes for your domestic happiness as well as public administrations and beleive me to be your most Obedient & very Humble Servant   MOSES ROBINSON

RC (DLC); at foot of text: "President Jefferson"; endorsed by TJ as received 29 Dec. and so recorded in SJL.

BENJAMIN ROBINSON made successful experiments with smallpox vaccinations in Vermont in 1800 and 1801. He relocated to Fayetteville, North Carolina, around 1805, where he was a prominent physician and civic leader until his death in 1857 (Abby Maria Hemenway, ed., *Vermont Historical Gazetteer*, 5 vols. [Burlington, 1868-91], 1:164, 180; *Vermont Gazette*, 2 Feb., 9 Nov. 1801; William S. Powell, ed., *Dictionary of North Carolina Biography*, 6 vols. [Chapel Hill, 1979-96], 5:233; John A. Oates, *The Story of Fayetteville and the Upper Cape Fear* [Charlotte, 1950], 856).

The brother-in-law in CHESTERFIELD COUNTY was probably Francis Eppes of Eppington. He was the husband of Elizabeth Wayles, who was the half-sister of TJ's wife, Martha Wayles Skelton, and the father of John Wayles Eppes (Malone, *Jefferson*, 1:432-3; Vol. 1:86-7).

ADDRESS TO YOUR SELF: Vermont House of Representatives to TJ, printed at 5 Nov. The address was adopted by a vote of 86 to 59 (*Journals of the General Assembly of the State of Vermont, at Their Session, Begun and Holden at Newbury, in the County of Orange, the Eighth Day of October, A.D. One Thousand Eight Hundred and One* [Windsor, 1802], 218).

REPLY TO GOVERNR. TICHENORS SPEECH: in their 21 Oct. reply to Federalist Governor Isaac Tichenor's 9 Oct. address to the General Assembly, the Republican-led House of Representatives rebuked the governor's speech of 10 Oct. 1800 to the assembly, in which he urged legislators to choose presidential electors who would select "an Independent American" rather than a candidate with a "predilection for foreign principles, or an ardor for foreign theories." In their 21 Oct. reply, the House congratulated the governor "on the spirit of true republicanism having so far regained its well merited ascendancy," and on the election of a man to the presidency, "who is not destitute of the sentiments of 'an independent American,' and who, you do not suspect, will be influenced in his administration by a predilection for foreign principles, or for the government of any foreign nation." The House approved the reply by a vote of 103 to 69 (E. P. Walton, ed., *Records of the Governor and Council of the State of Vermont*, 8 vols. [Montpelier, 1873-80; repr. New York, 1973], 4:516; *Journals of the General Assembly of the State of Vermont*, 10-16, 105-9; Shaw-Shoemaker, No. 3460).

MARYLAND RESOLUTIONS: on 17 Oct., Tichenor sent the Vermont house a set of resolutions passed by the Maryland assembly in December 1800. The resolutions called for a Constitutional amendment to create a uniform method for choosing presidential electors and representatives to Congress, recommending that they be chosen by district, rather than by statewide or legislative elections. The Vermont house approved Maryland's district plan and passed a virtually identical set of resolutions on 19 Oct. by votes of 126 to 41 and 105 to 55. In the election of 1800, the legislature had chosen Vermont's four presidential electors, all of whom were Federalists (*Journals of the General Assembly of the State of Vermont*, 77-80, 89-93; Stanley Elkins and Eric McKitrick, *The Age of Federalism* [New York, 1993], 905).

TJ appointed John WILLARD marshal for Vermont on 5 Mch., removing Federalist Jabez Fitch for "cruelty" and to increase the number of Republicans in the federal courts (Vol. 33:587, 673, 674).

[1] Preceding nine words interlined.

From James Sullivan

SIR   Boston Novr. 17th 1801

I have, frequently been requested to introduce my friends to you, but have uniformly refused[1] to comply. I have considered your time as the property of your country, and as being too important to be improved a moment on any thing I would propose. I cannot, however, refuse to join with many others in asking your attention to Colonel Lee of Marblehead. I formed an attachment to him on the plains of Cambrige, a few days after the battle of Lexington; his conduct since, as an officer, and as a private citizen, his sentiments in favour of a republican government, and the tenour of his life, combine to increase the opinion I had conceived of him. I can venture to pledge myself for his honor and integrety, in any office or place he may be called to in the government.

I ardently wish you the most perfect success in your exertions to restore the administration of our government to its constitutional channel; and that the American Nation, as a republic, may remember with gratitude an administration, which may have rescued them from the Jaws of Tyranny.

I continue with the warmest attachment to your person Your very humble Servant   JA SULLIVAN

RC (DNA: RG 59, LAR); at foot of text: "Thomas Jefferson President of the United States"; endorsed by TJ as received 29 Nov. and so recorded in SJL; also endorsed by TJ: "Colo. Lee of Marblehead to office."

Sullivan earlier in the year declined TJ's offer to serve as U.S. attorney for Massachusetts (Vol. 33:596, 675).

[1] MS: "refusted."

From Samuel Adams

MY DEAR FRIEND   Boston Novemr: 18th: 1801

Doctr: Eustis will be so kind as to deliver you this Letter.—I am perswaded, you will find him a man of a candid and fair Mind and liberal sentiments.—

I congratulate you on the return of Peace. The War both in America and Europe was designed by Tyrant Kings to exterminate those rights and liberties which the Gracious Creator has granted to Man, and to sink the happiness resulting therefrom in ruin and oblivion.—Is there not, my friend, reason to believe, that the principles of Democratic Republicanism are already better understood than they were before; and that by the continued efforts of Men of Science and Virtue, they will extend more, and more 'till the turbulent and destructive Spirit of War shall cease?—The proud oppressors over the Earth shall be totally broken down and those classes of Men, who have hitherto been the victims of their rage and cruelty shall perpetually enjoy perfect Peace and Safety 'till time shall be no more.—

I am Your cordial friend   SAML. ADAMS

RC (DLC); in John Avery's hand, signed by Adams; endorsed by TJ as received 7 Dec. and so recorded in SJL. Tr (NN).

William EUSTIS began serving two terms as a Massachusetts congressman in 1801 (*Biog. Dir. Cong.*).

To Aaron Burr

DEAR SIR   Washington Nov. 18. 1801.

Your favor of the 10th. has been recieved, as have been those also of Sep. 4. & 23. in due time. these letters all relating to office, fall within the general rule which even the very first week of my being engaged in the administration obliged me to establish, to wit, that of not answering letters on office[1] specifically, but leaving the answer to be found in what is done or not done on them. you will readily concieve into what scrapes one would get by saying *no*, either with or without reasons, by using a softer language which might excite false hopes or by saying *yes* prematurely. and to take away all offence from this silent answer, it is necessary to adhere to it in every case rigidly, as well with bosom friends as strangers.—Capt Sterritt is arrived here from the Mediterranean. Congress will have a question as to all the Barbary powers of some difficulty. we have had under consideration mr Pusy's plans of fortification. they are scientifically done, and expounded. he seems to prove that no works at either the Narrows or Governor's island can stop a vessel. but to stop them at the Hook by a fort of 8000. men & protecting army of 29,000. is beyond our present ideas of the scale of defence which we can adopt for all our seaport towns. his estimate of 4,000,000. D. which experience teaches us to double always, in a case where the law allows but (I believe) half a million, ties our hands at once. we refer the case back to Govr. Clinton to select half a dozen persons of judgment, of American ideas, and to present such a plan, within our limits, as these shall agree on. in the mean time the general subject will be laid before Congress. Accept assurances of my high respect & consideration.

TH: JEFFERSON

RC (PHi); addressed: "Aaron Burr esquire V.P. of the US. New York"; franked and postmarked; endorsed by Burr. PrC (DLC).

See Madison to TJ, 16 Nov., for Burr's FAVOR OF THE 10TH.

During John Adams's term, Alexander Hamilton had monitored plans for the FORTIFICATION of New York harbor. Following TJ's inauguration, Burr agreed to take on that role "of superintending a thorough examination of the port and harbour of New York for the purpose of enabling the President of the United States to decide on the most judicious modes of extending the fortifications at that place." In July, Burr sent a plan of the harbor, said that he would compile soundings of the water's depth, and suggested that Dearborn write Jean Xavier Bureaux

de Pusy "to urge dispatch" (Kline, *Burr*, 1:527-8).

HALF A MILLION: the expenditure for fortifications at New York City could not exceed $1,852,035, the amount of the state's debt to the United States (ASP, *Military Affairs*, 1:193).

REFER THE CASE BACK TO GOVR. CLINTON: see George Clinton to TJ, 14 Oct.

Burr also wrote to TJ on this day. In a brief note written at New York he stated: "Mr Burr's respectful Compliments—He has the honor herewith to enclose to the President of the U.S. the original Memoire of Monr. De Pusy on the Subject of the Defense of the Harbour of NYork" (RC in DLC; unsigned; endorsed by TJ as received 22 Nov. and so recorded in SJL).

[1] Preceding three words interlined in place of "them."

From a "Citizen"

Rhode Island Novr 18th 1801

The evil of which I have to complain will certainly interesting the feelings of our beloved President so far as to devise some immediate remedy.

The Supreme Court of Massachusetts have at length decreed that a Certificate of discharge under the insolvent or bankrupt Laws of the other States shall not be a bar in their Courts to demands originating before said insolvency or bankruptcy.—

The confusion that must follow such a decree I need not describe; not only the unfortunate who have obtained such Certificates in the several States are begining to be watched within the bounds of that State by "wolves in sheeps clothing"; but the heirs of the unfortunate who perhaps have shar'd some patrimonial estate which the Parent may have received in consequence of having obtained a Certificate of discharge and the property of all such Families must share the same fate.

That every blessing may attend your person & administration is the sincere prayer of a   CITIZEN

Two cases decided at Taunton October Term 1801—
Winsor vs Pease—Hodges vs Hodges—

RC (DLC); closing quotation mark supplied; endorsed by TJ as a letter of 11 Nov. received from "Anon." on 30 Nov. and so recorded in SJL.

On 18 Nov., the *Providence Journal* reported that the Supreme Judicial Court of MASSACHUSETTS had recently decided, "in conformity to their former decisions on similar questions," that a discharge under the insolvency act of Rhode Island did not prevent an action in Massachusetts in favor of a creditor "who resided there at the time the discharge was obtained."

From Thomas Newton

DR SIR   Norfolk Novr. 18. 1801

I Recieved your favor inclosing $20.75. for the charges of the things from Orleans, I hope they may give some incite, to the antient settlements on the Missisipi. Cyder in barrels from this will be the safest way of yr. getting it good, we have bottlers in plenty who will tell you they improve liquors, by mixtures, which I am not fond off, I like genuine best, the packets from this to Alexra. are respectable & but little danger of aduteration in them, from Alexr. to the City I am not acquainted, you'l please to direct who to deliver to that care may be taken between those places—

10 barrels cider will over run yr. qty. 60 doz some thing but suppose they will not be too much; as I shall be on our assembly I shall leave orders to have it sent. I, most sincerly wish to be clear of tribute to the Barbary powers, & am convinced it wou'd be better, to keep vessels in pay as cruisers, as it would cost as little as the tribute & the money imploy'd among oursilves. I have hopes Capt. Sterret brings good accounts of our little[1] & that we may be able to keep our fellow citizens from being taken. Accept my best wishes for yr health & happiness   THOS NEWTON

RC (DLC); endorsed by TJ as received 26 Nov. and so recorded in SJL.

[1] Word missing; remainder of letter written on verso.

YOUR FAVOR: TJ to Newton, 9 Nov.

From Martha Jefferson Randolph

DEAREST FATHER   Edgehill November 18 1801

Mr Trist who will deliver this can also give a better account of the children than (limited as I am for time) I possibly can. however I must write a few lines to you if it is only to wonder at your long silence. each successive post has been anxiously expected and desired, only to bring along with it fresh dissapointment. my sister left us on Monday with her little boy better than could be expected, but in a very precarious state of being. he is (altho healthy except the hooping cough), the most delicate creature I ever beheld. mine are doing well, all but poor Ellen, who looks wretchedly is much reduced and weakened by the cough which still continues upon her with extreme violence. little Virginia is recovering, still distressing us at times but the crisis seems to be over with all of them. it was a terible moment— Ellen and Cornelia were particularly ill both delirious one singing and laughing the other (Ellen) gloomy & terrified equally unconscious of the objects around them. my God what moment for a Parent the agonies of Mr Randolph's mind seemed to call forth every energy of mine I had to act in the double capacity of nurse to my children and comforter to their father. it is of service perhaps to be obliged to exert one self upon those occasions.[1] certainly the mind acquires strength by it to bear up against evils that in other circumstances would totally over come it. I am recovering from the fatigue which attended the illness of my children and I am at this moment in more perfect health than I have been for years. adieu beloved Father you would write oftener if you knew how much pleasure your letters give. there is not a child in the house that does not run at the return of the messenger to know if there is a letter from Grand Papa. Stewart your white smith is returned, the plaistering[2] at Monticello goes on, not as well as the first room which was elegantly done but better than the 3d & fourth, the two I think you would have been most anxious about, being below stairs. Moran goes on slowly every one the children with the hooping cough excepted is well and they are none of them bad but every thing upon the land (at Monticello) has it. once more adieu. believe me with ardent affection yours

M. RANDOLPH

to tell you it is past one o'clock will appologize for a great deal of incorectness in this scrawl and the hurried way in I generally write will account for the rest—

RC (MHi); endorsed by TJ as received 23 Nov. and so recorded in SJL.

[1] Preceding three words interlined.
[2] MS: "plaitering."

From Philip B. Bradley

SIR   Ridgfield November 19th. 1801

Want of health induces me to ask leave to resign the office of Marshall for the district of Connecticutt
The state of my health is such at present as prevents me from paying the necessary attention to the duties of the office, I therefore beg you to accept my resignation and that another person may be appointed in my stead Wishing that your administration may be prosperous to the people over whome you preside and honorable to your self, I take the liberty to subscribe my self with sentiment of great esteem and respect
    your Excellencys most Obedeint Humble Servant

PHILIP B BRADLEY

RC (DNA: RG 59, RD); at head of text: "His Excellcy Thomas Jefferson President of the United States"; endorsed by TJ as a letter of 9 Nov. received on 23 Nov. and so recorded in SJL.

Philip Burr Bradley (1738-1821) of Ridgefield, Connecticut, was a Yale grad-uate, a colonel during the American Revolution, and judge of the Fairfield County Court. He served as marshal for Connecticut from 1789 until his resignation in 1801. TJ replaced him with Joseph Willcox (Dexter, *Yale*, 2:515-16; JEP, 1:29, 397; Vol. 33:671, 674n).

To Aaron Burr

Dear Sir   Washington Nov. 19. 1801

In my letter of yesterday I forgot to put the inclosed and to ask the favor of you to address it to the proper place. it is in answer to one I received three months ago, dated in Dumfries, but the gentleman was there only as a traveller and did not advise me where to address the answer. I inclosed it to mr Gallatin having heard him speak of the writer. but he returned it to me two months ago, not knowing whither to address it. he has lately mentioned that you were acquainted with the person & would probably know his residence. this induces me to trouble you with superscribing the place where he is to be found and putting it into the post office. health and best wishes.   Th: Jefferson

PrC (DLC); in ink at foot of text: "A. Burr esq. V. P. of the US."; endorsed by TJ in ink on verso. Enclosure: TJ to John Davis, 11 Sep. 1801.

One i received three months ago: see John Davis to TJ, 31 Aug.

To Thomas Digges

Dear Sir   Washington Nov. 19. 1801.

My memory is so unfaithful that I am always afraid to affirm any thing on it's authority. but I believe I am not decieved in saying that a little before I went out of office in 1793, I did recieve from you the specimens of coins you describe, with an account of the falsifications going on in England, and that I published in the news papers what related to the latter in order to guard the public. the coins I must have left of course in the Secretary of states office, where it is also probable your letter is filed. if I am not mistaken you wrote also to Genl. Washington who communicated it to me. yet writing from memory I must be cautious. Accept my best wishes & respects.

                    Th: Jefferson

P.S. I return mr Pinckneys lre

PrC (DLC); at foot of text: "Thomas Digges esq. of Warburton"; endorsed by TJ in ink on verso.

mr pinckneys lre: see Digges to TJ, 17 Nov.

From Albert Gallatin

DEAR SIR   Treasury Department Nover. 19th 1801

Enclosed are the letters by this mail. The application of A. Bell, at all events, comes too late; the new collector Mr Marsh might have been informed, when appointed, that he must consider Mr Bell's removal as a resignation and claim only one half of the commission on uncollected outstanding duties; but he appears to me to have now acquired a legal right to the whole commission. The case of Mr Powell of Savannah where the removal has been considered as a resignation was different. He had, in fact, resigned before he received an account of his removal and whilst he was acting as collector.

Whether a row-boat should be allowed to Mr Marsh is a matter of detail which will be decided after a conference with the Comptroller. His letter is sent to show his opinion of the spirit of the courts.

Ought any notice be taken of A. M'Lane's letter? Brunson's news paper is the Gazette of the United States, lately "Wayne's." I have not seen the piece.

I enclose the navy estimate for the year 1802 amountg. to Drs. *1,101,000*. If it can be reduced to about six hundred thousand dollars, it is probable we may do without inter[nal] taxes. As connected with that question, I send it; the recapitulation of the two last pages shows the general items. But, it would be eligible to have it returned to me as early as Saturday. I will be fully ready to wait on you any day after Sunday next on the subject of finances.   The proceeds of the quarter ending 30th Septer. last are still greater than any former one—the impost having yielded Drs. 2,980,000 actually paid in the Treasury.

With sincere respect & attachment I have the honor to be Dear Sir Your most obedt. Servt.   ALBERT GALLATIN

RC (DLC); frayed at margin; at foot of text: "The President of the United States"; endorsed by TJ as received 19 Nov. and so recorded in SJL. Enclosures not found.

For the application of the 1799 act, which allowed the division of the COMMISSION between the collector leaving office and his successor, in the case of James POWELL, see TJ to Gallatin, 3 Oct. On 12 Nov., an article, signed "A Citizen of Delaware," appeared in the GA-ZETTE OF THE UNITED STATES. The writer accused Gallatin and the president of investigating charges made against Allen McLane, collector at Wilmington, in a devious, unconstitutional manner, designed to destroy his reputation and force him from office. The writer promised that he would resume the subject after McLane published "these scandalous proceedings." For the charges against McLane and the appointment of George Read, Jr., and James Tilton to investigate the case, see Gallatin to TJ, 23 May 1801.

From Philip Mazzei

A JEFFERSON   19 9bre, 1801.
Il Rè d'Etruria giunse finalmente in Firenze, e le persone illuminate
furono contente delle sue qualità dello spirito, come del cuore. Ma,
per disgrazia di questo paese, egli è soggetto ad accidenti epilettici,
che lo mettono per più giorni nell'incapacità di occuparsi agli affari;
e l'occupazione di mente, e più encora qualche scontentezza causata
dalle circostanze attuali, gli rendeno più frequenti.

Quando mancano i rimedi naturali, Ella sa bene quale straordinaria
forza di carattere si richiede, oltre una chiara idea dei veri e dei falsi,
per non cedere alla speranza d'aiuti invisibili a incomprensibili, che
nella prima educazione ci sono stati fatti credere onnipotenti, e che
nel cercare i mezzi d'ottenergli si cade facilmente in potere della
Teocrazia.[1]

Raccomando nuovamente un meglior provvedimento nei porti
d'Italia per gl'interessi dei naviganti e negozianti degli Stati Uniti, e
ripeto, che volendo creare un Console Generale, coll'incarico di so-
printendere a tutti gli altri Consoli e Viceconsoli, il mio voto sarebbe
per Mr. Appleton, giovane attivo, e molto ansioso (per quanto mi
pare) di farsi una buona reputazione in Patria.

EDITORS' TRANSLATION

To Jefferson   19 Nov. 1801
    The King of Etruria finally arrived in Florence and enlightened people
were pleased with the qualities of both his mind and heart. But unfortunately
for our country, he is subject to epileptic fits that prevent his attending to
state matters for days. These fits are rendered more frequent by mental strain
and some occasional disappointment caused by the present circumstances.
    In the absence of natural remedies, you know very well what extraordinary
strength of character—besides a clear idea of what are true remedies and
what are false—is required not to give in to the hope of those invisible and
incomprehensible aids which early in our upbringing we have been made to
believe omnipotent, and that, when we search for the means to obtain them,
make one easily fall into the power of Theocracy.
    Again I urge that better provisions be made in Italian ports for the benefit
of U.S. seamen and merchants. I repeat that, if it should be decided to have
a consul general to oversee all the other consuls and vice-consuls, my vote
would be for Mr. Appleton, who seems superlatively eager to earn a good
reputation back home.

FC (DLC: Mazzei Papers); in Mazzei's
hand; at foot of text, also in Mazzei's
hand, is a grocery list including expenses
for beef and bread. Dft (Archivio Filippo
Mazzei, Pisa, Italy); part of a conjoined
series of Mazzei's draft letters to TJ,
where it is an extract of the letter dated
15 Nov. 1801, see note 2 at that date

(Margherita Marchione and Barbara B. Oberg, eds., *Philip Mazzei: The Comprehensive Microform Edition of his Papers*, 9 reels [Millwood, N.Y., 1981], 6:906).

IL RÈ D'ETRURIA GIUNSE FINALMENTE IN FIRENZE: the new kingdom of Etruria in Tuscany was the product of the treaties of San Ildefonso (1 Oct. 1800) and Aranjuez (21 Mch. 1801), and part of the agreement between France and Spain that included the retrocession of Louisiana. Bonaparte agreed to make a son-in-law of King Carlos IV of Spain, Louis of Parma, the first king of Etruria. Louis entered Florence to begin his rule

on 12 Aug. 1801. TJ, Thomas Pinckney, and Charles Willson Peale corresponded with Louis about natural history topics beginning in 1795 (Howard R. Marraro, "Unpublished Mazzei Letters to Jefferson," WMQ, 3d Ser., 1 [1944], 390; Vol. 28:517-18; Vol. 29:27, 29n, 121, 136, 286-7, 389-92, 404, 481; Vol. 30:232-4; Vol. 31:61-2; Vol. 33:406n).

[1] In Dft, Mazzei added the following sentence to the end of this paragraph: "Per ora, s'io dicessi altro su questo Paese, agirei da indovino," meaning "As of now, were I to say anything more about this country, it would be sheer guesswork."

Memorandum on the Seneca Annuity

I. JOHN STEELE TO ALBERT GALLATIN, [19 NOV. 1801]

II. ALBERT GALLATIN'S REFERRAL, [19 NOV. 1801]

III. JEFFERSON'S MEMORANDUM, 19 NOV. 1801

EDITORIAL NOTE

In 1797, the Seneca Indians sold the last substantial tract of land held in the United States by any of the Six Nations Iroquois, approximately four million acres west of the Genesee River in western New York State. The negotiation at a place called Big Tree (now Geneseo, New York) was under the auspices of the United States government and overseen, nominally, by Jeremiah Wadsworth as U.S. commissioner. The transaction, however, was between the Senecas and Robert Morris. The Holland Land Company had purchased a pre-emption claim from Morris, but would not complete payment until he cleared the Indians' rights to the immense tract. Morris, who was hiding from his creditors in Philadelphia, had his son Thomas handle the talks at Big Tree. By manipulation and bribes to Seneca chiefs, the Morrises bought the land for $100,000. That money was not paid directly to the tribe, however, but was to be invested in shares of the Bank of the United States to be "held in the name of the President of the United States, for the use and behoof of the said nation of Indians." The Senecas, who then numbered approximately 1,700 to 1,800 in western New York and adjacent parts of Pennsylvania, were to receive expected annual earnings of up to six percent, or $6,000 a year, on the bank stock. They already received a smaller annual stipend from the federal government in the form of goods and services, and they retained 11 limited reservations around their principal settlements. Oliver Wolcott and Timothy Pickering, as secretary of the Treasury and secretary of state, respectively, handled the establishment of the stock trust. They rebuffed the elder Morris's wish to have the $100,000 principal revert to him or his heirs if "the Seneca nation" should ever "become extinct" (ASP, *Indian Affairs*, 1:626-8; Norman B. Wilkinson, "Robert Morris and the Treaty of Big Tree," *Mississippi Valley Historical Review*, 40 [1953], 257-78; Anthony F. C. Wallace, *The Death and Rebirth of the Seneca* [New York, 1973], 179-83; David Swatzler, *A Friend among the Senecas: The Quaker Mission to Cornplanter's People* [Mechanicsburg, Pa., 2000], 103-4, 137-44; Sturtevant, *Handbook*, 15:509; Syrett, *Hamilton*, 20:447-8n).

As documented below, the Senecas' annuity based on the Big Tree transaction became an issue for the Jefferson administration in November 1801, when the resigned treasurer of the United States, Samuel Meredith, submitted claims that included commissions for handling the dividends on the bank stock. The matter was quickly referred through the secretary of war, the comptroller, and the secretary of the Treasury to the president, who reached a decision on the same day the question came before him.

I. John Steele to Albert Gallatin

DEAR SIR,   Thursday Noon. [19 Nov. 1801]

Will you look over the enclosed, with my remarks, and if you concur, say whether it be fit that I shd. write an official letter on the subject to the Secrry. at war. If I understand the case one of the points can only be decided by the President not as President, but as Trustee, or Guardian of the Indians, the other by the Secrry. at War in his quality of Superintendant &ca. You know I suppose that the Bank dividends remitted to the Seneca Indians, are the proceeds of an investment made by Mr. Morris for their use.

Yours sincerely & respectfully   JNO. STEELE

RC (DLC); partially dated; addressed: "*Private* The Secrry. of the Treasury"; endorsed by Gallatin: "Mr Steele &c Mr Meredith's claim"; with Gallatin's referral written on the address panel and TJ's reply alongside. Enclosure: probably Henry Dearborn to Steele, 19 Nov. 1801, with other papers not found (see below).

On 18 Nov., Henry Dearborn received a letter from Samuel Meredith, written at Washington the previous day, stating Meredith's claim for commissions on funds he had paid as an agent for the War Department (not found, but recorded in DNA: RG 107, RLRMS). Dearborn wrote to Steele, the comptroller, on 19

Nov., enclosing papers from Meredith and asking if the claims "can or cannot be considered as a fair and proper charge against the Public if allowed at this Office." Dearborn informed Steele that he had let Meredith know "I shall have no objection to allowing him a reasonable compensation for any services he may have performed, that can be considered as unconnected with his duties as a public Officer, but I shall hold myself restricted by the established rules of the Treasury Department" (FC in Lb in DNA: RG 107, MLS; enclosures not found). On the 21st, Dearborn received another communication from Meredith on the subject. Also on 21 Nov., Steele sent an OFFICIAL

LETTER to Dearborn. Meredith wrote the secretary of war again on the 30th, this time enclosing an account of money he had paid for the War Department's Indian "factories," or trading houses. Meredith's and Steele's letters to Dearborn, recorded in correspondence registers of the War Department, have not been found (Meredith to Dearborn, 18, 30 Nov. 1801, and Steele to Dearborn, 21 Nov., all recorded in DNA: RG 107, RLRMS).

II. Albert Gallatin's Referral

[19 Nov. 1801]

Both are of a trifling nature; the objection to both is that a salary officer ought not to receive any compensation but his salary; the whole of his time being supposed to belong to the public. On the other hand the services are not such as, *by law*, could be considered as the Treasurer's official duty—Another objection lies against the claim for commissions on the Indian annuity arising from #Bank dividends; which is that it is not consistent with policy to detain any thing, from the Indians under name of commn., especially when it is recollected that the President is trustee—

Respectfully submitted to the President of the United States by his most obt. Servt.   ALBERT GALLATIN

The six nations sold the Genessee Country to R. Morris for an annuity which is vested in Bank stock, the dividends of which constitute the annuity—

MS (DLC); undated; entirely in Gallatin's hand; on verso of Document I, cross-written over address.

III. Jefferson's Memorandum

As trustee for the Seneca Indians it appears to me just that the charge of mr Meredith be allowed & be deducted from the dividends. at the same time, considering their want of familiarity with these subjects, and the natural jealousy of ignorance, it seems desireable that the US. should in future have their business transacted for them clear of expence, so that they may recieve their dividends without defalcation.   TH: JEFFERSON
Nov. 19. 1801.

MS (DLC); entirely in TJ's hand; written on verso of Document I alongside Gallatin's note.

On 2 Mch. 1802, Dearborn wrote to Meredith: "Not being able to procure that knowledge which is considered necessary relative to the Stock in the Bank of the United States, belonging to the Seneca Tribe of Indians, I request that you would give me all the information, your knowledge of the Subject will enable you to do." Meredith replied from Philadelphia on 5 Mch., but that letter has not been found (Dearborn to Meredith, 2 Mch. 1802, Lb in DNA: RG 107, MLS; Meredith to Dearborn, 5 Mch. 1802 received 9 Mch., recorded in DNA: RG 107, RLRMS).

From John Vaughan

DEAR SIR,   Philad: 19 Nov. 1801

I have the pleasure to inform you that D Coxe has himself taken the Vaccine Infection, & during the progress of the Disorder, has undergone uncommon fatigue, without any Inconvenience; two of his patients, one a child, one a laboring man, appear to have it finely; the latter has this day furnished fresh Virus; he has been obliged to work hard during the whole time, & found no other inconvenience than being obliged to work without his coat; the Symptoms & appearances correspond with Aikin's acct. except that clear Blistery appearance is not so exactly Defined—D Coxe has at the request of Dr Rush inoculated one of the Medical Students, & if the Case proves a favorable one, it may give rise to a Lecture; which is very much to be wished, as the Medical class is the Largest we have ever had, & from very distant & opposite quarters. D Coxe & myself both concieve a Very Valuable purpose would be answered (in quieting all Doubts) in this Country, if your letter on the Subject were permitted to be published; It seems highly important, to use the most powerful means within our reach, to Stamp with Authority & respectability, the Evedinces of a Discovery, more important than has been made for Centuries—& we concieve that your letter at this moment, would have a very decided & extensive effect, thro' means of the Medical Students, & we hope Sufficient Virus may soon be obtained to give them the means of Spreading it thro' the Continent—as soon as the Patients are completely over the Vaccine disease, Dr Coxe means to innoculate some of them for the Small Pox—He proposes, if he can Conveniently, to innoculate a Cow, & to try that Virus also. A new Edition (1801) of Jenner has come out—If there appears to be any new & Important matter in addition—I will get an abstract made by D Coxe—A Fresh Supply of Small Pox matter will be Sent for Dr Gantt when he meets with Some that is Satisfactory—

The third part of the Collection of Papers made by the Society of Naval Architecture in England, containing a Very Interesting report, relative to the preservation of timber &c; & being uncertain whether you might possess it, I take the Liberty of requesting your acceptance of it—The Work itself, I had not complete; it might be a Useful Work to the Secretary of the Navy, as it contains not only Interesting new Matter, but gives (I beleive) a list & acct. of authors on Naval Subjects.

Mr Peale is making progress in his Skeleton of the Non Descript, he puts in no other Bones, than those found together, & without any Doubt belonging to the Same animal;—Corresponding parts Deficient, he imitates in Wood—His Son is completing on the Same principle, another, from materials found in other Places, & proposes taking it to Europe. Our Society has made many Valuable additions to its Library from Dr Franklins & from Mr Bird's of Westover, particularly of the Lond: Phil: Trans.ts almost Complete to 1789 from Commencemt. As we propose making a Catalogue[1] our Members, are examining if they Have any Books Suitable to us which they can with Convenience Spare, after which the Catalogue will be made—Knowing your occupations at present, I shall not intrude further on Your time, nor wish you to do it so far as to impose upon Yourself the necessity of any reply.

I remain Your ob Serv & friend   JNO VAUGHAN

RC (DLC); at foot of text: "His Exy. Thomas Jefferson, Washington"; endorsed by TJ as received 23 Nov. and so recorded in SJL. FC (PPAmP). Enclosure: *A Collection of Papers on Naval Architecture, Originally Communicated through the . . . European Magazine,* Part III (London, 1801); see Sowerby, No. 1227.

YOUR LETTER ON THE SUBJECT: probably TJ to Vaughan, 5 Nov., in which TJ described his experiments with cowpox at Monticello.

A third EDITION of *An Inquiry into the Causes and Effects of the Variolæ Vaccinæ* by Edward JENNER was published in London in 1801.

Vaughan's brothers William and Benjamin were members of the SOCIETY for the Improvement of Naval Architecture in Britain. In 1792, William intended to send the second part of the *Collection of Papers* to TJ through his brother John (Vol. 23:99).

[1] Vaughan here canceled "immediately."

From William P. Gardner

SIR   Philadelphia 20 November 1801

I beg leave to address you upon a subject which has in some Degree involv'd my Character and reputation. I now enclose you sundry papers relative to the Transaction to which I refer. It is probable you have hitherto been unacquainted with the manner in which Mr. Campbell and myself brought forward the information relative to the public accounts and the motives and inducements which led thereto. I owe it to truth, I owe it to justice and to my own Character to state them to you. The publication of the accounts, to which the Enclos'd papers refer, was undertaken with the purest and best of motives. We knew the Sacrifices which we were about to make in the loss of places which we then held in the Treasury Department. We Knew that in Case a change shou'd not take place in the Administration that we cou'd never expect their Countenance or the Countenance and support of that Class of our fellow Citizens calling themselves Federalists. Knowing these things we notwithstanding came forward, voluntarily, and made every Sacrifice in the Cause of Republicanism. Had there been any Offers or persuasions made use of as an Inducement, then indeed wou'd the Transaction have worn a different aspect. It was an act springing purely from a Conciousness of the Duty which we owed to our Country and to ourselves. I wish the Letter of Mr. Israel to Colo. Burr to receive your Attention. I had not an Opportunity of seeing Colo. Burr, therefore the original is still in my possession. I had likewise a similar Letter to General Mason, which I forwarded under Cover to him as he was absent when I was at Washington. Much has been said of a Breach of trust and an Abuse of Confidence and from Quarters whence I should least of all expected it; I think it therefore not improper to give a Copy of the oath or Obligation administered on entering the Treasury Dept. It runs thus "I A.B. do swear that I will support the Constitution of the United States and faithfully discharge the Duties of Office." I think the Secretary of State's Office is the only one where an oath is administered as to secrecy. There was a transaction which lately occurred in this City not dissimilar to the One, on which I have now the Honor to address you, where several Clerks and among the rest, the cheif Clerk were dismiss'd for *not* giving information to the Directors of the Bank of Pennsylvania when the President of that Bank unwarrantably drew therefrom upwards of One hundred and twelve thousand Dollars. They were dismissed upon the plea, that, as the Stock of the Bank was the property of the stock holders, they should have had the earliest Information of the Act thro' the medium of the Board of Directors. In like manner I am of Opinion, that the people of the United States shou'd have been made acquainted with the Conduct of their public Agents, when such glaring misconduct occurs. I am well convinced that I have (tho' unknown to them) the thanks of a very great Majority of the people of the United States if we may judge from the Applause which Mr. Duane has obtained in Quality of RatCatcher to the People. I had the offer by Oliver Wolcott of being made his cheif Clerk provided I wou'd abandon my politicks and cordially embrace the Cause of Federalism; upon my Refusal, he told me, that if I had the Abilities of Sir Isaac Newton and all the Integrity requisite I should never have a place in his office.—

I have been a considerable looser upon this Occasion.—I might have remained in the Public Office, for it was not known to them that I was a principal in the Transaction. I considered it a point of Honor and resign'd my situation. I have been out of Employment at an Expense of at least six hundred Dollars, not to mention a loss of 2 or 300 Dollars ℔ Annum which I suffered during the last three years and a half when I was in public Employment on account of my principles. I cheerfully however make this sacrifice (tho' it falls extreemly hard upon me) convinc'd that I have contributed in no small Degree towards effecting the glorious Change which has taken place in this Country. For the purity of my intentions I appeal to Heaven and to my own Heart. Whatever may be my Condition in life; Whatever may be the Evils (and I have already in a pecuniary point of view experienced them) personally affecting me resulting from this Transaction, I shall have the pleasing Consolation of self-approbation. I might by a Dereliction of principle have placed myself in more prosperous Circumstances but Sir, I scorn the Idea and woud again and again. When the good of our Country demands personal sacrifices small indeed must be the Patriotism of that man who would not promptly and cheerfully make them. Not only have I suffered by my firm Adherrence to my political principles in my Native Country but also in Europe. I was compell'd at considerable loss in my Business to quit England in 1796 for being concerned in an affair of Honor on the part of my friend Mr. John Pride of Amelia County in Virginia, in the laudable attempt to vindicate the Characters of Mr. Giles and Mr. Madison against the Aspersions of Monarchists and Aristocrats. In this Affair the Calumniator of American Patriots lost his life. In short Sir, the whole tenor of my Conduct at all times and in all places has been that of an American and a Republican and I am Convinc'd that after the strictest Scrutiny and Enquiry it will be found to be that of a man of Honor and principle.

Had I have remained silent and thus cloathed with secrecy the Defalcations of Public Agents; Had I have remained silent when my Country was threatened with a savage and cruel Algerine War thro the misconduct of a public Agent, when the deerest interests of my Country were at stake and when the lives and liberties of my unsespecting and unofending fellow Citizens were endangered, then indeed shou'd I have considered my Conduct criminal. In the present

Case I cannot think so and I fain hope that you will be inclin'd, from the Reasons stated, to place this Act of mine in a favourable point of view. There is a duty which a man owes to his Country which in my mind is paramount to the Obligations which he owes to himself or to an Individual. Such Sir are my Sentiments in Regard to this matter. An Opinion seems to have gone abroad among the Republicans of this City, that I was offered a Cheif Clerkship in One of the Departments under Government. I declare to you Sir, that I never, either directly or indirectly, had such or any other offer.

I have the Mortification of seeing the man, who I am inform'd, offered a Bribe for the suppression of these Accts. still retain'd in Office as a cheif Clerk. I have the Mortification of seeing men retained in Office whom I have Known to be the Advocates of limited Monarchy in this Country, who have been the Revilers and slanders of those under whom they are now placed, who have been the Persecutors and tormentors of Republicans under the administration of Mr. Adams. No Doubt these things are unknown to the Heads of Departments. I mentioned to Mr. Gallatin my Connections, not that I derive any Honor therefrom but to shew that I was not a needy Adventurer destitute of Friends or Connections, wishing to bring myself into Notice by this Act of mine.

Among the papers which I now Enclose is a Copy of the Recommendation of the late Benjamin Fuller formerly a merchant of considerable Respectability in this City and one of the Directors of the Bank of North America, I believe from its earliest institution untill the time of his Death in the Year 1799. His Character stood eminently fair in the Estimation of his fellow Citizens, and I trust it will be deemd an honorable testimonial in favour of my Character. If it is found necessary I can forward the Signatures of all the respectable Citizens of Philadelphia in my favour To them I am generally known and to the greater part intimately so. I wou'd likewise refer you to Colo. John Hall, Governor of Delaware, who has an intimate Knowledge of my Connections and with whom I have the Honor of an acquaintance.

I should 'ere now have saild for Demerara but the Difficulty of obtaining a passage has prevented me.

My visit to Washington, in the month of June last, was with a view of obtaining some Employment under our Administration. You may recollect I did my self the Honor of handing you a letter and a small Box containing Medals of Buonaparte and the King of Prussia I remained at Washington about five weeks and having no prospect of obtaining a place I returnd to Philadelphia.

[702]

My Attachment to the Cause of Republicanism and my ardent Wishes for the prosperity of your Administration induce me to mention the names of some Persons who are now in Office under the General Government. Men who I know to be the bitterest and most violent Enemies of the Principles of our Constitution. Mr. Wagner Cheif Clerk in the Office of Mr. Madison has in my hearing frequently ridiculed Republicanism, declaring in the language of Mr. Adams, that it meant any thing or nothing. He has said that he never knew a man among the Republicans trust worthy, of probity or principle. About two years since he made a Bet with Mr. Jeremiah Pearsol of this City that Mr. Gallatin in the Course of one year from that Date wou'd either be hung or sent out of the Country, observing at the same time that he considered himself perfectly justified in making the Bet from the well known infamy of Mr. Gallatin's Character. When calld upon by Mr. Pearsol to pay the Bet he refused untill threatened with a Publication of the Transaction in the newspapers. He has declared that in Case you were elected to the Presidency he woud immediately resign his Situation under Government. Mr. Kimble if possible was more bitter than Mr. Wagner. Mr. Crawford I understand was One of the Party concerned in whipping Mr. Sneider the Republican Printer at Reading. He is in the same office. The late Mr. Robert Jones Heath informd me when I was at Washington that Edward Jones, Cheif Clerk in the Treasury Department was one, among a few Others, who at Trenton in the Year 1798, when the public Offices were there, gave Mr. Heath an invitation to drink a Glass of Wine and the first Toast given was "D——n to Thomas Jefferson." Mr. Heath immediately left the Room with those Expressions of Indignation which such Conduct must ever excite. If these men had the least particle of Honor and Honesty in their Composition they wou'd resign the situations which they now hold under those whose Characters they have uniformly abused and calumniated, But Sir, what can be expected of men, who would not only sacrifice their own principles but the Rights and liberties of their Country also at the shrine of self Interest.

I mention the following Persons as having been the Revilers and Slanderers of those under whom they are now placed and no less conspicuous for their unrelenting and persecuting Spirit. Mr. Ferrall of the Auditor's Office Colo. Thomas of the Navy Department, Thomas Turner Accountant do. and his Brother, Peter Hagner of the War Department, Major Rogers do. John Coyle of the Treasury Department. A worthy young Man with a Wife and One or two Children was dismissed by Mr. Wolcott to give Room for Mr. Coyle. There are a few Others who come under the Denomination of Trimmers, who have not intermeddled with politicks and who may be justly stiled harmless and innofensive Creatures. Permit me Sir, to assure you that I have never had any misunderstanding or personal Altercation with any of the foregoing Persons, but convinced as I am, from frequent Opportunities of knowing, that they are the irreconcilable Enemies of the present Administration, I have thought it right and proper to mention their Names to you.

Convinc'd Sir, that I am addressing an American, a Republican and the Head of a free People, I feel persuaded that you will readily, not only excuse the liberty which I have taken, but applaud the motive which has induced me to trouble you with this Letter.

Accept Sir, my ardent Wishes for your Health and Happiness and may a kind Providence long preserve you in the Hearts and affections of a free and a grateful People.   WM. P. GARDNER

RC (DNA: RG 59, LAR); addressed: "His Excellency Thomas Jefferson President of the United States"; endorsed by TJ as received 26 Nov. and so recorded in SJL. Enclosures: (1) Israel Israel to Aaron Burr, Philadelphia, 16 Mch. 1801, introducing Gardner, who was proceeding to Washington to obtain employment under the new administration, noting that Gardner, while a clerk in the Treasury Department, had come to his house in May or June 1800, carrying "a Beginning" of the accounts of Timothy Pickering and Jonathan Dayton and expressing indignation "at the Abuse of Public Trust and the Retention of the Public Monies by certain" public officers; he returned the same afternoon for further conversations with Israel and William Duane, but then proceeded with the move to Washington and left Anthony Campbell to complete the "Business of furnishing Mr. Duane and myself with the Treasury Report Book" from which the accounts were extracted in the presence of John Beckley, Israel, "and some others" and then published in the Aurora; Israel considers the publication "a most important Stroke against the Federal Party" and "productive of the happiest Effect upon the Minds of the People"; a short time later Gardner resigned his position at the Treasury Department, remaining "firm and unshaken in his Political Principles." (2) John Shee

to Gardner, 6 May 1801, wishing him success in his endeavors on his visit to Washington, noting that his length of time in public employment and the "patriotic Act" he performed "tending so much to unmask a weak and wicked Administration" would not be overlooked by "our first Majistrate" and heads of departments. (3) William Duane to Gardner, Philadelphia, 11 June 1801, assuring Gardner that the disappointments he had expressed about his trip to Washington and his interviews with Madison and Gallatin were not based on an understanding of the situation, explaining "I know that there is much Disgust felt by the Heads of Departments at the Conduct of the whole of the Clerks in the offices and that none of them that have misconducted themselves will ultimately be retaind"; noting that the Republican administration has been in power for only a short time and has to be careful in carrying out removals, Duane assures Gardner that Jacob Wagner, for one, will be removed soon and he knows who will succeed him; but Gardner is to tell no one, Duane only mentioning it to show "that you have suffered wrong impressions to be made upon you." (4) Gardner to Gallatin, Washington, D.C., 21 June 1801, requesting a passport and introduction for a trip to Demerara to recover an estate left by his uncle, John Patterson, Gardner notes that his father had taken "an early part in the American Revolution" and his mother was the sister of Samuel Patterson, a brigadier general in the American army in 1779 and later a loan officer and treasurer of the state of Delaware, and observes that his family was known to the present Pennsylvania governor and to Congressmen Michael Leib and William Jones; hearing it "whispered" that he would not receive an appointment in any government office because of his role in submitting the accounts of Timothy Pickering, Jonathan Dayton, and others to the press, Gardner explains that he did it only after Consul Richard O'Brien had inquired why treaties with the Mediterranean powers were not being fulfilled and promised supplies were not being sent; a review of Pickering's accounts indicated that while he had been advanced $374,000 "from the Public Treasury," he had expended only $27,000 to fulfill the treaties with the Barbary powers; Gardner assures Gallatin, "It does not follow that because I have publishd the accounts in Question, I make a Practice of these things," indeed he abhors "the Idea of such Conduct." (5) Gallatin to Gardner, Treasury Department, 24 June, wishing him a "safe and successful voyage" and enclosing a letter from the Treasury secretary to Nicholas Rousselet, U.S. consul for Demerara and Essequibo, 24 June, introducing Gardner as "a native of Philadelphia of respectable Connections" who is recommended "as a man of Talents and integrity" and requesting that he receive the full support of the American consul (all Trs in same, in Gardner's hand; for Enclosure No. 1, see Kline, *Burr*, 1:528-30). Other enclosure not found.

William P. Gardner, a Philadelphia native, had served as a government clerk for almost eight years, two of them with Joseph Nourse, register of the Treasury, "in his own Room and as his Confidential Clerk," and, after returning from Europe in 1796, as a clerk in the auditor's office. Although his role in delivering the Treasury Department records of Timothy Pickering, Jonathan Dayton, and others to William Duane was not known at the time, he resigned his clerkship in the de-

partment after the editor began publishing the accounts in the Philadelphia *Aurora* on 17 June 1800. On 10 Mch. 1802, TJ sent Gardner's nomination as consul at Demerara, a colony under British control in South America, to the Senate. By that time the Federalist press was aware of Gardner's role in the affair and described his appointment as "the reward of certain secret services." Upon his arrival at Demerara, Gardner found that the British would not recognize him in his official capacity, just as they had not recognized his predecessors. He returned to the United States in 1803 and found employment as a clerk in the General Post Office at Washington (Cunningham, *Process of Government*, 331; *Washington Federalist*, 27 Mch. 1802; JEP, 1:409; Kline, *Burr*, 528-30; Madison, *Papers, Sec. of State Ser.*, 3:589-90; Gardner to TJ, 14 Nov. 1803).

See Anthony CAMPBELL to TJ, 12 Oct., for another interpretation of the publication of the PUBLIC ACCOUNTS from the Treasury Department.

LETTER OF MR. ISRAEL TO COLO. BURR: see Enclosure No. 1, above.

Before he left for Europe in 1794, Gardner worked for a short time at the BANK OF PENNSYLVANIA, where he found he could make $200 more a year than as a Treasury Department clerk. By February 1798, Samuel M. Fox and Jonathan Smith had replaced John Barclay and Jonathan Mifflin as president and cashier, respectively, at the bank (Stafford, *Philadelphia Directory, for 1797*, 73; *The American Repository, and Annual Register of the United States, for the Year 1799* [Philadelphia, 1798], 87; *Philadelphia Gazette*, 9 Feb. 1798; Gardner to TJ, 14 Nov. 1803).

In October 1801, OLIVER WOLCOTT still thought Campbell was the only clerk involved in the publication of the accounts (Syrett, *Hamilton*, 25:423-4).

AFFAIR OF HONOR: on 20 Aug. 1796, John Pride and William Carpenter fought a duel in Hyde Park. Carpenter, described as an American, died that day of his wound and Pride was indicted for "wilful murder" (J. G. Millingen, *The History of Duelling: Including Narratives of the Most Remarkable Personal Encoun-*

ters *That Have Taken Place from the Earliest Period to the Present Time*, 2 vols. [London, 1841], 2:152).

MISCONDUCT OF A PUBLIC AGENT: for Gardner's contention that Timothy Pickering received public funds but did not purchase and send stores to Algiers as specified by treaty, see Enclosure No. 4, above.

In his letter of 11 June, Duane informed Gardner that he had heard rumors that after the resignation of Basil Wood, Gardner had been offered a CLERKSHIP in the Treasury secretary's office, but he "had objected to the labour of the situation," and consequently Doyle Sweeny received the appointment (see Enclosure No. 3, above).

I MENTIONED TO MR. GALLATIN MY CONNECTIONS: see Enclosure No. 4, above.

HONOR OF HANDING YOU A LETTER: see Duane to TJ, 10 May 1801.

For the WHIPPING of Jacob Schneider, THE REPUBLICAN PRINTER AT READING, see Tench Coxe to TJ, 24 and 25 June 1801.

Jacob Wagner, Edward JONES, Patrick FERRALL, Thomas TURNER, Samuel Turner, Jr., Peter HAGNER, Hezekiah ROGERS, and John COYLE continued to hold their government positions in 1807—Wagner, Jones, Ferrall, and Hagner as chief clerks (Cunningham, *Process of Government*, 328-32).

From Lewis Littlepage

SIR,   Rhodes Hotel Novbr. 20th. 1801.

I am this moment arrived, and wish to know at what hour tomorrow you will condescend to see me.—

I have the honor to be with the highest respect,

Sir, your most obedient humble Servant—

LEWIS LITTLEPAGE.

RC (DLC); at foot of text: "Thomas Jefferson—President of the United States"; endorsed by TJ as received from Washington on 20 Nov. and so recorded in SJL.

RHODES HOTEL: William Rhodes kept a hotel on F Street near 15th Street in Washington beginning in 1799. In 1801, Rhodes leased additional space at that intersection for a tavern (Bryan, *National Capital*, 1:313, 414, 517).

From William Maclure

Paris 20th Novemr. 1801

I wrote you from England last summer and have since been thro' Germany and on the Rhine I thought both the soil and climate in many places bore a greater resemblance to the soil and climate in the back parts of Pensylvania Maryland and Virginia than any part of Europe I have yet been in and finding that the farmers from the want of enclosures and pasture feed their cattle for some part of the year on roots induced me to forward to you by this opportunity some of the Beets and the Turnip Cabbage which they use principally as winter food for their cattle and hope they will arrive in time for you to make the experiment—am rather induced to believe that sufficient attention has not been paid in the Choice of seeds to the previouse habits of the vegitable depending much on the nature of the climate and perhaps something on the soil—in many of the experiments to rais winter food for the Cattle in Virginia such as turnips &c &c—the seeds have been brought from England & Holland where the climate is moist and not so variable in point of temperateture from their proximity to the Sea and Insolar situation for the same reason perhaps the Clover lucern & other grasses which growe in the upper parts of Germany might succeed with you where the English and Dutch seeds have failed and not improbably the Vine from the banks of the Rhine would thrive well on the Southwest mountains as the soil is much the same and the Climate equally warm—when I passed that country it was the Vintage and too early for the setts or I should have forwarded some from the different situations and exposures—They plant Tobacco very generally in Germany and have found it answere all the purposes of a Pulse crop in cleaning and ameliorating the soil in June they plant and take it up in Septemr when they immediately sowe wheat which experience has taught them yields a better crop than if the land had lain fallow the price is from 15/ to 16/ Stg ℔ 100 [lb.] at which the farmer makes little or nothing but as a Pulse crope in the rotation they are induced to plant it every five years Ive rather been of oppinion that the common idea in Virginia of the Tobacco being an impoverishing crop arrose from allowing the Soil to wash after having been well pulverised and suffering the Stalks to run to seed after they were cut—in the country round the Hartz mountains they use pulverised Gypsum as a tope dressing for their Luzern & Clover tho their soil is calcariouse and frequently cut the lusern seven times and the clover five times by sowing about a bushell to the acre after every cutting—both in Germany and this country they are turning their attention more to agriculture than they used to do the cheapness of labour facilitates their experiments and, is perhaps the only part of their improvements that can add to the prosperity of America by addopting only those that have succeeded—much is expected here from the consequences of an active commerce I fear the immediate effects of the Peace on the trade of America the withdrawing that half of their commerce that depended on the war will make an equall reduction of the circulating medium of paper necessary for which Im affraid neither the mercantile men nor the Banks are prepared the immediate effects may be injuriouse tho' the Ultimate result may be salutary the number of incorporated companies for the circulation of

a paper medium is an evill not easily cured its a morgage on future industry for the expenditure and perhaps the extravagance of the past
supported by a missplaced confidence its foundation vanishes at the
approach of reformation and truth and the edifice crumbles to pieces
in the hands of those that attemp the reform—as a protection for the
seeds I have sent an abstract of the Kantian Philosophie its much in
fashion in Germany tho I neither comprehend it nor have met with
any one that appeared capable of an explanation it may be a new tho
I scarce think it can be a usefull discovery youll excuse this scraul and
believe me to be with much Esteem yours Sincerely

WM MACLURE

RC (DLC); addressed: "Thomas Jefferson President of the United States";
endorsed by TJ as received 12 June 1802
and so recorded in SJL.

Maclure wrote TJ from ENGLAND on 3
July (printed above in this series) and 9
July 1801. In the latter communication, a
brief note from London, Maclure wrote:
"I took the liberty of writting you a few
lines by way of Norfolk and intended the
accompanying Pamplets to go by the
same conveyance but finding a passenger
for Baltimore thought it a more dirrect
conveyance and remain with much esteem Yours Sincerely." The pamphlets,
which Maclure's brother, Alexander

Maclure, referred to as "two Books," were
evidently parts of the *Projet de Code Civil*,
a two-volume précis of the intended new
code of laws for France (RC in MHi, at
foot of text: "His Excellency Thomas
Jefferson President of the United States,"
endorsed as received 8 Oct. and so recorded in SJL; Sowerby, No. 2216; Vol.
34:504n).

ABSTRACT OF THE KANTIAN PHILOSO-
PHIE: probably Charles François Do-
minique de Villers, *Philosophie de Kant:
Ou, Principes fondamentaux de la Philoso-
phie transcendentale* (Metz, 1801), which
TJ had bound in July 1802; see Sowerby,
No. 1364.

To Amos Marsh

SIR   Washington Nov. 20. 1801.
I recieve with great satisfaction the Address you have been pleased
to inclose me from the House of Representatives of the Freemen of
the state of Vermont. the friendly and favorable sentiments they are
so good as to express towards myself personally are high encouragement to perseverance in duty, & call for my sincere thanks.

With them I join cordially in admiring and revering the Constitution of the United States, the result of the collected wisdom of our
country. that wisdom has committed to us the important task of proving by example that a government, if organised in all it's parts on the
Representative principle unadulterated by the infusion of spurious
elements, if founded, not in the fears & follies of man, but on his reason, on his sense of right, on the predominance of the social, over

his dissocial passions, may be so free as to restrain him in no moral right, and so firm as to protect him from every moral wrong. To observe our fellow citizens gathering daily under the banners of this faith, devoting their powers to it's establishment, and strengthening with their confidence the instruments of their selection, cannot but give new animation to the zeal of those who, stedfast in the same belief, have seen no other object worthy the labours & losses we have all encountered.

To draw around the whole nation the strength of the General government as a barrier against foreign foes, to watch the borders of every state, that no external hand may intrude, or disturb the exercise of self-government reserved to itself, to equalize and moderate the public contributions, that while the requisite services are invited by due remuneration, nothing beyond this may exist to attract the attention of our citizens from the pursuits of useful industry, nor unjustly to burthen those who continue in those pursuits, these are functions of the General government on which you have a right to call. they are in unison with those principles[1] which have met the approbation of the Representatives of Vermont, as announced by myself on the former & recent occasions alluded to. these shall be faithfully pursued according to the plain & candid import of the expressions in which they were announced. no longer than they are so, will I ask that support which, through you, has been so respectfully tendered me: and I join in addressing him, whose kingdom ruleth over all, to direct the administration of their affairs to their own greatest good.

Praying you to be the channel of communicating these sentiments to the House of Representatives of the freemen of the state of Vermont, I beseech you to accept, for yourself personally, as well as for them, the homage of my high respect and consideration.

Th: Jefferson

PrC (DLC); at foot of first page: "Amos Marsh esquire."

The address TJ received from the

Vermont House of Representatives is printed at 5 Nov.

[1] Preceding word interlined.

From John Vaughan

Dear Sir.   Philad: 20 Nov. 1801

My anxiety not to Intrude upon your Time, made me omit in the closing Sentiment of my letter, one exception to it, by adding a request, that (to the Single point of publishing your very Interesting letter) I may be favor'd with a reply—Dr Rush to whom I have taken the liberty of shewing it, was much Struck with the weight & importance of it, & agrees in wishing Strongly that it may be published— He means to publish his own change of opinion, being now favorable to it, whereas in the Early Stage of the Discovery, he wanted to give an unfavorable one, in a letter to a Southern friend.—

Mr Peale permits two of his Children to be innoculated by Dr Coxe—I was pleased with his assent, as his Situation is peculiarly adapted to give publicity to the Experiment—

I remain Dr sir with the greatest Respect Your friend & Servant

Jn Vaughan

RC (DLC); at foot of text: "His Excy T. Jefferson"; endorsed by TJ as received 25 Nov. and so recorded in SJL.

MY LETTER: Vaughan to TJ, 19 Nov.

From Thomas Leiper

Dear Sir　　　　　　　　　Philada. [before 21] Novr. 1801

I have been about writing you for some months back but I was of the opinion Tobacco would be lower in this I have been mistaken—I want to be informed if your last years Crop is on hand and what will be the price and day of payment—

I have a letter from Richmond dated the 11th. that Quotes Prime Tobacco at 36/ to 37/6. inferior at 33/ V Currency—If your crop is unsold and at Richmond I will take it at the highest price viz 37/6 V Currency and pay an interest of six pr Ct. from the day it is ship't at Richmond—If those terms are agreeable you may order your Agent at Richmond to ship me your Tobacco' immediately for I am in immediate want of some 40 or Fifty Hhds and this market I am affraid will not produce this fall of the Quality I wish to purchase—

Indeed Sir to be candid with you I have not manufactured Fifty Hhds of Tobacco' equal in quality to those I purchased of you last ever since that period—If your last years Tobacco is sold I should thank you for an offer of your present Crop on its arrival at Richmond. I am with much esteem

Dear Sir Your most Obedient St.　　　　Thomas Leiper

RC (MHi); partially dated; endorsed by TJ as received 21 Nov. and so recorded in SJL. FC (Lb in Leiper Papers, Friends of the Thomas Leiper House, on deposit at PPL).

THOSE I PURCHASED OF YOU LAST: TJ sold his tobacco crop to Leiper in January 1800 (Vol. 31:341-2, 382-3).

From Albert Gallatin

DEAR SIR   Sat. 20 [i.e. 21] Nov. 1801

Please to read the enclosed letter from the collector of Nottingham (about 30 miles from this) and the intended answer. His servant waits & informs me verbally that a number of arms were, (since writing the letter) found on board. The Collector ought to have acted instead of writing for instructions. But it is necessary to dispatch immediately his messenger. If you think any alteration in the answer necessary, be good enough to mention the same. The bearer will wait for your answer—

With great respect Your obedt. Servt.   ALBERT GALLATIN

RC (DLC); partially misdated; addressed: "The President of the United States"; endorsed by TJ as a letter of "Nov. 20. 1801. for Nov. 21," received 21 Nov., and "Collector of Nottingham" and so recorded in SJL. Enclosures: (1) George Briscoe to Gallatin, Nottingham, Maryland, 19 Nov., describing a suspicious vessel brought into port "said to be the *Sally*," a 60-ton schooner, which sailed from Charleston on 10 Oct., commanded by Elias De Butts; upon landing in distress, the captain left for Baltimore and ordered the *Sally* to go 30 miles up the Patuxent River, instead of to Norfolk, where the vessel was said to belong; left without papers, the schooner's cargo includes tobacco, rum, flour, bread, crackers, and wine; an inspector and guard have been placed on board, but the cargo has not been landed "for want of a necessary warehouse"; in closing, Briscoe requests, "The man who delivers you this is a Special messenger, and by him you will be pleased to direct the proper mode for me to proceed in" (Gallatin, *Papers*, 6:56). (2) Probably Gallatin to Briscoe, Treasury Department, 20 Nov., noting that the vessel, under the circumstances as described by the collector, "is, even if no crime has been committed, liable to forfeiture if she has any distilled spirits of any kind, or any articles of foreign growth on board"; the master also being liable to penalties under several sections of the Coasting Act, Gallatin recommends that the collector "seize and dismantle the vessel and have the cargo landed and stored in any private Warehouse" and authorizes any expenses incurred; while the Treasury secretary cannot give advice as to proceedings to be pursued with civil authorities, he notes "if there are strong suspicions of any act of piracy having been committed, as this is an offence against the United States, it is your duty to apply to the proper Officer and forcibly represent the circumstances of the case in order that all the parties may be arrested and each of them privately examined by him"; further actions to be determined after the examination at the discretion of the judge (same, 6:85).

On 21 Nov., Gallatin also sent TJ the "Weekly list of Warrants issued on Treasurer Week ending *21 Nover. 1801*," reporting eight warrants, Nos. 134 to 141, inclusive, for a total of $206,626.25, including No. 136 for $4,534.26 issued to John Smith, the marshal of the Eastern District of Pennsylvania, for the census; four warrants under the military establishment, totaling more than $150,000, including No. 134 for $50,000 for fortifications; and one warrant, No. 137, for $50,000, for the navy (MS in DLC; entirely in Gallatin's hand; address clipped: "ted States"; endorsed by TJ as received from the Treasury Department on 21 Nov. and "Warrts" and so recorded in SJL).

From Lewis Littlepage

SIR, [21 Nov. 1801]

Be pleased to accept my thanks for the invitation with which you have honored me, but as I find nothing can be done in my pecuniary affairs here, I must proceed to Philadelphia while I have the means of so doing, as my monied friends and Agents in England made a strange blunder with respect to our Stocks, and I cannot draw from this place on London.—I shall set out tomorrow morning and regret that the state of my health will not permit me to assure again of the high respect with which I have the honor to be,

Sir, your most devoted Servant L. LITTLEPAGE.

RC (MHi); undated; at foot of page: "T. Jefferson, President of the United States"; endorsed by TJ as received 21 Nov. and so recorded in SJL.

On 30 Nov., Julian Ursin Niemcewicz wrote TJ briefly from Elizabeth, New Jersey, enclosing a letter for Littlepage at Littlepage's request. "Knowing, how particularly at this time all your moments are usefuly employed for the Good of our Commonwealth, I forbid myself the Pleasure to write longer to you," Niemcewicz wrote (RC in DLC; endorsed by TJ as received 4 Dec. and so recorded in SJL).

To James Madison

TH:J. TO J.M. Nov. 22. 1801.

The Virginia resolution inclosed was, I am sure, in full confidence that you would contribute your counsel as well as myself. I have only relieved you from the labour of the premier ebauche. I must you[1] to consider the subject thoroughly, and either make the inclosed what it should be, or a new draught. it should go on without delay, because I shall desire Monroe, if there is any thing in it he does not like, to send it back for alteration. and a fortnight is the whole time allowed for this. best wishes & affections.

RC (DLC: Madison Papers, Rives Collection); addressed: "Mr. Madison." Enclosures: (1) Resolution of the Virginia House of Delegates, 31 Dec. 1800, which James Monroe sent to TJ on 15 June 1801. (2) Dft, not found, of TJ to Monroe, 24 Nov. 1801 (second letter).

PREMIER EBAUCHE: first draft.

[1] Thus in MS.

From "An Observer & Friend to Justice"

Charleston South Carolina
SIR   23 Nov 1801—

I have this day written a letter to Mr Galatin respecting the official Conduct of James Simons Collector of this port & requested him to shew it to you as time will not permit me to send you a Copy—I remain with consideraton of the highest respect

Your Most Obed. Servt.

AN OBSERVER & FRIEND TO JUSTICE

PS. Policy will no doubt induce you to keep this communication as secret as possible—

If you think proper to receive any further information respecting the conduct of this Collector in his official Capacity it is in my power to give that which you have no idea off—& by your inserting a hint in the Gazettes I shall be able to know if you approve of my conduct in this business or not.

For instance. Sec. 53 & 55 of the Collection Law of 2 March 1799—Duty of Inspectors & Collectors as regards the returns of Cargoes landed at Charleston, liable to duty—From the manner in which this Business is conducted in the Collectors office it is impossible to Know what is landed or whether the government receives Duty on the whole Cargo or on only *a small part thereof*—the Inspectors in general are a set of ignorant Brutes in human shape who make their returns, *which are not compared by the Collector as the Law directs*—consequently it is impossible to Know whether the whole Duties are secured or not—again this Collector sets Clerks to calculate the Duties on Imports, who cannot copy a paper, and who are perfectly ignorant of the principles on which the duty is rated; this calculation is certified in the Naval office *as right,* by Clerks equally as ignorant as themselves, hence the United States may receive a Duty of only $12\frac{1}{2}$ pr Cent on a large Amount, when they are entitled to 15 or 20 pr Cent—The Collector here receives $\frac{3}{4}$ of 1 pr ct, the Collector at New York $\frac{1}{4}$ of 1 pr Cent therefore in the first instance the latter must receive three times the Amount of Duties as the former to be equal to him in this instance, hence it results that the latter must employ a greater number of Clerks to execute the Business (at a more liberal Salary I am told) which is to be deducted from his profits—which will make his office of less value to him than the Collectors office is to the Collector of Charleston.—In short, if you are disposed to notice this information, please direct for me under the fictitious name of *Jared* [*Irid*?] Charleston South Carolina

RC (DNA: RG 59, LAR); at foot of first page: "Thomas Jefferson Esqr President of the united States of America"; endorsed by TJ as received 9 Dec. and "Simmons. against him" and so recorded in SJL.

This is the first of several letters addressed to the president by an unidentified person or persons at Charleston using various pseudonyms, all critical of JAMES SIMONS. The second complaint, signed "An American," is printed at 11 Dec.

Section 53 of the 1799 COLLECTION LAW regarded the duties of inspectors, who were appointed by the customs collector and surveyor of the port to board a vessel and "suffer no goods, wares or merchandise of any nature or kind whatsoever to be landed or unladen or otherwise taken or removed" without a permit from the collector and naval officer of the port. Section 55 of the act provided the form of the return to be filled out and signed by the inspector "under whose superintendence the deliveries shall have been made." The return was to be examined and certified by the surveyor of the port and transmitted to the naval officer, who would compare it with the manifests and entries in his possession. He would note any differences and then transmit the return to the collector (U.S. Statutes at Large, 1:627, 667-9).

INSPECTORS IN GENERAL ARE A SET OF IGNORANT BRUTES: for the 32 port inspectors employed at Charleston in 1801, see ASP, *Miscellaneous*, 1:278.

On 2 Mch. 1799, a separate law was enacted "to establish the compensations of the officers employed in the collection of the duties on imports and tonnage," setting a fee for the entrance and clearance of each vessel and for the issuance of necessary documents and an additional compensation for collectors based on a percentage of the duties collected. On 10 May 1800, a supplementary act reduced the percentage of compensation for the collector at Charleston from $\frac{7}{8}$ to $\frac{3}{4}$ of one percent. Compensation for the COLLECTOR AT NEW YORK remained unchanged (U.S. Statutes at Large, 1:704-8, 2:72).

From Samuel Harrison Smith

SIR   [23 Nov. 1801]

I have the pleasure of communicating, what may in its details be *possibly* unknown to you, that the Preliminary Articles of peace between France & England were signed at London on the 1st of Oct. The terms agreed to are stated in the London Prints to be those proposed as the ultimatum of the British ministry, and acceded to by Buonaparte, without the least alteration.

The articles are not given, but they are stated to be the guarantee by France of the three Allies of England, viz Turkey, Portugal & Naples. Egypt to be evacuated by French & English, and Madeira restored. The Stadtholder, the King of Sardinia and the French princes are abandoned to their fate. Malta to be restored to the Knights, Minorca to be restored to Spain—Nothing is gained to England in the Mediterranean or in Europe; while France gains all Holland, the

Netherlands, a large part of Germany, Switzerland & ⅔rds. of Italy. In the West Indies England is to keep only Trinidad; the cape of Good Hope is to be a free port and Ceylon is to be ceded to England.

The English Prints condemn in the most indignant terms the conduct of ministers.

I am with sentiments of great respect   SAM. H. SMITH

RC (DLC); undated; endorsed by TJ as received 23 Nov. and so recorded in SJL.

LONDON PRINTS: Smith's summary of the presumed contents of the articles of peace echoed a paragraph from a special issue of the *London Gazette* published on 2 Oct., before the text of the articles was released. Smith reprinted that report and others from London in the next issue of the *National Intelligencer*, on 25 Nov.

Compensation to some of the hereditary monarchs who lost territorial possessions in the 1790s was an unresolved issue. The displaced rulers included the Dutch STADTHOLDER; the KING OF SARDINIA, who had retained control of that island but lost Piedmont, Savoy, and Nice; and the FRENCH PRINCES, Louis XVIII, Comte de Provence and titular king of France, and his brother Charles Philippe, Comte d'Artois (Grainger, *Amiens Truce*, 57, 70, 74, 116; Tulard,

Dictionnaire Napoléon, 405, 1087-9, 1332-4).

THE ENGLISH PRINTS CONDEMN: the *London Gazette* decried the secrecy of the peace negotiation for harming merchants while benefiting a few financial speculators who had advance warning of the terms of the pact. Lamenting that Britain had not acceded to a truce long before, the *Gazette* expressed hope that the government's ministers had finally recognized "the folly of attempting to conquer France." Henry Addington's government had faced the wrath of various factions since the new cabinet took over in March 1801, with economic malaise and poor harvests contributing to the discontent. The government's opponents in Parliament, including a group led by Grenville in the House of Lords, denounced the terms of the peace (*National Intelligencer*, 25 Nov. 1801; Grainger, *Amiens Truce*, 99-106; Vol. 33:90n).

From Joseph Elgar, Jr.

MY DEAR PRESIDENT   Brooke-ville Novemr. 24th. 1801—

It is the misfortune of those whose talents and virtues have raised them to eminence and power to be persecuted by a train of applicants and projectors.—I am sorry to add one to the number

But laying my confidence upon that amiable part of thy character, acknowleged even by political enemies as the warm friend to mankind and to every thing that can promote their happiness or convenience, I am encouraged to trouble thee with a subject and however trifling or foreign it may appear to thee I pray the good intentions with which it is dictated may in some measure interpose to procure my pardon—

In the course of my business, as a Surveyor, I have frequently experienced the great vexation and embarrassment to the artist, and law-suits and destruction of good neighbourhood among land holders, occasioned by local attractions influencing the magnetic Needle from the true point; and have been looking out with a kind of hopeless wish for something to remedy the evil. A paragraph from Tillocks Philosophical Magazine printed in London at length induced me to beleive that what I had regarded as a thing to be wished for but not expected was perhaps attainable. It is there stated on the authority of M. Humboldt that a species of Serpentine which he describes possesses polarity but is not Obedient to Iron. Taking the fact as stated and supposing the local attractions in this country to proceed from bodies of Iron oar lodged below the surface of the Earth, I inferred that if it were possible to procure a needle of this Serpentine it would be the desideratum I had in view—Considering Humboldt as authority sufficient respectable to justify an experiment I wrote to a member of the New York Mineralogical Society (Dr Mitchill) and recieved for answer that Serpentines exist in plenty and variety in the neighbourhood of New York City, that he thought the object I had in view was important but could not send me any Specimens.

This indifference to a Subject I had earnestly recommended, from a man who has professed himself a friend to the Arts—added to the information that Humboldt was engaged in traveling through South America which would render access to him extremely difficult if not impracticable to one in my sphere—and not being able to procure his description or one species of Serpentine— and pecuniary embarrassments forbiding any exertions on my part which would be attended with much expense—I began to dispair of my Object and abandon the pursuit.

But recollecting that I was within a few miles of the great patron of every usefull Art and improvement, and that a single dash of his pen might procure for me the Substances I wished to experiment upon, I have so far overcome my natural diffidence as to take the liberty of laying the Subject before him and will have the pleasure of submitting to any decision he may come to upon it—

While the great Interests of America and of man are revolveing in the mind of our worthy President I may be charged with want of patriotism for desiring to claim one moment of his attention, but I will cheerfully submit to this charge or any other for the presumption of troubling him with this address since it gives me an opportunity of declaring my love for the excellency of his character and the high respect with which

I am his friend   JOSEPH ELGAR JUNR.

RC (DLC); at foot of text: "Thomas Jefferson President of the United States"; endorsed by TJ as received 1 Dec. and so recorded in SJL.

Joseph Elgar, Jr., was probably born between 1772 and 1784. In 1807, when he wrote TJ again to recommend someone for office, he signed himself as surveyor of Montgomery County, Maryland. He later became a clerk under Samuel Lane, who was then the commissioner of public buildings for the District of Columbia. Benjamin H. Latrobe, who had an acrimonious relationship with Lane, described Elgar unflatteringly in 1816 as "a Schoolmaster, and Land surveyor." The next year Lane forced Latrobe out of the office of surveyor of Washington and replaced him with Elgar. Upon Lane's death in 1822, Elgar succeeded him as commissioner of public buildings. He held that position until 1834. His younger brother, John Elgar, was a foundryman and machinist, and their father built mills and forges (Alexander Crosby Brown, "Autobiographical Sketch of the Formative Years of John Elgar, 1784-1858, Builder of America's First Iron Ship," WMQ, 3d ser., 13 [1956], 87-93; John C. Van Horne, ed., *The Correspondence and Miscellaneous Papers of Benjamin Henry Latrobe*, 3 vols. [New Haven, 1984-88], 3:810, 694n; William C. Allen, *History of the United States Capitol: A Chronicle of Design, Construction, and Politics* [Washington, 2001], 146-7, 150-1, 165-6, 176; Charles Lanman, *Biographical Annals of the Civil Government of the United States, During its First Century* [Washington, 1876], 135).

BROOKE-VILLE: Brookeville, Maryland, was characterized in 1804 as a "post town" located about 20 miles northwest of Washington in Montgomery County (Jedidiah Morse, *The American Gazetteer*, 2d ed. [Charlestown, Mass., 1804]; T. H. S. Boyd, *The History of Montgomery County, Maryland, from its Earliest Settlement in 1650 to 1879* [Clarksburg, Md., 1879; repr. Baltimore, 1968], 122).

In the first volume of the PHILOSOPHICAL MAGAZINE, a scientific serial begun by English printer and inventor Alexander Tilloch in 1798, a brief notice about polarity of different substances reported that "Humboldt's serpentine" had magnetic poles but would not attract iron (*The Philosophical Magazine. Comprehending the Various Branches of Science, the Liberal and Fine Arts, Agriculture, Manufactures, and Commerce*, 1 [1798], 426; DNB, 54:790-1).

Alexander von Humboldt had embarked in 1799 on a scientific journey that took him through much of SOUTH AMERICA, Mexico, and Cuba. The trip lasted until 1804 (DSB, 6:550-1).

From B. T. Longbothom

SIR   Novr. 24th. 1801

Tho' ambitious of the pleasure to be known to you I am without the immediate means of arriving thereat, unless through this expedient which however it may differ from the usual routine of introductions I shall be gratified to find answer the effect.—You cannot but be aware how much a Gentleman in your Station influences the conduct of those around him—could I obtain the honor of your countenance at this present I do not doubt it would lead to a Practice in this Country which may establish my future independance Should you incline thereto I beg to assure you neither my past Situation in Life or future conduct will give you reason to regret having bestowed your favor

unworthily I have the honor to be Sir with much respect Your Obedt.
Hbl St   B. T. LONGBOTHOM

RC (MHi); endorsed by TJ as received from Washington on 24 Nov. and so recorded in SJL.

In a Washington newspaper advertisement for his services, B. T. Longbothom identified himself as a "surgeon dentist," with learning in London and experience in Jamaica. He published *Treatise on* *Dentistry, Explaining the Diseases of the Teeth and Gums, with the Most Effectual Means of Prevention and Remedy; to which is added, Dentition; with Rules to be Observed during that Interesting Period* (Baltimore, 1802; Shaw-Shoemaker, No. 2549; *National Intelligencer*, 23 Dec. 1801).

To James Monroe

TH:J. TO J.M.   Nov. 24. 1801. Washington.

The inclosed is the result of consideration & consultation between mr Madison & myself. if there be any thing you may think could be changed for the better, send it back, & it shall be altered.

I congratulate you on the certain event of peace, whatever it's conditions may be. health & happiness cum ceteris votis.

RC (DLC: Monroe Papers); addressed: "James Monroe Governor of Virginia Richmond"; franked and postmarked; endorsed by Monroe. Enclosure: the following document.

After seeing the enclosure, Monroe did not SEND IT BACK, but suggested a change. See note to the next document.

CUM CETERIS VOTIS: see TJ to Monroe, 14 Nov.

To James Monroe

DEAR SIR   Washington Nov. 24. 1801.

I had not been unmindful of your letter of June 15, covering a resolution of the House of Representatives of Virginia, and referred to in your's of the 17th. inst. the importance of the subject, and the belief that it gave us time for consideration till the next meeting of the legislature have induced me to defer the answer to this date. you will percieve that some circumstances, connected with the subject, & necessarily presenting themselves to view, would be improper but for your's & the legislative ear. their publication might have an ill effect in more than one quarter. in confidence of attention to this, I shall indulge greater freedom in writing.

Common malefactors, I presume, make no part of the object of that resolution. neither their numbers, nor the nature of their offences, seem to require any provisions beyond those practised heretofore, &

found adequate to the repression of ordinary crimes. Conspiracy, insurgency, treason, rebellion, among that description of persons who brought, on us the alarm, and on themselves the tragedy, of 1800, were doubtless within the view of every one: but many perhaps contemplated, and one expression of the resolution might comprehend, a much larger scope. respect to both opinions makes it my duty to understand the resolution in all the extent of which it is susceptible.

The idea seems to be to provide for these people by a purchase of lands; and it is asked Whether such a purchase can be made of the US. in their Western territory? a very great extent of country, North of the Ohio, has been laid off into townships, and is now at market, according to the provisions of the acts of Congress, with which you are acquainted. there is nothing which would restrain the state of Virginia either in the purchase or the application of these lands. but a purchase, by the acre, might perhaps be a more expensive provision than the H. of Representatives contemplated. questions would also arise whether the establishment of such a colony, within our limits, & to become a part of our Union, would be desireable to the state of Virginia itself, or to the other states, especially those who would be in it's vicinity?

Could we procure lands beyond the limits of the US. to form a receptacle for these people? on our Northern boundary, the country not occupied by British subjects, is the property of Indian nations, whose title would be to be extinguished, with the consent of Great Britain; & the new settlers would be British subjects. it is hardly to be believed that either Great Britain or the Indian proprietors have so disinterested a regard for us as to be willing to relieve us by recieving such a colony themselves; and as much to be doubted whether that race of men could long exist in so rigorous a climate. on our Western & Southern frontiers, Spain holds an immense country; the occupancy of which however is in the Indian nations; except a few insulated spots possessed by Spanish subjects. it is very questionable indeed Whether the Indians would sell? whether Spain would be willing to recieve these people? and nearly certain that she would not alienate the sovereignty. the same question to ourselves would recur here also, as did in the first case: should we be willing to have such a colony in contact with us? however our present interests may restrain us within our own limits, it is impossible not to look forward to distant times, when our rapid multiplication will expand itself beyond those limits, & cover the whole Northern, if not the Southern continent with a people speaking the same language, governed in similar forms, & by similar laws: nor can we contemplate, with satisfaction, either blot or mixture on that surface.   Spain, France, and Portugal hold possessions on the Southern continent, as to which I am not well enough informed to say how far they might meet our views. but either there, or in the Northern continent, should the constituted authorities of Virginia fix their attention, of preference, I will have the dispositions of those powers sounded in the first instance.

The West Indies offer a more probable & practicable retreat for them. inhabited already by a people of their own race & colour; climates congenial with their natural constitution; insulated from the other descriptions of men; Nature seems to have formed these islands to become the receptacle of the blacks transplanted into this hemisphere. whether we could obtain from the European sovereigns of those islands leave to send thither the persons under contemplation, I cannot say: but I think it more probable than the former propositions, because of their being already inhabited more or less by the same race. the most promising portion of them is the island of St. Domingo, where the blacks are established into a sovereignty de facto, & have organised themselves under regular laws & government. I should conjecture that their present ruler might be willing, on many considerations, to recieve even that description which would be exiled for acts deemed criminal by us, but meritorious perhaps by him. the possibility that these exiles might stimulate & conduct vindictive or predatory descents on our coasts, & facilitate concert with their brethren remaining here, looks to a state of things between that island & us[1] not probable on a contemplation of our relative strength, and of the disproportion daily growing: and it is over-weighed by the humanity of the measures proposed, & the advantages of disembarrassing ourselves of such dangerous characters.   Africa would offer a last & undoubted resort, if all others more desireable should fail us. Whenever the legislature of Virginia shall have brought it's mind to a point, so that I may know exactly what to propose to foreign authorities, I will execute their wishes with fidelity & zeal. I hope however they will pardon me for suggesting a single question for their own consideration. when we contemplate the variety of countries & of sovereigns towards which we may direct our views, the vast revolutions & changes of circumstance which are now in a course of progression, the possibilities that arrangements now to be made with a view to any particular place may, at no great distance of time, be totally deranged by a change of sovereignty, of government, or of other circumstances, it will be for the legislature to consider Whether, after they shall have made all those general provisions which may be fixed by legislative authority, it would be reposing too much confidence in their executive to leave the place of relegation to be decided on by him, & executed with the aid of the Federal executive? these could accomodate[2] their arrangements to the actual state of things, in which countries or powers may be found to exist at the day; and may prevent the effect of the law from being defeated by intervening[3] changes. this however is for them to decide. our duty will be to respect their decision.

Accept assurances[4] of my constant affection, & high consideration and respect.   TH: JEFFERSON

PrC (DLC); at foot of first page: "Governor Monroe"; with later emendation by TJ in ink, ca. 12-13 Dec. 1801 (see note 2 below). RC not found; altered by Monroe (see note 2) and transmitted to the Virginia General Assembly, 21 Dec. 1801 (ASP, *Miscellaneous*, 1:466); printed in same, 465, and in *Annals*, 16:995-8 (appendix), from documents communicated to the Senate on 16 Jan. 1807. Enclosed in the preceding document.

In the aftermath of the discovery of the slave conspiracy of 1800, the Virginia General Assembly passed legislation allowing for the eviction from the state, rather than the execution, of condemned slaves. By a RESOLUTION of 31 Dec. 1800, which Monroe enclosed to TJ on 15 June 1801, the legislature requested the governor to correspond with the president to find a place to send such transported criminals (Vol. 32:145n, 482n; Monroe to TJ, 15 June 1801, first letter). Years earlier, for the revisal of Virginia's laws begun in 1777, TJ had drafted "A Bill for Proportioning Crimes and Punishments in Cases Heretofore Capital" that included the provision: "Slaves guilty of any offence punishable in others by labor in the public works, shall be transported to such parts in the West Indies, S. America or Africa, as the Governor shall direct, there to be continued in slavery." Madison introduced the bill in the assembly, but it failed to pass in 1785 and 1786 (Vol. 2:314, 492, 504, 505-6n).

The Virginia House of Delegates passed resolutions in response to the letter above on 16 Jan. 1802, immediately after Monroe informed the legislature of the discovery of a new plot for a slave insurrection. In those resolutions, the legis-

lators repeated TJ's language to confirm that they were not interested in finding a destination for ordinary criminals, but for those who engaged in CONSPIRACY, INSURGENCY, TREASON, and REBELLION (ASP, *Miscellaneous*, 1:466; Douglas R. Egerton, *Gabriel's Rebellion: The Virginia Slave Conspiracies of 1800 and 1802* [Chapel Hill, 1993], 153).

As Monroe informed the General Assembly when he laid this letter before them, although there had been some initial intention to find a tract NORTH OF THE OHIO, he believed that "a liberal construction of the resolution admitted a greater scope." When Monroe asked for TJ's opinion he drew attention to the fact that the assembly's request did not "preclude" a site outside the United States (ASP, *Miscellaneous*, 1:466; Monroe to TJ, 15 June 1801).

PRESENT RULER: Toussaint-Louverture.

In the resolutions of 16 Jan. 1802, drafted by the House of Delegates and agreed to by the Virginia Senate, the lawmakers asked that the governor and the president give preference to AFRICA or South America as a destination for the rebellious slaves. The assembly also asked Monroe to correspond with the president to identify a place outside the United States where free blacks or mulattoes, or those who might be emancipated, could be sent "or choose to remove as a place of asylum." It was not the assembly's intention, according to the resolution, to acquire sovereignty over the locale on behalf of the people who might go there (ASP, *Miscellaneous*, 1:466; Egerton, *Gabriel's Rebellion*, 153-4). Monroe enclosed the legislature's resolutions in a letter he wrote to TJ on 13 Feb. 1802.

In both ASP, *Miscellaneous*, 1:464-7, and *Annals*, 16:994-1000 (appendix), TJ's letter above was printed as part of a set of documents that included the legislature's resolution of 31 Dec. 1800; Monroe's letter to TJ of 15 June 1801; Monroe's to the assembly, 21 Dec. 1801, conveying TJ's letter; a letter from TJ to Governor John Page, 27 Dec. 1804; a subsequent General Assembly resolution; and a letter from Page to Virginia's representatives in Congress, 2 Feb. 1805. The documents were reprinted in publications dealing with the colonization movement, such as Archibald Alexander, *A History of Colonization on the Western Coast of Africa* (Philadelphia, 1846), 63-72, and Philip Slaughter, *The Virginian History of African Colonization* (Richmond, 1855), 1-6.

[1] Preceding five words interlined.

[2] In response to a letter from Monroe, dated 8 Dec. 1801 and received 12 Dec., TJ used ink on the PrC to shorten and alter the preceding passage to read: "decided on by them. they could accomodate." Monroe emended the passage differently on the RC; when he laid TJ's letter before the legislature, the only alterations to the passage as TJ had originally written it were the substitution of "them" for "him" and "they" for "these" (ASP, *Miscellaneous*, 1:465; Monroe to TJ, 8, 21 Dec.; TJ to Monroe, 13 Dec.).

[3] TJ first wrote "by any changes in them" before altering the phrase to read as above.

[4] Remainder of closing replaced by "&c." in ASP, *Miscellaneous*, 1:465.

To John Vaughan

DEAR SIR   Washington Nov. 24. 1801.

I recieved last night your favor of the 19th. and with it the pamphlet of Naval architecture for which I thank you. it may be of use in our navy office where I shall deposit it. I am extremely glad to hear that the infection from the vaccine matter I sent has succeeded. but my great anxiety now is to know whether it prevents the small pox: and my anxiety arises not from any doubt that it would prevent it if taken in a proper stage, but from an incertainty whether it has been continued genuine. I have great confidence it was so when I brought it here. I suppose it from the uniformity of all the cases, & from the certainty with which the matter always took effect. I suspect that when effete, it oftener fails to give any disease, tho' it sometimes does give a spurious one. with respect to the publication of my letter, you observe it does not go at all to the only fact about which the world has any doubt, to wit, whether the vaccine disease prevents the small pox? I had no opportunity of trying that. it therefore would give no evidence on that subject. add to this that it is in a branch of science with which I have little acquaintance, have no pretensions to descant on, and that it gives no information sufficiently accurate to be of any service to a physician. I should therefore be entirely unwilling to have it presented to the public. the facts are free for use either in lectures, conversation or otherwise, and they may be mentioned on my observation if that will accredit them, because I believe them to be exact: but the publication of the letter would be entering an Arena on which I am not qualified to exhibit before the public. I shall be very glad to learn the effect of the variolous after the vaccine inoculation. Accept my respects & best wishes   TH: JEFFERSON

RC (PPAmP); addressed: "John Vaughan esq. Philadelphia"; franked and post-marked. PrC (DLC).

From Samuel Smith

SIR/   Baltimore 25th. Novemr 1801

I did myself the Honor to forward y[our] Box of Books by a Schooner bound to the Navy Yard—and by the same Opportunity I directed Peters & Johnson to send you one half Barrel of their best Beer—If it Should please you will know where you Can with Convenience supply yourself in future—I have this Day recieved from Malaga a Hhd of Wine sent to you from thence by order of Mr. Yznardi—Will you be pleased to direct what is to be done with it—

Peace in Europe will make more easy the Administration of the Government of the U.S. on which permit me to Congratulate you—Œconomic Changes may now be made with perfect Safety & [to] general satisfaction.—As to myself personally [it] will induce me to retire from my Commercial pur[suits] and put me at leisure to render your Administration every Service you may Concieve me Capable of—Our Relations with foreign Nations being Chiefly of a Commercial Nature has Induced me to suppose the Information & Knowledg of the Commercial Interest of our Country may at some Period be useful to our Nation in making Arrangements abroad—If they should I shall be prepared to give every Aid in my power—

My Brother is to be pitied—He has lost his Eldest Son, his next Cannot recover. he is expected to expire every Moment, and his third son is not perfectly recovered—I fear he will not be able to be with you soon—With the greatest Respect I am Sir/

your friend & servt.   S. SMITH

RC (DLC); frayed at margin; endorsed by TJ as received 28 Nov. and so recorded in SJL.

PETERS & JOHNSON operated a brewery in Baltimore on King George Street (Stafford, *Baltimore Directory, for 1802*, 84).

For the MALAGA wine sent to TJ by Joseph Yznardi, Sr., see Vol. 33:362, 441; Vol. 34:589; Yznardi to TJ, 15 Jan. 1802.

From Giuseppe Caracciolo di Brienza

Sigor. Baltimore a li 26. Novembre 1801

Mai mi sarei preso la libertà d'importunarlo con ques mia, se non fossi stato incoraggito, dalla grand stima, e venerazione che hanno tutti veri repubblicani per la persona di V:S: Troppo lungo sarebbe di descriverli la mia infelice istoria, e mai mi azzardarei di farlo un racconto, dove sarei sicuro di tediarlo. Solamente deve sapere, dopo che il Re delle due Sicilie, ha sacrificato i miei parenti sopra un patibolo, lungi d'esser contento d'aver sparso il sangue di tante vittime: ha vuoluto ancora in me dimostrare la sua crudeltà; non ostante che allora la mia età mi proteggeva, ma tutto questo, non mi avrebbe salvato al suo furore, se non avessi avuto la fortuna di salvarmi con la fuga. Dopo aver sofferto quasi piu di quello che un uomo può sopportare, sono arrivato in questa Città da più d'un mese, ove insegno la lingua Italiana: ma il troppo piccolo numero non mi basta per la mia sussistenza, e dall'altra parte la malinconia si è impatroni dello mio Spirito, e mi fa bramare di finire i miei giorni in una Solitudine. Da lei dipende di far felice una persona, che professera una eterna gratitudine a V:S: La mia preghiera è troppo temeraria, ma la di lei generosità è tanto più grande. Per trovare il riposo bramato, non so un'altro luogo che un convento, in questi Stati felici non ve ne sono, perciò sono costretto d'andare negli Stabilimenti Spagnoli: ma per far questo viaggio non ho il denaro necessario, perciò mi reccomando alla di lei generosità. Spero che V:S: mi voglia perdonare la mia temerita, butando un sguardo sopra lo stato infelice in cui mi trovo: in un paese, senza conoscere la lingua, senza amici, tutto abbandonato, a chi mi doveva indrizzare, che a un uomo dall quale per tutte le parti del mondo si parla con la più alta stima. La più grande consolazione sarebbe stata per me, di pregarlo a voce, ma la mancanza del denaro mi priva di questo piacere.

Tutta la mia Speranza e forse la vita dipende di lei, e resto con tutto il dovuto Rispetto

Suo umiliss.o e aff.mo Servo

Giuseppe Caracciolo di Brienza.

EDITORS' TRANSLATION

Sir, Baltimore, November 26 1801

I never would have taken the liberty of disturbing you with this letter, had I not been encouraged by the great esteem and veneration that all true republicans have for your person. It would be too long to recount my sad story, and I would never dare to give you a report that would certainly be boring to you. It suffices you to know that, after the king of the Two Sicilies sacrificed my relatives on the gallows, far from being sated by having shed the blood of so many victims, he wanted to exercise his cruelty on me as well; even if, at that point, my age protected me, yet all this would have not rescued me from his fury, had I not been lucky enough to save myself by taking flight. After having suffered more than any man can bear, I arrived in this city, one month ago, where I teach the Italian language. However, the exceedingly small number of pupils is not enough to support me; also, melancholy has taken hold of my spirit so that I desire to end my days in solitude. It rests on you to bring happiness to a person who will profess eternal gratitude to you. My plea is too daring, but your generosity is so much larger. I do not know any other place in which to find the rest I seek but a convent, but there are none in these happy states. Therefore, I am forced to pass into Spanish territory, but I do not have the money necessary to take this trip and thus I appeal to your generosity. I hope that you will forgive my daring if you just cast a glance at the sorry state in which I find myself: in a country where I do not know the language, without friends, utterly forsaken, whom should I have addressed if not a man of whom in the whole world people speak with the highest esteem? The greatest comfort to me would have been to present my plea in person, but the lack of money deprives me of this pleasure.

All my hope, and perhaps even my life, depends on you. I remain with all due Respect

Your most humble and affectionate servant

GIUSEPPE CARACCIOLO DI BRIENZA.

RC (DLC). Recorded in SJL as received 27 Nov.

Giuseppe Caracciolo de Brienza was probably a relative of the Neopolitan admiral Francesco Caracciolo de Brienza (1752-1799). The Caracciolos were an ancient noble family of Naples dating back to at least the thirteenth century (*Dizionario Biografico degli Italiani*, 66 vols. to date [Rome, 1960-   ], 19:304-465).

RE DELLA DUE SICILIE: late in 1798, an advancing French army combined with Neapolitan republicans to push Ferdinand, the king of Naples and of the Two Sicilies, out of Naples. In June of the fol-lowing year, royalist forces regained control of the city, allowing Ferdinand to return under the aegis of Lord Horatio Nelson and the British navy. At Nelson's instigation, Admiral Caracciolo, the commander of the republican forces, was hanged from the yardarm of the ship he had formerly commanded. More than one hundred people were hanged and over a thousand sentenced to prison terms (same, 19:360-2; DNB, s.v. "Nelson, Horatio"; Alan Palmer, "Naples," *An Encyclopedia of Napoleon's Europe* [London, 1984], 200; Samuel F. Scott and Barry Rothaus, eds., *Historical Dictionary of the French Revolution, 1789-1799*, 2 vols. [Westport, Conn., 1985], 2:749-51).

From Albert Gallatin

DEAR SIR   Treas. Dep. Thursday morning [26 Nov. 1801]

In relation to the within papers, it is proposed to transmit those concerning Latimer to Mr Dallas, with request that he should make a private enquiry into the facts & give this Depart. his opinion as to the Legality or illegality of the Collector's conduct. From his report we will be able to judge whether the subject deserves consideration. With respect to Jordan, it is proposed to write to him as advised by Mr Steele. Gen. Dearborne knows the parties—Sparks's case mentioned in Mr Steele's & Sparks's letters does not seem to require, and, indeed, he does not ask any investigation.

Respectfully Your obt. Servt. ALBERT GALLATIN

RC (DLC); partially dated; addressed: "The President"; endorsed by TJ as received on 26 Nov. and so recorded in SJL. Enclosures not found.

On 20 Nov., Gallatin sent letters regarding customs collectors George LATIMER and Melatiah JORDAN to John Steele and inquired if the comptroller knew anything about the transaction in the Latimer case, since his name was mentioned in SPARKS's letter. He noted that the complaints against Jordan "would have more weight was not the complainant anxious to get the office" and asked whether any of the "former complaints" mentioned had reached the comptroller's office. Gallatin continued: "Does Jordan appear to have acted generally with propriety? or, have there been any suspicious circumstances in his conduct?" If an investigation were necessary, who was the best officer "in that part of the country" to carry out the inquiry? (Gallatin, *Papers*, 6:90; endorsed and initialed by Steele: "Secty. of the

Treasy. Concerns Latimer & Jordan. Mr. Luffborough is directed to give me the papers in the 1st. and Mr. Underwood to investigate the accompts of the last. J.S.," and "Answd. and returned papers 25th. Nov. 1801").

Jordan had served as collector at Frenchman's Bay, in the district of Maine, since 1789, when the office was established (JEP, 1:10, 13). On 15 Aug., Jordan informed Henry Dearborn that he had learned through his friend Leonard Jarvis that Paul Dudley Sargent had brought charges against him to the Treasury Department. Jordan noted that Sargent wanted his office, and that five years earlier he had brought similar complaints against his "Character & Conduct," which, after an investigation, were dismissed. Jordan requested that Dearborn testify as to his character. The secretary of war sent the letter to Gallatin (Gallatin, *Papers*, 5:578-9; endorsed, in part, by Gallatin: "Melat. Jordan Collector applies to Gen. Dearborn to be continued").

To Peter Lyons

DEAR SIR Washington Nov. 26. 1801.

An old account between mr Wayles's & Bathurst Skelton's estate is shortly to be settled between the parties interested. in that account is the following item. '1792. July 3. To my assumpsit to pay your bond (i.e. B. Skelton's bond) to Thos. Moore assigned to Saml. Farmer who assigned to Peter Lyons £20. To interest on do. from 17[67. Nov. 3.-?]' at a meeting with Meriwether Skelton & Jerman Baker as his attorney about 1773, we went through these accounts. our voucher for this £20. & interest was an account in your handwriting,

I think, but not signed by you, of which the inclosed is a copy. this was disallowed as an insufficient voucher either of the paiment or of the discharge of B. Skelton's estate. tho' this is a very antient matter, yet I trust your exactness in business has been such that you can still turn to your papers concerning it, & either furnish us with B. Skelton's bond, or some equivalent voucher which may satisfy the representatives, and you will oblige me by doing it. if sent to me at this place by post it will come safely.

I am happy in an occasion of recalling myself to your recollection. it is now a great many years since we have seen one another or had any communication. I hope you have enjoyed all the health which your age will admit, & pray you to accept assurances of my constant esteem & great respect.   TH: JEFFERSON

PrC (ViW); faint and blurred; at foot of text: "The honble P. Lyons"; endorsed by TJ in ink on verso.

Peter Lyons (1735-1809), an old friend of George Washington's from Studley, Hanover County, was a judge in Virginia's General Court. In 1803 he became the second president of the Supreme

Court of Appeals in Virginia, serving in this role until his death (Washington, *Papers, Ret. Ser.*, 2:90n; David J. Mays, *Sketch of Peter Lyons The Second President of the Supreme Court of Appeals of Virginia* [Richmond, 1927], 1-3).

For SKELTON'S ESTATE, see TJ to William Fleming, 19 Sep.

From John Monroe

SIR   Staunton. Novr. 26th. 1801.

This letter will be addressed on a subject entirely private; and the motive has arisen in my observations on your private character only. To bring into review all the adverse causes of oppression which have for some years operated on me will be unpleasant to you to read & extreamly painfull for me to recapitulate.

The events which have passed I cannot now controle. The object is to try to command the future. Without the assistance of some benevolent hart I must fail in this object also.

I have, with a rational prospect of success, taken, as rented the Warm Springs; where, under the direction of my family & Son in Law, Mr. Smith I mean to open a tavern. This I cannot do, with any prospect of advantage without the command of a sum of ready money. where to obtain it I cannot tell, unless Sir, prompted by humanity, you will extend your fostering hand, & contribute to rear a Man & his family (who have Wrestled hard with adversity) once more into a state of competence. The sum necessary for the outfits will be at the least fifteen hundred Dollars. With this sum I can, fairly calculate on success & a handsom profit: without it, difficulty & labour, unattended by advantage—The manner of my application, will impress you with my high opinion of your character & my confidence, that (unless in this, as in every other important act of my life I shall be opposed by imperious circumstances) I shall succeed, is drawn from the same source. But should my adverse Destiny still prevail; and you be unable to gratify your own feelings by extending the aid I now solicit, I have the pleasant reflection of believing, that the application will remain a secret to the World.—

I will thank you for an answer as soon as may be convenient. But I had rather your letter should not be franked. I can with convenience wait on you when ever you may appoint—

Accept Sir my high respect & sincere Esteem   J, MONROE

RC (MHi); endorsed by TJ as received 2 Dec. and so recorded in SJL.

TJ considered the WARM SPRINGS and nearby Hot Springs, located in Bath County, to be the two "most efficacious" medicinal springs in Virginia (*Notes*, ed. Peden, 35).

From Benjamin Vaughan

DEAR SIR,   November 26, 1801.

Avocations, proceeding from rural & family concerns & a sickly season, have long suspended my letters. In resuming the pen, I feel more pleasure than I shall probably communicate.

By the present post, I have the honor to send a pamphlet with which you have had former occasions to be acquainted. It contains a section (p.   ) which may suggest or confirm the project of promoting American ship-building, through the medium of negotiations in Europe, at the present juncture.

It seems true, as a general principle, that a national maritime force for war, is better prepared, by attending to the formation of the *crews* of the vessels employed in the national carrying trade in time of peace, than by laying stress upon the *origin* (or built) of the vessels themselves. If foreign vessels are more advantageous to merchants, than such as are built at home, it seems wise to have recourse to them; since by checking the proceedings of merchants as to their vessels, the number of vessels may[1] be lessened, & consequently the number of seamen. If the merchant-service is to be burthened in any way, during peace, with a view to war, it seems more adviseable to insist on the employment of supernumerary seamen, or the successive introduction of fresh landsmen; than to limit the merchant as to the vehicles in which he is to convey his commodities. Contrary maxims, originating in times less enlightened than the present, continue in force perhaps chiefly as the result of habit & want of thought.

In any event, the present moment seems favorable, if not to a general, yet to a partial review of this subject.—The war just terminated, has destroyed many European merchant vessels, either by violence, by time, or by neglect; and new ones have never been built in sufficient numbers to replace them. Such seems the position justifying an attempt to obtain at least a temporary permission for the sale of American vessels, in certain countries in Europe. The quick revival of *commerce*, & its dependent public & private revenues, must eminently follow from the quick reinstatement of mercantile fleets. The persons also for the moment in power in France are not indisposed to novelties; & the Bishop of Autun in particular is well apprized of the opinions contained in the pamphlet above referred to, and was formerly not ill affected towards them; and the immediate renovation of every[2] concerning trade & the French colonies & settlements must deeply interest the personal interests both of himself & his principal.

By introducing into practice the doctrine here contended for, though only temporarily, results may occur to make its permanent establishment seem both desireable & easy. By inducing a single European nation, even for a time, to navigate in any degree with American vessels, the charm on this subject may be broken with other European nations. By providing a ready sale for American vessels in Europe, (& if possible in the foreign possessions of European nations,) & thus preventing the return to America of many empty vessels; the freights to & from America will be brought more upon a balance, to the advantage both of those who sell & of those who retain their vessels. By selling vessels at the close of an outward voyage, the citizens of the United States will be saved the anxiety of attending to them in foreign ports; & come into an earlier command of their capital, for other purposes, if they so choose. By a measure of this kind, the inhabitants of the Eastern states of the Union will also be gratified, who seek to receive a boon at your hands,[3] especially those among them who are disappointed adventurers at this instant. Such are a portion of the benefits which may be proposed on this occasion.

To facilitate the operation of the plan, indulgence may be given to American vessels having *alien* owners & *alien* crews, when by accident returning back to American ports; a measure, which as it depends upon Congress, may by Congress be provisionally legalized. This law will not commit Congress, and will strengthen the hands of your negotiators in Europe, & may prevent injurious delays.

Difficulties will still remain between European nations acceding to the plan, when trading to other European nations; the commercial conventions, now subsisting between European nations, having generally limited their indulgences to vessels *built*, as well as to vessels owned & principally navigated, by the parties to whom these indulgences relate. But should remedies be refused to these difficulties in the connections of European nations with each other, American vessels may still be used within the respective dominions of each nation.

It is perhaps not altogether easy to say, how the European timber-markets will be supplied at the present moment, considering the great changes lately made both in the ownership of landed property & in the possession of rivers connected with the places where timber is still growing. In Great Britain, navigable canals of recent construction have stripped the country of much wood; & the calls of government & the distresses or avarice of individuals in other states, have lately prostrated multitudes of trees. But what may be the balance of all these operations, & whether to last for a longer or a shorter time, is not for me at this distance to calculate.—It is easy however for foreign governments to perceive, that if they waste their timber upon merchant-shipping; they will have, for their national vessels, timber less in quantity, worse in quality, & dearer in price. It is also no less apparent, that the ship yards of foreign nations cannot supply vessels to their respective merchants so fast, as the calls of their commerce will require at the present instant. Nor can it be concealed from the most wilfully blind, that trees grow slowly; that little care has been taken to supply their waste, (little for example in England since the time of Cromwell which can avail the present generation;) & that the turn for navigation has become so much more extensive than ever, & is so rapidly on the increase, that few things next to pacific principles are more important to maritime nations, than a reserve of a domestic supply of timber, out of the reach of the caprice or of the hostility of foreign powers.

I send a French translation of the little work in question at the beginning of this letter, that it may be used, if needed. Our friends Messrs. Talleyrand & Gallois know where to obtain other copies, especially as there has been either a new edition of it or a new translation at Paris, since you resided there. As to the work itself, I know that the author wishes to strike out much, to add a little, & to new-model the rest.

I have the honor to be, Dear sir, With the highest esteem, Your respectful & sincere humble servt.

P.S. The books must follow by the next post.

RC (DLC); endorsed by TJ as a letter from Vaughan received 10 Dec. from "Holloway" (that is, Hallowell, Maine) and so recorded in SJL.

[1] Word interlined in place of "will."
[2] Vaughan apparently omitted a word here.
[3] Remainder of sentence interlined.

Albert Gallatin's Statement on the Bank of the United States

[after 26 Nov. 1801]

Bills discd. & bills of exchange		13,640,582
Due by Banks	#	804,690
" " Govt. temporary	2,940,000	6,030,756
funded debt	3,090,756	
Specie	#	5,246,863
		25,722,891
Bank notes in circulation		5,081,713
Deposited vizt.		
by Government	4,111,218	
Banks	374,193	9,156.690
dividends unpd.	304,051	
Individuals	4,367,228	
	#	14,238,403
Capital		1[1]0,000,000
		24,238,403
Amsterdam loans		746,000
		24,984,403
next dividend		400,000
		25,384,403
Contingt. fund		338,488
		25,722,891

Specie   5,246,863
Bank   804,690
On hand   6,051,553
Due   14,238,403
Proportion 1 to $2\frac{1}{3} - \frac{1}{2}$

MS (DLC: TJ Papers, 118:20337); in
Gallatin's hand; arranged by Gallatin
with the debit column to the left of the
credit column, with a wide arrow to the
left of the debit column, perhaps indicating that it belonged under the credit column giving the statement as reproduced
above; at foot of text: "State Bank U.
States 26th Nover. 1801"; endorsed by
TJ as received from the Treasury Department on 1 Dec. and "Banks" and so
recorded in SJL.

BILLS DISCD. & BILLS OF EXCHANGE:
Gallatin probably provided this consolidated weekly statement of the Bank of
United States and its branches in response to TJ's expressed interest in the
bank statements and TJ's previous effort
to organize the information (see Notes on
the Bank of the United States and Internal Revenues, printed above at 10 Nov.,
and TJ to Gallatin, 11 Nov.). Before com-
piling the statement above, Gallatin gath-

ered information from the reports of the
Bank of the United States at Philadelphia
and the five offices of discount and deposit
for the weeks ending 19 and 26 Nov. He
organized it in tabular form, adding the
amounts from the six banks in several cat-
egories, and thereby determined the totals for discounted bills, specie, and bank
notes in circulation, for the deposits by
government, banks, and individuals, and
for other designations (MS in NHi: Gallatin Papers; printed in James O. Wettereau, *Statistical Records of the First
Bank of the United States* [New York,
1985], 290-1). Gallatin used the consolidated totals of 26 Nov. to prepare the
statement above.

[1] Gallatin first wrote "2" and then reworked the preceding figure to "1." He
then altered the sum below reworking the
first digit from "3" to "2" to give the correct total.

From William C. C. Claiborne

MY DEAR SIR,   Natchez, November 27th. 1801

After a passage of 46 days from Nashville; I reached this Town, on
the Morning of the 23rd. Instant;—during the Voyge, I experienced
no misfortune; and Mrs. Claiborne; myself; and family enjoyed good
health.

The Affairs of this District, are greatly confused; in a Word, Anarchy is (nearly) the order of the day:—The restoration of Good Order;
and regular Government will be an arduous Work; and cannot be accomplished in a short period;—My whole time, however, shall be devoted to the service of this people, and I hope to be instrumental to
their happiness & prosperity.—

The *rage* of Party, in this little settlement, has been greater, than I
had supposed, but of *late*, *it* has assumed a Milder *Aspect*; I shall
avail myself of this Circumstance, & will endeavour to destroy *discord*
and *distrust*; and to rear on their *Ruins*, harmony and Confidence;—
I cannot promise myself, to be wholly successful; in that Attempt, but
I am sanguine in a hope, that under my Administration, the public
mind will experience a great Share of quietude.

May I be permitted to inform you Sir, that the conduct of my

Predecessor, has been such, as to furnish for me, an instructive Lesson; I shall profit by his Misfortunes, and observe a policy quite opposite to the one, heretofore pursued in this District.

The pamphlet published by Mr. Sergent, in vindication of his official Conduct, has reached this Territory;—I am told however, that it will have no effect, except to excite against Mr. S. still further the hatred of many Citizens.—I presume Sir, you have understood the Contents of this Production:—The *Abuse*, which the Writer has thought proper to bestow upon me, gives me no Concern; Conscious of *its* entire want of Truth, I cannot suppose, *that* it will operate "ought against my Good Name":—But I cannot conceal from you, how greatly I regret, that my Appointment should have encreased the torrent of Calumny, against the federal Executive.

I owe you an Apology, for introducing this subject;—perhaps it was improper;—But my feelings hurried me to notice thus far, the publication of Mr. S.

The Legislature of this Territory, will be in Session, on Tuesday next; they have much to perform;—The public Will, and the public Good will require many radical changes, in the present Code of *Laws*; *those* now existing seem to me (generally) to be in opposition, to the Interest of a young settlement, & illy suited to the preservation of good Order.

I wish, I had more experience in the Business of Legislation; But my best Talents & Reflection shall be employed in the discharge of my Duties.—

This Country is greatly extolled by its Inhabitants; I believe *it* has many Advantages, of which, I will acquaint you, when I have had an opportunity of visiting the Territory generally.—

With best Wishes for your happiness in public & private Life—I have the honor to be, With sincere Regard & great Respect Your mo: obt. sert. WILLIAM C. C. CLAIBORNE

RC (DLC); addressed: "His Excellency Thomas Jefferson President of the U. States"; closing quotation mark supplied; endorsed by TJ as received 15 Jan. 1802 and so recorded in SJL.

MRS. CLAIBORNE was Elizabeth W. Lewis Claiborne, originally of Nashville. The FAMILY on the journey to Natchez included an infant daughter named Cornelia Tennessee Claiborne, a sister of Mrs. Claiborne, and several servants (Joseph T. Hatfield, *William Claiborne:*

Jeffersonian Centurion in the American Southwest [Lafayette, La., 1976], 40, 47, 207).

PAMPHLET: in addition to *Political Intolerance*, Winthrop Sargent had also published *Papers, in Relation to the Official Conduct of Governour Sargent* (Boston, 1801).

The second SESSION of the first General Assembly of Mississippi Territory opened on 1 Dec. Although he had arrived too recently to make extensive recommendations, Claiborne did ask the legislature to make changes to the judiciary and the militia (Dunbar Rowland, ed., *Official Letter Books of W. C. C. Claiborne, 1801-1816*, 6 vols. [Jackson, Miss., 1917], 1:12-21).

To Thomas Newton

DEAR SIR   Washington Nov. 27. 1801.

I have just recieved your favor of the 18th and after due thanks for your attention to the procuring the cyder, I according to your desire mention that it may be consigned to mr John G. Ladd, merchant at Alexandria, who will receive & forward it to the address of mr John Barnes his correspondent & my agent here.

I sincerely congratulate you on the unexpected news of peace. it is a happy event for this country as well as the rest of the world, inasmuch as it restores business to a steady course, and [secures?] our peace, and thereby enables us to pursue with safety the financial operations which our interests require. accept assurances of my sincere esteem & respect.   TH: JEFFERSON

PrC (DLC); blurred; at foot of text: "Colo. Thos. Newton"; endorsed by TJ in ink on verso.

To Ellen Wayles Randolph

MY DEAR ELLEN   Washington Nov. 27. 1801.

I have recieved your letter and am very happy to find you have made such rapid progress in learning. when I left Monticello you could not read; and now I find you can not only read, but write also. I inclose you two little books as a mark of my satisfaction, and if you continue to learn as fast, you will become a learned lady and publish books yourself. I hope you will at the same time continue to be a very good girl, never getting angry with your playmates nor the servants, but always trying to be more good humored & more generous than they. if ever you find that one of them has been better tempered to you than you to them, you must blush, and be very much ashamed, and resolve not to let them excel you again. in this way you will make us all too fond of you, and I shall particularly think of nothing but what I can send you or carry you to shew you how much I love you. I hope you are getting the better of your whooping cough. you will learn to bear it patiently when you consider you can never have it again. I have given this letter 20. kisses[1] which it will deliver to you: half for yourself, & the other half you must give to Anne. Adieu my dear Ellen.

TH: JEFFERSON

PrC (MHi); at foot of text in ink: "Eleonor Randolph"; endorsed by TJ in ink on verso. Enclosures not identified.

YOUR LETTER: see Ellen Wayles Randolph to TJ, [before 10 Nov. 1801].

[1] TJ first wrote "I have kissed this letter 20. times," before altering it to read as above.

To Martha Jefferson Randolph

MY DEAR MARTHA   Washington Nov. 27. 1801.

Your's of Nov. 18. by mr Trist has been duly recieved. my business is become so intense that when post day comes, it is often out of my power to spare a moment. the post too, being now on the winter establishment is three days longer in carrying our letters. I am sincerely concerned at the situation of our dear little ones with the whooping cough, but much rejoiced that they have past the crisis of the disease safely. there is no disease whatever which I so much dread with children. I have not heard from Maria since she left you: but generally sucking children bear that disease better than those a little past that stage. I hope therefore her little Francis will do well. I am afraid, from what I hear that Moran & Perry have gone on badly with my works at Monticello. I am anxious to see the hull of the buildings once done with. we are all overjoyed with the news of peace. I consider it as the most fortunate thing which could have happened to place the present administration on advantageous ground. the only rock we feared was war; and it did not depend on ourselves but others whether we should keep out of it. we hope Great Britain will have so much to do at home that she will not have time to intrigue and plot against this country. we are now within 10. days of Congress when our campaign will begin & will probably continue to April. I hope I shall continue to hear from you often, and always that the children are doing well. my affections and contemplations are all with you, where indeed all my happiness centers. my cordial esteem to mr Randolph, kisses to the little ones, and tenderest love to yourself.

TH: JEFFERSON

RC (NNPM); at foot of text: "Mrs. Randolph." PrC (MHi); endorsed by TJ in ink on verso.

From Benjamin Rush

Philadelphia Novemr. 27th. 1801

Accept much honoured & dear sir of a Copy of the enclosed publication.

How joyful the Sound of Peace! It brings a thousand blessings in its train, among which the revival & diffusion of knowledge will not I hope be the least.

Receive again, and again Assurances of the friendship of Dear sir your Affectionate humble Servant   BENJN: RUSH

PS: *Vaccination* as you have happily called it, has taken root in our city, and will shortly supercede the Old mode of Inoculation. I consider it as a complete Antidote to the ravages of war in its influence upon population. It is computed 210,000 lives will annually be saved by it in Europe. It is only necessary to believe the plague *every where*, is the Offspring of *domestic* causes, & not propagated by Contagion, to extirpate it in like manner from the list of human evils.—

RC (DLC); endorsed by TJ as received 2 Dec. and so recorded in SJL. Enclosure: Benjamin Rush, *Six Introductory Lectures, to Courses of Lectures, upon the Institutes and Practice of Medicine, Delivered in the University of Pennsylvania* (Philadelphia, 1801; Sowerby, No. 979).

The origins of the word VACCINATION are obscure and are believed to be in France (Hervé Bazin, *The Eradication of Smallpox: Edward Jenner and the First and Only Eradication of a Human Infectious Disease*, trans. Andrew and Glenise Morgan [San Diego, 2000], 40, 208-10).

From David Austin

RESPECTED SIR—   Sat'y Even'g, Washingn, Novr. 28th A.D. 1801.

Having been educated to the science of Morals; & having been ever satisfied with those exercises which fall to the lott of a public teacher; it would never have been my wish, from private motives, to have turned my thoughts towards any other subject: But as providence would have it; my eyes have been directed towards the movings of the invisible finger of God, in the affairs of the late revolution. This invisible energy, it is the determination of the Most High, in due time, openly to illustrate. The interposition hath been upon a national scale, and determines towards a national illustration. The idea, I know is novel to some; but to those who believe in a Universal providence, the matter contains no mystery. The invisible energy insists, so to speak, on an alliance with national administration. This, again, may be thought strange; but to those who know, that "by him princes reign," & that at his nod kingdoms rise & fall, the matter is plain. The Universal power hath right to toutch such chord, in the mighty instrument of performance as seemeth him good. I now say, that the chord of American administration Almighty God is determined to toutch; & that it is not in my power to arrest the determination. However well pleased I may be in the entertainments of Literary & of moral pursuits on common subjects; I am not allowed to take my ease, by quieting myself, as indulgence might dictate. When I am ready to say, now will I be at peace; Heaven, again arrouses me to action, & demands obedience.

In a word, Sir, for I need not again explain, what I have so many times explained, I have now to ask a place in the Office of the Secretary of State: Let me be placed in such grade, as you may judge my talents may reputably fill. I am not ambitious of grade, of priority or of preeminence: but some kind of association with the system of national administration Heaven insists upon.

The Manifestation, this evening presented is accompanied by authority to say, that my request is to be supported under the pain of a cloud ready to burst upon the present state of things: the fire is shewn to me, & the wood made ready; & nothing is wanting but the breath of the Almighty to enkindle the flame. I could file a sheet in description; but let it suffice to say, there are combustibles still in the nation: they are ready to take fire: the forges & bellowes are ready to play: and howsoever, resistance may be attempted, by men, there is no successful fighting against God.

Your Excel'y will have the goodness to recollect what I have heretofore expressed; that the spirit that is now upon me dictated the fall of Mr Adams, wh. was duly noted to him before he left N. England: &, that the decision would be had in the Capitol was signified to Oliver Wolcot from Eliza. Town, of the date of the day on wh. the votes were dropped into the box of the Electors—Decr 3d. if I rightly recollect.—

A new scene now opens, & the same tide is still in flood.—

Your Ex'y hath my ideas, & with due acknowts for the favors & attention already afforded, subscribe with all due esteem

DAVID AUSTIN

RC (DNA: RG 59, LAR); addressed: "His Excel'y Thomas Jefferson Esqr. Pres: U: States Washington"; endorsed by TJ as received 30 Nov. and so recorded in SJL; also endorsed by TJ: "referred to Secy. of state to take order. Th:J."

From Albert Gallatin

DEAR SIR   T. Dt. Nover. 28th 1801

I had yesterday enclosed a rough draft of a letter to the Collector of New York in relation to the erection of the beacon at Sandy hook— You have returned it without remarks. Yet it is a delicate subject & I would wish to have your opinion on the propriety of the act. For that purpose it is returned together with a draft of the letter to the Govr. of N. Jersey to which I also request your attention. Is there any thing in it improper or disrespectful?

With great respect Your obt. Servt.   ALBERT GALLATIN

RC (DLC); at foot of text: "The President of the United States"; endorsed by TJ as received 28 Nov. and "beacon at Sandy hook" and so recorded in SJL. Enclosures not found.

David Gelston, customs COLLECTOR OF NEW YORK, became the superintendent of lighthouses in the state in the fall of 1801. His jurisdiction extended to the lighthouse and beacon at Sandy Hook, New Jersey. Built at the insistence of New York City merchants with New York funds, the lighthouse, at the southern entrance to New York harbor, was completed in 1764 and ceded to the United States in March 1790. Alexander Hamilton oversaw the erection of a beacon at Sandy Hook in the early 1790s, replacing one destroyed in a storm that struck New York City in November 1789 (George R. Putnam, *Lighthouses and Lightships of the United States* [Boston, 1933], 2-4, 11-14; Washington, *Papers, Pres. Ser.*, 5:544; Enclosure No. 13, at Gallatin to TJ, 24 Aug.).

GOVR. OF N. JERSEY: Joseph Bloomfield.

On this date, Gallatin also sent TJ the

"Weekly list of Warrants week ending 28th Nover. 1801," with information on 13 warrants, Nos. 142 to 154. Five under the civil list, totaling $2,729.70, included Nos. 142 to 144 to the assignee of Rufus Putnam, surveyor general, for surveying expenses of $2,412.39. Two under "Miscellaneous," totaling $1,800, included No. 151 to Jared Ingersoll for $300 for "fees in sundry suit—unprovd. claim." One warrant for $942.21 was specified for intercourse with foreign nations. Two warrants were issued, totaling $35,000, for the interest and reimbursement of the public debt. Three warrants, totaling $28,400, were issued for the purchase of bills on Holland at 40 cents per guilder for the payment of the Dutch debt, including No. 146 at New York for $4,000, No. 153 at Boston for $24,000, and No. 154 on Gallatin for $400. No warrants were issued for the military or navy. The warrants for the week totaled $68,871.91 (MS in DLC: TJ Papers, 118:20343; entirely in Gallatin's hand; endorsed by TJ as received from the Treasury Department on 28 Nov. and "Warrants" and so recorded in SJL).

From Albert Gallatin

DEAR SIR   Nover. 28th. 1801.

Some days ago a letter from Mr Briscoe Collector at Nottingham (Patuxent Riv.) was communicated to you. It related to the arrival of a vessel without captain or papers, which under those circumstances was directed to be seized & dismantled and the cargos landed.

The Captain is now here, and I enclose his papers which are so far regular and the Collector's letter enclosing the amount of the cargo— from whence it is inferred she was intended for the Slave trade.

The manifest of her cargo as entered at the custom house of Charleston agrees in every particular with the cargo found on board except in the articles of "glass beads" "hand cuffs," chains & bolts which are *omitted* in the manifest. The vessel cleared from Charleston S.C. for Cape Verd, was by stress of weather obliged to put in the Chesapeak, & without stopping at Norfolk where the vessel belongs or going to Baltimore where the Captain went taking the papers along with him was left in an obscure harbour at the mouth of Patuxent—

Under those circumstances, is the prima facie evidence strong enough to induce giving directions to the dist. attorney of Maryland to libel the vessel? More evidence, from the mariners, who should on that account be secured, may come out in the trial. The Attorney general thinks we may proceed—Mr Steele has some doubts though upon the whole he does not object. The law of March 22d 1794 (Vol. 3d. page 22) is the only one which applies; and it seems to embrace a forfeiture only of the vessel & not of the cargo. As the case is pressing, as speedy an opinion as practicable would be acceptable

Respectfully Your most obt. Servt.   ALBERT GALLATIN

RC (DLC); at foot of text: "The President of the United States"; endorsed by TJ as received from the Treasury Department on 28 Nov. and "The Schooner Sally. Slave trade" and so recorded in SJL. Enclosure: George Briscoe to Gallatin, Nottingham, Maryland, 27 Nov. 1801, assuring the Treasury secretary that he had complied with the instructions regarding the schooner *Sally*; the unloaded cargo, including plank and scantling, necessary to make partitions, indicates that the vessel was bound for the "coast of Africa and that Slaves was the object"; Elias De Butts, captain of the seized schooner, appeared that morning with his clearance paper from Charleston, "which has every appearance of regularity"; Briscoe states that he awaits further instructions regarding the *Sally* and encloses a "Return of the Cargo unladen at the port of Nottingham from the Schooner Sally," dated 27 Nov., listing "Stores" of beef and pork, port, wine, candles, "a Small quantity coffee Tea & Sugar," muskets, pistols, and gunpowder, and a "Cargo" of tobacco, rum, flour, bread, crackers, oars, 937 feet of plank, 241 feet of scantling, 54 pairs of handcuffs, chains, bolts, long bars, glass beads, and 37 shaken hogsheads (Gallatin, *Papers*, 5:958; 6:124). Other enclosures not found.

For the LETTER FROM George BRISCOE, see Enclosure No. 1 at Gallatin to TJ, 21 Nov.

DIST. ATTORNEY OF MARYLAND: Zebulon Hollingsworth.

The LAW of 22 Mch. 1794 prohibited the preparation of any vessel, within any port of the United States, "for the purpose of carrying on any trade or traffic in slaves." A vessel fitted out for the slave trade, with "her tackle, furniture, apparel and other appurtenances," was liable to

seizure, prosecution, and condemnation (U.S. Statutes at Large, 1:347-9).

To Albert Gallatin

TH:J. TO MR GALLATIN   Nov. 28. 1801.

Your own opinion & that of the Atty Genl. are sufficient authorities to me to approve of prosecuting in the case of the Schooner Sally. and I will candidly add that my judgment also concurs. the handcuffs & bolts are palpable testimonials of the intention of the voyage, & the concealment of them, & their omission in the statement of the cargo, strengthens the proof. the traffic too is so odious that no indulgences can be claimed.

RC (NHi); endorsed by Gallatin: "Schooner Sally." PrC (DLC).

To John G. Ladd

SIR   Washington Nov. 28. 1810 [i.e. 1801]

Having often occasion to have packages of various contents brought to Alexandria; to be forwarded here, & consequently to have some person at Alexandria to whom my correspondents may consign them, mr Barnes, who acts for me here in all pecuniary matters, has encouraged me to hope you would be so good as to recieve and forward my packages from time to time to his address. I have therefore taken the liberty of naming you to some correspondents, and particularly by a letter of yesterday to Colo. Newton of Norfolk to desire him to send to your address 10. barrels of Hughes's crab cyder he has procured for me. with respect to the articles of liquor generally I would ask the favor of your attention to forward them only by known persons who can be confided in not to adulterate them. all charges incurred will be thankfully replaced by mr Barnes for me on demand. I pray you to accept my best wishes & respects.

TH: JEFFERSON

PrC (MHi); partially misdated; at foot of text: "Mr. John G. Ladd"; endorsed by TJ in ink on verso as a letter of 28 Nov. 1801 and so recorded in SJL.

John G. Ladd (d. 1819), a native of Newport, Rhode Island, was a merchant in Alexandria from at least 1796 until the mid-1810s (Miller, *Alexandria Artisans*, 1:258-9; *Alexandria Gazette & Daily Advertiser*, 23 Feb. 1819).

From George Latimer

Sir,   Philadelphia 28th. November 1801

I have the honor to enclose a Letter this day handed to me for you and also a bill of lading for three cases directed to you per the Ship Pennsylvania, York Master from Hamburg, together with an extract of a Letter to Messrs. Wachsmuth & Soullier of this City respecting the cases

Permit me to request that you will have the goodness to endorse and return to me the bill of lading that I may hand it to Captn York

In mean time the cases shall be brought to this Office with all the care that is possable so as to prevent injury to their contents which are represented to be of a fragile nature

The extract from Messrs. Wachsmuth & Soullier's Letter shews that there is not any charge for freight to be made to you

It will afford me great pleasure to recieve whatever instructions you may be pleased to give respecting these cases

With the highest & most sincere respect, I have the honor to be Sir, Your obedient Servant   Geo Latimer

RC (MHi); at foot of text: "His Excellency Thomas Jefferson President of the United States"; endorsed by TJ as received 2 Dec. and so recorded in SJL. Enclosures: (1) Arnold Oelrichs to TJ, 14 Sep. (2) Extract of Barger Kramer & Rump to Wachsmuth & Soullier, 16 Sep. 1801, from Hamburg, regarding the shipping and freight charges as well as proper handling of three cases containing statuary for the president (Tr in DLC). Bill of lading not found.

George Latimer (1750-1825), a lifelong resident of Philadelphia, was a delegate to the Pennsylvania ratifying convention in 1787, a presidential elector in 1792, and a representative to the Pennsylvania Assembly from 1792 to 1799, serving as its speaker for five years. He lived at 85 South Sixth Street in 1801 and was the city's customs collector from 1798 until his resignation in 1802 (Stafford, *Philadelphia Directory, for 1801*, 67; PMHB, 11 [1887], 219-20; JEP, 1:282, 432; Vol. 33:458n, 670).

For the THREE CASES, see Arnold Oelrichs to TJ, 14 Sep.

From Albert Gallatin

Dear Sir   29th Nover. 1801

I enclosed yesterday papers relative to a vessel suspected of having been fitted out for slave trade.

The presumptive evidence is strong as she had on board, (& several of the same not inserted in her manifest,) handcuffs & bolts, scantling & boards fit to make partitions, 35 shaken hogsheads which would be necessary for water for the number of slaves she might bring back, a quantity of bread & biscuit for same purpose, and tobacco, rum, & beads being a cargo also suited for the purchase— The iron cuffs & bolts, shaken hogsheads, and beads were not in the manifest.

The master Eliah De Butts is here waiting for a decision & will take this letter to your house. If you have concluded on what is proper to be done, I wish to know it in order to be able, at all events, to give him an answer.

He says that the iron cuffs are old & rusty and have been as ballast in the schooner ever since he commanded her; that the proofs of his not being intended for the Coast are, his having no canon, (he had a few small arms) the smallness of the vessel *47 tons* & his nor any of his hands having ever been on the coast. The fact of his having left the vessel & taken the papers, he justifies by saying that his mate was worthless, that he could not trust the papers to him, & went to Baltimore in order to engage another mate. This is so far true that he brought such one from Baltimore to Nottingham and has discharged the old one.

It is important neither to distress on suspicion an innocent man, nor to suffer him to escape if he was guilty. What renders this case difficult is that the voyage not having been performed, the criminality consists in the intention; and that, unless some of the sailors will or can give evidence, can be proven only by circumstances & presumptive evidence. We may think that evidence sufficiently strong to libel the vessel. The jury may decide otherways.

I have the honor to be Very respectfully Dear Sir Your most obedt. Servt. ALBERT GALLATIN

If you have any doubts, I might empower the collector to decide after having examined the sailors A. G.

RC (DLC); postscript written on verso of address sheet; addressed: "The President of the United States"; endorsed by TJ as received from the Treasury Department on 29 Nov. and "Schooner Slave trade" and so recorded in SJL with notation "schooner Sally. slave trade."

GIVE HIM AN ANSWER: perhaps TJ's reply of 28 Nov. did not reach the Treasury secretary until after he dispatched this letter. No other reply has been found, but on 30 Nov., Gallatin wrote George Briscoe that the presumptive evidence that the schooner *Sally* was intended for the slave trade was "such as to make it the duty of the Executive to have a prosecution instituted, leaving it to the ordinary course of law to decide whether the equipment of the vessel was actually for that purpose or not." Gallatin informed the collector that papers and instructions were being forwarded to the district attorney who would institute the proper suits. Gallatin also instructed Briscoe to take steps to have the crew and others on board examined (Gallatin, *Papers*, 6:118).

On 2 Dec., John Steele sent Gallatin a memorandum on the "schooner lately arrested at Nottingham," along with an enclosure, probably a letter to Zebulon Hollingsworth, dated 1 Dec., providing the U.S. district attorney for Maryland with instructions and documents for the prosecution of the *Sally*. Steele reported that the enclosure was prepared the day before and that if approved would be dispatched immediately. Steele asked Gallatin to return, as soon as convenient, the documents with his or the president's approbation and with any desired changes noted. Gallatin submitted Steele's documents to the President. TJ wrote "Approved" on the memorandum and signed with his initials (MS in DLC: TJ Papers, 118:20354; partially dated; in Steele's hand; with submittal to president in Gallatin's hand and signed by him; endorsed by TJ as received from the Treasury Department on 2 Dec. and "Schooner. Sally" and so recorded in SJL). For Steele's letter to Hollingsworth, see Gallatin, *Papers*, 6:124.

JURY MAY DECIDE OTHERWAYS: on 11 Jan. 1802, Briscoe received notice of the trial and acquittal of the *Sally* in the court of admiralty for Maryland district and an order from the marshal to release the vessel and cargo to Captain De Butts. Hollingsworth informed Gallatin that the district court judge had thought proper to refer the case to the admiralty court, where, "without the intervention of a Jury," a decision was found against the United States (Gallatin, *Papers*, 6:443, 553). In February 1807, De Butts and others petitioned Congress for compensation for damages sustained by the seizure and detention of the ship (JHR, 6:203). For Gallatin's response, see ASP, *Commerce and Navigation*, 1:726-7.

James L. Henderson and Elizabeth Henderson Deed to Craven Peyton

this indenture made on the 29th day of Novemr. 1801. between James L. Henderson & Elizabeth his Wife on the one part and Craven Peyton on the other part all of the County of albemarle Witnesseth that the said James L. Henderson and Elizabeth his Wife in consideration of the Sum of Five Hundred Dollars to them in hand actually paid have given granted bargained and sold unto the said Craven all the part or property divided or undivided of the lands of the late Bennett Henderson deceased in the County of albermarle which descended on the said James L. Henderson As one of the children and heirs of the said Bennett meaning to include as well the revertion of those now held in dower as those vested in possession, with all these appertenences but excepting a mill which is now erected and standing on a part of the Above mentioned land which with its perquisites is reserved to the said James L. & excepting also his portion in the house & lott. in the Town of Milton now occupied by Henderson & Connard reserved to the said James L.

To have & to hold the said lands and appertenences to him the said Craven and his heirs and the said James L. Henderson & Elizabeth his Wife their heirs & administrators the said lands and appertenences to him the sd. Craven and his heirs will for ever warrant. & defend in witness where of the sd. James L. Henderson & Elizabeth his Wife have hereto set there hands and seals on the day & year above mentioned.

JAMES L. HENDERSON

ELIZABETH HENDERSON

MS (ViU); in Craven Peyton's hand, except signatures; with hand-drawn fascimile seals beside signatures; at foot of text in Peyton's hand: "signed sealed & delivard in presents of," followed by signatures of George W. Catlett and John L. Cosby with note that they had "before signed" and signature of Joel Shiflett with added notation "June 1803"; statement on verso in hand of and signed by John Nicholas, clerk of court for Albemarle County, that the indenture was produced in court on 4 Aug. 1802 and proved by Catlett's and Cosby's oaths, and in court on 6 June 1803 it was "fully proved" with the addition of Shiflett's oath, then ordered to be recorded; endorsed by Nicholas; endorsed by Peyton: "Deed James L. Henderson & Elizabeth his Wife to Craven Peyton"; endorsed by TJ: "James L. Henderson to Craven Peyton 1801. Nov. 29. 500 D. excepts mill, & house & lot in Milton occupd by Henderson & Cunnard."

The Elizabeth Henderson who signed this deed was James L. Henderson's wife. His mother was Elizabeth Lewis Henderson, and he also had a sister Elizabeth.

This deed follows the form that TJ wrote out for Peyton before the 1 Oct. partition of the estate of Bennett Henderson, but incorporating TJ's later modification of the language to make the indenture cover PROPERTY DIVIDED OR UNDIVIDED (Form of Deeds for Henderson Purchases, [September? 1801]; TJ to Peyton, 8 Oct.).

From Thomas Mann Randolph

DEAR SIR,   Edgehill Nov. 29. 1801

I am completely happy in being able to inform you that all our little family has passed safely through the worst stage of the Whooping cough: we have no apprehensions now about any of them: the cough has so much abated and all the serious symptoms so long disappeared that we boldly congratulate ourselves on our good fortune. The fourth week was the worst with all: with Cornelia and Ellen it was a period of considerable danger, with little Virginia of alarm for two days, but with the 3 eldest only of somewhat more trouble & pain in coughing. We consider that we have now only to fear injury to their lungs from protracted and occasionally exacerbated coughing by fresh colds, and we have full confidence in the efficacy of management against that: the morbid action once ceased or greatly abated there is certainly no room for anxiety. Little Francis now excites our anxious thoughts alone having heard nothing of him since his departure on the 16th. instant.

Being closely confined by the state of my children I have not seen much of Moorans conduct since your departure: attending Judge Stewart & his lady on the 24th. to show them your house and paintings &c. I observed that the work on the S'o. Flank was still so backward as not to promise completion this Autumn: that on the N'o. as you expected has not been thought of: the work appears well done tho' clearly, I think, stinted as to the Mortar. Mooran had then been 3 weeks nearly absent and the journeymen at times without Lime, sand, water & even provisions, I was informed. It would be rendering a service to the neighbourhood to bring some good stone Masons into it from the Northward: building in wood would soon be droped I believe the saving is so evident in the other. Every thing has gone on well at Mont'o.; Lillies ardor not in the smallest degree abating. I think Craven goes on rapidly to prove that his neighbours had not just ideas of industry & management in farming when they predicted him bankrupt on his taking Tufton.

With true affection   TH: M. RANDOLPH

RC (MHi); endorsed by TJ as received 9 Dec. and so recorded in SJL.

In August 1800, TJ leased fields at Monticello and Tufton to John H. CRAVEN (Vol. 32:108-10).

From Nathan Burrowes

DEAR SIR   Lexington Kent 30th Novm 1801

Excuse this intrusion. In addressing this scrol to you, And my presumption in aspiring to a situation which from my obscurity and abilities—I can scarcely hope for—I trust you will excuse this liberty—

I asure you I am actuated by the dictates of an honest heart, deaply impres'd with a sense of your eminent Virtues and Patriotism—

I wrote a letter about a year ago of nearly the same purports as the present Wherein in I anticipated your present elevated Situation with infinate pleasure—(Because in placing you there was the payment of a moiety due to your merit, And a faint acknowledgement of your preemminent Services in the cause of humanity, and National affairs) But declined forwarding it on reflecting, that your numerous, Subordinate offices might (Either of them) Be much better fil'd than by me—A juster reward of merit—and relief to the more indigent— But from adverse fortune, and the averice of man, I am desirous of droping all commurtial intercourse with them (At least untill I become better acquainted with their general disposetions.) And being a subordinate of, And nearer Allied to you—Under a republican Chief, I could serve any where with chearfulness, and pleasure. But the reverse I could not—The terror loss and efforts of my Parents in opposing the base incroachments of a proud Tyrant on our Liberties—With their ravages and slaughter is so ingraved on my mind, That it can never be errac'd, Altho I was but an infant—

I wish my abilities could intitle me to a Situation, in either the Army or Navy or else where, that, I might serve my Country, and gain a comfortable subsistance—And thereby become better acquainted with you whome, I love and respect as a Farther, And view as the Chaste Guardian of the good people of the United States—

I am Dear Sir with great Esteeme Your Most Obdnt Hbl St

NATHAN BURROWES

PS it may perhaps be properly in form to apply to the Secretary of War for Commissions, But from my little knowledge of him, I rest my hopes with you knowing that where fullness is nothing is lacking

N B

RC (DNA: RG 59, LAR); above postscript: "To Thomas Jefferson Esqr President of U States"; endorsed by TJ as received 22 Dec. and so recorded in SJL; also endorsed by TJ: "appmt in Army or Navy."

Merchant and inventor Nathan Burrowes (d. 1846) arrived in Lexington around 1792. After a failed attempt at hemp manufacturing in the 1790s, he later found success as the manufacturer of a popular brand of table mustard (George W. Ranck, *History of Lexington, Kentucky, Its Early Annals and Recent Progress* [Cincinnati, 1872], 184-5; Charles R. Staples, *The History of Pioneer Lexington, 1779-1806* [Lexington, 1939; repr., 1996], 123-4, 138, 143, 158, 161).

From John G. Ladd

SIR   Alexandria Nov. 30th. 1801

I have this morning had the pleasure to receive your favor of the 28th Instant, and to observe your wishes respecting any Articles or Packages of yours which may come to my address at this place—and now to assure you that I shall with great cheerfulness on every occasion particularly attend thereto in the best possible manner agreeable to your desire.—I have the honor to be with perfect Respect

Sir Your Obed. Servant   JNO. G. LADD

RC (MHi); at foot of text: "The President of the United States"; endorsed by TJ as received 1 Dec. and so recorded in SJL.

Proclamation Offering a Reward for Murderers of a Cherokee Woman

By the President of the United States of America

A Proclamation:

Whereas information has been received that an atrocious murder was in the month of August last committed on an Indian Woman of the Cherokee Tribe in the peace and friendship of the United States, in the County of Knox in the State of Tenessee, aggravated also by the consideration that it was committed at a moment when a friendly meeting was about to be held by Commissioners of the United States with the Chiefs of the said Tribe of Indians, for the purpose of making certain arrangements favorable to the tranquility and advantage of the Frontier Settlers, as well as just and eligible to the Indians themselves; And Whereas the apprehension and punishment of the murderers and their accessaries will be an example due to justice and humanity, and every way salutary in its operation; I have therefore thought fit to issue this my proclamation hereby exhorting the citizens of the United States, and requiring all the Officers thereof, according to their respective stations, to use their utmost endeavors to apprehend and bring the principals and accessaries to the said murder to justice: and I do moreover offer a reward of one thousand dollars each principal, and five hundred dollars for each accessary to the same before the fact, who shall be apprehended and brought to justice.

In Testimony whereof, I have caused the seal of the United States of America to be affixed to these Presents and signed the same with my hand,

Done at the City of Washington the thirtieth day of November in the year of our Lord one thousand eight hundred and one, and of the Independence of the United States of America the twenty sixth.

TH: JEFFERSON

MS (DNA: RG 11, Presidential Proclamations); in a clerk's hand, signed by TJ; at foot of text: "By the President," followed by signature of James Madison alongside "Secretary of State" in the clerk's hand; endorsed by Jacob Wagner: "Proclamation offering a reward for the apprehension of the murderers of the Indian Woman in Knox County Tennessee. 30 Novr. 1801."

The WOMAN OF THE CHEROKEE TRIBE, whose name does not appear in the documents, was killed near Knoxville on 12 Aug. The Cherokees had already expressed concern over the government's failure to apprehend murderers, and this killing in August was mentioned by chiefs later that month and in September as a factor in their refusal to negotiate with the government's commissioners. Newspapers reported that the woman's murder was one reason the Cherokee leaders were "highly displeased." The

Cherokees suspected a man named Peter Wheeler of the crime. Benjamin Hawkins and James Wilkinson understood that Wheeler, who was "said to be of bad character," had fled, but on 13 Nov., Return Jonathan Meigs wrote to Henry Dearborn that Wheeler had apparently been apprehended, examined at Knoxville, and released for lack of evidence. The Cherokees "are very apt to charge us with partiality in matters relating breaches of Law where they are concerned," Meigs wrote to a federal judge in January 1802. "They are still complaining of the murder of the Indian Woman, & for want of knowledge of the value of our Laws, are apt to consider our prudent proceedings as a dereliction of Justice." In language drafted by TJ, Dearborn had assured The Glass and other Cherokee chiefs visiting the capital in July 1801 that the government would "certainly punish" those who robbed or killed Cherokees, provided the wrongdoers could be caught (Foster, *Hawkins*, 371, 373, 382, 383; Return J. Meigs, "Journal of [O]ccurences &c—relating to the Cherokee Nation," 1801, Meigs to Dearborn, 13 Nov. 1801, Meigs to John McNairy, 1 Jan. 1802, all in DNA: RG 75, RCIAT; *Philadelphia Gazette*, 6 Oct. 1801; *Washington Federalist*, 12 Oct. 1801; Salem, Mass., *Salem Impartial Register*, 15 Oct. 1801; Vol. 34:505-6, 509, 511; Wilkinson and Hawkins to TJ, 1 Sep. 1801; TJ to Wilkinson, Hawkins, and Andrew Pickens, 16 Sep. 1801).

On 2 Dec., Dearborn sent Meigs a copy of this proclamation with the request that he have it published in Tennessee newspapers. Dearborn also asked Meigs to have "copies of it stuck up at public places, and use your best endeavours to have its contents explained throughout the Cherokee Nation." On 25 Dec., Meigs reported that he was distributing copies of the proclamation. "It has been explained to some of the Chiefs, they say that it is Good," Meigs informed Dearborn. "Will endeavor to have it explaind throughout the nation & the proper impression made, & have reason to believe that it will have a good effect on the Indians." EXHORTING THE CITIZENS OF THE UNITED STATES: several newspapers printed the text of the proclamation, and other publications summarized or took notice of it (Dearborn to Meigs, 2 Dec. 1801, DNA: RG 75, RCIAT, enclosing a copy of the proclamation attested by John Newman; Meigs to Dearborn, 25 Dec., Dft in same; *National Intelligencer*, 7 Dec.; *Federal Gazette & Baltimore Daily Advertiser*, 8 Dec.; *Gazette of the United States*, 8 Dec.; *New-York Evening Post*, 9 Dec.; Boston *Columbian Centinel*, 16 Dec.; Norwich, Conn., *Courier*, 16 Dec.; Hartford, Conn., *American Mercury*, 24 Dec.).

When TJ issued this proclamation, he and Dearborn knew that the commissioners' attempt to negotiate with the Cherokees had failed. TJ and Dearborn were probably not yet aware that the commissioners had successfully concluded talks with the Chickasaws (ASP, *Indian Affairs*, 1:648-53; Hawkins to Dearborn, 6 Sep., 28 Oct., Wilkinson, Hawkins, and Pickens to Dearborn, 6 Sep., Wilkinson to Dearborn, 8, 28 Sep., 13 Oct. 1801, recorded in DNA: RG 107, RLRMS).

Appendix I

Letters Not Printed in Full

In keeping with the editorial method established for this edition, the chronological series includes "in one form or another every available letter known to have been written by or to Thomas Jefferson" (Vol. 1:xv). Beginning with Volume 33, when Jefferson's substantial presidential correspondence necessitated greater selectivity, the Editors summarized or briefly described in annotation a larger proportion of letters than had been their practice in recent volumes. The situation was like that which our predecessors faced as they edited Jefferson's papers from his tenure as governor of Virginia or secretary of state. The present Editors are following their guidelines, but have also chosen to prepare an appendix of the letters falling within the period covered by the volume that are not printed in full. Arranged in chronological order, the list includes for each letter the correspondent, date, and location in the volume where it is noted. Among the letters to Jefferson that are not printed in full are brief letters of transmittal, multiple testimonials recommending a particular candidate for office, repetitive letters from a candidate seeking a post, and official correspondence that the president saw in only a cursory way. While letters written by Jefferson typically are printed in full, in some instances the brevity and routine nature of his reply or the near illegibility of an especially blurred press copy, when it is the only extant text, suggest the advantage of summarizing the letter in annotation.

Using the list in this appendix, the table of contents, and Appendix II (correspondence not found but recorded in Jefferson's Summary Journal of Letters), readers will be able to reconstruct Jefferson's chronological epistolary record from 1 Aug. to 30 Nov. 1801. Letters falling outside of this span, but that are most usefully discussed in annotation here, will be listed in an appendix to their chronologically appropriate volume.

From Gibson & Jefferson, 3 Aug. Noted at TJ to George Jefferson, 29 July.
From Robert Smith, 3 Aug. Noted at TJ to Albert Gallatin, 7 Aug.
From Charles D. Coxe, 7 Aug. Noted at Thomas McKean to TJ, 10 Aug.
From George Helmbold, 7 Aug. Noted at Helmbold to TJ, 30 July.
From "Nics Jeffroy," 7 Aug. Noted at "Nicholas Geffroy" to TJ, 1 Aug.
From Archibald Stuart, 7 Aug. Noted at TJ to Stuart, 5 Aug.
John Newman to Meriwether Lewis, 8 Aug. Noted at TJ to Albert Gallatin, 14 Aug.
From David Meade Randolph, 8 Aug. Noted at Randolph to TJ, 13 Sep.
From Abishai Thomas, 10 Aug. Noted at TJ to Robert Smith, 14 Aug.
From John Kemp, 11 Aug. Noted at Samuel Latham Mitchill to TJ, 23 July.
From Wilson Cary Nicholas, 12 Aug. Noted at TJ to Nicholas, 4 Aug.
From George Gilpin, 17 Aug. Noted at Tobias Lear to TJ, 25 July.
From William Scales, 18 Aug. Noted at Scales to TJ, 5 May.
From Absalom Bainbridge, 20 Aug. Noted at Edward Gantt to TJ, 17 Aug.

APPENDIX I

From Alexander White, 20 Aug. Noted at District of Columbia Commissioners to TJ, 24 Aug.
To George Booker, 21 Aug. Noted at TJ to Samuel Sheild, 21 Aug.
To Edward Gantt, 21 Aug. Noted at TJ to Benjamin Waterhouse, 21 Aug.
From Abishai Thomas, 24 Aug. Noted at Robert Smith to TJ, 17 Aug.
From James Monroe, [25 Aug.]. Noted at Samuel Fulton to TJ, 29 Apr.
From David Austin, 26 Aug. Noted at Austin to TJ, 25 Aug.
From Daniel Ludlow, John Broome, Brockholst Livingston, and John B. Prevost, 26 Aug. Noted at Henry Remsen to TJ, 25 Aug.
From Robert Smith, 27 Aug. Noted at TJ to Smith, 5 Sep.
To George Gilpin, 28 Aug. Noted at Tobias Lear to TJ, 25 July.
From Jean Chas, 29 Aug. Noted at TJ to Chas, 3 Sep.
From Thomas Calvert, 30 Aug. Noted at Richard Richardson to TJ, 20 July.
To William Foushee, 30 Aug. Noted at Foushee to TJ, 13 Sep.
From George Jefferson, 31 Aug. Noted at Jefferson to TJ, 29 Aug.
From Robert Smith, 31 Aug. Noted at TJ to Smith, 5 Sep.
To District of Columbia Commissioners, 3 Sep. Noted at TJ to John Carroll, 3 Sep.
From David Austin, 4 Sep. Noted at Austin to TJ, 31 Aug.
From Isaac Ledyard, 7 Sep. Noted at Ledyard to TJ, 7 Sep.
From Abishai Thomas, 7 Sep. Noted at TJ to Robert Smith, 19 Sep.
From Robert Smith, 8 Sep. Noted at TJ to Smith, 19 Sep.
To St. George Tucker, 11 Sep. Noted at Tucker to TJ, 5 Sep.
From David Austin, 12 Sep. Noted at Austin to TJ, 14 Sep.
From Matthew Clarkson, 12 Sep. Noted at DeWitt Clinton to TJ, 14 Sep.
From the Executive Directory of the Batavian Republic, 12 Sep. Noted at TJ to Executive Directory, 30 May.
From George Jefferson, 14 Sep. Noted at TJ to Jefferson, 12 Sep.
From Richard Parrott, 14 Sep. Noted at Albert Gallatin to TJ, 14 Sep.
From Abishai Thomas, 14 Sep. Noted at TJ to Robert Smith, 19 Sep.
From Edward Livingston, [17 Sep.]. Noted at Albert Gallatin to TJ, 12 Sep.
From Alexander Maclure, 19 Sep. Noted at William Maclure to TJ, 3 July.
From John Mitchell, 19 Sep. Noted at Mitchell to TJ, 9 Mch.
To Gibson & Jefferson, 26 Sep. Noted at TJ to Gibson & Jefferson, 26 Sep.
From James Monroe, 28 Sep. Noted at Monroe to TJ, 28 Sep.
From John H. Barney, 1 Oct. Noted at Joseph Habersham to TJ, 23 Mch.
To Fulwar Skipwith, 3 Oct. Noted at TJ to Robert R. Livingston, 3 Oct. (first letter).
From Anthony Butler, 5 Oct. Noted at Butler to TJ, 29 July.
From John Mitchell, 8 Oct. Noted at Mitchell to TJ, 9 Mch.
From Nathaniel Macon, 9 Oct. Noted at Macon to TJ, 25 Sep.
From Robert Smith, 9 Oct. Noted at TJ to Smith, 9 Oct.
From Robert Williams, 9 Oct. Noted at Albert Gallatin to TJ, 19 Oct.
From John Thomson Mason, 10 Oct. Noted at Mason to TJ, 5 Oct.
To Albert Gallatin, 15 Oct. Noted at Benjamin Rittenhouse to TJ, 8 Oct.
From Gideon Granger, 18 Oct. Noted at TJ to Granger, 7 Oct.
From Robert Smith, 26 Oct. Noted at Smith to TJ, 26 Oct. (second letter).

To Robert Patton, 31 Oct. Noted at TJ to Thomas Tudor Tucker, 31 Oct.

From Robert Patton, 4 Nov. Noted at Thomas Tudor Tucker to TJ, 5 Nov.

From Abishai Thomas, 4 Nov. Noted at Robert Smith to TJ, 26 Oct. (first letter).

From Matthew Clarkson, 5 Nov. Noted at DeWitt Clinton to TJ, 14 Sep.

From Amos Marsh, 5 Nov. Noted at Vermont House of Representatives to TJ, 5 Nov.

To Samuel Meredith, 9 Nov. Noted at Thomas Tudor Tucker to TJ, 5 Nov.

From Nicolas Gouin Dufief, 13 Nov. Noted at TJ to Dufief, 1 Nov.

From David Hopkins, 14 Nov. Noted at Hopkins to TJ, 31 Aug. (enclosed in Peter Freneau to TJ, 11 Sep.).

From Navy Department, 17 Nov. Noted at Notes on Consultation with Robert Smith, 15 Nov.

From Aaron Burr, 18 Nov. Noted at TJ to Burr, 18 Nov.

From J. P. G. Muhlenberg, 19 Nov. Noted at Isaac Cox Barnet to TJ, 10 Sep.

From Julian Ursin Niemcewicz, 30 Nov. Noted at Lewis Littlepage to TJ, [21 Nov.].

From John Richards and others, undated. Noted at Benjamin Rittenhouse to TJ, 8 Oct.

Appendix II

Letters Not Found

EDITORIAL NOTE

This appendix lists chronologically letters written by and to Jefferson during the period covered by this volume for which no text is known to survive. Jefferson's Summary Journal of Letters provides a record of the missing documents. For incoming letters, Jefferson typically recorded in SJL the date that the letter was sent and the date on which he received it. He sometimes included the location from which it was dispatched and an abbreviated notation indicating the government department to which it pertained: "N" for Navy, "P" for the Postmaster General's Office, "S" for State, "T" for Treasury, and "W" for War. "Off." designated a person seeking office.

From Christopher Ellery, 1 Aug.; received 20 Aug. from Newport.

From Anthony W. White, 1 Aug.; received 13 Aug. from New Brunswick; notation: "T."

From William Cooch, 3 Aug.; received 13 Aug. from Christiana Bridge; notation: "Off."

From David Austin, 4 Aug.; received 13 Aug. from Washington; notation: "Off."

From Christopher Ellery, 4 Aug.; received 20 Aug. from Newport.

From Samuel Quarrier, 4 Aug.; received 13 Aug. from Washington; notation: "Off. W."

From Amos and Ethan Stillman, 4 Aug.; received 20 Aug. from Farmington; notation: "W."

From Samuel Thurber, Jr., 5 Aug.; received 20 Aug. from Providence; notation: "Off."

From Bowling Clark, 6 Aug.; received 27 Aug.

From Joshua Key, 6 Aug.; received 6 Aug.

To Joshua Key, 7 Aug.

To Joseph Moran, 7 Aug.

From Gilbert Giberson, 10 Aug.; received 5 Dec. from "on board the Cumberland Capt Baynton Port royal bay"; notation: "S." TJ drew a brace connecting this letter's entry with entries for letters received the same day from James Driskell of 14 Aug., William Hawker of 17 Aug., Benjamin Tucker of 17 Aug., and Peleg Whiten of 17 Aug.

To Anne S. Marks, 10 Aug.

From William Wood, 10 Aug.; received 25 Aug.

From Bishop John Carroll and others; received 13 Aug.

To Henry Duke, 13 Aug.; notation: "£47.15 plus int. Sep. 3."

From Anonymous, 14 Aug.; received 10 Sep. from Boston.

From Pierce Butler, 14 Aug.; received 20 Aug. from Philadelphia.

From James Driskell, 14 Aug.; received 5 Dec. from "on board the Cumberland Capt Baynton Port royal bay"; notation: "S." TJ drew a brace connecting this letter's entry with entries for letters received the same day from Gilbert Giberson of 10 Aug., William Hawker of 17 Aug., Benjamin Tucker of 17 Aug., and Peleg Whiten of 17 Aug.

To David Meade Randolph, 14 Aug.

To Bowling Clark, 17 Aug.

From William Hawker, 17 Aug.; received 5 Dec. from "on board the Cumberland Capt Baynton Port royal bay"; notation: "S." TJ drew a brace connecting this letter's entry with entries for letters received the same day from James Driskell of 14 Aug., Gilbert Giberson of 10 Aug., Benjamin Tucker of 17 Aug., and Peleg Whiten of 17 Aug.

From Philip Landais, 17 Aug.; received 3 Sep. from Albany; notation: "W."

From Charles L. Lewis, 17 Aug.; received 18 Aug.

From Benjamin Tucker, 17 Aug.; received 5 Dec. from "on board the Cumberland Capt Baynton Port royal bay"; notation: "S." TJ drew a brace connecting this letter's entry with entries for letters received the same day from James Driskell of 14 Aug., Gilbert Giberson of 10 Aug., William Hawker of 17 Aug., and Peleg Whiten of 17 Aug.

From Peleg Whiten, 17 Aug.; received 5 Dec. from "on board the Cumberland Capt Baynton Port royal bay"; notation: "S." TJ drew a brace connecting this letter's entry with entries for letters received the same day from James Driskell of 14 Aug., Gilbert Giberson of 10 Aug., William Hawker of 17 Aug., and Benjamin Tucker of 17 Aug.

To Thomas Claxton, 18 Aug.

To Nicolas Gouin Dufief, 18 Aug.

To John Barnes, 21 Aug.

From Bowling Clark, 22 Aug.; received 25 Aug.

From William Killen, Jr., 23 Aug.; received 3 Sep. from Dover.

From John Caton, 24 Aug.; received 3 Sep. from Dover.

From John Rowe, 24 Aug.; received 3 Sep. from Boston; notation: "W."

From John Frederic Wrede, 24 Aug.; received 28 Oct. from Oldenburg; notation: "S."

From Martin Dawson for Brown, Rives & Co., 26 Aug.; received 25 Aug. from Milton.

To John Barnes, 28 Aug.

To Roberts & Jones, 28 Aug.

To Henry Sheaff, 28 Aug.

From George Booker, 29 Aug.; received 3 Sep. from "Backriver."

To Edmund Randolph, 30 Aug.; notation: "ads. Gilliam et ux."

To Bowling Clark, 31 Aug.

From John Henry Purviance, 31 Aug.; received 3 Sep. from Washington.

From George Walton, 2 Sep.; received 17 Sep. from Augusta; notation: "Off."

From Samuel L. Mitchill, 3 Sep.; received 18 Sep. from New York. TJ drew a brace connecting this letter's entry with entries of eight other letters received the same day and wrote outside the brace: "Davis to be Naval officer."

From William Few, 5 Sep.; received 18 Sep. from New York. TJ drew a brace connecting this letter's entry with entries of eight other letters received the same day and wrote outside the brace: "Davis to be Naval officer."

From Edmund Randolph, 7 Sep.; received 10 Sep.

From William Thornton, 8 Sep.; received 17 Sep. from Washington; notation: "Off."

From Claudine Cenas, 9 Sep.; received 13 Feb. 1802 from Lyons.

From James M. Lingan, 11 Sep.; received 17 Sep. from Georgetown.

From Henry Sheaff, 11 Sep.; received 17 Sep. from Philadelphia.

From Frederic Liebnau, 12 Sep.; received 24 Sep. from New York.

From Roberts & Jones, 12 Sep.; received 24 Sep. from Philadelphia; notation: "sash-weights."

From James Traquair, 15 Sep.; received 24 Sep. from Philadelphia.

From Bowling Clark, 17 Sep.; received 24 Sep.

From Elbridge Gerry, 18 Sep.; received 3 Oct. from Cambridge; notation: "Wm. Lee to be collectr Salem." TJ drew a brace connecting this letter's entry with that of a letter from William Heath of 18 Sep. received the same day.

To Francis Eppes, 19 Sep.

To Christopher Smith, 21 Sep.

From Rodolphe Tillier, 22 Sep.; received 1 Oct. from New York; notation: "S."

From David Ross, 24 Sep.; received 26 Sep. from Richmond.

From John Coalter, 25 Sep.; received 6 Oct. from Staunton.

From James Neail, 25 Sep.; received 1 Oct. from Philadelphia; notation: "to be midshipmn.   N."

To Bowling Clark, 26 Sep.

To John H. Craven, 26 Sep.

From John Langdon, 28 Sep.; received 12 Oct. from Portsmouth.

From Amos and Ethan Stillman, 29 Sep.; received 6 Oct. from Farmington.

From General William Hull; received 1 Oct. from Newton, Massachusetts; notation: "Cunha to be Consul Madeira."

From Sylvanus Bourne, 2 Oct.; received 4 Jan. 1802 from Amsterdam; notation: "S."

From War Department, 3 Oct.; received 5 Oct.; notation: "Warrants."

From Henry Clay, 4 Oct.; received 4 Jan. 1802 from "Portroyal Jama. Brit. ship Cumbld."; notation: "S."

To John Wayles Eppes, 5 Oct.

From George Jefferson, 5 Oct.; received 8 Oct.

To Gabriel Lilly, 5 Oct.

From William Davis, 6 Oct.; received 6 Nov. from Boston.

From John Lamb, 6 Oct.; received 12 Oct. from New London; notation: "T."

From Navy Department, 6 Oct.; received 6 Oct.; notation: "warrts."

From Pierce Butler, 8 Oct.; received 10 Oct. from Philadelphia.

To David Higginbotham, 8 Oct.; notation: "500."

To John Watson, 8 Oct.; notation: "143.73."

From Gabriel Lilly, 9 Oct.; received 13 Oct. from Monticello.

From Pierpont Edwards and Gideon Granger, 10 Oct.; received 16 Oct. from "New H."; notation: "Andrews to be Consul in Barbary or Med."

From Pierpont Edwards and Gideon Granger, 10 Oct.; received 16 Oct. from "New H."; notation: "Lyman to be P.M:G."

From William Wingate, 12 Oct.; received 21 Oct. from Haverhill.

From George Clinton, 13 Oct.; received 22 Oct. from New York.

From Cornelius Coningham, 13 Oct.; received 13 Oct. from Washington; notation: "N."

From Navy Department, 13 Oct.; received 13 Oct.; notation: "warrants."

From War Department, 13 Oct.; received 13 Oct.; notation: "warrants."

From Edmund Randolph, 14 Oct.; received 17 Oct. from Richmond.

From Benjamin Tucker, 14 Oct.; received 4 Jan. 1802 from "Portroyal Jamaica. Brit. ship Cumbld."; notation: "S."

To Francis Eppes, 16 Oct.

From David Higginbotham, 17 Oct.; received 20 Oct. from Milton.

To Gabriel Lilly, 19 Oct.

From Thomas Paul, 19 Oct.; received 20 Oct. from Baltimore.

From Samuel Quarrier, 19 Oct.; received 22 Oct. from Baltimore; notation: "W."

To Edmund Randolph, 19 Oct.

From Navy Department, 19 Oct.; received 19 Oct.; notation: "Warrants."

From Henry Clay; received 20 Oct. from "Brit. ship Cumberld. Portroyal Jamaica."

From War Department, 20 Oct.; received 20 Oct.; notation: "Warrants."

From Robert Fulton, 22 Oct.; received 11 Feb. 1802 from Paris.

From John Mercer, 23 Oct.; received 28 Oct. from Fredericksburg; notation: "Chas. Benson to be Midshipmn.   N." TJ drew a brace connecting this letter's entry with entries for letters from John Minor of 25 Oct. and Mann Page of 24 Oct. received the same day.

From Augustus B. Woodward, 23 Oct.; received 23 Oct. from Washington; notation: "N."

From Mann Page, 24 Oct.; received 28 Oct. from Mannsfield; notation: "Chas. Benson to be Midshipmn.   N." TJ drew a brace connecting this letter's entry with entries for letters from John Mercer of 23 Oct. and John Minor of 25 Oct. received the same day.

To Bowling Clark, 25 Oct.

To Burgess Griffin, 25 Oct.

From John Minor, 25 Oct.; received 28 Oct. from Fredericksburg; notation: "Chas. Benson to be Midshipmn.   N." TJ drew a brace connecting this letter's entry with entries for letters from John Mercer of 23 Oct. and Mann Page of 24 Oct. received the same day.

From Joseph Pulis, 25 Oct.; received 29 Apr. 1802 from Malta.

From Anonymous; received 26 Oct.

From Enoch Edwards, 26 Oct.; received 29 Oct. from Frankford.

From H. Frederic Liebenau, 26 Oct.; received 29 Oct. from New York; notation: "W."

From Navy Department, 26 Oct.; received 26 Oct.; notation: "Warrants."

From War Department, 26 Oct.; received 26 Oct.; notation: "Warrants."

From Martha Jefferson Randolph, Oct.; received 27 Oct. from Monticello.

From William Stewart (Stuart), 27 Oct.; received 2 Nov. from Philadelphia.

From Treasury Department, 27 Oct.; received 27 Oct.; notation: "Collectors N.Y. & Wilmington."

From Henry Clay; received 28 Oct. from "the Cumberld. Port royal Jamaica"; notation: "S."

From Oliveras y Foris, 28 Oct.; received 7 Dec. from Havana; notation: "S."

From Roberts & Jones, 28 Oct.; received 23 Dec.

From Hy. Cheriot, 31 Oct.; received 29 Nov. from New York; notation: "S."

From Thomas Mann Randolph, 31 Oct.; received 3 Nov. 1801 from Edgehill.

From Francis Eppes, 1 Nov.; received 6 Nov. from Eppington.

From Hudson M. Garland, 1 Nov.; received 11 Nov. from New Glasgow.
To Henry Sheaff, 1 Nov.
From War Department, 2 Nov.; received 3 Nov.; notation: "Warrants."
From Burgess Griffin, 4 Nov.; received 15 Nov.
From War Department; received 4 Nov.; notation: "court martl. on Capt. Lyman."
From Elizabeth House Trist, 5 Nov.; received 14 Nov. from Birdwood; notation: "Easton."
From James Dinsmore, 7 Nov.; received 18 Nov. from Monticello.
From Navy Department, 7 Nov.; received 9 Nov.; notation: "Warrants."
To James Dinsmore, 9 Nov.
From Aaron Burr, 10 Nov.; received 13 Nov. from New York.
From Gabriel Lilly; received 10 Nov. from Monticello.
From Thomas Mann Randolph; received 10 Nov. from Edgehill.
From William H. Graham, 11 Nov.; received 27 Nov.
From William Jones, 13 Nov.; received 18 Nov. from Philadelphia.
From William Newsum, 13 Nov.; received 13 Nov.
From George Bruce, 14 Nov.; received Nov. 18.
From Navy Department, 14 Nov.; received 16 Nov.; notation: "Warrants."
From John Drayton, 16 Nov.; received 27 Nov. from Columbia; notation: "Darrel's death   T."
To Gabriel Lilly, 16 Nov.
From War Department, 16 Nov.; received 17 Nov.; notation: "warrants."
From Charles Benson, 19 Nov.; received 22 Nov. from Fredericksburg.
From John Frederic Wrede, 20 Nov.; received 3 Jun. 1802 from Oldenburg.
From James Dinsmore, 21 Nov.; received 25 Nov. from Monticello.
From John Wayles Eppes, 21 Nov.; received 28 Nov. from Eppington.
From Reuben Perry, 21 Nov.; received 25 Nov.
From Peter Derieux, 23 Nov.; received 9 Dec. from Sweet Springs.
From Navy Department, 23 Nov.; received 23 Nov.; notation: "Warrts."
From War Department, 23 Nov.; received 23 Nov.; notation: "Warrts."
From Henry Sheaff, 24 Nov.; received 28 Nov. from Philadelphia; notation: "30 doz. Sauterne."
To Francis Eppes, 25 Nov.
To Edmund Randolph, 25 Nov.
To Francis Eppes, 27 Nov.
To George Bruce, 28 Nov.
To James Dinsmore, 28 Nov.
From David Higginbotham, 28 Nov.; received 2 Dec.
From John Brown, 30 Nov.; received 9 Dec. from Providence; notation: "in favr. Howell."

Appendix III

Financial Documents

E D I T O R I A L   N O T E

This appendix briefly describes, in chronological order, the documents pertaining to Jefferson's finances during the period covered by this volume that are not printed in full or accounted for elsewhere in this volume. These include orders for payment, invoices, and receipts. Because Jefferson was responsible for the costs of running the President's House, his financial documents include receipts of payment submitted by the stewards Joseph Rapin and Étienne Lemaire (Lucia Stanton, "'A Well-Ordered Household': Domestic Servants in Jefferson's White House," *White House History*, 17 [2006], 10). The *Memorandum Books* are cited when relevant to a specific document and provide additional information.

Certificate by TJ acknowledging purchase of 50 barrels of corn, at £0.11.0 per barrel, from Major John Key on 31 Oct. 1796, for which TJ made payment in full, according to Key's wishes, with an order on Charles Johnston of Richmond for $91.67 in favor of Tarlton Woodson on 13 Nov. 1796, the amount debited to TJ's account with Johnston on 16 [Nov.], which TJ allowed him on settlement this day, 8 Sep. 1801 (MS in Albemarle County Circuit Court, Charlottesville; damaged; in TJ's hand and signed by him). See MB, 2:948.

Invoice submitted by Middleton Bett to Étienne Lemaire, with seven entries for milk from 11 to 17 Sep., at £0.0.5½ per quart, totaling £0.10.10½ (MS in CSmH; in Bett's hand and signed by him acknowledging payment).

Statement of account with Gibson & Jefferson from 31 Aug. to 26 Sep., showing credit in TJ's favor of £599.8.10 plus £200 "to error in Statement of acct. as pr. your letter," on 31 Aug., followed by a list of debits, specifically, a remittance of £300 or $1000 to John Barnes on 12 Sep., an order for payment of £114.15.0 or $382.52 to Joel Yancey on 20 Sep., an order for payment of £158.4.1 or $527.38 to Alexander Garrett on 26 Sep., an order for payment of £144.19.2 to Bowling Clark on 26 Sep., an order for payment of £15 or $50 to John Snead on 26 Sep., and an order for payment of £4.10.0 or $15 to Anthony Robinson on 26 Sep. (MS in MHi; entirely in TJ's hand). See MB, 2:1050-2.

List of seven sums for travel expenses from Monticello to Washington from 27 to 30 Sep., corresponding to TJ's entries in his financial memoranda, with a total sum of $28.655; followed by a list of four sums, with TJ's total of $60.075, being the amount recorded in his financial memoranda as cash on hand on 30 Sep. (MS in MHi; in TJ's hand; at head of figures: "tavern bills. Sep. 27-30 Monto. to Washn."; written on verso of invoice for oats, four dinners, wine, and spirits, totaling £0.16.6, dated 30 Sep., in an unidentified hand, at the head of which TJ wrote "Wren's"). See MB, 2:1053.

Order on John Barnes for payment of $21.425 to Joseph Dougherty, 5 Oct. (MS owned by Charles Retz, Inc., New York City, 1946; in TJ's hand

and signed by him; signed by Dougherty acknowledging payment; endorsed by Barnes). See MB, 2:1054.

Order on John Barnes for payment of $376.17 to Étienne Lemaire, 5 Sep. [i.e. Oct.] (MS in ViU: Edgehill-Randolph Papers; in TJ's hand and signed by him; signed by Lemaire acknowledging payment on 9 Oct.; endorsed by Barnes). See MB, 2:1054.

Order on John Barnes for payment of $27 to Edward Maher "in lieu of a suit of clothes," 6 Oct. (MS in MHi; in TJ's hand and signed by him; signed by Maher acknowledging payment on 8 Oct.; endorsed by TJ and Barnes). See MB, 2:1054.

Order on John Barnes for payment of $17 to Joseph Dougherty, Washington, 11 Oct. (MS in ViU: Edgehill-Randolph Papers; in TJ's hand and signed by him; signed by Dougherty acknowledging payment; endorsed by Barnes). See MB, 2:1055.

Order on John Barnes for payment of $51.66 to Étienne Lemaire, Washington, 11 Oct. (MS in CSmH; in TJ's hand and signed by him; signed by Joseph Dougherty acknowledging payment; endorsed by Barnes). See MB, 2:1055.

Receipt of payment submitted by A. Joucherez to Thomas Claxton for purchase of nine pans, totaling £0.7.6, 13 Oct. (MS in CSmH; in Joucherez's hand and signed by him acknowledging payment).

Receipt of payment submitted by William Morgan to TJ for purchase of seven bushels of oats, at $0.62½ per bushel, totaling $4.375, Georgetown, 25 Oct. [1801?] (MS in CSmH; in Mordi. Morgan's hand and signed by him acknowledging payment).

Order on John Barnes for payment of $46.87 to Joseph Dougherty, Washington, 2 Nov. (MS in MHi; in TJ's hand and signed by him; signed by Dougherty acknowledging payment; endorsed by TJ; endorsed by Barnes: "Presidents Househd"). See MB, 2:1057.

Order on John Barnes for payment of $240.94 to Étienne Lemaire, Washington, 2 Nov. (MS in MHi; in TJ's hand and signed by him; signed by Lemaire acknowledging payment; endorsed by Barnes). See MB, 2:1056-7.

Order on John Barnes for payment of $60 to Dr. William Baker for hay, Washington, 4 Nov. (MS in MHi; in TJ's hand and signed by him; signed by Joseph Dougherty acknowledging payment; endorsed by Barnes, who altered "Oct." to "Novr" in the dateline). See MB, 2:1057.

Order on John Barnes for payment of $24 to Étienne Lemaire, Washington, 7 Nov. (MS in ViU: Edgehill-Randolph Papers; in TJ's hand and signed by him; signed by Lemaire acknowledging payment; endorsed by Barnes). See MB, 2:1057.

Order on John Barnes for payment of $31.23 to Joseph Dougherty, Washington, 9 Nov. (MS in MHi; in TJ's hand and signed by him; signed by Dougherty acknowledging payment; endorsed in an unidentified hand: "Stable Use"; endorsed by Barnes). See MB, 2:1058.

Order on John Barnes for payment of $202.64 to Étienne Lemaire, Washington, 9 Nov. (MS in ViU: Edgehill-Randolph Papers; in TJ's hand and signed by him; signed by Lemaire acknowledging payment on 12 Nov.; endorsed by Barnes). See MB, 2:1057.

Invoice submitted by Joseph Dyson to Étienne Lemaire for 30 bushels of potatoes, at £0.4.3 per bushel, and drayage at £0.1.6, totaling £6.9.0, or $21.50, Alexandria, 9 Nov. (MS in CSmH; in Dyson's hand and signed by him).

Invoice submitted by Peter Billy to Étienne Lemaire for one "amarant flower" at $3, one barrel of parsley at $3, three bushels of carrots for $3, a barrel at $0.33, and drayage at $0.25, totaling $9.58, Alexandria, 14 Nov. (MS in CSmH; in Billy's hand and signed by him acknowledging payment).

Order on John Barnes for payment of $187.12 to Étienne Lemaire, Washington, 16 Nov. (MS in ViU: Edgehill-Randolph Papers; in TJ's hand and signed by him; signed by Lemaire acknowledging payment on 18 Nov.; endorsed by Barnes). See MB, 2:1059.

Order on John Barnes for payment of $65.17 to Étienne Lemaire, Washington, 23 Nov. (MS in MHi; in TJ's hand and signed by him; acknowledgement of payment on 25 Nov. marked by a crosshatch, alongside which Barnes wrote "Julian"; endorsed by Barnes). See MB, 2:1059.

Order on John Barnes for payment of $56 to Dr. William Baker, 25 Nov. (MS owned by Barb and John Pengelly, Fort Washington, Pennsylvania, 1994; in TJ's hand and signed by him; signed by Baker acknowledging payment on 26 Nov.; endorsed by Barnes). See MB, 2:1059.

Invoice submitted by William Thomson to TJ, for tinning "peases" and for making and tinning four "panes," a "Wotrenpot," and a "Coffy boyler," with entries dated 15 Oct. and 20 Nov., totaling $17, Washington, 25 Nov. (MS in CSmH; in Samuel [Mackel]'s hand and signed by him acknowledging payment).

Invoice submitted by Middleton Bett to Étienne Lemaire, with seven entries, probably for milk, from 22 to 28 Nov., at £0.8.0 per quart, totaling £0.11.8 (MS in CSmH; in Bett's hand and signed by him acknowledging payment; endorsed by TJ on verso: "LeMaire Nov. 22-28. 1801 vouchers").

Invoice submitted by James D. Barry to TJ for 12 cords of firewood, at $4.50 per cord, totaling $54, Washington, 28 Nov. (MS in CSmH; in Edmund Scannell's hand and signed by him acknowledging payment; endorsed by Scannell on verso).

Order on John Barnes for payment of $29.46 to Joseph Dougherty, 30 Nov. (MS in MHi; in TJ's hand and signed by him; signed by Dougherty acknowledging payment; endorsed by Barnes). See MB, 2:1059.

INDEX

Abigail & Rebecca (sloop), 11, 95
Abram (b. 1794, TJ's slave), 35
accountants, 215n, 628-9, 636, 703
Adams, Abigail, 3, 237n

ADAMS, JOHN

Minister to Great Britain
negotiates treaties, 245n

Politics
and election of 1800, 256; meets with
L. Lincoln, 299

President
criticism of, xlv, 21, 33n, 456; and fortifications at Newport, 3; and Fergusson, 51; makes appointments,
54, 57n, 58, 320n, 460n, 469n, 493,
494n, 601n; administration praised,
86n; late-term appointments, 252n,
301n, 371n; removals by, 263n,
277n, 654; absences of, from capital, 315, 577; and surveyors for
D.C., 349n; and term limits for foreign missions, 381; leaves horses
and carriages for TJ, 391; and President's House accounts, 391; and
Spain, 393n; method of communicating with heads of departments,
577; annual address to Congress,
612; applications to, for appointments, 676n; removal from office
an act of God, 737

Adams, Samuel: letter from, 687; por-
trait of, 115; congratulates TJ on re-
turn of peace, 687
Adams, Fort, 308n, 549, 550, 560n
Adams, Fort (R.I.), 3
Adams (U.S. frigate), 663, 668
Addington, Henry, 715n
Adet, Pierre Auguste, 189n
Adriatic Sea, 398n
Aeolus, 294
Africa: removal of condemned slaves
to, x, 720, 721n; smallpox in, 199;
Africans compared to American Indi-
ans, 556; and slave trade, 561n, 739n
Aggy. *See* Gillette, Agnes (b. 1798,
Aggy, TJ's slave)
agriculture: U.S. an agricultural nation,
240, 652; measurement of bushels,
280-1, 659, 660n, 679; "artificial"
meadows, 326; viticulture, 326n;

books on, 605; one of four pillars of
prosperity, 647; comparison of European to American, 706-7; erosion, 707
Aikin, Charles Rochemont: *Concise
View,* 490, 491n, 573, 698
Alabama Indians, 555, 561n
Albemarle Co., Va.: descriptions of, 22n,
461-3; land taxes, 350n; surveyor,
455n; midwives in, 511n; clerk of
court, 744n
alcoholism: among Monticello artisans,
50; among candidates for office, 184,
347n, 350; among Irish immigrants,
350; as cause of suicide, 570; among
mariners, 653n
Alembert, Jean Le Rond d': *Synonymes
Français,* 203
Alès, France, 345n
Alexandria, Bank of, 682
Alexandria, Egypt, 239n, 296, 297n,
341
Alexandria, Va.: collector at, 43, 46n,
682, 683n; surveyor at, 43; merchants, 82n, 734, 740; packet service
to, from, 453, 454n, 689-90; stage
lines to, from, 486n; breweries, 592;
banks, 682
*Alexandria Advertiser and Commercial
Intelligencer,* 46n
Alfred (Continental ship), 674-5
Algeciras, Spain: naval battle near, 192,
194n, 239, 407n; American vessels
taken to, 406, 407n, 425, 488, 507,
545, 593-5, 660-1
Alger, James, 229n, 570, 580
Algiers: consuls at, 109n, 163; tribute
for, 148, 163, 456, 474, 643, 690,
705n, 706n; U.S. warships depart for,
219n; support for military action
against, 474; attacks U.S. shipping,
701. *See also* Mediterranean Sea;
Mustafa Baba, Dey of Algiers
Alicante, Spain, 498
Alien Enemies Act (1798), 621n
Alien Friends Act (1798), 26n, 621n
aliens. *See* immigrants
Allan (Allen), John, 653n
Allen, Captain. *See* Takinowtha (Captain
Allen, Delaware chief)
Allen, John, 598
Allison, Patrick (Baltimore), 406, 407n
Almon, John: *Remembrancer,* 482-4
almonds, 12, 95, 96n

Alston, Theodosia Burr, 539
Altona, 17
alum water, 16
amaranth, 759
American Academy of Arts and Sciences, 299, 516
American and Daily Advertiser (Baltimore), 355, 356n
American Citizen and General Advertiser (New York), 409n, 439, 589n, 607. *See also* Denniston & Cheetham
American Philosophical Society: elects members, xlv, 165n, 490, 491n, 670n; receives communications, specimens, 122, 124n, 412n, 423, 424n, 491n; publishes *Transactions,* 124n; secretary, 165n; vice president, 213n; loans money to C. W. Peale, 434-5; displays mastodon skeleton, 436n; library, 699
American Revolution: Eastern Navy Board, 6n; relief efforts for troops, 23n; women in, 23n; veterans of, 26n, 36, 37n, 68-9, 83n, 144, 172n, 249, 257, 262, 279n, 302n, 315-16, 332, 335, 339n, 352n, 429n, 447n, 456-7, 460n, 473-4, 476n, 477n, 485, 502-3, 591n, 592n, 608, 691n; Loyalists, 62, 253n, 274n, 332, 481n, 601, 655, 679; and France, 68-9; persistent principles and spirit of, 127, 203, 338; privateers, 160n, 249; chaplains, 183n; histories of, 203; in S.C., 257; and West Indies, 257n, 332; and Louisiana, 328n; in Va., 328n, 502-3; in N.Y., 337n; quartermasters, 447n; hospitals, 531n; physicians, 592n; in Vt., 601; naval affairs, 654, 674-6; Sons of Liberty, 654n
"Americanus" (pseudonym): argues against unwarranted removals, 229-30n
Americanus (schooner), 547
Ames, Fisher, 299-300
Amsterdam: bills of exchange on, 228, 229n, 597; C. Pinckney at, 239, 295; banks, 371n; consul at, 401-2; prospects for revival of trade, 540. *See also* Batavian Republic; Netherlands
Anacostia River: road to, 167-8, 172; wharves on, 349n; navy yard at, 641n, 646
Anderson, Charles, 429n
Anderson, David, 343n, 380n
Anderson, James, 298-9
Anderson, Joseph, 404n
Andrews, George, 30-1, 95, 127, 418

Andrews, Hannah Shelton, 71
Andrews, Joseph (La.), 557
Andrews, Philo: letter from, 71; seeks consular appointment, 71; identified, 71n; recommended for office, 754
Andrews, Samuel, 71
Anmours, Charles François, Chevalier d', 558-9, 562n
Annapolis Convention (1786), 206, 208n
Annual Message to Congress (1801): drafting of, x-xi, 611-52; fair copy, 641-50
Annual Register, and Virginian Repository, for the Year 1800 (George Douglas), 8-9
Anomabo, Africa, 561n
anonymous letters: and proposals for government reform, 246-7; recommend aspirants for office, 364; recorded in SJL, 752, 755
António, Prince of Beira, 441-2
Antwerp, 252n, 540
Apollo Belvedere (sculpture), 538, 539n
Appleton, Thomas, 664n, 666, 667, 694
Aranjuez, Treaty of, 695n
architects, 92n
Argument Against Continuing the War (James Workman), 670-1n
Argus (revenue cutter), 675n
Arkansas Territory, 175n
Armstrong, Gen. John: advises on appointments, 62, 63n; letter from cited, 63n; political influence in N.Y., 287
Armstrong, John (Nassau), 547, 548n
Army, U.S. *See* War, U.S. Department of
Arnold, Benedict, 674
art: lack of patronage for, 388n; France collects, from Europe, 538, 539n
Artois, Charles Philippe, Comte d', 714, 715n
Ash, James, 582, 584n
Ashe, John Baptista, 390
Ashley, Warren, 406, 487
Aspinwall, William, 681n
Ast, William Frederick, 103-4
astronomy, 411-12, 423, 424n, 548-9
attorneys: mentioned, 5n, 42n, 71, 136n, 155, 165n, 207n, 288n, 337, 355n, 516, 517n, 547-8, 559n, 661n; overabundance of, 155; deemed an unproductive profession, 246; seek admission to the bar, 335-6; conveyancers, 336n, 367
auctions, 602, 604n

INDEX

Augean stable, 5
Auldjo, Thomas: letter from, 280-1;
sends news from England, 280-1
Aurora (brigantine), 546-7, 548n
Aurora (Philadelphia): delivery of, in
Va., 41; prints T. Coxe's writings,
263; subscriptions to, 310; publishes
accounts from Egypt, 415n; reports
misuse of public funds, 438-41, 700,
704-5n; as source of news and information, 455. *See also* Duane, William
Austin, David: letters from, 138-41, 176-
8, 281-2, 736-7; observations on Barbary affairs, 138, 140n; offers plans,
advice, 138-41, 176-8; removes to
Washington, 140; letters from cited,
140-1n, 178n, 282n, 750, 752; sends
draft of message to Congress, 140-1n;
seeks appointment, 178n, 281-2, 736-7
Austria, 192, 396
Auvergne, France, 326, 461-5
Avery, John, 687n

Bache, Benjamin Franklin, 23
Bache, Richard, 100, 102n
Bache, Sarah Franklin: letter from, 23;
recommends Joseph Clay, 23; identi-
fied, 23n
Bache, William: arrives in Washington,
96; carries letters to TJ, 107, 132, 153,
162; seeks appointment, 330, 374
Bagwell (TJ's slave), 35
Bahamas, 546-8, 559n, 674, 675n
Bailey, Theodorus: seeks appointment,
62-3, 204, 323-4, 331-3, 518-19
Bainbridge, Absalom: forwards vaccine
matter, 103n; letter from cited, 103n,
749; and E. Gantt, 430n
Bainbridge, William, 163, 488
Baker, Dr. William (Md.), 758, 759
Baker, Jerman (attorney), 320, 446, 726
Baldwin, Abraham: letter from, 71-3; advises on appointments, 53, 85, 133,
226; and settlement of western land
claims by Ga., 71-3; as reference, 144;
elected to U.S. Senate, 144n; C. Pinckney sends regards to, 398, 538
Balfour, George, 221n, 358n
Ballow, Charles, 524
Baltic Sea, 192
Baltimore, Md.: Spanish consul at, 40;
merchants, 96, 203n, 445n, 665;
Catholics in, 202-3n; Mediterranean
trade of, 219n; roads to, from, 270;
conveyancers, 336; churches, 351,

407n; newspapers, 355, 356n; collector at, 364n, 587n; banks in, 374n,
375n, 602-4; surveyor, 445n; Female
Humane Association, 471, 475;
schools, 471, 475; census in, 532n;
trade with New Orleans, 550; growth
of, 631; Republicans in, 665; breweries, 723
Bank of the United States: drafts on, 11,
12n, 283; directors, 42, 44-5, 46-7n,
132, 133-4n, 136n, 166-7, 190-1, 321;
establishment of branch in Washington, 43, 132, 133-4n, 135-6n, 166,
191n, 304-5, 412; cashiers, 44-5, 134n,
166-7, 229n, 303-5, 597n; relationship
with Treasury Department, 135-6n,
191n, 602-4, 628; branches, 229n,
602-4; impact of yellow fever epi-
demic on, 304; influence of, 474; and
Dutch loan, 597n; TJ's notes on,
599n, 602-4, 606n, 612; statements of
assets and obligations, 602-4, 731-2;
notes of, 603; weekly returns by,
604n, 606; shares in, 628, 695-8;
and Seneca annuity, 695-8
bankruptcy, 565, 689
banks: shares in, 17, 565, 568n; purchase of bills from, 54; clerks, 102n;
proposed taxes on, 335n; circular to,
on appointment of T. T. Tucker,
606; and reduction of paper medium,
707-8. *See also* Columbia, Bank of
(Georgetown); North America, Bank
of; Pennsylvania, Bank of
Baptists, 407-9
Barbados, W.I., 259n, 562n
Barbary states: threat from, 78, 425,
588, 593-5; consuls to, 101; payments
to, 163. *See also* Algiers; Mediterranean Sea; Tripoli; Tunis
Barbé de Marbois, François, 175, 396,
397, 535
Barber, Joseph, 435n
Barclay, John, 705n
Barger, Kramer & Rump, 740n
Barlow, Joel: letters from, 141-2, 385-6,
509-10; plans return to U.S., 141, 385,
510; promotes improvement of Amer-
ica, 141-2; sends news of preliminary
peace treaty, 385-6; recommends Ful-
ton, sends thoughts on naval matters,
509-10
Barnaby. *See* Gillette, Barnaby (b. 1783,
TJ's slave)
Barnes, David L., 4, 5n, 6n, 80
Barnes, Jacob, 452n

Carroll, William, 681
carrots, 759
Carter, Edward, 581n
Carter, John, 522n
Carter, John, Jr., 521, 522n
Caruthers, John, 26, 27
Cary (b. 1785, TJ's slave), 34
Cary, Wilson Jefferson, 266n
Catahoula River, 554
Cathalan, Stephen, Jr., 189n, 494, 495n
Cathcart, James Leander, 163, 188, 189n, 477, 663-4
Catholic Church: in Pa., xlvi; in France, 194n; in Washington, D.C., 202-3; education, 202-3n; in Spain, 494; in Africa, 556; Irish, 671n
Catlett, George W., 744n
Catlett, Kemp, 581n
Caton, John: letter from cited, 753
cattle: for Tunisian minister, 148, 149n, 162; feed for, 326; in France, 461; in Europe, 706-7
Cayes, Saint-Domingue, 312-13
Cenas, Claudine: letter from cited, 754
census: returns for 1800 delayed, 19, 49, 255, 531; in Tenn., 19, 531, 532n; in Va., 49, 255, 570n; in Conn., 288n; expense of, 288n, 375n, 624n, 711n; in N.C., 288n; in S.C., 288n; shows population increase, 382, 507, 531-3, 545, 627, 643, 661; in N.J., 469n; in Md., 531, 532n; in Pa., 711n
Ceracchi, Giuseppe, 293, 294n, 482-4, 542
Ceylon, 398n, 715
chairs, 23-4, 137, 232
Chancellor, William, 46n
Chancognie, Simon Jude, 114-15, 258, 268
chandeliers, viii, 153
Chanlas. See De Chanlas, Monsieur
Channing, Walter, 595n
Chapman, John, 481n
Chaptal, Jean Antoine, 542n
Charles Emmanuel IV, Duke of Savoy and King of Sardinia, 714, 715n
Charleston, S.C.: Federalists in, 14n; Republicans in, 14n; attorneys, 42n; marine hospital, 53, 108; collector at, 53-4, 85, 713-14; Spanish consul at, 114, 115n; French prisoners at, 114-15, 268; election of 1800 in, 202; lighthouses, 202n; merchants, 202n, 257, 453n; custom house, 229n, 713-14, 739; and American Revolution, 257; British influence in, 257; and Jay

Treaty, 257; navy agent at, 259n; revenue cutter at, 596n; banks, 602-4; anonymous letters from, 714n
Charlottesville, Va.: mail service to, from, 41; whooping cough in, 373; descriptions of, 462-3; travel to, from, 568-9, 581
Charlton, John, 46n
Chas, Jean: letter to, 203-4; TJ receives books from, 203-4; letter from cited, 203-4n, 750; wishes to visit U.S., 203-4n; R. R. Livingston carries letter to, 292n
Chastellux, François Jean de Bauvoir, Marquis de, 179-80
cheese, 461
chemistry, 212-13, 269, 542n
Cheriot, Henry: letter from cited, 755
Cherokee Indians: demand new negotiation site, 196n, 308, 402, 747n; land cessions sought from, 196n; murder of, 196n, 308, 747-8; send delegation to Washington, 308; inns on land of, 308n; road through lands of, 308n; consult with Hawkins, 325n; hold negative view of TJ's administration, 402-3; agent to, 403, 404n; trading houses, factories, 554; removal of, 559n
Chesapeake (U.S. frigate), 663, 668
Chesapeake and Delaware Canal, 207n
chess, 81
Chew, Benjamin, 42
Chickasaw Bluffs, 196n, 518n
Chickasaw Indians, 196n, 403, 518n, 559n, 748n
China, 105n, 180
Chisholm, Hugh, 34
Chisman, Mount Edward: recommended, appointed to office, 53, 85, 86n, 89, 92, 112, 119, 127, 157-8, 169, 185-6, 216, 263
Choctaw Indians: agent to, 55, 86, 108, 403; proposed conference with, 196, 308, 324; trading houses, factories, 554; removal of, 559n
Chribbs, William, 392
Christian VII, King of Denmark, 111n
Church, Edward, 277
Church, Jonathan, 512-13
Cicero, 428, 429n
cider, 453-4, 588, 689-90, 734, 740
Cilley, Bradbury, 601
Cincinnati, Society of the, 69n
ciphers, 340n
"Citizen" (pseudonym): letter from,

689; complains about bankruptcy laws in Mass., 689

"Citizen of Delaware" (pseudonym), 693n

Claiborne, Clarissa Duralde, 562n

Claiborne, Cornelia Tennessee, 733n

Claiborne, Elizabeth W. Lewis, 732, 733n

Claiborne, William C. C.: letters from, 17-19, 402-4, 732-4; prepares to assume governorship of Miss. Terr., 17-19, 402; and census in Tenn., 19, 532n; withdraws as candidate for Congress, 19, 402, 403-4n; rumored to have declined governorship, 154; recommends aspirants for office, 392; advises on Indian affairs, 402-4; as reference, 478; and DeLacy, 559n; and Workman, 670n; sends news of Miss. Terr. politics, 732-4

Clark, Bowling: letter from, 659-60; leaves TJ's employment, 21, 22n, 525; TJ's account with, 349, 350n, 375, 660, 757; letters to cited, 350n, 753, 754, 755; surveys Poplar Forest lands, 414, 419, 659; reports on harvest at Poplar Forest, 659-60; letters from cited, 752, 753, 754

Clark, Daniel: and Claiborne, 18, 670n; consul at New Orleans, 327, 560n; shipments for TJ, 454n; and DeLacy, 557

Clark, Jonas, 54, 57n, 85, 108, 158

Clark (Clarke), Elijah, Jr., 144

Clark (Clarke), Elijah (d. 1799), 144

Clarke, Samuel, 409-10

Clarkson, Matthew: bank director, 46n; letters from cited, 284n, 750, 751; resigns as loan commissioner, 284n, 518; as reference, 345

Claxton, Thomas: letters to, 204-5, 480; letters from, 23-4, 152-3, 466; and furnishings for Monticello, 23-4, 152-3, 204-5; and furnishings for President's House, 152-3, 391, 466, 469n, 480, 588n, 758; letter to cited, 153n, 753; account with TJ, 391; forwards letter to TJ, 400

Clay, Charles: letter from cited, 22n; recommends overseer to TJ, 22n; examines Poplar Forest lands, 659

Clay, Henry: letters from cited, 754, 755

Clay, Joseph (Pa.): recommended for office, 23, 100-1, 102n, 118, 125, 148; declines consular appointment, 107, 157; as reference, 440n

Clayton, Solomon, 452n

Clérisseau, Charles Louis: letter from cited, 175n

clerks: Treasury Department, 55, 108, 170n, 284-5, 288-9n, 388n, 437-40, 477n, 570n, 629, 630n, 681, 700-1, 703, 705n, 706n; Navy Department, 60n, 703; bank, 102n, 700, 705n; War Department, 108, 703; Continental Congress, 165n; Pa. senate, 165n; applications for clerkships, 214, 479, 496; territorial, 229n; State Department, 311n, 370, 371n, 378, 379n, 445n; for D.C. commissioners, 372; illness among, 423-4; political sympathies of, 477n; House of Representatives, 479, 513; custom house, 481n, 713; revenue, 582; salaries, 582, 629, 630n, 705n; removal of, 700, 704n, 706n; offered bribes, 700-1, 702; Federalists as, 702, 703, 704n; postal service, 705n

Clermont-Ferrand, France, 461-3, 465n

Clinch River, 344n

Clinton, DeWitt: letter from, 283-4; member of council of appointment, 275n; recommends aspirants for office, 283-4; identified, 284n; opposes M. L. Davis's appointment, 311; and Iroquois resettlement, 316, 317n

Clinton, George: letter from, 447-8; as reference, 142; elected governor, 235n; removal policies of, 275n, 287; secretary for, 284n; and harbor fortifications at New York, 447-8, 688; letter from cited, 754

Clopton, John, 214

clover, 326, 707

Clymer, George: letter from, 610-11; seeks patent for pump, 610-11; identified, 611n

Clymer, George E., 610-11

Clymer, Henry, 118n

Clymer, Mary Willing, 118n

coal: ordered by TJ, 171, 232, 275-6, 375, 470; mining of, in Va., 233n; in France, 345n

Coalter, John: letter to, 409-10; obtains judgment against S. Clarke, 409-10; letter from cited, 410n, 754

Coates, Samuel, 46n

Cobb, Henry J., 325n

Cobbett, William, xlv

Cocke, William, 404n

cod, 134n

coffee: ordered by TJ, 83, 87, 118, 128; cargoes of, 134n; from Saint-Domingue, 312
Coffyn, Mr., 534
Cohen, Jacob J., 104n
Coiffier de Verseux, Henri Louis, Baron: *Dictionnaire,* 484n
coins, 15-16, 681-3, 692
Colbert, Brown (1785-1833, TJ's slave), 34
Colbert, Burwell (TJ's slave), 34, 35n
Coleman, Mary Littlepage, 473n
Coleman, Nathan: letter to, 486; letter from, 457-8; presents "Mammoth Veal" to TJ, 457-8, 479; thanked by TJ, 486, 513
Coleman, Robert S.: letter to, 491; letter from, 473; and L. Littlepage, 473, 491; identified, 473n
Coleman, William, 460n
Colles, Raymond, 134n
Collier, Thomas, 519n
Columbia, Bank of (Georgetown): directors of, 44, 46n, 56n, 254, 400n, 545n; presidents of, 56n; TJ's account with, 128, 178-9, 283n; distrusted by Gallatin, 135n, 191n, 545-6n; cashier, 166; Madison's note with, 179; stockholders, 191; TJ predicts demise of, 399, 412, 545-6, 580; notes of, 412, 413n, 454, 545-6, 580
Columbia College, 190n, 284n, 662n
Columbian Centinel (Boston), 147n
Columella, Lucius Junius Moderatus, 326
Comanche Indians, 555, 561n
commerce: one of four pillars of prosperity, 647
Complete Collection of All the Protests of the Peers in Parliament Entered on their Journals, Since the Year 1774 (House of Lords), 482-4
Complete Collection of the Lords' Protests (House of Lords), 482-4
Concise View of All the Most Important Facts which have Hitherto Appeared Concerning the Cow-Pox (Charles Rochemont Aikin), 490, 491n, 573, 698
Congregationalists, 409n, 516, 517n

CONGRESS, U.S.

Confederation
and western land claims, 72; members, 172n; instructions to treaty

commissioners, 244, 245-6n; journals of, 310

Continental
TJ as member of, 14; appoints TJ peace commissioner, 126n; clerks, 165n; and the *Hope,* 300, 301n; journals of, 310; commercial agent for, at New Orleans, 328n; members, 531n

House of Representatives
chamber, viii-ix; and Lehman's petition, 10-11; committees, 10-11n; temporary building for, 97, 132, 153, 167, 176; and spoliations by Spain, 407n; clerk of, 479, 513; and L'Enfant's petition, 567n

Legislation
relief of Lehman, 10-11n; exoneration from French treaties, 38, 39n; and District of Columbia, 47-8, 98, 99n; Indian cessions, 73; western land claims, 76; lighthouses, 91, 92n; Logan Act, 162, 163n; and Barbary states, 163, 588, 688; Marine barracks, 168, 172-3, 187n, 217; and Northwest Terr., 170n, 587n, 719; President may not forward petitions to, 201; court fee bills, 215, 216n; marine hospitals, 220; excise tax, 262; election reform, 289n; commissions busts of Washington, 293; compensation of collectors, 374n, 693n, 714n; appropriation for naval galleys, 488n; and Sterett's victory, 589n; naturalization, 618, 621n; communications from secretary of the Treasury, 623-4, 633-4, 635-6n, 645; construction of 74-gun ships, 640-1n, 646; and fortifications, 650n, 688; regulation of coasting trade, 711n; collection laws, 714n; and slave trade, 739-40; and the *Sally,* 743n. *See also* Alien Enemies Act (1798); Alien Friends Act (1798); Judiciary Act (1801); Peace Establishment Act (1801); Sedition Act (1798); Stamp Act (1797)

Public Opinion
proposal to reorganize, 247; president's communications should be by letter, 612; need to guard against misapplication of public money, 635

CONGRESS, U.S. (*cont.*)

Senate

and L. Lehman's petition, 10-11n; and Convention of 1800, 105n, 188, 189n, 316, 501, 506, 519, 525, 609; Republicans gain majority in, 147, 269, 303, 324; and TJ's nominations, 299n, 327, 377n, 382, 539n; and Adams's nominations, 494n; secretary of, 513-14; may reject TJ's nominations, 538; L'Enfant's petition to, 567n; and Sedition Act, 613, 635, 652, 653-4n, 655-7

Congress (U.S. frigate), 668

Coningham, Cornelius: letter to, 611; letter from, 592; seeks government loan, 592, 611; identified, 592n; letter from cited, 592n, 754

Connecticut: elections in, ix, 169, 409n, 506, 519-20n; union of clergy and Federalists in, 33, 338; attorneys, 71; Wallingford, 71; Episcopalians in, 71n, 409n; Falkner Island lighthouse, 91-2, 118n, 492; Farmington, 117n; need for removals in, 147; Hartford, 169; Middletown collectorship, 260n; census, 288n; letters to, from the 12th Regiment, 338-9, 517; Lebanon, 339n; legislature, 339n, 475-6; militia, 339n, 475-6; physicians, 369; smallpox vaccination in, 369, 430; Baptists, 407-9; calls for disestablishment in, 407-9; Universalists, 409n; and American Revolution, 457n; marshal for, 475-6, 484-6, 691; Killingworth, 476n; emigrants from, 477-8; Whitneyville, 514n; newspapers, 519-20; Litchfield, 597-9; postmasters, 597-9; supervisor for, 598, 599n; circuit court cases in, 658; courts, 691n. *See also* Danbury Baptist Association; Federalists; New Haven, Conn.; Republicans

Connelly, John (Pa.), 100, 102n

Conrad, Frederic, 416n

Conrad & McMunn (Washington), 12n, 96

Constantinople, 163n, 341-2

Constellation (U.S. frigate), 663, 668

Constitution (U.S. frigate), 663, 668

Constitution of the United States: and Sedition Act, xi, 647-8, 652, 655-6; ratification of, 26n, 679n, 740n; and revenue collection, 264; Federalists threaten, 265, 528, 576; revision and amendment called for, 286, 289n, 314; oaths to uphold, 439; and use of *nolle prosequi,* 480-1; and citizenship, 559n, 649; signers of, 610n; and president's annual message to Congress, 612; and executive authority to call on departments for information, 634; declaring war, enacting peace, 642-3; freedom of the press, 656; TJ's opinion of, 708

Convention of 1800: ratification of, 56, 101, 105n, 161, 173-4, 176-8, 186-8, 189n, 191, 193-4n, 211-12, 216, 217, 228, 245n, 265, 268, 276, 291, 303, 311, 314-15, 316, 410-11, 492-3, 501-2, 506, 519, 525, 545, 593; spoliation claims, 105n, 186, 187-8n, 188, 189n, 211-12, 228, 268, 276, 316, 501-2, 519, 527; restitution of prizes, 146, 316, 410-11; impact of, on commerce, 492-3; proclamation of, 609; execution of, 609n

Cooch, William: letter from cited, 752

Cook, Johnson: letters from, 455-7, 473-4, 477-8; seeks back pay, 455-7; identified, 457n; reports on Ohio politics, 473-4, 477-8

Cook, Thomas Jefferson, 456

Cooke (Cook), John Travers, 386-7

cooks, 542-3

Coolidge, Joseph, Jr., 589n

Cooper, Thomas, 23n, 533n

copper, 587n, 596-7, 681-2

Corcoran, Thomas: letter from, 457; and pardon for T. Leach, 457

Corey, Isaac, & Sons (Newry), 274n

Corey, Trevor, 274n

corn, 659-60, 757

Corny, Marguerite Victoire de Palerne de, 189n

Corsica, 105n

Cosby, John L., 744n

cotton, 451, 518, 527, 535

cotton gin, 514-15, 662-3

Coulon, Paul, 56n

counterfeiting, 681-3, 692-3

counterpanes, 270

COURTS, U.S.

Circuit

District of Columbia, 46n; and the *Hope,* 160n, 299-300; and Marchant's case, 302n; TJ's notes concerning cases of, 599n, 612, 658

Davis, Matthew L.: recommended, opposed for appointment, vii, 62, 143-4, 161, 204, 233-5, 237, 238, 272-5, 307, 311, 332, 333n, 753; visits Monticello, vii, 272-3, 286, 287, 289n, 307, 311, 314, 316, 340; relationship with Burr, 63-4n, 287; *Oration,* 234n

Davis, Thomas T.: letter from, 154-5; seeks appointment, 154-5; advises on appointments, 277

Davis, William (Boston): letter from cited, 754

Davy. *See* Hern, David (b. 1784, Davy, TJ's slave)

Davy (b. 1785, TJ's slave), 34

Dawes, Abijah, 46n

Dawson, Mr., 331

Dawson, John: letter from, 105; returns to U.S., 101, 105n, 142, 385; forwards letter from Volney, 105; sends dispatches to U.S., 105, 161, 187n, 188, 193-4n, 217, 445n; carries letters, news to Europe, 141, 380, 381; proposed as peace negotiator, 173-4n; carries ratified convention to France, 178n; appointment of, criticized, 288; letter from cited, 473; letter to cited, 473n

Dawson, Martin: letter from cited, 753

Dayton, Jonathan: accused of misusing public funds, 55, 108, 437-41, 704n, 705n; and S. A. Otis, 514n

Deakins, Francis, 417n

Deakins, William, Jr., 46n

Deane (Continental frigate), 654

Dearborn, Dorcas Osgood Marble, 195

Dearborn, Henry: letters to, 83-4, 116-17, 215-16, 271-2; letters from, 74, 195, 254-5; absent from Washington, viii, 90, 275n, 330; advises on annual message to Congress, xi, 614-15, 622; and fortifications, 6n, 83-4, 195, 271-2, 309, 448n, 688n; advises on Mediterranean squadron, 74; family of, 74, 169, 170n, 195, 215, 216; and military contracts, 74, 116-17, 254-5; and Indian affairs, 76, 196-7, 307, 324, 325n, 404n, 696-8, 748n; forwards information, pamphlets, 86n, 600n; acting secretary of the navy, 168n; advises on appointments, 195, 227, 229n, 314, 440n; cases of Landais and Rowe, 215-16; as reference, 352; and Barraud's removal, 358; applications to, for appointments, 452; attends

cabinet meetings, 488-9, 609; and Ellicott's map of southwestern U.S., 549n; and L'Enfant's claim, 564, 567n; method of communication with the president, 576-8; TJ praises, 577; conveys thanks to Lorimier, 599; and War Department appropriations and expenditures, 636n, 638n, 645; and Jordan, 726

debt. *See* United States: Economy; United States: Public Finance

De Butts, Elias, 711n, 739n, 742, 743n

Decatur, Stephen, Sr., 488

De Chanlas, Monsieur: letter from, 325-6; offers to manage TJ's farms, 325-6; letter from cited, 326n

Decisions of Cases in Virginia, By The High Court of Chancery (George Wythe), 466-7

Declaration of Independence, 6n, 15n, 165n, 610n

deeds, 310, 359-61, 379

DeLacy, John Devereux: letter from, 549-62; sends news, descriptions of southwestern territories, 549-62; identified, 559-60n

Delage de Volude, Nathalie. *See* Sumter, Nathalie Delage de Volude

Delaware: marshal for, 32-3; Kent Co., 69, 70, 428, 429n; elections in, 69-70, 147, 207n, 324, 427-9; need for removals in, 147; French consul for, 161n; attorneys in, 207-8n; governor, 427-9; legislature, 427-9; district attorney, 428; sheriffs, 428, 429n; Sussex Co., 428, 429n; and American Revolution, 429n; New Castle Co., 429n; circuit court cases in, 658. *See also* Federalists; Republicans; Wilmington, Del.

Delaware Indians, 599-600

Delaware River, 23n

Demerara, 702, 704-5n

Democratic-Republican societies, 275n

Democratic Society of the City of New-York, 275n

Den Helder, 239, 295

Denison (Dennison), Jabez, 594, 595n

Denmark: U.S. relations with, 13, 14n, 31, 148, 149n, 163n, 189n; armistice with Britain, 32n; prisoners of war, 39n, 110, 111n, 125

Denniston & Cheetham: letter from, 480-1; supports halt to Duane's sedition trial, 480-1, 543-4, 607.

INDEX

Denniston & Cheetham (*cont.*)
See also *American Citizen and General Advertiser* (New York)
Densley, Hugh, 95
Dent, George, 303, 330, 374, 426
Derieux, Justin Pierre Plumard: letter from cited, 756
Dering, Henry P., 52, 57n
Description topographique, physique, civile, politique et historique de la partie française de l'Isle Saint-Domingue (Médéric Louis Elie Moreau de St. Méry), 356
De Senectute (Cicero), 429n
desertion, 81n, 215, 216n, 219n
Dexter, Samuel, 447-8
Dickerson, Mahlon, 440n
Dickinson, John, 206
Dickson, William, 19n
Dictionnaire Biographique et Historique des Hommes Marquans de la Fin du Dix-Huitième Siècle (attributed to Baron Coiffier de Verseux), 482-4, 542
Diderot, Denis: *Synonymes Français,* 203
Didot, Pierre and Firmin, 20
Digges, Edward, 502-3
Digges, Elizabeth, 502
Digges, Maria (Molly): letter from, 502-3; asks TJ for money, 502-3; identified, 503n; letters to, from cited, 503n
Digges, Susannah, 502
Digges, Thomas: letter to, 692; letter from, 681-3; forwards information on coins and counterfeiting, 681-3, 692
Dinmore, Richard, 487n
Dinsmore, Andrew, 11, 12n, 31
Dinsmore, James: and brother's account, 11; letters to, from cited, 756
Direct Tax (1798), 54, 628
Discorso del Signor Tommaso Jefferson (Philip Mazzei), 666, 667, 668n
Dissertation on the Freedom of Navigation and Maritime Commerce (William Barton), 610n
distilleries, 22n
District of Columbia: Rock Creek, ix, 131, 168, 209; streets and roads in, ix, 97, 131-2, 167-8, 172-3, 176, 208-9, 372, 450; commissioners, 46n, 113; U.S. circuit court, 46n; alterations to plan of, 47-8; letters to, from commissioners, 97-100, 129-30, 131-2, 167-8, 208-9, 371-3, 450; Maryland loan to, 97-100, 113, 129-30, 175-6, 208,

371-3; sale of lots in, 113, 129-30, 373, 384-5, 450; TJ on the functions of commissioners, 130; marshal for, 191n, 290; U.S. attorney for, 191n; education in, 203n; letter to commissioners cited, 203n, 750; communications between commissioners and the president, 297-8; survey of lots in, 348-9; estimate of commissioners' debts, 371-3, 384-5; superintendent of public buildings, 372; canals in, 373; James Creek, 373; Tiber Creek, 373; TJ's notes on commissioners' accounts, 384-5; divided into counties, 444; taxes, 444; and L'Enfant, 562-8; maps of, 564, 568n; commissioner of public buildings, 717n. *See also* Georgetown, D.C.; Washington, D.C.
Dixon, Roger, 552, 560-1n
Dobrée, Pierre Frédéric, 494, 495n
Dodge, Nehemiah: letter from, 407-9; supports religious liberty, 407-9; identified, 409n
Doll (b. 1757, TJ's slave), 35
Dolly (b. 1794, TJ's slave), 35
Dolton, Mr., 301-2
Donath, Joseph, 225, 676n
donkeys, 105n
Donnell, John, 469n, 665
Dorsey, Mr., 95
Dorsey, William H., 136n
Dougherty, Joseph: handles payments, 128; and delivery of TJ's carriage, 224, 270, 282, 328-9, 421; and E. Maher, 421n; hauls coal, 470n; stable accounts, 757-9
Douglas, George: letter from, 8-9; and engraving of Va. Capitol, 8-9; writings, 9n
D'Oyley, Daniel: advises on appointments, 13-14n, 32, 53; reports on S.C. politics, 100, 101-2n; recommended for office, 320n
drapery, viii
Drayton, John: letter to, 258-9; letter from, 114-15; appoints commissioner of Direct Tax, 54; and recognition of Chancognie, 114-15, 258-9; and return of French prisoners, 114-15, 259, 268; letter from cited, 756
Drayton, Stephen, 189n
Dresden, 237n
Driskell, James: letter from cited, 752
Duane, William: letter to, 41; forwards books to TJ, 20; recommends aspirants for office, 23n, 55, 57n, 108, 285;

INDEX

TJ advises on postal schedules in Va.,
41; urges removals, 100; sedition trial
of, 125, 148, 480-1, 543-4, 607, 613,
617, 651n, 652, 653-4n, 655-7; as reference, 326n; alleges misuse of public
funds, 438, 440-1n, 700-1, 704n,
706n; printing and binding contract,
469n; evaluates political sympathies of
government clerks, 477n; TJ pledges
support for, 479; sends regards to TJ,
513. See also *Aurora* (Philadelphia)
Dublin, Ireland, 93
Ducarne de Blangy, Jacques Joseph,
194n
duels, 551, 560n, 701, 705-6n
Dufief, Nicolas Gouin: letter to, 542; letters from, 20, 482-4; bookseller, 20;
offers books from Franklin's library,
482-4, 542; letter to cited, 483n, 753;
letter from cited, 542n, 751; sends
books to TJ, 542n
Dugnani, Antonio: letter from cited,
189n
Duhamel du Monceau, M.: *Traité des
arbres fruitiers,* xlix
Duke, Henry: letter to cited, 752
Dunbar, William: letter from, 121-4; TJ
recommends, 18; meteorological observations, 121, 124n; scientific pursuits, 121-4
Dunkirk, France, 65, 280
Dunlop, James, 190, 191n
Dunlop, John, 136n
Dunwoody's Tavern (Philadelphia),
118n
du Pont, Victor Marie, 464, 465n
du Pont de Nemours, Éleuthère Irénée,
74
Du Pont de Nemours, Pierre Samuel,
74, 448n
Duralde, Martin Milony, 121-2, 124n
DuVal, William, 104n
Dwight, Timothy, 369, 370n, 497
Dyson, Joseph, 759

Eagle (British brig), 132, 134n
Early, Joshua, 659
Eastern Branch. *See* Anacostia River
Easton, David, 82-3, 500
Easton, Sarah Harrison, 82, 83n
Eaton, William: dispatches from, 108,
109n, 162, 189-90n; charters vessel,
148, 149n, 162-3; consul at Tunis,
240; estimates marine force of Tunis,
664

eclipses, 423, 424n
economics, 341
Eddins, Samuel: seeks appointment,
112; letter from cited, 112n
Edgehill (Randolph estate), 373, 471,
578, 579
Edinburgh, 103n, 278n, 279n, 425n,
531n
education: legal, 144, 335-6, 670n;
Catholic, 202-3n; of women, 471, 475.
See also medicine
Edwards, Enoch: letters to, 155, 309,
429-30; letters from, 115-16, 181-2;
TJ orders carriage from, viii, 115-16,
155, 181-2, 224, 282, 309, 429-30;
and G. Stuart's portrait of TJ, 225,
282-3, 329; health of, 329; TJ's account with, 418; letter from cited, 755
Edwards, Frances Gordon, 181, 309,
429
Edwards, John, 229n
Edwards, Pierpont: letters from, 259-
60, 484-6, 514-15; as reference, 71;
family of, 229n; recommends aspirants for office, 259-60, 484-6, 511,
754; letters from cited, 260n, 511n,
754; recommends E. Whitney, 514-15;
advises on appointments, 515
Edwin (b. 1793; TJ's slave), 34
Egypt: donkeys from, 105n; accounts
from, 108, 192, 239, 295, 415; France
attempts to reinforce, 194n; French
army in, capitulates, 239n, 296, 297n,
415n; restored to Ottoman Empire,
395, 398n; pyramids, 426; Britain
and France to evacuate, 714
Elam, Samuel: letter from, 593-5; and
Spanish seizures of U.S. vessels, 593-
5; identified, 595n
election of 1800: in Va., 185, 256; in
S.C., 201-2; in Del., 207n; in N.Y.,
233, 234n, 332; in New York City,
235n; in Md., 303n; in Miss. Terr.,
553; in Vt., 686n
election of 1804, xi, 286
Elgar, John, 717n
Elgar, Joseph, Jr.: letter from, 715-17;
seeks to acquire sample of serpentine,
715-17; identified, 717n
Elgin, Thomas Bruce, Earl of, 415
Eliza (sloop), 454n
Elk Island, Va., 321n
Elk Run Church (Fauquier Co., Va.),
568, 581
Ellery, Christopher: letter to, 309-10;
letter from, 156-7; recommended for

INDEX

GREAT BRITAIN (*cont.*)
237n; use of fraudulent ship registers by British, 236-8; resolution of debt claims, 506-7, 519, 525, 545, 615, 628, 630, 635n, 660; and Florida, 557; share of U.S. funded debt, 672; refuses to issue exequatur, 705n; and removal of condemned slaves from Va., 719

War with France
preliminary articles of peace signed, ix, 193-4n, 385-6, 395-8, 401, 641-2, 687, 707-8, 714-15, 723, 734, 735, 736; and the *Windsor,* 39n; defense against French invasion, 192, 194n, 297n; and Egypt, 192, 239, 415n; may threaten Portuguese colonies, 192; prospects for peace, 228, 239, 295-7; peace with northern powers, 239

Greenleaf, James, 401, 402n
Gregorie, John, 279-80
Gregory of Tours, 462, 465n
Grenada, W.I., 82n
Grenville, William Wyndham, Lord, 715n
Griffin, Burgess: hired as overseer at Poplar Forest, 21-2, 525, 659-60; letter to cited, 507n, 755; letter from cited, 756
Griffin, Cyrus, 72, 73n
Griffing, Joseph, 492n
Griffith, Dennis: letter from, 411-12; theory for calculating longitude, 411-12
Grigsby, Joseph, 27-8
Grove, William Barry, 376
Guadeloupe, W.I., 134n
Guerard, Robert G., 109n
guilders, 228
Guinea, Gulf of, 561n
Guion, Isaac, 551, 560n
Gulf of Mexico, 106
gunboats, 192
gunpowder: manufacture of, 74; ordered by TJ, 118, 137, 171; for dey of Algiers, 148, 163; price of, 171
gypsum, 707

Habersham, Joseph: letter to, 209-10; letters from, 291, 330-1; as postmaster general, 77-8; offered new appointment, 169, 209-10, 216, 288, 291, 307, 330; declines appointment, 330-1, 405n; resigns as postmaster

general, 334, 364, 374, 460, 529; college classmates of, 516; and Litchfield postmastership, 598-9
Haden, George, 383n
Hagner, Peter, 703, 706n
Halifax, Nova Scotia, 134n
Hall, David, 427-9
Hall, Edward (Marine officer), 218n
Hall, John (Del.), 702
Hall, John (Marine officer), 218n
Hamburg, Germany: firearms imported from, 10n; consul at, 82, 83n, 500; smallpox vaccination at, 199; rags imported from, 214
Hamilton, Alexander: as secretary of the Treasury, 26n, 634; and Alexandria collectorship, 43, 46n; as opposition leader, 101, 460n; and American neutrality, 111n; and the *Hope,* 160n; attends Annapolis Convention, 206; praises R. Rogers, 333n; visits Pearce's factory, 451; advises on Washington's annual address, 614; and fortification of New York harbor, 688n; and beacon at Sandy Hook, 738n
Hamilton, William, 42
Hamilton & Wilkinson (Nassau), 546-7
Hammell, William: petition from, 492; seeks appointment, 492
Hammer, Frédéric L., 351-2
Hammond, Abijah, 46n
Hammond, George, 368n
Hammuda Bey (of Tunis): letter to, 240-1; jewels for, 148, 189-90n; requests cannon from U.S., 148, 149n, 162, 189; TJ affirms peace and friendship with, 240-1, 265. *See also* Tunis
Hampden-Sydney College, 499n
hams, 137, 171, 406
Hancock, Mr., 404, 410-11, 420
Hand, Edward, 164, 165n
Hannibal, 319n
Hannibal (British ship-of-war), 192
Hanover, Germany, 295, 296n
Hans, Mr., 42
Hanse, Conrad: letter from, 421; builds carriage for TJ, 115, 116, 181-2; account with TJ, 182, 224, 270, 282-3, 309, 328-9; sends new harness to TJ, 421
Hanson, Samuel: letter to, 321-2; letter from, 42-7; seeks cashier's appointment, offers political advice, 42-7; Bank of Columbia cashier, 128; TJ recommends, 166-7, 303-5, 321-2, 399,

Hanson, Samuel (*cont.*)
479; recommended by J. T. Mason,
223; seeks appointment as treasurer,
321; dismissed as cashier, 399-400;
Forrest's suit against, 399-400, 479;
Beckley promises clerkship to, 513
Hardware River (Albemarle Co.), 310
Hare, Charles Willing, 301n
Harmony (British sloop), 404, 410-11,
420, 677
harnesses, 115, 224, 282, 283n, 421
Harper, Robert Goodloe: *Letter,* 521,
522n
Harris, Charles, 288n
Harrison, Jesse, 599-600
Harrison, Richard: and restoration of
W. P. Gardner and A. Campbell, 108,
158, 284-5; and settlement of delin-
quent Treasury accounts, 133, 134-5n;
rumored resignation of, 364; offered
appointment as treasurer, 405n
Harrison, Robert Hanson, 82, 83n
Harrison, William Henry, 599, 600n
Harvie, John, 373
Haskel, Michael, 516
Hastings, Seth, 306n
Haswell, Anthony: letter to, 265; pub-
lisher of *Vermont Gazette,* 37n; seeks
printing contract, 265
Hatheway, Mr. (Vt.), 685
hatmakers, 256
Havana, Cuba, 138n, 388n, 534, 547-8
Hawker, William: letter from cited, 753
Hawkesbury, Robert Banks Jenkinson,
Baron, 281n, 297n, 386n, 398n, 507n
Hawkins, Benjamin: letters to, 305, 307-
8; letters from, 196-7, 518; appointed
Indian commissioner, 75, 305n, 307;
forwards correspondence with Dear-
born, 196-7; correspondence with
E. Trist, 305, 518; and treaty negotiations, 307-8, 402, 518n; arrives at
Southwest Point, 325; as Creek agent,
403; observations on cotton's impact
on the South, 518; and murder of
Cherokee woman, 748n
hay, 758
Hay, George: letter from, 136; borrows
book from TJ, 136; *Essay,* 136n; identified, 136n
Heard, John: confusion over appointment of, 101, 102n, 117, 118n, 622;
advises on appointments, 226, 314
Heath, Robert Jones, 703
Heath, William: letter from, 315-16; recommends W. R. Lee, 315-16, 754

Helder, Den. *See* Den Helder
Helmbold, George: seeks contract to
print laws in German, 79, 80n; letter
from cited, 749
Hemings, Betsy (1783-1857, Eppes
slave), 34, 579, 580n
Hemings, Critta (1769-1850), 34, 35n,
579, 580n
Hemings, Elizabeth (Betty), 580n
Hemings, James: suicide of, viii, 542-3,
569-70
Hemings, James (b. 1787, Jamy, TJ's
slave), 34
Hemings, Mary, 580n
Hemings, Sally, 580n
hemp, 746n
Henderson, Archibald, 376
Henderson, Bennett (d. 1793), xlvi-xlvii,
342, 343n, 360-1, 379n, 413, 454,
580-1, 743-4
Henderson, Charles, xlviii, 342, 343n,
361, 413n, 455n, 581n
Henderson, Elizabeth (daughter of Ben-
nett Henderson), 744n
Henderson, Elizabeth (Mrs. James L.
Henderson), 743-4
Henderson, Elizabeth Lewis (Mrs. Ben-
nett Henderson), xlvii, 362-4, 413n,
546n, 581n, 744n
Henderson, Isham, xlviii, 342, 343n,
360-1, 413n, 455n, 581n
Henderson, James L., xlviii, 342, 343n,
360, 379, 380n, 413n, 455, 581n,
743-4
Henderson, John, 171, 343n, 361n, 362,
380n, 413, 454, 455n
Henderson, Sally (Sarah). *See* Kerr,
Sarah (Sally) Henderson
Henderson, Samuel, 416n
Henderson, William, 343n
Henderson, William (Pa.), 23n
Henderson & Connard, 360-1, 743
Henderson lands: TJ purchases, xlvi,
342-4, 412-14, 454-5; plat of allotments of, xlvi-xlviii, 382 (illus.);
dower lands, xlvii, 362-4, 413n, 454,
581n, 743; mill seat, xlvii, 343n, 361n,
362, 363n, 379-80, 413, 454, 455n,
581n, 743; statement of accounts regarding, 343-4n; deeds for purchase
of, 359-61, 380n, 413, 743-4; division
of, 361n, 363n, 379-80, 412-13, 580-1;
form of deeds for purchase of, 379
Henry, Patrick, 344n, 663n
Hepburn, Alexander, 354n
Hepburn, Samuel, 444n

INDEX

JEFFERSON, THOMAS (*cont.*)
595-6; letters of introduction requested from, 684. *See also* Summary Journal of Letters

Governor of Virginia
and Gálvez, 328n

Inauguration
descriptions of, 180n

Law
and rights of neutral vessels, 81, 86, 90, 108, 609-10, 649; opposes excessive court fees, 215; use of *nolle prosequi,* 543-4

Library
books obtained for, 12, 20, 95, 310, 406, 426, 491n, 533n, 542, 605, 698-9, 708n, 723; works on moral philosophy, 20; books borrowed from, 136, 346; book subscriptions, 283n, 356, 489; cookbooks, 355; letter cases, 355; music books, 355; pays for bookbinding, 355-6; catalog of books, 356n; offered books from Franklin's library, 482-4, 542; scrapbooks, 589n; books on finance, 626n

Minister to France
offered passage on the *Romulus,* 125, 126n; meets various people, 142; negotiates treaties, 245n; returns to U.S., 381

Nailery
slaves at, vaccinated, 35n; nailrod and iron stock for, 226n; account with S. Clarke, 409-10; new nailery to be built, 579

Opinions
on slave trade, x, 740; avoids determining hypothetical cases, 80-1, 86, 90, 132; unreliability of newspapers, 81, 86, 90, 260; enemy to waste and extravagance, 90; private passengers on public vessels, 125, 126n; opposes tributes and douceurs, 162-3; public vs. private character, 166-7; American Revolution an example to the world, 203; impact of popular opinion, 203; U.S. an agricultural nation, 240; peaceable coercion preferable to war, 244; on servants, 421n; family the source of happiness, 471, 510-11; on Washington society, 511; loan

of public funds to individuals, 611; burden of debt, 677-8; Constitution the "collected wisdom of our country," 708

Patronage and Appointments
difficulty of making appointments and removals, ix, 32, 33n, 146; moderate approach toward, 12, 32, 85, 117, 145, 146-7, 265, 381-2, 501, 618-19; sends blank commissions, 26, 88, 227; relies on friends, congressmen for advice on, 27, 30, 32, 85, 89, 92, 347; and postal appointments, 30, 612, 619; and appointment of Joel Lewis, 32; removals due to misconduct and delinquency, 53, 57n, 89, 92, 118, 119, 195n, 223n, 263n, 317, 366n, 374, 381, 601, 655, 686n; reappointment of W. P. Gardner and A. Campbell, 55, 86, 108, 158, 284-5, 314, 449; reduction of useless offices, 55, 86, 644; and "midnight appointments," 80, 252n, 300-1n, 371n, 618-19; Republicans entitled to share of offices, 80, 85, 145, 146, 317, 618, 686n; and "electioneering" by Federal officers, 85, 601; will not appoint Federalists, 85, 108, 580; reappoints Republicans, 86, 158, 263n, 654n; cabinet unanimous on removal policy, 146; judiciary removals, 147, 619, 686n; and Barraud's removal, 221n, 358; principles regarding removals, 263n, 381-2, 459, 612, 618-19; can only appoint offices of first grade, 264; offers advice to office seekers, 264; promises printing contracts, 265, 392n; geographic balance sought, 426, 488, 508; and W. Sargent's removal, 501-2; maintains silence on all applications, 530, 687-8; notes on patronage, 601; diplomatic appointments, 619. *See also* New Haven, Conn.

Personal Affairs
suicide of James Hemings, viii, 542-3, 569-70; assembles household staff, 7, 24-5, 31, 66-7, 83, 89-90, 543n; made executor of L. Littlepage, 17, 491; friendship with Franklin, 23; private secretary, 31, 395n; seeks portrait of S. Adams, 115; health of, 119, 133, 216-17; friendship with

INDEX

JEFFERSON, THOMAS (*cont.*)
J. Page, 157-8; orders wine, 165, 226n, 255, 317, 348, 568, 588-9, 723, 756; makes recommendations, 166-7, 303-5, 321-2, 350-1, 377-8, 399-400, 479, 662-3; receives liqueurs and sweetmeats, 282, 283n; receives sculpture, statuary, 292-5, 454n, 588, 689, 741; expense of outfit in Washington, 414; gives Poplar Forest land to sons-in-law, 414-15, 418-20, 503-4, 510, 658, 677-8; receives model of Egyptian pyramid, 426; Madisons reside with, at President's House, 471; sends gifts to grandchildren, 471, 677; strangers ask for money, 475, 724-5; inquires about G. Morris's silver service, 492; lacks free time, 677. *See also* President's House

Political Theories
neutral rights, ix, 86, 90, 241-6, 266, 276, 382, 420; freedom of the press, 67-8n; application of presidential pardons, 84; both parties are republican, 85, 146, 147, 399; function of D.C. commissioners, 130; economy in public expense, 162-3, 217-18, 276-7, 382, 644-5; on entangling foreign alliances, American isolation, 216, 217, 265, 268, 316, 382; states' rights, 259; amending the Constitution regarding elections, 314; term limits for foreign missions, 381; militia preferable to standing army, 628, 639, 643-4, 645; strength of republican government, 708-9

Politics
potential successors to, xi, 286; fears divisions among Republicans, 85, 118, 146, 427, 607; Federalist leaders incurable, isolated, 145, 146-7, 399, 501; anticipates "concert of action" with Congress, 147; absence from Washington criticized, 288, 315; pledges support for Duane, 479; receives newspapers from Federalist printers, 519-20; and rumored removal of federal arms from Springfield, 521, 522n; need to assemble phalanx of talents and virtue, 528-9; supports the rights of aliens, 612-13, 618, 620, 639, 648-9. *See also* Federalists; Republicans

Portraits
by R. Peale, 128; by Stuart, 225, 226n, 282-3, 329; by Polk, 388n

President
assembles cabinet, viii, 528-9; and D.C., ix, 129-30, 167-8, 172-3, 175-6, 217; and departure of R. R. Livingston, ix, 216, 217, 218, 270-1, 276, 314-15; and peace in Europe, ix, 734, 735; and removal of condemned slaves from Va., ix-x, 718-22; communications with heads of departments, x, 571, 576-8, 586, 595-6; and the *Sally,* x, 711, 738-9, 740, 741-3; halts prosecutions under Sedition Act, xi, 480-1, 543-4, 607, 613, 616-17, 640, 647-8, 650, 652, 653-4n, 655-7; relations with Spain, xlv, 392-3, 488, 545; and Geffroy letters, 3-6, 83-4, 87, 89, 90, 156-7, 271-2, 309-10; salary, 11, 12n, 96, 178-9, 225, 226n, 288, 469n, 588n; granting of passports, 13, 31; and warrants drawn on Treasury, 13, 31, 86, 90, 100, 102n, 117, 133, 135n, 169, 216, 218n, 227, 229n, 288, 324, 325n, 329-30, 374-5n, 447n, 469n, 512n, 570-1n, 587-8n, 595-6, 597, 606, 738n; calls for reconciliation and harmony, 64, 85, 145, 146-7, 382, 399, 501, 619, 639; and the *Windsor,* 80-1, 86, 124-5, 158; relations with Great Britain, 80-2, 86, 163; issues pardons, 84, 86n, 109, 158-9, 216n, 261n, 391, 457n; and funding of marine hospitals, 84-5; and naval prizes, 86, 90, 108, 111n, 124-5, 158, 159n; and lighthouses, 91-2, 118n, 159; demands quarterly accounts from collectors, 109n; and Stillman musket contract, 116-17; and the *Hope,* 124, 126, 159-60, 163, 299-301; and Duane's legal trials, 125, 148, 480-1, 543-4, 607, 650n, 652, 653-4n, 655-7; and letters of credence, 125, 126n, 270-1; and Prussia, 126; capture and restoration of the *Berceau,* 145-6; reduces diplomatic establishment, 157, 159n, 382, 507, 519, 644; relations with France, 161, 258-9; and Blicher Olsen's exequatur, 162, 163n; and Barbary affairs, 162-3, 240-1, 265, 474, 588, 642-3; orders navy vessels to Mediterranean, 163,

[789]

INDEX

JEFFERSON, THOMAS (*cont.*)
    Independence; Inaugural Address
    (1801); *Manual of Parliamentary
    Practice. For the Use of the Senate
    of the United States;* New Haven,
    Conn.: TJ's reply to merchants of;
    Notes on the State of Virginia

Jenkins, Elisha, 62
Jenner, Edward: develops smallpox vac-
    cine, vii, 200; *Inquiry,* xlix, 425n,
    698, 699n; sends vaccine matter to
    Waterhouse, 8, 89, 170, 174, 278, 495,
    572; receives gold medal, 231; advises
    on vaccination methods, 369-70; *Ori-
    gin of the Vaccine Inoculation,* 430
Jenny (daughter of Bagwell, TJ's slave),
    35
Jerry (b. 1777; TJ's slave), 35
Jerusalem, 478
Jessie (brigantine), 82n
João, Prince Regent of Portugal: letter
    to, 441-2; consul general of, 137, 267;
    family, 441-2; identified, 442n; letters
    to, from cited, 442n
Joe. *See* Fossett, Joseph (1780-1858,
    Joe, TJ's slave)
John (b, 1753, TJ's slave), 34
John (b. 1785, Bedford John, TJ's
    slave), 34
John Adams (U.S. frigate), 668
Johnny (Delaware Indian), 599-600
Johns, Kensey, 428
Johnson, Charles, 460
Johnson, Joshua, 682
Johnson, Thomas de Mattos: recom-
    mended, appointed collector, 53, 54,
    85, 226, 229n, 288; settlement of pre-
    decessor's accounts, 374n
Johnston, Charles, 757
Johnston, Peter, 501
Johnston, Samuel, 46n, 459
Jones, Edward (N.C.), 469n
Jones, Edward (Treasury clerk), 630n,
    703, 706n
Jones, Evan, 549-50, 560n
Jones, Meriwether: letter from cited,
    112n; recommends aspirants for office,
    112n; as reference, 214; TJ's subscrip-
    tion to the *Examiner,* 233
Jones, Thomas, 185, 186n
Jones, Walter, 267
Jones, William (mariner), 111n
Jones, William (Pa.): recommends aspi-
    rants to office, 65; advises on appoint-
    ments, 100-1, 102n; as reference,

440n, 609, 705n; letter from cited,
    756
Jordan, Melatiah, 726
Jordon, John, 83n
Joucherez, A., 758
Jouett, John, Jr., 14n
*Journal of Andrew Ellicott, Late Com-
    missioner on Behalf of the United
    States* (Andrew Ellicott), 107n
Judiciary Act (1801), 27, 620
Julien, Honoré, 759
juries, 620, 635, 639, 648
"Juris Consultus" (pseudonym), 480-1,
    607n

Kant, Immanuel, 708
Karankawa Indians, 561n
Kelsall, John, 547, 548n
Kemp, John: letter from cited, 749
Kentucky: marshal for, 14n, 155n;
    Washington Co., 21; Republicans in,
    74-5; descriptions of, 75; immigrants
    to, 75, 78n, 183n, 190n, 363n, 446n;
    seeks Indian cessions, 75-7; postal
    service in, 77-8; lands in, claimed by
    Indians, 78-9n; Eddyville, 78n; Big
    Bone Lick, 121; attorneys, 155; elec-
    tions in, 155; supervisor for, 170n;
    newspapers, 392n; and smallpox vac-
    cination, 472, 523; circuit court cases
    in, 657, 658n
Keppel, Augustus, 293, 294n
Ker, David: letter from, 376-7; seeks ap-
    pointment, 376-7; identified, 376-7n
Kerr, John R., 342, 359-60, 454
Kerr, Sarah (Sally) Henderson, xlvii,
    342, 343n, 359-60, 380n, 413n, 581n
Kerr (Ker), James (Philadelphia), 440n
Kersey, William, 551, 560n
Keteltas, Abraham, 337
Keteltas, William: letters from, 345-6,
    518-19; as reference, 10; seeks ap-
    pointment, 337-8, 345-6; recommends
    T. Bailey, 518-19
Key, John, 757
Key, Joshua: letters to, from cited, 752
Kilgore, Charles, 229n
Killen, William, Jr.: letter from cited,
    753
Kilty, Charles, 387, 388n
Kimball, Hazen, 370, 371n, 378, 379n,
    703
Kin (King), Mathias: letter from, 351-2;
    forwards letter, requests seeds, 351-2;
    identified, 351-2n

Kindred, Edward, 137n
Kindred, Thomas, 137
kinepox. *See* smallpox
King, Mr. (plasterer), 49-51, 95
King, Nicholas: letter from, 657; as surveyor, 349n; sends drawing to TJ, 657
King, Robert, Sr., 349
King, Rufus: minister to Great Britain, 138-9, 178n; and blockade of French ports, 280, 281n; secretary to, 313n; negotiates settlement of British debt claims, 506-7, 519, 545, 615, 628, 630, 635n, 660
King's College, 661n
Kirby, Ephraim: letters from, 33, 484-6, 597-9; forwards "Brutus" essay, 33; as reference, 71; recommends aspirants for office, 484-6; reports abuse of postal service by Federalists, 597-9
Kirby, William: removal of, 53, 89, 92, 119, 126; appointment of, 186n
Kittera, John Wilkes, 263n
Knox, Henry, 3, 89, 195n, 567n, 614, 663n
Knox, Samuel, 387-8
Koasati Indians, 561n
Kosciuszko, Tadeusz, 50n

Lacci, Dr., 199
Ladd, John G.: letter to, 740; letter from, 746; receives shipments for TJ, 734, 740, 746; identified, 740n
Ladies Association of Philadelphia, 23n
Lafayette, Marie Adrienne Françoise de Noailles, Marquise de, 69n, 201
Lafayette, Marie Joseph Paul Yves Roch Gilbert du Motier, Marquis de: and Poirey, 69n, 201; letter from cited, 189n; patron of J. E. Caldwell, 253n; as reference, 344n
La Forest, Antoine René Charles Mathurin de, 161, 292, 396, 397, 535
Laird, John, 190-1
La Luzerne, Anne César, Chevalier de, 125, 126n
Lamb, John: letter from cited, 754
Lancaster Journal, 263n
Landais, Philip: claim on War Department, 215-16; letters from cited, 215n, 753
land speculation, 352n, 402n, 560n, 565, 568n
Lane, Samuel, 717n
Langdon, John: advises on appointments, 54, 56n, 85, 601, 675n; offered,

declines secretaryship of the navy, 78; presents L'Enfant's petition, 567n; as bank president, 653n; as reference, 653n; as superintendent of navy yard, 654; letter from cited, 754
Langdon, Woodbury, 601
Laocoon (sculpture), 538, 539n
La Rochefoucauld, Alexandrine Charlotte Sophie de Rohan-Chabot, Duchesse de, 383, 461, 465n
La Rochefoucauld d'Enville, Louis Alexandre, Duc de La Roche-Guyon et de, 378
La Salle, Robert de Cavelier, Sieur de, 561n
Latimer, George: letter from, 741; removal of, sought, 57n, 725-6; as Federalist partisan, 102n; collector at Philadelphia, 404; and the *Harmony*, 410-11; receives sculpture for TJ, 741; identified, 741n
Latrobe, Benjamin Henry, 412n, 559-60n, 717n
Lavinia (Randolph slave), 34
law: and neutral rights, 37-9, 110, 241-6, 609-10; and smallpox inoculation, 47; court fee bills, 215, 216n; revenue, 261-2; intestate estates, 343n; dower rights, 362-4, 454, 455n, 581n; guardianships, 455n; *nolle prosequi,* 480-1, 543-4, 607n, 617, 640, 650, 653n; books, 489; naturalization, 612-13, 618, 620-1, 639, 648-9; inconsistent application of, 620; quarantine, 624n; common law, 655; bankruptcy, 689
Law, Thomas, 190, 191n, 417n
Lawrence, James, 422n
Lawson, Alexander, 9
Lazaria (b. 1791, TJ's slave), 35
Leach, Thomas, Jr., 457
Leake, John G., 46n
Lear, Tobias: letter from, 322-3; commission refused by Toussaint, 125, 126n; forwards liqueurs and sweetmeats to TJ, 283n, 437n; and Dandridge, 312-13, 322; and relocation of seat of government on Saint-Domingue, 322-3
Leclerc, Victoire Emmanuel, 398n, 528, 539n
Ledyard, Isaac: letter from, 233-4; recommends M. L. Davis, 233-4; forwards pamphlet, 234n; letter from cited, 234n, 750
Ledyard, John, 234n

London Gazette, 715n
Longbothom, B. T.: letter from, 717-18; seeks TJ's acquaintance, 717-18; identified, 718n; *Treatise on Dentistry,* 718n
Long Island, battle of, 338n
longitude, 411-12, 549n
L'Orient (Lorient), France, 249, 371
Lorimier, Louis, 599-600
Louis Ferdinand (of Prussia), 293
Louis I, King of Etruria, 694-5
Louisiana: ceded to France by Spain, 18, 228, 340, 396, 507, 509, 527, 535, 540, 669-70, 695n; boundary of, 106; fossils found in, 121-2, 124n; immigration to, 144n; and American Revolution, 328n; C. Pinckney's instructions regarding, 340; French plans to colonize, 527, 535; descriptions of, 553-5; Indians in, 554-5, 561n; U.S. occupation of, urged, 669-70; settlement of emancipated slaves in, 669; legal system, 670n; U.S. acquisition of, 670n
Louis of Parma, 436n, 695n
Louis XIV, King of France, 81
Louis XVIII, King of France, 714, 715n
Louvre (Paris), 538, 539n
Lowndes, Francis, 417n
Lowry, Thomas, 101, 469n
Loyalists. *See* American Revolution
Lucas, John B. C., 184
lucerne (alfalfa), 326
Ludlow, Daniel: letter from cited, 143-4n, 750; recommends M. L. Davis, 143-4n; family of, 180n; and grounding of the *Boston,* 446
Lufborough, Nathan, 726n
lumber, 527
Lunéville, Treaty of, 192, 295, 296n, 297n, 539n
lupine, 326
Lyman, Cornelius, 756
Lyman, William, 511, 754
Lynchburg, Va., 487, 488n
Lyon, James: letter from, 487-8; plan for establishing country newspapers, 487-8
Lyon, Matthew: letter from, 74-9; and election of 1800, 33n; advises on Indian affairs, 74-9; moves to Ky., 78n
Lyons, Peter: letter to, 726-7; debt to Edmund Randolph, 380-1, 383n; and settlement of Wayles estate, 726-7; identified, 727n

McCall, Archibald, 46n
McClary (McCleary), Michael, 601n
McClenachan, Blair, 57n
McComb, John, Jr., 91-2
MacCreery, William, 495n
McDonogh, Thomas, 111n
McDowell, James, 525
McDowell, Sarah Preston, 525
McGuire, William, 551, 560n
McHenry, James, 10n, 195, 445n
McHoy, Mr., 559
Mackay, Adam, 367, 368n
McKean, Thomas: letter from, 64-6; Irujo's father-in-law, xlvi, 393; and Pa. politics, 64; advises on appointments, 64-6; election of, 184; patronage practices, 202; Republican support for, 424; McKeanites, 553; as reference, 609, 705n
McKee, John (mariner), 134n
McKeen, Levi: letters from, 323-4, 331-3; recommends Bailey, 323-4, 331-3; identified, 324n
Mackel, Samuel, 759
McKnight, Washington, 406, 407n
McLane, Allen, 693
Maclure, Alexander: forwards letter and books to TJ, 708n; letter from cited, 750
McLure, Brydie & Co., 28
Maclure, William: letter from, 706-8; observations on European agriculture and economy, 706-8; letter from cited, 708n; sends pamphlets to TJ, 708n
McLurg, James, 46n
McMillan, William, 392n
McNeill, Daniel, 56n, 187, 268n, 291, 446-7, 488, 661
Macon, Nathaniel: letter from, 347; and J. P. Williams, 347; letter from cited, 347n, 750; recommends aspirants for office, 467, 468n; and Wilmington collectorship, 496-7
McPherson, William, 102n
McRee, Griffith J., 132, 134n, 159n, 389, 390n, 468n
Maddux, John W.: letter from, 21; declares support for TJ, 21
Madeira: consul at, 148, 154, 754; to be restored to Portugal, 714. *See also* wine
Madison, Dolley Payne Todd: visits Monticello, 79, 81, 374n; returns to Washington, 389; resides at President's House, 471; invited to dine with TJ, 677

INDEX

Manhattan Company, 62, 143

Manual of Parliamentary Practice. For the Use of the Senate of the United States (Thomas Jefferson), 501

manufacturing: of paper, 214; cotton, 451; muskets, 514n, 599-600, 662-3; and principle of interchangeable parts, 514n, 600n, 662-3; one of four pillars of prosperity, 647; hemp, 746n; mustard, 746n

manure, 247

maps: of southwestern U.S., 106-7, 423-4, 548-9; of Federal District, 564, 568n

marble: Carrara, 293-4, 482-3

March, John: account with TJ, 355-6, 418; identified, 356n

Marchant, Elihu, 301-2

Marchant, Sarah Norton, 301, 302n

Maria I, Queen of Portugal, 442n

Maria Theresa, Archduchess of Austria, 297n

Marie Antoinette, Queen of France, 297n

Marines, U.S.: barracks for, 167-8, 172-3, 187, 211, 217, 417-18, 512; officers' commissions, 218n; resignations from, 512-13; appropriations for, 637

Marks, Anna Scott Jefferson (Mrs. Hastings Marks, TJ's sister): TJ's affection for, 419; letter to cited, 752

Marks, Peter S., 551, 560n

Marseilles, France, 59, 251, 494

Marsh, Amos: letter to, 708-9; letter from, 574-5; congratulatory address from, 574-5; identified, 575n; letter from cited, 575n, 751; thanked by TJ, 708-9

Marsh, Daniel, 118n, 693

Marshall, Andrew: letter from, 442-4; criticizes St. Clair, 442-4; identified, 444n

Marshall, John, 46n, 493, 494n

Martin, Thomas, 135n, 159n, 263n

Martinique, W.I., 160n, 395

Mary (ship), 60n

Maryland: elections in, 22, 147, 169, 223, 269, 273, 303, 324, 529, 684, 686n; Harford Co., 22; Charles Co., 83n; legislature, 97-8, 99-100n, 384; loan to D.C. commissioners, 97-100, 113, 129-30, 175-6, 371-3; Bladensburg, 109n; Frederick, 168, 387, 388n; Calvert Co., 223; Frederick Co., 223; Prince George's Co., 223, 289-90, 444; ferries, 225, 328; Havre de Grace, 225, 270, 328; Oldtown, 228n; roads in, 270; smallpox vaccination in, 289-90; courts, 335-6, 452n; U.S. district court, 336; Portuguese vice consul in, 349n; Nottingham collectorship, 364, 711, 738, 743n; medical societies, 384n; presidential electors, 384n; inspectors of revenue in, 388n; Presbyterians in, 388n; maps of, 412n; too many federal appointees from, 426, 508; Montgomery Co., 444, 717n; taxes in, 444; Queen Anne's Co., 451, 452n; registers of wills, 451, 452n; Anne Arundel Co., 499; census in, 531, 532n; French consul for, 562n; circuit court cases in, 658n; agriculture, 706; smuggling, 711; Brookeville, 717n; surveyors, 717n; U.S. attorney for, 739, 742-3n; admiralty court, 743n. *See also* Baltimore, Md.; Federalists; Republicans

Maryland (U.S. sloop): ordered to give passage to T. Paine, 125, 126n; returns to U.S., 173, 174n, 175n, 176, 187n, 188, 189, 216, 263, 268, 394, 445n, 587n

Mason, Mr. (Georgetown, D.C.), 289-90

Mason, George, 224n, 387n

Mason, John (Georgetown merchant), 46n, 191, 223-4, 290

Mason, John Thomson: letters from, 223-4, 387-8, 444; as bank director, 136n, 191n; as attorney, 144; Notes on Candidates for Bank Director, 190-1; recommends aspirants for office, 223-4, 290, 387-8; as reference, 386; letter from cited, 388n, 750; sends tax estimates, 444

Mason, Mary Elizabeth Armistead, 519, 520n

Mason, Mary Thomson, 387n

Mason, Stevens Thomson: letter to, 519-20; and S.C. appointments, 12, 13-14n, 31, 53; C. Pinckney sends regards to, 398, 538; TJ sends newspapers, foreign news to, 519-20; and Miss. Terr., 553; and W. P. Gardner, 700

Mason, Thomson, 224n

masons. *See* Freemasons

Massac: customs district, 391-2

Massac, Fort (Illinois), 77, 560n

Massachusetts: union of clergy and Federalists in, 4; Plymouth collectorship, 53, 56n, 221-3; Marblehead

INDEX

Massachusetts (*cont.*)
collectorship, 108, 587n; roads in, 155; U.S. attorney for, 160, 687n; courts, 160n, 299, 689; privateers from, 160n; heat wave in, 198; kinepox reported in, 199, 430; Massachusetts Medical Society, 199; paper manufacturing in, 214; smuggling in, 222; Dedham, 300, 301n; Martha's Vineyard, 302n; postmasters, 302n; elections in, 305, 498; newspapers, 305-6; Worcester, 305-6; Salem and Beverly collectorship, 315-16, 352, 498; legislature, 498; attorneys in, 516, 517n; Congregationalists in, 516, 517n; Marblehead, 516; Brookfield, 520-1; Springfield armory, 521, 522n; Stockbridge, 521, 522n; circuit court cases in, 658; hospitals, 681n; smallpox vaccination in, 681n; American Revolution in, 686; bankruptcy laws in, 689. *See also* Boston; Federalists; Republicans

Massachusetts Spy (Worcester), 147n, 306n

Massena, André, 528

Masten, John, 435n

mastodon: C. W. Peale's painting of exhumation of, xlviii-xlix, 382 (illus.); remains discovered in Hudson Valley, 107, 430-6, 699

Matagorda Bay, 555, 561n

mathematics: geometric progressions, xi, 531-3, 545, 643; logarithms, 531-3, 625

Mathews, Mr. (Nassau attorney), 547

Matilda (slave of Randolph Lewis), 346n

Matlock, Timothy: letter from, 164-5; reports on Federalists in Pa., 164-5; identified, 165n

mattresses, 205

Maurepas, Lake, 106

Maximilian Franz, Elector of Cologne, 295, 296-7n

Maxwell, Robert: letter to, 30; removed as postmaster, 30

Mazzei, Philip: letters from, 353-4, 666-8, 694-5; exchanges seeds, plants with TJ, 353-4, 666, 667; finances of, 666-8; prints Italian translation of inaugural address, 666-7; seeks U.S. position in Italy, 666-7; reports arrival of king of Etruria, 694-5

Mease, James: letter from, 341-2; seeks appointment, 341-2

medals, 231, 599, 681, 683n, 702

Medical and Chirurgical Faculty of the State of Maryland, 384n

medicine: rheumatism, 52n, 334; mental illness, 74, 170n, 195, 406, 407n, 442n, 502-3; seasoning, 75, 77, 350, 357; hygiene, 77; surgeons, 93, 183n, 358n; medical schools, education, 103n, 200, 278n, 279n, 490, 491n, 531n, 605, 698; physicians, 103n, 119n, 198-9, 252n, 278n, 279n, 289n, 369, 592n, 684-5; anatomists, 183n; eyesight, 197, 383-4; medical societies, 199, 384n; chicken pox, 200, 578; diarrhea, 297; autumnal diseases, 318; ruptures, 334; importation, cost of drugs, 341; head inflammation, 346n; strokes, 348; fraud, unethical behavior by physicians, 369; deafness, 382; fevers, 433; childbirth, 498; influenza, 500; invalids, 505; midwives, 510, 511n; gout, 513, 523; worms, 590; epilepsy, 694-5; dentists, 718n. *See also* hospitals; smallpox; whooping cough; yellow fever

Mediterranean Sea: Mediterranean passes, 13, 14n, 31; British navy bases in, 74; navy squadron sent to, 74, 108-9, 163, 187, 188n, 211, 240, 277, 422, 638-9, 663-4; squadron arrives at, 219, 228, 303, 630-1, 638; U.S. trade in, 341-2, 593-5, 630-1, 638-9, 642, 664; Britain to withdraw from, 398n, 714

Meeks, Richard, 383n

Meeks, William, 383n

Meigs, Return Jonathan, 403, 404n, 456, 473-4, 748n

Melinda (b. 1787, Eppes slave), 34

Mello e Castro, João de Almeida de, 442n

"Memorandum on the Vaccine Disease" (Samuel L. Mitchill), 430

Menou, Jacques François de Boussay, Baron de, 296, 297n

Mercer, Mr., 11

Mercer, John (Va.): letter from cited, 755

Mercer, John F.: letter to, 529-30; letter from, 499; invites TJ and Madison to visit, 499, 529-30

Mercer, Sophia Sprigg, 499, 530

Mercury and New-England Palladium (Boston), 146-7, 519, 521, 598

Meredith, Margaret Cadwalader, 172

Meredith, Samuel: letter to, 210; letter from, 172; warrants issued on, 56n,

[798]

169n; resigns as treasurer of the U.S., 169, 172, 209-10, 216, 223, 253, 281-2, 303, 307, 321, 330, 364, 530, 571-2; identified, 172n; letter to cited, 572n, 751; commission on Seneca annuity, 696-8

Merrick, Pliny, 521

Merry, Anthony, 295, 297n

"Metempsychosis Doctrine, in a Limited Sense, Defended" (Isaac Story), 516-17

Mexican Association, 670n

Mexico, 122, 561n, 717n

Michaux, François André, 352n

Michilimackinac: collection district, 13, 31

microscopes, 198

Middleton, James R., 218n

Mifflin, Jonathan, 705n

militia: fines for non-service, 246; preferable to standing armies, 645

milk, 757, 759

Milledge, John: advises on appointments, 53, 85, 133, 226, 229n, 287-8, 314, 570, 580; recommends E. Clark, Jr., 144n

Miller, Henry, 263n

Miller, John, Jr., 46n

Miller, Lillian B., xlviii

Miller, William: commissioner of the revenue, 91, 92n, 101, 117, 133, 135n, 159n, 584n

mills: Warren, 22n; Somerville's, 568; Poindexter's, 659. *See also* Henderson lands

Mills, Jared, 409n

Millspaw, Peter, 435n

Milton, Va.: creation of, xlvii; and Henderson lands, xlvii, 343n, 360-1, 363n, 379, 380n, 581n, 743; merchants, 28; roads to, from, 36; post office, 41, 173, 510; shipments received at, 171, 210, 361n; tobacco sent from, 232; whooping cough in, 373; demand for firewood in, 580

mineralogy, 212

Minor, John, Jr.: letter from cited, 755

Minorca, 199, 714

Mint, U.S.: coining process at, 15; treasurer of, 135n, 375n, 597n; salaries of officers, 375n; applications for appointment in, 416n; rumored to be discontinued, 530; copper for, 587n, 596-7; expense of, 628; establishment of, 682

mirrors: ordered by TJ, 12, 96

Mississippi River: as transportation system, 77; Spanish settlements along, 106; Dunbar studies, 121; maps of, 423; defense of, 562n; French interest in, 670

Mississippi Territory: relations with Spain, 17-18; politics, 18, 732-3; descriptions of, 121, 550; U.S. attorney for, 149n, 162; governor of, 154; collection of internal revenues in, 264; immigrants to, 376, 377n; salaries in, 376; courts, 376-7, 550-1, 552, 560n, 734n; trade with New Orleans, 549-50; military in, 550-2, 550-3, 734n; Adams Co., 553, 561n; attorney general, 553; election of 1800 in, 553; Federalists in, 553; Republicans in, 553; sheriffs, 553, 561n; code of laws, 733; legislature, 733-4. *See also* Adams, Fort; Claiborne, William C. C.; Natchez

Missouri River, 553-4

Mitchell, John (Georgetown): letters from cited, 750

Mitchell, Nathaniel, 428

Mitchill, Samuel Latham: and New York City Republicans, 235n; "Memorandum on the Vaccine Disease," 430; and New York Mineralogical Society, 716; letter from cited, 753

Mobile, W. Fla., 106, 557, 561n

molasses, 134n

Molly (servant), 178

Molly (ship), 594-5

Moniteur (Paris), 527

Monitor (Litchfield, Conn.), 519-20

Monroe, James: letters to, 662-3, 718-22; letters from, 354-5, 683; and removal of condemned slaves, ix-x, 683, 712, 718-22; recommends aspirants for office, 59, 354-5, 478, 496; travels between Albemarle and Richmond, 81, 110-11; and Hay, 136n; and I. C. Barnet, 249-50, 252-3n; *View*, 253n; applications to, for appointment, 298-9n; Albemarle Co. property, 309; letters from cited, 355n, 750; as reference, 356, 357n; and J. H. Purviance, 445n, 683; secretaries for, 445n; advises on appointments, 494n; service in the American Revolution, 502; TJ recommends Whitney to, 662-3

Monroe, John: letter from, 727-8; seeks loan to open tavern, 727-8

Monticello: M. L. Davis visits, vii, 272-3, 286, 287, 289n, 307, 311, 314, 316;

INDEX

Natchez, 76, 196n, 308n, 553, 558, 560n, 732

National Aegis (Worcester), 306, 521-2

National Gazette (Philadelphia), 533n

National Intelligencer (Washington): prints TJ's reply to New Haven merchants, 46n; prints list of Bank of the U.S. branch directors, 136n; reports news from overseas, 189n, 219n, 589n, 715n; reports on smallpox vaccination, 430, 472

National Magazine, or Cabinet of the United States (Georgetown), 487-8

Natural Bridge, Va., 179, 180n

natural history, 435, 436n

naturalization, 612-13, 618, 620-1, 639, 648-9, 671n

Nautical Almanac and Astronomical Ephemeris, 355, 356n

naval stores, 535

Navy, U.S.: warrants drawn on Treasury by, 14n, 31, 90-1, 101n, 104, 218n, 324, 325n, 375n, 447n, 512n, 570n, 711n; chief clerk of, 60n, 447n, 703; British open Mediterranean bases to, 74, 663; sends squadrons to Mediterranean, 74, 108-9, 187, 188n, 219, 240, 277, 303, 422, 630-1, 638-9, 642, 645-6, 663-4, 668; search for secretary, 78; abuses, improprieties in, 83-4, 89; applications for commissions, 93, 746, 754; warehouses for, 187n; arsenals and magazines, 217-18, 512n; contract with J. Lloyd, 277; officers' commissions and warrants, 324, 325n, 422-3n, 668n; inspectors of naval stores, 389; galleys, 488; reduction of, 488, 624n, 628, 632, 634, 639, 640-1n, 644, 646, 661n; need to strengthen, 509-10; courts-martial in, 513n; and *Warren* mission to Veracruz, 534; yellow fever in, 534; appointment of navy agents, 601n; accountant of, 628-9, 636, 703; navy yards, 634, 637, 641n, 646; appropriations and expenditures for, 637, 693; clothing, 637; docks and wharves, 637, 641n; medical expenses, 637; pay for navy, 637; construction of 74-gun ships, 639, 640-1, 646, 651; expense of maintaining frigates in service, 641n; and American Revolution, 654, 674-6; arrangement of, for 1802, 668; vessels laid up, 668; letters from cited, 668n, 751, 754, 755, 756; six percent stocks, 672-3; naval architecture,

698-9, 722; timber for, 698-9, 730. *See also* Marines, U.S.; Peace Establishment Act (1801); Smith, Robert

Neail, James: letter from cited, 754

Ned. *See* Gillette, Edward (b. 1760, Ned, TJ's slave)

Nelson, Horatio, 295, 297n, 725n

Nelson, John, 226

Nelson, Stephen S.: letter from, 407-9; supports religious liberty, 407-9; identified, 409n

Netherlands: immigrants from, 10; U.S. debt to, 14n, 54, 101n, 227-8, 229n, 276, 288n, 330n, 374n, 375n, 469n, 570-1n, 588n, 597n, 623, 672, 731, 738n; and neutral rights, 81, 111n; prisoners of war, 125; bills of exchange on, 229n, 288n, 330n, 374n, 375n, 469n, 570-1n, 588n, 597n, 738n; U.S. treaty of amity and commerce with, 244, 245n; descriptions of, 295; and slave trade, 561n; agriculture in, 707; France to acquire, 714. *See also* Amsterdam; Batavian Republic

Neue Philadelphische Correspondenz, 80n

neutrality, league of armed, 31, 32n, 191-2

neutral rights: TJ's opinion on, ix, 81, 124-5, 241-6, 609-10, 641-2; naval prizes in neutral ports, 37-9, 56, 57n, 79, 81, 86, 90, 108, 110-11, 124-5, 132-3, 134n, 153-4, 158, 247; privateers in neutral ports, 56, 57n, 79-80; R. R. Livingston's opinion on, 393-4; need strong navy to protect, 509-10; works on, 523-4, 609-10; misrepresenting foreign vessels as American-owned, 621n, 649

Neutral Rights; or, An Impartial Examination of the Right of Search of Neutral Vessels Under Convoy (J. F. W. Schlegel), 81, 82n

Neville, John, 184

New, Anthony, 183

New and Universal Gazetteer; or, Modern Geographical Dictionary (Joseph T. Scott), 267

New Calabar, 556, 561n

New England: Republicans in, 4; religion in, 78; kinepox reported in, 199; Federalists in, 520-1; newspapers in, 521-2; subordinated to southern, Virginia interests, 522n; importance of commerce to, 652

Newfoundland, 199

INDEX

New Hampshire: union of clergy and Federalists in, 4; Concord, 37n; newspapers, 37n; postmasters, 37n; physicians, 369; smallpox vaccination in, 369; marshal for, 601; supervisor, 601, 652-3, 655; banks, 652-3; Sons of Liberty in, 654n; U.S. attorney for, 655n; circuit court cases in, 658. *See also* Federalists; Portsmouth, N.H.; Republicans

New Hampshire Bank, 652-3

New Haven, Conn.: TJ's reply to merchants of, ix, 4, 6n, 31, 33n, 42-3, 54-5, 56n, 57n, 64, 69-70, 79, 80, 80n, 85, 88, 100, 118, 138, 146, 169, 234, 272, 459, 460n, 574; Remonstrance of the Merchants of, 4-5, 6n, 42-3, 80n, 146, 459, 460n, 478

New Jersey: New Brunswick surveyorship, 84, 86n, 107, 157, 226; marshal for, 101, 102n, 117, 162; Trenton, 115-16; Perth Amboy collectorship, 118n, 693; need for removals in, 147; French consul for, 161n; Federalists in, 226, 365, 591n; Republicans in, 226, 365, 590-1; Elizabeth, 248, 252n, 253n; and American Revolution, 249; physicians, 252n; Presbyterians in, 253n, 499n; elections in, 365, 591; Burlington Co., 365n; postmasters, 365n; shipbuilding, 365n; Tuckerton, 365n; Sandy Hook, 448n, 738; census in, 469n; attorney general, 591n; governor, 591n; circuit court cases in, 658. *See also* Little Egg Harbor, N.J.

New Jersey, College of (Princeton): graduates of, 103n, 516, 517n, 575n, 662n; president of, 497, 499n

New London, Conn.: Falkner Island lighthouse, 91-2; carpenters, 92n; Fort Trumbull, 592n

Newman, John: forwards pamphlets, 86n; letter from cited, 86n, 749; chief clerk of the War Department, 325n

Newman, Morris, 422n

Newman, Timothy, 534n

Newman, William (midshipman), 325n

New Orleans: consul at, 18, 327-8, 549-50; and U.S.-Spanish relations, 18, 106-7, 550; trade of, 549-50

Newport, R.I.: coffeehouses, 3; harbor defenses, 3-4, 6n, 83-4, 87, 88, 90, 157, 195, 271-2, 309; collector at, 4, 6n; TJ and Washington visit, 5, 6n; jewelers, 5n, 156; watchmakers, 5n;

156; merchants, 6n, 593-5; postmaster, 156-7; insurance companies, 593-5

Newport Insurance Company, 593-5

newspapers: Federalist, viii, 4, 56n, 80, 126n, 146-7, 263n, 265, 288, 305-6, 324n, 338, 381-2, 399, 460n, 480-1, 497, 519-20, 521-2, 598, 705n; Republican, 37n, 265, 306, 356n, 392n, 480, 521-2, 598, 703; delivery of, 41; TJ urged to disseminate information through, 55, 86; British gather information from, 57n; German, in Pa., 79, 80n; unreliability of, 81, 86, 90, 260; European, 189; seek printing contracts, 265, 392n; printing presses, 611n; postage on, 616, 643, 649-50n, 651; British, 715

Newsum, William: recommended by T. Newton, 568; letter from cited, 568n, 756

Newton, Isaac, 123, 701

Newton, Thomas: letters to, 89, 317, 588-9, 734; letters from, 126-7, 127, 347-8, 350, 357-8, 453-4, 568, 689-90; advises on appointments, 86n, 89, 126-7, 317, 347-8, 350, 449; reseals letter to TJ, 127; supplies wine to TJ, 348, 568, 588-9; sends news, observations from Norfolk, 357-8; forwards plants and curiosities, 453-4, 568, 588, 689; TJ orders cider from, 453-4, 588, 689-90, 734, 740; introduces W. Newsum, 568

Newton, Thomas, Jr., 169, 226

New York: U.S. attorney for, 33n; Sag Harbor collectorship, 52; supervisor, 56n, 101, 102n, 204, 323-4, 332; comptroller, 62; attorneys, 71, 337; lighthouses, 92n; need for removals in, 147; French consul for, 161n; Cayuga collectorship, 227, 314; elections in, 233, 234n, 286-7, 324n, 332; boundary, 249, 253n; Council of Appointment, 273, 275n, 337-8; legislature, 275n, 284n, 332; marshals for, 275n; commissioner of loans, 283-4, 323-4, 332-3, 345, 518; governors, 284n; Clintonians, 287; physicians, 289n; secretary of state, 289n; merchants, 324n; postmasters, 324n; Poughkeepsie, 324n; Quakers in, 324n; agriculture in, 326; Dutchess Co., 331-3; courts, 337-8, 518; American Revolution in, 337n; and Indian affairs, 434, 695-8; debt to U.S.,

INDEX

448n; land speculation in, 568n; circuit court cases in, 658; weights and measures in, 679. *See also* Federalists; Republicans

New York (U.S. frigate), 668

New York City: naval officer at, vii, 62, 63n, 100, 143, 204, 233-4, 234-5, 236-7, 238, 272-5, 291-2, 316, 323-4, 331-3, 481n; trade of, 28, 550; as center of finance, 54; merchants, 62-3, 96, 238n, 249, 291-2, 481n, 548n; architects, 92n; city hall, 92n; collector at, 100, 159, 236-7, 275n, 291, 713-14, 755; physicians, 103n; lighthouses, 135n, 159, 738; publishing, 152n; banks, 229n, 375n, 602-4; custom house, 235-7, 481n; surveyor at, 235-7; breweries, 235n; elections in, 235n; Republicans in, 235n, 236-7, 238, 272-5, 284n; Federalists in, 236-7, 238; fraudulent ship registers at, 236-8; harbor defenses, 238, 447-8, 688; Governor's Island, 238n; Democratic Society, 275n; mayors, 284n, 544n; political influence of, 285-6; council, 568n; post office, 572n; revenue cutter at, 596n; growth of, 631; navy yard at, 641n

New-York Evening Post, 460n

New York Mineralogical Society, 716

New-York Missionary Magazine, and Repository of Religious Intelligence, 152n

Nicholas, John, Jr. (clerk of Albemarle County Court), 744n

Nicholas, Philip Norborne, 93-4, 112

Nicholas, Wilson Cary: letters to, 21-2, 92, 506-7; letters from, 112, 525; sells plantations, property, 21, 22n; recommends overseer to TJ, 21-2, 525; letter from cited, 22n, 749; advises on appointments, 86n, 92, 112, 525; as reference, 356; C. Pinckney sends regards to, 398, 538; as congressman, 455n; TJ sends copy of ratified convention, foreign news to, 506-7

Nicholson, James, 235n, 283-4

Nicholson, James Witter, 170n

Nicholson, John, 113n, 384, 401, 402n

Nicholson, Joseph H., 452

Nicholson, Maria, 168, 170n

Nicholson, Samuel, 488

Niemcewicz, Julian Ursin: forwards letter from L. Littlepage, 712n; letter from cited, 712n, 751

Niger River, 561n

Nixon, Jacob: letter from, 93; seeks appointment, 93; identified, 93n

Nolan, Philip, 122, 124n

Nones, Benjamin: letter from, 608-9; seeks appointment, 608-9

Norfolk, Va.: marine hospital, 53, 108, 219-21, 357-8, 449; aldermen, 81n; physicians, 93n; packet service to, from, 95, 453, 454n, 689-90; climate, 127, 453; trade of, 127; common council, 127n; smallpox vaccination in, 312; collector at, 348; health of, 350, 357, 453; Irish in, 350, 357; attorneys, 355n; banks, 355n, 602-4; Republicans in, 355n; courthouse, 357; population, 357; prisons, 357; revenue cutter at, 596n; navy yard at, 641n; bottlers, 689

Norman's ford (Rappahannock River), 568

Norris, Mr., 453

Norris, Kezia: letter to, 475; letter from, 471; and plan for charity school, 471, 475

North America, Bank of, 101, 102n, 172n, 702

North Carolina: collection of internal revenues in, 54; attorneys, 71, 662n; New Bern, 71; Freemasons in, 71n; migrants to Ky. from, 75; western land claims, 76; lighthouses, 92n; and camels, 105n; Republicans in, 145, 389-90; census, 288n; Presbyterians in, 376n; Lumberton, 377n; elections in, 389-90; Federalists in, 389-90; Brunswick Co., 390; claim on U.S., 447n; marshal for, 459, 460n; opposition to Jay Treaty in, 459, 461n; Edenton, 459-61; Albemarle Sound, 460n; American Revolution in, 460n; galleys in, 488n; revenue inspectors in, 655n; circuit court cases in, 658; weights and measures in, 679; Bertie Co., 679n; legislature, 679n; and ratification of the U.S. Constitution, 679n; physicians, 685n. *See also* Wilmington, N.C.

North Carolina, University of, 377n

Northwest Territory: supervisor for, 169, 170n; collection of internal revenues in, 170n, 264; receiver of public monies, 170n, 227, 392n; register of land office, 170n, 227, 229n; revenue inspectors, 227, 229n; Erie

[803]

INDEX

Randolph, Anne Cary (TJ's granddaughter): health of, vii, 589, 590,
677, 690-1, 735, 744; TJ's affection
for, 415, 472, 678, 735; TJ sends gifts
to, 471, 677; affection for TJ, 691

Randolph, Cornelia Jefferson (TJ's
granddaughter): health of, vii, 579,
589, 590, 677, 690-1, 735, 744; vaccinated, 34; TJ's affection for, 415, 472,
678, 735; affection for TJ, 691

Randolph, David Meade: letter from,
279-80; and census of 1800, 49; recommends J. Gregorie, 279-80; letter
from cited, 280n, 749; letter to cited,
280n, 753

Randolph, Edmund: as attorney general,
160n, 614; as reference, 214; letters
from cited, 214n, 753, 755; and
Short's salary, 380, 383n, 463; letters
to cited, 753, 755, 756

Randolph, Ellen Wayles, II (TJ's granddaughter): letter to, 734-5; letter
from, 589; asks TJ for books, vii, 589,
677, 734-5; health of, vii, 579, 590,
677, 690-1, 734, 735, 744; vaccinated,
34; TJ's affection for, 415, 472, 678,
735; TJ sends gifts to, 471; identified,
589n; affection for TJ, 691

Randolph, Jane Cary, 508n

Randolph, John (of Roanoke), 218n

Randolph, Martha Jefferson (Patsy,
Mrs. Thomas Mann Randolph, TJ's
daughter): letters to, 471-2, 735; letters from, 590, 690-1; invited to Monticello, vii; in-laws of, 266n; TJ's
affection for, 415, 472, 511, 678;
Poplar Forest lands given to, 415n; invited to Washington, 471; TJ wishes
to spend more time with, 471-2; returns to Edgehill, 579; and family's
health, 590, 690-1, 735; health of,
690-1; letter from cited, 755

Randolph, Thomas Eston, 507-8, 580

Randolph, Thomas Jefferson (TJ's
grandson): TJ's affection for, 415,
472, 678, 735; health of, 590, 677,
690-1, 735, 744; affection for TJ, 690

Randolph, Thomas Mann (TJ's son-in-
law): letters to, 414-15, 677-8; letter
from, 744-5; and D. Ross, 94, 339;
and smallpox vaccinations, 278, 495,
572; cares for TJ's affairs at Monticello, Shadwell, 319, 346n, 507, 524,
745; indebted to G. Jefferson, 414; TJ
gives Poplar Forest land to, 414-15,

419, 659, 677-8; and family's plan to
visit Washington, 471; TJ's affection
for, 472, 511, 735; family of, 508n; letters from cited, 590n, 678n, 755, 756;
wheat harvest of, 659; health of, 690;
and family's health, 744-5

Randolph, Thomas Mann, Sr., 266n

Randolph, Virginia (sister of Thomas
Mann Randolph), 265, 266n

Randolph, Virginia Jefferson (TJ's
granddaughter): birth of, vii, 266n;
health of, vii, 579, 589, 590, 677, 690-
1, 735, 744; TJ's affection for, 415,
472, 678, 735

Randolph, William (TJ's uncle), 508n

Ranger (brig), 302n

Rapin, Joseph: letters to, 89-90, 436-7;
letter from, 66-7; leaves TJ's service,
viii, 7, 11, 24-5, 31, 50, 66-7, 83, 89-
90, 96, 225, 436-7; TJ's account with,
67n, 90, 282, 283n, 418, 436-7; steward of the President's House, 95; and
President's House accounts, 128, 178,
757

Rapine, Conrad & Co. (Washington,
D.C.): letter from, 489; seeks book
subscription from TJ, 489; identified,
489n

Rapine, Daniel, 489n

Rathbone, John, 274n

Raynal, Guillaume Thomas François,
Abbé de, 105n

Read, George, Jr., 428, 693n

Read, Jacob, 46n

Read, James, 467-9, 622, 653n, 655, 656n

Read, John K., 81-2n

Red River, 554, 558

Reeve, Tapping, 598

Reily, John, 392n

religion: involvement of clergy in politics, 33, 147, 338, 497, 521; in New
England, 78; religious publications,
152n; clergy encourage smallpox vaccinations, 199; clergy considered an
unproductive profession, 246; benefits
of, to society, 335n; separation of
church and state, 388n, 407-9; deism,
429n; salaries for ministers, 516; atheism, 520n; as means to promote civilization, 556-7. *See also* Jefferson,
Thomas: Religion

*Remembrancer, or Impartial Repository
of Public Events* (John Almon), 482-4

Remsen, Henry: letter from, 143-4; recommends M. L. Davis, 143-4

Sons of Liberty, 654n
Sophia (brig), 453, 454n
South America, 435, 436n, 717n, 720, 721n
South Carolina: appointments and removals in, 12-14, 31-2, 53-4, 85, 100, 101-2n, 117, 145, 201-2, 319-20; elections in, 32, 100, 101-2n, 118, 147, 201-2; attorneys, 42n; commissioners of Direct Tax, 54; migrants to Ky. from, 75; banks, 101n; and camels, 105n; Beaufort collectorship, 109n; French commercial agent at, 114-15; supervisor for, 201-2; lighthouses, 202n; and American Revolution, 257-8; Chester District, 262n; legislature, 262n, 531n; census, 288n; Spanish agent in, 453n; galleys in, 488n; and Whitney's cotton gin patent, 514n, 663; Camden, 531n; medical societies, 531n; Ninety Six District, 531n; physicians, 531n; circuit court cases in, 658. *See also* Charleston, S.C.; Federalists; Republicans
South Carolina Medical Society, 531n
South-Carolina State Gazette, and Timothy's Daily Advertiser (Charleston), 229n, 519, 520n
southern states: demand few removals, 145, 618; prejudice against, 267; New England subordinated to, 522n; perceived as hostile to navigation and commerce, 652
Southwest Point, Tenn., 78n, 196n, 308n, 325n
Spain: and Irujo's recall, xlv; U.S. relations with, xlv, 17-18, 72, 73n, 106-7, 392-3, 488, 550, 670n; cedes Louisiana to France, 18, 340, 396, 507, 527, 535, 695n; trade with U.S., 18; consul at Baltimore, 40; immigrants to Spanish territories, 75; sheep from, 105n, 463-4; and Florida, 106-7, 559-60n; naval prizes in U.S. ports, 110, 111n, 125, 132-3, 134n, 154, 158, 159n; prisoners of war, 110, 125; secretary of U.S. legation, 189, 190n; declares blockade of Gibraltar, 406, 407n, 425, 488, 507, 545, 593-5, 660-1; and C. W. Peale's petition to collect specimens, 435, 436n; agent in S.C., 453n; agriculture, 462; Valencia, 462; Catholics in, 494; privateers, 494n; and New Orleans, 550; and Nuevo León, 553-4, 561n; horses imported by, 555; and Indian relations,

555; missionaries, 556; possessions in the Americas, 670n, 719; relations with France, 695n; and preliminary peace, 714; removal of condemned slaves to territories of, 719. *See also* Algeciras, Spain; Cadiz, Spain
Spanish language, xlv, 197, 328
Sparks, Mr., 726
Spectator (London), 562n
Spence, John, 318
Spooner, Alden, 265n
Sprigg, Osborn, 228n
springs, 727-8
Sproat, Ebenezer, 169, 216
stagecoaches, 52n, 486n
Stamp Act (1797), 104n, 602, 604n, 633, 643
Stanton, Joseph, Jr., 4, 5n
Stanwix, Fort, 76, 78n
Stark, Theodore, 148, 149n, 162
stars, 549n
State, U.S. Department of: passports, 13, 14n, 31; warrants drawn on Treasury by, 31; consular appointments, 57-60, 65-6n, 71, 82-3, 101, 107, 125, 148, 157, 247-53, 259, 277, 279-80, 298-9, 312-13, 322, 327, 341-2, 371, 388n, 493-5, 498, 500, 526-7, 528n, 585, 705n, 754; contracts sought from, 79, 80n, 265, 570n; publication of laws in German, 79, 80n; letters of credence, 125, 217n, 258, 266, 270-1; secretaries of legation, 144n, 189, 190n, 237n; and exequaturs, 148, 162, 163n, 258; and abuses by British admiralty courts, 163; and Dutch loan, 276-7; clerks, 311n, 378, 379n, 445n; compensation of consuls, 327, 401, 633; uses ciphers, 340n; reduction of diplomatic establishment, 382, 519, 633, 644; and blockade of Gibraltar, 406; revised system for making expenditures, 629, 630n; expenses of, 633, 738n; accountant of, 636; oaths required by, 700. *See also* Madison, James; United States: Foreign Relations; Wagner, Jacob
Staunton, Va., 49
staves, 277n
steamboats, 560n
Steele, John (comptroller of Treasury): and A. W. White's resignation, 107; forwards letters from Simons, 227, 229n; and Richard Harrison's appointment offer, 405n; and Wilmington collectorship, 468, 496-7; and

INDEX

Vindication of the Religion of Mr. Jefferson and a Statement of his Services in the Cause of Religious Liberty (Samuel Knox), 388n
Virgil, 180n

VIRGINIA

Agriculture
camels, 105n; suitability for olive trees, 105n; hams from, 137, 406; Ravensworth tract, 569n; compared with Europe, 706-7; cattle, 707

Constitution of the U.S.
ratification of, 26n

Council of State
members of, 279n

Courts
High Court of Chancery, 343n; Court of Appeals, 446n, 727n; General Court, 446n, 727n; circuit court cases in, 658

Economy
distilleries, 22n; mills, 22n, 568; taverns, inns, 22n, 185, 568-9, 727-8, 757; Warren, 22n; Blandford, 52n; merchants, 52n, 185, 280, 344, 345n; smuggling, 226, 317, 347; coal mining, 232, 233n; Manchester, 232, 233n; hatmakers, 256; Petersburg, 345n, 405, 487; roads, 568-9, 581-2; Thomas's crossroads, 569n. *See also* Alexandria, Va.; Milton, Va.; Norfolk, Va.; Richmond, Va.

Education and Science
smallpox vaccination in, 47, 174, 198, 213, 278, 279, 311-12, 318, 321, 339, 340n, 369; Hampden-Sydney College, 499n; physicians, 684

General Assembly
removal of condemned slaves, ix-x, 683, 712, 718-22; members, 26n, 120n, 186n, 228n, 279n, 319n, 355n, 357n, 455n, 501n, 568, 665n; supports Va. Resolutions, 26n

Laws
and smallpox inoculation, 47; taxes, 52n; to restore county records, 310; and intestate estates, 343n; education, 499n; juries, 639

Military
militia, 26n, 319n, 663n; bounties for Revolutionary War veterans, 76, 78-

9n; navy, 127n; and American Revolution, 328n, 335, 502-3

Politics
Hampton collectorship, 53, 85, 89, 92, 108, 112, 119-20, 126-7, 157, 169, 185-6, 216, 263; Old Point Comfort lighthouse, 112n; Cape Henry lighthouse, 127n; election of 1800 in, 185, 256; York Co., 185; Cherrystone collectorship, 226, 314, 317, 347-8, 350, 449, 468, 469n, 570, 580, 606, 653n, 655, 665, 674; Petersburg collectorship, 278n; Henrico Co., 279n; national influence of, 286, 639; Eastern Shore, 347-8; Portuguese vice consul in, 349n; governors, 357n; postmasters, 357n; too many federal appointees from, 426, 508; New England subordinated to, 522n; TJ's visits misinterpreted by Federalists, 529; French consul for, 562n; Accomac Co., 665; Northampton Co., 665, 674. *See also* Federalists; Republicans

Relations with U.S.
U.S. marshals, 26, 27, 32, 49, 371; postal service, 41, 49, 186n, 217, 218; census, 49, 255, 570n; western land claims, 76, 79n; collection of internal revenues in, 356, 525

Society
Scots-Irish in, 26n; immigrants to, 52n, 344-5n; attorneys, 136n, 355n; churches, religious groups, 183, 184n, 350-1, 446, 568-9; Russell Co., 344n; horse racing, 500; population growth in, 533n; Chesterfield Co., 684, 685n; Warm Springs, 727-8; Hot Springs, 728n. *See also* Charlottesville, Va.

State Institutions
Capitol, 9; hospital for the insane, 503n

Virginia and North Carolina Almanack for the Year 1802 (George Douglas), 9n
Virginia Manufactory of Arms, 663
Virginia Resolutions, 26n
"Voice of A Sybil" (pseudonym): letter from, 575-6; advises on Pa. politics, 575-6
Voigt, Henry, 15

135-6n, 166, 191n, 304-5; President's Square, 48, 131, 168, 209; financial markets, 54; smallpox vaccination at, 103n, 230-1, 369, 495, 573; government relocates to, 108, 133, 285, 288-9n, 438, 440n, 570n, 629; Capitol Hill, 109, 131, 133, 167, 209; bridges, 131, 167-8; Capitol Square, 131, 209; New Jersey Ave., 131, 167-8, 176, 209; Pennsylvania Ave., 131, 167-8, 176, 209; Washington Navy Yard, 187; Catholics in, 202-3; St. Mary's Church, 203n, 349n; Seven Buildings, 209; justices of the peace, 254n, 592n; mayors, 254n; Orphan's Court, 254n; office-seeking in, 264; surveyors for, 349n, 372, 373, 717n; wharves, 349n; land development, speculation, 402n; F Street, 449; drought at, 471-2; newspapers, 487-8; booksellers, 489; social life, 511; immigrants to, 543; packet service to, from, 543; longitude of, 549n; L'Enfant's plan of, 562-8; breweries, 592n; images of, 657n; hotels, boardinghouses, 706n; taverns, 706n. *See also* Anacostia River; District of Columbia

Washington, Fort, 477n

Washington (British packet), 543

Washington Federalist, 275n, 282

Washingtoniana: A Collection of Papers Relative to the Death and Character of General George Washington (George Douglas), 9n

Washington Printing and Bookselling Company, 487-8

Waterhouse, Benjamin: letters to, 47, 91, 120-1, 311-12; letters from, 8, 166, 198-200, 213-14, 369-70, 680-1; supplies vaccine matter to TJ, vii, 8, 35n, 47, 89, 103, 120, 170, 174, 277-8, 311, 495, 572; and TJ's vaccination experiments, vii, xlix, 91, 120-1, 166, 311-12, 472, 495, 680-1; supplies vaccine matter to others, 198, 231, 290, 318; successful spread of vaccination, 198-200, 213-14; as professor, 200; *Prospect of Exterminating the Small Pox*, 200n; reports fraud, rivalry among physicians, 369-70, 680-1; and Lettsom, 425n

Watson, James, 10n, 101

Watson, John: enters trade with Higginbotham, 28; payments to, 400; letter to cited, 400n, 754

Watson, Josiah, 196

Watson, William (Mass.), 53, 56n, 222-3

Watson, William (N.J.), 365-6

Watt, James, 681-2

Wayles, John (TJ's father-in-law), 320-1, 726

Wayles estate, 320-1, 726

Wayne, Caleb P., 693

Wealth of Nations (Adam Smith), xlv

weather: heat, 198; gales, 224, 674; drought, 471-2, 500, 659, 678

Webster, Noah, 79, 80, 80n

weddings, 178

Wedgwood & Bentley, 294

Weems, John, 119

weights and measures, 462, 465n, 659, 660n, 679

Wessel, Gerhard George, 293, 294n

West, Benjamin, xlviii

West, John S., 460n

West Indies: export of firearms to, prevented, 10n; and American Revolution, 257n, 332; and Great Britain, 396; Quakers in, 425n; and Louisiana, 527; American prizes taken to, 546-8; and preliminary peace, 715; removal of condemned slaves to, 720

Weston, Abijah, 325n

whale oil, 60n

Wharton, Isaac, 46n

wheat: price of, 104, 280-1, 659-60; bearded, 504; Hessian fly destroys wheat, 678; grown in Germany, 707

Wheeler, Peter, 748n

Whelan, Patrick, 373

Whelen, Israel, 57n

Whipple, Joseph, 135n, 263n, 652-3, 654

Whiskey Insurrection, 184n

White, Alexander: letters from, 47-8, 297-8; as D.C. commissioner, 46n, 97-100, 132, 349n, 371-3, 450; and S. Davidson's claim, 47-8; and Maryland loan, 113; absent from Washington, 132n; letter from cited, 132n, 750; communications between D.C. commissioners and president, 297-8; and survey of D.C. lots, 349n; estimate of commissioners' debts, 371-3

White, Anthony Walton: resigns as surveyor, 84, 86n, 107, 157, 226, 314; letter from cited, 752

White, Bishop William, 42

White, Samuel, 205, 207-8n

A comprehensive index of Volumes 1-20 of the
First Series has been issued as Volume 21.
Each subsequent volume has its own index,
as does each volume or set of volumes
in the Second Series.

THE PAPERS OF THOMAS JEFFERSON are composed in Monticello, a font based on the "Pica No. 1" created in the early 1800s by Binny & Ronaldson, the first successful typefounding company in America. The face is considered historically appropriate for The Papers of Thomas Jefferson because it was used extensively in American printing during the last quarter-century of Jefferson's life, and because Jefferson himself expressed cordial approval of Binny & Ronaldson types. It was revived and rechristened Monticello in the late 1940s by the Mergenthaler Linotype Company, under the direction of C. H. Griffith and in close consultation with P. J. Conkwright, specifically for the publication of the Jefferson Papers. The font suffered some losses in its first translation to digital format in the 1980s to accommodate computerized typesetting. Matthew Carter's reinterpretation in 2002 restores the spirit and style of Binny & Ronaldson's original design of two centuries earlier.

✧